The Oxford Spanish Minidictionary

The Oxford Spanish Minidictionary

Spanish–English
English–Spanish

Español–Inglés
Inglés–Español

Christine Lea

Second Edition
edited by
Carol Styles Carvajal
Michael Britton
Jane Horwood

OXFORD
UNIVERSITY PRESS

OXFORD
UNIVERSITY PRESS

Great Clarendon Street, Oxford OX2 6DP

Oxford University Press is a department of the University of Oxford. It furthers the University's objective of excellence in research, scholarship, and education by publishing worldwide in

Oxford New York

Athens Auckland Bangkok Bogotá Buenos Aires Calcutta Cape Town Chennai Dar es Salaam Delhi Florence Hong Kong Istanbul Karachi Kuala Lumpur Madrid Melbourne Mexico City Mumbai Nairobi Paris São Paulo Singapore Taipei Tokyo Toronto Warsaw

and associated companies in Berlin Ibadan

Published in the United States by Oxford University Press Inc., New York

British Library Cataloguing in Publication Data
Data available

Library of Congress Cataloging in Publication Data
Data available

ISBN 0-19-8602316
ISBN 0-19-8602642 (Spanish cover edition)

10 9 8 7 6 5

Typeset in Nimrod and Arial
by Tradespools Ltd
Printed in Great Britain
by Charles Letts (Scotland) Ltd

Contents/Índice

Proprietary terms

This dictionary includes some words which have, or are asserted to have, proprietary status as trademarks. Their inclusion does not imply that they have acquired for legal purposes a non-proprietary or general significance, nor any other judgement concerning their legal status. In cases where the editorial staff have some evidence that a word has proprietary status this is indicated in the entry for that word by the symbol (P), but no judgement concerning the legal status of such words is made or implied thereby.

Marcas registradas

Este diccionario incluye algunas palabras que son o pretenden ser marcas registradas. No debe atribuirse ningún valor jurídico ni a la presencia ni a la ausencia de tal designación.

Contributors/Colaboradores

Second Edition

Editors/Editores
Carol Styles Carvajal
Michael Britton
Jane Horwood

First Edition

Editor/Editora
Christine Lea

Phrasefinder/Índice temático de frases
Idoia Noble
Neil and Roswitha Morris

Data input/Entrada de datos
Muriel Ranivoalison
Susan Wilkin

Introduction

This major new edition of the *Oxford Spanish Minidictionary* is designed as an effective and practical reference tool for the student, adult learner, traveller, and business professional.

The wordlist has been comprehensively revised to reflect recent additions to both languages. The central *Phrasefinder* section aims to provide the user with the confidence to communicate in the most commonly encountered social situations such as travel, shopping, eating out, and organizing leisure activities.

A further new feature of the dictionary is the special status given to more complex grammatical words which provide the basic structure of both languages. Boxed entries in the text for these *function words* provide extended treatment, including notes to warn of possible pitfalls.

The dictionary has an easy-to-use, streamlined layout. Bullets separate each new part of speech within an entry. Nuances of sense or usage are pinpointed by indicators or by typical collocates with which the word frequently occurs. Extra help is given in the form of symbols to mark the register of words and phrases. An exclamation mark [!] indicates colloquial language, and a cross [✖] indicates slang.

Each English headword is followed by its phonetic transcription between slashes. The symbols used are those of the International Phonetic Alphabet. Pronunciation is also shown for derivatives and compounds where it is not easily deduced from that of a headword. The rules for pronunciation of Spanish are given on pages viii–ix.

The swung dash (~) is used to replace a headword or that part of a headword preceding the vertical bar (|).

In both English and Spanish only irregular plurals are given. Normally Spanish nouns and adjectives ending in an unstressed vowel form the plural by adding *s* (e.g. *libro, libros*). Nouns and adjectives ending in a stressed vowel or a consonant add *es* (e.g. *rubí, rubíes, pared, paredes*). An accent on the final syllable is not required when *es* is added (e.g. *nación, naciones*). Final *z* becomes *ces* (e.g. *vez, veces*).

Spanish nouns and adjectives ending in *o* form the feminine by changing the final *o* to *a* (e.g. *hermano, hermana*). Most Spanish nouns and adjectives ending in anything other than final *o* do not have a separate feminine form, with the exception of those denoting nationality etc.; these add *a* to the masculine singular form (e.g. *español, española*). An accent on the final syllable is then not required (e.g. *inglés, inglesa*). Adjectives ending in *án, ón*, or *or* behave like those denoting nationality, with the following exceptions: *inferior, mayor, mejor, menor, peor, superior*, where the feminine has the same form as the masculine. Spanish verb tables will be found at the back of the book.

The Spanish alphabet

In Spanish *ñ* is considered a separate letter and in the Spanish–English section, therefore, is alphabetized after *ny*.

Introducción

Esta importante nueva edición del *Minidiccionario de Oxford* ha sido concebida a fin de proporcionar una herramienta de referencia práctica y eficaz al estudiante, joven y adulto, al viajero y a la persona de negocios.

Se ha revisado exhaustivamente la lista de palabras con el objeto de incorporar nuevos términos en ambos idiomas. La sección central contiene una *Lista temática de frases*, destinada a que el usuario adquiera la confianza necesaria para comunicarse en las situaciones más normales de la vida diaria, como las que se encuentran al viajar, hacer compras, comer fuera y organizar actividades recreativas.

Otro nuevo aspecto del diccionario es la importancia especial que se da a palabras con una función más compleja dentro de la gramática y que proveen la estructura básica de ambos idiomas. Estos *vocablos clave* están contenidos en recuadros dentro del texto, donde se les da un tratamiento amplio y se incluyen notas para advertir sobre posibles escollos.

El diccionario tiene una presentación clara y es fácil de usar. Símbolos distintivos separan las diferentes categorías gramaticales dentro de cada entrada. Los matices de sentido y de uso se muestran con precisión mediante indicadores o por colocaciones típicas con las que la palabra se usa frecuentemente. Se encuentra ayuda adicional en los signos que indican el registro idiomático de las palabras y frases. Un signo de exclamación [!] señala el uso coloquial y una cruz [✖] el uso argot.

Cada palabra cabeza de artículo en inglés va seguida de su transcripción fonética entre barras oblicuas. Los símbolos que se usan son los del Alfabeto Fonético Internacional. También aparece la pronunciación de derivados y nombres compuestos cuando no es posible deducirla de la palabra cabeza de artículo. Las reglas sobre pronunciación española se encuentran en las páginas viii–ix.

La tilde (~) se emplea para sustituir la palabra cabeza de artículo o aquella parte de tal palabra que precede a la barra vertical (|).

Tanto en inglés como en español se dan los plurales solamente si son irregulares. Para formar el plural regular en inglés se añade la letra *s* al sustantivo singular, pero se añade *es* cuando se trata de una palabra que termina en *ch, sh, s, ss, us, x, o, z* (p.ej. *sash, sashes*). En el caso de una palabra que termine en *y* precedida por una consonante, la *y* se transforma en *ies* (p.ej. *baby, babies*). Para formar el tiempo pasado y el participio pasado se añade *ed* al infinitivo de los verbos regulares ingleses (p.ej. *last, lasted*). En el caso de los verbos ingleses que terminan en *e* muda se añade sólo la *d* (p.ej. *move, moved*). En el caso de los verbos ingleses que terminan en *y*, se debe cambiar la *y* por *ied* (p.ej. *carry, carried*). Los verbos irregulares se encuentran en el diccionario por orden alfabético remitidos al infinitivo, y también en la lista que aparece en las últimas páginas del diccionario.

Pronunciation of Spanish

Vowels

a between pronunciation of *a* in English *cat* and *arm*

e like *e* in English *bed*

i like *ee* in English *see* but a little shorter

o like *o* in English *hot* but a little longer

u like *oo* in English *too*

y when a vowel is as Spanish **i**

Consonants

b (1) in initial position or after a nasal consonant is like English *b*

(2) in other positions is between English *b* and English *v*

c (1) before **e** or **i** is like *th* in English *thin*. In Latin American Spanish is like English *s*.

(2) in other positions is like *c* in English *cat*

ch like *ch* in English *chip*

d (1) in initial position, after nasal consonants and after **l** is like English *d*

(2) in other positions is like *th* in English *this*

f like English *f*

g (1) before **e** or **i** is like *ch* in Scottish *loch*

(2) in initial position is like *g* in English *get*

(3) in other positions is like (2) but a little softer

h silent in Spanish but see also **ch**

Pronunciación Inglesa

Símbolos fonéticos

Vocales y diptongos

iː	*see*	ɔː	*saw*	əɪ	*page*	ɔɪ	*join*
ɪ	*sit*	ʊ	*put*	əʊ	*home*	ɪə	*near*
e	*ten*	uː	*too*	aɪ	*five*	eə	*hair*
æ	*hat*	ʌ	*cup*	aɪə	*fire*	ʊə	*poor*
ɑː	*arm*	ɜː	*fur*	aʊ	*now*		
ɒ	*got*	ə	*ago*	aʊə	*flour*		

Consonantes

p	*pen*	tʃ	*chin*	s	*so*	n	*no*
b	*bad*	dʒ	*June*	z	*zoo*	ŋ	*sing*
t	*tea*	f	*fall*	ʃ	*she*	l	*leg*
d	*dip*	v	*voice*	ʒ	*measure*	r	*red*
k	*cat*	θ	*thin*	h	*how*	j	*yes*
g	*got*	ð	*then*	m	*man*	w	*wet*

Abbreviations/Abreviaturas

adjective	*a*	adjetivo
abbreviation	*abbr/abrev*	abreviatura
administration	*admin*	administración
adverb	*adv*	adverbio
American	*Amer*	americano
anatomy	*Anat*	anatomía
architecture	*Archit/Arquit*	arquitectura
definite article	*art def*	artículo definido
indefinite article	*art indef*	artículo indefinido
astrology	*Astr*	astrología
motoring	*Auto*	automóvil
auxiliary	*aux*	auxiliar
aviation	*Aviat/Aviac*	aviación
biology	*Biol*	biología
botany	*Bot*	botánica
British	*Brit*	británico
commerce	*Com*	comercio
conjunction	*conj*	conjunción
cookery	*Culin*	cocina
electricity	*Elec*	electricidad
school	*Escol*	enseñanza
Spain	*Esp*	España
feminine	*f*	femenino
familiar	*fam*	familiar
figurative	*fig*	figurado
philosophy	*Fil*	filosofía
photography	*Foto*	fotografía
geography	*Geog*	geografía
geology	*Geol*	geología

grammar	*Gram*	gramática
humorous	*hum*	humorístico
interjection	*int*	interjección
interrogative	*inter*	interrogativo
invariable	*invar*	invariable
legal, law	*Jurid*	jurídico
Latin American	*LAm*	latinoamericano
language	*Lang*	lengua(je)
masculine	*m*	masculino
mathematics	*Mat(h)*	matemáticas
mechanics	*Mec*	mecánica
medicine	*Med*	medicina
Mexico	*Mex*	México
military	*Mil*	militar
music	*Mus*	música
mythology	*Myth*	mitología
noun	*n*	nombre
nautical	*Naut*	náutica
oneself	*o. s.*	uno mismo, se
proprietary term	*P*	marca registrada
pejorative	*pej*	peyorativo
philosophy	*Phil*	filosofía
photography	*Photo*	fotografía
plural	*pl*	plural
politics	*Pol*	política
possessive	*poss*	posesivo
past participle	*pp*	participio pasado
prefix	*pref*	prefijo
preposition	*prep*	preposición
present participle	*pres p*	participio de presente

pronoun	*pron*	pronombre
psychology	*Psych*	psicología
past tense	*pt*	tiempo pasado
railroad	*Rail*	ferrocarril
relative	*rel*	relativo
religion	*Relig*	religión
school	*Schol*	enseñanza
singular	*sing*	singular
slang	*sl*	argot
someone	*s. o.*	alguien
something	*sth*	algo
subjunctive	*subj*	subjuntivo
technical	*Tec*	técnico
television	*TV*	televisión
university	*Univ*	universidad
auxiliary verb	*v aux*	verbo auxiliar
verb	*vb*	verbo
intransitive verb	*vi*	verbo intransitivo
pronominal verb	*vpr*	verbo pronominal
transitive verb	*vt*	verbo transitivo
transitive & intransitive verb	*vti*	verbo transitivo e intransitivo
vulgar	*vulg*	vulgar

Aa

a

● *preposición*

Note that **a** followed by **el** becomes **al**, e.g. **vamos al cine**

....➤ (dirección) to. **fui a México** I went to Mexico. **muévete a la derecha** move to the right

....➤ (posición) **se sentaron a la mesa** they sat at the table. **al lado del banco** next to the bank. **a orillas del río** on the banks of the river

....➤ (distancia) **queda a 5 km** it's 5 km away. **a pocos metros de aquí** a few metres from here

....➤ (fecha) **hoy estamos a 5** today is the 5th. **¿a cuánto estamos?**, (LAm) **¿a cómo estamos?** what's the date?

....➤ (hora, momento) at. **a las 2** at 2 o'clock. **a fin de mes** at the end of the month. **a los 21 años** at the age of 21; (después de) after 21 years

....➤ (precio) **¿a cómo están las peras?** how much are the pears? **están a 500 pesetas el kilo** they're 500 pesetas a kilo. **salen a 30 pesetas cada uno** they work out at 30 pesetas each.

....➤ (medio, modo) **fuimos a pie** we went on foot. **hecho a mano** handmade. **pollo al horno** (LAm) roast chicken

....➤ (cuando precede al objeto directo de persona) *no se traduce*. **conocí a Juan** I met Juan. **quieren mucho a sus hijos** they love their children very much

....➤ (con objeto indirecto) to. **se lo di a Juan** I gave it to Juan. **le vendí el coche a mi amigo** I sold my friend the car, I sold the car to my friend. **se lo compré a mi madre** I bought it from my mother; (para) I bought it for my mother

⇨ Cuando la preposición **a** se emplea precedida de ciertos verbos como **empezar, faltar, ir, llegar** etc., ver bajo el respectivo verbo

ábaco *m* abacus

abadía *f* abbey

abajo *adv* (down) below; (dirección) down(wards); (en casa) downstairs. ● *int* down with. **~ de** (LAm) under(neath). **calle ~** down the street. **el ~ firmante** the undersigned. **escaleras ~** down the stairs. **la parte de ~** the bottom (part). **los de ~** those at the bottom. **más ~** further down

abalanzarse [10] *vpr* rush (**hacia** towards)

abanderado *m* standard-bearer; (Mex, en fútbol) linesman

abandon|ado *adj* abandoned; (descuidado) neglected; *<persona>* untidy. **~ar** *vt* leave *<un lugar>*; abandon *<persona, cosa>*. ● *vi* give up. □ **~arse** *vpr* give in; (descuidarse) let o.s. go. **~o** *m* abandonment; (estado) neglect

abani|car [7] *vt* fan. **~co** *m* fan

abaratar *vt* reduce

abarcar [7] *vt* put one's arms around, embrace; (comprender) embrace

abarrotar *vt* overfill, pack full

abarrotes *mpl* (LAm) groceries; (tienda) grocer's shop

abast|ecer [11] *vt* supply. **~ecimiento** *m* supply; (acción) supplying. **~o** *m* supply. **no dar ~o** be unable to cope (**con** with)

abati|do *a* depressed. **~miento** *m* depression

abdicar [7] *vt* give up. ● *vi* abdicate

abdom|en *m* abdomen. **~inal** *a* abdominal

abec|é *m* ⓘ alphabet, ABC. **~edario** *m* alphabet

abedul *m* birch (tree)

abej|a *f* bee. **~orro** *m* bumble-bee

aberración *f* aberration

abertura *f* opening

abeto *m* fir (tree)

abierto *pp* ⇒ABRIR. ● *a* open

abism|al *a* abysmal; (profundo) deep. **~ar** *vt* throw into an abyss; (fig, abatir) humble. □ **~arse** *vpr* be absorbed (**en** in), be lost (**en** in). **~o** *m* abyss; (fig, diferencia) world of difference

ablandar *vt* soften. □ **~se** *vpr* soften

abnega|ción *f* self-sacrifice. **~do** *a* self-sacrificing

abochornar *vt* embarrass. □ **~se** *vpr* feel embarrassed

abofetear *vt* slap

aboga|cía *f* law. **~do** *m* lawyer, solicitor; (ante tribunal superior) barrister (Brit), attorney (Amer). **~r** [12] *vi* plead

abolengo *m* ancestry

aboli|ción *f* abolition. **~cionismo** *m* abolitionism. **~cionista** *m & f* abolitionist. **~r** [24] *vt* abolish

abolla|dura *f* dent. **~r** *vt* dent

abolsado *a* baggy

abomba|do *a* convex; (LAm, atontado) dopey. **~r** *vt* make convex. □ **~rse** *vpr* (LAm, descomponerse) go bad

abominable *a* abominable

abona|ble *a* payable. **~do** *a* paid. ● *m* subscriber. **~r** *vt* pay; (en agricultura) fertilize. □ **~rse** *vpr* subscribe. **~o** *m* payment; (estiércol) fertilizer; (a un periódico) subscription

aborda|ble *a* reasonable; <*persona*> approachable. **~je** *m* boarding. **~r** *vt* tackle <*un asunto*>; approach <*una persona*>; (Naut) come alongside; (Mex, Aviac) board

aborigen *a & m* native

aborrec|er [11] *vt* loathe. **~ible** *a* loathsome. **~ido** *a* loathed. **~imiento** *m* loathing

abort|ar *vi* have a miscarriage. **~ivo** *a* abortive. **~o** *m* miscarriage; (voluntario) abortion. **hacerse un ~o** have an abortion

abotonar *vt* button (up). □ **~se** *vpr* button (up)

abovedado *a* vaulted

abrasa|dor *a* burning. **~r** *vt* burn. □ **~rse** *vpr* burn

abraz|ar *vt* [10] embrace. **~arse** *vpr* embrace. **~o** *m* hug. **un fuerte ~o de** (en una carta) with best wishes from

abre|botellas *m invar* bottle-opener. **~cartas** *m invar* paper-knife. **~latas** *m invar* tin opener (Brit), can opener

abrevia|ción *f* abbreviation; (texto abreviado) abridged text. **~do** *a* brief; *<texto>* abridged. **~r** *vt* abbreviate; abridge *<texto>*; cut short *<viaje etc>*. ● *vi* be brief. **~tura** *f* abbreviation

abrig|ado *a* *<lugar>* sheltered; *<persona>* well wrapped up. **~ador** *a* (Mex, ropa) warm. **~ar** [12] *vt* shelter; cherish *<esperanza>*; harbour *<duda, sospecha>*. □ **~arse** *vpr* (take) shelter; (con ro-pa) wrap up. **~o** *m* (over)coat; (lu-gar) shelter

abril *m* April. **~eño** *a* April

abrillantar *vt* polish

abrir (*pp* **abierto**) *vt/i* open. □ **~se** *vpr* open; (extenderse) open out; *<el tiempo>* clear

abrochar *vt* do up; (con botones) button up

abruma|dor *a* overwhelming. **~r** *vt* overwhelm

abrupto *a* steep; (áspero) harsh

abrutado *a* brutish

absentismo *m* absenteeism

absolución *f* (Relig) absolution; (Jurid) acquittal

absolut|amente *adv* absolutely, completely. **~o** *a* absolute. **en ~o** (not) at all

absolver [2] (*pp* **absuelto**) *vt* (Relig) absolve; (Jurid) acquit

absor|bente *a* absorbent; (fig, interesante) absorbing. **~ber** *vt* absorb. **~ción** *f* absorption. **~to** *a* absorbed

abstemio *a* teetotal. ● *m* teetotaller

absten|ción *f* abstention. □ **~erse** [40] *vpr* abstain, refrain (**de** from)

abstinencia *f* abstinence

abstra|cción *f* abstraction. **~cto** *a* abstract. **~er** [41] *vt* abstract. □ **~erse** *vpr* be lost in thought. **~ído** *a* absent-minded

absuelto *a* (Relig) absolved; (Jurid) acquitted

absurdo *a* absurd. ● *m* absurd thing

abuche|ar *vt* boo. **~o** *m* booing

abuel|a *f* grandmother. **~o** *m* grandfather. **~os** *mpl* grandparents

ab|ulia *f* apathy. **~úlico** *a* apathetic

abulta|do *a* bulky. **~r** *vt* (fig, exagerar) exaggerate. ● *vi* be bulky

abunda|ncia *f* abundance. **nadar en la ~ncia** be rolling in money. **~nte** *a* abundant, plentiful. **~r** *vi* be plentiful

aburguesarse *vpr* become middle-class

aburri|do *a* (*con estar*) bored; (*con ser*) boring. **~dor** *a* (LAm) boring. **~miento** *m* boredom; (cosa pesada) bore. **~r** *vt* bore. □ **~rse** *vpr* get bored

abus|ar *vi* take advantage. **~ar de la bebida** drink too much. **~ivo** *a* excessive. **~o** *m* abuse

acá *adv* here. **~ y allá** here and there. **de ~ para allá** to and fro. **de ayer ~** since yesterday. **más ~** nearer

acaba|do *a* finished; (perfecto) perfect. ● *m* finish. **~r** *vt/i* finish. □ **~rse** *vpr* finish; (agotarse) run out; (morirse) die. **~r con** put an end to. **~r de** (+ *infinitivo*) have just (+ *pp*). **~ de llegar** he has just arrived. **~r por** (+ *infinitivo*) end up (+ *gerundio*). **¡se acabó!** that's it!

acabóse *m*. **ser el ~** be the end, be the limit

acad|emia *f* academy. **~émico** *a* academic

acallar *vt* silence

acalora|do *a* heated; <*persona*> hot. □ **~rse** *vpr* get hot; (fig, excitarse) get excited

acampar *vi* camp

acantilado *m* cliff

acapara|r *vt* hoard; (monopolizar) monopolize. **~miento** *m* hoarding; (monopolio) monopolizing

acariciar *vt* caress; <*animal*> stroke; <*idea etc*> nurture

ácaro *m* mite

acarre|ar *vt* transport; <*desgracias etc*> cause. **~o** *m* transport

acartona|do *a* <*piel*> wizened. □ **~rse** *vpr* (ponerse rígido) go stiff; <*piel*> become wizened

acaso *adv* maybe, perhaps. ● *m* chance. **~ llueva mañana** perhaps it will rain tomorrow. **por si ~** (just) in case

acata|miento *m* compliance (**de** with). **~r** *vt* comply with

acatarrarse *vpr* catch a cold, get a cold

acaudalado *a* well off

acceder *vi* agree; (tener acceso) have access

acces|ible *a* accessible; <*persona*> approachable. **~o** *m* access, entry; (Med, ataque) attack

accesorio *a & m* accessory

accident|ado *a* <*terreno*> uneven; (agitado) troubled; <*persona*> injured. **~al** *a* accidental. □ **~arse** *vpr* have an accident. **~e** *m* accident

acci|ón *f* (incl Jurid) action; (hecho) deed; (Com) share. **~onar** *vt* work. ● *vi* gesticulate. **~onista** *m & f* shareholder

acebo *m* holly (tree)

acech|ar *vt* lie in wait for. **~o** *m* spying. **al ~o** on the look-out

aceit|ar *vt* oil; (Culin) add oil to. **~e** *m* oil. **~e de oliva** olive oil. **~te de ricino** castor oil. **~era** *f* cruet; (para engrasar) oilcan. **~ero** *a* oil. **~oso** *a* oily

aceitun|a *f* olive. **~ado** *a* olive. **~o** *m* olive tree

acelera|dor *m* accelerator. **~r** *vt* accelerate; (fig) speed up, quicken

acelga *f* chard

acent|o *m* accent; (énfasis) stress. **~uación** *f* accentuation. **~uar** [21] *vt* stress; (fig) emphasize. □ **~uarse** *vpr* become noticeable

acepción *f* meaning, sense

acepta|ble *a* acceptable. **~ción** *f* acceptance; (éxito) success. **~r** *vt* accept

acequia *f* irrigation channel

acera *f* pavement (Brit), sidewalk (Amer)

acerca de *prep* about

acerca|miento *m* approach; (fig) reconciliation. **~r** [7] *vt* bring near. □ **~rse** *vpr* approach

acero *m* steel. **~ inoxidable** stainless steel

acérrimo *a* (fig) staunch

acert|ado *a* right, correct; (apropiado) appropriate. **~ar** [1] *vt* (adivinar) get right, guess. ● *vi* get right; (en el blanco) hit. **~ar a** happen to. **~ar con** hit on. **~ijo** *m* riddle

achacar [7] *vt* attribute

achacoso *a* sickly

achaque *m* ailment

achatar *vt* flatten

achicar [7] *vt* make smaller; (fig, [I], empequeñecer) belittle; (Naut) bale out. □ **~rse** *vpr* become smaller; (humillarse) be intimidated

achicharra|r *vt* burn; (fig) pester. □ **~rse** *vpr* burn

achichincle *m & f* (Mex) hanger-on

achicopalado *a* (Mex) depressed

achicoria *f* chicory

achiote *m* (LAm) annatto

achispa|do *a* tipsy. □ **~rse** *vpr* get tipsy

achulado *a* cocky

acicala|do *a* dressed up. **~r** *vt* dress up. □ **~rse** *vpr* get dressed up

acicate *m* spur

acidez *f* acidity; (Med) heartburn

ácido *a* sour. ● *m* acid

acierto *m* success; (idea) good idea; (habilidad) skill

aclama|ción *f* acclaim; (aplausos) applause. **~r** *vt* acclaim; (aplaudir) applaud

aclara|ción *f* explanation. **~r** *vt* lighten <*colores*>; (explicar) clarify; (enjuagar) rinse. ● *vi* <*el tiempo*> brighten up. □ **~rse** *vpr* become clear. **~torio** *a* explanatory

aclimata|ción *f* acclimatization, acclimation (Amer). **~r** *vt* acclimatize, acclimate (Amer). □ **~rse** *vpr* become acclimatized, become acclimated (Amer)

acné *m* acne

acobardar *vt* intimidate. □ **~se** *vpr* lose one's nerve

acocil *m* (Mex) freshwater shrimp

acog|edor *a* welcoming; <*ambiente*> friendly. **~er** [14] *vt* welcome; (proteger) shelter; (recibir) receive. □ **~erse** *vpr* take refuge. **~ida** *f* welcome; (refugio) refuge

acolcha|do *a* quilted. **~r** *vt* quilt, pad

acomedido *a* (Mex) obliging

acomet|er *vt* attack; (emprender) undertake **~ida** *f* attack

acomod|ado *a* well off. **~ador** *m* usher. **~adora** *f* usherette. **~ar** *vt* arrange; (adaptar) adjust. ● *vi* be suitable. □ **~arse** *vpr* settle down; (adaptarse) conform

acompaña|miento *m* accompaniment. **~nte** *m & f* companion; (Mus) accompanist. **~r** *vt* go with; (hacer compañía) keep company; (adjuntar) enclose

acondicionar *vt* fit out; (preparar) prepare

aconseja|ble *a* advisable. **~do** *a* advised. **~r** *vt* advise. □ **~rse** *vpr* **~rse con** consult

acontec|er [11] *vi* happen. **~imiento** *m* event

acopla|miento *m* coupling; (Elec) connection. **~r** *vt* fit; (Elec) connect; (Rail) couple

acorazado *a* armour-plated. ● *m* battleship

acord|ar [2] *vt* agree (upon); (decidir) decide; (recordar) remind. □ **~arse** *vpr* remember. **~e** *a* in agreement; (Mus) harmonious. ● *m* chord

acorde|ón *m* accordion. **~onista** *m & f* accordionist

acordona|do *a* <*lugar*> cordoned off; <*zapatos*> lace-up. **~r** *vt* lace (up); (rodear) cordon off

acorralar *vt* round up <*animales*>; corner <*personas*>

acortar *vt* shorten; cut short <*permanencia*>. □ **~se** *vpr* get shorter

acos|ar *vt* hound; (fig) pester. **~o** *m* pursuit; (fig) pestering

acostar [2] *vt* put to bed; (Naut) bring alongside. ● *vi* (Naut) reach land. ◻ **~se** *vpr* go to bed; (echarse) lie down. **~se con** (fig) sleep with

acostumbra|do *a* (habitual) usual. **~do a** used to. **~r** *vt* get used. **me ha ~do a levantarme por la noche** he's got me used to getting up at night. ● *vi*. **~r a** be accustomed to. **acostumbro a comer a la una** I usually have lunch at one o'clock. ◻ **~rse** *vpr* become accustomed, get used (**a** to)

acota|ción *f* (nota) margin note; (en el teatro) stage direction; (cota) elevation mark. **~miento** *m* (Mex) hard shoulder

acrecentar [1] *vt* increase. ◻ **~se** *vpr* increase

acredita|do *a* reputable; (Pol) accredited. **~r** *vt* prove; accredit <*diplomático*>; (garantizar) guarantee; (autorizar) authorize. ◻ **~rse** *vpr* make one's name

acreedor *a* worthy (**de** of). ● *m* creditor

acribillar *vt* (a balazos) riddle (**a** with); (a picotazos) cover (**a** with); (fig, a preguntas etc) bombard (**a** with)

acr|obacia *f* acrobatics. **~obacias aéreas** aerobatics. **~óbata** *m* & *f* acrobat. **~obático** *a* acrobatic

acta *f* minutes; (certificado) certificate

actitud *f* posture, position; (fig) attitude, position

activ|ar *vt* activate; (acelerar) speed up. **~idad** *f* activity. **~o** *a* active. ● *m* assets

acto *m* act; (ceremonia) ceremony. **en el ~** immediately

act|or *m* actor. **~riz** *f* actress

actuación *f* action; (conducta) behaviour; (Theat) performance

actual *a* present; <*asunto*> topical. **~idad** *f* present; (de asunto) topicality. **en la ~idad** (en este momento) currently; (hoy en día) nowadays. **~idades** *fpl* current affairs. **~ización** *f* modernization. **~izar** [10] *vt* modernize. **~mente** *adv* now, at the present time

actuar [21] *vi* act. **~ de** act as

acuarel|a *f* watercolour. **~ista** *m* & *f* watercolourist

acuario *m* aquarium. **A~** Aquarius

acuartelar *vt* quarter, billet; (mantener en cuartel) confine to barracks

acuático *a* aquatic

acuchillar *vt* slash; stab <*persona*>

acuci|ante *a* urgent. **~ar** *vt* urge on; (dar prisa a) hasten. **~oso** *a* keen

acudir *vi*. **~ a** go to; (asistir) attend; turn up for <*a una cita*>. **~ en auxilio** go to help

acueducto *m* aqueduct

acuerdo *m* agreement. ● *vb* ⇨ACORDAR. **¡de ~!** OK! **de ~ con** in accordance with. **estar de ~** agree. **ponerse de ~** agree

acuesto *vb* ⇨ACOSTAR

acumula|dor *m* accumulator. **~r** *vt* accumulate. ◻ **~rse** *vpr* accumulate

acunar *vt* rock

acuñar *vt* mint, coin

acupuntura *f* acupuncture

acurrucarse [7] *vpr* curl up

acusa|do *a* accused; (destacado) marked. ● *m* accused. **~r** *vt* accuse; (mostrar) show; (denunciar) denounce; acknowledge <*recibo*>

acuse *m.* ~ **de recibo** acknowledgement of receipt

acus|ica *m & f* ⊡ telltale. **~ón** *m* ⊡ telltale

acústic|a *f* acoustics. **~o** *a* acoustic

adapta|ble *a* adaptable. **~ción** *f* adaptation. **~dor** *m* adapter. **~r** *vt* adapt; (ajustar) fit. □ **~rse** *vpr* adapt o.s.

adecua|do *a* suitable. **~r** *vt* adapt, make suitable

adelant|ado *a* advanced; <*niño*> precocious; <*reloj*> fast. **por ~ado** in advance. **~amiento** *m* advance(ment); (Auto) overtaking. **~ar** *vt* advance, move forward; (acelerar) speed up; put forward <*reloj*>; (Auto) overtake. ● *vi* advance, go forward; <*reloj*> gain, be fast. □ **~arse** *vpr* advance, move forward; <*reloj*> gain; (Auto) overtake. **~e** *adv* forward. ● *int* come in!; (¡siga!) carry on! **más ~e** (lugar) further on; (tiempo) later on. **~o** *m* advance; (progreso) progress

adelgaza|miento *m* slimming. **~r** [10] *vt* make thin; lose <*kilos*>. ● *vi* lose weight; (adrede) slim. □ **~rse** *vpr* lose weight; (adrede) slim

ademán *m* gesture. **en ~ de** as if to. **ademanes** *mpl* (modales) manners.

además *adv* besides; (también) also; (lo que es más) what's more. **~ de** besides

adentr|arse *vpr*. **~arse en** penetrate into; study thoroughly <*tema etc*>. **~o** *adv* in(side). **~ de** (LAm) in(side). **mar ~o** out at sea. **tierra ~o** inland

adepto *m* supporter

aderez|ar [10] *vt* flavour <*bebidas*>; (condimentar) season; dress <*ensalada*>. **~o** *m* flavouring; (con condimentos) seasoning; (para ensalada) dressing

adeud|ar *vt* owe. **~o** *m* debit

adhe|rir [4] *vt/i* stick. □ **~rirse** *vpr* stick; (fig) follow. **~sión** *f* adhesion; (fig) support. **~sivo** *a & m* adhesive

adici|ón *f* addition. **~onal** *a* additional. **~onar** *vt* add

adicto *a* addicted. ● *m* addict; (seguidor) follower

adiestra|do *a* trained. **~miento** *m* training. **~r** *vt* train. □ **~rse** *vpr* practise

adinerado *a* wealthy

adiós *int* goodbye!; (al cruzarse con alguien) hello!

adit|amento *m* addition; (accesorio) accessory. **~ivo** *m* additive

adivin|anza *f* riddle. **~ar** *vt* foretell; (acertar) guess. **~o** *m* fortuneteller

adjetivo *a* adjectival. ● *m* adjective

adjudica|ción *f* award. **~r** [7] *vt* award. □ **~rse** *vpr* appropriate. **~tario** *m* winner of an award

adjunt|ar *vt* enclose. **~o** *a* enclosed; (auxiliar) assistant. ● *m* assistant

administra|ción *f* administration; (gestión) management. **~dor** *m* administrator; (gerente) manager. **~dora** *f* administrator; manageress. **~r** *vt* administer. **~tivo** *a* administrative

admira|ble *a* admirable. **~ción** *f* admiration. **~dor** *m* admirer. **~r** *vt* admire; (sorprender) amaze. □ **~rse** *vpr* be amazed

admi|sibilidad *f* admissibility. **~sible** *a* acceptable. **~sión** *f* admission; (aceptación) acceptance. **~tir** *vt* admit; (aceptar) accept

adobar *vt* (Culin) pickle; (condimentar) marinade

adobe *m* sun-dried brick

adobo *m* pickle; (condimento) marinade

adoctrinar *vt* indoctrinate

adolecer [11] *vi*. **~ de** suffer from

adolescen|cia *f* adolescence. **~te** *a* adolescent. ● *m* & *f* teenager, adolescent

adonde *adv* where

adónde *adv* where?

adop|ción *f* adoption. **~tar** *vt* adopt. **~tivo** *a* adoptive; <*hijo*> adopted; <*patria*> of adoption

adoqu|ín *m* paving stone; (imbécil) idiot. **~inado** *m* paving. **~inar** *vt* pave

adora|ción *f* adoration. **~r** *vt* adore

adormec|er [11] *vt* send to sleep; (fig, calmar) calm, soothe. □ **~erse** *vpr* fall asleep; <*un miembro*> go to sleep. **~ido** *a* sleepy; <*un miembro*> numb

adormilarse *vpr* doze

adorn|ar *vt* adorn (**con, de** with). **~o** *m* decoration

adosar *vt* lean (**a** against); (Mex, adjuntar) to enclose

adquiri|r [4] *vt* acquire; (comprar) purchase. **~sición** *f* acquisition; (compra) purchase. **~sitivo** *a* purchasing

adrede *adv* on purpose

adrenalina *f* adrenalin

aduan|a *f* customs. **~ero** *a* customs. ● *m* customs officer

aducir [47] *vt* allege

adueñarse *vpr* take possession

adul|ación *f* flattery. **~ador** *a* flattering. ● *m* flatterer. **~ar** *vt* flatter

ad|ulterar *vt* adulterate. **~últero** *a* adulterous. **~ulterio** *m* adultery

adulto *a* & *m* adult, grown-up

advenedizo *a* & *m* upstart

advenimiento *m* advent, arrival; (subida al trono) accession

adverbio *m* adverb

advers|ario *m* adversary. **~idad** *f* adversity. **~o** *a* adverse, unfavourable

advert|encia *f* warning. **~ir** [4] *vt* warn; (notar) notice

adviento *m* Advent

adyacente *a* adjacent

aéreo *a* air; <*foto*> aerial; <*ferrocarril*> overhead

aeróbico *a* aerobic

aerodeslizador *m* hovercraft

aero|lito *m* meteorite. **~moza** *f* (LAm) flight attendant. **~puerto** *m* airport. **~sol** *m* aerosol

afab|ilidad *f* affability. **~le** *a* affable

afamado *a* famous

af|án *m* hard work; (deseo) desire. **~nador** *m* (Mex) cleaner. **~anar** *vt* ⊠ pinch [I]. □ **~anarse** *vpr* strive (**en, por** to)

afear *vt* disfigure, make ugly; (censurar) censure

afecta|ción *f* affectation. **~do** *a* affected. **~r** *vt* affect

afect|ivo *a* sensitive. **~o** *m* (cariño) affection. ● *a*. **~o a** attached to. **~uoso** *a* affectionate. **con un ~uoso saludo** (en cartas) with kind regards. **suyo ~ísimo** (en cartas) yours sincerely

afeita|do *m* shave. **~dora** *f* electric razor. **~r** *vt* shave. □ **~rse** *vpr* shave, have a shave

afeminado *a* effeminate. ● *m* effeminate person

aferrar *vt* grasp. □ **~se** *vpr* to cling (**a** to)

afianza|miento *m* (refuerzo) strengthening; (garantía) guarantee. □ **~rse** [10] *vpr* become established

afiche *m* (LAm) poster

afici|ón *f* liking; (conjunto de aficionados) fans. **por ~ón** as a hobby. **~onado** *a* keen (**a** on), fond (**a** of). ● *m* fan. **~onar** *vt* make fond. □ **~onarse** *vpr* take a liking to

afila|do *a* sharp. **~dor** *m* knife-grinder. **~r** *vt* sharpen

afilia|ción *f* affiliation. **~do** *a* affiliated. □ **~rse** *vpr* become a member (**a** of)

afín *a* similar; (contiguo) adjacent; <*personas*> related

afina|ción *f* (Auto, Mus) tuning. **~do** *a* (Mus) in tune. **~dor** *m* tuner. **~r** *vt* (afilar) sharpen; (Auto, Mus) tune. □ **~rse** *vpr* become thinner

afincarse [7] *vpr* settle

afinidad *f* affinity; (parentesco) relationship by marriage

afirma|ción *f* affirmation. **~r** *vt* make firm; (asentir) affirm. □ **~rse** *vpr* steady o.s. **~tivo** *a* affirmative

aflicción *f* affliction

afligi|do *a* distressed. **~r** [14] *vt* distress. □ **~rse** *vpr* distress o.s.

aflojar *vt* loosen; (relajar) ease. ● *vi* let up. □ **~se** *vpr* loosen

aflu|encia *f* flow. **~ente** *a* flowing. ● *m* tributary. **~ir** [17] *vi* flow (**a** into)

afónico *a* hoarse

aforismo *m* aphorism

aforo *m* capacity

afortunado *a* fortunate, lucky

afrancesado *a* Frenchified

afrenta *f* insult; (vergüenza) disgrace

África *f* Africa. **~ del Sur** South Africa

africano *a* & *m* African

afrodisíaco, afrodisiaco *a* & *m* aphrodisiac

afrontar *vt* bring face to face; (enfrentar) face, confront

afuera *adv* out(side) **¡~!** out of the way! **~ de** (LAm) outside. **~s** *fpl* outskirts

agachar *vt* lower. □ **~se** *vpr* bend over

agalla *f* (de los peces) gill. **~s** *fpl* (fig) guts

agarradera *f* (LAm) handle

agarr|ado *a* (fig, [I]) mean. **~ar** *vt* grasp; (esp LAm) take; (LAm, pillar) catch. □ **~arse** *vpr* hold on; ([I], reñirse) have a fight. **~ón** *m* tug; (LAm [I], riña) row

agarrotar *vt* tie tightly; <*el frío*> stiffen; garotte <*un reo*>. □ **~se** *vpr* go stiff; (Auto) seize up

agasaj|ado *m* guest of honour. **~ar** *vt* look after well. **~o** *m* good treatment

agazaparse *vpr* crouch

agencia *f* agency. **~ de viajes** travel agency. **~ inmobiliaria** estate agency (Brit), real estate agency (Amer). □ **~rse** *vpr* find (out) for o.s.

agenda *f* diary (Brit), appointment book (Amer); (programa) agenda

agente *m* agent; (de policía) policeman. ● *f* agent; (de policía) policewoman. **~ de aduanas** customs officer. **~ de bolsa** stockbroker

ágil *a* agile

agili|dad *f* agility. **~zación** *f* speeding up. **~zar** *vt* speed up

agita|ción *f* waving; (de un líquido) stirring; (intranquilidad) agitation. **~do** *a* <*el mar*> rough; (fig) agitated. **~dor** *m* (Pol) agitator

agitar *vt* wave; shake <*botellas etc*>; stir <*líquidos*>; (fig) stir up. □ **~se** *vpr* wave; <*el mar*> get rough; (fig) get excited

aglomera|ción *f* agglomeration; (de tráfico) traffic jam. **~r** *vt* amass. □ **~rse** *vpr* form a crowd

agnóstico *a* & *m* agnostic

agobi|ante *a* <*trabajo*> exhausting; <*calor*> oppressive. **~ar** *vt* weigh down; (fig, abrumar) overwhelm. **~o** *m* weight; (cansancio) exhaustion; (opresión) oppression

agolparse *vpr* crowd together

agon|ía *f* death throes; (fig) agony. **~izante** *a* dying; <*luz*> failing. **~izar** [10] *vi* be dying

agosto *m* August. **hacer su ~** feather one's nest

agota|do *a* exhausted; (todo vendido) sold out; <*libro*> out of print. **~dor** *a* exhausting. **~miento** *m* exhaustion. **~r** *vt* exhaust. □ **~rse** *vpr* be exhausted; <*existencias*> sell out; <*libro*> go out of print

agracia|do *a* attractive; (que tiene suerte) lucky. **~r** *vt* make attractive

agrada|ble *a* pleasant, nice. **~r** *vt/i* please. **esto me ~** I like this

agradec|er [11] *vt* thank <*persona*>; be grateful for <*cosa*>. **~ido** *a* grateful. **¡muy ~ido!** thanks a lot! **~imiento** *m* gratitude

agrado *m* pleasure; (amabilidad) friendliness

agrandar *vt* enlarge; (fig) exaggerate. □ **~se** *vpr* get bigger

agrario *a* agrarian, land; <*política*> agricultural

agrava|nte *a* aggravating. ● *f* additional problem. **~r** *vt* aggravate; (aumentar el peso) make heavier. □ **~rse** *vpr* get worse

agravi|ar *vt* offend; (perjudicar) wrong. **~o** *m* offence

agredir [24] *vt* attack. **~ de palabra** insult

agrega|do *m* aggregate; (diplomático) attaché. **~r** [12] *vt* add; appoint <*persona*>. □ **~se** *vpr* to join

agres|ión *f* aggression; (ataque) attack. **~ividad** *f* aggressiveness. **~ivo** *a* aggressive. **~or** *m* aggressor

agreste *a* country; <*terreno*> rough

agriar *regular, o raramente* [20] *vt* sour. □ **~se** *vpr* turn sour; (fig) become embittered

agr|ícola *a* agricultural. **~icultor** *m* farmer. **~icultura** *f* agriculture, farming

agridulce *a* bitter-sweet; (Culin) sweet-and-sour

agrietar *vt* crack. □ **~se** *vpr* crack; <*piel*> chap

agrio *a* sour. **~s** *mpl* citrus fruits

agro|nomía *f* agronomy. **~pecuario** *a* farming

agrupa|ción *f* group; (acción) grouping. **~r** *vt* group. □ **~rse** *vpr* form a group

agruras *fpl* (Mex) heartburn

agua *f* water; (lluvia) rain; (marea) tide; (vertiente del tejado) slope. **~ abajo** downstream. **~ arriba** upstream. **~ bendita** holy water. **~ corriente** running water. **~ de colonia** eau-de-cologne. **~ dulce** fresh water. **~ mineral con gas** fizzy mineral water. **~ mineral sin gas**

still mineral water. ~ **potable** drinking water. ~ **salada** salt water. **hacer** ~ (Naut) leak. **se me hizo** ~ **la boca** (LAm) it made my mouth water

aguacate *m* avocado pear; (árbol) avocado pear tree

aguacero *m* downpour, heavy shower

aguado *a* watery; (Mex, aburrido) boring

agua|fiestas *m & f invar* spoilsport, wet blanket. **~mala** *f* (Mex), **~mar** *m* jellyfish. **~marina** *f* aquamarine

aguant|ar *vt* put up with, bear; (sostener) support. ● *vi* hold out. □ **~arse** *vpr* restrain o.s. **~e** *m* patience; (resistencia) endurance

aguar [15] *vt* water down

aguardar *vt* wait for. ● *vi* wait

agua|rdiente *m* (cheap) brandy. **~rrás** *m* turpentine, turps [I]

agud|eza *f* sharpness; (fig, perspicacia) insight; (fig, ingenio) wit. **~izar** [10] *vt* sharpen. □ **~izarse** *vpr* *<enfermedad>* get worse. **~o** *a* sharp; *<ángulo, enfermedad>* acute; *<voz>* high-pitched

agüero *m* omen. **ser de mal** ~ be a bad omen

aguijón *m* sting; (vara) goad

águila *f* eagle; (persona perspicaz) astute person; (Mex, de moneda) heads. **¿~ o sol?** heads or tails?

aguileño *a* aquiline

aguinaldo *m* Christmas box; (LAm, paga) Christmas bonus

aguja *f* needle; (del reloj) hand; (Arquit) steeple. **~s** *fpl* (Rail) points

agujer|ear *vt* make holes in. **~o** *m* hole

agujetas *fpl* stiffness; (Mex, de zapatos) shoe laces. **tener** ~ be stiff

aguzado *a* sharp

ah *int* ah!, oh!

ahí *adv* there. ~ **nomás** (LAm) just there. **de** ~ **que** that is why. **por** ~ that way; (aproximadamente) thereabouts

ahija|da *f* god-daughter, godchild. **~do** *m* godson, godchild. **~dos** *mpl* godchildren

ahínco *m* enthusiasm; (empeño) insistence

ahog|ado *a* (en el agua) drowned; (asfixiado) suffocated. **~ar** [12] *vt* (en el agua) drown; (asfixiar) suffocate; put out *<fuego>*. □ **~arse** *vpr* (en el agua) drown; (asfixiarse) suffocate. **~o** *m* breathlessness; (fig, angustia) distress

ahondar *vt* deepen. ● *vi* go deep. ~ **en** (fig) examine in depth. □ **~se** *vpr* get deeper

ahora *adv* now; (hace muy poco) just now; (dentro de poco) very soon. ~ **bien** however. ~ **mismo** right now. **de** ~ **en adelante** from now on, in future. **por** ~ for the time being

ahorcar [7] *vt* hang. □ **~se** *vpr* hang o.s.

ahorita *adv* (esp LAm [I]) now. ~ **mismo** right now

ahorr|ador *a* thrifty. **~ar** *vt* save. □ **~arse** *vpr* save o.s. **~o** *m* saving. **~os** *mpl* savings

ahuecar [7] *vt* hollow; fluff up *<colchón>*; deepen *<la voz>*

ahuizote *m* (Mex) scourge

ahuma|do *a* (Culin) smoked; (de colores) smoky. **~r** *vt* (Culin) smoke; (llenar de humo) fill with smoke. ● *vi* smoke. □ **~rse** *vpr* become smoky; *<comida>* acquire a smoky taste

ahuyentar *vt* drive away; banish *<pensamientos etc>*

aimará *a* & *m* Aymara. ● *m* & *f* Aymara Indian

airado *a* annoyed

aire *m* air; (viento) breeze; (corriente) draught; (aspecto) appearance; (Mus) tune, air. ~ **acondicionado** air-conditioning. **al ~ libre** outdoors. **darse ~s** give o.s. airs. **~ar** *vt* air; (ventilar) ventilate; (fig, publicar) make public. □ **~arse** *vpr*. **salir para ~arse** go out for some fresh air

airoso *a* graceful; (exitoso) successful

aisla|do *a* isolated; (Elec) insulated. **~dor** *a* (Elec) insulating. **~nte** *a* insulating. **~r** [23] *vt* isolate; (Elec) insulate

ajar *vt* crumple; (estropear) spoil

ajedre|cista *m* & *f* chess-player. **~z** *m* chess

ajeno *a* (de otro) someone else's; (de otros) other people's; (extraño) alien

ajetre|ado *a* hectic, busy. **~o** *m* bustle

ají *m* (LAm) chilli; (salsa) chilli sauce

aj|illo *m* garlic. **al ~illo** cooked with garlic. **~o** *m* garlic. **~onjolí** *m* sesame

ajuar *m* furnishings; (de novia) trousseau; (de bebé) layette

ajust|ado *a* right; <*vestido*> tight. **~ar** *vt* fit; (adaptar) adapt; (acordar) agree; settle <*una cuenta*>; (apretar) tighten. ● *vi* fit. □ **~arse** *vpr* fit; (adaptarse) adapt o.s.; (acordarse) come to an agreement. **~e** *m* fitting; (adaptación) adjustment; (acuerdo) agreement; (de una cuenta) settlement

al = **a** + **el**

ala *f* wing; (de sombrero) brim. ● *m* & *f* (deportes) winger

alaba|nza *f* praise. **~r** *vt* praise

alacena *f* cupboard (Brit), closet (Amer)

alacrán *m* scorpion

alambr|ada *f* wire fence. **~ado** *m* (LAm) wire fence. **~e** *m* wire. **~e de púas** barbed wire

alameda *f* avenue; (plantío de álamos) poplar grove

álamo *m* poplar. ~ **temblón** aspen

alarde *m* show. **hacer ~ de** boast of

alarga|do *a* long. **~dor** *m* extension. **~r** [12] *vt* lengthen; stretch out <*mano etc*>; (dar) give, pass. □ **~rse** *vpr* get longer

alarido *m* shriek

alarm|a *f* alarm. **~ante** *a* alarming. **~ar** *vt* alarm, frighten. □ **~arse** *vpr* be alarmed. **~ista** *m* & *f* alarmist

alba *f* dawn

albacea *m* & *f* executor

albahaca *f* basil

albanés *a* & *m* Albanian

Albania *f* Albania

albañil *m* builder; (que coloca ladrillos) bricklayer

albarán *m* delivery note

albaricoque *m* apricot. **~ro** *m* apricot tree

albedrío *m* will. **libre ~** free will

alberca *f* tank, reservoir; (Mex, piscina) swimming pool

alberg|ar [12] *vt* (alojar) put up; <*vivienda*> house; (dar refugio) shelter. □ **~arse** *vpr* stay; (refugiarse) shelter. **~ue** *m* accommodation; (refugio) shelter. **~ue de juventud** youth hostel

albino *a* & *m* albino

albóndiga *f* meatball, rissole

albornoz *m* bathrobe

alborot|ado *a* excited; (aturdido) hasty. **~ador** *a* rowdy. ● *m* trouble-maker. **~ar** *vt* disturb, upset. ● *vi* make a racket. □ **~arse** *vpr* get excited; *<el mar>* get rough. **~o** *m* row, uproar

álbum *m* (*pl* **~es** *o* **~s**) album

alcachofa *f* artichoke

alcald|e *m* mayor. **~esa** *f* mayoress. **~ía** *f* mayoralty; (oficina) mayor's office

alcance *m* reach; (de arma, telescopio etc) range; (déficit) deficit

alcancía *f* money-box; (LAm, de niño) piggy bank

alcantarilla *f* sewer; (boca) drain

alcanzar [10] *vt* (llegar a) catch up; (coger) reach; catch *<un autobús>*; *<bala etc>* strike, hit. ● *vi* reach; (ser suficiente) be enough. **~ a** manage

alcaparra *f* caper

alcázar *m* fortress

alcoba *f* bedroom

alcoh|ol *m* alcohol. **~ol desnaturalizado** methylated spirits, meths **~ólico** *a* & *m* alcoholic. **~olímetro** *m* Breathalyser. **~olismo** *m* alcoholism

alcornoque *m* cork-oak; (persona torpe) idiot

aldaba *f* door-knocker

aldea *f* village. **~no** *a* village. ● *m* villager

alea|ción *f* alloy. **~r** *vt* alloy

aleatorio *a* uncertain

aleccionar *vt* instruct

aledaños *mpl* outskirts

alega|ción *f* allegation; (LAm, disputa) argument. **~r** [12] *vt* claim; (Jurid) plead. ● *vi* (LAm) argue. **~ta** *f* (Mex) argument. **~to** *m* plea

alegoría *f* allegory

alegr|ar *vt* make happy; (avivar) brighten up. □ **~arse** *vpr* be happy; (emborracharse) get merry. **~e** *a* happy; (achispado) merry, tight. **~ía** *f* happiness

aleja|do *a* distant. **~miento** *m* removal; (entre personas) estrangement; (distancia) distance. **~r** *vt* remove; (ahuyentar) get rid of; (fig, apartar) separate. □ **~rse** *vpr* move away

alemán *a* & *m* German

Alemania *f* Germany. **~ Occidental** (historia) West Germany. **~ Oriental** (historia) East Germany

alenta|dor *a* encouraging. **~r** [1] *vt* encourage. ● *vi* breathe

alerce *m* larch

al|ergia *f* allergy. **~érgico** *a* allergic

alero *m* (del tejado) eaves

alerta *a* alert. ¡**~**! look out! **estar ~** be alert; (en guardia) be on the alert. **~r** *vt* alert

aleta *f* wing; (de pez) fin

aletarga|do *a* lethargic. **~r** [12] *vt* make lethargic. □ **~rse** *vpr* become lethargic

alet|azo *m* (de un ave) flap of the wings; (de un pez) flick of the fin. **~ear** *vi* flap its wings, flutter

alevosía *f* treachery

alfab|ético *a* alphabetical. **~etizar** [10] *vt* alphabetize; teach to read and write. **~eto** *m* alphabet. **~eto Morse** Morse code

alfalfa *f* alfalfa

alfarería *m* pottery. **~ero** *m* potter

alféizar *m* (window)sill

alférez *m* second lieutenant

alfil *m* (en ajedrez) bishop

alfile|r *m* pin. **~tero** *m* pincushion; (estuche) pin-case

alfombr|a *f* (grande) carpet; (pequeña) rug, mat. **~ado** *a* (LAm) carpeted. **~ar** *vt* carpet. **~illa** *f* rug, mat; (Med) type of measles

alforja *f* saddle-bag

algarabía *f* hubbub

algas *fpl* seaweed

álgebra *f* algebra

álgido *a* (fig) decisive

algo *pron* something; (en frases interrogativas, condicionales) anything. ● *adv* rather. **¿~ más?** anything else? **¿quieres tomar ~?** would you like a drink?; (de comer) would you like something to eat?

algod|ón *m* cotton. **~ón de azúcar** candy floss (Brit), cotton candy (Amer). **~ón hidrófilo** cotton wool. **~onero** *a* cotton. ● *m* cotton plant

alguacil *m* bailiff

alguien *pron* someone, somebody; (en frases interrogativas, condicionales) anyone, anybody

alguno *a* (delante de nombres masculinos en singular **algún**) some; (en frases interrogativas, condicionales) any; (pospuesto al nombre en frases negativas) at all. **no tiene idea alguna** he hasn't any idea at all. **alguna que otra vez** from time to time. **algunas veces, alguna vez** sometimes. ● *pron* one; (en plural) some; (alguien) someone

alhaja *f* piece of jewellery; (fig) treasure. **~s** *fpl* jewellery

alharaca *f* fuss

alhelí *m* wallflower

alia|do *a* allied. ● *m* ally. **~nza** *f* alliance; (anillo) wedding ring. **~r** [20] *vt* combine. □ **~rse** *vpr* be combined; (formar una alianza) form an alliance

alias *adv* & *m* alias

alicaído *a* (fig, débil) weak; (fig, abatido) depressed

alicates *mpl* pliers

aliciente *m* incentive; (de un lugar) attraction

alienado *a* mentally ill

aliento *m* breath; (ánimo) courage

aligerar *vt* make lighter; (aliviar) alleviate, ease; (apresurar) quicken

alijo *m* (de contrabando) consignment

alimaña *f* pest. **~s** *fpl* vermin

aliment|ación *f* diet; (acción) feeding. **~ar** *vt* feed; (nutrir) nourish. ● *vi* be nourishing. □ **~arse** *vpr* feed (**con, de** on). **~icio** *a* nourishing. **productos** *mpl* **~icios** foodstuffs. **~o** *m* food. **~os** *mpl* (Jurid) alimony

alinea|ción *f* alignment; (en deportes) line-up. **~r** *vt* align, line up

aliñ|ar *vt* (Culin) season; dress <*ensalada*>. **~o** *m* seasoning; (para ensalada) dressing

alioli *m* garlic mayonnaise

alisar *vt* smooth

alistar *vt* put on a list; (Mil) enlist. □ **~se** *vpr* enrol; (Mil) enlist; (LAm, prepararse) get ready

alivi|ar *vt* lighten; relieve <*dolor, etc*>; (⊠, hurtar) steal, pinch Ⅰ. □ **~arse** *vpr* <*dolor*> diminish; <*persona*> get better. **~o** *m* relief

aljibe *m* tank

allá *adv* (over) there. **¡~ él!** that's his business. **~ fuera** out there. **~ por 1970** back in 1970. **el más ~** the beyond. **más ~** further on. **más ~ de** beyond. **por ~** that way

allana|miento *m*. **~miento (de morada)** breaking and entering;

(LAm, por la autoridad) raid. **~r** *vt* level; remove <*obstáculos*>; (fig) iron out <*dificultades etc*>; break into <*una casa*>; (LAm, por la autoridad) raid

allega|do *a* close. ● *m* close friend; (pariente) close relative. **~r** [12] *vt* collect

allí *adv* there; (tiempo) then. **~ fuera** out there. **por ~** that way

alma *f* soul; (habitante) inhabitant

almac|én *m* warehouse; (LAm, tienda) grocer's shop; (de un arma) magazine. **~enes** *mpl* department store. **~enaje** *m* storage; (derechos) storage charges. **~enar** *vt* store; stock up with <*provisiones*>

almanaque *m* almanac

almeja *f* clam

almendr|a *f* almond. **~ado** *a* almond-shaped. **~o** *m* almond tree

alm|íbar *m* syrup. **~ibarar** *vt* cover in syrup

almid|ón *m* starch. **~onado** *a* starched; (fig, estirado) starchy

almirante *m* admiral

almizcle *m* musk. **~ra** *f* muskrat

almohad|a *f* pillow. **consultar con la ~a** sleep on it. **~illa** *f* small cushion. **~ón** *m* large pillow, bolster

almorranas *fpl* haemorrhoids, piles

alm|orzar [2 & 10] *vt* (a mediodía) have for lunch; (desayunar) have for breakfast. ● *vi* (a mediodía) have lunch; (desayunar) have breakfast. **~uerzo** *m* (a mediodía) lunch; (desayuno) breakfast

alocado *a* scatter-brained

aloja|miento *m* accommodation. **~r** *vt* put up. □ **~rse** *vpr* stay

alondra *f* lark

alpaca *f* alpaca

alpargata *f* canvas shoe, espadrille

alpin|ismo *m* mountaineering, climbing. **~ista** *m & f* mountaineer, climber. **~o** *a* Alpine

alpiste *m* birdseed

alquil|ar *vt* (tomar en alquiler) hire <*vehículo*>, rent <*piso, casa*>; (dar en alquiler) hire (out) <*vehículo*>, rent (out) <*piso, casa*>. **se alquila** to let (Brit), for rent (Amer.) **~er** *m* (acción — de alquilar un piso etc) renting; (— de alquilar un vehículo) hiring; (precio — por el que se alquila un piso etc) rent; (— por el que se alquila un vehículo) hire charge. **de ~er** for hire

alquimi|a *f* alchemy. **~sta** *m* alchemist

alquitrán *m* tar

alrededor *adv* around. **~ de** around; (con números) about. **~es** *mpl* surroundings; (de una ciudad) outskirts

alta *f* discharge

altaner|ía *f* (arrogancia) arrogance. **~o** *a* arrogant, haughty

altar *m* altar

altavoz *m* loudspeaker

altera|ble *a* changeable. **~ción** *f* change, alteration. **~r** *vt* change, alter; (perturbar) disturb; (enfadar) anger, irritate. □ **~rse** *vpr* change, alter; (agitarse) get upset; (enfadarse) get angry; <*comida*> go off

altercado *m* argument

altern|ar *vt/i* alternate. □ **~arse** *vpr* take turns. **~ativa** *f* alternative. **~ativo** *a* alternating. **~o** *a* alternate; (Elec) alternating

Alteza *f* (título) Highness

altibajos *mpl* (de terreno) unevenness; (fig) ups and downs

altiplanicie *f*, **altiplano** *m* high plateau

altisonante *a* pompous

altitud *f* altitude

altiv|ez *f* arrogance. **~o** *a* arrogant

alto *a* high; <*persona, edificio*> tall; <*voz*> loud; (fig, elevado) lofty; (Mus) <*nota*> high(-pitched); (Mus) <*voz, instrumento*> alto; <*horas*> early. ● *adv* high; (de sonidos) loud(ly). ● *m* height; (de un edificio) top floor; (viola) viola; (voz) alto; (parada) stop. ● *int* halt!, stop! **en lo ~ de** on the top of. **tiene 3 metros de ~** it is 3 metres high

altoparlante *m* (esp LAm) loudspeaker

altruis|mo *m* altruism. **~ta** *a* altruistic. ● *m & f* altruist

altura *f* height; (Aviac, Geog) altitude; (de agua) depth; (fig, cielo) sky. **a estas ~s** at this stage. **tiene 3 metros de ~** it is 3 metres high

alubia *f* (haricot) bean

alucinación *f* hallucination

alud *m* avalanche

aludi|do *a* in question. **darse por ~do** take it personally. **no darse por ~do** turn a deaf ear. **~r** *vi* mention

alumbra|do *a* lit. ● *m* lighting. **~miento** *m* lighting; (parto) childbirth. **~r** *vt* light

aluminio *m* aluminium (Brit), aluminum (Amer)

alumno *m* pupil; (Univ) student

aluniza|je *m* landing on the moon. **~r** [10] *vi* land on the moon

alusi|ón *f* allusion. **~vo** *a* allusive

alza *f* rise. **~da** *f* (de caballo) height; (Jurid) appeal. **~do** *a* raised; (Mex, soberbio) vain; <*precio*> fixed. **~miento** *m* (Pol) uprising. **~r** [10] *vt* raise, lift (up); raise <*precios*>. □ **~rse** *vpr* (Pol) rise up

ama *f* lady of the house. **~ de casa** housewife. **~ de cría** wet-nurse. **~ de llaves** housekeeper

amab|ilidad *f* kindness. **~le** *a* kind; (simpático) nice

amaestra|do *a* trained. **~r** *vt* train

amag|ar [12] *vt* (mostrar intención de) make as if to; (Mex, amenazar) threaten. ● *vi* threaten; <*algo bueno*> be in the offing. **~o** *m* threat; (señal) sign; (Med) symptom

amainar *vi* let up

amalgama *f* amalgam. **~r** *vt* amalgamate

amamantar *vt/i* breast-feed; <*animal*> to suckle

amanecer *m* dawn. ● *vi* dawn; <*persona*> wake up. **al ~** at dawn, at daybreak. □ **~se** *vpr* (Mex) stay up all night

amanera|do *a* affected. □ **~rse** *vpr* become affected

amansar *vt* tame; break in <*un caballo*>; soothe <*dolor etc*>. □ **~se** *vpr* calm down

amante *a* fond. ● *m & f* lover

amapola *f* poppy

amar *vt* love

amara|je *m* landing on water; (de astronave) splash-down. **~r** *vi* land on water; <*astronave*> splash down

amarg|ado *a* embittered. **~ar** [12] *vt* make bitter; embitter <*persona*>. □ **~arse** *vpr* become bitter. **~o** *a* bitter. **~ura** *f* bitterness

amariconado *a* 🄸 effeminate

amarill|ento *a* yellowish; <*tez*> sallow. **~o** *a & m* yellow

amarra|s *fpl*. **soltar las ~s** cast off. **~do** *a* (LAm) mean. **~r** *vt* moor;

(esp LAm, atar) tie. □ **~rse** *vpr* LAm tie up

amas|ar *vt* knead; (acumular) to amass. **~ijo** *m* dough; (acción) kneading; (fig, ▣, mezcla) hotchpotch

amate *m* (Mex) fig tree

amateur *a & m & f* amateur

amazona *f* Amazon; (jinete) horsewoman

ámbar *m* amber

ambici|ón *f* ambition. **~onar** *vt* aspire to. **~onar ser** have an ambition to be. **~oso** *a* ambitious. ● *m* ambitious person

ambidextro *a* ambidextrous. ● *m* ambidextrous person

ambient|ar *vt* give an atmosphere to. □ **~arse** *vpr* adapt o.s. **~e** *m* atmosphere; (entorno) environment

ambig|üedad *f* ambiguity. **~uo** *a* ambiguous

ámbito *m* sphere; (alcance) scope

ambos *a & pron* both

ambulancia *f* ambulance

ambulante *a* travelling

ambulatorio *m* out-patients' department

amedrentar *vt* frighten, scare. □ **~se** *vpr* be frightened

amén *m* amen. ● *int* amen! **en un decir ~** in an instant

amenaza *f* threat. **~r** [10] *vt* threaten

amen|idad *f* pleasantness. **~izar** [10] *vt* brighten up. **~o** *a* pleasant

América *f* America. **~ Central** Central America. **~ del Norte** North America. **~ del Sur** South America. **~ Latina** Latin America

american|a *f* jacket. **~ismo** *m* Americanism. **~o** *a* American

amerita|do *a* (LAm) meritorious. **~r** *vt* (LAm) deserve

amerizaje *m* ⇒AMARAJE

ametralla|dora *f* machine-gun. **~r** *vt* machine-gun

amianto *m* asbestos

amig|a *f* friend; (novia) girl-friend; (amante) lover. **~able** *a* friendly. **~ablemente** *adv* amicably

am|ígdala *f* tonsil. **~igdalitis** *f* tonsillitis

amigo *a* friendly. ● *m* friend; (novio) boyfriend; (amante) lover. **ser ~ de** be fond of. **ser muy ~s** be close friends

amilanar *vt* daunt. □ **~se** *vpr* be daunted

aminorar *vt* lessen; reduce *<velocidad>*

amist|ad *f* friendship. **~ades** *fpl* friends. **~oso** *a* friendly

amn|esia *f* amnesia. **~ésico** *a* amnesiac

amnist|ía *f* amnesty. **~iar** [20] *vt* grant an amnesty to

amo *m* master; (dueño) owner

amodorrarse *vpr* feel sleepy

amoldar *vt* mould; (adaptar) adapt; (acomodar) fit. □ **~se** *vpr* adapt

amonestar *vt* rebuke, reprimand; (anunciar la boda) publish the banns of

amoniaco, **amoníaco** *m* ammonia

amontonar *vt* pile up; (fig, acumular) accumulate. □ **~se** *vpr* pile up; *<gente>* crowd together

amor *m* love. **~es** *mpl* (relaciones amorosas) love affairs. **~ propio** pride. **con mil ~es, de mil ~es** with (the greatest of) pleasure. **hacer el ~** make love. **por (el) ~ de Dios** for God's sake

amoratado *a* purple; (de frío) blue

amordazar [10] *vt* gag; (fig) silence

amorfo *a* amorphous, shapeless

amor|ío *m* affair. **~oso** *a* loving; <*cartas*> love; (LAm, encantador) cute

amortajar *vt* shroud

amortigua|dor *a* deadening. ● *m* (Auto) shock absorber. **~r** [15] *vt* deaden <*ruido*>; dim <*luz*>; cushion <*golpe*>; tone down <*color*>

amortiza|ble *a* redeemable. **~ción** *f* (de una deuda) repayment; (de bono etc) redemption. **~r** [10] *vt* repay <*una deuda*>

amotinar *vt* incite to riot. □ **~se** *vpr* rebel; (Mil) mutiny

ampar|ar *vt* help; (proteger) protect. □ **~arse** *vpr* seek protection; (de la lluvia) shelter. **~o** *m* protection; (de la lluvia) shelter. **al ~o de** under the protection of

amperio *m* ampere, amp

amplia|ción *f* extension; (photo) enlargement. **~r** [20] *vt* enlarge, extend; (photo) enlarge

amplifica|ción *f* amplification. **~dor** *m* amplifier. **~r** [7] amplify

ampli|o *a* wide; (espacioso) spacious; <*ropa*> loose-fitting. **~tud** *f* extent; (espaciosidad) spaciousness; (espacio) space

ampolla *f* (Med) blister; (de medicamento) ampoule, phial

ampuloso *a* pompous

amputar *vt* amputate; (fig) delete

amueblar *vt* furnish

amuleto *m* charm, amulet

amuralla|do *a* walled. **~r** *vt* build a wall around

anacr|ónico *a* anachronistic. **~onismo** *m* anachronism

anales *mpl* annals

analfabet|ismo *m* illiteracy. **~o** *a* & *m* illiterate

analgésico *a* analgesic. ● *m* painkiller

an|álisis *m invar* analysis. **~álisis de sangre** blood test. **~alista** *m* & *f* analyst. **~alítico** *a* analytical. **~alizar** [10] *vt* analyze

an|alogía *f* analogy. **~álogo** *a* analogous

anaranjado *a* orangey

an|arquía *f* anarchy. **~árquico** *a* anarchic. **~arquismo** *m* anarchism. **~arquista** *a* anarchistic. ● *m* & *f* anarchist

anat|omía *f* anatomy. **~ómico** *a* anatomical

anca *f* haunch; (parte superior) rump; ([I], nalgas) bottom. **en ~s** (LAm) on the crupper

ancestro *m* ancestor

ancho *a* wide; <*ropa*> loose-fitting; (fig) relieved; (demasiado grande) too big; (ufano) smug. ● *m* width; (Rail) gauge. **a mis anchas, a sus anchas** *etc* comfortable, relaxed. **tiene 3 metros de ~** it is 3 metres wide

anchoa *f* anchovy

anchura *f* width; (medida) measurement

ancian|o *a* elderly, old. ● *m* elderly man, old man. **~a** *f* elderly woman, old woman. **los ~os** old people

ancla *f* anchor. **echar ~s** drop anchor. **levar ~s** weigh anchor. **~r** *vi* anchor

andad|eras *fpl* (Mex) baby-walker. **~or** *m* baby-walker

Andalucía *f* Andalusia

andaluz *a* & *m* Andalusian

andamio *m* platform. **~s** *mpl* scaffolding

and|anzas *fpl* adventures. **~ar** [25] *vt* (recorrer) cover, go. ● *vi* walk; <*máquina*> go, work; (estar) be; (moverse) move. **~ar a caballo** (LAm) ride a horse. **~ar en bicicleta** (LAm) ride a bicycle. **¡anda!** go on!, come on! **~ar por** be about. ◻ **~arse** *vpr* (LAm, en imperativo) **¡ándate!** go away!. ● *m* walk. **~ariego** *a* fond of walking

andén *m* platform

Andes *mpl.* **los ~** the Andes

andin|o *a* Andean. **~ismo** *m* (LAm) mountaineering, climbing. **~ista** *m & f* (LAm) mountaineer, climber

andrajo *m* rag. **~so** *a* ragged

anduve *vb* ⇨ANDAR

anécdota *f* anecdote

anecdótico *a* anecdotal

anegar [12] *vt* flood. ◻ **~rse** *vpr* be flooded, flood

anejo *a* ⇨ANEXO

an|emia *f* anaemia. **~émico** *a* anaemic

anest|esia *f* anaesthesia; (droga) anaesthetic. **~esiar** *vt* anaesthetize. **~ésico** *a & m* anaesthetic. **~esista** *m & f* anaesthetist

anex|ar *vt* annex. **~o** *a* attached. ● *m* annexe

anfibio *a* amphibious. ● *m* amphibian

anfiteatro *m* amphitheatre; (en un teatro) upper circle

anfitri|ón *m* host. **~ona** *f* hostess

ángel *m* angel; (encanto) charm

angelical *a*, **angélico** *a* angelic

angina *f.* **~ de pecho** angina (pectoris). **tener ~s** have tonsillitis

anglicano *a & m* Anglican

angl|icismo *m* Anglicism. **~ófilo** *a & m* Anglophile. **~ohispánico** *a* Anglo-Spanish. **~osajón** *a & m* Anglo-Saxon

angosto *a* narrow

angu|ila *f* eel. **~la** *f* elver, baby eel

ángulo *m* angle; (rincón, esquina) corner; (curva) bend

angusti|a *f* anguish. **~ar** *vt* distress; (inquietar) worry. ◻ **~arse** *vpr* get distressed; (inquietarse) get worried. **~oso** *a* anguished; (que causa angustia) distressing

anhel|ar *vt* (+ *nombre*) long for; (+ *verbo*) long to. **~o** *m* (fig) yearning

anidar *vi* nest

anill|a *f* ring. **~o** *m* ring. **~o de boda** wedding ring

ánima *f* soul

anima|ción *f* (de personas) life; (de cosas) liveliness; (bullicio) bustle; (en el cine) animation. **~do** *a* lively; <*sitio etc*> busy. **~dor** *m* host. **~dora** *f* hostess; (de un equipo) cheerleader

animadversión *f* ill will

animal *a* animal; (fig, ⊡, torpe) stupid. ● *m* animal; (fig, ⊡, idiota) idiot; (fig, ⊡, bruto) brute

animar *vt* give life to; (dar ánimo) encourage; (dar vivacidad) liven up. ◻ **~se** *vpr* (decidirse) decide; (ponerse alegre) cheer up. **¿te animas a ir al cine?** do you feel like going to the cinema?

ánimo *m* soul; (mente) mind; (valor) courage; (intención) intention. **¡~!** come on!, cheer up! **dar ~s** encourage

animos|idad *f* animosity. **~o** *a* brave; (resuelto) determined

aniquilar *vt* annihilate; (acabar con) ruin

anís *m* aniseed; (licor) anisette

aniversario *m* anniversary

anoche *adv* last night, yesterday evening

anochecer [11] *vi* get dark. **anochecí en Madrid** I was in Madrid at dusk. ● *m* nightfall, dusk. **al ~** at nightfall

anodino *a* bland

an|omalía *f* anomaly. **~ómalo** *a* anomalous

an|onimato *m* anonymity. **~ónimo** *a* anonymous; <*sociedad*> limited. ● *m* (carta) anonymous letter

anormal *a* abnormal. ● *m & f* Ⓘ idiot. **~idad** *f* abnormality

anota|ción *f* (nota) note; (acción de poner notas) annotation. **~r** *vt* (poner nota) annotate; (apuntar) make a note of; (LAm) score <*un gol*>

anquilosa|miento *m* (fig) paralysis. □ **~rse** *vpr* become paralyzed

ansi|a *f* anxiety, worry; (anhelo) yearning. **~ar** [20] *vt* long for. **~edad** *f* anxiety. **~oso** *a* anxious; (deseoso) eager

antag|ónico *a* antagonistic. **~onismo** *m* antagonism. **~onista** *m & f* antagonist

antaño *adv* in days gone by

antártico *a & m* Antarctic

ante *prep* in front of, before; (frente a) in the face of; (en vista de) in view of. ● *m* elk; (piel) suede. **~anoche** *adv* the night before last. **~ayer** *adv* the day before yesterday. **~brazo** *m* forearm

antece|dente *a* previous. ● *m* antecedent. **~dentes** *mpl* history, background. **~dentes penales** criminal record. **~der** *vt* precede. **~sor** *m* predecessor; (antepasado) ancestor

antelación *f* (advance) notic
con ~ in advance

antemano *adv*. **de ~** beforehan

antena *f* antenna; (radio, TV) aeria

antenoche *adv* (LAm) the nigh before last

anteoj|eras *fpl* blinkers. **~jo** *r* telescope. **~os** *mpl* binoculars (LAm, gafas) glasses, spectacles. **~os de sol** sunglasses

ante|pasados *mpl* forebears, an cestors. **~poner** [34] *vt* put ir front (a of); (fig) put before, prefer **~proyecto** *m* preliminary sketch; (fig) blueprint

anterior *a* previous; (delantero front. **~idad** *f*. **con ~idad** previ ously. **con ~idad a** prior to

antes *adv* before; (antiguamente) in the past; (mejor) rather; (primero first. **~ de** before. **~ de ayer** the day before yesterday. **~ de que** + *subj* before. **~ de quellegue** befor he arrives. **cuanto ~, lo ~ posibl** as soon as possible

anti|aéreo *a* anti-aircraft **~biótico** *a & m* antibiotic **~ciclón** *m* anticyclone

anticip|ación *f*. **con ~ación** in advance. **con mediahora d ~ación** half an hour early. **~ad** *a* advance. **por ~ado** in advance **~ar** *vt* bring forward; advanc <*dinero*>. □ **~arse** *vpr* be early **~o** *m* (dinero) advance; (fig) fore taste

anti|conceptivo *a & m* contra ceptive. **~congelante** *m* anti freeze

anticua|do *a* old-fashioned **~rio** *m* antique dealer

anticuerpo *m* antibody

antídoto *m* antidote

anti|estético *a* ugly. **~faz** *m* mask

antig|ualla *f* old relic. **~uamente** *adv* formerly; (hace mucho tiempo) long ago. **~üedad** *f* antiquity; (objeto) antique; (en un empleo) length of service. **~uo** *a* old; *<ruinas>* ancient; *<mueble>* antique

Antillas *fpl.* **las ~** the West Indies

antílope *m* antelope

antinatural *a* unnatural

antip|atía *f* dislike; (cualidad de antipático) unpleasantness. **~ático** *a* unpleasant, unfriendly

anti|semita *m & f* anti-Semite. **~séptico** *a & m* antiseptic. **~social** *a* antisocial

antítesis *f invar* antithesis

antoj|adizo *a* capricious. □ **~arse** *vpr* fancy. **se le ~a un caramelo** he fancies a sweet. **~itos** *mpl* (Mex) snacks bought at street stands. **~o** *m* whim; (de embarazada) craving

antología *f* anthology

antorcha *f* torch

antro *m* (fig) dump, hole. **~ de perversión** den of iniquity

antrop|ología *f* anthropology. **~ólogo** *m* anthropologist

anua|l *a* annual. **~lidad** *f* annuity. **~lmente** *adv* yearly. **~rio** *m* yearbook

anudar *vt* tie, knot. □ **~se** *vpr* tie

anula|ción *f* annulment, cancellation. **~r** *vt* annul, cancel. ● *a* *<dedo>* ring. ● *m* ring finger

anunci|ante *m & f* advertiser. **~ar** *vt* announce; advertise *<producto comercial>*; (presagiar) be a sign of. **~o** *m* announcement; (para vender algo) advertisement, advert ▣; (cartel) poster

anzuelo *m* (fish)hook; (fig) bait. **tragar el ~** swallow the bait

añadi|dura *f* addition. **por ~dura** in addition. **~r** *vt* add

añejo *a* *<vino>* mature

añicos *mpl.* **hacer(se) ~** smash to pieces

año *m* year. **~ bisiesto** leap year. **~ nuevo** new year. **al ~** per year, a year. **¿cuántos ~s tiene?** how old is he? **tiene 5 ~s** he's 5 (years old). **el ~ pasado** last year. **el ~ que viene** next year. **entrado en ~s** elderly. **los ~s 60** the sixties

añora|nza *f* nostalgia. **~r** *vt* miss

apabulla|nte *a* overwhelming. **~r** *vt* overwhelm

apacible *a* gentle; *<clima>* mild

apaciguar [15] *vt* pacify; (calmar) calm; relieve *<dolor etc>*. □ **~se** *vpr* calm down

apadrinar *vt* sponsor; be godfather to *<a un niño>*

apag|ado *a* extinguished; *<color>* dull; *<aparato eléctrico, luz>* off; *<persona>* lifeless; *<sonido>* muffled. **~ar** [12] *vt* put out *<fuego, incendio>*; turn off, switch off *<aparato eléctrico, luz>*; quench *<sed>*; muffle *<sonido>*. □ **~arse** *vpr* *<fuego, luz>* go out; *<sonido>* die away. **~ón** *m* blackout

apalabrar *vt* make a verbal agreement; (contratar) engage

apalear *vt* winnow *<grano>*; beat *<alfombra, frutos, persona>*

apantallar *vt* (Mex) impress

apañar *vt* (arreglar) fix; (remendar) mend; (agarrar) grasp, take hold of. □ **~se** *vpr* get along, manage

apapachar *vt* (Mex) cuddle

aparador *m* sideboard; (Mex, de tienda) shop window

aparato *m* apparatus; (máquina) machine; (doméstico) appliance; (teléfono) telephone; (radio, TV) set; (ostentación) show, pomp. **~so** *a* showy, ostentatious; <*caída*> spectacular

aparca|miento *m* car park (Brit), parking lot (Amer). **~r** [7] *vt/i* park

aparear *vt* mate <*animales*>.□ **~se** *vpr* mate

aparecer [11] *vi* appear. □ **~se** *vpr* appear

aparej|ado *a*. **llevar ~ado, traer ~ado** mean, entail. **~o** *m* (avíos) equipment; (de caballo) tack; (de pesca) tackle

aparent|ar *vt* (afectar) feign; (parecer) look. ● *vi* show off. **~a 20 años** she looks like she's 20. **~e** *a* apparent

apari|ción *f* appearance; (visión) apparition. **~encia** *f* appearance; (fig) show. **guardar las ~encias** keep up appearances

apartado *a* separated; (aislado) isolated. ● *m* (de un texto) section. **~ (de correos)** post-office box, PO box

apartamento *m* apartment, flat (Brit)

apart|ar *vt* separate; (alejar) move away; (quitar) remove; (guardar) set aside. □ **~arse** *vpr* leave; (quitarse de en medio) get out of the way; (aislarse) cut o.s. off. **~e** *adv* apart; (por separado) separately; (además) besides. ● *m* aside; (párrafo) new paragraph. **~e de** apart from. **dejar ~e** leave aside. **eso ~e** apart from that

apasiona|do *a* passionate; (entusiasta) enthusiastic; (falto de objetividad) biased. ● *m*. **~do de** lover. **~miento** *m* passion. **~r** *vt* excite. □ **~rse** *vpr* be mad (**por** about) (ser parcial) become biased

ap|atía *f* apathy. **~ático** *a* apathetic

apea|dero *m* (Rail) halt. □ **~rse** *vpr* get off

apechugar [12] *vi* **T** **~ con** put up with

apedrear *vt* stone

apeg|ado *a* attached (**a** to). **~o** *m* **T** attachment. **tener ~o a** be fond of

apela|ción *f* appeal. **~r** *vi* appeal; (recurrir) resort (**a** to). ● *vt* (apodar) call. **~tivo** *m* (nick)name

apellid|ar *vt* call. □ **~arse** *vpr* be called. **¿cómo te apellidas?** what's your surname? **~o** *m* surname

apelmazarse *vpr* <*lana*> get matted

apenar *vt* sadden; (LAm, avergonzar) embarrass. □ **~se** *vpr* be sad; (LAm, avergonzarse) be embarrassed

apenas *adv* hardly, scarcely; (Mex, sólo) only. ● *conj* (esp LAm, en cuanto) as soon as. **~ si** **T** hardly

ap|éndice *m* appendix. **~endicitis** *f* appendicitis

apergaminado *a* <*piel*> wrinkled

aperitivo *m* (bebida) aperitif; (comida) appetizer

aperos *mpl* implements; (de labranza) agricultural equipment; (LAm, de un caballo) tack

apertura *f* opening

apesadumbrar *vt* upset. □ **~se** *vpr* sadden

apestar *vt* infect. ● *vi* stink (**a** of)

apet|ecer [11] *vi*. **¿te ~ece una copa?** do you fancy a drink? do you feel like a drink?. **no me ~ece** I don't feel like it. **~ecible** *a* attractive. **~ito** *m* appetite; (fig) desire. **~itoso** *a* appetizing

apiadarse *vpr* feel sorry (**de** for)

ápice *m* (nada, en frases negativas) anything. **no ceder un ~** not give an inch

apilar *vt* pile up

apiñar *vt* pack in. □ **~se** *vpr* <*personas*> crowd together; <*cosas*> be packed tight

apio *m* celery

aplacar [7] *vt* placate; soothe <*dolor*>

aplanar *vt* level. **~ calles** (LAm [I]) loaf around

aplasta|nte *a* overwhelming. **~r** *vt* crush. □ **~rse** *vpr* flatten o.s.

aplau|dir *vt* clap, applaud; (fig) applaud. **~so** *m* applause; (fig) praise

aplaza|miento *m* postponement. **~r** [10] *vt* postpone; defer <*pago*>

aplica|ble *a* applicable. **~ción** *f* application. **~do** *a* <*persona*> diligent. **~r** [7] *vt* apply. ● *vi* (LAm, a un puesto) apply (for). □ **~rse** *vpr* apply o.s.

aplom|ado *a* composed. **~o** *m* composure

apocado *a* timid

apocar [7] *vt* belittle <*persona*>. □ **~se** *vpr* feel small

apodar *vt* nickname

apodera|do *m* representative. □ **~rse** *vpr* seize

apodo *m* nickname

apogeo *m* (fig) height

apolilla|do *a* moth-eaten. □ **~rse** *vpr* get moth-eaten

apolítico *a* non-political

apología *f* defence

apoltronarse *vpr* settle o.s. down

apoplejía *f* stroke

aporrear *vt* hit, thump; beat up <*persona*>

aport|ación *f* contribution. **~ar** *vt* contribute. **~e** *m* (LAm) contribution

aposta *adv* on purpose

apostar¹ [2] *vt/i* bet

apostar² *vt* station. □ **~se** *vpr* station o.s.

apóstol *m* apostle

apóstrofo *m* apostrophe

apoy|ar *vt* lean (**en** against); (descansar) rest; (asentar) base; (reforzar) support. □ **~arse** *vpr* lean, rest. **~o** *m* support

apreci|able *a* appreciable; (digno de estima) worthy. **~ación** *f* appreciation; (valoración) appraisal. **~ar** *vt* value; (estimar) appreciate. **~o** *m* appraisal; (fig) esteem

apremi|ante *a* urgent, pressing. **~ar** *vt* urge; (obligar) compel; (dar prisa a) hurry up. ● *vi* be urgent. **~o** *m* urgency; (obligación) obligation

aprender *vt/i* learn. □ **~se** *vpr* learn

aprendiz *m* apprentice. **~aje** *m* learning; (período) apprenticeship

aprensi|ón *f* apprehension; (miedo) fear. **~vo** *a* apprehensive, fearful

apresar *vt* seize; (capturar) capture

aprestar *vt* prepare. □ **~se** *vpr* prepare

apresura|do *a* in a hurry; (hecho con prisa) hurried. **~r** *vt* hurry. □ **~rse** *vpr* hurry up

apret|ado *a* tight; (difícil) difficult; (tacaño) stingy, mean. **~ar** [1] *vt* tighten; press <*botón*>; squeeze <*persona*>; (comprimir) press down. ● *vi* be too tight. □ **~arse** *vpr* crowd together. **~ón** *m* squeeze. **~ón de manos** handshake

aprieto *m* difficulty. **verse en un ~** be in a tight spot

aprisa *adv* quickly

aprisionar *vt* trap

aproba|ción *f* approval. **~r** [2] *vt* approve (of); pass <*examen*>. ● *vi* pass

apropia|ción *f* appropriation. **~do** *a* appropriate. **~rse** *vpr*. **~rse de** appropriate, take

aprovecha|ble *a* usable. **~do** *a* (aplicado) diligent; (ingenioso) resourceful; (oportunista) opportunist. **bien ~do** well spent. **~miento** *m* advantage; (uso) use. **~r** *vt* take advantage of; (utilizar) make use of. ● *vi* make the most of it. **¡que aproveche!** enjoy your meal! □ **~rse** *vpr*. **~rse de** take advantage of

aprovisionar *vt* provision (**con, de** with). □ **~se** *vpr* stock up

aproxima|ción *f* approximation; (proximidad) closeness; (en la lotería) consolation prize. **~damente** *adv* roughly, approximately. **~do** *a* approximate, rough. **~r** *vt* bring near; (fig) bring together <*personas*>. □ **~rse** *vpr* come closer, approach

apt|itud *f* suitability; (capacidad) ability. **~o** *a* (capaz) capable; (adecuado) suitable

apuesta *f* bet

apuesto *m* handsome. ● *vb* ⇒APOSTAR

apuntalar *vt* shore up

apunt|ar *vt* aim <*arma*>; (señalar) point at; (anotar) make a note of, note down; (inscribir) enrol; (en el teatro) prompt. ● *vi* (con un arma) to aim (**a** at). □ **~arse** *vpr* put one's name down; score <*triunfo, tanto etc*>. **~e** *m* note; (bosquejo) sketch. **tomar ~s** take notes

apuñalar *vt* stab

apur|ado *a* difficult; (sin dinero) hard up; (LAm, con prisa) in a hurry. **~ar** *vt* (acabar) finish; drain <*vaso etc*>; (causar vergüenza) embarrass; (LAm, apresurar) hurry. □ **~arse** *vpr* worry; (LAm, apresurarse) hurry up. **~o** *m* tight spot, difficult situation; (vergüenza) embarrassment; (estrechez) hardship, want; (LAm, prisa) hurry

aquejar *vt* afflict

aquel *a* (*f* **aquella**, *mpl* **aquellos**, *fpl* **aquellas**) that; (en plural) those

aquél *pron* (*f* **aquélla**, *mpl* **aquéllos**, *fpl* **aquéllas**) that one; (en plural) those

aquello *pron* that; (asunto) that business

aquí *adv* here. **de ~** from here. **de ~ a 15 días** in a fortnight's time. **~ mismo** right here. **de ~ para allá** to and fro. **de ~ que** that is why. **hasta ~** until now. **por ~** around here

aquietar *vt* calm (down)

árabe *a & m & f* Arab; (lengua) Arabic

Arabia *f* Arabia. **~ Saudita, ~ Saudí** Saudi Arabia

arado *m* plough. **~r** *m* ploughman

arancel *m* tariff; (impuesto) duty. **~ario** *a* tariff

arandela *f* washer

araña *f* spider; (lámpara) chandelier. **~r** *vt* scratch

arar *vt* plough

arbitra|je *m* arbitration; (en deportes) refereeing. **~r** *vt/i* arbitrate; (en fútbol etc) referee; (en tenis etc) umpire

arbitr|ariedad *f* arbitrariness. **~ario** *a* arbitrary. **~io** *m* (free) will

árbitro *m* arbitrator; (en fútbol etc) referee; (en tenis etc) umpire

árbol *m* tree; (eje) axle; (palo) mast. **~ genealógico** family tree. **~ de Navidad** Christmas tree

arbol|ado *m* trees. **~eda** *f* wood

arbusto *m* bush

arca *f* (caja) chest. **~ de Noé** Noah's ark

arcada *f* arcade; (de un puente) arch; (náuseas) retching

arcaico *a* archaic

arce *m* maple (tree)

arcén *m* (de autopista) hard shoulder; (de carretera) verge

archipiélago *m* archipelago

archiv|ador *m* filing cabinet. **~ar** *vt* file (away). **~o** *m* file; (de documentos históricos) archives

arcilla *f* clay

arco *m* arch; (Elec, Mat) arc; (Mus, arma) bow; (LAm, en fútbol) goal. **~ iris** rainbow

arder *vi* burn; (LAm, escocer) sting; (fig, de ira) seethe. **estar que arde** be very tense

ardid *m* trick, scheme

ardiente *a* burning

ardilla *f* squirrel

ardor *m* heat; (fig) ardour; (LAm, escozor) smarting. **~ de estómago** heartburn

arduo *a* arduous

área *f* area

arena *f* sand; (en deportes) arena; (en los toros) (bull)ring. **~ movediza** quicksand

arenoso *a* sandy

arenque *m* herring. **~ ahumado** kipper

arete *m* (Mex) earring

Argel *m* Algiers. **~ia** *f* Algeria

Argentina *f* Argentina

argentino *a* Argentinian, Argentine. ● *m* Argentinian

argolla *f* ring. **~ de matrimonio** (LAm) wedding ring

arg|ot *m* slang. **~ótico** *a* slang

argucia *f* cunning argument

argüir [19] *vt* (probar) prove, show; (argumentar) argue. ● *vi* argue

argument|ación *f* argument. **~ar** *vt/i* argue. **~o** *m* argument; (de libro, película etc) story, plot

aria *f* aria

aridez *f* aridity, dryness

árido *a* arid, dry. **~s** *mpl* dry goods

Aries *m* Aries

arisco *a* unfriendly

arist|ocracia *f* aristocracy. **~ócrata** *m & f* aristocrat. **~ocrático** *a* aristocratic

aritmética *f* arithmetic

arma *f* arm, weapon; (sección) section. **~ de fuego** firearm. **~da** *f* navy; (flota) fleet. **~do** *a* armed (**de** with). **~dura** *f* armour; (de gafas etc) frame; (Tec) framework. **~mentismo** *m* build-up of arms. **~mento** *m* arms, armaments; (acción de armar) armament. **~r** *vt* arm (**de** with); (montar) put together. **~r un lío** kick up a fuss

armario *m* cupboard; (para ropa) wardrobe (Brit), closet (Amer)

armatoste *m* huge great thing

armazón *m & f* frame(work)

armiño *m* ermine

armisticio *m* armistice

armonía *f* harmony

armónica *f* harmonica, mouth organ

armoni|oso *a* harmonious. **~zar** [10] *vt* harmonize. ● *vi* harmonize; <*personas*> get on well (**con** with); <*colores*> go well (**con** with)

arn|és *m* armour. **~eses** *mpl* harness

aro *m* ring, hoop

arom|a *m* aroma; (de flores) scent; (de vino) bouquet. **~ático** *a* aromatic

arpa *f* harp

arpía *f* harpy; (fig) hag

arpillera *f* sackcloth, sacking

arpón *m* harpoon

arquear *vt* arch, bend. ▫ **~se** *vpr* arch, bend

arque|ología *f* archaeology. **~ológico** *a* archaeological. **~ólogo** *m* archaeologist

arquero *m* archer; (LAm, en fútbol) goalkeeper

arquitect|o *m* architect. **~ónico** *a* architectural. **~ura** *f* architecture

arrabal *m* suburb; (barrio pobre) poor area. **~es** *mpl* outskirts. **~ero** *a* suburban; (de modales groseros) common

arraiga|do *a* deeply rooted. **~r** [12] *vi* take root. ▫ **~rse** *vpr* take root; (fig) settle

arran|car [7] *vt* pull up <*planta*>; pull out <*diente*>; (arrebatar) snatch; (Auto) start. ● *vi* start. ▫ **~carse** *vpr* pull out. **~que** *m* sudden start; (Auto) start; (fig) outburst

arras *fpl* deposit, security

arrasar *vt* level, smooth; raze to the ground <*edificio etc*>; (llenar) fill to the brim. ● *vi* (en deportes) sweep to victory; (en política) win a landslide victory

arrastr|ar *vt* pull; (por el suelo) drag (along); give rise to <*consecuencias*>. ● *vi* trail on the ground. ▫ **~arse** *vpr* crawl; (humillarse) grovel. **~e** *m* dragging; (transporte) haulage. **estar para el ~e** 🄸 be done in

arre *int* gee up! **~ar** *vt* urge on

arrebat|ado *a* (irreflexivo) impetuous. **~ar** *vt* snatch (away); (fig) win (over); captivate <*corazón etc*>. ▫ **~arse** *vpr* get carried away. **~o** *m* (de cólera etc) fit; (éxtasis) extasy

arrech|ar *vt* (LAm 🄸, enfurecer) to infuriate. ▫ **~se** *vpr* get furious. **~o** *a* furious

arrecife *m* reef

arregl|ado *a* neat; (bien vestido) well-dressed; (LAm, amañado) fixed. **~ar** *vt* arrange; (poner en orden) tidy up; sort out <*asunto, problema etc*>; (reparar) mend. ▫ **~arse** *vpr* (solucionarse) get sorted out; (prepararse) get ready; (apañarse) manage, make do; (ponerse de acuerdo) come to an agreement. **~árselas** manage, get by. **~o** *m* (incl Mus) arrangement; (acción de reparar) repair; (acuerdo) agreement; (solución) solution. **con ~o a** according to

arrellanarse *vpr* settle o.s. (**en** into)

arremangar [12] *vt* roll up <*mangas*>; tuck up <*falda*>. ▫ **~se** *vpr* roll up one's sleeves

arremeter *vi* charge (**contra** at); (atacar) attack

arremolinarse *vpr* mill about; <*el agua*> to swirl

arrenda|dor *m* landlord. **~dora** *f* landlady. **~miento** *m* renting; (contrato) lease; (precio) rent. **~r** [1] *vt* (dar casa en alquiler) let; (dar cosa en alquiler) hire out; (tomar en alquiler) rent. **~tario** *m* tenant

arreos *mpl* tack

arrepenti|miento *m* repentance, regret. **~rse** [4] *vpr* (retractarse) to change one's mind; (lamentarse) be sorry. **~rse de** regret; repent of *<pecados>*

arrest|ar *vt* arrest, detain; (encarcelar) imprison. **~o** *m* arrest; (encarcelamiento) imprisonment

arriar [20] *vt* lower *<bandera, vela>*

arriba *adv* up; (dirección) up(wards); (en casa) upstairs. ● *int* up with; (¡levántate!) up you get!; (¡ánimo!) come on! **¡~ España!** long live Spain! **~ de** (LAm) on top of. **~ mencionado** aforementioned. **calle ~** up the street. **de ~ abajo** from top to bottom. **de 100 pesetas para ~** over 100 pesetas. **escaleras ~** upstairs. **la parte de ~** the top part. **los de ~** those at the top. **más ~** higher up

arrib|ar *vi <barco>* reach port; (esp LAm, llegar) arrive. **~ista** *m & f* social climber. **~o** *m* (esp LAm) arrival

arriero *m* muleteer

arriesga|do *a* risky; *<person>* daring. **~r** [12] *vt* risk; (aventurar) venture. □ **~rse** *vpr* take a risk

arrim|ar *vt* bring close(r). □ **~arse** *vpr* come closer, approach; (apoyarse) lean (**a** on). **~o** *m* protection. **al ~o de** with the help of

arrincona|do *a* forgotten; (acorralado) cornered. **~r** *vt* put in a corner; (perseguir) corner (arrumbar) put aside. □ **~rse** *vpr* become a recluse

arrocero *a* rice

arrodillarse *vpr* kneel (down)

arrogan|cia *f* arrogance; (orgullo) pride. **~te** *a* arrogant; (orgulloso) proud

arroj|ar *vt* throw; (emitir) give off, throw out; (producir) produce. ● *vi* (esp LAm, vomitar) throw up. □ **~arse** *vpr* throw o.s. **~o** *m* courage

arrollar *vt* roll (up); (atropellar) run over; (vencer) crush

arropar *vt* wrap up; (en la cama) tuck up. □ **~se** *vpr* wrap (o.s.) up

arroy|o *m* stream; (de una calle) gutter. **~uelo** *m* small stream

arroz *m* rice. **~ con leche** rice pudding. **~al** *m* rice field

arruga *f* (en la piel) wrinkle, line; (en tela) crease. **~r** [12] *vt* wrinkle; crumple *<papel>*; crease *<tela>*. □ **~rse** *vpr <la piel>* become wrinkled; *<tela>* crease, get creased

arruinar *vt* ruin; (destruir) destroy. □ **~se** *vpr <persona>* be ruined

arrullar *vt* lull to sleep. ● *vi <palomas>* coo

arrumbar *vt* put aside

arsenal *m* (astillero) shipyard; (de armas) arsenal; (fig) mine

arsénico *m* arsenic

arte *m* (*f en plural*) art; (habilidad) skill; (astucia) cunning. **bellas ~s** fine arts. **con ~** skilfully. **malas ~s** trickery. **por amor al ~** for the fun of it

artefacto *m* device

arteria *f* artery; (fig, calle) main road

artesan|al *a* craft. **~ía** *f* handicrafts. **objeto** *m* **de ~ía** traditional craft object. **~o** *m* artisan, craftsman

ártico *a* Arctic. **Á~** *m*. **el Á~** the Arctic

articula|ción *f* joint; (pronunciación) articulation. **~do** *a* articulated; *<lenguaje>* articulate. **~r** *vt* articulate

artículo *m* article. **~s** *mpl* (géneros) goods. **~ de exportación** export product. **~ de fondo** editorial, leader

artífice *m & f* artist; (creador) architect

artifici|al *a* artificial. **~o** *m* (habilidad) skill; (dispositivo) device; (engaño) trick

artiller|ía *f* artillery. **~o** *m* artilleryman, gunner

artilugio *m* gadget

artimaña *f* trick

art|ista *m & f* artist. **~ístico** *a* artistic

artritis *f* arthritis

arveja *f* (LAm) pea

arzobispo *m* archbishop

as *m* ace

asa *f* handle

asado *a* roast(ed) ● *m* roast (meat), joint; (LAm, reunión) barbecue. **~o a la parrilla** grilled meat; (LAm) barbecued meat

asalariado *a* salaried. ● *m* employee

asalt|ante *m* attacker; (de un banco) robber. **~ar** *vt* storm *<fortaleza>*; attack *<persona>*; raid *<banco etc>*; (fig) *<duda>* assail; (fig) *<idea etc>* cross one's mind. **~o** *m* attack; (robo) robbery; (en boxeo) round

asamblea *f* assembly; (reunión) meeting

asar *vt* roast. □ **~se** *vpr* be very hot. **~ a la parrilla** grill; (LAm) barbecue. **~ al horno** (sin grasa) bake; (con grasa) roast

asbesto *m* asbestos

ascend|encia *f* descent; (LAm, influencia) influencia. **~ente** *a* ascending. **~er** [1] *vt* promote. ● *vi* go up, ascend; *<cuenta etc>* come to, amount to; (ser ascendido) be promoted. **~iente** *m & f* ancestor; (influencia) influence

ascens|ión *f* ascent; (de grado) promotion. **día de la A~ión** Ascension Day. **~o** *m* ascent; (de grado) promotion

ascensor *m* lift (Brit), elevator (Amer). **~ista** *m & f* lift attendant (Brit), elevator operator (Amer)

asco *m* disgust. **dar ~** be disgusting; (fig, causar enfado) be infuriating. **estar hecho un ~** be disgusting. **me da ~** it makes me feel sick. **¡qué ~!** how disgusting! **ser un ~** be disgusting

ascua *f* ember. **estar en ~s** be on tenterhooks

asea|do *a* clean; (arreglado) neat. **~r** *vt* (lavar) wash; (limpiar) clean; (arreglar) tidy up

asedi|ar *vt* besiege; (fig) pester. **~o** *m* siege

asegura|do *a & m* insured. **~dor** *m* insurer. **~r** *vt* secure, make safe; (decir) assure; (concertar un seguro) insure; (preservar) safeguard. □ **~rse** *vpr* make sure

asemejarse *vpr* be alike

asenta|do *a* situated; (arraigado) established. **~r** [1] *vt* place; (asegurar) settle; (anotar) note down; (Mex, afirmar) state. □ **~rse** *vpr* settle; (estar situado) be situated; (esp LAm, sentar cabeza) settle down

asentir [4] *vi* agree (a to). **~ con la cabeza** nod

aseo *m* cleanliness. **~s** *mpl* toilets

asequible *a* obtainable; *<precio>* reasonable; *<persona>* approachable

asesin|ar *vt* murder; (Pol) assassinate. **~ato** *m* murder; (Pol) as sassination. **~o** *m* murderer; (Pol) assassin

asesor *m* adviser, consultant. **~ar** *vt* advise. □ **~arse** *vpr*. **~arse con** consult. **~ía** *f* consultancy; (oficina) consultant's office

asfalt|ado *a* asphalt. **~ar** *vt* asphalt. **~o** *m* asphalt

asfixia *f* suffocation. **~nte** *a* suffocating. **~r** *vt* suffocate. □ **~rse** *vpr* suffocate

así *adv* (de esta manera) like this, like that. ● *a* such. **~ ~** so-so. **~ como** just as. **~ como ~**, (LAm) **~ nomás** just like that. **~ ... como** both ... and. **~ pues** so. **~ que** so; (en cuanto) as soon as. **~ sea** so be it. **~ y todo** even so. **aun ~** even so. **¿no es ~?** isn't that right? **si es ~** if that is the case. **y ~** (**sucesivamente**) and so on

Asia *f* Asia

asiático *a & m* Asian

asidero *m* handle; (fig, pretexto) excuse

asidu|amente *adv* regularly. **~o** *a & m* regular

asiento *m* seat; (en contabilidad) entry. **~ delantero** front seat. **~ trasero** back seat

asignar *vt* assign; allot <*porción, tiempo etc*>

asignatura *f* subject. **~ pendiente** (Escol) failed subject; (fig) matter still to be resolved

asil|ado *m* inmate; (Pol) refugee. **~o** *m* asylum; (fig) shelter; (de ancianos etc) home. **pedir ~o político** ask for political asylum

asimétrico *a* asymmetrical

asimila|ción *f* assimilation. **~r** *vt* assimilate

asimismo *adv* also; (igualmente) in the same way, likewise

asir [45] *vt* grasp

asist|encia *f* attendance; (gente) people (present); (en un teatro etc) audience; (ayuda) assistance. **~encia médica** medical care. **~enta** *f* (mujer de la limpieza) cleaning lady. **~ente** *m & f* assistant. **~ente social** social worker. **~ido** *a* assisted. **~ir** *vt* assist, help. ● *vi*. **~ir a** attend, be present at

asm|a *f* asthma. **~ático** *a & m* asthmatic

asno *m* donkey; (fig) ass

asocia|ción *f* association; (Com) partnership. **~do** *a* associated; <*socio*> associate. ● *m* associate. **~r** *vt* associate; (Com) take into partnership. □ **~rse** *vpr* associate; (Com) become a partner

asolar [1] *vt* devastate

asomar *vt* show. ● *vi* appear, show. □ **~se** *vpr* <*persona*> lean out (**a, por** of); <*cosa*> appear

asombr|ar *vt* (pasmar) amaze; (sorprender) surprise. □ **~arse** *vpr* be amazed; (sorprenderse) be surprised. **~o** *m* amazement, surprise. **~oso** *a* amazing, astonishing

asomo *m* sign. **ni por ~** by no means

aspa *f* cross, X-shape; (de molino) (windmill) sail. **en ~** X-shaped

aspaviento *m* show, fuss. **~s** *mpl* gestures. **hacer ~s** make a big fuss

aspecto *m* look, appearance; (fig) aspect

aspereza *f* roughness; (de sabor etc) sourness

áspero *a* rough; <*sabor etc*> bitter

aspersión *f* sprinkling

aspiración *f* breath; (deseo) ambition

aspirador *m*, **aspiradora** *f* vacuum cleaner

aspira|nte *m & f* candidate. **~r** *vt* breathe in; <*máquina*> suck up. ● *vi* breathe in; <*máquina*> suck. **~r** a aspire to

aspirina *f* aspirin

asquear *vt* sicken. ● *vi* be sickening. ▫ **~se** *vpr* be disgusted

asqueroso *a* disgusting

asta *f* spear; (de la bandera) flagpole; (cuerno) horn. **a media ~** at half-mast. **~bandera** *f* (Mex) flagpole

asterisco *m* asterisk

astilla *f* splinter. **~s** *fpl* firewood

astillero *m* shipyard

astringente *a & m* astringent

astr|o *m* star. **~ología** *f* astrology. **~ólogo** *m* astrologer. **~onauta** *m & f* astronaut. **~onave** *f* spaceship. **~onomía** *f* astronomy. **~ónomo** *m* astronomer

astu|cia *f* cleverness; (ardid) cunning trick. **~to** *a* astute; (taimado) cunning

asumir *vt* assume

asunción *f* assumption. **la A~** the Assumption

asunto *m* (cuestión) matter; (de una novela) plot; (negocio) business. **~s** *mpl* **exteriores** foreign affairs. **el ~ es que** the fact is that

asusta|dizo *a* easily frightened. **~r** *vt* frighten. ▫ **~rse** *vpr* be frightened

ataca|nte *m & f* attacker. **~r** [7] *vt* attack

atad|o *a* tied. ● *m* bundle. **~ura** *f* tie

ataj|ar *vi* take a short cut; (Mex, en tenis) pick up the balls. ● *vt* (LAm, agarrar) catch. **~o** *m* short cut

atañer [22] *vt* concern

ataque *m* attack; (Med) fit, attack. **~ al corazón** heart attack. **~ de nervios** fit of hysterics

atar *vt* tie. ▫ **~se** *vpr* tie up

atarantar *vt* (LAm) fluster. ▫ **~se** *vpr* (LAm) get flustered

atardecer [11] *vi* get dark. ● *m* dusk. **al ~** at dusk

atareado *a* busy

atasc|ar [7] *vt* block; (fig) hinder. ▫ **~arse** *vpr* get stuck; <*tubo etc*> block. **~o** *m* blockage; (Auto) traffic jam

ataúd *m* coffin

atav|iar [20] *vt* dress up. ▫ **~iarse** *vpr* dress up, get dressed up. **~ío** *m* dress, attire

atemorizar [10] *vt* frighten. ▫ **~se** *vpr* be frightened

atención *f* attention; (cortesía) courtesy, kindness; (interés) interest. **¡~!** look out! **llamar la ~** attract attention, catch the eye. **prestar ~** pay attention

atender [1] *vt* attend to; (cuidar) look after. ● *vi* pay attention

atenerse [40] *vpr* abide (**a** by)

atentado *m* (ataque) attack; (afrenta) affront (**contra** to). **~ contra la vida de uno** attempt on s.o.'s life

atentamente *adv* attentively; (con cortesía) politely; (con amabilidad) kindly. **lo saluda ~** (en cartas) yours faithfully

atentar *vi*. **~ contra** threaten. **~ contra la vida de uno** make an attempt on s.o.'s life

atento *a* attentive; (cortés) polite; (amable) kind

atenua|nte *a* extenuating. ● *f* extenuating circumstance. **~r** [21] *vt* attenuate; (hacer menor) diminish, lessen

~rse *vpr* lie across; (en la garganta) get stuck, stick

atrayente *a* attractive

atrev|erse *vpr* dare. **~erse con** tackle. **~ido** *a* daring; (insolente) insolent. **~imiento** *m* daring; (descaro) insolence

atribu|ción *f* attribution. **~ciones** *fpl* authority. **~uir** [17] *vt* attribute; confer <*función*>. □ **~irse** *vpr* claim

atribulado *a* afflicted

atributo *m* attribute

atril *m* lectern; (Mus) music stand

atrocidad *f* atrocity. **¡qué ~!** how awful!

atrofiarse *vpr* atrophy

atropell|ado *a* hasty. **~ar** *vt* knock down; (por encima) run over; (empujar) push aside; (fig) outrage, insult. □ **~arse** *vpr* rush. **~o** *m* (Auto) accident; (fig) outrage

atroz *a* appalling; (fig) atrocious

atuendo *m* dress, attire

atún *m* tuna (fish)

aturdi|do *a* bewildered; (por golpe) stunned. **~r** *vt* bewilder; <*golpe*> stun; <*ruido*> deafen

auda|cia *f* boldness, audacity. **~z** *a* bold

audi|ble *a* audible. **~ción** *f* hearing; (prueba) audition. **~encia** *f* audience; (tribunal) court; (sesión) hearing

auditor *m* auditor. **~io** *m* audience; (sala) auditorium

auge *m* peak; (Com) boom

augur|ar *vt* predict; <*cosas*> augur. **~io** *m* prediction. **con nuestros mejores ~ios para** with our best wishes for. **mal ~** bad omen

aula *f* class-room; (Univ) lecture room

aull|ar [23] *vi* howl. **~ido** *m* howl

aument|ar *vt* increase; magnify <*imagen*>. ● *vi* increase. **~o** *m* increase; (de sueldo) rise

aun *adv* even. **~ así** even so. **~ cuando** although. **más ~** even more. **ni ~** not even

aún *adv* still, yet. **~ no ha llegado** it still hasn't arrived, it hasn't arrived yet

aunar [23] *vt* join. □ **~se** *vpr* join together

aunque *conj* although, (even) though

aúpa *int* up! **de ~** wonderful

aureola *f* halo

auricular *m* (de teléfono) receiver. **~es** *mpl* headphones

aurora *f* dawn

ausen|cia *f* absence. **en ~cia de** in the absence of. □ **~tarse** *vpr* leave. **~te** *a* absent. ● *m & f* absentee; (Jurid) missing person. **~tismo** *m* (LAm) absenteeism

auspici|ador *m* sponsor. **~ar** *vt* sponsor. **~o** *m* sponsorship; (signo) omen. **bajo los ~s de** sponsored by

auster|idad *f* austerity. **~o** *a* austere

austral *a* southern

Australia *m* Australia

australiano *a & m* Australian

Austria *f* Austria

austriaco, **austríaco** *a & m* Austrian

aut|enticar [7] authenticate. **~enticidad** *f* authenticity. **~éntico** *a* authentic

auto *m* (Jurid) decision; (orden) order; (Auto, [I]) car. **~s** *mpl* proceedings

auto|abastecimiento *m* self-sufficiency. **~biografía** *f* autobiography
autobús *m* bus. **en ~** by bus
autocar *m* (long-distance) bus, coach (Brit)
autocontrol *m* self-control
autóctono *a* indigenous
auto|determinación *f* self-determination. **~didacta** *a* self-taught. ● *m & f* self-taught person. **~escuela** *f* driving school. **~financiamiento** *m* self-financing
autógrafo *m* autograph
autómata *m* robot
autom|ático *a* automatic. ● *m* press-stud. **~atización** *f* automation
automotor *m* diesel train
autom|óvil *a* motor. ● *m* car. **~ovilismo** *m* motoring. **~ovilista** *m & f* driver, motorist
aut|onomía *f* autonomy. **~onómico** *a*, **~ónomo** *a* autonomous
autopista *f* motorway (Brit), freeway (Amer)
autopsia *f* autopsy
autor *m* author. **~a** *f* author(ess)
autori|dad *f* authority. **~tario** *a* authoritarian
autoriza|ción *f* authorization. **~do** *a* authorized, official; <*opinión etc*> authoritative. **~r** [10] *vt* authorize
auto|rretrato *m* self-portrait. **~servicio** *m* self-service restaurant. **~stop** *m* hitch-hiking. **hacer ~stop** hitch-hike
autosuficiente *a* self-sufficient
autovía *f* dual carriageway
auxili|ar *a* auxiliary; <*profesor*> assistant. ● *m & f* assistant. ● *vt* help. **~o** *m* help. **¡~o!** help! **en ~o de** in aid of. **pedir ~o** shout for help. **primeros ~os** first aid
Av. *abrev* (**Avenida**) Ave
aval *m* guarantee
avalancha *f* avalanche
avalar *vt* guarantee
aval|uar *vt* [21] (LAm) value. **~úo** *m* valuation
avance *m* advance; (en el cine) trailer. **~s** *mpl* (Mex) trailer
avanzar [10] *vt* move forward. ● *vi* advance
avar|icia *f* avarice. **~icioso** *a*, **~iento** *a* greedy; (tacaño) miserly. **~o** *a* miserly. ● *m* miser
avasallar *vt* dominate
Avda. *abrev* (**Avenida**) Ave
ave *f* bird. **~ de paso** (incl fig) bird of passage. **~ de rapiña** bird of prey
avecinarse *vpr* approach
avejentar *vt* age
avellan|a *f* hazel-nut. **~o** *m* hazel (tree)
avemaría *f* Hail Mary
avena *f* oats
avenida *f* (calle) avenue
avenir [53] *vt* reconcile. □ **~se** *vpr* come to an agreement; (entenderse) get on well (**con** with)
aventaja|do *a* outstanding. **~r** *vt* be ahead of; (superar) surpass
avent|ar [1] *vt* fan; winnow <*grano etc*>; (Mex, lanzar) throw; (Mex, empujar) push. □ **~arse** *vpr* (Mex) throw o.s.; (atreverse) dare. **~ón** *m* (Mex) ride, lift (Brit)
aventur|a *f* adventure. **~a amorosa** love affair. **~ado** *a* risky. **~ero** *a* adventurous. ● *m* adventurer
avergonzar [10 & 16] *vt* shame; (abochornar) embarrass. □ **~se** *vpr*

be ashamed; (abochornarse) be embarrassed

aver|ía *f* (Auto) breakdown; (en máquina) failure. **~iado** *a* broken down. □ **~iarse** [20] *vpr* break down

averigua|ción *f* inquiry; (Mex, disputa) argument. **~r** [15] *vt* find out. ● *vi* (Mex) argue

aversión *f* aversion (**a, hacia, por** to)

avestruz *m* ostrich

avia|ción *f* aviation; (Mil) air force. **~dor** *m* (piloto) pilot

av|ícola *a* poultry. **~icultura** *f* poultry farming

avidez *f* eagerness, greed

ávido *a* eager, greedy

avinagra|do *a* sour. □ **~rse** *vpr* go sour; (fig) become embittered

avi|ón *m* aeroplane (Brit), airplane (Amer); (Mex, juego) hopscotch. **~onazo** *m* (Mex) plane crash

avis|ar *vt* warn; (informar) notify, inform; call <*médico etc*>. **~o** *m* warning; (comunicación) notice; (LAm, anuncio, cartel) advertisement; (en televisión) commercial. **estar sobre ~o** be on the alert. **sin previo ~o** without prior warning

avisp|a *f* wasp. **~ado** *a* sharp. **~ero** *m* wasps' nest; (fig) mess. **~ón** *m* hornet

avistar *vt* catch sight of

avivar *vt* stoke up <*fuego*>; brighten up <*color*>; arouse <*interés, pasión*>; intensify <*dolor*>. □ **~se** *vpr* revive; (animarse) cheer up; (LAm, despabilarse) wise up

axila *f* armpit, axilla

axioma *m* axiom

ay *int* (de dolor) ouch!; (de susto) oh!; (de pena) oh dear! **¡~ de ti!** poor you!

aya *f* governess

ayer *adv* yesterday. ● *m* past. **antes de ~** the day before yesterday. **~ por la mañana,** (LAm) **~ en la mañana** yesterday morning

ayuda *f* help, aid. **~ de cámara** valet. **~nta** *f*, **~nte** *m* assistant; (Mil) adjutant. **~r** *vt* help

ayun|ar *vi* fast. **~as** *fpl*. **estar en ~as** have had nothing to eat or drink; (fig, 🅘) be in the dark. **~o** *m* fasting

ayuntamiento *m* town council, city council; (edificio) town hall

azabache *m* jet

azad|a *f* hoe. **~ón** *m* (large) hoe

azafata *f* air hostess

azafate *m* (LAm) tray

azafrán *m* saffron

azahar *m* orange blossom; (del limonero) lemon blossom

azar *m* chance; (desgracia) misfortune. **al ~** at random. **por ~** by chance. **~es** *mpl* ups and downs

azaros|amente *adv* hazardously. **~o** *a* hazardous, risky; <*vida*> eventful

azorar *vt* embarrass. □ **~rse** *vpr* be embarrassed

Azores *fpl*. **las ~** the Azores

azotador *m* (Mex) caterpillar

azot|ar *vt* whip, beat; (Mex, puerta) slam. **~e** *m* whip; (golpe) smack; (fig, calamidad) calamity

azotea *f* flat roof

azteca *a* & *m* & *f* Aztec

az|úcar *m* & *f* sugar. **~ucarado** *a* sweet, sugary. **~ucarar** *vt* sweeten. **~ucarero** *m* sugar bowl

azucena *f* (white) lily

azufre *m* sulphur

azul *a* & *m* blue. **~ado** *a* bluish. **~ marino** navy blue

azulejo *m* tile

azuzar [10] *vt* urge on, incite

Bb

bab|a *f* spittle. **~ear** *vi* drool, slobber; <*niño*> dribble. **caérsele la ~a a uno** be delighted. **~eo** *m* drooling; (de un niño) dribbling. **~ero** *m* bib

babor *m* port. **a ~** to port, on the port side

babosa *f* slug

babosada *f* (Mex) drivel

babos|ear *vt* slobber over; <*niño*> dribble over. ● *vi* (Mex) day dream. **~o** *a* slimy; (LAm, tonto) silly

babucha *f* slipper

baca *f* luggage rack

bacalao *m* cod

bache *m* pothole; (fig) bad patch

bachillerato *m* school-leaving examination

bacteria *f* bacterium

bagaje *m*. **~ cultural** cultural knowledge; (de un pueblo) cultural heritage

bahía *f* bay

bail|able *a* dance. **~aor** *m* Flamenco dancer. **~ar** *vt/i* dance. **ir a ~ar** go dancing. **~arín** *m* dancer. **~arina** *f* dancer; (de ballet) ballerina. **~e** *m* dance; (actividad) dancing. **~e de etiqueta** ball

baja *f* drop, fall; (Mil) casualty. **~ por maternidad** maternity leave. **darse de ~** take sick leave. **~da** *f* slope; (acto de bajar) descent; (camino) way down. **~r** *vt* lower; (llevar abajo) get down; go down <*escalera*>; bow <*la cabeza*>. ● *vi* go down; <*temperatura, precio*> fall. □ **~rse** *vpr* pull down <*pantalones*>. **~r(se) de** get out of <*coche*>; get off <*autobús, caballo, tren, bicicleta*>

bajeza *f* vile deed

bajío *m* shallows; (de arena) sandbank; (LAm, terreno bajo) low-lying area

bajo *a* low; (de estatura) short, small; <*cabeza, ojos*> lowered; (humilde) humble, low; (vil) vile, low; <*voz*> low; (Mus) deep. ● *m* lowland; (Mus) bass. ● *adv* quietly; <*volar*> low. ● *prep* under. **~ cero** below zero. **~ la lluvia** in the rain. **los ~s** (LAm) ground floor (Brit), first floor (Amer); **los ~s fondos** the underworld

bajón *m* sharp drop; (de salud) sudden decline

bala *f* bullet; (de algodón etc) bale. (LAm, en atletismo) shot. **como una ~** like a shot. **lanzamiento de ~** (LAm) shot put

balada *f* ballad

balan|ce *m* balance; (documento) balance sheet; (resultado) outcome. **~cear** *vt* balance. □ **~cearse** *vpr* swing. **~ceo** *m* swinging. **~cín** *m* rocking chair; (de niños) seesaw. **~za** *f* scales; (Com) balance

balar *vi* bleat

balazo *m* (disparo) shot; (herida) bullet wound

balboa *f* (unidad monetaria panameña) balboa

balbuc|ear *vt/i* stammer; <*niño*> babble. **~eo** *m* stammering; (de niño) babbling. **~ir** [24] *vt/i* stammer; <*niño*> babble

balcón *m* balcony

balda *f* shelf

balde *m* bucket. **de ~** free (of charge). **en ~** in vain
baldío *a* <*terreno*> waste
baldosa *f* (floor) tile; (losa) flagstone
bale|ar *a* Balearic. **las (Islas) B~ares** the Balearics, the Balearic Islands. ● *vt* (LAm) to shoot. **~o** *m* (LAm, tiroteo) shooting
balero *m* (Mex) cup and ball toy; (rodamiento) bearing
balido *m* bleat; (varios sonidos) bleating
balística *f* ballistics
baliza *f* (Naut) buoy; (Aviac) beacon
ballena *f* whale
ballet /ba'le/ (*pl* **~s**) *m* ballet
balneario *m* spa; (con playa) seaside resort
balompié *m* soccer, football (Brit)
bal|ón *m* ball. **~oncesto** *m* basketball. **~onmano** *m* handball. **~onvolea** *m* volleyball
balotaje *m* (LAm) voting
balsa *f* (de agua) pool; (plataforma flotante) raft
bálsamo *m* balsam; (fig) balm
baluarte *m* (incl fig) bastion
bambalina *f* drop curtain. **entre ~s** behind the scenes
bambole|ar *vi* sway. □ **~arse** *vpr* sway; <*mesa etc*> wobble; <*barco*> rock. **~o** *m* swaying; (de mesa etc) wobbling; (de barco) rocking
bambú *m* (*pl* **~es**) bamboo
banal *a* banal. **~idad** *f* banality
banan|a *f* (esp LAm) banana. **~ero** *a* banana. **~o** *m* (LAm) banana tree
banc|a *f* banking; (conjunto de bancos) banks; (en juegos) bank; (LAm, asiento) bench. **~ario** *a* bank, banking. **~arrota** *f* bankruptcy. **hacer ~arrota, ir a la ~arrota** go bankrupt. **~o** *m* (asiento) bench; (Com) bank; (bajío) sandbank; (de peces) shoal
banda *f* (incl Mus, Radio) band; (Mex, para el pelo) hair band; (raya ancha) stripe; (cinta ancha) sash; (grupo) gang, group. **~ sonora** soundtrack. **~da** *f* (de pájaros) flock; (de peces) shoal
bandeja *f* tray
bandejón *m* (Mex) central reservation (Brit), median strip (Amer)
bander|a *f* flag. **~illa** *f* banderilla. **~ear** *vt* stick the banderillas in. **~ero** *m* banderillero. **~ín** *m* pennant, small flag
bandido *m* bandit
bando *m* edict, proclamation; (facción) camp, side. **~s** *mpl* banns. **pasarse al otro ~** go over to the other side
bandolero *m* bandit
bandoneón *m* large accordion
banjo *m* banjo
banquero *m* banker
banquete *m* banquet; (de boda) wedding reception
banquillo *m* bench; (Jurid) dock; (taburete) footstool
bañ|ador *m* (de mujer) swimming costume; (de hombre) swimming trunks. **~ar** *vt* bath <*niño*>; (Culin, recubrir) coat. □ **~arse** *vpr* go swimming, have a swim; (en casa) have a bath. **~era** *f* bath(tub). **~ista** *m & f* bather. **~o** *m* bath; (en piscina, mar etc) swim; (cuarto) bathroom; (LAm, wáter) toilet; (bañera) bath(tub); (capa) coat(ing)
baqueano, (LAm) **baquiano** *m* guide
bar *m* bar

baraja *f* pack of cards. **~r** *vt* shuffle; juggle <*cifras etc*>; consider <*posibilidades*>; (Mex, explicar) explain

baranda, **barandilla** *f* rail; (de escalera) banisters

barat|a *f* (Mex) sale. **~ija** *f* trinket. **~illo** *m* junk shop; (géneros) cheap goods. **~o** *a* cheap. ● *adv* cheap(ly)

barba *f* chin; (pelo) beard

barbacoa *f* barbecue; (carne) barbecued meat

barbari|dad *f* atrocity; (🅸, mucho) awful lot 🅸. **¡qué ~dad!** how awful! **~e** *f* barbarity; (fig) ignorance. **~smo** *m* barbarism

bárbaro *a* barbaric, cruel; (bruto) uncouth; (🅸, estupendo) terrific 🅸 ● *m* barbarian. **¡qué ~!** how marvellous!

barbear *vt* (Mex, lisonjear) suck up to

barbecho *m*. **en ~** fallow

barber|ía *f* barber's (shop). **~o** *m* barber; (Mex, adulador) creep

barbilla *f* chin

barbitúrico *m* barbiturate

barbudo *a* bearded

barca *f* (small) boat. **~ de pasaje** ferry. **~za** *f* barge

barcelonés *a* of Barcelona, from Barcelona. ● *m* native of Barcelona

barco *m* boat; (navío) ship. **~ cisterna** tanker. **~ de vapor** steamer. **~ de vela** sailing boat. **ir en ~** go by boat

barda *f* (Mex) wall; (de madera) fence

barítono *a & m* baritone

barman *m* (*pl* **~s**) barman

barniz *m* varnish; (para loza etc) glaze; (fig) veneer. **~ar** [10] *vt* varnish; glaze <*loza etc*>

barómetro *m* barometer

bar|ón *m* baron. **~onesa** *f* baroness

barquero *m* boatman

barquillo *m* wafer; (Mex, de helado) ice-cream cone

barra *f* bar; (pan) loaf of French bread; (palanca) lever; (de arena) sandbank; (LAm, de hinchas) supporters. **~ de labios** lipstick

barrabasada *f* mischief, prank

barraca *f* hut; (vivienda pobre) shack, shanty

barranco *m* ravine, gully; (despeñadero) cliff, precipice

barrer *vt* sweep; thrash <*rival*>

barrera *f* barrier. **~ del sonido** sound barrier

barriada *f* district; (LAm, barrio marginal) slum

barrial *m* (LAm) quagmire

barrida *f* sweep; (LAm, redada) police raid

barrig|a *f* belly. **~ón** *a*, **~udo** *a* pot-bellied

barril *m* barrel

barrio *m* district, area. **~s bajos** poor quarter, poor area. **el otro ~** (fig, 🅸) the other world. **~bajero** *a* vulgar, common

barro *m* mud; (arcilla) clay; (arcilla cocida) earthenware

barroco *a* Baroque. ● *m* Baroque style

barrote *m* bar

bartola *f*. **tirarse a la ~** take it easy

bártulos *mpl* things. **liar los ~** pack one's bags

barullo *m* racket; (confusión) confusion. **a ~** galore

basar *vt* base. □ **~se** *vpr*. **~se en** be based on

báscula *f* scales

base *f* base; (fig) basis, foundation. **a ~ de** thanks to; (mediante) by means of; (en una receta) mainly consisting of. **~ de datos** database. **partiendo de la ~ de, tomando como ~** on the basis of

básico *a* basic

basílica *f* basilica

básquetbol, **basquetbol** *m* (LAm) basketball

---

bastante

● *adjetivo/pronombre*

····➤ (suficiente) enough. **¿hay ~s sillas?** are there enough chairs? **ya tengo ~** I have enough already

····➤ (mucho) quite a lot. **vino ~ gente** quite a lot of people came. **tiene ~s amigos** he has quite a lot of friends **¿te gusta?- sí, ~** do you like it? - yes, quite a lot

● *adverbio*

····➤ (suficientemente) enough. **no has estudiado ~** you haven't studied enough. **no es lo ~ inteligente** he's not clever enough (**como para** to)

····➤ **bastante** + *adjetivo/adverbio* (modificando la intensidad) quite, fairly. **parece ~ simpático** he looks quite friendly. **es ~ fácil de hacer** it's quite easy to do. **canta ~ bien** he sings quite well

····➤ **bastante** *con verbo* (considerablemente) quite a lot. **el lugar ha cambiado ~** the place has changed quite a lot

---

bastar *vi* be enough. **¡basta!** that's enough! **basta con decir que** suffice it to say that. **basta y sobra** that's more than enough

bastardilla *f* italics

bastardo *a & m* bastard

bastidor *m* frame; (Auto) chassis **~es** *mpl* (en el teatro) wings. **entre ~es** behind the scenes

basto *a* coarse. **~s** *mpl* (naipes) clubs

bast|ón *m* walking stick; (de esquí) ski pole. **~onazo** *m* blow with a stick; (de mando) staff of office

basur|a *f* rubbish, garbage (Amer); (en la calle) litter. **~al** *m* (LAm, lugar) rubbish dump. **~ero** *m* dustman (Brit), garbage collector (Amer); (sitio) rubbish dump; (Mex, recipiente) dustbin (Brit), garbage can (Amer)

bata *f* dressing-gown; (de médico etc) white coat; (esp LAm, de baño) bathrobe

batahola *f* (LAm) pandemonium

batall|a *f* battle. **~a campa[l]** pitched battle. **de ~a** everyday. **~ador** *a* fighting. ● *m* fighter. **~ar** *vi* battle, fight. **~ón** *m* battalion.

batata *f* sweet potato

bate *m* bat. **~ador** *m* batter, (cricket) batsman. **~ar** *vi* bat

batería *f* battery; (Mus) drums. ● *m & f* drummer. **~ de cocina** kitchen utensils, pots and pans

baterista *m & f* drummer

batido *a* beaten; <*nata*> whipped. ● *m* batter; (bebida) milk shake. **~ra** *f* (food) mixer

batir *vt* beat; break <*récord*>; whip <*nata*>. **~ palmas** clap. □ **~se** *vpr* fight

batuta *f* baton. **llevar la ~** be in command, be the boss

baúl *m* trunk

bauti|smal *a* baptismal. **~smo** *m* baptism, christening. **~zar** [10] *vt* baptize, christen. **~zo** *m* christening

baya *f* berry

bayeta *f* cloth

bayoneta *f* bayonet

baza *f* (naipes) trick; (fig) advantage. **meter ~** interfere

bazar *m* bazaar

bazofia *f* revolting food; (fig) rubbish

beato *a* blessed; (piadoso) devout; (pey) overpious

bebé *m* baby

beb|edero *m* drinking trough; (sitio) watering place. **~edizo** *m* potion; (veneno) poison. **~edor** *m* heavy drinker. **~er** *vt/i* drink. **~ida** *f* drink. **~ido** *a* drunk

beca *f* grant, scholarship. **~do** *m* (LAm) scholarship holder, scholar. **~r** [7] *vt* give a scholarship to. **~rio** *m* scholarship holder, scholar

beige /beis, beʒ/ *a* & *m* beige

béisbol, (Mex) **beisbol** *m* baseball

belén *m* crib, nativity scene

belga *a* & *m* & *f* Belgian

Bélgica *f* Belgium

bélico *a*, **belicoso** *a* warlike

bell|eza *f* beauty. **~o** *a* beautiful. **~as artes** *fpl* fine arts

bellota *f* acorn

bemol *m* flat. **tener (muchos) ~es** be difficult

bend|ecir [46] (*pero imperativo* **bendice**, *futuro, condicional y pp regulares*) *vt* bless. **~ición** *f* blessing. **~ito** *a* blessed; (que tiene suerte) lucky; (feliz) happy

benefactor *m* benefactor

benefic|encia *f* charity. **de ~encia** charitable. **~iar** *vt* benefit. □ **~iarse** *vpr* benefit. **~iario** *m* beneficiary; (de un cheque etc) payee. **~io** *m* benefit; (ventaja) advantage; (ganancia) profit, gain. **~ioso** *a* beneficial

benéfico *a* beneficial; (de beneficencia) charitable

ben|evolencia *f* benevolence. **~évolo** *a* benevolent

bengala *f* flare. **luz** *f* **de ~** flare

benigno *a* kind; (moderado) gentle, mild; <*tumor*> benign

berberecho *m* cockle

berenjena *f* aubergine (Brit), eggplant (Amer)

berr|ear *vi* <*animales*> bellow; <*niño*> bawl. **~ido** *m* bellow; (de niño) bawling

berrinche *m* temper; (de un niño) tantrum

berro *m* watercress

besamel(a) *f* white sauce

bes|ar *vt* kiss. □ **~arse** *vpr* kiss (each other). **~o** *m* kiss

bestia *f* beast; (bruto) brute; (idiota) idiot. **~ de carga** beast of burden. **~l** *a* bestial, animal; (fig, [I]) terrific. **~lidad** *f* (acción brutal) horrid thing; (insensatez) stupidity

besugo *m* red bream

besuquear *vt* cover with kisses

betabel *f* (Mex) beetroot

betún *m* (para el calzado) shoe polish

biberón *m* feeding-bottle

Biblia *f* Bible

bibliografía *f* bibliography

biblioteca *f* library; (mueble) bookcase. **~ de consulta** reference library. **~rio** *m* librarian

bicarbonato *m* bicarbonate

bicho *m* insect, bug; (animal) small animal, creature. **~ raro** odd sort

bici *f* [I] bike. **~cleta** *f* bicycle. **ir en ~cleta** cycle. **~moto** (LAm) moped

bidé, **bidet** *m* /bi'ðe/ bidet

bidón *m* drum, can

bien *adv* well; (muy) very, quite; (correctamente) right; (de buena gana) willingly. ● *m* good; (efectos) property. **¡~!** fine!, OK!, good! **~... (o) ~** either... or. **¡está ~!** fine!, alright!; (basta) that is enough!. **más ~** rather. **¡muy ~!** good! **no ~** as soon as. **¡qué ~!** marvellous!, great! [T]. **si ~** although

bienal *a* biennial

bien|aventurado *a* fortunate. **~estar** *m* well-being. **~hablado** *a* well-spoken. **~hechor** *m* benefactor. **~intencionado** *a* well-meaning

bienio *m* two-year period

bienvenid|a *f* welcome. **dar la ~a a uno** welcome s.o. **~o** *a* welcome. **¡~o!** welcome!

bifurca|ción *f* junction. ▫ **~rse** [7] *vpr* fork; (rail) branch off

b|igamia *f* bigamy. **~ígamo** *a* bigamous. ● *m* bigamist

bigot|e *m* moustache. **~ón** *a* (Mex), **~udo** *a* with a big moustache

bikini *m* bikini

bilingüe *a* bilingual

billar *m* billiards

billete *m* ticket; (de banco) (bank) note (Brit), bill (Amer). **~ de ida y vuelta** return ticket (Brit), round-trip ticket (Amer). **~ sencillo** single ticket (Brit), one-way ticket (Amer). **~ra** *f*, **~ro** *m* wallet, billfold (Amer)

billón *m* billion (Brit), trillion (Amer)

bi|mensual *a* fortnightly, twice-monthly. **~mestral** *a* two-monthly. **~mestre** *m* two-month period. **~motor** *a* twin-engined. ● *m* twin-engined plane

binoculares *mpl* binoculars

bi|ografía *f* biography. **~ográfico** *a* biographical

bi|ología *f* biology. **~ológico** *a* biological. **~ólogo** *m* biologist

biombo *m* folding screen

biopsia *f* biopsy

biplaza *m* two-seater

biquini *m* bikini

birlar *vt* [T] steal, pinch [T]

bis *m* encore. **¡~!** encore! **vivo en el 3 ~** I live at 3A

bisabuel|a *f* great-grandmother. **~o** *m* great-grandfather. **~os** *mpl* great-grandparents

bisagra *f* hinge

bisiesto *a*. **año** *m* **~** leap year

bisniet|a *f* great-granddaughter. **~o** *m* great-grandson. **~os** *mpl* great-grandchildren

bisonte *m* bison

bisoño *a* inexperienced

bisté, **bistec** *m* steak

bisturí *m* scalpel

bisutería *f* imitation jewellery, costume jewellery

bitácora *f* binnacle

bizco *a* cross-eyed

bizcocho *m* sponge (cake)

bizquear *vi* squint

blanc|a *f* white woman; (Mus) minim. **~o** *a* white; <*tez*> fair. ● *m* white; (persona) white man; (espacio) blank; (objetivo) target. **dar en el ~o** hit the mark. **dejar en ~o** leave blank. **pasar la noche en ~o** have a sleepless night. **~ura** *f* whiteness

blandir [24] *vt* brandish

bland|o *a* soft; <*carácter*> weak; (cobarde) cowardly; <*carne*> tender. **~ura** *f* softness; (de la carne) tenderness

blanque|ar *vt* whiten; whitewash <*paredes*>; bleach <*tela*>; launder

<dinero>. ● *vi* turn white. **~o** *m* whitening; (de dinero) laundering

blasón *m* coat of arms

bledo *m*. **me importa un ~** I couldn't care less

blinda|je *m* armour (plating). **~r** *vt* armour(-plate)

bloc *m* (*pl* **~s**) pad

bloque *m* block; (Pol) bloc. **en ~** en bloc. **~ar** *vt* block; (Mil) blockade; (Com) freeze. **~o** *m* blockade; (Com) freezing

blusa *f* blouse

bob|ada *f* silly thing. **decir ~adas** talk nonsense. **~ería** *f* silly thing

bobina *f* reel; (Elec) coil

bobo *a* silly, stupid. ● *m* idiot, fool

boca *f* mouth; (fig, entrada) entrance; (de buzón) slot; (de cañón) muzzle. **~ abajo** face down. **~ arriba** face up. **a ~ de jarro** point-blank. **con la ~ abierta** dumbfounded. **se me hizo la ~ agua** it made my mouth water

bocacalle *f* junction. **la primera ~ a la derecha** the first turning on the right

bocad|illo *m* (filled) roll; ([I], comida ligera) snack. **~o** *m* mouthful; (mordisco) bite; (de caballo) bit

boca|jarro. **a ~jarro** point-blank. **~manga** *f* cuff

bocanada *f* puff; (de vino etc) mouthful; (ráfaga) gust

bocazas *m & f invar* big mouth

boceto *m* sketch; (de proyecto) outline

bochinche *m* row; (alboroto) racket. **~ro** *a* (LAm) rowdy

bochorno *m* sultry weather; (fig, vergüenza) embarrassment. **¡qué ~!** how embarrassing!. **~so** *a* oppressive; (fig) embarrassing

bocina *f* horn; (LAm, auricular) receiver. **tocar la ~** sound one's horn. **~zo** *m* toot

boda *f* wedding

bodeg|a *f* cellar; (de vino) wine cellar; (LAm, almacén) warehouse; (de un barco) hold. **~ón** *m* cheap restaurant; (pintura) still life

bodoque *m & f* ([I], tonto) thickhead; (Mex, niño) kid

bofes *mpl* lights. **echar los ~** slog away

bofet|ada *f* slap; (fig) blow. **~ón** *m* punch

boga *f* (moda) fashion. **estar en ~** be in fashion, be in vogue. **~r** [12] *vt* row. **~vante** *m* (crustáceo) lobster

Bogotá *f* Bogotá

bogotano *a* from Bogotá. ● *m* native of Bogotá

bohemio *a & m* Bohemian

bohío *m* (LAm) hut

boicot *m* (*pl* **~s**) boycott. **~ear** *vt* boycott. **~eo** *m* boycott. **hacer un ~** boycott

boina *f* beret

bola *f* ball; (canica) marble; (mentira) fib; (Mex, reunión desordenada) rowdy party; (Mex, montón). **una ~ de** a bunch of; (Mex, revolución) revolution; (Mex, brillo) shine

boleadoras (LAm) *fpl* bolas

bolear *vt* (Mex) polish, shine

bolera *f* bowling alley

bolero *m* (baile, chaquetilla) bolero; (fig, [I], mentiroso) liar; (Mex, limpiabotas) bootblack

bole|ta *f* (LAm, de rifa) ticket; (Mex, de notas) (school) report; (Mex, electoral) ballot paper. **~taje** *m* (Mex) tickets. **~tería** *f* (LAm) ticket office; (de teatro, cine) box office. **~tero** *m* (LAm) ticket-seller

boletín *m* bulletin; (publicación periódica) journal; (de notas) report

boleto *m* (esp LAm) ticket; (Mex, de avión) (air) ticket. **~ de ida y vuelta**, (Mex) **~ redondo** return ticket (Brit), round-trip ticket (Amer). **~ sencillo** single ticket (Brit), one-way ticket (Amer)

boli *m* 🅸 Biro (P), ball-point pen

boliche *m* (juego) bowls; (bolera) bowling alley

bolígrafo *m* Biro (P), ball-point pen

bolillo *m* bobbin; (Mex, pan) (bread) roll

bolívar *m* (unidad monetaria venezolana) bolívar

Bolivia *f* Bolivia

boliviano *a* Bolivian. ● *m* Bolivian; (unidad monetaria de Bolivia) boliviano

boll|ería *f* baker's shop. **~o** *m* roll; (con azúcar) bun

bolo *m* skittle; (Mex, en bautizo) coins. **~s** *mpl* (juego) bowling

bols|a *f* bag; (Mex, bolsillo) pocket; (Mex, de mujer) handbag; (Com) stock exchange; (cavidad) cavity. **~a de agua caliente** hot-water bottle. **~illo** *m* pocket. **de ~illo** pocket. **~o** *m* (de mujer) handbag. **~o de mano, ~o de viaje** (overnight) bag

bomba *f* bomb; (máquina) pump; (noticia) bombshell. **~ de aceite** (Auto) oil pump. **~ de agua** (Auto) water pump. **pasarlo ~** have a marvellous time

bombachos *mpl* baggy trousers, baggy pants (Amer)

bombarde|ar *vt* bombard; (desde avión) bomb. **~o** *m* bombardment; (desde avión) bombing. **~ro** *m* (avión) bomber

bombazo *m* explosion

bombear *vt* pump

bombero *m* fireman. **cuerpo** *m* **de ~s** fire brigade (Brit), fire department (Amer)

bombilla *f* (light) bulb; (LAm, para mate) pipe for drinking maté

bombín *m* pump; (🅸, sombrero) bowler (hat) (Brit), derby (Amer)

bombo *m* (tambor) bass drum. **a ~ y platillos** with a lot of fuss

bomb|ón *m* chocolate; (Mex, malvavisco) marshmallow. **~ona** *f* gas cylinder

bonachón *a* easygoing; (bueno) good-natured

bonaerense *a* from Buenos Aires. ● *m* native of Buenos Aires

bondad *f* goodness; (amabilidad) kindness; (del clima) mildness. **tenga la ~ de** would you be kind enough to. **~oso** *a* kind

boniato *m* sweet potato

bonito *a* nice; (mono) pretty. **¡muy ~!, ¡qué ~!** that's nice!, very nice! ● *m* bonito

bono *m* voucher; (título) bond. **~ del Tesoro** government bond

boñiga *f* dung

boqueada *f* gasp. **dar la última ~** be dying

boquerón *m* anchovy

boquete *m* hole; (brecha) breach

boquiabierto *a* open-mouthed; (fig) amazed, dumbfounded. **quedarse ~** be amazed

boquilla *f* mouthpiece; (para cigarillos) cigarette-holder; (filtro de cigarillo) tip

borbotón *m*. **hablar a borbotones** gabble. **salir a borbotones** gush out

borda|do *a* embroidered. ● *m* embroidery. **~r** *vt* embroider

bord|e *m* edge; (de carretera) side; (de plato etc) rim; (de un vestido) hem. **al ~e de** on the edge of; (fig) on the brink of. **~ear** *vt* go round; (fig) border on. **~illo** *m* kerb (Brit), curb (esp Amer)

bordo *m*. **a ~** on board

borla *f* tassel

borrach|era *f* drunkenness. **pegarse una ~era** get drunk. **~ín** *m* drunk; (habitual) drunkard. **~o** *a* drunk. ● *m* drunkard. **estar ~o** be drunk. **ser ~o** be a drunkard

borrador *m* rough draft; (de contrato) draft; (para la pizarra) (black)-board rubber; (goma) eraser

borrar *vt* rub out; (tachar) cross out; delete *<información>*

borrasc|a *f* depression; (tormenta) storm. **~oso** *a* stormy

borrego *m* year-old lamb; (Mex, noticia falsa) canard

borrico *m* donkey; (fig, 🅘) ass

borrón *m* smudge; (de tinta) inkblot. **~ y cuenta nueva** let's forget about it!

borroso *a* blurred; (fig) vague

bos|coso *a* wooded. **~que** *m* wood, forest

bosquej|ar *vt* sketch; outline *<plan>*. **~o** *m* sketch; (de plan) outline

bosta *f* dung

bostez|ar [10] *vi* yawn. **~o** *m* yawn

bota *f* boot; (recipiente) wineskin

botana *f* (Mex) snack, appetizer

botánic|a *f* botany. **~o** *a* botanical. ● *m* botanist

botar *vt* launch; bounce *<pelota>*; (esp LAm, tirar) throw away. ● *vi* bounce

botarate *m* irresponsible person; (esp LAm, derrochador) spendthrift

bote *m* boat; (de una pelota) bounce; (lata) tin, can; (vasija) jar. **~ de la basura** (Mex) rubbish bin (Brit), trash can (Amer). **~ salvavidas** lifeboat. **de ~ en ~** packed

botella *f* bottle

botica *f* chemist's (shop) (Brit), drugstore (Amer). **~rio** *m* chemist (Brit), druggist (Amer)

botijo *m* earthenware jug

botín *m* half boot; (de guerra) booty; (de ladrones) haul

botiquín *m* medicine chest; (de primeros auxilios) first aid kit

bot|ón *m* button; (yema) bud; (LAm, insignia) badge. **~ones** *m invar* bellboy (Brit), bellhop (Amer)

bóveda *f* vault

boxe|ador *m* boxer. **~ar** *vi* box. **~o** *m* boxing

boya *f* buoy; (corcho) float. **~nte** *a* buoyant

bozal *m* (de perro etc) muzzle; (de caballo) halter

bracear *vi* wave one's arms; (nadar) swim, crawl

bracero *m* seasonal farm labourer

braga(s) *f(pl)* panties, knickers (Brit)

bragueta *f* flies

bram|ar *vi* bellow. **~ido** *m* bellowing

branquia *f* gill

bras|a *f* ember. **a la ~a** grilled. **~ero** *m* brazier

brasier *m* (Mex) bra

Brasil *m*. **(el) ~** Brazil

brasile|ño *a* & *m* Brazilian. **~ro** *a* & *m* (LAm) Brazilian

bravío *a* wild

brav|o *a* fierce; (valeroso) brave; <*mar*> rough. **¡~o!** *int* well done!, bravo! **~ura** *f* ferocity; (valor) bravery

braz|a *f* fathom. **nadar a ~a** swim breast-stroke. **~ada** *f* (en natación) stroke. **~alete** *m* bracelet; (brazal) arm-band. **~o** *m* arm; (de caballo) foreleg; (rama) branch. **~o derecho** right-hand man. **del ~o** arm in arm

brea *f* tar, pitch

brebaje *m* potion; (pej) concoction

brecha *f* opening; (Mil) breach; (Med) gash. **~ generacional** generation gap. **estar en la ~** be in the thick of it

brega *f* struggle. **andar a la ~** work hard

breva *f* early fig

breve *a* short. **en ~** soon, shortly. **en ~s momentos** soon. **~dad** *f* shortness

brib|ón *m* rogue, rascal. **~onada** *f* dirty trick

brida *f* bridle

brigad|a *f* squad; (Mil) brigade. **~ier** *m* brigadier (Brit), brigadier-general (Amer)

brill|ante *a* bright; (lustroso) shiny; <*persona*> brilliant. ● *m* diamond. **~ar** *vi* shine; (centellear) sparkle. **~o** *m* shine; (brillantez) brilliance; (centelleo) sparkle. **sacar ~o** polish. **~oso** *a* (LAm) shiny

brinc|ar [7] *vi* jump up and down. **~o** *m* jump. **dar un ~o, pegar un ~o** jump

brind|ar *vt* offer. ● *vi.* **~ar por** toast, drink a toast to. **~is** *m* toast

br|ío *m* energy; (decisión) determination. **~ioso** *a* spirited; (garboso) elegant

brisa *f* breeze

británico *a* British. ● *m* Briton, British person

brocha *f* paintbrush; (para afeitarse) shaving-brush

broche *m* clasp, fastener; (joya) brooch; (Mex, para el pelo) hairslide (Brit), barrete (Amer)

brocheta *f* skewer; (plato) kebab

brócoli *m* broccoli

brom|a *f* joke. **~a pesada** practical joke. **en ~a** in fun. **ni de ~a** no way. **~ear** *vi* joke. **~ista** *a* fond of joking. ● *m & f* joker

bronca *f* row; (reprensión) telling-off; (LAm, rabia) foul mood. **dar ~ a uno** bug s.o.

bronce *m* bronze; (LAm) brass. **~ado** *a* bronze; (por el sol) tanned. **~ar** *vt* tan <*piel*>. □ **~arse** *vpr* get a suntan

bronquitis *f* bronchitis

brot|ar *vi* (plantas) sprout; (Med) break out; <*líquido*> gush forth; <*lágrimas*> well up. **~e** *m* shoot; (Med) outbreak

bruces: **de ~** face down(wards). **caer de ~** fall flat on one's face

bruj|a *f* witch. **~ería** *f* witchcraft. **~o** *m* wizard, magician. ● *a* (Mex) broke

brújula *f* compass

brum|a *f* mist; (fig) confusion. **~oso** *a* misty, foggy

brusco *a* (repentino) sudden; <*persona*> brusque

Bruselas *f* Brussels

brusquedad *f* roughness; (de movimiento) abruptness

brut|al *a* brutal. **~alidad** *f* brutality; (estupidez) stupidity. **~o** *a* ignorant; (tosco) rough; <*peso, sueldo*> gross

bucal *a* oral; <*lesión*> mouth

buce|ar *vi* dive; (nadar) swim under water. **~o** *m* diving; (natación) underwater swimming

bucle *m* ringlet

budín *m* pudding

budis|mo *m* Buddhism. **~ta** *m & f* Buddhist

buen ⇒BUENO

buenaventura *f* good luck; (adivinación) fortune

bueno *a* (delante de nombre masculino en singular **buen**) good; (agradable) nice; <*tiempo*> fine. ● *int* well!; (de acuerdo) OK!, very well! **¡buena la has hecho!** you've gone and done it now! **¡buenas noches!** good night! **¡buenas tardes!** (antes del atardecer) good afternoon!; (después del atardecer) good evening! **¡~s días!** good morning! **estar de buenas** be in a good mood. **por las buenas** willingly. **¡qué bueno!** (LAm) great!

Buenos Aires *m* Buenos Aires

buey *m* ox

búfalo *m* buffalo

bufanda *f* scarf

bufar *vi* snort

bufete *m* (mesa) writing-desk; (despacho) lawyer's office

buf|o *a* comic. **~ón** *a* comical. ● *m* buffoon; (Historia) jester

buhardilla *f* attic; (ventana) dormer window

búho *m* owl

buhonero *m* pedlar

buitre *m* vulture

bujía *f* (Auto) spark plug

bulbo *m* bulb

bulevar *m* avenue, boulevard

Bulgaria *f* Bulgaria

búlgaro *a* & *m* Bulgarian

bull|a *f* noise. **~icio** *m* hubbub; (movimiento) bustle. **~icioso** *a* bustling; (ruidoso) noisy

bullir [22] *vi* boil; (burbujear) bubble; (fig) bustle

bulto *m* (volumen) bulk; (forma) shape; (paquete) package; (maleta etc) piece of luggage; (protuberancia) lump

buñuelo *m* fritter

BUP *abrev* (**Bachillerato Unificado Polivalente**) secondary school education

buque *m* ship, boat

burbuj|a *f* bubble. **~ear** *vi* bubble; <*vino*> sparkle

burdel *m* brothel

burdo *a* rough, coarse; <*excusa*> clumsy

burgu|és *a* middle-class, bourgeois. ● *m* middle-class person. **~esía** *f* middle class, bourgeoisie

burla *f* taunt; (broma) joke; (engaño) trick. **~r** *vt* evade. □ **~rse** *vpr*. **~rse de** mock, make fun of

burlesco *a* (en literatura) burlesque

burlón *a* mocking

bur|ocracia *f* bureaucracy; (Mex, funcionariado) civil service. **~ócrata** *m & f* bureaucrat; (Mex, funcionario) civil servant. **~ocrático** *a* bureaucratic; (Mex) <*empleado*> government

burro *a* stupid; (obstinado) pigheaded. ● *m* donkey; (fig) ass

bursátil *a* stock-exchange

bus *m* bus

busca *f* search. **a la ~ de** in search of. **en ~ de** in search of. ● *m* beeper

buscapleitos *m & f invar* (LAm) trouble-maker

buscar [7] *vt* look for. ● *vi* look. **buscársela** ask for it; **ir a ~ a uno** fetch s.o.

búsqueda *f* search

busto *m* bust

butaca *f* armchair; (en el teatro etc) seat

buzo *m* diver

buzón *m* postbox (Brit), mailbox (Amer)

Cc

C/ *abrev* (**Calle**) St, Rd

cabal *a* exact; (completo) complete. **no estar en sus ~es** not be in one's right mind

cabalga|dura *f* mount, horse. **~r** [12] *vt* ride. ● *vi* ride, go riding. **~ta** *f* ride; (desfile) procession

caballa *f* mackerel

caballerango *m* (Mex) groom

caballeresco *a* gentlemanly. **literatura** *f* **caballeresca** books of chivalry

caballer|ía *f* mount, horse. **~iza** *f* stable. **~izo** *m* groom

caballero *m* gentleman; (de orden de caballería) knight; (tratamiento) sir. **~so** *a* gentlemanly

caballete *m* (del tejado) ridge; (para mesa) trestle; (de pintor) easel

caballito *m* pony. **~ del diablo** dragonfly. **~ de mar** sea-horse. **~s** *mpl* (carrusel) merry-go-round

caballo *m* horse; (del ajedrez) knight; (de la baraja española) queen. **~ de fuerza** horsepower. **a ~** on horseback

cabaña *f* hut

cabaret /kaba're/ *m* (*pl* **~s**) night-club

cabecear *vi* nod off; (en fútbol) head the ball; <*caballo*> toss its head

cabecera *f* (de la cama) headboard; (de la mesa) head; (en un impreso) heading

cabecilla *m* ringleader

cabello *m* hair. **~s** *mpl* hair

caber [28] *vi* fit (**en** into). **no cabe duda** there's no doubt

cabestr|illo *m* sling. **~o** *m* halter

cabeza *f* head; (fig, inteligencia) intelligence. **andar de ~** have a lot to do. **~da** *f* nod. **dar una ~da** nod off. **~zo** *m* butt; (en fútbol) header

cabida *f* capacity; (extensión) area; (espacio) room. **dar ~ a** have room for, accommodate

cabina *f* (de pasajeros) cabin; (de pilotos) cockpit; (electoral) booth; (de camión) cab. **~ telefónica** telephone box (Brit), telephone booth (Amer)

cabizbajo *a* crestfallen

cable *m* cable

cabo *m* end; (trozo) bit; (Mil) corporal; (mango) handle; (Geog) cape; (Naut) rope. **al ~ de** after. **de ~ a rabo** from beginning to end. **llevar a ~** carry out

cabr|a *f* goat. **~iola** *f* jump, skip. **~itilla** *f* kid. **~ito** *m* kid

cábula *m* (Mex) crook

cacahuate, (Mex) **cacahuete** *m* peanut

cacalote *m* (Mex) crow

cacao *m* (planta y semillas) cacao; (polvo) cocoa; (fig) confusion

cacarear *vt* boast about. ● *vi* <*gallo*> crow; <*gallina*> cluck

cacería *f* hunt. **ir de ~** go hunting

cacerola *f* saucepan, casserole

cacharro *m* (earthenware) pot; (coche estropeado) wreck; (cosa inútil) piece of junk; (chisme) thing. **~s** *mpl* pots and pans

cachear *vt* frisk

cachemir *m*, **cachemira** *f* cashmere

cacheo *m* frisking

cachetada *f* (LAm) slap

cache|te *m* slap; (esp LAm, mejilla) cheek. **~tear** *vt* (LAm) slap. **~tón** *a* (LAm) chubby-cheeked

cachimba *f* pipe

cachiporra *f* club, truncheon

cachivache *m* piece of junk. **~s** *mpl* junk

cacho *m* bit, piece; (LAm, cuerno) horn

cachondeo *m* 🅘 joking, joke

cachorro *m* (perrito) puppy; (de león, tigre) cub

cachucha *f* (Mex) cup

caciqu|e *m* cacique, chief; (Pol) local political boss; (hombre poderoso) tyrant. **~il** *a* despotic. **~ismo** *m* despotism

caco *m* thief

cacofonía *f* cacophony

cacto *m*, **cactus** *m invar* cactus

cada *a invar* each, every. **~ uno** each one, everyone. **uno de ~ cinco** one in five. **~ vez más** more and more

cadáver *m* corpse

cadena *f* chain; (TV) channel. **~ de fabricación** production line. **~ de montañas** mountain range. **~ perpetua** life imprisonment

cadera *f* hip

cadete *m* cadet

caduc|ar [7] *vi* expire. **~idad** *f*. **fecha** *f* **de ~idad** sell-by date. **~o** *a* outdated

cae|r [29] *vi* fall. **dejar ~r** drop. **este vestido no me ~ bien** this dress doesn't suit me. **hacer ~r** knock over. **Juan me ~ bien** I like Juan. **su cumpleaños cayó en martes** his birthday fell on a Tuesday. □ **~rse** *vpr* fall (over). **se le cayó** he dropped it

café *m* coffee; (cafetería) café; (Mex, marrón) brown. ● *a*. **color ~** coffee-coloured. **~ con leche** white coffee. **~ cortado** coffee with a little milk. **~ negro** (LAm) expresso. **~ solo** black coffee

cafe|ína *f* caffeine. **~tal** *m* coffee plantation. **~tera** *f* coffee-pot. **~tería** *f* café. **~tero** *a* coffee

caíd|a *f* fall; (disminución) drop; (pendiente) slope. **~o** *a* fallen

caigo *vb* ⇒CAER

caimán *m* cayman, alligator

caj|a *f* box; (de botellas) case; (ataúd) coffin; (en tienda) cash desk; (en supermercado) check-out; (en banco) cashier's desk. **~a de ahorros** savings bank. **~a de cambios** gearbox. **~a de caudales**, **~a fuerte** safe. **~a registradora** till. **~ero** *m* cashier. **~ero automático** cash dispenser. **~etilla** *f* packet. **~ita** *f* small box. **~ón** *m* (de mueble) drawer; (caja grande) crate; (LAm, ataúd) coffin; (Mex, en estacionamiento) parking space. **ser de ~ón** be obvious. **~uela** *f* (Mex) boot (Brit), trunk (Amer)

cal *m* lime

cala *f* cove

calaba|cín *m*, **~cita** *f* (Mex) courgette (Brit), zucchini (Amer). **~za** *f* pumpkin; (fig, [I], idiota) idiot. **dar ~zas a uno** give s.o. the brush-off

calabozo *m* prison; (celda) cell

calado *a* soaked. **estar ~ hasta los huesos** be soaked to the skin. ● *m* (Naut) draught

calamar *m* squid

calambre *m* cramp

calami|dad *f* calamity, disaster. **~toso** *a* calamitous

calaña *f* sort

calar *vt* soak; (penetrar) pierce; (fig, penetrar) see through; rumble <*persona*>; sample <*fruta*>. □ **~se** *vpr* get soaked; <*zapatos*> leak; (Auto) stall

calavera *f* skull; (Mex, Auto) tail-light

calcar [7] *vt* trace; (fig) copy

calcet|a *f*. **hacer ~** knit. **~ín** *m* sock

calcetín *m* sock

calcinar *vt* burn

calcio *m* calcium

calcomanía *f* transfer

calcula|dor *a* calculating. **~dora** *f* calculator. **~r** *vt* calculate; (suponer) reckon, think; (imaginar) imagine

cálculo *m* calculation; (Med) stone

caldear *vt* heat, warm. □ **~se** *vpr* get hot

caldera *f* boiler

calderilla *f* small change

caldo *m* stock; (sopa) clear soup, broth

calefacción *f* heating. **~ central** central heating

caleidoscopio *m* kaleidoscope

calendario *m* calendar; (programa) schedule

calent|ador *m* heater. **~amiento** *m* warming; (en deportes) warm-up. **~ar** [1] *vt* heat; (templar) warm. □ **~arse** *vpr* get hot; (templarse) warm up; (LAm, enojarse) get mad. **~ura** *f* fever, (high) temperature. **~uriento** *a* feverish

calibr|ar *vt* calibrate; (fig) weigh up. **~e** *m* calibre; (diámetro) diameter; (fig) importance

calidad *f* quality; (condición) capacity. **en ~ de** as

calidez *f* (LAm) warmth

cálido *a* warm

caliente *a* hot; <*habitación, ropa*> warm; (LAm, enojado) angry

califica|ción *f* qualification; (evaluación) assessment; (nota) mark. **~do** *a* (esp LAm) qualified; (mano de obra) skilled. **~r** [7] *vt* qualify; (evaluar) assess; mark <*examen etc*>. **~r de** describe as, label

cáliz *m* chalice; (Bot) calyx

caliz|a *f* limestone. **~o** *a* lime

calla|do *a* quiet. **~r** *vt* silence; keep <*secreto*>; hush up <*asunto*>. ● *vi* be quiet, keep quiet, shut up [I]. □ **~rse** *vpr* be quiet, keep quiet, shut up [I] **¡cállate!** be quiet!, shut up! [I]

calle *f* street, road; (en deportes, autopista) lane. **~ de dirección única** one-way street. **~ mayor** high street, main street. **de ~** everyday. **~ja** *f* narrow street. **~jear** *vi* hang out on the streets. **~jero** *a* street. ● *m* street plan. **~jón** *m* alley. **~jón sin salida** dead end. **~juela** *f* back street, side street

call|ista *m & f* chiropodist. **~o** *m* corn, callus. **~os** *mpl* tripe. **~osidad** *f* callus

calm|a *f* calm. **¡~a!** calm down!. **en ~a** calm. **perder la ~a** lose one's composure. **~ante** *m* tranquilizer; (para el dolor) painkiller. **~ar** *vt* calm; (aliviar) soothe. ● *vi* <*viento*> abate. □ **~arse** *vpr* calm down; <*viento*> abate. **~o** *a* calm. **~oso** *a* calm; (🅸, flemático) slow

calor *m* heat; (afecto) warmth. **hace ~** it's hot. **tener ~** be hot. **~ía** *f* calorie. **~ífero** *a* heat-producing. **~ico** *a* calorific

calumni|a *f* calumny; (oral) slander; (escrita) libel. **~ar** *vt* slander; (por escrito) libel. **~oso** *a* slanderous; <*cosa escrita*> libellous

caluroso *a* warm; <*clima*> hot

calv|a *f* bald head; (parte sin pelo) bald patch. **~icie** *f* baldness. **~o** *a* bald

calza *f* wedge

calzada *f* road; (en autopista) carriageway

calza|do *a* wearing shoes. ● *m* footwear, shoe. **~dor** *m* shoehorn. **~r** [10] *vt* put shoes on; (llevar) wear. **¿qué número calza Vd?** what size shoe do you take? ● *vi* wear shoes. □ **~rse** *vpr* put on

calz|ón *m* shorts. **~ones** *mpl* shorts; (LAm, ropa interior) panties. **~oncillos** *mpl* underpants

cama *f* bed. **~ de matrimonio** double bed. **~ individual** single bed. **guardar ~** stay in bed

camada *f* litter

camafeo *m* cameo

camaleón *m* chameleon

cámara *f* (aposento) chamber; (fotográfica) camera. **~ fotográfica** camera. **a ~ lenta** in slow motion

camarad|a *m & f* colleague; (de colegio) schoolfriend; (Pol) comrade. **~ería** *f* camaraderie

camarer|a *f* chambermaid; (de restaurante etc) waitress. **~o** *m* waiter

camarógrafo *m* cameraman

camarón *m* shrimp

camarote *m* cabin

cambi|able *a* changeable; (Com etc) exchangeable. **~ante** *a* variable; <*persona*> moody. **~ar** *vt* change; (trocar) exchange. ● *vi* change. **~ar de idea** change one's mind. □ **~arse** *vpr* change. **~o** *m* change; (Com) exchange rate; (moneda menuda) (small) change; (Auto) gear. **en ~o** on the other hand

camello *m* camel

camellón *m* (Mex) traffic island

camerino *m* dressing room

camilla *f* stretcher

camin|ante *m* traveller. **~ar** *vt/i* walk. **~ata** *f* long walk. **~o** *m* road; (sendero) path, track; (dirección, ruta) way. **~o de** towards, on the way to. **abrir ~o** make way. **a medio ~o, a la mitad del ~o** half-way. **de ~o** on the way

cami|ón *m* lorry; (Mex, autobús) bus. **~onero** *m* lorry-driver; (Mex, de autobús) bus driver. **~oneta** *f* van; (LAm, coche familiar) estate car

camis|a *f* shirt. **~a de fuerza** strait-jacket. **~ería** *f* shirtmaker's. **~eta** *f* T-shirt; (ropa interior) vest. **~ón** *m* nightdress

camorra *f* 🅸 row. **buscar ~** look for a fight

camote *m* (LAm) sweet potato

campamento *m* camp. **de ~** *a* camping

campan|a *f* bell. **~ada** *f* stroke. **~ario** *m* bell tower, belfry. **~illa** *f* bell

campaña *f* campaign

campe|ón *a* & *m* champion. **~onato** *m* championship

campes|ino *a* country. ● *m* peasant. **~tre** *a* country

camping /'kampin/ *m* (*pl* **~s**) camping; (lugar) campsite. **hacer ~** go camping

camp|iña *f* countryside. **~o** *m* country; (agricultura, fig) field; (de fútbol) pitch; (de golf) course. **~osanto** *m* cemetery

camufla|je *m* camouflage. **~r** *vt* camouflage

cana *f* grey hair, white hair. **peinar ~s** be getting old

Canadá *m*. **el ~** Canada

canadiense *a* & *m* & *f* Canadian

canal *m* (incl TV) channel; (artificial) canal; (del tejado) gutter. **~ de la Mancha** English Channel. **~ de Panamá** Panama Canal. **~ón** *m* (horizontal) gutter; (vertical) drain-pipe

canalla *f* rabble. ● *m* (fig, [I]) swine. **~da** *f* dirty trick

canapé *m* sofa, couch; (Culin) canapé

Canarias *fpl*. **las (islas) ~** the Canary Islands, the Canaries

canario *a* of the Canary Islands. ● *m* native of the Canary Islands; (pájaro) canary

canast|a *f* (large) basket **~illa** *f* small basket; (para un bebé) layette. **~illo** *m* small basket. **~o** *m* (large) basket

cancela|ción *f* cancellation. **~r** *vt* cancel; write off <*deuda*>

cáncer *m* cancer. **C~** Cancer

cancha *f* court; (LAm, de fútbol, rugby) pitch, ground

canciller *m* chancellor; (LAm, ministro) Minister of Foreign Affairs

canci|ón *f* song. **~ón de cuna** lullaby. **~onero** *m* song-book

candado *m* padlock

candel|a *f* candle. **~abro** *m* candelabra. **~ero** *m* candlestick

candente *a* (rojo) red-hot; (fig) burning

candidato *m* candidate

candidez *f* innocence; (ingenuidad) naivety

cándido *a* naive

candil *m* oil lamp. **~ejas** *fpl* footlights

candor *m* innocence; (ingenuidad) naivety

canela *f* cinnamon

cangrejo *m* crab. **~ de río** crayfish

canguro *m* kangaroo. ● *m* & *f* (persona) baby-sitter

caníbal *a* & *m* & *f* cannibal

canica *f* marble

canijo *a* weak; (Mex, terco) stubborn; (Mex, intenso) incredible

canilla *f* (LAm) shinbone

canino *a* canine. ● *m* canine (tooth)

canje *m* exchange. **~ar** *vt* exchange

cano *a* grey. **de pelo ~** grey-haired

canoa *f* canoe

can|ónigo *m* canon. **~onizar** [10] *vt* canonize

canoso *a* grey-haired

cansa|do *a* tired; (que cansa) tiring. **~dor** (LAm) tiring. **~ncio** *m* tiredness. **~r** *vt* tire; (aburrir) bore. ● *vi* be tiring; (aburrir) get boring. □ **~rse** *vpr* get tired

canta|nte *a* singing. ● *m* & *f* singer. **~or** *m* Flamenco singer. **~r** *vt/i* sing. **~rlas claras** speak frankly. ● *m* singing; (poema) poem

cántaro *m* pitcher. **llover a ~s** pour down

cante *m* folk song. **~ flamenco, ~ jondo** Flamenco singing

cantera *f* quarry

cantidad *f* quantity; (número) number; (de dinero) sum. **una ~ de** lots of

cantimplora *f* water-bottle

cantina *f* canteen; (Rail) buffet; (LAm, bar) bar

cant|inela *f* song. **~o** *m* singing; (canción) chant; (borde) edge; (de un cuchillo) blunt edge. **~o rodado** boulder; (guijarro) pebble. **de ~o** on edge

canturre|ar *vt/i* hum. **~o** *m* humming

canuto *m* tube

caña *f* (planta) reed; (del trigo) stalk; (del bambú) cane; (de pescar) rod; (de la bota) leg; (vaso) glass. **~ de azúcar** sugar-cane. **~da** *f* ravine; (camino) track; (LAm, arroyo) stream

cáñamo *m* hemp. **~ indio** cannabis

cañ|ería *f* pipe; (tubería) piping. **~o** *m* pipe, tube; (de fuente) jet. **~ón** *m* (de pluma) quill; (de artillería) cannon; (de arma de fuego) barrel; (desfiladero) canyon. **~onera** *f* gunboat

caoba *f* mahogany

ca|os *m* chaos. **~ótico** *a* chaotic

capa *f* layer; (de pintura) coat; (Culin) coating; (prenda) cloak; (más corta) cape; (Geol) stratum

capaci|dad *f* capacity; (fig) ability. **~tar** *vt* qualify, enable; (instruir) train

caparazón *m* shell

capataz *m* foreman

capaz *a* capable, able

capcioso *a* sly, insidious

capellán *m* chaplain

caperuza *f* hood; (de bolígrafo) cap

capilla *f* chapel

capital *a* capital, very important. ● *m* (dinero) capital. ● *f* (ciudad) capital. **~ de provincia** county town. **~ino** *a* (LAm) of/from the capital. **~ismo** *m* capitalism. **~ista** *a & m & f* capitalist. **~izar** [10] *vt* capitalize

capit|án *m* captain; (de pesquero) skipper. **~anear** *vt* lead, command; skipper <*pesquero*>; captain <*un equipo*>

capitel *m* (Arquit) capital

capitulaci|ón *f* surrender. **~ones** *fpl* marriage contract

capítulo *m* chapter; (de serie) episode

capó *m* bonnet (Brit), hood (Amer)

capón *m* (pollo) capon

caporal *m* (Mex) foreman

capot|a *f* (de mujer) bonnet; (Auto) folding top; (de cochecito) hood. **~e** *m* cape; (Mex, de coche) bonnet (Brit), hood (Amer)

capricho *m* whim. **~so** *a* capricious, whimsical

Capricornio *m* Capricorn

cápsula *f* capsule

captar *vt* harness <*agua*>; grasp <*sentido*>; capture <*atención*>; win <*confianza*>; (radio) pick up

captura *f* capture. **~r** *vt* capture

capucha *f* hood

capullo *m* bud; (de insecto) cocoon

caqui *m* khaki

cara *f* face; (de una moneda) heads; (de un objeto) side; (aspecto) look, appearance; (descaro) cheek. **~ a** facing. **~ a ~** face to face. **~ dura** ⇨ CARADURA. **~ o cruz** heads or tails. **dar la ~ a** face up to. **hacer ~ a** face. **tener mala ~** look ill. **volver la ~** look the other way

carabela *f* caravel

carabina *f* carbine; (fig, ⓘ, señora) chaperone

caracol *m* snail; (de mar) winkle; (LAm, concha) conch; (de pelo) curl. **¡~es!** Good Heavens!. **~a** *f* conch

carácter *m* (*pl* **caracteres**) character; (indole) nature. **con ~ de** as

característic|a *f* characteristic. **~o** *a* characteristic, typical

caracteriza|do *a* characterized; (prestigioso) distinguished. **~r** [10] *vt* characterize

caradura *f* cheek, nerve. ● *m & f* cheeky person

caramba *int* good heavens!

carambola *f* (en billar) cannon; (Mex, choque múltiple) pile-up. **de ~** by pure chance

caramelo *m* sweet (Brit), candy (Amer); (azúcar fundido) caramel

caraqueño *a* from Caracas

carátula *f* (de disco) sleeve (Brit), jacket (Amer); (de video) case; (de libro) cover; (Mex, del reloj) face

caravana *f* caravan; (de vehículos) convoy; (Auto) long line, traffic jam; (remolque) caravan (Brit), trailer (Amer); (Mex, reverencia) bow

caray *int* ⓘ good heavens!

carb|ón *m* coal; (para dibujar) charcoal. **~ de leña** charcoal. **~oncillo** *m* charcoal. **~onero** *a* coal. ● *m* coal-merchant. **~onizar** [10] *vt* (fig) burn (to a cinder). **~ono** *m* carbon

carbura|dor *m* carburettor. **~nte** *m* fuel

carcajada *f* guffaw. **reírse a ~s** roar with laughter. **soltar una ~** burst out laughing

cárcel *f* prison, jail

carcelero *m* jailer

carcom|er *vt* eat away; (fig) undermine. □ **~erse** *vpr* be eaten away; (fig) waste away

cardenal *m* cardinal; (contusión) bruise

cardiaco, cardíaco *a* cardiac, heart

cardinal *a* cardinal

cardo *m* thistle

carear *vt* bring face to face <*personas*>; compare <*cosas*>

care|cer [11] *vi*. **~cer de** lack. **~cer de sentido** not to make sense. **~ncia** *f* lack. **~nte** *a* lacking

care|ro *a* pricey. **~stía** *f* (elevado) high cost

careta *f* mask

carey *m* tortoiseshell

carga *f* load; (fig) burden; (acción) loading; (de barco, avión) cargo; (de tren) freight; (de arma) charge; (Elec, ataque) charge; (obligación) obligation. **llevar la ~ de algo** be responsible for sth. **~da** *f* (Mex, Pol) supporters. **~do** *a* loaded; (fig) burdened; <*atmósfera*> heavy; <*café*> strong; <*pila*> charged. **~mento** *m* load; (acción) loading; (de un barco) cargo. **~r** [12] *vt* load; (fig) burden; (Elec, atacar) charge; fill <*pluma etc*>. ● *vi* load. **~r con** carry. □ **~rse** *vpr* <*pila*> charge. **~rse de** to load s.o. down with

cargo *m* (puesto) post; (acusación) charge. **a ~ de** in the charge of. **hacerse ~ de** take responsibility for. **tener a su ~** be in charge of

carguero *m* (Naut) cargo ship

caria|do *a* decayed. □ **~rse** *vpr* decay

caribeño *a* Caribbean

caricatura *f* caricature

caricia *f* caress; (a animal) stroke

caridad *f* charity. **¡por ~!** for goodness sake!

caries *f invar* tooth decay; (lesión) cavity

cariño *m* affection; (caricia) caress. **~ mío** my darling. **con mucho ~** (en carta) with love from. **tener ~ a** be fond of. **tomar ~ a** become fond of. **~so** *a* affectionate

carisma *m* charisma

caritativo *a* charitable

cariz *m* look

carmesí *a & m* crimson

carmín *m* (de labios) lipstick; (color) red

carnal *a* carnal. **primo ~** first cousin

carnaval *m* carnival. **~esco** *a* carnival

carne *f* meat; (Anat, de frutos, pescado) flesh. **~ de cerdo** pork. **~ de cordero** lamb. **~ de gallina** goose pimples. **~ molida** (LAm), **~ picada** mince (Brit), ground beef (Amer). **~ de ternera** veal. **~ de vaca** beef. **me pone la ~ de gallina** it gives me the creeps. **ser de ~ y hueso** be only human

carné, **carnet** *m* card. **~ de conducir** driving licence (Brit), driver's license (Amer) **~ de identidad** identity card. **~ de manejar** (LAm) driving license (Brit), driver's license (Amer). **~ de socio** membership card

carnero *m* ram

carnicer|ía *f* butcher's (shop); (fig) massacre. **~o** *a* carnivorous. ● *m* butcher

carnívoro *a* carnivorous. ● *m* carnivore

carnoso *a* fleshy; <*pollo*> meaty

caro *a* expensive. ● *adv* dear, dearly. **costar ~ a uno** cost s.o. dear.

carpa *f* carp; (LAm, tienda) tent

carpeta *f* folder, file. **~zo** *m*. **dar ~zo a** shelve

carpinter|ía *f* carpentry. **~o** *m* carpinter, joiner

carraspe|ar *vi* clear one's throat. **~ra** *f*. **tener ~ra** have a frog in one's throat

carrera *f* run; (prisa) rush; (concurso) race; (estudios) degree course; (profesión) career; (de taxi) journey

carreta *f* cart. **~da** *f* cartload

carrete *m* reel; (película) film

carretear *vi* (LAm) taxi

carretera *f* road. **~ de circunvalación** bypass, ring road. **~ nacional** A road (Brit), highway (Amer)

carretilla *f* wheelbarrow

carril *m* lane; (Rail) rail

carrito *m* (en supermercado, para equipaje) trolley (Brit), cart (Amer)

carro *m* cart; (LAm, coche) car; (Mex, vagón) coach. **~ de combate** tank. **~cería** *f* (Auto) bodywork

carroña *f* carrion

carroza *f* coach, carriage; (en desfile de fiesta) float

carruaje *m* carriage

carrusel *m* merry-go-round

cart|a *f* letter; (lista de platos) menu; (lista de vinos) list; (Geog) map; (naipe) card. **~a blanca** free hand. **~a de crédito** letter of credit. **~earse** *vpr* correspond

cartel *m* poster; (letrero) sign. **~era** *f* hoarding; (en periódico) listings; (LAm en escuela, oficina) notice board (Brit), bulletin board (Amer). **de ~** celebrated

carter|a *f* wallet; (de colegial) satchel; (para documentos) briefcase; (LAm, de mujer) handbag (Brit), purse (Amer). **∼ista** *m & f* pickpocket

cartero *m* postman, mailman (Amer)

cartílago *m* cartilage

cartilla *f* first reading book. **∼ de ahorros** savings book. **leerle la ∼ a uno** tell s.o. off

cartón *m* cardboard

cartucho *m* cartridge

cartulina *f* card

casa *f* house; (hogar) home; (empresa) firm. **∼ de huéspedes** boarding-house. **∼ de socorro** first aid post. **ir a ∼** go home. **salir de ∼** go out

casaca *f* jacket

casado *a* married. **los recién ∼os** the newly-weds

casa|mentero *m* matchmaker. **∼miento** *m* marriage; (ceremonia) wedding. **∼r** *vt* marry. □ **∼rse** *vpr* get married

cascabel *m* small bell; (de serpiente) rattle

cascada *f* waterfall

casca|nueces *m invar* nutcrackers. **∼r** [7] *vt* crack *<nuez, huevo>*; (pegar) beat. □ **∼rse** *vpr* crack

cáscara *f* (de huevo, nuez) shell; (de naranja) peel; (de plátano) skin

cascarrabias *a invar* grumpy

casco *m* helmet; (de cerámica etc) piece, fragment; (cabeza) scalp; (de barco) hull; (envase) empty bottle; (de caballo) hoof; (de una ciudad) part, area

cascote *m* piece of rubble. **∼s** *mpl* rubble

caserío *m* country house; (poblado) hamlet

casero *a* home-made; (doméstico) domestic; (amante del hogar) home-loving; *<reunión>* family. ● *m* owner; (vigilante) caretaker

caseta *f* hut; (puesto) stand. **∼ de baño** bathing hut

casete *m & f* cassette

casi *adv* almost, nearly; (en frases negativas) hardly. **∼ ∼** very nearly. **∼ nada** hardly any. **¡∼ nada!** is that all? **∼ nunca** hardly ever

casill|a *f* hut; (en ajedrez etc) square; (en formulario) box; (compartimento) pigeonhole. **∼ electrónica** e-mail address. **∼ero** *m* pigeonholes; (compartimento) pigeonhole

casino *m* casino; (club social) club

caso *m* case. **el ∼ es que** the fact is that. **en ∼ de** in the event of. **en cualquier ∼** in any case, whatever happens. **en ese ∼** in that case. **en todo ∼** in any case. **en último ∼** as a last resort. **hacer ∼ de** take notice of. **poner por ∼** suppose

caspa *f* dandruff

casquivana *f* flirt

cassette *m & f* cassette

casta *f* (de animal) breed; (de persona) descent; (grupo social) caste

castaña *f* chestnut

castañetear *vi <dientes>* chatter

castaño *a* chestnut; *<ojos>* brown. ● *m* chestnut (tree)

castañuela *f* castanet

castellano *a* Castilian. ● *m* (persona) Castilian; (lengua) Castilian, Spanish. **∼parlante** *a* Castilian-speaking, Spanish-speaking. **¿habla Vd ∼?** do you speak Spanish?

castidad *f* chastity

castig|ar [12] *vt* punish; (en deportes) penalize. **∼o** *m* punishment; (en deportes) penalty

castillo *m* castle

cast|izo *a* traditional; (puro) pure. **~o** *a* chaste

castor *m* beaver

castrar *vt* castrate

castrense *m* military

casual *a* chance, accidental. **~idad** *f* chance, coincidence. **dar la ~idad** happen. **de ~idad, por ~idad** by chance. **¡qué ~idad!** what a coincidence!. **~mente** *adv* by chance; (precisamente) actually

cataclismo *m* cataclysm

catador *m* taster

catalán *a & m* Catalan

catalizador *m* catalyst

cat|alogar [12] *vt* catalogue; (fig) classify. **~álogo** *m* catalogue

Cataluña *f* Catalonia

catamarán *m* catamaran

catapulta *f* catapult

catar *vt* taste, try

catarata *f* waterfall, falls; (Med) cataract

catarro *m* cold

cat|ástrofe *m* catastrophe. **~astrófico** *a* catastrophic

catecismo *m* catechism

cátedra *f* (en universidad) professorship, chair; (en colegio) post of head of department

catedral *f* cathedral

catedrático *m* professor; (de colegio) teacher, head of department

categ|oría *f* category; (clase) class. **de ~oría** important. **de primera ~oría** first-class. **~órico** *a* categorical

cat|olicismo *m* catholicism. **~ólico** *a* (Roman) Catholic ● *m* (Roman) Catholic

catorce *a & m* fourteen

cauce *m* river bed; (fig, artificial) channel

caucho *m* rubber

caudal *m* (de río) volume of flow; (riqueza) wealth. **~oso** *a* <*río*> large

caudillo *m* leader

causa *f* cause; (motivo) reason; (Jurid) trial. **a ~ de, por ~ de** because of. **~r** *vt* cause

cautel|a *f* caution. **~oso** *a* cautious, wary

cauterizar [10] *vt* cauterize

cautiv|ar *vt* capture; (fig, fascinar) captivate. **~erio** *m*, **~idad** *f* captivity. **~o** *a & m* captive

cauto *a* cautious

cavar *vt/i* dig

caverna *f* cave, cavern

caviar *m* caviare

cavidad *f* cavity

caza *f* hunting; (con fusil) shooting; (animales) game. ● *m* fighter. **andar a (la) ~ de** be in search of. **~ mayor** game hunting. **dar ~** chase, go after. **ir de ~** go hunting/shooting. **~dor** *m* hunter. **~dora** *f* jacket. **~r** [10] *vt* hunt; (con fusil) shoot; (fig) track down; (obtener) catch, get

caz|o *m* saucepan; (cucharón) ladle. **~oleta** *f* (small) saucepan. **~uela** *f* casserole

cebada *f* barley

ceb|ar *vt* fatten (up); bait <*anzuelo*>; prime <*arma de fuego*>. **~o** *m* bait; (de arma de fuego) charge

ceboll|a *f* onion. **~eta** *f* spring onion (Brit), scallion (Amer). **~ino** *m* chive

cebra *f* zebra

cece|ar *vi* lisp. **~o** *m* lisp

cedazo *m* sieve

ceder *vt* give up; (transferir) transfer. ● *vi* give in; (disminuir) ease off;

(romperse) give way, collapse. **ceda el paso** give way (Brit), yield (Amer)

cedro *m* cedar

cédula *f* bond. ~ **de identidad** identity card

CE(E) *abrev* (**Comunidad** (**Económica**) **Europea**) E(E)C

ceg|ador *a* blinding. ~**ar** [1 & 12] *vt* blind; (tapar) block up. □ ~**arse** *vpr* be blinded (**de** by). ~**uera** *f* blindness

ceja *f* eyebrow

cejar *vi* give way

celada *f* ambush; (fig) trap

cela|dor *m* (de cárcel) prison warder; (de museo etc) security guard. ~**r** *vt* watch

celda *f* cell

celebra|ción *f* celebration. ~**r** *vt* celebrate; (alabar) praise. □ ~**rse** *vpr* take place

célebre *a* famous

celebridad *f* fame; (persona) celebrity

celest|e *a* heavenly; <*vestido*> pale blue. **azul** ~**e** sky-blue. ~**ial** *a* heavenly

celibato *m* celibacy

célibe *a* celibate

celo *m* zeal; (de las hembras) heat; (de los machos) rut; (cinta adhesiva) Sellotape (P) (Brit), Scotch (P) tape (Amer). ~**s** *mpl* jealousy. **dar** ~**s** make jealous. **tener** ~**s** be jealous

celofán *m* cellophane

celoso *a* conscientious; (que tiene celos) jealous

celta *a* & *m* (lengua) Celtic. ● *m* & *f* Celt

célula *f* cell

celular *a* cellular. ● *m* (LAm) mobile phone

celulosa *f* cellulose

cementerio *m* cemetery

cemento *m* cement; (hormigón) concrete; (LAm, cola) glue

cena *f* dinner; (comida ligera) supper

cenag|al *m* marsh, bog; (fig) tight spot. ~**oso** *a* boggy

cenar *vt* have for dinner; (en cena ligera) have for supper. ● *vi* have dinner; (tomar cena ligera) have supper

cenicero *m* ashtray

ceniza *f* ash

censo *m* census. ~ **electoral** electoral roll

censura *f* censure; (de prensa etc) censorship. ~**r** *vt* censure; censor <*prensa etc*>

centavo *a* & *m* hundredth; (moneda) centavo

centell|a *f* flash; (chispa) spark. ~**ar**, ~**ear** *vi* sparkle

centena *f* hundred. ~**r** *m* hundred. **a** ~**res** by the hundred. ~**rio** *a* centenarian. ● *m* centenary; (persona) centenarian

centeno *m* rye

centésim|a *f* hundredth. ~**o** *a* hundredth

cent|ígrado *a* centigrade, Celsius. ● *m* centigrade. ~**igramo** *m* centigram. ~**ilitro** *m* centilitre. ~**ímetro** *m* centimetre

céntimo *a* hundredth. ● *m* cent

centinela *f* sentry

centolla *f*, **centollo** *m* spider crab

central *a* central. ● *f* head office. ~ **de correos** general post office. ~ **eléctrica** power station. ~ **nuclear** nuclear power station. ~ **telefónica** telephone exchange. ~**ita** *f* switchboard

centraliza|ción *f* centralization. **~r** [10] *vt* centralize

centrar *vt* centre

céntrico *a* central

centrífugo *a* centrifugal

centro *m* centre. **~ comercial** shopping centre (Brit), shopping mall (Amer)

Centroamérica *f* Central America

centroamericano *a* & *m* Central American

ceñi|do *a* tight. **~r** [5 & 22] *vt* take <*corona*>; <*vestido*> cling to. □ **~rse** *vpr* limit o.s. (**a** to)

ceñ|o *m* frown. **fruncir el ~o** frown. **~udo** *a* frowning

cepill|ar *vt* brush; (en carpintería) plane. **~o** *m* brush; (en carpintería) plane. **~o de dientes** toothbrush

cera *f* wax

cerámic|a *f* ceramics; (materia) pottery; (objeto) piece of pottery. **~o** *a* ceramic

cerca *f* fence; (de piedra) wall. ● *adv* near, close. **~ de** close to, close up, closely

cercan|ía *f* nearness, proximity. **~ías** *fpl* vicinity. **tren** *m* **de ~ías** local train. **~o** *a* near, close.

cercar [7] *vt* fence in, enclose; <*gente*> surround; (asediar) besiege

cerciorar *vt* convince. □ **~se** *vpr* make sure

cerco *m* (asedio) siege; (círculo) ring; (LAm, valla) fence; (LAm, seto) hedge

cerdo *m* pig; (carne) pork

cereal *m* cereal

cerebr|al *a* cerebral. **~o** *m* brain; (persona) brains

ceremoni|a *f* ceremony. **~al** *a* ceremonial. **~oso** *a* ceremonious

cerez|a *f* cherry. **~o** *m* cherry tree

cerill|a *f* match. **~o** *m* (Mex) match

cern|er [1] *vt* sieve. □ **~erse** *vpr* hover. **~idor** *m* sieve

cero *m* nought, zero; (fútbol) nil (Brit), zero (Amer); (tenis) love; (persona) nonentity

cerquillo *m* (LAm, flequillo) fringe (Brit), bangs (Amer)

cerra|do *a* shut, closed; (espacio) shut in, enclosed; <*cielo*> overcast; <*curva*> sharp. **~dura** *f* lock; (acción de cerrar) shutting, closing. **~jero** *m* locksmith. **~r** [1] *vt* shut, close; (con llave) lock; (cercar) enclose; turn off <*grifo*>; block up <*agujero etc*>. ● *vi* shut, close. □ **~rse** *vpr* shut, close; <*herida*> heal. **~r con llave** lock

cerro *m* hill

cerrojo *m* bolt. **echar el ~** bolt

certamen *m* competition, contest

certero *a* accurate

certeza, **certidumbre** *f* certainty

certifica|do *a* <*carta etc*> registered. ● *m* certificate. **~r** [7] *vt* certify

certitud *f* certainty

cervatillo, **cervato** *m* fawn

cerve|cería *f* beerhouse, bar; (fábrica) brewery. **~za** *f* beer. **~za de barril** draught beer. **~za rubia** lager

cesa|ción *f* cessation, suspension. **~nte** *a* redundant. **~r** *vt* stop. ● *vi* stop, cease; (dejar un empleo) resign. **sin ~r** incessantly

cesárea *f* caesarian (section)

cese *m* cessation; (de un empleo) dismissal. **~ del fuego** (LAm) ceasefire

césped *m* grass, lawn

cest|a *f* basket. **~o** *m* basket. **~o de los papeles** waste-paper basket

chabacano *a* common; <*chiste etc*> vulgar. ● *m* (Mex, albaricoque) apricot

chabola *f* shack. **~s** *fpl* shanty town

cháchara *f* [I] chatter; (Mex, objetos sin valor) junk

chacharear *vt* (Mex) sell. ● *vi* [I] chatter

chacra *f* (LAm) farm

chal *m* shawl

chalado *a* [I] crazy

chalé *m* house (with a garden), villa

chaleco *m* waistcoat, vest (Amer). **~ salvavidas** life-jacket

chalet *m* (*pl* **~s**) house (with a garden), villa

chalote *m* shallot

chamac|a *f* (esp Mex) girl. **~o** *m* (esp Mex) boy

chamarra *f* sheepskin jacket; (Mex, chaqueta corta) jacket

chamb|a *f* (Mex, trabajo) work. **por ~a** by fluke. **~ear** *vi* (Mex, [I]) work

champán *m*, **champaña** *m & f* champagne

champiñón *m* mushroom

champú *m* (*pl* **~es** *o* **~s**) shampoo

chamuscar [7] *vt* scorch

chance *m* (esp LAm) chance

chancho *m* (LAm) pig

chanchullo *m* [I] swindle, fiddle [I]

chanclo *m* clog; (de caucho) rubber overshoe

chándal *m* (*pl* **~s**) tracksuit

chantaje *m* blackmail. **~ar** *vt* blackmail

chanza *f* joke

chapa *f* plate, sheet; (de madera) plywood; (de botella) metal top; (carrocería) bodywork; (LAm cerradura) lock. **~do** *a* plated. **~do a la antigua** old-fashioned. **~do en oro** gold-plated

chaparro *a* (LAm) short, squat

chaparrón *m* downpour

chapopote *m* (Mex) tar

chapotear *vi* splash

chapucero *a* <*persona*> slapdash; <*trabajo*> shoddy

chapulín *m* (Mex) locust; (saltamontes) grasshopper

chapurrar, **chapurrear** *vt* have a smattering of, speak a little

chapuza *f* botched job; (trabajo ocasional) odd job

chaquet|a *f* jacket. **cambiar de ~a** change sides. **~ón** *m* three-quarter length coat

charc|a *f* pond, pool. **~o** *m* puddle, pool

charcutería *f* delicatessen

charla *f* chat; (conferencia) talk. **~dor** *a* talkative. **~r** *vi* [I] chat. **~tán** *a* talkative. ● *m* chatterbox; (vendedor) cunning hawker; (curandero) charlatan

charol *m* varnish; (cuero) patent leather. **~a** *f* (Mex) tray

charr|a *f* (Mex) horsewoman, cowgirl. **~o** *m* (Mex) horseman, cowboy

chascar [7] *vt* crack <*látigo*>; click <*lengua*>; snap <*dedos*>. ● *vi* <*madera*> creak. **~ con la lengua** click one's tongue

chasco *m* disappointment

chasis *m* (Auto) chassis

chasqu|ear *vt* crack <*látigo*>; click <*lengua*>; snap <*dedos*>. ● *vi*

<madera> creak. **~ con la lengua** click one's tongue. **~ido** *m* crack; (de la lengua) click; (de los dedos) snap

chatarra *f* scrap iron; (fig) scrap

chato *a* *<nariz>* snub; *<objetos>* flat. ● *m* wine glass

chav|a *f* (Mex) girl, lass. **~al** *m* [I] boy, lad. **~o** *m* (Mex) boy, lad.

checa|da *f* (Mex) check; (Mex, Med) checkup. **~r** [7] *vt* (Mex) check; (vigilar) check up on. **~r tarjeta** clock in

checo *a & m* Czech. **~slovaco** *a & m* (History) Czechoslovak

chelín *m* shilling

chelo *m* cello

cheque *m* cheque. **~ de viaje** traveller's cheque. **~ar** *vt* check; (LAm) check in *<equipaje>*. **~o** *m* check; (Med) checkup. **~ra** *f* cheque-book

chévere *a* (LAm) great

chica *f* girl; (criada) maid, servant

chicano *a & m* Chicano, Mexican-American

chícharo *m* (Mex) pea

chicharra *f* cicada; (timbre) buzzer

chichón *m* bump

chicle *m* chewing-gum

chico *a* [I] small; (esp LAm, de edad) young. ● *m* boy. **~s** *mpl* children

chicoria *f* chicory

chifla|do *a* [I] crazy, daft. **~r** *vt* whistle at, boo. ● *vi* (LAm) whistle; ([I], gustar mucho) **me chifla el chocolate** I'm mad about chocolate. □ **~rse** *vpr* be mad (**por** about)

chilango *a* (Mex) from Mexico City

chile *m* chilli

Chile *m* Chile

chileno *a & m* Chilean

chill|ar *vi* scream, shriek; *<ratón>* squeak; *<cerdo>* squeal. **~ido** *m* scream, screech. **~ón** *a* noisy; *<colores>* loud; *<sonido>* shrill

chimenea *f* chimney; (hogar) fireplace

chimpancé *m* chimpanzee

china *f* Chinese (woman)

China *f* China

chinche *m* drawing-pin (Brit), thumbtack (Amer); (insecto) bedbug; (fig) nuisance. **~eta** *f* drawing-pin (Brit), thumbtack (Amer)

chinela *f* slipper

chino *a* Chinese; (Mex rizado) curly. ● *m* Chinese (man); (Mex, de pelo rizado) curly-haired person

chipriota *a & m & f* Cypriot

chiquero *m* pen; (LAm, pocilga) pigsty (Brit), pigpen (Amer)

chiquillo *a* childish. ● *m* child, kid [I]

chirimoya *f* custard apple

chiripa *f* fluke

chirri|ar [20] *vi* creak; *<frenos>* screech; *<pájaro>* chirp. **~do** *m* creaking; (de frenos) screech; (de pájaros) chirping

chis *int* sh!, hush!; ([I], para llamar a uno) hey!, psst!

chism|e *m* gadget, thingumajig [I]; (chismorreo) piece of gossip. **~es** *mpl* things, bits and pieces. **~orreo** *m* gossip. **~oso** *a* gossipy. ● *m* gossip

chisp|a *f* spark; (pizca) drop; (gracia) wit; (fig) sparkle. **estar que echa ~a(s)** be furious. **~eante** *a* sparkling. **~ear** *vi* spark; (lloviznar) drizzle; (fig) sparkle. **~orrotear** *vt* throw out sparks; *<fuego>* crackle; *<aceite>* spit

chistar *vi*. **ni chistó** he didn't say a word. **sin ~** without saying a word

chiste *m* joke, funny story. **tener ~** be funny

chistera *f* top hat
chistoso *a* funny
chiva|rse *vpr* tip-off; <*niño*> tell. **~tazo** *m* tip-off. **~to** *m* informer; (niño) telltale
chivo *m* kid; (LAm, macho cabrío) billy goat
choca|nte *a* shocking; (Mex, desagradable) unpleasant. **~r** [7] *vt* clink <*vasos*>; (LAm) crash <*vehículo*>. **¡chócala!** give me five! ● *vi* collide, hit. **~r con, ~r contra** crash into
choch|ear *vi* be gaga. **~o** *a* gaga; (fig) soft
chocolate *m* chocolate. **tableta** *f* **de ~** bar of chocolate
chófer, (LAm) **chofer** *m* chauffeur; (conductor) driver
cholo *a* & *m* (LAm) half-breed
chopo *m* poplar
choque *m* collision; (fig) clash; (eléctrico) shock; (Auto, Rail etc) crash, accident; (sacudida) jolt
chorizo *m* chorizo
chorro *m* jet, stream; (caudal pequeño) trickle; (fig) stream. **a ~** <*avión*> jet. **a ~os** (fig) in abundance
chovinista *a* chauvinistic. ● *m* & *f* chauvinist
choza *f* hut
chubas|co *m* squall, heavy shower. **~quero** *m* raincoat, anorak
chuchería *f* trinket
chueco *a* (LAm) crooked
chufa *f* tiger nut
chuleta *f* chop
chulo *a* cocky; (bonito) lovely (Brit), neat (Amer); (Mex, atractivo) cute. ● *m* tough guy; (proxeneta) pimp
chup|ada *f* suck; (al helado) lick; (al cigarro) puff. **~ado** *a* skinny; (🅃, fácil) very easy. **~ar** *vt* suck; puff at <*cigarro etc*>; (absorber) absorb. **~ete** *m* dummy (Brit), pacifier (Amer). **~ón** *m* sucker; (LAm) dummy (Brit), pacifier (Amer); (Mex, del biberón) teat
churro *m* fritter; 🅃 mess
chusma *f* riff-raff
chut|ar *vi* shoot. **~e** *m* shot
cianuro *m* cyanide
cibernética *f* cibernetics
cicatriz *f* scar. **~ar** [10] *vt/i* heal. □ **~arse** *vpr* heal
cíclico *a* cyclic(al)
ciclis|mo *m* cycling. **~ta** *a* cycle. ● *m* & *f* cyclist
ciclo *m* cycle; (de películas, conciertos) season; (de conferencias) series
ciclomotor *m* moped
ciclón *m* cyclone
ciego *a* blind. ● *m* blind man, blind person. **a ciegas** in the dark
cielo *m* sky; (Relig) heaven; (persona) darling. **¡~s!** good heavens!, goodness me!
ciempiés *m invar* centipede
cien *a* a hundred. **~ por ~** one hundred per cent
ciénaga *f* bog, swamp
ciencia *f* science; (fig) knowledge. **~s** *fpl* (Univ etc) science. **~s empresariales** business studies. **a ~ cierta** for certain
cieno *m* mud
científico *a* scientific. ● *m* scientist
ciento *a* & *m* a hundred, one hundred. **~s de** hundreds of. **por ~** per cent
cierre *m* fastener; (acción de cerrar) shutting, closing; (LAm, cremallera) zip, zipper (Amer)
cierro *vb* ⇒CERRAR

cierto *a* certain; (verdad) true. **estar en lo ~** be right. **lo ~ es que** the fact is that. **no es ~** that's not true. **¿no es ~?** isn't that right? **por ~** by the way. **si bien es ~ que** although

ciervo *m* deer

cifra *f* figure, number; (cantidad) sum. **en ~** coded, in code. **~do** *a* coded. **~r** *vt* code; place <*esperanzas*>

cigala *f* crayfish

cigarra *f* cicada

cigarr|illera *f* cigarette box; (de bolsillo) cigarette case. **~illo** *m* cigarette. **~o** *m* (cigarrillo) cigarette; (puro) cigar

cigüeña *f* stork

cilantro *m* coriander

cil|índrico *a* cylindrical. **~indro** *m* cylinder

cima *f* top; (fig) summit

cimbr|ear *vt* shake. □ **~earse** *vpr* sway. **~onada** *f*, **~onazo** *m* (LAm) jolt; (de explosión) blast

cimentar [1] *vt* lay the foundations of; (fig, reforzar) strengthen

cimientos *mpl* foundations

cinc *m* zinc

cincel *m* chisel. **~ar** *vt* chisel

cinco *a* & *m* five; (en fechas) fifth

cincuent|a *a* & *m* fifty; (quincuagésimo) fiftieth. **~ón** *a* in his fifties

cine *m* cinema; (local) cinema (Brit), movie theater (Amer). **~asta** *m* & *f* film maker (Brit), movie maker (Amer). **~matográfico** *a* film (Brit), movie (Amer)

cínico *a* cynical. ● *m* cynic

cinismo *m* cynicism

cinta *f* ribbon; (película) film (Brit), movie (Amer); (para grabar, en carreras) tape. **~ aislante** insulating tape. **~ métrica** tape measure. **~ virgen** blank tape

cintur|a *f* waist. **~ón** *m* belt. **~ón de seguridad** safety belt. **~ón salvavidas** lifebelt

ciprés *m* cypress (tree)

circo *m* circus

circuito *m* circuit; (viaje) tour. **~ cerrado** closed circuit. **corto ~** short circuit

circula|ción *f* circulation; (vehículos) traffic. **~r** *a* circular. ● *vi* circulate; <*líquidos*> flow; (conducir) drive; (caminar) walk; <*autobús*> run

círculo *m* circle. **~ vicioso** vicious circle. **en ~** in a circle

circunci|dar *vt* circumcise. **~sión** *f* circumcision

circunferencia *f* circumference

circunflejo *m* circumflex

circunscri|bir (*pp* **circunscrito**) *vt* confine. □ **~birse** *vpr* confine o.s. (a to). **~pción** *f* (distrito) district. **~pción electoral** constituency

circunspecto *a* circumspect

circunstancia *f* circumstance

circunv|alar *vt* bypass. **~olar** *vt* [2] circle

cirio *m* candle

ciruela *f* plum. **~ pasa** prune

ciru|gía *f* surgery. **~jano** *m* surgeon

cisne *m* swan

cisterna *f* tank, cistern

cita *f* appointment; (entre chico y chica) date; (referencia) quotation. **~ción** *f* quotation; (Jurid) summons. **~do** *a* aforementioned. **~r** *vt* make an appointment with; (mencionar) quote; (Jurid) summons. □ **~rse** *vpr* arrange to meet

cítara *f* zither

ciudad *f* town; (grande) city. ~ **balneario** (LAm) coastal resort. ~ **perdida** (Mex) shanty town. ~ **universitaria** university campus. ~**anía** *f* citizenship; (habitantes) citizens. ~**ano** *a* civic. ● *m* citizen, inhabitant

cívico *a* civic

civil *a* civil. ● *m & f* civil guard; (persona no militar) civilian

civiliza|ción *f* civilization. ~**r** [10] *vt* civilize. □ ~**rse** *vpr* become civilized

civismo *m* community spirit

clam|ar *vi* cry out, clamour. ~**or** *m* clamour; (protesta) outcry. ~**oroso** *a* noisy; (éxito) resounding

clandestino *a* clandestine, secret; <*periódico*> underground

clara *f* (de huevo) egg white

claraboya *f* skylight

clarear *vi* dawn; (aclarar) brighten up

clarete *m* rosé

claridad *f* clarity; (luz) light

clarifica|ción *f* clarification. ~**r** [7] *vt* clarify

clar|ín *m* bugle. ~**inete** *m* clarinet. ~**inetista** *m & f* clarinettist

clarividen|cia *f* clairvoyance; (fig) far-sightedness. ~**te** *a* clairvoyant; (fig) far-sighted

claro *a* clear; (luminoso) bright; <*colores*> light; <*líquido*> thin. ● *m* (en bosque etc) clearing; (espacio) gap. ● *adv* clearly. ● *int* of course! **¡~ que sí!** yes, of course! **¡~ que no!** of course not!

clase *f* class; (tipo) kind, sort; (aula) classroom. ~ **media** middle class. ~ **obrera** working class. ~ **social** social class. **dar ~s** teach

clásico *a* classical; (típico) classic. ● *m* classic

clasifica|ción *f* classification; (deportes) league. ~**r** [7] *vt* classify; (seleccionar) sort

claudicar [7] give in

claustro *m* cloister; (Univ) staff

claustrof|obia *f* claustrophobia. ~**óbico** *a* claustrophobic

cláusula *f* clause

clausura *f* closure; (ceremonia) closing ceremony. ~**r** *vt* close

clava|do *a* fixed; (con clavo) nailed. **es ~do a su padre** he's the spitting image of his father. ● *m* (LAm) dive. ~**r** *vt* knock in <*clavo*>; stick in <*cuchillo*>; (fijar) fix; (juntar) nail together

clave *f* key; (Mus) clef; (instrumento) harpsichord. ~**cín** *m* harpsichord

clavel *m* carnation

clavícula *f* collarbone, clavicle

clav|ija *f* peg; (Elec) plug. ~**o** *m* nail; (Culin) clove

claxon *m* /'klakson/ (*pl* ~**s**) horn

clemencia *f* clemency, mercy

clementina *f* clementine

cleptómano *m* kleptomaniac

clerical *a* clerical

clérigo *m* priest

clero *m* clergy

cliché *m* cliché; (Foto) negative

cliente *m* customer; (de médico) patient; (de abogado) client. ~**la** *f* clientele, customers; (de médico) patients

clim|a *m* climate; (ambiente) atmosphere. ~**ático** *a* climatic. ~**atizado** *a* air-conditioned

clínic|a *f* clinic. ~**o** *a* clinical

cloaca *f* drain, sewer

cloro *m* chlorine

club *m* (*pl* ~**s** *o* ~**es**) club

coacci|ón *f* coercion. **~onar** *vt* coerce

coagular *vt* coagulate; clot <*sangre*>; curdle <*leche*>. □ **~se** *vpr* coagulate; <*sangre*> clot; <*leche*> curdle

coalición *f* coalition

coarta|da *f* alibi. **~r** *vt* hinder; restrict <*libertad etc*>

cobard|e *a* cowardly. ● *m* coward. **~ía** *f* cowardice

cobert|izo *m* shed. **~ura** *f* covering

cobij|a *f* (Mex, manta) blanket. **~as** *fpl* (LAm, ropa de cama) bedclothes. **~ar** *vt* shelter. □ **~arse** *vpr* (take) shelter. **~o** *m* shelter

cobra *f* cobra

cobra|dor *m* collector; (de autobús) conductor. **~r** *vt* collect; (ganar) earn; charge <*precio*>; cash <*cheque*>; (recuperar) recover. ● *vi* be paid

cobr|e *m* copper. **~izo** *a* coppery

cobro *m* collection; (de cheque) cashing; (pago) payment. **presentar al ~** cash

cocaína *f* cocaine

cocción *f* cooking; (Tec) firing

coc|er [2 & 9] *vt/i* cook; (hervir) boil; (Tec) fire. **~ido** *m* stew

coche *m* car, automobile (Amer); (de tren) coach, carriage; (de bebé) pram (Brit), baby carriage (Amer). **~-cama** sleeper. **~ fúnebre** hearse. **~ restaurante** dining-car. **~s de choque** dodgems. **~ra** *f* garage; (de autobuses) depot

cochin|ada *f* dirty thing. **~o** *a* dirty, filthy. ● *m* pig

cociente *m* quotient. **~ intelectual** intelligence quotient, IQ

cocin|a *f* kitchen; (arte) cookery, cuisine; (aparato) cooker. **~a de gas** gas cooker. **~a eléctrica** electric cooker. **~ar** *vt/i* cook. **~ero** *m* cook

coco *m* coconut; (árbol) coconut palm; (cabeza) head; (que mete miedo) bogeyman. **comerse el ~** think hard

cocoa *f* (LAm) cocoa

cocodrilo *m* crocodile

cocotero *m* coconut palm

cóctel *m* (*pl* **~s** *o* **~es**) cocktail

cod|azo *m* nudge (with one's elbow). **~ear** *vt/i* elbow, nudge. □ **~arse** *vpr* rub shoulders (**con** with)

codici|a *f* greed. **~ado** *a* coveted, sought after. **~ar** *vt* covet. **~oso** *a* greedy

código *m* code. **~ de la circulación** Highway Code

codo *m* elbow; (dobladura) bend. **~ a ~** side by side. **hablar (hasta) por los ~s** talk too much

codorniz *m* quail

coeficiente *m* coefficient. **~ intelectual** intelligence quotient, IQ

coerción *f* constraint

coetáneo *a & m* contemporary

coexist|encia *f* coexistence. **~ir** *vi* coexist

cofradía *f* brotherhood

cofre *m* chest; (Mex, capó) bonnet (Brit), hood (Amer)

coger [14] *vt* (esp Esp) take; catch <*tren, autobús, pelota, catarro*>; (agarrar) take hold of; (del suelo) pick up; pick <*frutos etc*>. □ **~se** *vpr* trap, catch; (agarrarse) hold on

cogollo *m* (de lechuga etc) heart; (brote) bud

cogote *m* nape; (LAm, cuello) neck

cohech|ar *vt* bribe. **~o** *m* bribery

cohe|rente *a* coherent. **~sión** *f* cohesion

cohete *m* rocket

cohibi|do *a* shy; (inhibido) awkward; (incómodo) awkward. **~r** *vt* inhibit; (incomodar) make s.o. feel embarrassed. □ **~rse** *vpr* feel inhibited

coincid|encia *f* coincidence. **dar la ~encia** happen. **~ir** *vt* coincide

coje|ar *vt* limp; <*mueble*> wobble. **~ra** *f* lameness

coj|ín *m* cushion. **~inete** *m* small cushion

cojo *a* lame; <*mueble*> wobbly. ● *m* lame person

col *f* cabbage. **~es de Bruselas** Brussel sprouts

cola *f* tail; (fila) queue; (para pegar) glue. **a la ~** at the end. **hacer ~** queue (up) (Brit), line up (Amer). **tener ~, traer ~** have serious consequences

colabora|ción *f* collaboration. **~dor** *m* collaborator. **~r** *vi* collaborate

colada *f* washing. **hacer la ~** do the washing

colador *m* strainer

colapso *m* collapse; (fig) standstill

colar [2] *vt* strain; pass <*moneda falsa etc*>. ● *vi* <*líquido*> seep through; (fig) be believed. □ **~se** *vpr* slip; (en una cola) jump the queue; (en fiesta) gatecrash

colch|a *f* bedspread. **~ón** *m* mattress. **~oneta** *f* air bed; (en gimnasio) mat.

colear *vi* wag its tail; <*asunto*> not be resolved. **vivito y coleando** alive and kicking

colecci|ón *f* collection. **~onar** *vt* collect. **~onista** *m & f* collector

colecta *f* collection

colectivo *a* collective

colega *m & f* colleague

colegi|al *m* schoolboy. **~ala** *f* schoolgirl. **~o** *m* school; (de ciertas profesiones) college. **~o mayor** hall of residence

cólera *m* cholera. ● *f* anger, fury. **montar en ~** fly into a rage

colérico *a* furious, irate

colesterol *m* cholesterol

coleta *f* pigtail

colga|nte *a* hanging. ● *m* pendant. **~r** [2 & 12] *vt* hang; hang out <*ropa lavada*>; hang up <*abrigo etc*>; put down <*teléfono*>. ● *vi* hang; (teléfono) hang up. □ **~rse** *vpr* hang o.s. **dejar a uno ~do** let s.o. down

colibrí *m* hummingbird

cólico *m* colic

coliflor *f* cauliflower

colilla *f* cigarette end

colina *f* hill

colinda|nte *a* adjoining. **~r** *vt* border (**con** on)

colisión *f* collision, crash; (fig) clash

collar *m* necklace; (de perro) collar

colmar *vt* fill to the brim; try <*paciencia*>; (fig) fulfill. **~ a uno de atenciones** lavish attention on s.o.

colmena *f* beehive, hive

colmillo *m* eye tooth, canine (tooth); (de elefante) tusk; (de carnívoro) fang

colmo *m* height. **ser el ~** be the limit, be the last straw

coloca|ción *f* positioning; (empleo) job, position. **~r** [7] *vt* put, place; (buscar empleo) find work for. □ **~rse** *vpr* find a job

Colombia *f* Colombia

colombiano *a & m* Colombian

colon *m* colon

colón *m* (unidad monetaria de Costa Rica y El Salvador) colon

colon|ia *f* colony; (comunidad) community; (agua de colonia) cologne; (Mex, barrio) residential suburb. **~a de verano** holiday camp. **~iaje** *m* (LAm) colonial period. **~ial** *a* colonial. **~ialista** *m & f* colonialist. **~ización** *f* colonization. **~izar** [10] colonize. **~o** *m* colonist, settler; (labrador) tenant farmer

coloqui|al *a* colloquial. **~o** *m* conversation; (congreso) conference

color *m* colour. **de ~** colour. **en ~(es)** <*fotos, película*> colour. **~ado** *a* (rojo) red. **~ante** *m* colouring. **~ear** *vt/i* colour. **~ete** *m* blusher. **~ido** *m* colour

colosal *a* colossal; (fig, I, magnífico) terrific

columna *f* column; (Anat) spine. **~ vertebral** spinal column; (fig) backbone

columpi|ar *vt* swing. □ **~arse** *vpr* swing. **~o** *m* swing

coma *f* comma; (Mat) point. ● *m* (Med) coma

comadre *f* (madrina) godmother; (amiga) friend. **~ar** *vi* gossip

comadreja *f* weasel

comadrona *f* midwife

comal *m* (Mex) griddle

comand|ancia *f* command. **~ante** *m & f* commander. **~o** *m* command; (Mil, soldado) commando; (de terroristas) cell

comarca *f* area, region

comba *f* bend; (juguete) skipping-rope; (de viga) sag. **saltar a la ~** skip. □ **~rse** *vpr* bend; <*viga*> sag

combat|e *m* combat; (pelea) fight. **~iente** *m* fighter. **~ir** *vt/i* fight

combina|ción *f* combination; (enlace) connection; (prenda) slip. **~r** *vt* combine; put together <*colores*>

combustible *m* fuel

comedia *f* comedy; (cualquier obra de teatro) play; (LAm, telenovela) soap (opera)

comedi|do *a* restrained; (LAm, atento) obliging. □ **~rse** [5] *vpr* show restrain

comedor *m* dining-room; (restaurante) restaurant

comensal *m* companion at table, fellow diner

comentar *vt* comment on; discuss <*tema*>; (mencionar) mention. **~io** *m* commentary; (observación) comment. **~ios** *mpl* gossip. **~ista** *m & f* commentator

comenzar [1 & 10] *vt/i* begin, start

comer *vt* eat; (a mediodía) have for lunch; (esp LAm, cenar) have for dinner; (corroer) eat away; (en ajedrez) take. ● *vi* eat; (a mediodía) have lunch; (esp LAm, cenar) have dinner. **dar de ~ a** feed. □ **~se** *vpr* eat (up)

comerci|al *a* commercial; <*ruta*> trade; <*nombre, trato*> business. ● *m* (LAm) commercial, ad. **~ante** *m* trader; (de tienda) shopkeeper. **~ar** *vi* trade (**con** with, **en** in); (con otra persona) do business. **~o** *m* commerce; (actividad) trade; (tienda) shop; (negocios) business

comestible *a* edible. **~s** *mpl* food. **tienda de ~s** grocer's (shop) (Brit), grocery (Amer)

cometa *m* comet. ● *f* kite

comet|er *vt* commit; make <*falta*>. **~ido** *m* task

comezón *m* itch

comicios *mpl* elections

cómico *a* comic; (gracioso) funny. ● *m* comic actor; (humorista) comedian

comida *f* food; (a mediodía) lunch; (esp LAm, cena) dinner; (acto) meal

comidilla *f*. **ser la ~ del pueblo** be the talk of the town

comienzo *m* beginning, start

comillas *fpl* inverted commas

comil|ón *a* greedy. **~ona** *f* feast

comino *m* cumin. **(no) me importa un ~** I couldn't care less

comisar|ía *f* police station. **~io** *m* commissioner; (deportes) steward

comisión *f* assignment; (organismo) commission, committee; (Com) commission

comisura *f* corner. **~ de los labios** corner of the mouth

comité *m* committee

como *prep* as; (comparación) like. ● *adv* about. ● *conj* as. **~ quieras** as you like. **~ si** as if

---

cómo

● *adverbio*

····➤ how. **¿~ se llega?** how do you get there? **¿~ es de alto?** how tall is it? **sé ~ pasó** I know how it happened

> **!** Cuando **cómo** va seguido del verbo **llamar** se traduce por *what*, p. ej. **¿~ te llamas?** *what's your name?*

····➤ **cómo + ser** (sugiriendo descripción) **¿~ es su marido?** what's her husband like?; (físicamente) what does her husband look like? **no sé ~ es la comida** I don't know what the food's like

····➤ (por qué) why. **¿~ no actuaron antes?** why didn't they act sooner?

····➤ (pidiendo que se repita) sorry?, pardon? **¿~? no te escuché** sorry? I didn't hear you

····➤ (en exclamaciones) **¡ ~ llueve!** it's really pouring! **¡~! ¿que no lo sabes?** what! you mean you don't know? **¡~ no!** of course!

---

cómoda *f* chest of drawers

comodidad *f* comfort. **a su ~** at your convenience

cómodo *a* comfortable; (conveniente) convenient

comoquiera *conj*. **~ que sea** however it may be

compacto *a* compact; (denso) dense; <*líneas etc*> close

compadecer [11] *vt* feel sorry for. □ **~se** *vpr*. **~se de** feel sorry for

compadre *m* godfather; (amigo) friend

compañ|ero *m* companion; (de trabajo) colleague; (de clase) classmate; (pareja) partner. **~ía** *f* company. **en ~ía de** with

compara|ble *a* comparable. **~ción** *f* comparison. **~r** *vt* compare. **~tivo** *a* & *m* comparative

comparecer [11] *vi* appear

comparsa *f* group. ● *m* & *f* (en el teatro) extra

compartim(i)ento *m* compartment

compartir *vt* share

compás *m* (instrumento) (pair of) compasses; (ritmo) rhythm; (división) bar (Brit), measure (Amer); (Naut) compass. **a ~** in time

compasi|ón *f* compassion, pity. **tener ~ón de** feel sorry for. **~vo** *a* compassionate

compatib|ilidad *f* compatibility. **~le** *a* compatible

compatriota *m & f* compatriot

compendio *m* summary

compensa|ción *f* compensation. **~ción por despido** redundancy payment. **~r** *vt* compensate

competen|cia *f* competition; (capacidad) competence; (poder) authority; (incumbencia) jurisdiction. **~te** *a* competent

competi|ción *f* competition. **~dor** *m* competitor. **~r** [5] *vi* compete

compinche *m* accomplice; (🅸, amigo) friend, mate 🅸

complac|er [32] *vt* please. □ **~erse** *vpr* be pleased. **~iente** *a* obliging; *<marido>* complaisant

complej|idad *f* complexity. **~o** *a & m* complex

complement|ario *a* complementary. **~o** *m* complement; (Gram) object, complement

complet|ar *vt* complete. **~o** *a* complete; (lleno) full; (exhaustivo) comprehensive

complexión *f* build

complica|ción *f* complication; (esp AmL, implicación) involvement. **~r** [7] *vt* complicate; involve *<persona>*. □ **~rse** *vpr* become complicated; (implicarse) get involved

cómplice *m & f* accomplice

complot *m* (*pl* **~s**) plot

compon|ente *a* component. ● *m* component; (miembro) member. **~er** [34] *vt* make up; (Mus, Literatura etc) write, compose; (esp LAm, reparar) mend; (LAm) set *<hueso>*; settle *<estómago>*. □ **~erse** *vpr* be made up; (arreglarse) get better. **~érselas** manage

comporta|miento *m* behaviour. □ **~rse** *vpr* behave. **~rse mal** misbehave

composi|ción *f* composition. **~tor** *m* composer

compostura *f* composure; (LAm, arreglo) repair

compota *f* stewed fruit

compra *f* purchase. **~ a plazos** hire purchase. **hacer la(s) ~(s)** do the shopping. **ir de ~s** go shopping. **~dor** *m* buyer. **~r** *vt* buy. **~venta** *f* buying and selling; (Jurid) sale and purchase contract. **negocio** *m* **de ~venta** second-hand shop

compren|der *vt* understand; (incluir) include. **~sión** *f* understanding. **~sivo** *a* understanding

compresa *f* compress; (de mujer) sanitary towel

compr|esión *f* compression. **~imido** *a* compressed. ● *m* pill, tablet. **~imir** *vt* compress

comproba|nte *m* proof; (recibo) receipt. **~r** *vt* check; (demostrar) prove

comprom|eter *vt* compromise; (arriesgar) jeopardize. □ **~eterse** *vpr* compromise o.s.; (obligarse) agree to; *<novios>* get engaged. **~etido** *a* *<situación>* awkward, delicate; *<autor>* politically committed. **~iso** *m* obligation; (apuro) predicament; (cita) appointment; (acuerdo) agreement. **sin ~iso** without obligation

compuesto *a* compound; *<persona>* smart. ● *m* compound

computa|ción *f* (esp LAm) computing. **curso** *m* **de ~ción** computer course. **~dor** *m*, **~dora** *f* computer. **~r** *vt* calculate. **~rizar, computerizar** [10] *vt* computerize

cómputo *m* calculation

comulgar [12] *vi* take Communion

común *a* common; (compartido) joint. **en ~** in common. **por lo ~** generally. ● *m*. **el ~ de** most

comunal *a* communal

comunica|ción *f* communication. **~do** *m* communiqué. **~do de prensa** press release. **~r** [7] *vt* communicate; (informar) inform; (LAm, por teléfono) put through. **está ~ndo** <*teléfono*> it's engaged. □ **~rse** *vpr* communicate; (ponerse en contacto) get in touch. **~tivo** *a* communicative

comunidad *f* community. **~ de vecinos** residents' association. **C~ (Económica) Europea** European (Economic) Community. **en ~** together

comunión *f* communion; (Relig) (Holy) Communion

comunis|mo *m* communism. **~ta** *a* & *m* & *f* communist

con *prep* with; (+ *infinitivo*) by. **~ decir la verdad** by telling the truth. **~ que** so. **~ tal que** as long as

concebir [5] *vt/i* conceive

conceder *vt* concede, grant; award <*premio*>; (admitir) admit

concej|al *m* councillor. **~ero** *m* (LAm) councillor. **~o** *m* council

concentra|ción *f* concentration; (Pol) rally. **~r** *vt* concentrate; assemble <*personas*>. □ **~rse** *vpr* concentrate

concep|ción *f* conception. **~to** *m* concept; (opinión) opinion. **bajo ningún ~to** in no way

concerniente *a*. **en lo ~ a** with regard to

concertar [1] *vt* arrange; agree (upon) <*plan*>

concesión *f* concession

concha *f* shell; (carey) tortoiseshell

conciencia *f* conscience; (conocimiento) awareness. **~ limpia** clear conscience. **~ sucia** guilty conscience. **a ~ de que** fully aware that. **en ~** honestly. **tener ~ de** be aware of. **tomar ~ de** become aware of. **~r** *vt* make aware. **~rse** *vpr* become aware

concientizar [10] *vt* (esp LAm) make aware. □ **~se** *vpr* become aware

concienzudo *a* conscientious

concierto *m* concert; (acuerdo) agreement; (Mus, composición) concerto

concilia|ción *f* reconciliation. **~r** *vt* reconcile. **~r el sueño** get to sleep. □ **~rse** *vpr* gain

concilio *m* council

conciso *m* concise

conclu|ir [17] *vt* finish; (deducir) conclude. ● *vi* finish, end. **~sión** *f* conclusion. **~yente** *a* conclusive

concord|ancia *f* agreement. **~ar** [2] *vt* reconcile. ● *vi* agree. **~e** *a* in agreement. **~ia** *f* harmony

concret|amente *adv* specifically, to be exact. **~ar** *vt* make specific. **~arse** *vpr* become definite; (limitarse) confine o.s. **~o** *a* concrete; (determinado) specific, particular. **en ~o** definite; (concretamente) to be exact; (en resumen) in short. ● *m* (LAm, hormigón) concrete

concurr|encia *f* concurrence; (reunión) audience. **∼ido** *a* crowded, busy. **∼ir** *vi* meet; ; (coincidir) agree. **∼ a** (asistir a) attend

concurs|ante *m & f* competitor, contestant. **∼ar** *vi* compete, take part. **∼o** *m* competition; (ayuda) help

cond|ado *m* county. **∼e** *m* earl, count

condena *f* sentence. **∼ción** *f* condemnation. **∼do** *m* convicted person. **∼r** *vt* condemn; (Jurid) convict

condensa|ción *f* condensation. **∼r** *vt* condense

condesa *f* countess

condescende|ncia *f* condescension; (tolerancia) indulgence. **∼r** [1] *vi* agree; (dignarse) condescend

condici|ón *f* condition. **a ∼ón de (que)** on condition that. **∼onal** *a* conditional. **∼onar** *vt* condition

condiment|ar *vt* season. **∼o** *m* seasoning

condolencia *f* condolence

condominio *m* joint ownership; (LAm, edificio) block of flats (Brit), condominium (esp Amer)

condón *m* condom

condonar *vt* (perdonar) reprieve; cancel <*deuda*>

conducir [47] *vt* drive <*vehículo*>; carry <*electricidad, gas, agua*>. ● *vi* drive; (fig, llevar) lead. **¿a qué conduce?** what's the point? ▫ **∼se** *vpr* behave

conducta *f* behaviour

conducto *m* pipe, tube; (Anat) duct. **por ∼ de** through. **∼r** *m* driver; (jefe) leader; (Elec) conductor

conduzco *vb* ⇒CONDUCIR

conectar *vt/i* connect

conejo *m* rabbit

conexión *f* connection

confabularse *vpr* plot

confecci|ón *f* (de trajes) tailoring; (de vestidos) dressmaking. **∼ones** *fpl* clothing, clothes. **de ∼ón** ready-to-wear. **∼onar** *vt* make

confederación *f* confederation

conferencia *f* conference; (al teléfono) long-distance call; (Univ) lecture. **∼ en la cima, ∼ (en la) cumbre** summit conference. **∼nte** *m & f* lecturer

conferir [4] *vt* confer; award <*premio*>

confes|ar [1] *vt/i* confess. ▫ **∼arse** *vpr* confess. **∼ión** *f* confession. **∼ionario** *m* confessional. **∼or** *m* confessor

confeti *m* confetti

confia|do *a* trusting; (seguro de sí mismo) confident. **∼nza** *f* trust; (en sí mismo) confidence; (intimidad) familiarity. **∼r** [20] *vt* entrust. ● *vi*. **∼r en** trust

confiden|cia *f* confidence, secret. **∼cial** *a* confidential. **∼te** *m* confidant. ● *f* confidante

conf|ín *m* border. **∼ines** *mpl* outermost parts. **∼inar** *vt* confine; (desterrar) banish

confirma|ción *f* confirmation. **∼r** *vt* confirm

confiscar [7] *vt* confiscate

confit|ería *f* sweet-shop (Brit), candy store (Amer). **∼ura** *f* jam

conflict|ivo *a* difficult; <*época*> troubled; (polémico) controversial. **∼o** *m* conflict

confluencia *f* confluence

conform|ación *f* conformation, shape. **∼ar** *vt* (acomodar) adjust. ● *vi* agree. ▫ **∼arse** *vpr* conform.

~e *a* in agreement; (contento) happy, satisfied; (según) according (con to). **~e a** in accordance with, according to. ● *conj* as. ● *int* OK!. **~idad** *f* agreement; (tolerancia) resignation. **~ista** *m & f* conformist

conforta|ble *a* comfortable. **~nte** *a* comforting. **~r** *vt* comfort

confronta|ción *f* confrontation. **~r** *vt* confront

confu|ndir *vt* (equivocar) mistake, confuse; (mezclar) mix up, confuse; (turbar) embarrass. □ **~ndirse** *vpr* become confused; (equivocarse) make a mistake. **~sión** *f* confusion; (vergüenza) embarrassment. **~so** *a* confused; (borroso) blurred

congela|do *a* frozen. **~dor** *m* freezer. **~r** *vt* freeze

congeniar *vi* get on

congesti|ón *f* congestion. **~onado** *a* congested. □ **~onarse** *vpr* become congested

congoja *f* distress; (pena) grief

congraciarse *vpr* ingratiate o.s.

congratular *vt* congratulate

congrega|ción *f* gathering; (Relig) congregation. □ **~rse** [12] *vpr* gather, assemble

congres|ista *m & f* delegate, member of a congress. **~o** *m* congress, conference. **C~** Parliament. **C~o de los Diputados** Chamber of Deputies

cónico *a* conical

conífer|a *f* conifer. **~o** *a* coniferous

conjetura *f* conjecture, guess. **~r** *vt* conjecture, guess

conjuga|ción *f* conjugation. **~r** [12] *vt* conjugate

conjunción *f* conjunction

conjunto *a* joint. ● *m* collection; (Mus) band; (ropa) suit, outfit. **en ~** altogether

conjurar *vt* exorcise; avert *<peligro>*. ● *vi* plot, conspire

conllevar *vt* to entail

conmemora|ción *f* commemoration. **~r** *vt* commemorate

conmigo *pron* with me

conmo|ción *f* shock; (tumulto) upheaval. **~ cerebral** concussion. **~cionar** *vt* shock. **~ver** [2] *vt* shake; (emocionar) move

conmuta|dor *m* switch; (LAm, de teléfonos) switchboard. **~r** *vt* exchange

connota|ción *f* connotation. **~do** *a* (LAm, destacado) distinguished. **~r** *vt* connote

cono *m* cone

conoc|edor *a & m* expert. **~er** [11] *vt* know; (por primera vez) meet; (reconocer) recognize, know. **se conoce que** apparently. **dar a ~er** make known. □ **~erse** *vpr* know o.s.; *<dos personas>* know each other; (notarse) be obvious. **~ido** *a* well-known. ● *m* acquaintance. **~imiento** *m* knowledge; (sentido) consciousness. **sin ~imiento** unconscious. **tener ~imiento de** know about

conozco *vb* ⇒CONOCER

conque *conj* so

conquista *f* conquest. **~dor** *a* conquering. ● *m* conqueror; (de América) conquistador. **~r** *vt* conquer, win

consabido *a* usual, habitual

consagra|ción *f* consecration. **~r** *vt* consecrate; (fig) devote. □ **~rse** *vpr* devote o.s.

consanguíneo *m* blood relation

consciente *a* conscious

consecuen|cia *f* consequence; (coherencia) consistency. **a ~cia de** as a result of. **~te** *a* consistent

consecutivo *a* consecutive

conseguir [5 & 13] *vt* get, obtain; (lograr) manage; achieve <*objetivo*>

consej|ero *m* adviser; (miembro de consejo) member. **~o** *m* piece of advice; (Pol) council. **~o de ministros** cabinet

consenso *m* assent, consent

consenti|do *a* <*niño*> spoilt. **~miento** *m* consent. **~r** [4] *vt* allow; spoil <*niño*>. ● *vi* consent

conserje *m* porter, caretaker. **~ría** *f* porter's office

conserva *f* (mermelada) preserve; (en lata) tinned food. **en ~** tinned (Brit), canned. **~ción** *f* conservation; (de alimentos) preservation

conservador *a* & *m* (Pol) conservative

conservar *vt* keep; preserve <*alimentos*>. □ **~se** *vpr* keep; <*costumbre*> survive

conservatorio *m* conservatory

considera|ble *a* considerable. **~ción** *f* consideration; (respeto) respect. **de ~ción** serious. **de mi ~ción** (LAm, en cartas) Dear Sir. **~do** *a* considerate; (respetado) respected. **~r** *vt* consider; (respetar) respect

consigna *f* order; (para equipaje) left luggage office (Brit), baggage room (Amer); (eslogan) slogan

consigo *pron* (él) with him; (ella) with her; (Ud, Uds) with you; (uno mismo) with o.s.

consiguiente *a* consequent. **por ~** consequently

consist|encia *f* consistency. **~ente** *a* consisting (**en** of); (firme) solid; (LAm, congruente) consistent. **~ir** *vi*. **~ en** consist of; (radicar en) be due to

consola|ción *f* consolation. **~r** [2] *vt* console, comfort. □ **~rse** *vpr* console o.s.

consolidar *vt* consolidate. □ **~se** *vpr* consolidate

consomé *m* clear soup, consommé

consonante *a* consonant. ● *f* consonant

consorcio *m* consortium

conspira|ción *f* conspiracy. **~dor** *m* conspirator. **~r** *vi* conspire

consta|ncia *f* constancy; (prueba) proof; (LAm, documento) written evidence. **~nte** *a* constant. **~r** *vi* be clear; (figurar) appear, figure; (componerse) consist. **hacer ~r** state; (por escrito) put on record. **me ~ que** I'm sure that. **que conste que** believe me

constatar *vt* check; (confirmar) confirm

constipa|do *m* cold. ● *a*. **estar ~do** have a cold; (LAm, estreñido) be constipated. □ **~rse** *vpr* catch a cold

constitu|ción *f* constitution; (establecimiento) setting up. **~cional** *a* constitutional. **~ir** [17] *vt* constitute; (formar) form; (crear) set up, establish. □ **~irse** *vpr* set o.s. up (**en** as). **~tivo** *a*, **~yente** *a* constituent

constru|cción *f* construction. **~ctor** *m* builder. **~ir** [17] *vt* construct; build <*edificio*>

consuelo *m* consolation

consuetudinario *a* customary

cónsul *m* & *f* consul

consulado *m* consulate

consult|a *f* consultation. **horas** *fpl* **de ~a** surgery hours. **obra** *f* **de ~a** reference book. **~ar** *vt* consult. **~orio** *m* surgery

consumar *vt* complete; commit <*crimen*>; carry out <*robo*>; consummate <*matrimonio*>

consum|ición *f* consumption; (bebida) drink; (comida) food. **~ición mínima** minimum charge. **~ido** *a* <*persona*> skinny, wasted. **~idor** *m* consumer. **~ir** *vt* consume. □ **~irse** *vpr* <*persona*> waste away; <*vela, cigarillo*> burn down; <*líquido*> dry up. **~ismo** *m* consumerism. **~o** *m* consumption; (LAm, en restaurante etc) (bebida) drink; (comida) food. **~o mínimo** minimum charge

contab|ilidad *f* book-keeping; (profesión) accountancy. **~le** *m & f* accountant

contacto *m* contact. **ponerse en ~ con** get in touch with

conta|do *a*. **al ~** cash. **~s** *a pl* few. **tiene los días ~s** his days are numbered. **~dor** *m* meter; (LAm, persona) accountant

contagi|ar *vt* infect <*persona*>; pass on <*enfermedad*>; (fig) contaminate. **~o** *m* infection; (directo) contagion. **~oso** *a* infectious; (por contacto directo) contagious

contamina|ción *f* contamination, pollution. **~r** *vt* contaminate, pollute

contante *a*. **dinero** *m* **~** cash

contar [2] *vt* count; tell <*relato*>. **se cuenta que** it's said that. ● *vi* count. **~ con** rely on, count on. □ **~se** *vpr* be included (**entre** among)

contempla|ción *f* contemplation. **sin ~ciones** unceremoniously. **~r** *vt* look at; (fig) contemplate

contemporáneo *a & m* contemporary

conten|er [40] *vt* contain; hold <*respiración*>. □ **~erse** *vpr* contain o.s. **~ido** *a* contained. ● *m* contents

content|ar *vt* please. □ **~arse** *vpr*. **~arse con** be satisfied with, be pleased with. **~o** *a* (alegre) happy; (satisfecho) pleased

contesta|ción *f* answer. **~dor** *m*. **~ automático** answering machine. **~r** *vt/i* answer; (replicar) answer back

contexto *m* context

contienda *f* conflict; (lucha) contest

contigo *pron* with you

contiguo *a* adjacent

continen|tal *a* continental. **~te** *m* continent

continu|ación *f* continuation. **a ~ación** immediately after. **~ar** [21] *vt* continue, resume. ● *vi* continue. **~idad** *f* continuity. **~o** *a* continuous; (frecuente) continual. **corriente** *f* **~a** direct current

contorno *m* outline; (de árbol) girth; (de caderas) measurement. **~s** *mpl* surrounding area

contorsión *f* contortion

contra *prep* against. **en ~** against. ● *m* cons. ● *f* snag. **llevar la ~** contradict

contraata|car [7] *vt/i* counter-attack. **~que** *m* counter-attack

contrabaj|ista *m & f* double-bass player. **~o** *m* double-bass; (persona) double-bass player

contraband|ista *m & f* smuggler. **~o** *m* contraband

contracción *f* contraction

contrad|ecir [46] *vt* contradict. **~icción** *f* contradiction. **~ictorio** *a* contradictory

contraer [41] *vt* contract. **~ matrimonio** marry. □ **~se** *vpr* contract

contralto *m* counter tenor. ● *f* contralto

contra|mano. **a ~** in the wrong direction. **~partida** *f* compensation. **~pelo**. **a ~** the wrong way

contrapes|ar *vt* counterweight. **~o** *m* counterweight

contraproducente *a* counterproductive

contrari|a *f*. **llevar la ~a** contradict. **~ado** *a* upset; (enojado) annoyed. **~ar** [20] *vt* upset; (enojar) annoy. **~edad** *f* setback; (disgusto) annoyance. **~o** *a* contrary (**a** to); *<dirección>* opposite. **al ~o** on the contrary. **al ~o de** contrary to. **de lo ~o** otherwise. **por el ~o** on the contrary. **ser ~o a** be opposed to, be against

contrarrestar *vt* counteract

contrasentido *m* contradiction

contraseña *f* (palabra) password; (en cine) stub

contrast|ar *vt* check, verify. ● *vi* contrast. **~e** *m* contrast; (en oro, plata) hallmark

contratar *vt* contract *<servicio>*; hire, take on *<empleados>*; sign up *<jugador>*

contratiempo *m* setback; (accidente) mishap

contrat|ista *m & f* contractor. **~o** *m* contract

contraven|ción *f* contravention. **~ir** [53] *vt* contravene

contraventana *f* shutter

contribu|ción *f* contribution; (tributo) tax. **~ir** [17] *vt/i* contribute. **~yente** *m & f* contributor; (que paga impuestos) taxpayer

contrincante *m* rival, opponent

control *m* control; (vigilancia) check; (lugar) checkpoint. **~ar** *vt* control; (vigilar) check. □ **~se** *vpr* control s.o.

controversia *f* controversy

contundente *a* *<arma>* blunt; *<argumento>* convincing

contusión *f* bruise

convalec|encia *f* convalescence. **~er** [11] *vi* convalesce. **~iente** *a & m & f* convalescent

convalidar *vt* recognize *<título>*

convenc|er [9] *vt* convince. **~imiento** *m* conviction

convenci|ón *f* convention. **~onal** *a* conventional

conveni|encia *f* convenience; (aptitud) suitability. **~ente** *a* suitable; (aconsejable) advisable; (provechoso) useful. **~o** *m* agreement. **~r** [53] *vt* agree. ● *vi* agree (**en** on); (ser conveniente) be convenient for, suit; (ser aconsejable) be advisable

convento *m* (de monjes) monastery; (de monjas) convent

conversa|ción *f* conversation. **~ciones** *fpl* talks. **~r** *vi* converse, talk

conver|sión *f* conversion. **~so** *a* converted. ● *m* convert. **~tible** *a* convertible. ● *m* (LAm) convertible. **~tir** [4] *vt* convert. □ **~tirse** *vpr*. **~tirse en** turn into; (Relig) convert

convic|ción *f* conviction. **~to** *a* convicted

convida|do *m* guest. **~r** *vt* invite

convincente *a* convincing

conviv|encia *f* coexistence; (de parejas) life together. **~ir** *vi* live together; (coexistir) coexist

convocar [7] *vt* call <*huelga, elecciones*>; convene <*reunión*>; summon <*personas*>

convulsión *f* convulsion

conyugal *a* marital, conjugal; <*vida*> married

cónyuge *m* spouse. **~s** *mpl* married couple

coñac *m* (*pl* **~s**) brandy

coopera|ción *f* cooperation. **~r** *vi* cooperate. **~tiva** *f* cooperative. **~tivo** *a* cooperative

coordinar *vt* coordinate

copa *f* glass; (deportes, fig) cup; (de árbol) top. **~s** *fpl* (naipes) hearts. **tomar una ~** have a drink

copia *f* copy. **~ en limpio** fair copy. **sacar una ~** make a copy. **~r** *vt* copy

copioso *a* copious; <*lluvia, nevada etc*> heavy

copla *f* verse; (canción) folksong

copo *m* flake. **~ de nieve** snowflake. **~s de maíz** cornflakes

coquet|a *f* flirt; (mueble) dressing-table. **~ear** *vi* flirt. **~o** *a* flirtatious

coraje *m* courage; (rabia) anger

coral *a* choral. ● *m* coral; (Mus) chorale

coraza *f* cuirass; (Naut) armour-plating; (de tortuga) shell

coraz|ón *m* heart; (persona) darling. **sin ~ón** heartless. **tener buen ~ón** be good-hearted. **~onada** *f* hunch; (impulso) impulse

corbata *f* tie, necktie (esp Amer). **~ de lazo** bow tie

corche|a *f* quaver. **~te** *m* fastener, hook and eye; (gancho) hook; (paréntesis) square bracket

corcho *m* cork. **~lata** *f* (Mex) (crown) cap

corcova *f* hump. **~do** *a* hunchbacked

cordel *m* cord, string

cordero *m* lamb

cordial *a* cordial, friendly. ● *m* tonic. **~idad** *f* cordiality, warmth

cordillera *f* mountain range

córdoba *m* (unidad monetaria de Nicaragua) córdoba

cordón *m* string; (de zapatos) lace; (cable) cord; (fig) cordon. **~ umbilical** umbilical cord

coreografía *f* choreography

corista *f* (bailarina) chorus girl

cornet|a *f* bugle; (Mex, de coche) horn. **~ín** *m* cornet

cornudo *a* horned. ● *m* cuckold

coro *m* (Arquit, Mus) choir; (en teatro) chorus

corona *f* crown; (de flores) wreath, garland. **~ción** *f* coronation. **~r** *vt* crown

coronel *m* colonel

coronilla *f* crown. **estar hasta la ~** be fed up

corpora|ción *f* corporation. **~l** *a* <*castigo*> corporal; <*trabajo*> physical

corpulento *a* stout

corral *m* farmyard. **aves** *fpl* **de ~** poultry

correa *f* strap; (de perro) lead; (cinturón) belt

correc|ción *f* correction; (cortesía) good manners. **~to** *a* correct; (cortés) polite

corre|dizo *a* running. **nudo** *m* **~dizo** slip knot. **puerta** *f* **~diza** sliding door. **~dor** *m* runner; (pasillo) corridor; (agente) agent, broker. **~dor de coches** racing driver

corregir [5 & 14] *vt* correct

correlación *f* correlation

correo *m* post, mail; (persona) courier; (LAm, oficina) post office. **~s** *mpl* post office. **~ electrónico** e-mail. **echar al ~** post

correr *vt* run; (mover) move; draw *<cortinas>*. ● *vi* run; *<agua, electricidad etc>* flow; *<tiempo>* pass. □ **~se** *vpr* (apartarse) move along; *<colores>* run

correspond|encia *f* correspondence. **~er** *vi* correspond; (ser adecuado) be fitting; (contestar) reply; (pertenecer) belong; (incumbir) fall to. □ **~erse** *vpr* (amarse) love one another. **~iente** *a* corresponding

corresponsal *m* correspondent

corrid|a *f* run. **~a de toros** bullfight. **de ~a** from memory. **~o** *a* (continuo) continuous

corriente *a* *<agua>* running; *<monedas, publicación, cuenta, año>* current; (ordinario) ordinary. ● *f* current; (de aire) draught; (fig) tendency. ● *m* current month. **al ~** (al día) up-to-date; (enterado) aware

corr|illo *m* small group. **~o** *m* circle

corroborar *vt* corroborate

corroer [24 & 37] *vt* corrode; (Geol) erode; (fig) eat away

corromper *vt* corrupt, rot *<materia>*. □ **~se** *vpr* become corrupted; *<materia>* rot; *<alimentos>* go bad

corrosi|ón *f* corrosion. **~vo** *a* corrosive

corrupción *f* corruption; (de materia etc) rot

corsé *m* corset

corta|do *a* cut; *<carretera>* closed; *<leche>* curdled; (avergonzado) embarrassed; (confuso) confused. ● *m* coffee with a little milk. **~dura** *f* cut. **~nte** *a* sharp; *<viento>* biting; *<frío>* bitter. **~r** *vt* cut; (recortar) cut out; (aislar, separar, interrumpir) cut off. ● *vi* cut; *<novios>* break up. □ **~rse** *vpr* cut o.s.; *<leche etc>* curdle; (fig) be embarrassed. **~rse el pelo** have one's hair cut. **~rse las uñas** cut one's nails. **~uñas** *m invar* nail-clippers

corte *m* cut; (de tela) length. **~ de luz** power cut. **~ y confección** dressmaking. ● *f* court; (LAm, tribunal) Court of Appeal. **hacer la ~** court. **las C~s** the Spanish parliament. **la C~ Suprema** the Supreme Court

cortej|ar *vt* court. **~o** *m* (de rey etc) entourage. **~o fúnebre** cortège, funeral procession

cortés *a* polite

cortesía *f* courtesy

corteza *f* bark; (de queso) rind; (de pan) crust

cortijo *m* farm; (casa) farmhouse

cortina *f* curtain

corto *a* short; (apocado) shy. **~ de** short of. **~ de alcances** dim, thick. **~ de vista** short-sighted. **a la corta o a la larga** sooner or later. **quedarse ~** fall short; (miscalcular) underestimate. **~circuito** *m* short circuit

Coruña *f*. **La ~** Corunna

cosa *f* thing; (asunto) business; (idea) idea. **como si tal ~** just like that; (como si no hubiera pasado nada) as if nothing had happened. **decirle a uno cuatro ~s** tell s.o. a thing or two

cosecha *f* harvest; (de vino) vintage. **~r** *vt* harvest

coser *vt* sew; sew on *<botón>*; stitch *<herida>*. ● *vi* sew. □ **~se** *vpr* stick to s.o.

cosmético *a* & *m* cosmetic

cósmico *a* cosmic
cosmo|polita *a & m & f* cosmopolitan. **~s** *m* cosmos
cosquillas *fpl*. **dar ~** tickle. **hacer ~** tickle. **tener ~** be ticklish
costa *f* coast. **a ~ de** at the expense of. **a toda ~** at any cost
costado *m* side
costal *m* sack
costar [2] *vt* cost. ● *vi* cost; (resultar difícil) to be hard. **~ caro** be expensive. **cueste lo que cueste** at any cost
costarricense *a & m*, **costarriqueño** *a & m* Costa Rican
cost|as *fpl* (Jurid) costs. **~e** *m* cost. **~ear** *vt* pay for; (Naut) sail along the coast
costero *a* coastal
costilla *f* rib; (chuleta) chop
costo *m* cost. **~so** *a* expensive
costumbre *f* custom; (de persona) habit. **de ~** usual; (como adv) usually
costur|a *f* sewing; (línea) seam; (confección) dressmaking. **~era** *f* dressmaker. **~ero** *m* sewing box
cotejar *vt* compare
cotidiano *a* daily
cotille|ar *vt* gossip. **~o** *m* gossip
cotiza|ción *f* quotation, price. **~r** [10] *vt* (en la bolsa) quote. ● *vi* pay contributions. □ **~rse** *vpr* fetch; (en la bolsa) stand at; (fig) be valued
coto *m* enclosure; (de caza) preserve. **~ de caza** game preserve
cotorr|a *f* parrot; (fig) chatterbox. **~ear** *vi* chatter
coyuntura *f* joint
coz *f* kick
cráneo *m* skull
cráter *m* crater
crea|ción *f* creation. **~dor** *a* creative. ● *m* creator. **~r** *vt* create
crec|er [11] *vi* grow; (aumentar) increase; <*río*> rise. **~ida** *f* (de río) flood. **~ido** *a* <*persona*> grown-up; <*número*> large, considerable; <*plantas*> fully-grown. **~iente** *a* growing; <*luna*> crescent. **~imiento** *m* growth
credencial *f* document. ● *a*. **cartas** *fpl* **~es** credentials
credibilidad *f* credibility
crédito *m* credit; (préstamo) loan. **digno de ~** reliable
credo *m* creed
crédulo *a* credulous
cre|encia *f* belief. **~er** [18] *vt/i* believe; (pensar) think. **~o que no** I don't think so, I think not. **~o que sí** I think so. **no ~o** I don't think so. **¡ya lo ~o!** I should think so!. □ **~erse** *vpr* consider o.s. **no me lo ~o** I don't believe it. **~íble** *a* credible
crema *f* cream; (Culin) custard; (LAm, de la leche) cream. **~ batida** (LAm) whipped cream. **~ bronceadora** sun-tan cream
cremallera *f* zip (Brit), zipper (Amer)
crematorio *m* crematorium
crepitar *vi* crackle
crepúsculo *m* twilight
crespo *a* frizzy; (LAm, rizado) curly. ● *m* (LAm) curl
cresta *f* crest; (de gallo) comb
creyente *m* believer
cría *f* breeding; (animal) baby animal. **las ~s** the young
cria|da *f* maid, servant. **~dero** *m* (de pollos etc) farm; (de ostras) bed; (Bot) nursery. ● *m* servant. **~dor** *m* breeder. **~nza** *f* breeding. **~r** [20] *vt* suckle; grow <*plantas*>;

breed <*animales*>; (educar) bring up (Brit), raise (esp Amer). □ **~rse** *vpr* grow up

criatura *f* creature; (niño) baby

crim|en *m* (serious) crime; (asesinato) murder; (fig) crime. **~inal** *a & m & f* criminal

crin *f* mane

crío *m* child

criollo *a* Creole; (LAm), <*música, comida*> traditional. ● *m* Creole; (LAm, nativo) Peruvian, Chilean etc

crisantemo *m* chrysanthemum

crisis *f invar* crisis

crispar *vt* twitch; (Ⓘ, irritar) annoy. **~le los nervios a uno** get on s.o.'s nerves

cristal *m* crystal; (Esp, vidrio) glass; (Esp, de una ventana) pane of glass. **limpiar los ~es** (Esp) clean the windows. **~ino** *a* crystalline; (fig) crystal-clear. **~izar** [10] crystallize. □ **~izarse** *vpr* crystallize

cristian|dad *f* Christendom. **~ismo** *m* Christianity. **~o** *a* Christian. **ser ~o** be a Christian. ● *m* Christian

cristo *m* crucifix

Cristo *m* Christ

criterio *m* criterion; (discernimiento) judgement; (opinión) opinion

cr|ítica *f* criticism; (reseña) review. **~iticar** [7] *vt* criticize. **~ítico** *a* critical. ● *m* critic

croar *vi* croak

crom|ado *a* chromium-plated. **~o** *m* chromium, chrome

crónic|a *f* chronicle; (de radio, TV) report; (de periódico) feature. **~a deportiva** sport section. **~o** *a* chronic

cronista *m & f* reporter

cronología *f* chronology

cron|ometrar *vt* time. **~ómetro** *m* (en deportes) stop-watch

croqueta *f* croquette

cruce *m* crossing; (de calles, carreteras) crossroads; (de peatones) (pedestrian) crossing

crucial *a* crucial

crucifi|car [7] *vt* crucify. **~jo** *m* crucifix

crucigrama *m* crossword (puzzle)

crudo *a* raw; (fig) harsh. ● *m* crude (oil)

cruel *a* cruel. **~dad** *f* cruelty

cruji|do *m* (de seda, de hojas secas) rustle; (de muebles) creak. **~r** *vi* <*seda, hojas secas*> rustle; <*muebles*> creak

cruz *f* cross; (de moneda) tails. **~ gamada** swastika. **la C~ Roja** the Red Cross

cruza|da *f* crusade. **~r** [10] *vt* cross; exchange <*palabras*>. □ **~rse** *vpr* cross; (pasar en la calle) pass each other. **~rse con** pass

cuaderno *m* exercise book; (para apuntes) notebook

cuadra *f* (caballeriza) stable; (LAm, distancia) block

cuadrado *a & m* square

cuadragésimo *a* fortieth

cuadr|ar *vt* square. ● *vi* suit; <*cuentas*> tally. □ **~arse** *vpr* (Mil) stand to attention; (fig) dig one's heels in. **~ilátero** *m* quadrilateral; (Boxeo) ring

cuadrilla *f* group; (pandilla) gang

cuadro *m* square; (pintura) painting; (Teatro) scene; (de números) table; (de mando etc) panel; (conjunto del personal) staff. **~ de distribución** switchboard. **a ~s, de ~s** check. **¡qué ~!, ¡vaya un ~!** what a sight!

cuadrúpedo *m* quadruped

cuádruple *a & m* quadruple

cuajar *vt* congeal <*sangre*>; curdle <*leche*>; (llenar) fill up. ● *vi* <*nieve*> settle; (fig, [I]) work out. **cuajado de** full of. □ **~se** *vpr* coagulate; <*sangre*> clot; <*leche*> curdle

cual *pron*. **el ~, la ~ etc** (animales y cosas) that, which; (personas, sujeto) who, that; (personas, objeto) whom. ● *a* (LAm, qué) what. **~ si** as if. **cada ~** everyone. **lo ~** which. **por lo ~** because of which. **sea ~ sea** whatever

cuál *pron* which

cualidad *f* quality

cualquiera *a* (delante de nombres **cualquier,** *pl* **cualesquiera**) any. ● *pron* (*pl* **cualesquiera**) anyone, anybody; (cosas) whatever, whichever. **un ~** a nobody. **una ~** a slut

cuando *adv* when. ● *conj* when; (si) if. **~ más** at the most. **~ menos** at the least. **aun ~** even if. **de ~ en ~** from time to time

cuándo *adv & conj* when. **¿de ~ acá?, ¿desde ~?** since when? **¡~ no!** (LAm) as usual!, typical!

cuant|ía *f* quantity; (extensión) extent. **~ioso** *a* abundant. **~o** *a* as much ... as, as many ... as. ● *pron* as much as, as many as. ● *adv* as much as. **~o antes** as soon as possible. **~o más, mejor** the more the merrier. **en ~o** as soon as. **en ~o a** as for. **por ~o** since. **unos ~os** a few, some

cuánto *a* (interrogativo) how much?; (interrogativo en plural) how many?; (exclamativo) what a lot of! ● *pron* how much?; (en plural) how many? ● *adv* how much. **¿~ mides?** how tall are you? **¿~ tiempo?** how long? **¡~ tiempo sin verte!** it's been a long time! **¿a ~s estamos?** what's the date today? **un Sr. no sé ~s** Mr So-and-So

cuáquero *m* Quaker

cuarent|a *a & m* forty; (cuadragésimo) fortieth. **~ena** *f* (Med) quarantine. **~ón** *a* about forty

cuaresma *f* Lent

cuarta *f* (palmo) span

cuartel *m* (Mil) barracks. **~ general** headquarters

cuarteto *m* quartet

cuarto *a* fourth. ● *m* quarter; (habitación) room. **~ de baño** bathroom. **~ de estar** living room. **~ de hora** quarter of an hour. **estar sin un ~** be broke. **y ~** (a) quarter past

cuarzo *m* quartz

cuate *m* (Mex) twin; (amigo) friend; ([I], tipo) guy

cuatro *a & m* four. **~cientos** *a & m* four hundred

Cuba *f* Cuba

cuba|libre *m* rum and Coke (P). **~no** *a & m* Cuban

cúbico *a* cubic

cubículo *m* cubicle

cubiert|a *f* cover; (neumático) tyre; (Naut) deck. **~o** *a* covered; <*cielo*> overcast. ● *m* place setting, piece of cutlery; (en restaurante) cover charge. **a ~o** under cover

cubilete *m* bowl; (molde) mould; (para los dados) cup

cubis|mo *m* cubism. **~ta** *a & m & f* cubist

cubo *m* bucket; (Mat) cube

cubrecama *m* bedspread

cubrir (*pp* **cubierto**) *vt* cover; fill <*vacante*>. □ **~se** *vpr* cover o.s.; (ponerse el sombrero) put on one's hat; <*el cielo*> cloud over, become overcast

cucaracha *f* cockroach

cuchar|a *f* spoon. **~ada** *f* spoonful. **~adita** *f* teaspoonful. **~illa**, **~ita** *f* teaspoon. **~ón** *m* ladle

cuchichear *vi* whisper

cuchill|a *f* large knife; (de carnicero) cleaver; (hoja de afeitar) razor blade. **~ada** *f* stab; (herida) knife wound. **~o** *m* knife

cuchitril *m* (fig) hovel

cuclillas: **en ~** *adv* squatting

cuco *a* shrewd; (mono) pretty, nice. ● *m* cuckoo

cucurucho *m* cornet

cuello *m* neck; (de camisa) collar. **cortar(le) el ~ a uno** cut s.o.'s throat

cuenc|a *f* (del ojo) (eye) socket; (Geog) basin. **~o** *m* hollow; (vasija) bowl

cuenta *f* count; (acción de contar) counting; (cálculo) calculation; (factura) bill; (en banco, relato) account; (de collar) bead. **~ corriente** current account, checking account (Amer). **dar ~ de** give an account of. **darse ~ de** realize. **en resumidas ~s** in short. **por mi propia ~** on my own account. **tener en ~** bear in mind

cuentakilómetros *m invar* milometer

cuent|ista *m & f* story-writer; (de mentiras) fibber. **~o** *m* story; (mentira) fib, tall story. **~ de hadas** fairy tale. ● *vb* ⇒CONTAR

cuerda *f* rope; (más fina) string; (Mus) string. **~ floja** tightrope. **dar ~ a** wind up *<un reloj>*

cuerdo *a <persona>* sane; *<acción>* sensible

cuerno *m* horn

cuero *m* leather; (piel) skin; (del grifo) washer. **~ cabelludo** scalp. **en ~s (vivos)** stark naked

cuerpo *m* body

cuervo *m* crow

cuesta *f* slope, hill. **~ abajo** downhill. **~ arriba** uphill. **a ~s** on one's back

cuestión *f* matter; (problema) problem; (cosa) thing

cueva *f* cave

cuida|do *m* care; (preocupación) worry. **~do!** watch out!. **tener ~do** be careful. **~doso** *a* careful. **~r** *vt* look after. ● *vi*. **~r de** look after. □ **~rse** *vpr* look after o.s. **~rse de** be careful to

culata *f* (de revólver, fusil) butt. **~zo** *m* recoil

culebr|a *f* snake. **~ón** *m* soap opera

culinario *a* culinary

culminar *vi* culminate

culo *m* [!] bottom; (LAm vulg) arse (Brit vulg), ass (Amer vulg)

culpa *f* fault. **echar la ~** blame. **por ~ de** because of. **tener la ~** be to blame (**de** for). **~bilidad** *f* guilt. **~ble** *a* guilty. ● *m & f* culprit. **~r** *vt* blame (**de** for)

cultiv|ar *vt* farm; grow *<plantas>*; (fig) cultivate. **~o** *m* farming; (de plantas) growing

cult|o *a <persona>* educated. ● *m* cult; (homenaje) worship. **~ura** *f* culture. **~ural** *a* cultural

culturismo *m* body-building

cumbre *f* summit

cumpleaños *m invar* birthday

cumplido *a* perfect; (cortés) polite. ● *m* compliment. **de ~** courtesy. **por ~** out of a sense of duty. **~r** *a* reliable

cumpli|miento *m* fulfilment; (de ley) observance; (de orden) carrying out. **~r** *vt* carry out; observe *<ley>*; serve *<condena>*; reach *<años>*;

keep *<promesa>*. **hoy cumple 3 años** he's 3 (years old) today. ● *vi* do one's duty. **por ~r** as a mere formality. □ **~rse** *vpr* expire; (realizarse) be fulfilled

cuna *f* cradle; (fig, nacimiento) birthplace

cundir *vi* spread; (rendir) go a long way

cuneta *f* ditch

cuña *f* wedge

cuñad|a *f* sister-in-law. **~o** *m* brother-in-law

cuño *m* stamp. **de nuevo ~** new

cuota *f* quota; (de sociedad etc) membership, fee; (LAm, plazo) instalment; (Mex, peaje) toll

cupe *vb* ⇒CABER

cupo *m* cuota; (LAm, capacidad) room; (Mex, plaza) place

cupón *m* coupon

cúpula *f* dome

cura *f* cure; (tratamiento) treatment. ● *m* priest. **~ción** *f* healing. **~ndero** *m* faith-healer. **~r** *vt* (incl Culin) cure; dress *<herida>*; (tratar) treat; (fig) remedy; tan *<pieles>*. □ **~rse** *vpr* get better

curios|ear *vi* pry; (mirar) browse. **~idad** *f* curiosity. **~o** *a* curious; (raro) odd, unusual. ● *m* onlooker; (fisgón) busybody

curita *f* (LAm) (sticking) plaster

curriculum (**vitae**) *m* curriculum vitae, CV

cursar *vt* issue; (estudiar) study

cursi *a* pretentious, showy

cursillo *m* short course

cursiva *f* italics

curso *m* course; (Univ etc) year. **en ~** under way; *<año etc>* current

cursor *m* cursor

curtir *vt* tan; (fig) harden. □ **~se** *vpr* become tanned; (fig) become hardened

curv|a *f* curve; (de carretera) bend. **~ar** *vt* bend; bow *<estante>*. **~arse** *vpr* bend; *<estante>* bow; *<madera>* warp. **~ilíneo** *a* curvilinear; *<mujer>* curvaceous. **~o** *a* curved

cúspide *f* top; (fig) pinnacle

custodi|a *f* safe-keeping; (Jurid) custody. **~ar** *vt* guard; (guardar) look after. **~o** *m* guardian

cutáneo *a* skin

cutis *m* skin, complexion

cuyo *pron* (de persona) whose, of whom; (de cosa) whose, of which. **en ~ caso** in which case

Dd

dactilógrafo *m* typist

dado *m* dice. ● *a* given. **~ que** since, given that

daltónico *a* colour-blind

dama *f* lady. **~ de honor** bridesmaid. **~s** *fpl* draughts (Brit), checkers (Amer)

damasco *m* damask; (LAm, fruta) apricot

danés *a* Danish. ● *m* Dane; (idioma) Danish

danza *f* dance; (acción) dancing. **~r** [10] *vt/i* dance

dañ|ar *vt* damage. □ **~se** *vpr* get damaged. **~ino** *a* harmful. **~o** *m* damage; (a una persona) harm. **~os y perjuicios** damages. **hacer ~o a** harm, hurt. **hacerse ~o** hurt o.s.

dar [26] *vt* give; bear <*frutos*>; give out <*calor*>; strike <*la hora*>. ● *vi* give. **da igual** it doesn't matter. **¡dale!** go on! **da lo mismo** it doesn't matter. **~ a** <*ventana*> look on to; <*edificio*> face. **~ a luz** give birth. **~ con** meet <*persona*>; find <*cosa*>. **¿qué más da?** it doesn't matter! □ **~se** *vpr* have <*baño*>. **dárselas de** make o.s. out to be. **~se por** consider o.s.

dardo *m* dart

datar *vi*. **~ de** date from

dátil *m* date

dato *m* piece of information. **~s** *mpl* data, information. **~s personales** personal details

de

● *preposición*

Note that **de** before **el** becomes **del**, e.g. **es del norte**

····➤ (contenido, material) of. **un vaso de agua** a glass of water. **es de madera** it's made of wood

····➤ (pertenencia) **el coche de Juan** Juan's car. **es de ella** it's hers. **es de María** it's María's. **las llaves del coche** the car keys

····➤ (procedencia, origen, época) from. **soy de Madrid** I'm from Madrid. **una llamada de Lima** a call from Lima. **es del siglo V** it's from the 5th century

····➤ (causa, modo) **se murió de cáncer** he died of cancer. **temblar de miedo** to tremble with fear. **de dos en dos** two by two

····➤ (parte del día, hora) **de noche** at night. **de madrugada** early in the morning. **las diez de la mañana** ten (o'clock) in the morning. **de 9 a 12** from 9 to 12

····➤ (en oraciones pasivas) by. **rodeado de agua** surrounded by water. **va seguido de coma** it's followed by a comma. **es de Mozart** it's by Mozart

····➤ (al especificar) **el cajón de arriba** the top drawer. **la clase de inglés** the English lesson. **la chica de verde** the girl in green. **el de debajo** the one underneath

····➤ (en calidad de) as. **trabaja de oficinista** he works as a clerk. **vino de chaperón** he came as a chaperon

····➤ (en comparaciones) than. **pesa más de un kilo** it weighs more than a kilo

····➤ (con superlativo) **el más alto del mundo** the tallest in the world. **el mejor de todos** the best of all

····➤ (sentido condicional) if. **de haberlo sabido** if I had known. **de continuar así** if this goes on

⇨ Cuando la preposición **de** se emplea como parte de expresiones como **de prisa, de acuerdo** etc., y de nombres compuestos como **hombre de negocios, saco de dormir** etc., ver bajo el respectivo nombre

deambular *vi* roam (**por** about)

debajo *adv* underneath. **~ de** under(neath). **el de ~** the one underneath. **por ~** underneath. **por ~ de** below

debat|e *m* debate. **~ir** *vt* debate

deber *vt* owe. ● *v aux* have to, must; (en condicional) should. **debo marcharme** I must go, I have to go. ● *m* duty. **~es** *mpl* homework. □ **~se** *vpr*. **~se a** be due to

debido *a* due; (correcto) proper. **~ a** due to. **como es ~** as is proper

débil *a* weak; *<sonido>* faint; *<luz>* dim

debili|dad *f* weakness. **~tar** *vt* weaken. □ **~tarse** *vpr* weaken, get weak

débito *m* debit. **~ bancario** (LAm) direct debit

debutar *vi* make one's debut

década *f* decade

deca|dencia *f* decline. **~dente** *a* decadent. **~er** [29] *vi* decline; (debilitarse) weaken. **~ído** *a* in low spirits. **~imiento** *m* decline, weakening

decano *m* dean; (miembro más antiguo) senior member

decapitar *vt* behead

decena *f* ten. **una ~ de** about ten

decencia *f* decency

decenio *m* decade

decente *a* decent; (decoroso) respectable; (limpio) clean, tidy

decepci|ón *f* disappointment. **~onar** *vt* disappoint

decidi|do *a* decided; *<persona>* determined, resolute. **~r** *vt* decide; settle *<cuestión etc>*. ● *vi* decide. □ **~rse** *vpr* make up one's mind

decimal *a* & *m* decimal

décimo *a* & *m* tenth. ● *m* (de lotería) tenth part of a lottery ticket

decir [46] *vt* say; (contar) tell. ● *m* saying. **~ que no** say no. **~ que sí** say yes. **dicho de otro modo** in other words. **dicho y hecho** no sooner said than done. **¿dígame?** can I help you? **¡dígame!** (al teléfono) hello! **digamos** let's say. **es ~** that is to say. **mejor dicho** rather. **¡no me digas!** you don't say!, really! **por así ~, por ~lo así** so to speak, as it were. **querer ~** mean. **se dice que** it is said that, they say that

decisi|ón *f* decision. **~vo** *a* decisive

declara|ción *f* declaration; (a autoridad, prensa) statement. **~ción de renta** income tax return. **~r** *vt/i* declare. □ **~rse** *vpr* declare o.s.; *<epidemia etc>* break out

declinar *vt* turn down; (Gram) decline

declive *m* slope; (fig) decline. **en ~** sloping

decola|je *m* (LAm) take-off. **~r** *vi* (LAm) take off

decolorarse *vpr* become discoloured, fade

decora|ción *f* decoration. **~do** *m* (en el teatro) set. **~r** *vt* decorate. **~tivo** *a* decorative

decoro *m* decorum. **~so** *a* decent, respectable

decrépito *a* decrepit

decret|ar *vt* decree. **~o** *m* decree

dedal *m* thimble

dedica|ción *f* dedication. **~r** [7] *vt* dedicate; devote *<tiempo>*. □ **~rse** *vpr*. **~rse a** devote o.s. to. **¿a qué se dedica?** what does he do? **~toria** *f* dedication

dedo *m* finger; (del pie) toe. **~ anular** ring finger. **~ corazón** middle finger. **~gordo** thumb; (del pie) big toe. **~ índice** index finger. **~ meñique** little finger. **~ pulgar** thumb

deduc|ción *f* deduction. **~ir** [47] *vt* deduce; (descontar) deduct

defect|o *m* fault, defect. **~uoso** *a* defective

defen|der [1] *vt* defend. **~sa** *f* defence. □ **~derse** *vpr* defend o.s. **~sivo** *a* defensive. **~sor** *m* defender. **abogado** *m* **~sor** defence counsel

defeño *m* (Mex) person from the Federal District

deficien|cia *f* deficiency. **~cia mental** mental handicap. **~te** *a* poor, deficient. ● *m & f.* **~te mental** mentally handicapped person

déficit *m invar* deficit

defini|ción *f* definition. **~do** *a* defined. **~r** *vt* define. **~tivo** *a* definitive. **en ~tiva** all in all

deform|ación *f* deformation; (de imagen etc) distortion. **~ar** *vt* deform; distort <*imagen, metal*>. □ **~arse** *vpr* go out of shape. **~e** *a* deformed

defraudar *vt* defraud; (decepcionar) disappoint

defunción *f* death

degenera|ción *f* degeneration; (cualidad) degeneracy. **~do** *a* degenerate. **~r** *vi* degenerate

degollar [16] *vt* cut s.o.'s throat

degradar *vt* degrade; (Mil) demote. □ **~se** *vpr* demean o.s..

degusta|ción *f* tasting. **~r** *vt* taste

dehesa *f* pasture

deja|dez *f* slovenliness; (pereza) laziness. **~do** *a* slovenly; (descuidado) slack, negligent. **~r** *vt* leave; (abandonar) abandon; give up <*estudios*>; (prestar) lend; (permitir) let. **~r a un lado** leave aside. **~r de** stop

dejo *m* aftertaste; (tonillo) slight accent; (toque) touch

del = **de** + **el**

delantal *m* apron

delante *adv* in front. **~ de** in front of. **de ~** front. **~ra** *f* front; (de teatro etc) front row; (ventaja) lead; (de equipo) forward line. **llevar la ~ra** be in the lead. **~ro** *a* front. ● *m* forward

delat|ar *vt* denounce. **~or** *m* informer

delega|ción *f* delegation; (oficina) regional office; (Mex, comisaría) police station. **~do** *m* delegate; (Com) agent, representative. **~r** [12] *vt* delegate

deleit|ar *vt* delight. **~e** *m* delight

deletrear *vt* spell (out)

delfín *m* dolphin

delgad|ez *f* thinness. **~o** *a* thin; (esbelto) slim. **~ucho** *a* skinny

delibera|ción *f* deliberation. **~do** *a* deliberate. **~r** *vi* deliberate (**sobre** on)

delicad|eza *f* gentleness; (fragilidad) frailty; (tacto) tact. **falta de ~eza** tactlessness. **tener la ~ de** have the courtesy to. **~o** *a* delicate; (refinado) refined; (sensible) sensitive

delici|a *f* delight. **~oso** *a* delightful; <*sabor etc*> delicious

delimitar *vt* delimit

delincuen|cia *f* delinquency. **~te** *m & f* criminal, delinquent

delinquir [8] *vi* commit a criminal offence

delir|ante *a* delirious. **~ar** *vi* be delirious; (fig) talk nonsense. **~io** *m* delirium; (fig) frenzy

delito *m* crime, offence

demacrado *a* haggard

demagogo *m* demagogue

demanda *f* demand; (Jurid) lawsuit. **~do** *m* defendant. **~nte** *m & f* (Jurid) plaintiff. **~r** *vt* (Jurid) sue; (LAm, requerir) require

demarcación *f* demarcation

demás *a* rest of the, other. ● *pron* rest, others. **lo ~** the rest. **por ~** extremely. **por lo ~** otherwise

demas|ía *f*. **en ~ía** in excess. **~iado** *a* too much; (en plural) too many. ● *adv* too much; (con adjetivo) too

demen|cia *f* madness. **~te** *a* demented, mad

dem|ocracia *f* democracy. **~ócrata** *m & f* democrat. **~ocrático** *a* democratic

demol|er [2] *vt* demolish. **~ición** *f* demolition

demonio *m* devil, demon. **¡~s!** hell! **¿cómo ~s?** how the hell? **¡qué ~s!** what the hell!

demora *f* delay. **~r** *vt* delay. ● *vi* stay on. ◻ **~rse** *vpr* be too long; (LAm, cierto tiempo). **se ~ una hora en llegar** it takes him an hour to get there

demostra|ción *f* demonstration, show. **~r** [2] *vt* demonstrate; (mostrar) show; (probar) prove. **~tivo** *a* demonstrative

dengue *m* dengue fever

denigrar *vt* denigrate

dens|idad *f* density. **~o** *a* dense, thick

denta|dura *f* teeth. **~dura postiza** dentures, false teeth. **~l** *a* dental

dent|era *f*. **darle ~era a uno** set s.o.'s teeth on edge. **~ífrico** *m* toothpaste. **~ista** *m & f* dentist

dentro *adv* inside; (de un edificio) indoors. **~ de** in. **~ de poco** soon. **por ~** inside

denuncia *f* report; (acusación) accusation. **~r** *vt* report; <*periódico etc*> denounce

departamento *m* department; (LAm, apartamento) flat (Brit), apartment (Amer)

depend|encia *f* dependence; (sección) section; (oficina) office. **~encias** *fpl* buildings. **~er** *vi* depend (**de** on). **~ienta** *f* shop assistant. **~iente** *a* dependent (**de** on). ● *m* shop assistant

depila|r *vt* depilate. **~torio** *a* depilatory

deplora|ble *a* deplorable. **~r** *vt* deplore, regret

deponer [34] *vt* remove from office; depose <*rey*>; lay down <*armas*>. ● *vi* give evidence

deporta|ción *f* deportation. **~r** *vt* deport

deport|e *m* sport. **hacer ~e** take part in sports. **~ista** *m* sportsman. ● *f* sportswoman. **~ivo** *a* sports. ● *m* sports car

dep|ositante *m & f* depositor. **~ositar** *vt* deposit; (poner) put, place. **~ósito** *m* deposit; (almacén) warehouse; (Mil) depot; (de líquidos) tank

depravado *a* depraved

deprecia|ción *f* depreciation. **~r** *vt* depreciate. ◻ **~rse** *vpr* depreciate

depr|esión *f* depression. **~imido** *a* depressed. **~imir** *vt* depress. ◻ **~imirse** *vpr* get depressed

depura|ción *f* purification. **~do** *a* refined. **~r** *vt* purify; (Pol) purge; refine <*estilo*>

derech|a *f* (mano) right hand; (lado) right. **a la ~a** on the right; (hacia el lado derecho) to the right. **~ista** *a* right-wing. ● *m & f* right-winger. **~o** *a* right; (vertical) upright; (recto) straight. ● *adv* straight. **todo ~o** straight on. ● *m* right; (Jurid) law; (lado) right side. **~os** *mpl* dues. **~os de autor** royalties

deriva *f* drift. **a la ~** drifting, adrift

deriva|do *a* derived. ● *m* derivative, by-product. **~r** *vt* divert. ● *vi*. **~r de** derive from, be derived from. ◻ **~rse** *vpr*. **~se de** be derived from

derram|amiento *m* spilling. **~amiento de sangre** bloodshed. **~ar** *vt* spill; shed <*lágrimas*>. □ **~arse** *vpr* spill. **~e** *m* spilling; (pérdida) leakage; (Med) discharge; (Med, de sangre) haemorrhage

derretir [5] *vt* melt

derribar *vt* knock down; bring down, overthrow <*gobierno etc*>

derrocar [7] *vt* bring down, overthrow <*gobierno etc*>

derroch|ar *vt* squander. **~e** *m* waste

derrot|a *f* defeat. **~ar** *vt* defeat. **~ado** *a* defeated. **~ero** *m* course

derrumba|r *vt* knock down. □ **~rse** *vpr* collapse; <*persona*> go to pieces

desabotonar *vt* unbutton, undo. □ **~se** *vpr* come undone; <*persona*> undo

desabrido *a* tasteless; <*persona*> surly; (LAm) dull

desabrochar *vt* undo. □ **~se** *vpr* come undone; <*persona*> undo

desacato *m* defiance; (Jurid) contempt of court

desac|ertado *a* ill-advised; (erróneo) wrong. **~ierto** *m* mistake

desacreditar *vt* discredit

desactivar *vt* defuse

desacuerdo *m* disagreement

desafiar [20] *vt* challenge; (afrontar) defy

desafina|do *a* out of tune. **~r** *vi* be out of tune. □ **~rse** *vpr* go out of tune

desafío *m* challenge; (a la muerte) defiance; (combate) duel

desafortunad|amente *adv* unfortunately. **~o** *a* unfortunate

desagrada|ble *a* unpleasant. **~r** *vt* displease. ● *vi* be unpleasant. **me ~ el sabor** I don't like the taste

desagradecido *a* ungrateful

desagrado *m* displeasure. **con ~** unwillingly

desagüe *m* drain; (acción) drainage. **tubo** *m* **de ~** drain-pipe

desahog|ado *a* roomy; (acomodado) comfortable. **~ar** [12] *vt* vent. □ **~arse** *vpr* let off steam. **~o** *m* comfort; (alivio) relief

desahuci|ar *vt* declare terminally ill <*enfermo*>; evict <*inquilino*>. **~o** *m* eviction

desair|ar *vt* snub. **~e** *m* snub

desajuste *m* maladjustment; (desequilibrio) imbalance

desal|entador *a* disheartening. **~entar** [1] *vt* discourage. **~iento** *m* discouragement

desaliñado *a* slovenly

desalmado *a* heartless

desalojar *vt* <*ocupantes*> evacuate; <*policía*> to clear; (LAm) evict <*inquilino*>

desampar|ado *a* helpless; <*lugar*> unprotected. **~ar** *vt* abandon. **~o** *m* helplessness; (abandono) lack of protection

desangrar *vt* bleed. □ **~se** *vpr* bleed

desanima|do *a* down-hearted. **~r** *vt* discourage. □ **~rse** *vpr* lose heart

desapar|ecer [11] *vi* disappear; <*efecto*> wear off. **~ecido** *a* missing. ● *m* missing person. **~ición** *f* disappearance

desapego *m* indifference

desapercibido *a*. **pasar ~** go unnoticed

desaprobar [2] *vt* disapprove of

desarm|able *a* collapsible; <*estante*> easy to dismantle. **~ar** *vt* disarm; (desmontar) dismantle; take apart; (LAm) take down <*carpa*>. **~e** *m* disarmament

desarraig|ado *a* rootless. **~ar** [12] *vt* uproot. **~o** *m* uprooting

desarregl|ar *vt* mess up; (alterar) disrupt. **~o** *m* disorder

desarroll|ar *vt* develop. □ **~arse** *vpr* (incl Foto) develop; <*suceso*> take place. **~o** *m* development

desaseado *a* dirty; (desordenado) untidy

desasosiego *m* anxiety; (intranquilidad) restlessness

desastr|ado *a* scruffy. **~e** *m* disaster. **~oso** *a* disastrous

desatar *vt* untie; (fig, soltar) unleash. □ **~se** *vpr* come undone; to undo <*zapatos*>

desatascar [7] *vt* unblock

desaten|der [1] *vt* not pay attention to; neglect <*deber etc*>. **~to** *a* inattentive; (descortés) discourteous

desatin|ado *a* silly. **~o** *m* silliness; (error) mistake

desatornillar *vt* unscrew

desautorizar [10] *vt* declare unauthorized; discredit <*persona*>; (desmentir) deny

desavenencia *f* disagreement

desayun|ar *vt* have for breakfast. ● *vi* have breakfast. **~o** *m* breakfast

desazón *m* (fig) unease

desbandarse *vpr* (Mil) disband; (dispersarse) disperse

desbarajust|ar *vt* mess up. **~e** *m* mess

desbaratar *vt* spoil; (Mex) mess up <*papeles*>

desbloquear *vt* clear; release <*mecanismo*>; unfreeze <*cuenta*>

desbocado *a* <*caballo*> runaway; <*escote*> wide

desbordarse *vpr* overflow; <*río*> burst its banks

descabellado *a* crazy

descafeinado *a* decaffeinated. ● *m* decaffeinated coffee

descalabro *m* disaster

descalificar [7] *vt* disqualify; (desacreditar) discredit

descalz|ar [10] *vt* take off <*zapatos*>. **~o** *a* barefoot

descampado *m* open ground. **al ~** (LAm) in the open air

descans|ado *a* rested; <*trabajo*> easy. **~ar** *vt/i* rest. **~illo** *m* landing. **~o** *m* rest; (del trabajo) break; (LAm, rellano) landing; (en deportes) half-time; (en el teatro etc) interval

descapotable *a* convertible

descarado *a* cheeky; (sin vergüenza) shameless

descarg|a *f* unloading; (Mil, Elec) discharge. **~ar** [12] *vt* unload; (Mil, Elec) discharge; (Informática) download. **~o** *m* (recibo) receipt; (Jurid) evidence

descaro *m* cheek, nerve

descarriarse [20] *vpr* go the wrong way; <*res*> stray; (fig) go astray

descarrila|miento *m* derailment. **~r** *vi* be derailed. □ **~se** *vpr* (LAm) be derailed

descartar *vt* rule out

descascararse *vpr* <*pintura*> peel; <*taza*> chip

descen|dencia *f* descent; (personas) descendants. **~der** [1] *vt* go down <*escalera etc*>. ● *vi* go down; <*temperatura*> fall, drop; (provenir) be descended (**de** from). **~diente**

m & f descendant. **~so** *m* descent; (de temperatura, fiebre etc) fall, drop

descifrar *vt* decipher; decode <*clave*>

descolgar [2 & 12] *vt* take down; pick up <*el teléfono*>. □ **~se** *vpr* lower o.s.

descolor|ar *vt* discolour, fade. **~ido** *a* discoloured, faded; <*persona*> pale

descomp|oner [34] *vt* break down; decompose <*materia*>; upset <*estómago*>; (esp LAm, estropear) break; (esp LAm, desarreglar) mess up. □ **~onerse** *vpr* decompose; (esp LAm, estropearse) break down; <*persona*> feel sick. **~ostura** *f* (esp LAm, de máquina) breakdown; (esp LAm, náuseas) sickness; (esp LAm, diarrea) diarrhoea; (LAm, falla) fault. **~uesto** *a* decomposed; (encolerizado) angry; (esp LAm, estropeado) broken. **estar ~uesto** (del estómago) have diarrhoea

descomunal *a* enormous

desconc|ertante *a* disconcerting. **~ertar** [1] *vt* disconcert; (dejar perplejo) puzzle. □ **~ertarse** *vpr* be put out, be disconcerted

desconectar *vt* disconnect

desconfia|do *a* distrustful. **~nza** *f* distrust, suspicion. **~r** [20] *vi*. **~r de** mistrust; (no creer) doubt

descongelar *vt* defrost; (Com) unfreeze

desconoc|er [11] *vt* not know, not recognize. **~ido** *a* unknown; (cambiado) unrecognizable. ● *m* stranger. **~imiento** *m* ignorance

desconsidera|ción *f* lack of consideration. **~do** *a* inconsiderate

descons|olado *a* distressed. **~uelo** *m* distress; (tristeza) sadness

desconta|do *a*. **dar por ~do** (**que**) take for granted (that). **~r** [2] *vt* discount; deduct <*impuestos etc*>

descontento *a* unhappy (**con** with), dissatisfied (**con** with). ● *m* discontent

descorazonar *vt* discourage. □ **~se** *vpr* lose heart

descorchar *vt* uncork

descorrer *vt* draw <*cortina*>. **~ el cerrojo** unbolt the door

descort|és *a* rude, discourteous. **~esía** *f* rudeness

descos|er *vt* unpick. □ **~erse** *vpr* come undone. **~ido** *a* unstitched

descrédito *m* disrepute. **ir en ~ de** damage the reputation of

descremado *a* skimmed

descri|bir (*pp* **descrito**) *vt* describe. **~pción** *f* description

descuartizar [10] *vt* cut up

descubierto *a* discovered; (no cubierto) uncovered; <*vehículo*> open-top; <*piscina*> open-air; <*cielo*> clear; <*cabeza*> bare. ● *m* overdraft. **poner al ~** expose

descubri|miento *m* discovery. **~r** (*pp* **descubierto**) *vt* discover; (destapar) uncover; (revelar) reveal; unveil <*estatua*>. □ **~rse** *vpr* (quitarse el sombrero) take off one's hat

descuento *m* discount; (del sueldo) deduction

descuid|ado *a* careless; <*aspecto etc*> untidy; (desprevenido) unprepared. **~ar** *vt* neglect. ● *vi* not worry. **¡~a!** don't worry! □ **~arse** *vpr* be careless **~o** *m* carelessness; (negligencia) negligence

desde *prep* (lugar etc) from; (tiempo) since, from. **~ ahora** from now on. **~ hace un mes** for a month. **~ luego** of course. **~ Madrid hasta**

Barcelona from Madrid to Barcelona. **~ niño** since childhood

desdecirse [46] *vpr*. **~ de** take back <*palabras etc*>; go back on <*promesa*>

desd|én *m* scorn. **~eñable** *a* insignificant. **nada ~eñable** significant. **~eñar** *vt* scorn

desdicha *f* misfortune. **por ~** unfortunately. **~do** *a* unfortunate

desdoblar *vt* (desplegar) unfold

desear *vt* want; wish <*suerte etc*>. **le deseo un buen viaje** I hope you have a good journey. **¿qué desea Vd?** can I help you?

desech|able *a* disposable. **~ar** *vt* throw out; (rechazar) reject. **~o** *m* waste

desembalar *vt* unpack

desembarcar [7] *vt* unload. ● *vi* disembark

desemboca|dura *f* (de río) mouth; (de calle) opening. **~r** [7] *vi*. **~r en** <*río*> flow into; <*calle*> lead to

desembolso *m* payment

desembragar [12] *vi* declutch

desempaquetar *vt* unwrap

desempat|ar *vi* break a tie. **~e** *m* tie-breaker

desempeñ|ar *vt* redeem; play <*papel*>; hold <*cargo*>; perform, carry out <*deber etc*>. □ **~arse** *vpr* (LAm) perform. **~arse bien** manage well. **~o** *m* redemption; (de un deber, una función) discharge; (LAm, actuación) performance

desemple|ado *a* unemployed. ● *m* unemployed person. **los ~ados** the unemployed. **~o** *m* unemployment

desencadenar *vt* unchain <*preso*>; unleash <*perro*>; (causar) trigger. □ **~se** *vpr* be triggered off; <*guerra etc*> break out

desencajar *vt* dislocate; (desconectar) disconnect. □ **~se** *vpr* become dislocated

desenchufar *vt* unplug

desenfad|ado *a* uninhibited; (desenvuelto) self-assured. **~o** *m* lack of inhibition; (desenvoltura) self-assurance

desenfocado *a* out of focus

desenfren|ado *a* unrestrained. **~o** *m* licentiousness

desenganchar *vt* unhook; uncouple <*vagón*>

desengañ|ar *vt* disillusion. □ **~arse** *vpr* become disillusioned; (darse cuenta) realize. **~o** *m* disillusionment, disappointment

desenlace *m* outcome

desenmascarar *vt* unmask

desenredar *vt* untangle. □ **~se** *vpr* untangle

desenro|llar *vt* unroll, unwind. **~scar** [7] *vt* unscrew

desentend|erse [1] *vpr* want nothing to do with. **~ido** *m*. **hacerse el ~ido** (fingir no oír) pretend not to hear; (fingir ignorancia) pretend not to know

desenterrar [1] *vt* exhume; (fig) unearth

desentonar *vi* be out of tune; <*colores*> clash

desenvoltura *f* ease; (falta de timidez) confidence

desenvolver [2] (*pp* **desenvuelto**) *vt* unwrap; expound <*idea etc*>. □ **~se** *vpr* perform; (manejarse) manage

deseo *m* wish, desire. **~so** *a* eager. **estar ~so de** be eager to

desequilibr|ado *a* unbalanced. **~io** *m* imbalance

des|ertar *vt* desert; (Pol) defect. **~értico** *a* desert-like. **~ertor** *m* deserter; (Pol) defector

desespera|ción *f* despair. **~do** *a* desperate. **~nte** *a* infuriating. **~r** *vt* drive to despair. □ **~rse** *vpr* despair

desestimar *vt* (rechazar) reject

desfachat|ado *a* brazen, shameless. **~ez** *f* nerve, cheek

desfallec|er [11] *vt* weaken. ● *vi* become weak; (desmayarse) faint. **~imiento** *m* weakness; (desmayo) faint

desfasado *a* out of phase; <*idea*> outdated; <*persona*> out of touch

desfavorable *a* unfavourable

desfil|adero *m* narrow mountain pass; (cañón) narrow gorge. **~ar** *vi* march (past). **~e** *m* procession, parade. **~e de modelos** fashion show

desgana *f*, (LAm) **desgano** *m* (falta de apetito) lack of appetite; (Med) weakness, faintness; (fig) unwillingness

desgarr|ador *a* heart-rending. **~ar** *vt* tear; (fig) break <*corazón*>. **~o** *m* tear, rip

desgast|ar *vt* wear away; wear out <*ropa*>. □ **~arse** *vpr* wear away; <*ropa*> be worn out; <*persona*> wear o.s. out. **~e** *m* wear

desgracia *f* misfortune; (accidente) accident; **por ~** unfortunately. **¡qué ~!** what a shame!. **~do** *a* unlucky; (pobre) poor. ● *m* unfortunate person, poor devil [I]

desgranar *vt* shell <*habas etc*>

desgreñado *a* ruffled, dishevelled

deshabitado *a* uninhabited; <*edificio*> unoccupied

deshacer [31] *vt* undo; strip <*cama*>; unpack <*maleta*>; (desmontar) take to pieces; break <*trato*>; (derretir) melt; (disolver) dissolve. □ **~se** *vpr* come undone; (disolverse) dissolve; (derretirse) melt. **~se de algo** get rid of sth. **~se en lágrimas** dissolve into tears. **~se por hacer algo** go out of one's way to do sth

desheredar *vt* disinherit

deshidratarse *vpr* become dehydrated

deshielo *m* thaw

deshilachado *a* frayed

deshincha|do *a* <*neumático*> flat. **~r** *vt* deflate; (Med) reduce the swelling in. □ **~rse** *vpr* go down

deshollinador *m* chimney sweep

deshon|esto *a* dishonest; (obsceno) indecent. **~ra** *f* disgrace. **~rar** *vt* dishonour

deshora *f*. **a ~** out of hours. **comer a ~s** eat between meals

deshuesar *vt* bone <*carne*>; stone <*fruta*>

desidia *f* slackness; <*pereza*> laziness

desierto *a* deserted. ● *m* desert

designar *vt* designate; (fijar) fix

desigual *a* unequal; <*terreno*> uneven; (distinto) different. **~dad** *f* inequality

desilusi|ón *f* disappointment; (pérdida de ilusiones) disillusionment. **~onar** *vt* disappoint; (quitar las ilusiones) disillusion. □ **~onarse** *vpr* be disappointed; (perder las ilusiones) become disillusioned

desinfecta|nte *m* disinfectant. **~r** *vt* disinfect

desinflar *vt* deflate. □ **~se** *vpr* go down

desinhibido *a* uninhibited

desintegrar *vt* disintegrate. ▫ **~se** *vpr* disintegrate

desinter|és *m* lack of interest; (generosidad) unselfishness. **~esado** *a* uninterested; (liberal) unselfish

desistir *vi*. **~ de** give up

desleal *a* disloyal. **~tad** *f* disloyalty

desligar [12] *vt* untie; (separar) separate; (fig, librar) free. ▫ **~se** *vpr* break away; (de un compromiso) free o.s. (**de** from)

desliza|dor *m* (Mex) hang glider. **~r** [10] *vt* slide, slip. ▫ **~se** *vpr* slide, slip; <*patinador*> glide; <*tiempo*> slip by, pass; (fluir) flow

deslucido *a* tarnished; (gastado) worn out; (fig) undistinguished

deslumbrar *vt* dazzle

desmadr|arse *vpr* get out of control. **~e** *m* excess

desmán *m* outrage

desmanchar *vt* (LAm) remove the stains from

desmantelar *vt* dismantle; (despojar) strip

desmaquillador *m* make-up remover

desmay|ado *a* unconscious. ▫ **~arse** *vpr* faint. **~o** *m* faint

desmedido *a* excessive

desmemoriado *a* forgetful

desmenti|do *m* denial. **~r** [4] *vt* deny; (contradecir) contradict

desmenuzar [10] *vt* crumble; shred <*carne etc*>

desmerecer [11] *vi*. **no ~ de** compare favourably with

desmesurado *a* excessive; (enorme) enormous

desmonta|ble *a* collapsible; <*armario*> easy to dismantle; (separable) removable. **~r** *vt* (quitar) remove; (desarmar) dismantle, take apart. ● *vi* dismount

desmoralizar [10] *vt* demoralize

desmoronarse *vpr* crumble; <*edificio*> collapse

desnatado *a* skimmed

desnivel *m* unevenness; (fig) difference, inequality

desnud|ar *vt* strip; undress, strip <*persona*>. ▫ **~arse** *vpr* undress. **~ez** *f* nudity. **~o** *a* naked; (fig) bare. ● *m* nude

desnutri|ción *f* malnutrition. **~do** *a* undernourished

desobed|ecer [11] *vt* disobey. **~iencia** *f* disobedience

desocupa|do *a* <*asiento etc*> vacant, free; (sin trabajo) unemployed; (ocioso) idle. **~r** *vt* vacate; (vaciar) empty; (desalojar) clear

desodorante *m* deodorant

desolado *a* desolate; <*persona*> sorry, sad

desorbitante *a* excessive

desorden *m* disorder, untidiness; (confusión) confusion. **~ado** *a* untidy. **~ar** *vt* disarrange, make a mess of

desorganizar [10] *vt* disorganize; (trastornar) disturb

desorienta|do *a* confused. **~r** *vt* disorientate. ▫ **~rse** *vpr* lose one's bearings

despabila|do *a* wide awake; (listo) quick. **~r** *vt* (despertar) wake up; (avivar) wise up. ▫ **~rse** *vpr* wake up; (avivarse) wise up

despach|ar *vt* finish; (tratar con) deal with; (atender) serve; (vender) sell; (enviar) send; (despedir) fire. **~o** *m* dispatch; (oficina) office; (venta) sale; (de localidades) box office

despacio *adv* slowly

despampanante *a* stunning
desparpajo *m* confidence; (descaro) impudence
desparramar *vt* scatter; spill <*líquidos*>
despavorido *a* terrified
despecho *m* spite. **a ~ de** in spite of. **por ~** out of spite
despectivo *a* contemptuous; <*sentido etc*> pejorative
despedazar [10] *vt* tear to pieces
despedi|da *f* goodbye, farewell. **~da de soltero** stag-party. **~r** [5] *vt* say goodbye to, see off; dismiss <*empleado*>; evict <*inquilino*>; (arrojar) throw; give off <*olor etc*>. □ **~rse** *vpr* say goodbye (**de** to)
despeg|ar [12] *vt* unstick. ● *vi* <*avión*> take off. **~ue** *m* take-off
despeinar *vt* ruffle the hair of
despeja|do *a* clear; <*persona*> wide awake. **~r** *vt* clear; (aclarar) clarify. ● *vi* clear. □ **~rse** *vpr* (aclararse) become clear; <*tiempo*> clear up
despellejar *vt* skin
despensa *f* pantry, larder
despeñadero *m* cliff
desperdici|ar *vt* waste. **~o** *m* waste. **~os** *mpl* rubbish
desperta|dor *m* alarm clock. **~r** [1] *vt* wake (up); (fig) awaken. □ **~rse** *vpr* wake up
despiadado *a* merciless
despido *m* dismissal
despierto *a* awake; (listo) bright
despilfarr|ar *vt* waste. **~o** *m* squandering; (gasto innecesario) extravagance
despintarse *vpr* (Mex) run
despista|do *a* (con estar) confused; (con ser) absent-minded. **~r** *vt* throw off the scent; (fig) mislead. □ **~rse** *vpr* go wrong; (fig) get confused
despiste *m* mistake; (confusión) muddle
desplaza|miento *m* displacement; (de opinión etc) swing, shift. **~r** [10] *vt* displace. □ **~rse** *vpr* travel
desplegar [1 & 12] *vt* open out; spread <*alas*>; (fig) show
desplomarse *vpr* collapse
despoblado *m* deserted area
despoj|ar *vt* deprive <*persona*>; strip <*cosa*>. **~os** *mpl* remains; (de res) offal; (de ave) giblets
despreci|able *a* despicable; <*cantidad*> negligible. **~ar** *vt* despise; (rechazar) scorn. **~o** *m* contempt; (desaire) snub
desprender *vt* remove; give off <*olor*>. □ **~se** *vpr* fall off; (fig) part with; (deducirse) follow
despreocupa|do *a* unconcerned; (descuidado) careless. □ **~rse** *vpr* not worry
desprestigiar *vt* discredit
desprevenido *a* unprepared. **pillar a uno ~** catch s.o. unawares
desproporcionado *a* disproportionate
desprovisto *a*. **~ de** lacking in, without
después *adv* after, afterwards; (más tarde) later; (a continuación) then. **~ de** after. **~ de comer** after eating. **~ de todo** after all. **~ (de) que** after. **poco ~** soon after
desquit|arse *vpr* get even (**de** with). **~e** *m* revenge
destaca|do *a* outstanding. **~r** [7] *vt* emphasize. ● *vi* stand out. □ **~rse** *vpr* stand out. **~se en** excel at

destajo *m*. **trabajar a ~** do piece-work

destap|ar *vt* uncover; open <*botella*>. □ **~arse** *vpr* reveal one's true self. **~e** *m* (fig) permissiveness

destartalado *a* <*coche*> clapped-out; <*casa*> ramshackle

destello *m* sparkle; (de estrella) twinkle; (fig) glimmer

destemplado *a* discordant; <*nervios*> frayed

desteñir [5 & 22] *vt* fade. ● *vi* fade; <*color*> run. □ **~se** *vpr* fade; <*color*> run

desterra|do *m* exile. **~r** [1] *vt* banish

destetar *vt* wean

destiempo *m*. **a ~** at the wrong moment; (Mus) out of time

destierro *m* exile

destil|ar *vt* distil. **~ería** *f* distillery

destin|ar *vt* destine; (nombrar) post. **~atario** *m* addressee. **~o** *m* (uso) use, function; (lugar) destination; (suerte) destiny. **con ~o a** (going) to

destituir [17] *vt* dismiss

destornilla|dor *m* screwdriver. **~r** *vt* unscrew

destreza *f* skill

destroz|ar [10] *vt* destroy; (fig) shatter. **~os** *mpl* destruction, damage

destru|cción *f* destruction. **~ir** [17] *vt* destroy

desus|ado *a* old-fashioned; (insólito) unusual. **~o** *m* disuse. **caer en ~o** fall into disuse

desvalido *a* needy, destitute

desvalijar *vt* rob; ransack <*casa*>

desvalorizar [10] *vt* devalue

desván *m* loft

desvanec|er [11] *vt* make disappear; (borrar) blur; (fig) dispel. □ **~erse** *vpr* disappear; (desmayarse) faint. **~imiento** *m* (Med) faint

desvariar [20] *vi* be delirious; (fig) talk nonsense

desvel|ar *vt* keep awake. □ **~arse** *vpr* stay awake, have a sleepless night. **~o** *m* sleeplessness

desvencijado *a* <*mueble*> rickety

desventaja *f* disadvantage

desventura *f* misfortune. **~do** *a* unfortunate

desverg|onzado *a* impudent, cheeky. **~üenza** *f* impudence, cheek

desvestirse [5] *vpr* undress

desv|iación *f* deviation; (Auto) diversion. **~iar** [20] *vt* divert; deflect <*pelota*>. □ **~iarse** *vpr* <*carretera*> branch off; (del camino) make a detour; (del tema) stray. **~ío** *m* diversion

desvivirse *vpr*. **~se por** be completely devoted to; (esforzarse) go out of one's way to

detall|ar *vt* relate in detail. **~e** *m* detail; (fig) gesture. **al ~e** retail. **entrar en ~es** go into detail. **¡qué ~e!** how thoughtful! **~ista** *m & f* retailer

detect|ar *vt* detect. **~ive** *m* detective

deten|ción *f* stopping; (Jurid) arrest; (en la cárcel) detention. **~er** [40] *vt* stop; (Jurid) arrest; (encarcelar) detain; (retrasar) delay. □ **~erse** *vpr* stop; (entretenerse) spend a lot of time. **~idamente** *adv* at length. **~ido** *a* (Jurid) under arrest. ● *m* prisoner

detergente *a & m* detergent

deterior|ar *vt* damage, spoil. □ **~arse** *vpr* deteriorate. **~o** *m* deterioration

determina|ción *f* determination; (decisión) decison. **~nte** *a* decisive. **~r** *vt* determine; (decidir) decide

detestar *vt* detest

detrás *adv* behind; (en la parte posterior) on the back. **~ de** behind. **por ~** at the back; (por la espalda) from behind

detrimento *m* detriment. **en ~ de** to the detriment of

deud|a *f* debt. **~or** *m* debtor

devalua|ción *f* devaluation. **~r** [21] *vt* devalue. □ **~se** *vpr* depreciate

devastador *a* devastating

devoción *f* devotion

devol|ución *f* return; (Com) repayment, refund. **~ver** [5] (*pp* **devuelto**) *vt* return; (Com) repay, refund. ● *vi* be sick

devorar *vt* devour

devoto *a* devout; <*amigo etc*> devoted. ● *m* admirer

di *vb* ⇒DAR, DECIR

día *m* day. **~ de fiesta** (public) holiday. **~ del santo** saint's day. **~ feriado** (LAm), **~ festivo** (public) holiday. **al ~** up to date. **al ~ siguiente** (on) the following day. **¡buenos ~s!** good morning! **de ~** by day. **el ~ de hoy** today. **el ~ de mañana** tomorrow. **un ~ sí y otro no** every other day. **vivir al ~** live from hand to mouth

diab|etes *f* diabetes. **~ético** *a* diabetic

diab|lo *m* devil. **~lura** *f* mischief. **~ólico** *a* diabolical

diadema *f* diadem

diáfano *a* diaphanous; <*cielo*> clear

diafragma *m* diaphragm

diagn|osis *f* diagnosis. **~osticar** [7] *vt* diagnose. **~óstico** *m* diagnosis

diagonal *a* & *f* diagonal

diagrama *m* diagram

dialecto *m* dialect

di|alogar [12] *vi* talk. **~álogo** *m* dialogue; (Pol) talks

diamante *m* diamond

diámetro *m* diameter

diana *f* reveille; (blanco) bull's-eye

diapositiva *f* slide, transparency

diario *a* daily. ● *m* newspaper; (libro) diary. **a ~o** daily. **de ~o** everyday, ordinary

diarrea *f* diarrhoea

dibuj|ante *m* draughtsman. ● *f* draughtswoman. **~ar** *vt* draw. **~o** *m* drawing. **~os animados** cartoons

diccionario *m* dictionary

dich|a *f* happiness. **por ~a** fortunately. **~o** *a* said; (tal) such. ● *m* saying. **~o y hecho** no sooner said than done. **mejor ~o** rather. **propiamente ~o** strictly speaking. **~oso** *a* happy; (afortunado) fortunate

diciembre *m* December

dicta|do *m* dictation. **~dor** *m* dictator. **~dura** *f* dictatorship. **~men** *m* opinion; (informe) report. **~r** *vt* dictate; pronounce <*sentencia etc*>; (LAm) give <*clase*>

didáctico *a* didactic

dieci|nueve *a* & *m* nineteen. **~ocho** *a* & *m* eighteen. **~séis** *a* & *m* sixteen. **~siete** *a* & *m* seventeen

diente *m* tooth; (de tenedor) prong; (de ajo) clove. **~ de león** dandelion. **hablar entre ~s** mumble

diestro *a* right-handed; (hábil) skilful

dieta *f* diet

diez *a & m* ten

diezmar *vt* decimate

difamación *f* (con palabras) slander; (por escrito) libel

diferen|cia *f* difference; (desacuerdo) disagreement. **~ciar** *vt* differentiate between. □ **~ciarse** *vpr* differ. **~te** *a* different; (diversos) various

diferido *a* (TV etc). **en ~** recorded

dif|ícil *a* difficult; (poco probable) unlikely. **~icultad** *f* difficulty. **~icultar** *vt* make difficult

difteria *f* diphtheria

difundir *vt* spread; (TV etc) broadcast

difunto *a* late, deceased. ● *m* deceased

difusión *f* spreading

dige|rir [4] *vt* digest. **~stión** *f* digestion. **~stivo** *a* digestive

digital *a* digital; (de los dedos) finger

dign|arse *vpr* deign to. **~atario** *m* dignitary. **~idad** *f* dignity. **~o** *a* honourable; (decoroso) decent; (merecedor) worthy (**de** of). **~ de elogio** praiseworthy

digo *vb* ⇒DECIR

dije *vb* ⇒DECIR

dilatar *vt* expand; (Med) dilate; (prolongar) prolong. □ **~se** *vpr* expand; (Med) dilate; (extenderse) extend; (Mex, demorarse) be late

dilema *m* dilemma

diligen|cia *f* diligence; (gestión) job; (carruaje) stagecoach. **~te** *a* diligent

dilucidar *vt* clarify; solve *<misterio>*

diluir [17] *vt* dilute

diluvio *m* flood

dimensión *f* dimension; (tamaño) size

diminut|ivo *a & m* diminutive. **~o** *a* minute

dimitir *vt/i* resign

Dinamarca *f* Denmark

dinamarqués *a* Danish. ● *m* Dane

dinámic|a *f* dynamics. **~o** *a* dynamic

dinamita *f* dynamite

dínamo *m* dynamo

dinastía *f* dynasty

diner|al *m* fortune. **~o** *m* money. **~o efectivo** cash. **~o suelto** change

dinosaurio *m* dinosaur

dios *m* god. **~a** *f* goddess. **¡D~ mío!** good heavens! **¡gracias a D~!** thank God!

diplom|a *m* diploma. **~acia** *f* diplomacy. **~ado** *a* qualified. □ **~arse** *vpr* (LAm) graduate. **~ático** *a* diplomatic. ● *m* diplomat

diptongo *m* diphthong

diputa|ción *f* delegation. **~ción provincial** county council. **~do** *m* deputy; (Pol, en España) member of the Cortes; (Pol, en Inglaterra) Member of Parliament; (Pol, en Estados Unidos) congressman

dique *m* dike

direc|ción *f* direction; (señas) address; (los que dirigen) management; (Pol) leadership; (Auto) steering. **~ción prohibida** no entry. **~ción única** one-way. **~ta** *f* (Auto) top gear. **~tiva** *f* board; (Pol) executive committee. **~tivas** *fpl* guidelines.

~to *a* direct; <*línea*> straight; <*tren*> through. **en ~to** (TV etc) live. **~tor** *m* director; (Mus) conductor; (de escuela) headmaster; (de periódico) editor; (gerente) manager. **~tora** *f* (de escuela etc) headmistress. **~torio** *m* board of directors; (LAm, de teléfonos) telephone directory

dirig|ente *a* ruling. ● *m & f* leader; (de empresa) manager. **~ir** [14] *vt* direct; (Mus) conduct; run <*empresa etc*>; address <*carta etc*>. □ **~irse** *vpr* make one's way; (hablar) address

disciplina *f* discipline. **~r** *vt* discipline. **~rio** *a* disciplinary

discípulo *m* disciple; (alumno) pupil

disco *m* disc; (Mus) record; (deportes) discus; (de teléfono) dial; (de tráfico) sign; (Rail) signal. **~ duro** hard disk. **~ flexible** floppy disk

disconforme *a* not in agreement

discord|e *a* discordant. **~ia** *f* discord

discoteca *f* discothèque, disco [I]; (colección de discos) record collection

discreción *f* discretion

discrepa|ncia *f* discrepancy; (desacuerdo) disagreement. **~r** *vi* differ

discreto *a* discreet; (moderado) moderate

discrimina|ción *f* discrimination. **~r** *vt* (distinguir) discriminate between; (tratar injustamente) discriminate against

disculpa *f* apology; (excusa) excuse. **pedir ~s** apologize. **~r** *vt* excuse, forgive. □ **~rse** *vpr* apologize

discurs|ar *vi* speak (**sobre** about). **~o** *m* speech

discusión *f* discussion; (riña) argument

discuti|ble *a* debatable. **~r** *vt* discuss; (contradecir) contradict. ● *vi* argue (**por** about)

disecar [7] *vt* stuff; (cortar) dissect

diseminar *vt* disseminate, spread

disentir [4] *vi* disagree (**de** with, **en** on)

diseñ|ador *m* designer. **~ar** *vt* design. **~o** *m* design; (fig) sketch

disertación *f* dissertation

disfraz *m* fancy dress; (para engañar) disguise. **~ar** [10] *vt* dress up; (para engañar) disguise. □ **~arse** *vpr*. **~arse de** dress up as; (para engañar) disguise o.s. as.

disfrutar *vt* enjoy. ● *vi* enjoy o.s. **~ de** enjoy

disgust|ar *vt* displease; (molestar) annoy. □ **~arse** *vpr* get annoyed, get upset; <*dos personas*> fall out. **~o** *m* annoyance; (problema) trouble; (riña) quarrel; (dolor) sorrow, grief

disidente *a & m & f* dissident

disimular *vt* conceal. ● *vi* pretend

disipar *vt* dissipate; (derrochar) squander

dislocarse [7] *vpr* dislocate

disminu|ción *f* decrease. **~ir** [17] *vi* diminish

disolver [2] (*pp* **disuelto**) *vt* dissolve. □ **~se** *vpr* dissolve

dispar *a* different

disparar *vt* fire; (Mex, pagar) buy. ● *vi* shoot (**contra** at)

disparate *m* silly thing; (error) mistake. **decir ~s** talk nonsense. **¡qué ~!** how ridiculous!

disparidad *f* disparity

disparo *m* (acción) firing; (tiro) shot

dispensar *vt* give; (eximir) exempt. ● *vi*. **¡Vd dispense!** forgive me

dispers|ar *vt* scatter, disperse. □ **~arse** *vpr* scatter, disperse. **~ión** *f* dispersion. **~o** *a* scattered

dispon|er [34] *vt* arrange; (Jurid) order. ● *vi*. **~er de** have; (vender etc) dispose of. □ **~erse** *vpr* prepare (**a** to). **~ibilidad** *f* availability. **~ible** *a* available

disposición *f* arrangement; (aptitud) talent; (disponibilidad) disposal; (Jurid) order, decree. **~ de ánimo** frame of mind. **a la ~ de** at the disposal of. **a su ~** at your service

dispositivo *m* device

dispuesto *a* ready; <*persona*> disposed (**a** to); (servicial) helpful

disputa *f* dispute; (pelea) argument

disquete *m* diskette, floppy disk

dista|ncia *f* distance. **a ~ncia** from a distance. **guardar las ~ncias** keep one's distance. **~nciar** *vt* space out; distance <*amigos*>. □ **~nciarse** *vpr* <*dos personas*> fall out. **~nte** *a* distant. **~r** *vi* be away; (fig) be far. **~ 5 kilómetros** it's 5 kilometres away

distin|ción *f* distinction; (honor) award. **~guido** *a* distinguished. **~guir** [13] *vt/i* distinguish. □ **~guirse** *vpr* distinguish o.s.; (diferenciarse) differ. **~tivo** *a* distinctive. ● *m* badge. **~to** *a* different, distinct

distra|cción *f* amusement; (descuido) absent-mindedness, inattention. **~er** [41] *vt* distract; (divertir) amuse. □ **~erse** *vpr* amuse o.s.; (descuidarse) not pay attention. **~ído** *a* (desatento) absent-minded

distribu|ción *f* distribution. **~idor** *m* distributor. **~ir** [17] *vt* distribute

distrito *m* district

disturbio *m* disturbance

disuadir *vt* deter, dissuade

diurno *a* daytime

divagar [12] *vi* digress; (hablar sin sentido) ramble

diván *m* settee, sofa

diversi|dad *f* diversity. **~ficar** [7] *vt* diversify

diversión *f* amusement, entertainment; (pasatiempo) pastime

diverso *a* different

diverti|do *a* amusing; (que tiene gracia) funny. **~r** [4] *vt* amuse, entertain. □ **~rse** *vpr* enjoy o.s.

dividir *vt* divide; (repartir) share out

divino *a* divine

divisa *f* emblem. **~s** *fpl* currency

divisar *vt* make out

división *f* division

divorci|ado *a* divorced. ● *m* divorcee. **~ar** *vt* divorce. □ **~arse** *vpr* get divorced. **~o** *m* divorce

divulgar [12] *vt* spread; divulge <*secreto*>

dizque *adv* (LAm) apparently; (supuestamente) supposedly

do *m* C; (solfa) doh

dobl|adillo *m* hem; (de pantalón) turn-up (Brit), cuff (Amer). **~ar** *vt* double; (plegar) fold; (torcer) bend; turn <*esquina*>; dub <*película*>. ● *vi* turn; <*campana*> toll. □ **~arse** *vpr* double; (curvarse) bend. **~e** *a* double. ● *m* double. **el ~e** twice as much (**de**, **que** as). **~egar** [12] *vt* (fig) force to give in. □ **~egarse** *vpr* give in

doce *a* & *m* twelve. **~na** *f* dozen

docente *a* teaching. ● *m* & *f* teacher

dócil *a* obedient

doctor *m* doctor. **~ado** *m* doctorate

doctrina *f* doctrine

document|ación *f* documentation, papers. **~al** *a* & *m* documentary. **~o** *m* document. **D~o Nacional de Identidad** national identity card

dólar *m* dollar

dol|er [2] *vi* hurt, ache; (fig) grieve. **me duele la cabeza** I have a headache. **le duele el estómago** he has (a) stomach-ache. **~or** *m* pain; (sordo) ache; (fig) sorrow. **~or de cabeza** headache. **~or de muelas** toothache. **~oroso** *a* painful

domar *vt* tame; break in <*caballo*>

dom|esticar [7] *vt* domesticate. **~éstico** *a* domestic

domicili|ar *vt*. **~ar los pagos** pay by direct debit. **~o** *m* address. **~o particular** home address. **reparto a ~o** home delivery service

domina|nte *a* dominant; <*persona*> domineering. **~r** *vt* dominate; (contener) control; (conocer) have a good command of. ● *vi* dominate. □ **~rse** *vpr* control o.s.

domingo *m* Sunday

dominio *m* authority; (territorio) domain; (fig) command

dominó *m* (*pl* **~s**) dominoes; (ficha) domino

don *m* talent, gift; (en un sobre) Mr. **~ Pedro** Pedro

donación *f* donation

donaire *m* grace, charm

dona|nte *m* & *f* (de sangre) donor. **~r** *vt* donate

doncella *f* maiden; (criada) maid

donde *adv* where

dónde *adv* where?; (LAm, cómo) how; **¿hasta ~?** how far? **¿por ~?** whereabouts?; (por qué camino?) which way? **¿a ~ vas?** where are you going? **¿de ~ eres?** where are you from?

dondequiera *adv*. **~ que** wherever. **por ~** everywhere

doña *f* (en un sobre) Mrs. **~ María** María

dora|do *a* golden; (cubierto de oro) gilt. **~r** *vt* gilt; (Culin) brown

dormi|do *a* asleep. **quedarse ~do** fall asleep; (no despertar) oversleep. **~r** [6] *vt* send to sleep. **~r la siesta** have an afternoon nap, have a siesta. ● *vi* sleep. □ **~rse** *vpr* fall asleep. **~tar** *vi* doze. **~torio** *m* bedroom

dors|al *a* back. ● *m* (en deportes) number. **~o** *m* back. **nadar de ~** (Mex) do (the) backstroke

dos *a* & *m* two. **de ~ en ~** in twos, in pairs. **los ~, las ~** both (of them). **~cientos** *a* & *m* two hundred

dosi|ficar [7] *vt* dose; (fig) measure out. **~s** *f invar* dose

dot|ado *a* gifted. **~ar** *vt* give a dowry; (proveer) provide (**de** with). **~e** *m* dowry

doy *vb* ⇒DAR

dragar [12] *vt* dredge

drama *m* drama; (obra de teatro) play. **~turgo** *m* playwright

drástico *a* drastic

droga *f* drug. **~dicto** *m* drug addict. **~do** *m* drug addict. **~r** [12] *vt* drug. □ **~rse** *vpr* take drugs

droguería *f* hardware store

ducha *f* shower. □ **~rse** *vpr* have a shower

dud|a *f* doubt. **poner en ~a** question. **sin ~a (alguna)** without a doubt. **~ar** *vt/i* doubt. **~oso** *a* doubtful; (sospechoso) dubious

duelo *m* duel; (luto) mourning

duende *m* imp

dueñ|a *f* owner, proprietress; (de una pensión) landlady. **~o** *m* owner, proprietor; (de una pensión) landlord

duermo *vb* ⇒DORMIR

dul|ce *a* sweet; <*agua*> fresh; (suave) soft, gentle. ● *m* (LAm) sweet. **~zura** *f* sweetness; (fig) gentleness

duna *f* dune

dúo *m* duet, duo

duplica|do *a* duplicated. **por ~** in duplicate. ● *m* duplicate. **~r** [7] *vt* duplicate. □ **~rse** *vpr* double

duque *m* duke. **~sa** *f* duchess

dura|ción *f* duration, length. **~dero** *a* lasting. **~nte** *prep* during; (medida de tiempo) for. **~ todo el año** all year round. **~r** *vi* last

durazno *m* (LAm, fruta) peach

dureza *f* hardness; (Culin) toughness; (fig) harshness

duro *a* hard; (Culin) tough; (fig) harsh. ● *adv* (esp LAm) hard. ● *m* five-peseta coin

Ee

e *conj* and

ebrio *a* drunk

ebullición *f* boiling

eccema *m* eczema

echar *vt* throw; post <*carta*>; give off <*olor*>; pour <*líquido*>; (expulsar) expel; (de recinto) throw out; fire <*empleado*>; (poner) put on; get <*gasolina*>; put out <*raíces*>; show <*película*>. **~ a** start. **~ a perder** spoil. **~ de menos** miss. **~se atrás** (fig) back down. **echárselas de** feign. □ **~se** *vpr* throw o.s.; (tumbarse) lie down

eclesiástico *a* ecclesiastical

eclipse *m* eclipse

eco *m* echo. **hacerse ~ de** echo

ecolog|ía *f* ecology. **~ista** *m & f* ecologist

economato *m* cooperative store

econ|omía *f* economy; (ciencia) economics. **~ómico** *a* economic; (no caro) inexpensive. **~omista** *m & f* economist. **~omizar** [10] *vt/i* economize

ecuación *f* equation

ecuador *m* equator. **el E~** the Equator. **E~** (país) Ecuador

ecuánime *a* level-headed; (imparcial) impartial

ecuatoriano *a & m* Ecuadorian

ecuestre *a* equestrian

edad *f* age. **~ avanzada** old age. **E~ de Piedra** Stone Age. **E~ Media** Middle Ages. **¿qué ~ tiene?** how old is he?

edición *f* edition; (publicación) publication

edicto *m* edict

edific|ación *f* building. **~ante** *a* edifying. **~ar** [7] *vt* build; (fig) edify. **~io** *m* building; (fig) structure

edit|ar *vt* edit; (publicar) publish. **~or** *a* publishing. ● *m* editor; (que publica) publisher. **~orial** *a* editorial. ● *m* leading article. ● *f* publishing house

edredón *m* duvet

educa|ción *f* upbringing; (modales) (good) manners; (enseñanza) education. **falta de ~ción** rudeness, bad manners. **~do** *a* polite. **bien ~do** polite. **mal ~do** rude. **~r**

[7] *vt* bring up; (enseñar) educate. **~tivo** *a* educational

edulcorante *m* sweetener

EE.UU. *abrev* (**Estados Unidos**) USA

efect|ivamente *adv* really; (por supuesto) indeed. **~ivo** *a* effective; (auténtico) real. ● *m* cash. **~o** *m* effect; (impresión) impression. **en ~o** really; (como respuesta) indeed. **~os** *mpl* belongings; (Com) goods. **~uar** [21] *vt* carry out; make *<viaje, compras etc>*

efervescente *a* effervescent; *<bebidas>* fizzy

efica|cia *f* effectiveness; (de persona) efficiency. **~z** *a* effective; *<persona>* efficient

eficien|cia *f* efficiency. **~te** *a* efficient

efímero *a* ephemeral

efusi|vidad *f* effusiveness. **~vo** *a* effusive; *<persona>* demonstrative

egipcio *a & m* Egyptian

Egipto *m* Egypt

ego|ísmo *m* selfishness, egotism. **~ísta** *a* selfish

egresar *vi* (LAm) graduate; (de colegio) leave school, graduate Amer

eje *m* axis; (Tec) axle

ejecu|ción *f* execution; (Mus) performance. **~tar** *vt* carry out; (Mus) perform; (matar) execute. **~tivo** *m* executive

ejempl|ar *a* exemplary; (ideal) model. ● *m* specimen; (libro) copy; (revista) issue, number. **~ificar** [7] *vt* exemplify. **~o** *m* example. **dar (el) ~o** set an example. **por ~o** for example

ejerc|er [9] *vt* exercise; practise *<profesión>*; exert *<influencia>*. ● *vi* practise. **~icio** *m* exercise; (de profesión) practice. **hacer ~icios** take exercise. **~itar** *vt* exercise

ejército *m* army

ejido *m* (Mex) cooperative

ejote *m* (Mex) green bean

---

el

● *artículo definido masculino* (*pl* **los**)

> The masculine article **el** is also used before feminine nouns which begin with stressed **a** or **ha**, e.g. **el ala derecha, el hada madrina.** Also, preceded by **de, el** becomes **del**, and preceded by **a, el** becomes **al**

····➤ the. **el tren de las seis** the six o'clock train. **el vecino de al lado** the next-door neighbour. **cerca del hospital** near the hospital

No se traduce en los siguientes casos:

····➤ (con nombre abstracto, genérico) **el tiempo vuela** time flies. **odio el queso** I hate cheese. **el hilo es muy durable** linen is very durable

····➤ (con colores, días de la semana) **el rojo está de moda** red is in fashion. **el lunes es fiesta** Monday is a holiday

····➤ (con algunas instituciones) **termino el colegio mañana** I finish school tomorrow. **lo ingresaron en el hospital** he was admitted to hospital

····➤ (con nombres propios) **el Sr. Díaz** Mr Díaz. **el doctor Lara** Doctor Lara

····➤ (antes de infinitivo) **es muy cuidadosa en el vestir** she takes great care in the way she dresses. **me di**

cuenta al verlo I realized when I saw him

····➤(con partes del cuerpo, artículos personales) *se traduce por un posesivo*. **apretó el puño** he clenched his fist. **tienes el zapato desatado** your shoe is undone

····➤**el + de. es el de Pedro** it's Pedro's. **el del sombrero** the one with the hat

····➤**el + que** (persona) **el que me atendió** the one who served me. (cosa) **el que se rompió** the one that broke.

····➤**el + que** + *subjuntivo* (quienquiera) whoever. **el que gane la lotería** whoever wins the lottery. (cualquiera) whichever. **compra el que sea más barato** buy whichever is cheaper

él *pron* (persona) he; (persona con prep) him; (cosa) it. **es de ~** it's his

elabora|ción *f* elaboration; (fabricación) manufacture. **~r** *vt* elaborate; manufacture <*producto*>; (producir) produce

el|asticidad *f* elasticity. **~ástico** *a & m* elastic

elec|ción *f* choice; (de político etc) election. **~ciones** *fpl* (Pol) election. **~tor** *m* voter. **~torado** *m* electorate. **~toral** *a* electoral; <*campaña*> election

electrici|dad *f* electricity. **~sta** *m & f* electrician

eléctrico *a* electric; <*aparato*> electrical

electri|ficar [7] *vt*, electrify. **~zar** [10] *vt* electrify

electrocutar *vt* electrocute. □ **~se** *vpr* be electrocuted

electrodoméstico *a* electrical appliance

electrónic|a *f* electronics. **~o** *a* electronic

elefante *m* elephant

elegan|cia *f* elegance. **~te** *a* elegant

elegía *f* elegy

elegi|ble *a* eligible. **~do** *a* chosen. **~r** [5 & 14] *vt* choose; (por votación) elect

element|al *a* elementary; (esencial) fundamental. **~o** *m* element; (persona) person, bloke (Brit, [I]). **~os** *mpl* (nociones) basic principles

elenco *m* (en el teatro) cast

eleva|ción *f* elevation; (de precios) rise, increase; (acción) raising. **~dor** *m* (Mex) lift (Brit), elevator (Amer). **~r** *vt* raise; (promover) promote

elimina|ción *f* elimination. **~r** *vt* eliminate; (Informática) delete. **~toria** *f* preliminary heat

élite /e'lit, e'lite/ *f* elite

ella *pron* (persona) she; (persona con prep) her; (cosa) it. **es de ~** it's hers. **~s** *pron pl* they; (con prep) them. **es de ~s** it's theirs

ello *pron* it

ellos *pron pl* they; (con prep) them. **es de ~** it's theirs

elocuen|cia *f* eloquence. **~te** *a* eloquent

elogi|ar *vt* praise. **~o** *m* praise

elote *m* (Mex) corncob; (Culin) corn on the cob

eludir *vt* avoid, elude

emanar *vi* emanate (**de** from); (originarse) originate (**de** from, in)

emancipa|ción *f* emancipation. **~r** *vt* emancipate. □ **~rse** *vpr* become emancipated

embadurnar *vt* smear

embajad|a *f* embassy. **~or** *m* ambassador

embalar *vt* pack

embaldosar *vt* tile

embalsamar *vt* embalm

embalse *m* reservoir

embaraz|ada *a* pregnant. ● *f* pregnant woman. **~ar** [10] *vt* get pregnant. **~o** *m* pregnancy; (apuro) embarrassment; (estorbo) hindrance. **~oso** *a* awkward, embarrassing

embar|cación *f* vessel. **~cadero** *m* jetty, pier. **~car** [7] *vt* load <*mercancías etc*>. □ **~carse** *vpr* board. **~carse en** (fig) embark upon

embargo *m* embargo; (Jurid) seizure. **sin ~** however

embarque *m* loading; (de pasajeros) boarding

embaucar [7] *vt* trick

embelesar *vt* captivate

embellecer [11] *vt* make beautiful

embesti|da *f* charge. **~r** [5] *vt/i* charge

emblema *m* emblem

embolsarse *vpr* pocket

embonar *vt* (Mex) fit

emborrachar *vt* get drunk. □ **~se** *vpr* get drunk

emboscada *f* ambush

embotar *vt* dull

embotella|miento *m* (de vehículos) traffic jam. **~r** *vt* bottle

embrague *m* clutch

embriag|arse [12] *vpr* get drunk. **~uez** *f* drunkenness

embrión *m* embryo

embroll|ar *vt* mix up; involve <*persona*>. □ **~arse** *vpr* get into a muddle; (en un asunto) get involved. **~o** *m* tangle; (fig) muddle

embruj|ado *a* bewitched; <*casa*> haunted. **~ar** *vt* bewitch. **~o** *m* spell

embrutecer [11] *vt* brutalize

embudo *m* funnel

embuste *m* lie. **~ro** *a* deceitful. ● *m* liar

embuti|do *m* (Culin) sausage. **~r** *vt* stuff

emergencia *f* emergency

emerger [14] *vi* appear, emerge

emigra|ción *f* emigration. **~nte** *a & m & f* emigrant. **~r** *vi* emigrate

eminen|cia *f* eminence. **~te** *a* eminent

emisario *m* emissary

emi|sión *f* emission; (de dinero) issue; (TV etc) broadcast. **~sor** *a* issuing; (TV etc) broadcasting. **~sora** *f* radio station. **~tir** *vt* emit, give out; (TV etc) broadcast; cast <*voto*>; (poner en circulación) issue

emoci|ón *f* emotion; (excitación) excitement. **¡qué ~ón!** how exciting! **~onado** *a* moved. **~onante** *a* exciting; (conmovedor) moving. **~onar** *vt* move. □ **~onarse** *vpr* get excited; (conmoverse) be moved

emotivo *a* emotional; (conmovedor) moving

empacar [7] *vt* (LAm) pack

empacho *m* indigestion

empadronar *vt* register. □ **~se** *vpr* register

empalagoso *a* sickly; <*persona*> cloying

empalizada *f* fence

empalm|ar *vt* connect, join. ● *vi* meet. **~e** *m* junction; (de trenes) connection

empan|ada *f* (savoury) pie; (LAm, individual) pasty. **~adilla** *f* pasty

empantanarse *vpr* become swamped; <*coche*> get bogged down

empañar *vt* steam up; (fig) tarnish. □ **~se** *vpr* steam up

empapar *vt* soak. □ **~se** *vpr* get soaked

empapela|do *m* wallpaper. **~r** *vt* wallpaper

empaquetar *vt* package

emparedado *m* sandwich

emparentado *a* related

empast|ar *vt* fill <*muela*>. **~e** *m* filling

empat|ar *vi* draw. **~e** *m* draw

empedernido *a* confirmed; <*bebedor*> inveterate

empedrar [1] *vt* pave

empeine *m* instep

empeñ|ado *a* in debt; (decidido) determined (**en** to). **~ar** *vt* pawn; pledge <*palabra*>. □ **~arse** *vpr* get into debt; (estar decidido a) be determined (**en** to). **~o** *m* pledge; (resolución) determination. **casa** *f* **de ~s** pawnshop. **~oso** *a* (LAm) hard-working

empeorar *vt* make worse. ● *vi* get worse. □ **~se** *vpr* get worse

empequeñecer [11] *vt* become smaller; (fig) belittle

empera|dor *m* emperor. **~triz** *f* empress

empezar [1 & 10] *vt/i* start, begin. **para ~** to begin with

empina|do *a* <*cuesta*> steep. **~r** *vt* raise. □ **~rse** *vpr* <*persona*> stand on tiptoe

empírico *a* empirical

emplasto *m* plaster

emplaza|miento *m* (Jurid) summons; (lugar) site. **~r** [10] *vt* summon; (situar) site

emple|ada *f* employee; (doméstica) maid. **~ado** *m* employee. **~ar** *vt* use; employ <*persona*>; spend <*tiempo*>. □ **~arse** *vpr* get a job. **~o** *m* use; (trabajo) employment; (puesto) job

empobrecer [11] *vt* impoverish. □ **~se** *vpr* become poor

empoll|ar *vt* incubate <*huevos*>; (⊠, estudiar) cram Ⓣ. ● *vi* <*ave*> sit; <*estudiante*> ⊠ cram. **~ón** *m* ⊠ swot (Brit Ⓣ), grind (Amer Ⓣ)

empolvarse *vpr* powder

empotra|do *a* built-in, fitted. **~r** *vt* fit

emprende|dor *a* enterprising. **~r** *vt* undertake; set out on <*viaje*>. **~rla con uno** pick a fight with s.o.

empresa *f* undertaking; (Com) company, firm. **~rio** *m* businessman; (patrón) employer; (de teatro etc) impresario

empuj|ar *vt* push. **~e** *m* (fig) drive. **~ón** *m* push, shove

empuña|dura *f* handle. **~r** *vt* take up <*pluma, espada*>

emular *vt* emulate

en *prep* in; (sobre) on; (dentro) inside, in; (medio de transporte) by. **~ casa** at home. **~ coche** by car. **~ 10 días** in 10 days. **de pueblo ~ pueblo** from town to town

enagua *f* petticoat

enajena|ción *f* alienation. **~ción mental** insanity. **~r** *vt* alienate; (volver loco) derange

enamora|do *a* in love. ● *m* lover. **~r** *vt* win the love of. □ **~rse** *vpr* fall in love (**de** with)

enano *a* & *m* dwarf

enardecer [11] *vt* inflame. □ **~se** *vpr* get excited (**por** about)

encabeza|do *m* (Mex) headline. **~miento** *m* heading; (de periódico) headline. **~r** [10] *vt* head; lead <*revolución etc*>

encabritarse *vpr* rear up

encadenar *vt* chain; (fig) tie down

encaj|ar *vt* fit; fit together <*varias piezas*>. ● *vi* fit; (cuadrar) tally. □ **~arse** *vpr* put on. **~e** *m* lace; (Com) reserve

encaminar *vt* direct. □ **~se** *vpr* make one's way

encandilar *vt* dazzle; (estimular) stimulate

encant|ado *a* enchanted; <*persona*> delighted. ¡**~ado!** pleased to meet you! **~ador** *a* charming. **~amiento** *m* spell. **~ar** *vt* bewitch; (fig) charm, delight. **me ~a la leche** I love milk. **~o** *m* spell; (fig) delight

encapricharse *vpr*. **~ con** take a fancy to

encarar *vt* face; (LAm) stand up to <*persona*>. □ **~se** *vpr*. **~se con** stand up to

encarcelar *vt* imprison

encarecer [11] *vt* put up the price of. □ **~se** *vpr* become more expensive

encarg|ado *a* in charge. ● *m* manager, person in charge. **~ar** [12] *vt* entrust; (pedir) order. □ **~arse** *vpr* take charge (**de** of). **~o** *m* job; (Com) order; (recado) errand. **hecho de ~o** made to measure

encariñarse *vpr*. **~ con** take to, become fond of

encarna|ción *f* incarnation. **~do** *a* incarnate; (rojo) red; <*uña*> ingrowing. ● *m* red

encarnizado *a* bitter

encarpetar *vt* file; (LAm, dar carpetazo) shelve

encarrilar *vt* put back on the rails; (fig) direct, put on the right track

encasillar *vt* classify; (fig) pigeonhole

encauzar [10] *vt* channel

enceguecer *vt* [11] (LAm) blind

encend|edor *m* lighter. **~er** [1] *vt* light; switch on, turn on <*aparato eléctrico*>; start <*motor*>; (fig) arouse. □ **~erse** *vpr* light; <*aparato eléctrico*> come on; (excitarse) get excited; (ruborizarse) blush. **~ido** *a* lit; <*aparato eléctrico*> on; (rojo) bright red. ● *m* (Auto) ignition

encera|do *a* waxed. ● *m* (pizarra) blackboard. **~r** *vt* wax

encerr|ar [1] *vt* shut in; (con llave) lock up; (fig, contener) contain. **~ona** *f* trap

enchilar *vt* (Mex) add chili to

enchinar *vt* (Mex) perm

enchuf|ado *a* switched on. **~ar** *vt* plug in; fit together <*tubos etc*>. **~e** *m* socket; (clavija) plug; (de tubos etc) joint; (🄸, influencia) contact. **tener ~e** have friends in the right places

encía *f* gum

enciclopedia *f* encyclopaedia

encierro *m* confinement; (cárcel) prison

encim|a *adv* on top; (arriba) above. **~ de** on, on top of; (sobre) over; (además de) besides, as well as. **por ~** on top; (*a* la ligera) superficially. **por ~ de todo** above all. **~ar** *vt* (Mex) stack up. **~era** *f* worktop

encina *f* holm oak

encinta *a* pregnant

enclenque *a* weak; (enfermizo) sickly

encoger [14] *vt* shrink; (contraer) contract. □ **~se** *vpr* shrink. **~erse de hombros** shrug one's shoulders

encolar *vt* glue; (pegar) stick

encolerizar [10] *vt* make angry. □ **~se** *vpr* get furious

encomendar [1] *vt* entrust

encomi|ar *vt* praise. **~o** *m* praise. **~oso** *a* (LAm) complimentary

encono *m* bitterness, ill will

encontra|do *a* contrary, conflicting. **~r** [2] *vt* find; (tropezar con) meet. □ **~rse** *vpr* meet; (hallarse) be. **no ~rse** feel uncomfortable

encorvar *vt* hunch. □ **~se** *vpr* stoop

encrespa|do *a* <*pelo*> curly; <*mar*> rough. **~r** *vt* curl <*pelo*>; make rough <*mar*>

encrucijada *f* crossroads

encuaderna|ción *f* binding. **~dor** *m* bookbinder. **~r** *vt* bind

encub|ierto *a* hidden. **~rir** (*pp* **encubierto**) *vt* hide, conceal; cover up <*delito*>; shelter <*delincuente*>

encuentro *m* meeting; (en deportes) match; (Mil) encounter

encuesta *f* survey; (investigación) inquiry

encumbrado *a* eminent; (alto) high

encurtidos *mpl* pickles

endeble *a* weak

endemoniado *a* possessed; (muy malo) wretched

enderezar [10] *vt* straighten out; (poner vertical) put upright; (fig, arreglar) put right, sort out; (dirigir) direct. □ **~se** *vpr* straighten out

endeudarse *vpr* get into debt

endiablado *a* possessed; (malo) terrible; (difícil) difficult

endosar *vt* endorse <*cheque*>

endulzar [10] *vt* sweeten; (fig) soften

endurecer [11] *vt* harden. □ **~se** *vpr* harden

enemi|go *a* enemy. ● *m* enemy. **~stad** *f* enmity. **~star** *vt* make an enemy of. □ **~starse** *vpr* fall out (**con** with)

en|ergía *f* energy. **~érgico** *a* <*persona*> lively; <*decisión*> forceful

energúmeno *m* madman

enero *m* January

enésimo *a* nth, umpteenth [T]

enfad|ado *a* angry; (molesto) annoyed. **~ar** *vt* make cross, anger; (molestar) annoy. □ **~arse** *vpr* get angry; (molestarse) get annoyed. **~o** *m* anger; (molestia) annoyance

énfasis *m invar* emphasis, stress. **poner ~ en** stress, emphasize

enfático *a* emphatic

enferm|ar *vi* fall ill. □ **~arse** *vpr* (LAm) fall ill. **~edad** *f* illness. **~era** *f* nurse. **~ería** *f* sick bay; (carrera) nursing. **~ero** *m* (male) nurse **~izo** *a* sickly. **~o** *a* ill. ● *m* patient

enflaquecer [11] *vt* make thin. ● *vi* lose weight

enfo|car [7] *vt* shine on; focus <*lente*>; (fig) approach. **~que** *m* focus; (fig) approach

enfrentar *vt* face, confront; (poner frente a frente) bring face to face. □ **~se** *vpr*. **~se con** confront; (en deportes) meet

enfrente *adv* opposite. **~ de** opposite. **de ~** opposite

enfria|miento *m* cooling; (catarro) cold. **~r** [20] *vt* cool (down); (fig) cool down. □ **~rse** *vpr* go cold; (fig) cool off

enfurecer [11] *vt* infuriate. □ **~se** *vpr* get furious

engalanar *vt* adorn. □ **~se** *vpr* dress up

enganchar *vt* hook; hang up <*ropa*>. □ **~se** *vpr* get caught; (Mil) enlist

engañ|ar *vt* deceive, trick; (ser infiel) be unfaithful. □ **~arse** *vpr* be wrong, be mistaken; (no admitir la verdad) deceive o.s. **~o** *m* deceit, trickery; (error) mistake. **~oso** *a* deceptive; <*persona*> deceitful

engarzar [10] *vt* string <*cuentas*>; set <*joyas*>

engatusar *vt* [I] coax

engendr|ar *vt* father; (fig) breed. **~o** *m* (monstruo) monster; (fig) brainchild

englobar *vt* include

engomar *vt* glue

engordar *vt* fatten, gain <*kilo*>. ● *vi* get fatter, put on weight

engorro *m* nuisance

engranaje *m* (Auto) gear

engrandecer [11] *vt* (enaltecer) exalt, raise

engrasar *vt* grease; (con aceite) oil; (ensuciar) get grease on

engreído *a* arrogant

engullir [22] *vt* gulp down

enhebrar *vt* thread

enhorabuena *f* congratulations. **dar la ~** congratulate

enigm|a *m* enigma. **~ático** *a* enigmatic

enjabonar *vt* soap. □ **~se** *vpr* to soap o.s.

enjambre *m* swarm

enjaular *vt* put in a cage

enjuag|ar [12] *vt* rinse. **~ue** *m* rinsing; (para la boca) mouthwash

enjugar [12] *vt* wipe (away)

enjuiciar *vt* pass judgement on

enjuto *a* <*persona*> skinny

enlace *m* connection; (matrimonial) wedding

enlatar *vt* tin, can

enlazar [10] *vt* link; tie together <*cintas*>; (Mex, casar) marry

enlodar *vt*, **enlodazar** [10] *vt* cover in mud

enloquecer [11] *vt* drive mad. ● *vi* go mad. □ **~se** *vpr* go mad

enlosar *vt* (con losas) pave; (con baldosas) tile

enmarañar *vt* tangle (up), entangle; (confundir) confuse. □ **~se** *vpr* get into a tangle; (confundirse) get confused

enmarcar [7] *vt* frame

enm|endar *vt* correct. □ **~endarse** *vpr* mend one's ways. **~ienda** *f* correction; (de ley etc) amendment

enmohecerse [11] *vpr* (con óxido) go rusty; (con hongos) go mouldy

enmudecer [11] *vi* be dumbstruck; (callar) fall silent

ennegrecer [11] *vt* blacken

ennoblecer [11] *vt* ennoble; (fig) add style to

enoj|adizo *a* irritable. **~ado** *a* angry; (molesto) annoyed. **~ar** *vt* anger; (molestar) annoy. □ **~arse** *vpr* get angry; (molestarse) get annoyed. **~o** *m* anger; (molestia) annoyance. **~oso** *a* annoying

enorgullecerse [11] *vpr* be proud

enorm|e *a* huge, enormous. **~emente** *adv* enormously.

~idad *f* immensity; (de crimen) enormity

enraizado *a* deeply rooted

enrarecido *a* rarefied

enred|adera *f* creeper. **~ar** *vt* tangle (up), entangle; (confundir) confuse; (involucrar) involve. □ **~arse** *vpr* get tangled; (confundirse) get confused; <*persona*> get involved (**con** with). **~o** *m* tangle; (fig) muddle, mess

enrejado *m* bars

enriquecer [11] *vt* make rich; (fig) enrich. □ **~se** *vpr* get rich

enrojecerse [11] *vpr* <*persona*> go red, blush

enrolar *vt* enlist

enrollar *vt* roll (up), wind <*hilo etc*>

enroscar [7] *vt* coil; (atornillar) screw in

ensalad|a *f* salad. **armar una ~a** make a mess. **~era** *f* salad bowl. **~illa** *f* Russian salad

ensalzar [10] *vt* praise; (enaltecer) exalt

ensambla|dura *f*, **ensamblaje** *m* (acción) assembling; (efecto) joint. **~r** *vt* join

ensanch|ar *vt* widen; (agrandar) enlarge. □ **~arse** *vpr* get wider. **~e** *m* widening

ensangrentar [1] *vt* stain with blood

ensañarse *vpr*. **~ con** treat cruelly

ensartar *vt* string <*cuentas etc*>

ensay|ar *vt* test; rehearse <*obra de teatro etc*>. **~o** *m* test, trial; (composición literaria) essay

enseguida *adv* at once, immediately

ensenada *f* inlet, cove

enseña|nza *f* education; (acción de enseñar) teaching. **~nza media** secondary education. **~r** *vt* teach; (mostrar) show

enseres *mpl* equipment

ensillar *vt* saddle

ensimismarse *vpr* be lost in thought

ensombrecer [11] *vt* darken

ensordecer [11] *vt* deafen. ● *vi* go deaf

ensuciar *vt* dirty. □ **~se** *vpr* get dirty

ensueño *m* dream

entablar *vt* (empezar) start

entablillar *vt* put in a splint

entallar *vt* tailor <*un vestido*>. ● *vi* fit

entarimado *m* parquet; (plataforma) platform

ente *m* entity, being; ([T], persona rara) weirdo; (Com) firm, company

entend|er [1] *vt* understand; (opinar) believe, think. ● *vi* understand. **~er de** know about. **a mi ~er** in my opinion. **dar a ~er** hint. **darse a ~er** (LAm) make o.s. understood □ **~erse** *vpr* make o.s. understood; (comprenderse) be understood. **~erse con** get on with. **~ido** *a* understood; (enterado) well-informed. **no darse por ~ido** pretend not to understand. ● *interj* agreed!, OK! [T]. **~imiento** *m* understanding

entera|do *a* well-informed; (que sabe) aware. **darse por ~do** take the hint. **~r** *vt* inform (**de** of). □ **~rse** *vpr*. **~rse de** find out about, hear of. **¡entérate!** listen! **¿te ~s?** do you understand?

entereza *f* (carácter) strength of character

enternecer [11] *vt* (fig) move, touch. □ **~se** *vpr* be moved, be touched

entero *a* entire, whole. **por ~** entirely, completely

enterra|dor *m* gravedigger. **~r** [1] *vt* bury

entibiar *vt* (enfriar) cool; (calentar) warm (up). □ **~se** *vpr* (enfriarse) cool down; (fig) cool; (calentarse) get warm

entidad *f* entity; (organización) organization; (Com) company; (importancia) significance

entierro *m* burial; (ceremonia) funeral

entona|ción *f* intonation. **~r** *vt* intone; sing *<nota>*. ● *vi* (Mus) be in tune; *<colores>* match. □ **~rse** *vpr* (emborracharse) get tipsy

entonces *adv* then. **en aquel ~** at that time, then

entorn|ado *a* *<puerta>* ajar; *<ventana>* slightly open. **~o** *m* environment; (en literatura) setting

entorpecer [11] *vt* dull; slow down *<tráfico>*; (dificultar) hinder

entra|da *f* entrance; (incorporación) admission, entry; (para cine etc) ticket; (de datos, Tec) input; (de una comida) starter. **de ~da** right away. **~do** *a*. **~do en años** elderly. **ya ~da la noche** late at night. **~nte** *a* next, coming

entraña *f* (fig) heart. **~s** *fpl* entrails; (fig) heart. **~ble** *a* *<cariño>* deep; *<amigo>* close. **~r** *vt* involve

entrar *vt* (traer) bring in; (llevar) take in. ● *vi* go in, enter; (venir) come in, enter; (empezar) start, begin; (incorporarse) join. **~ en**, (LAm) **~ a** go into

entre *prep* (dos personas o cosas) between; (más de dos) among(st)

entre|abierto *a* half-open. **~abrir** (*pp* **entreabierto**) *vt* half open. **~acto** *m* interval. **~cejo** *m* forehead. **fruncir el ~cejo** frown. **~cerrar** [1] *vt* (LAm) half close. **~cortado** *a* *<voz>* faltering; *<respiración>* laboured. **~cruzar** [10] *vt* intertwine

entrega *f* handing over; (de mercancías etc) delivery; (de novela etc) instalment; (dedicación) commitment. **~r** [12] *vt* deliver; (dar) give; hand in *<deberes>*; hand over *<poder>*. □ **~rse** *vpr* surrender, give o.s. up; (dedicarse) devote o.s. (**a** to)

entre|lazar [10] *vt* intertwine. **~més** *m* hors-d'oeuvre; (en el teatro) short comedy. **~mezclar** *vt* intermingle

entrena|dor *m* trainer. **~miento** *m* training. **~r** *vt* train. □ **~rse** *vpr* train

entre|pierna *f* crotch. **~piso** *m* (LAm) mezzanine. **~sacar** [7] *vt* pick out. **~suelo** *m* mezzanine. **~tanto** *adv* meanwhile. **~tejer** *vt* interweave

entreten|ción *f* (LAm) entertainment. **~er** [40] *vt* entertain, amuse; (detener) delay, keep. □ **~erse** *vpr* amuse o.s.; (tardar) delay, linger. **~ido** *a* (con ser) entertaining; (con estar) busy. **~imiento** *m* entertainment

entrever [43] *vt* make out, glimpse

entrevista *f* interview; (reunión) meeting. □ **~rse** *vpr* have an interview

entristecer [11] *vt* sadden, make sad. □ **~se** *vpr* grow sad

entromet|erse *vpr* interfere. **~ido** *a* interfering

entumec|erse [11] *vpr* go numb. **~ido** *a* numb

enturbiar *vt* cloud

entusi|asmar *vt* fill with enthusiasm; (gustar mucho) delight. □ **~asmarse** *vpr*. **~asmarse con** get enthusiastic about. **~asmo** *m* enthusiasm. **~asta** *a* enthusiastic. ● *m & f* enthusiast

enumerar *vt* enumerate

envalentonar *vt* encourage. □ **~se** *vpr* become bolder

envas|ado *m* packaging; (en latas) canning; (en botellas) bottling. **~ar** *vt* package; (en latas) tin, can; (en botellas) bottle. **~e** *m* packing; (lata) tin, can; (botella) bottle

envejec|er [11] *vt* make (look) older. ● *vi* age, grow old. □ **~erse** *vpr* age, grow old

envenenar *vt* poison

envergadura *f* importance

envia|do *m* envoy; (de la prensa) correspondent. **~r** [20] *vt* send

enviciarse *vpr* become addicted (**con** to)

envidi|a *f* envy; (celos) jealousy. **~ar** *vt* envy, be envious of. **~oso** *a* envious; (celoso) jealous. **tener ~a a** envy

envío *m* sending, dispatch; (de mercancías) consignment; (de dinero) remittance. **~ contra reembolso** cash on delivery. **gastos** *mpl* **de ~** postage and packing (costs)

enviudar *vi* be widowed

env|oltura *f* wrapping. **~olver** [2] (*pp* **envuelto**) *vt* wrap; (cubrir) cover; (rodear) surround; (fig, enredar) involve. **~uelto** *a* wrapped (up)

enyesar *vt* plaster; (Med) put in plaster

épica *f* epic

épico *a* epic

epid|emia *f* epidemic. **~émico** *a* epidemic

epil|epsia *f* epilepsy. **~éptico** *a* epileptic

epílogo *m* epilogue

episodio *m* episode

epístola *f* epistle

epitafio *m* epitaph

época *f* age; (período) period. **hacer ~** make history, be epoch-making

equidad *f* equity

equilibr|ado *a* (well-)balanced. **~ar** *vt* balance. **~io** *m* balance; (de balanza) equilibrium. **~ista** *m & f* tightrope walker

equinoccio *m* equinox

equipaje *m* luggage (esp Brit), baggage (esp Amer)

equipar *vt* equip; (de ropa) fit out

equiparar *vt* make equal; (comparar) compare

equipo *m* equipment; (de personas) team

equitación *f* riding

equivale|nte *a* equivalent. **~r** [42] *vi* be equivalent; (significar) mean

equivoca|ción *f* mistake, error. **~do** *a* wrong. □ **~rse** *vpr* make a mistake; (estar en error) be wrong, be mistaken. **~rse de** be wrong about. **~rse de número** dial the wrong number. **si no me equivoco** if I'm not mistaken

equívoco *a* equivocal; (sospechoso) suspicious ● *m* misunderstanding; (error) mistake

era *f* era. ● *vb* ⇒SER

erario *m* treasury

erección *f* erection

eres *vb* ⇒SER

erguir [48] *vt* raise. □ **~se** *vpr* raise

erigir [14] *vt* erect. □ **~se** *vpr*. **~se en** set o.s. up as; (llegar a ser) become

eriza|do *a* prickly. □ **~rse** [10] *vpr* stand on end; (LAm) <*persona*> get goose pimples

erizo *m* hedgehog; (de mar) sea urchin. **~ de mar** sea urchin

ermita *f* hermitage. **~ño** *m* hermit

erosi|ón *f* erosion. **~onar** *vt* erode

er|ótico *a* erotic. **~otismo** *m* eroticism

err|ar [1] (*la* **i** *inicial pasa a ser* **y**) *vt* miss. ● *vi* wander; (equivocarse) make a mistake, be wrong. **~ata** *f* misprint. **~óneo** *a* erroneous, wrong. **~or** *m* error, mistake. **estar en un ~or** be wrong, be mistaken

eruct|ar *vi* belch. **~o** *m* belch

erudi|ción *f* learning, erudition. **~to** *a* learned; <*palabra*> erudite

erupción *f* eruption; (Med) rash

es *vb* ⇒SER

esa *a* ⇒ESE

ésa *pron* ⇒ÉSE

esbelto *a* slender, slim

esboz|ar [10] *vt* sketch, outline. **~o** *m* sketch, outline

escabeche *m* brine. **en ~** pickled

escabroso *a* <*terreno*> rough; <*asunto*> difficult; (atrevido) crude

escabullirse [22] *vpr* slip away

escafandra *f* diving-suit

escala *f* scale; (escalera de mano) ladder; (Aviac) stopover. **hacer ~ en** stop at. **vuelo sin ~s** non-stop flight. **~da** *f* climbing; (Pol) escalation. **~r** *vt* climb; break into <*una casa*>. ● *vi* climb, go climbing

escaldar *vt* scald

escalera *f* staircase, stairs; (de mano) ladder. **~ de caracol** spiral staircase. **~ de incendios** fire escape. **~ de tijera** step-ladder. **~ mecánica** escalator

escalfa|do *a* poached. **~r** *vt* poach

escalinata *f* flight of steps

escalofrío *m* shiver. **tener ~s** be shivering

escalón *m* step, stair; (de escala) rung

escalope *m* escalope

escam|a *f* scale; (de jabón, de la piel) flake. **~oso** *a* scaly; <*piel*> flaky

escamotear *vt* make disappear; (robar) steal, pinch

escampar *vi* stop raining

esc|andalizar [10] *vt* scandalize, shock. □ **~andalizarse** *vpr* be shocked. **~ándalo** *m* scandal; (alboroto) commotion, racket. **armar un ~** make a scene. **~andaloso** *a* scandalous; (alborotador) noisy

escandinavo *a* & *m* Scandinavian

escaño *m* bench; (Pol) seat

escapa|da *f* escape; (visita) flying visit. **~r** *vi* escape. **dejar ~r** let out. □ **~rse** *vpr* escape; <*líquido, gas*> leak

escaparate *m* (shop) window

escap|atoria *f* (fig) way out. **~e** *m* (de gas, de líquido) leak; (fuga) escape; (Auto) exhaust

escarabajo *m* beetle

escaramuza *f* skirmish

escarbar *vt* scratch; pick <*dientes, herida*>; (fig, escudriñar) pry (**en** into). □ **~se** *vpr* pick

escarcha *f* frost. **~do** *a* <*fruta*> crystallized

escarlat|a *a invar* scarlet. **~ina** *f* scarlet fever

escarm|entar [1] *vt* teach a lesson to. ● *vi* learn one's lesson. **~iento** *m* punishment; (lección) lesson

escarola *f* endive

escarpado *a* steep

escas|ear *vi* be scarce. **~ez** *f* scarcity, shortage; (pobreza) poverty. **~o** *a* scarce; (poco) little; (muy justo) barely. **~o de** short of

escatimar *vt* be sparing with

escayola *f* plaster

esc|ena *f* scene; (escenario) stage. **~enario** *m* stage; (fig) scene. **~énico** *a* stage. **~enografía** *f* set design

esc|epticismo *m* scepticism. **~éptico** *a* sceptical. ● *m* sceptic

esclarecer [11] *vt* (fig) throw light on, clarify

esclav|itud *f* slavery. **~izar** [10] *vt* enslave. **~o** *m* slave

esclusa *f* lock; (de presa) floodgate

escoba *f* broom

escocer [2 & 9] *vi* sting

escocés *a* Scottish. ● *m* Scot

Escocia *f* Scotland

escog|er [14] *vt* choose. **~ido** *a* chosen; <*mercancía*> choice; <*clientela*> select

escolar *a* school. ● *m* schoolboy. ● *f* schoolgirl

escolta *f* escort

escombros *mpl* rubble

escond|er *vt* hide. □ **~erse** *vpr* hide. **~idas** *fpl* (LAm, juego) hide-and-seek. **a ~idas** secretly. **~ite** *m* hiding place; (juego) hide-and-seek. **~rijo** *m* hiding place

escopeta *f* shotgun

escoria *f* slag; (fig) dregs

escorpión *m* scorpion

Escorpión *m* Scorpio

escot|ado *a* low-cut. **~e** *m* low neckline. **pagar a ~e** share the expenses

escozor *m* stinging

escri|bano *m* clerk. **~bir** (*pp* **escrito**) *vt/i* write. **~bir a máquina** type. **¿cómo se escribe...?** how do you spell...? □ **~birse** *vpr* write to each other. **~to** *a* written. **por ~to** in writing. ● *m* document. **~tor** *m* writer. **~torio** *m* desk; (oficina) office; (LAm, en una casa) study. **~tura** *f* (hand)writing; (Jurid) deed

escr|úpulo *m* scruple. **~upuloso** *a* scrupulous

escrut|ar *vt* scrutinize; count <*votos*>. **~inio** *m* count

escuadr|a *f* (instrumento) square; (Mil) squad; (Naut) fleet. **~ón** *m* squadron

escuálido *a* skinny

escuchar *vt* listen to; (esp LAm, oír) hear. ● *vi* listen

escudo *m* shield. **~ de armas** coat of arms

escudriñar *vt* examine

escuela *f* school. **~ normal** teachers' training college

escueto *a* simple

escuincle *m* (Mex 🅸) kid 🅸

escul|pir *vt* sculpture. **~tor** *m* sculptor. **~tora** *f* sculptress. **~tura** *f* sculpture

escupir *vt/i* spit

escurr|eplatos *m invar* plate rack. **~idizo** *a* slippery. **~ir** *vt* drain; wring out *<ropa>*. ● *vi* drain; *<ropa>* drip. □ **~irse** *vpr* slip

ese *a* (*f* **esa**) that; (*mpl* **esos**, *fpl* **esas**) those

ése *pron* (*f* **ésa**) that one: (*mpl* **ésos**, *fpl* **ésas**) those; (primero de dos) the former

esencia *f* essence. **~l** *a* essential. **lo ~l** the main thing

esf|era *f* sphere; (de reloj) face. **~érico** *a* spherical

esf|orzarse [2 & 10] *vpr* make an effort. **~uerzo** *m* effort

esfumarse *vpr* fade away; *<persona>* vanish

esgrim|a *f* fencing. **~ir** *vt* brandish; (fig) use

esguince *m* sprain

eslabón *m* link

eslavo *a* Slavic, Slavonic

eslogan *m* slogan

esmalt|ar *vt* enamel. **~e** *m* enamel. **~e de uñas** nail polish

esmerado *a* careful; *<persona>* painstaking

esmeralda *f* emerald

esmer|arse *vpr* take care (**en** over). **~o** *m* care

esmero *m* care

esmoquin (*pl* **esmóquines**) *m* dinner jacket, tuxedo (Amer)

esnob *a invar* snobbish. ● *m & f* (*pl* **~s**) snob. **~ismo** *m* snobbery

esnórkel *m* snorkel

eso *pron* that. **¡~ es!** that's it! **~ mismo** exactly. **a ~ de** about. **en ~** at that moment. **¿no es ~?** isn't that right? **por ~** that's why. **y ~ que** even though

esos *a pl* ⇒ESE

ésos *pron pl* ⇒ÉSE

espabila|do *a* bright; (despierto) awake. **~r** *vt* (avivar) brighten up; (despertar) wake up. □ **~rse** *vpr* wake up; (avivarse) wise up; (apresurarse) hurry up

espaci|al *a* space. **~ar** *vt* space out. **~o** *m* space. **~oso** *a* spacious

espada *f* sword. **~s** *fpl* (en naipes) spades

espaguetis *mpl* spaghetti

espald|a *f* back. **a ~as de uno** behind s.o.'s back. **volver la(s) ~a(s) a uno** give s.o. the cold shoulder. **~illa** *f* shoulder-blade

espant|ajo *m*, **~apájaros** *m invar* scarecrow. **~ar** *vt* frighten; (ahuyentar) frighten away. □ **~arse** *vpr* be frightened; (ahuyentarse) be frightened away. **~o** *m* terror; (horror) horror. **¡qué ~o!** how awful! **~oso** *a* horrific; (terrible) terrible

España *f* Spain

español *a* Spanish. ● *m* (persona) Spaniard; (lengua) Spanish. **los ~es** the Spanish. **~izado** *a* Hispanicized

esparadrapo *m* (sticking) plaster

esparcir [9] *vt* scatter; (difundir) spread. □ **~rse** *vpr* be scattered; (difundirse) spread; (divertirse) enjoy o.s.

espárrago *m* asparagus

espasm|o *m* spasm. **~ódico** *a* spasmodic

espátula *f* spatula; (en pintura) palette knife

especia *f* spice

especial *a* special. **en ~** especially. **~idad** *f* speciality (Brit), specialty (Amer). **~ista** *a & m & f* specialist. **~ización** *f* specialization. □ **~izarse** [10] *vpr* specialize. **~mente** *adv* especially

especie *f* kind, sort; (Biol) species. **en ~** in kind

especifica|ción *f* specification. **~r** [7] *vt* specify

específico *a* specific

espect|áculo *m* sight; (de circo etc) show. **~acular** *a* spectacular. **~ador** *m & f* spectator

espectro *m* spectre; (en física) spectrum

especula|dor *m* speculator. **~r** *vi* speculate

espej|ismo *m* mirage. **~o** *m* mirror. **~o retrovisor** (Auto) rear-view mirror

espeluznante *a* horrifying

espera *f* wait. **a la ~** waiting (**de** for). **~nza** *f* hope. **~r** *vt* hope; (aguardar) wait for; expect *<visita, carta, bebé>*. **espero que no** I hope not. **espero que sí** I hope so. ● *vi* (aguardar) wait. □ **~rse** *vpr* hang on; (prever) expect

esperma *f* sperm

esperpento *m* fright

espes|ar *vt/i* thicken. □ **~arse** *vpr* thicken. **~o** *a* thick. **~or** *m* thickness

espetón *m* spit

esp|ía *f* spy. **~iar** [20] *vt* spy on. ● *vi* spy

espiga *f* (de trigo etc) ear

espina *f* thorn; (de pez) bone; (Anat) spine. **~ dorsal** spine

espinaca *f* spinach

espinazo *m* spine

espinilla *f* shin; (Med) blackhead; (LAm, grano) spot

espino *m* hawthorn. **~so** *a* thorny; (fig) difficult

espionaje *m* espionage

espiral *a & f* spiral

esp|iritista *m & f* spiritualist. **~íritu** *m* spirit; (mente) mind. **~iritual** *a* spiritual

espl|éndido *a* splendid; *<persona>* generous. **~endor** *m* splendour

espolear *vt* spur (on)

espolvorear *vt* sprinkle

esponj|a *f* sponge. **~oso** *a* spongy

espont|aneidad *f* spontaneity. **~áneo** *a* spontaneous

esporádico *a* sporadic

espos|a *f* wife. **~as** *fpl* handcuffs. **~ar** *vt* handcuff. **~o** *m* husband

espuela *f* spur; (fig) incentive

espum|a *f* foam; (en bebidas) froth; (de jabón) lather; (de las olas) surf. **echar ~a** foam, froth. **~oso** *a <vino>* sparkling

esqueleto *m* skeleton; (estructura) framework

esquema *m* outline

esqu|í *m* (*pl* **~is**, **~íes**) ski; (deporte) skiing. **~iar** [20] *vi* ski

esquilar *vt* shear

esquimal *a & m* Eskimo

esquina *f* corner

esquiv|ar *vt* avoid; dodge *<golpe>*. **~o** *a* elusive

esquizofrénico *a & m* schizophrenic

esta *a* ⇒ESTE

ésta *pron* ⇒ÉSTE

estab|ilidad *f* stability. **~le** *a* stable

establec|er [11] *vt* establish. □ **~erse** *vpr* settle; (Com) set up. **~imiento** *m* establishment

establo *m* cattleshed

estaca *f* stake

estación *f* station; (del año) season. ~ **de invierno** winter (sports) resort. ~ **de servicio** service station

estaciona|miento *m* parking; (LAm, lugar) car park (Brit), parking lot (Amer). **~r** *vt* station; (Auto) park. **~rio** *a* stationary

estadía *f* (LAm) stay

estadio *m* stadium; (fase) stage

estadista *m* statesman. ● *f* stateswoman

estadístic|a *f* statistics; (cifra) statistic. **~o** *a* statistical

estado *m* state; (Med) condition. ~ **civil** marital status. ~ **de ánimo** frame of mind. ~ **de cuenta** bank statement. ~ **mayor** (Mil) staff. **en buen** ~ in good condition

Estados Unidos *mpl* United States

estadounidense *a* American, United States. ● *m & f* American

estafa *f* swindle. **~r** *vt* swindle

estafeta *f* (oficina de correos) (sub-) post office

estala|ctita *f* stalactite. **~gmita** *f* stalagmite

estall|ar *vi* explode; <*olas*> break; <*guerra etc*> break out; (fig) burst. **~ar en llanto** burst into tears. **~ar de risa** burst out laughing. **~ido** *m* explosion; (de guerra etc) outbreak

estamp|a *f* print; (aspecto) appearance. **~ado** *a* printed. ● *m* printing; (motivo) pattern; (tela) cotton print. **~ar** *vt* stamp; (imprimir) print

estampido *m* bang

estampilla *f* (LAm, de correos) (postage) stamp

estanca|do *a* stagnant. **~r** [7] *vt* stem. □ **~rse** *vpr* stagnate

estancia *f* stay; (cuarto) large room

estanco *a* watertight. ● *m* tobacconist's (shop)

estandarte *m* standard, banner

estanque *m* pond; (depósito de agua) (water) tank

estanquero *m* tobacconist

estante *m* shelf. **~ría** *f* shelves; (para libros) bookcase

estaño *m* tin

---

estar [27]

● *verbo intransitivo*

····➤ to be. **¿cómo estás?** how are you? **estoy enfermo** I'm ill. **está muy cerca** it's very near. **¿está Pedro?** is Pedro in? **¿cómo está el tiempo?** what's the weather like? **ya estamos en invierno** it's winter already

····➤ (quedarse) to stay. **sólo ~é una semana** I'll only be staying for a week. **estoy en un hotel** I'm staying in a hotel

····➤ (con fecha) **¿a cuánto estamos?** what's the date today? **estamos a 8 de mayo** it's the 8th of May.

····➤ (en locuciones) **¿estamos?** all right? **¡ahí está!** that's it! ~ **por** (apoyar a) to support; (LAm, encontrarse a punto de) to be about to; (quedar por) **eso está por verse** that remains to be seen. **son cuentas que están por pagar** they're bills still to be paid

● *verbo auxiliar*

····➤ (con gerundio) **estaba estudiando** I was studying

····➤ (con participio) **está condenado a muerte** he's been sentenced to death. **está mal traducido** it's wrongly translated.

□ **estarse** *verbo pronominal* to stay. **no se está quieto** he won't stay still

➡ Cuando el verbo **estar** forma parte de expresiones como **estar de acuerdo, estar a la vista, estar constipado,** etc., ver bajo el respectivo nombre o adjetivo

estatal *a* state

estático *a* static

estatua *f* statue

estatura *f* height

estatuto *m* statute; (norma) rule

este *a* <*región*> eastern; <*viento, lado*> east. ● *m* east. ● *a* (*f* **esta**) this; (*mpl* **estos**, *fpl* **estas**) these; (LAm, como muletilla) well, er

éste *pron* (*f* **ésta**) this one; (*mpl* **éstos**, *fpl* **éstas**) these; (segundo de dos) the latter

estela *f* wake; (de avión) trail; (Arquit) carved stone

estera *f* mat; (tejido) matting

est|éreo *a* stereo. **~ereofónico** *a* stereo, stereophonic

estereotipo *m* stereotype

estéril *a* sterile; <*terreno*> barren

esterilla *f* mat

esterlina *a*. **libra** *f* **~** pound sterling

estético *a* aesthetic

estiércol *m* dung; (abono) manure

estigma *m* stigma. **~s** *mpl* (Relig) stigmata

estil|arse *vpr* be used. **~o** *m* style; (en natación) stroke. **~ mariposa** butterfly. **~ pecho** (LAm) breaststroke. **por el ~o** of that sort

estilográfica *f* fountain pen

estima *f* esteem. **~do** *a* <*amigo, colega*> valued. **~do señor** (en cartas) Dear Sir. **~r** *vt* esteem; have great respect for <*persona*>; (valorar) value; (juzgar) consider

est|imulante *a* stimulating. ● *m* stimulant. **~imular** *vt* stimulate; (incitar) incite. **~ímulo** *m* stimulus

estir|ado *a* stretched; <*persona*> haughty. **~ar** *vt* stretch; (fig) stretch out. **~ón** *m* pull, tug; (crecimiento) sudden growth

estirpe *m* stock

esto *pron neutro* this; (este asunto) this business. **en ~** at this point. **en ~ de** in this business of. **por ~** therefore

estofa|do *a* stewed. ● *m* stew. **~r** *vt* stew

estómago *m* stomach. **dolor** *m* **de ~** stomach ache

estorb|ar *vt* obstruct; (molestar) bother. ● *vi* be in the way. **~o** *m* hindrance; (molestia) nuisance

estornud|ar *vi* sneeze. **~o** *m* sneeze

estos *a mpl* ⇒ESTE

éstos *pron mpl* ⇒ÉSTE

estoy *vb* ⇒ESTAR

estrabismo *m* squint

estrado *m* stage; (Mus) bandstand

estrafalario *a* eccentric; <*ropa*> outlandish

estrago *m* devastation. **hacer ~os** devastate

estragón *m* tarragon

estrambótico *a* eccentric; <*ropa*> outlandish

estrangula|dor *m* strangler; (Auto) choke. **~r** *vt* strangle

estratagema *f* stratagem

estrat|ega *m* & *f* strategist. **~egia** *f* strategy. **~égico** *a* strategic

estrato *m* stratum

estrech|ar *vt* make narrower; take in <*vestido*>; embrace <*persona*>. **~ar la mano a uno** shake hands with s.o. □ **~arse** *vpr* become narrower; (abrazarse) embrace. **~ez** *f* narrowness. **~eces** *fpl* financial difficulties. **~o** *a* narrow; <*vestido etc*> tight; (fig, íntimo) close. **~o de miras** narrow-minded. ● *m* strait(s)

estrella *f* star. **~ de mar** starfish. **~ado** *a* starry

estrellar *vt* smash; crash <*coche*>. □ **~se** *vpr* crash (**contra** into)

estremec|er [11] *vt* shake. □ **~erse** *vpr* shake; (de emoción etc) tremble (**de** with). **~imiento** *m* shaking

estren|ar *vt* wear for the first time <*vestido etc*>; show for the first time <*película*>. □ **~arse** *vpr* make one's début. **~o** *m* (de película) première; (de obra de teatro) first night; (de persona) debut

estreñi|do *a* constipated. **~miento** *m* constipation

estrés *m* stress

estría *f* groove; (de la piel) stretch mark

estribillo *m* (incl Mus) refrain

estribo *m* stirrup; (de coche) step. **perder los ~s** lose one's temper

estribor *m* starboard

estricto *a* strict

estridente *a* strident, raucous

estrofa *f* stanza, verse

estropajo *m* scourer

estropear *vt* damage; (plan) spoil; ruin <*ropa*>. □ **~se** *vpr* be damaged; (averiarse) break down; <*ropa*> get ruined; <*fruta etc*> go bad; (fracasar) fail

estructura *f* structure. **~l** *a* structural

estruendo *m* roar; (de mucha gente) uproar

estrujar *vt* squeeze; wring (out) <*ropa*>; (fig) drain

estuario *m* estuary

estuche *m* case

estudi|ante *m* & *f* student. **~antil** *a* student. **~ar** *vt* study. **~o** *m* study; (de artista) studio. **~oso** *a* studious

estufa *f* heater; (Mex, cocina) cooker

estupefac|iente *m* narcotic. **~to** *a* astonished

estupendo *a* marvellous; <*persona*> fantastic; ¡~! that's great!

est|upidez *f* stupidity; (acto) stupid thing. **~úpido** *a* stupid

estupor *m* amazement

estuve *vb* ⇒ESTAR

etapa *f* stage. **por ~s** in stages

etc *abrev* (**etcétera**) etc. **~étera** *adv* et cetera

etéreo *a* ethereal

etern|idad *f* eternity. **~o** *a* eternal

étic|a *f* ethics. **~o** *a* ethical

etimología *f* etymology

etiqueta *f* ticket, tag; (ceremonial) etiquette. **de ~** formal

étnico *a* ethnic

eucalipto *m* eucalyptus

eufemismo *m* euphemism

euforia *f* euphoria

Europa *f* Europe

europeo *a* & *m* European

eutanasia *f* euthanasia

evacua|ción *f* evacuation. **~r** [21] *vt* evacuate

evadir *vt* avoid; evade <*impuestos*>. □ **~se** *vpr* escape

evaluar [21] *vt* assess; evaluate <*datos*>

evangeli|o *m* gospel. **~sta** *m & f* evangelist; (Mex, escribiente) scribe

evapora|ción *f* evaporation. □ **~rse** *vpr* evaporate; (fig) disappear

evasi|ón *f* evasion; (fuga) escape. **~vo** *a* evasive

evento *m* event; (caso) case

eventual *a* possible. **~idad** *f* eventuality

eviden|cia *f* evidence. **poner en ~cia a uno** show s.o. up. **~ciar** *vt* show. □ **~ciarse** *vpr* be obvious. **~te** *a* obvious. **~temente** *adv* obviously

evitar *vt* avoid; (ahorrar) spare; (prevenir) prevent

evocar [7] *vt* evoke

evoluci|ón *f* evolution. **~onar** *vi* evolve; (Mil) manoeuvre

ex *pref* ex-, former

exacerbar *vt* exacerbate

exact|amente *adv* exactly. **~itud** *f* exactness. **~o** *a* exact; (preciso) accurate; (puntual) punctual. ¡**~**! exactly!

exagera|ción *f* exaggeration. **~do** *a* exaggerated. **~r** *vt/i* exaggerate

exalta|do *a* exalted; (excitado) (over-)excited; (fanático) hot-headed. **~r** *vt* exalt. □ **~rse** *vpr* get excited

exam|en *m* exam, examination. **~inar** *vt* examine. □ **~inarse** *vpr* take an exam

exasperar *vt* exasperate. □ **~se** *vpr* get exasperated

excarcela|ción *f* release (from prison). **~r** *vt* release

excava|ción *f* excavation. **~dora** *f* digger. **~r** *vt* excavate

excede|ncia *f* leave of absence. **~nte** *a & m* surplus. **~r** *vi* exceed. □ **~rse** *vpr* go too far

excelen|cia *f* excellence; (tratamiento) Excellency. **~te** *a* excellent

exc|entricidad *f* eccentricity. **~éntrico** *a & m* eccentric

excepci|ón *f* exception. **~onal** *a* exceptional. **a ~ón de, con ~ón de** except (for)

except|o *prep* except (for). **~uar** [21] *vt* except

exces|ivo *a* excessive. **~o** *m* excess. **~o de equipaje** excess luggage (esp Brit), excess baggage (esp Amer)

excita|ción *f* excitement. **~r** *vt* excite; (incitar) incite. □ **~rse** *vpr* get excited

exclama|ción *f* exclamation. **~r** *vi* exclaim

exclu|ir [17] *vt* exclude. **~sión** *f* exclusion. **~siva** *f* sole right; (reportaje) exclusive (story). **~sivo** *a* exclusive

excomu|lgar [12] *vt* excommunicate. **~nión** *f* excommunication

excremento *m* excrement

excursi|ón *f* excursion, outing. **~onista** *m & f* day-tripper

excusa *f* excuse; (disculpa) apology. **presentar sus ~s** apologize. **~r** *vt* excuse

exento *a* exempt; (libre) free

exhalar *vt* exhale, breath out; give off <*olor etc*>

exhaust|ivo *a* exhaustive. **~o** *a* exhausted

exhibi|ción *f* exhibition; (demostración) display. **~cionista** *m & f* exhibitionist. **~r** *vt* exhibit. □ **~rse** *vpr* show o.s.; (hacerse notar) draw attention to o.s.

exhumar *vt* exhume; (fig) dig up

exig|encia *f* demand. **~ente** *a* demanding. **~ir** [14] *vt* demand

exiguo *a* meagre

exil|(i)ado *a* exiled. ● *m* exile. □ **~(i)arse** *vpr* go into exile. **~io** *m* exile

exim|ente *m* reason for exemption; (Jurid) grounds for acquittal. **~ir** *vt* exempt

existencia *f* existence. **~s** *fpl* stock. **~lismo** *m* existentialism

exist|ente *a* existing. **~ir** *vi* exist

éxito *m* success. **no tener ~** fail. **tener ~** be successful

exitoso *a* successful

éxodo *m* exodus

exonerar *vt* exonerate

exorbitante *a* exorbitant

exorci|smo *m* exorcism. **~zar** [10] *vt* exorcise

exótico *a* exotic

expan|dir *vt* expand; (fig) spread. □ **~dirse** *vpr* expand. **~sión** *f* expansion. **~sivo** *a* expansive

expatria|do *a* & *m* expatriate. □ **~rse** *vpr* emigrate; (exiliarse) go into exile

expectativa *f* prospect; (esperanza) expectation. **estar a la ~** be waiting

expedi|ción *f* expedition; (de documento) issue; (de mercancías) dispatch. **~ente** *m* record, file; (Jurid) proceedings. **~r** [5] *vt* issue; (enviar) dispatch, send. **~to** *a* clear; (LAm, fácil) easy

expeler *vt* expel

expend|edor *m* dealer. **~dor automático** vending machine. **~io** *m* (LAm) shop; (venta) sale

expensas *fpl* (Jurid) costs. **a ~ de** at the expense of. **a mis ~** at my expense

experiencia *f* experience

experiment|al *a* experimental. **~ar** *vt* test, experiment with; (sentir) experience. **~o** *m* experiment

experto *a* & *m* expert

expiar [20] *vt* atone for

expirar *vi* expire

explanada *f* levelled area; (paseo) esplanade

explayarse *vpr* speak at length; (desahogarse) unburden o.s. (**con** to)

explica|ción *f* explanation. **~r** [7] *vt* explain. □ **~rse** *vpr* understand; (hacerse comprender) explain o.s. **no me lo explico** I can't understand it

explícito *a* explicit

explora|ción *f* exploration. **~dor** *m* explorer; (muchacho) boy scout. **~r** *vt* explore

explosi|ón *f* explosion; (fig) outburst. **~onar** *vt* blow up. **~vo** *a* & *m* explosive

explota|ción *f* working; (abuso) exploitation. **~r** *vt* work <*mina*>; farm <*tierra*>; (abusar) exploit. ● *vi* explode

expone|nte *m* exponent. **~r** [34] *vt* expose; display <*mercancías*>; present <*tema*>; set out <*hechos*>; exhibit <*cuadros etc*>; (arriesgar) risk. ● *vi* exhibit. □ **~rse** *vpr.* **~se a que** run the risk of

exporta|ción *f* export. **~dor** *m* exporter. **~r** *vt* export

exposición *f* exposure; (de cuadros etc) exhibition; (de hechos) exposition

expres|ar *vt* express. □ **~arse** *vpr* express o.s. **~ión** *f* expression. **~ivo** *a* expressive; (cariñoso) affectionate

expreso *a* express. ● *m* express; (café) expresso

exprimi|dor *m* squeezer. **~r** *vt* squeeze

expropiar *vt* expropriate

expuesto *a* on display; <*lugar etc*> exposed; (peligroso) dangerous. **estar ~ a** be exposed to

expuls|ar *vt* expel; throw out <*persona*>; send off <*jugador*>. **~ión** *f* expulsion

exquisito *a* exquisite; (de sabor) delicious

éxtasis *m invar* ecstasy

extend|er [1] *vt* spread (out); (ampliar) extend; issue <*documento*>. ▫ **~erse** *vpr* spread; <*paisaje etc*> extend, stretch. **~ido** *a* spread out; (generalizado) widespread; <*brazos*> outstretched

extens|amente *adv* widely; (detalladamente) in full. **~ión** *f* extension; (área) expanse; (largo) length. **~o** *a* extensive

extenuar [21] *vt* exhaust

exterior *a* external, exterior; (del extranjero) foreign; <*aspecto etc*> outward. ● *m* outside, exterior; (países extranjeros) abroad

extermin|ación *f* extermination. **~ar** *vt* exterminate. **~io** *m* extermination

externo *a* external; <*signo etc*> outward. ● *m* day pupil

extin|ción *f* extinction. **~guidor** *m* (LAm) fire extinguisher. **~guir** [13] *vt* extinguish. ▫ **~guirse** *vpr* die out; <*fuego*> go out. **~to** *a* <*raza etc*> extinct. **~tor** *m* fire extinguisher

extirpar *vt* eradicate; remove <*tumor*>

extorsión *f* extortion

extra *a invar* extra; (de buena calidad) good-quality; <*huevos*> large. **paga** *f* **~** bonus

extracto *m* extract

extradición *f* extradition

extraer [41] *vt* extract

extranjero *a* foreign. ● *m* foreigner; (países) foreign countries. **del ~** from abroad. **en el ~**, **por el ~** abroad

extrañ|ar *vt* surprise; (encontrar extraño) find strange; (LAm, echar de menos) miss. ▫ **~arse** *vpr* be surprised (**de** at). **~eza** *f* strangeness; (asombro) surprise. **~o** *a* strange. ● *m* stranger

extraoficial *a* unofficial

extraordinario *a* extraordinary

extrarradio *m* outlying districts

extraterrestre *a* extraterrestrial. ● *m* alien

extravagan|cia *f* oddness, eccentricity. **~te** *a* odd, eccentric

extrav|iado *a* lost. **~iar** [20] *vt* lose. ▫ **~iarse** *vpr* get lost; <*objetos*> go missing. **~ío** *m* loss

extremar *vt* take extra <*precauciones*>; tighten up <*vigilancia*>. ▫ **~se** *vpr* make every effort

extremeño *a* from Extremadura

extrem|idad *f* end. **~idades** *fpl* extremities. **~ista** *a* & *m* & *f* extremist. **~o** *a* extreme. ● *m* end; (colmo) extreme. **en ~o** extremely. **en último ~o** as a last resort

extrovertido *a* & *m* extrovert

exuberan|cia *f* exuberance. **~te** *a* exuberant

eyacular *vt/i* ejaculate

Ff

fa *m* F; (solfa) fah

fabada *f* bean and pork stew

fábrica *f* factory. **marca** *f* **de ~** trade mark

fabrica|ción *f* manufacture. **~ción en serie** mass production. **~nte** *m* & *f* manufacturer. **~r** [7] *vt* manufacture

fábula *f* fable; (mentira) fabrication

fabuloso *a* fabulous

facci|ón *f* faction. **~ones** *fpl* (de la cara) features

faceta *f* facet

facha *f* (Ⅱ, aspecto) look. **~da** *f* façade

fácil *a* easy; (probable) likely

facili|dad *f* ease; (disposición) aptitude. **~dades** *fpl* facilities. **~tar** *vt* facilitate; (proporcionar) provide

factible *a* feasible

factor *m* factor

factura *f* bill, invoice. **~r** *vt* (hacer la factura) invoice; (Aviat) check in

faculta|d *f* faculty; (capacidad) ability; (poder) power. **~tivo** *a* optional

faena *f* job. **~s domésticas** housework

faisán *m* pheasant

faja *f* (de tierra) strip; (corsé) corset; (Mil etc) sash

fajo *m* bundle; (de billetes) wad

falda *f* skirt; (de montaña) side

falla *f* fault; (defecto) flaw. **~ humana** (LAm) human error. **~r** *vi* fail. **me falló** he let me down. **sin ~r** without fail. ● *vt* (errar) miss

fallec|er [11] *vi* die. **~ido** *m* deceased

fallido *a* vain; (fracasado) unsuccessful

fallo *m* (defecto) fault; (error) mistake. **~ humano** human error; (en certamen) decision; (Jurid) ruling

falluca *f* (Mex) smuggled goods

fals|ear *vt* falsify, distort. **~ificación** *f* forgery. **~ificador** *m* forger. **~ificar** [7] *vt* forge. **~o** *a* false; (falsificado) forged; <*joya*> fake

falt|a *f* lack; (ausencia) absence; (escasez) shortage; (defecto) fault, defect; (culpa) fault; (error) mistake; (en fútbol etc) foul; (en tenis) fault. **a ~a de** for lack of. **echar en ~a** miss. **hacer ~a** be necessary. **me hace ~a** I need. **sacar ~as** find fault. **~o** *a* lacking (**de** in

faltar

● *verbo intransitivo*

> **!** Cuando el verbo **faltar** va precedido del complemento indirecto **le** (o **les, nos** etc) el sujeto en español pasa a ser el objeto en inglés p.ej: **les falta experiencia** *they lack experience*

....➤ (no estar) to be missing **¿quién falta?** who's missing? **falta una de las chicas** one of the girls is missing. **al abrigo le faltan 3 botones** the coat has three buttons missing. **~ a algo** (no asistir) to be absent from sth; (no acudir) to miss sth

....➤ (no haber suficiente) **va a ~ leche** there won't be enough milk. **nos**

faltó tiempo we didn't have enough time

····➤ (no tener) **le falta cariño** he lacks affection

····➤ (hacer falta) **le falta sal** it needs more salt. **¡es lo que nos faltaba!** that's all we needed!

····➤ (quedar) **¿te falta mucho?** are you going to be much longer? **falta poco para Navidad** it's not long until Christmas. **aún falta mucho** (distancia) there's a long way to go yet **¡no faltaba más!** of course!

fama *f* fame; (reputación) reputation

famélico *a* starving

familia *f* family; (hijos) children. **~ numerosa** large family. **~r** *a* familiar; (de la familia) family; (sin ceremonia) informal; <*lenguaje*> colloquial. ● *m & f* relative. **~ridad** *f* familiarity. □ **~rizarse** [10] *vpr* become familiar (**con** with)

famoso *a* famous

fanático *a* fanatical. ● *m* fanatic

fanfarr|ón *a* boastful. ● *m* braggart. **~onear** *vi* show off

fango *m* mud. **~so** *a* muddy

fantasía *f* fantasy. **de ~** fancy; <*joya*> imitation

fantasma *m* ghost

fantástico *a* fantastic

fardo *m* bundle

faringe *f* pharynx

farmac|eútico *m* chemist (Brit), pharmacist, druggist (Amer). **~ia** *f* (ciencia) pharmacy; (tienda) chemist's (shop) (Brit), pharmacy

faro *m* lighthouse; (Aviac) beacon; (Auto) headlight

farol *m* lantern; (de la calle) street lamp. **~a** *f* street lamp

farr|a *f* partying. **~ear** *vi* (LAm) go out partying

farsa *f* farce. **~nte** *m & f* fraud

fascículo *m* instalment

fascinar *vt* fascinate

fascis|mo *m* fascism. **~ta** *a & m & f* fascist

fase *f* phase

fastidi|ar *vt* annoy; (estropear) spoil. □ **~arse** *vpr* <*máquina*> break down; hurt <*pierna*>; (LAm, molestarse) get annoyed. **¡para que te ~es!** so there!. **~o** *m* nuisance; (aburrimiento) boredom. **~oso** *a* annoying

fatal *a* fateful; (mortal) fatal; (Ⓘ, pésimo) terrible. **~idad** *f* fate; (desgracia) misfortune

fatig|a *f* fatigue. **~ar** [12] *vt* tire. □ **~arse** *vpr* get tired. **~oso** *a* tiring

fauna *f* fauna

favor *m* favour. **a ~ de, en ~ de** in favour of. **haga el ~ de** would you be so kind as to, please. **por ~** please

favorec|er [11] *vt* favour; <*vestido, peinado etc*> suit. **~ido** *a* favoured

favorito *a & m* favourite

faz *f* face

fe *f* faith. **dar ~ de** certify. **de buena ~** in good faith

fealdad *f* ugliness

febrero *m* February

febril *a* feverish

fecha *f* date. **a estas ~s** now; (todavía) still. **hasta la ~** so far. **poner la ~** date. **~r** *vt* date

fecund|ación *f* fertilization **~ación artificial** artificial insemination. **~ar** *vt* fertilize. **~o** *a* fertile; (fig) prolific

federa|ción *f* federation. **~l** *a* federal

felici|dad *f* happiness. **~dades** *fpl* best wishes; (congratulaciones) congratulations. **~tación** *f* letter of congratulation. **¡~taciones!** (LAm) congratulations! **~tar** *vt* congratulate

feligrés *m* parishioner

feliz *a* happy; (afortunado) lucky. **¡Felices Pascuas!** Happy Christmas! **¡F~ Año Nuevo!** Happy New Year!

felpudo *m* doormat

fem|enil *a* (Mex) women's. **~inino** *a* feminine; <*equipo*> women's; (Biol, Bot) female. ● *m* feminine. **~inista** *a* & *m* & *f* feminist.

fen|omenal *a* phenomenal. **~ómeno** *m* phenomenon; (monstruo) freak

feo *a* ugly; (desagradable) nasty. ● *adv* (LAm, mal) bad

feria *f* fair; (verbena) carnival; (Mex, cambio) small change. **~do** *m* (LAm) public holiday

ferment|ar *vt/i* ferment. **~o** *m* ferment

fero|cidad *f* ferocity. **~z** *a* fierce

férreo *a* iron; <*disciplina*> strict

ferreter|ía *f* hardware store, ironmonger's (Brit). **~o** *m* hardware dealer, ironmonger (Brit)

ferro|carril *m* railway (Brit), railroad (Amer). **~viario** *a* rail. ● *m* railwayman (Brit), railroader (Amer)

fértil *a* fertile

fertili|dad *f* fertility. **~zante** *m* fertilizer. **~zar** [10] *vt* fertilize

ferv|iente *a* fervent. **~or** *m* fervour

festej|ar *vt* celebrate; entertain <*persona*>. **~o** *m* celebration

festiv|al *m* festival. **~idad** *f* festivity. **~o** *a* festive. ● *m* public holiday

fétido *a* stinking

feto *m* foetus

fiable *a* reliable

fiado *m*. **al ~** on credit. **~r** *m* (Jurid) guarantor

fiambre *m* cold meat. **~ría** *f* (LAm) delicatessen

fianza *f* (dinero) deposit; (objeto) surety. **bajo ~** on bail

fiar [20] *vt* (vender) sell on credit. ● *vi* give credit. **ser de ~** be trustworthy. □ **~se** *vpr*. **~se de** trust

fibra *f* fibre. **~ de vidrio** fibreglass

fic|ción *f* fiction. **~ticio** *a* fictitious; (falso) false

fich|a *f* token; (tarjeta) index card; (en juegos) counter. **~ar** *vt* open a file on. **estar ~ado** have a (police) record. **~ero** *m* card index

fidedigno *a* reliable

fidelidad *f* faithfulness. **alta ~** hi-fi [T], high fidelity

fideos *mpl* noodles

fiebre *f* fever. **~ del heno** hay fever. **tener ~** have a temperature

fiel *a* faithful; <*memoria, relato etc*> reliable. ● *m* believer; (de balanza) needle. **los ~es** the faithful

fieltro *m* felt

fier|a *f* wild animal. **~o** *a* fierce

fierro *m* (LAm) metal bar; (hierro) iron

fiesta *f* party; (día festivo) holiday. **~s** *fpl* celebrations

figura *f* figure; (forma) shape. **~r** *vi* appear; (destacar) show off. □ **~rse** *vpr* imagine. **¡figúrate!** just imagine!

fij|ación *f* fixing; (obsesión) fixation. **~ar** *vt* fix; establish <*residencia*>. □ **~arse** *vpr* (poner atención) pay attention; (percatarse) notice. **¡fíjate!** just imagine! **~o** *a* fixed; (firme) stable; (permanente) permanent. ● *adv*. **mirar ~o** stare

fila *f* line; (de soldados etc) file; (en el teatro, cine etc) row; (cola) queue. **ponerse en ~** line up

filántropo *m* philanthropist

filat|elia *f* stamp collecting, philately. **~élico** *a* philatelic. ● *m* stamp collector, philatelist

filete *m* fillet

filial *a* filial. ● *f* subsidiary

Filipinas *fpl*. **las (islas) ~** the Philippines

filipino *a* Philippine, Filipino

filmar *vt* film; shoot <*película*>

filo *m* edge; (de hoja) cutting edge. **al ~ de las doce** at exactly twelve o'clock. **sacar ~ a** sharpen

filología *f* philology

filón *m* vein; (fig) gold-mine

fil|osofía *f* philosophy. **~ósofo** *m* philosopher

filtr|ar *vt* filter. □ **~arse** *vpr* filter; <*dinero*> disappear; <*noticia*> leak. **~o** *m* filter; (bebida) philtre. **~ solar** sunscreen

fin *m* end; (objetivo) aim. **~ de semana** weekend. **a ~ de** in order to. **a ~ de cuentas** at the end of the day. **a ~ de que** in order that. **a ~es de** at the end of. **al ~** finally. **al ~ y al cabo** after all. **dar ~ a** end. **en ~** in short. **por ~** finally. **sin ~** endless

final *a* final. ● *m* end. ● *f* final. **~idad** *f* aim. **~ista** *m & f* finalist. **~izar** [10] *vt* finish. ● *vi* end

financi|ación *f* financing; (fondos) funds; (facilidades) credit facilities. **~ar** *vt* finance. **~ero** *a* financial. ● *m* financier

finca *f* property; (tierras) estate; (rural) farm; (de recreo) country house

fingir [14] *vt* feign; (simular) simulate. ● *vi* pretend. □ **~se** *vpr* pretend to be

finlandés *a* Finnish. ● *m* (persona) Finn; (lengua) Finnish

Finlandia *f* Finland

fino *a* fine; (delgado) thin; <*oído*> acute; (de modales) refined; (sútil) subtle

firma *f* signature; (acto) signing; (empresa) firm

firmar *vt/i* sign

firme *a* firm; (estable) stable, steady; <*color*> fast. ● *m* (pavimento) (road) surface. ● *adv* hard. **~za** *f* firmness

fisc|al *a* fiscal, tax. ● *m & f* public prosecutor. **~o** *m* treasury

fisg|ar [12] *vi* snoop (around). **~ón** *a* nosy. ● *m* snooper

físic|a *f* physics. **~o** *a* physical. ● *m* physique; (persona) physicist

fisonomista *m & f*. **ser buen ~** be good at remembering faces

fistol *m* (Mex) tiepin

flaco *a* thin, skinny; (débil) weak

flagelo *m* scourge

flagrante *a* flagrant. **en ~** red-handed

flama *f* (Mex) flame

flamante *a* splendid; (nuevo) brand-new

flamear *vi* flame; <*bandera etc*> flap

flamenco *a* flamenco; (de Flandes) Flemish. ● *m* (ave) flamingo; (música etc) flamenco; (idioma) Flemish

flan *m* crème caramel

flaqueza *f* thinness; (debilidad) weakness

flauta *f* flute

flecha *f* arrow. **~zo** *m* love at first sight

fleco *m* fringe; (Mex, en el pelo) fringe (Brit), bangs (Amer)

flem|a *f* phlegm. **~ático** *a* phlegmatic

flequillo *m* fringe (Brit), bangs (Amer)

fletar *vt* charter; (LAm, transportar) transport

flexible *a* flexible

flirte|ar *vi* flirt. **~o** *m* flirting

floj|ear *vi* flag; (holgazanear) laze around. **~o** *a* loose; (poco fuerte) weak; (perezoso) lazy

flor *f* flower. **la ~ y nata** the cream. **~a** *f* flora. **~ecer** [11] *vi* flower, bloom; (fig) flourish. **~eciente** *a* (fig) flourishing. **~ero** *m* flower vase. **~ista** *m & f* florist

flot|a *f* fleet. **~ador** *m* float; (de niño) rubber band. **~ar** *vi* float. **~e** *m*. **a ~e** afloat

fluctua|ción *f* fluctuation. **~r** [21] *vi* fluctuate

flu|idez *f* fluidity; (fig) fluency. **~ido** *a* fluid; (fig) fluent. ● *m* fluid. **~ir** [17] *vi* flow

fluoruro *m* fluoride

fluvial *a* river

fobia *f* phobia

foca *f* seal

foco *m* focus; (lámpara) floodlight; (LAm, de coche) (head)light; (Mex, bombilla) light bulb

fogón *m* cooker; (LAm, fogata) bonfire

folio *m* sheet

folklórico *a* folk

follaje *m* foliage

follet|ín *m* newspaper serial. **~o** *m* pamphlet

follón *m* [I] mess; (alboroto) row; (problema) trouble

fomentar *vt* promote; boost <*ahorro*>; stir up <*odio*>

fonda *f* (pensión) boarding-house; (LAm, restaurant) cheap restaurant

fondo *m* bottom; (de calle, pasillo) end; (de sala etc) back; (de escenario, pintura etc) background. **~s** *mpl* funds, money. **a ~** thoroughly. **en el ~** deep down

fonétic|a *f* phonetics. **~o** *a* phonetic

fontanero *m* plumber

footing /'futin/ *m* jogging

forastero *m* stranger

forcejear *vi* struggle

forense *a* forensic. ● *m & f* forensic scientist

forjar *vt* forge. □ **~se** *vpr* forge; build up <*ilusiones*>

forma *f* form; (contorno) shape; (modo) way; (Mex, formulario) form. **~s** *fpl* conventions. **de todas ~s** anyway. **estar en ~** be in good form. **~ción** *f* formation; (educación) training. **~l** *a* formal; (de fiar) reliable; (serio) serious. **~lidad** *f* formality; (fiabilidad) reliability; (seriedad) seriousness. **~r** *vt* form; (componer) make up; (enseñar) train. □ **~rse** *vpr* form; (desarrollarse) develop; (educarse) to be educated. **~to** *m* format

formidable *a* formidable; (muy grande) enormous

fórmula *f* formula; (sistema) way. **~ de cortesía** polite expression

formular *vt* formulate; make <*queja etc*>. **~io** *m* form

fornido *a* well-built

forr|ar *vt* (en el interior) line; (en el exterior) cover. **~o** *m* lining; (cubierta) cover

fortale|cer [11] *vt* strengthen. **~za** *f* strength; (Mil) fortress; (fuerza moral) fortitude

fortuito *a* fortuitous; *<encuentro>* chance

fortuna *f* fortune; (suerte) luck

forz|ar [2 & 10] *vt* force; strain *<vista>*. **~osamente** *adv* necessarily. **~oso** *a* necessary

fosa *f* ditch; (tumba) grave. **~s nasales** nostrils

fósforo *m* phosphorus; (cerilla) match

fósil *a & m* fossil

foso *m* ditch; (en castillo) moat; (de teatro) pit

foto *f* photo. **sacar ~s** take photos

fotocopia *f* photocopy. **~dora** *f* photocopier. **~r** *vt* photocopy

fotogénico *a* photogenic

fot|ografía *f* photography; (Foto) photograph. **~ografiar** [20] *vt* photograph. **~ógrafo** *m* photographer

foul /faʊl/ *m* (*pl* **~s**) (LAm) foul

frac *m* (*pl* **~s** *o* **fraques**) tails

fracas|ar *vi* fail. **~o** *m* failure

fracción *f* fraction; (Pol) faction

fractura *f* fracture. **~r** *vt* fracture. ▫ **~rse** *vpr* fracture

fragan|cia *f* fragrance. **~te** *a* fragrant

frágil *a* fragile

fragmento *m* fragment; (de canción etc) extract

fragua *f* forge. **~r** [15] *vt* forge; (fig) concoct. ● *vi* set

fraile *m* friar; (monje) monk

frambuesa *f* raspberry

franc|és *a* French. ● *m* (persona) Frenchman; (lengua) French. **~esa** *f* Frenchwoman

Francia *f* France

franco *a* frank; (evidente) marked; (Com) free. ● *m* (moneda) franc

francotirador *m* sniper

franela *f* flannel

franja *f* border; (banda) stripe; (de terreno) strip

franque|ar *vt* clear; (atravesar) cross; pay the postage on *<carta>*. **~o** *m* postage

franqueza *f* frankness

frasco *m* bottle; (de mermelada etc) jar

frase *f* phrase; (oración) sentence. **~ hecha** set phrase

fratern|al *a* fraternal. **~idad** *f* fraternity

fraud|e *m* fraud. **~ulento** *a* fraudulent

fray *m* brother, friar

frecuen|cia *f* frequency. **con ~cia** frequently. **~tar** *vt* frequent. **~te** *a* frequent

frega|dero *m* sink. **~r** [1 & 12] *vt* scrub; wash *<los platos>*; mop *<el suelo>*; (LAm, 🅃, molestar) annoy

freír [51] (*pp* **frito**) *vt* fry. ▫ **~se** *vpr* fry; *<persona>* roast

frenar *vt* brake; (fig) check

frenético *a* frenzied; (furioso) furious

freno *m* (de caballería) bit; (Auto) brake; (fig) check

frente *m* front. **~ a** opposite. **~ a ~** face to face. **al ~** at the head; (hacia delante) forward. **chocar de ~** crash head on. **de ~ a** (LAm) facing. **hacer ~ a** face *<cosa>*; stand up to *<persona>*. ● *f* forehead. **arrugar la ~** frown

fresa *f* strawberry

fresc|o *a* (frío) cool; (reciente) fresh; (descarado) cheeky. ● *m* fresh air; (frescor) coolness; (mural) fresco; (persona) impudent person. **al ~o** in the open air. **hacer ~o** be cool. **tomar el ~o** get some fresh air. **~or** *m* coolness. **~ura** *f* freshness; (frío) coolness; (descaro) cheek

frialdad *f* coldness; (fig) indifference

fricci|ón *f* rubbing; (fig, Tec) friction; (masaje) massage. **~onar** *vt* rub

frigidez *f* frigidity

frígido *a* frigid

frigorífico *m* fridge, refrigerator

frijol *m* (LAm) bean. **~es refritos** (Mex) fried purée of beans

frío *a & m* cold. **tomar ~** catch cold. **hacer ~** be cold. **tener ~** be cold

frito *a* fried; (I, harto) fed up. **me tiene ~** I'm sick of him

fr|ivolidad *f* frivolity. **~ívolo** *a* frivolous

fronter|a *f* border, frontier. **~izo** *a* border; <*país*> bordering

frontón *m* pelota court; (pared) fronton

frotar *vt* rub; strike <*cerilla*>

fructífero *a* fruitful

fruncir [9] *vt* gather <*tela*>. **~ el ceño** frown

frustra|ción *f* frustration. **~r** *vt* frustrate. □ **~rse** *vpr* (fracasar) fail. **quedar ~do** be disappointed

frut|a *f* fruit. **~al** *a* fruit. **~ería** *f* fruit shop. **~ero** *m* fruit seller; (recipiente) fruit bowl. **~icultura** *f* fruit-growing. **~o** *m* fruit

fucsia *f* fuchsia. ● *m* fuchsia

fuego *m* fire. **~s artificiales** fireworks. **a ~ lento** on a low heat. **tener ~** have a light

fuente *f* fountain; (manantial) spring; (plato) serving dish; (fig) source

fuera *adv* out; (al exterior) outside; (en otra parte) away; (en el extranjero) abroad. **~ de** outside; (excepto) except for, besides. **por ~** on the outside. ● *vb* ⇒IR y SER

fuerte *a* strong; <*color*> bright; <*sonido*> loud; <*dolor*> severe; (duro) hard; (grande) large; <*lluvia, nevada*> heavy. ● *m* fort; (fig) strong point. ● *adv* hard; (con hablar etc) loudly; <*llover*> heavily; (mucho) a lot

fuerza *f* strength; (poder) power; (en física) force; (Mil) forces. **~ de voluntad** will-power. **a ~ de** by (dint of). **a la ~** by necessity. **por ~** by force; (por necesidad) by necessity. **tener ~s para** have the strength to

fuese *vb* ⇒IR *y* SER

fug|a *f* flight, escape; (de gas etc) leak; (Mus) fugue. □ **~arse** [12] *vpr* flee, escape. **~az** *a* fleeting. **~itivo** *a & m* fugitive

fui *vb* ⇒IR, SER

fulano *m* so-and-so. **~, mengano y zutano** every Tom, Dick and Harry

fulminar *vt* (fig, con mirada) look daggers at

fuma|dor *a* smoking. ● *m* smoker. **~r** *vt/i* smoke. **~r en pipa** smoke a pipe. □ **~rse** *vpr* smoke. **~rada** *f* puff of smoke

funci|ón *f* function; (de un cargo etc) duty; (de teatro) show, performance. **~onal** *a* functional. **~onar** *vi* work, function. **no ~ona** out of order. **~onario** *m* civil servant

funda *f* cover. ~ **de almohada** pillowcase

funda|ción *f* foundation. **~mental** *a* fundamental. **~mentar** *vt* base (**en** on). **~mento** *m* foundation. **~r** *vt* found; (fig) base. □ **~rse** *vpr* be based

fundi|ción *f* melting; (de metales) smelting; (taller) foundry. **~r** *vt* melt; smelt <*metales*>; cast <*objeto*>; blend <*colores*>; (fusionar) merge; (Elec) blow; (LAm) seize up <*motor*>. □ **~rse** *vpr* melt; (unirse) merge

fúnebre *a* funeral; (sombrío) gloomy

funeral *a* funeral. ● *m* funeral. **~es** *mpl* funeral

funicular *a* & *m* funicular

furg|ón *m* van. **~oneta** *f* van

fur|ia *f* fury; (violencia) violence. **~ibundo** *a* furious. **~ioso** *a* furious. **~or** *m* fury

furtivo *a* furtive. **cazador ~** poacher

furúnculo *m* boil

fusible *m* fuse

fusil *m* rifle. **~ar** *vt* shoot

fusión *f* melting; (unión) fusion; (Com) merger

fútbol *m*, (Mex) **futbol** *m* football

futbolista *m* & *f* footballer

futur|ista *a* futuristic. ● *m* & *f* futurist. **~o** *a* & *m* future

Gg

gabardina *f* raincoat

gabinete *m* (Pol) cabinet; (en museo etc) room; (de dentista, médico etc) consulting room

gaceta *f* gazette

gafa *f* hook. **~s** *fpl* glasses, spectacles. **~s de sol** sunglasses

gaf|ar *vt* 🅸 bring bad luck to. **~e** *m* jinx

gaita *f* bagpipes

gajo *m* segment

gala *f* gala. **~s** *fpl* finery, best clothes. **estar de ~** be dressed up. **hacer ~ de** show off

galán *m* (en el teatro) (romantic) hero; (enamorado) lover

galante *a* gallant. **~ar** *vt* court. **~ría** *f* gallantry

galápago *m* turtle

galardón *m* award

galaxia *f* galaxy

galera *f* galley

galer|ía *f* gallery. **~ía comercial** (shopping) arcade. **~ón** *m* (Mex) hall

Gales *m* Wales. **país de ~** Wales

gal|és *a* Welsh. ● *m* Welshman; (lengua) Welsh. **~esa** *f* Welshwoman

galgo *m* greyhound

Galicia *f* Galicia

galimatías *m invar* gibberish

gallard|ía *f* elegance. **~o** *a* elegant

gallego *a* & *m* Galician

galleta *f* biscuit (Brit), cookie (Amer)

gall|ina *f* hen, chicken; (fig, [I]) coward. **~o** *m* cock

galón *m* gallon; (cinta) braid; (Mil) stripe

galop|ar *vi* gallop. **~e** *m* gallop

gama *f* scale; (fig) range

gamba *f* prawn (Brit), shrimp (Amer)

gamberro *m* hooligan

gamuza *f* (piel) chamois leather; (de otro animal) suede

gana *f* wish, desire; (apetito) appetite. **de buena ~** willingly. **de mala ~** reluctantly. **no me da la ~** I don't feel like it. **tener ~s de** (+ *infinitivo*) feel like (+ *gerundio*)

ganad|ería *f* cattle raising; (ganado) livestock. **~o** *m* livestock. **~o lanar** sheep. **~o porcino** pigs. **~o vacuno** cattle

gana|dor *a* winning. ● *m* winner. **~ncia** *f* gain; (Com) profit. **~r** *vt* earn; (en concurso, juego etc) win; (alcanzar) reach. ● *vi* (vencer) win; (mejorar) improve. **~rle a uno** beat s.o. **~rse la vida** earn a living. **salir ~ndo** come out better off

ganch|illo *m* crochet. **hacer ~illo** crochet. **~o** *m* hook; (LAm, colgador) hanger. **tener ~o** be very attractive

ganga *f* bargain

ganso *m* goose

garabat|ear *vt/i* scribble. **~o** *m* scribble

garaje *m* garage

garant|e *m & f* guarantor. **~ía** *f* guarantee. **~izar** [10] *vt* guarantee

garapiña *f* (Mex) pineapple squash. **~do** *a*. **almendras** *fpl* **~das** sugared almonds

garbanzo *m* chick-pea

garbo *m* poise; (de escrito) style. **~so** *a* elegant

garganta *f* throat; (Geog) gorge

gárgaras *fpl*. **hacer ~** gargle

garita *f* hut; (de centinela) sentry box

garra *f* (de animal) claw; (de ave) talon

garrafa *f* carafe

garrafal *a* huge

garrapata *f* tick

garrapat|ear *vi* scribble. **~o** *m* scribble

garrote *m* club, cudgel; (tormento) garrotte

gar|úa *f* (LAm) drizzle. **~uar** *vi* [21] (LAm) drizzle

garza *f* heron

gas *m* gas. **con ~** fizzy. **sin ~** still

gasa *f* gauze

gaseosa *f* fizzy drink

gas|óleo *m* diesel. **~olina** *f* petrol (Brit), gasoline (Amer), gas (Amer). **~olinera** *f* petrol station (Brit), gas station (Amer)

gast|ado *a* spent; <*vestido etc*> worn out. **~ador** *m* spendthrift. **~ar** *vt* spend; (consumir) use; (malgastar) waste; (desgastar) wear out; wear <*vestido etc*>; crack <*broma*>. □ **~arse** *vpr* wear out. **~o** *m* expense; (acción de gastar) spending

gastronomía *f* gastronomy

gat|a *f* cat. **a ~as** on all fours. **~ear** *vi* crawl

gatillo *m* trigger

gat|ito *m* kitten. **~o** *m* cat. **dar ~o por liebre** take s.o. in

gaucho *m* Gaucho

gaveta *f* drawer

gaviota *f* seagull

gazpacho *m* gazpacho

gelatina *f* gelatine; (jalea) jelly

gema *f* gem

gemelo *m* twin. **~s** *mpl* (anteojos) binoculars; (de camisa) cuff-links

gemido *m* groan

Géminis *m* Gemini

gemir [5] *vi* moan; <*animal*> whine, howl

gen *m*, **gene** *m* gene

geneal|ogía *f* genealogy. **~ógico** *a* genealogical. **árbol** *m* **~ógico** family tree

generaci|ón *f* generation. **~onal** *a* generation

general *a* general. **en ~** in general. **por lo ~** generally. ● *m* general. **~izar** [10] *vt/i* generalize. **~mente** *adv* generally

generar *vt* generate

género *m* type, sort; (Biol) genus; (Gram) gender; (en literatura etc) genre; (producto) product; (tela) material. **~s de punto** knitwear. **~ humano** mankind

generos|idad *f* generosity. **~o** *a* generous

genétic|a *f* genetics. **~o** *a* genetic

geni|al *a* brilliant; (divertido) funny. **~o** *m* temper; (carácter) nature; (talento, persona) genius

genital *a* genital. **~es** *mpl* genitals

gente *f* people; (nación) nation; ([I], familia) family, folks; (Mex, persona) person. ● *a* (LAm) respectable; (amable) kind

gentil *a* charming. **~eza** *f* kindness. **tener la ~eza de** be kind enough to

gentío *m* crowd

genuflexión *f* genuflection

genuino *a* genuine

ge|ografía *f* geography. **~ográfico** *a* geographical.

ge|ología *f* geology. **~ólogo** *m* geologist

geom|etría *f* geometry. **~étrico** *a* geometrical

geranio *m* geranium

geren|cia *f* management. **~ciar** *vt* (LAm) manage. **~te** *m & f* manager

germen *m* germ

germinar *vi* germinate

gestación *f* gestation

gesticula|ción *f* gesticulation. **~r** *vi* gesticulate

gesti|ón *f* step; (administración) management. **~onar** *vt* take steps to arrange; (dirigir) manage

gesto *m* expression; (ademán) gesture; (mueca) grimace

gibraltareño *a & m* Gibraltarian

gigante *a* gigantic. ● *m* giant. **~sco** *a* gigantic

gimn|asia *f* gymnastics. **~asio** *m* gymnasium, gym [I]. **~asta** *m & f* gymnast. **~ástic** *a* gymnastic

gimotear *vi* whine

ginebra *f* gin

ginecólogo *m* gynaecologist

gira *f* tour. **~r** *vt* spin; draw <*cheque*>; transfer <*dinero*>. ● *vi* rotate, go round; <*en camino*> turn

girasol *m* sunflower

gir|atorio *a* revolving. **~o** *m* turn; (Com) draft; (locución) expression. **~o postal** money order

gitano *a & m* gypsy

glacia|l *a* icy. **~r** *m* glacier

glándula *f* gland

glasear *vt* glaze; (Culin) ice

glob|al *a* global; (fig) overall. **~o** *m* globe; (aerostato, juguete) balloon

glóbulo *m* globule

gloria *f* glory; (placer) delight. □ **~rse** *vpr* boast (**de** about)

glorieta *f* square; (Auto) roundabout (Brit), (traffic) circle (Amer)

glorificar [7] *vt* glorify

glorioso *a* glorious

glotón *a* gluttonous. ● *m* glutton

gnomo /'nomo/ *m* gnome

gob|ernación *f* government. **Ministerio** *m* **de la G~ernación** Home Office (Brit), Department of the Interior (Amer). **~ernador** *a* governing. ● *m* governor. **~ernante** *a* governing. ● *m* & *f* leader. **~ernar** [1] *vt* govern. **~ierno** *m* government

goce *m* enjoyment

gol *m* goal

golf *m* golf

golfo *m* gulf; (niño) urchin; (holgazán) layabout

golondrina *f* swallow

golos|ina *f* titbit; (dulce) sweet. **~o** *a* fond of sweets

golpe *m* blow; (puñetazo) punch; (choque) bump; (de emoción) shock; (⊠, atraco) job ⊡; (en golf, en tenis, de remo) stroke. **~ de estado** coup d'etat. **~ de fortuna** stroke of luck. **~ de vista** glance. **~ militar** military coup. **de ~** suddenly. **de un ~** in one go. **~ar** *vt* hit; (dar varios golpes) beat; (con mucho ruido) bang; (con el puño) punch. ● *vi* knock

goma *f* rubber; (para pegar) glue; (banda) rubber band; (de borrar) eraser. **~a de mascar** chewing gum. **~a espuma** foam rubber

gord|a *f* (Mex) small thick tortilla. **~o** *a* <*persona*> (con ser) fat; (con estar) have put on weight; <*carne*> fatty; (grueso) thick; (grande) large, big. ● *m* first prize. **~ura** *f* fatness; (grasa) fat

gorila *f* gorilla

gorje|ar *vi* chirp. **~o** *m* chirping

gorra *f* cap. **~ de baño** (LAm) bathing cap

gorrión *m* sparrow

gorro *m* cap; (de niño) bonnet. **~ de baño** bathing cap

got|a *f* drop; (Med) gout. **ni ~a** nothing. **~ear** *vi* drip. **~era** *f* leak

gozar [10] *vt* enjoy. ● *vi*. **~ de** enjoy

gozne *m* hinge

gozo *m* pleasure; (alegría) joy. **~so** *a* delighted

graba|ción *f* recording. **~do** *m* engraving, print; (en libro) illustration. **~dora** *f* tape-recorder. **~r** *vt* engrave; record <*discos etc*>

graci|a *f* grace; (favor) favour; (humor) wit. **~as** *fpl* thanks. **¡~as!** thank you!, thanks! **dar las ~as** thank. **hacer ~a** amuse; (gustar) please. **¡muchas ~as!** thank you very much! **tener ~a** be funny. **~oso** *a* funny. ● *m* fool, comic character

grad|a *f* step. **~as** *fpl* stand(s). **~ación** *f* gradation. **~o** *m* degree; (Escol) year (Brit), grade (Amer). **de buen ~o** willingly

gradua|ción *f* graduation; (de alcohol) proof. **~do** *m* graduate. **~l** *a* gradual. **~r** [21] *vt* graduate; (regular) adjust. □ **~rse** *vpr* graduate

gráfic|a *f* graph. **~o** *a* graphic. ● *m* graph

gram|ática *f* grammar. **~atical** *a* grammatical

gramo *m* gram, gramme (Brit)

gran *a véase* GRANDE

grana *f* (color) deep red

granada *f* pomegranate; (Mil) grenade

granate *m* (color) maroon

Gran Bretaña *f* Great Britain

grande *a* (*delante de nombre en singular* **gran**) big, large; (alto) tall; (fig) great; (LAm, de edad) grown up. **~za** *f* greatness

grandioso *a* magnificent

granel *m*. **a ~** in bulk; (suelto) loose; (fig) in abundance

granero *m* barn

granito *m* granite; (grano) small grain

graniz|ado *m* iced drink. **~ar** [10] *vi* hail. **~o** *m* hail

granj|a *f* farm. **~ero** *m* farmer

grano *m* grain; (semilla) seed; (de café) bean; (Med) spot. **~s** *mpl* cereals

granuja *m & f* rogue

grapa *f* staple. **~r** *vt* staple

gras|a *f* grease; (Culin) fat. **~iento** *a* greasy

gratifica|ción *f* (de sueldo) bonus (recompensa) reward. **~r** [7] *vt* reward

grat|is *adv* free. **~itud** *f* gratitude. **~o** *a* pleasant **~uito** *a* free; (fig) uncalled for

grava|men *m* tax; (carga) burden; (sobre inmueble) encumbrance. **~r** *vt* tax; (cargar) burden

grave *a* serious; <*voz*> deep; <*sonido*> low; <*acento*> grave. **~dad** *f* gravity

gravilla *f* gravel

gravitar *vi* gravitate; (apoyarse) rest (**sobre** on); <*peligro*> hang (**sobre** over)

gravoso *a* costly

graznar *vi* <*cuervo*> caw; <*pato*> quack; honk <*ganso*>

Grecia *f* Greece

gremio *m* union

greña *f* mop of hair

gresca *f* rumpus; (riña) quarrel

griego *a & m* Greek

grieta *f* crack

grifo *m* tap, faucet (Amer)

grilletes *mpl* shackles

grillo *m* cricket. **~s** *mpl* shackles

gringo *m* (LAm) foreigner; (norteamericano) Yankee 🄸

gripe *f* flu

gris *a* grey. ● *m* grey; (🄸, policía) policeman

grit|ar *vi* shout. **~ería** *f*, **~erío** *m* uproar. **~o** *m* shout; (de dolor, sorpresa) cry; (chillido) scream. **dar ~s** shout

grosella *f* redcurrant. **~ negra** blackcurrant

groser|ía *f* rudeness; (ordinariez) coarseness; (comentario etc) coarse remark; (palabra) swearword. **~o** *a* coarse; (descortés) rude

grosor *m* thickness

grotesco *a* grotesque

grúa *f* crane

grueso *a* thick; <*persona*> fat, stout. ● *m* thickness; (fig) main body

grumo *m* lump

gruñi|do *m* grunt; (de perro) growl. **~r** [22] *vi* grunt; <*perro*> growl

grupa *f* hindquarters

grupo *m* group

gruta *f* grotto

guacamole *m* guacamole

guadaña *f* scythe

guaje *m* (Mex) gourd

guajolote *m* (Mex) turkey

guante *m* glove

guapo *a* good-looking; <*chica*> pretty; (elegante) smart

guarda *m & f* guard; (de parque etc) keeper. **~barros** *m invar* mudguard. **~bosque** *m* gamekeeper.

~costas *m invar* coastguard vessel. **~espaldas** *m invar* bodyguard. **~meta** *m* goalkeeper. **~r** *vt* keep; (proteger) protect; (en un lugar) put away; (reservar) save, keep. □ **~rse** *vpr*. **~rse de** (+ *infinitivo*) avoid (+ *gerundio*). **~rropa** *m* wardrobe; (en local público) cloakroom. **~vallas** *m invar* (LAm) goalkeeper

guardería *f* nursery

guardia *f* guard; (policía) policewoman; (de médico) shift. **G~ Civil** Civil Guard. **~ municipal** police. **estar de ~** be on duty. **estar en ~** be on one's guard. **montar la ~** mount guard. ● *m* policeman. **~ jurado** *m & f* security guard. **~ de tráfico** *m* traffic policeman. ● *f* traffic policewoman

guardián *m* guardian; (de parque etc) keeper; (de edificio) security guard

guar|ecer [11] *vt* (albergar) give shelter to. □ **~ecerse** *vpr* take shelter. **~ida** *f* den, lair; (de personas) hideout

guarn|ecer [11] *vt* (adornar) adorn; (Culin) garnish. **~ición** *m* adornment; (de caballo) harness; (Culin) garnish; (Mil) garrison; (de piedra preciosa) setting

guas|a *f* joke. **~ón** *a* humorous. ● *m* joker

Guatemala *f* Guatemala

guatemalteco *a & m* Guatemalan

guateque *m* party, bash

guayab|a *f* guava; (dulce) guava jelly. **~era** *f* lightweight jacket

gubernatura *f* (Mex) government

güero *a* (Mex) fair

guerr|a *f* war; (método) warfare. **dar ~a** annoy. **~ero** *a* warlike; (belico so) fighting. ● *m* warrior. **~illa** *f* band of guerrillas. **~illero** *m* guerrilla

guía *m & f* guide. ● *f* guidebook; (de teléfonos) directory

guiar [20] *vt* guide; (llevar) lead; (Auto) drive. □ **~se** *vpr* be guided (**por** by)

guijarro *m* pebble

guillotina *f* guillotine

guind|a *f* morello cherry. **~illa** *f* chilli

guiñapo *m* rag; (fig, persona) wreck

guiñ|ar *vt/i* wink. **~o** *m* wink. **hacer ~os** wink

gui|ón *m* hyphen, dash; (de película etc) script. **~onista** *m & f* scriptwriter

guirnalda *f* garland

guisado *m* stew

guisante *m* pea. **~ de olor** sweet pea

guis|ar *vt/i* cook. **~o** *m* stew

guitarr|a *f* guitar. **~ista** *m & f* guitarist

gula *f* gluttony

gusano *m* worm; (larva de mosca) maggot

gustar

● *verbo intransitivo*

! Cuando el verbo **gustar** va precedido del complemento indirecto **le** (o **les**, **nos** etc), el sujeto en español pasa a ser el objeto en inglés. **me gusta mucho la música** *I like music very much.* **le gustan los helados** *he likes ice cream.* **a Juan**

no le gusta *Juan doesn't like it* (or *her* etc)

····➤ **gustar** + *infinitivo*. **les gusta ver televisión** they like watching television

····➤ **gustar que** + *subjuntivo*. **me ~ía que vinieras** I'd like you to come. **no le gusta que lo corrijan** he doesn't like being corrected. **¿te ~ía que te lo comprara?** would you like me to buy it for you?

····➤ **gustar de algo** to like sth. **gustan de las fiestas** they like parties

····➤ (tener acogida) to go down well. **ese tipo de cosas siempre gusta** those sort of things always go down well. **el libro no gustó** the book didn't go down well

····➤ (en frases de cortesía) to wish. **como guste** as you wish. **cuando gustes** whenever you wish

● *verbo transitivo*

····➤ (LAm, querer) **¿gusta un café?** would you like a coffee? **¿gustan pasar?** would you like to come in?

□ **gustarse** *verbo pronominal* to like each other

gusto *m* taste; (placer) pleasure. **a ~** comfortable. **a mi ~** to my liking. **buen ~** good taste. **con mucho ~** with pleasure. **dar ~** please. **mucho ~** pleased to meet you. **~so** *a* tasty; (de buen grado) willingly

gutural *a* guttural

Hh

ha *vb* ⇒HABER

haba *f* broad bean

Habana *f*. **La ~** Havana

habano *m* (puro) Havana

haber *v aux* [30] have. ● *v impersonal* (*presente s & pl* **hay**, *imperfecto s & pl* **había**, *pretérito s & pl* **hubo**). **hay una carta para ti** there's a letter for you. **hay 5 bancos en la plaza** there are 5 banks in the square. **hay quehacerlo** it must be done, you have to do it. **he aquí** here is, here are. **no hay de qué** don't mention it, not at all. **¿qué hay?** (¿qué pasa?) what's the matter?; (¿qué tal?) how are you?

habichuela *f* bean

hábil *a* skilful; (listo) clever; <*día*> working; (Jurid) competent

habili|dad *f* skill; (astucia) cleverness; (Jurid) competence. **~tar** *vt* qualify

habita|ción *f* room; (dormitorio) bedroom; (en biología) habitat. **~ción de matrimonio**, **~ción doble** double room. **~ción individual**, **~ción sencilla** single room. **~do** *a* inhabited. **~nte** *m* inhabitant. **~r** *vt* live in. ● *vi* live

hábito *m* habit

habitua|l *a* usual, habitual; <*cliente*> regular. **~r** [21] *vt* accustom. □ **~rse** *vpr*. **~rse a** get used to

habla *f* speech; (idioma) language; (dialecto) dialect. **al ~** (al teléfono) speaking. **ponerse al ~ con** get in touch with. **~dor** *a* talkative. ● *m* chatterbox. **~duría** *f* rumour. **~durías** *fpl* gossip. **~nte** *a* speaking. ● *m & f* speaker. **~r** *vt* speak. ● *vi* speak, talk (**con** to); (Mex, por teléfono) call. **¡ni ~r!** out of the question! **se ~ español** Spanish spoken

hacend|ado *m* landowner; (LAm) farmer. **~oso** *a* hard-working

hacer [31]

● *verbo transitivo*

····➤ to do. **¿qué haces?** what are you doing? **~ los deberes** to do one's homework. **no sé qué ~** I don't know what to do. **hazme un favor** can you do me a favour?

····➤ (fabricar, preparar, producir) to make. **me hizo un vestido** she made me a dress. **~ un café** to make a (cup of) coffee. **no hagas tanto ruido** don't make so much noise

····➤ (construir) to build *<casa, puente>*

····➤ **hacer que uno haga algo** to make s.o. do sth. **haz que se vaya** make him leave. **hizo que se equivocara** he made her go wrong

····➤ **hacer hacer algo** to have sth done. **hizo arreglar el techo** he had the roof repaired

➡ Cuando el verbo **hacer** se emplea en expresiones como **hacer una pregunta, hacer trampa** etc., ver bajo el respectivo nombre

● *verbo intransitivo*

····➤ (actuar, obrar) to do. **hiciste bien en llamar** you did the right thing to call. **¿cómo haces para parecer tan joven?** what do you do to look so young?

····➤ (fingir, simular) **hacer como que** to pretend. **hizo como que no me conocía** he pretended not to know me. **haz como que estás dormido** pretend you're asleep

····➤ **hacer de** (en teatro) to play the part of; (ejercer la función de) to act as

····➤ (LAm, sentar) **tanta sal hace mal** so much salt is not good for you. **dormir le hizo bien** the sleep did him good. **el pepino me hace mal** cucumber doesn't agree with me

● *verbo impersonal*

····➤ (hablando del tiempo atmosférico) to be. **hace sol** it's sunny. **hace 3 grados** it's 3 degrees

····➤ (con expresiones temporales) **hace una hora que espero** I've been waiting for an hour. **llegó hace 3 días** he arrived 3 days ago. **hace mucho tiempo** a long time ago. **hasta hace poco** until recently

□ **hacerse** *verbo pronominal*

····➤ (para sí) to make o.s. *<falda, café>*

····➤ (hacer que otro haga) **se hizo la permanente** she had her hair permed. **me hice una piscina** I had a swimming pool built

····➤ (convertirse en) to become. **se hicieron amigos** they became friends

····➤ (acostumbrarse) **~se a algo** to get used to sth

····➤ (fingirse) to pretend. **~se el enfermo** to pretend to be ill

····➤ (moverse) to move. **hazte para atrás** move back

····➤ **hacerse de** (LAm) to make *<amigo, dinero>*

hacha *f* axe; (antorcha) torch

hacia *prep* towards; (cerca de) near; (con tiempo) at about. ~ **abajo** downwards. ~ **arriba** upwards. ~ **atrás** backwards. ~ **las dos** (at) about two o'clock

hacienda *f* country estate; (en LAm) ranch; **la ~ pública** the Treasury. **Ministerio** *m* **de H~** Ministry of Finance; (en Gran Bretaña) Exchequer; (en Estados Unidos) Treasury

hada *f* fairy. **el ~ madrina** the fairy godmother

hago *vb* ⇒HACER

Haití *m* Haiti

halag|ar [12] *vt* flatter. **~üeño** *a* flattering; (esperanzador) promising

halcón *m* falcon

halla|r *vt* find; (descubrir) discover. □ **~rse** *vpr* be. **~zgo** *m* discovery

hamaca *f* hammock; (asiento) deck-chair

hambr|e *f* hunger; (de muchos) famine. **tener ~e** be hungry. **~iento** *a* starving

hamburguesa *f* hamburger

harag|án *a* lazy, idle. ● *m* layabout. **~anear** *vi* laze around

harap|iento *a* in rags. **~o** *m* rag

harina *f* flour

hart|ar *vt* (fastidiar) annoy. **me estás ~ando** you're annoying me. □ **~arse** *vpr* (llenarse) gorge o.s. (**de** on); (cansarse) get fed up (**de** with). **~o** *a* full; (cansado) tired; (fastidiado) fed up (**de** with). ● *adv* (LAm) (muy) very; (mucho) a lot

hasta *prep* as far as; (en el tiempo) until, till; (Mex) not until. ● *adv* even. **¡~ la vista!** goodbye!, see you! 🄵 **¡~ luego!** see you later! **¡~ mañana!** see you tomorrow! **¡~ pronto!** see you soon!

hast|iar [20] *vt* (cansar) weary, tire; (aburrir) bore. □ **~iarse** *vpr* get fed up (**de** with). **~ío** *m* weariness; (aburrimiento) boredom

haya *f* beech (tree). ● *vb* ⇒HABER

hazaña *f* exploit

hazmerreír *m* laughing stock

he *vb* ⇒HABER

hebilla *f* buckle

hebra *f* thread; (fibra) fibre

hebreo *a* & *m* Hebrew

hechi|cera *f* witch. **~cería** *f* witchcraft. **~cero** *m* wizard. **~zar** [10] *vt* cast a spell on; (fig) captivate. **~zo** *m* spell; (fig) charm

hech|o *pp de* **hacer**. ● *a* (manufacturado) made; (terminado) done; <*vestidos etc*> ready-made; (Culin) done. ● *m* fact; (acto) deed; (cuestión) matter; (suceso) event. **de ~o** in fact. **~ura** *f* making; (forma) form; (del cuerpo) build; (calidad de fabricación) workmanship

hed|er [1] *vi* stink. **~iondez** *f* stench. **~iondo** *a* stinking, smelly. **~or** *m* stench

hela|da *f* frost. **~dera** *f* (LAm) fridge, refrigerator. **~dería** *f* ice-cream shop. **~do** *a* freezing; (congelado) frozen; (LAm, bebida) chilled. ● *m* ice-cream. **~r** [1] *vt/i* freeze. **anoche heló** there was a frost last night. □ **~rse** *vpr* freeze

helecho *m* fern

hélice *f* propeller

helicóptero *m* helicopter

hembra *f* female; (mujer) woman

hemorr|agia *f* haemorrhage. **~oides** *fpl* haemorrhoids

hendidura *f* crack, split; (Geol) fissure

heno *m* hay

heráldica *f* heraldry

hered|ar *vt/i* inherit. **~era** *f* heiress. **~ero** *m* heir. **~itario** *a* hereditary

herej|e *m* heretic. **~ía** *f* heresy

herencia *f* inheritance; (fig) heritage

heri|da *f* injury; (con arma) wound. **~do** *a* injured; (con arma) wounded; (fig) hurt. ● *m* injured person. **~r** [4] *vt* injure; (con arma) wound; (fig) hurt. □ **~rse** *vpr* hurt o.s.

herman|a *f* sister. **~a política** sister-in-law. **~astra** *f* stepsister. **~astro** *m* stepbrother. **~o** *m* brother. **~o político** brother-in-law. **~os** *mpl* brothers; (chicos y chicas) brothers and sisters. **~os gemelos** twins

hermético *a* hermetic; (fig) watertight

hermos|o *a* beautiful; (espléndido) splendid. **~ura** *f* beauty

héroe *m* hero

hero|ico *a* heroic. **~ína** *f* heroine; (droga) heroin. **~ísmo** *m* heroism

herr|adura *f* horseshoe. **~amienta** *f* tool. **~ero** *m* blacksmith

herv|idero *m* (fig) hotbed; (multitud) throng. **~ir** [4] *vt/i* boil. **~or** *m* (fig) ardour. **romper el ~** come to the boil

hiberna|ción *f* hibernation. **~r** *vi* hibernate

híbrido *a & m* hybrid

hice *vb* ⇒HACER

hidalgo *m* nobleman

hidrata|nte *a* moisturizing. **~r** *vt* hydrate; <*crema etc*> moisturize

hidráulico *a* hydraulic

hid|roavión *m* seaplane. **~oeléctrico** *a* hydroelectric. **~ofobia** *f* rabies. **~ófobo** *a* rabid. **~ógeno** *m* hydrogen

hiedra *f* ivy

hielo *m* ice

hiena *f* hyena

hierba *f* grass; (Culin, Med) herb. **mala ~** weed. **~buena** *f* mint

hierro *m* iron

hígado *m* liver

higi|ene *f* hygiene. **~énico** *a* hygienic

hig|o *m* fig. **~uera** *f* fig tree

hij|a *f* daughter. **~astra** *f* stepdaughter. **~astro** *m* stepson. **~o** *m* son. **~os** *mpl* sons; (chicos y chicas) children

hilar *vt* spin. **~ delgado** split hairs

hilera *f* row; (Mil) file

hilo *m* thread; (Elec) wire; (de líquido) trickle; (lino) linen

hilv|án *m* tacking. **~anar** *vt* tack; (fig) put together

himno *m* hymn. **~ nacional** anthem

hincapié *m*. **hacer ~ en** stress, insist on

hincar [7] *vt* drive <*estaca*> **(en** into). □ **~se** *vpr*. **~se de rodillas** kneel down

hincha *f* [I] grudge. ● *m & f* ([I], aficionado) fan

hincha|do *a* inflated; (Med) swollen. **~r** *vt* inflate, blow up. □ **~rse** *vpr* swell up; (fig, [I], comer mucho) gorge o.s. **~zón** *f* swelling

hinojo *m* fennel

hiper|mercado *m* hypermarket. **~sensible** *a* hypersensitive. **~tensión** *f* high blood pressure

hípic|a *f* horse racing. **~o** *a* horse

hipn|osis *f* hypnosis. **~otismo** *m* hypnotism. **~otizar** [10] *vt* hypnotize

hipo *m* hiccup. **tener ~** have hiccups

hipo|alérgeno *a* hypoallergenic. **~condríaco** *a & m* hypochondriac

hip|ocresía *f* hypocrisy. **~ócrita** *a* hypocritical. ● *m & f* hypocrite

hipódromo *m* racecourse

hipopótamo *m* hippopotamus

hipoteca *f* mortgage. **~r** [7] *vt* mortgage

hip|ótesis *f invar* hypothesis. **~otético** *a* hypothetical

hiriente *a* offensive, wounding

hirsuto *a* <*barba*> bristly; <*pelo*> wiry

hispánico *a* Hispanic

Hispanoamérica *f* Spanish America

hispano|americano *a* Spanish American. **~hablante** *a* Spanish-speaking

hist|eria *f* hysteria. **~érico** *a* hysterical

hist|oria *f* history; (relato) story; (excusa) tale, excuse. **pasar a la ~oria** go down in history. **~oriador** *m* historian. **~órico** *a* historical. **~orieta** *f* tale; (con dibujos) strip cartoon

hito *m* milestone

hizo *vb* ⇒HACER

hocico *m* snout

hockey /ˈ(x)oki/ *m* hockey. **~ sobre hielo** ice hockey

hogar *m* home; (chimenea) hearth. **~eño** *a* domestic; <*persona*> home-loving

hoguera *f* bonfire

hoja *f* leaf; (de papel, metal etc) sheet; (de cuchillo, espada etc) blade. **~ de afeitar** razor blade. **~lata** *f* tin

hojaldre *m* puff pastry

hojear *vt* leaf through

hola *int* hello!

Holanda *f* Holland

holand|és *a* Dutch. ● *m* Dutchman; (lengua) Dutch. **~esa** *f* Dutchwoman. **los ~eses** the Dutch

holg|ado *a* loose; (fig) comfortable. **~ar** [2 & 12] *vi*. **huelga decir que** needless to say. **~azán** *a* lazy. ● *m* idler. **~ura** *f* looseness; (fig) comfort

hollín *m* soot

hombre *m* man; (especiehumana) man(kind). ● *int* Good Heavens!; (de duda) well. **~ de negocios** businessman. **~ rana** frogman

hombr|era *f* shoulder pad. **~o** *m* shoulder

homenaje *m* homage, tribute. **rendir ~ a** pay tribute to

home|ópata *m* homoeopath. **~opatía** *f* homoeopathy. **~opático** *a* homoeopathic

homicid|a *a* murderous. ● *m & f* murderer. **~io** *m* murder

homosexual *a & m & f* homosexual. **~idad** *f* homosexuality

hond|o *a* deep. **~onada** *f* hollow

Honduras *f* Honduras

hondureño *a & m* Honduran

honest|idad *f* honesty. **~o** *a* honest

hongo *m* fungus; (LAm, Culin) mushroom; (venenoso) toadstool

hon|or *m* honour. **~orable** *a* honourable. **~orario** *a* honorary. **~orarios** *mpl* fees. **~ra** *f* honour; (buena fama) good name. **~radez** *f* honesty. **~rado** *a* honest. **~rar** *vt* honour

hora *f* hour; (momento puntual) time; (cita) appointment. **~ pico, ~ punta** rush hour. **~s** *fpl* **de trabajo** working hours. **~s** *fpl* **extraordinarias** overtime. **~s** *fpl* **libres** free time. **a**

estas **~s** now. **¿a qué ~?** (at) what time? **a última ~** at the last moment. **de última ~** last-minute. **en buena ~** at the right time. **media ~** half an hour. **pedir ~** to make an appointment. **¿qué ~ es?** what time is it?

horario *a* hourly. ● *m* timetable. **~ de trabajo** working hours

horca *f* gallows

horcajadas *fpl.* **a ~** astride

horchata *f* tiger-nut milk

horizont|al *a & f* horizontal. **~e** *m* horizon

horma *f* mould; (para fabricar calzado) last; (para conservar su forma) shoe-tree. **de ~ ancha** broad-fitting

hormiga *f* ant

hormigón *m* concrete

hormigue|ar *vi* tingle; (bullir) swarm. **me ~a la mano** I've got pins and needles in my hand. **~o** *m* tingling; (fig) anxiety

hormiguero *m* anthill; (de gente) swarm

hormona *f* hormone

horn|ada *f* batch. **~illa** *f* (LAm) burner. **~illo** *m* burner; (cocina portátil) portable electric cooker. **~o** *m* oven; (para cerámica etc) kiln; (Tec) furnace

horóscopo *m* horoscope

horquilla *f* pitchfork; (para el pelo) hairpin

horr|endo *a* awful. **~ible** *a* horrible. **~ipilante** *a* terrifying. **~or** *m* horror; (atrocidad) atrocity. **¡qué ~or!** how awful!. **~orizar** [10] *vt* horrify. □ **~orizarse** *vpr* be horrified. **~oroso** *a* horrifying

hort|aliza *f* vegetable. **~elano** *m* market gardener

hosco *a* surly

hospeda|je *m* accommodation. **~r** *vt* put up. □ **~rse** *vpr* stay

hospital *m* hospital. **~ario** *a* hospitable. **~idad** *f* hospitality

hostal *m* boarding-house

hostería *f* inn

hostia *f* (Relig) host

hostigar [12] *vt* whip; (fig, molestar) pester

hostil *a* hostile. **~idad** *f* hostility

hotel *m* hotel. **~ero** *a* hotel. ● *m* hotelier

hoy *adv* today. **~ (en) día** nowadays. **~ por ~** at the present time. **de ~ en adelante** from now on

hoy|o *m* hole. **~uelo** *m* dimple

hoz *f* sickle

hube *vb* ⇒HABER

hucha *f* money box

hueco *a* hollow; <*palabras*> empty; <*voz*> resonant; <*persona*> superficial. ● *m* hollow; (espacio) space; (vacío) gap

huelg|a *f* strike. **~a de brazos caídos** sit-down strike. **~a de hambre** hunger strike. **declararse en ~a** come out on strike. **~uista** *m & f* striker

huella *f* footprint; (de animal, vehículo etc) track. **~ digital** fingerprint

huelo *vb* ⇒OLER

huérfano *a* orphaned. ● *m* orphan. **~ de** without

huert|a *f* market garden (Brit), truck farm (Amer); (terreno de regadío) irrigated plain. **~o** *m* vegetable garden; (de árboles frutales) orchard

hueso *m* bone; (de fruta) stone

huésped *m* guest; (que paga) lodger

huesudo *a* bony

huev|a *f* roe. **~o** *m* egg. **~o duro** hard-boiled egg. **~o escalfado**

poached egg. **~o estrellado**, **~o frito** fried egg. **~o pasado por agua** boiled egg. **~os revueltos** scrambled eggs. **~o tibio** (Mex) boiled egg

hui|da *f* flight, escape. **~dizo** *a* (tímido) shy; (esquivo) elusive

huipil *m* (Mex) traditional embroidered smock

huir *vi* [17] flee, run away; (evitar). **~ de** avoid. **me huye** he avoids me

huitlacoche *m* (Mex) edible black fungus

hule *m* oilcloth; (Mex, goma) rubber

human|idad *f* mankind; (fig) humanity. **~itario** *a* humanitarian. **~o** *a* human; (benévolo) humane

humareda *f* cloud of smoke

humed|ad *f* dampness; (en meteorología) humidity; (gotitas de agua) moisture. **~ecer** [11] *vt* moisten. □ **~ecerse** *vpr* become moist

húmedo *a* damp; <*clima*> humid; <*labios*> moist; (mojado) wet

humil|dad *f* humility. **~de** *a* humble. **~llación** *f* humiliation. **~llar** *vt* humiliate. □ **~llarse** *vpr* lower o.s.

humo *m* smoke; (vapor) steam; (gas nocivo) fumes. **~s** *mpl* airs

humor *m* mood, temper; (gracia) humour. **estar de mal ~** be in a bad mood. **~ista** *m & f* humorist. **~ístico** *a* humorous

hundi|miento *m* sinking. **~r** *vt* sink; destroy <*persona*>. □ **~rse** *vpr* sink; <*edificio*> collapse

húngaro *a & m* Hungarian

Hungría *f* Hungary

huracán *m* hurricane

huraño *a* unsociable

hurgar [12] *vi* rummage (en through). □ **~se** *vpr*. **~se la nariz** pick one's nose

hurra *int* hurray!

hurtadillas *fpl*. **a ~** stealthily

hurt|ar *vt* steal. **~o** *m* theft; (cosa robada) stolen object

husmear *vt* sniff out; (fig) pry into

huyo *vb* ⇒HUIR

Ii

iba *vb* ⇒IR

ibérico *a* Iberian

iberoamericano *a & m* Latin American

iceberg /iθ'ber/ *m* (*pl* **~s**) iceberg

ictericia *f* jaundice

ida *f* outward journey; (partida) departure. **de ~ y vuelta** <*billete*> return (Brit), round-trip (Amer); <*viaje*> round

idea *f* idea; (opinión) opinion. **cambiar de ~** change one's mind. **no tener la más remota ~, no tener la menor ~** not have the slightest idea, not have a clue [I]

ideal *a & m* ideal. **~ista** *m & f* idealist. **~izar** [10] *vt* idealize

idear *vt* think up, conceive; (inventar) invent

ídem *pron & adv* the same

idéntico *a* identical

identi|dad *f* identity. **~ficación** *f* identification. **~ficar** [7] *vt* identify. □ **~ficarse** *vpr* identify o.s. **~ficarse con** identify with

ideol|ogía *f* ideology. **~ógico** *a* ideological

idílico *a* idyllic

idilio *m* idyll

idiom|a *m* language. **~ático** *a* idiomatic

idiosincrasia *f* idiosyncrasy

idiot|a *a* idiotic. ● *m & f* idiot. **~ez** *f* stupidity

idolatrar *vt* worship; (fig) idolize

ídolo *m* idol

idóneo *a* suitable (**para** for)

iglesia *f* church

iglú *m* igloo

ignora|ncia *f* ignorance. **~nte** *a* ignorant. ● *m* ignoramus. **~r** *vt* not know, be unaware of; (no hacer caso de) ignore

igual *a* equal; (mismo) the same; (similar) like; (llano) even; (liso) smooth. ● *adv* the same. ● *m* equal. **~ que** (the same) as. **al ~ que** the same as. **da ~**, **es ~** it doesn't matter. **sin ~** unequalled

igual|ar *vt* make equal; equal <*éxito, récord*>; (allanar) level. □ **~arse** *vpr* be equal. **~dad** *f* equality. **~mente** *adv* equally; (también) also, likewise; (respuesta de cortesía) the same to you

ilegal *a* illegal

ilegible *a* illegible

ilegítimo *a* illegitimate

ileso *a* unhurt

ilícito *a* illicit

ilimitado *a* unlimited

ilógico *a* illogical

ilumina|ción *f* illumination; (alumbrado) lighting. **~r** *vt* light (up). □ **~rse** *vpr* light up

ilusi|ón *f* illusion; (sueño) dream; (alegría) joy. **hacerse ~ones** build up one's hopes. **me hace ~ón** I'm thrilled; I'm looking forward to <*algo en el futuro*>. **~onado** *a* excited. **~onar** *vt* give false hope. □ **~onarse** *vpr* have false hopes

ilusionis|mo *m* conjuring. **~ta** *m & f* conjurer

iluso *a* naive. ● *m* dreamer. **~rio** *a* illusory

ilustra|ción *f* learning; (dibujo) illustration. **~do** *a* learned; (con dibujos) illustrated. **~r** *vt* explain; (instruir) instruct; (añadir dibujos etc) illustrate. □ **~rse** *vpr* acquire knowledge. **~tivo** *a* illustrative

ilustre *a* illustrious

imagen *f* image; (TV etc) picture

imagina|ble *a* imaginable. **~ción** *f* imagination. **~r** *vt* imagine. □ **~rse** *vpr* imagine. **~rio** *m* imaginary. **~tivo** *a* imaginative

imán *m* magnet

imbécil *a* stupid. ● *m & f* idiot

imborrable *a* indelible; <*recuerdo etc*> unforgettable

imita|ción *f* imitation. **~r** *vt* imitate

impacien|cia *f* impatience. □ **~tarse** *vpr* lose one's patience. **~te** *a* impatient

impacto *m* impact; (huella) mark. **~ de bala** bullet hole

impar *a* odd

imparcial *a* impartial. **~idad** *f* impartiality

impartir *vt* impart, give

impasible *a* impassive

impávido *a* fearless; (impasible) impassive

impecable *a* impeccable

impedi|do *a* disabled. **~mento** *m* impediment. **~r** [5] *vt* prevent; (obstruir) hinder

impenetrable *a* impenetrable

impensa|ble *a* unthinkable. **~do** *a* unexpected

impera|r *vi* prevail. **~tivo** *a* imperative; <*necesidad*> urgent

imperceptible *a* imperceptible

imperdible *m* safety pin

imperdonable *a* unforgivable

imperfec|ción *f* imperfection. **~to** *a* imperfect

imperi|al *a* imperial. **~alismo** *m* imperialism. **~o** *m* empire; (poder) rule. **~oso** *a* imperious

impermeable *a* waterproof. ● *m* raincoat

impersonal *a* impersonal

impertinen|cia *f* impertinence. **~te** *a* impertinent

imperturbable *a* imperturbable

ímpetu *m* impetus; (impulso) impulse; (violencia) force

impetuos|idad *f* impetuosity. **~o** *a* impetuous

implacable *a* implacable

implantar *vt* introduce

implica|ción *f* implication. **~r** [7] *vt* implicate; (significar) imply

implícito *a* implicit

implorar *vt* implore

impon|ente *a* imposing; 🅸 terrific. **~er** [34] *vt* impose; (requerir) demand; deposit <*dinero*>. □ **~erse** *vpr* (hacerse obedecer) assert o.s.; (hacerse respetar) command respect; (prevalecer) prevail. **~ible** *a* taxable

importa|ción *f* importation; (artículo) import. **~ciones** *fpl* imports. **~dor** *a* importing. ● *m* importer

importa|ncia *f* importance. **~nte** *a* important; (en cantidad) considerable. **~r** *vt* import; (ascender a) amount to. ● *vi* be important, matter. **¿le ~ría...?** would you mind...? **no ~** it doesn't matter

importe *m* price; (total) amount

importun|ar *vt* bother. **~o** *a* troublesome; (inoportuno) inopportune

imposib|ilidad *f* impossibility. **~le** *a* impossible. **hacer lo ~le para** do all one can to

imposición *f* imposition; (impuesto) tax

impostor *m* impostor

impoten|cia *f* impotence. **~te** *a* impotent

impracticable *a* impracticable; (intransitable) unpassable

imprecis|ión *f* vagueness; (error) inaccuracy. **~o** *a* imprecise

impregnar *vt* impregnate; (empapar) soak

imprenta *f* printing; (taller) printing house, printer's

imprescindible *a* indispensable, essential

impresi|ón *f* impression; (acción de imprimir) printing; (tirada) edition; (huella) imprint. **~onable** *a* impressionable. **~onante** *a* impressive; (espantoso) frightening. **~onar** *vt* impress; (negativamente) shock; (conmover) move; (Foto) expose. □ **~onarse** *vpr* be impressed; (negativamente) be shocked; (conmover) be moved

impresionis|mo *m* impressionism. **~ta** *a & m & f* impressionist

impreso *a* printed. ● *m* form. **~s** *mpl* printed matter. **~ra** *f* printer

imprevis|ible *a* unforeseeable. **~to** *a* unforeseen

imprimir (*pp* **impreso**) *vt* print <*libro etc*>

improbab|ilidad *f* improbability. **~le** *a* unlikely, improbable

improcedente *a* inadmissible; *<conducta>* improper; *<despido>* unfair

improductivo *a* unproductive

improperio *m* insult. **~s** *mpl* abuse

impropio *a* improper

improvis|ación *f* improvisation. **~ado** *a* improvised. **~ar** *vt* improvise. **~o** *a*. **de ~o** unexpectedly

impruden|cia *f* imprudence. **~te** *a* imprudent

imp|udicia *f* indecency; (desvergüenza) shamelessness. **~údico** *a* indecent; (desvergonzado) shameless. **~udor** *m* indecency; (desvergüenza) shamelessness

impuesto *a* imposed. ● *m* tax. **~ a la renta** income tax. **~ sobre el valor agregado** (LAm), **~ sobre el valor añadido** VAT, value added tax

impuls|ar *vt* propel; drive *<persona>*; boost *<producción etc>*. **~ividad** *f* impulsiveness. **~ivo** *a* impulsive. **~o** *m* impulse

impun|e *a* unpunished. **~idad** *f* impunity

impur|eza *f* impurity. **~o** *a* impure

imputa|ción *f* charge. **~r** *vt* attribute; (acusar) charge

inaccesible *a* inaccessible

inaceptable *a* unacceptable

inactiv|idad *f* inactivity. **~o** *a* inactive

inadaptado *a* maladjusted

inadecuado *a* inadequate; (inapropiado) unsuitable

inadmisible *a* inadmissible; (inaceptable) unacceptable

inadvertido *a* distracted. **pasar ~** go unnoticed

inagotable *a* inexhaustible

inaguantable *a* unbearable

inaltera|ble *a* impassive; *<color>* fast; *<convicción>* unalterable. **~do** *a* unchanged

inapreciable *a* invaluable; (imperceptible) imperceptible

inapropiado *a* inappropriate

inasequible *a* out of reach

inaudito *a* unprecedented

inaugura|ción *f* inauguration. **~l** *a* inaugural. **~r** *vt* inaugurate

inca *a* & *m* & *f* Inca. **~ico** *a* Inca

incalculable *a* incalculable

incandescente *a* incandescent

incansable *a* tireless

incapa|cidad *f* incapacity; (física) disability. **~citado** *a* disabled. **~citar** *vt* incapacitate. **~z** *a* incapable

incauto *a* unwary; (fácil de engañar) gullible

incendi|ar *vt* set fire to. □ **~arse** *vpr* catch fire. **~ario** *a* incendiary. ● *m* arsonist. **~o** *m* fire

incentivo *m* incentive

incertidumbre *f* uncertainty

incesante *a* incessant

incest|o *m* incest. **~uoso** *a* incestuous

inciden|cia *f* incidence; (efecto) impact; (incidente) incident. **~tal** *a* incidental. **~te** *m* incident

incidir *vi* fall (**en** into); (influir) influence

incienso *m* incense

incierto *a* uncertain

incinera|dor *m* incinerator. **~r** *vt* incinerate; cremate *<cadáver>*

incipiente *a* incipient

incisi|ón *f* incision. **~vo** *a* incisive. ● *m* incisor

incitar *vt* incite

inclemen|cia *f* harshness. **~te** *a* harsh

inclina|ción *f* slope; (de la cabeza) nod; (fig) inclination. **~r** *vt* tilt; (inducir) incline. **~rse** *vpr* lean; (en saludo) bow; (tender) be inclined (**a** to)

inclu|ido *a* included; <*precio*> inclusive. **~ir** [17] *vt* include; (en cartas) enclose. **~sión** *f* inclusion. **~sive** *adv* inclusive. **hasta el lunes ~sive** up to and including Monday. **~so** *adv* even

incógnito *a* unknown. **de ~** incognito

incoheren|cia *f* incoherence. **~te** *a* incoherent

incoloro *a* colourless

incomestible *a*, **incomible** *a* uneatable, inedible

incomodar *vt* inconvenience; (causar vergüenza) make feel uncomfortable. □ **~se** *vpr* feel uncomfortable; (enojarse) get angry

incómodo *a* uncomfortable; (inconveniente) inconvenient

incomparable *a* incomparable

incompatib|ilidad *f* incompatibility. **~le** *a* incompatible

incompeten|cia *f* incompetence. **~te** *a & m & f* incompetent

incompleto *a* incomplete

incompren|dido *a* misunderstood. **~sible** *a* incomprehensible. **~sión** *f* incomprehension

incomunicado *a* cut off; <*preso*> in solitary confinement

inconcebible *a* inconceivable

inconcluso *a* unfinished

incondicional *a* unconditional

inconfundible *a* unmistakable

incongruente *a* incoherent; (contradictorio) inconsistent

inconmensurable *a* immeasurable

inconscien|cia *f* unconsciousness; (irreflexión) recklessness. **~te** *a* unconscious; (irreflexivo) reckless

inconsecuente *a* inconsistent

inconsistente *a* flimsy

inconsolable *a* unconsolable

inconstan|cia *f* lack of perseverance. **~te** *a* changeable; <*persona*> lacking in perseverance; (voluble) fickle

incontable *a* countless

incontenible *a* irrepressible

incontinen|cia *f* incontinence. **~te** *a* incontinent

inconvenien|cia *f* inconvenience. **~te** *a* inconvenient; (inapropiado) inappropriate; (incorrecto) improper. ● *m* problem; (desventaja) drawback

incorpora|ción *f* incorporation. **~r** *vt* incorporate; (Culin) add. □ **~rse** *vpr* sit up; join <*sociedad, regimiento etc*>

incorrecto *a* incorrect; (descortés) discourteous

incorregible *a* incorrigible

incorruptible *a* incorruptible

incrédulo *a* sceptical; <*mirada, gesto*> incredulous

increíble *a* incredible

increment|ar *vt* increase. **~o** *m* increase

incriminar *vt* incriminate

incrustar *vt* encrust

incuba|ción *f* incubation. **~dora** *f* incubator. **~r** *vt* incubate; (fig) hatch

incuestionable *a* unquestionable

inculcar [7] *vt* inculcate
inculpar *vt* accuse
inculto *a* uneducated
incumplimiento *m* non-fulfilment; (de un contrato) breach
incurable *a* incurable
incurrir *vi*. ~ **en** incur <*gasto*>; fall into <*error*>; commit <*crimen*>
incursión *f* raid
indagar [12] *vt* investigate
indebido *a* unjust; <*uso*> improper
indecen|cia *f* indecency. **~te** *a* indecent
indecible *a* indescribable
indecis|ión *f* indecision. **~o** *a* (con ser) indecisive; (con estar) undecided
indefenso *a* defenceless
indefini|ble *a* indefinable. **~do** *a* indefinite; (impreciso) undefined
indemnizar [10] *vt* compensate
independ|encia *f* independence. **~iente** *a* independent. **~izarse** [10] *vpr* become independent
indes|cifrable *a* indecipherable. **~criptible** *a* indescribable
indeseable *a* undesirable
indestructible *a* indestructible
indetermina|ble *a* indeterminable. **~do** *a* indeterminate; <*tiempo*> indefinite
India *f*. **la ~** India
indica|ción *f* indication; (señal) signal. **~ciones** *fpl* directions. **~dor** *m* indicator; (Tec) gauge. **~r** [7] *vt* show, indicate; (apuntar) point at; (hacer saber) point out; (aconsejar) advise. **~tivo** *a* indicative. ● *m* indicative; (al teléfono) dialling code
índice *m* index; (dedo) index finger; (catálogo) catalogue; (indicación) indication; (aguja) pointer
indicio *m* indication, sign; (vestigio) trace
indiferen|cia *f* indifference. **~te** *a* indifferent. **me es ~te** it's all the same to me
indígena *a* indigenous. ● *m & f* native
indigen|cia *f* poverty. **~te** *a* needy
indigest|ión *f* indigestion. **~o** *a* indigestible
indign|ación *f* indignation. **~ado** *a* indignant. **~ar** *vt* make indignant. □ **~arse** *vpr* become indignant. **~o** *a* unworthy; (despreciable) contemptible
indio *a & m* Indian
indirect|a *f* hint. **~o** *a* indirect
indisciplinado *a* undisciplined
indiscre|ción *f* indiscretion. **~to** *a* indiscreet
indiscutible *a* unquestionable
indisoluble *a* indissoluble
indispensable *a* indispensable
indisp|oner [34] *vt* (enemistar) set against. □ **~onerse** *vpr* fall out; (ponerse enfermo) fall ill. **~osición** *f* indisposition. **~uesto** *a* indisposed
individu|al *a* individual; <*cama*> single. ● *m* (en tenis etc) singles. **~alidad** *f* individuality. **~alista** *m & f* individualist. **~alizar** [10] *vt* individualize. **~o** *m* individual
índole *f* nature; (clase) type
indolen|cia *f* indolence. **~te** *a* indolent
indoloro *a* painless
indomable *a* untameable
inducir [47] *vt* induce. **~ a error** be misleading
indudable *a* undoubted

indulgen|cia *f* indulgence. **~te** *a* indulgent

indult|ar *vt* pardon. **~o** *m* pardon

industria *f* industry. **~l** *a* industrial. ● *m & f* industrialist. **~lización** *f* industrialization. **~lizar** [10] *vt* industrialize

inédito *a* unpublished; (fig) unknown

inefable *a* indescribable

ineficaz *a* ineffective; <*sistema etc*> inefficient

ineficiente *a* inefficient

ineludible *a* inescapable, unavoidable

inept|itud *f* ineptitude. **~o** *a* inept

inequívoco *a* unequivocal

inercia *f* inertia

inerte *a* inert; (sin vida) lifeless

inesperado *a* unexpected

inestable *a* unstable

inestimable *a* inestimable

inevitable *a* inevitable

inexistente *a* non-existent

inexorable *a* inexorable

inexper|iencia *f* inexperience. **~to** *a* inexperienced

inexplicable *a* inexplicable

infalible *a* infallible

infam|ar *vt* defame. **~atorio** *a* defamatory. **~e** *a* infamous; (fig, [I], muy malo) awful. **~ia** *f* infamy

infancia *f* infancy

infant|a *f* infanta, princess. **~e** *m* infante, prince. **~ería** *f* infantry. **~il** *a* children's; <*población*> child; <*actitud etc*> childish, infantile

infarto *m* heart attack

infec|ción *f* infection. **~cioso** *a* infectious. **~tar** *vt* infect. □ **~tarse** *vpr* become infected. **~to** *a* infected; [I] disgusting

infeli|cidad *f* unhappiness. **~z** *a* unhappy

inferior *a* inferior. ● *m & f* inferior. **~idad** *f* inferiority

infernal *a* infernal, hellish

infestar *vt* infest; (fig) inundate

infi|delidad *f* unfaithfulness. **~el** *a* unfaithful

infierno *m* hell

infiltra|ción *f* infiltration. □ **~rse** *vpr* infiltrate

ínfimo *a* lowest; <*calidad*> very poor

infini|dad *f* infinity. **~tivo** *m* infinitive. **~to** *a* infinite. ● *m*. **el ~to** the infinite; (en matemáticas) infinity. **~dad de** countless

inflación *f* inflation

inflama|ble *a* (in)flammable **~ción** *f* inflammation. **~r** *vt* set on fire; (fig, Med) inflame. □ **~rse** *vpr* catch fire; (Med) become inflamed

inflar *vt* inflate; blow up <*globo*>; (fig, exagerar) exaggerate

inflexi|ble *a* inflexible. **~ón** *f* inflexion

influ|encia *f* influence (en on). **~ir** [17] *vt* influence. ● *vi*. **~ en** influence. **~jo** *m* influence. **~yente** *a* influential

informa|ción *f* information; (noticias) news; (en aeropuerto etc) information desk; (de teléfonos) directory enquiries. **~dor** *m* informant

informal *a* informal; <*persona*> unreliable

inform|ante *m & f* informant. **~ar** *vt/i* inform. □ **~arse** *vpr* find out. **~ática** *f* information technology, computing. **~ativo** *a* in formative; <*programa*> news. **~atizar** [10] *vt* computerize

informe *a* shapeless. ● *m* report. **~s** *fpl* references, information

infracción *f* infringement. **~ de tráfico** traffic offence

infraestructura *f* infrastructure

infranqueable *a* impassable; (fig) insuperable

infrarrojo *a* infrared

infringir [14] *vt* infringe

infructuoso *a* fruitless

ínfulas *fpl*. **darse ~** give o.s. airs. **tener ~ de** fancy o.s. as

infundado *a* unfounded

infu|ndir *vt* instil. **~sión** *f* infusion

ingeni|ar *vt* invent. **~árselas para** find a way to

ingenier|ía *f* engineering. **~o** *m* engineer

ingenio *m* ingenuity; (agudeza) wit; (LAm, de azúcar) refinery. **~so** *a* ingenious

ingenu|idad *f* naivety. **~o** *a* naive

Inglaterra *f* England

ingl|és *a* English. ● *m* Englishman; (lengua) English. **~esa** *f* Englishwoman. **los ~eses** the English

ingrat|itud *f* ingratitude. **~o** *a* ungrateful; (desagradable) thankless

ingrediente *m* ingredient

ingres|ar *vt* deposit. ● *vi*. **~ar en** come in, enter; join <*sociedad*>. **~o** *m* entrance; (de dinero) deposit; (en sociedad, hospital) admission. **~os** *mpl* income

inh|ábil *a* unskilful; (no apto) unfit. **~abilidad** *f* unskilfulness; (para cargo) ineligibility

inhabitable *a* uninhabitable

inhala|dor *m* inhaler. **~r** *vt* inhale

inherente *a* inherent

inhibi|ción *f* inhibition. **~r** *vt* inhibit

inhóspito *a* inhospitable

inhumano *a* inhuman

inici|ación *f* beginning. **~al** *a* & *f* initial. **~ar** *vt* initiate; (comenzar) begin, start. **~ativa** *f* initiative. **~o** *m* beginning

inigualado *a* unequalled

ininterrumpido *a* uninterrupted

injert|ar *vt* graft. **~to** *m* graft

injuri|a *f* insult. **~ar** *vt* insult. **~oso** *a* insulting

injust|icia *f* injustice. **~o** *a* unjust, unfair

inmaculado *a* immaculate

inmaduro *a* unripe; <*persona*> immature

inmediaciones *fpl*. **las ~** the vicinity, the surrounding area

inmediat|amente *adv* immediately. **~o** *a* immediate; (contiguo) next. **de ~o** immediately

inmejorable *a* excellent

inmemorable *a* immemorial

inmens|idad *f* immensity. **~o** *a* immense

inmersión *f* immersion

inmigra|ción *f* immigration. **~nte** *a* & *m* & *f* immigrant. **~r** *vt* immigrate

inminen|cia *f* imminence. **~te** *a* imminent

inmiscuirse [17] *vpr* interfere

inmobiliario *a* property

inmolar *vt* sacrifice

inmoral *a* immoral. **~idad** *f* immorality

inmortal *a* immortal. **~izar** [10] *vt* immortalize

inmóvil *a* immobile

inmueble *a*. **bienes ~s** property

inmund|icia *f* filth. **~o** *a* filthy

inmun|e *a* immune. **~idad** *f* immunity. **~ización** *f* immunization. **~izar** [10] *vt* immunize

inmuta|ble *a* unchangeable. □ **~rse** *vpr* be perturbed. **sin ~rse** unperturbed

innato *a* innate

innecesario *a* unnecessary

innegable *a* undeniable

innova|ción *f* innovation. **~r** *vi* innovate. ● *vt* make innovations in

innumerable *a* innumerable

inocen|cia *f* innocence. **~tada** *f* practical joke. **~te** *a* innocent. **~tón** *a* naïve

inocuo *a* innocuous

inodoro *a* odourless. ● *m* toilet

inofensivo *a* inoffensive

inolvidable *a* unforgettable

inoperable *a* inoperable

inoportuno *a* untimely; <*comentario*> ill-timed

inoxidable *a* stainless

inquiet|ar *vt* worry. □ **~arse** *vpr* get worried. **~o** *a* worried; (agitado) restless. **~ud** *f* anxiety

inquilino *m* tenant

inquirir [4] *vt* enquire into, investigate

insaciable *a* insatiable

insalubre *a* unhealthy

insatisfecho *a* unsatisfied; (descontento) dissatisfied

inscri|bir (*pp* **inscrito**) *vt* (en registro) register; (en curso) enrol; (grabar) inscribe. □ **~birse** *vpr* register. **~pción** *f* inscription; (registro) registration

insect|icida *m* insecticide. **~o** *m* insect

insegur|idad *f* insecurity. **~o** *a* insecure; <*ciudad*> unsafe, dangerous

insemina|ción *f* insemination. **~r** *vt* inseminate

insensato *a* foolish

insensible *a* insensitive

inseparable *a* inseparable

insertar *vt* insert

insidi|a *f* malice. **~oso** *a* insidious

insigne *a* famous

insignia *f* badge; (bandera) flag

insignificante *a* insignificant

insinu|ación *f* insinuation. **~ante** *a* insinuating. **~ar** [21] *vt* imply; insinuate <*algo ofensivo*>. □ **~arse** *vpr*. **~ársele a** make a pass at

insípido *a* insipid

insist|encia *f* insistence. **~ente** *a* insistent. **~ir** *vi* insist; (hacer hincapié) stress

insolación *f* sunstroke

insolen|cia *f* rudeness, insolence. **~te** *a* rude, insolent

insólito *a* unusual

insolven|cia *f* insolvency. **~te** *a* & *m* & *f* insolvent

insomn|e *a* sleepless. ● *m* & *f* insomniac. **~io** *m* insomnia

insondable *a* unfathomable

insoportable *a* unbearable

insospechado *a* unexpected

insostenible *a* untenable

inspec|ción *f* inspection. **~cionar** *vt* inspect. **~tor** *m* inspector

inspira|ción *f* inspiration. **~r** *vt* inspire. □ **~rse** *vpr* be inspired

instala|ción *f* installation. **~r** *vt* install. □ **~rse** *vpr* settle

instancia *f* request. **en última ~** as a last resort

instant|ánea *f* snapshot. **~áneo** *a* instantaneous; <*café etc*> instant. **~e** *m* instant. **a cada ~e** constantly. **al ~e** immediately

instaura|ción *f* establishment. **~r** *vt* establish

instiga|ción *f* instigation. **~dor** *m* instigator. **~r** [12] *vt* instigate; (incitar) incite

instint|ivo *a* instinctive. **~o** *m* instinct

institu|ción *f* institution. **~cional** *a* institutional. **~ir** [17] *vt* establish. **~to** *m* institute; (Escol) (secondary) school. **~triz** *f* governess

instru|cción *f* education; (Mil) training. **~cciones** *fpl* instruction. **~ctivo** *a* instructive; <*película etc*> educational. **~ctor** *m* instructor. **~ir** [17] *vt* instruct, teach; (Mil) train

instrument|ación *f* instrumentation. **~al** *a* instrumental. **~o** *m* instrument; (herramienta) tool

insubordina|ción *f* insubordination. **~r** *vt* stir up. □ **~rse** *vpr* rebel

insuficien|cia *f* insufficiency; (inadecuación) inadequacy. **~te** *a* insufficient

insufrible *a* insufferable

insular *a* insular

insulina *f* insulin

insulso *a* tasteless; (fig) insipid

insult|ar *vt* insult. **~o** *m* insult

insuperable *a* insuperable; (inmejorable) unbeatable

insurgente *a* insurgent

insurrec|ción *f* insurrection. **~to** *a* insurgent

intachable *a* irreproachable

intacto *a* intact

intangible *a* intangible

integra|ción *f* integration. **~l** *a* integral; (completo) complete; (incorporado) built-in; <*pan*> wholemeal (Brit), wholewheat (Amer). **~r** *vt* make up

integridad *f* integrity; (entereza) wholeness

íntegro *a* complete; (fig) upright

intelect|o *m* intellect. **~ual** *a* & *m* & f intellectual

inteligen|cia *f* intelligence. **~te** *a* intelligent

inteligible *a* intelligible

intemperie *f*. **a la ~** in the open

intempestivo *a* untimely

intenci|ón *f* intention. **con doble ~ón** implying sth else. **~onado** *a* deliberate. **bien ~onado** well-meaning. **mal ~onado** malicious. **~onal** *a* intentional

intens|idad *f* intensity. **~ificar** [7] *vt* intensify. **~ivo** *a* intensive. **~o** *a* intense

intent|ar *vt* try. **~o** *m* attempt; (Mex, propósito) intention

inter|calar *vt* insert. **~cambio** *m* exchange. **~ceder** *vt* intercede

interceptar *vt* intercept

interdicto *m* ban

inter|és *m* interest; (egoísmo) self-interest. **~esado** *a* interested; (parcial) biassed; (egoísta) selfish. **~esante** *a* interesting. **~esar** *vt* interest; (afectar) concern. ● *vi* be of interest. □ **~esarse** *vpr* take an interest (**por** in)

interfer|encia *f* interference. **~ir** [4] *vi* interfere

interfono *m* intercom

interino *a* temporary; <*persona*> acting. ● *m* stand-in; (médico) locum

interior *a* interior; <*comercio etc*> domestic. ● *m* inside. **Ministerio del I~** Home Office (Brit), Department of the Interior (Amer)

interjección *f* interjection

inter|locutor *m* speaker. **~mediario** *a & m* intermediary. **~medio** *a* intermediate. ● *m* interval

interminable *a* interminable

intermitente *a* intermittent. ● *m* indicator

internacional *a* international

intern|ado *m* (Escol) boarding-school. **~ar** *vt* (en manicomio) commit; (en hospital) admit. □ **~arse** *vpr* penetrate

Internet *m* Internet

interno *a* internal; (Escol) boarding. ● *m* (Escol) boarder

interponer [34] *vt* interpose. □ **~se** *vpr* intervene

int|erpretación *f* interpretation. **~erpretar** *vt* interpret; (Mús etc) play. **~érprete** *m* interpreter; (Mus) performer

interroga|ción *f* interrogation; (signo) question mark. **~r** [12] *vt* question. **~tivo** *a* interrogative

interru|mpir *vt* interrupt; cut off <*suministro*>; cut short <*viaje etc*>; block <*tráfico*>. **~pción** *f* interruption. **~ptor** *m* switch

inter|sección *f* intersection. **~urbano** *a* inter-city; <*llamada*> long-distance

intervalo *m* interval; (espacio) space. **a ~s** at intervals

interven|ir [53] *vt* control; (Med) operate on. ● *vi* intervene; (participar) take part. **~tor** *m* inspector; (Com) auditor

intestino *m* intestine

intim|ar *vi* become friendly. **~idad** *f* intimacy

intimidar *vt* intimidate

íntimo *a* intimate; <*amigo*> close. ● *m* close friend

intolera|ble *a* intolerable. **~nte** *a* intolerant

intoxicar [7] *vt* poison

intranquilo *a* worried

intransigente *a* intransigent

intransitable *a* impassable

intransitivo *a* intransitive

intratable *a* impossible

intrépido *a* intrepid

intriga *f* intrigue. **~nte** *a* intriguing. **~r** [12] *vt* intrigue

intrincado *a* intricate

intrínseco *a* intrinsic

introduc|ción *f* introduction. **~ir** [47] *vt* introduce; (meter) insert. □ **~irse** *vpr* get into

intromisión *f* interference

introvertido *a* introverted. ● *m* introvert

intruso *m* intruder

intui|ción *f* intuition. **~r** [17] *vt* sense. **~tivo** *a* intuitive

inunda|ción *f* flooding. **~r** *vt* flood

inusitado *a* unusual

in|útil *a* useless; (vano) futile. **~utilidad** *f* uselessness

invadir *vt* invade

inv|alidez *f* invalidity; (Med) disability. **~álido** *a & m* invalid

invariable *a* invariable

invas|ión *f* invasion. **~or** *a* invading. ● *m* invader

invencible *a* invincible

inven|ción *f* invention. **~tar** *vt* invent

inventario *m* inventory

invent|iva *f* inventiveness. **~ivo** *a* inventive. **~or** *m* inventor

invernadero *m* greenhouse

invernal *a* winter

inverosímil *a* implausible

inversión *f* inversion; (Com) investment

inverso *a* inverse; (contrario) opposite. **a la inversa** the other way round. **a la inversa de** contrary to

invertir [4] *vt* reverse; (Com) invest; put in <*tiempo*>

investidura *f* investiture

investiga|ción *f* investigation; (Univ) research. **~dor** *m* investigator; (Univ) researcher. **~r** [12] *vt* investigate; (Univ) research

investir [5] *vt* invest

invicto *a* unbeaten

invierno *m* winter

inviolable *a* inviolate

invisible *a* invisible

invita|ción *f* invitation. **~do** *m* guest. **~r** *vt* invite. **te invito a una copa** I'll buy you a drink

invocar [7] *vt* invoke

involuntario *a* involuntary

invulnerable *a* invulnerable

inyec|ción *f* injection. **~tar** *vt* inject

---

ir [49]

● *verbo intransitivo*

····➤ to go. **fui a verla** I went to see her. **ir a pie** to go on foot. **ir en coche** to go by car. **vamos a casa** let's go home. **fue (a) por el pan** he went to get some bread

! Cuando la acción del verbo **ir** significa trasladarse hacia o con el interlocutor la traducción es *to come*, p.ej: **¡ya voy!** *I'm coming!* **yo voy contigo** *I'll come with you*

····➤ (estar) to be. **iba con su novio** she was with her boyfriend. **¿cómo te va?** how are you?

····➤ (sentar) to suit. **ese color no le va** that colour doesn't suit her. **no me va ni me viene** I don't mind at all

····➤ (Méx, apoyar) **irle a** to support. **le va al equipo local** he supports the local team

····➤ (en exclamaciones) **¡vamos!** come on! **¡vaya!** what a surprise!; (contrariedad) oh, dear! **¡vaya noche!** what a night! **¡qué va!** nonsense!

⇨ Cuando el verbo intransitivo se emplea con expresiones como **ir de paseo, ir de compras, ir tirando** etc., ver bajo el respectivo nombre, verbo etc.

● *verbo auxiliar*

····➤ **ir a** + *infinitivo* (para expresar futuro, propósito) to be going to + *infinitive;* (al prevenir) **no te vayas a caer** be careful you don't fall. **no vaya a ser quellueva** in case it rains. (en sugerencias) **vamos a dormir** let's go to sleep. **vamos a ver** let's see

····➤ **ir** + *gerundio*. **ve arreglándote** start getting ready. **el tiempo va mejorando** the weather is gradually getting better.

□ **irse** *verbo pronominal*

····➤ to go. **vete a la cama** go to bed. **se ha ido a casa** he's gone home

····➤ (marcharse) to leave. **se fue sin despedirse** he left without saying goodbye. **se fue de casa** she left home

ira *f* anger. **~cundo** *a* irascible

Irak *m* Iraq

Irán *m* Iran

iraní *a* & *m* & *f* Iranian

iraquí *a* & *m* & *f* Iraqi

iris *m* (Anat) iris

Irlanda *f* Ireland

irland|és *a* Irish. ● *m* Irishman; (lengua) Irish. **~esa** *f* Irishwoman. **los ~eses** the Irish

ir|onía *f* irony. **~ónico** *a* ironic

irracional *a* irrational

irradiar *vt* radiate

irreal *a* unreal. **~idad** *f* unreality

irrealizable *a* unattainable

irreconciliable *a* irreconcilable

irreconocible *a* unrecognizable

irrecuperable *a* irretrievable

irreflexión *f* impetuosity

irregular *a* irregular. **~idad** *f* irregularity

irreparable *a* irreparable

irreprimible *a* irrepressible

irreprochable *a* irreproachable

irresistible *a* irresistible

irrespetuoso *a* disrespectful

irresponsable *a* irresponsible

irriga|ción *f* irrigation. **~r** [12] *vt* irrigate

irrisorio *a* derisory

irrita|ble *a* irritable. **~ción** *f* irritation. **~r** *vt* irritate. □ **~rse** *vpr* get annoyed

irrumpir *vi* burst (**en** in)

isla *f* island. **las I~s Británicas** the British Isles

islámico *a* Islamic

islandés *a* Icelandic. ● *m* Icelander; (lengua) Icelandic

Islandia *f* Iceland

isleño *a* island. ● *m* islander

Israel *m* Israel

israelí *a* & *m* Israeli

Italia *f* Italy

italiano *a* & *m* Italian

itinerario *a* itinerary

IVA *abrev* (**impuesto sobre el valor agregado** (LAm), **impuesto sobre el valor añadido**) VAT

izar [10] *vt* hoist

izquierd|a *f*. **la ~a** the left hand; (Pol) left. **a la ~a** on the left; (con movimiento) to the left. **de ~a** left-wing. **~ista** *m* & *f* leftist. **~o** *a* left

Jj

ja *int* ha!

jabalí *m* (*pl* **~es**) wild boar

jabalina *f* javelin

jab|ón *m* soap. **~onar** *vt* soap. **~onoso** *a* soapy

jaca *f* pony

jacinto *m* hyacinth

jactarse *vpr* boast

jadea|nte *a* panting. **~r** *vi* pant

jaguar *m* jaguar

jaiba *f* (LAm) crab

jalar *vt* (LAm) pull

jalea *f* jelly

jaleo *m* row, uproar. **armar un ~** kick up a fuss

jalón *m* (LAm, tirón) pull; (Mex 🅘, trago) drink; (Mex, tramo) stretch

jamás *adv* never. **nunca ~** never ever

jamelgo *m* nag

jamón *m* ham. **~ de York** boiled ham. **~ serrano** cured ham

Japón *m*. **el ~** Japan

japonés *a* & *m* Japanese

jaque *m* check. **~ mate** checkmate

jaqueca *f* migraine

jarabe *m* syrup

jardín *m* garden. **~ de la infancia**, (Mex) **~ de niños** kindergarten, nursery school

jardiner|ía *f* gardening. **~o** *m* gardener

jarr|a *f* jug. **en ~as** with hands on hips. **~o** *m* jug. **caer como un ~o de agua fría** come as a shock. **~ón** *m* vase

jaula *f* cage

jauría *f* pack of hounds

jazmín *m* jasmine

jef|a *f* boss. **~atura** *f* leadership; (sede) headquarters. **~e** *m* boss; (Pol etc) leader. **~e de camareros** head waiter. **~e de estación** station-master. **~e de ventas** sales manager

jengibre *m* ginger

jer|arquía *f* hierarchy. **~árquico** *a* hierarchical

jerez *m* sherry. **al ~** with sherry

jerga *f* coarse cloth; (argot) jargon

jerigonza *f* jargon; (galimatías) gibberish

jeringa *f* syringe; (LAm 🅘, molestia) nuisance. **~r** [12] *vt* (fig, 🅘, molestar) annoy

jeroglífico *m* hieroglyph(ic)

jersey *m* (*pl* **~s**) jersey

Jesucristo *m* Jesus Christ. **antes de ~** BC, before Christ

jesuita *a* & *m* Jesuit

Jesús *m* Jesus. ● *int* good heavens!; (al estornudar) bless you!

jícara *f* (Mex) gourd

jilguero *m* goldfinch

jinete *m* & *f* rider

jipijapa *m* panama hat

jirafa *f* giraffe

jirón *m* shred, tatter

jitomate *m* (Mex) tomato

jorna|da *f* working day; (viaje) journey; (etapa) stage. **~l** *m* day's wage. **~lero** *m* day labourer

joroba *f* hump. **~do** *a* hunchbacked. ● *m* hunchback. **~r** *vt* 🅘 annoy

jota *f* letter J; (danza) jota, popular dance. **ni ~** nothing

joven (*pl* **jóvenes**) *a* young. ● *m* young man. ● *f* young woman

jovial *a* jovial

joy|a *f* jewel. **~as** *fpl* jewellery. **~ería** *f* jeweller's (shop). **~ero** *m* jeweller; (estuche) jewellery box

juanete *m* bunion

jubil|ación *f* retirement. **~ado** *a* retired. **~ar** *vt* pension off. □ **~arse** *vpr* retire. **~eo** *m* jubilee

júbilo *m* joy

judaísmo *m* Judaism

judía *f* Jewish woman; (alubia) bean. **~ blanca** haricot bean. **~ escarlata** runner bean. **~ verde** French bean

judicial *a* judicial

judío *a* Jewish. ● *m* Jewish man

judo *m* judo

juego *m* play; (de mesa, niños) game; (de azar) gambling; (conjunto) set. **estar en ~** be at stake. **estar fuera de ~** be offside. **hacer ~** match. **~s**

mpl **malabares** juggling. **J~s** *mpl* **Olímpicos** Olympic Games. ● *vb* ⇒JUGAR

juerga *f* spree

jueves *m invar* Thursday

juez *m* judge. **~ de instrucción** examining magistrate. **~ de línea** linesman

juga|dor *m* player; (habitual, por dinero) gambler. **~r** [3] *vt* play. ● *vi* play; (apostar fuerte) gamble. □ **~rse** *vpr* risk. **~r al fútbol**, (LAm) **~r fútbol** play football

juglar *m* minstrel

jugo *m* juice; (de carne) gravy; (fig) substance. **~so** *a* juicy; (fig) substantial

juguet|e *m* toy. **~ear** *vi* play. **~ón** *a* playful

juicio *m* judgement; (opinión) opinion; (razón) reason. **a mi ~** in my opinion. **~so** *a* wise

juliana *f* vegetable soup

julio *m* July

junco *m* rush, reed

jungla *f* jungle

junio *m* June

junt|a *f* meeting; (consejo) board, committee; (Pol) junta; (Tec) joint. **~ar** *vt* join; (reunir) collect. □ **~arse** *vpr* join; <*gente*> meet. **~o** *a* joined; (en plural) together. **~o a** next to. **~ura** *f* joint

jura|do *a* sworn. ● *m* jury; (miembro de jurado) juror. **~mento** *m* oath. **prestar ~mento** take an oath. **~r** *vt/i* swear. **~r en falso** commit perjury. **jurárselas a uno** have it in for s.o.

jurel *m* (type of) mackerel

jurídico *a* legal

juris|dicción *f* jurisdiction. **~prudencia** *f* jurisprudence

justamente *a* exactly; (con justicia) fairly

justicia *f* justice

justifica|ción *f* justification. **~r** [7] *vt* justify

justo *a* fair, just; (exacto) exact; <*ropa*> tight. ● *adv* just. **~ a tiempo** just in time

juven|il *a* youthful. **~tud** *f* youth; (gente joven) young people

juzga|do *m* (tribunal) court. **~r** [12] *vt* judge. **a ~r por** judging by

Kk

kilo *m*, **kilogramo** *m* kilo, kilogram

kil|ometraje *m* distance in kilometres, mileage. **~ométrico** *a* Ⓘ endless. **~ómetro** *m* kilometre. **~ómetro cuadrado** square kilometre

kilovatio *m* kilowatt

kiosco *m* kiosk

Ll

la

● *artículo definido femenino* (*pl* **las**)

····➤ the. **la flor azul** the blue flower. **la casa de al lado** the house next door. **cerca de la iglesia** near the church

No se traduce en los siguientes casos:

····▸ (con nombre abstracto, genérico) **la paciencia es una virtud** patience is a virtue. **odio la leche** I hate milk. **la madera es muy versátil** wood is very versatile

····▸ (con algunas instituciones) **termino la universidad mañana** I finish university tomorrow. **no va nunca a la iglesia** he never goes to church. **está en la cárcel** he's in jail

····▸ (con nombres propios) **la Sra. Díaz** Mrs Díaz. **la doctora Lara** doctor Lara

····▸ (antes de infinitivo) **es muy cuidadosa en el vestir** she takes great care in the way she dresses. **me di cuenta al verla** I realized when I saw her

····▸ (con partes del cuerpo, artículos personales) *se traduce por un posesivo.* **apretó la mano** he clenched his fist. **tienes la camisa desabrochada** your shirt is undone

····▸ **la + de. es la de Ana** it's Ana's. **la del sombrero** the one with the hat

····▸ **la + que** (persona) **la que me atendió** the one who served me. (cosa) **la que se rompió** the one that broke

····▸ **la + que** + *subjuntivo* (quienquiera) whoever. **la que gane pasará a la final** whoever wins will go to the final. (cualquiera) whichever. **compra la que sea más barata** buy whichever is cheaper

laberinto *m* labyrinth, maze

labia *f* gift of the gab

labio *m* lip

labor *f* work. **~es de aguja** needlework. **~es de ganchillo** crochet. **~es de punto** knitting. **~es domésticas** housework. **~able** *a* working. **~ar** *vi* work

laboratorio *m* laboratory

laborioso *a* laborious

laborista *a* Labour. • *m & f* member of the Labour Party

labra|do *a* worked; *<madera>* carved; *<metal>* wrought; *<tierra>* ploughed. **~dor** *m* farmer; (obrero) farm labourer. **~nza** *f* farming. **~r** *vt* work; carve *<madera>*; cut *<piedra>*; till *<la tierra>*. □ **~rse** *vpr*. **~rse un porvenir** carve out a future for o.s.

labriego *m* peasant

laca *f* lacquer

lacayo *m* lackey

lacio *a* straight; (flojo) limp

lacón *m* shoulder of pork

lacónico *a* laconic

lacr|ar *vt* seal. **~e** *m* sealing wax

lactante *a <niño>* still on milk

lácteo *a* milky. **productos** *mpl* **~s** dairy products

ladear *vt* tilt. □ **~se** *vpr* lean

ladera *f* slope

ladino *a* astute

lado *m* side. **al ~** near. **al ~ de** next to, beside. **de ~** sideways. **en todos ~s** everywhere. **los de al ~** the next-door neighbours. **por otro ~** on the other hand. **por todos ~s** everywhere. **por un ~** on the one hand

ladr|ar *vi* bark. **~ido** *m* bark

ladrillo *m* brick

ladrón *m* thief, robber; (de casas) burglar

lagart|ija *f* (small) lizard. **~o** *m* lizard

lago *m* lake

lágrima *f* tear

lagrimoso *a* tearful

laguna *f* small lake; (fig, omisión) gap

laico *a* lay

lament|able *a* deplorable; (que da pena) pitiful; <*pérdida*> sad. **~ar** *vt* be sorry about. □ **~arse** *vpr* lament; (quejarse) complain. **~o** *m* moan

lamer *vt* lick

lámina *f* sheet; (ilustración) plate; (estampa) picture card

lamina|do *a* laminated. **~r** *vt* laminate

lámpara *f* lamp. **~ de pie** standard lamp

lamparón *m* stain

lampiño *a* beardless; <*cuerpo*> hairless

lana *f* wool. **de ~** wool(len)

lanceta *f* lancet

lancha *f* boat. **~ motora** motor boat. **~ salvavidas** lifeboat

langost|a *f* (de mar) lobster; (insecto) locust. **~ino** *m* king prawn

languide|cer [11] *vi* languish. **~z** *f* languor

lánguido *a* languid; (decaído) listless

lanilla *f* nap; (tela fina) flannel

lanudo *a* woolly; <*perro*> shaggy

lanza *f* lance, spear

lanza|llamas *m invar* flamethrower. **~miento** *m* throw; (acción de lanzar) throwing; (de proyectil, de producto) launch. **~miento de peso**, (LAm) **~miento de bala** shot put. **~r** [10] *vt* throw; (de un avión) drop; launch <*proyectil, producto*>. □ **~rse** *vpr* throw o.s.

lapicero *m* (propelling) pencil

lápida *f* tombstone; (placa conmemorativa) memorial tablet

lapidar *vt* stone

lápiz *m* pencil. **~ de labios** lipstick. **a ~** in pencil

lapso *m* lapse

larg|a *f*. **a la ~a** in the long run. **dar ~as** put off. **~ar** [12] *vt* (Naut) let out; ([I], dar) give; [I] deal <*bofetada etc*>. □ **~arse** *vpr* [I] beat it [I]. **~o** *a* long. ● *m* length. **¡~o!** go away! **a lo ~o** lengthwise. **a lo ~o de** along. **tener 100 metros de ~o** be 100 metres long

laring|e *f* larynx. **~itis** *f* laryngitis

larva *f* larva

las *art def fpl* the. *véase tb* LA. ● *pron* them. **~ de** those, the ones. **~ de Vd** your ones, yours. **~ que** whoever, the ones

láser *m* laser

lástima *f* pity; (queja) complaint. **da ~ verlo así** it's sad to see him like that. **ella me da ~** I feel sorry for her. **¡qué ~!** what a pity!

lastim|ado *a* hurt. **~ar** *vt* hurt. □ **~arse** *vpr* hurt o.s. **~ero** *a* doleful. **~oso** *a* pitiful

lastre *m* ballast; (fig) burden

lata *f* tinplate; (envase) tin (esp Brit), can; ([I], molestia) nuisance. **dar la ~** be a nuisance. **¡qué ~!** what a nuisance!

latente *a* latent

lateral *a* side, lateral

latido *m* beating; (cada golpe) beat

latifundio *m* large estate

latigazo *m* (golpe) lash; (chasquido) crack

látigo *m* whip

latín *m* Latin. **saber ~** [I] know what's what [I]

latino *a* Latin. **L~américa** *f* Latin America. **~americano** *a & m* Latin American

latir *vi* beat; <*herida*> throb

latitud *f* latitude

latón *m* brass

latoso *a* annoying; (pesado) boring

laúd *m* lute

laureado *a* honoured; (premiado) prize-winning

laurel *m* laurel; (Culin) bay

lava *f* lava

lava|ble *a* washable. **~bo** *m* wash-basin; (retrete) toilet. **~dero** *m* sink. **~do** *m* washing. **~do de cerebro** brainwashing. **~do en seco** dry-cleaning. **~dora** *f* washing machine. **~ndería** *f* laundry. **~ndería automática** launderette, laundromat (esp Amer). **~platos** *m & f invar* dishwasher. ● *m* (Mex, fregadero) sink. **~r** *vt* wash. **~r en seco** dry-clean. □ **~rse** *vpr* have a wash. **~rse las manos** (incl fig) wash one's hands. **~tiva** *f* enema. **~vajillas** *m invar* dishwasher; (detergente) washing-up liquid (Brit), dishwashing liquid (Amer)

laxante *a & m* laxative

lazada *f* bow

lazarillo *m* guide for a blind person

lazo *m* knot; (lazada) bow; (fig, vínculo) tie; (con nudo corredizo) lasso; (Mex, cuerda) rope

le *pron* (acusativo, él) him; (acusativo, Vd) you; (dativo, él) (to) him; (dativo, ella) (to) her; (dativo, cosa) (to) it; (dativo, Vd) (to) you

leal *a* loyal; (fiel) faithful. **~tad** *f* loyalty; (fidelidad) faithfulness

lección *f* lesson

leche *f* milk; (golpe) bash. **~ condensada** condensed milk. **~ desnatada** skimmed milk. **~ en polvo** powdered milk. **~ sin desnatar** whole milk. **tener mala ~** be spiteful. **~ra** *f* (vasija) milk jug. **~ría** *f* dairy. **~ro** *a* milk, dairy. ● *m* milkman

lecho *m* (en literatura) bed. **~ de río** river bed

lechoso *a* milky

lechuga *f* lettuce

lechuza *f* owl

lect|or *m* reader; (Univ) language assistant. **~ura** *f* reading

leer [18] *vt/i* read

legación *f* legation

legado *m* legacy; (enviado) legate

legajo *m* bundle, file

legal *a* legal. **~idad** *f* legality. **~izar** [10] *vt* legalize; (certificar) authenticate. **~mente** *adv* legally

legar [12] *vt* bequeath

legible *a* legible

legi|ón *f* legion. **~onario** *m* legionary

legisla|ción *f* legislation. **~dor** *m* legislator. **~r** *vi* legislate. **~tura** *f* term (of office); (año parlamentario) session; (LAm, cuerpo) legislature

leg|itimidad *f* legitimacy. **~ítimo** *a* legitimate; (verdadero) real

lego *a* lay; (ignorante) ignorant. ● *m* layman

legua *f* league

legumbre *f* vegetable

lejan|ía *f* distance. **~o** *a* distant

lejía *f* bleach

lejos *adv* far. **~ de** far from. **a lo ~** in the distance. **desde ~** from a distance, from afar

lema *m* motto

lencería *f* linen; (de mujer) lingerie

lengua *f* tongue; (idioma) language. **irse de la ~** talk too much. **morderse la ~** hold one's tongue
lenguado *m* sole
lenguaje *m* language
lengüeta *f* (de zapato) tongue. **~da** *f*, **~zo** *m* lick
lente *f* lens. **~s** *mpl* glasses. **~s de contacto** contact lenses
lentej|a *f* lentil. **~uela** *f* sequin
lentilla *f* contact lens
lent|itud *f* slowness. **~o** *a* slow
leñ|a *f* firewood. **~ador** *m* woodcutter. **~o** *m* log
Leo *m* Leo
le|ón *m* lion. **~ona** *f* lioness
leopardo *m* leopard
leotardo *m* thick tights
lepr|a *f* leprosy. **~oso** *m* leper
lerdo *a* dim; (torpe) clumsy
les *pron* (acusativo) them; (acusativo, Vds) you; (dativo) (to) them; (dativo, Vds) (to) you
lesbiana *f* lesbian
lesi|ón *f* wound. **~onado** *a* injured. **~onar** *vt* injure; (dañar) damage
letal *a* lethal
let|árgico *a* lethargic. **~argo** *m* lethargy
letr|a *f* letter; (escritura) handwriting; (de una canción) words, lyrics. **~a de cambio** bill of exchange. **~a de imprenta** print. **~ado** *a* learned. **~ero** *m* notice; (cartel) poster
letrina *f* latrine
leucemia *f* leukaemia
levadura *f* yeast. **~ en polvo** baking powder
levanta|miento *m* lifting; (sublevación) uprising. **~r** *vt* raise, lift; (construir) build; (recoger) pick up. □ **~rse** *vpr* get up; (ponerse de pie) stand up; (erguirse, sublevarse) rise up
levante *m* east; (viento) east wind
levar *vt*. **~ anclas** weigh anchor
leve *a* light; <*sospecha etc*> slight; <*enfermedad*> mild; (de poca importancia) trivial. **~dad** *f* lightness; (fig) slightness
léxico *m* vocabulary
lexicografía *f* lexicography
ley *f* law; (parlamentaria) act
leyenda *f* legend
liar [20] *vt* tie; (envolver) wrap up; roll <*cigarrillo*>; (fig, confundir) confuse; (fig, enredar) involve. □ **~se** *vpr* get involved
libanés *a* & *m* Lebanese
libelo *m* (escrito) libellous article; (Jurid) petition
libélula *f* dragonfly
libera|ción *f* liberation. **~dor** *a* liberating. ● *m* liberator
liberal *a* & *m* & *f* liberal. **~idad** *f* liberality
liber|ar *vt* free. **~tad** *f* freedom. **~tad de cultos** freedom of worship. **~tad de imprenta** freedom of the press. **~tad provisional** bail. **en ~tad** free. **~tador** *m* liberator. **~tar** *vt* free
libertino *m* libertine
libido *f* libido
libio *a* & *m* Libyan
libra *f* pound. **~ esterlina** pound sterling
Libra *m* Libra
libra|dor *m* (Com) drawer. **~r** *vt* free; (de un peligro) save. □ **~rse** *vpr* free o.s. **~rse de** get rid of
libre *a* free. **estilo ~** (en natación) freestyle. **~ de impuestos** tax-free
librea *f* livery

libr|ería *f* bookshop (Brit), bookstore (Amer); (mueble) bookcase. **~ero** *m* bookseller; (Mex, mueble) bookcase. **~eta** *f* notebook. **~o** *m* book. **~o de bolsillo** paperback. **~o de ejercicios** exercise book. **~o de reclamaciones** complaints book

licencia *f* permission; (documento) licence. **~do** *m* graduate; (Mex, abogado) lawyer. **~ para manejar** (Mex) driving licence. **~r** *vt* (Mil) discharge; (echar) dismiss. **~tura** *f* degree

licencioso *a* licentious

licitar *vt* bid for

lícito *a* legal; (permisible) permissible

licor *m* liquor; (dulce) liqueur

licua|dora *f* blender. **~r** [21] liquefy; (Culin) blend

lid *f* fight. **en buena ~** by fair means. **~es** *fpl* matters

líder *m* leader

liderato *m*, **liderazgo** *m* leadership

lidia *f* bullfighting; (lucha) fight. **~r** *vt/i* fight

liebre *f* hare

lienzo *m* linen; (del pintor) canvas; (muro, pared) wall

liga *f* garter; (alianza) league; (LAm, gomita) rubber band. **~dura** *f* bond; (Mus) slur; (Med) ligature. **~mento** *m* ligament. **~r** [12] *vt* bind; (atar) tie; (Mus) slur. ● *vi* mix. **~r con** (fig) pick up. □ **~rse** *vpr* (fig) commit o.s.

liger|eza *f* lightness; (agilidad) agility; (rapidez) swiftness; (de carácter) fickleness. **~o** *a* light; (rápido) quick; (ágil) agile; (superficial) superficial; (de poca importancia) slight. ● *adv* quickly. **a la ~a** lightly, superficially

liguero *m* suspender belt

lija *f* dogfish; (papel de lija) sandpaper. **~r** *vt* sand

lila *f* lilac. ● *m* (color) lilac

lima *f* file; (fruta) lime. **~duras** *fpl* filings. **~r** *vt* file (down)

limita|ción *f* limitation. **~do** *a* limited. **~r** *vt* limit. **~r con** border on. **~tivo** *a* limiting

límite *m* limit. **~ de velocidad** speed limit

limítrofe *a* bordering

lim|ón *m* lemon; (Mex) lime. **~onada** *f* lemonade

limosn|a *f* alms. **pedir ~a** beg. **~ear** *vi* beg

limpia|botas *m invar* bootblack. **~parabrisas** *m invar* windscreen wiper (Brit), windshield wiper (Amer). **~pipas** *m invar* pipe-cleaner. **~r** *vt* clean; (enjugar) wipe. **~vidrios** *m invar* (LAm) window cleaner.

limpi|eza *f* cleanliness; (acción de limpiar) cleaning. **~eza en seco** dry-cleaning. **~o** *a* clean; <*cielo*> clear; (fig, honrado) honest; (neto) net. **pasar a ~o**, (LAm) **pasar en ~o** make a fair copy. ● *adv* fairly. **jugar ~o** play fair

linaje *m* lineage; (fig, clase) kind

lince *m* lynx

linchar *vt* lynch

lind|ar *vi* border (**con** on). **~e** *f* boundary. **~ero** *m* border

lindo *a* pretty, lovely. **de lo ~** [I] a lot

línea *f* line. **en ~s generales** broadly speaking. **guardar la ~** watch one's figure

lingote *m* ingot

lingü|ista *m & f* linguist. **~ística** *f* linguistics. **~ístico** *a* linguistic

lino *m* flax; (tela) linen

linterna *f* lantern; (de bolsillo) torch, flashlight (Amer)

lío *m* bundle; (jaleo) fuss; (embrollo) muddle; (amorío) affair

liquida|ción *f* liquidation; (venta especial) sale. **~r** *vt* liquify; (Com) liquidate; settle *<cuenta>*

líquido *a* liquid; (Com) net. ● *m* liquid; (Com) cash

lira *f* lyre; (moneda italiana) lira

líric|a *f* lyric poetry. **~o** *a* lyric(al)

lirio *m* iris

lirón *m* dormouse; (fig) sleepyhead. **dormir como un ~** sleep like a log

lisiado *a* crippled

liso *a* smooth; *<pelo>* straight; *<tierra>* flat; (sencillo) plain

lisonj|a *f* flattery. **~eador** *a* flattering. ● *m* flatterer. **~ear** *vt* flatter. **~ero** *a* flattering

lista *f* stripe; (enumeración) list. **~ de correos** poste restante. **a ~s** striped. **pasar ~** take the register. **~do** *a* striped

listo *a* clever; (preparado) ready

listón *m* strip; (en saltos) bar; (Mex, cinta) ribbon

litera *f* (en barco, tren) berth; (en habitación) bunk bed

literal *a* literal

litera|rio *a* literary. **~tura** *f* literature

litig|ar [12] *vi* dispute; (Jurid) litigate. **~io** *m* dispute; (Jurid) litigation

litografía *f* (arte) lithography; (cuadro) lithograph

litoral *a* coastal. ● *m* coast

litro *m* litre

lituano *a & m* Lithuanian

liturgia *f* liturgy

liviano *a* fickle; (LAm, de poco peso) light

lívido *a* livid

llaga *f* wound; (úlcera) ulcer

llama *f* flame; (animal) llama

llamada *f* call

llama|do *a* called. ● *m* (LAm) call. **~miento** *m* call. **~r** *vt* call; (por teléfono) phone. ● *vi* call; (golpear en la puerta) knock; (tocar el timbre) ring. **~r por teléfono** phone, telephone. □ **~rse** *vpr* be called. **¿cómo te ~s?** what's your name?

llamarada *f* sudden blaze; (fig, de pasión etc) outburst

llamativo *a* flashy; *<color>* loud; *<persona>* striking

llamear *vi* blaze

llano *a* flat, level; *<persona>* natural; (sencillo) plain. ● *m* plain

llanta *f* (Auto) (wheel) rim; (LAm, neumático) tyre

llanto *m* crying

llanura *f* plain

llave *f* key; (para tuercas) spanner; (LAm, del baño etc) tap (Brit), faucet (Amer); (Elec) switch. **~ inglesa** monkey wrench. **cerrar con ~** lock. **echar la ~** lock up. **~ro** *m* key-ring

llega|da *f* arrival. **~r** [12] *vi* arrive, come; (alcanzar) reach; (bastar) be enough. **~r a** (conseguir) manage to. **~r a saber** find out. **~r a ser** become. **~r hasta** go as far as

llen|ar *vt* fill (up); (rellenar) fill in; (cubrir) cover (**de** with). **~o** *a* full. ● *m* (en el teatro etc) full house. **de ~** entirely

lleva|dero *a* tolerable. **~r** *vt* carry; (inducir, conducir) lead; (acompañar) take; wear *<ropa>*. **¿cuánto tiempo ~s aquí?** how long have you been here? **llevo 3 años estu-**

diando inglés I've been studying English for 3 years. □ **~rse** *vpr* take away; win <*premio etc*>; (comprar) take. **~rse bien** get on well together

llor|ar *vi* cry; <*ojos*> water. **~iquear** *vi* whine. **~iqueo** *m* whining. **~o** *m* crying. **~ón** *a* whining. • *m* cry-baby. **~oso** *a* tearful

llov|er [2] *vi* rain. **~izna** *f* drizzle. **~iznar** *vi* drizzle

llueve *vb* ⇒LLOVER

lluvi|a *f* rain; (fig) shower. **~oso** *a* rainy; <*clima*> wet

lo *art def neutro*. **~ importante** what is important, the important thing. • *pron* (él) him; (cosa) it. **~ que** what, that which

loa *f* praise. **~ble** *a* praiseworthy. **~r** *vt* praise

lobo *m* wolf

lóbrego *a* gloomy

lóbulo *m* lobe

local *a* local. • *m* premises. **~idad** *f* locality; (de un espectáculo) seat; (entrada) ticket. **~izar** [10] *vt* find, locate

loción *f* lotion

loco *a* mad, crazy. • *m* lunatic. **~ de alegría** mad with joy. **estar ~ por** be crazy about. **volverse ~** go mad

locomo|ción *f* locomotion. **~tora** *f* locomotive

locuaz *a* talkative

locución *f* expression

locura *f* madness; (acto) crazy thing. **con ~** madly

locutor *m* broadcaster

lod|azal *m* quagmire. **~o** *m* mud

lógic|a *f* logic. **~o** *a* logical

logr|ar *vt* get; win <*premio*>. **~ hacer** manage to do. **~o** *m* achievement; (de premio) winning; (éxito) success

loma *f* small hill

lombriz *f* worm

lomo *m* back; (de libro) spine. **~ de cerdo** loin of pork

lona *f* canvas

loncha *f* slice; (de tocino) rasher

londinense *a* from London. • *m* Londoner

Londres *m* London

loneta *f* thin canvas

longaniza *f* sausage

longev|idad *f* longevity. **~o** *a* long-lived

longitud *f* length; (Geog) longitude

lonja *f* slice; (de tocino) rasher; (Com) market

lord *m* (*pl* **lores**) lord

loro *m* parrot

los *art def mpl* the. *véase tb* EL. • *pron* them. **~ de Antonio** Antonio's. **~ que** whoever, the ones

losa *f* (baldosa) flagstone. **~ sepulcral** tombstone

lote *m* share; (de productos) batch; (terreno) plot (Brit), lot (Amer)

lotería *f* lottery

loto *m* lotus

loza *f* crockery; (fina) china

lozano *a* fresh; <*vegetación*> lush; <*persona*> healthy-looking

lubrica|nte *a* lubricating. • *m* lubricant. **~r** [7] *vt* lubricate

lucero *m* bright star. **~ del alba** morning star

lucha *f* fight; (fig) struggle. **~dor** *m* fighter. **~r** *vi* fight; (fig) struggle

lucid|ez *f* lucidity. **~o** *a* splendid

lúcido *a* lucid

luciérnaga *f* glow-worm

lucimiento *m* brilliance

lucir [11] *vt* (fig) show off. ● *vi* shine; *<joya>* sparkle; (LAm, mostrarse) look. □ **~se** *vpr* (fig) shine, excel; (presumir) show off

lucr|ativo *a* lucrative. **~o** *m* gain

luego *adv* then; (más tarde) later (on); (Mex, pronto) soon. ● *conj* therefore. **~ que** as soon as. **desde ~** of course

lugar *m* place; (espacio libre) room. **~ común** cliché. **dar ~ a** give rise to. **en ~ de** instead of. **en primer ~** first. **hacer ~** make room. **tener ~** take place. **~eño** *a* local, village

lugarteniente *m* deputy

lúgubre *a* gloomy

lujo *m* luxury. **de ~** luxury. **~so** *a* luxurious

lujuria *f* lust

lumbago *m* lumbago

lumbre *f* fire; (luz) light

luminoso *a* luminous; (fig) bright; *<letrero>* illuminated

luna *f* moon; (espejo) mirror. **~ de miel** honeymoon. **claro de ~** moonlight. **estar en la ~** be miles away. **~r** *a* lunar. ● *m* mole; (en tela) spot

lunes *m invar* Monday

lupa *f* magnifying glass

lustr|abotas *m invar* (LAm) bootblack. **~ar** *vt* shine, polish. **~e** *m* shine; (fig, esplendor) splendour. **dar ~e a, sacar ~e a** polish. **~oso** *a* shining

luto *m* mourning. **estar de ~** be in mourning

luz *f* light; (electricidad) electricity. **luces altas** (LAm) headlights on full beam. **luces bajas** (LAm), **luces cortas** dipped headlights. **luces antiniebla** fog light. **luces largas** headlights on full beam. **a la ~ de** in the light of. **a todas luces** obviously. **dar a ~** give birth. **hacer la ~ sobre** shed light on. **sacar a la ~** bring to light

Mm

macabro *a* macabre

macaco *m* macaque (monkey)

macanudo *a* [I] great[I]

macarrones *mpl* macaroni

macerar *vt* macerate *<fruta>*; marinade *<carne etc>*

maceta *f* mallet; (tiesto) flowerpot

machacar [7] *vt* crush. ● *vi* go on (**sobre** about)

machamartillo. **a ~** *adj* ardent; (como adv) firmly

machet|azo *m* blow with a machete; (herida) wound from a machete. **~e** *m* machete

mach|ista *m* male chauvinist. **~o** *a* male; (varonil) macho

machu|car [7] *vt* bruise; (aplastar) crush. **~cón** *m* (LAm) bruise

macizo *a* solid. ● *m* mass; (de plantas) bed

madeja *f* skein

madera *m* (vino) Madeira. ● *f* wood; (naturaleza) nature. **~ble** *a* yielding timber. **~men** *m* woodwork

madero *m* log; (de construcción) timber

madona *f* Madonna

madr|astra *f* stepmother. **~e** *f* mother. **~eperla** *f* mother-of-pearl. **~eselva** *f* honeysuckle

madrigal *m* madrigal

madriguera *f* den; (de conejo) burrow

madrileño *a* of Madrid. ● *m* person from Madrid

madrina *f* godmother; (en una boda) matron of honour

madrug|ada *f* dawn. **de ~ada** at dawn. **~ador** *a* who gets up early. ● *m* early riser. **~ar** [12] *vi* get up early

madur|ación *f* maturing; (de fruta) ripening. **~ar** *vt/i* mature; <*fruta*> ripen. **~ez** *f* maturity; (de fruta) ripeness. **~o** *a* mature; <*fruta*> ripe

maestr|ía *f* skill; (Univ) master's degree. **~o** *m* master; (de escuela) schoolteacher

mafia *f* mafia

magdalena *f* fairy cake (Brit), cup cake (Amer)

magia *f* magic

mágico *a* magic; (maravilloso) magical

magist|erio *m* teaching (profession); (conjunto de maestros) teachers. **~rado** *m* magistrate; (juez) judge. **~ral** *a* teaching; (bienhecho) masterly. **~ratura** *f* magistracy

magn|animidad *f* magnanimity. **~ánimo** *a* magnanimous. **~ate** *m* magnate, tycoon

magnavoz *m* (Mex) megaphone

magnético *a* magnetic

magneti|smo *m* magnetism. **~zar** [10] *vt* magnetize

magn|ificar *vt* extol; (LAm) magnify <*objeto*>. **~ificencia** *f* magnificence. **~ífico** *a* magnificent. **~itud** *f* magnitude

magnolia *f* magnolia

mago *m* magician; (en cuentos) wizard

magro *a* lean; <*tierra*> poor

magulla|dura *f* bruise. **~r** *vt* bruise. □ **~rse** *vpr* bruise

mahometano *a* Islamic

maíz *m* maize, corn (Amer)

majada *f* sheepfold; (estiércol) manure; (LAm) flock of sheep

majader|ía *f* silly thing. **~o** *m* idiot. ● *a* stupid

majest|ad *f* majesty. **~uoso** *a* majestic

majo *a* nice

mal *adv* badly; (poco) poorly; (difícilmente) hardly; (equivocadamente) wrongly; (desagradablemente) bad. ● *a*. **estar ~** be ill; (anímicamente) be in a bad way; (incorrecto) be wrong. **estar ~ de** (escaso de) be short of. *véase tb* MALO. ● *m* evil; (daño) harm; (enfermedad) illness. **~ que bien** somehow (or other). **de ~ en peor** from bad to worse. **hacer ~ en** be wrong to. **¡menos ~!** thank goodness!

malabaris|mo *m* juggling. **~ta** *m & f* juggler

mala|consejado *a* ill-advised. **~costumbrado** *a* spoilt. **~crianza** *f* (LAm) rudeness. **~gradecido** *a* ungrateful

malagueño *a* of Málaga. ● *m* person from Málaga

malaria *f* malaria

Malasia *f* Malaysia

malavenido *a* incompatible

malaventura *a* unfortunate

malayo *a* Malay(an)

malbaratar *vt* sell off cheap; (malgastar) squander

malcarado *a* nasty looking

malcriado *a* <*niño*> spoilt

maldad *f* evil; (acción) wicked thing

maldecir [46] (*pero imperativo* **maldice**, *futuro y condicional regulares, pp* **maldecido** *o* **maldito**) *vt* curse. ● *vi* curse; speak ill (**de** of)

maldi|ciente *a* backbiting; (que blasfema) foul-mouthed. **~ción** *f* curse. **~to** *a* damned. **¡~to sea!** damn (it)!

maleab|ilidad *f* malleability. **~le** *a* malleable

malea|nte *m* criminal. **~r** *vt* damage; (pervertir) corrupt. □ **~rse** *vpr* be spoilt; (pervertirse) be corrupted

malecón *m* breakwater; (embarcadero) jetty; (Rail) embankment; (LAm, paseo marítimo) seafront

maledicencia *f* slander

mal|eficio *m* curse. **~éfico** *a* evil

malestar *m* discomfort; (fig) uneasiness

malet|a *f* (suit)case. **hacer la ~a** pack (one's case). **~ero** *m* porter; (Auto) boot, trunk (Amer). **~ín** *m* small case; (para documentos) briefcase

mal|evolencia *f* malevolence. **~évolo** *a* malevolent

maleza *f* weeds; (matorral) undergrowth

mal|gastar *vt* waste. **~hablado** *a* foul-mouthed. **~hechor** *m* criminal. **~humorado** *a* bad-tempered

malici|a *f* malice; (picardía) mischief. □ **~arse** *vpr* suspect. **~oso** *a* malicious; (pícaro) mischievous

maligno *a* malignant; <*persona*> evil

malintencionado *a* malicious

malla *f* mesh; (de armadura) mail; (de gimnasia) leotard

Mallorca *f* Majorca.

mallorquín *a* & *m* Majorcan

malmirado *a* (con estar) frowned upon

malo *a* (*delante de nombre masculino en singular* **mal**) bad; (enfermo) ill. **~ de** difficult to. **estar de malas** (malhumorado) be in a bad mood; (LAm, con mala suerte) be out of luck. **lo ~ es que** the trouble is that. **por las malas** by force

malogr|ar *vt* waste; (estropear) spoil. □ **~arse** *vpr* fall through

maloliente *a* smelly

malpensado *a* nasty, malicious

malsano *a* unhealthy

malsonante *a* ill-sounding; (grosero) offensive

malt|a *f* malt. **~eada** *f* (LAm) milk shake. **~ear** *vt* malt

maltr|atar *vt* ill-treat; (pegar) batter; mistreat <*juguete etc*>. **~echo** *a* battered

malucho *a* 🅸 under the weather

malva *f* mallow. **(color de) ~** *a invar* mauve

malvado *a* wicked

malvavisco *m* marshmallow

malversa|ción *f* embezzlement. **~dor** *a* embezzling. ● *m* embezzler. **~r** *vt* embezzle

Malvinas *fpl.* **las (islas) ~** the Falklands, the Falkland Islands

mama *f* mammary gland; (de mujer) breast

mamá *f* mum; (usado por niños) mummy

mama|da *f* sucking. **~r** *vt* suck; (fig) grow up with. ● *vi* <*bebé*> feed; <*animal*> suckle. **dar de ~** breastfeed

mamario *a* mammary

mamarracho *m* clown; (cosa ridícula) (ridiculous) sight; (cosa mal hecha) botch; (cosa fea) mess. **ir hecho un ~** look a sight

mameluco *m* (LAm) overalls; (de niño) rompers

mamífero *a* mammalian. ● *m* mammal

mamila *f* (Mex) feeding bottle

mamotreto *m* (libro) hefty volume; (armatoste) huge thing

mampara *f* screen

mampostería *f* masonry

mamut *m* mammoth

manada *f* herd; (de lobos) pack; (de leones) pride. **en ~** in crowds

mana|ntial *m* spring; (fig) source. **~r** *vi* flow; (fig) abound. ● *vt* drip with

manaza *f* big hand

mancha *f* stain; (en la piel) blotch. **~do** *a* stained; (sucio) dirty; <*animal*> spotted. **~r** *vt* stain; (ensuciar) dirty. □ **~rse** *vpr* get stained; (ensuciarse) get dirty

manchego *a* of la Mancha. ● *m* person from la Mancha

manchón *m* large stain

mancilla *f* blemish. **~r** *vt* stain

manco *a* (de una mano) one-handed; (de las dos manos) handless; (de un brazo) one-armed; (de los dos brazos) armless

mancomun|adamente *adv* jointly. **~ar** *vt* unite; (Jurid) make jointly liable. □ **~arse** *vpr* unite. **~idad** *f* union

manda *f* (Mex) religious offering

manda|dero *m* messenger. **~do** *m* (LAm) shopping; (diligencia) errand. **hacer los ~dos** (LAm) do the shopping. **~miento** *m* order; (Relig) commandment. **~r** *vt* order; (enviar) send; (gobernar) rule. ● *vi* be in command. **¿mande?** (Mex) pardon?

mandarin|a *f* (naranja) mandarin (orange). **~o** *m* mandarin tree

mandat|ario *m* attorney; (Pol) head of state. **~o** *m* mandate; (Pol) term of office

mandíbula *f* jaw

mando *m* command. **~ a distancia** remote control. **al ~ de** in charge of. **altos ~s** *mpl* high-ranking officers

mandolina *f* mandolin

mandón *a* bossy

manducar [7] *vt* 🅘 stuff oneself with

manecilla *f* hand

manej|able *a* manageable. **~ar** *vt* use; handle <*asunto etc*>; (fig) manage; (LAm, conducir) drive. □ **~arse** *vpr* get by. **~o** *m* handling. **~os** *mpl* scheming

manera *f* way. **~s** *fpl* manners. **de alguna ~** somehow. **de ~ que** so (that). **de ninguna ~** by no means. **de otra ~** otherwise. **de todas ~s** anyway

manga *f* sleeve; (tubo de goma) hose; (red) net; (para colar) filter; (LAm, de langostas) swarm

mango *m* handle; (fruta) mango. **~near** *vt* boss about. ● *vi* (entrometerse) interfere

manguera *f* hose(pipe)

manguito *m* muff

maní *m* (*pl* **~es**) (LAm) peanut

manía *f* mania; (antipatía) dislike. **tener la ~ de** have an obsession with

maniaco *a*, **maníaco** *a* maniac(al). ● *m* maniac

maniatar *vt* tie s.o.'s hands

maniático *a* maniac(al); (obsesivo) obsessive; (loco) crazy; (delicado) finicky

manicomio *m* lunatic asylum

manicura *f* manicure; (mujer) manicurist

manido *a* stale

manifesta|ción *f* manifestation, sign; (Pol) demonstration. **~nte** *m* demonstrator. **~r** [1] *vt* show; (Pol) state. □ **~rse** *vpr* show; (Pol) demonstrate

manifiesto *a* clear; <*error*> obvious; <*verdad*> manifest. ● *m* manifesto

manilargo *a* light-fingered

manilla *f* (de cajón etc) handle; (de reloj) hand. **~r** *m* handlebar(s)

maniobra *f* manoeuvre. **~r** *vt* operate; (Rail) shunt. ● *vt/i* manoeuvre. **~s** *fpl* (Mil) manoeuvres

manipula|ción *f* manipulation. **~r** *vt* manipulate

maniquí *m* dummy. ● *m & f* model

mani|rroto *a & m* spendthrift. **~ta** *f*, (LAm) **~to** *m* little hand

manivela *f* crank

manjar *m* delicacy

mano *f* hand; (de animales) front foot; (de perros, gatos) front paw. **~ de obra** work force. **~s arriba!** hands up! **a ~** by hand; (próximo) handy. **a ~ derecha** on the right. **de segunda ~** second hand. **echar una ~** lend a hand. **tener buena ~ para** be good at. ● *m* (LAm, [I]) mate (Brit), buddy (Amer)

manojo *m* bunch

manose|ar *vt* handle. **~o** *m* handling

manotada *f*, **manotazo** *m* slap

manote|ar *vi* gesticulate. **~o** *m* gesticulation

mansalva: **a ~** *adv* without risk

mansarda *f* attic

mansión *f* mansion. **~ señorial** stately home

manso *a* gentle; <*animal*> tame

manta *f* blanket

mantec|a *f* fat. **~oso** *a* greasy

mantel *m* tablecloth; (del altar) altar cloth. **~ería** *f* table linen

manten|er [40] *vt* support; (conservar) keep; (sostener) maintain. □ **~erse** *vpr* support o.s.; (permanecer) remain. **~se de/con** live off. **~imiento** *m* maintenance

mantequ|era *f* butter churn. **~illa** *f* butter

mant|illa *f* mantilla. **~o** *m* cloak. **~ón** *m* shawl

manual *a & m* manual

manubrio *m* crank; (LAm, de bicicleta) handlebars

manufactura *f* manufacture. **~r** *vt* manufacture, make

manuscrito *a* handwritten. ● *m* manuscript

manutención *f* maintenance

manzana *f* apple; (de edificios) block. **~ de Adán** (LAm) Adam's apple. **~r** *m* (apple) orchard

manzan|illa *f* camomile tea. ● *m* manzanilla, pale dry sherry. **~o** *m* apple tree

maña *f* skill. **~s** *fpl* cunning

mañan|a *f* morning. **~a por la ~a** tomorrow morning. **pasado ~a** the day after tomorrow. **en la ~a** (LAm), **por la ~a** in the morning. ● *m* future. ● *adv* tomorrow. **~ero** *a* who gets up early. ● *m* early riser

mañoso *a* clever; (astuto) crafty; (LAm, caprichoso) difficult

mapa *m* map

mapache *m* racoon

maqueta *f* scale model

maquiladora *f* (Mex) cross-border assembly plant

maquilla|je *m* make-up. **~r** *vt* make up. □ **~rse** *vpr* make up

máquina *f* machine; (Rail) engine. **~ de afeitar** shaver. **~ de escribir** typewriter. **~ fotográfica** camera

maquin|ación *f* machination. **~al** *a* mechanical. **~aria** *f* machinery. **~ista** *m & f* operator; (Rail) engine driver

mar *m & f* sea. **alta ~** high seas. **la ~ de** Ⓘ lots of

maraña *f* thicket; (enredo) tangle; (embrollo) muddle

maratón *m & f* marathon

maravill|a *f* wonder. **a las mil ~as, de ~as** marvellously. **contar/decir ~as de** speak wonderfully of. **hacer ~as** work wonders. **~ar** *vt* astonish. □ **~arse** *vpr* be astonished (**de** at). **~oso** *a* marvellous, wonderful

marca *f* mark; (de coches etc) make; (de alimentos, cosméticos) brand; (Deportes) record. **~ de fábrica** trade mark. **de ~** brand name; (fig) excellent. **de ~ mayor** Ⓘ absolute. **~do** *a* marked. **~dor** *m* marker; (Deportes) scoreboard. **~r** [7] *vt* mark; (señalar) show; score *<un gol>*; dial *<número de teléfono>*. ● *vi* score

marcha *f* (incl Mus) march; (Auto) gear; (desarrollo) course; (partida) departure. **a toda ~** at full speed. **dar/hacer ~ atrás** put into reverse. **poner en ~** start; (fig) set in motion

marchante *m* (*f* **marchanta**) art dealer; (Mex, en mercado) stall holder

marchar *vi* go; (funcionar) work, go; (Mil) march. □ **~se** *vpr* leave

marchit|ar *vt* wither. □ **~arse** *vpr* wither. **~o** *a* withered

marcial *a* martial

marciano *a & m* Martian

marco *m* frame; (moneda alemana) mark; (deportes) goal-posts

marea *f* tide. **~do** *a* sick; (en el mar) seasick; (aturdido) dizzy; (borracho) drunk. **~r** *vt* make feel sick; (aturdir) make feel dizzy; (confundir) confuse. □ **~rse** *vpr* feel sick; (en un barco) get seasick; (estar aturdido) feel dizzy; (irse la cabeza) feel faint; (emborracharse) get slightly drunk; (confundirse) get confused

marejada *f* swell; (fig) wave

mareo *m* sickness; (en el mar) seasickness; (aturdimiento) dizziness; (confusión) muddle

marfil *m* ivory

margarina *f* margarine

margarita *f* daisy; (cóctel) margarita

marg|en *m* margin; (de un camino) side. ● *f* (de un río) bank. **~inado** *a* excluded. ● *m* outcast. **al ~en** (fig) outside. **~inal** *a* marginal. **~inar** *vt* (excluir) exclude; (fijar márgenes) set margins

mariachi *m* (Mex) (música popular de Jalisco) Mariachi music; (conjunto) Mariachi band; (músico) Mariachi musician

maric|a *m* Ⓘ sissy Ⓘ. **~ón** *m* Ⓘ homosexual, queer Ⓘ; (LAm, cobarde) wimp

marido *m* husband

mariguana *f*, **marihuana** *f* marijuana

marimacho *f* mannish woman

marimba *f* (type of) drum (LAm, especie de xilofón) marimba

marin|a *f* navy; (barcos) fleet; (cuadro) seascape. **~a de guerra** navy. **~a mercante** merchant navy. **~ería** *f* seamanship; (marineros) sailors. **~ero** *a* marine; <*barco*> seaworthy. ● *m* sailor. **a la ~era** in tomato and garlic sauce. **~o** *a* marine

marioneta *f* puppet. **~s** *fpl* puppet show

maripos|a *f* butterfly. **~a nocturna** moth. **~ear** *vi* be fickle; (galantear) flirt. **~ón** *m* flirt

mariquita *f* ladybird (Brit), ladybug (Amer). ● *m* [I] sissy [I]

mariscador *m* shell-fisher

mariscal *m* marshal

maris|car *vt* fish for shellfish. **~co** *m* seafood, shellfish. **~quero** *m* (pescador de mariscos) seafood fisherman; (vendedor de mariscos) seafood seller

marital *a* marital; <*vida*> married

marítimo *a* maritime; <*ciudad etc*> coastal, seaside

marmita *f* cooking pot

mármol *m* marble

marmota *f* marmot

maroma *f* rope; (Mex, voltereta) somersault

marqu|és *m* marquess. **~esa** *f* marchioness. **~esina** *f* glass canopy; (en estadio) roof

marran|a *f* sow. **~ada** *f* filthy thing; (cochinada) dirty trick. **~o** *a* filthy. ● *m* hog

marrón *a* & *m* brown

marroqu|í *a* & *m* & *f* Moroccan. ● *m* (leather) morocco. **~inería** *f* leather goods

Marruecos *m* Morocco

marsopa *f* porpoise

marsupial *a* & *m* marsupial

marta *f* marten

martajar *vt* (Mex) crush <*maíz*>

Marte *m* Mars

martes *m invar* Tuesday. **~ de carnaval** Shrove Tuesday

martill|ar *vt* hammer. **~azo** *m* blow with a hammer. **~ear** *vt* hammer. **~eo** *m* hammering. **~o** *m* hammer

martín pescador *m* kingfisher

martinete *m* (del piano) hammer; (ave) heron

martingala *f* (ardid) trick

mártir *m* & *f* martyr

martir|io *m* martyrdom; (fig) torment. **~izar** [10] *vt* martyr; (fig) torment, torture

marxis|mo *m* Marxism. **~ta** *a* & *m* & *f* Marxist

marzo *m* March

más *adv* & *a* (comparativo) more; (superlativo) most. **~ caro** dearer. **~ doloroso** more painful. **el ~ caro** the dearest; (de dos) the dearer. **el ~ curioso** the most curious; (de dos) the more curious. ● *prep* plus. ● *m* plus (sign). **~ bien** rather. **~ de** (cantidad indeterminada) more than. **~ o menos** more or less. **~ que** more than. **~ y ~** more and more. **a lo ~** at (the) most. **dos ~ dos** two plus two. **de ~** too many. **es ~** moreover. **nadie ~** nobody else. **no ~** no more

masa *f* mass; (Culin) dough. **en ~** en masse

masacre *f* massacre

masaj|e *m* massage. **~ear** *vt* massage. **~ista** *m* masseur. ● *f* masseuse

mascada *f* (Mex) scarf

mascar [7] *vt* chew

máscara *f* mask

mascar|ada *f* masquerade. **~illa** *f* mask. **~ón** *m* (Naut) figurehead

mascota *f* mascot

masculin|idad *f* masculinity. **~o** *a* masculine; <*sexo*> male. ● *m* masculine

mascullar [3] *vt* mumble

masilla *f* putty

masivo *a* massive, large-scale

mas|ón *m* Freemason. **~onería** *f* Freemasonry. **~ónico** *a* Masonic

masoquis|mo *m* masochism. **~ta** *a* masochistic. ● *m* & *f* masochist

mastica|ción *f* chewing. **~r** [7] *vt* chew

mástil *m* (Naut) mast; (de bandera) flagpole; (de guitarra, violín) neck

mastín *m* mastiff

mastodonte *m* mastodon; (fig) giant

masturba|ción *f* masturbation. ▫ **~rse** *vpr* masturbate

mata *f* (arbusto) bush; (LAm, planta) plant

matad|ero *m* slaughterhouse. **~or** *a* killing. ● *m* (torero) matador

matamoscas *m invar* fly swatter

mata|nza *f* killing. **~r** *vt* kill <*personas*>; slaughter <*reses*>. **~rife** *m* butcher. ▫ **~rse** *vpr* kill o.s.; (en un accidente) be killed; (Mex, para un examen) cram. **~rse trabajando** work like mad

mata|polillas *m invar* moth killer. **~rratas** *m invar* rat poison

matasanos *m invar* quack

matasellos *m invar* postmark

mate *a* matt. ● *m* (ajedrez) (check) mate (LAm, bebida) maté

matemátic|as *fpl* mathematics, maths (Brit), math (Amer). **~o** *a* mathematical. ● *m* mathematician

materia *f* matter; (material) material; (LAm, asignatura) subject. **~ prima** raw material. **en ~ de** on the question of

material *a* & *m* material. **~idad** *f* material nature. **~ismo** *m* materialism. **~ista** *a* materialistic. ● *m* & *f* materialist; (Mex, constructor) building contractor. **~izar** [10] *vt* materialize. ▫ **~izarse** *vpr* materialize. **~mente** *adv* materially; (absolutamente) absolutely

matern|al *a* maternal; <*amor*> motherly. **~idad** *f* motherhood; (hospital) maternity hospital; (sala) maternity ward. **~o** *a* motherly; <*lengua*> mother

matin|al *a* morning. **~ée** *m* matinée

matiz *m* shade; (fig) nuance. **~ación** *f* combination of colours. **~ar** [10] *vt* blend <*colores*>; (introducir variedad) vary; (teñir) tinge (**de** with)

mat|ón *m* bully; (de barrio) thug. **~onismo** *m* bullying; (de barrio) thuggery

matorral *m* scrub; (conjunto de matas) thicket

matraca *f* rattle. **dar ~** pester

matraz *m* flask

matriarca *f* matriarch. **~do** *m* matriarchy. **~l** *a* matriarchal

matr|ícula *f* (lista) register, list; (inscripción) registration; (Auto) registration number; (placa) licence plate. **~icular** *vt* register. ▫ **~icularse** *vpr* enrol, register

matrimoni|al *a* matrimonial. **~o** *m* marriage; (pareja) married couple

matriz *f* matrix; (molde) mould; (Anat) womb, uterus

matrona *f* matron; (partera) midwife

matutino *a* morning

maull|ar *vi* miaow. **~ido** *m* miaow

mausoleo *m* mausoleum

maxilar *a* maxillary. ● *m* jaw(bone)

máxim|a *f* maxim. **~e** *adv* especially. **~o** *a* maximum; <*punto*> highest. ● *m* maximum

maya *f* daisy. ● *a* Mayan. ● *m & f* (persona) Maya

mayo *m* May

mayonesa *f* mayonnaise

mayor *a* (más grande, comparativo) bigger; (más grande, superlativo) biggest; (de edad, comparativo) older; (de edad, superlativo) oldest; (adulto) grown-up; (principal) main, major; (Mus) major. ● *m & f* (adulto) adult. **al por ~** wholesale. **~al** *m* foreman. **~azgo** *m* entailed estate

mayordomo *m* butler

mayor|ía *f* majority. **~ista** *m & f* wholesaler. **~itario** *a* majority; <*socio*> principal. **~mente** *adv* especially

mayúscul|a *f* capital (letter). **~o** *a* capital; (fig, grande) big

mazacote *m* hard mass

mazapán *m* marzipan

mazmorra *f* dungeon

mazo *m* mallet; (manojo) bunch; (LAm, de naipes) pack (Brit), deck (Amer)

mazorca *f* cob. **~ de maíz** corncob

me *pron* (acusativo) me; (dativo) (to) me; (reflexivo) (to) myself

mecánic|a *f* mechanics. **~o** *a* mechanical. ● *m* mechanic

mecani|smo *m* mechanism. **~zación** *f* mechanization. **~zar** [10] *vt* mechanize

mecanograf|ía *f* typing. **~iado** *a* typed, typewritten. **~iar** [20] *vt* type

mecanógrafo *m* typist

mecate *m* (Mex) string; (más grueso) rope

mecedora *f* rocking chair

mecenas *m & f invar* patron

mecer [9] *vt* rock; swing <*columpio*>. □ **~se** *vpr* rock; (en un columpio) swing

mecha *f* (de vela) wick; (de explosivo) fuse. **~s** *fpl* highlights

mechar *vt* stuff, lard

mechero *m* (cigarette) lighter

mechón *m* (de pelo) lock

medall|a *f* medal. **~ón** *m* medallion; (relicario) locket

media *f* stocking; (promedio) average. **a ~s** half each

mediación *f* mediation

mediado *a* half full; (a mitad de) halfway through. **~s** *mpl.* **a ~s de marzo** in mid-March

mediador *m* mediator

medialuna *f* (*pl* **mediaslunas**) croissant

median|a *f* (Auto) central reservation (Brit), median strip (Amer). **~amente** *adv* fairly. **~era** *f* party wall. **~ero** *a* <*muro*> party. **~o** *a* medium; (mediocre) average, mediocre

medianoche *f* (*pl* **mediasnoches**) midnight; (Culin) *type of roll*

mediante *prep* through, by means of

mediar *vi* mediate; (llegar a la mitad) be halfway through; (interceder) intercede (**por** for)

medic|ación *f* medication. **~amento** *m* medicine. **~ina** *f* medicine. **~inal** *a* medicinal

medición *f* measurement

médico *a* medical. ● *m* doctor. **~ de cabecera** GP, general practitioner

medid|a *f* measurement; (unidad) measure; (disposición) measure, step; (prudencia) moderation. **a la ~a** made to measure. **a ~a que** as. **en cierta ~a** to a certain extent. **~or** *m* (LAm) meter

medieval *a* medieval. **~ista** *m & f* medievalist

medio *a* half (a); (mediano) average. **dos horas y media** two and a half hours. **~ litro** half a litre. **las dos y media** half past two. ● *m* middle; (Math) half; (manera) means; (en deportes) half(-back). **en ~** in the middle (**de** of). **por ~ de** through. **~ ambiente** *m* environment

medioambiental *a* environmental

mediocr|e *a* mediocre. **~idad** *f* mediocrity

mediodía *m* midday, noon; (sur) south

medioevo *m* Middle Ages

Medio Oriente *m* Middle East

medir [5] *vt* measure; weigh up <*palabras etc*>. ● *vi* measure, be. **¿cuánto mide de alto?** how tall is it? □ **~se** *vpr* (moderarse) measure o.s.; (Mex, probarse) try on

medita|bundo *a* thoughtful. **~ción** *f* meditation. **~r** *vt* think about. ● *vi* meditate

mediterráneo *a* Mediterranean

Mediterráneo *m* Mediterranean

médium *m & f* medium

médula *f* marrow

medusa *f* jellyfish

megáfono *m* megaphone

megalómano *m* megalomaniac

mejicano *a & m* Mexican

Méjico *m* Mexico

mejilla *f* cheek

mejillón *m* mussel

mejor *a & adv* (comparativo) better; (superlativo) best. **~ dicho** rather. **a lo ~** perhaps. **tanto ~** so much the better. **~a** *f* improvement. **~able** *a* improvable. **~amiento** *m* improvement

mejorana *f* marjoram

mejorar *vt* improve, better. ● *vi* get better. □ **~se** *vpr* get better

mejunje *m* mixture

melanc|olía *f* melancholy. **~ólico** *a* melancholic

melaza *f* molasses

melen|a *f* long hair; (de león) mane. **~udo** *a* long-haired

melindr|es *mpl* affectation. **hacer ~es con la comida** be picky about food. **~oso** *a* affected

mellizo *a & m* twin

melocot|ón *m* peach. **~onero** *m* peach tree

mel|odía *f* melody. **~ódico** *a* melodic. **~odioso** *a* melodious

melodram|a *m* melodrama. **~ático** *a* melodramatic

melómano *m* music lover

melón *m* melon

meloso *a* sickly-sweet; <*canción*> slushy

membran|a *f* membrane. **~oso** *a* membranous

membrete *m* letterhead

membrill|ero *m* quince tree. **~o** *m* quince

memo *a* stupid. ● *m* idiot

memorable *a* memorable

memorando *m*, **memorándum** *m* notebook; (nota) memorandum, memo

memori|a *f* memory; (informe) report; (tesis) thesis. **~as** *fpl* (autobiografía) memoirs. **de ~a** by heart; <*citar*> from memory. **~al** *m* memorial. **~ón** *m* good memory. **~zación** *f* memorizing. **~zar** [10] *vt* memorize

menaje *m* household goods. **~ de cocina** kitchenware

menci|ón *f* mention. **~onado** *a* aforementioned. **~onar** *vt* mention

mendi|cidad *f* begging. **~gar** [12] *vt* beg for. ● *vi* beg. **~go** *m* beggar

mendrugo *m* piece of stale bread

mene|ar *vt* wag <*rabo*>; shake <*cabeza*>; wiggle <*caderas*>. □ **~arse** *vpr* move; (con inquietud) fidget; (balancearse) swing). **~o** *m* movement; <*sacudida*> shake

menester *m* occupation. **ser ~** be necessary. **~oso** *a* needy

menestra *f* vegetable stew

mengano *m* so-and-so

mengua *f* decrease; (falta) lack. **~do** *a* diminished. **~nte** *a* <*luna*> waning; <*marea*> ebb. **~r** [15] *vt/i* decrease, diminish

meningitis *f* meningitis

menjurje *m* mixture

menopausia *f* menopause

menor *a* (más pequeño, comparativo) smaller; (más pequeño, superlativo) smallest; (más joven, comparativo) younger; (más joven, superlativo) youngest; (Mus) minor. ● *m & f* (menor de edad) minor. **al por ~** retail

menos *a* (comparativo) less; (comparativo, con plural) fewer; (superlativo) least; (superlativo, con plural) fewest. ● *adv* (comparativo) less; (superlativo) least. ● *prep* except. **al ~** at least. **a ~ que** unless. **las dos ~ diez** ten to two. **ni mucho ~** far from it. **por lo ~** at least. **~cabar** *vt* lessen; (fig, estropear) damage. **~cabo** *m* lessening. **~preciable** *a* contemptible. **~preciar** *vt* despise. **~precio** *m* contempt

mensaje *m* message. **~ro** *m* messenger

menso *a* (LAm, [I]) stupid

menstru|ación *f* menstruation. **~al** *a* menstrual. **~ar** [21] *vi* menstruate

mensual *a* monthly. **~idad** *f* monthly pay; (cuota) monthly payment

mensurable *a* measurable

menta *f* mint

mental *a* mental. **~idad** *f* mentality. **~mente** *adv* mentally

mentar [1] *vt* mention, name

mente *f* mind

mentecato *a* stupid. ● *m* idiot

mentir [4] *vi* lie. **~a** *f* lie. **~ijillas** *fpl*. **de ~ijillas** for a joke. **~oso** *a* lying. ● *m* liar

mentís *m invar* denial

mentor *m* mentor

menú *m* menu

menud|ear *vi* happen frequently; (Mex, Com) sell retail. **~encia** *f* trifle. **~encias** *fpl* (LAm) giblets. **~eo** *m* (Mex) retail trade. **~illos** *mpl* giblets. **~o** *a* small; <*lluvia*> fine. **a ~o** often. **~os** *mpl* giblets

meñique *a* <*dedo*> little. ● *m* little finger

meollo *m* (médula) marrow; (de tema etc) heart

merca|chifle *m* hawker; (fig) profiteer. **~der** *m* merchant.

~dería *f* (LAm) merchandise. **~do** *m* market. **M~do Común** Common Market. **~do negro** black market

mercan|cía(s) *f(pl)* goods, merchandise. **~te** *a* merchant. ● *m* merchant ship. **~til** *a* mercantile, commercial. **~tilismo** *m* mercantilism

merced *f* favour. **su/vuestra ~** your honour

mercenario *a* & *m* mercenary

mercer|ía *f* haberdashery (Brit), notions (Amer). **~io** *m* mercury

mercurial *a* mercurial

Mercurio *m* Mercury

merec|edor *a* worthy (**de** of). **~er** [11] *vt* deserve. □ **~erse** *vpr* deserve. **~idamente** *adv* deservedly. **~ido** *a* well deserved. **~imiento** *m* (mérito) merit

merend|ar [1] *vt* have as an afternoon snack. ● *vi* have an afternoon snack. **~ero** *m* snack bar; (lugar) picnic area

merengue *m* meringue

meridi|ano *a* midday; (fig) dazzling. ● *m* meridian. **~onal** *a* southern. ● *m* southerner

merienda *f* afternoon snack

merino *a* merino

mérito *m* merit; (valor) worth

meritorio *a* praiseworthy. ● *m* unpaid trainee

merluza *f* hake

merma *f* decrease. **~r** *vt/i* decrease, reduce

mermelada *f* jam

mero *a* mere; (Mex, verdadero) real. ● *adv* (Mex, precisamente) exactly; (Mex, casi) nearly. ● *m* grouper

merode|ador *m* prowler. **~ar** *vi* prowl

mes *m* month

mesa *f* table; (para escribir o estudiar) desk. **poner la ~** lay the table

mesarse *vpr* tear at one's hair

meser|a *f* (LAm) waitress. **~o** *m* (LAm) waiter

meseta *f* plateau; (descansillo) landing

Mesías *m* Messiah

mesilla *f*, **mesita** *f* small table. **~ de noche** bedside table

mesón *m* inn

mesoner|a *f* landlady. **~o** *m* landlord

mestiz|aje *m* crossbreeding. **~o** *a* <*persona*> half-caste; <*animal*> cross-bred. ● *m* (persona) half-caste; (animal) cross-breed

mesura *f* moderation. **~do** *a* moderate

meta *f* goal; (de una carrera) finish

metabolismo *m* metabolism

metafísic|a *f* metaphysics. **~o** *a* metaphysical

met|áfora *f* metaphor. **~afórico** *a* metaphorical

met|al *m* metal; (de la voz) timbre. **~ales** *mpl* (instrumentos de latón) brass. **~álico** *a* <*objeto*> metal; <*sonido*> metallic

metal|urgia *f* metallurgy. **~úrgico** *a* metallurgical

metamorfosis *f invar* metamorphosis

metedura de pata *f* blunder

mete|órico *a* meteoric. **~orito** *m* meteorite. **~oro** *m* meteor. **~orología** *f* meteorology. **~orológico** *a* meteorological. **~orólogo** *m* meteorologist

meter *vt* put; score <*un gol*>; (enredar) involve; (causar) make. □ **~se**

vpr get involved (**en** in); (entrometerse) meddle. **~se con uno** pick a quarrel with s.o.

meticulos|idad *f* meticulousness. **~o** *a* meticulous

metida de pata *f* (LAm) blunder

metido *m* reprimand. ● *a*. **~ en años** getting on. **estar ~ en algo** be involved in sth. **estar muy ~ con uno** be well in with s.o.

metódico *a* methodical

metodis|mo *m* Methodism. **~ta** *a & m & f* Methodist

método *m* method

metodología *f* methodology

metraje *m* length. **de largo ~** <*película*> feature

metrall|a *f* shrapnel. **~eta** *f* submachine gun

métric|a *f* metrics. **~o** *a* metric; <*verso*> metrical

metro *m* metre; (tren) underground (Brit), subway (Amer). **~ cuadrado** square metre

metrónomo *m* metronome

metr|ópoli *f* metropolis. **~opolitano** *a* metropolitan. ● *m* metropolitan; (tren) underground (Brit), subway (Amer)

mexicano *a & m* Mexican

México *m* Mexico. **~ D. F.** Mexico City

mezcal *m* (Mex) mescal

mezc|la *f* (acción) mixing; (substancia) mixture; (argamasa) mortar. **~lador** *m* mixer. **~lar** *vt* mix; shuffle <*los naipes*>. □ **~larse** *vpr* mix; (intervenir) interfere. **~olanza** *f* mixture

mezquin|dad *f* meanness. **~o** *a* mean; (escaso) meagre. ● *m* mean person

mezquita *f* mosque

mi *a* my. ● *m* (Mus) E; (solfa) mi

mí *pron* me

miau *m* miaow

mica *f* (silicato) mica

mico *m* (long-tailed) monkey

microbio *m* microbe

micro|biología *f* microbiology. **~cosmos** *m invar* microcosm. **~film(e)** *m* microfilm

micrófono *m* microphone

microonda *f* microwave. **~s** *m invar* microwave oven

microordenador *m* microcomputer

micros|cópico *a* microscopic. **~copio** *m* microscope. **~urco** *m* long-playing record

miedo *m* fear (**a** for). **dar ~** frighten. **morirse de ~** be scared to death. **tener ~** be frightened. **~so** *a* fearful

miel *f* honey

miembro *m* limb; (persona) member

mientras *conj* while. ● *adv* meanwhile. **~ que** whereas. **~ tanto** in the meantime

miércoles *m invar* Wednesday. **~ de ceniza** Ash Wednesday

mierda *f* (vulgar) shit

mies *f* ripe, grain

miga *f* crumb; (fig, meollo) essence. **~jas** *fpl* crumbs; (sobras) scraps. **~r** [12] *vt* crumble

migra|ción *f* migration. **~torio** *a* migratory

mijo *m* millet

mil *a & m* a/one thousand. **~es de** thousands of. **~ novecientos noventa y nueve** nineteen ninety-nine. **~ pesetas** a thousand pesetas

milagro *m* miracle. **~so** *a* miraculous

milen|ario *a* millenial. **~io** *m* millennium

milésimo *a* & *m* thousandth

mili *f* [I] military service. **~cia** *f* soldiering; (gente armada) militia

mili|gramo *m* milligram. **~litro** *m* millilitre

milímetro *m* millimetre

militante *a* & *m* & *f* activist

militar *a* military. ● *m* soldier. **~ismo** *m* militarism. **~ista** *a* militaristic. ● *m* & *f* militarist. **~izar** [10] *vt* militarize

milla *f* mile

millar *m* thousand. **a ~es** by the thousand

mill|ón *m* million. **un ~ón de libros** a million books. **~onada** *f* fortune. **~onario** *m* millionaire. **~onésimo** *a* & *m* millionth

milonga *f popular dance and music from the River Plate region*

milpa *f* (Mex) maize field, cornfield (Amer)

milpies *m invar* woodlouse

mimar *vt* spoil

mimbre *m* & *f* wicker. □ **~arse** *vpr* sway. **~ra** *f* osier. **~ral** *m* osier-bed

mimetismo *m* mimicry

mímic|a *f* mime. **~o** *a* mimic

mimo *m* mime; (*a un niño*) spoiling; (caricia) cuddle

mimosa *f* mimosa

mina *f* mine. **~r** *vt* mine; (fig) undermine

minarete *m* minaret

mineral *m* mineral; (mena) ore. **~ogía** *f* mineralogy. **~ogista** *m* & *f* mineralogist

miner|ía *f* mining. **~o** *a* mining. ● *m* miner

miniatura *f* miniature

minifundio *m* smallholding

minimizar [10] *vt* minimize

mínim|o *a* & *m* minimum. **como ~** at least. **~um** *m* minimum

minino *m* [I] cat, puss [I]

minist|erial *a* ministerial; <*reunión*> cabinet. **~erio** *m* ministry. **~ro** *m* minister

minor|ía *f* minority. **~idad** *f* minority. **~ista** *m* & *f* retailer

minuci|a *f* trifle. **~osidad** *f* thoroughness. **~oso** *a* thorough; (detallado) detailed

minúscul|a *f* lower case letter. **~o** *a* tiny

minuta *f* draft copy; (de abogado) bill

minut|ero *m* minute hand. **~o** *m* minute

mío *a* & *pron* mine. **un amigo ~** a friend of mine

miop|e *a* short-sighted. ● *m* & *f* short-sighted person. **~ía** *f* short-sightedness

mira *f* sight; (fig, intención) aim. **a la ~** on the lookout. **con ~s a** with a view to. **~da** *f* look. **echar una ~da a** glance at. **~do** *a* careful with money; (comedido) considerate. **bien ~do** highly regarded. **no estar bien ~do** be frowned upon. **~dor** *m* viewpoint. **~miento** *m* consideration. **~r** *vt* look at; (observar) watch; (considerar) consider. **~r fijamente a** stare at. ● *vi* look <*edificio etc*>. **~ hacia** face. □ **~rse** *vpr* <*personas*> look at each other

mirilla *f* peephole

miriñaque *m* crinoline

mirlo *m* blackbird

mirón *a* nosey. ● *m* nosy parker; (espectador) onlooker

mirto *m* myrtle

misa *f* mass. **~l** *m* missal

misántropo *m* misanthropist

miscelánea *f* miscellany; (Mex, tienda) corner shop (Brit), small general store (Amer)

miser|able *a* very poor; (lastimoso) miserable; (tacaño) mean. **~ia** *f* extreme poverty; (suciedad) squalor

misericordi|a *f* pity; (piedad) mercy. **~oso** *a* merciful

mísero *a* miserable; (tacaño) mean; (malvado) wicked

misil *m* missile

misi|ón *f* mission. **~onero** *m* missionary

misiva *f* missive

mism|ísimo *a* very same. **~o** *a* same; (después de pronombre personal) myself, yourself, himself, herself, itself, ourselves, yourselves, themselves; (enfático) very. ● *adv*. **ahora ~** right now. **aquí ~** right here. **lo ~** the same

misterio *m* mystery. **~so** *a* mysterious

místic|a *f* mysticism. **~o** *a* mystical. ● *m* mystic

mistifica|ción *f* mystification. **~r** [7] *vt* mystify

mitad *f* half; (centro) middle. **cortar algo por la ~** cut sth in half

mitigar [12] *vt* mitigate; quench *<sed>*; relieve *<dolor etc>*

mitin *m*, **mitín** *m* meeting

mito *m* myth. **~logía** *f* mythology. **~lógico** *a* mythological

mitón *m* mitten

mitote *m* (Mex) Aztec dance

mixt|o *a* mixed. **educación mixta** coeducation

mobiliario *m* furniture

moce|dad *f* youth. **~río** *m* young people. **~tón** *m* strapping lad. **~tona** *f* strapping girl

mochales *a invar*. **estar ~** be round the bend

mochila *f* rucksack

mocho *a* blunt. ● *m* butt end

mochuelo *m* little owl

moción *f* motion

moco *m* mucus. **limpiarse los ~s** blow one's nose

moda *f* fashion. **estar de ~** be in fashion. **~l** *a* modal. **~les** *mpl* manners. **~lidad** *f* kind

model|ado *m* modelling. **~ador** *m* modeller. **~ar** *vt* model; (fig, configurar) form. **~o** *m* & *f* model

módem *m* modem

modera|ción *f* moderation. **~do** *a* moderate. **~r** *vt* moderate; reduce *<velocidad>*. □ **~rse** *vpr* control oneself

modern|idad *f* modernity. **~ismo** *m* modernism. **~ista** *m* & *f* modernist. **~izar** [10] *vt* modernize. **~o** *a* modern; (a la moda) fashionable

modest|ia *f* modesty. **~o** *a* modest

módico *a* moderate

modifica|ción *f* modification. **~r** [7] *vt* modify

modismo *m* idiom

modist|a *f* dressmaker. **~o** *m* designer

modo *m* manner, way; (Gram) mood; (Mus) mode. **~ de ser** character. **de ~ que** so that. **de ningún ~** certainly not. **de todos ~s** anyhow. **ni ~** (LAm) no way

modorra *f* drowsiness

modula|ción *f* modulation. **~dor** *m* modulator. **~r** *vt* modulate

módulo *m* module

mofa *f* mockery. □ **~rse** *vpr*. **~rse de** make fun of

mofeta *f* skunk

moflet|e *m* chubby cheek. **~udo** *a* with chubby cheeks

mohín *m* grimace. **hacer un ~** pull a face

moho *m* mould; (óxido) rust. **~so** *a* mouldy; <*metales*> rusty

moisés *m* Moses basket

mojado *a* wet

mojar *vt* wet; (empapar) soak; (humedecer) moisten, dampen

mojigat|ería *f* prudishness. **~o** *m* prude. ● *a* prudish

mojón *m* boundary post; (señal) signpost

molar *m* molar

mold|e *m* mould; (aguja) knitting needle. **~ear** *vt* mould, shape; (fig) form. **~ura** *f* moulding

mole *f* mass, bulk. ● *m* (Mex, salsa) chilli sauce with chocolate and sesame

mol|écula *f* molecule. **~ecular** *a* molecular

mole|dor *a* grinding. ● *m* grinder. **~r** [2] grind

molest|ar *vt* annoy; (incomodar) bother. **¿le ~a que fume?** do you mind if I smoke? ● *vi* be a nuisance. **no ~ar** do not disturb. □ **~arse** *vpr* bother; (ofenderse) take offence. **~ia** *f* bother, nuisance; (inconveniente) inconvenience; (incomodidad) discomfort. **~o** *a* annoying; (inconveniente) inconvenient; (ofendido) offended

molicie *f* softness; (excesiva comodidad) easy life

molido *a* ground; (fig, muy cansado) worn out

molienda *f* grinding

molin|ero *m* miller. **~ete** *m* toy windmill. **~illo** *m* mill; (juguete) toy windmill. **~o** *m* mill. **~ de agua** watermill. **~o de viento** windmill

molleja *f* gizzard

mollera *f* (de la cabeza) crown; (fig, sesera) brains

molusco *m* mollusc

moment|áneamente *adv* momentarily. **~áneo** *a* (breve) momentary; (pasajero) temporary. **~o** *m* moment; (ocasión) time. **al ~o** at once. **de ~o** for the moment

momi|a *f* mummy. **~ficar** [7] *vt* mummify. □ **~ficarse** *vpr* become mummified

monacal *a* monastic

monada *f* beautiful thing; (niño bonito) cute kid; (acción tonta) silliness

monaguillo *m* altar boy

mon|arca *m* & *f* monarch. **~arquía** *f* monarchy. **~árquico** *a* monarchical

monasterio *m* monastery

monda *f* peeling; (piel) peel. **~dientes** *m invar* toothpick. **~adura** *f* peeling; (piel) peel. **~ar** *vt* peel <*fruta etc*>. **~o** *a* (sin pelo) bald

mondongo *m* innards

moned|a *f* coin; (de un país) currency. **~ero** *m* purse (Brit), change purse (Amer)

monetario *a* monetary

mongolismo *m* Down's syndrome

monigote *m* weak character; (muñeco) rag doll; (dibujo) doodle

monitor *m* monitor

monj|a *f* nun. **~e** *m* monk. **~il** *a* nun's; (como de monja) like a nun

mono *m* monkey; (sobretodo) overalls. ● *a* pretty

monocromo *a* & *m* monochrome

monóculo *m* monocle

mon|ogamia *f* monogamy. **~ógamo** *a* monogamous

monogra|fía *f* monograph. **~ma** *m* monogram

mon|ologar [12] *vi* soliloquize. **~ólogo** *m* monologue

monoplano *m* monoplane

monopoli|o *m* monopoly. **~zar** [10] *vt* monopolize

monos|ilábico *a* monosyllabic. **~ílabo** *m* monosyllable

monoteís|mo *m* monotheism. **~ta** *a* monotheistic. ● *m* & *f* monotheist

mon|otonía *f* monotony. **~ótono** *a* monotonous

monseñor *m* monsignor

monstruo *m* monster. **~sidad** *f* monstrosity; (atrocidad) atrocity. **~so** *a* monstrous

monta *f* mounting; (valor) total value

montacargas *m invar* service lift (Brit), service elevator (Amer)

monta|dor *m* fitter. **~je** *m* assembly; (Cine) montage; (teatro) staging, production

montañ|a *f* mountain. **~a rusa** roller coaster. **~ero** *a* mountaineer. **~és** *a* mountain. ● *m* highlander. **~ismo** *m* mountaineering. **~oso** *a* mountainous

montaplatos *m invar* dumb waiter

montar *vt* ride; (subirse a) get on; (ensamblar) assemble; cock <*arma*>; set up <*una casa, un negocio*>. ● *vi* ride; (subirse) mount. **~ a caballo** ride a horse

monte *m* (montaña) mountain; (terreno inculto) scrub; (bosque) woodland. **~ de piedad** pawnshop

montepío *m* charitable fund for dependents

montés *a* wild

montevideano *a* & *m* Montevidean

montículo *m* hillock

montón *m* heap, pile. **a montones** in abundance. **un ~ de** loads of

montura *f* mount; (silla) saddle

monument|al *a* monumental; (fig, muy grande) enormous. **~o** *m* monument

monzón *m* & *f* monsoon

moñ|a *f* ribbon. **~o** *m* bun; (LAm, lazo) bow

moque|o *m* runny nose. **~ro** *m* [T] handkerchief

moqueta *f* fitted carpet

moquillo *m* distemper

mora *f* mulberry; (de zarzamora) blackberry; (Jurid) default

morada *f* dwelling

morado *a* purple

morador *m* inhabitant

moral *m* mulberry tree. ● *f* morals. ● *a* moral. **~eja** *f* moral. **~idad** *f* morality. **~ista** *m* & *f* moralist. **~izador** *a* moralizing. ● *m* moralist. **~izar** [10] *vt* moralize

morar *vi* live

moratoria *f* moratorium

mórbido *a* soft; (malsano) morbid

morbo *m* illness. **~sidad** *f* morbidity. **~so** *a* unhealthy

morcilla *f* black pudding

morda|cidad *f* sharpness. **~z** *a* scathing

mordaza *f* gag

morde|dura *f* bite. **~r** [2] *vt* bite; (Mex, exigir soborno a) extract a bribe from. ● *vi* bite. □ **~rse** *vpr* bite o.s. **~rse las uñas** bite one's nails

mordi|da *f* (Mex) bribe. **~sco** *m* bite. **~squear** *vt* nibble (at)

moreno *a* (con ser) dark; (de pelo obscuro) dark-haired; (de raza negra) dark-skinned; (con estar) brown, tanned

morera *f* white mulberry tree

moretón *m* bruise

morfema *m* morpheme

morfin|a *f* morphine. **~ómano** *m* morphine addict

morfol|ogía *f* morphology. **~ógico** *a* morphological

moribundo *a* dying

morir [6] (*pp* **muerto**) *vi* die; (fig, extinguirse) die away; (fig, terminar) end. **~ ahogado** drown. □ **~se** *vpr* die. **~se de hambre** starve to death; (fig) be starving. **se muere por una flauta** she's dying to have a flute

morisco *a* Moorish. ● *m* Moor

morm|ón *m* Mormon. **~ónico** *a* Mormon. **~onismo** *m* Mormonism

moro *a* Moorish. ● *m* Moor

morral *m* (mochila) rucksack; (de cazador) gamebag; (para caballos) nosebag

morrillo *m* nape of the neck

morriña *f* homesickness

morro *m* snout

morrocotudo *a* [I] (tremendo) terrible; (estupendo) terrific [I]

morsa *f* walrus

mortaja *f* shroud

mortal *a* & *m* & *f* mortal. **~idad** *f* mortality. **~mente** *adv* mortally

mortandad *f* loss of life; (Mil) carnage

mortecino *a* failing; <color> pale

mortero *m* mortar

mortífero *a* deadly

mortifica|ción *f* mortification. **~r** [7] *vt* (atormentar) torment. □ **~rse** *vpr* distress o.s.

mortuorio *a* death

mosaico *m* mosaic; (Mex, baldosa) floor tile

mosca *f* fly. **~rda** *f* blowfly. **~rdón** *m* botfly; (de cuerpo azul) bluebottle

moscatel *a* muscatel

moscón *m* botfly; (mosca de cuerpo azul) bluebottle

moscovita *a* & *m* & *f* Muscovite

mosque|arse *vpr* get cross. **~o** *m* resentment

mosquete *m* musket. **~ro** *m* musketeer

mosquit|ero *m* mosquito net. **~o** *m* mosquito

mostacho *m* moustache

mostaza *f* mustard

mosto *m* must, grape juice

mostrador *m* counter

mostrar [2] *vt* show. □ **~se** *vpr* (show oneself to) be. **se mostró muy amable** he was very kind

mota *f* spot, speck

mote *m* nickname

motea|do *a* speckled. **~r** *vt* speckle

motejar *vt* call

motel *m* motel

motete *m* motet

motín *m* riot; (de tropas, tripulación) mutiny

motiv|ación *f* motivation. **~ar** *vt* motivate. **~o** *m* reason. **con ~o de** because of

motocicl|eta *f* motor cycle, motor bike ⊡. **~ista** *m & f* motorcyclist

motoneta *f* (LAm) (motor) scooter

motor *a* motor. ● *m* motor, engine. **~ de arranque** starter motor. **~a** *f* motor boat. **~ismo** *m* motorcycling. **~ista** *m & f* motorist; (de una moto) motorcyclist. **~izar** [10] *vt* motorize

motriz *a* motor

move|dizo *a* movable; (poco firme) unstable; <*persona*> fickle. **~r** [2] *vt* move; shake <*la cabeza*>; (provocar) cause. ◻ **~rse** *vpr* move; (darse prisa) hurry up

movi|ble *a* movable. **~do** *a* moved; (Foto) blurred

móvil *a* mobile. ● *m* motive

movili|dad *f* mobility. **~zación** *f* mobilization. **~zar** [10] *vt* mobilize

movimiento *m* movement, motion; (agitación) bustle

moza *f* young girl. **~lbete** *m* lad

mozárabe *a* Mozarabic. ● *m & f* Mozarab

moz|o *m* young boy. **~uela** *f* young girl. **~uelo** *m* young boy/ lad

mucam|a *f* (LAm) servant. **~o** *m* (LAm) servant

muchach|a *f* girl; (sirvienta) servant, maid. **~o** *m* boy, lad

muchedumbre *f* crowd

mucho *a* a lot of; (en negativas, preguntas) much, a lot of. **~s** a lot of; (en negativas, preguntas) many, a lot of. ● *pron* a lot; (personas) many (people). **como ~** at the most. **ni ~ menos** by no means. **por ~ que** however much. ● *adv* a lot, very much; (tiempo) long, a long time

mucos|idad *f* mucus. **~o** *a* mucous

muda *f* change of clothing; (de animales) shedding. **~ble** *a* changeable; <*personas*> fickle. **~nza** *f* move, removal (Brit). **~r** *vt* change; shed <*piel*>. **~rse** *vpr* (de ropa) change one's clothes; (de casa) move (house)

mudéjar *a & m & f* Mudejar

mud|ez *f* dumbness. **~o** *a* dumb; (callado) silent

mueble *a* movable. ● *m* piece of furniture. **~s** *mpl* furniture

mueca *f* grimace, face. **hacer una ~** pull a face

muela *f* back tooth, molar; (piedra de afilar) grindstone; (piedra de molino) millstone. **~ del juicio** wisdom tooth

muelle *a* soft. ● *m* spring; (Naut) wharf; (malecón) jetty

muérdago *m* mistletoe

muero *vb* ⇒MORIR

muert|e *f* death; (homicidio) murder. **~o** *a* dead. ● *m* dead person

muesca *f* nick; (ranura) slot

muestra *f* sample; (prueba) proof; (modelo) model; (señal) sign. **~rio** *m* collection of samples

muestro *vb* ⇒MOSTRAR

muevo *vb* ⇒MOVER

mugi|do *m* moo. **~r** [14] *vi* moo

mugr|e *m* dirt. **~iento** *a* dirty, filthy

mugrón *m* sucker

mujer *f* woman; (esposa) wife. ● *int* my dear! **~iego** *a* fond of the women. ● *m* womanizer. **~zuela** *f* prostitute

mula *f* mule. **~da** *f* drove of mules

mulato *a* of mixed race (black and white). ● *m* person of mixed race

mulero *m* muleteer

muleta *f* crutch; (toreo) stick with a red flag

mulli|do *a* soft. **~r** [22] *vt* soften

mulo *m* mule

multa *f* fine. **~r** *vt* fine

multi|color *a* multicoloured. **~copista** *m* duplicator. **~forme** *a* multiform. **~lateral** *a* multilateral. **~lingüe** *a* multilingual. **~millonario** *m* multimillionaire

múltiple *a* multiple

multiplic|ación *f* multiplication. **~ar** [7] *vt* multiply. □ **~arse** *vpr* multiply. **~idad** *f* multiplicity

múltiplo *m* multiple

multitud *f* multitude, crowd. **~inario** *a* mass; <*concierto*> with mass audience

mund|ano *a* wordly; (de la sociedad elegante) society. **~ial** *a* worldwide. **la segunda guerra ~ial** the Second World War. **~illo** *m* world, circles. **~o** *m* world. **todo el ~o** everybody

munición *f* ammunition; (provisiones) supplies

municip|al *a* municipal. **~alidad** *f* municipality. **~io** *m* municipality; (ayuntamiento) town council

muñe|ca *f* (Anat) wrist; (juguete) doll; (maniquí) dummy. **~co** *m* doll. **~quera** *f* wristband

muñón *m* stump

mura|l *a* mural, wall. ● *m* mural. **~lla** *f* (city) wall. **~r** *vt* wall

murciélago *m* bat

murga *f* street band

murmullo *m* (incl fig) murmur

murmura|ción *f* gossip. **~dor** *a* gossiping. ● *m* gossip. **~r** *vi* murmur; (criticar) gossip

muro *m* wall

murria *f* depression

mus *m* card game

musa *f* muse

musaraña *f* shrew

muscula|r *a* muscular. **~tura** *f* muscles

músculo *m* muscle

musculoso *a* muscular

muselina *f* muslin

museo *m* museum. **~ de arte** art gallery

musgo *m* moss. **~so** *a* mossy

música *f* music

musical *a* & *m* musical

músico *a* musical. ● *m* musician

music|ología *f* musicology. **~ólogo** *m* musicologist

muslo *m* thigh

mustio *a* <*plantas*> withered; <*cosas*> faded; <*personas*> gloomy; (Mex, hipócrita) two-faced

musulmán *a* & *m* Muslim

muta|bilidad *f* mutability. **~ción** *f* mutation

mutila|ción *f* mutilation. **~do** *a* crippled. ● *m* cripple. **~r** *vt* mutilate; maim <*persona*>

mutis *m* (en el teatro) exit. **~mo** *m* silence

mutu|alidad *f* mutuality; (asociación) friendly society. **~amente** *adv* mutually. **~o** *a* mutual

muy *adv* very; (demasiado) too

Nn

nabo *m* turnip

nácar *m* mother-of-pearl

nac|er [11] *vi* be born; <*pollito*> hatch out; <*planta*> sprout. **~ido** *a* born. **recien ~ido** newborn. **~iente** *a* <*sol*> rising. **~imiento** *m* birth; (de río) source; (belén) crib. **lugar** *m* **de ~imiento** place of birth

naci|ón *f* nation. **~onal** *a* national. **~onalidad** *f* nationality. **~onalismo** *m* nationalism. **~onalista** *m* & *f* nationalist. **~onalizar** [10] *vt* nationalize. □ **~onalizarse** *vpr* become naturalized

nada *pron* nothing, not anything. ● *adv* not at all. **¡~ de eso!** nothing of the sort! **antes que ~** first of all. **¡de ~!** (después de 'gracias') don't mention it! **para ~** (not) at all. **por ~ del mundo** not for anything in the world

nada|dor *m* swimmer. **~r** *vi* swim. **~r de espalda(s)** do (the) backstroke

nadería *f* trifle

nadie *pron* no one, nobody

nado *m* (Mex) swimming. ● *adv* **a ~** swimming

naipe *m* (playing) card. **juegos** *mpl* **de ~s** card games

nalga *f* buttock. **~s** *fpl* bottom. **~da** *f* (Mex) smack on the bottom

nana *f* lullaby

naranj|a *f* orange. **~ada** *f* orangeade. **~al** *m* orange grove. **~ero** *m* orange tree

narcótico *a* & *m* narcotic

nariz *f* nose. **¡narices!** rubbish!

narra|ción *f* narration. **~dor** *m* narrator. **~r** *vt* tell. **~tivo** *a* narrative

nasal *a* nasal

nata *f* cream

natación *f* swimming

natal *a* native; <*pueblo etc*> home. **~idad** *f* birth rate

natillas *fpl* custard

nativo *a* & *m* native

nato *a* born

natural *a* natural. ● *m* native. **~eza** *f* nature. **~eza muerta** still life. **~idad** *f* naturalness. **~ista** *m* & *f* naturalist. **~izar** [10] *vt* naturalize. □ **~izarse** *vpr* become naturalized. **~mente** *adv* naturally. ● *int* of course!

naufrag|ar [12] *vi* <*barco*> sink; <*persona*> be shipwrecked; (fig) fail. **~io** *m* shipwreck

náufrago *a* shipwrecked. ● *m* shipwrecked person

náuseas *fpl* nausea. **dar ~s a uno** make s.o. feel sick. **sentir ~s** feel sick

náutico *a* nautical

navaja *f* penknife; (de afeitar) razor. **~zo** *m* slash

naval *a* naval

nave *f* ship; (de iglesia) nave. **~ espacial** spaceship. **quemar las ~s** burn one's boats

navega|ble *a* navigable; <*barco*> seaworthy. **~ción** *f* navigation; (tráfico) shipping. **~dor** *m* (Informática) browser. **~nte** *m* & *f* naviga tor. **~r** [12] *vi* sail; (Informática) browse

Navid|ad *f* Christmas. **~eño** *a* Christmas. **en ~ades** at Christmas. **¡feliz ~ad!** Happy Christmas! **por ~ad** at Christmas

nazi *a & m & f* Nazi. **~smo** *m* Nazism

neblina *f* mist

nebuloso *a* misty; (fig) vague

necedad *f* foolishness. **decir ~es** talk nonsense. **hacer una ~** do sth stupid

necesari|amente *adv* necessarily. **~o** *a* necessary

necesi|dad *f* need; (cosa esencial) necessity; (pobreza) poverty. **~dades** *fpl* hardships. **no hay ~dad** there's no need. **por ~dad** (out) of necessity. **~tado** *a* in need (**de** of). **~tar** *vt* need. ● *vi*. **~tar de** need

necio *a* silly. ● *m* idiot

néctar *m* nectar

nectarina *f* nectarine

nefasto *a* unfortunate; *<consecuencia>* disastrous; *<influencia>* harmful

nega|ción *f* denial; (Gram) negative. **~do** *a* useless. **~r** [1 & 12] *vt* deny; (rehusar) refuse. □ **~rse** *vpr* refuse (**a** to). **~tiva** *f* (acción) denial; (acción de rehusar) refusal. **~tivo** *a & m* negative

negligen|cia *f* negligence. **~te** *a* negligent

negoci|able *a* negotiable. **~ación** *f* negotiation. **~ante** *m & f* dealer. **~ar** *vt/i* negotiate. **~ar en** trade in. **~o** *m* business; (Com, trato) deal. **~os** *mpl* business. **hombre** *m* **de ~os** businessman

negr|a *f* black woman; (Mus) crotchet. **~o** *a* black; *<ojos>* dark. ● *m* (color) black; (persona) black man. **~ura** *f* blackness. **~uzco** *a* blackish

nen|a *f* little girl. **~o** *m* little boy

nenúfar *m* water lily

neocelandés *a* from New Zealand. ● *m* New Zealander

neón *m* neon

nepotismo *m* nepotism

nervio *m* nerve; (tendón) sinew; (Bot) vein. **~sidad** *f*, **~sismo** *m* nervousness; (impaciencia) impatience. **~so** *a* nervous; (de temperamento) highly-strung. **ponerse ~so** get nervous

neto *a* clear; *<verdad>* simple; (Com) net

neumático *a* pneumatic. ● *m* tyre

neumonía *f* pneumonia

neur|algia *f* neuralgia. **~ología** *f* neurology. **~ólogo** *m* neurologist. **~osis** *f* neurosis. **~ótico** *a* neurotic

neutr|al *a* neutral. **~alidad** *f* neutrality. **~alizar** [10] *vt* neutralize. **~o** *a* neutral; (Gram) neuter

neva|da *f* snowfall. **~r** [1] *vi* snow. **~sca** *f* blizzard

nevera *f* refrigerator, fridge (Brit)

nevisca *f* light snowfall

nexo *m* link

ni *conj*. **~... ~** neither... nor. **~ aunque** not even if. **~ siquiera** not even. **sin... ~ ...** without ... or...

Nicaragua *f* Nicaragua

nicaragüense *a & m & f* Nicaraguan

nicho *m* niche

nicotina *f* nicotine

nido *m* nest; (de ladrones) den

niebla *f* fog. **hay ~** it's foggy. **un día de ~** a foggy day

niet|a *f* granddaughter. **~o** *m* grandson. **~os** *mpl* grandchildren

nieve *f* snow; (Mex, helado) sorbet

niki *m* polo shirt

nimi|edad *f* triviality. **~o** *a* insignificant

ninfa *f* nymph

ningún ⇒ NINGUNO

ninguno *a* (*delante de nombre masculino en singular* **ningún**) no; (con otro negativo) any. **de ninguna manera, de ningún modo** by no means. **en ninguna parte** nowhere. **sin ningún amigo** without any friends. ● *pron* (de dos) neither; (de más de dos) none; (nadie) no-one, nobody

niñ|a *f* (little) girl. **~era** *f* nanny. **~ería** *f* childish thing. **~ez** *f* childhood. **~o** *a* childish. ● *m* (little) boy **de ~o** as a child. **desde ~o** from childhood

níquel *m* nickel

níspero *m* medlar

nitidez *f* clarity; (de foto, imagen) sharpness

nítido *a* clear; (foto, imagen) sharp

nitrógeno *m* nitrogen

nivel *m* level; (fig) standard. **~ de vida** standard of living. **~ar** *vt* level. □ **~arse** *vpr* become level

no *adv* not; (como respuesta) no. **¿~?** isn't it? **¡a que ~!** I bet you don't! **¡cómo ~!** of course! **Felipe ~ tiene hijos** Felipe has no children. **¡que ~!** certainly not!

nob|iliario *a* noble. **~le** *a & m & f* noble. **~leza** *f* nobility

noche *f* night. **~ vieja** New Year's Eve. **de ~** at night. **hacerse de ~** get dark. **hacer ~** spend the night. **media ~** midnight. **en la ~** (LAm), **por la ~** at night

Nochebuena *f* Christmas Eve

noción *f* notion. **nociones** *fpl* rudiments

nocivo *a* harmful

nocturno *a* nocturnal; <*clase*> evening; <*tren etc*> night. ● *m* nocturne

nodriza *f* wet nurse

nogal *m* walnut tree; (madera) walnut

nómada *a* nomadic. ● *m & f* nomad

nombr|ado *a* famous; (susodicho) aforementioned. **~amiento** *m* appointment. **~ar** *vt* appoint; (citar) mention. **~e** *m* name; (Gram) noun; (fama) renown. **~e de pila** Christian name. **en ~e de** in the name of. **no tener ~e** be unspeakable. **poner de ~e** call

nomeolvides *m invar* forget-me-not

nómina *f* payroll

nomina|l *a* nominal. **~tivo** *a & m* nominative. **~tivo a** <*cheque etc*> made out to

non *a* odd. ● *m* odd number. **pares y ~es** odds and evens

nono *a* ninth

nordeste *a* <*región*> north-eastern; <*viento*> north-easterly. ● *m* northeast

nórdico *a* Nordic. ● *m* Northern European

noria *f* water-wheel; (en una feria) big wheel (Brit), Ferris wheel (Amer)

norma *f* rule

normal *a* normal. ● *f* teachers' training college. **~idad** *f* normality (Brit), normalcy (Amer). **~izar** [10] *vt* normalize. **~mente** *adv* normally, usually

noroeste *a* <*región*> north-western; <*viento*> north-westerly. ● *m* northwest

norte *a* <*región*> northern; <*viento, lado*> north. ● *m* north; (fig, meta) aim

Norteamérica *f* (North) America

norteamericano *a* & *m* (North) American

norteño *a* northern. ● *m* northerner

Noruega *f* Norway

noruego *a* & *m* Norwegian

nos *pron* (acusativo) us; (dativo) (to) us; (reflexivo) (to) ourselves; (recíproco) (to) each other

nosotros *pron* we; (con prep) us

nost|algia *f* nostalgia; (de casa, de patria) homesickness. **~álgico** *a* nostalgic

nota *f* note; (de examen etc) mark. **de ~** famous. **de mala ~** notorious. **digno de ~** notable. **~ble** *a* notable. **~ción** *f* notation. **~r** *vt* notice. **es de ~r** it should be noted. **hacerse ~r** stand out

notario *m* notary

notici|a *f* (piece of) news. **~as** *fpl* news. **atrasado de ~as** behind with the news. **tener ~as de** hear from. **~ario**, (LAm) **~ero** *m* news

notifica|ción *f* notification. **~r** [7] *vt* notify

notori|edad *f* notoriety. **~o** *a* well-known; (evidente) obvious; (notable) marked

novato *a* inexperienced. ● *m* novice

novecientos *a* & *m* nine hundred

noved|ad *f* newness; (cosa nueva) innovation; (cambio) change; (moda) latest fashion. **llegar sin ~ad** arrive safely. **~oso** *a* novel

novel|a *f* novel. **~ista** *m* & *f* novelist

noveno *a* ninth

noventa *a* & *m* ninety; (nonagésimo) ninetieth

novia *f* girlfriend; (prometida) fiancée; (en boda) bride. **~r** *vi* (LAm) go out together. **~zgo** *m* engagement

novicio *m* novice

noviembre *m* November

novill|a *f* heifer. **~o** *m* bullock. **hacer ~os** play truant

novio *m* boyfriend; (prometido) fiancé; (en boda) bridegroom. **los ~s** the bride and groom

nub|arrón *m* large dark cloud. **~e** *f* cloud; (de insectos etc) swarm. **~lado** *a* cloudy, overcast. ● *m* cloud. **~lar** *vt* cloud. □ **~larse** *vpr* become cloudy; <*vista*> cloud over. **~oso** *a* cloudy

nuca *f* back of the neck

nuclear *a* nuclear

núcleo *m* nucleus

nudillo *m* knuckle

nudis|mo *m* nudism. **~ta** *m* & *f* nudist

nudo *m* knot; (de asunto etc) crux. **tener un ~ en la garganta** have a lump in one's throat. **~so** *a* knotty

nuera *f* daughter-in-law

nuestro *a* our. ● *pron* ours. **~ amigo** our friend. **un coche ~** a car of ours

nueva *f* (piece of) news. **~s** *fpl* news. **~mente** *adv* again

Nueva Zelanda, (LAm) **Nueva Zelandia** *f* New Zealand

nueve *a* & *m* nine

nuevo *a* new. **de ~** again. **estar ~** be as good as new

nuez *f* walnut. **~ de Adán** Adam's apple. **~ moscada** nutmeg

nul|idad *f* nullity; (Ⓘ, persona) dead loss Ⓘ. **~o** *a* useless; (Jurid) null and void

num|eración *f* numbering. **~eral** *a* & *m* numeral. **~erar** *vt* number. **~érico** *a* numerical

número *m* number; (arábigo, romano) numeral; (de zapatos etc) size; (billete de lotería) lottery ticket; (de publicación) issue. **sin ~** countless

numeroso *a* numerous

nunca *adv* never. **~ (ja)más** never again. **casi ~** hardly ever. **como ~** like never before. **más que ~** more than ever

nupcial *a* nuptial. **banquete ~** wedding breakfast

nutria *f* otter

nutri|ción *f* nutrition. **~do** *a* nourished, fed; (fig) large; <*aplausos*> loud; <*fuego*> heavy. **~r** *vt* nourish, feed; (fig) feed. **~tivo** *a* nutritious. **valor** *m* **~tivo** nutritional value

nylon *m* nylon

Ññ

ñapa *f* (LAm) *extra goods given free*

ñato *adj* (LAm) snub-nosed

ñoñ|ería *f*, **~ez** *f* insipidity. **~o** *a* insipid; (tímido) bashful; (quisquilloso) prudish

Oo

o *conj* or. **~ bien** rather. **~... ~** either ... or

oasis *m invar* oasis

obed|ecer [11] *vt/i* obey. **~iencia** *f* obedience. **~iente** *a* obedient

obes|idad *f* obesity. **~o** *a* obese

obispo *m* bishop

obje|ción *f* objection. **~tar** *vt/i* object

objetivo *a* objective. ● *m* objective; (foto etc) lens

objeto *m* object. **~r** *m* objector. **~r de conciencia** conscientious objector

oblicuo *a* oblique

obliga|ción *f* obligation; (Com) bond. **~do** *a* obliged; (forzoso) obligatory; **~r** [12] *vt* force, oblige. □ **~rse** *vpr*. **~rse a** undertake to. **~torio** *a* obligatory

oboe *m* oboe. ● *m* & *f* (músico) oboist

obra *f* work; (acción) deed; (de teatro) play; (construcción) building work. **~ maestra** masterpiece. **en ~s** under construction. **por ~ de** thanks to. **~r** *vt* do

obrero *a* labour; <*clase*> working. ● *m* workman; (de fábrica, construcción) worker

obscen|idad *f* obscenity. **~o** *a* obscene

obscu... ⇒ OSCU...

obsequi|ar *vt* lavish attention on. **~ar con** give, present with. **~o** *m* gift, present; (agasajo) attention. **~oso** *a* obliging

observa|ción *f* observation. **hacer una ~ción** make a remark. **~dor** *m* observer. **~ncia** *f* observance. **~r** *vt* observe; (notar) notice. **~torio** *m* observatory

obses|ión *f* obsession. **~ionar** *vt* obsess. **~ivo** *a* obsessive. **~o** *a* obsessed

obst|aculizar [10] *vt* hinder; hold up <*tráfico*>. **~áculo** *m* obstacle

obstante: **no ~** *adv* however, nevertheless; (como prep) in spite of

obstar *vi*. **eso no obsta para que vaya** that should not prevent him from going

obstina|do *a* obstinate. □ **~rse** *vpr*. **~rse en** (+ *infinitivo*) insist on (+ *gerundio*)

obstru|cción *f* obstruction. **~ir** [17] *vt* obstruct

obtener [40] *vt* get, obtain

obtura|dor *m* (Foto) shutter. **~r** *vt* plug; fill <*muela etc*>

obvio *a* obvious

oca *f* goose

ocasi|ón *f* occasion; (oportunidad) opportunity. **aprovechar la ~ón** take the opportunity. **con ~ón de** on the occasion of. **de ~ón** bargain; (usado) second-hand. **en ~ones** sometimes. **perder una ~ón** miss a chance. **~onal** *a* chance. **~onar** *vt* cause

ocaso *m* sunset; (fig) decline

occident|al *a* western. ● *m & f* westerner. **~e** *m* west

océano *m* ocean

ochenta *a & m* eighty

ocho *a & m* eight. **~cientos** *a & m* eight hundred

ocio *m* idleness; (tiempo libre) leisure time. **~sidad** *f* idleness. **~so** *a* idle; (inútil) pointless

oct|agonal *a* octagonal. **~ágono** *m* octagon

octano *m* octane

octav|a *f* octave. **~o** *a & m* eighth

octogenario *a & m* octogenarian

octubre *m* October

ocular *a* eye

oculista *m & f* ophthalmologist, ophthalmic optician

ocult|ar *vt* hide. □ **~arse** *vpr* hide. **~o** *a* hidden; (secreto) secret

ocupa|ción *f* occupation. **~do** *a* occupied; <*persona*> busy. **estar ~do** <*asiento*> be taken; <*línea telefónica*> be engaged (Brit), be busy (Amer). **~nte** *m & f* occupant. **~r** *vt* occupy, take up <*espacio*>. □ **~rse** *vpr* look after

ocurr|encia *f* occurrence, event; (idea) idea; (que tiene gracia) witty remark. **~ir** *vi* happen. **¿qué ~e?** what's the matter? □ **~irse** *vpr* occur. **se me ~e que** it occurs to me that

oda *f* ode

odi|ar *vt* hate. **~o** *m* hatred. **~oso** *a* hateful; <*persona*> horrible

oeste *a* <*región*> western; <*viento, lado*> west. ● *m* west

ofen|der *vt* offend; (insultar) insult. □ **~derse** *vpr* take offence. **~sa** *f* offence. **~siva** *f* offensive. **~sivo** *a* offensive

oferta *f* offer; (en subasta) bid. **~s de empleo** situations vacant. **en ~** on (special) offer

oficial *a* official. ● *m* skilled worker; (Mil) officer

oficin|a *f* office. **~a de colocación** employment office. **~a de turismo** tourist office. **horas** *fpl* **de ~a**

business hours. **~ista** *m & f* office worker

oficio *m* trade. **~so** *a* (no oficial) unofficial

ofrec|er [11] *vt* offer; give <*fiesta, banquete etc*>; (prometer) promise. □ **~erse** *vpr* <*persona*> volunteer. **~imiento** *m* offer

ofrenda *f* offering. **~r** *vt* offer

ofuscar [7] *vt* blind; (confundir) confuse. □ **~se** *vpr* get worked up

oí|ble *a* audible. **~do** *m* hearing; (Anat) ear. **al ~do** in one's ear. **de ~das** by hearsay. **conocer de ~das** have heard of. **de ~do** by ear. **duro de ~do** hard of hearing

oigo *vb* ⇨OÍR

oír [50] *vt* hear. **¡oiga!** listen!; (al teléfono) hello!

ojal *m* buttonhole

ojalá *int* I hope so! ● *conj* if only

ojea|da *f* glance. **dar una ~da a, echar una ~da a** have a quick glance at. **~r** *vt* have a look at

ojeras *fpl* rings under one's eyes

ojeriza *f* ill will. **tener ~ a** have a grudge against

ojo *m* eye; (de cerradura) keyhole; (de un puente) span. **¡~!** careful!

ola *f* wave

olé *int* bravo!

olea|da *f* wave. **~je** *m* swell

óleo *m* oil; (cuadro) oil painting

oleoducto *m* oil pipeline

oler [2] (*las formas que empezarían por* **ue** *se escriben* **hue**) *vt* smell. ● *vi* smell (a of). **me huele mal** (fig) it sounds fishy to me

olfat|ear *vt* sniff; scent <*rastro*>. **~o** *m* (sense of) smell (fig) intuition

olimpiada *f*, **olimpíada** *f* Olympic games, Olympics

olímpico *a* Olympic; (fig, Ⓘ) total

oliv|a *f* olive. **~ar** *m* olive grove. **~o** *m* olive tree

olla *f* pot, casserole. **~ a/de presión, ~ exprés** pressure cooker

olmo *m* elm (tree)

olor *m* smell. **~oso** *a* sweet-smelling

olvid|adizo *a* forgetful. **~ar** *vt* forget. □ **~arse** *vpr* forget. **~arse de** forget. **se me ~ó** I forgot. **~o** *m* oblivion; (acto) omission

ombligo *m* navel

omi|sión *f* omission. **~tir** *vt* omit

ómnibus *a* omnibus

omnipotente *a* omnipotent

omóplato *m*, **omoplato** *m* shoulder blade

once *a & m* eleven

ond|a *f* wave. **~a corta** short wave. **~a larga** long wave. **longitud** *f* **de ~a** wavelength. **~ear** *vi* wave; <*agua*> ripple. **~ulación** *f* undulation; (del pelo) wave. **~ular** *vi* wave

onomásti|co *a* <*índice*> of names. ● *m* (LAm) saint's day. **~ca** *f* saint's day

ONU *abrev* (**Organización de las Naciones Unidas**) UN

opac|ar [7] (LAm) make opaque; (deslucir) mar; (anular) overshadow. **~o** *a* opaque; (fig) dull

opci|ón *f* option. **~onal** *a* optional

ópera *f* opera

opera|ción *f* operation; (Com) transaction. **~dor** *m* operator; (TV) cameraman; (Mex, obrero) machinist. **~r** *vt* operate on; work <*milagro etc*>; (Mex) operate <*máquina*>. ● *vi* operate; (Com) deal. **~rio** *m* machinist. □ **~rse** *vpr* take place; (Med) have an operation. **~torio** *a* operative

opereta *f* operetta

opin|ar *vi* express one's opinion. ● *vt* think. **~ que** think that. **¿qué opinas?** what do you think? **~ión** *f* opinion. **la ~ión pública** public opinion

opio *m* opium

opone|nte *a* opposing. ● *m & f* opponent. **~r** *vt* oppose; offer <*resistencia*>; raise <*objeción*>. □ **~rse** *vpr* be opposed; <*dos personas*> oppose each other

oporto *m* port (wine)

oportun|idad *f* opportunity; (cualidad de oportuno) timeliness; (LAm, ocasión) occasion. **~ista** *m & f* opportunist. **~o** *a* opportune; (apropiado) suitable

oposi|ción *f* opposition. **~ciones** *fpl* public examination. **~tor** *m* candidate; (Pol) opponent

opres|ión *f* oppression; (ahogo) difficulty in breathing. **~ivo** *a* oppressive. **~or** *m* oppressor

oprimir *vt* squeeze; press <*botón etc*>; <*ropa*> be too tight for; (fig) oppress

optar *vi* choose. **~ por** opt for

óptic|a *f* optics; (tienda) optician's (shop). **~o** *a* optic(al). ● *m* optician

optimis|mo *m* optimism. **~ta** *a* optimistic. ● *m & f* optimist

óptimo *a* ideal; <*condiciones*> perfect

opuesto *a* opposite; <*opiniones*> conflicting

opulen|cia *f* opulence. **~to** *a* opulent

oración *f* prayer; (Gram) sentence

ora|dor *m* speaker. **~l** *a* oral

órale *int* (Mex) come on!; (de acuerdo) OK!

orar *vi* pray (**por** for)

órbita *f* orbit

orden *f* order. **~ del día** agenda. **órdenes** *fpl* **sagradas** Holy Orders. **a sus órdenes** (esp Mex) can I help you? **~ de arresto** arrest warrant. **en ~** in order. **por ~** in turn. **~ado** *a* tidy

ordenador *m* computer

ordena|nza *f* ordinance. ● *m* (Mil) orderly. **~r** *vt* put in order; (mandar) order; (Relig) ordain; (LAm, en restaurante) order

ordeñar *vt* milk

ordinario *a* ordinary; (grosero) common; (de mala calidad) poor-quality

orear *vt* air

orégano *m* oregano

oreja *f* ear

orfanato *m* orphanage

orfebre *m* goldsmith, silversmith

orfeón *m* choral society

orgánico *a* organic

organillo *m* barrel-organ

organismo *m* organism

organista *m & f* organist

organiza|ción *f* organization. **~dor** *m* organizer. **~r** [10] *vt* organize. □ **~rse** *vpr* get organized

órgano *m* organ

orgasmo *m* orgasm

orgía *f* orgy

orgullo *m* pride. **~so** *a* proud

orientación *f* orientation; (guía) guidance; (Archit) aspect

oriental *a & m & f* oriental

orientar *vt* position; advise <*persona*>. □ **~se** *vpr* point; <*persona*> find one's bearings

oriente *m* east

orificio *m* hole

orig|en *m* origin. **dar ~en a** give rise to. **~inal** *a* original; (excéntrico) odd. **~inalidad** *f* originality. **~inar** *vt* give rise to. **~inario** *a* original; (nativo) native. **ser ~inario de** come from. □ **~inarse** *vpr* originate; <*incendio*> start

orilla *f* (del mar) shore; (de río) bank; (borde) edge. **a ~s del mar** by the sea

orina *f* urine. **~l** *m* chamber-pot. **~r** *vi* urinate

oriundo *a* native. **ser ~ de** <*persona*> come from; <*especie etc*> native to

ornamental *a* ornamental

ornitología *f* ornithology

oro *m* gold. **~s** *mpl* Spanish card suit. **~ de ley** 9 carat gold. **hacerse de ~** make a fortune. **prometer el ~ y el moro** promise the moon

orquesta *f* orchestra. **~l** *a* orchestral. **~r** *vt* orchestrate

orquídea *f* orchid

ortiga *f* nettle

ortodoxo *a* orthodox

ortografía *f* spelling

ortopédico *a* orthopaedic

oruga *f* caterpillar

orzuelo *m* sty

os *pron* (acusativo) you; (dativo) (to) you; (reflexivo) (to) yourselves; (recíproco) (to) each other

osad|ía *f* boldness. **~o** *a* bold

oscila|ción *f* swinging; (de precios) fluctuation; (Tec) oscillation. **~r** *vi* swing; <*precio*> fluctuate; (Tec) oscillate

oscur|ecer [11] *vi* get dark. ● *vt* darken; (fig) obscure. □ **~ecerse** *vpr* grow dark; (nublarse) cloud over. **~idad** *f* darkness; (fig) obscurity. **~o** *a* dark; (fig) obscure. **a ~as** in the dark

óseo *a* bone

oso *m* bear. **~ de felpa, ~ de peluche** teddy bear

ostensible *a* obvious

ostent|ación *f* ostentation. **~ar** *vt* show off; (mostrar) show. **~oso** *a* ostentatious

osteópata *m & f* osteopath

ostión *m* (esp Mex) oyster

ostra *f* oyster

ostracismo *m* ostracism

Otan *abrev* (**Organización del Tratado del Atlántico Norte**) NATO, North Atlantic Treaty Organization

otitis *f* inflammation of the ear

otoño *m* autumn, fall (Amer)

otorga|miento *m* granting. **~r** [12] *vt* give; grant <*préstamo*>; (Jurid) draw up <*testamento*>

otorrinolaringólogo *m* ear, nose and throat specialist

otro, otra

● *adjetivo*

····➤ another; (con artículo, posesivo) other. **come ~ pedazo** have another piece. **el ~ día** the other day. **mi ~ coche** my other car. **otra cosa** something else. **otra persona** somebody else. **otra vez** again

····➤ (en plural) other; (con numeral) another. **en otras ocasiones** on other occasions. **~s 3 vasos** another 3 glasses

····➤ (siguiente) next. **al ~ día** the next day. **me bajo en la otra estación** I get off at the next station

● *pronombre*

····➤ (cosa) another one. **lo cambié por ~** I changed it for another one

····➤ (persona) someone else. **invitó a ~** she invited someone else

····➤ (en plural) (some) others. **tengo ~s en casa** I have (some) others at home. **~s piensan lo contrario** others think the opposite

····➤ (con artículo) **el ~** the other one. **los ~s** the others. **uno detrás del ~** one after the other. **los ~s no vinieron** the others didn't come. **esta semana no, la otra** not this week, next week. **de un día para el ~** from one day to the next

⇨ Para usos complementarios ver **uno, tanto**

ovación *f* ovation

oval *a*, **ovalado** *a* oval

óvalo *m* oval

ovario *m* ovary

oveja *f* sheep; (hembra) ewe

overol *m* (LAm) overalls

ovillo *m* ball. **hacerse un ~** curl up

OVNI *abrev* (**objeto volante no identificado**) UFO

ovulación *f* ovulation

oxida|ción *f* rusting. **~r** *vi* rust. □ **~rse** *vpr* go rusty

óxido *m* rust; (en química) oxide

oxígeno *m* oxygen

oye *vb* ⇒ OÍR

oyente *a* listening. ● *m* & *f* listener; (Univ) occasional student

ozono *m* ozone

Pp

pabellón *m* pavilion; (en jardín) summerhouse; (en hospital) block; (de instrumento) bell; (bandera) flag

pacer [11] *vi* graze

pachucho *a* <*fruta*> overripe; <*persona*> poorly

pacien|cia *f* patience. **perder la ~cia** lose patience. **~te** *a* & *m* & *f* patient

pacificar [7] *vt* pacify. □ **~se** *vpr* calm down

pacífico *a* peaceful. **el (Océano) P~** the Pacific (Ocean)

pacifis|mo *m* pacifism. **~ta** *a* & *m* & *f* pacifist

pact|ar *vi* agree, make a pact. **~o** *m* pact, agreement

padec|er [11] *vt/i* suffer (**de** from); (soportar) bear. **~cer del corazón** have heart trouble. **~imiento** *m* suffering

padrastro *m* stepfather

padre *a* Ⓘ terrible; (Mex, estupendo) great. ● *m* father. **~s** *mpl* parents

padrino *m* godfather; (en boda) *man who gives away the bride*

padrón *m* register. **~ electoral** (LAm) electoral roll

paella *f* paella

paga *f* payment; (sueldo) pay. **~dero** *a* payable

pagano *a* & *m* pagan

pagar [12] *vt* pay; pay for <*compras*>. ● *vi* pay. **~é** *m* IOU

página *f* page

pago *m* payment

país *m* country; (ciudadanos) nation. ~ **natal** native land. **el P~ Vasco** the Basque Country. **los P~es Bajos** the Low Countries

paisaje *m* landscape, scenery

paisano *m* compatriot

paja *f* straw; (en texto) padding

pájaro *m* bird. ~ **carpintero** woodpecker

paje *m* page

pala *f* shovel; (para cavar) spade; (para basura) dustpan; (de pimpón) bat

palabr|a *f* word; (habla) speech. **pedir la ~a** ask to speak. **tomar la ~a** take the floor. **~ota** *f* swear-word. **decir ~otas** swear

palacio *m* palace

paladar *m* palate

palanca *f* lever; (fig) influence. ~ **de cambio (de velocidades)** gear lever (Brit), gear shift (Amer)

palangana *f* washbasin (Brit), washbowl (Amer)

palco *m* (en el teatro) box

palestino *a* & *m* Palestinian

paleta *f* (de pintor) palette; (de albañil) trowel

paleto *m* yokel

paliativo *a* & *m* palliative

palide|cer [11] *vi* turn pale. **~z** *f* paleness

pálido *a* pale. **ponerse ~** turn pale

palillo *m* (de dientes) toothpick; (para comer) chopstick

paliza *f* beating

palma *f* (de la mano) palm; (árbol) palm (tree); (de dátiles) date palm. **dar ~s** clap. **~da** *f* pat; (LAm) slap. **~das** *fpl* applause

palmera *f* palm tree

palmo *m* span; (fig) few inches. **~ a ~** inch by inch

palmote|ar *vi* clap. **~o** *m* clapping, applause

palo *m* stick; (de valla) post; (de golf) club; (golpe) blow; (de naipes) suit; (mástil) mast

paloma *f* pigeon; (blanca, símbolo) dove

palomitas *fpl* popcorn

palpar *vt* feel

palpita|ción *f* palpitation. **~nte** *a* throbbing. **~r** *vi* beat; (latir con fuerza) pound; <*vena, sien*> throb

palta *f* (LAm) avocado (pear)

paludismo *m* malaria

pamp|a *f* pampas. **~ero** *a* of the pampas

pan *m* bread; (barra) loaf. ~ **integral** wholewheat bread, wholemeal bread (Brit). ~ **tostado** toast. ~ **rallado** breadcrumbs. **ganarse el ~** earn one's living

pana *f* corduroy

panader|ía *f* bakery; (tienda) baker's (shop). **~o** *m* baker

panal *m* honeycomb

panameño *a* & *m* Panamanian

pancarta *f* banner, placard

panda *m* panda

pander|eta *f* (small) tambourine **~o** *m* tambourine

pandilla *f* gang

panecillo *m* (bread) roll

panel *m* panel

panfleto *m* pamphlet

pánico *m* panic. **tener ~** be terrified (a of)

panor|ama *m* panorama. **~ámico** *a* panoramic

panque *m* (Mex) sponge cake

pantaletas *fpl* (Mex) panties, knickers (Brit)

pantalla *f* screen; (de lámpara) (lamp)shade

pantalón *m*, **pantalones** *mpl* trousers

pantano *m* marsh; (embalse) reservoir. **~so** *a* marshy

pantera *f* panther

panti *m*, (Mex) **pantimedias** *fpl* tights (Brit), pantyhose (Amer)

pantomima *f* pantomime

pantorrilla *f* calf

pantufla *f* slipper

panz|a *f* belly. **~udo** *a* pot-bellied

pañal *m* nappy (Brit), diaper (Amer)

paño *m* material; (de lana) woollen cloth; (trapo) cloth. **~o de cocina** dishcloth; (para secar) tea towel. **~o higiénico** sanitary towel. **en ~os menores** in one's underclothes

pañuelo *m* handkerchief; (de cabeza) scarf

papa *m* pope. ● *f* (LAm) potato. **~s fritas** (LAm) chips (Brit), French fries (Amer); (de paquete) crisps (Brit), chips (Amer)

papá *m* dad(dy). **~s** *mpl* parents. **P~ Noel** Father Christmas

papada *f* (de persona) double chin

papagayo *m* parrot

papalote *m* (Mex) kite

papanatas *m invar* simpleton

paparrucha *f* (tontería) silly thing

papaya *f* papaya, pawpaw

papel *m* paper; (en el teatro etc) role. **~ carbón** carbon paper. **~ de calcar** tracing paper. **~ de envolver** wrapping paper. **~ de plata** silver paper. **~ higiénico** toilet paper. **~ pintado** wallpaper. **~ secante** blotting paper. **~eo** *m* paperwork. **~era** *f* waste-paper basket. **~ería** *f* stationer's (shop). **~eta** *f* (para votar) (ballot) paper

paperas *fpl* mumps

paquete *m* packet; (bulto) parcel; (LAm, de papas fritas) bag; (Mex, problema) headache. **~ postal** parcel

Paquistán *m* Pakistan

paquistaní *a* & *m* Pakistani

par *a* <*número*> even. ● *m* couple; (dos cosas iguales) pair. **a ~es** two by two. **de ~ en ~** wide open. **~es y nones** odds and evens. **sin ~** without equal. ● *f* par. **a la ~** (Com) at par. **a la ~ que** at the same time

para

● *preposición*

····➤ for. **es ~ ti** it's for you. **~ siempre** for ever. **¿~ qué?** what for? **~ mi cumpleaños** for my birthday

····➤ (con infinitivo) to. **es muy tarde ~ llamar** it's too late to call. **salió ~ para divertirse** he went out to have fun. **lo hago ~ ahorrar** I do it (in order) to save money

····➤ (dirección) **iba ~ la oficina** he was going to the office. **empújalo ~ atrás** push it back. **¿vas ~ casa?** are you going home?

····➤ (tiempo) by. **debe estar listo ~ el 5** it must be ready by the 5th. **~ entonces** by then

····➤ (LAm, hora) to. **son 5 para la una** it's 5 to one

····➤ **para que** so (that). **grité ~ que me oyera** I shouted so (that) he could hear me.

Note that **para que** is always followed by a verb in the subjunctive

parabienes *mpl* congratulations

parábola *f* (narración) parable

parabólica *f* satellite dish

para|brisas *m invar* windscreen (Brit), windshield (Amer). **~caídas** *m invar* parachute. **~caidista** *m & f* parachutist; (Mil) paratrooper. **~choques** *m invar* bumper (Brit), fender (Amer); (Rail) buffer

parad|a *f* (acción) stop; (lugar) bus stop; (de taxis) rank; (Mil) parade. **~ero** *m* whereabouts; (LAm, lugar) bus stop. **~o** *a* stationary; <*desempleado*> unemployed. **estar ~** (LAm, de pie) be standing

paradoja *f* paradox

parador *m* state-owned hotel

parafina *f* paraffin

paraguas *m invar* umbrella

Paraguay *m* Paraguay

paraguayo *a & m* Paraguayan

paraíso *m* paradise; (en el teatro) gallery

paralel|a *f* parallel (line). **~as** *fpl* parallel bars. **~o** *a & m* parallel

par|álisis *f invar* paralysis. **~alítico** *a* paralytic. **~alizar** [10] *vt* paralyse

paramilitar *a* paramilitary

páramo *m* bleak upland

parangón *m* comparison.

paraninfo *m* main hall

paranoi|a *f* paranoia. **~co** *a* paranoiac

parar *vt/i* stop. **sin ~** continuously. □ **~se** *vpr* stop; (LAm, ponerse de pie) stand

pararrayos *m invar* lightning conductor

parásito *a* parasitic. ● *m* parasite

parcela *f* plot. **~r** *vt* divide into plots

parche *m* patch

parcial *a* partial. **a tiempo ~** part-time. **~idad** *f* prejudice

parco *a* laconic; (sobrio) sparing, frugal

parear *vt* put into pairs

parec|er *m* opinion. **al ~er** apparently. **a mi ~er** in my opinion. ● *vi* [11] seem; (asemejarse) look like; (tener aspecto de) look. **me ~e** I think. **~e fácil** it looks easy. **¿qué te ~e?** what do you think? **según ~e** apparently. □ **~erse** *vpr* resemble, look like. **~ido** *a* similar. **bien ~ido** good-looking. ● *m* similarity

pared *f* wall. **~ por medio** next door. **~ón** *m* (de fusilamiento) wall. **llevar al ~ón** shoot

parej|a *f* pair; (hombre y mujer) couple; (compañero) partner. **~o** *a* the same; (LAm, sin desniveles) even; (LAm, liso) smooth; (Mex, equitativo) equal. ● *adv* (LAm) evenly

parente|la *f* relations. **~sco** *m* relationship

paréntesis *m invar* parenthesis, bracket (Brit); (intervalo) break. **entre ~** in brackets (Brit), in parenthesis: (fig) by the way

paria *m & f* outcast

paridad *f* equality; (Com) parity

pariente *m & f* relation, relative

parir *vt* give birth to. ● *vi* give birth

parisiense *a & m & f*, **parisino** *a & m* Parisian

parking /'parkin/ *m* car park (Brit), parking lot (Amer)

parlament|ar *vi* talk. **~ario** *a* parliamentary. ● *m* member of parliament (Brit), congressman (Amer). **~o** *m* parliament

parlanchín *a* talkative. ● *m* chatterbox

parlante *m* (LAm) loudspeaker

paro *m* stoppage; (desempleo) unemployment; (subsidio) unemploy ment benefit; (LAm, huelga) strike. ~ **cardíaco** cardiac arrest

parodia *f* parody

parpadear *vi* blink; <*luz*> flicker

párpado *m* eyelid

parque *m* park. ~ **de atracciones** funfair. ~ **infantil** playground. ~ **zoológico** zoo, zoological gardens

parquímetro *m* parking meter

parra *f* grapevine

párrafo *m* paragraph

parrilla *f* grill; (LAm, Auto) luggage rack. **a la** ~ grilled. ~**da** *f* grill

párroco *m* parish priest

parroquia *f* parish; (iglesia) parish church. ~**no** *m* parishioner; (cliente) customer

parte *m* (informe) report. **dar** ~ report. **de mi** ~ for me ● *f* part; (porción) share; (Jurid) party; (Mex, repuesto) spare (part). **de** ~ **de** from. **¿de** ~ **de quién?** (al teléfono) who's speaking? **en cualquier** ~ anywhere. **en gran** ~ largely. **en** ~ partly. **en todas** ~**s** everywhere. **la mayor** ~ the majority. **la** ~ **superior** the top. **ninguna** ~ nowhere. **por otra** ~ on the other hand. **por todas** ~**s** everywhere

partera *f* midwife

partición *f* division; (Pol) partition

participa|ción *f* participation; (noticia) announcement; (de lotería) share. ~**nte** *a* participating. ● *m* & *f* participant. ~**r** *vt* announce. ● *vi* take part

participio *m* participle

particular *a* particular; <*clase*> private. **nada de** ~ nothing special. ● *m* private individual.

partida *f* departure; (en registro) entry; (documento) certificate; (de mercancías) consignment; (juego) game; (de gente) group

partidario *a* & *m* partisan. ~ **de** in favour of

parti|do *m* (Pol) party; (encuentro) match, game; (LAm, de ajedrez) game. ~**r** *vt* cut; (romper) break; crack <*nueces*>. ● *vi* leave. **a** ~**r de** from. ~ **de** start from. □ ~**rse** *vpr* (romperse) break; (dividirse) split

partitura *f* (Mus) score

parto *m* labour. **estar de** ~ be in labour

parvulario *m* kindergarten, nursery school (Brit)

pasa *f* raisin. ~ **de Corinto** currant

pasa|da *f* passing; (de puntos) row. **de** ~**da** in passing. ~**dero** *a* passable. ~**dizo** *m* passage. ~**do** *a* past; <*día, mes etc*> last; (anticuado) old-fashioned; <*comida*> bad, off. ~**do mañana** the day after tomorrow. ~**dos tres días** after three days. ~**dor** *m* bolt; (de pelo) hair-slide

pasaje *m* passage; (pasajeros) passengers; (LAm, de avión etc) ticket. ~**ro** *a* passing. ● *m* passenger

pasamano(s) *m* handrail; (barandilla de escalera) banister(s)

pasamontañas *m invar* balaclava

pasaporte *m* passport

pasar *vt* pass; (atravesar) go through; (filtrar) strain; spend <*tiempo*>; show <*película*>; (tolerar) tolerate; give <*mensaje, enfermedad*>. ● *vi* pass; (suceder) happen; (ir) go; (venir) come; <*tiempo*> go by. ~ **de** have no interest in. ~**lo bien** have a good time. ~ **frío** be cold. ~ **la aspiradora** vacuum. ~ **por alto** leave out. **lo que pasa es que** the fact is that. **pase lo que pase**

whatever happens. **¡pase Vd!** come in!, go in! **¡que lo pases bien!** have a good time! **¿qué pasa?** what's the matter?, what's happening? □ **~se** *vpr* pass; <*dolor*> go away; <*flores*> wither; <*comida*> go bad; spend <*tiempo*>; (excederse) go too far

pasarela *f* footbridge; (Naut) gangway

pasatiempo *m* hobby, pastime

Pascua *f* (fiesta de los hebreos) Passover; (de Resurrección) Easter; (Navidad) Christmas. **~s** *fpl* Christmas

pase *m* pass

pase|ante *m & f* passer-by. **~ar** *vt* walk <*perro*>; (exhibir) show off. ● *vi* walk. **ir a ~ar, salir a ~ar** walk. □ **~arse** *vpr* walk. **~o** *m* walk; (en coche etc) ride; (calle) avenue. **~o marítimo** promenade. **dar un ~o, ir de ~** go for a walk. **¡vete a ~o!** [I] get lost! [I]

pasillo *m* corridor; (de cine, avión) aisle

pasión *f* passion

pasivo *a* passive

pasm|ar *vt* astonish. □ **~arse** *vpr* be astonished

paso *m* step; (acción de pasar) passing; (camino) way; (entre montañas) pass; (estrecho) strait(s). **~ a nivel** level crossing (Brit), grade crossing (Amer). **~ de cebra** zebra crossing. **~ de peatones** pedestrian crossing. **~ elevado** flyover (Brit), overpass (Amer). **a cada ~** at every turn. **a dos ~s** very near. **de ~** in passing. **de ~ por** just passing through. **oír ~s** hear footsteps. **prohibido el ~** no entry

pasota *m & f* drop-out

pasta *f* paste; (masa) dough; ([▣], dinero) dough [▣]. **~s** *fpl* pasta; (pasteles) pastries. **~ de dientes, ~ dentífrica** toothpaste

pastel *m* cake; (empanada) pie; (lápiz) pastel. **~ería** *f* cake shop

pasteurizado *a* pasteurized

pastilla *f* pastille; (de jabón) bar; (de chocolate) piece

pasto *m* pasture; (hierba) grass; (LAm, césped) lawn. **~r** *m* shepherd; (Relig) minister. **~ra** *f* shepherdess

pata *f* leg; (pie de perro, gato) paw; (de ave) foot. **~s arriba** upside down. **a cuatro ~s** on all fours. **meter la ~** put one's foot in it. **tener mala ~** have bad luck. **~da** *f* kick. **~lear** *vi* stamp one's feet; <*niño pequeño*> kick

patata *f* potato. **~s fritas** chips (Brit), French fries (Amer); (de bolsa) (potato) crisps (Brit), (potato) chips (Amer)

patente *a* obvious. ● *f* licence

patern|al *a* paternal; <*cariño etc*> fatherly. **~idad** *f* paternity. **~o** *a* paternal; <*cariño etc*> fatherly

patético *a* moving

patillas *fpl* sideburns

patín *m* skate; (con ruedas) roller skate

patina|dor *m* skater. **~je** *m* skating. **~r** *vi* skate; (resbalar) slide; <*coche*> skid

patio *m* patio. **~ de butacas** stalls (Brit), orchestra (Amer)

pato *m* duck

patológico *a* pathological

patoso *a* clumsy

patraña *f* hoax

patria *f* homeland

patriarca *m* patriarch

patrimonio *m* patrimony; (fig) heritage

patri|ota *a* patriotic. ● *m & f* patriot. **~otismo** *m* patriotism

patrocin|ar *vt* sponsor. **~io** *m* sponsorship

patrón *m* (jefe) boss; (de pensión etc) landlord; (en costura) pattern

patrulla *f* patrol; (fig, cuadrilla) group. **~r** *vt/i* patrol

pausa *f* pause. **~do** *a* slow

pauta *f* guideline

paviment|ar *vt* pave. **~o** *m* pavement

pavo *m* turkey. **~ real** peacock

pavor *m* terror

payas|ada *f* buffoonery. **~o** *m* clown

paz *f* peace

peaje *m* toll

peatón *m* pedestrian

peca *f* freckle

peca|do *m* sin; (defecto) fault. **~dor** *m* sinner. **~minoso** *a* sinful. **~r** [7] *vi* sin

pech|o *m* chest; (de mujer) breast; (fig, corazón) heart. **dar el ~o a un niño** breast-feed a child. **tomar a ~o** take to heart. **~uga** *f* breast

pecoso *a* freckled

peculiar *a* peculiar, particular. **~idad** *f* peculiarity

pedal *m* pedal. **~ear** *vi* pedal

pedante *a* pedantic

pedazo *m* piece, bit. **a ~s** in pieces. **hacer(se) ~s** smash

pediatra *m & f* paediatrician

pedicuro *m* chiropodist

pedi|do *m* order; (LAm, solicitud) request. **~r** [5] *vt* ask for; (Com, en restaurante) order. ● *vi* ask. **~r prestado** borrow

pega|dizo *a* catchy. **~joso** *a* sticky

pega|mento *m* glue. **~r** [12] *vt* stick (on); (coser) sew on; give <*enfermedad etc*>; (juntar) join; (golpear) hit; (dar) give. **~r fuego a** set fire to. ● *vi* stick. □ **~rse** *vpr* stick; (pelearse) hit each other. **~tina** *f* sticker

pein|ado *m* hairstyle. **~ar** *vt* comb. □ **~arse** *vpr* comb one's hair. **~e** *m* comb. **~eta** *f* ornamental comb

p.ej. *abrev* (**por ejemplo**) e.g.

pelado *a* <*fruta*> peeled; <*cabeza*> bald; <*terreno*> bare

pela|je *m* (de animal) fur; (fig, aspecto) appearance. **~mbre** *m* (de animal) fur; (de persona) thick hair

pelar *vt* peel; shell <*habas*>; skin <*tomates*>; pluck <*ave*>

peldaño *m* step; (de escalera de mano) rung

pelea *f* fight; (discusión) quarrel. **~r** *vi* fight; (discutir) quarrel. □ **~rse** *vpr* fight; (discutir) quarrel

peletería *f* fur shop

peliagudo *a* difficult, tricky

pelícano *m* pelican

película *f* film (esp Brit), movie (esp Amer). **~ de dibujos animados** cartoon (film)

peligro *m* danger; (riesgo) hazard, risk. **poner en ~** endanger. **~so** *a* dangerous

pelirrojo *a* red-haired

pellejo *m* skin

pellizc|ar [7] *vt* pinch. **~o** *m* pinch

pelma *m & f*, **pelmazo** *m* bore, nuisance

pelo *m* hair. **no tener ~os en la lengua** be outspoken. **tomar el ~o a uno** pull s.o.'s leg

pelota *f* ball. **~ vasca** pelota. **hacer la ~ a uno** suck up to s.o.

pelotera *f* squabble

peluca *f* wig

peludo *a* hairy

peluquer|ía *f* hairdresser's. **~o** *m* hairdresser

pelusa *f* down

pena *f* sadness; <*lástima*> pity; (LAm, vergüenza) embarrassment; (Jurid) sentence. **~ de muerte** death penalty. **a duras ~s** with difficulty. **da ~ que** it's a pity that. **me da ~** it makes me sad. **merecer la ~** be worthwhile. **pasar ~s** suffer hardship. **¡qué ~!** what a pity! **valer la ~** be worthwhile

penal *a* penal; <*derecho*> criminal. ● *m* prison; (LAm, penalty) penalty. **~idad** *f* suffering; (Jurid) penalty. **~ty** *m* penalty

pendiente *a* hanging; <*cuenta*> outstanding; <*asunto etc*> pending. ● *m* earring. ● *f* slope

péndulo *m* pendulum

pene *m* penis

penetra|nte *a* penetrating; <*sonido*> piercing; <*viento*> bitter. **~r** *vt* penetrate; (fig) pierce. ● *vi*. **~r en** penetrate; (entrar) go into

penicilina *f* penicillin

pen|ínsula *f* peninsula. **~insular** *a* peninsular

penique *m* penny

penitencia *f* penitence; (castigo) penance

penoso *a* painful; (difícil) difficult; (LAm, tímido) shy; (LAm, embarazoso) embarrassing

pensa|do *a*. **bien ~do** all things considered. **menos ~do** least expected. **~dor** *m* thinker. **~miento** *m* thought. **~r** [1] *vt* think; (considerar) consider. **cuando menos se piensa** when least expected. **¡ni ~rlo!** no way! **pienso que sí** I think so. ● *vi* think. **~r en** think about. **~tivo** *a* thoughtful

pensi|ón *f* pension; (casa de huéspedes) guest-house. **~ón completa** full board. **~onista** *m & f* pensioner; (huésped) lodger

penúltimo *a & m* penultimate, last but one

penumbra *f* half-light

penuria *f* shortage. **pasar ~s** suffer hardship

peñ|a *f* rock; (de amigos) group; (LAm, club) folk club. **~ón** *m* rock. **el P~ón de Gibraltar** The Rock (of Gibraltar)

peón *m* labourer; (en ajedrez) pawn; (en damas) piece

peonza *f* (spinning) top

peor *a* (comparativo) worse; (superlativo) worst. ● *adv* worse. **de mal en ~** from bad to worse. **lo ~** the worst thing. **tanto ~** so much the worse

pepin|illo *m* gherkin. **~o** *m* cucumber. **(no) me importa un ~o** I couldn't care less

pepita *f* pip; (de oro) nugget

pequeñ|ez *f* smallness; (minucia) trifle. **~o** *a* small, little; (de edad) young; (menor) younger. ● *m* little one. **es el ~o** he's the youngest

pera *f* (fruta) pear. **~l** *m* pear (tree)

percance *m* mishap

percatarse *vpr*. **~ de** notice

perc|epción *f* perception. **~ibir** *vt* perceive; earn <*dinero*>

percha *f* hanger; (de aves) perch

percusión *f* percussion

perde|dor *a* losing. ● *m* loser. **~r** [1] *vt* lose; (malgastar) waste; miss <*tren etc*>. ● *vi* lose. □ **~rse** *vpr* get lost; (desaparecer) disappear; (desperdiciarse) be wasted; (estropearse) be spoilt. **echar(se) a ~r** spoil

pérdida *f* loss; (de líquido) leak; (de tiempo) waste
perdido *a* lost
perdiz *f* partridge
perd|ón *m* pardon, forgiveness. **pedir ~ón** apologize. ● *int* sorry! **~onar** *vt* excuse, forgive; (Jurid) pardon. **¡~one (Vd)!** sorry!
perdura|ble *a* lasting. **~r** *vi* last
perece|dero *a* perishable. **~r** [11] *vi* perish
peregrin|ación *f* pilgrimage. **~o** *a* strange. ● *m* pilgrim
perejil *m* parsley
perengano *m* so-and-so
perenne *a* everlasting; (Bot) perennial
perez|a *f* laziness. **~oso** *a* lazy
perfec|ción *f* perfection. **a la ~ción** perfectly, to perfection. **~cionar** *vt* perfect; (mejorar) improve. **~cionista** *m & f* perfectionist. **~to** *a* perfect; (completo) complete
perfil *m* profile; (contorno) outline. **~ado** *a* well-shaped
perfora|ción *f* perforation. **~dora** *f* punch. **~r** *vt* pierce, perforate; punch <*papel, tarjeta etc*>
perfum|ar *vt* perfume. □ **~arse** *vpr* put perfume on. **~e** *m* perfume, scent. **~ería** *f* perfumery
pericia *f* skill
perif|eria *f* (de ciudad) outskirts. **~érico** *a* <*barrio*> outlying. ● *m* (Mex, carretera) ring road
perilla *f* (barba) goatee
perímetro *m* perimeter
periódico *a* periodic(al). ● *m* newspaper
periodis|mo *m* journalism. **~ta** *m & f* journalist
período *m*, **periodo** *m* period
periquito *m* budgerigar
periscopio *m* periscope
perito *a & m* expert
perju|dicar [7] *vt* damage; (desfavorecer) not suit. **~dicial** *a* damaging. **~icio** *m* damage. **en ~icio de** to the detriment of
perla *f* pearl. **de ~s** *adv* very well
permane|cer [11] *vi* remain. **~ncia** *f* permanence; (estancia) stay. **~nte** *a* permanent. ● *f* perm. ● *m* (Mex) perm
permi|sivo *a* permissive. **~so** *m* permission; (documento) licence; (Mil etc) leave. **~so de conducir** driving licence (Brit), driver's license (Amer). **con ~so** excuse me. **~tir** *vt* allow, permit. **¿me ~te?** may I? □ **~tirse** *vpr* allow s.o.
pernicioso *a* pernicious; <*persona*> wicked
perno *m* bolt
pero *conj* but. ● *m* fault; (objeción) objection
perogrullada *f* platitude
perpendicular *a & f* perpendicular
perpetrar *vt* perpetrate
perpetu|ar [21] *vt* perpetuate. **~o** *a* perpetual
perplejo *a* perplexed
perr|a *f* (animal) bitch; (moneda) coin, penny (Brit), cent (Amer); (rabieta) tantrum. **estar sin una ~a** be broke. **~era** *f* dog pound; (vehículo) dog catcher's van. **~o** *a* awful. ● *m* dog. **~o galgo** greyhound. **de ~os** awful
persa *a & m & f* Persian
perse|cución *f* pursuit; (política etc) persecution. **~guir** [5 & 13] *vt* pursue; (por ideología etc) persecute
persevera|nte *a* persevering. **~r** *vi* persevere

persiana *f* blind; (LAm, contraventana) shutter

persignarse *vpr* cross o.s.

persist|ente *a* persistent. **~ir** *vi* persist

person|a *f* person. **~as** *fpl* people. **~aje** *m* (persona importante) important figure; (de obra literaria) character. **~al** *a* personal. ● *m* staff. **~alidad** *f* personality. □ **~arse** *vpr* appear in person. **~ificar** [7] *vt* personify

perspectiva *f* perspective

perspica|cia *f* shrewdness; (de vista) keen eyesight. **~z** *a* shrewd; <*vista*> keen

persua|dir *vt* persuade. **~sión** *f* persuasion. **~sivo** *a* persuasive

pertenecer [11] *vi* belong

pértiga *f* pole. **salto** *m* **con ~** pole vault

pertinente *a* relevant

perturba|ción *f* disturbance. **~ción del orden público** breach of the peace. **~r** *vt* disturb; disrupt <*orden*>

Perú *m*. **el ~** Peru

peruano *a* & *m* Peruvian

perver|so *a* evil. ● *m* evil person. **~tir** [4] *vt* pervert

pesa *f* weight. **~dez** *f* weight; (de cabeza etc) heaviness; (lentitud) sluggishness; (cualidad de fastidioso) tediousness; (cosa fastidiosa) bore, nuisance

pesadilla *f* nightmare

pesado *a* heavy; <*sueño*> deep; <*viaje*> tiring; (duro) hard; (aburrido) boring, tedious

pésame *m* sympathy, condolences

pesar *vt* weigh. ● *vi* be heavy. ● *m* sorrow; (remordimiento) regret. **a ~ de (que)** in spite of. **pese a (que)** in spite of

pesca *f* fishing; (peces) fish; (pescado) catch. **ir de ~** go fishing. **~da** *f* hake. **~dería** *f* fish shop. **~dilla** *f* whiting. **~do** *m* fish. **~dor** *a* fishing. ● *m* fisherman. **~r** [7] *vt* catch. ● *vi* fish

pescuezo *m* neck

pesebre *m* manger

pesero *m* (Mex) minibus

peseta *f* peseta

pesimista *a* pessimistic. ● *m* & *f* pessimist

pésimo *a* very bad, awful

peso *m* weight; (moneda) peso. **~ bruto** gross weight. **~ neto** net weight. **al ~** by weight. **de ~** influential

pesquero *a* fishing

pestañ|a *f* eyelash. **~ear** *vi* blink

pest|e *f* plague; (hedor) stench. **~icida** *m* pesticide

pestillo *m* bolt; (de cerradura) latch

petaca *f* cigarette case; (Mex, maleta) suitcase

pétalo *m* petal

petardo *m* firecracker

petición *f* request; (escrito) petition

petirrojo *m* robin

petrificar [7] *vt* petrify

petr|óleo *m* oil. **~olero** *a* oil. ● *m* oil tanker

petulante *a* smug

peyorativo *a* pejorative

pez *f* fish; (substancia negruzca) pitch. **~ espada** swordfish

pezón *m* nipple

pezuña *f* hoof

piadoso *a* compassionate; (devoto) devout

pian|ista *m & f* pianist. **~o** *m* piano. **~o de cola** grand piano

piar [20] *vi* chirp

picad|a *f.* **caer en ~a** (LAm) nosedive. **~o** *a* perforated; <*carne*> minced (Brit), ground (Amer); (ofendido) offended; <*mar*> choppy; <*diente*> bad. ● *m.* **caer en ~o** nosedive. **~ura** *f* bite, sting; (de polilla) moth hole

picaflor *m* (LAm) hummingbird

picante *a* hot; <*chiste etc*> risqué

picaporte *m* door-handle; (aldaba) knocker

picar [7] *vt* <*ave*> peck; <*insecto, pez*> bite; <*abeja, avispa*> sting; (comer poco) pick at; mince (Brit), grind (Amer) <*carne*>; chop (up) <*cebolla etc*>; (Mex, pinchar) prick. ● *vi* itch; <*ave*> peck; <*insecto, pez*> bite; <*sol*> scorch; <*comida*> be hot

picardía *f* craftiness; (travesura) naughty thing

pícaro *a* crafty; <*niño*> mischievous. ● *m* rogue

picazón *f* itch

pichón *m* pigeon; (Mex, novato) beginner

pico *m* beak; (punta) corner; (herramienta) pickaxe; (cima) peak. **y ~** (con tiempo) a little after; (con cantidad) a little more than. **~tear** *vt* peck; (🅸, comer) pick at

picudo *a* pointed

pido *vb* ⇒PEDIR

pie *m* foot; (Bot, de vaso) stem. **~ cuadrado** square foot. **a cuatro ~s** on all fours. **al ~ de la letra** literally. **a ~** on foot. **a ~(s) juntillas** (fig) firmly. **buscarle tres ~s al gato** split hairs. **de ~** standing (up). **de ~s a cabeza** from head to toe. **en ~** standing (up). **ponerse de ~** stand up

piedad *f* pity; (Relig) piety

piedra *f* stone; (de mechero) flint

piel *f* skin; (cuero) leather

pienso *vb* ⇒PENSAR

pierdo *vb* ⇒PERDER

pierna *f* leg

pieza *f* piece; (parte) part; (obra teatral) play; (moneda) coin; (habitación) room. **~ de recambio** spare part

pijama *m* pyjamas

pila *f* (montón) pile; (recipiente) basin; (eléctrica) battery. **~ bautismal** font. **~r** *m* pillar

píldora *f* pill

pilla|je *m* pillage. **~r** *vt* catch

pillo *a* wicked. ● *m* rogue

pilot|ar *vt* pilot. **~o** *m* pilot

pim|entero *m* (vasija) pepperpot. **~entón** *m* paprika; (LAm, fruto) pepper. **~ienta** *f* pepper. **grano** *m* **de ~ienta** peppercorn. **~iento** *m* pepper

pináculo *m* pinnacle

pinar *m* pine forest

pincel *m* paintbrush. **~ada** *f* brush-stroke. **la última ~ada** (fig) the finishing touch

pinch|ar *vt* pierce, prick; puncture <*neumático*>; (fig, incitar) push; (Med, 🅸) give an injection to. **~azo** *m* prick; (en neumático) puncture. **~itos** *mpl* kebab(s); (tapas) savoury snacks. **~o** *m* point

ping-pong *m* table tennis, ping-pong

pingüino *m* penguin

pino *m* pine (tree)

pint|a *f* spot; (fig, aspecto) appearance. **tener ~a de** look like. **~ada** *f* graffiti. **~ar** *vt* paint. **no ~a nada** (fig) it doesn't count. □ **~arse** *vpr* put on make-up. **~or** *m* painter.

~oresco *a* picturesque. **~ura** *f* painting; (material) paint

pinza *f* (clothes-)peg (Brit), clothes-pin (Amer); (de cangrejo etc) claw. **~s** *fpl* tweezers

piñ|a *f* pine cone; (fruta) pineapple. **~ón** *m* (semilla) pine nut

pío *a* pious. ● *m* chirp. **no decir ni ~** not say a word

piojo *m* louse

pionero *m* pioneer

pipa *f* pipe; (semilla) seed; (de girasol) sunflower seed

pique *m* resentment; (rivalidad) rivalry. **irse a ~** sink

piquete *m* picket; (Mex, herida) prick; (Mex, de insecto) sting

piragua *f* canoe

pirámide *f* pyramid

pirata *a invar* pirate. ● *m* & *f* pirate

Pirineos *mpl.* **los ~**the Pyrenees

piropo *m* flattering comment

pirueta *f* pirouette

pirulí *m* lollipop

pisa|da *f* footstep; (huella) footprint. **~papeles** *m invar* paperweight. **~r** *vt* tread on. ● *vi* tread

piscina *f* swimming pool

Piscis *m* Pisces

piso *m* floor; (vivienda) flat (Brit), apartment (Amer); (de autobús) deck

pisotear *vt* trample (on)

pista *f* track; (fig, indicio) clue. **~ de aterrizaje** runway. **~ de baile** dance floor. **~ de carreras** racing track. **~ de hielo** ice-rink. **~ de tenis** tennis court

pistol|a *f* pistol. **~era** *f* holster. **~ero** *m* gunman

pistón *m* piston

pit|ar, (LAm) **~ear** *vt* whistle at; *<conductor>* hoot at; award *<falta>*. ● *vi* blow a whistle; (Auto) sound one's horn. **~ido** *m* whistle

pitill|era *f* cigarette case. **~o** *m* cigarette

pito *m* whistle; (Auto) horn

pitón *m* python

pitorre|arse *vpr*. **~arse de** make fun of. **~o** *m* teasing

pitorro *m* spout

piyama *m* (LAm) pyjamas

pizarr|a *f* slate; (en aula) blackboard. **~ón** *m* (LAm) blackboard

pizca *f* ⊞ tiny piece; (de sal) pinch. **ni ~** not at all

placa *f* plate; (con inscripción) plaque; (distintivo) badge. **~ de matrícula** number plate

place|ntero *a* pleasant. **~r** [32] *vi*. **haz lo que te plazca** do as you please. **me ~ hacerlo** I'm pleased to do it. ● *m* pleasure

plácido *a* placid

plaga *f* (also fig) plague. **~do** *a*. **~do de** filled with

plagio *m* plagiarism

plan *m* plan. **en ~ de** as

plana *f* page. **en primera ~** on the front page

plancha *f* iron; (lámina) sheet. **a la ~** grilled. **tirarse una ~** put one's foot in it. **~do** *m* ironing. **~r** *vt* iron. ● *vi* do the ironing

planeador *m* glider

planear *vt* plan. ● *vi* glide

planeta *m* planet

planicie *f* plain

planifica|ción *f* planning. **~r** [7] *vt* plan

planilla *f* (LAm) payroll; (personal) staff

plano *a* flat. ● *m* plane; (de edificio) plan; (de ciudad) street plan. **primer ~** foreground; (Foto) close-up

planta *f* (Anat) sole; (Bot, fábrica) plant; (plano) ground plan; (piso) floor. **~ baja** ground floor (Brit), first floor (Amer)

planta|ción *f* plantation. **~r** *vt* plant; deal <*golpe*>. **~r en la calle** throw out. □ **~rse** *vpr* stand; (fig) stand firm

plantear *vt* (exponer) expound; (causar) create; raise <*cuestión*>

plantilla *f* insole; (nómina) payroll; (personal) personnel

plaqué *m* plating. **de ~** plated

plástico *a* & *m* plastic

plata *f* silver; (fig, [I], dinero) money. **~ de ley** hallmarked silver

plataforma *f* platform

plátano *m* plane (tree); (fruta) banana. **platanero** *m* banana tree

platea *f* stalls (Brit), orchestra (Amer)

plateado *a* silver-plated; (color de plata) silver

pl|ática *f* talk. **~aticar** [7] *vi* (Mex) talk. ● *vt* (Mex) tell

platija *f* plaice

platillo *m* saucer; (Mus) cymbal. **~ volador** (LAm), **~ volante** flying saucer

platino *m* platinum. **~s** *mpl* (Auto) points

plato *m* plate; (comida) dish; (parte de una comida) course

platónico *a* platonic

playa *f* beach; (fig) seaside

plaza *f* square; (mercado) market (place); (sitio) place; (empleo) job. **~ de toros** bullring

plazco *vb* ⇒PLACER

plazo *m* period; (pago) instalment; (fecha) date. **comprar a ~s** buy on hire purchase (Brit), buy on the installment plan (Amer)

plazuela *f* little square

pleamar *f* high tide

pleb|e *f* common people. **~eyo** *a* & *m* plebeian. **~iscito** *m* plebiscite

plega|ble *a* pliable; <*silla*> folding. **~r** [1 & 12] *vt* fold. □ **~rse** *vpr* bend; (fig) yield

pleito *m* (court) case; (fig) dispute

plenilunio *m* full moon

plen|itud *f* fullness; (fig) height. **~o** *a* full. **en ~o día** in broad daylight. **en ~o verano** at the height of the summer

plieg|o *m* sheet. **~ue** *m* fold; (en ropa) pleat

plisar *vt* pleat

plom|ero *m* (LAm) plumber. **~o** *m* lead; (Elec) fuse. **con ~o** leaded. **sin ~o** unleaded

pluma *f* feather; (para escribir) pen. **~ atómica** (Mex) ballpoint pen. **~ estilográfica** fountain pen. **~je** *m* plumage

plum|ero *m* feather duster; (para plumas, lápices etc) pencil-case. **~ón** *m* down; (edredón) down-filled quilt

plural *a* & *m* plural. **en ~** in the plural

pluriempleo *m* having more than one job

plus *m* bonus

pluscuamperfecto *m* pluperfect

plusvalía *f* capital gain

pluvial *a* rain

pobla|ción *f* population; (ciudad) city, town; (pueblo) village. **~do** *a* populated. ● *m* village. **~r** [2] *vt* populate; (habitar) inhabit. □ **~rse** *vpr* get crowded

pobre *a* poor. ● *m* & *f* poor person; (fig) poor thing. **¡~cito!** poor (little) thing! ¡~ de mí! poor (old) me! **~za** *f* poverty

pocilga *f* pigsty

poción *f* potion

poco

● *adjetivo/pronombre*

····➤ **poco, poca** little, not much. **tiene poca paciencia** he has little patience. **¿cuánta leche queda? - poca** how much milk is there left? - not much

····➤ **pocos, pocas** few. **muy ~s días** very few days. **unos ~s dólares** a few dollars. **compré unos ~s** I bought a few. **aceptaron a muy ~s** very few (people) were accepted

····➤ **a ~ de llegar** soon after he arrived. **¡a ~ !** (Mex) really? **dentro de ~** soon. **~ a ~**, (LAm) **de a ~** gradually, little by little. **hace ~** recently, not long ago. **por ~** nearly. **un ~** (cantidad) a little; (tiempo) a while. **un ~ de** a (little) bit of, a little, some

● *adverbio*

····➤ (con verbo) not much. **lee muy ~** he doesn't read very much

····➤ (con adjetivo) **un lugar ~ conocido** a little known place. **es ~ inteligente** he's not very intelligent

! Cuando **poco** modifica a un adjetivo, muchas veces el inglés prefiere el uso del prefijo *un-*, p. ej. **poco amistoso** *unfriendly*. **poco agradecido** *ungrateful*

podar *vt* prune

poder [33] *v aux* be able to. **no voy a ~ terminar** I won't be able to finish. **no pudo venir** he couldn't come. **¿puedo hacer algo?** can I do anything? **¿puedo pasar?** may I come in? **no ~ con** not be able to cope with; (no aguantar) not be able to stand. **no ~ más** be exhausted; (estar harto de algo) not be able to manage any more. **no ~ menos que** have no alternative but. **puede que** it is possible that. **puede ser** it is possible. **¿se puede ...?** may I...? ● *m* power. **en el ~** in power. **~es** *mpl* **públicos** authorities. **~oso** *a* powerful

podrido *a* rotten

po|ema *m* poem. **~esía** *f* poetry; (poema) poem. **~eta** *m & f* poet. **~ético** *a* poetic

polaco *a* Polish. ● *m* Pole; (lengua) Polish

polar *a* polar. **estrella ~** polestar

polea *f* pulley

pol|émica *f* controversy. **~emizar** [10] *vi* argue

polen *m* pollen

policía *f* police (force); (persona) policewoman. ● *m* policeman. **~co** *a* police; <*novela etc*> detective

policromo *a*, **polícromo** *a* polychrome

polideportivo *m* sports centre

polietileno *m* polythene

poligamia *f* polygamy

polígono *m* polygon

polilla *f* moth

polio(mielitis) *f* polio(myelitis)

polític|a *f* politics; (postura) policy; (mujer) politician. **~ interior** domestic policy. **~o** *a* political. **familia ~a** in-laws. ● *m* politician

póliza *f* (de seguros) policy

poll|o *m* chicken; (gallo joven) chick. **~uelo** *m* chick

polo *m* pole; (helado) ice lolly (Brit), Popsicle (P) (Amer); (juego) polo. **P~ norte** North Pole

Polonia *f* Poland

poltrona *f* armchair

polución *f* pollution

polv|areda *f* dust cloud; (fig, escándalo) uproar. **~era** *f* compact. **~o** *m* powder; (suciedad) dust. **~os** *mpl* powder. **en ~o** powdered. **estar hecho ~o** be exhausted. **quitar el ~o** dust

pólvora *f* gunpowder; (fuegos artificiales) fireworks

polvoriento *a* dusty

pomada *f* ointment

pomelo *m* grapefruit

pómez *a*. **piedra** *f* **~** pumice stone

pomp|a *f* bubble; (esplendor) pomp. **~as fúnebres** funeral. **~oso** *a* pompous; (espléndido) splendid

pómulo *m* cheekbone

ponchar *vt* (Mex) puncture

ponche *m* punch

poncho *m* poncho

ponderar *vt* (alabar) speak highly of

poner [34] *vt* put; put on *<ropa, obra de teatro, TV etc>*; lay *<la mesa, un huevo>*; set *<examen, deberes>*; (contribuir) contribute; give *<nombre>*; make *<nervioso>*; pay *<atención>*; show *<película, interés>*; open *<una tienda>*; equip *<una casa>*. **~ con** (al teléfono) put through to. **~ por escrito** put into writing. **~ una multa** fine. **pongamos** let's suppose. ● *vi* lay. □ **~se** *vpr* put o.s.; (volverse) get; put on *<ropa>*; *<sol>* set. **~se a** start to. **~se a mal con uno** fall out with s.o.

pongo *vb* ⇒PONER

poniente *m* west; (viento) west wind

pont|ificar [7] *vi* pontificate. **~ífice** *m* pontiff

popa *f* stern

popote *m* (Mex) (drinking) straw

popul|acho *m* masses. **~ar** *a* popular; *<costumbre>* traditional; *<lenguaje>* colloquial. **~aridad** *f* popularity. **~arizar** [10] *vt* popularize.

póquer *m* poker

poquito *m*. **un ~** a little bit. ● *adv* a little

por

● *preposición*

····➤ for. **es ~ tu bien** it's for your own good. **lo compró ~ 5 dólares** he bought it for 5 dollars. **si no fuera ~ ti** if it weren't for you. **vino ~ una semana** he came for a week

⇨ Para expresiones como **por la mañana, por la noche** etc., ver bajo el respectivo nombre

····➤ (causa) because of. **se retrasó ~ la lluvia** he was late because of the rain. **no hay trenes ~ la huelga** there aren't any trains because of the strike

····➤ (medio, agente) by. **lo envié ~ correo** I sent it by post. **fue destruida ~ las bombas** it was destroyed by the bombs

····➤ (a través de) through. **entró ~ la ventana** he got in through the window. **me enteré ~ un amigo** I found out through a friend. **~ todo el país** throughout the country

····➤ (a lo largo de) along. **caminar ~ la playa** to walk along the beach.

cortar ~ la línea de puntos cut along the dotted line

····➤ (proporción) per. **cobra 30 dólares ~ hora** he charges 30 dollars per hour. **uno ~ persona** one per person. **10 ~ ciento** 10 per cent

····➤ (Mat) times. **dos ~ dos (son) cuatro** two times two is four

····➤ (modo) in. **~ escrito** in writing. **pagar ~ adelantado** to pay in advance

⇨ Para expresiones como **por dentro, por fuera** etc., ver bajo el respectivo adverbio

····➤ (en locuciones) **~ más que** no matter how much. **¿~ qué?** why? **~ si** in case. **~ supuesto** of course

porcelana *f* china

porcentaje *m* percentage

porcino *a* pig

porción *f* portion; (de chocolate) piece

pordiosero *m* beggar

porfia|do *a* stubborn. **~r** [20] *vi* insist

pormenor *m* detail

pornogr|afía *f* pornography. **~áfico** *a* pornographic

poro *m* pore; (Mex, puerro) leek. **~so** *a* porous

porque *conj* because; (para que) so that

porqué *m* reason

porquería *f* filth; (basura) rubbish; (grosería) dirty trick

porra *f* club

porrón *m* wine jug (with a long spout)

portaaviones *m invar* aircraft carrier

portada *f* (de libro) title page; (de revista) cover

portadocumentos *m invar* (LAm) briefcase

portador *m* bearer

portaequipaje(s) *m invar* boot (Brit), trunk (Amer); (encima del coche) roof-rack

portal *m* hall; (puerta principal) main entrance. **~es** *mpl* arcade

porta|ligas *m invar* suspender belt. **~monedas** *m invar* purse

portarse *vpr* behave

portátil *a* portable

portavoz *m* spokesman. ● *f* spokeswoman

portazo *m* bang. **dar un ~** slam the door

porte *m* transport; (precio) carriage; (LAm, tamaño) size. **~ador** *m* carrier

portento *m* marvel

porteño *a* (from Buenos Aires

porter|ía *f* porter's lodge; (en deportes) goal. **~o** *m* caretaker, porter; (en deportes) goalkeeper. **~o automático** entryphone

pórtico *m* portico

portorriqueño *a* & *m* Puerto Rican

Portugal *m* Portugal

portugués *a* & *m* Portuguese

porvenir *m* future

posada *f* inn. **dar ~** give shelter

posar *vt* put. ● *vi* pose. □ **~se** *vpr* <*pájaro*> perch; <*avión*> land

posdata *f* postscript

pose|edor *m* owner; (de récord, billete, etc) holder. **~er** [18] *vt* own; hold <*récord*>; have <*conocimientos*>. **~sión** *f* possession. □ **~sionarse** *vpr*. **~sionarse de** take possession of. **~sivo** *a* possessive

posgraduado *a & m* postgraduate

posguerra *f* post-war years

posib|ilidad *f* possibility. **~le** *a* possible. **de ser ~le** if possible. **en lo ~le** as far as possible. **si es ~le** if possible

posición *f* position; (en sociedad) social standing

positivo *a* positive

poso *m* sediment

posponer [34] *vt* put after; (diferir) postpone

posta *f*. **a ~** on purpose

postal *a* postal. ● *f* postcard

poste *m* pole; (de valla) post

póster *m* (*pl* **~s**) poster

postergar [12] *vt* pass over; (diferir) postpone

posteri|dad *f* posterity. **~or** *a* back; <*años*> later; <*capítulos*> subsequent. **~ormente** *adv* later

postigo *m* door; (contraventana) shutter

postizo *a* false, artificial. ● *m* hairpiece

postrarse *vpr* prostrate o.s.

postre *m* dessert, pudding (Brit)

postular *vt* postulate; (LAm) nominate <*candidato*>

póstumo *a* posthumous

postura *f* position, stance

potable *a* drinkable; <*agua*> drinking

potaje *m* vegetable stew

potasio *m* potassium

pote *m* pot

poten|cia *f* power. **~cial** *a & m* potential. **~te** *a* powerful

potro *m* colt; (en gimnasia) horse

pozo *m* well; (hoyo seco) pit; (de mina) shaft; (fondo común) pool

práctica *f* practice. **en la ~** in practice

practica|nte *m & f* nurse. **~r** [7] *vt* practise; play <*deportes*>; (ejecutar) carry out

práctico *a* practical; (conveniente, útil) handy. ● *m* practitioner

prad|era *f* meadow; (terreno grande) prairie. **~o** *m* meadow

pragmático *a* pragmatic

preámbulo *m* preamble

precario *a* precarious; <*medios*> scarce

precaución *f* precaution; (cautela) caution. **con ~** cautiously

precaverse *vpr* take precautions

precede|ncia *f* precedence; (prioridad) priority. **~nte** *a* preceding. ● *m* precedent. **~r** *vt/i* precede

precepto *m* precept. **~r** *m* tutor

precia|do *a* valued; <*don*> valuable. □ **~rse** *vpr*. **~rse de** pride o.s. on

precio *m* price. **~ de venta al público** retail price. **al ~ de** at the cost of. **no tener ~** be priceless. **¿qué ~ tiene?** how much is it?

precios|idad *f* (cosa preciosa) beautiful thing. **¡es una ~idad!** it's beautiful! **~o** *a* precious; (bonito) beautiful

precipicio *m* precipice

precipita|ción *f* precipitation; (prisa) rush. **~damente** *adv* hastily. **~do** *a* hasty. **~r** *vt* (apresurar) hasten; (arrojar) hurl. □ **~rse** *vpr* throw o.s.; (correr) rush; (actuar sin reflexionar) act rashly

precis|amente *a* exactly. **~ar** *vt* require; (determinar) determine. **~ión** *f* precision. **~o** *a* precise; (necesario) necessary. **si es ~o** if necessary

preconcebido *a* preconceived

precoz *a* early; <*niño*> precocious

precursor *m* forerunner

predecesor *m* predecessor

predecir [46], (*pero imperativo* **predice**, *futuro y condicional regulares*) *vt* foretell

predestinado *a* predestined

prédica *f* sermon

predicar [7] *vt/i* preach

predicción *f* prediction; (del tiempo) forecast

predilec|ción *f* predilection. **~to** *a* favourite

predisponer [34] *vt* predispose

predomin|ante *a* predominant. **~ar** *vi* predominate. **~io** *m* predominance

preeminente *a* pre-eminent

prefabricado *a* prefabricated

prefacio *m* preface

prefer|encia *f* preference; (Auto) right of way. **de ~encia** preferably. **~ente** *a* preferential. **~ible** *a* preferable. **~ido** *a* favourite. **~ir** [4] *vt* prefer

prefijo *m* prefix; (telefónico) dialling code

pregonar *vt* announce

pregunta *f* question. **hacer una ~** ask a question. **~r** *vt/i* ask (**por** about). □ **~rse** *vpr* wonder

prehistórico *a* prehistoric

preju|icio *m* prejudice. **~zgar** [12] *vt* prejudge

preliminar *a* & *m* preliminary

preludio *m* prelude

premarital *a*, **prematrimonial** *a* premarital

prematuro *a* premature

premedita|ción *f* premeditation. **~r** *vt* premeditate

premi|ar *vt* give a prize to; (recompensar) reward. **~o** *m* prize; (recompensa) reward. **~o gordo** jackpot

premonición *f* premonition

prenatal *a* antenatal

prenda *f* garment; (garantía) surety; (en juegos) forfeit. **en ~ de** as a token of. **~r** *vt* captivate. □ **~rse** *vpr* fall in love (**de** with)

prende|dor *m* brooch. **~r** *vt* capture; (sujetar) fasten; light <*cigarrillo*>; (LAm) turn on <*gas, radio, etc*>. ● *vi* catch; (arraigar) take root. □ **~se** *vpr* (encenderse) catch fire

prensa *f* press. **~r** *vt* press

preñado *a* pregnant; (fig) full

preocupa|ción *f* worry. **~do** *a* worried. **~r** *vt* worry. □ **~rse** *vpr* worry. **~rse de** look after

prepara|ción *f* preparation. **~do** *a* prepared. ● *m* preparation. **~r** *vt* prepare. □ **~rse** *vpr* get ready. **~tivos** *mpl* preparations. **~torio** *a* preparatory

preposición *f* preposition

prepotente *a* arrogant; <*actitud*> high-handed

prerrogativa *f* prerogative

presa *f* (cosa) prey; (embalse) dam

presagi|ar *vt* presage. **~o** *m* omen

presb|iteriano *a* & *m* Presbyterian. **~ítero** *m* priest

prescindir *vi*. **~ de** do without; (deshacerse de) dispense with

prescri|bir (*pp* **prescrito**) *vt* prescribe. **~pción** *f* prescription

presencia *f* presence; (aspecto) appearance. **en ~ de** in the presence of. **~r** *vt* be present at; (ver) witness

presenta|ble *a* presentable. **~ción** *f* presentation; (de una persona a otra) introduction. **~dor** *m* presenter. **~r** *vt* present; (ofrecer) offer; (entregar) hand in; (hacer cono cer) introduce; show <*película*>. ▫ **~rse** *vpr* present o.s.; (hacerse conocer) introduce o.s.; (aparecer) turn up

presente *a* present; (actual) this. ● *m* present. **los ~s** those present. **tener ~** remember

presenti|miento *m* premonition. **~r** [4] *vt* have a feeling (**que** that)

preserva|r *vt* preserve. **~tivo** *m* condom

presiden|cia *f* presidency; (de asamblea) chairmanship. **~cial** *a* presidential. **~ta** *f* (woman) president. **~te** *m* president; (de asamblea) chairman. **~te del gobierno** prime minister

presidi|ario *m* convict. **~o** *m* prison

presidir *vt* be president of; preside over <*tribunal*>; chair <*reunión, comité*>

presi|ón *f* pressure. **a ~ón** under pressure. **hacer ~ón** press. **~onar** *vt* press; (fig) put pressure on

preso *a*. **estar ~** be in prison. **llevarse ~ a uno** take s.o. away under arrest. ● *m* prisoner

presta|do *a* (de uno) lent; (a uno) borrowed. **pedir ~do** borrow. **~mista** *m & f* moneylender

préstamo *m* loan; (acción de pedir prestado) borrowing; (acción de prestar) lending

prestar *vt* lend; give <*ayuda etc*>; pay <*atención*>. ▫ **~se** *vpr*. **~se a** be open to; (ser apto) be suitable (**para** for)

prestidigita|ción *f* conjuring. **~dor** *m* conjurer

prestigio *m* prestige. **~so** *a* prestigious

presu|mido *a* conceited. **~mir** *vi* show off. boast (**de** about). **~nción** *f* conceit; (suposición) presumption. **~nto** *a* alleged. **~ntuoso** *a* conceited

presup|oner [34] *vt* presuppose. **~uesto** *m* budget; (precio estimado) estimate

preten|cioso *a* pretentious. **~der** *vt* try to; (afirmar) claim; (solicitar) apply for; (cortejar) court. **~diente** *m* pretender; (a una mujer) suitor. **~sión** *f* pretension; (aspiración) aspiration

pretérito *m* preterite, past

pretexto *m* pretext. **con el ~ de** on the pretext of

prevalecer [11] *vi* prevail (**sobre** over)

preven|ción *f* prevention; (prejuicio) prejudice. **~ido** *a* ready; (precavido) cautious. **~ir** [53] *vt* prevent; (advertir) warn. **~tiva** *f* (Mex) amber light. **~tivo** *a* preventive

prever [43] *vt* foresee; (planear) plan

previo *a* previous

previs|ible *a* predictable. **~ión** *f* forecast; (prudencia) precaution

prima *f* (pariente) cousin; (cantidad) bonus

primario *a* primary

primavera *f* spring. **~l** *a* spring

primer *a* ⇒PRIMERO. **~a** *f* (Auto) first (gear); (en tren etc) first class. **~o** *a* (*delante de nombre masculino en singular* **primer**) first; (mejor) best; (principal) leading. **la ~a fila** the front row. **lo ~o es** the most important thing is. **~a enseñanza** primary education. **a ~os de** at the beginning of. **de ~a** first-class. ● *n* (the) first. ● *adv* first

primitivo *a* primitive

primo *m* cousin; ⓘ fool. **hacer el ~** be taken for a ride

primogénito *a & m* first-born, eldest

primor *m* delicacy; (cosa) beautiful thing

primordial *a* fundamental; <*interés*> paramount

princesa *f* princess

principal *a* main. **lo ~ es que** the main thing is that

príncipe *m* prince

principi|ante *m & f* beginner. **~o** *m* beginning; (moral, idea) principle; (origen) origin. **al ~o** at first. **a ~o(s) de** at the beginning of. **desde el ~o** from the start. **en ~o** in principle. **~os** *mpl* (nociones) rudiments

prioridad *f* priority

prisa *f* hurry, haste. **a ~** quickly. **a toda ~** as quickly as possible. **darse ~** hurry (up). **de ~** quickly. **tener ~** be in a hurry

prisi|ón *f* prison; (encarcelamiento) imprisonment. **~onero** *m* prisoner

prismáticos *mpl* binoculars

priva|ción *f* deprivation. **~da** *f* (Mex) private road. **~do** *a* (particular) private. **~r** *vt* deprive (**de** of). **~tivo** *a* exclusive (**de** to)

privilegi|ado *a* privileged; (muy bueno) exceptional. **~o** *m* privilege

pro *prep.* **en ~ de** for, in favour of. • *m* advantage. **los ~s y los contras** the pros and cons

proa *f* bow

probab|ilidad *f* probability. **~le** *a* probable, likely. **~lemente** *adv* probably

proba|dor *m* fitting-room. **~r** [2] *vt* try; try on <*ropa*>; (demostrar) prove. • *vi* try. ▫ **~rse** *vpr* try on

probeta *f* test-tube

problema *m* problem. **hacerse ~as** (LAm) worry

procaz *a* indecent

proced|encia *f* origin. **~ente** *a* (razonable) reasonable. **~ente de** (coming) from. **~er** *m* conduct. • *vi* proceed. **~er contra** start legal proceedings against. **~er de** come from. **~imiento** *m* procedure; (sistema) process; (Jurid) proceedings

proces|ador *m*. **~ de textos** word processor. **~al** *a* procedural. **costas ~ales** legal costs. **~amiento** *m* processing; (Jurid) prosecution. **~amiento de textos** word-processing. **~ar** *vt* process; (Jurid) prosecute

procesión *f* procession

proceso *m* process; (Jurid) trial; (transcurso) course

proclamar *vt* proclaim

procrea|ción *f* procreation. **~r** *vt* procreate

procura|dor *m* attorney, solicitor; (asistente) clerk (Brit), paralegal (Amer). **~r** *vt* try; (obtener) obtain

prodigar [12] *vt* lavish

prodigio *m* prodigy; (maravilla) wonder; (milagro) miracle. **~ioso** *a* prodigious

pródigo *a* prodigal

produc|ción *f* production. **~ir** [47] *vt* produce; (causar) cause. ▫ **~irse** *vpr* (suceder) happen. **~tivo** *a* productive. **~to** *m* product. **~tos agrícolas** farm produce. **~tos alimenticios** foodstuffs. **~tos de belleza** cosmetics. **~tos de consumo** consumer goods. **~tor** *m* producer.

proeza *f* exploit

profan|ación *f* desecration. **~ar** *vt* desecrate. **~o** *a* profane

profecía *f* prophecy

proferir [4] *vt* utter; hurl <*insultos etc*>

profes|ión *f* profession. **~ional** *a* professional. **~or** *m* teacher; (en universidad) lecturer. **~orado** *m* teaching profession; (conjunto de profesores) staff

prof|eta *m* prophet. **~etizar** [10] *vt/i* prophesize

prófugo *a* & *m* fugitive

profund|idad *f* depth. **~o** *a* deep; (fig) profound. **poco ~** shallow

progenitor *m* ancestor

programa *m* programme; (de estudios) syllabus. **~ concurso** quiz show. **~ de entrevistas** chat show. **~ción** *f* programming; (TV etc) programmes; (en periódico) TV guide. **~r** *vt* programme. **~dor** *m* computer programmer

progres|ar *vi* (make) progress. **~ión** *f* progression. **~ista** *a* progressive. **~ivo** *a* progressive. **~o** *m* progress. **hacer ~os** make progress

prohibi|ción *f* prohibition. **~do** *a* forbidden. **prohibido fumar** no smoking. **~r** *vt* forbid. **~tivo** *a* prohibitive

prójimo *m* fellow man

prole *f* offspring

proletari|ado *m* proletariat. **~o** *a* & *m* proletarian

prol|iferación *f* proliferation. **~iferar** *vi* proliferate. **~ífico** *a* prolific

prolijo *a* long-winded

prólogo *m* prologue

prolongar [12] *vt* prolong; (alargar) lengthen. ◻ **~se** *vpr* go on

promedio *m* average. **como ~** on average

prome|sa *f* promise. **~ter** *vt* promise. ● *vi* show promise. ◻ **~terse** *vpr* <*novios*> get engaged. **~tida** *f* fiancée. **~tido** *a* promised; <*novios*> engaged. ● *m* fiancé

prominente *f* prominence

promiscu|idad *f* promiscuity. **~o** *a* promiscuous

promo|ción *f* promotion. **~tor** *m* promoter. **~ver** [2] *vt* promote; (causar) cause

promulgar [12] *vt* promulgate

pronombre *m* pronoun

pron|osticar [7] *vt* predict; forecast <*tiempo*>. **~óstico** *m* prediction; (del tiempo) forecast; (Med) prognosis

pront|itud *f* promptness. **~o** *a* quick. ● *adv* quickly; (dentro de poco) soon; (temprano) early. **de ~o** suddenly. **por lo ~o** for the time being. **tan ~o como** as soon as

pronuncia|ción *f* pronunciation. **~miento** *m* revolt. **~r** *vt* pronounce; deliver <*discurso*>. ◻ **~rse** *vpr* (declararse) declare o.s.; (sublevarse) rise up

propagación *f* propagation

propaganda *f* propaganda; (anuncios) advertising

propagar [12] *vt/i* propagate. ◻ **~se** *vpr* spread

propasarse *vpr* go too far

propens|ión *f* inclination. **~o** *a* inclined

propici|ar *vt* favour; (provocar) bring about. **~o** *a* favourable

propie|dad *f* property. **~tario** *m* owner

propina *f* tip

propio *a* own; (característico) typical; (natural) natural; (apropiado) proper. **el ~ médico** the doctor himself

proponer [34] *vt* propose; put forward <*persona*>. □ **~se** *vpr*. **~se hacer** intend to do

proporci|ón *f* proportion. **~onado** *a* proportioned. **~onal** *a* proportional. **~onar** *vt* provide

proposición *f* proposition

propósito *m* intention. **a ~** (adrede) on purpose; (de paso) by the way. **a ~ de** with regard to

propuesta *f* proposal

propuls|ar *vt* propel; (fig) promote. **~ión** *f* propulsion. **~ión a chorro** jet propulsion

prórroga *f* extension

prorrogar [12] *vt* extend

prosa *f* prose. **~ico** *a* prosaic

proscri|bir (*pp* **proscrito**) *vt* exile; (prohibir) ban. **~to** *a* banned. ● *m* exile; (bandido) outlaw

proseguir [5 & 13] *vt/i* continue

prospecto *m* prospectus; (de fármaco) directions for use

prosper|ar *vi* prosper; <*persona*> do well. **~idad** *f* prosperity

próspero *a* prosperous. **¡P~ Año Nuevo!** Happy New Year!

prostit|ución *f* prostitution. **~uta** *f* prostitute

protagonista *m & f* protagonist

prote|cción *f* protection. **~ctor** *a* protective. ● *m* protector; (benefactor) patron. **~ger** [14] *vt* protect. **~gida** *f* protegée. **~gido** *a* protected. ● *m* protegé

proteína *f* protein

protesta *f* protest; (manifestación) demonstration; (Mex, promesa) promise; (Mex, juramento) oath

protestante *a & m & f* Protestant

protestar *vt/i* protest

protocolo *m* protocol

provecho *m* benefit. **¡buen ~!** enjoy your meal! **de ~** useful. **en ~ de** to the benefit of. **sacar ~ de** benefit from

proveer [18] (*pp* **proveído** *y* **provisto**) *vt* supply, provide

provenir [53] *vi* come (**de** from)

proverbi|al *a* proverbial. **~o** *m* proverb

provincia *f* province. **~l** *a*, **~no** *a* provincial

provisional *a* provisional

provisto *a* provided (**de** with)

provoca|ción *f* provocation. **~r** [7] *vt* provoke; (causar) cause. **~tivo** *a* provocative

proximidad *f* proximity

próximo *a* next; (cerca) near

proyec|ción *f* projection. **~tar** *vt* hurl; cast <*luz*>; show <*película*>. **~til** *m* missile. **~to** *m* plan. **~to de ley** bill. **en ~to** planned. **~tor** *m* projector

pruden|cia *f* prudence; (cuidado) caution. **~te** *a* prudent, sensible

prueba *f* proof; (examen) test; (de ropa) fitting. **a ~** on trial. **a ~ de** proof against. **a ~ de agua** waterproof. **poner a ~** test

pruebo *vb* ⇒PROBAR

psicoan|álisis *f* psychoanalysis. **~alista** *m & f* psychoanalyst. **~alizar** [10] *vt* psychoanalyse

psic|ología *f* psychology. **~ológico** *a* psychological. **~ólogo** *m* psychologist. **~ópata** *m & f* psychopath. **~osis** *f invar* psychosis

psiqu|e *f* psyche. **~iatra** *m & f* psychiatrist. **~iátrico** *a* psychiatric

psíquico *a* psychic
ptas, **pts** *abrev* (**pesetas**) pesetas
púa *f* sharp point; (Bot) thorn; (de erizo) quill; (de peine) tooth; (Mus) plectrum
pubertad *f* puberty
publica|ción *f* publication. **~r** [7] *vt* publish
publici|dad *f* publicity; (Com) advertising. **~tario** *a* advertising
público *a* public. ● *m* public; (de espectáculo etc) audience
puchero *m* cooking pot; (guisado) stew. **hacer ~s** (fig, Ⓘ) pout
pude *vb* ⇒PODER
pudor *m* modesty. **~oso** *a* modest
pudrir (*pp* **podrido**) *vt* rot; (fig, molestar) annoy. □ **~se** *vpr* rot
puebl|ecito *m* small village. **~erino** *m* country bumpkin. **~o** *m* town; (aldea) village; (nación) nation, people
puedo *vb* ⇒PODER
puente *m* bridge; (fig, Ⓘ) long weekend. **~ colgante** suspension bridge. **~ levadizo** drawbridge. **hacer ~** Ⓘ have a long weekend
puerco *a* filthy; (grosero) coarse. ● *m* pig. **~ espín** porcupine
puerro *m* leek
puerta *f* door; (en deportes) goal; (de ciudad, en jardín) gate. **~ principal** main entrance. **a ~ cerrada** behind closed doors
puerto *m* port; (fig, refugio) refuge; (entre montañas) pass. **~ franco** free port
puertorriqueño *a* & *m* Puerto Rican
pues *adv* (entonces) then; (bueno) well. ● *conj* since
puest|a *f* setting; (en juegos) bet. **~a de sol** sunset. **~a en escena** staging. **~a en marcha** starting. **~o** *a* put; (vestido) dressed. ● *m* place; (empleo) position, job; (en mercado etc) stall. ● *conj*. **~o que** since
pugna *f* struggle. **~r** *vi*. **~r por** strive to
puja *f* struggle (**por** to); (en subasta) bid. **~r** *vt* struggle; (en subasta) bid
pulcro *a* neat
pulga *f* flea. **tener malas ~s** be bad-tempered
pulga|da *f* inch. **~r** *m* thumb; (del pie) big toe
puli|do *a* polished; <*modales*> refined. **~r** *vt* polish; (suavizar) smooth
pulla *f* gibe
pulm|ón *m* lung. **~onar** *a* pulmonary. **~onía** *f* pneumonia
pulpa *f* pulp
pulpería *f* (LAm) grocer's shop (Brit), grocery store (Amer)
púlpito *m* pulpit
pulpo *m* octopus
pulque *m* (Mex) pulque, alcoholic Mexican drink. **~ría** *f* bar
pulsa|ción *f* pulsation. **~dor** *m* button. **~r** *vt* press; (Mus) pluck
pulsera *f* bracelet
pulso *m* pulse; (firmeza) steady hand. **echar un ~** arm wrestle. **tomar el ~ a uno** take s.o.'s pulse
pulular *vi* teem with
puma *m* puma
puna *f* puna, high plateau
punitivo *a* punitive
punta *f* point; (extremo) tip. **estar de ~** be in a bad mood. **ponerse de ~ con uno** fall out with s.o. **sacar ~ a** sharpen
puntada *f* stitch
puntaje *m* (LAm) score

puntal *m* prop, support

puntapié *m* kick

puntear *vt* mark; (Mus) pluck; (LAm, en deportes) lead

puntería *f* aim; (destreza) marksmanship

puntiagudo *a* pointed; (afilado) sharp

puntilla *f* (encaje) lace. **en ~s** (LAm), **de ~s** on tiptoe

punto *m* point; (señal, trazo) dot; (de examen) mark; (lugar) spot, place; (de taxis) stand; (momento) moment; (punto final) full stop (Brit), period (Amer); (puntada) stitch. **~ de vista** point of view. **~ final** full stop (Brit), period (Amer). **~ muerto** (Auto) neutral (gear). **~ y aparte** full stop, new paragraph (Brit), period, new paragraph (Amer). **~ y coma** semicolon. **a ~** on time; (listo) ready. **a ~ de** on the point of. **de ~** knitted. **dos ~s** colon. **en ~** exactly. **hacer ~** knit. **hasta cierto ~** to a certain extent

puntuación *f* punctuation; (en deportes, acción) scoring; (en deportes, número de puntos) score

puntual *a* punctual; (exacto) accurate. **~idad** *f* punctuality; (exactitud) accuracy

puntuar [21] *vt* punctuate; mark (Brit), grade (Amer) <*examen*>. ● *vi* score (points)

punza|da *f* sharp pain; (fig) pang. **~nte** *a* sharp. **~r** [10] *vt* prick

puñado *m* handful. **a ~s** by the handful

puñal *m* dagger. **~ada** *f* stab

puñ|etazo *m* punch. **~o** *m* fist; (de ropa) cuff; (mango) handle. **de su ~o (y letra)** in his own handwriting

pupa *f* (F, en los labios) cold sore

pupila *f* pupil

pupitre *m* desk

puré *m* purée; (sopa) thick soup. **~ de papas** (LAm), **~ de patatas** mashed potatoes

pureza *f* purity

purga *f* purge. **~torio** *m* purgatory

puri|ficación *f* purification. **~ficar** [7] *vt* purify. **~sta** *m & f* purist. **~tano** *a* puritanical. ● *m* puritan

puro *a* pure; <*cielo*> clear. **de pura casualidad** by sheer chance. **de ~ tonto** out of sheer stupidity. ● *m* cigar

púrpura *f* purple

pus *m* pus

puse *vb* ⇒PONER

pusilánime *a* fainthearted

puta *f* (vulg) whore

Qq

que *pron rel* (personas, sujeto) who; (personas, complemento) whom; (cosas) which, that. ● *conj* that. **¡~ tengan Vds buen viaje!** have a good journey! **¡~ venga!** let him come! **~ venga o no venga** whether he comes or not. **creo ~ tiene razón** I think (that) he is right. **más ~** more than. **lo ~** what. **yo ~ tú** if I were you

qué *a* (con sustantivo) what; (con a o adv) how. ● *pron* what. **¡~ bonito!** how nice! **¿en ~ piensas?** what are you thinking about?

quebra|da *f* gorge; (paso) pass. **~dizo** *a* fragile. **~do** *a* broken; (Com) bankrupt. ● *m* (Math) fraction. **~ntar** *vt* break; disturb <*paz*>. **~nto** *m* (pérdida) loss; (daño) damage. **~r** [1] *vt* break. ● *vi* break; (Com) go bankrupt. □ **~rse** *vpr* break

quechua *a* Quechua. ● *m & f* Quechan. ● *m* (lengua) Quecha

quedar *vi* stay, remain; (estar) be; (haber todavía) be left. **~ bien** come off well. □ **~se** *vpr* stay. **~ con** arrange to meet. **~ en** agree to. **~ en nada** come to nothing. **~ por** (+ *infinitivo*) remain to be (+ *pp*)

quehacer *m* work. **~es domésticos** household chores

quej|a *f* complaint; (de dolor) moan. □ **~arse** *vpr* complain (**de** about); (gemir) moan. **~ido** *m* moan

quema|do *a* burnt; (LAm, bronceado) tanned; (fig) annoyed. **~dor** *m* burner. **~dura** *f* burn. **~r** *vt/i* burn. □ **~rse** *vpr* burn o.s.; (consumirse) burn up; (con el sol) get sunburnt. **~rropa** *adv*. **a ~rropa** point-blank

quena *f* Indian flute

quepo *vb* ⇒CABER

querella *f* (riña) quarrel, dispute; (Jurid) criminal action

quer|er [35] *vt* want; (amar) love; (necesitar) need. **~er decir** mean. ● *m* love; (amante) lover. **como quiera que** however. **cuando quiera que** whenever. **donde quiera** wherever. **¿quieres darme ese libro?** would you pass me that book? **¿quieres un helado?** would you like an ice-cream? **quisiera ir a la playa** I'd like to go to the beach. **sin ~er** without meaning to. **~ido** *a* dear; (amado) loved

querosén *m*, **queroseno** *m* kerosene

querubín *m* cherub

ques|adilla *f* (Mex) tortilla filled with cheese. **~o** *m* cheese

quetzal *m* (unidad monetaria ecuatoriana) quetzal

quicio *m* frame. **sacar de ~ a uno** infuriate s.o.

quiebra *f* (Com) bankruptcy

quien *pron rel* (sujeto) who; (complemento) whom

quién *pron interrogativo* (sujeto) who; (tras preposición) **¿con ~?** who with ?, to whom? **¿de ~ son estos libros?** whose are these books?

quienquiera *pron* whoever

quiero *vb* ⇒QUERER

quiet|o *a* still; (inmóvil) motionless; <*carácter etc*> calm. **~ud** *f* stillness

quijada *f* jaw

quilate *m* carat

quilla *f* keel

quimera *f* (fig) illusion

químic|a *f* chemistry. **~o** *a* chemical. ● *m* chemist

quince *a & m* fifteen. **~ días** a fortnight. **~na** *f* fortnight. **~nal** *a* fortnightly

quincuagésimo *a* fiftieth

quiniela *f* pools coupon. **~s** *fpl* (football) pools

quinientos *a & m* five hundred

quinquenio *m* (period of) five years

quinta *f* (casa) villa

quintal *m* a hundred kilograms

quinteto *m* quintet

quinto *a & m* fifth

quiosco *m* kiosk; (en jardín) summerhouse; (en parque etc) bandstand

quirúrgico *a* surgical

quise *vb* ⇒QUERER

quisquill|a *f* trifle; (camarón) shrimp. **~oso** *a* irritable; (exigente) fussy

quita|esmalte *m* nail polish remover. **~manchas** *m invar* stain remover. **~nieves** *m invar* snow plough. **~r** *vt* remove, take away; take off <*ropa*>; (robar) steal. **~ndo** (🅃, a excepción de) apart from. □ **~rse** *vpr* get rid of <*dolor*>; take off <*ropa*>. **~rse de** (no hacerlo más) stop. **~rse de en medio** get out of the way. **~sol** *m* sunshade

quizá(s) *adv* perhaps

quórum *m* quorum

Rr

rábano *m* radish. **~ picante** horseradish. **me importa un ~** I couldn't care less

rabi|a *f* rabies; (fig) rage. **~ar** *vi* (de dolor) be in great pain; (estar enfadado) be furious. **dar ~a** infuriate. **~eta** *f* tantrum

rabino *m* rabbi

rabioso *a* rabid; (furioso) furious

rabo *m* tail

racha *f* gust of wind; (fig) spate. **pasar por una mala ~** go through a bad patch

racial *a* racial

racimo *m* bunch

ración *f* share, ration; (de comida) portion

raciona|l *a* rational. **~lizar** [10] *vt* rationalize. **~r** *vt* (limitar) ration; (repartir) ration out

racis|mo *m* racism. **~ta** *a* racist

radar *m* radar

radiación *f* radiation

radiactiv|idad *f* radioactivity. **~o** *a* radioactive

radiador *m* radiator

radiante *a* radiant; (brillante) brilliant

radical *a* & *m* & *f* radical

radicar [7] *vi* lie (**en** in). □ **~se** *vpr* settle

radio *m* radius; (de rueda) spoke; (LAm) radio. ● *f* radio. **~actividad** *f* radioactivity. **~activo** *a* radioactive. **~difusión** *f* broadcasting. **~emisora** *f* radio station. **~escucha** *m* & *f* listener. **~grafía** *f* radiography

radi|ólogo *m* radiologist. **~oterapia** *f* radiotherapy

radioyente *m* & *f* listener

raer [36] *vt* scrape; (quitar) scrape off

ráfaga *f* (de viento) gust; (de ametralladora) burst

rafia *f* raffia

raído *a* threadbare

raíz *f* root. **a ~ de** as a result of. **echar raíces** (fig) settle

raja *f* split; (Culin) slice. **~r** *vt* split. □ **~rse** *vpr* split; (fig) back out

rajatabla. **a ~** rigorously

ralea *f* sort

ralla|dor *m* grater. **~r** *vt* grate

ralo *a* <*pelo*> thin

rama *f* branch. **~je** *m* branches. **~l** *m* branch

rambla *f* watercourse; (avenida) avenue

ramera *f* prostitute

ramifica|ción *f* ramification. □ **~rse** [7] *vpr* branch out

ram|illete *m* bunch. **~o** *m* branch; (de flores) bunch, bouquet

rampa *f* ramp, slope

rana *f* frog

ranch|era *f* (Mex) folk song. **~ero** *m* cook; (Mex, hacendado) rancher. **~o** *m* (LAm, choza) hut; (LAm, casucha) shanty; (Mex, hacienda) ranch

rancio *a* rancid; <*vino*> old; (fig) ancient

rango *m* rank

ranúnculo *m* buttercup

ranura *f* groove; (para moneda) slot

rapar *vt* shave; crop <*pelo*>

rapaz *a* rapacious; <*ave*> of prey

rapidez *f* speed

rápido *a* fast, quick. ● *adv* quickly. ● *m* (tren) express. **~s** *mpl* rapids

rapiña *f* robbery. **ave** *f* **de ~** bird of prey

rapsodia *f* rhapsody

rapt|ar *vt* kidnap. **~o** *m* kidnapping; (de ira etc) fit

raqueta *f* racquet

rar|eza *f* rarity; (cosa rara) oddity. **~o** *a* rare; (extraño) odd. **es ~o que** it is strange that. **¡qué ~o!** how strange!

ras *m*. **a ~ de** level with

rasca|cielos *m invar* skyscraper. **~r** [7] *vt* scratch; (raspar) scrape

rasgar [12] *vt* tear

rasgo *m* characteristic; (gesto) gesture; (de pincel) stroke. **~s** *mpl* (facciones) features

rasguear *vt* strum

rasguñ|ar *vt* scratch. **~o** *m* scratch

raso *a* <*cucharada etc*> level; <*vuelo etc*> low. **al ~** in the open air. ● *m* satin

raspa|dura *f* scratch; (acción) scratching. **~r** *vt* scratch; (rozar) scrape

rastr|a. **a ~as** dragging. **~ear** *vt* track. **~ero** *a* creeping. **~illar** *vt* rake. **~illo** *m* rake. **~o** *m* track; (señal) sign. **ni ~o** not a trace

rata *f* rat

ratero *m* petty thief

ratifica|ción *f* ratification. **~r** [7] *vt* ratify

rato *m* moment, short time. **~s libres** spare time. **a ~s** at times. **a cada ~** (LAm) always. **hace un ~** a moment ago. **pasar un mal ~** have a rough time

rat|ón *m* mouse. **~onera** *f* mousetrap; (madriguera) mouse hole

raudal *m* torrent. **a ~les** in abundance

raya *f* line; (lista) stripe; (de pelo) parting. **a ~s** striped. **pasarse de la ~** go too far. **~r** *vt* scratch. **~r en** border on

rayo *m* ray; (descarga eléctrica) lightning. **~ de luna** moonbeam. **~ láser** laser beam. **~s X** X-rays

raza *f* race; (de animal) breed. **de ~** <*caballo*> thoroughbred; <*perro*> pedigree

raz|ón *f* reason. **a ~ón de** at the rate of. **perder la ~ón** go out of one's mind. **tener ~ón** be right. **~onable** *a* reasonable. **~onamiento** *m* reasoning. **~onar** *vt* reason out. ● *vi* reason

re *m* D; (solfa) re

reac|ción *f* reaction; (LAm, Pol) right wing. **~ción en cadena** chain reaction. **~cionario** *a* & *m* reactionary. **~tor** *m* reactor; (avión) jet

real *a* real; (de rey etc) royal; *<hecho>* true. ● *m* real, old Spanish coin

realidad *f* reality; (verdad) truth. **en ~** in fact. **hacerse ~** come true

realis|mo *m* realism. **~ta** *a* realistic. ● *m & f* realist

realiza|ción *f* fulfilment. **~r** [10] *vt* carry out; make *<viaje>*; fulfil *<ilusión>*; (vender) sell. □ **~rse** *vpr* *<sueño, predicción etc>* come true; *<persona>* fulfil o.s.

realzar [10] *vt* (fig) enhance

reanimar *vt* revive. □ **~se** *vpr* revive

reanudar *vt* resume; renew *<amistad>*

reavivar *vt* revive

rebaja *f* reduction. **en ~s** in the sale. **~do** *a* *<precio>* reduced. **~r** *vt* lower; lose *<peso>*

rebanada *f* slice

rebaño *m* herd; (de ovejas) flock

rebasar *vt* exceed; (dejar atrás) leave behind; (Mex, Auto) overtake

rebatir *vt* refute

rebel|arse *vpr* rebel. **~de** *a* rebellious; *<grupo>* rebel. ● *m* rebel. **~día** *f* rebelliousness. **~ión** *f* rebellion

rebosa|nte *a* brimming (de with). **~r** *vi* overflow; (abundar) abound

rebot|ar *vt* bounce; (rechazar) repel. ● *vi* bounce; *<bala>* ricochet. **~e** *m* bounce, rebound. **de ~e** on the rebound

reboz|ar [10] *vt* wrap up; (Culin) coat in batter. **~o** *m* (LAm) shawl

rebusca|do *a* affected; (complicado) over-elaborate. **~r** [7] *vt* search through

rebuznar *vi* bray

recado *m* errand; (mensaje) message

reca|er [29] *vi* fall back; (Med) relapse; (fig) fall. **~ída** *f* relapse

recalcar [7] *vt* stress

recalcitrante *a* recalcitrant

recalentar [1] *vt* reheat; (demasiado) overheat

recámara *f* small room; (de arma de fuego) chamber; (Mex, dormitorio) bedroom

recambio *m* (Mec) spare (part); (de pluma etc) refill. **de ~** spare

recapitular *vt* sum up

recarg|ar [12] *vt* overload; (aumentar) increase; recharge *<batería>*. **~o** *m* increase

recat|ado *a* modest. **~o** *m* prudence; (modestia) modesty. **sin ~o** openly

recauda|ción *f* (cantidad) takings. **~dor** *m* tax collector. **~r** *vt* collect

recel|ar *vt* suspect. ● *vi* be suspicious (de of). **~o** *m* distrust; (temor) fear. **~oso** *a* suspicious

recepci|ón *f* reception. **~onista** *m & f* receptionist

receptáculo *m* receptacle

receptor *m* receiver

recesión *f* recession

receta *f* recipe; (Med) prescription

rechaz|ar [10] *vt* reject; defeat *<moción>*; repel *<ataque>*; (no aceptar) turn down. **~o** *m* rejection

rechifla *f* booing

rechinar *vi* squeak. **le rechinan los dientes** he grinds his teeth

rechoncho *a* stout

recib|imiento *m* (acogida) welcome. **~ir** *vt* receive; (acoger) welcome. ● *vi* entertain. □ **~irse** *vpr* graduate. **~o** *m* receipt. **acusar ~o** acknowledge receipt

reci|én *adv* recently; (LAm, hace poco) just. ~ **casado** newly married. ~ **nacido** newborn. **~ente** *a* recent; (Culin) fresh

recinto *m* enclosure; (local) premises

recio *a* strong; <*voz*> loud. ● *adv* hard; (en voz alta) loudly

recipiente *m* receptacle. ● *m & f* recipient

recíproco *a* reciprocal; <*sentimiento*> mutual

recita|l *m* recital; (de poesías) reading. **~r** *vt* recite

reclama|ción *f* claim; (queja) complaint. **~r** *vt* claim. ● *vi* appeal

réclame *m* (LAm) advertisement

reclamo *m* (LAm) complaint

reclinar *vi* lean. □ **~se** *vpr* lean

reclus|ión *f* imprisonment. **~o** *m* prisoner

recluta *m & f* recruit. **~miento** *m* recruitment. **~r** *vt* recruit

recobrar *vt* recover. □ **~se** *vpr* recover

recodo *m* bend

recog|er [14] *vt* collect; pick up <*cosa caída*>; (cosechar) harvest. □ **~erse** *vpr* withdraw; (ir a casa) go home; (acostarse) go to bed. **~ida** *f* collection; (cosecha) harvest

recomenda|ción *f* recommendation. **~r** [1] *vt* recommend; (encomendar) entrust

recomenzar [1 & 10] *vt/i* start again

recompensa *f* reward. **~r** *vt* reward

reconcilia|ción *f* reconciliation. **~r** *vt* reconcile. □ **~rse** *vpr* be reconciled

reconoc|er [11] *vt* recognize; (admitir) acknowledge; (examinar) examine. **~imiento** *m* recognition; (admisión) acknowledgement; (agradecimiento) gratitude; (examen) examination

reconozco *vb* ⇨RECONOCER

reconquista *f* reconquest. **~r** *vt* reconquer; (fig) win back

reconsiderar *vt* reconsider

reconstruir [17] *vt* reconstruct

récord /'rekor/ *m* (*pl* **~s**) record

recordar [2] *vt* remember; (hacer acordar) remind. ● *vi* remember. **que yo recuerde** as far as I remember. **si mal no recuerdo** if I remember rightly

recorr|er *vt* tour <*país*>; go round <*zona, museo*>; cover <*distancia*>. ~ **mundo** travel all around the world. **~ido** *m* journey; (trayecto) route

recort|ar *vt* cut (out). **~e** *m* cutting (out); (de periódico etc) cutting

recostar [2] *vt* lean. □ **~se** *vpr* lie down

recoveco *m* bend; (rincón) nook

recre|ación *f* recreation. **~ar** *vt* recreate; (divertir) entertain. □ **~arse** *vpr* amuse o.s. **~ativo** *a* recreational. **~o** *m* recreation; (Escol) break

recrudecer [11] *vi* intensify

recta *f* straight line. ~ **final** home stretch

rect|angular *a* rectangular. **~ángulo** *a* rectangular; <*triángulo*> right-angled. ● *m* rectangle

rectifica|ción *f* rectification. **~r** [7] *vt* rectify

rect|itud *f* straightness; (fig) honesty. **~o** *a* straight; (fig, justo) fair; (fig, honrado) honest. **todo ~o** straight on. ● *m* rectum

rector *a* governing. ● *m* rector

recubrir (*pp* **recubierto**) *vt* cover (**con, de** with)

recuerdo *m* memory; (regalo) souvenir. **~s** *mpl* (saludos) regards. ● *vb* ⇒RECORDAR

recupera|ción *f* recovery. **~r** *vt* recover. **~r el tiempo perdido** make up for lost time. □ **~rse** *vpr* recover

recur|rir *vi*. **~rir a** resort to <*cosa*>; turn to <*persona*>. **~so** *m* resort; (medio) resource; (Jurid) appeal. **~sos** *mpl* resources

red *f* network; (malla) net; (para equipaje) luggage rack; (Com) chain; (Elec, gas) mains. **la R~** the Net

redac|ción *f* writing; (lenguaje) wording; (conjunto de redactores) editorial staff; (oficina) editorial office; (Escol, Univ) essay. **~tar** *vt* write. **~tor** *m* writer; (de periódico) editor

redada *f* catch; (de policía) raid

redecilla *f* small net; (para el pelo) hairnet

redentor *a* redeeming

redimir *vt* redeem

redoblar *vt* redouble; step up <*vigilancia*>

redomado *a* utter

redond|a *f* (de imprenta) roman (type); (Mus) semibreve (Brit), whole note (Amer). **a la ~a** around. **~ear** *vt* round off. **~el** *m* circle; (de plaza de toros) arena. **~o** *a* round; (completo) complete; (Mex, boleto) return, round-trip (Amer). **en ~o** round; (categóricamente) flatly

reduc|ción *f* reduction. **~ido** *a* reduced; (limitado) limited; (pequeño) small; <*precio*> low. **~ir** [47] *vt* reduce. □ **~irse** *vpr* be reduced; (fig) amount

reduje *vb* ⇒REDUCIR

redundan|cia *f* redundancy. **~te** *a* redundant

reduzco *vb* ⇒REDUCIR

reembols|ar *vt* reimburse. **~o** *m* repayment. **contra ~o** cash on delivery

reemplaz|ar [10] *vt* replace. **~o** *m* replacement

refacci|ón *f* (LAm) refurbishment; (Mex, Mec) spare part. **~onar** *vt* (LAm) refurbish. **~onaria** *f* (Mex) repair shop

referencia *f* reference; (información) report. **con ~ a** with reference to. **hacer ~ a** refer to

referéndum *m* (*pl* **~s**) referendum

referir [4] *vt* tell; (remitir) refer. □ **~se** *vpr* refer. **por lo que se refiere a** as regards

refiero *vb* ⇒REFERIR

refilón. **de ~** obliquely

refin|amiento *m* refinement. **~ar** *vt* refine. **~ería** *f* refinery

reflector *m* reflector; (proyector) searchlight

reflej|ar *vt* reflect. **~o** *a* reflex. ● *m* reflection; (Med) reflex; (en el pelo) highlights

reflexi|ón *f* reflection. **sin ~ón** without thinking. **~onar** *vi* reflect. **~vo** *a* <*persona*> thoughtful; (Gram) reflexive

reforma *f* reform. **~s** *fpl* (reparaciones) repairs. **~r** *vt* reform. □ **~rse** *vpr* reform

reforzar [2 & 10] *vt* reinforce

refrac|ción *f* refraction. **~tario** *a* heat-resistant

refrán *m* saying

refregar [1 & 12] *vt* scrub

refresc|ar [7] *vt* refresh; (enfriar) cool. ● *vi* get cooler. □ **~arse** *vpr* refresh o.s. **~o** *m* cold drink. **~os** *mpl* refreshments

refrigera|ción *f* refrigeration; (aire acondicionado) air-conditioning; (de motor) cooling. **~r** *vt* refrigerate; air-condition <*lugar*>; cool <*motor*>. **~dor** *m* refrigerator

refuerzo *m* reinforcement

refugi|ado *m* refugee. □ **~arse** *vpr* take refuge. **~o** *m* refuge, shelter

refunfuñar *vi* grumble

refutar *vt* refute

regadera *f* watering-can; (Mex, ducha) shower

regala|do *a* as a present, free; (cómodo) comfortable. **~r** *vt* give

regalo *m* present, gift

regañ|adientes. **a ~adientes** reluctantly. **~ar** *vt* scold. ● *vi* moan; (dos personas) quarrel. **~o** *m* (reprensión) scolding

regar [1 & 12] *vt* water

regata *f* boat race; (serie) regatta

regate|ar *vt* haggle over; (economizar) economize on. ● *vi* haggle; (en deportes) dribble. **~o** *m* haggling; (en deportes) dribbling

regazo *m* lap

regenerar *vt* regenerate

régimen *m* (*pl* **regímenes**) regime; (Med) diet; (de lluvias) pattern

regimiento *m* regiment

regi|ón *f* region. **~onal** *a* regional

regir [5 & 14] *vt* govern. ● *vi* apply, be in force

registr|ado *a* registered. **~ar** *vt* register; (Mex) check in <*equipaje*>; (grabar) record; (examinar) search. □ **~arse** *vpr* register; (darse) be reported. **~o** *m* (acción de registrar) registration; (libro) register; (cosa anotada) entry; (inspección) search. **~o civil** (oficina) registry office

regla *f* ruler; (norma) rule; (menstruación) period. **en ~** in order. **por ~ general** as a rule. **~mentación** *f* regulation. **~mentar** *vt* regulate. **~mentario** *a* regulation; <*horario*> set. **~mento** *m* regulations

regocij|arse *vpr* be delighted. **~o** *m* delight

regode|arse *vpr* (+ *gerundio*) delight in (+ *gerund*). **~o** *m* delight

regordete *a* chubby

regres|ar *vi* return; (LAm) send back <*persona*>. □ **~arse** *vpr* (LAm) return. **~ivo** *a* backward. **~o** *m* return

regula|ble *a* adjustable. **~dor** *m* control. **~r** *a* regular; (mediano) average; (no bueno) so-so. ● *vt* regulate; adjust <*volumen etc*>. **~ridad** *f* regularity. **con ~ridad** regularly

rehabilita|ción *f* rehabilitation; (en empleo etc) reinstatement. **~r** *vt* rehabilitate; (en cargo) reinstate

rehacer [31] *vt* redo; (repetir) repeat; rebuild <*vida*>. □ **~se** *vpr* recover

rehén *m* hostage

rehogar [12] *vt* sauté

rehuir [17] *vt* avoid

rehusar *vt/i* refuse

reimpr|esión *f* reprinting. **~imir** (*pp* **reimpreso**) *vt* reprint

reina *f* queen. **~do** *m* reign. **~nte** *a* ruling; (fig) prevailing. **~r** *vi* reign; (fig) prevail

reincidir *vi* (Jurid) reoffend

reino *m* kingdom. **R~ Unido** United Kingdom

reintegr|ar *vt* reinstate <*persona*>; refund <*cantidad*>. □ **~arse** *vpr* return. **~o** *m* refund

reír [51] *vi* laugh. □ **~se** *vpr* laugh. **~se de** laugh at. **echarse a ~** burst out laughing

reivindica|ción *f* claim. **~r** [7] *vt* claim; (rehabilitar) restore

rej|a *f* grille; (verja) railing. **entre ~as** behind bars. **~illa** *f* grille, grating; (red) luggage rack

rejuvenecer [11] *vt/i* rejuvenate. □ **~se** *vpr* be rejuvenated

relaci|ón *f* connection; (trato) relation(ship); (relato) account; (lista) list. **con ~ón a, en ~ón a** in relation to. **~onado** *a* related. **bien ~onado** well-connected. **~onar** *vt* relate (**con** to). □ **~onarse** *vpr* be connected; (tratar) mix (**con** with)

relaja|ción *f* relaxation; (aflojamiento) slackening. **~do** *a* relaxed. **~r** *vt* relax; (aflojar) slacken. □ **~rse** *vpr* relax

relamerse *vpr* lick one's lips

relámpago *m* (flash of) lightning

relatar *vt* tell, relate

relativ|idad *f* relativity. **~o** *a* relative

relato *m* tale; (relación) account

relegar [12] *vt* relegate. **~ al olvido** consign to oblivion

relev|ante *a* outstanding. **~ar** *vt* relieve; (substituir) replace. **~o** *m* relief. **carrera** *f* **de ~os** relay race

relieve *m* relief; (fig) importance. **de ~** important. **poner de ~** emphasize

religi|ón *f* religion. **~osa** *f* nun. **~oso** *a* religious. ● *m* monk

relinch|ar *vi* neigh. **~o** *m* neigh

reliquia *f* relic

rellano *m* landing

rellen|ar *vt* refill; (Culin) stuff; fill in <*formulario*>. **~o** *a* full up; (Culin) stuffed. ● *m* filling; (Culin) stuffing

reloj *m* clock; (de bolsillo o pulsera) watch. **~ de caja** grandfather clock. **~ de pulsera** wrist-watch. **~ de sol** sundial. **~ despertador** alarm clock. **~ería** *f* watchmaker's (shop). **~ero** *m* watchmaker

reluci|ente *a* shining. **~r** [11] *vi* shine; (destellar) sparkle

relumbrar *vi* shine

remach|ar *vt* rivet. **~e** *m* rivet

remangar [12] *vt* roll up

remar *vi* row

remat|ado *a* (total) complete. **~ar** *vt* finish off; (agotar) use up; (Com) sell off cheap; (LAm, subasta) auction; (en tenis) smash. **~e** *m* end; (fig) finishing touch; (LAm, subastar) auction; (en tenis) smash. **de ~e** completely

remedar *vt* imitate

remedi|ar *vt* remedy; repair <*daño*>; (fig, resolver) solve. **no lo pude ~ar** I couldn't help it. **~o** *m* remedy; (fig) solution; (LAm, medicamento) medicine. **como último ~o** as a last resort. **no hay más ~o** there's no other way. **no tener más ~o** have no choice

remedo *m* poor imitation

rem|endar [1] *vt* repair. **~iendo** *m* patch

remilg|ado *a* fussy; (afectado) affected. **~o** *m* fussiness; (afectación) affectation. **~oso** *a* (Mex) fussy

reminiscencia *f* reminiscence

remisión *f* remission; (envío) sending; (referencia) reference

remit|e *m* sender's name and address. **~ente** *m* sender. **~ir** *vt* send; (referir) refer ● *vi* diminish

remo *m* oar

remoj|ar *vt* soak; (fig, [I]) celebrate. **~o** *m* soaking. **poner a ~o** soak

remolacha *f* beetroot. **~ azucarera** sugar beet

remolcar [7] *vt* tow

remolino *m* swirl; (de aire etc) whirl

remolque *m* towing; (cabo) towrope; (vehículo) trailer. **a ~** on tow. **dar ~ a** tow

remontar *vt* overcome. **~ el vuelo** soar up; *<avión>* gain height. □ **~se** *vpr* soar up; (en el tiempo) go back to

remord|er [2] *vi*. **eso le remuerde** he feels guilty for it. **me remuerde la conciencia** I have a guilty conscience. **~imiento** *m* remorse. **tener ~imientos** feel remorse

remoto *a* remote; *<época>* distant

remover [2] *vt* stir *<líquido>*; turn over *<tierra>*; (quitar) remove; (fig, activar) revive

remunera|ción *f* remuneration. **~r** *vt* remunerate

renac|er [11] *vi* be reborn; (fig) revive. **~imiento** *m* rebirth. **R~imiento** Renaissance

renacuajo *m* tadpole; (fig) tiddler

rencilla *f* quarrel

rencor *m* bitterness. **guardar ~ a** have a grudge against. **~oso** *a* resentful

rendi|ción *f* surrender. **~do** *a* submissive; (agotado) exhausted

rendija *f* crack

rendi|miento *m* performance; (Com) yield. **~r** [5] *vt* yield; (agotar) exhaust; pay *<homenaje>*; present *<informe>*. ● *vi* pay; (producir) produce. □ **~rse** *vpr* surrender

renegar [1 & 12] *vt* deny. ● *vi* grumble. **~r de** renounce *<fe etc>*; disown *<personas>*

renglón *m* line; (Com) item. **a ~ seguido** straight away

reno *m* reindeer

renombr|ado *a* renowned. **~e** *m* renown

renova|ción *f* renewal; (de edificio) renovation; (de mobiliario) complete change. **~r** *vt* renew; renovate *<edificio>*; change *<mobiliario>*

rent|a *f* income; (Mex, alquiler) rent. **~a vitalicia** (life) annuity. **~able** *a* profitable. **~ar** *vt* yield; (Mex, alquilar) rent, hire. **~ista** *m & f* person of independent means

renuncia *f* renunciation; (dimisión) resignation. **~r** *vi*. **~r a** renounce, give up; (dimitir) resign

reñi|do *a* hard-fought. **estar ~do con** be incompatible with *<cosa>*; be on bad terms with *<persona>*. **~r** [5 & 22] *vt* scold. ● *vi* quarrel

reo *m & f* (Jurid) accused; (condenado) convicted offender

reojo. **mirar de ~** look out of the corner of one's eye at

reorganizar [10] *vt* reorganize

repar|ación *f* repair; (acción) repairing (fig, compensación) reparation. **~ar** *vt* repair; (fig) make amends for; (notar) notice. ● *vi*. **~ar en** notice; (hacer caso de) pay attention to. **~o** *m* fault; (objeción) objection. **poner ~os** raise objections

repart|ición *f* distribution. **~idor** *m* delivery man. **~imiento** *m* distribution. **~ir** *vt* distribute, share out; deliver *<cartas, leche etc>*; hand out *<folleto, premio>*. **~o** *m* distribution; (de cartas, leche etc) delivery; (actores) cast

repas|ar *vt* go over; check *<cuenta>*; revise *<texto>*; (leer a la ligera) glance through; (coser) mend. ● *vi* revise. **~o** *m* revision; (de ropa) mending. **dar un ~o** look through

repatria|ción *f* repatriation. **~r** *vt* repatriate

repele|nte *a* repulsive. ● *m* insect repellent. **~r** *vt* repel

repent|e. **de ~** suddenly. **~ino** *a* sudden

repercu|sión *f* repercussion. **~tir** *vi* reverberate; (fig) have repercussions (**en** on)

repertorio *m* repertoire

repeti|ción *f* repetition; (de programa) repeat. **~damente** *adv* repeatedly. **~r** [5] *vt* repeat; have a second helping of <*plato*>; (imitar) copy. ● *vi* have a second helping of

repi|car [7] *vt* ring <*campanas*>. **~que** *m* peal

repisa *f* shelf. **~ de chimenea** mantlepiece

repito *vb* ⇒REPETIR

replegarse [1 & 12] *vpr* withdraw

repleto *a* full up. **~ de gente** packed with people

réplica *a* reply; (copia) replica

replicar [7] *vi* reply

repollo *m* cabbage

reponer [34] *vt* replace; revive <*obra de teatro*>; (contestar) reply. ▫ **~se** *vpr* recover

report|aje *m* report; (LAm, entrevista) interview. **~ar** *vt* yield; (LAm, denunciar) report. **~e** *m* (Mex, informe) report; (Mex, queja) complaint. **~ero** *m* reporter

repos|ado *a* quiet; (sin prisa) unhurried. **~ar** *vi* rest; <*líquido*> settle. **~o** *m* rest

repost|ar *vt* replenish. ● *vi* (Aviac) refuel; (Auto) fill up. **~ería** *f* pastrymaking

reprender *vt* reprimand

represalia *f* reprisal. **tomar ~s** retaliate

representa|ción *f* representation; (en el teatro) performance. **en ~ción de** representing. **~nte** *m* representative. **~r** *vt* represent; perform <*obra de teatro*>; play <*papel*>; (aparentar) look. ▫ **~rse** *vpr* imagine. **~tivo** *a* representative

represi|ón *f* repression. **~vo** *a* repressive

reprimenda *f* reprimand

reprimir *vt* supress. ▫ **~se** *vpr* control o.s.

reprobar [2] *vt* condemn; (LAm, Univ, etc) fail

reproch|ar *vt* reproach. **~e** *m* reproach

reproduc|ción *f* reproduction. **~ir** [47] *vt* reproduce. **~tor** *a* reproductive; <*animal*> breeding

reptil *m* reptile

rep|ública *f* republic. **~ublicano** *a* & *m* republican

repudiar *vt* condemn; (Jurid) repudiate

repuesto *m* (Mec) spare (part). **de ~** spare

repugna|ncia *f* disgust. **~nte** *a* repugnant; <*olor*> disgusting. **~r** *vt* disgust

repuls|a *f* rebuff. **~ión** *f* repulsion. **~ivo** *a* repulsive

reputa|ción *f* reputation. **~do** *a* reputable. **~r** *vt* consider

requeri|miento *m* request; (necesidad) requirement. **~r** [4] *vt* require; summons <*persona*>

requesón *m* curd cheese

requete... *pref* extremely

requis|a *f* requisition; (confiscación) seizure; (inspección) inspection; (Mil) requisition. **~ar** *vt* requisition;

(confiscar) seize; (inspeccionar) inspect. **~ito** *m* requirement

res *f* animal. **~ lanar** sheep. **~ vacuna** (vaca) cow; (toro) bull; (buey) ox. **carne de ~** (Mex) beef

resabido *a* well-known; <*persona*> pedantic

resaca *f* undercurrent; (después de beber) hangover

resaltar *vi* stand out. **hacer ~** emphasize

resarcir [9] *vt* repay; (compensar) compensate. □ **~se** *vpr* make up for

resbal|adilla *f* (Mex) slide. **~adizo** *a* slippery. **~ar** *vi* slip; (Auto) skid; <*líquido*> trickle. □ **~arse** *vpr* slip; (Auto) skid; <*líquido*> trickle. **~ón** *m* slip; (de vehículo) skid. **~oso** *a* (LAm) slippery

rescat|ar *vt* rescue; (fig) recover. **~e** *m* ransom; (recuperación) recovery; (salvamento) rescue

rescoldo *m* embers

resecar [7] *vt* dry up. □ **~se** *vpr* dry up

resenti|do *a* resentful. **~miento** *m* resentment. □ **~rse** *vpr* feel the effects; (debilitarse) be weakened; (ofenderse) take offence (**de** at)

reseña *f* summary; (de persona) description; (en periódico) report, review. **~r** *vt* describe; (en periódico) report on, review

reserva *f* reservation; (provisión) reserve(s). **de ~** in reserve. **~ción** *f* (LAm) reservation. **~do** *a* reserved. **~r** *vt* reserve; (guardar) keep, save. □ **~rse** *vpr* save o.s.

resfria|do *m* cold. □ **~rse** *vpr* catch a cold

resguard|ar *vt* protect. □ **~arse** *vpr* protect o.s.; (fig) take care. **~o** *m* protection; (garantía) guarantee; (recibo) receipt

resid|encia *f* residence; (Univ) hall of residence (Brit), dormitory (Amer); (de ancianos etc) home. **~encial** *a* residential. **~ente** *a* & *m* & *f* resident. **~ir** *vi* reside; (fig) lie (**en** in)

residu|al *a* residual. **~o** *m* residue. **~os** *mpl* waste

resigna|ción *f* resignation. □ **~rse** *vpr* resign o.s. (**a** to)

resist|encia *f* resistence. **~ente** *a* resistent. **~ir** *vt* resist; (soportar) bear. ● *vi* resist. **ya no resisto más** I can't take it any more

resol|ución *f* resolution; (solución) solution; (decisión) decision. **~ver** [2] (*pp* **resuelto**) resolve; solve <*problema etc*>. □ **~verse** *vpr* resolve itself; (resultar bien) work out; (decidir) decide

resona|ncia *f* resonance. **tener ~ncia** cause a stir. **~nte** *a* resonant; (fig) resounding. **~r** [2] *vi* resound

resorte *m* spring; (Mex, elástico) elastic. **tocar (todos los) ~s** (fig) pull strings

respald|ar *vt* back; (escribir) endorse. □ **~arse** *vpr* lean back. **~o** *m* backing; (de asiento) back

respect|ar *vi*. **en lo que ~a a** with regard to. **en lo que a mí ~a** as far as I'm concerned. **~ivo** *a* respective. **~o** *m* respect. **al ~o** on this matter. **(con) ~o a** with regard to

respet|able *a* respectable. ● *m* audience. **~ar** *vt* respect. **~o** *m* respect. **faltar al ~o a** be disrespectful to. **~uoso** *a* respectful

respir|ación *f* breathing; (ventilación) ventilation. **~ar** *vi* breathe; (fig) breathe a sigh of relief. **~o** *m* breathing; (fig) rest

resplandǀecer [11] *vi* shine. **~eciente** *a* shining. **~or** *m* brilliance; (de llamas) glow

responder *vi* answer; (replicar) answer back; (reaccionar) respond. **~ de** be responsible for. **~ por uno** vouch for s.o.

responsabǀilidad *f* responsibility. **~le** *a* responsible

respuesta *f* reply, answer

resquebrajar *vt* crack. □ **~se** *vpr* crack

resquemor *m* (fig) uneasiness

resquicio *m* crack; (fig) possibility

resta *f* subtraction

restablecer [11] *vt* restore. □ **~se** *vpr* recover

restǀante *a* remaining. **lo ~nte** the rest. **~ar** *vt* take away; (substraer) subtract. ● *vi* be left

restauraǀción *f* restoration. **~nte** *m* restaurant. **~r** *vt* restore

restituǀción *f* restitution. **~ir** [17] *vt* return; (restaurar) restore

resto *m* rest, remainder; (en matemática) remainder. **~s** *mpl* remains; (de comida) leftovers

restorán *m* restaurant

restregar [1 & 12] *vt* rub

restriǀcción *f* restriction. **~ngir** [14] *vt* restrict, limit

resucitar *vt* resuscitate; (fig) revive. ● *vi* return to life

resuello *m* breath; (respiración) heavy breathing

resuelto *a* resolute

resultaǀdo *m* result (en in). **~r** *vi* result; (salir) turn out; (dar resultado) work; (ser) be; (costar) come to

resumǀen *m* summary. **en ~en** in short. **~ir** *vt* summarize; (recapitular) sum up

resurǀgir [14] *vi* re-emerge; (fig) revive. **~gimiento** *m* resurgence. **~rección** *f* resurrection

retaguardia *f* (Mil) rearguard

retahíla *f* string

retar *vt* challenge

retardar *vt* slow down; (demorar) delay

retazo *m* remnant; (fig) piece, bit

retenǀción *f* retention. **~er** [40] *vt* keep; (en la memoria) retain; (no dar) withhold

reticencia *f* insinuation; (reserva) reluctance

retina *f* retina

retirǀada *f* withdrawal. **~ado** *a* remote; <*vida*> secluded; (jubilado) retired. **~ar** *vt* move away; (quitar) remove; withdraw <*dinero*>; (jubilar) pension off. □ **~arse** *vpr* draw back; (Mil) withdraw; (jubilarse) retire; (acostarse) go to bed. **~o** *m* retirement; (pensión) pension; (lugar apartado) retreat; (LAm, de apoyo, fondos) withdrawal

reto *m* challenge

retocar [7] *vt* retouch

retoño *m* shoot; (fig) kid

retoque *m* (acción) retouching; (efecto) finishing touch

retorcǀer [2 & 9] *vt* twist; wring <*ropa*>. □ **~erse** *vpr* get twisted up; (de dolor) writhe. **~ijón** *m* (LAm) stomach cramp

retóricǀa *f* rhetoric; (grandilocuencia) grandiloquence. **~o** *m* rhetorical

retornǀar *vt/i* return. **~o** *m* return

retortijón *m* twist; (de tripas) stomach cramp

retractarse *vpr* retract. **~se de lo dicho** withdraw what one said

retransmitir *vt* repeat; (radio, TV) broadcast. **~ en directo** broadcast live

retras|ado *a* (*con ser*) mentally handicapped; (*con estar*) behind; *<reloj>* slow; (poco desarrollado) backward; (anticuado) old-fashioned. **~ar** *vt* delay; put back *<reloj>*; (retardar) slow down; (posponer) postpone. ● *vi* *<reloj>* be slow. □ **~arse** *vpr* be late; *<reloj>* be slow. **~o** *m* delay; (poco desarrollo) backwardness; (de reloj) slowness. **traer ~o** be late. **~os** *mpl* arrears

retrato *m* portrait; (fig, descripción) description. **ser el vivo ~o de** be the living image of

retrete *m* toilet

retribu|ción *f* payment; (recompensa) reward. **~ir** [17] *vt* pay; (recompensar) reward; (LAm) return *<favor>*

retroce|der *vi* move back; (fig) back down. **~so** *m* backward movement; (de arma de fuego) recoil; (Med) relapse

retrógrado *a* & *m* (Pol) reactionary

retrospectivo *a* retrospective

retrovisor *m* rear-view mirror

retumbar *vt* echo; *<trueno etc>* boom

reum|a *m*, **reúma** *m* rheumatism. **~ático** *a* rheumatic. **~atismo** *m* rheumatism

reuni|ón *f* meeting; (entre amigos) reunion. **~r** [23] *vt* join together; (recoger) gather (together); raise *<fondos>*. □ **~rse** *vpr* meet; *<amigos etc>* get together

revalidar *vt* confirm; (Mex, estudios) validate

revalorizar [10] *vt*, (LAm) **revaluar** [21] *vt* revalue; increase *<pensiones>*. □ **~se** *vpr* appreciate

revancha *f* revenge; (en deportes) return match. **tomar la ~** get one's own back

revela|ción *f* revelation. **~do** *m* developing. **~dor** *a* revealing. **~r** *vt* reveal; (Foto) develop

revent|ar [1] *vi* burst; (tener ganas) be dying to. □ **~arse** *vpr* burst. **~ón** *m* burst; (Auto) blow out; (Mex, fiesta) party

reveren|cia *f* reverence; (de hombre, niño) bow; (de mujer) curtsy. **~ciar** *vt* revere. **~do** *a* (Relig) reverend. **~te** *a* reverent

revers|ible *a* reversible. **~o** *m* reverse; (de papel) back

revertir [4] *vi* revert (**a** to)

revés *m* wrong side; (de prenda) inside; (contratiempo) setback; (en deportes) backhand. **al ~** the other way round; (con lo de arriba abajo) upside down; (con lo de dentro fuera) inside out

revesti|miento *m* coating. **~r** [5] *vt* cover

revis|ar *vt* check; overhaul *<mecanismo>*; service *<coche etc>*; (LAm, equipaje) search. **~ión** *f* check(ing); (Med) checkup; (de coche etc) service; (LAm, de equipaje) inspection. **~or** *m* inspector

revista *f* magazine; (inspección) inspection; (artículo) review; (espectáculo) revue. **pasar ~ a** inspect

revivir *vi* revive

revolcar [2 & 7] *vt* knock over. □ **~se** *vpr* roll around

revolotear *vi* flutter

revoltijo *m*, **revoltillo** *m* mess

revoltoso *a* rebellious; <*niño*> naughty

revoluci|ón *f* revolution. **~onar** *vt* revolutionize. **~onario** *a & m* revolutionary

revolver [2] (*pp* **revuelto**) *vt* mix; stir <*líquido*>; (desordenar) mess up

revólver *m* revolver

revuelo *m* fluttering; (fig) stir

revuelt|a *f* revolt; (conmoción) disturbance. **~o** *a* mixed up; <*líquido*> cloudy; <*mar*> rough; <*tiempo*> unsettled; <*huevos*> scrambled

rey *m* king. **los ~es** the king and queen. **los R~es Magos** the Three Wise Men

reyerta *f* brawl

rezagarse [12] *vpr* fall behind

rez|ar [10] *vt* say. ● *vi* pray; (decir) say. **~o** *m* praying; (oración) prayer

rezongar [12] *vi* grumble

ría *f* estuary

riachuelo *m* stream

riada *f* flood

ribera *f* bank

ribete *m* border; (fig) embellishment

rico *a* rich; (Culin, [I]) good, nice. ● *m* rich person

rid|ículo *a* ridiculous. **~iculizar** [10] *vt* ridicule

riego *m* watering; (irrigación) irrigation

riel *m* rail

rienda *f* rein

riesgo *m* risk. **correr (el) ~ de** run the risk of

rifa *f* raffle. **~r** *vt* raffle

rifle *m* rifle

rigidez *f* rigidity; (fig) inflexibility

rígido *a* rigid; (fig) inflexible

rig|or *m* strictness; (exactitud) exactness; (de clima) severity. **de ~or** compulsory. **en ~or** strictly speaking. **~uroso** *a* rigorous

rima *f* rhyme. **~r** *vt/i* rhyme

rimbombante *a* resounding; <*lenguaje*> pompous; (fig, ostentoso) showy

rímel *m* mascara

rin *m* (Mex) rim

rincón *m* corner

rinoceronte *m* rhinoceros

riña *f* quarrel; (pelea) fight

riñón *m* kidney

río *m* river; (fig) stream. **~ abajo** downstream. **~ arriba** upstream. ● *vb* ⇒REÍR

riqueza *f* wealth; (fig) richness. **~s** *fpl* riches

ris|a *f* laugh. **desternillarse de ~a** split one's sides laughing. **la ~a** laughter. **~otada** *f* guffaw. **~ueño** *a* smiling; (fig) cheerful

rítmico *a* rhythmic(al)

ritmo *m* rhythm; (fig) rate

rit|o *m* rite; (fig) ritual. **~ual** *a & m* ritual

rival *a & m & f* rival. **~idad** *f* rivalry. **~izar** [10] *vi* rival

riz|ado *a* curly. **~ar** [10] *vt* curl; ripple <*agua*>. **~o** *m* curl; (en agua) ripple

róbalo *m* bass

robar *vt* steal <*cosa*>; rob <*banco*>; (raptar) kidnap

roble *m* oak (tree)

robo *m* theft; (de banco, museo) robbery; (en vivienda) burglary

robusto *a* robust

roca *f* rock

roce *m* rubbing; (señal) mark; (fig, entre personas) regular contact; (Pol) friction. **tener un ~ con uno** have a brush with s.o.

rociar [20] *vt* spray

rocín *m* nag

rocío *m* dew

rodaballo *m* turbot

rodaja *f* slice. **en ~s** sliced

roda|je *m* (de película) shooting; (de coche) running in. **~r** [2] *vt* shoot <*película*>; run in <*coche*>. ● *vi* roll; <*coche*> run; (hacer una película) shoot

rode|ar *vt* surround; (LAm) round up <*ganado*>. □ **~arse** *vpr* surround o.s. (**de** with). **~o** *m* detour; (de ganado) round-up. **andar con ~os** beat about the bush. **sin ~os** plainly

rodill|a *f* knee. **ponerse de ~as** kneel down. **~era** *f* knee-pad

rodillo *m* roller; (Culin) rolling-pin

roe|dor *m* rodent. **~r** [37] *vt* gnaw

rogar [2 & 12] *vt/i* beg; (Relig) pray; **se ruega a los Sres. pasajeros...** passengers are requested.... **se ruega no fumar** please do not smoke

roj|izo *a* reddish. **~o** *a* & *m* red. **ponerse ~o** blush

roll|izo *a* plump; <*bebé*> chubby. **~o** *m* roll; (de cuerda) coil; (Culin, rodillo) rolling-pin; (fig, Ⓘ, pesadez) bore

romance *a* Romance. ● *m* (idilio) romance; (poema) ballad

romano *a* & *m* Roman. **a la ~a** (Culin) (deep-)fried in batter

rom|anticismo *m* romanticism. **~ántico** *a* romantic

romería *f* pilgrimage; (LAm, multitud) mass

romero *m* rosemary

romo *a* blunt; <*nariz*> snub

rompe|cabezas *m invar* puzzle; (de piezas) jigsaw (puzzle). **~olas** *m invar* breakwater

romp|er (*pp* **roto**) *vt* break; tear <*hoja, camisa etc*>; break off <*relaciones etc*>. ● *vi* break; <*novios*> break up. **~er a** burst out. □ **~erse** *vpr* break

ron *m* rum

ronc|ar [7] *vi* snore. **~o** *a* hoarse

roncha *f* lump; (por alergia) rash

ronda *f* round; (patrulla) patrol; (serenata) serenade. **~r** *vt* patrol. ● *vi* be on patrol; (merodear) hang around

ronqu|era *f* hoarseness. **~ido** *m* snore

ronronear *vi* purr

roñ|a *f* (suciedad) grime. **~oso** *a* dirty; (oxidado) rusty; (tacaño) mean

rop|a *f* clothes, clothing. **~a blanca** linen, underwear. **~a de cama** bedclothes. **~a interior** underwear. **~aje** *m* robes; (excesivo) heavy clothing. **~ero** *m* wardrobe

ros|a *a invar* pink. ● *f* rose. ● *m* pink. **~áceo** *a* pinkish. **~ado** *a* pink; <*mejillas*> rosy. ● *m* (vino) rosé. **~al** *m* rose-bush

rosario *m* rosary; (fig) series

ros|ca *f* (de tornillo) thread; (de pan) roll; (bollo) type of doughnut. **~co** *m* roll. **~quilla** *f* type of doughnut

rostro *m* face

rota|ción *f* rotation. **~r** *vt/i* rotate. □ **~rse** *vpr* take turns. **~tivo** *a* rotary

roto *a* broken

rótula *f* kneecap

rotulador *m* felt-tip pen

rótulo *m* sign; (etiqueta) label; (logotipo) logo

rotundo *a* categorical

rotura *f* tear; (grieta) crack
rozadura *f* scratch
rozagante *a* (LAm) healthy
rozar [10] *vt* rub against; (ligeramente) brush against; (raspar) graze. □ **~se** *vpr* rub; (con otras personas) mix
Rte. *abrev* (**Remite(nte)**) sender
rubéola *f* German measles
rubí *m* ruby
rubicundo *a* ruddy
rubio *a* <*pelo*> fair; <*persona*> fair-haired; <*tabaco*> Virginia
rubor *m* blush; (Mex, cosmético) blusher. □ **~izarse** [10] *vpr* blush
rúbrica *f* (de firma) flourish; (firma) signature; (título) heading
rudeza *f* roughness
rudiment|ario *a* rudimentary. **~os** *mpl* rudiments
rueca *f* distaff
rueda *f* wheel; (de mueble) castor; (de personas) ring; (Culin) slice. **~ de prensa** press conference
ruedo *m* edge; (redondel) bullring
ruego *m* request; (súplica) entreaty. ● *vb* ⇒ROGAR
rufián *m* pimp; (granuja) rogue
rugby *m* rugby
rugi|do *m* roar. **~r** [14] *vi* roar
ruibarbo *m* rhubarb
ruido *m* noise. **~so** *a* noisy; (fig) sensational
ruin *a* despicable; (tacaño) mean
ruin|a *f* ruin; (colapso) collapse. **~oso** *a* ruinous
ruiseñor *m* nightingale
ruleta *f* roulette
rulo *m* curler
rumano *a* & *m* Romanian
rumbo *m* direction; (fig) course; (fig, esplendidez) lavishness. **con ~ a** in the direction of. **~so** *a* lavish
rumia|nte *a* & *m* ruminant. **~r** *vt* chew; (fig) brood over. ● *vi* ruminate
rumor *m* rumour; (ruido) murmur. **~ear** *vt.* **se ~ea que** rumour has it that. **~oso** *a* murmuring
runrún *m* (de voces) murmur; (de motor) whirr
ruptura *f* breakup; (de relaciones etc) breaking off; (de contrato) breach
rural *a* rural
ruso *a* & *m* Russian
rústico *a* rural; (de carácter) coarse. **en rústica** paperback
ruta *f* route; (fig) course
rutina *f* routine. **~rio** *a* routine; <*trabajo*> monotonous

Ss

S.A. *abrev* (**Sociedad Anónima**) Ltd, plc, Inc (Amer)
sábado *m* Saturday
sábana *f* sheet
sabañón *m* chilblain
sabático *a* sabbatical
sab|elotodo *m* & *f invar* know-all [!]. **~er** [38] *vt* know; (ser capaz de) be able to, know how to; (enterarse de) find out. ● *vi* know. **~er a** taste of. **hacer ~er** let know. **¡qué sé yo!** how should I know? **que yo sepa** as far as I know. **¿~es nadar?** can you swim? **un no sé qué** a certain sth. **¡yo qué sé!** how should I know? **¡vete a ~er!** who knows?

● *m* knowledge. **~ido** *a* well-known. **~iduría** *f* wisdom; (conocimientos) knowledge

sabi|endas. a **~** knowingly; (a propósito) on purpose. **~hondo** *m* know-all [I]. **~o** *a* learned; (prudente) wise

sabor *m* taste, flavour; (fig) flavour. **~ear** *vt* taste; (fig) savour

sabot|aje *m* sabotage. **~eador** *m* saboteur. **~ear** *vt* sabotage

sabroso *a* tasty; *<chisme>* juicy; (LAm, agradable) pleasant

sabueso *m* (perro) bloodhound; (fig, detective) detective

saca|corchos *m invar* corkscrew. **~puntas** *m invar* pencil-sharpener

sacar [7] *vt* take out; put out *<parte del cuerpo>*; (quitar) remove; take *<foto>*; win *<premio>*; get *<billete, entrada>*; withdraw *<dinero>*; reach *<solución>*; draw *<conclusión>*; make *<copia>*. **~ adelante** bring up *<niño>*; carry on *<negocio>*

sacarina *f* saccharin

sacerdo|cio *m* priesthood. **~te** *m* priest

saciar *vt* satisfy; quench *<sed>*

saco *m* sack; (LAm, chaqueta) jacket. **~ de dormir** sleeping-bag

sacramento *m* sacrament

sacrific|ar [7] *vt* sacrifice; slaughter *<res>*; put to sleep *<perro, gato>*. □ **~arse** *vpr* sacrifice o.s. **~io** *m* sacrifice; (de res) slaughter

sacr|ilegio *m* sacrilege. **~ílego** *a* sacrilegious

sacudi|da *f* shake; (movimiento brusco) jolt, jerk; (fig) shock. **~da eléctrica** electric shock. **~r** *vt* shake; (golpear) beat. □ **~rse** *vpr* shake off; (fig) get rid of

sádico *a* sadistic. ● *m* sadist

sadismo *m* sadism

safari *m* safari

sagaz *a* shrewd

Sagitario *m* Sagittarius

sagrado *a* *<lugar>* holy, sacred; *<altar, escrituras>*) holy; (fig) sacred

sal *f* salt. ● *vb* ⇒SALIR

sala *f* room; (en casa) living room; (en hospital) ward; (para reuniones etc) hall; (en teatro) house; (Jurid) courtroom. **~ de embarque** departure lounge. **~ de espera** waiting room. **~ de estar** living room. **~ de fiestas** nightclub

salado *a* salty; *<agua del mar>* salt; (no dulce) savoury; (fig) witty

salario *m* wage

salchich|a *f* (pork) sausage. **~ón** *m* salami

sald|ar *vt* settle *<cuenta>*; (vender) sell off. **~o** *m* balance. **~os** *mpl* sales. **venta de ~os** clearance sale

salero *m* salt-cellar

salgo *vb* ⇒SALIR

sali|da *f* departure; (puerta) exit, way out; (de gas, de líquido) leak; (de astro) rising; (Com, venta) sale; (chiste) witty remark; (fig) way out; **~da de emergencia** emergency exit. **~ente** *a* (Archit) projecting; *<pómulo etc>* prominent. **~r** [52] *vi* leave; (ir afuera) go out; (Informática) exit; *<revista etc>* be published; (resultar) turn out; *<astro>* rise; (aparecer) appear. **~r adelante** get by. □ **~rse** *vpr* leave; *<recipiente, líquido etc>* leak. **~rse con la suya** get one's own way

saliva *f* saliva

salmo *m* psalm

salm|ón *m* salmon. **~onete** *m* red mullet

salón *m* living-room, lounge. ~ **de actos** assembly hall. ~ **de clases** classroom. ~ **de fiestas** dancehall

salpica|dera *f* (Mex) mudguard. ~**dero** *m* (Auto) dashboard. ~**dura** *f* splash; (acción) splashing. ~**r** [7] *vt* splash; (fig) sprinkle

sals|a *f* sauce; (para carne asada) gravy; (Mus) salsa. ~**a verde** parsley sauce. ~**era** *f* sauce-boat

salt|amontes *m invar* grasshopper. ~**ar** *vt* jump (over); (fig) miss out. ● *vi* jump; (romperse) break; <*líquido*> spurt out; (desprenderse) come off; <*pelota*> bounce; (estallar) explode. ~**eador** *m* highwayman. ~**ear** *vt* (Culin) sauté

salt|o *m* jump; (al agua) dive. ~**o de agua** waterfall. ~ **mortal** somersault. **de un** ~**o** with one jump. ~**ón** *a* <*ojos*> bulging

salud *f* health. ● *int* cheers!; (LAm, al estornudar) bless you! ~**able** *a* healthy

salud|ar *vt* greet, say hello to; (Mil) salute. **lo** ~**a atentamente** (en cartas) yours faithfully. ~ **con la mano** wave. ~**o** *m* greeting; (Mil) salute. ~**os** *mpl* best wishes

salva *f* salvo. **una** ~ **de aplausos** a burst of applause

salvación *f* salvation

salvado *m* bran

salvaguardia *f* safeguard

salvaje *a* (planta, animal) wild; (primitivo) savage. ● *m & f* savage

salva|mento *m* rescue. ~**r** *vt* save, rescue; (atravesar); cross (recorrer); travel (fig) overcome. □ ~**rse** *vpr* save o.s. ~**vidas** *m & f invar* lifeguard. ● *m* lifebelt. **chaleco** *m* ~**vidas** life-jacket

salvo *a* safe. ● *adv & prep* except (for). **a** ~ out of danger. **poner a** ~ put in a safe place. ~ **que** unless. ~**conducto** *m* safe-conduct

San *a* Saint, St. ~ **Miguel** St Michael

sana|r *vt* cure. ● *vi* recover; heal <*herida*>. ~**torio** *m* sanatorium

sanci|ón *f* sanction. ~**onar** *vt* sanction

sandalia *f* sandal

sandía *f* watermelon

sándwich /'saŋgwitʃ/ *m* (*pl* ~**s,** ~**es**) sandwich

sangr|ante *a* bleeding; (fig) flagrant ~**ar** *vt/i* bleed. ~**e** *f* blood. **a** ~**e fría** in cold blood

sangría *f* (bebida) sangria

sangriento *a* bloody

sangu|ijuela *f* leech. ~**íneo** *a* blood

san|idad *f* health. ~**itario** *a* sanitary. ● *m* (Mex) toilet. ~**o** *a* healthy; <*mente*> sound. ~**o y salvo** safe and sound. **cortar por lo** ~**o** settle things once and for all

santiamén *m.* **en un** ~ in an instant

sant|idad *f* sanctity. ~**ificar** [7] *vt* sanctify. □ ~**iguarse** [15] *vpr* cross o.s. ~**o** *a* holy; (delante de nombre) Saint, St. ● *m* saint; (día) saint's day, name day. ~**uario** *m* sanctuary. ~**urrón** *a* sanctimonious

saña *f* viciousness. **con** ~ viciously

sapo *m* toad

saque *m* (en tenis) service; (inicial en fútbol) kick-off. ~ **de banda** throw-in; (en rugby) line-out. ~ **de esquina** corner (kick)

saque|ar *vt* loot. ~**o** *m* looting

sarampión *m* measles

sarape *m* (Mex) colourful blanket

sarc|asmo *m* sarcasm. **~ástico** *a* sarcastic

sardina *f* sardine

sargento *m* sergeant

sarpullido *m* rash

sartén *f or m* frying-pan (Brit), fry-pan (Amer)

sastre *m* tailor. **~ría** *f* tailoring; (tienda) tailor's (shop)

Sat|anás *m* Satan. **~ánico** *a* satanic

satélite *m* satellite

satinado *a* shiny

sátira *f* satire

satírico *a* satirical. ● *m* satirist

satisf|acción *f* satisfaction. **~acer** [31] *vt* satisfy; (pagar) pay; (gustar) please; meet <*gastos, requisitos*>. □ **~acerse** *vpr* satisfy o.s.; (vengarse) take revenge. **~actorio** *a* satisfactory. **~echo** *a* satisfied. **~echo de sí mismo** smug

satura|ción *f* saturation. **~r** *vt* saturate

Saturno *m* Saturn

sauce *m* willow. **~ llorón** weeping willow

sauna *f*, (LAm) **sauna** *m* sauna

saxofón *m*, **saxófono** *m* saxophone

sazona|do *a* ripe; (Culin) seasoned. **~r** *vt* ripen; (Culin) season

se

● *pronombre*

⟶ (en lugar de le, les) **se lo di** (a él) I gave it to him; (a ella) I gave it to her; (a usted, ustedes) I gave it to you; (a ellos, ellas) I gave it to them. **se lo compré** I bought it for him (*or* her *etc*). **se lo quité** I took it away from him (*or* her *etc*). **se lo dije** I told him (*or* her *etc*)

⟶ (reflexivo) **se secó** (él) he dried himself; (ella) she driedherself; (usted) you dried yourself; (sujeto no humano) it dried itself. **se secaron** (ellos, ellas) they dried themselves; (ustedes) you dried yourselves. (con partes del cuerpo) **se lavó la cara** (él) he washed his face. (con efectos personales) **se limpian los zapatos** they clean their shoes

⟶ (recíproco) each other, one another. **se ayudan mucho** they help each other a lot. **no se hablan** they don't speak to each other

⟶ (cuando otro hace la acción) **va a operarse** she's going to have an operation. **se cortó el pelo** he had his hair cut

⟶ (enfático) **se bebió el café** he drank his coffee. **se subió al tren** he got on the train

⇨ **se** also forms part of certain pronominal verbs such as **equivocarse, arrepentirse, caerse** etc., which are treated under the respective entries

⟶ (voz pasiva) **se construyeron muchas casas** many houses were built. **se vendió rápidamente** it was sold very quickly

⟶ (impersonal) **antes se escuchaba más radio** people used to listen to the radio more in the past. **no se puede entrar** you can't get in. **se está bien aquí** it's very nice here

⟶ (en instrucciones) **sírvase frío** serve cold

sé *vb* ⇒SABER *y* SER

sea *vb* ⇒SER

seca|dor *m* drier; (de pelo) hair-drier. **~nte** *a* drying. ● *m* blotting-paper. **~r** [7] *vt* dry. □ **~rse** *vpr* dry; <*río etc*> dry up; <*persona*> dry o.s.

sección *f* section

seco *a* dry; <*frutos, flores*> dried; (flaco) thin; <*respuesta*> curt. **a secas** just. **en ~** (bruscamente) suddenly. **lavar en ~** dry-clean

secretar|ía *f* secretariat; (Mex, ministerio) ministry. **~io** *m* secretary; (Mex, Pol) minister

secreto *a* & *m* secret

secta *f* sect. **~rio** *a* sectarian

sector *m* sector

secuela *f* consequence

secuencia *f* sequence

secuestr|ar *vt* confiscate; kidnap <*persona*>; hijack <*avión*>. **~o** *m* seizure; (de persona) kidnapping; (de avión) hijack(ing)

secundar *vt* second, help. **~io** *a* secondary

sed *f* thirst. ● *vb* ⇒SER. **tener ~** be thirsty. **tener ~ de** (fig) be hungry for

seda *f* silk. **~ dental** dental floss

sedante *a* & *m* sedative

sede *f* seat; (Relig) see; (de organismo) headquarters; (de congreso, juegos etc) venue

sedentario *a* sedentary

sedici|ón *f* sedition. **~oso** *a* seditious

sediento *a* thirsty

seduc|ción *f* seduction. **~ir** [47] *vt* seduce; (atraer) attract. **~tor** *a* seductive. ● *m* seducer

seglar *a* secular. ● *m* layman

segrega|ción *f* segregation. **~r** [12] *vt* segregate

segui|da *f*. **en ~da** immediately. **~do** *a* continuous; (en plural) consecutive. **~ de** followed by. ● *adv* straight; (LAm, a menudo) often. **todo ~do** straight ahead. **~dor** *m* follower; (en deportes) supporter. **~r** [5 & 13] *vt* follow. ● *vi* (continuar) continue; (por un camino) go on. **~ adelante** carry on

según *prep* according to. ● *adv* it depends; (a medida que) as

segunda *f* (Auto) second gear; (en tren, avión etc) second class. **~o** *a* & *m* second

segur|amente *adv* certainly; (muy probablemente) surely. **~idad** *f* security; (ausencia de peligro) safety; (certeza) certainty; (aplomo) confidence. **~idad en sí mismo** self-confidence. **~idad social** social security. **~o** *a* safe; (cierto) certain, sure; (estable) secure; (de fiar) reliable. ● *adv* for certain. ● *m* insurance; (dispositivo de seguridad) safety device. **~o de sí mismo** self-confident. **~o contra terceros** third-party insurance

seis *a* & *m* six. **~cientos** *a* & *m* six hundred

seísmo *m* earthquake

selec|ción *f* selection. **~cionar** *vt* select, choose. **~tivo** *a* selective. **~to** *a* selected; (fig) choice

sell|ar *vt* stamp; (cerrar) seal. **~o** *m* stamp; (precinto) seal; (fig, distintivo) hallmark; (LAm, en moneda) reverse

selva *f* forest; (jungla) jungle

semáforo *m* (Auto) traffic lights; (Rail) signal; (Naut) semaphore

semana *f* week. **S~ Santa** Holy Week. **~l** *a* weekly. **~rio** *a* & *m* weekly

semántic|a *f* semantics. **~o** *a* semantic

semblante *m* face; (fig) look

sembrar [1] *vt* sow; (fig) scatter

semeja|nte *a* similar; (tal) such. ● *m* fellow man. **~nza** *f* similarity. **a ~nza de** like. **~r** *vi.* **~ a** resemble

semen *m* semen. **~tal** *a* stud. ● *m* stud animal

semestr|al *a* half-yearly. **~e** *m* six months

semi|circular *a* semicircular. **~círculo** *m* semicircle. **~final** *f* semifinal

semill|a *f* seed. **~ero** *m* seedbed; (fig) hotbed

seminario *m* (Univ) seminar; (Relig) seminary

sémola *f* semolina

senado *m* senate. **~r** *m* senator

sencill|ez *f* simplicity. **~o** *a* simple; (para viajar) single ticket; (disco) single; (LAm, dinero suelto) change

senda *f*, **sendero** *m* path

sendos *a pl* each

seno *m* bosom. **~ materno** womb

sensaci|ón *f* sensation; (percepción, impresión) feeling. **~onal** *a* sensational

sensat|ez *f* good sense. **~o** *a* sensible

sensi|bilidad *f* sensibility. **~ble** *a* sensitive; (notable) notable; (lamentable) lamentable. **~tivo** *a* <*órgano*> sense

sensual *a* sensual. **~idad** *f* sensuality

senta|do *a* sitting (down); **dar algo por ~do** take something for granted. **~dor** *a* (LAm) flattering. **~r** [1] *vt* sit; (establecer) establish. ● *vi* suit; (de medidas) fit; <*comida*> agree with. □ **~rse** *vpr* sit (down)

sentencia *f* (Jurid) sentence. **~r** *vt* sentence (**a** to)

sentido *a* heartfelt; (sensible) sensitive. ● *m* sense; (dirección) direction; (conocimiento) consciousness. **~ común** common sense. **~ del humor** sense of humour. **~ único** one-way. **doble ~** double meaning. **no tener ~** not make sense. **perder el ~** faint. **sin ~** senseless

sentim|ental *a* sentimental. **~iento** *m* feeling; (sentido) sense; (pesar) regret

sentir [4] *vt* feel; (oír) hear; (lamentar) be sorry for. **lo siento mucho** I'm really sorry. ● *m* (opinión) opinion. □ **~se** *vpr* feel; (Mex, ofenderse) be offended

seña *f* sign. **~s** *fpl* (dirección) address; (descripción) description. **dar ~s de** show signs of

señal *f* signal; (letrero, aviso) sign; (telefónica) tone; (Com) deposit. **dar ~es de** show signs of. **en ~ de** as a token of. **~ado** *a* <*hora, día*> appointed. **~ar** *vt* signal; (poner señales en) mark; (apuntar) point out; <*manecilla, aguja*> point to; (determinar) fix. □ **~arse** *vpr* stand out

señor *m* man, gentleman; (delante de nombre propio) Mr; (tratamiento directo) sir. **~a** *f* lady, woman; (delante de nombre propio) Mrs; (esposa) wife; (tratamiento directo) madam. **el ~** Mr. **muy ~ mío** Dear Sir. **¡no ~!** certainly not!. **~ial** *a* <*casa*> stately. **~ita** *f* young lady; (delante de nombre propio) Miss; (tratamiento directo) miss. **~ito** *m* young gentleman

señuelo *m* lure

sepa *vb* ⇒SABER

separa|ción *f* separation. **~do** *a* separate. **por ~do** separately. **~r** *vt* separate; (de empleo) dismiss. □

~rse *vpr* separate; <*amigos*> part. **~tista** *a* & *m* & *f* separatist

septentrional *a* north(ern)

septiembre *m* September

séptimo *a* seventh

sepulcro *m* sepulchre

sepult|ar *vt* bury. **~ura** *f* burial; (tumba) grave. **~urero** *m* gravedigger

sequ|edad *f* dryness. **~ía** *f* drought

séquito *m* entourage; (fig) train

ser [39]

● *verbo intransitivo*

····➤ to be. **es bajo** he's short. **es abogado** he's a lawyer. **ábreme, soy yo** open up, it's me. **¿cómo es?** (como persona) what's he like?; (físicamente) what does he look like? **era invierno** it was winter

····➤ **ser de** (indicando composición) to be made of. **es de hierro** it's made of iron. (provenir de) to be from. **es de México** he's from Mexico. (pertenecer a) to belong to. **el coche es de Juan** the car belongs to Juan, it's Juan's car

····➤ (sumar) **¿cuánto es todo?** how much is that altogether? **son 40 dólares** that's 40 dollars. **somos 10** there are 10 of us

····➤ (con la hora) **son las 3** it's 3 o'clock. **~ía la una** it must have been one o'clock

····➤ (tener lugar) to be held. **~á en la iglesia** it will be held in the church

····➤ (ocurrir) to happen **¿dónde fue el accidente?** where did the accident happen? **me contó cómo fue** he told me how it happened

····➤ (en locuciones) **a no ~ que** unless. **como sea** no matter what. **cuando sea** whenever. **donde sea** wherever **¡eso es!** that's it! **es que** the thing is. **lo que sea** anything. **no sea que, no vaya a ~ que** in case. **o sea** in other words. **sea ... sea ...** either ... or ... **sea como sea** at all costs

● *nombre masculino*

····➤ being; (persona) person. **el ~ humano** the human being. **un ~ amargado** a bitter person. **los ~es queridos** the loved ones

seren|ar *vt* calm down. ▫ **~arse** *vpr* calm down. **~ata** *f* serenade. **~idad** *f* serenity. **~o** *a* serene; <*cielo*> clear; <*mar*> calm. ● *m* night watchman. **al ~o** in the open

seri|al *m* serial. **~e** *f* series. **fuera de ~e** (fig) out of this world. **producción** *f* **en ~e** mass production

seri|edad *f* seriousness. **~o** *a* serious; (confiable) reliable; **en ~o** seriously. **poco ~o** frivolous

sermón *m* sermon; (fig) lecture

serp|enteante *a* winding. **~entear** *vi* wind. **~iente** *f* snake. **~iente de cascabel** rattlesnake

serr|ar [1] *vt* saw. **~ín** *m* sawdust. **~uchar** *vt* (LAm) saw. **~ucho** *m* (hand)saw

servi|cial *a* helpful. **~cio** *m* service; (conjunto) set; (aseo) toilet; **~cio a domicilio** delivery service. **~dor** *m* servant. **su (seguro) ~dor** (en cartas) yours faithfully. **~dumbre** *f* servitude; (criados) servants, staff. **~l** *a* servile

servilleta *f* napkin, serviette

servir [5] *vt* serve; (en restaurante) wait on. ● *vi* serve; (ser útil) be of use. ▫ **~se** *vpr* help o.s. **~se de**

use. **no ~ de nada** be useless. **para ~le** at your service. **sírvase sentarse** please sit down

sesent|a *a & m* sixty. **~ón** *a & m* sixty-year-old

seseo *m* pronunciation of the Spanish *c* as an *s*

sesión *f* session; (en el cine, teatro)

seso *m* brain

seta *f* mushroom

sete|cientos *a & m* seven hundred. **~nta** *a & m* seventy. **~ntón** *a & m* seventy-year-old

setiembre *m* September

seto *m* fence; (de plantas) hedge. **~ vivo** hedge

seudónimo *m* pseudonym

sever|idad *f* severity; (de profesor etc) strictness. **~o** *a* severe; *<profesor etc>* strict

sevillan|as *fpl* popular dance from Seville. **~o** *m* person from Seville

sexo *m* sex

sext|eto *m* sextet. **~o** *a* sixth

sexual *a* sexual. **~idad** *f* sexuality

si *m* (Mus) B; (solfa) te. ● *conj* if; (dubitativo) whether; **~ no** otherwise. **por ~ (acaso)** in case

sí[1] *pron reflexivo* (él) himself; (ella) herself; (de cosa) itself; (uno) oneself; (Vd) yourself; (ellos, ellas) themselves; (Vds) yourselves; (recíproco) each other

sí[2] *adv* yes. ● *m* consent

sida *m* Aids

sidra *f* cider

siembra *f* sowing; (época) sowing time

siempre *adv* always; (LAm, todavía) still; (Mex, por fin) after all. **~ que** if; (cada vez) whenever. **como ~** as usual. **de ~** (acostumbrado) usual. **lo de ~** the usual thing. **para ~** for ever

sien *f* temple

siento *vb* ⇒SENTAR *y* SENTIR

sierra *f* saw; (cordillera) mountain range

siesta *f* nap, siesta

siete *a & m* seven

sífilis *f* syphilis

sifón *m* U-bend; (de soda) syphon

sigilo *m* stealth; (fig) secrecy

sigla *f* abbreviation

siglo *m* century; (época) age. **hace ~s que no escribe** he hasn't written for ages

significa|ción *f* significance. **~do** *a* (conocido) well-known. ● *m* meaning; (importancia) significance. **~r** [7] *vt* mean; (expresar) express. **~tivo** *a* meaningful; (importante) significant

signo *m* sign. **~ de admiración** exclamation mark. **~ de interrogación** question mark

sigo *vb* ⇒SEGUIR

siguiente *a* following, next. **lo ~** the following

sílaba *f* syllable

silb|ar *vt/i* whistle. **~ato** *m*, **~ido** *m* whistle

silenci|ador *m* silencer. **~ar** *vt* hush up. **~o** *m* silence. **~oso** *a* silent

sill|a *f* chair; (de montar) saddle; (Relig) see. **~a de ruedas** wheelchair. **~ín** *m* saddle. **~ón** *m* armchair

silueta *f* silhouette; (dibujo) outline

silvestre *a* wild

simb|ólico *a* symbolic(al). **~olismo** *m* symbolism. **~olizar** [10] *vt* symbolize

símbolo *m* symbol

sim|etría *f* symmetry. **~étrico** *a* symmetric(al)

similar *a* similar (a to)

simp|atía *f* friendliness; (cariño) affection. **~ático** *a* nice, likeable; <*ambiente*> pleasant. **~atizante** *m & f* sympathizer. **~atizar** [10] *vi* get on (well together)

simpl|e *a* simple; (mero) mere. **~eza** *f* simplicity; (tontería) stupid thing; (insignificancia) trifle. **~icidad** *f* simplicity. **~ificar** [7] *vt* simplify. **~ista** *a* simplistic. **~ón** *m* simpleton

simula|ción *f* simulation. **~r** *vt* simulate; (fingir) feign

simultáneo *a* simultaneous

sin *prep* without. **~ saber** without knowing. **~ querer** accidentally

sinagoga *f* synagogue

sincer|idad *f* sincerity. **~o** *a* sincere

sincronizar [10] *vt* synchronize

sindica|l *a* (trade-)union. **~lista** *m & f* trade-unionist. **~to** *m* trade union

síndrome *m* syndrome

sinfín *m* endless number (**de** of)

sinfonía *f* symphony

singular *a* singular; (excepcional) exceptional. □ **~izarse** *vpr* stand out

siniestro *a* sinister. ● *m* disaster; (accidente) accident

sinnúmero *m* endless number (**de** of)

sino *m* fate. ● *conj* but

sinónimo *a* synonymous. ● *m* synonym (**de** for)

sintaxis *f* syntax

síntesis *f invar* synthesis; (resumen) summary

sint|ético *a* synthetic. **~etizar** [10] *vt* synthesize; (resumir) summarize

síntoma *f* sympton

sintomático *a* symptomatic

sinton|ía *f* tuning; (Mus) signature tune. **~izar** [10] *vt* (con la radio) tune (in) to

sinvergüenza *m & f* crook

siquiera *conj* even if. ● *adv* at least. **ni ~** not even

sirena *f* siren; (en cuentos) mermaid

sirio *a & m* Syrian

sirvient|a *f* maid. **~e** *m* servant

sirvo *vb* ⇒SERVIR

sísmico *a* seismic

sismo *m* earthquake

sistem|a *m* system. **por ~a** as a rule. **~ático** *a* systematic

sitiar *vt* besiege; (fig) surround

sitio *m* place; (espacio) space; (Mil) siege; (Mex, parada de taxi) taxi rank. **en cualquier ~** anywhere. **~ web** website

situa|ción *f* situation; (estado, condición) position. **~r** [21] *vt* place, put; locate <*edificio*>. □ **~rse** *vpr* be successful, establish o.s.

slip /es'lip/ *m* (*pl* **~s**) underpants, briefs

smoking /es'mokin/ *m* (*pl* **~s**) dinner jacket (Brit), tuxedo (Amer)

sobaco *m* armpit

sobar *vt* handle; knead <*masa*>

soberan|ía *f* sovereignty. **~o** *a* sovereign; (fig) supreme. ● *m* sovereign

soberbi|a *f* pride; (altanería) arrogance. **~o** *a* proud; (altivo) arrogant

soborn|ar *vt* bribe. **~o** *m* bribe

sobra *f* surplus. **de ~** more than enough. **~s** *fpl* leftovers. **~do** *a* more than enough. **~nte** *a* sur plus. **~r** *vi* be left over; (estorbar) be in the way

sobre *prep* on; (encima de) on top of; (más o menos) about; (por encima de) above; (sin tocar) over. **~ todo** above all, especially. ● *m* envelope. **~cargar** [12] *vt* overload. **~coger** [14] *vt* startle; (conmover) move. **~cubierta** *f* dustcover. **~dosis** *f invar* overdose. **~entender** [1] *vt* understand, infer. **~girar** *vt* (LAm) overdraw. **~giro** *m* (LAm) overdraft. **~humano** *a* superhuman. **~llevar** *vt* bear. **~mesa** *f*. **de ~mesa** after-dinner. **~natural** *a* supernatural. **~nombre** *m* nickname. **~pasar** *vt* exceed. **~peso** *m* (LAm) excess baggage. **~poner** [34] *vt* superimpose. □ **~ponerse** *vpr* overcome. **~saliente** *a* (fig) outstanding. ● *m* excellent mark. **~salir** [52] *vi* stick out; (fig) stand out. **~saltar** *vt* startle. **~salto** *m* fright. **~sueldo** *m* bonus. **~todo** *m* overcoat. **~venir** [53] *vi* happen. **~viviente** *a* surviving. ● *m & f* survivor. **~vivir** *vi* survive. **~volar** *vt* fly over

sobriedad *f* moderation; (de estilo) simplicity

sobrin|a *f* niece. **~o** *m* nephew. **~os** (varones) nephews; (varones y mujeres) nieces and nephews

sobrio *a* moderate, sober

socavar *vt* undermine

soci|able *a* sociable. **~al** *a* social. **~aldemócrata** *m & f* social democrat. **~alismo** *m* socialism. **~alista** *a & m & f* socialist. **~edad** *f* society; (Com) company. **~edad anónima** limited company. **~o** *m* member; (Com) partner. **~ología** *f* sociology. **~ólogo** *m* sociologist

socorr|er *vt* help. **~o** *m* help

soda *f* (bebida) soda (water)

sodio *m* sodium

sofá *m* sofa, settee

sofistica|ción *f* sophistication. **~do** *a* sophisticated

sofo|cante *a* suffocating; (fig) stifling. **~r** [7] *vt* smother <*fuego*>; (fig) stifle. □ **~rse** *vpr* get upset

soga *f* rope

soja *f* soya (bean)

sojuzgar [12] *vt* subdue

sol *m* sun; (luz) sunlight; (Mus) G; (solfa) soh. **al ~** in the sun. **día** *m* **de ~** sunny day. **hace ~, hay ~** it is sunny. **tomar el ~** sunbathe

solamente *adv* only

solapa *f* lapel; (de bolsillo etc) flap. **~do** *a* sly

solar *a* solar. ● *m* plot

solariego *a* <*casa*> ancestral

soldado *m* soldier. **~ raso** private

solda|dor *m* welder; (utensilio) soldering iron. **~r** [2] *vt* weld, solder

soleado *a* sunny

soledad *f* solitude; (aislamiento) loneliness

solemn|e *a* solemn. **~idad** *f* solemnity

soler [2] *vi* be in the habit of. **suele despertarse a las 6** he usually wakes up at 6 o'clock

sol|icitar *vt* request, ask for; apply for <*empleo*>. **~ícito** *a* solicitous. **~icitud** *f* request; (para un puesto) application; (formulario) application form; (preocupación) concern

solidaridad *f* solidarity

solid|ez *f* solidity; (de argumento etc) soundness. □ **~ificarse** [7] *vpr* solidify

sólido *a* solid; <*argumento etc*> sound. ● *m* solid

soliloquio *m* soliloquy

solista *m & f* soloist

solitario *a* solitary; (aislado) lonely. ● *m* loner; (juego, diamante) solitaire

solloz|ar [10] *vi* sob. **~o** *m* sob

solo *a* (sin compañía) alone; (aislado) lonely; (sin ayuda) by oneself; (único) only; (Mus) solo; *<café>* black. ● *m* solo; (juego) solitaire. **a solas** alone

sólo *adv* only. **~ que** except that. **no ~... sino también** not only... but also.... **tan ~** only

solomillo *m* sirloin

soltar [2] *vt* let go of; (dejar ir) release; (dejar caer) drop; (dejar salir, decir) let out; give *<golpe etc>*. □ **~se** *vpr* come undone; (librarse) break loose

solter|a *f* single woman. **~o** *a* single. ● *m* bachelor

soltura *f* looseness; (fig) ease, fluency

solu|ble *a* soluble. **~ción** *f* solution. **~cionar** *vt* solve; settle *<huelga, asunto>*

solvente *a & m* solvent

sombr|a *f* shadow; (lugar sin sol) shade. **a la ~a** in the shade. **~eado** *a* shady

sombrero *m* hat. **~ hongo** bowler hat

sombrío *a* sombre

somero *a* superficial

someter *vt* subdue; subject *<persona>*; (presentar) submit. □ **~se** *vpr* give in

somn|oliento *a* sleepy. **~ífero** *m* sleeping-pill

somos *vb* ⇒SER

son *m* sound. ● *vb* ⇒SER

sonámbulo *m* sleepwalker. **ser ~** walk in one's sleep

sonar [2] *vt* blow; ring *<timbre>*. ● *vi* sound; *<timbre, teléfono etc>* ring; *<despertador>* go off; (Mus) play; (fig, ser conocido) be familiar. **~ a** sound like. □ **~se** *vpr* blow one's nose

sonde|ar *vt* sound out; explore *<espacio>*; (Naut) sound. **~o** *m* poll; (Naut) sounding

soneto *m* sonnet

sonido *m* sound

sonoro *a* sonorous; (ruidoso) loud

sonr|eír [51] *vi* smile. □ **~eírse** *vpr* smile. **~isa** *f* smile

sonroj|arse *vpr* blush. **~o** *m* blush

sonrosado *a* rosy, pink

sonsacar [7] *vt* wheedle out

soñ|ado *a* dream. **~ador** *m* dreamer. **~ar** [2] *vi* dream (**con** of). **¡ni ~arlo!** not likely!

sopa *f* soup

sopesar *vt* (fig) weigh up

sopl|ar *vt* blow; blow out *<vela>*; blow off *<polvo>*; (inflar) blow up. ● *vi* blow. **~ete** *m* blowlamp. **~o** *m* puff

soport|al *m* porch. **~ales** *mpl* arcade. **~ar** *vt* support; (fig) bear, put up with. **~e** *m* support

soprano *f* soprano

sor *f* sister

sorb|er *vt* sip; (con ruido) slurp; (absorber) absorb. **~ por la nariz** sniff. **~ete** *m* sorbet, water-ice. **~o** *m* (pequeña cantidad) sip; (trago grande) gulp

sordera *f* deafness

sórdido *a* squalid; *<asunto>* sordid

sordo *a* deaf; *<ruido etc>* dull. ● *m* deaf person. **hacerse el ~** turn a deaf ear. **~mudo** *a* deaf and dumb

soroche *m* (LAm) mountain sickness

sorpre|ndente *a* surprising. **~nder** *vt* surprise. □ **~nderse** *vpr* be surprised. **~sa** *f* surprise

sorte|ar *vt* draw lots for; (fig) avoid. **~o** *m* draw. **por ~o** by drawing lots

sortija *f* ring; (de pelo) ringlet

sortilegio *m* sorcery; (embrujo) spell

sos|egar [1 & 12] *vt* calm. **~iego** *m* calmness

soslayo. **de ~** sideways

soso *a* tasteless; (fig) dull

sospech|a *f* suspicion. **~ar** *vt* suspect. ● *vi*. **~ de** suspect. **~oso** *a* suspicious. ● *m* suspect

sost|én *m* support; (prenda femenina) bra 🅸, brassière. **~ener** [40] *vt* support; bear <*peso*>; (sujetar) hold; (sustentar) maintain; (alimentar) sustain. □ **~enerse** *vpr* support o.s.; (continuar) remain. **~enido** *a* sustained; (Mus) sharp. ● *m* (Mus) sharp

sota *f* (de naipes) jack

sótano *m* basement

soviético *a* (Historia) Soviet

soy *vb* ⇒SER

Sr. *abrev* (**Señor**) Mr. **~a.** *abrev* (**Señora**) Mrs. **~ta.** *abrev* (**Señorita**) Miss

su *a* (de él) his; (de ella) her; (de animal, objeto) its; (de uno) one's; (de Vd) your; (de ellos, de ellas) their; (de Vds) your

suav|e *a* smooth; (fig) gentle; <*color, sonido*> soft; <*tabaco, sedante*> mild. **~idad** *f* smoothness, softness. **~izante** *m* conditioner; (para ropa) softener. **~izar** [10] *vt* smooth, soften

subalimentado *a* underfed

subarrendar [1] *vt* sublet

subasta *f* auction. **~r** *vt* auction

sub|campeón *m* runner-up. **~consciencia** *f* subconscious. **~consciente** *a* & *m* subconscious. **~continente** *m* subcontinent. **~desarrollado** *a* underdeveloped. **~director** *m* assistant manager

súbdito *m* subject

sub|dividir *vt* subdivide. **~estimar** *vt* underestimate

subi|da *f* rise; (a montaña) ascent; (pendiente) slope. **~do** *a* <*color*> intense. **~r** *vt* go up; climb <*mountain*>; (llevar) take up; (aumentar) raise; turn up <*radio, calefacción*>. ● *vi* go up. **~r a** get into <*coche*>; get on <*autobús, avión, barco, tren*>; (aumentar) rise. **~ a pie** walk up. □ **~rse** *vpr* climb up. **~rse a** get on <*tren etc*>

súbito *a* sudden. **de ~** suddenly

subjetivo *a* subjective

subjuntivo *a* & *m* subjunctive

subleva|ción *f* uprising. □ **~rse** *vpr* rebel

sublim|ar *vt* sublimate. **~e** *a* sublime

submarino *a* underwater. ● *m* submarine

subordinado *a* & *m* subordinate

subrayar *vt* underline

subsanar *vt* rectify; overcome <*dificultad*>; make up for <*carencia*>

subscri|bir *vt* (*pp* **subscrito**) sign. □ **~birse** *vpr* subscribe (a to). **~pción** *f* subscription

subsidi|ario *a* subsidiary. **~o** *m* subsidy. **~o de desempleo**, **~ de paro** unemployment benefit

subsiguiente *a* subsequent

subsist|encia *f* subsistence. **~ir** *vi* subsist; (perdurar) survive
substraer [41] *vt* take away
subterráneo *a* underground
subtítulo *m* subtitle
suburb|ano *a* suburban. **~io** *m* suburb; (barrio pobre) depressed area
subvenci|ón *f* subsidy. **~onar** *vt* subsidize
subver|sión *f* subversion. **~sivo** *a* subversive. **~tir** [4] *vt* subvert
succi|ón *f* suction. **~onar** *vt* suck
suce|der *vi* happen; (seguir) **~ a** follow. ● *vt* (substituir) succeed. **lo que ~de es que** the trouble is that. **¿qué ~de?** what's the matter? **~sión** *f* succession. **~sivo** *a* successive; (consecutivo) consecutive. **en lo ~sivo** in future. **~so** *m* event; (incidente) incident. **~sor** *m* successor
suciedad *f* dirt; (estado) dirtiness
sucinto *a* concise; <*prenda*> scanty
sucio *a* dirty; <*conciencia*> guilty. **en ~** in rough
sucre *m* (unidad monetaria del Ecuador) sucre
suculento *a* succulent
sucumbir *vi* succumb (**a** to)
sucursal *f* branch (office)
Sudáfrica *f* South Africa
sudafricano *a* & *m* South African
Sudamérica *f* South America
sudamericano *a* & *m* South American
sudar *vi* sweat
sud|este *m* south-east. **~oeste** *m* south-west
sudor *m* sweat
Suecia *f* Sweden
sueco *a* Swedish. ● *m* (persona) Swede; (lengua) Swedish. **hacerse el ~** pretend not to hear
suegr|a *f* mother-in-law. **~o** *m* father-in-law. **mis ~os** my in-laws
suela *f* sole
sueldo *m* salary
suelo *m* ground; (dentro de edificio) floor; (territorio) soil; (en la calle etc) road surface. ● *vb* ⇒SOLER
suelto *a* loose; <*cordones*> undone; (sin pareja) odd; <*lenguaje*> fluent. **con el pelo ~** with one's hair down. ● *m* change
sueño *m* sleep; (lo soñado, ilusión) dream. **tener ~** be sleepy
suerte *f* luck; (destino) fate; (azar) chance. **de otra ~** otherwise. **de ~ que** so. **echar ~s** draw lots. **por ~** fortunately. **tener ~** be lucky
suéter *m* sweater, jersey
suficien|cia *f* (aptitud) aptitude; (presunción) smugness. **~te** *a* enough, sufficient; (presumido) smug. **~temente** *adv* sufficiently
sufijo *m* suffix
sufragio *m* (voto) vote
sufrimiento *m* suffering. **~r** *vt* suffer; undergo <*cambio*>; have <*accident*>. ● *vi* suffer
suge|rencia *f* suggestion. **~rir** [4] *vt* suggest. **~stión** *f* (Psych) suggestion. **es pura ~stión** it's all in one's mind. **~stionable** *a* impressionable. **~stionar** *vt* influence. **~stivo** *a* (estimulante) stimulating; (atractivo) sexy
suicid|a *a* suicidal. ● *m* & *f* suicide victim; (fig) maniac. □ **~arse** *vpr* commit suicide. **~io** *m* suicide
Suiza *f* Switzerland
suizo *a* & *m* Swiss

suje|ción *f* subjection. **con ~ a** in accordance with. **~tador** *m* bra [T], brassière. **~tapapeles** *m invar* paper-clip. **~tar** *vt* fasten; (agarrar) hold. □ **~tarse** *vpr*. **~se a** hold on to; (someterse) abide by. **~to** *a* fastened; (susceptible) subject (a to). ● *m* individual; (Gram) subject.

suma *f* sum; (Math) addition; (combinación) combination. **en ~** in short. **~mente** *adv* extremely. **~r** *vt* add (up); (totalizar) add up to. ● *vi* add up. □ **~rse** *vpr*. **~rse a** join in

sumario *a* brief; (Jurid) summary. ● *m* table of contents; (Jurid) pre-trial proceedings

sumergi|ble *a* submersible. **~r** [14] *vt* submerge

suministr|ar *vt* supply. **~o** *m* supply; (acción) supplying

sumir *vt* sink; (fig) plunge

sumis|ión *f* submission. **~o** *a* submissive

sumo *a* great; (supremo) supreme. **a lo ~** at the most

suntuoso *a* sumptuous

supe *vb* ⇒SABER

superar *vt* surpass; (vencer) overcome; beat *<marca>*; (dejar atrás) get over. □ **~se** *vpr* better o.s.

superchería *f* swindle

superfici|al *a* superficial. **~e** *f* surface; (extensión) area. **de ~e** surface

superfluo *a* superfluous

superior *a* superior; (más alto) higher; (mejor) better; *<piso>* upper. ● *m* superior. **~idad** *f* superiority

superlativo *a* & *m* superlative

supermercado *m* supermarket

supersticí|ón *f* superstition. **~oso** *a* superstitious

supervis|ar *vt* supervise. **~ión** *f* supervision. **~or** *m* supervisor

superviv|encia *f* survival. **~iente** *a* surviving. ● *m* & *f* survivor

suplantar *vt* supplant

suplement|ario *a* supplementary. **~o** *m* supplement

suplente *a* & *m* & *f* substitute

súplica *f* entreaty; (Jurid) request

suplicar [7] *vt* beg

suplicio *m* torture

suplir *vt* make up for; (reemplazar) replace

supo|ner [34] *vt* suppose; (significar) mean; involve *<gasto, trabajo>*. **~sición** *f* supposition

suprem|acía *f* supremacy. **~o** *a* supreme

supr|esión *f* suppression; (de impuesto) abolition; (de restricción) lifting. **~imir** *vt* suppress; abolish *<impuesto>*; lift *<restricción>*; delete *<párrafo>*

supuesto *a* supposed; *<falso>* false. ● *m* assumption. **¡por ~!** of course!

sur *m* south; (viento) south wind

surc|ar [7] *vt* plough; cut through *<agua>*. **~o** *m* furrow; (de rueda) rut

surfear *vi* (Informática) surf

surgir [14] *vi* spring up; (elevarse) loom up; (aparecer) appear; *<dificultad, oportunidad>* arise

surrealis|mo *m* surrealism. **~ta** *a* & *m* & *f* surrealist

surti|do *a* well-stocked; (variado) assorted. ● *m* assortment, selection. **~dor** *m* (de gasolina) petrol pump (Brit), gas pump (Amer). **~r** *vt* supply; have *<efecto>*. □ **~rse** *vpr* provide o.s. (**de** with)

susceptib|ilidad *f* sensitivity. **~le** *a* susceptible; (sensible) sensitive

suscitar *vt* provoke; arouse <*curiosidad, interés*>

suscr... ⇒SUBSCR...

susodicho *a* aforementioned

suspen|der *vt* suspend; stop <*tratamiento*>; call off <*viaje*>; (Escol) fail; (colgar) hang (**de** from). **~se** *m* suspense. **novela de ~se** thriller. **~sión** *f* suspension. **~so** *m* fail; (LAm, en libro, película) suspense. **en ~so** suspended

suspir|ar *vi* sigh. **~o** *m* sigh

sust... ⇒SUBST...

sustanci|a *f* substance. **~al** *a* substantial. **~oso** *a* substantial

sustantivo *m* noun

sustent|ación *f* support. **~ar** *vt* support; (alimentar) sustain; (mantener) maintain. **~o** *m* support; (alimento) sustenance

sustitu|ción *f* substitution; (permanente) replacement. **~ir** [17] *vt* substitute, replace. **~to** *m* substitute; (permanente) replacement

susto *m* fright

susurr|ar *vi* <*persona*> whisper; <*agua*> murmur; <*hojas*> rustle

sutil *a* fine; (fig) subtle. **~eza** *f* subtlety

suyo *a & pron* (de él) his; (de ella) hers; (de animal) its; (de Vd) yours; (de ellos, de ellas) theirs; (de Vds) yours. **un amigo ~** a friend of his, a friend of theirs, etc

Tt

tabac|alera *f* (state) tobacco monopoly. **~o** *m* tobacco; (cigarillos) cigarettes

tabern|a *f* bar. **~ero** *m* barman; (dueño) landlord

tabique *m* partition wall; (Mex, ladrillo) brick

tabl|a *f* plank; (del suelo) floorboard; (de vestido) pleat; (índice) index; (gráfico, en matemática etc) table. **hacer ~as** (en ajedrez) draw. **~a de surf** surfboard. **~ado** *m* platform; (en el teatro) stage. **~ao** *m* place where flamenco shows are held. **~ero** *m* board. **~ero de mandos** dashboard

tableta *f* tablet; (de chocolate) bar

tabl|illa *f* splint; (Mex, de chocolate) bar. **~ón** *m* plank. **~ón de anuncios** notice board (esp Brit), bulletin board (Amer)

tabú *m* (*pl* **~es**, **~s**) taboo

tabular *vt* tabulate

taburete *m* stool

tacaño *a* mean

tacha *f* stain, blemish. **sin ~** unblemished; <*conducta*> irreproachable. **~r** *vt* (con raya) cross out; (Jurid) impeach. **~ de** accuse of

tácito *a* tacit

taciturno *a* taciturn; (triste) glum

taco *m* plug; (LAm, tacón) heel; (de billar) cue; (de billetes) book; (fig, [!], lío) mess; (palabrota) swearword; (Mex, Culin) taco, filled tortilla

tacón *m* heel

táctic|a *f* tactics. **~o** *a* tactical

táctil *a* tactile
tacto *m* touch; (fig) tact
tahúr *m* card-sharp
Tailandia *f* Thailand
tailandés *a & m* Thai
taimado *a* sly
taj|ada *f* slice. **sacar ~ada** profit. **~ante** *a* categorical; *<tono>* sharp. **~ear** *vt* (LAm) slash. **~o** *m* cut; (en mina) face
tal *a* such. **de ~ manera** in such a way. **un ~** someone called. ● *pron.* **como ~** as such. **y ~** and things like that. ● *adv.* **con ~ de que** as long as. **~ como** the way. **~ para cual** ⓘ two of a kind. **~ vez** maybe. **¿qué ~?** how are you? **¿qué ~ es ella?** what's she like?
taladr|ar *vt* drill. **~o** *m* drill
talante *m* mood. **de buen ~** *<estar>* in a good mood; *<ayudar>* willingly
talar *vt* fell
talco *m* talcum powder
talega *f*, **talego** *m* sack
talento *m* talent; (fig) talented person
talismán *m* talisman
talla *f* carving; (de diamante etc) cutting; (estatura) height; (tamaño) size. **~do** *m* carving; (de diamante etc) cutting. **~dor** *m* carver; (cortador) cutter; (LAm, de naipes) dealer. **~r** *vt* carve; sculpt *<escultura>*; cut *<diamante>*; (Mex, restregar) scrub. □ **~rse** *vpr* (Mex) rub o.s.
tallarín *m* noodle
talle *m* waist; (figura) figure
taller *m* workshop; (de pintor etc) studio; (Auto) garage
tallo *m* stem, stalk
tal|ón *m* heel; (recibo) counterfoil; (cheque) cheque. **~onario** *m* receipt book; (de cheques) cheque book
tamal *m* (LAm) tamale
tamaño *a* such a. ● *m* size. **de ~ natural** life-size
tambalearse *vpr* (persona) stagger; *<cosa>* wobble
también *adv* also, too
tambor *m* drum. **~ del freno** brake drum. **~ilear** *vi* drum
tamiz *m* sieve. **~ar** [10] *vt* sieve
tampoco *adv* neither, nor, not either. **yo ~ fui** I didn't go either
tampón *m* tampon; (para entintar) ink-pad
tan *adv* so. **~... como** as... as. **¿qué ~...?** (LAm) how...?
tanda *f* group; (de obreros) shift
tang|ente *a & f* tangent. **~ible** *a* tangible
tango *m* tango
tanque *m* tank
tante|ar *vt* estimate; sound up *<persona>*; (ensayar) test; (fig) weigh up; (LAm, palpar) feel. ● *vi* (LAm) feel one's way. **~o** *m* estimate; (prueba) test; (en deportes) score
tanto *a* (en singular) so much; (en plural) so many; (comparación en singular) as much; (comparación en plural) as many. ● *pron* so much; (en plural) so many. ● *adv* so; (con verbo) so much. **hace ~ tiempo** it's been so long. **~... como** both...and. **¿qué ~...?** (LAm) how much...? **~ como** as well as; (cantidad) as much as. **~ más... cuanto que** all the more ... because. **~ si... como si** whether ... or. **a ~s de** sometime in. **en ~** meanwhile. **en ~ que** while. **entre ~** meanwhile. **hasta ~ que** until. **no es para ~** it's not as bad as all that. **otro ~** the same; (el doble) as much again. **por (lo) ~** therefore.

● *m* certain amount; (punto) point; (gol) goal. **estar al ~ de** be up to date with

tañer [22] *vi* peal

tapa *f* lid; (de botella) top; (de libro) cover. **~s** *fpl* savoury snacks. **~dera** *f* cover, lid; (fig) cover. **~r** *vt* cover; (abrigar) wrap up; (obturar) plug. **~rrabos** *m invar* loincloth

tapete *m* (de mesa) table cover; (Mex, alfombra) rug

tapia *f* wall. **~r** *vt* enclose

tapi|cería *f* tapestry; (de muebles) upholstery. **~z** *m* tapestry. **~ar** [10] *vt* upholster <*muebles*>

tapón *m* stopper; (Tec) plug

taqu|igrafía *f* shorthand. **~ígrafo** *m* shorthand writer

taquill|a *f* ticket office; (fig, dinero) takings. **~ero** *a* box-office

tara *f* (peso) tare; (defecto) defect

tarántula *f* tarantula

tararear *vt/i* hum

tarda|nza *f* delay. **~r** *vt* take. ● *vi* (retrasarse) be late; (emplear mucho tiempo) take a long time. **a más ~r** at the latest. **sin ~r** without delay

tard|e *adv* late. ● *f* (antes del atardecer) afternoon; (después del atardecer) evening. **~e o temprano** sooner or later. **de ~e en ~e** from time to time. **en la ~e** (LAm), **por la ~e** in the afternoon. **~ío** *a* late

tarea *f* task, job

tarifa *f* rate; (en transporte) fare; (lista de precios) tariff

tarima *f* dais

tarjeta *f* card. **~ de crédito** credit card. **~ postal** postcard

tarro *m* jar; (Mex, taza) mug

tarta *f* cake; (con base de masa) tart. **~ helada** ice-cream gateau

tartamud|ear *vi* stammer. **~o** *a*. **es ~o** he stammers

tasa *f* valuation; (impuesto) tax; (índice) rate. **~r** *vt* value; (limitar) ration

tasca *f* bar

tatarabuel|a *f* great-great-grandmother. **~o** *m* great-great-grandfather. **~os** *mpl* great-great-grandparents

tatua|je *m* (acción) tattooing; (dibujo) tattoo. **~r** [21] *vt* tattoo

taurino *a* bullfighting

Tauro *m* Taurus

tauromaquia *f* bullfighting

taxi *m* taxi. **~ista** *m* & *f* taxi-driver

taz|a *f* cup. **~ón** *m* bowl

te *pron* (acusativo) you; (dativo) (to) you; (reflexivo) (to) yourself

té *m* tea; (LAm, reunión) tea party

teatr|al *a* theatre; (exagerado) theatrical. **~o** *m* theatre; (literatura) drama

tebeo *m* comic

tech|ado *m* roof. **~ar** *vt* roof. **~o** *m* (interior) ceiling; (LAm, tejado) roof. **~umbre** *f* roof

tecl|a *f* key. **~ado** *m* keyboard. **~ear** *vt* key in

técnica *f* technique

tecnicismo *m* technical nature; (palabra) technical term

técnico *a* technical. ● *m* technician; (en deportes) trainer

tecnol|ogía *f* technology. **~ógico** *a* technological

tecolote *m* (Mex) owl

teja *f* tile. **~s de pizarra** slates. **~do** *m* roof. **a toca ~** cash

teje|dor *m* weaver. **~r** *vt* weave; (hacer punto) knit

tejemaneje *m* [I] intrigue. **~s** *mpl* scheming

tejido *m* material; (Anat, fig) tissue. **~s** *mpl* textiles

tejón *m* badger

tela *f* material, fabric; (de araña) web; (en líquido) skin

telar *m* loom. **~es** *mpl* textile mill

telaraña *f* spider's web, cobweb

tele *f* [T] TV, telly

tele|comunicación *f* telecommunication. **~diario** *m* television news. **~dirigido** *a* remote-controlled; <*misil*> guided. **~férico** *m* cable-car

tel|efonear *vt/i* telephone. **~efónico** *a* telephone. **~efonista** *m & f* telephonist. **~éfono** *m* telephone. **al ~éfono** on the phone

tel|egrafía *f* telegraphy. **~égrafo** *m* telegraph. **~egrama** *m* telegram

telenovela *f* television soap opera

teleobjetivo *m* telephoto lens

telep|atía *f* telepathy. **~ático** *a* telepathic

telesc|ópico *a* telescopic. **~opio** *m* telescope

telesilla *m & f* chair-lift

telespectador *m* viewer

telesquí *m* ski-lift

televi|dente *m & f* viewer. **~sar** *vt* televise. **~sión** *f* television. **~sor** *m* television (set)

télex *m invar* telex

telón *m* curtain

tema *m* subject; (Mus) theme

tembl|ar [1] *vi* shake; (de miedo) tremble; (de frío) shiver. **~or** *m* shaking; (de miedo) trembling; (de frío) shivering; **~or de tierra** earth tremor. **~oroso** *a* trembling

tem|er *vt* be afraid (of). ● *vi* be afraid. □ **~erse** *vpr* be afraid. **~erario** *a* reckless. **~eroso** *a* frightened. **~ible** *a* fearsome. **~or** *m* fear

témpano *m* floe

temperamento *m* temperament

temperatura *f* temperature

tempest|ad *f* storm. **~uoso** *a* stormy

templ|ado *a* (tibio) warm; <*clima, tiempo*> mild; (valiente) courageous. **~anza** *f* mildness. **~ar** *vt* temper; (calentar) warm up. **~e** *m* tempering; <*coraje*> courage; (humor) mood

templo *m* temple

tempora|da *f* season. **~l** *a* temporary. ● *m* storm

tempran|ero *a* <*frutos*> early. **ser ~ero** be an early riser. **~o** *a & adv* early

tenacidad *f* tenacity

tenacillas *fpl* tongs

tenaz *a* tenacious

tenaza *f*, **tenazas** *fpl* pliers; (de chimenea, Culin) tongs; (de cangrejo) pincer

tende|ncia *f* tendency. **~nte** *a*. **~nte a** aimed at. **~r** [1] *vt* spread (out); hang out <*ropa a secar*>; (colocar) lay. ● *vi* tend (a to). □ **~rse** *vpr* lie down

tender|ete *m* stall. **~o** *m* shopkeeper

tendido *a* spread out; <*ropa*> hung out; <*persona*> lying down. ● *m* (en plaza de toros) front rows

tendón *m* tendon

tenebroso *a* gloomy; <*asunto*> sinister

tenedor *m* fork; (poseedor) holder

tener [40]

● *verbo transitivo*

> ! El presente del verbo **tener** admite dos traducciones: *to have* y *to have got*, este último de uso más extendido en el inglés británico

····➤ to have. **¿tienen hijos?** do you have any children?, have you got any children? **no tenemos coche** we don't have a car, we haven't got a car. **tiene gripe** he has (the) flu, he's got (the) flu

····➤ to be <*dimensiones, edad*>. **tiene 1 metro de largo** it's 1 metre long. **tengo 20 años** I'm 20 (years old)

····➤ (sentir) **tener** + *nombre* to be + *adjective*. **~ celos** to be jealous. **~ frío** to be cold

····➤ (sujetar, sostener) to hold. **tenme la escalera** hold the ladder for me

····➤ (indicando estado) **tiene las manos sucias** his hands are dirty. **me tiene preocupada** I'm worried about him. **me tuvo esperando** he kept me waiting

····➤ (llevar puesto) to be wearing, to have on. **¡qué zapatos más elegantes tienes!** those are very smart shoes you're wearing! **tienes el suéter al revés** you have your sweater on inside out

····➤ (considerar) **~ a uno por algo** to think s.o. is sth. **lo tenía por tímido** I thought he was shy

● *verbo auxiliar*

····➤ **~ quehacer algo** to have to do sth. **tengo que irme** I have to go

····➤ **tener** + *participio pasado*. **tengo pensado comprarlo** I'm thinking of buying it. **tenía entendido otra cosa** I understood something else

····➤ (LAm, con expresiones temporales) **tienen 2 años de estar aquí** they've been here for 2 months. **tiene mucho tiempo sin verlo** she hasn't seen him for a long time

····➤ (en locuciones) **aquí tiene** here you are. **¿qué tienes?** what's the matter with you? **¿ y eso qué tiene?** (LAm) and what's wrong with that?

□ **tenerse** *verbo pronominal*

····➤ (sostenerse) **no podía ~se en pie** (de cansancio) he was dead on his feet; (de borracho) he could hardly stand

····➤ (considerarse) to consider o.s. **se tiene por afortunado** he considers himself lucky

tengo *vb* ⇒TENER

teniente *m* lieutenant

tenis *m* tennis. **~ de mesa** table tennis. **~ta** *m & f* tennis player

tenor *m* sense; (Mus) tenor. **a ~ de** according to

tens|ión *f* tension; (arterial) blood pressure; (Elec) voltage; (estrés) strain. **~o** *a* tense

tentación *f* temptation

tentáculo *m* tentacle

tenta|dor *a* tempting. **~r** [1] *vt* tempt; (palpar) feel

tentativa *f* attempt

tenue *a* thin; <*luz, voz*> faint; <*color*> subdued

teñi|r [5 & 22] *vt* dye; (fig) tinge (**de** with). □ **~rse** *vpr* dye one's hair

teología *f* theology

te|oría *f* theory. **~órico** *a* theoretical

tequila *f* tequila

terap|euta *m & f* therapist. **~éutico** *a* therapeutic. **~ia** *f* therapy

terc|er *a* véase TERCERO. **~era** *f* (Auto) third (gear). **~ero** *a* (*delante de nombre masculino en singular* **tercer**) third. ● *m* third party. **~io** *m* third

terciopelo *m* velvet

terco *a* obstinate

tergiversar *vt* distort

termal *a* thermal

térmico *a* thermal

termina|ción *f* ending; (conclusión) conclusion. **~l** *a & m* terminal. **~nte** *a* categorical. **~r** *vt* finish, end. **~r por** end up. □ **~rse** *vpr* come to an end

término *m* end; (palabra) term; (plazo) period. **~ medio** average. **dar ~ a** finish off. **en primer ~** first of all. **en último ~** as a last resort. **estar en buenos ~s con** be on good terms with. **llevar a ~** carry out

terminología *f* terminology

termita *f* termite

termo *m* Thermos (P) flask, flask

termómetro *m* thermometer

termo|nuclear *a* thermonuclear. **~stato** *m* thermostat

terner|a *f* (carne) veal. **~o** *m* calf

ternura *f* tenderness

terquedad *f* stubbornness

terrado *m* flat roof

terraplén *m* embankment

terrateniente *m & f* landowner

terraza *f* terrace; (balcón) balcony; (terrado) flat roof

terremoto *m* earthquake

terre|no *a* earthly. ● *m* land; (solar) plot (fig) field. **~stre** *a* land; (Mil) ground

terrible *a* terrible. **~mente** *adv* awfully

territori|al *a* territorial. **~o** *m* territory

terrón *m* (de tierra) clod; (Culin) lump

terror *m* terror. **~ífico** *a* terrifying. **~ismo** *m* terrorism. **~ista** *m & f* terrorist

terso *a* smooth

tertulia *f* gathering

tesina *f* dissertation

tesón *m* tenacity

tesor|ería *f* treasury. **~ero** *m* treasurer. **~o** *m* treasure; (tesorería) treasury; (libro) thesaurus

testaferro *m* figurehead

testa|mento *m* will. **T~mento** (Relig) Testament. **~r** *vi* make a will

testarudo *a* stubborn

testículo *m* testicle

testi|ficar [7] *vt/i* testify. **~go** *m* witness. **~go ocular, ~go presencial** eyewitness. **ser ~go de** witness. **~monio** *m* testimony

teta *f* tit (🅃 o vulg); (de biberón) teat

tétanos *m* tetanus

tetera *f* (para el té) teapot

tetilla *f* nipple; (de biberón) teat

tétrico *a* gloomy

textil *a & m* textile

text|o *m* text. **~ual** *a* textual; <*traducción*> literal; <*palabras*> exact

textura *f* texture

tez *f* complexion

ti *pron* you

tía *f* aunt; 🅃 woman

tiara *f* tiara

tibio *a* lukewarm

tiburón *m* shark

tiempo *m* time; (atmosférico) weather; (Mus) tempo; (Gram) tense; (en partido) half. **a su ~** in due course. **a ~** in time. **¿cuánto ~?**

how long? **hace buen ~** the weather is fine. **hace ~** some time ago. **mucho ~** a long time. **perder el ~** waste time

tienda *f* shop (esp Brit), store (esp Amer); (de campaña) tent. **~ de comestibles, ~ de ultramarinos** grocer's (shop) (Brit), grocery store (Amer)

tiene *vb* ⇒TENER

tienta. **andar a ~s** feel one's way

tierno *a* tender; (joven) young

tierra *f* land; (planeta, Elec) earth; (suelo) ground; (Geol) soil, earth; (LAm, polvo) dust. **por ~** overland, by land

tieso *a* stiff; (engreído) conceited

tiesto *m* flowerpot

tifón *m* typhoon

tifus *m* typhus; (fiebre tifoidea) typhoid (fever)

tigre *m* tiger. **~sa** *f* tigress

tijera *f*, **tijeras** *fpl* scissors; (de jardín) shears

tijeretear *vt* snip

tila *f* (infusión) lime tea

tild|ar *vt*. **~ar de** (fig) brand as. **~e** *f* tilde

tilo *m* lime(-tree)

timar *vt* swindle

timbal *m* kettledrum; (Culin) timbale, meat pie. **~es** *mpl* (Mus) timpani

timbr|ar *vt* stamp. **~e** *m* (sello) fiscal stamp; (Mex) postage stamp; (Elec) bell; (sonido) timbre

timidez *f* shyness

tímido *a* shy

timo *m* swindle

timón *m* rudder; (rueda) wheel; (fig) helm

tímpano *m* eardrum

tina *f* tub. **~co** *m* (Mex) water tank. **~ja** *f* large earthenware jar

tinglado *m* mess; (asunto) racket

tinieblas *fpl* darkness; (fig) confusion

tino *f* good sense; (tacto) tact

tint|a *f* ink. **de buena ~a** on good authority. **~e** *m* dyeing; (color) dye; (fig) tinge. **~ero** *m* ink-well

tintinear *vi* tinkle; <*vasos*> chink, clink

tinto *a* <*vino*> red

tintorería *f* dry cleaner's

tintura *f* dyeing; (color) dye

tío *m* uncle; [I] man. **~s** *mpl* uncle and aunt

tiovivo *m* merry-go-round

típico *a* typical

tipo *m* type; ([I], persona) person; (figura de mujer) figure; (figura de hombre) build; (Com) rate

tip|ografía *f* typography. **~ográfico** *a* typographic(al)

tira *f* strip. **la ~ de** lots of

tirabuzón *m* corkscrew; (de pelo) ringlet

tirad|a *f* distance; (serie) series; (de periódico etc) print-run. **de una ~a** in one go. **~o** *a* (barato) very cheap; ([I], fácil) very easy. **~or** *m* (asa) handle

tiran|ía *f* tyranny. **~izar** [10] *vt* tyrannize. **~o** *a* tyrannical. ● *m* tyrant

tirante *a* tight; (fig) tense; <*relaciones*> strained. ● *m* strap. **~s** *mpl* braces (esp Brit), suspenders (Amer)

tirar *vt* throw; (desechar) throw away; (derribar) knock over; drop <*bomba*>; fire <*cohete*>; (imprimir) print. ● *vi* (disparar) shoot. **~ a** tend to (be); (parecerse a) resemble. **~ abajo** knock down. **~ de** pull. **a todo ~** at the most. **ir tirando** get by. □ **~se** *vpr* throw o.s.; (tumbarse) lie down

tirita *f* (sticking) plaster
tiritar *vi* shiver (**de** with)
tiro *m* throw; (disparo) shot. **~ libre** free kick. **a ~** within range. **errar el ~** miss. **pegarse un ~** shoot o.s.
tiroides *m* thyroid (gland)
tirón *m* tug. **de un ~** in one go
tirote|ar *vt* shoot at. **~o** *m* shooting
tisana *f* herb tea
tisú *m* (*pl* **~s**, **~es**) tissue
títere *m* puppet. **~s** *mpl* puppet show
titilar *vi* <*estrella*> twinkle
titiritero *m* puppeteer; (acróbata) acrobat
titube|ante *a* faltering; (fig) hesitant. **~ar** *vi* falter. **~o** *m* hesitation
titula|do *a* <*libro*> entitled; <*persona*> qualified. **~r** *m* headline; (persona) holder. ● *vt* call. □ **~rse** *vpr* be called; <*persona*> graduate
título *m* title; (académico) qualification; (Univ) degree. **a ~ de** as, by way of
tiza *f* chalk
tiz|nar *vt* dirty. **~ne** *m* soot
toall|a *f* towel. **~ero** *m* towel-rail
tobillo *m* ankle
tobogán *m* slide; (para la nieve) toboggan
tocadiscos *m invar* record-player
toca|do *a* touched Ⓘ. ● *m* headdress. **~dor** *m* dressing-table. **~nte** *a*. **en lo ~nte a** with regard to. **~r** [7] *vt* touch; (palpar) feel; (Mus) play; ring <*timbre*>; (mencionar) touch on; <*barco*> stop at. ● *vi* ring; (corresponder a uno). **te ~ a ti** it's your turn. **en lo que ~ a** as for. □ **~rse** *vpr* touch; <*personas*>; touch each other
tocayo *m* namesake
tocino *m* bacon
tocólogo *m* obstetrician
todavía *adv* still; (con negativos) yet. **~ no** not yet

todo, toda

● *adjetivo*

....➤ (la totalidad) all. **~ el vino** all the wine. **~s los edificios** all the buildings. **~ ese dinero** all that money. **~ el mundo** everyone. (como adv) **está toda sucia** it's all dirty

....➤ (entero) whole. **~ el día** the whole day, all day. **toda su familia** his whole family. **~ el tiempo** the whole time, all the time

....➤ (cada, cualquiera) every. **~ tipo de coche** every type of car. **~s los días** every day

....➤ (enfático) **a toda velocidad** at top speed. **es ~ un caballero** he's a real gentleman

....➤ (en locuciones) **ante ~** above all. **a ~ esto** meanwhile. **con ~** even so. **del ~** totally. **~ lo contrario** quite the opposite

⇨ Para expresiones como **todo recto, todo seguido** etc., ver bajo el respectivo adjetivo

● *pronombre*

....➤ all; (todas las cosas) everything. **eso es ~** that's all. **lo perdieron ~** they lost everything. **quiere comprar ~** he wants to buy everything

····➤ **todos, todas** all; (todo el mundo) everyone. **los compró ~s** he bought them all, he bought all of them. **~s queríamos ir** we all wanted to go. **vinieron ~s** everyone came

● *nombre masculino*

····➤ **el/un ~** the/a whole

toldo *m* awning

tolera|ncia *f* tolerance. **~nte** *a* tolerant. **~r** *vt* tolerate

toma *f* taking; (de universidad etc) occupation; (Med) dose; (de agua) intake; (Elec) socket; (LAm, acequia) irrigation channel. ● *int* well!, fancy that! **~ de corriente** power point. **~dura** *f*. **~dura de pelo** hoax. **~r** *vt* take; catch <*autobús, tren*>; occupy <*universidad etc*>; (beber) drink, have; (comer) eat, have. ● *vi* take; (esp LAm, beber) drink; (LAm, dirigirse) go. **~r a bien** take well. **~r a mal** take badly. **~r en serio** take seriously. **~rla con uno** pick on s.o. **~r por** take for. **~ y daca** give and take. **¿qué va a ~r?** what would you like? ◻ **~rse** *vpr* take; (beber) drink, have; (comer) eat, have

tomate *m* tomato

tomillo *m* thyme

tomo *m* volume

ton: **sin ~ ni son** without rhyme or reason

tonad|a *f* tune; (canción) popular song; (LAm, acento) accent. **~illa** *f* tune

tonel *m* barrel. **~ada** *f* ton. **~aje** *m* tonnage

tónic|a *f* trend; (bebida) tonic water. **~o** *a* tonic; <*sílaba*> stressed. ● *m* tonic

tonificar [7] *vt* invigorate

tono *m* tone; (Mus, modo) key; (color) shade

tont|ería *f* silliness; (cosa) silly thing; (dicho) silly remark. **dejarse de ~erías** stop fooling around. **~o** *a* silly. ● *m* fool, idiot; (payaso) clown. **hacer el ~o** act the fool. **hacerse el ~o** act dumb

topacio *m* topaz

topar *vi*. **~ con** run into

tope *a* maximum. ● *m* end; (de tren) buffer; (Mex, Auto) speed bump. **hasta los ~s** crammed full. **ir a ~** go flat out

tópico *a* trite. **de uso ~** (Med) for external use only. ● *m* cliché

topo *m* mole

topogr|afía *f* topography. **~áfico** *a* topographical

toque *m* touch; (sonido) sound; (de campana) peal; (de reloj) stroke. **~ de queda** curfew. **dar los últimos ~s a** put the finishing touches to. **~tear** *vt* fiddle with

toquilla *f* shawl

tórax *m invar* thorax

torcer [2 & 9] *vt* twist; (doblar) bend; wring out <*ropa*>. ● *vi* turn. ◻ **~se** *vpr* twist

tordo *a* dapple grey. ● *m* thrush

tore|ar *vt* fight; (evitar) dodge. ● *vi* fight (bulls). **~o** *m* bullfighting. **~ro** *m* bullfighter

torment|a *f* storm. **~o** *m* torture. **~oso** *a* stormy

tornado *m* tornado

tornasolado *a* irridescent

torneo *m* tournament

tornillo *m* screw

torniquete *m* (Med) tourniquet; (entrada) turnstile

torno *m* lathe; (de alfarero) wheel. **en ~ a** around

toro *m* bull. **los ~s** *mpl* bullfighting. **ir a los ~s** go to a bullfight

toronja *f* (LAm) grapefruit

torpe *a* clumsy; (estúpido) stupid

torpedo *m* torpedo

torpeza *f* clumsiness; (de inteligencia) slowness. **una ~** a blunder

torre *f* tower; (en ajedrez) castle, rook; (Elec) pylon; (edificio) tower block (Brit), apartment block (Amer)

torren|cial *a* torrential. **~te** *m* torrent; (circulatorio) bloodstream; (fig) flood

tórrido *a* torrid

torsión *f* twisting

torso *m* torso

torta *f* tart; (LAm, de verduras) pie; (golpe) slap, punch; (Mex, bocadillo) filled roll. **no entender ni ~** not understand a thing. **~zo** *m* slap, punch. **pegarse un ~zo** have a bad accident

tortícolis *f* stiff neck

tortilla *f* omelette; (Mex, de maíz) tortilla

tórtola *f* turtle-dove

tortuga *f* tortoise; (de mar) turtle

tortuoso *a* winding; (fig) devious

tortura *f* torture. **~r** *vt* torture

tos *f* cough. **~ ferina** whooping cough

tosco *a* crude; <*persona*> coarse

toser *vi* cough

tost|ada *f* piece of toast. **~adas** *fpl* toast; (Mex, de tortilla) fried tortillas. **~ado** *a* <*pan*> toasted; <*café*> roasted; <*persona, color*> tanned. **~ar** *vt* toast <*pan*>; roast <*café*>; tan <*piel*>

total *a* total. ● *adv* after all. **~ que** so, to cut a long story short. ● *m* total; (totalidad) whole. **~idad** *f* whole. **~itario** *a* totalitarian. **~izar** [10] *vt* total

tóxico *a* toxic

toxi|cómano *m* drug addict. **~na** *f* toxin

tozudo *a* stubborn

traba *f* catch; (fig, obstáculo) obstacle. **poner ~s a** hinder

trabaj|ador *a* hard-working. ● *m* worker. **~ar** *vt* work; knead <*masa*>. ● *vi* work (**de** as); <*actor*> act. **¿en qué ~as?** what do you do? **~o** *m* work. **costar ~o** be difficult. **~oso** *a* hard

trabalenguas *m invar* tongue-twister

traba|r *vt* (sujetar) fasten; (unir) join; (entablar) strike up. □ **~rse** *vpr* get stuck. **trabársele la lengua** get tongue-tied

trácala *m* (Mex) cheat. ● *f* (Mex) trick

tracción *f* traction

tractor *m* tractor

tradici|ón *f* tradition. **~onal** *a* traditional

traduc|ción *f* translation. **~ir** [47] *vt* translate (**a** into). **~tor** *m* translator

traer [41] *vt* bring; (llevar) carry; (causar) cause. **traérselas** be difficult

trafica|nte *m & f* dealer. **~r** [7] *vi* deal

tráfico *m* traffic; (Com) trade

traga|luz *m* skylight. **~perras** *f invar* slot-machine. **~r** [12] *vt* swallow; (comer mucho) devour; (soportar) put up with. **no lo trago** I can't stand him. □ **~rse** *vpr* swallow; (fig) swallow up

tragedia *f* tragedy

trágico *a* tragic. ● *m* tragedian

trag|o *m* swallow, gulp; (pequeña porción) sip; (fig, disgusto) blow; (LAm, bebida alcohólica) drink. **echar(se) un ~o** have a drink. **~ón** *a* greedy. ● *m* glutton.

trai|ción *f* treachery; (Pol) treason. **~cionar** *vt* betray. **~cionero** *a* treacherous. **~dor** *a* treacherous. ● *m* traitor

traigo *vb* ⇒TRAER

traje *m* dress; (de hombre) suit. **~ de baño** swimming-costume. **~ de etiqueta, ~ de noche** evening dress. ● *vb* ⇒TRAER

traj|ín *m* coming and going; (ajetreo) hustle and bustle. **~inar** *vi* bustle about

trama *f* weft; (fig, argumento) plot. **~r** *vt* weave; (fig) plot

tramitar *vt* negotiate

trámite *m* step. **~s** *mpl* procedure

tramo *m* (parte) section; (de escalera) flight

tramp|a *f* trap; (fig) trick. **hacer ~a** cheat. **~illa** *f* trapdoor

trampolín *m* trampoline; (de piscina) springboard; (rígido) diving board

tramposo *a* cheating. ● *m* cheat

tranca *f* bar. **~r** *vt* bar

trance *m* moment; (hipnótico etc) trance

tranco *m* stride

tranquil|idad *f* peace; (de espíritu) peace of mind. **con ~** calmly. **~izar** [10] *vt* calm down; (reconfortar) reassure. **~o** *a* calm; <*lugar*> quiet; <*conciencia*> clear. **estáte ~o** don't worry

transa|cción *f* transaction; (acuerdo) settlement. **~r** *vi* (LAm) compromise

transatlántico *a* transatlantic. ● *m* (ocean) liner

transbord|ador *m* ferry. **~ar** *vt* transfer. **~o** *m* transfer. **hacer ~o** change (**en** at)

transcri|bir (*pp* **transcrito**) *vt* transcribe. **~pción** *f* transcription

transcur|rir *vi* pass. **~so** *m* course

transeúnte *m* & *f* passer-by

transfer|encia *f* transfer. **~ir** [4] *vt* transfer

transforma|ción *f* transformation. **~dor** *m* transformer. **~r** *vt* transform

transfusión *f* transfusion

transgre|dir *vt* transgress. **~sión** *f* transgression

transición *f* transition

transigir [14] *vi* give in, compromise

transistor *m* transistor

transita|ble *a* passable. **~r** *vi* go

transitivo *a* transitive

tránsito *m* transit; (tráfico) traffic

transitorio *a* transitory

transmi|sión *f* transmission; (radio, TV) broadcast **~sor** *m* transmitter. **~sora** *f* broadcasting station. **~tir** *vt* transmit; (radio, TV) broadcast; (fig) pass on

transparen|cia *f* transparency. **~tar** *vt* show. **~te** *a* transparent

transpira|ción *f* perspiration. **~r** *vi* transpire; (sudar) sweat

transport|ar *vt* transport. **~e** *m* transport. **empresa** *f* **de ~es** removals company

transversal *a* transverse. **una calle ~ a la Gran Vía** a street which crosses the Gran Vía

tranvía *m* tram

trapear *vt* (LAm) mop

trapecio *m* trapeze; (Math) trapezium

trapo *m* cloth. **~s** *mpl* rags; (Ⓘ, ropa) clothes. **a todo ~** out of control

tráquea *f* windpipe, trachea

traquete|ar *vt* bang, rattle; <*persona*> rush around. **~o** *m* banging, rattle

tras *prep* after; (detrás) behind

trascende|ncia *f* significance; (alcance) implication. **~ntal** *a* transcendental; (importante) important. **~r** [1] *vi* (saberse) become known; (extenderse) spread

trasero *a* back, rear. ● *m* (Anat) bottom

trasfondo *m* background

traslad|ar *vt* move; transfer <*empleado etc*>; (aplazar) postpone. **~o** *m* transfer; (copia) copy. (mudanza) removal. **dar ~o** notify

trasl|úcido *a* translucent. □ **~ucirse** [11] *vpr* be translucent; (dejarse ver) show through; (fig, revelarse) be revealed. **~uz** *m*. **al ~uz** against the light

trasmano. **a ~** out of the way

trasnochar *vt* (acostarse tarde) go to bed late; (no acostarse) stay up all night; (no dormir) be unable to sleep

traspas|ar *vt* go through; (transferir) transfer; go beyond <*límite*>. **se ~a** for sale. **~o** *m* transfer

traspié *m* trip; (fig) slip. **dar un ~** stumble; (fig) slip up

trasplant|ar *vt* transplant. **~e** *m* transplant

trastada *f* prank; (jugada) dirty trick

traste *m* fret. **dar al ~ con** ruin. **ir al ~** fall through. **~s** *mpl* (Mex) junk

trastero *m* storeroom

trasto *m* piece of junk. ● **~s** *mpl* junk

trastorn|ado *a* mad. **~ar** *vt* upset; (volver loco) drive mad; (fig, Ⓘ, gustar mucho) delight. □ **~arse** *vpr* get upset; (volverse loco) go mad. **~o** *m* (incl Med) upset; (Pol) disturbance; (fig) confusion

trat|able *a* friendly; (Med) treatable. **~ado** *m* treatise; (acuerdo) treaty. **~amiento** *m* treatment; (título) title. **~ante** *m & f* dealer. **~ar** *vt* (incl Med) treat; deal with <*asunto etc*>; (manejar) handle; (de tú, de Vd) address (**de** as). ● *vi* deal (with). **~ar con** have to do with; (Com) deal in. **~ar de** be about; (intentar) try. **¿de qué se ~a?** what's it about? **~o** *m* treatment; (acuerdo) agreement; (título) title; (relación) relationship. **¡~o hecho!** agreed! **~os** *mpl* dealings

traum|a *m* trauma. **~ático** *a* traumatic

través: **a ~ de** through; (de lado a lado) crossways

travesaño *m* crossbeam; (de portería) crossbar

travesía *f* crossing; (calle) side street

trav|esura *f* prank. **~ieso** *a* <*niño*> mischievous, naughty

trayecto *m* (tramo) stretch; (ruta) route; (viaje) journey. **~ria** *f* trajectory; (fig) course

traz|a *f* (aspecto) appearance. **~as** *fpl* signs. **~ado** *m* plan. **~ar** [10] *vt* draw; (bosquejar) sketch. **~o** *m* stroke; (línea) line

trébol *m* clover. **~es** *mpl* (en naipes) clubs

trece *a & m* thirteen

trecho *m* stretch; (distancia) distance; (tiempo) while. **a ~s** here and there. **de ~ en ~** at intervals

tregua *f* truce; (fig) respite

treinta *a & m* thirty

tremendo *a* terrible; (extraordinario) terrific

tren *m* train. **~ de aterrizaje** landing gear. **~ de vida** lifestyle

tren|cilla *f* braid. **~za** *f* braid; (de pelo) plait. **~zar** [10] *vt* plait

trepa|dor *a* climbing. **~dora** *f* climber. **~r** *vt/i* climb. □ **~rse** *vpr*. **~rse a** climb <*árbol*>; climb onto <*silla etc*>

tres *a & m* three. **~cientos** *a & m* three hundred. **~illo** *m* three-piece suite; (Mus) triplet

treta *f* trick

tri|angular *a* triangular. **~ángulo** *m* triangle

trib|al *a* tribal. **~u** *f* tribe

tribuna *f* platform; (de espectadores) stand. **~l** *m* court; (de examen etc) board; (fig) tribunal

tribut|ar *vt* pay. **~o** *m* tribute; (impuesto) tax

triciclo *m* tricycle

tricolor *a* three-coloured

tricotar *vt/i* knit

tridimensional *a* three-dimensional

trig|al *m* wheat field. **~o** *m* wheat

trigésimo *a* thirtieth

trigueño *a* olive-skinned; <*pelo*> dark blonde

trilla|do *a* (fig, manoseado) trite; (fig, conocido) well-known. **~r** *vt* thresh

trilogía *f* trilogy

trimestr|al *a* quarterly. **~e** *m* quarter; (Escol, Univ) term

trinar *vi* warble. **estar que trina** be furious

trinchar *vt* carve

trinchera *f* ditch; (Mil) trench; (abrigo) trench coat

trineo *m* sledge

trinidad *f* trinity

trino *m* warble

trío *m* trio

tripa *f* intestine; (fig, vientre) tummy, belly. **~s** *fpl* (de máquina etc) parts, workings. **revolver las ~s** turn one's stomach

tripl|e *a* triple. ● *m*. **el ~e (de)** three times as much (as). **~icado** *a*. **por ~icado** in triplicate. **~icar** [7] *vt* treble

tripula|ción *f* crew. **~nte** *m & f* member of the crew. **~r** *vt* man

tris *m*. **estar en un ~** be on the point of

triste *a* sad; <*paisaje, tiempo etc*> gloomy; (fig, insignificante) miserable. **~za** *f* sadness

triturar *vt* crush

triunf|al *a* triumphal. **~ante** *a* triumphant. **~ar** *vi* triumph (**de, sobre** over). **~o** *m* triumph

trivial *a* trivial. **~idad** *f* triviality

trizas. **hacer algo ~** smash sth to pieces. **hacerse ~** smash

trocear *vt* cut up, chop

trocha *f* narrow path; (LAm, rail) gauge

trofeo *m* trophy

tromba *f* whirlwind; (marina) waterspout. **~ de agua** heavy downpour

trombón *m* trombone

trombosis *f invar* thrombosis

trompa *f* horn; (de orquesta) French horn; (de elefante) trunk; (hocico) snout; (Anat) tube. **coger una ~** [I] get drunk. **~zo** *m* bump

trompet|a *f* trumpet; (músico) trumpet player; (Mil) trumpeter. **~illa** *f* ear-trumpet

trompo *m* (juguete) (spinning) top

tronar *vt* (Mex) shoot. ● *vi* thunder

tronchar *vt* bring down; (fig) cut short. **~se de risa** laugh a lot

tronco *m* trunk. **dormir como un ~** sleep like a log

trono *m* throne

trop|a *f* troops. **~el** *m* mob

tropez|ar [1 & 10] *vi* trip; (fig) slip up. **~ar con** run into. **~ón** *m* stumble; (fig) slip

tropical *a* tropical

trópico *a* tropical. ● *m* tropic

tropiezo *m* slip; (desgracia) hitch

trot|ar *vi* trot. **~e** *m* trot; (fig) toing and froing. **al ~e** at a trot; (de prisa) in a rush. **de mucho ~e** hard-wearing

trozo *m* piece, bit. **a ~s** in bits

trucha *f* trout

truco *m* trick. **coger el ~** get the knack

trueno *m* thunder; (estampido) bang

trueque *m* exchange; (Com) barter

trufa *f* truffle

truhán *m* rogue

truncar [7] *vt* truncate; (fig) cut short

tu *a* your

tú *pron* you

tuba *f* tuba

tubérculo *m* tuber

tuberculosis *f* tuberculosis

tub|ería *f* pipes; (oleoducto etc) pipeline. **~o** *m* tube. **~o de ensayo** test tube. **~o de escape** (Auto) exhaust (pipe). **~ular** *a* tubular

tuerca *f* nut

tuerto *a* one-eyed, blind in one eye. ● *m* one-eyed person

tuétano *m* marrow; (fig) heart. **hasta los ~s** completely

tufo *m* stench

tugurio *m* hovel

tul *m* tulle

tulipán *m* tulip

tulli|do *a* paralysed. **~r** [22] *vt* cripple

tumba *f* grave, tomb

tumb|ar *vt* knock over, knock down *<estructura>*; (fig, 🅘, en examen) fail. ◻ **~arse** *vpr* lie down. **~o** *m* jolt. **dar un ~o** tumble. **~ona** *f* sun lounger

tumor *m* tumour

tumulto *m* turmoil; (Pol) riot

tuna *f* prickly pear; (de estudiantes) student band

tunante *m & f* rogue

túnel *m* tunnel

túnica *f* tunic

tupé *m* toupee; (fig) nerve

tupido *a* thick

turba *f* peat; (muchedumbre) mob

turbado *a* upset

turbante *m* turban

turbar *vt* upset; (molestar) disturb. ◻ **~se** *vpr* be upset

turbina *f* turbine

turbi|o *a* cloudy; *<vista>* blurred; *<asunto etc>* shady. **~ón** *m* squall

turbulen|cia *f* turbulence; (disturbio) disturbance. **~te** *a* turbulent

turco *a* Turkish. ● *m* Turk; (lengua) Turkish

tur|ismo *m* tourism; (coche) car. **hacer ~** travel around. **~ista** *m & f* tourist. **~ístico** *a* tourist

turn|arse *vpr* take turns (**para** to). **∼o** *m* turn; (de trabajo) shift. **de ∼** on duty

turquesa *f* turquoise

Turquía *f* Turkey

turrón *m* nougat

tutear *vt* address as *tú*. ◻ **∼se** *vpr* be on familiar terms

tutela *f* (Jurid) guardianship; (fig) protection

tutor *m* guardian; (Escol) form master

tuve *vb* ⇒TENER

tuyo *a & pron* yours. **un amigo ∼** a friend of yours

Uu

u *conj* or

ubic|ar *vt* (LAm) place; (localizar) find. ◻ **∼arse** *vpr* (LAm) be situated; (orientarse) find one's way around

ubre *f* udder

Ud. *abrev* (**Usted**) you

uf *int* phew!; (de repugnancia) ugh!

ufan|arse *vpr* be proud (**con, de** of); (jactarse) boast (**con, de** about). **∼o** *a* proud

úlcera *f* ulcer

ulterior *a* later; *<lugar>* further

últimamente *adv* (recientemente) recently; (finalmente) finally

ultim|ar *vt* complete; (LAm, matar) kill. **∼átum** *m* ultimatum

último *a* last; (más reciente) latest; (más lejano) furthest; (más alto) top; (más bajo) bottom; (definitivo) final. ● *m* last one. **estar en las últimas** be on one's last legs; (sin dinero) be down to one's last penny. **por ∼** finally. **vestido a la última** dressed in the latest fashion

ultra *a* ultra, extreme

ultraj|ante *a* offensive. **∼e** *m* insult, outrage

ultramar *m*. **de ∼** overseas; *<productos>* foreign. **∼inos** *mpl* groceries. **tienda de ∼inos** grocer's (shop) (Brit), grocery store (Amer)

ultranza. **a ∼** (con decisión) decisively; (extremo) out-and-out

ultravioleta *a invar* ultraviolet

umbilical *a* umbilical

umbral *m* threshold

un, una

● *artículo indefinido*

! The masculine article **un** is also used before feminine nouns which begin with stressed **a** or **ha**, e.g. **un alma piadosa, un hada madrina**

····➤ (en sing) a; (antes de sonido vocálico) an. **un perro** a dog. **una hora** an hour

····➤ **unos, unas** (cantidad incierta) some. **compré ∼os libros** I bought some books. (cantidad cierta) **tiene ∼os ojos preciosos** she has beautiful eyes. **tiene ∼os hijos muy buenos** her children are very good. (en aproximaciones) about. **en ∼as 3 horas** in about 3 hours

⇨ For further information see **uno**

un|ánime *a* unanimous. **~animidad** *f* unanimity

undécimo *a* eleventh

ungüento *m* ointment

únic|amente *adv* only. **~o** *a* only; (fig, incomparable) unique

unicornio *m* unicorn

unid|ad *f* unit; (cualidad) unity. **~ad de disco** disk drive. **~o** *a* united

unifica|ción *f* unification. **~r** [7] *vt* unite, unify

uniform|ar *vt* standardize. **~e** *a* & *m* uniform. **~idad** *f* uniformity

unilateral *a* unilateral

uni|ón *f* union; (cualidad) unity; (Tec) joint. **~r** *vt* join; mix *<líquidos>*. □ **~rse** *vpr* join together; *<caminos>* converge; *<compañías>* merge

unísono *m* unison. **al ~** in unison

univers|al *a* universal. **~idad** *f* university. **~itario** *a* university. **~o** *m* universe

uno, una

● *adjetivo*

Note that **uno** becomes **un** before masculine nouns

····➤ one. **una peseta** one peseta. **un dólar** one dollar. **ni una persona** not one person, not a single person. **treinta y un años** thirty-one years

● *pronombre*

····➤ one. **~ es mío** one (of them) is mine. **es la una** it's one o'clock. **se ayudan el ~ al otro** they help one another, they help each other. **lo que sienten el ~ por el otro** what they feel for each other

····➤ ([I], alguien) someone. **le pregunté a ~** I asked someone

····➤ **unos, unas** some. **no tenía vasos así es que le presté ~s** she didn't have any glasses so I lent her some. **a ~s les gusta, a otros no** some like it, others don't. **los ~s a los otros** one another, each other.

····➤ (impersonal) you. **~ no sabe qué decir** you don't know what to say

untar *vt* grease; (cubrir) spread; (fig, [I], sobornar) bribe

uña *f* nail; (de animal) claw; (casco) hoof

uranio *m* uranium

Urano *m* Uranus

urban|idad *f* politeness. **~ismo** *m* town planning. **~ización** *f* development. **~izar** [10] *vt* develop. **~o** *a* urban

urbe *f* big city

urdir *vt* (fig) plot

urg|encia *f* urgency; (emergencia) emergency. **~ente** *a* urgent; *<carta>* express. **~ir** [14] *vi* be urgent.

urinario *m* urinal

urna *f* urn; (Pol) ballot box

urraca *f* magpie

URSS *abrev* (Historia) (**Unión de Repúblicas Socialistas Soviéticas**) USSR

Uruguay *m*. **el ~** Uruguay

uruguayo *a* & *m* Uruguayan

us|ado *a* (con estar) used; *<ropa etc>* worn; (con ser) secondhand. **~ar** *vt* use; (llevar) wear. □ **~arse** *vpr* (LAm) be in fashion. **~o** *m* use; (costumbre) custom. **al ~o de** in the style of

usted *pron* you. **~es** you

usual *a* usual
usuario *a* user
usur|a *f* usury. **~ero** *m* usurer
usurpar *vt* usurp
utensilio *m* utensil; (herramienta) tool
útero *m* womb, uterus
útil *a* useful. **~es** *mpl* implements; (equipo) equipment
utili|dad *f* usefulness. **~dades** *fpl* (LAm) profits. **~zación** *f* use, utilization. **~zar** [10] *vt* use, utilize
utopía *f* Utopia
uva *f* grape. **~ pasa** raisin. **mala ~** bad mood

Vv

vaca *f* cow. **carne de ~** beef
vacaciones *fpl* holiday(s), vacation(s) (Amer). **de ~** on holiday, on vacation (Amer)
vacante *a* vacant. ● *f* vacancy
vaciar [20] *vt* empty; (ahuecar) hollow out; (en molde) cast
vacila|ción *f* hesitation. **~nte** *a* unsteady; (fig) hesitant. **~r** *vi* hesitate (🅃, bromear) tease; (LAm, divertirse) have fun
vacío *a* empty; (frívolo) frivolous. ● *m* empty space; (estado) emptiness; (en física) vacuum; (fig) void
vacuna *f* vaccine. **~ción** *f* vaccination. **~r** *vt* vaccinate
vacuno *a* bovine
vad|ear *vt* ford. **~o** *m* ford
vaga|bundear *vi* wander. **~bundo** *a* vagrant; <perro> stray. **niño ~bundo** street urchin. ● *m* tramp, vagrant. **~ncia** *f* vagrancy; (fig) laziness. **~r** [12] *vi* wander (about)
vagina *f* vagina
vago *a* vague; (holgazán) lazy. ● *m* layabout
vag|ón *m* coach, carriage; (de mercancías) wagon. **~ón restaurante** dining-car. **~oneta** *f* small freight wagon; (Mex, para pasajeros) van
vaho *m* breath; (vapor) steam. **~s** *mpl* inhalation
vain|a *f* sheath; (Bot) pod. **~illa** *f* vanilla
vaiv|én *m* swinging; (de tren etc) rocking. **~enes** *mpl* (fig, de suerte) swings
vajilla *f* dishes, crockery
vale *m* voucher; (pagaré) IOU. **~dero** *a* valid
valenciano *a* from Valencia
valentía *f* bravery, courage
valer [42] *vt* be worth; (costar) cost; (fig, significar) mean. ● *vi* be worth; (costar) cost; (servir) be of use; (ser valedero) be valid; (estar permitido) be allowed. **~ la pena** be worthwhile, be worth it. **¿cuánto vale?** how much is it? **no ~ para nada** be useless. **eso no me vale** (Mex, 🅃) I don't give a damn about that. **¡vale!** all right!, OK! 🅃
valeroso *a* courageous
valgo *vb* ⇨ VALER
valía *f* worth
validez *f* validity. **dar ~ a** validate
válido *a* valid
valiente *a* brave; (en sentido irónico) fine. ● *m* brave person
valija *f* suitcase. **~ diplomática** diplomatic bag
valioso *a* valuable

valla *f* fence; (en atletismo) hurdle

valle *m* valley

valor *m* value, worth; (coraje) courage. **objetos** *mpl* **de ~** valuables. **sin ~** worthless. **~es** *mpl* securities. **~ación** *f* valuation. **~ar** *vt* value

vals *m invar* waltz

válvula *f* valve

vampiro *m* vampire

vanagloriarse *vpr* boast

vandalismo *m* vandalism

vándalo *m & f* vandal

vanguardia *f* vanguard. **de ~** (en arte, música etc) avant-garde

vani|dad *f* vanity. **~doso** *a* vain. **~o** *a* vain; (inútil) futile; <*palabras*> empty. **en ~** in vain

vapor *m* steam, vapour; (Naut) steamer. **al ~** (Culin) steamed. **~izador** *m* vaporizer. **~izar** [10] vaporize

vaquer|o *m* cowherd, cowboy. **~os** *mpl* jeans

vara *f* stick; (de autoridad) staff (medida) yard

varar *vi* run aground

varia|ble *a & f* variable. **~ción** *f* variation. **~do** *a* varied. **~nte** *f* variant; (Auto) by-pass. **~ntes** *fpl* hors d'oeuvres. **~r** [20] *vt* change; (dar variedad a) vary. ● *vi* vary; (cambiar) change

varicela *f* chickenpox

variedad *f* variety

varilla *f* stick; (de metal) rod

varios *a* several

varita *f* wand

variz *f* (*pl* **varices**, (LAm) **várices**) varicose vein

var|ón *a* male. ● *m* man; (niño) boy. **~onil** *a* manly

vasco *a & m* Basque

vaselina *f* Vaseline (P), petroleum jelly

vasija *f* vessel, pot

vaso *m* glass; (Anat) vessel

vástago *m* shoot; (descendiente) descendant

vasto *a* vast

vaticin|ar *vt* forecast. **~io** *m* prediction, forecast

vatio *m* watt

vaya *vb* ⇒IR

Vd. *abrev* (**Usted**) you

vecin|al *a* local. **~dad** *f* neighbourhood; (vecinos) residents; (Mex, edificio) tenement house. **~dario** *m* neighbourhood; (vecinos) residents. **~o** *a* neighbouring. ● *m* neighbour; (de barrio, edificio) resident

veda *f* close season. **~do** *m* reserve. **~do de caza** game reserve. **~r** *vt* prohibit

vega *f* fertile plain

vegeta|ción *f* vegetation. **~l** *a & m* plant, vegetable. **~r** *vi* grow; <*persona*> vegetate. **~riano** *a & m* vegetarian

vehemente *a* vehement

vehículo *m* vehicle

veinte *a & m* twenty

veinti|cinco *a & m* twenty-five. **~cuatro** *a & m* twenty-four. **~dós** *a & m* twenty-two. **~nueve** *a & m* twenty-nine; **~ocho** *a & m* twenty-eight. **~séis** *a & m* twenty-six. **~siete** *a & m* twenty-seven. **~trés** *a & m* twenty-three. **~uno** *a & m* (*delante de nombre masculino* **veintiún**) twenty-one

vejar *vt* ill-treat

veje|storio *m* old crock; (LAm, cosa) old relic. **~z** *f* old age

vejiga *f* bladder

vela *f* (Naut) sail; (de cera) candle; (vigilia) vigil. **pasar la noche en ~** have a sleepless night

velada *f* evening

vela|do *a* veiled; (Foto) exposed. **~r** *vt* watch over; hold a wake over <*difunto*>; (encubrir) veil; (Foto) expose. ● *vi* stay awake. **~r por** look after. □ **~rse** *vpr* (Foto) get exposed

velero *m* sailing-ship

veleta *f* weather vane

vell|o *m* hair; (pelusa) down. **~ón** *m* fleece

velo *m* veil

veloc|idad *f* speed; (Auto, Mec) gear. **a toda ~idad** at full speed. **~ímetro** *m* speedometer. **~ista** *m & f* sprinter

velódromo *m* cycle-track

veloz *a* fast, quick

vena *f* vein; (en madera) grain. **estar de/en ~** be in the mood

venado *m* deer; (Culin) venison

vencedor *a* winning. ● *m* winner

venc|er [9] *vt* defeat; (superar) overcome. ● *vi* win; <*pasaporte*> expire. □ **~erse** *vpr* collapse; (LAm, pasaporte) expire. **~ido** *a* beaten; <*pasaporte*> expired; (Com, atrasado) in arrears. **darse por ~ido** give up. **~imiento** *m* due date; (de pasaporte) expiry date

venda *f* bandage. **~je** *m* dressing. **~r** *vt* bandage

vendaval *m* gale

vende|dor *a* selling. ● *m* seller; (en tienda) salesperson. **~dor ambulante** pedlar. **~r** *vt* sell. **se ~** for sale. □ **~rse** *vpr* <*persona*> sell out

vendimia *f* grape harvest

veneciano *a* Venetian

veneno *m* poison; (malevolencia) venom. **~so** *a* poisonous

venera|ble *a* venerable. **~ción** *f* reverence. **~r** *vt* revere

venéreo *a* venereal

venezolano *a & m* Venezuelan

Venezuela *f* Venezuela

venga|nza *f* revenge. **~r** [12] *vt* avenge. □ **~rse** *vpr* take revenge (**de, por** for) (**en** on). **~tivo** *a* vindictive

vengo *vb* ⇒VENIR

venia *f* (permiso) permission. **~l** *a* venial

veni|da *f* arrival; (vuelta) return. **~dero** *a* coming. **~r** [53] *vi* come. **~r bien** suit. **la semana que viene** next week. **¡venga!** come on!

venta *f* sale; (posada) inn. **en ~** for sale

ventaj|a *f* advantage. **~oso** *a* advantageous

ventan|a *f* (inc informática) window; (de la nariz) nostril. **~illa** *f* window

ventarrón *m* 🅸 strong wind

ventila|ción *f* ventilation. **~dor** *m* fan. **~r** *vt* air

vent|isca *f* blizzard. **~olera** *f* gust of wind. **~osa** *f* sucker. **~osidad** *f* wind, flatulence. **~oso** *a* windy

ventrílocuo *m* ventriloquist

ventur|a *f* happiness; (suerte) luck. **a la ~a** with no fixed plan. **echar la buena ~a a uno** tell s.o.'s fortune. **por ~a** fortunately; (acaso) perhaps. **~oso** *a* happy, lucky

Venus *m* Venus

ver [43] *vt* see; watch <*televisión*>. ● *vi* see. **a mi modo de ~** in my view. **a ~** let's see. **dejarse ~** show. **no lo puedo ~** I can't stand him. **no tener nada que ~ con** have nothing to do with. **vamos a ~** let's see.

ya lo veo that's obvious. **ya ~emos** we'll see. □ **~se** *vpr* see o.s.; (encontrarse) find o.s.; <*dos personas*> meet; (LAm, parecer) look

veran|eante *m & f* holidaymaker, vacationer (Amer). **~ear** *vi* spend one's summer holiday. **~eo** *m*. **ir de ~eo** spend one's summer holiday. **lugar** *m* **de ~eo** summer resort. **~iego** *a* summer. **~o** *m* summer

vera|s. **de ~s** really; (verdadero) real. **~z** *a* truthful

verbal *a* verbal

verbena *f* (fiesta) fair; (baile) dance

verbo *m* verb. **~so** *a* verbose

verdad *f* truth. **¿~?** isn't it?, aren't they?, won't it? etc. **a decir ~** to tell the truth. **de ~** really. **~eramente** *adv* really. **~ero** *a* true; (fig) real

verd|e *a* green; <*fruta*> unripe; <*chiste*> dirty. ● *m* green; (hierba) grass. **~or** *m* greenness

verdugo *m* executioner; (fig) tyrant

verdu|lería *f* greengrocer's (shop). **~lero** *m* greengrocer

vereda *f* path; (LAm, acera) pavement (Brit), sidewalk (Amer)

veredicto *m* verdict

verg|onzoso *a* shameful; (tímido) shy. **~üenza** *f* shame; (bochorno) embarrassment. **¡es una ~üenza!** it's a disgrace! **me da ~üenza** I'm ashamed/embarrassed. **tener ~üenza** be ashamed/embarrassed

verídico *a* true

verifica|ción *f* verification. **~r** [7] *vt* check. □ **~rse** *vpr* take place; (resultar verdad) come true

verja *f* (cerca) railings; (puerta) iron gate

vermú *m*, **vermut** *m* vermouth

verosímil *a* likely; <*relato*> credible

verruga *f* wart

versa|do *a* versed. **~r** *vi*. **~ sobre** deal with

versátil *a* versatile; (fig) fickle

versión *f* version; (traducción) translation

verso *m* verse; (poema) poem

vértebra *f* vertebra

verte|dero *m* dump; (desagüe) drain **~r** [1] *vt* pour; (derramar) spill ● *vi* flow

vertical *a & f* vertical

vértice *f* vertex

vertiente *f* slope

vertiginoso *a* dizzy

vértigo *m* (Med) vertigo. **dar ~** make dizzy

vesícula *f* vesicle. **~ biliar** gall bladder

vespertino *a* evening

vestíbulo *m* hall; (de hotel, teatro) foyer

vestido *m* dress

vestigio *m* trace. **~s** *mpl* remains

vest|imenta *f* clothes. **~ir** [5] *vt* (llevar) wear; dress <*niño etc*>. ● *vi* dress. **~ir de** wear. □ **~irse** *vpr* get dressed. **~irse de** wear; (disfrazarse) dress up as. **~uario** *m* wardrobe; (en gimnasio etc) changing room (Brit), locker room (Amer)

vetar *vt* veto

veterano *a* veteran

veterinari|a *f* veterinary science. **~o** *a* veterinary. ● *m* vet 🄸, veterinary surgeon (Brit), veterinarian (Amer)

veto *m* veto

vez *f* time; (turno) turn. **a la ~** at the same time. **alguna ~** sometimes; (en preguntas) ever. **algunas veces**

sometimes. **a su ~** in turn. **a veces** sometimes. **cada ~** each time. **cada ~ más** more and more. **de una ~** in one go. **de una ~ para siempre** once and for all. **de ~ en cuando** from time to time. **dos veces** twice. **en ~ de** instead of. **érase una ~, había una ~** once upon a time there was. **otra ~** again. **pocas veces, rara ~** seldom. **una ~ (que)** once

vía *f* road; (Rail) line; (Anat) tract; (fig) way. **estar en ~s de** be in the process of. ● *prep* via. **~ aérea** by air. **~ de comunicación** means of communication. **~ férrea** railway (Brit), railroad (Amer). **~ rápida** fast lane

viab|ilidad *f* viability. **~le** *a* viable

viaducto *m* viaduct

viaj|ante *m & f* commercial traveller. **~ar** *vi* travel. **~e** *m* journey; (corto) trip. **~e de novios** honeymoon. **¡buen ~e!** have a good journey!. **estar de ~** be away. **salir de ~** go on a trip. **~ero** *m* traveller; (pasajero) passenger

víbora *f* viper

vibra|ción *f* vibration. **~nte** *a* vibrant. **~r** *vt/i* vibrate

vicario *m* vicar

viceversa *adv* vice versa

vici|ado *a* <*texto*> corrupt; <*aire*> stale. **~ar** *vt* corrupt; (estropear) spoil. **~o** *m* vice; (mala costumbre) bad habit. **~oso** *a* dissolute; <*círculo*> vicious

víctima *f* victim; (de un accidente) casualty

victori|a *f* victory. **~oso** *a* victorious

vid *f* vine

vida *f* life; (duración) lifetime. **¡~ mía!** my darling! **de por ~** for life. **en mi ~** never (in my life). **estar con ~** be still alive

vídeo *m*, (LAm) **video** *m* video; (cinta) videotape; (aparato) video recorder

videojuego *m* video game

vidri|era *f* stained glass window; (puerta) glass door; (LAm, escaparate) shop window. **~ería** *f* glass works. **~ero** *m* glazier. **~o** *m* glass; (LAm, en ventana) window pane. **limpiar los ~os** clean the windows. **~oso** *a* glassy

vieira *f* scallop

viejo *a* old. ● *m* old person

viene *vb* ⇒VENIR

viento *m* wind. **hacer ~** be windy

vientre *m* stomach; (cavidad) abdomen; (matriz) womb; (intestino) bowels; (de vasija etc) belly

viernes *m invar* Friday. **V~ Santo** Good Friday

viga *f* beam; (de metal) girder

vigen|cia *f* validity. **~te** *a* valid; <*ley*> in force. **entrar en ~cia** come into force

vigésimo *a* twentieth

vigía *f* watch-tower. ● *m & f* (persona) lookout

vigil|ancia *f* vigilance. **~ante** *a* vigilant. ● *m & f* security guard; (nocturno) watchman. **~ar** *vt* keep an eye on. ● *vi* be vigilant; <*vigía*> keep watch. **~ia** *f* vigil; (Relig) fasting

vigor *m* vigour; (vigencia) force. **entrar en ~** come into force. **~oso** *a* vigorous

vil *a* vile. **~eza** *f* vileness; (acción) vile deed

villa *f* (casa) villa; (Historia) town. **la V~** Madrid

villancico *m* (Christmas) carol

villano *a* villanous; (Historia) peasant

vilo. **en ~** in the air

vinagre *m* vinegar. **~ra** *f* vinegar bottle. **~ras** *fpl* cruet. **~ta** *f* vinaigrette

vincular *vt* bind

vínculo *m* tie, bond

vindicar [7] *vt* (rehabilitar) vindicate

vine *vb* ⇒VENIR

vinicult|or *m* wine-grower. **~ura** *f* wine growing

vino *m* wine. **~ de la casa** house wine. **~ de mesa** table wine. **~ tinto** red wine

viñ|a *f* vineyard. **~atero** *m* (LAm) wine-grower. **~edo** *m* vineyard

viola *f* viola

viola|ción *f* violation; (de una mujer) rape. **~r** *vt* violate; break *<ley>*; rape *<mujer>*

violen|cia *f* violence; (fuerza) force. □ **~tarse** *vpr* get embarrassed. **~to** *a* violent; (fig) awkward

violeta *a invar* & *f* violet

viol|ín *m* violin. ● *m & f* (músico) violinist. **~inista** *m & f* violinist. **~ón** *m* double bass. **~onc(h)elista** *m & f* cellist. **~onc(h)elo** *m* cello

vira|je *m* turn. **~r** *vt* turn. ● *vi* turn; (fig) change direction. **~r bruscamente** swerve

virg|en *a*. **ser ~en** be a virgin. ●*f* virgin. **~inal** *a* virginal. **~inidad** *f* virginity

Virgo *m* Virgo

viril *a* virile. **~idad** *f* virility

virtu|al *a* virtual. **~d** *f* virtue; (capacidad) power. **en ~d de** by virtue of. **~oso** *a* virtuous. ● *m* virtuoso

viruela *f* smallpox

virulento *a* virulent

virus *m invar* virus

visa *f* (LAm) visa. **~ado** *m* visa. **~r** *vt* endorse

vísceras *fpl* entrails

viscoso *a* viscous

visera *f* visor; (de gorra) peak

visib|ilidad *f* visibility. **~le** *a* visible

visillo *m* (cortina) net curtain

visi|ón *f* vision; (vista) sight. **~onario** *a* & *m* visionary

visita *f* visit; (visitante) visitor; (invitado) guest. **~nte** *m & f* visitor. **~r** *vt* visit

vislumbrar *vt* glimpse

viso *m* sheen; (aspecto) appearance

visón *m* mink

visor *m* viewfinder

víspera *f* day before, eve

vista *f* sight, vision; (aspecto, mirada) look; (panorama) view. **apartar la ~** look away. **a primera ~**, **a simple ~** at first sight. **con ~s a** with a view to. **en ~ de** in view of. **estar a la ~** be obvious. **hacer la ~ gorda** turn a blind eye. **perder la ~** lose one's sight. **tener a la ~** have in front of one. **volver la ~ atrás** look back. **~zo** *m* glance. **dar/echar un ~zo a** glance at

visto *a* seen; (poco original) common (considerado) considered. **~ que** since. **bien ~** acceptable. **está ~ que** it's obvious that. **mal ~** unacceptable. **por lo ~** apparently. ● *vb* ⇒VESTIR. **~ bueno** *m* approval. **~so** *a* colourful, bright

visual *a* visual. **campo ~** field of vision

vital *a* vital. **~icio** *a* life; *<cargo>* held for life. **~idad** *f* vitality

vitamina *f* vitamin

viticult|or *m* wine-grower. **~ura** *f* wine growing

vitorear *vt* cheer

vítreo *a* vitreous

vitrina *f* showcase; (en casa) glass cabinet; (LAm, escaparate) shop window

viud|a *f* widow. **~ez** *f* widowhood. **~o** *a* widowed. ● *m* widower

viva *m* cheer. **~cidad** *f* liveliness. **~mente** *adv* vividly. **~z** *a* lively

víveres *mpl* supplies

vivero *m* nursery; (de peces) hatchery; (de moluscos) bed

viveza *f* vividness; (de inteligencia) sharpness; (de carácter) liveliness

vívido *a* vivid

vividor *m* pleasure seeker

vivienda *f* housing; (casa) house; (piso) flat (Brit), apartment (esp Amer). **sin ~** homeless

viviente *a* living

vivificar [7] *vt* (animar) enliven

vivir *vt* live through. ● *vi* live; (estar vivo) be alive. **~ de** live on. **¡viva!** hurray! **¡viva el rey!** long live the king! ● *m* life. **de mal ~** dissolute

vivisección *f* vivisection

vivo *a* alive; (viviente) living; *<color>* bright; (listo) clever; (fig) lively. ● *m* sharp operator

vocab|lo *m* word. **~ulario** *m* vocabulary

vocación *f* vocation

vocal *a* vocal. ● *f* vowel. ● *m & f* member. **~ista** *m & f* vocalist

voce|ar *vt* call *<mercancías>*; (fig) proclaim; (Mex) page *<persona>*. ● *vi* shout. **~río** *m* shouting. **~ro** *m* (LAm) spokeperson

vociferar *vi* shout

vola|dor *a* flying. ● *m* rocket. **~ndas. en ~ndas** in the air. **~nte** *a* flying. ● *m* (Auto) steering-wheel; (nota) note; (rehilete) shuttlecock. **~r** [2] *vt* blow up. ● *vi* fly; (🅸, desaparecer) disappear

volátil *a* volatile

volcán *m* volcano. **~ico** *a* volcanic

volcar [2 & 7] *vt* knock over; (vaciar) empty out; turn over *<molde>*. ● *vi* overturn. □ **~se** *vpr* fall over; *<vehículo>* overturn; (fig) do one's utmost. **~se en** throw o.s. into

vóleibol *m*, (Mex) **volibol** *m* volleyball

voltaje *m* voltage

volte|ar *vt* turn over; (en el aire) toss; ring *<campanas>*; (LAm) turn over *<colchón etc>*. □ **~arse** *vpr* (LAm) turn around; *<carro>* overturn. **~reta** *f* somersault

voltio *m* volt

voluble *a* (fig) fickle

volum|en *m* volume. **~inoso** *a* voluminous

voluntad *f* will; (fuerza de voluntad) willpower; (deseo) wish; (intención) intention. **buena ~** goodwill. **mala ~** ill will

voluntario *a* voluntary. ● *m* volunteer

voluptuoso *a* voluptuous

volver [2] (*pp* **vuelto**) *vt* turn; (de arriba a abajo) turn over; (devolver) restore. ● *vi* return; (fig) revert. **~ a hacer algo** do sth again. **~ en sí** come round. □ **~se** *vpr* turn round; (hacerse) become

vomit|ar *vt* bring up. ● *vi* be sick, vomit. **~ivo** *a* disgusting

vómito *m* vomit; (acción) vomiting

voraz *a* voracious

vos *pron* (LAm) you. **~otros** *pron* you; (reflexivo) yourselves

vot|ación *f* voting; (voto) vote. **~ante** *m & f* voter. **~ar** *vt* vote for. ● *vi* vote (**por** for). **~o** *m* vote; (Relig) vow

voy *vb* ⇒IR

voz *f* voice; (rumor) rumour; (palabra) word. **~ pública** public opinion. **a media ~** softly. **a una ~** unanimously. **dar voces** shout. **en ~ alta** loudly

vuelco *m* upset. **el corazón me dio un ~** my heart missed a beat

vuelo *m* flight; (acción) flying; (de ropa) flare. **al ~** in flight; (fig) in passing

vuelta *f* turn; (curva) bend; (paseo) walk; (revolución) revolution; (regreso) return; (dinero) change. **a la ~** on one's return. **a la ~ de la esquina** round the corner. **dar la ~ al mundo** go round the world. **dar una ~** go for a walk. **estar de ~** be back

vuelvo *vb* ⇒VOLVER

vuestro *a* your. ● *pron* yours. **un amigo ~** a friend of yours

vulg|ar *a* vulgar; <*persona*> common. **~aridad** *f* vulgarity. **~arizar** [10] *vt* popularize. **~o** *m* common people

vulnerable *a* vulnerable

Ww

wáter /'(g)water/ *m* toilet

Web *m* /'(g)web/. **el ~** the Web

whisky /'(g)wiski/ *m* whisky

Xx

xenofobia *f* xenophobia

xilófono *m* xylophone

Yy

y *conj* and

ya *adv* already; (ahora) now; (con negativos) any more; (para afirmar) yes, sure; (en seguida) immediately; (pronto) soon. **~ mismo** (LAm) right away. ● *int* of course! **~ no** no longer. **~ que** since. ¡~, ~! oh sure!

yacaré *m* (LAm) alligator

yac|er [44] *vi* lie. **~imiento** *m* deposit; (de petróleo) oilfield

yanqui *m & f* American, Yank(ee)

yate *m* yacht

yegua *f* mare

yelmo *m* helmet

yema *f* (Bot) bud; (de huevo) yolk; (golosina) sweet. **~ del dedo** fingertip

yerba *f* (LAm) grass; (Med) herb

yergo *vb* ⇒ERGUIR

yermo *a* uninhabited; (no cultivable) barren. ● *m* wasteland

yerno *m* son-in-law

yerro *m* mistake. ● *vb* ⇒ERRAR

yeso *m* plaster; (mineral) gypsum

yo *pron* I. **~ mismo** myself. **¿quién, ~?** who, me? **soy ~** it's me

yodo *m* iodine

yoga *m* yoga

yogur *m* yog(h)urt

yuca *f* yucca

yugo *m* yoke

Yugoslavia *f* Yugoslavia

yugoslavo *a & m* Yugoslav

yunque *m* anvil

yunta *f* yoke

Zz

zafarrancho *m* (confusión) mess; (riña) quarrel

zafarse *vpr* escape; get out of <*obligación etc*>; (Mex, dislocarse) dislocate

zafiro *m* sapphire

zaga *f* rear; (en deportes) defence. **a la ~** behind

zaguán *m* hall

zaherir [4] *vt* hurt

zahorí *m* dowser

zaino *a* <*caballo*> chestnut; <*vaca*> black

zalamer|ía *f* flattery. **~o** *a* flattering. ● *m* flatterer

zamarra *f* (piel) sheepskin; (prenda) sheepskin jacket

zamarrear *vt* shake

zamba *f* South American dance

zambulli|da *f* dive; (baño) dip. □ **~rse** *vpr* dive

zamparse *vpr* gobble up

zanahoria *f* carrot

zancad|a *f* stride. **~illa** *f* trip. **hacer una ~illa a uno** trip s.o. up

zanc|o *m* stilt. **~udo** *a* long-legged; <*ave*> wading. ● *m* (LAm) mosquito

zanganear *vi* idle

zángano *m* drone. ● *m & f* (persona) idler

zangolotear *vt* shake. ● *vi* rattle; <*persona*> fidget

zanja *f* ditch; (para tuberías etc) trench. **~r** *vt* (fig) settle

zapat|ear *vi* tap with one's feet. **~ería** *f* shoe shop; (arte) shoemaking. **~ero** *m* shoemaker; (el que remienda zapatos) cobbler. **~illa** *f* slipper; (de deportes) trainer. **~ de ballet** ballet shoe. **~o** *m* shoe

zarand|a *f* sieve. **~ear** *vt* (sacudir) shake

zarcillo *m* earring

zarpa *f* paw

zarpar *vi* set sail, weigh anchor

zarza *f* bramble. **~mora** *f* blackberry

zarzuela *f* Spanish operetta

zigzag *m* zigzag. **~uear** *vi* zigzag

zinc *m* zinc

zócalo *m* skirting-board; (pedestal) plinth; (Mex, plaza) main square

zodiaco *m*, **zodíaco** *m* zodiac

zona *f* zone; (área) area

zoo *m* zoo. **~logía** *f* zoology. **~lógico** *a* zoological

zoólogo *m* zoologist

zopenco *a* stupid. ● *m* idiot

zoquete *m* blockhead

zorr|a *f* vixen **~illo** *m* (LAm) skunk. **~o** *m* fox

zorzal *m* thrush

zozobra *f* (fig) anxiety. **~r** *vi* founder

zueco *m* clog

zumb|ar *vt* [I] give <*golpe etc*>. ● *vi* buzz. **~ido** *m* buzzing

zumo *m* juice

zurci|do *m* darning. **~r** [9] *vt* darn

zurdo *a* left-handed; <*mano*> left

zurrar *vt* (fig, [I], dar golpes) beat (up)

zutano *m* so-and-so

Phrasefinder

Useful phrases	Expresiones útiles
yes, please/no, thank you	sí, por favor/no, gracias
sorry	perdone
excuse me	disculpe
I'm sorry, I don't understand	perdone, pero no le entiendo
Meeting people	**Saludos**
hello/goodbye	hola/adiós
how are you?	¿cómo está usted?
nice to meet you	mucho gusto
Asking questions	**Preguntas**
do you speak English/Spanish?	¿habla usted inglés/español?
what's your name?	¿cómo se llama?
where are you from?	¿de dónde es?
how much is it?	¿cuánto es?
where is...?	¿dónde está...?
can I have...?	¿me da...?
would you like...?	¿quiere usted...?
Statements about yourself	**Información personal**
my name is...	me llamo...
I'm American/I'm Mexican	soy americano/-a/mexicano/-a
I don't speak Spanish/English	no hablo español/inglés
I live near Seville/Chester	vivo cerca de Sevilla/Chester
I'm a student	soy estudiante
I work in an office	trabajo en una oficina
Emergencies	**Emergencias**
can you help me, please?	¿me ayuda, por favor?
I'm lost	me he perdido
I'm ill	no me encuentro bien
call an ambulance	llamen a una ambulancia
Reading signs	**Carteles y señales**
no entry	prohibido el paso
no smoking	prohibido fumar
fire exit	salida de emergencia
for sale	en venta

❶ Going Places

On the road	Por carretera
where's the nearest garage/petrol station, (*Amer*) gas station	¿dónde está el taller más cercano/la gasolinera más cercana?
what's the best way to get there?	¿cuál es la mejor forma de llegar allí?
I've got a puncture	he pinchado, (*Mex*) se nos ponchó una llanta
I'd like to hire a bike/car	quisiera alquilar, (*Mex*) rentar una bicicleta/un coche
there's been an accident	ha habido un accidente
my car's broken down	se me ha estropeado el coche, (*Lam*) se me descompuso el carro
the car won't start	el coche no arranca

By rail	En tren
where can I buy a ticket?	¿dónde se sacan los billetes, (*Lam*) boletos?
what time is the next train to Barcelona/York?	¿a qué hora sale el próximo tren para Barcelona/York?
do I have to change?	¿tengo que hacer algún transbordo?
can I take my bike on the train?	¿puedo llevar la bicicleta en el tren?
which platform for the train to San Sebastian/Bath?	¿de qué andén sale el tren para San Sebastián/Bath?
there's a train to London at 10 o'clock	hay un tren que sale para Londres a las 10
a single/return to Leeds/Valencia, please	un billete, (*Lam*) boleto de ida/ida y vuelta para Leeds/Valencia, por favor
I'd like an all-day ticket	quiero un billete, (*Lam*) boleto que valga para todo el día
I'd like to reserve a seat	quisiera reservar una plaza

At the airport	En el aeropuerto
when's the next flight to Paris/Rome?	¿cuándo sale el próximo vuelo para París/Roma?
where do I check in?	¿dónde puedo facturar, (*Lam*) chequear, (*Mex*) registrar el equipaje?
I'd like to confirm my flight	quisiera confirmar mi vuelo
I'd like a window seat/ an aisle seat	quisiera un asiento de ventanilla/pasillo
I want to change/cancel my reservation	quiero cambiar/cancelar mi reserva

Getting there	Cómo llegar a los sitios
could you tell me the way to the castle?	¿me podría decir cómo se llega al castillo?
how long will it take to get there?	¿cuánto tiempo se tarda en llegar?
how far is it from here?	¿a qué distancia está?
which bus do I take for the cathedral?	¿qué autobús debo tomar para ir a la catedral?
can you tell me where to get off?	¿podría decirme dónde me tengo que bajar?
what time is the last bus?	¿a qué hora sale el último autobús?
how do I get to the airport?	¿cómo se llega al aeropuerto?
where's the nearest underground station, (*Amer*) subway station?	¿dónde está la estación de metro más cercana?
can you call me a taxi?	¿me puede pedir un taxi?
take the first turning right	gire por la primera (calle) a la derecha
turn left at the traffic lights/just past the church	al llegar al semáforo/después de pasar la iglesia, gire a la izquierda
I'll take a taxi	tomaré un taxi

❷ Keeping in touch

On the phone	Por teléfono
where can I buy a phone card?	¿dónde puedo comprar una tarjeta para el teléfono?
may I use your phone?	¿puedo llamar por teléfono?
do you have a mobile?	¿tiene usted un móvil, (*Lam*) un celular?
what is the code for Alava/ Cardiff?	¿cuál es el prefijo de Álava/ Cardiff?
I want to make a phone call	quiero hacer una llamada
I'd like to reverse the charges, (*Amer*) call collect	quisiera hacer una llamada a cobro revertido, (*Lam*) una llamada por cobrar
the line's engaged, busy (*Amer*)	está comunicando, (esp *Lam*) está ocupado
there's no answer	no contestan
hello, this is Natalia	hola, soy, (esp *Lam*) habla Natalia
is Juan there, please?	¿está Juan, por favor?
who's calling?	¿de parte de quién?
sorry, wrong number	perdone, se ha confundido
just a moment, please	un momento, por favor
would you like to hold?	¿quiere esperar?
please tell him/her I called	dígale que lo/la he llamado, por favor
I'd like to leave a message for him/her	quisiera dejarle un mensaje
...I'll try again later	lo/la voleré a llamar más tarde
please tell him/her that Maria called	dígale que lo/la ha llamado María, por favor
can he/she ring me back?	¿le puede decir que me llame?
my home number is...	mi número (de teléfono) es el...
my business number is...	el número del trabajo es el...
my fax number is...	mi número de fax es el...
we were cut off	se ha cortado

Cómo mantenerse en contacto ❷

Writing	Por carta
what's your address?	¿cuál es su dirección?
where is the nearest post office?	¿dónde está la oficina de correos más cercana?, (*Lam*) ¿dónde está el correo más cercano?
could I have a stamp for Argentina/Italy, please?	¿me da un sello, (*Lam*) una estampilla, (*Mex*) un timbre para Argentina/Italia, por favor?
I'd like to send a parcel/ a telegram	quisiera mandar un paquete/ telegrama

On line	En línea
are you on the Internet?	¿está conectado/-a a Internet?
what's your e-mail address?	¿cuál es su dirección de correo electrónico*?
we could send it by e-mail	lo podríamos mandar por correo electrónico*
I'll e-mail it to you on Tuesday	se lo mandaré por correo electrónico* el martes
I looked it up on the Internet	lo he mirado en Internet
the information is on their website	la información está en su página web

Meeting up	Citas, encuentros
what shall we do this evening?	¿qué hacemos esta tarde?
where shall we meet?	¿dónde podemos encontrarnos?
I'll see you outside the café at 6 o'clock	nos vemos a las 6 en la puerta de la cafetería
see you later	hasta luego
I can't today, I'm busy	hoy no puedo, estoy ocupado/-a

* e-mail (*informal*) is now commonly used in Spanish instead of 'correo electrónico'

❸ Food and drink

Booking a restaurant	Reservar mesa en un restaurante
can you recommend a good restaurant?	¿me puede recomendar un buen restaurante?
I'd like to reserve a table for four	quisiera reservar una mesa para cuatro
a reservation for tomorrow evening at eight o'clock	una reserva para mañana a las ocho de la tarde

Ordering	Pedir la comida
could we see the menu/wine list, please?	¿nos enseña el menú/la carta de vinos, por favor?
do you have a vegetarian/ children's menu?	¿tienen un menú especial para vegetarianos/niños?
could we have some more bread/rice?	¿nos puede traer más pan/arroz?
could I have the bill, (*Amer*) check, please?	¿nos trae la cuenta, por favor?
a bottle/glass of mineral water, please	una botella/un vaso de agua mineral, por favor
as a starter... and to follow...	de primero... y de segundo...
a black/white coffee	un café solo, (*Lam*) negro/ con leche

Reading a menu	El Menú
starters	entrantes, (*Lam*) entradas
soups/salads	sopas/ensaladas
dish/menu of the day	plato/menú del día
seafood	marisco, (*Lam*) mariscos
meat	carne
fish	pescado
desserts	postres
drinks	bebidas

Any complaints?	¿Algún problema?
there's a mistake in the bill, (*Amer*) check	hay un error en la cuenta
the meat isn't cooked/ is overdone	la carne no está bien hecha/está demasiado hecha
I asked for a small/large portion	he pedido una ración, (*Lam*) porción pequeña/grande
we are waiting to be served	estamos esperando a que nos sirvan
the wine is not chilled	el vino no está fresco, (*Lam*) frío

Food shopping	La(s) compra(s)
where is the nearest supermarket?	¿dónde está el supermercado más cercano?
is there a baker's/butcher's near here?	¿hay alguna panadería/ carnicería por aquí?
can I have a carrier bag, please?	¿me da una bolsa, por favor?
how much is it?	¿cuánto es?
I'll have this/that one	me llevo éste/-a/ése/-a

On the shopping list	La lista de la(s) compra(s)
I'd like some bread	un pan, por favor
that's all, thank you	eso es todo, gracias
a bit more/less, please	póngame un poco más/quíteme un poco, por favor
that's enough, thank you	así es suficiente, gracias
100 grams of salami/cheese	100 gramos de salchichón/queso
half a kilo of tomatoes	medio kilo de tomates
a packet of tea/coffee	un paquete de té/café
a carton/litre of milk	un cartón/litro de leche
a can/bottle of beer	una lata/botella de cerveza

❹ Places to stay

Camping	Campings
can we pitch our tent here?	¿podemos montar la tienda (de campaña) aquí?
can we park our caravan here?	¿podemos aparcar la caravana aquí?, (*Lam*) ¿podemos estacionar el tráiler aquí?
what are the facilities like?	¿cómo son las instalaciones?
how much is it per night?	¿cuánto cobran por (pasar la) noche?
where do we park the car?	¿dónde podemos aparcar, (esp *Lam*) estacionar?
we're looking for a campsite	estamos buscando un camping
this is a list of local campsites	ésta es una lista de los campings de la zona
we go on a camping holiday every year	todos los años pasamos las vacaciones en un camping

At the hotel	Hoteles
I'd like a double/single room with bath	quisiera una habitación individual/doble con baño
we have a reservation in the name of Morris	tenemos una reserva a nombre de Morris
we'll be staying three nights, from Friday to Sunday	nos quedaremos tres noches, de viernes a domingo
how much does the room cost?	¿cuánto cuesta la habitación?
I'd like to see the room	quisiera ver la habitación
what time is breakfast?	¿a qué hora se sirve el desayuno?
can I leave this in your safe?	¿puedo dejar esto en la caja fuerte?
bed and breakfast	(lugar donde dan) alojamiento y desayuno
we'd like to stay another night	nos gustaría quedarnos una noche más
please call me at 7:30	¿me podría despertar a las 7:30, por favor?
are there any messages for me?	¿hay algún mensaje para mí?

Hostels	Albergues
could you tell me where the youth hostel is?	¿me podría indicar dónde está el albergue?
what time does the hostel close?	¿a qué hora cierra el albergue?
I'm staying in a hostel	me alojaré en un albergue
the hostel we're staying in is great value	el albergue donde nos alojamos ofrece una buena relación calidad-precio
I know a really good hostel in Dublin	conozco un albergue estupendo en Dublín
I'd like to go backpacking in Australia	me gustaría irme a Australia con la mochila al hombro

Rooms to let	Alquiler de habitaciones
I'm looking for a room with a reasonable rent	quiero alquilar, (*Mex*) rentar una habitación que tenga un precio razonable
I'd like to rent an apartment for a few weeks	me gustaría alquilar, (*Mex*) rentar un apartamento para unas cuantas semanas
where do I find out about rooms to let?	¿dónde me puedo informar sobre alquileres, (*Mex*) rentas de habitaciones?
what's the weekly rent?	¿cuánto cuesta el alquiler, (*Mex*) la renta semanal?
I'm staying with friends at the moment	en este momento estoy alojado en casa de unos amigos
I rent an apartment on the outskirts of town	vivo en un apartamento alquilado, (*Mex*) rentado en las afueras
the room's fine — I'll take it	la habitación está muy bien, me la quedo
the deposit is one month's rent in advance	como depósito, se paga un mes de alquiler, (*Mex*) renta por adelantado

❺ Shopping and money

At the bank	En el banco
I'd like to change some money	quisiera cambiar dinero
I want to change some pounds into Spanish pesetas	quisiera cambiar libras esterlinas a pesetas
do you take Eurocheques?	¿acepan Eurocheques?
what's the exchange rate today?	¿a cuánto está hoy el cambio?
I prefer traveller's cheques, (*Amer*) traveler's checks to cash	prefiero cheques de viaje que dinero en metálico, (esp *Lam*) en efectivo
I'd like to transfer some money from my account	quisiera hacer una transferencia desde mi cuenta corriente
I'll get some money from the cash machine	sacaré dinero del cajero (automático)
I usually pay by direct debit, (*Amer*) direct billing	suelo domiciliar los pagos en mi cuenta, (*Lam*) acostumbro a pagar por débito bancario
I'm with another bank	no soy cliente/-a de este banco

Finding the right shop	Dar con la tienda adecuada
where's the main shopping district?	¿dónde está la zona de tiendas?
where can I buy batteries/postcards?	¿dónde puedo comprar unas pilas/postales?
where's the nearest chemist/bookshop?	¿dónde está la farmacia/librería más cercana?
is there a good food shop around here?	¿hay una buena tienda de comestibles por aquí?
what time do the shops open/close?	¿a qué hora abren/cierran las tiendas?
where did you get those?	¿dónde los/las ha comprado?
I'm looking for presents for my family	estoy buscando regalos para mi familia
we'll do all our shopping on Saturday	(nosotros) haremos las compras el sábado
I love shopping	me encanta ir de compras

Are you being served?	¿Lo/La atienden?
how much does that cost?	¿cuánto cuesta?
can I try it on?	¿me lo puedo probar?
could you wrap it for me, please?	¿me lo envuelve, por favor?
can I pay by credit card/ cheque, (*Amer*) check?	¿puedo pagar con tarjeta/ cheque?
do you have this in another colour, (*Amer*) color?	¿tiene éste/-a en otro color?
could I have a bag, please?	¿me da una bolsa, por favor?
I'm just looking	sólo estoy mirando
I'll think about it	me lo voy a pensar
I'd like a receipt, please	¿me da el recibo, por favor?
I need a bigger/smaller size	necesito una talla más grande/ más pequeña
I take a size 10/a medium	uso la talla 38/mediana
it doesn't suit me	no me queda bien
I'm sorry, I don't have any change/anything smaller	perdone, pero no tengo cambio/billetes más pequeños
that's all, thank you	nada más, gracias

Changing things	Devoluciones
can I have a refund?	¿me podría devolver el dinero?
can you mend it for me?	¿me lo/la podrían arreglar?
can I speak to the manager?	quisiera hablar con el encargado/la encargada
it doesn't work	no funciona
I'd like to change it, please	quisiera cambiarlo/-a, por favor
I bought this here yesterday	compré esto ayer

❻ Sport and leisure

Keeping fit	Mantenerse en forma
where can we play football/squash?	¿dónde se puede jugar al fútbol/squash, (*Lam*) jugar fútbol/squash?
where is the local sports centre, (*Amer*) center?	¿dónde está el polideportivo?
what's the charge per day?	¿cuánto cobran (al día)?
is there a reduction for children/a student discount?	¿hacen descuentos a niños/estudiantes?
I'm looking for a swimming pool/tennis court	estoy buscando una piscina, (*Mex*) alberca/un club de tenis
you have to be a member	(para entrar) hace falta ser socio
I play tennis on Mondays	los lunes juego al tenis, (*Lam*) juego tenis
I would like to go fishing/riding	me gustaría ir a pescar/montar a caballo
I want to do aerobics	quiero hacer aerobic
I love swimming/rollerblading	me encanta nadar/patinar con patines en línea
we want to hire skis/snowboards	queremos alquilar unos esquís/unas tablas de nieve

Watching sport	Ver espectáculos deportivos
is there a football match on Saturday?	¿hay algún partido de fútbol el sábado?
which teams are playing?	¿qué equipos juegan?
where can I get tickets?	¿dónde se compran las entradas?
I'd like to see a rugby/football match	me gustaría ver un partido de rugby/fútbol
my favourite, (*Amer*) favorite team is...	mi equipo favorito es el...
let's watch the match on TV	veamos el partido en la tele

Going to the cinema/theatre/club	Cine/Teatro/Discotecas
what's on?	¿qué ponen, (esp *Lam*) dan (en el cine/teatro)?
when does the box office open/close?	¿a qué hora abren/cierran la taquilla, (*Lam*) boletería?
what time does the concert/performance start?	¿a qué hora empieza el concierto/la representación?
when does it finish?	¿a qué hora termina?
are there any seats left for tonight?	¿quedan entradas para esta noche?
how much are the tickets?	¿cuánto cuestan las entradas?
where can I get a programme, (*Amer*) program?	¿dónde puedo conseguir un programa?
I want to book tickets for tonight's performance	quiero reservar entradas para esta noche
I'll book seats in the circle	reservaré entradas de platea
I'd rather have seats in the stalls	prefiero el patio de butacas
somewhere in the middle, but not too far back	que sean centrales, pero no demasiado atrás
four, please	cuatro, por favor
for Saturday	para el sábado
we'd like to go to a club	nos gustaría ir a una discoteca
I go clubbing every weekend	voy a la discoteca todos los fines de semana

Hobbies	Aficiones y hobbies
what do you do at the weekend?	¿qué hace los fines de semana?
I like yoga/listening to music	me gusta el yoga/escuchar música
I spend a lot of time surfing the Net	me paso mucho tiempo navegando por la Red
I read a lot	leo mucho
I collect musical instruments	colecciono instrumentos musicales

❼ Good timing

Telling the time	La hora
what time is it?	¿qué hora es?
it's 2 o'clock	son las 2
at about 8 o'clock	hacia las 8
from 10 o'clock onwards	a partir de las 10
at 5 o'clock in the morning/ afternoon	a las cinco de la mañana/tarde
it's five past/quarter past/ half past one	es la una y cinco/y cuarto/ y media
it's twenty-five to/quarter to one	es la una menos veinticinco/ menos cuarto/(*Lam*) son veinticinco/un cuarto para la una
a quarter/three quarters of an hour	un cuarto/tres cuartos de hora

Days and dates	Días y fechas
Sunday*, Monday, Tuesday, Wednesday, Thursday, Friday, Saturday	domingo, lunes, martes, miércoles, jueves, viernes, sábado

* Para los anglosajones la semana empieza un domingo y acaba el domingo siguiente, mientras que los latinos solemos empezar la semana el lunes.

January, February, March, April, May, June, July, August, September, October, November, December	enero**, febrero, marzo, abril, mayo, junio, julio, agosto, septiembre, octubre, noviembre, diciembre

**In Spanish, days of the week and months of the year are always spelt with a lower case.

what's the date?	¿qué fecha es hoy?
it's the second of June	(es el) dos de junio
we meet up every Monday	nos vemos todos los lunes
we're going away in August	nos vamos fuera en agosto
on November 8th	el 8 de noviembre

Public holidays and special days	Fiestas y celebraciones especiales
Bank holiday	día festivo durante el cual los bancos cierran por ley
Bank holiday Monday	lunes de puente
New Year's Day (Jan 1)	Año Nuevo (1 de enero)
Epiphany (Jan 6)	Reyes (6 de enero)
St Valentine's Day (Feb 14)	San Valentín (14 de febrero)
Shrove Tuesday/Pancake Day	Martes de Carnaval (este día es tradicional merendar crêpes con azúcar y zumo de limón)
Ash Wednesday	Miércoles de Ceniza
Independence Day	4 de julio, fiesta de la independencia de los EEUU
Maundy Thursday	Jueves Santo
Good Friday	Viernes Santo
May Day (May 1)	1 de mayo, día del trabajador
Thanksgiving	día de Acción de Gracias, fiesta típica de EEUU y Canadá
Halloween (Oct 31)	Halloween (fiesta de fantasmas y brujas que se celebra la víspera de Todos los Santos)
All Saints' Day	Todos los Santos
Guy Fawkes Day/Bonfire Night (Nov 5)	fiesta de Guy Fawkes/de las hogueras (5 de noviembre: se celebra que el católico Guy Fawkes fracasó en su intento de incendiar el parlamento)
Remembrance Sunday	fiesta en recuerdo a los caídos en las dos guerras mundiales
St Nicholas' Day (Dec 6)	San Nicolás (6 de diciembre)
Christmas Eve (Dec 24)	Nochebuena (24 de diciembre)
Christmas Day (Dec 25)	Navidad (25 de diciembre)
Boxing Day (Dec 26)	día de fiesta que sigue al día de Navidad
New Year's Eve (Dec 31)	Nochevieja (31 de diciembre)

❽ Weights and measures/Pesos y medidas

Length/Longitud

inches/pulgadas	0.39	3.9	7.8	11.7	15.6	19.7	39
cm/centímetros	1	10	20	30	40	50	100

Distance/Distancia

miles/millas	0.62	6.2	12.4	18.6	24.9	31	62
km/km	1	10	20	30	40	50	100

Weight/Peso

pounds/libras	2.2	22	44	66	88	110	220
kg/kilos	1	10	20	30	40	50	100

Capacity/Capacidad

gallons/galones	0.22	2.2	4.4	6.6	8.8	11	22
litres/litros	1	10	20	30	40	50	100

Temperature/Temperatura

°C	0	5	10	15	20	25	30	37	38	40
°F	32	41	50	59	68	77	86	98.4	100	104

Clothing and shoe sizes/Tallas de ropa y calzado

Women's clothing sizes/Ropa de señora

UK	8	10	12	14	16	18
US	6	8	10	12	14	16
Continent	36	38	40	42	44	46

Men's clothing sizes/Ropa de caballero

UK/US	36	38	40	42	44	46
Continent	46	48	50	52	54	56

Men's and women's shoes/Calzado de señora y caballero

UK women	4	5	6	7	7.5	8			
UK men				6	7	8	9	10	11
US	6.5	7.5	8.5	9.5	10.5	11.5	12.5	13.5	14.5
Continent	37	38	39	40	41	42	43	44	45

Aa

a /ə/, *stressed form* /eɪ/

before vowel sound or silent 'h' **an**

● *indefinite article*

····➤ un (*m*), una (*f*). **a problem** un problema. **an apple** una manzana. **have you got a pencil?** ¿tienes un lápiz?

! Feminine singular nouns beginning with stressed or accented *a* or *ha* take the article *un* instead of *una*, e.g. *un águila, un hada*

····➤ (when talking about prices and quantities) por. **30 miles an hour** 30 millas por hora. **twice a week** dos veces por semana, dos veces a la semana

! There are many cases in which **a** is not translated, such as when talking about people's professions, in exclamations, etc: **she's a lawyer** *es abogada.* **what a beautiful day!** *¡qué día más precioso!.* **have you got a car?** *¿tienes coche?* **half a cup** *media taza*

aback /əˈbæk/ *adv.* **be taken ~** quedar desconcertado

abandon /əˈbændən/ *vt* abandonar. ● *n* abandono *m*, desenfado *m*. **~ed** *a* abandonado. **~ment** *n* abandono *m*

abashed /əˈbæʃt/ *a* confuso

abate /əˈbeɪt/ *vi* disminuir; <*storm etc*> calmarse

abattoir /ˈæbətwɑː(r)/ *n* matadero *m*

abbess /ˈæbɪs/ *n* abadesa *f*

abbey /ˈæbɪ/ *n* abadía *f*

abbot /ˈæbət/ *n* abad *m*

abbreviat|e /əˈbriːvɪeɪt/ *vt* abreviar. **~ion** /-ˈeɪʃn/ *n* abreviatura *f*; (act) abreviación *f*

abdicat|e /ˈæbdɪkeɪt/ *vt/i* abdicar. **~ion** /-ˈeɪʃn/ *n* abdicación *f*

abdom|en /ˈæbdəmən/ *n* abdomen *m*. **~inal** /-ˈdɒmɪnl/ *a* abdominal

abduct /æbˈdʌkt/ *vt* secuestrar. **~ion** /-ʃn/ *n* secuestro *m*

abhor /əbˈhɔː(r)/ *vt* (*pt* **abhorred**) aborrecer. **~rence** /-ˈhɒrəns/ *n* aborrecimiento *m*. **~rent** /-ˈhɒrənt/ *a* aborrecible

abide /əˈbaɪd/ *vt* (*pt* **abided**) soportar. ● *vi* (old use, *pt* **abode**) morar. □ **~ by** *vt* atenerse a; cumplir <*promise*>

ability /əˈbɪlətɪ/ *n* capacidad *f*; (cleverness) habilidad *f*

abject /ˈæbdʒekt/ *a* (wretched) miserable

ablaze /əˈbleɪz/ *a* en llamas

able /ˈeɪbl/ *a* (**-er**, **-est**) capaz. **be ~** poder; (know how to) saber. **~-bodied** /-ˈbɒdɪd/ *a* sano, no discapacitado

ably /ˈeɪblɪ/ *adv* hábilmente

abnormal /æb'nɔ:ml/ *a* anormal. **~ity** /-'mælətɪ/ *n* anormalidad *f*

aboard /ə'bɔ:d/ *adv* a bordo. ● *prep* a bordo de

abode /ə'bəʊd/ ⇒ABIDE. ● *n* (old use) domicilio *m*

aboli|sh /ə'bɒlɪʃ/ *vt* abolir. **~tion** /æbə'lɪʃn/ *n* abolición *f*

abominable /ə'bɒmɪnəbl/ *a* abominable

aborigin|al /æbə'rɪdʒənl/ *a & n* aborigen (*m & f*), indígena (*m & f*). **~es** /-i:z/ *npl* aborígenes *mpl*

abort /ə'bɔ:t/ *vt* hacer abortar. **~ion** /-ʃn/ *n* aborto *m* provocado; (fig) aborto *m*. **have an ~ion** hacerse un aborto. **~ive** *a* fracasado

abound /ə'baʊnd/ *vi* abundar (in en)

about /ə'baʊt/ *adv* (approximately) alrededor de; (here and there) por todas partes; (in existence) por aquí. **~ here** por aquí. **be ~ to** estar a punto de. ● *prep* sobre; (around) alrededor de; (somewhere in) en. **talk ~** hablar de. **~-face**, **~-turn** *n* (fig) cambio *m* rotundo

above /ə'bʌv/ *adv* arriba. ● *prep* encima de; (more than) más de. **~ all** sobre todo. **~ board** *a* legítimo. ● *adv* abiertamente. **~-mentioned** *a* susodicho

abrasi|on /ə'breɪʒn/ *n* abrasión *f*. **~ve** /-sɪv/ *a* abrasivo

abreast /ə'brest/ *adv*. **march four ~** marchar en columna de cuatro en fondo. **keep ~ of** mantenerse al corriente de

abroad /ə'brɔ:d/ *adv* (be) en el extranjero; (go) al extranjero; (far and wide) por todas partes

abrupt /ə'brʌpt/ *a* brusco. **~ly** *adv* (suddenly) repentinamente; (curtly) bruscamente

abscess /'æbsɪs/ *n* absceso *m*

abscond /əb'skɒnd/ *vi* fugarse

absen|ce /'æbsəns/ *n* ausencia *f*; (lack) falta *f*. **~t** /'æbsənt/ *a* ausente. **~t-minded** /-'maɪndɪd/ *a* distraído. **~t-mindedness** *n* distracción *f*, despiste *m*. **~tee** /-'ti:/ *n* ausente *m & f*. **~teeism** *n* absentismo *m*, ausentismo (LAm)

absolute /'æbsəlu:t/ *a* absoluto. **~ly** *adv* absolutamente

absolve /əb'zɒlv/ *vt* (from sin) absolver; (from obligation) liberar

absor|b /əb'zɔ:b/ *vt* absorber. **~bent** /-bent/ *a* absorbente. **~bent cotton** *n* (Amer) algodón *m* hidrófilo. **~ption** /əb'zɔ:pʃən/ *n* absorción *f*

abstain /əb'steɪn/ *vi* abstenerse (from de)

abstemious /əb'sti:mɪəs/ *a* abstemio

abstention /əb'stenʃn/ *n* abstención *f*

abstract /'æbstrækt/ *a* abstracto. ● *n* (summary) resumen *m*; (painting) cuadro *m* abstracto. ● /əb'strækt/ *vt* extraer; (summarize) resumir. **~ion** /-ʃn/ *n* abstracción *f*

absurd /əb'sɜ:d/ *a* absurdo. **~ity** *n* absurdo *m*, disparate *m*

abundan|ce /ə'bʌndəns/ *n* abundancia *f*. **~t** *a* abundante

abus|e /ə'bju:z/ *vt* (misuse) abusar de; (ill-treat) maltratar; (insult) insultar. ● /ə'bju:s/ *n* abuso *m*; (insults) insultos *mpl*. **~ive** /ə'bju:sɪv/ *a* injurioso

abysmal /ə'bɪzməl/ *a* Ⓘ pésimo

abyss /ə'bɪs/ *n* abismo *m*

academic /ækə'demɪk/ *a* académico; (pej) teórico. ● *n* universitario *m*, catedrático *m*

academy /ə'kædəmɪ/ *n* academia *f*.

accelerat|e /ək'seləreɪt/ *vt* acelerar. ● *vi* acelerar; (Auto) apretar el acelerador. **~ion** /-'reɪʃn/ *n* aceleración *f*. **~or** *n* acelerador *m*

accent /'æksənt/ *n* acento *m*

accept /ək'sept/ *vt* aceptar. **~able** *a* aceptable. **~ance** *n* aceptación *f*; (approval) aprobación *f*

access /'ækses/ *n* acceso *m*. **~ible** /ək'sesəbl/ *a* accesible; <*person*> tratable

accession /æk'seʃn/ *n* (to power, throne etc) ascenso *m*; (thing added) adquisición *f*

accessory /ək'sesərɪ/ *a* accesorio. ● *n* accesorio *m*, complemento *m*; (Jurid) cómplice *m & f*

accident /'æksɪdənt/ *n* accidente *m*; (chance) casualidad *f*. **by ~** sin querer; (by chance) por casualidad. **~al** /-'dentl/ *a* accidental, fortuito. **~ally** /-'dentəlɪ/ *adv* sin querer; (by chance) por casualidad. **~-prone** *a* propenso a los accidentes

acclaim /ə'kleɪm/ *vt* aclamar. ● *n* aclamación *f*

accolade /'ækəleɪd/ *n* (praise) encomio *m*

accommodat|e /ə'kɒmədeɪt/ *vt* (give hospitality to) alojar; (adapt) acomodar; (oblige) complacer. **~ing** *a* complaciente. **~ion** /-'deɪʃn/ *n*, **~ions** *npl* (Amer) alojamiento *m*

accompan|iment /ə'kʌmpənɪmənt/ *n* acompañamiento *m*. **~ist** *n* acompañante *m & f*. **~y** /ə'kʌmpənɪ/ *vt* acompañar

accomplice /ə'kʌmplɪs/ *n* cómplice *m & f*

accomplish /ə'kʌmplɪʃ/ *vt* (complete) acabar; (achieve) realizar; (carry out) llevar a cabo. **~ed** *a* consumado. **~ment** *n* realización *f*; (ability) talento *m*; (thing achieved) triunfo *m*, logro *m*

accord /ə'kɔ:d/ *vi* concordar. ● *vt* conceder. ● *n* acuerdo *m*; (harmony) armonía *f*. **of one's own ~** espontáneamente. **~ance** *n*. **in ~ance with** de acuerdo con. **~ing** *adv*. **~ing to** según. **~ingly** *adv* en conformidad; (therefore) por consiguiente

accordion /ə'kɔ:dɪən/ *n* acordeón *m*

accost /ə'kɒst/ *vt* abordar

account /ə'kaʊnt/ *n* cuenta *f*; (description) relato *m*. **~s** *npl* (in business) contabilidad *f*. **on ~ of** a causa de. **on no ~** de ninguna manera. **on this ~** por eso. **take into ~** tener en cuenta. ● *vt* considerar. □ **~ for** *vt* dar cuenta de, explicar

accountan|cy /ə'kaʊntənsɪ/ *n* contabilidad *f*. **~t** *n* contable *m & f*, contador *m* (LAm)

accumulat|e /ə'kju:mjʊleɪt/ *vt* acumular. ● *vi* acumularse. **~ion** /-'leɪʃn/ *n* acumulación *f*

accura|cy /'ækjərəsɪ/ *n* exactitud *f*, precisión *f*. **~te** /-ət/ *a* exacto, preciso

accus|ation /ækju:'zeɪʃn/ *n* acusación *f*. **~e** /ə'kju:z/ *vt* acusar

accustom /ə'kʌstəm/ *vt* acostumbrar. **~ed** *a*. **be ~ed (to)** estar acostumbrado (a). **get ~ed (to)** acostumbrarse (a)

ace /eɪs/ *n* as *m*

ache /eɪk/ *n* dolor *m*. ● *vi* doler. **my leg ~s** me duele la pierna

achieve /ə'tʃi:v/ *vt* realizar; lograr <*success*>. **~ment** *n* realización *f*; (feat) proeza *f*; (thing achieved) logro *m*

acid /'æsɪd/ *a & n* ácido (*m*). **~ic** *a* /ə'sɪdɪk/ *a* ácido. **~ rain** *n* lluvia *f* ácida

acknowledge /ək'nɒlɪdʒ/ *vt* reconocer. **~ receipt of** acusar recibo de. **~ment** *n* reconocimiento *m*; (Com) acuse *m* de recibo

acne /'æknɪ/ *n* acné *m*

acorn /'eɪkɔ:n/ *n* bellota *f*

acoustic /ə'ku:stɪk/ *a* acústico. **~s** *npl* acústica *f*

acquaint /ə'kweɪnt/ *vt*. **~ s.o. with** poner a uno al corriente de. **be ~ed with** conocer <*person*>; saber <*fact*>. **~ance** *n* conocimiento *m*; (person) conocido *m*

acquiesce /ækwɪ'es/ *vi* consentir (**in** en). **~nce** *n* aquiescencia *f*, consentimiento *m*

acqui|re /ə'kwaɪə(r)/ *vt* adquirir; aprender <*language*>. **~re a taste for** tomar gusto a. **~sition** /ækwɪ'zɪʃn/ *n* adquisición *f*. **~sitive** /ə'kwɪzətɪv/ *a* codicioso

acquit /ə'kwɪt/ *vt* (*pt* **acquitted**) absolver. **~tal** *n* absolución *f*

acre /'eɪkə(r)/ *n* acre *m*

acrid /'ækrɪd/ *a* acre

acrimonious /ækrɪ'məʊnɪəs/ *a* cáustico, mordaz

acrobat /'ækrəbæt/ *n* acróbata *m & f*. **~ic** /-'bætɪk/ *a* acrobático. **~ics** *npl* acrobacia *f*

acronym /'ækrənɪm/ *n* acrónimo *m*, siglas *fpl*

across /ə'krɒs/ *adv & prep* (side to side) de un lado al otro; (on other side) al otro lado de; (crosswise) a través. **it is 20 metres ~** tiene 20 metros de ancho. **go** *or* **walk ~** atravesar, cruzar

act /ækt/ *n* acto *m*; (action) acción *f*; (in variety show) número *m*; (decree) decreto *m*. ● *vt* hacer <*part, role*>. ● *vi* actuar; (pretend) fingir. **~ as** actuar de; <*object*> servir de. **~ for** representar. **~ing** *a* interino. ● *n* (of play) representación *f*; (by actor) interpretación *f*; (profession) profesión *f* de actor

action /'ækʃn/ *n* acción *f*; (Jurid) demanda *f*; (plot) argumento *m*. **out of ~** (on sign) no funciona. **put out of ~** inutilizar. **take ~** tomar medidas. **~ replay** *n* repetición *f* de la jugada

activate /'æktɪveɪt/ *vt* activar

activ|e /'æktɪv/ *a* activo; (energetic) lleno de energía; <*volcano*> en actividad. **~ist** *n* activista *m & f*. **~ity** /-'tɪvətɪ/ *n* actividad *f*

act|or /'æktə(r)/ *n* actor *m*. **~ress** /-trɪs/ *n* actriz *f*

actual /'æktʃʊəl/ *a* verdadero. **~ly** *adv* en realidad, efectivamente; (even) incluso

acute /ə'kju:t/ *a* agudo. **~ly** *adv* agudamente

ad /æd/ *n* [T] anuncio *m*, aviso *m* (LAm)

AD /eɪ'di:/ *abbr* (= **Anno Domini**) d. de J.C.

Adam's apple /ædəmz'æpl/ *n* nuez *f* (de Adán)

adapt /ə'dæpt/ *vt* adaptar. ● *vi* adaptarse. **~ability** /-ə'bɪlətɪ/ *n* adaptabilidad *f*. **~able** /-əbl/ *a* adaptable. **~ation** /ædæp'teɪʃn/ *n* adaptación *f*; (of book etc) versión *f*. **~or** /ə'dæptə(r)/ *n* (Elec, with several sockets) enchufe *m* múltiple; (Elec, for different sockets) adaptador *m*

add /æd/ *vt* añadir. ● *vi* sumar. □ ~ **up** *vt* sumar; (fig) tener sentido. ~ **up to** equivaler a

adder /ˈædə(r)/ *n* víbora *f*

addict /ˈædɪkt/ *n* adicto *m*; (fig) entusiasta *m & f*. **~ed** /əˈdɪktɪd/ *a*. **~ed to** adicto a; (fig) fanático de. **~ion** /əˈdɪkʃn/ *n* (Med) dependencia *f*; (fig) afición *f*. **~ive** /əˈdɪktɪv/ *a* que crea adicción; (fig) que crea hábito

addition /əˈdɪʃn/ *n* suma *f*. **in ~** además. **~al** *a* suplementario

address /əˈdres/ *n* dirección *f*; (on form) domicilio *m*; (speech) discurso *m*. ● *vt* poner la dirección en; (speak to) dirigirse a. **~ book** *n* libreta *f* de direcciones. **~ee** /ædreˈsiː/ *n* destinatario *m*

adept /ˈædept/ *a & n* experto (*m*)

adequa|cy /ˈædɪkwəsɪ/ *n* suficiencia *f*. **~te** /-ət/ *a* suficiente, adecuado. **~tely** *adv* suficientemente, adecuadamente

adhere /ədˈhɪə(r)/ *vi* adherirse (**to** a); observar <*rule*>. **~nce** /-rəns/ *n* adhesión *f*; (to rules) observancia *f*

adhesi|on /ədˈhiːʒn/ *n* adherencia *f*. **~ve** /-sɪv/ *a & n* adhesivo (*m*)

adjacent /əˈdʒeɪsnt/ *a* contiguo

adjective /ˈædʒɪktɪv/ *n* adjetivo *m*

adjourn /əˈdʒɜːn/ *vt* aplazar; suspender <*meeting etc*>. ● *vi* suspenderse

adjust /əˈdʒʌst/ *vt* ajustar <*machine*>; (arrange) arreglar. ● *vi*. **~ (to)** adaptarse (a). **~able** *a* ajustable. **~ment** *n* adaptación *f*; (Tec) ajuste *m*

administer /ədˈmɪnɪstə(r)/ *vt* administrar

administrat|ion /ədmɪnɪˈstreɪʃn/ *n* administración *f*. **~ive** /ədˈmɪnɪstrətɪv/ *a* administrativo. **~or** /ədˈmɪnɪstreɪtə(r)/ *n* administrador *m*

admirable /ˈædmərəbl/ *a* admirable

admiral /ˈædmərəl/ *n* almirante *m*

admir|ation /ædməˈreɪʃn/ *n* admiración *f*. **~e** /ədˈmaɪə(r)/ *vt* admirar. **~er** /ədˈmaɪərə(r)/ *n* admirador *m*

admission /ədˈmɪʃn/ *n* admisión *f*; (entry) entrada *f*

admit /ədˈmɪt/ *vt* (*pt* **admitted**) dejar entrar; (acknowledge) admitir, reconocer. **~ to** confesar. **be ~ted** (to hospital etc) ingresar. **~tance** *n* entrada *f*. **~tedly** *adv* es verdad que

admonish /ədˈmɒnɪʃ/ *vt* reprender; (advise) aconsejar

ado /əˈduː/ *n* alboroto m; (trouble) dificultad *f*. **without more** *or* **further ~** en seguida, sin más

adolescen|ce /ædəˈlesns/ *n* adolescencia *f*. **~t** *a & n* adolescente (*m & f*)

adopt /əˈdɒpt/ *vt* adoptar. **~ed** *a* <*child*> adoptivo. **~ion** /-ʃn/ *n* adopción *f*

ador|able /əˈdɔːrəbl/ *a* adorable. **~ation** /ædəˈreɪʃn/ *n* adoración *f*. **~e** /əˈdɔː(r)/ *vt* adorar

adorn /əˈdɔːn/ *vt* adornar. **~ment** *n* adorno *m*

adrift /əˈdrɪft/ *a & adv* a la deriva

adult /ˈædʌlt/ *a & n* adulto (*m*)

adulter|er /əˈdʌltərə(r)/ *n* adúltero *m*. **~ess** /-ɪs/ *n* adúltera *f*. **~y** *n* adulterio *m*

advance /ədˈvɑːns/ *vt* adelantar. ● *vi* adelantarse. ● *n* adelanto *m*. **in ~** con anticipación, por adelantado. **~d** *a* avanzado; <*studies*> superior

advantage /əd'vɑ:ntɪdʒ/ *n* ventaja *f*. **take ~ of** aprovecharse de; abusar de <*person*>. **~ous** /ædvən'teɪdʒəs/ *a* ventajoso

advent /'ædvənt/ *n* venida *f*. **A~** *n* adviento *m*

adventur|e /əd'ventʃə(r)/ *n* aventura *f*. **~er** *n* aventurero *m*. **~ous** *a* <*person*> aventurero; <*thing*> arriesgado; (fig, bold) audaz

adverb /'ædvɜ:b/ *n* adverbio *m*

adversary /'ædvəsərɪ/ *n* adversario *m*

advers|e /'ædvɜ:s/ *a* adverso, contrario, desfavorable. **~ity** /əd'vɜ:sətɪ/ *n* infortunio *m*

advert /'ædvɜ:t/ *n* ⊞ anuncio *m*, aviso *m* (LAm). **~ise** /'ædvətaɪz/ *vt* anunciar. ● *vi* hacer publicidad; (seek, sell) poner un anuncio. **~isement** /əd'vɜ:tɪsmənt/ *n* anuncio *m*, aviso *m* (LAm). **~iser** /'ædvətaɪzə(r)/ *n* anunciante *m & f*

advice /əd'vaɪs/ *n* consejo *m*; (report) informe *m*

advis|able /əd'vaɪzəbl/ *a* aconsejable. **~e** /əd'vaɪz/ *vt* aconsejar; (inform) avisar. **~e against** aconsejar en contra de. **~er** *n* consejero *m*; (consultant) asesor *m*. **~ory** *a* consultivo

advocate /'ædvəkət/ *n* defensor *m*; (Jurid) abogado *m*. ● /'ædvəkeɪt/ *vt* recomendar

aerial /'eərɪəl/ *a* aéreo. ● *n* antena *f*

aerobics /eə'rəʊbɪks/ *npl* aeróbica *f*

aerodrome /'eərədrəʊm/ *n* aeródromo *m*

aerodynamic /eərəʊdaɪ'næmɪk/ *a* aerodinámico

aeroplane /'eərəpleɪn/ *n* avión *m*

aerosol /'eərəsɒl/ *n* aerosol *m*

aesthetic /i:s'θetɪk/ *a* estético

afar /ə'fɑ:(r)/ *adv* lejos

affable /'æfəbl/ *a* afable

affair /ə'feə(r)/ *n* asunto *m*. (**love**) **~** aventura *f*, amorío *m*. **~s** *npl* (business) negocios *mpl*

affect /ə'fekt/ *vt* afectar; (pretend) fingir. **~ation** /æfek'teɪʃn/ *n* afectación *f*. **~ed** *a* afectado, amanerado

affection /ə'fekʃn/ *n* cariño *m*. **~ate** /-ət/ *a* cariñoso

affiliate /ə'fɪlɪeɪt/ *vt* afiliar

affirm /ə'fɜ:m/ *vt* afirmar. **~ative** /-ətɪv/ *a* afirmativo. ● *n* respuesta *f* afirmativa

afflict /ə'flɪkt/ *vt* afligir. **~ion** /-ʃn/ *n* aflicción *f*, pena *f*

affluen|ce /'æfluəns/ *n* riqueza *f*. **~t** *a* rico.

afford /ə'fɔ:d/ *vt* permitirse; (provide) dar. **he can't ~ a car** no le alcanza el dinero para comprar un coche

affront /ə'frʌnt/ *n* afrenta *f*, ofensa *f*. ● *vt* afrentar, ofender

afield /ə'fi:ld/ *adv*. **far ~** muy lejos

afloat /ə'fləʊt/ *adv* a flote

afraid /ə'freɪd/ *a*. **be ~** tener miedo (**of** a); (be sorry) sentir, lamentar

afresh /ə'freʃ/ *adv* de nuevo

Africa /'æfrɪkə/ *n* África *f*. **~n** *a & n* africano (*m*). **~n-American** *a & n* norteamericano (*m*) de origen africano

after /'ɑ:ftə(r)/ *adv* después; (behind) detrás. ● *prep* después de; (behind) detrás de. **it's twenty ~ four** (Amer) son las cuatro y veinte. **be ~** (seek) andar en busca de. ● *conj* después de que. ● *a* posterior. **~-effect** *n* consecuencia *f*, efecto *m* secundario. **~math** /'ɑ:ftəmæθ/ *n* secuelas *fpl*. **~noon**

/-'nu:n/ *n* tarde *f*. **~shave** *n* loción *f* para después de afeitarse. **~thought** *n* ocurrencia *f* tardía. **~wards** /-wədz/ *adv* después

again /ə'gen/ *adv* otra vez; (besides) además. **do ~** volver a hacer, hacer otra vez. **~ and ~** una y otra vez

against /ə'genst/ *prep* contra; (in opposition to) en contra de, contra

age /eɪdʒ/ *n* edad *f*. **at four years of ~** a los cuatro años. **under ~** menor de edad. **~s** *npl* 🅸 siglos *mpl*. ● *vt/i* (*pres p* **ageing**) envejecer. **~d** /'eɪdʒd/ *a* de ... años. **~d 10** de 10 años. **~d** /'eɪdʒɪd/ *a* viejo, anciano

agency /'eɪdʒənsɪ/ *n* agencia *f*; (department) organismo *m*

agenda /ə'dʒendə/ *n* orden *m* del día

agent /'eɪdʒənt/ *n* agente *m* & *f*; (representative) representante *m* & *f*

aggravat|e /'ægrəveɪt/ *vt* agravar; (🅸, irritate) irritar. **~ion** /-'veɪʃn/ *n* agravación *f*; (🅸, irritation) irritación *f*

aggress|ion /ə'greʃn/ *n* agresión *f*. **~ive** *a* agresivo. **~iveness** *n* agresividad *f*. **~or** *n* agresor *m*

aggrieved /ə'gri:vd/ *a* apenado, ofendido

aghast /ə'gɑ:st/ *a* horrorizado

agil|e /'ædʒaɪl/ *a* ágil. **~ity** /ə'dʒɪlətɪ/ *n* agilidad *f*

aging /'eɪdʒɪŋ/ *a* envejecido. ● *n* envejecimiento *m*

agitat|e /'ædʒɪteɪt/ *vt* agitar. **~ed** *a* nervioso. **~ion** /-'teɪʃn/ *n* agitación *f*, excitación *f*. **~or** *n* agitador *m*

ago /ə'gəʊ/ *adv*. **a long time ~** hace mucho tiempo. **3 days ~** hace 3 días

agon|ize /'ægənaɪz/ *vi* atormentarse. **~izing** *a* <*pain*> atroz; <*experience*> angustioso. **~y** *n* dolor *m* (agudo); (mental) angustia *f*

agree /ə'gri:/ *vt* acordar. ● *vi* estar de acuerdo; (of figures) concordar; (get on) entenderse. □ **~ on** *vt* acordar <*date, details*>. □ **~ with** *vt* (of food etc) sentarle bien a. **~able** /ə'gri:əbl/ *a* agradable. **be ~able** (willing) estar de acuerdo. **~d** *a* <*time, place*> convenido. **~ment** /-mənt/ *n* acuerdo *m*. **in ~ment** de acuerdo

agricultur|al /ægrɪ'kʌltʃərəl/ *a* agrícola. **~e** /'ægrɪkʌltʃə(r)/ *n* agricultura *f*

aground /ə'graʊnd/ *adv*. **run ~** (of ship) varar, encallar

ahead /ə'hed/ *adv* delante; (in time) antes de. **be ~** ir delante

aid /eɪd/ *vt* ayudar. ● *n* ayuda *f*. **in ~ of** a beneficio de

AIDS /eɪdz/ *n* sida *m*

ailment /'eɪlmənt/ *n* enfermedad *f*

aim /eɪm/ *vt* apuntar; (fig) dirigir. ● *vi* apuntar; (fig) pretender. ● *n* puntería *f*; (fig) objetivo *m*. **~less** *a*, **~lessly** *adv* sin objeto, sin rumbo

air /eə(r)/ *n* aire *m*. **be on the ~** (Radio, TV) estar en el aire. **put on ~s** darse aires. ● *vt* airear. **~ bag** *n* (Auto) bolsa *f* de aire. **~ base** *n* base *f* aérea. **~borne** *a* en el aire; (Mil) aerotransportado. **~-conditioned** *a* climatizado, con aire acondicionado. **~ conditioning** *n* aire *m* acondicionado. **~craft** *n* (*pl invar*) avión *m*. **~craft carrier** *n* portaaviones *m*. **~field** *n* aeródromo *m*. **A~ Force** *n* fuerzas *fpl* aéreas. **~ freshener** *n* ambientador *m*. **~gun** *n* escopeta *f* de aire comprimido. **~ hostess**

n azafata *f*, aeromoza *f* (LAm). **~line** *n* línea *f* aérea. **~ mail** *n* correo *m* aéreo. **~plane** *n* (Amer) avión *m*. **~port** *n* aeropuerto *m*. **~sick** *a* mareado (*en un avión*). **~tight** *a* hermético. **~ traffic controller** *n* controlador *m* aéreo. **~y** *a* (**-ier**, **-iest**) aireado; <*manner*> desenfadado

aisle /aɪl/ *n* nave *f* lateral; (gangway) pasillo *m*

ajar /əˈdʒɑː(r)/ *a* entreabierto

alarm /əˈlɑːm/ *n* alarma *f*. ● *vt* asustar. **~ clock** *n* despertador *m*. **~ist** *n* alarmista *m* & *f*

Albania /ælˈbeɪmɪə/ *n* Albania *f*. **~n** *a* & *n* albanés (*m*)

albatross /ˈælbətrɒs/ *n* albatros *m*

album /ˈælbəm/ *n* álbum *m*

alcohol /ˈælkəhɒl/ *n* alcohol *m*. **~ic** /-ˈhɒlɪk/ *a* & *n* alcohólico (*m*)

alcove /ˈælkəʊv/ *n* nicho *m*

ale /eɪl/ *n* cerveza *f*

alert /əˈlɜːt/ *a* vivo; (watchful) vigilante. ● *n* alerta *f*. **on the ~** alerta. ● *vt* avisar

algebra /ˈældʒɪbrə/ *n* álgebra *f*

Algeria /ælˈdʒɪərɪə/ *n* Argelia *f*. **~n** *a* & *n* argelino (*m*)

alias /ˈeɪlɪəs/ *n* (*pl* **-ases**) alias *m*. ● *adv* alias

alibi /ˈælɪbaɪ/ *n* (*pl* **-is**) coartada *f*

alien /ˈeɪlɪən/ *n* extranjero *m*. ● *a* ajeno. **~ate** /-eɪt/ *vt* enajenar. **~ation** /-ˈneɪʃn/ *n* enajenación *f*

alienat|e /ˈeɪlɪəneɪt/ *vt* enajenar. **~ion** /-ˈneɪʃn/ *n* enajenación *f*

alight /əˈlaɪt/ *a* ardiendo; <*light*> encendido

align /əˈlaɪn/ *vt* alinear. **~ment** *n* alineación *f*

alike /əˈlaɪk/ *a* parecido, semejante. **look** *or* **be ~** parecerse. ● *adv* de la misma manera

alive /əˈlaɪv/ *a* vivo. **~ with** lleno de

alkali /ˈælkəlaɪ/ *n* (*pl* **-is**) álcali *m*. **~ne** *a* alcalino

all /ɔːl/

● *adjective*

····➤ todo, -da; (pl) todos, -das. **~ day** todo el día. **~ the windows** todas las ventanas. **~ four of us went** fuimos los cuatro

● *pronoun*

····➤ (everything) todo. **that's ~** eso es todo. **I did ~ I could to persuade her** hice todo lo que pude para convencerla

····➤ (after pronoun) todo, -da; (pl) todos, -das. **he helped us ~** nos ayudó a todos

····➤ **all of** todo, -da, (pl) todos, -das. **~ of the paintings** todos los cuadros. **~ of the milk** toda la leche

····➤ (in phrases) **all in all** en general. **not at all** (in no way) de ninguna manera; (after thanks) de nada, no hay de qué. **it's not at ~ bad** no está nada mal. **I don't like it at ~** no me gusta nada

● *adverb*

····➤ (completely) completamente. **she was ~ alone** estaba completamente sola. **I got ~ dirty** me ensucié todo/toda. **I don't know him ~ that well** no lo conozco tan bien

····➤ (in scores) **the score was one ~** iban empatados uno a uno

····➤ (in phrases) **to be all for sth** estar completamente a favor de algo. **to be all in** 🅸 estar rendido

all-around /ɔːlə'raʊnd/ *a* (Amer) completo

allay /ə'leɪ/ *vt* aliviar <*pain*>; aquietar <*fears etc*>

all-clear /ɔːl'klɪə(r)/ *n* fin *m* de (la) alarma; (permission) visto *m* bueno

alleg|ation /ælɪ'geɪʃn/ *n* alegato *m*. **~e** /ə'ledʒ/ *vt* alegar. **~edly** /-ɪdlɪ/ *adv* según se dice, supuestamente

allegiance /ə'liːdʒəns/ *n* lealtad *f*

allegory /'ælɪgərɪ/ *n* alegoría *f*

allerg|ic /ə'lɜːdʒɪk/ *a* alérgico (**to** a). **~y** /'ælədʒɪ/ *n* alergia *f*

alleviate /ə'liːvɪeɪt/ *vt* aliviar

alley /'ælɪ/ (*pl* **-eys**), **~way** *ns* callejuela *f*

alliance /ə'laɪəns/ *n* alianza *f*

alligator /'ælɪgeɪtə(r)/ *n* caimán *m*

allocat|e /'æləkeɪt/ *vt* asignar; (share out) repartir. **~ion** /-'keɪʃn/ *n* asignación *f*; (distribution) reparto *m*

allot /ə'lɒt/ *vt* (*pt* **allotted**) asignar. **~ment** *n* asignación *f*; (land) parcela *f*

allow /ə'laʊ/ *vt* permitir; (grant) conceder; (reckon on) prever; (agree) admitir. □ **~ for** *vt* tener en cuenta. **~ance** /ə'laʊəns/ *n* concesión *f*; (pension) pensión *f*; (Com) rebaja *f*. **make ~ances for** ser indulgente con <*person*>; (take into account) tener en cuenta

alloy /'ælɔɪ/ *n* aleación *f*

all: ~ right *adj & adv* bien. ● *int* ¡vale!, ¡okey! (esp LAm), ¡órale! (Mex). **~-round** *a* completo

allusion /ə'luːʒn/ *n* alusión *f*

ally /'ælaɪ/ *n* aliado *m*. ● /ə'laɪ/ *vt*. **~ o.s.** aliarse (**with** con)

almighty /ɔːl'maɪtɪ/ *a* todopoderoso

almond /'ɑːmənd/ *n* almendra *f*

almost /'ɔːlməʊst/ *adv* casi

alms *npl* limosnas *fpl*

alone /ə'ləʊn/ *a* solo. ● *adv* sólo, solamente

along /ə'lɒŋ/ *prep* por, a lo largo de. ● *adv*. **~ with** junto con. **all ~** todo el tiempo. **come ~** venga. **~side** /-'saɪd/ *adv* (Naut) al costado. ● *prep* al lado de

aloof /ə'luːf/ *adv* apartado. ● *a* reservado

aloud /ə'laʊd/ *adv* en voz alta

alphabet /'ælfəbet/ *n* alfabeto *m*. **~ical** /-'betɪkl/ *a* alfabético

Alps /ælps/ *npl*. **the ~** los Alpes

already /ɔːl'redɪ/ *adv* ya

Alsatian /æl'seɪʃn/ *n* pastor *m* alemán

also /'ɔːlsəʊ/ *adv* también; (moreover) además

altar /'ɔːltə(r)/ *n* altar *m*

alter /'ɔːltə(r)/ *vt* cambiar. ● *vi* cambiarse. **~ation** /-'reɪʃn/ *n* modificación *f*; (to garment) arreglo *m*

alternate /ɔːl'tɜːnət/ *a* alterno; (Amer) ⇒ALTERNATIVE. ● /'ɔːltəneɪt/ *vt/i* alternar. **~ly** /ɔːl'tɜːnətlɪ/ *adv* alternativamente

alternative /ɔːl'tɜːnətɪv/ *a* alternativo. ● *n* alternativa *f*. **~ly** *adv* en cambio, por otra parte

although /ɔːl'ðəʊ/ *conj* aunque

altitude /'æltɪtjuːd/ *n* altitud *f*

altogether /ɔːltə'geðə(r)/ *adv* completamente; (on the whole) en total

aluminium /ælјʊ'mɪnɪəm/, **aluminum** /ə'lu:mɪnəm/ (Amer) *n* aluminio *m*

always /'ɔ:lweɪz/ *adv* siempre

am /æm/ ⇒BE

a.m. *abbr* (= **ante meridiem**) de la mañana

amalgamate /ə'mælgəmeɪt/ *vt* amalgamar. ● *vi* amalgamarse

amass /ə'mæs/ *vt* acumular

amateur /'æmətə(r)/ *a & n* amateur (*m & f*). **~ish** *a* (pej) torpe, chapucero

amaz|e /ə'meɪz/ *vt* asombrar. **~ed** *a* asombrado, estupefacto. **be ~ed at** quedarse asombrado de, asombrarse de. **~ement** *n* asombro *m*. **~ing** *a* increíble

ambassador /æm'bæsədə(r)/ *n* embajador *m*

ambigu|ity /æmbɪ'gju:ətɪ/ *n* ambigüedad *f*. **~ous** /æm'bɪgjʊəs/ *a* ambiguo

ambiti|on /æm'bɪʃn/ *n* ambición *f*. **~ous** /-ʃəs/ *a* ambicioso

ambivalent /æm'bɪvələnt/ *a* ambivalente

amble /'æmbl/ *vi* andar despacio, andar sin prisa

ambulance /'æmbjʊləns/ *n* ambulancia *f*

ambush /'æmbʊʃ/ *n* emboscada *f*. ● *vt* tender una emboscada a

amen /ɑ:'men/ *int* amén

amend /ə'mend/ *vt* enmendar. **~ment** *n* enmienda *f*. **~s** *npl*. **make ~s** reparar

amenities /ə'mi:nətɪz/ *npl* servicios *mpl*; (of hotel, club) instalaciones *fpl*

America /ə'merɪkə/ *n* (continent) América; (North America) Estados *mpl* Unidos, Norteamérica *f*. **~n** *a & n* americano (*m*); (North American) estadounidense (*m & f*), norteamericano (*m*). **~nism** *n* americanismo *m*

amiable /'eɪmɪəbl/ *a* simpático

amicable /'æmɪkəbl/ *a* amistoso

amid(st) /ə'mɪd(st)/ *prep* entre, en medio de

ammonia /ə'məʊnɪə/ *n* amoníaco *m*, amoniaco *m*

ammunition /æmjʊ'nɪʃn/ *n* municiones *fpl*

amnesty /'æmnəstɪ/ *n* amnistía *f*

amok /ə'mɒk/ *adv*. **run ~** volverse loco

among(st) /ə'mʌŋ(st)/ *prep* entre

amount /ə'maʊnt/ *n* cantidad *f*; (total) total *m*, suma *f*. □ **~ to** *vt* sumar; (fig) equivaler a, significar

amp(ere) /'amp(eə(r))/ *n* amperio *m*

amphibi|an /æm'fɪbɪən/ *n* anfibio *m*. **~ous** /-əs/ *a* anfibio

amphitheatre /'æmfɪθɪətə(r)/ *n* anfiteatro *m*

ampl|e /'æmpl/ *a* (**-er**, **-est**) amplio; (enough) suficiente; (plentiful) abundante. **~y** *adv* ampliamente, bastante

amplif|ier /'æmplɪfaɪə(r)/ *n* amplificador *m*. **~y** /'æmplɪfaɪ/ *vt* amplificar

amputat|e /'æmpjʊteɪt/ *vt* amputar. **~ion** /-'teɪʃn/ *n* amputación *f*

amus|e /ə'mju:z/ *vt* divertir. **~ed** *a* <expression> divertido. **keep s.o. ~ed** entretener a uno. **~ement** *n* diversión *f*. **~ing** *a* divertido

an /ən, æn/ ⇒A

anaemi|a /ə'ni:mɪə/ *n* anemia *f*. **~c** *a* anémico

anaesthe|tic /ænɪs'θetɪk/ *n* anestésico *m*. **~tist** /ə'ni:sθɪtɪst/ *n* anestesista *m & f*

anagram /'ænəgræm/ *n* anagrama *m*

analogy /ə'nælədʒɪ/ *n* analogía *f*

analy|se /'ænəlaɪz/ *vt* analizar. **~sis** /ə'næləsɪs/ *n* (*pl* **-ses** /-si:z/) *n* análisis *m*. **~st** /'ænəlɪst/ *n* analista *m & f*. **~tic(al)** /ænə'lɪtɪk(əl)/ *a* analítico

anarch|ist /'ænəkɪst/ *n* anarquista *m & f*. **~y** *n* anarquía *f*

anatom|ical /ænə'tɒmɪkl/ *a* anatómico. **~y** /ə'nætəmɪ/ *n* anatomía *f*

ancest|or /'ænsestə(r)/ *n* antepasado *m*. **~ral** /-'sestrəl/ *a* ancestral. **~ry** /'ænsestrɪ/ *n* ascendencia *f*

anchor /'æŋkə(r)/ *n* ancla *f*. ● *vt* anclar; (fig) sujetar. ● *vi* anclar. **~man** *n* (on TV) presentador *m*. **~woman** *n* (on TV) presentadora *f*.

ancient /'eɪnʃənt/ *a* antiguo, viejo

ancillary /æn'sɪlərɪ/ *a* auxiliar

and /ənd, ænd/ *conj* y; (before **i-** and **hi-**) e. **bread ~ butter** pan *m* con mantequilla. **go ~ see him** ve a verlo. **more ~ more** cada vez más. **try ~ come** trata de venir

anecdot|al /ænɪk'dəʊtl/ *a* anecdótico. **~e** /'ænɪkdəʊt/ *n* anécdota *f*

anew /ə'nju:/ *adv* de nuevo

angel /'eɪndʒl/ *n* ángel *m*. **~ic** /æn'dʒelɪk/ *a* angélico

anger /'æŋgə(r)/ *n* ira *f*. ● *vt* enfadar, (esp LAm) enojar

angle /'æŋgl/ *n* ángulo *m*; (fig) punto *m* de vista. **~r** /'æŋglə(r)/ *n* pescador *m*

Anglican /'æŋglɪkən/ *a & n* anglicano (*m*)

angr|ily /'æŋgrɪlɪ/ *adv* con enfado, (esp LAm) con enojo. **~y** /'æŋgrɪ/ *a* (**-ier**, **-iest**) enfadado, (esp LAm) enojado. **get ~y** enfadarse, enojarse (esp LAm)

anguish /'æŋgwɪʃ/ *n* angustia *f*

animal /'ænɪməl/ *a & n* animal (*m*)

animat|e /'ænɪmeɪt/ *vt* animar. **~ion** /-'meɪʃn/ *n* animación *f*

animosity /ænɪ'mɒsətɪ/ *n* animosidad *f*

ankle /'æŋkl/ *n* tobillo *m*. **~ boot** botín *m*. **~ sock** calcetín *m* corto

annexe /'æneks/ *n* anexo *m*

annihilat|e /ə'naɪəleɪt/ *vt* aniquilar. **~ion** /-'leɪʃn/ *n* aniquilación *f*

anniversary /ænɪ'vɜ:sərɪ/ *n* aniversario *m*

announce /ə'naʊns/ *vt* anunciar, comunicar. **~ment** *n* anuncio *m*; (official) comunicado *m*. **~r** *n* (Radio, TV) locutor *m*

annoy /ə'nɔɪ/ *vt* molestar. **~ance** *n* molestia *m*. **~ed** *a* enfadado, enojado (LAm). **~ing** *a* molesto

annual /'ænjʊəl/ *a* anual. ● *n* anuario *m*. **~ly** *adv* cada año

annul /ə'nʌl/ *vt* (*pt* **annulled**) anular. **~ment** *n* anulación *f*

anonymous /ə'nɒnɪməs/ *a* anónimo

anorak /'ænəræk/ *n* anorac *m*

another /ə'nʌðə(r)/ *a & pron* otro. **~ 10 minutes** 10 minutos más. **in ~ way** de otra manera. **one ~** el uno al otro; (*pl*) unos a otros

answer /'ɑ:nsə(r)/ *n* respuesta *f*; (solution) solución *f*. ● *vt* contestar; escuchar, oír <*prayer*>. **~ the door** abrir la puerta. ● *vi* contestar. □ **~ back** *vi* contestar. □ **~ for** *vt* ser responsable de. **~able** *a* responsable. **~ing machine** *n* contestador *m* automático

ant /ænt/ *n* hormiga *f*

antagoni|sm /æn'tægənɪzəm/ *n* antagonismo *m*. **~stic** /-'nɪstɪk/ *a* antagónico, opuesto. **~ze** /æn'tægənaɪz/ *vt* provocar la enemistad de

Antarctic /æn'tɑ:ktɪk/ *a* antártico. ● *n* **the ~** la región antártica

antelope /'æntɪləʊp/ *n* antílope *m*

antenatal /'æntɪneɪtl/ *a* prenatal

antenna /æn'tenə/ (*pl* **-nae** /-ni:/) (of insect etc) *n* antena *f*; (*pl* **-nas**) (of radio, TV) antena *f*

anthem /'ænθəm/ *n* himno *m*

anthology /æn'θɒlədʒɪ/ *n* antología *f*

anthropolog|ist /ænθrə'pɒlədʒɪst/ *n* antropológo *m*. **~y** *n* antropología *f*

anti-... /æntɪ/ *pref* anti... **~aircraft** /-'eəkrɑ:ft/ *a* antiaéreo

antibiotic /æntɪbaɪ'ɒtɪk/ *a* & *n* antibiótico (*m*)

anticipat|e /æn'tɪsɪpeɪt/ *vt* anticiparse a; (foresee) prever; (forestall) prevenir. **~ion** /-'peɪʃn/ *n* (foresight) previsión *f*; (expectation) expectativa *f*

anti: ~climax /-'klaɪmæks/ *n* decepción *f*. **~clockwise** /-'klɒkwaɪz/ *adv* & *a* en sentido contrario al de las agujas del reloj

antidote /'æntɪdəʊt/ *m* antídoto *m*

antifreeze /'æntɪfri:z/ *n* anticongelante *m*

antiperspirant /æntɪ'pɜ:spɪrənt/ *n* antitranspirante *m*

antiquated /'æntɪkweɪtɪd/ *a* anticuado

antique /æn'ti:k/ *a* antiguo. ● *n* antigüedad *f*. **~ dealer** anticuario *m*. **~ shop** tienda *f* de antigüedades

antiquity /æn'tɪkwətɪ/ *n* antigüedad *f*

anti: ~septic /-'septɪk/ *a* & *n* antiséptico (*m*). **~social** /-'səʊʃl/ *a* antisocial

antlers /'æntləz/ *npl* cornamenta *f*

anus /'eɪnəs/ *n* ano *m*

anvil /'ænvɪl/ *n* yunque *m*

anxi|ety /æŋ'zaɪətɪ/ *n* ansiedad *f*; (worry) inquietud *f*; (eagerness) anhelo *m*. **~ous** /'æŋkʃəs/ *a* inquieto; (eager) deseoso. **~ously** *adv* con inquietud; (eagerly) con impaciencia

any /'enɪ/ *a* algún; (negative) ningún *m*; (whatever) cualquier; (every) todo. **at ~ moment** en cualquier momento. **have you ~ wine?** ¿tienes vino? ● *pron* alguno; (negative) ninguno. **have we ~?** ¿tenemos algunos? **not ~** ninguno. ● *adv* (a little) un poco, algo. **is it ~ better?** ¿está algo mejor?

anybody /'enɪbɒdɪ/ *pron* alguien; (*after negative*) nadie. **~ can do it** cualquiera puede hacerlo

anyhow /'enɪhaʊ/ *adv* de todas formas; (in spite of all) a pesar de todo; (badly) de cualquier manera

anyone /'enɪwʌn/ *pron* ⇒ANYBODY

anything /'enɪθɪŋ/ *pron* algo; (whatever) cualquier cosa; (*after negative*) nada. **~ but** todo menos

anyway /'enɪweɪ/ *adv* de todas formas

anywhere /'enɪweə(r)/ *adv* en cualquier parte; (*after negative*) en ningún sitio. **~ else** en cualquier otro lugar. **~ you go** dondequiera que vayas

apart /ə'pɑ:t/ *adv* aparte; (separated) separado. **~ from** aparte de.

come ~ romperse. **take** ~ desmontar

apartheid /ə'pɑ:theɪt/ *n* apartheid *m*

apartment /ə'pɑ:tmənt/ *n* (Amer) apartamento *m*, piso *m*. ~ **building** *n* (Amer) edificio *m* de apartamentos, casa *f* de pisos

apath|etic /æpə'θetɪk/ *a* apático. ~**y** /'æpəθɪ/ *n* apatía *f*

ape /eɪp/ *n* mono *m*. ● *vt* imitar

aperitif /ə'perətɪf/ *n* aperitivo *m*

aperture /'æpətʃʊə(r)/ *n* abertura *f*

apex /'eɪpeks/ *n* ápice *m*

aphrodisiac /æfrə'dɪzɪæk/ *a & n* afrodisíaco (*m*), afrodisiaco (*m*)

apolog|etic /əpɒlə'dʒetɪk/ *a* lleno de disculpas. **be** ~**etic** disculparse. ~**ize** /ə'pɒlədʒaɪz/ *vi* disculparse (**for** de). ~**y** /ə'pɒlədʒɪ/ *n* disculpa *f*

apostle /ə'pɒsl/ *n* apóstol *m*

apostrophe /ə'pɒstrəfɪ/ *n* apóstrofo *m*

appal /ə'pɔ:l/ *vt* (*pt* **appalled**) horrorizar. ~**ling** *a* espantoso

apparatus /æpə'reɪtəs/ *n* aparato *m*

apparel /ə'pærəl/ *n* (Amer) ropa *f*

apparent /ə'pærənt/ *a* aparente; (clear) evidente. ~**ly** *adv* por lo visto

apparition /æpə'rɪʃn/ *n* aparición *f*

appeal /ə'pi:l/ *vi* apelar; (attract) atraer. ● *n* llamamiento *m*; (attraction) atractivo *m*; (Jurid) apelación *f*. ~**ing** *a* atrayente

appear /ə'pɪə(r)/ *vi* aparecer; (seem) parecer; (in court) comparecer. ~**ance** *n* aparición *f*; (aspect) aspecto *m*; (in court) comparecencia *f*

appease /ə'pi:z/ *vt* aplacar; (pacify) apaciguar

append /ə'pend/ *vt* adjuntar

appendicitis /əpendɪ'saɪtɪs/ *n* apendicitis *f*

appendix /ə'pendɪks/ *n* (*pl* **-ices** /-ɪsi:z/) (of book) apéndice *m*. (*pl* **-ixes**) (Anat) apéndice *m*

appetite /'æpɪtaɪt/ *n* apetito *m*

applau|d /ə'plɔ:d/ *vt/i* aplaudir. ~**se** /ə'plɔ:z/ *n* aplausos *mpl*. **round of** ~**se** aplauso *m*

apple /'æpl/ *n* manzana *f*. ~ **tree** *n* manzano *m*

appliance /ə'plaɪəns/ *n* aparato *m*. **electrical** ~ electrodoméstico *m*

applic|able /'æplɪkəbl/ *a* aplicable; (relevant) pertinente. ~**ant** /'æplɪkənt/ *n* candidato *m*, solicitante *m & f*. ~**ation** /æplɪ'keɪʃn/ *n* aplicación *f*; (request) solicitud *f*. ~**ation form** formulario *m* (de solicitud)

appl|ied /ə'plaɪd/ *a* aplicado. ~**y** /ə'plaɪ/ *vt* aplicar. ● *vi* aplicarse; (ask) presentar una solicitud. ~**y for** solicitar <*job etc*>

appoint /ə'pɔɪnt/ *vt* nombrar; (fix) señalar. ~**ment** *n* cita *f*

apprais|al /ə'preɪzl/ *n* evaluación *f*. ~**e** /ə'preɪz/ *vt* evaluar

appreciable /ə'pri:ʃəbl/ *a* (considerable) considerable

appreciat|e /ə'pri:ʃɪeɪt/ *vt* (value) apreciar; (understand) comprender; (be grateful for) agradecer. ~**ion** /-'eɪʃn/ *n* aprecio *m*; (gratitude) agradecimiento *m*. ~**ive** /ə'pri:ʃɪətɪv/ *a* agradecido

apprehen|sion /æprɪ'henʃn/ *n* (fear) recelo *f*. ~**sive** *a* aprensivo

apprentice /ə'prentɪs/ *n* aprendiz *m*. ● *vt*. **be** ~**d to s.o.** estar de aprendiz con uno. **~ship** *n* aprendizaje *m*

approach /ə'prəʊtʃ/ *vt* acercarse a. ● *vi* acercarse. ● *n* acercamiento *m*; (to problem) enfoque *m*; (access) acceso *m*

appropriate /ə'prəʊprɪət/ *a* apropiado. ● /ə'prəʊprɪeɪt/ *vt* apropiarse de. **~ly** /-ətli/ *adv* apropiadamente

approv|al /ə'pru:vl/ *n* aprobación *f*. **on ~al** a prueba. **~e** /ə'pru:v/ *vt/i* aprobar. **~ingly** *adv* con aprobación

approximat|e /ə'prɒksɪmət/ *a* aproximado. ● /ə'prɒksɪmeɪt/ *vt* aproximarse a. **~ely** /-ətlɪ/ *adv* aproximadamente. **~ion** /-'meɪʃn/ *n* aproximación *f*

apricot /'eɪprɪkɒt/ *n* albaricoque *m*, chabacano *m* (Mex)

April /'eɪprəl/ *n* abril *m*. **~ fool!** ¡inocentón!

apron /'eɪprən/ *n* delantal *m*

apt /æpt/ *a* apropiado. **be ~ to** tener tendencia a. **~itude** /'æptɪtju:d/ *n* aptitud *f*. **~ly** *adv* acertadamente

aquarium /ə'kweərɪəm/ *n* (*pl* **-ums**) acuario *m*

Aquarius /ə'kweərɪəs/ *n* Acuario *m*

aquatic /ə'kwætɪk/ *a* acuático

aqueduct /'ækwɪdʌkt/ *n* acueducto *m*

Arab /'ærəb/ *a & n* árabe (*m & f*). **~ian** /ə'reɪbɪən/ *a* árabe. **~ic** /'ærəbɪk/ *a & n* árabe (*m*). **~ic numerals** números *mpl* arábigos

arable /'ærəbl/ *a* cultivable

arbitrary /'ɑ:bɪtrərɪ/ *a* arbitrario

arbitrat|e /'ɑ:bɪtreɪt/ *vi* arbitrar. **~ion** /-'treɪʃn/ *n* arbitraje *m*. **~or** *n* árbitro *m*

arc /ɑ:k/ *n* arco *m*

arcade /ɑ:'keɪd/ *n* arcada *f*; (around square) soportales *mpl*; (shops) galería *f*

arch /ɑ:tʃ/ *n* arco *m*. ● *vt* arquear. ● *vi* arquearse

archaeolog|ical /ɑ:kɪə'lɒdʒɪkl/ *a* arqueológico. **~ist** /ɑ:kɪ'ɒlədʒɪst/ *n* arqueólogo *m*. **~y** /ɑ:kɪ'ɒlədʒɪ/ *n* arqueología *f*

archaic /ɑ:'keɪɪk/ *a* arcaico

archbishop /ɑ:tʃ'bɪʃəp/ *n* arzobispo *m*

archer /'ɑ:tʃə(r)/ *n* arquero *m*. **~y** *n* tiro *m* con arco

architect /'ɑ:kɪtekt/ *n* arquitecto *m*. **~ure** /-tʃə(r)/ *n* arquitectura *f*. **~ural** /-'tektʃərəl/ *a* arquitectónico

archives /'ɑ:kaɪvz/ *npl* archivo *m*

archway /'ɑ:tʃweɪ/ *n* arco *m*

Arctic /'ɑ:ktɪk/ *a* ártico. ● *n*. **the ~** el Ártico

ard|ent /'ɑ:dənt/ *a* fervoroso; <*supporter, lover*> apasionado. **~our** /'ɑ:də(r)/ *n* fervor *m*; (love) pasión *f*

arduous /'ɑ:djʊəs/ *a* arduo

are /ɑ:(r)/ ⇒BE

area /'eərɪə/ *n* (Math) superficie *f*; (of country) zona *f*; (of city) barrio *m*

arena /ə'ri:nə/ *n* arena *f*; (scene of activity) ruedo *m*

aren't /ɑ:nt/ = **are not**

Argentin|a /ɑ:dʒən'ti:nə/ *n* Argentina *f*. **~ian** /-'tɪnɪən/ *a & n* argentino (*m*)

argu|able /'ɑ:gjʊəbl/ *a* discutible. **~e** /'ɑ:gju:/ *vi* discutir; (reason) razonar. **~ment** /'ɑ:gjʊmənt/ *n* disputa *f*; (reasoning) argumento *m*. **~mentative** /ɑ:gjʊ'mentətɪv/ *a* discutidor

arid /'ærɪd/ *a* árido

Aries /'eəri:z/ *n* Aries *m*

arise /ə'raɪz/ *vi* (*pt* **arose**, *pp* **arisen**) surgir (from de)

aristocra|cy /ærɪ'stɒkrəsɪ/ *n* aristocracia *f*. **~t** /'ærɪstəkræt/ *n* aristócrata *m & f*. **~tic** /-'krætɪk/ *a* aristocrático

arithmetic /ə'rɪθmətɪk/ *n* aritmética *f*

ark /ɑ:k/ *n* (Relig) arca *f*

arm /ɑ:m/ *n* brazo *m*; (of garment) manga *f*. **~s** *npl* armas *fpl*. ● *vt* armar

armament /'ɑ:məmənt/ *n* armamento *m*

arm: ~band *n* brazalete *m*. **~chair** *n* sillón *m*

armed /ɑ:md/ *a* armado. **~ robbery** *n* robo *m* a mano armada

armful /'ɑ:mfʊl/ *n* brazada *f*

armour /'ɑ:mə(r)/ *n* armadura *f*. **~ed** /'ɑ:məd/ *a* blindado. **~y** /'ɑ:mərɪ/ *n* arsenal *m*

armpit /'ɑ:mpɪt/ *n* sobaco *m*, axila *f*

army /'ɑ:mɪ/ *n* ejército *m*

aroma /ə'rəʊmə/ *n* aroma *m*

arose /ə'rəʊz/ ⇒ARISE

around /ə'raʊnd/ *adv* alrededor; (near) cerca. **all ~** por todas partes. ● *prep* alrededor de; (with time) a eso de

arouse /ə'raʊz/ *vt* despertar

arrange /ə'reɪndʒ/ *vt* arreglar; (fix) fijar. **~ment** *n* arreglo *m*; (agreement) acuerdo *m*. **~ments** *npl* (plans) preparativos *mpl*

arrears /ə'rɪəz/ *npl* atrasos *mpl*. **in ~** atrasado en el pago (with de)

arrest /ə'rest/ *vt* detener. ● *n* detención *f*. **under ~** detenido

arriv|al /ə'raɪvl/ *n* llegada *f*. **new ~al** recién llegado *m*. **~e** /ə'raɪv/ *vi* llegar

arrogan|ce /'ærəgəns/ *n* arrogancia *f*. **~t** *a* arrogante. **~tly** *adv* con arrogancia

arrow /'ærəʊ/ *n* flecha *f*

arse /ɑ:s/ *n* (vulg) culo *m*

arsenal /'ɑ:sənl/ *n* arsenal *m*

arsenic /'ɑ:snɪk/ *n* arsénico *m*

arson /'ɑ:sn/ *n* incendio *m* provocado. **~ist** *n* incendiario *m*

art[1] /ɑ:t/ *n* arte *m*. **A~s** *npl* (Univ) Filosofía y Letras *fpl*. **fine ~s** bellas artes *fpl*

art[2] /ɑ:t/ (*old use, with* **thou**) ⇒ARE

artery /'ɑ:tərɪ/ *n* arteria *f*

art gallery *n* museo *m* de arte, pinacoteca *f*; *<commercial>* galería *f* de arte

arthritis /ɑ:'θraɪtɪs/ *n* artritis *f*

article /'ɑ:tɪkl/ *n* artículo *m*. **~ of clothing** prenda *f* de vestir

articulat|e /ɑ:'tɪkjʊlət/ *a <utterance>* articulado; *<person>* que sabe expresarse. ● /ɑ:'tɪkjʊleɪt/ *vt/i* articular. **~ed lorry** *n* camión *m* articulado. **~ion** /-'leɪʃn/ *n* articulación *f*

artificial /ɑ:tɪ'fɪʃl/ *a* artificial. **~ respiration** respiración *f* artificial

artillery /ɑ:'tɪlərɪ/ *n* artillería *f*

artist /'ɑ:tɪst/ *n* artista *m & f*. **~tic** /ɑ:'tɪstɪk/ *a* artístico. **~ry** /'ɑ:tɪstrɪ/ *n* arte *m*, habilidad *f*

as /æz, əz/ *adv & conj* como; (since) ya que; (while) mientras. **~ big ~** tan grande como. **~ far ~** (distance) hasta; (qualitative) en cuanto a. **~ far ~ I know** que yo sepa. **~ if** como si. **~ long ~** mientras. **~ much ~** tanto como. **~ soon ~** tan pronto como. **~ well** también

asbestos /æz'bestɒs/ *n* amianto *m*, asbesto *m*

ascen|d /ə'send/ *vt/i* subir. **A~sion** /ə'senʃn/ *n*. **the A~sion** la Ascensión. **~t** /ə'sent/ *n* subida *f*

ascertain /æsə'teɪn/ *vt* averiguar

ash /æʃ/ *n* ceniza *f*. ● *n*. **~** (tree) fresno *m*

ashamed /ə'ʃeɪmd/ *a* avergonzado (of de). **be ~ of s.o.** avergonzarse de uno

ashore /ə'ʃɔ:(r)/ *adv* a tierra. **go ~** desembarcar

ash: ~tray *n* cenicero *m*. **A~ Wednesday** *n* Miércoles *m* de Ceniza

Asia /'eɪʃə/ *n* Asia *f*. **~n** *a* & *n* asiático (*m*). **~tic** /-ɪ'ætɪk/ *a* asiático

aside /ə'saɪd/ *adv* a un lado. ● *n* (in theatre) aparte *m*

ask /ɑ:sk/ *vt* pedir; hacer *<question>*; (invite) invitar. **~ about** enterarse de. **~ s.o. to do something** pedirle a uno que haga algo. □ **~ after** *vt* preguntar por. □ **~ for** *vt*. **~ for help** pedir ayuda. **~ for trouble** buscarse problemas. □ **~ in** *vt*. **~ s.o. in** invitar a uno a pasar

askew /ə'skju:/ *adv* & *a* torcido

asleep /ə'sli:p/ *adv* & *a* dormido. **fall ~** dormirse

asparagus /ə'spærəgəs/ *n* espárrago *m*

aspect /'æspekt/ *n* aspecto *m*

asphalt /'æsfælt/ *n* asfalto *m*. ● *vt* asfaltar

aspir|ation /æspə'reɪʃn/ *n* aspiración *f*. **~e** /əs'paɪə(r)/ *vi* aspirar

aspirin /'æsprɪn/ *n* aspirina *f*

ass /æs/ *n* asno *m*; (fig, 🄸) imbécil *m*; (Amer vulg) culo *m*

assassin /ə'sæsɪn/ *n* asesino *m*. **~ate** /-eɪt/ *vt* asesinar. **~ation** /-'eɪʃn/ *n* asesinato *m*

assault /ə'sɔ:lt/ *n* (Mil) ataque *m*; (Jurid) atentado *m*. ● *vt* asaltar

assembl|e /ə'sembl/ *vt* reunir; (Mec) montar. ● *vi* reunirse. **~y** *n* reunión *f*; (Pol etc) asamblea *f*. **~y line** *n* línea *f* de montaje

assent /ə'sent/ *n* asentimiento *m*. ● *vi* asentir

assert /ə'sɜ:t/ *vt* afirmar; hacer valer *<one's rights>*. **~ion** /-ʃn/ *n* afirmación *f*. **~ive** *a* positivo, firme

assess /ə'ses/ *vt* evaluar; (determine) determinar; fijar *<tax etc>*. **~ment** *n* evaluación *f*

asset /'æset/ *n* (advantage) ventaja *f*. **~s** *npl* (Com) bienes *mpl*

assign /ə'saɪn/ *vt* asignar; (appoint) nombrar. **~ment** *n* asignación *f*; (mission) misión *f*; (task) función *f*; (for school) trabajo *m*

assimilate /ə'sɪmɪleɪt/ *vt* asimilar. ● *vi* asimilarse

assist /ə'sɪst/ *vt/i* ayudar. **~ance** *n* ayuda *f*. **~ant** *n* ayudante *m* & *f*; (shop) dependienta *f*, dependiente *m*. ● *a* auxiliar, adjunto

associat|e /ə'səʊʃɪeɪt/ *vt* asociar. ● *vi* asociarse. ● /ə'səʊʃɪət/ *a* asociado. ● *n* colega *m* & *f*; (Com) socio *m*. **~ion** /-'eɪʃn/ *n* asociación *f*.

assort|ed /ə'sɔ:tɪd/ *a* surtido. **~ment** *n* surtido *m*

assum|e /ə'sju:m/ *vt* suponer; tomar *<power, attitude>*; asumir *<role, burden>*. **~ption** /ə'sʌmpʃn/ *n* suposición *f*

assur|ance /ə'ʃʊərəns/ *n* seguridad *f*; (insurance) seguro *m*. **~e** /ə'ʃʊə(r)/ *vt* asegurar. **~ed** *a* seguro

asterisk /ˈæstərɪsk/ *n* asterisco *m*

asthma /ˈæsmə/ *n* asma *f*. **~tic** /-ˈmætɪk/ *a & n* asmático (*m*)

astonish /əˈstɒnɪʃ/ *vt* asombrar. **~ed** *adj* asombrado. **~ing** *a* asombroso. **~ment** *n* asombro *m*

astound /əˈstaʊnd/ *vt* asombrar. **~ed** *adj* atónito. **~ing** *adj* increíble

astray /əˈstreɪ/ *adv*. **go ~** extraviarse. **lead ~** llevar por mal camino

astrology /əˈstrɒlədʒɪ/ *n* astrología *f*

astronaut /ˈæstrənɔːt/ *n* astronauta *m & f*

astronom|er /əˈstrɒnəmə(r)/ *n* astrónomo *m*. **~ical** /æstrəˈnɒmɪkl/ *a* astronómico. **~y** /əˈstrɒnəmɪ/ *n* astronomía *f*

astute /əˈstjuːt/ *a* astuto

asylum /əˈsaɪləm/ *n* asilo *m*. **lunatic ~** manicomio *m*

at /æt/, *unstressed form* /ət/

● *preposition*

····➤ (location) en. **she's at the office** está en la oficina. **at home** en casa. **call me at the office** llámame a la oficina

⇨ For translations of phrases such as **at the top, at the front of, at the back of** see entries **top, front** etc

····➤ (at the house of) en casa de. **I'll be at Rachel's** estaré en casa de Rachel, voy a estar donde Rachel (LAm)

····➤ (talking about time) **at 7 o'clock** a las siete. **at night** por la noche, de noche, en la noche (LAm). **at Christmas** en Navidad

····➤ (talking about age) a. **at six (years of age)** a los seis años

····➤ (with measurements, numbers etc) a. **at 60 miles an hour** a 60 millas por hora. **at a depth of** a una profundidad de. **three at a time** de tres en tres

⇨ For translations of phrasal verbs with **at**, such as **look at**, see entries for those verbs

ate /et/ ⇨EAT

atheis|m /ˈeɪθɪɪzəm/ *n* ateísmo *m*. **~t** *n* ateo *m*

athlet|e /ˈæθliːt/ *n* atleta *m & f*. **~ic** /-ˈletɪk/ *a* atlético. **~ics** *npl* atletismo *m*; (Amer, Sport) deportes *mpl*

Atlantic /ətˈlæntɪk/ *a* atlántico. ● *n*. **the ~ (Ocean)** el (Océano) Atlántico

atlas /ˈætləs/ *n* atlas *m*

ATM *abbr* (= **automated teller machine**) cajero *m* automático

atmospher|e /ˈætməsfɪə(r)/ *n* atmósfera *f*; (fig) ambiente *m*. **~ic** /-ˈferɪk/ *a* atmosférico

atom /ˈætəm/ *n* átomo *m*. **~ic** /əˈtɒmɪk/ *a* atómico

atroci|ous /əˈtrəʊʃəs/ *a* atroz. **~ty** /əˈtrɒsətɪ/ *n* atrocidad *f*

attach /əˈtætʃ/ *vt* sujetar; adjuntar <*document etc*>. **be ~ed to** (be fond of) tener cariño a. **~ment** *n* (affection) cariño *m*; (tool) accesorio *m*

attack /əˈtæk/ *n* ataque *m*. ● *vt/i* atacar. **~er** *n* agresor *m*

attain /əˈteɪn/ *vt* conseguir. **~able** *a* alcanzable

attempt /əˈtempt/ *vt* intentar. ● *n* tentativa *f*; (attack) atentado *m*

attend /ə'tend/ *vt* asistir a; (escort) acompañar. ● *vi* prestar atención. □ ~ **to** *vt* (look after) ocuparse de. ~**ance** *n* asistencia *f*; (people present) concurrencia *f*

atten|tion /ə'tenʃn/ *n* atención *f*. ~**tion!** (Mil) ¡firmes! **pay ~tion** prestar atención. ~**tive** *a* atento

attic /'ætɪk/ *n* desván *m*

attire /ə'taɪə(r)/ *n* atavío *m*. ● *vt* ataviar

attitude /'ætɪtju:d/ *n* postura *f*

attorney /ə'tɜ:nɪ/ *n* (*pl* **-eys**) (Amer) abogado *m*

attract /ə'trækt/ *vt* atraer. ~**ion** /-ʃn/ *n* atracción *f*; (charm) atractivo *m*. ~**ive** *a* atractivo; (interesting) atrayente

attribute /ə'trɪbju:t/ *vt* atribuir. ● /'ætrɪbju:t/ *n* atributo *m*

aubergine /'əʊbəʒi:n/ *n* berenjena *f*

auction /'ɔ:kʃn/ *n* subasta *f*. ● *vt* subastar. ~**eer** /-ə'nɪə(r)/ *n* subastador *m*

audaci|ous /ɔ:'deɪʃəs/ *a* audaz. ~**ty** /ɔ:'dæsətɪ/ *n* audacia *f*

audible /'ɔ:dəbl/ *a* audible

audience /'ɔ:dɪəns/ *n* (at play, film) público *m*; (TV) audiencia *f*; (interview) audiencia *f*

audiovisual /ɔ:dɪəʊ'vɪʒʊəl/ *a* audiovisual

audit /'ɔ:dɪt/ *n* revisión *f* de cuentas. ● *vt* revisar

audition /ɔ:'dɪʃn/ *n* audición *f*. ● *vt* hacerle una audición a. ● *vi* dar una audición (**for** para)

auditor /'ɔ:dɪtə(r)/ *n* interventor *m* de cuentas

auditorium /ɔ:dɪ'tɔ:rɪəm/ (*pl* **-riums** *or* **-ria** /-rɪə/) *n* sala *f*, auditorio *m*

augment /ɔ:g'ment/ *vt* aumentar

augur /'ɔ:gə(r)/ *vt* augurar. **it ~s well** es de buen agüero

August /'ɔ:gəst/ *n* agosto *m*

aunt /ɑ:nt/ *n* tía *f*

au pair /əʊ'peə(r)/ *n* chica *f* au pair

aura /'ɔ:rə/ *n* aura *f*, halo *m*

auster|e /ɔ:'stɪə(r)/ *a* austero. ~**ity** /ɔ:'sterətɪ/ *n* austeridad *f*

Australia /ɒ'streɪlɪə/ *n* Australia *f*. ~**n** *a* & *n* australiano (*m*)

Austria /'ɒstrɪə/ *n* Austria *f*. ~**n** *a* & *n* austríaco (*m*)

authentic /ɔ:'θentɪk/ *a* auténtico. ~**ate** /-keɪt/ *vt* autenticar. ~**ity** /-ən'tɪsətɪ/ *n* autenticidad *f*

author /'ɔ:θə(r)/ *n* autor *m*. ~**ess** /-ɪs/ *n* autora *f*

authoritative /ɔ:'θɒrɪtətɪv/ *a* autorizado; <*manner*> autoritario

authority /ɔ:'θɒrətɪ/ *n* autoridad *f*; (permission) autorización *f*

authoriz|ation /ɔ:θəraɪ'zeɪʃn/ *n* autorización *f*. ~**e** /'ɔ:θəraɪz/ *vt* autorizar

autobiography /ɔ:təʊbaɪ'ɒgrəfɪ/ *n* autobiografía *f*

autograph /'ɔ:təgrɑ:f/ *n* autógrafo *m*. ● *vt* firmar, autografiar

automat|e /'ɔ:təmeɪt/ *vt* automatizar. ~**ic** /-'mætɪk/ *a* automático. ~**ion** /-'meɪʃn/ *n* automatización *f*. ~**on** /ɔ:'tɒmətən/ *n* (*pl* **-tons** *or* **-ta** /-tə/) autómata *m*

automobile /'ɔ:təməbi:l/ *n* (Amer) coche *m*, carro *m* (LAm), automóvil *m*

autonom|ous /ɔ:'tɒnəməs/ *a* autónomo. ~**y** *n* autonomía *f*

autopsy /'ɔ:tɒpsɪ/ *n* autopsia *f*

autumn /'ɔ:təm/ *n* otoño *m*. ~**al** /ɔ:'tʌmnəl/ *a* otoñal

auxiliary /ɔːgˈzɪlɪərɪ/ *a & n* auxiliar (*m & f*)

avail /əˈveɪl/ *n*. to no ~ inútil

availab|ility /əveɪləˈbɪlətɪ/ *n* disponibilidad *f*. **~le** /əˈveɪləbl/ *a* disponible

avalanche /ˈævəlɑːnʃ/ *n* avalancha *f*

avaric|e /ˈævərɪs/ *n* avaricia *f*. **~ious** /-ˈrɪʃəs/ *a* avaro

avenue /ˈævənjuː/ *n* avenida *f*; (fig) vía *f*

average /ˈævərɪdʒ/ *n* promedio *m*. on ~ por término medio. ● *a* medio

avers|e /əˈvɜːs/ *a*. be **~e** to ser reacio a. **~ion** /-ʃn/ *n* repugnancia *f*

avert /əˈvɜːt/ *vt* (turn away) apartar; (ward off) desviar

aviation /eɪvɪˈeɪʃn/ *n* aviación *f*

avid /ˈævɪd/ *a* ávido

avocado /ævəˈkɑːdəʊ/ *n* (*pl* **-os**) aguacate *m*

avoid /əˈvɔɪd/ *vt* evitar. **~able** *a* evitable. **~ance** *n* el evitar

await /əˈweɪt/ *vt* esperar

awake /əˈweɪk/ *vt/i* (*pt* **awoke**, *pp* **awoken**) despertar. ● *a* despierto. wide ~ completamente despierto; (fig) despabilado. **~n** /əˈweɪkən/ *vt/i* despertar. **~ning** *n* el despertar

award /əˈwɔːd/ *vt* otorgar; (Jurid) adjudicar. ● *n* premio *m*; (Jurid) adjudicación *f*; (scholarship) beca *f*

aware /əˈweə(r)/ *a*. be ~ of sth ser consciente de algo, darse cuenta de algo

awash /əˈwɒʃ/ *a* inundado

away /əˈweɪ/ *adv* (absent) fuera. far ~ muy lejos. ● *a* ~ match partido *m* fuera de casa

awe /ɔː/ *n* temor *m*. **~-inspiring** *a* impresionante. **~some** /-səm/ *a* imponente

awful /ˈɔːfʊl/ *a* terrible, malísimo. feel ~ sentirse muy mal

awkward /ˈɔːkwəd/ *a* difícil; (inconvenient) inoportuno; (clumsy) desmañado; (embarrassed) incómodo. **~ness** *n* dificultad *f*; (discomfort) molestia *f*; (clumsiness) torpeza *f*

awning /ˈɔːnɪŋ/ *n* toldo *m*

awoke /əˈwəʊk/, **awoken** /əˈwəʊkən/ ⇒AWAKE

axe /æks/ *n* hacha *f*. ● *vt* (*pres p* **axing**) cortar con hacha; (fig) recortar

axis /ˈæksɪs/ *n* (*pl* **axes** /-iːz/) eje *m*

axle /ˈæksl/ *n* eje *m*

Bb

BA /biːˈeɪ/ *abbr* ⇒BACHELOR

babble /ˈbæbl/ *vi* balbucir; (chatter) parlotear; <*stream*> murmullar.

baboon /bəˈbuːn/ *n* mandril *m*

baby /ˈbeɪbɪ/ *n* niño *m*, bebé *m*. ~ **buggy**, ~ **carriage** *n* (Amer) cochecito *m*. **~ish** /ˈbeɪbɪɪʃ/ *a* infantil. **~-sit** *vi* cuidar a los niños, hacer de canguro. **~-sitter** *n* baby sitter *m & f*, canguro *m & f*

bachelor /ˈbætʃələ(r)/ *n* soltero *m*. **B~ of Arts** (**BA**) licenciado *m* en filosofía y letras. **B~ of Science** (**BSc**) licenciado *m* en ciencias

back /bæk/ *n* espalda *f*; (of car) parte *f* trasera; (of chair) respaldo *m*; (of cloth) revés *m*; (of house) parte *f* de atrás; (of animal, book) lomo *m*; (of hand, document) dorso *m*; (football) defensa *m & f*. **in the ~ of beyond** en el quinto infierno. ● *a* trasero. **the ~ door** la puerta trasera. ● *adv* atrás; (returned) de vuelta. ● *vt* apoyar; (betting) apostar a; dar marcha atrás a <*car*>. ● *vi* retroceder; <*car*> dar marcha atrás. □ **~ down** *vi* volverse atrás. □ **~ out** *vi* retirarse. □ **~ up** *vt* apoyar; (Comp) hacer una copia de seguridad de. **~ache** *n* dolor *m* de espalda. **~bone** *n* columna *f* vertebral; (fig) pilar *m*. **~date** /-'deɪt/ *vt* antedatar. **~er** *n* partidario *m*; (Com) financiador *m*. **~fire** /-'faɪə(r)/ *vi* (Auto) petardear; (fig) fallar. **his plan ~fired on him** le salió el tiro por la culata. **~ground** *n* fondo *m*; (environment) antecedentes *mpl*. **~hand** *n* (Sport) revés *m*. **~ing** *n* apoyo *m*. **~lash** *n* reacción *f*. **~log** *n* atrasos *mpl*. **~side** /-'saɪd/ *n* 🅃 trasero *m*. **~stage** /-'steɪdʒ/ *a* de bastidores. ● *adv* entre bastidores. **~stroke** *n* (tennis etc) revés *m*; (swimming) estilo *m* espalda, estilo *m* dorso (Mex). **~-up** *n* apoyo *m*; (Comp) copia *f* de seguridad. **~ward** /-wəd/ *a* <*step etc*> hacia atrás; (retarded) retrasado; (undeveloped) atrasado. ● *adv* (Amer) ⇒BACKWARDS. **~wards** *adv* hacia atrás; (fall) de espaldas; (back to front) al revés. **go ~wards and forwards** ir de acá para allá. **~water** *n* agua *f* estancada; (fig) lugar *m* apartado

bacon /'beɪkən/ *n* tocino *m*

bacteria /bæk'tɪərɪə/ *npl* bacterias *fpl*

bad /bæd/ *a* (**worse**, **worst**) malo, (before masculine singular noun) mal; (serious) grave; (harmful) nocivo; <*language*> indecente. **feel ~** sentirse mal

bade /beɪd/ ⇒BID

badge /bædʒ/ *n* distintivo *m*, chapa *f*

badger /'bædʒə(r)/ *n* tejón *m*. ● *vt* acosar

bad: ~ly *adv* mal. **want ~ly** desear muchísimo. **~ly injured** gravemente herido. **~ly off** mal de dinero. **~-mannered** /-'mænəd/ *a* mal educado

badminton /'bædmɪntən/ *n* bádminton *m*

bad-tempered /bæd'tempəd/ *a* (always) de mal carácter; (temporarily) de mal humor

baffle /'bæfl/ *vt* desconcertar. **~d** *a* perplejo

bag /bæg/ *n* bolsa *f*; (handbag) bolso *m*. ● *vt* (*pt* **bagged**) ensacar; (take) coger (esp Spain), agarrar (LAm). **~s** *npl* (luggage) equipaje *m*. **~s of** 🅃 montones de

baggage /'bægɪdʒ/ *n* equipaje *m*. **~ room** *n* (Amer) consigna *f*

baggy /'bægɪ/ *a* <*clothes*> holgado

bagpipes /'bægpaɪps/ *npl* gaita *f*

bail[1] /beɪl/ *n* fianza *f*. ● *vt* poner en libertad bajo fianza. **~ s.o. out** pagar la fianza a uno

bail[2] *vt*. **~ out** (Naut) achicar

bait /beɪt/ *n* cebo *m*

bak|e /beɪk/ *vt* cocer al horno. ● *vi* cocerse. **~er** *n* panadero *m*. **~ery** *n* panadería *f*

balance /'bæləns/ *n* equilibrio *m*; (Com) balance *m*; (sum) saldo *m*; (scales) balanza *f*; (remainder) resto *m*. ● *vt* equilibrar <*load*>; mantener en equilibrio <*object*>; nivelar <*budget*>. ● *vi* equilibrarse; (Com) cuadrar. **~d** *a* equilibrado

balcony /'bælkənɪ/ *n* balcón *m*

bald /bɔ:ld/ *a* (**-er**, **-est**) calvo, pelón (Mex)

bale /beɪl/ *n* bala *f*, fardo *m*. ● *vi*. ~ out lanzarse en paracaídas

Balearic /bælɪ'ærɪk/ *a*. **the ~ Islands** las Islas *fpl* Baleares

ball /bɔ:l/ *n* bola *f*; (tennis etc) pelota *f*; (football etc) balón *m*, pelota *f* (esp LAm); (of yarn) ovillo *m*; (*dance*) baile *m*

ballad /'bæləd/ *n* balada *f*

ballast /'bæləst/ *n* lastre *m*

ball bearing *n* cojinete *m* de bolas

ballerina /bælə'ri:nə/ *f* bailarina *f*

ballet /'bæleɪ/ *n* ballet *m*. **~ dancer** *n* bailarín *m* de ballet, bailarina *f* de ballet

balloon /bə'lu:n/ *n* globo *m*

ballot /'bælət/ *n* votación *f*. **~ box** *n* urna *f*. **~ paper** *n* papeleta *f*.

ball: ~point *n*. **~point** (pen) bolígrafo *m*, pluma *f* atómica (Mex). **~room** *n* salón *m* de baile

bamboo /bæm'bu:/ *n* bambú *m*

ban /bæn/ *vt* (*pt* **banned**) prohibir. **~ s.o. from sth** prohibir algo a uno. ● *n* prohibición *f*

banal /bə'nɑ:l/ *a* banal. **~ity** /bə'nælətɪ/ *n* banalidad *f*

banana /bə'nɑ:nə/ *n* plátano *m*

band /bænd/ *n* (strip) banda *f*. ● *n* (Mus) orquesta *f*; (military, brass) banda *f*. □ **~ together** *vi* juntarse

bandage /'bændɪdʒ/ *n* venda *f*. ● *vt* vendar

Band-Aid /'bændeɪd/ *n* (Amer, P) tirita *f*, curita *f* (LAm)

B & B /'bi:ənbi:/ *abbr* (= **bed and breakfast**) cama *f* y desayuno; (place) pensión *f*

bandit /'bændɪt/ *n* bandido *m*

band: ~stand *n* quiosco *m* de música. **~wagon** *n*. **jump on the ~wagon** (fig) subirse al carro

bandy /'bændɪ/ *a* (**-ier**, **-iest**) patizambo

bang /bæŋ/ *n* (noise) ruido *m*; (blow) golpe *m*; (of gun) estampido *m*; (of door) golpe *m*. ● *vt* (strike) golpear. **~ the door** dar un portazo. ● *adv* exactamente. ● *int* ¡pum! **~s** *npl* (Amer) flequillo *m*, cerquillo *m* (LAm), fleco *m* (Mex)

banger /'bæŋə(r)/ *n* petardo *m*; (🅘, Culin) salchicha *f*

bangle /'bæŋgl/ *n* brazalete *m*

banish /'bænɪʃ/ *vt* desterrar

banisters /'bænɪstəz/ *npl* pasamanos *m*

banjo /'bændʒəʊ/ *n* (*pl* **-os**) banjo *m*

bank /bæŋk/ *n* (Com) banco *m*; (of river) orilla *f*. ● *vt* depositar. ● *vi* (Aviat) ladearse. □ **~ on** *vt* contar con. □ **~ with** *vi* tener una cuenta con. **~ card** *n* tarjeta *f* bancaria; (Amer) tarjeta *f* de crédito (expedida por un banco). **~er** *n* banquero *m*. **~ holiday** *n* día *m* festivo, día *m* feriado (LAm). **~ing** *n* (Com) banca *f*. **~note** *n* billete *m* de banco

bankrupt /'bæŋkrʌpt/ *a* & *n* quebrado (*m*). **go ~** quebrar. ● *vt* hacer quebrar. **~cy** /-rʌpsɪ/ *n* bancarrota *f*, quiebra *f*

bank statement *n* estado *m* de cuenta

banner /'bænə(r)/ *n* bandera *f*; (in demonstration) pancarta *f*

banquet /'bæŋkwɪt/ *n* banquete *m*

banter /'bæntə(r)/ *n* chanza *f*

bap /bæp/ *n* panecillo *m* blando

baptism /'bæptɪzəm/ *n* bautismo *m*; (act) bautizo *m*

Baptist /'bæptɪst/ *n* bautista *m* & *f*

baptize /bæp'taɪz/ *vt* bautizar

bar /bɑ:(r)/ *n* barra *f*; (on window) reja *f*; (of chocolate) tableta *f*; (of soap) pastilla *f*; (pub) bar *m*; (Mus) compás *m*; (Jurid) abogacía *f*; (fig) obstáculo *m*. ● *vt* (*pt* **barred**) atrancar <*door*>; (exclude) excluir; (prohibit) prohibir. ● *prep* excepto

barbar|ian /bɑ:'beərɪən/ *a & n* bárbaro (*m*). **~ic** /bɑ:'bærɪk/ *a* bárbaro

barbecue /'bɑ:bɪkju:/ *n* barbacoa *f*. ● *vt* asar a la parilla

barbed wire /bɑ:bd 'waɪə(r)/ *n* alambre *m* de púas

barber /'bɑ:bə(r)/ *n* peluquero *m*, barbero *m*

barbwire /'bɑ:b'waɪə(r)/ *n* (Amer) ⇒BARBED WIRE

bare /beə(r)/ *a* (**-er**, **-est**) desnudo; (room) con pocos muebles; (mere) simple; (empty) vacío. ● *vt* desnudar; (uncover) descubrir. **~ one's teeth** mostrar los dientes. **~back** *adv* a pelo. **~faced** *a* descarado. **~foot** *a* descalzo. **~headed** /-'hedɪd/ *a* descubierto. **~ly** *adv* apenas.

bargain /'bɑ:gɪn/ *n* (agreement) pacto *m*; (good buy) ganga *f*. ● *vi* negociar; (haggle) regatear. □ **~ for** *vt* esperar, contar con

barge /bɑ:dʒ/ *n* barcaza *f*. ● *vi*. **~ in** irrumpir

baritone /'bærɪtəʊn/ *n* barítono *m*

bark /bɑ:k/ *n* (of dog) ladrido *m*; (of tree) corteza *f*. ● *vi* ladrar

barley /'bɑ:lɪ/ *n* cebada *f*

bar: ~maid *n* camarera *f*. **~man** /-mən/ *n* camarero *m*, barman *m*

barmy /'bɑ:mɪ/ *a* ⊠ chiflado

barn /bɑ:n/ *n* granero *m*

barometer /bə'rɒmɪtə(r)/ *n* barómetro *m*

baron /'bærən/ *n* barón *m*. **~ess** /-ɪs/ *n* baronesa *f*

barracks /'bærəks/ *npl* cuartel *m*

barrage /'bærɑ:ʒ/ *n* (Mil) barrera *f*; (dam) presa *f*. **a ~ of questions** un aluvión de preguntas

barrel /'bærəl/ *n* barril *m*; (of gun) cañón *m*

barren /'bærən/ *a* estéril

barrette /bə'ret/ *n* (Amer) pasador *m*

barricade /bærɪ'keɪd/ *n* barricada *f*. ● *vt* cerrar con barricadas

barrier /'bærɪə(r)/ *n* barrera *f*

barring /'bɑ:rɪŋ/ *prep* salvo

barrister /'bærɪstə(r)/ *n* abogado *m*

bartender /'bɑ:tendə(r)/ *n* (Amer) (male) camarero *m*, barman *m*; (female) camarera *f*

barter /'bɑ:tə(r)/ *n* trueque *m*. ● *vt* trocar

base /beɪs/ *n* base *f*. ● *vt* basar. **~ball** *n* béisbol *m*, beisbol *m* (Mex)

basement /'beɪsmənt/ *n* sótano *m*

bash /bæʃ/ *vt* golpear. ● *n* golpe *m*. **have a ~** [I] probar

bashful /'bæʃfl/ *a* tímido

basic /'beɪsɪk/ *a* básico, fundamental. **~ally** *adv* fundamentalmente

basin /'beɪsn/ *n* (for washing) palangana *f*; (for food) cuenco *m*; (Geog) cuenca *f*

basis /'beɪsɪs/ *n* (*pl* **bases** /-si:z/) base *f*

bask /bɑ:sk/ *vi* asolearse; (fig) gozar (in de)

basket /'bɑ:skɪt/ *n* cesta *f*; (big) cesto *m*. **~ball** *n* baloncesto *m*, básquetbol *m* (LAm)

bass /beɪs/ *a* bajo. ● *n* (Mus) bajo *m*

bassoon /bə'su:n/ *n* fagot *m*

bastard /'bɑ:stəd/ *n* bastardo *m*. **you ~!** (▯ or vulg) ¡cabrón! (▯ or vulg)

bat /bæt/ *n* (for baseball, cricket) bate *m*; (for table tennis) raqueta *f*; (mammal) murciélago *m*. **off one's own ~** por sí solo. ● *vt* (*pt* **batted**) golpear. **without ~ting an eyelid** sin pestañear. ● *vi* batear

batch /bætʃ/ *n* (of people) grupo *m*; (of papers) pila *f*; (of goods) remesa *f*; (of bread) hornada *f*; (Comp) lote *m*

bated /'beɪtɪd/ *a*. **with ~ breath** con aliento entrecortado

bath /bɑ:θ/ *n* (*pl* **-s** /bɑ:ðz/) baño *m*; (tub) bañera *f*, tina *f* (LAm). **~s** *npl* (swimming pool) piscina *f*, alberca *f* (LAm). **have a ~, take a ~** (Amer) bañarse. ● *vt* bañar. ● *vi* bañarse

bathe /beɪð/ *vt* bañar. ● *vi* bañarse. ● *n* baño *m*. **~r** *n* bañista *m & f*

bathing /'beɪðɪŋ/ *n* baños *mpl*. **~ costume, ~ suit** *n* traje *m* de baño

bathroom /'bɑ:θrʊm/ *n* cuarto *m* de baño; (Amer, toilet) servicio *m*, baño *m* (LAm)

batsman /'bætsmən/ *n* (*pl* **-men**) bateador *m*

battalion /bə'tælɪən/ *n* batallón *m*

batter /'bætə(r)/ *vt* (beat) apalear; (cover with batter) rebozar. ● *n* batido *m* para rebozar; (Amer, for cake) masa *f*. **~ed** /'bætəd/ *a* <*car etc*> estropeado; <*wife etc*> maltratado

battery /'bætərɪ/ *n* (Mil, Auto) batería *f*; (of torch, radio) pila *f*

battle /'bætl/ *n* batalla *f*; (fig) lucha *f*. ● *vi* luchar. **~field** *n* campo *m* de batalla. **~ship** *n* acorazado *m*

bawl /bɔ:l/ *vt/i* gritar

bay /beɪ/ *n* (Geog) bahía *f*. **keep at ~** mantener a raya

bayonet /'beɪənet/ *n* bayoneta *f*

bay window /beɪ 'wɪndəʊ/ *n* ventana *f* saledIza

bazaar /bə'zɑ:(r)/ *n* bazar *m*

BC *abbr* (= **before Christ**) a. de C., antes de Cristo

---

be /bi:/

present **am, are, is**; past **was, were**; past participle **been**

● *intransitive verb*

! Spanish has two verbs meaning **be**, *ser* and *estar*. See those entries for further information about the differences between them.

····➤ (position, changed condition or state) estar. **where is the library?** ¿dónde está la biblioteca? **she's tired** está cansada. **how are you?** ¿cómo estás?

····➤ (identity, nature or permanent characteristics) ser. **she's tall** es alta. **he's Scottish** es escocés. **I'm a journalist** soy periodista. **he's very kind** es muy bondadoso

····➤ (feel) **to be** + *adjective* tener + *sustantivo*. **to be cold/hot** tener frío/calor. **he's hungry/thirsty** tiene hambre/sed

····➤ (age) **he's thirty** tiene treinta años

····➤ (weather) **it's cold/hot** hace frío/calor. **it was 40 degrees** hacía 40 grados

● *auxiliary verb*

····➤(in tenses) estar. **I'm working** estoy trabajando. **they were singing** estaban cantando, cantaban

····➤(in tag questions) **it's a beautiful house, isn't it?** es una casa preciosa, ¿verdad? *or* ¿no? *or* ¿no es cierto?

····➤(in short answers) **are you disappointed? - yes, I am** ¿estás desilusionado? - sí (,lo estoy). **I'm surprised, aren't you?** estoy sorprendido, ¿tú no?

····➤(in passive sentences) **it was built in 1834** fue construido en 1834, se construyó en 1834. **she was told that ...** le dijeron que..., se le dijo que ...

! Note that passive sentences in English are often translated using the pronoun *se* or using the third person plural.

beach /biːtʃ/ *n* playa *f*

beacon /ˈbiːkən/ *n* faro *m*

bead /biːd/ *n* cuenta *f*; (of glass) abalorio *m*

beak /biːk/ *n* pico *m*

beaker /ˈbiːkə(r)/ *n* taza *f* (alta y sin asa)

beam /biːm/ *n* (of wood) viga *f*; (of light) rayo *m*; (Naut) bao *m*. ● *vt* emitir. ● *vi* irradiar; (smile) sonreír

bean /biːn/ *n* alubia *f*, frijol *m* (LAm); (broad bean) haba *f*; (of coffee) grano *m*

bear /beə(r)/ *vt* (*pt* **bore**, *pp* **borne**) llevar; parir <*niño*>; (endure) soportar. ~ **right** torcer a la derecha. ~ **in mind** tener en cuenta. □ ~ **with** *vt* tener paciencia con. ● *n* oso *m*. ~**able** *a* soportable

beard /bɪəd/ *n* barba *f*. ~**ed** *a* barbudo

bearer /ˈbeərə(r)/ *n* portador *m*; (of passport) titular *m & f*

bearing /ˈbeərɪŋ/ *n* comportamiento *m*; (relevance) relación *f*; (Mec) cojinete *m*. **get one's ~s** orientarse. **lose one's ~s** desorientarse

beast /biːst/ *n* bestia *f*; (person) bruto *m*. ~**ly** *a* (**-ier**, **-iest**) bestial; [I] horrible

beat /biːt/ *vt* (*pt* **beat**, *pp* **beaten**) (hit) pegar; (Culin) batir; (defeat) derrotar; (better) sobrepasar; batir <*record*>; (baffle) dejar perplejo. ~ **it** [I] largarse. ● *vi* <*heart*> latir. ● *n* latido *m*; (Mus) ritmo *m*; (of policeman) ronda *f*. □ ~ **up** *vt* darle una paliza a; (Culin) batir. ~ **up on** (Amer, [I]) darle una paliza a.. ~**er** *n* batidor *m*. ~**ing** *n* paliza *f*

beautician /bjuːˈtɪʃn/ *n* esteticista *m & f*

beautiful /ˈbjuːtɪfl/ *a* hermoso. ~**ly** *adv* maravillosamente

beauty /ˈbjuːtɪ/ *n* belleza *f*. ~ **salon**, ~ **shop** (Amer) *n* salón *m* de belleza. ~ **spot** *n* (on face) lunar *m*; (site) lugar *m* pintoresco

beaver /ˈbiːvə(r)/ *n* castor *m*

became /bɪˈkeɪm/ ⇨BECOME

because /bɪˈkɒz/ *conj* porque. ● *adv*. ~ **of** por, a causa de

beckon /ˈbekən/ *vt/i*. ~ (**to**) hacer señas (a)

become /bɪˈkʌm/ *vi* (*pt* **became**, *pp* **become**) hacerse, llegar a ser, volverse, convertirse en. **what has ~ of her?** ¿qué es de ella?

bed /bed/ *n* cama *f*; (layer) estrato *m*; (of sea, river) fondo *m*; (of flowers) macizo *m*. **go to ~** acostarse. ~ **and breakfast** (**B & B**) cama y desayuno; (place) pensión *f*. **~bug** *n* chinche *f*. **~clothes** *npl*, **~ding** *n* ropa *f* de cama, cobijas *fpl* (LAm); **~room** *n* dormitorio *m*, cuarto *m*, habitación *f*, recámara *f* (Mex). **~-sitter** /-'sɪtə(r)/ *n* habitación *f* con cama y uso de cocina y baño compartidos, estudio *m*. **~spread** *n* colcha *f*. **~time** *n* hora *f* de acostarse

bee /bi:/ *n* abeja *f*; (Amer, social gathering) círculo *m*

beech /bi:tʃ/ *n* haya *f*

beef /bi:f/ *n* carne *f* de vaca, carne *f* de res (Mex). ● *vi* 🅸 quejarse. **~burger** *n* hamburguesa *f*. **~y** *a* (**-ier**, **-iest**) musculoso

bee: ~hive *n* colmena *f*. **~line** *n*. **make a ~line for** ir en línea recta hacia

been /bi:n/ ⇒BE

beer /bɪə(r)/ *n* cerveza *f*

beet /bi:t/ *n* (Amer) remolacha *f*, betabel *f* (Mex)

beetle /'bi:tl/ *n* escarabajo *m*

beetroot /'bi:tru:t/ *n invar* remolacha *f*, betabel *f* (Mex)

befall /bɪ'fɔ:l/ *vt* (*pt* **befell**, *pp* **befallen**) ocurrirle a. ● *vi* ocurrir

before /bɪ'fɔ:(r)/ *prep* (time) antes de; (place) delante de. **~ leaving** antes de marcharse. ● *adv* (place) delante; (time) antes. **a week ~** una semana antes. **the week ~** la semana anterior. ● *conj* (time) antes de que. **~ he leaves** antes de que se vaya. **~hand** *adv* de antemano

befriend /bɪ'frend/ *vt* hacerse amigo de

beg /beg/ *vt/i* (*pt* **begged**) mendigar; (entreat) suplicar; (ask) pedir. **~ s.o.'s pardon** pedir perdón a uno. **I ~ your pardon!** ¡perdone Vd! **I ~ your pardon?** ¿cómo?

began /bɪ'gæn/ ⇒BEGIN

beggar /'begə(r)/ *n* mendigo *m*

begin /bɪ'gɪn/ *vt/i* (*pt* **began**, *pp* **begun**, *pres p* **beginning**) comenzar, empezar. **~ner** *n* principiante *m & f*. **~ning** *n* principio *m*

begrudge /bɪ'grʌdʒ/ *vt* envidiar; (give) dar de mala gana

begun /bɪ'gʌn/ ⇒BEGIN

behalf /bɪ'hɑ:f/ *n*. **on ~ of, in ~ of** (Amer) de parte de, en nombre de

behav|e /bɪ'heɪv/ *vi* comportarse, portarse. **~e (o.s.)** portarse bien. **~iour** /bɪ'heɪvjə(r)/ *n* comportamiento *m*

behead /bɪ'hed/ *vt* decapitar

behind /bɪ'haɪnd/ *prep* detrás de, atrás de (LAm). ● *adv* detrás; (late) atrasado. ● *n* 🅸 trasero *m*

beige /beɪʒ/ *a & n* beige (*m*)

being /'bi:ɪŋ/ *n* ser *m*. **come into ~** nacer

belated /bɪ'leɪtɪd/ *a* tardío

belch /beltʃ/ *vi* eructar. □ **~ out** *vt* arrojar <*smoke*>

belfry /'belfrɪ/ *n* campanario *m*

Belgi|an /'beldʒən/ *a & n* belga (*m & f*). **~um** /'beldʒəm/ *n* Bélgica *f*

belie|f /bɪ'li:f/ *n* (trust) fe *f*; (opinion) creencia *f*. **~ve** /bɪ'li:v/ *vt/i* creer. **~ve in** creer en. **make ~ve** fingir

belittle /bɪ'lɪtl/ *vt* menospreciar <*achievements*>; denigrar <*person*>

bell /bel/ *n* campana *f*; (on door, bicycle) timbre *m*

belligerent /bɪ'lɪdʒərənt/ *a* beligerante

bellow /'beləʊ/ *vt* gritar. ● *vi* bramar. **~s** *npl* fuelle *m*

bell pepper *n* (Amer) pimiento *m*

belly /'belɪ/ *n* barriga *f*

belong /bɪ'lɒŋ/ *vi* pertenecer (**to** a); (club) ser socio (**to** de); (have as usual place) ir. **~ings** /bɪ'lɒŋɪŋz/ *npl* pertenencias *fpl*. **personal ~ings** efectos *mpl* personales

beloved /bɪ'lʌvɪd/ *a* querido

below /bɪ'ləʊ/ *prep* debajo de, abajo de (LAm); (fig) inferior a. ● *adv* abajo

belt /belt/ *n* cinturón *m*; (area) zona *f*. ● *vt* (fig) rodear; ⊠ darle una paliza a. **~way** *n* (Amer) carretera *f* de circunvalación

bench /bentʃ/ *n* banco *m*

bend /bend/ *n* curva *f*. ● *vt* (*pt & pp* **bent**) doblar; torcer <*arm, leg*>. ● *vi* doblarse; <*road*> torcerse. □ **~ down** *vi* inclinarse □ **~ over** *vi* agacharse

beneath /bɪ'ni:θ/ *prep* debajo de; (fig) inferior a. ● *adv* abajo

beneficial /benɪ'fɪʃl/ *a* provechoso

beneficiary /benɪ'fɪʃərɪ/ *n* beneficiario *m*

benefit /'benɪfɪt/ *n* provecho *m*, ventaja *f*; (allowance) prestación *f*; (for unemployed) subsidio *m*; (perk) beneficio *m*. ● *vt* (*pt* **benefited**, *pres p* **benefiting**) beneficiar. ● *vi* beneficiarse

benevolent /bə'nevələnt/ *a* benévolo

benign /bɪ'naɪn/ *a* benigno

bent /bent/ ⇒BEND. ● *n* inclinación *f*. ● *a* torcido; (⊠, corrupt) corrompido

bereave|d /bɪ'ri:vd/ *n*. **the ~d** la familia del difunto. **~ment** *n* pérdida *f*; (mourning) luto *m*

beret /'bereɪ/ *n* boina *f*

berry /'berɪ/ *n* baya *f*

berserk /bə'sɜ:k/ *a*. **go ~** volverse loco

berth /bɜ:θ/ *n* litera *f*; (anchorage) amarradero *m*. **give a wide ~ to** evitar. ● *vt/i* atracar

beside /bɪ'saɪd/ *prep* al lado de. **be ~ o.s.** estar fuera de sí

besides /bɪ'saɪdz/ *prep* además de; (except) excepto. ● *adv* además

besiege /bɪ'si:dʒ/ *vt* sitiar, asediar; (fig) acosar

best /best/ *a* (el) mejor. **the ~ thing is to...** lo mejor es... ● *adv* mejor. **like ~** preferir. ● *n* lo mejor. **at ~** a lo más. **do one's ~** hacer todo lo posible. **make the ~ of** contentarse con. **~ man** *n* padrino *m* (de boda)

bestow /bɪ'stəʊ/ *vt* conceder

bestseller /best'selə(r)/ *n* éxito *m* de librería, bestseller *m*

bet /bet/ *n* apuesta *f*. ● *vt/i* (*pt* **bet** *or* **betted**) apostar

betray /bɪ'treɪ/ *vt* traicionar. **~al** *n* traición *f*

better /'betə(r)/ *a & adv* mejor. **~ off** en mejores condiciones; (richer) más rico. **get ~** mejorar. **all the ~** tanto mejor. **I'd ~ be off** me tengo que ir. **the ~ part of** la mayor parte de. ● *vt* mejorar; (beat) sobrepasar. **~ o.s.** superarse. ● *n* superior *m*. **get the ~ of** vencer a. **my ~s** mis superiores *mpl*

between /bɪ'twi:n/ *prep* entre. ● *adv* en medio

beverage /'bevərɪdʒ/ *n* bebida *f*

beware /bɪ'weə(r)/ *vi* tener cuidado. ● *int* ¡cuidado!

bewilder /bɪ'wɪldə(r)/ *vt* desconcertar. **~ment** *n* aturdimiento *m*

bewitch /bɪ'wɪtʃ/ *vt* hechizar; (delight) cautivar

beyond /bɪ'jɒnd/ *prep* más allá de; (fig) fuera de. **~ doubt** sin lugar a duda. ● *adv* más allá

bias /'baɪəs/ *n* tendencia *f*; (prejudice) prejuicio *m*. ● *vt* (*pt* **biased**) influir en. **~ed** *a* parcial

bib /bɪb/ *n* babero *m*

Bible /'baɪbl/ *n* Biblia *f*

biblical /'bɪblɪkl/ *a* bíblico

bibliography /bɪblɪ'ɒgrəfɪ/ *n* bibliografía *f*

biceps /'baɪseps/ *n invar* bíceps *m*

bicker /'bɪkə(r)/ *vi* altercar

bicycle /'baɪsɪkl/ *n* bicicleta *f*

bid /bɪd/ *n* (offer) oferta *f*; (attempt) tentativa *f*. ● *vi* hacer una oferta. ● *vt* (*pt & pp* **bid**, *pres p* **bidding**) ofrecer; (*pt* **bid**, *pp* **bidden**, *pres p* **bidding**) mandar; dar <*welcome, good day etc*>. **~der** *n* postor *m*. **~ding** *n* (at auction) ofertas *fpl*; (order) mandato *m*

bide /baɪd/ *vt*. **~ one's time** esperar el momento oportuno

bifocals /baɪ'fəʊklz/ *npl* gafas *fpl* bifocales, anteojos *mpl* bifocales (LAm)

big /bɪg/ *a* (**bigger**, **biggest**) grande, (before singular noun) gran. ● *adv*. **talk ~** fanfarronear

bigam|ist /'bɪgəmɪst/ *n* bígamo *m*. **~ous** /'bɪgəməs/ *a* bígamo. **~y** *n* bigamia *f*

big-headed /-'hedɪd/ *a* engreído

bigot /'bɪgət/ *n* fanático *m*. **~ed** *a* fanático

bike /baɪk/ *n* [I] bici *f* [I]

bikini /bɪ'ki:nɪ/ *n* (*pl* **-is**) bikini *m*

bile /baɪl/ *n* bilis *f*

bilingual /baɪ'lɪŋgwəl/ *a* bilingüe

bill /bɪl/ *n* cuenta *f*; (invoice) factura *f*; (notice) cartel *m*; (Amer, banknote) billete *m*; (Pol) proyecto *m* de ley; (of bird) pico *m*

billet /'bɪlɪt/ *n* (Mil) alojamiento *m*. ● *vt* alojar

billfold /'bɪlfəʊld/ *n* (Amer) cartera *f*, billetera *f*

billiards /'bɪlɪədz/ *n* billar *m*

billion /'bɪlɪən/ *n* billón *m*; (Amer) mil millones *mpl*

bin /bɪn/ *n* recipiente *m*; (for rubbish) cubo *m* de basura, bote *m* de basura (Mex); (for waste paper) papelera *f*

bind /baɪnd/ *vt* (*pt* **bound**) atar; encuadernar <*book*>; (Jurid) obligar. ● *n* [I] lata *f*. **~ing** *n* (of books) encuadernación *f*; (braid) ribete *m*

binge /bɪndʒ/ *n* [▣] (of food) comilona *f*; (of drink) borrachera *f*. **go on a ~** ir de juerga

bingo /'bɪŋgəʊ/ *n* bingo *m*

binoculars /bɪ'nɒkjʊləz/ *npl* gemelos *mpl*

biograph|er /baɪ'ɒgrəfə(r)/ *n* biógrafo *m*. **~y** *n* biografía *f*

biolog|ical /baɪə'lɒdʒɪkl/ *a* biológico. **~ist** /baɪ'ɒlədʒɪst/ *n* biólogo *m*. **~y** /baɪ'ɒlədʒɪ/ *n* biología *f*

birch /bɜ:tʃ/ *n* (tree) abedul *m*

bird /bɜ:d/ *n* ave *f*; (small) pájaro *m*; ([▣], girl) chica *f*

Biro /'baɪərəʊ/ *n* (*pl* **-os**) (P) bolígrafo *m*

birth /bɜ:θ/ *n* nacimiento *m*. **give ~** dar a luz. **~ certificate** *n* partida *f* de nacimiento. **~ control** *n* control *m* de la natalidad. **~day** *n* cumpleaños *m*. **~mark** *n* marca *f* de nacimiento. **~place** *n* lugar *m* de nacimiento. **~ rate** *n* natalidad *f*

biscuit /'bɪskɪt/ *n* galleta *f*

bisect /baɪ'sekt/ *vt* bisecar

bishop /'bɪʃəp/ *n* obispo *m*; (Chess) alfil *m*

bit /bɪt/ ⇒BITE. ● *n* trozo *m*; (quantity) poco *m*; (of horse) bocado *m*; (Mec) broca *f*; (Comp) bit *m*

bitch /bɪtʃ/ *n* perra *f*; (Ⓘ, woman) bruja *f* Ⓘ

bit|e /baɪt/ *vt/i* (*pt* **bit**, *pp* **bitten**) morder; (insect) picar. **~e one's nails** morderse las uñas. ● *n* mordisco *m*; (mouthful) bocado *m*; (of insect etc) picadura *f*. **~ing** /ˈbaɪtɪŋ/ *a* mordaz

bitter /ˈbɪtə(r)/ *a* amargo; <*weather*> glacial. ● *n* cerveza *f* amarga. **~ly** *adv* amargamente. **it's ~ly cold** hace un frío glacial. **~ness** *n* amargor *m*; (resentment) amargura *f*

bizarre /bɪˈzɑ:(r)/ *a* extraño

black /blæk/ *a* (**-er**, **-est**) negro. **~ and blue** amoratado. ● *n* negro *m*; (coffee) solo, negro (LAm). ● *vt* ennegrecer; limpiar <*shoes*>. **~ out** *vi* desmayarse. **~ and white** *n* blanco y negro *m*. **~-and-white** *adj* en blanco y negro. **~berry** /-bərɪ/ *n* zarzamora *f*. **~bird** *n* mirlo *m*. **~board** *n* pizarra *f*. **~currant** /-ˈkʌrənt/ *n* grosella *f* negra. **~en** *vt* ennegrecer. **~ eye** *n* ojo *m* morado. **~list** *vt* poner en la lista negra. **~mail** *n* chantaje *m*. ● *vt* chantajear. **~mailer** *n* chantajista *m & f*. **~out** *n* apagón *m*; (Med) desmayo *m*; (of news) censura *f*. **~smith** *n* herrero *m*

bladder /ˈblædə(r)/ *n* vejiga *f*

blade /bleɪd/ *n* (of knife, sword) hoja *f*. **~ of grass** brizna *f* de hierba

blame /bleɪm/ *vt* echar la culpa a. **be to ~** tener la culpa. ● *n* culpa *f*. **~less** *a* inocente

bland /blænd/ *a* (**-er**, **-est**) suave

blank /blæŋk/ *a* <*page, space*> en blanco; <*cassette*> virgen; <*cartridge*> sin bala; (fig) vacío. ● *n* blanco *m*

blanket /ˈblæŋkɪt/ *n* manta *f*, cobija *f* (LAm), frazada (LAm); (fig) capa *f*. ● *vt* (*pt* **blanketed**) (fig) cubrir (**in, with** de)

blare /bleə(r)/ *vi* sonar muy fuerte. ● *n* estrépito *m*

blasphem|e /blæsˈfi:m/ *vt/i* blasfemar. **~ous** /ˈblæsfəməs/ *a* blasfemo. **~y** /ˈblæsfəmɪ/ *n* blasfemia *f*

blast /blɑ:st/ *n* explosión *f*; (gust) ráfaga *f*; (sound) toque *m*. ● *vt* volar. **~ed** *a* maldito. **~-off** *n* (of missile) despegue *m*

blatant /ˈbleɪtnt/ *a* patente; (shameless) descarado

blaze /ˈbleɪz/ *n* llamarada *f*; (of light) resplandor *m*; (fig) arranque *m*. ● *vi* arder en llamas; (fig) brillar

blazer /ˈbleɪzə(r)/ *n* chaqueta *f*

bleach /bli:tʃ/ *n* lejía *f*, cloro *m* (LAm), blanqueador *m* (LAm). ● *vt* blanquear; decolorar <*hair*>.

bleak /bli:k/ *a* (**-er**, **-est**) desolado; (fig) sombrío

bleat /bli:t/ *n* balido *m*. ● *vi* balar

bleed /bli:d/ *vt/i* (*pt* **bled** /bled/) sangrar

bleep /bli:p/ *n* pitido *m*

blemish /ˈblemɪʃ/ *n* mancha *f*

blend /blend/ *n* mezcla *f*. ● *vt* mezclar. ● *vi* combinarse. **~er** *n* licuadora *f*

bless /bles/ *vt* bendecir. **~ you!** (on sneezing) ¡Jesús!, ¡salud! (Mex). **~ed** /ˈblesɪd/ *a* bendito. **~ing** *n* bendición *f*; (advantage) ventaja *f*

blew /blu:/ ⇒BLOW

blight /blaɪt/ *n* añublo *m*, tizón *m*; (fig) plaga *f*. ● *vt* añublar, atizonar; (fig) destrozar

blind /blaɪnd/ *a* ciego. **~ alley** callejón *m* sin salida. ● *n* persiana *f*; (fig) pretexto *m*. ● *vt* dejar ciego; (dazzle) deslumbrar. **~fold** *a & adv* con los ojos vendados. ● *n* venda *f*.

● *vt* vendar los ojos a. **~ly** *adv* a ciegas. **~ness** *n* ceguera *f*

blink /blɪŋk/ *vi* parpadear; *<light>* centellear. **~ers** *npl* (on horse) anteojeras *fpl*

bliss /blɪs/ *n* felicidad *f*. **~ful** *a* feliz

blister /ˈblɪstə(r)/ *n* ampolla *f*

blizzard /ˈblɪzəd/ *n* ventisca *f*

bloated /ˈbləʊtɪd/ *a* hinchado (with de)

blob /blɒb/ *n* (drip) gota *f*; (stain) mancha *f*

bloc /blɒk/ *n* (Pol) bloque *m*

block /blɒk/ *n* bloque *m*; (of wood) zoquete *m*; (of buildings) manzana *f*, cuadra *f* (LAm). **in ~ letters** en letra de imprenta. **~ of flats** edificio *m* de apartamentos, casa *f* de pisos. ● *vt* bloquear. **~ade** /blɒˈkeɪd/ *n* bloqueo *m*. ● *vt* bloquear. **~age** /-ɪdʒ/ *n* obstrucción *f*. **~head** *n* [I] zopenco *m*

bloke /bləʊk/ *n* [I] tipo *m*, tío *m* [I]

blond /blɒnd/ *a & n* rubio (*m*), güero (*m*) (Mex [I]). **~e** *a & n* rubia (*f*), güera (*f*) (Mex [I])

blood /blʌd/ *n* sangre *f*. **~bath** *n* masacre *m*. **~-curdling** /-kɜːdlɪŋ/ *a* horripilante. **~hound** *n* sabueso *m*. **~ pressure** *n* tensión *f* arterial. **high ~ pressure** hipertensión *f*. **~shed** *n* derramamiento *m* de sangre. **~shot** *a* sanguinolento; *<eye>* inyectado de sangre. **~stream** *n* torrente *m* sanguíneo. **~thirsty** *a* sanguinario. **~y** *a* (**-ier**, **-iest**) sangriento; (stained) ensangrentado; [x] maldito

bloom /bluːm/ *n* flor *f*. ● *vi* florecer

blossom /ˈblɒsəm/ *n* flor *f*. ● *vi* florecer. **~ (out) into** (fig) llegar a ser

blot /blɒt/ *n* borrón *m*. ● *vt* (*pt* **blotted**) manchar; (dry) secar. □ **~ out** *vt* oscurecer

blotch /blɒtʃ/ *n* mancha *f*. **~y** *a* lleno de manchas

blotting-paper /ˈblɒtɪŋ/ *n* papel *m* secante

blouse /blaʊz/ *n* blusa *f*

blow /bləʊ/ *vt* (*pt* **blew**, *pp* **blown**) soplar; fundir *<fuse>*; tocar *<trumpet>*. ● *vi* soplar; *<fuse>* fundirse; (sound) sonar. ● *n* golpe *m*. □ **~ down** *vt* derribar. □ **~ out** *vi* apagar *<candle>*. □ **~ over** *vi* pasar. □ **~ up** *vt* inflar; (explode) volar; (Photo) ampliar. *vi* (explode) estallar; (burst) reventar. **~-dry** *vt* secar con secador. **~lamp** *n* soplete *m*. **~out** *n* (of tyre) reventón *m*. **~torch** *n* soplete *m*

blue /bluː/ *a* (**-er**, **-est**) azul; *<joke>* verde. ● *n* azul *m*. **out of the ~** totalmente inesperado. **~s** *npl*. **have the ~s** tener tristeza. **~bell** *n* campanilla *f*. **~bottle** *n* moscarda *f*. **~print** *n* plano *m*; (fig, plan) programa *m*

bluff /blʌf/ *n* (poker) farol *m*, bluff *m* (LAm), blof *m* (Mex). ● *vt* engañar. ● *vi* tirarse un farol, hacer un bluf (LAm), blofear (Mex)

blunder /ˈblʌndə(r)/ *vi* cometer un error. ● *n* metedura *f* de pata

blunt /blʌnt/ *a* desafilado; *<person>* directo, abrupto. ● *vt* desafilar. **~ly** *adv* francamente

blur /blɜː(r)/ *n* impresión *f* indistinta. ● *vt* (*pt* **blurred**) hacer borroso

blurb /blɜːb/ *n* resumen *m* publicitario

blurt /blɜːt/ *vt*. **~ out** dejar escapar

blush /blʌʃ/ *vi* ruborizarse. ● *n* rubor *m*

boar /bɔ:(r)/ *n* verraco *m*. **wild ~** jabalí *m*

board /bɔ:d/ *n* tabla *f*, tablero *m*; (for notices) tablón *m* de anuncios, tablero *m* de anuncios (LAm); (blackboard) pizarra *f*; (food) pensión *f*; (Admin) junta *f*. **~ and lodging** casa y comida. **full ~** pensión *f* completa. **go by the ~** ser abandonado. ● *vt* alojar; **~ a ship** embarcarse. ● *vi* alojarse (**with** en casa de); (at school) ser interno. **~er** *n* huésped *m* & *f*; (school) interno *m*. **~ing card** *n* tarjeta *f* de embarque. **~ing house** *n* casa *f* de huéspedes, pensión *f*. **~ing pass** *n* ⇨~ING CARD. **~ing school** *n* internado *m*

boast /bəʊst/ *vt* enorgullecerse de. ● *vi* jactarse. ● *n* jactancia *f*. **~ful** *a* jactancioso

boat /bəʊt/ *n* barco *m*; (small) bote *m*, barca *f*

bob /bɒb/ *vi* (*pt* **bobbed**) menearse, subir y bajar. □ **~ up** *vi* presentarse súbitamente

bobbin /ˈbɒbɪn/ *n* carrete *m*; (in sewing machine) canilla *f*, bobina *f*

bobby /ˈbɒbɪ/: **~ pin** *n* (Amer) horquilla *f*, pasador *m* (Mex). **~ sox** /sɒks/ *npl* (Amer) calcetines *mpl* cortos

bobsleigh /ˈbɒbsleɪ/ *n* bob(sleigh) *m*

bode /bəʊd/ *vi*. **~ well/ill** ser de buen/mal agüero

bodice /ˈbɒdɪs/ *n* corpiño *m*

bodily /ˈbɒdɪlɪ/ *a* físico, corporal. ● *adv* físicamente

body /ˈbɒdɪ/ *n* cuerpo *m*; (dead) cadáver *m*. **~guard** *n* guardaespaldas *m*. **~work** *n* carrocería *f*

bog /bɒg/ *n* ciénaga *f*. □ **~ down** *vt* (*pt* **bogged**). **get ~ged down** empantanarse

boggle /ˈbɒgl/ *vi* sobresaltarse. **the mind ~s** uno se queda atónito

bogus /ˈbəʊgəs/ *a* falso

boil /bɔɪl/ *vt/i* hervir. **be ~ing hot** estar ardiendo; <*weather*> hacer mucho calor. ● *n* furúnculo *m*. □ **~ away** *vi* evaporarse. □ **~ down to** *vt* reducirse a. □ **~ over** *vi* rebosar. **~ed** *a* hervido; <*egg*> pasado por agua. **~er** *n* caldera *f*. **~er suit** *n* mono *m*, overol *m* (LAm)

boisterous /ˈbɔɪstərəs/ *a* ruidoso, bullicioso

bold /bəʊld/ *a* (**-er**, **-est**) audaz. **~ly** *adv* con audacia, audazmente

Bolivia /bəˈlɪvɪə/ *n* Bolivia *f*. **~n** *a* & *n* boliviano (*m*)

bolster /ˈbəʊlstə(r)/ □ **~ up** *vt* sostener

bolt /bəʊlt/ *n* (on door) cerrojo *m*; (for nut) perno *m*; (lightning) rayo *m*; (leap) fuga *f*. ● *vt* echar el cerrojo a <*door*>; engullir <*food*>. ● *vi* fugarse. ● *adv*. **~ upright** rígido

bomb /bɒm/ *n* bomba *f*. ● *vt* bombardear. **~ard** /bɒmˈbɑ:d/ *vt* bombardear **~er** /ˈbɒmə(r)/ *n* (plane) bombardero *m*; (terrorist) terrorista *m* & *f*. **~ing** /ˈbɒmɪŋ/ *n* bombardeo *m*. **~shell** *n* bomba *f*

bond /bɒnd/ *n* (agreement) obligación *f*; (link) lazo *m*; (Com) bono *m*. ● *vi* (stick) adherirse. **~age** /-ɪdʒ/ *n* esclavitud *f*

bone /bəʊn/ *n* hueso *m*; (of fish) espina *f*. ● *vt* deshuesar; quitar las espinas a <*fish*>. **~-dry** *a* completamente seco. **~ idle** *a* holgazán

bonfire /ˈbɒnfaɪə(r)/ *n* hoguera *f*, fogata *f*

bonnet /ˈbɒnɪt/ *n* gorra *f*; (Auto) capó *m*, capote *m* (Mex)

bonus /ˈbəʊnəs/ *n* (payment) bonificación *f*; (fig) ventaja *f*

bony /ˈbəʊnɪ/ *a* (**-ier**, **-iest**) huesudo; <*fish*> lleno de espinas

boo /buː/ *int* ¡bu! ● *vt/i* abuchear

boob /buːb/ *n* (🅃, mistake) metedura *f* de pata. ● *vi* 🅃 meter la pata

booby /ˈbuːbɪ/ **:** ~ **prize** *n* premio *m* al peor. ~ **trap** *n* trampa *f*; (bomb) bomba *f* trampa.

book /bʊk/ *n* libro *m*; (of cheques etc) talonario *m*, chequera *f*; (notebook) libreta *f*; (exercise book) cuaderno *m*. ~**s** (*mpl*) (Com) cuentas *fpl*. ● *vt* (enter) registrar; (reserve) reservar. ● *vi* reservar. ~**case** *n* biblioteca *f*, librería *f*, librero *m* (Mex). ~**ing** *n* reserva *f*, reservación *f* (LAm). ~**ing office** *n* (in theatre) taquilla *f*, boletería *f* (LAm). ~**keeping** *n* contabilidad *f*. ~**let** /ˈbʊklɪt/ *n* folleto *m*. ~**maker** *n* corredor *m* de apuestas. ~**mark** *n* señal *f*. ~**seller** *n* librero *m*. ~**shop**, (Amer) ~**store** *n* librería *f*. ~**worm** *n* (fig) ratón *m* de biblioteca

boom /buːm/ *vi* retumbar; (fig) prosperar. ● *n* estampido *m*; (Com) boom *m*

boost /buːst/ *vt* estimular; reforzar <*morale*>. ● *n* empuje *m*. ~**er** *n* (Med) revacunación *f*. ~**er cable** *n* (Amer) cable *m* de arranque

boot /buːt/ *n* bota *f*; (Auto) maletero *m*, cajuela *f* (Mex). □ ~ **up** *vt* (Comp) cargar

booth /buːð/ *n* cabina *f*; (at fair) puesto *m*

booze /buːz/ *vi* 🅃 beber mucho. ● *n* 🅃 alcohol *m*

border /ˈbɔːdə(r)/ *n* borde *m*; (frontier) frontera *f*; (in garden) arriate *m*. □ ~ **on** *vt* lindar con. ~**line** *n* línea *f* divisoria. ~**line case** *n* caso *m* dudoso

bor|e /bɔː(r)/ ⇒BEAR. ● *vt* (annoy) aburrir; (Tec) taladrar. ● *vi* taladrar. ● *n* (person) pelmazo *m*; (thing) lata *f*. ~**ed** *a* aburrido. **be** ~**ed** estar aburrido. **get** ~**ed** aburrirse. ~**edom** /ˈbɔːdəm/ *n* aburrimiento *m*. ~**ing** *a* aburrido, pesado

born /bɔːn/ *a* nato. **be** ~ nacer

borne /bɔːn/ ⇒BEAR

borough /ˈbʌrə/ *n* municipio *m*

borrow /ˈbɒrəʊ/ *vt* pedir prestado

Bosnia /ˈbɒznɪə/**:** ~ **Herzegovina** /hɜːtsəgəʊˈviːnə/ *n* Bosnia Herzegovina *f*. ~**n** *a* & *n* bosnio (*m*)

boss /bɒs/ *n* 🅃 jefe *m*. ● *vt*. ~ (**about**) 🅃 dar órdenes a. ~**y** *a* mandón

botan|ical /bəˈtænɪkl/ *a* botánico. ~**ist** /ˈbɒtənɪst/ *n* botánico *m*. ~**y** /ˈbɒtənɪ/ *n* botánica *f*

both /bəʊθ/ *a & pron* ambos (*mpl*), los dos (*mpl*). ● *adv* al mismo tiempo, a la vez. ~ **Ann and Brian came** tanto Ann como Bob vinieron

bother /ˈbɒðə(r)/ *vt* (inconvenience) molestar; (worry) preocupar. ~ **it!** ¡caramba! ● *vi* molestarse. ~ **about** preocuparse de. ~ **doing** tomarse la molestia de hacer. ● *n* molestia *f*

bottle /ˈbɒtl/ *n* botella, mamila *f* (Mex); (for baby) biberón *m*. ● *vt* embotellar. □ ~ **up** *vt* (fig) reprimir. ~**neck** *n* (traffic jam) embotellamiento *m*. ~ **opener** *n* abrebotellas *m*, destapador *m* (LAm)

bottom /ˈbɒtəm/ *n* fondo *m*; (of hill) pie *m*; (buttocks) trasero *m*. ● *a* de más abajo; <*price*> más bajo; <*lip, edge*> inferior. **~less** *a* sin fondo

bough /baʊ/ *n* rama *f*

bought /bɔːt/ ⇒BUY

boulder /ˈbəʊldə(r)/ *n* canto *m*

bounce /baʊns/ *vt* hacer rebotar. ● *vi* rebotar; <*person*> saltar; Ⓘ <*cheque*> ser rechazado. ● *n* rebote *m*

bound /baʊnd/ ⇒BIND. ● *vi* saltar. ● *n* (jump) salto *m*. **~s** *npl* (limits) límites *mpl*. **out of ~s** zona *f* prohibida. ● *a*. **be ~ for** dirigirse a. **~ to** obligado a; (certain) seguro de

boundary /ˈbaʊndərɪ/ *n* límite *m*

bouquet /bʊˈkeɪ/ *n* ramo *m*; (of wine) buqué *m*, aroma *m*

bout /baʊt/ *n* período *m*; (Med) ataque *m*; (Sport) encuentro *m*

bow[1] /bəʊ/ *n* (weapon, mus) arco *m*; (knot) lazo *m*, moño *m* (LAm)

bow[2] /baʊ/ *n* reverencia *f*; (Naut) proa *f*. ● *vi* inclinarse. ● *vt* inclinar

bowels /ˈbaʊəlz/ *npl* intestinos *mpl*; (fig) entrañas *fpl*

bowl /bəʊl/ *n* (container) cuenco *m*; (for washing) palangana *f*; (ball) bola *f*. ● *vt* (cricket) arrojar. ● *vi* (cricket) arrojar la pelota. □ **~ over** *vt* derribar

bowl: ~er *n* (cricket) lanzador *m*. **~er** (hat) sombrero *m* de hongo, bombín *m*. **~ing** *n* bolos *mpl*. **~ing alley** *n* bolera *f*

bow tie /bəʊ ˈtaɪ/ *n* corbata *f* de lazo, pajarita *f*

box /bɒks/ *n* caja *f*; (for jewels etc) estuche *m*; (in theatre) palco *m*. ● *vt* boxear contra. **~ s.o.'s ears** dar una manotada a uno. ● *vi* boxear. **~er** *n* boxeador *m*. **~ing** *n* boxeo *m*. **B~ing Day** *n* el 26 de diciembre. **~ office** *n* taquilla *f*, boletería *f* (LAm). **~ room** *n* trastero *m*

boy /bɔɪ/ *n* chico *m*, muchacho *m*; (young) niño *m*

boycott /ˈbɔɪkɒt/ *vt* boicotear. ● *n* boicoteo *m*

boy: ~friend *n* novio *m*. **~hood** *n* niñez *f*. **~ish** *a* de muchacho; (childish) infantil

bra /brɑː/ *n* sostén *m*, sujetador *m*, brasier *m* (Mex)

brace /breɪs/ *n* abrazadera *f*. ● *vt* asegurar. **~ o.s.** prepararse. **~s** *npl* tirantes *mpl*; (Amer, dental) aparato(s) *m(pl)*

bracelet /ˈbreɪslɪt/ *n* pulsera *f*

bracken /ˈbrækən/ *n* helecho *m*

bracket /ˈbrækɪt/ *n* soporte *m*; (group) categoría *f*; (parenthesis) paréntesis *m*. **square ~s** corchetes *mpl*. ● *vt* poner entre paréntesis; (join together) agrupar

brag /bræg/ *vi* (*pt* **bragged**) jactarse (**about** de)

braid /breɪd/ *n* galón *m*; (Amer, in hair) trenza *f*

brain /breɪn/ *n* cerebro *m*. ● *vt* romper la cabeza a. **~child** *n* invento *m*. **~ drain** *n* Ⓘ fuga *f* de cerebros. **~storm** *n* ataque *m* de locura; (Amer, brainwave) idea *f* genial. **~wash** *vt* lavar el cerebro. **~wave** *n* idea *f* genial. **~y** *a* (**-ier, -iest**) inteligente

brake /breɪk/ *n* freno *m*. ● *vt/i* frenar. **~ fluid** *n* líquido *m* de freno. **~ lights** *npl* luces *fpl* de freno

bramble /ˈbræmbl/ *n* zarza *f*

bran /bræn/ *n* salvado *m*

branch /brɑːntʃ/ *n* rama *f*; (of road) bifurcación *f*; (Com) sucursal *m*; (fig) ramo *m*. □ **~ off** *vi* bifurcarse. □ **~ out** *vi* ramificarse

brand /brænd/ *n* marca *f*. ● *vt* marcar; (label) tildar de

brandish /ˈbrændɪʃ/ *vt* blandir

brand: ~ name *n* marca *f*. **~-new** /-ˈnjuː/ *a* flamante

brandy /ˈbrændɪ/ *n* coñac *m*

brash /bræʃ/ *a* descarado

brass /brɑːs/ *n* latón *m*. **get down to ~ tacks** (fig) ir al grano. **~ band** *n* banda *f* de música

brassière /ˈbræsjeə(r)/ *n* ⇒BRA

brat /bræt/ *n* (pej) mocoso *m*

bravado /brəˈvɑːdəʊ/ *n* bravata *f*

brave /breɪv/ *a* (**-er**, **-est**) valiente. ● *n* (North American Indian) guerrero *m* indio. **the ~** *npl* los valientes. ● *vt* afrontar. **~ry** /-ərɪ/ *n* valentía *f*, valor *m*

brawl /brɔːl/ *n* alboroto *m*. ● *vi* pelearse

brazen /ˈbreɪzn/ *a* descarado

Brazil /brəˈzɪl/ *n* Brasil *m*. **~ian** /-jən/ *a* & *n* brasileño (*m*)

breach /briːtʃ/ *n* infracción *f*, violación *f*; (of contract) incumplimiento *m*; (gap) brecha *f*. **~ of the peace** alteración *f* del orden público. ● *vt* abrir una brecha en

bread /bred/ *n* pan *m*. **a loaf of ~** un pan. **~crumbs** *npl* migajas *fpl*; (Culin) pan *m* rallado, pan *m* molido (Mex)

breadth /bredθ/ *n* anchura *f*

breadwinner /ˈbredwɪnə(r)/ *n* sostén *m* de la familia

break /breɪk/ *vt* (*pt* **broke**, *pp* **broken**) romper; infringir, violar <*law*>; batir <*record*>; comunicar <*news*>; interrumpir <*journey*>. ● *vi* romperse; <*news*> divulgarse. ● *n* ruptura *f*; (interval) intervalo *m*; (Ⓘ, chance) oportunidad *f*; (in weather) cambio *m*. □ **~ away** *vi* escapar. □ **~ down** *vt* derribar; analizar <*figures*>. *vi* estropearse, descomponerse (LAm); (Auto) averiarse; (cry) deshacerse en lágrimas. □ **~ in** *vi* <*intruder*> entrar (para robar). □ **~ into** *vt* entrar en (para robar) <*house etc*>; (start doing) ponerse a. □ **~ off** *vi* interrumpirse. □ **~ out** *vi* <*war, disease*> estallar; (run away) escaparse. □ **~ up** *vi* romperse; <*band, lovers*> separarse; <*schools*> terminar. **~able** *a* frágil. **~age** /-ɪdʒ/ *n* rotura *f*. **~down** *n* (Tec) falla *f*; (Med) colapso *m*, crisis *f* nerviosa; (of figures) análisis *f*. **~er** *n* (wave) ola *f* grande

breakfast /ˈbrekfəst/ *n* desayuno *m*. **have ~** desayunar

break: ~through *n* adelanto *m*. **~water** *n* rompeolas *m*

breast /brest/ *n* pecho *m*; (of chicken etc) pechuga *f*. (estilo *m*) **~stroke** *n* braza *f*, (estilo *m*) pecho *m* (LAm)

breath /breθ/ *n* aliento *m*, respiración *f*. **be out of ~** estar sin aliento. **hold one's ~** aguantar la respiración. **under one's ~** a media voz

breath|e /briːð/ *vt/i* respirar. **~er** *n* descanso *m*, pausa *f*. **~ing** *n* respiración *f*

breathtaking /ˈbreθteɪkɪŋ/ *a* impresionante

bred /bred/ ⇒BREED

breed /briːd/ *vt* (*pt* **bred**) criar; (fig) engendrar. ● *vi* reproducirse. ● *n* raza *f*

breez|e /briːz/ *n* brisa *f*. **~y** *a* de mucho viento

brew /bruː/ *vt* hacer <*beer*>; preparar <*tea*>. ● *vi* hacer cerveza; <*tea*> reposar; (fig) prepararse. ● *n* infusión *f*. **~er** *n* cervecero *m*. **~ery** *n* cervecería *f*, fábrica *f* de cerveza

bribe /braɪb/ *n* soborno *m*. ● *vt* sobornar. **~ry** /'braɪbərɪ/ *n* soborno *m*

brick /brɪk/ *n* ladrillo *m*. **~layer** *n* albañil *m*

bridal /'braɪdl/ *a* nupcial

bride /braɪd/ *m* novia *f*. **~groom** *n* novio *m*. **~smaid** /'braɪdzmeɪd/ *n* dama *f* de honor

bridge /brɪdʒ/ *n* puente *m*; (of nose) caballete *m*; (Cards) bridge *m*. ● *vt* tender un puente sobre. **~ a gap** llenar un vacío

bridle /'braɪdl/ *n* brida *f*. **~ path** *n* camino *m* de herradura

brief /bri:f/ *a* (**-er**, **-est**) breve. ● *n* (Jurid) escrito *m*. ● *vt* dar instrucciones a. **~case** *n* maletín *m*, portafolio(s) *m* (LAm). **~ly** *adv* brevemente. **~s** *npl* (man's) calzoncillos *mpl*; (woman's) bragas *fpl*, calzones *mpl* (LAm), pantaletas *fpl* (Mex)

brigade /brɪ'geɪd/ *n* brigada *f*

bright /braɪt/ *a* (**-er**, **-est**) brillante, claro; (clever) listo; (cheerful) alegre. **~en** *vt* aclarar; hacer más alegre *<house etc>*. ● *vi* (weather) aclararse; *<face>* illuminarse

brillian|ce /'brɪljəns/ *n* brillantez *f*, brillo *m*. **~t** *a* brillante

brim /brɪm/ *n* borde *m*; (of hat) ala *f*. □ **~ over** *vi* (*pt* **brimmed**) desbordarse

brine /braɪn/ *n* salmuera *f*

bring /brɪŋ/ *vt* (*pt* **brought**) traer; (lead) llevar. □ **~ about** *vt* causar. □ **~ back** *vt* devolver. □ **~ down** *vt* derribar. □ **~ off** *vt* lograr. □ **~ on** *vt* causar. □ **~ out** *vt* sacar; lanzar *<product>*; publicar *<book>*. □ **~ round/to** *vt* hacer volver en sí. □ **~ up** *vt* (Med) vomitar; educar *<children>*; plantear *<question>*

brink /brɪŋk/ *n* borde *m*

brisk /brɪsk/ *a* (**-er**, **-est**) enérgico, vivo

bristle /'brɪsl/ *n* cerda *f*. ● *vi* erizarse

Brit|ain /'brɪtən/ *n* Gran Bretaña *f*. **~ish** /'brɪtɪʃ/ *a* británico. ● *npl* **the ~ish** los británicos. **~on** /'brɪtən/ *n* británico *m*

Brittany /'brɪtənɪ/ *n* Bretaña *f*

brittle /'brɪtl/ *a* frágil, quebradizo

broach /brəʊtʃ/ *vt* abordar

broad /brɔ:d/ *a* (**-er**, **-est**) ancho. **in ~ daylight** a plena luz del día. **~ bean** *n* haba *f* **~cast** *n* emisión *f*. ● *vt* (*pt* **broadcast**) emitir. ● *vi* hablar por la radio. **~caster** *n* locutor *m*. **~casting** *n* radiodifusión *f*. **~en** *vt* ensanchar. ● *vi* ensancharse. **~ly** *adv* en general. **~-minded** /-'maɪndɪd/ *a* de miras amplias, tolerante

broccoli /'brɒkəlɪ/ *n invar* brécol *m*

brochure /'brəʊʃə(r)/ *n* folleto *m*

broil /brɔɪl/ *vt* (Amer) asar a la parrilla. **~er** *n* (Amer) parrilla *f*

broke /brəʊk/ ⇒BREAK. ● *a* 🅸 sin blanca, en la ruina

broken /'brəʊkən/ ⇒BREAK. ● *a* roto

broker /'brəʊkə(r)/ *n* corredor *m*

brolly /'brɒlɪ/ *n* 🅸 paraguas *m*

bronchitis /brɒŋ'kaɪtɪs/ *n* bronquitis *f*

bronze /brɒnz/ *n* bronce *m*. ● *a* de bronce

brooch /brəʊtʃ/ *n* broche *m*

brood /bru:d/ *n* cría *f*; (hum) prole *m*. ● *vi* empollar; (fig) meditar

brook /brʊk/ *n* arroyo *m*. ● *vt* soportar

broom /bru:m/ *n* escoba *f*. **~stick** *n* palo *m* de escoba

broth /brɒθ/ *n* caldo *m*

brothel /ˈbrɒθl/ *n* burdel *m*

brother /ˈbrʌðə(r)/ *n* hermano *m*. **~hood** *n* fraternidad *f*. **~-in-law** (*pl* **~s-in-law**) *n* cuñado *m*. **~ly** *a* fraternal

brought /brɔːt/ ⇒BRING

brow /braʊ/ *n* frente *f*; (of hill) cima *f*. **~beat** *vt* (*pt* **-beaten**, *pp* **-beat**) intimidar

brown /braʊn/ *a* (**-er**, **-est**) marrón, café (Mex); <*hair*> castaño; <*skin*> moreno; (tanned) bronceado. ● *n* marrón *m*, café *m* (Mex). ● *vt* poner moreno; (Culin) dorar. **~ bread** *n* pan *m* integral **~ sugar** /braʊn ˈʃʊgə(r)/ *n* azúcar *m* moreno, azúcar *f* morena

browse /braʊz/ *vi* (in a shop) curiosear; <*animal*> pacer; (Comp) navegar. **~r** (Comp) browser *m*, navegador *m*

bruise /bruːz/ *n* magulladura *f*. ● *vt* magullar; machucar <*fruit*>

brunch /brʌntʃ/ *n* [I] desayuno *m* tardío

brunette /bruːˈnet/ *n* morena *f*

brunt /brʌnt/ *n*. **bear** *o* **take the ~ of sth** sufrir algo

brush /brʌʃ/ *n* cepillo *m*; (large) escoba; (for decorating) brocha *f*; (artist's) pincel; (skirmish) escaramuza *f*. ● *vt* cepillar. □ **~ against** *vt* rozar. □ **~ aside** *vt* rechazar. □ **~ off** *vt* (rebuff) desairar. □ **~ up (on)** *vt* refrescar

brusque /bruːsk/ *a* brusco. **~ly** *adv* bruscamente

Brussels /ˈbrʌslz/ *n* Bruselas *f*. **~ sprout** *n* col *f* de Bruselas

brutal /ˈbruːtl/ *a* brutal. **~ity** /-ˈtælətɪ/ *n* brutalidad *f*. **~ly** *adv* brutalmente

brute /bruːt/ *n* bestia *f*. **~ force** fuerza *f* bruta

BSc *abbr* ⇒BACHELOR

bubbl|e /ˈbʌbl/ *n* burbuja *f*. ● *vi* burbujear. □ **~ over** *vi* desbordarse. **~y** *a* burbujeante

buck /bʌk/ *a* macho. ● *n* (deer) ciervo *m*; (Amer [I]) dólar *m*. **pass the ~** pasar la pelota

bucket /ˈbʌkɪt/ *n* balde *m*, cubo *m*, cubeta *f* (Mex)

buckle /ˈbʌkl/ *n* hebilla *f*. ● *vt* abrochar. ● *vi* torcerse

bud /bʌd/ *n* brote *m*. ● *vi* (*pt* **budded**) brotar.

Buddhis|m /ˈbʊdɪzəm/ *n* budismo *m*. **~t** *a & n* budista (*m & f*)

budding /ˈbʌdɪŋ/ *a* (fig) en ciernes

buddy /ˈbʌdɪ/ *n* [I] amigo *m*, cuate *m* (Mex)

budge /bʌdʒ/ *vt* mover. ● *vi* moverse

budgerigar /ˈbʌdʒərɪgɑː(r)/ *n* periquito *m*

budget /ˈbʌdʒɪt/ *n* presupuesto *m*

buffalo /ˈbʌfələʊ/ *n* (*pl* **-oes** *or* **-o**) búfalo *m*

buffer /ˈbʌfə(r)/ *n* parachoques *m*

buffet[1] /ˈbʊfeɪ/ *n* (meal) buffet *m*; (in train) bar *m*

buffet[2] /ˈbʌfɪt/ *n* golpe *m*; (slap) bofetada *f*. ● *vt* (*pt* **buffeted**) golpear

bug /bʌg/ *n* bicho *m*; [I], (germ) microbio *m*; (device) micrófono *m* oculto. ● *vt* (*pt* **bugged**) ocultar un micrófono en; ([I], bother) molestar

buggy /ˈbʌgɪ/ *n*. **baby ~** sillita *f* de paseo (plegable); (Amer) cochecito *m*

bugle /ˈbjuːgl/ *n* corneta *f*

build /bɪld/ *vt/i* (*pt* **built**) construir. ● *n* (of person) figura *f*, tipo *m*.

□ ~ **up** *vt/i* fortalecer; (increase) aumentar. **~er** *n* (contractor) contratista *m & f*; (labourer) albañil *m*. **~ing** *n* edificio *m*; (construction) construcción *f*. **~up** *n* aumento *m*; (of gas etc) acumulación *f*

built /bɪlt/ ⇒BUILD. **~-in** *a* empotrado. **~-up area** *n* zona *f* urbanizada

bulb /bʌlb/ *n* bulbo *m*; (Elec) bombilla *f*, foco *m* (Mex)

Bulgaria /bʌl'geərɪə/ *n* Bulgaria *f*. **~n** *a & n* búlgaro (*m*)

bulg|e /bʌldʒ/ *n* protuberancia *f*. ● *vi* pandearse. **~ing** *a* abultado; <*eyes*> saltón

bulk /bʌlk/ *n* bulto *m*, volumen *m*. **in ~** a granel; (loose) suelto. **the ~ of** la mayor parte de. **~y** *a* voluminoso

bull /bʊl/ *n* toro *m*. **~dog** *n* bulldog *m*. **~dozer** /-dəʊzə(r)/ *n* bulldozer *m*

bullet /'bʊlɪt/ *n* bala *f*

bulletin /'bʊlətɪn/ *n* anuncio *m*; (journal) boletín *m*. **~ board** *n* (Amer) tablón *m* de anuncios, tablero *m* de anuncios (LAm)

bulletproof /'bʊlɪtpru:f/ *a* a prueba de balas

bullfight /'bʊlfaɪt/ *n* corrida *f* (de toros). **~er** *n* torero *m*. **~ing** *n* (deporte *m* de) los toros

bull: ~ring *n* plaza *f* de toros. **~'s-eye** *n* diana *f*. **~shit** *n* (vulg) sandeces *fpl* [I], gilipolleces *fpl* [X]

bully /'bʊlɪ/ *n* matón *m*. ● *vt* intimidar. **~ing** *n* intimidación *f*

bum /bʌm/ *n* ([I], backside) trasero *m*; (Amer [I]) holgazán *m*

bumblebee /'bʌmblbi:/ *n* abejorro *m*

bump /bʌmp/ *vt* chocar contra. ● *vi* dar sacudidas. ● *n* (blow) golpe *m*; (jolt) sacudida *f*. □ ~ **into** *vt* chocar contra; (meet) encontrar.

bumper /'bʌmpə(r)/ *n* parachoques *m*. ● *a* récord. **~ edition** *n* edición *f* especial

bun /bʌn/ *n* bollo *m*; (bread roll) panecillo *m*, bolillo *m* (Mex); (hair) moño *m*, chongo *m* (Mex)

bunch /bʌntʃ/ *n* (of people) grupo *m*; (of bananas, grapes) racimo *m*; (of flowers) ramo *m*

bundle /'bʌndl/ *n* bulto *m*; (of papers) legajo *m*. □ ~ **up** *vt* atar

bungalow /'bʌŋgələʊ/ *n* casa *f* de un solo piso

bungle /'bʌŋgl/ *vt* echar a perder

bunk /bʌŋk/ *n* litera *f*

bunker /'bʌŋkə(r)/ *n* carbonera *f*; (Golf, Mil) búnker *m*

bunny /'bʌnɪ/ *n* conejito *m*

buoy /bɔɪ/ *n* boya *f*. □ ~ **up** *vt* hacer flotar; (fig) animar

buoyant /'bɔɪənt/ *a* flotante; (fig) optimista

burden /'bɜ:dn/ *n* carga *f*. ● *vt* cargar (with de)

bureau /'bjʊərəʊ/ *n* (*pl* **-eaux** /-əʊz/) agencia *f*; (desk) escritorio *m*; (Amer, chest of drawers) cómoda *f*

bureaucra|cy /bjʊə'rɒkrəsɪ/ *n* burocracia *f*. **~t** /'bjʊərəkræt/ *n* burócrata *m & f*. **~tic** /-'krætɪk/ *a* burocrático

burger /'bɜ:gə(r)/ *n* [I] hamburguesa *f*

burgl|ar /'bɜ:glə(r)/ *n* ladrón *m*. **~ar alarm** *n* alarma *f* antirrobo. **~ary** *n* robo *m* (*en casa o edificio*). **~e** /'bɜ:gl/ *vt* entrar a robar en. **we were ~ed** nos entraron a robar

burial /'berɪəl/ *n* entierro *m*

burly /'bɜ:lɪ/ *a* (**-ier, -iest**) corpulento

burn /bɜ:n/ *vt* (*pt* **burned** *or* **burnt**) quemar. ● *vi* quemarse. ● *n* quemadura *f*. □ ~ **down** *vt* incendiar. *vi* incendiarse

burnt /bɜ:nt/ ⇒BURN

burp /bɜ:p/ *n* [I] eructo *m*. ● *vi* [I] eructar

burrow /ˈbʌrəʊ/ *n* madriguera *f*. ● *vt* excavar

burst /bɜ:st/ *vt* (*pt* **burst**) reventar. ● *vi* reventarse. ~ **into tears** echarse a llorar. ~ **out laughing** echarse a reír. ● *n* (Mil) ráfaga *f*; (of activity) arrebato; (of applause) salva *f*

bury /ˈberɪ/ *vt* enterrar; (hide) ocultar

bus /bʌs/ *n* (*pl* **buses**) autobús *m*, camión *m* (Mex)

bush /bʊʃ/ *n* arbusto *m*; (land) monte *m*. **~y** *a* espeso

business /ˈbɪznɪs/ *n* negocio *m*; (Com) negocios *mpl*; (profession) ocupación *f*; (fig) asunto *m*. **mind one's own** ~ ocuparse de sus propios asuntos. **~like** *a* práctico, serio. **~man** /-mən/ *n* hombre *m* de negocios. **~woman** *n* mujer *f* de negocios

busker /ˈbʌskə(r)/ *n* músico *m* ambulante

bus stop *n* parada *f* de autobús, paradero *m* de autobús (LAm)

bust /bʌst/ *n* busto *m*; (chest) pecho *m*. ● *vt* (*pt* **busted** *or* **bust**) [I] romper. ● *vi* romperse. ● *a* roto. **go** ~ [I] quebrar

bust-up /ˈbʌstʌp/ *n* [I] riña *f*

busy /ˈbɪzɪ/ *a* (**-ier**, **-iest**) ocupado; *<street>* concurrido. **be** ~ (Amer) *<phone>* estar comunicando, estar ocupado (LAm). ● *vt*. ~ **o.s. with** ocuparse de. **~body** *n* entrometido *m*

but /bʌt/ *conj* pero; (*after negative*) sino. ● *prep* menos. ~ **for** si no fuera por. **last** ~ **one** penúltimo

butcher /ˈbʊtʃə(r)/ *n* carnicero *m*. ● *vt* matar; (fig) hacer una carnicería con

butler /ˈbʌtlə(r)/ *n* mayordomo *m*

butt /bʌt/ *n* (of gun) culata *f*; (of cigarette) colilla *f*; (target) blanco *m*; (Amer [I], backside) trasero *m*. ● *vi* topar. □ ~ **in** *vi* interrumpir

butter /ˈbʌtə(r)/ *n* mantequilla *f*. ● *vt* untar con mantequilla. **~cup** *n* ranúnculo *m*. **~fingers** *n* manazas *m*, torpe *m*. **~fly** *n* mariposa *f*; (swimming) estilo *m* mariposa

buttock /ˈbʌtək/ *n* nalga *f*

button /ˈbʌtn/ *n* botón *m*. ● *vt* abotonar. ● *vi* abotonarse. **~hole** *n* ojal *m*. ● *vt* (fig) detener

buy /baɪ/ *vt/i* (*pt* **bought**) comprar. ● *n* compra *f*. **~er** *n* comprador *m*

buzz /bʌz/ *n* zumbido *m*. ● *vi* zumbar. □ ~ **off** *vi* [x] largarse. **~er** *n* timbre *m*

by /baɪ/ *prep* por; (near) cerca de; (before) antes de; (according to) según. ~ **and large** en conjunto, en general. ~ **car** en coche. ~ **oneself** por sí solo

bye /baɪ/, **bye-bye** /ˈbaɪbaɪ/ *int* [I] ¡adiós!

by: **~-election** *n* elección *f* parcial. **~-law** *n* reglamento *m* (local). **~pass** *n* carretera *f* de circunvalación. ● *vt* eludir; *<road>* circunvalar. **~-product** *n* subproducto *m*. **~stander** /-stændə(r)/ *n* espectador *m*

byte /baɪt/ *n* (Comp) byte *m*, octeto *m*

Cc

cab /kæb/ *n* taxi *m*; (of lorry, train) cabina *f*

cabaret /ˈkæbəreɪ/ *n* cabaret *m*

cabbage /ˈkæbɪdʒ/ *n* col *f*, repollo *m*

cabin /ˈkæbɪn/ *n* (house) cabaña *f*; (in ship) camarote *m*; (in plane) cabina *f*

cabinet /ˈkæbɪnɪt/ *n* (cupboard) armario *m*; (for display) vitrina *f*. **C~** (Pol) gabinete *m*

cable /ˈkeɪbl/ *n* cable *m*. **~ car** *n* teleférico *m*. **~ TV** *n* televisión *f* por cable, cablevisión *f* (LAm)

cackle /ˈkækl/ *n* (of hen) cacareo *m*; (laugh) risotada *f*. ● *vi* cacarear; (laugh) reírse a carcajadas

cactus /ˈkæktəs/ *n* (*pl* **-ti** /-taɪ/ *or* **-tuses**) cacto *m*

caddie, **caddy** /ˈkædɪ/ *n* (golf) portador *m* de palos

cadet /kəˈdet/ *n* cadete *m*

cadge /kædʒ/ *vt/i* gorronear

café /ˈkæfeɪ/ *n* cafetería *f*

cafeteria /kæfɪˈtɪərɪə/ *n* restaurante *m* autoservicio

caffeine /ˈkæfiːn/ *n* cafeína *f*

cage /keɪdʒ/ *n* jaula *f*. ● *vt* enjaular

cake /keɪk/ *n* pastel *m*, tarta *f*; (sponge) bizcocho *m*. **~ of soap** pastilla *f* de jabón

calamity /kəˈlæmətɪ/ *n* calamidad *f*

calcium /ˈkælsɪəm/ *n* calcio *m*

calculat|e /ˈkælkjʊleɪt/ *vt/i* calcular. **~ion** /-ˈleɪʃn/ *n* cálculo *m*. **~or** *n* calculadora *f*

calculus /ˈkælkjʊləs/ *n* (Math) cálculo *m*

calendar /ˈkælɪndə(r)/ *n* calendario *m*

calf /kɑːf/ *n* (*pl* **calves**) (animal) ternero *m*; (of leg) pantorrilla *f*

calibre /ˈkælɪbə(r)/ *n* calibre *m*

call /kɔːl/ *vt/i* llamar. ● *n* llamada *f*; (shout) grito *m*; (visit) visita *f*. **be on ~** estar de guardia. **long-distance ~** llamada *f* de larga distancia, conferencia *f*. □ **~ back** *vt* hacer volver; (on phone) volver a llamar. *vi* volver; (on phone) volver a llamar. □ **~ for** *vt* pedir; (fetch) ir a buscar. □ **~ off** *vt* suspender. □ **~ on** *vt* pasar a visitar. □ **~ out** *vi* dar voces. □ **~ together** *vt* convocar. □ **~ up** *vt* (Mil) llamar al servicio militar; (phone) llamar. **~ box** *n* cabina *f* telefónica. **~er** *n* visita *f*; (phone) el que llama *m*. **~ing** *n* vocación *f*

callous /ˈkæləs/ *a* insensible, cruel

calm /kɑːm/ *a* (**-er**, **-est**) tranquilo; <*sea*> en calma. ● *n* tranquilidad *f*, calma *f*. ● *vt* calmar. ● *vi* calmarse. **~ down** *vi* tranquilizarse. *vt* calmar. **~ly** *adv* con calma

calorie /ˈkælərɪ/ *n* caloría *f*

calves /kɑːvz/ *npl* ⇒CALF

camcorder /ˈkæmkɔːdə(r)/ *n* videocámara *f*, camcórder *m*

came /keɪm/ ⇒COME

camel /ˈkæml/ *n* camello *m*

camera /ˈkæmərə/ *n* cámara *f*, máquina *f* fotográfica **~man** /-mən/ *n* camarógrafo *m*, cámara *m*

camouflage /'kæməflɑːʒ/ *n* camuflaje *m*. ● *vt* camuflar

camp /kæmp/ *n* campamento *m*. ● *vi* acampar. **go ~ing** hacer camping

campaign /kæm'peɪn/ *n* campaña *f*. ● *vi* hacer campaña

camp: ~bed *n* catre *m* de tijera. **~er** *n* campista *m* & *f*; (vehicle) cámper *m*. **~ground** *n* (Amer) ⇒~SITE. **~ing** *n* camping *m*. **~site** *n* camping *m*

campus /'kæmpəs/ *n* (*pl* **-puses**) campus *m*, ciudad *f* universitaria

can[1] /kæn/, *unstressed form* /kən/

negative **can't, cannot** (formal); past **could**

● *auxiliary verb*

····➤ (be able to) poder. **I ~'t lift it** no lo puedo levantar. **she says she ~ come** dice que puede venir

····➤ (be allowed to) poder. **~ I smoke?** ¿puedo fumar?

····➤ (know how to) saber. **~ you swim?** ¿sabes nadar?

····➤ (with verbs of perception) *not translated*. **I ~'t see you** no te veo. **I ~ hear you better now** ahora te oigo mejor

····➤ (in requests) **~ I have a glass of water, please?** ¿me trae un vaso de agua, por favor?. **~ I have a kilo of cheese, please?** ¿me da un kilo de queso, por favor?

····➤ (in offers) **~ I help you?** ¿te ayudo?; (in shop) ¿lo/la atienden?

can[2] /kæn/ *n* lata *f*, bote *m*. ● *vt* (*pt* **canned**) enlatar. **~ned music** música *f* grabada

Canad|a /'kænədə/ *n* (el) Canadá *m*. **~ian** /kə'neɪdɪən/ *a* & *n* canadiense (*m* & *f*)

canal /kə'næl/ *n* canal *m*

Canaries /kə'neərɪz/ *npl* = CANARY ISLANDS

canary /kə'neərɪ/ *n* canario *m*. **C~ Islands** *npl*. **the C~ Islands** las Islas Canarias

cancel /'kænsl/ *vt* (*pt* **cancelled**) cancelar; anular <*command, cheque*>; (delete) tachar. **~lation** /-'leɪʃn/ *n* cancelación *f*

cancer /'kænsə(r)/ *n* cáncer *m*. **C~** *n* (Astr) Cáncer *m*. **~ous** *a* canceroso

candid /'kændɪd/ *a* franco

candidate /'kændɪdeɪt/ *n* candidato *m*

candle /'kændl/ *n* vela *f*. **~stick** *n* candelero *m*

candour /'kændə(r)/ *n* franqueza *f*

candy /'kændɪ/ *n* (Amer) caramelo *m*, dulce *f* (LAm). **~floss** /-flɒs/ *n* algodón *m* de azúcar

cane /keɪn/ *n* caña *f*; (for baskets) mimbre *m*; (stick) bastón *m*; (for punishment) palmeta *f*. ● *vt* castigar con palmeta

canister /'kænɪstə(r)/ *n* bote *m*

cannabis /'kænəbɪs/ *n* cáñamo *m* índico, hachís *m*, cannabis *m*

cannibal /'kænɪbl/ *n* caníbal *m*. **~ism** *n* canibalismo *m*

cannon /'kænən/ *n invar* cañón *m*. **~ ball** *n* bala *f* de cañón

cannot /'kænət/ ⇒CAN[1]

canoe /kə'nuː/ *n* canoa *f*, piragua *f*. ● *vi* ir en canoa

canon /'kænən/ *n* canon *m*; (person) canónigo *m*. **~ize** *vt* canonizar

can opener *n* abrelatas *m*

canopy /'kænəpɪ/ *n* dosel *m*

can't /kɑ:nt/ ⇒CAN[1]

cantankerous /kæn'tæŋkərəs/ *a* mal humorado

canteen /kæn'ti:n/ *n* cantina *f*; (of cutlery) juego *m* de cubiertos

canter /'kæntə(r)/ *n* medio galope *m*. ● *vi* ir a medio galope

canvas /'kænvəs/ *n* lona *f*; (artist's) lienzo *m*

canvass /'kænvəs/ *vi* hacer campaña, solicitar votos. **~ing** *n* solicitación *f* (de votos)

canyon /'kænjən/ *n* cañón *m*

cap /kæp/ *n* gorra *f*; (lid) tapa *f*; (of cartridge) cápsula *f*; (of pen) capuchón *m*. ● *vt* (*pt* **capped**) tapar, poner cápsula a; (outdo) superar

capab|ility /keɪpə'bɪlətɪ/ *n* capacidad *f*. **~le** /'keɪpəbl/ *a* capaz

capacity /kə'pæsətɪ/ *n* capacidad *f*; (function) calidad *f*

cape /keɪp/ *n* (cloak) capa *f*; (Geog) cabo *m*

capital /'kæpɪtl/ *a* capital. **~ letter** mayúscula *f*. ● *n* (town) capital *f*; (money) capital *m*. **~ism** *n* capitalismo *m*. **~ist** *a* & *n* capitalista (*m* & *f*.) **~ize** *vt* capitalizar; escribir con mayúsculas <*word*>. ● *vi*. **~ize on** aprovechar

capitulat|e /kə'pɪtʃʊleɪt/ *vi* capitular. **~ion** /-'leɪʃn/ *n* capitulación *f*

Capricorn /'kæprɪkɔ:n/ *n* Capricornio *m*

capsize /kæp'saɪz/ *vt* hacer volcar. ● *vi* volcarse

capsule /'kæpsju:l/ *n* cápsula *f*

captain /'kæptɪn/ *n* capitán *m*; (of plane) comandante *m* & *f*. ● *vt* capitanear

caption /'kæpʃn/ *n* (heading) título *m*; (of cartoon etc) leyenda *f*

captivate /'kæptɪveɪt/ *vt* encantar

captiv|e /'kæptɪv/ *a* & *n* cautivo (*m*). **~ity** /-'tɪvətɪ/ *n* cautiverio *m*, cautividad *f*

capture /'kæptʃə(r)/ *vt* capturar; atraer <*attention*>; (Mil) tomar. ● *n* apresamiento *m*; (Mil) toma *f*

car /kɑ:(r)/ *n* coche *m*, carro *m* (LAm); (Amer, of train) vagón *m*

caramel /'kærəmel/ *n* azúcar *m* quemado; (sweet) caramelo *m*, dulce *m* (LAm)

caravan /'kærəvæn/ *n* caravana *f*

carbohydrate /kɑ:bəʊ'haɪdreɪt/ *n* hidrato *m* de carbono

carbon /'kɑ:bən/ *n* carbono *m*; (paper) carbón *m*. **~ copy** copia *f* al carbón. **~ dioxide** /daɪ'ɒksaɪd/ *n* anhídrido *m* carbónico. **~ monoxide** /mə'nɒksaɪd/ *n* monóxido de carbono

carburettor /kɑ:bjʊ'retə(r)/ *n* carburador *m*

carcass /'kɑ:kəs/ *n* cuerpo *m* de animal muerto; (for meat) res *f* muerta

card /kɑ:d/ *n* tarjeta *f*; (for games) carta *f*; (membership) carnet *m*; (records) ficha *f*. **~board** *n* cartón *m*

cardigan /'kɑ:dɪgən/ *n* chaqueta *f* de punto, rebeca *f*

cardinal /'kɑ:dɪnəl/ *a* cardinal. ● *n* cardenal *m*

care /keə(r)/ *n* cuidado *m*; (worry) preocupación *f*; (protection) cargo *m*. **~ of** a cuidado de, en casa de. **take ~** tener cuidado. **take ~ of** cuidar de <*person*>; ocuparse de <*matter*>. ● *vi* interesarse. **I don't ~** me da igual. □ **~ about** *vt* preocuparse por. □ ~ **for** *vt* cuidar de; (like) querer

career /kə'rɪə(r)/ *n* carrera *f*. ● *vi* correr a toda velocidad

care: ~**free** *a* despreocupado. ~**ful** *a* cuidadoso; (cautious) prudente. **be** ~**ful** tener cuidado. ~**fully** *adv* con cuidado. ~**less** *a* negligente; (not worried) indiferente. ~**lessly** *adv* descuidadamente. ~**lessness** *n* descuido *m*

caress /kə'res/ *n* caricia *f*. ● *vt* acariciar

caretaker /'keəteɪkə(r)/ *n* vigilante *m*; (of flats etc) portero *m*

car ferry *n* transbordador *m* de coches

cargo /'kɑːgəʊ/ *n* (*pl* **-oes**) carga *f*

Caribbean /kærɪ'biːən/ *a* caribeño. **the** ~ (**Sea**) *n* el mar Caribe

caricature /'kærɪkətʃʊə(r)/ *n* caricatura *f*. ● *vt* caricaturizar

carnage /'kɑːnɪdʒ/ *n* carnicería *f*, matanza *f*

carnation /kɑː'neɪʃn/ *n* clavel *m*

carnival /'kɑːnɪvl/ *n* carnaval *m*

carol /'kærəl/ *n* villancico *m*

carousel /kærə'sel/ *n* tiovivo *m*, carrusel *m* (LAm); (for baggage) cinta *f* transportadora

carp /kɑːp/ *n invar* carpa *f*. □ ~ **at** *vi* quejarse de

car park *n* aparcamiento *m*, estacionamiento *m*

carpent|er /'kɑːpɪntə(r)/ *n* carpintero *m*. ~**ry** /-trɪ/ *n* carpintería *f*

carpet /'kɑːpɪt/ *n* alfombra *f*. ~ **sweeper** *n* cepillo *m* mecánico

carriage /'kærɪdʒ/ *n* coche *m*; (Mec) carro *m*; (transport) transporte *m*; (cost, bearing) porte *m*; (of train) vagón *m*. ~**way** *n* calzada *f*, carretera *f*

carrier /'kærɪə(r)/ *n* transportista *m* & *f*; (company) empresa *f* de transportes; (Med) portador *m*. ~ **bag** *n* bolsa *f*

carrot /'kærət/ *n* zanahoria *f*

carry /'kærɪ/ *vt* llevar; transportar *<goods>*; (involve) llevar consigo, implicar. ● *vi* *<sounds>* llegar, oírse. □ ~ **off** *vt* llevarse. □ ~ **on** *vi* seguir, continuar. □ ~ **out** *vt* realizar; cumplir *<promise, threat>*. ~ **cot** *n* cuna *f* portátil

carsick /'kɑːsɪk/ *a* mareado (*por viajar en coche*)

cart /kɑːt/ *n* carro *m*; (Amer, in supermarket, airport) carrito *m*. ● *vt* acarrear; (🅸, carry) llevar

carton /'kɑːtən/ *n* caja *f* de cartón

cartoon /kɑː'tuːn/ *n* caricatura *f*, chiste *m*; (strip) historieta *f*; (film) dibujos *mpl* animados

cartridge /'kɑːtrɪdʒ/ *n* cartucho *m*

carve /kɑːv/ *vt* tallar; trinchar *<meat>*

cascade /kæs'keɪd/ *n* cascada *f*. ● *vi* caer en cascadas

case /keɪs/ *n* caso *m*; (Jurid) proceso *m*; (crate) cajón *m*; (box) caja *f*; (suitcase) maleta *f*, petaca *f* (Mex). **in any** ~ en todo caso. **in** ~ **he comes** por si viene. **in** ~ **of** en caso de

cash /kæʃ/ *n* dinero *m* efectivo. **pay (in)** ~ pagar al contado. ● *vt* cobrar. ~ **in (on)** aprovecharse de. ~ **desk** *n* caja *f*. ~ **dispenser** *n* cajero *m* automático

cashier /kæ'ʃɪə(r)/ *n* cajero *m*

cashpoint /'kæʃpɔɪnt/ *n* cajero *m* automático

casino /kə'siːnəʊ/ *n* (*pl* **-os**) casino *m*

cask /kɑːsk/ *n* barril *m*

casket /'kɑ:skɪt/ *n* cajita *f*; (Amer) ataúd *m*, cajón *m* (LAm)

casserole /'kæsərəʊl/ *n* cacerola *f*; (stew) guiso *m*, guisado *m* (Mex)

cassette /kə'set/ *n* cassette *m* & *f*

cast /kɑ:st/ *vt* (*pt* **cast**) arrojar; fundir *<metal>*; emitir *<vote>*. ● *n* lanzamiento *m*; (in play) reparto *m*; (mould) molde *m*

castanets /kæstə'nets/ *npl* castañuelas *fpl*

castaway /'kɑ:stəweɪ/ *n* náufrago *m*

caster /'kɑ:stə(r)/ *n* ruedecita *f*. **~ sugar** *n* azúcar *m* extrafino

Castil|e /kæ'sti:l/ *n* Castilla *f*. **~ian** /kæ'stɪlɪən/ *a* & *n* castellano (*m*)

cast: ~ iron *n* hierro *m* fundido. **~-iron** *a* (fig) sólido

castle /'kɑ:sl/ *n* castillo *m*; (Chess) torre *f*

cast-offs /'kɑ:stɒfs/ *npl* desechos *mpl*

castrat|e /kæ'streɪt/ *vt* castrar. **~ion** /-ʃn/ *n* castración *f*

casual /'kæʒʊəl/ *a* casual; *<meeting>* fortuito; *<work>* ocasional; *<attitude>* despreocupado; *<clothes>* informal, de sport. **~ly** *adv* de paso

casualt|y /'kæʒʊəltɪ/ *n* (injured) herido *m*; (dead) víctima *f*; (in hospital) urgencias *fpl*. **~ies** *npl* (Mil) bajas *fpl*

cat /kæt/ *n* gato *m*

Catalan /'kætəlæn/ *a* & *n* catalán (*m*)

catalogue /'kætəlɒg/ *n* catálogo *m*. ● *vt* catalogar

Catalonia /kætə'ləʊnɪə/ *n* Cataluña *f*

catalyst /'kætəlɪst/ *n* catalizador *m*

catamaran /kætəmə'ræn/ *n* catamarán *m*

catapult /'kætəpʌlt/ *n* catapulta *f*; (child's) tirachinas *f*, resortera *f* (Mex)

catarrh /kə'tɑ:(r)/ *n* catarro *m*

catastroph|e /kə'tæstrəfɪ/ *n* catástrofe *m*. **~ic** /kætə'strɒfɪk/ *a* catastrófico

catch /kætʃ/ *vt* (*pt* **caught**) coger (esp Spain), agarrar; tomar *<train, bus>*; (unawares) sorprender, pillar; (understand) entender; contagiarse de *<disease>*. **~ a cold** resfriarse. **~ sight of** avistar. ● *vi* (get stuck) engancharse; *<fire>* prenderse. ● *n* (by goalkeeper) parada *f*; (of fish) pesca *f*; (on door) pestillo *m*; (on window) cerradura *f*. □ **~ on** *vi* 🅘 hacerse popular. □ **~ up** *vi* poner al día. **~ up with** alcanzar; ponerse al corriente de *<news etc>*. **~ing** *a* contagioso. **~phrase** *n* eslogan *m*. **~y** *a* pegadizo

categor|ical /kætɪ'gɒrɪkl/ *a* categórico. **~y** /'kætɪgərɪ/ *n* categoría *f*

cater /'keɪtə(r)/ *vi* encargarse del servicio de comida. **~ for** proveer a *<needs>*. **~er** *n* proveedor *m*

caterpillar /'kætəpɪlə(r)/ *n* oruga *f*, azotador *m* (Mex)

cathedral /kə'θi:drəl/ *n* catedral *f*

catholic /'kæθəlɪk/ *a* universal. **C~** *a* & *n* católico (*m*). **C~ism** /kə'θɒlɪsɪzəm/ *n* catolicismo *m*

cat: ~nap *n* sueñecito *m*. **C~seyes** *npl* (P) catafaros *mpl*

cattle /'kætl/ *npl* ganado *m*

catwalk *n* pasarela *f*

Caucasian /kɔ:'keɪʒən/ *n*. **a male ~** (Amer) un hombre de raza blanca

caught /kɔ:t/ ⇒CATCH

cauliflower /ˈkɒlɪflaʊə(r)/ *n* coliflor *f*

cause /kɔːz/ *n* causa *f*, motivo *m*. ● *vt* causar

cautio|n /ˈkɔːʃn/ *n* cautela *f*; (warning) advertencia *f*. ● *vt* advertir; (Jurid) amonestar. **~us** /-ʃəs/ *a* cauteloso, prudente

cavalry /ˈkævəlrɪ/ *n* caballería *f*

cave /keɪv/ *n* cueva *f*. □ **~ in** *vi* hundirse. **~man** *n* troglodita *m*

cavern /ˈkævən/ *n* caverna *f*

caviare /ˈkævɪɑː(r)/ *n* caviar *m*

cavity /ˈkævətɪ/ *n* cavidad *f*; (in tooth) caries *f*

CD *abbr* (= **compact disc**) CD *m*. **~ player** (reproductor *m* de) compact-disc *m*. **~-ROM** *n* CD-ROM

cease /siːs/ *vt/i* cesar. **~fire** *n* alto *m* el fuego, cese *m* del fuego (LAm)

cedar /ˈsiːdə(r)/ *n* cedro *m*

ceiling /ˈsiːlɪŋ/ *n* techo *m*

celebrat|e /ˈselɪbreɪt/ *vt* celebrar. ● *vi* divertirse. **~ed** *a* célebre. **~ion** /-ˈbreɪʃn/ *n* celebración *f*; (party) fiesta *f*

celebrity /sɪˈlebrətɪ/ *n* celebridad *f*

celery /ˈselərɪ/ *n* apio *m*

cell /sel/ *n* celda *f*; (Biol, Elec) célula *f*

cellar /ˈselə(r)/ *n* sótano *m*; (for wine) bodega *f*

cello /ˈtʃeləʊ/ *n* (*pl* **-os**) violonc(h)elo *m*, chelo *m*

Cellophane /ˈseləfeɪn/ *n* (P) celofán *m* (P)

celluloid /ˈseljʊlɔɪd/ *n* celuloide *m*

Celsius /ˈselsɪəs/ *a*. **20 degrees ~** 20 grados centígrados *or* Celsio(s)

cement /sɪˈment/ *n* cemento *m*. ● *vt* cementar

cemetery /ˈsemətrɪ/ *n* cementerio *m*

cens|or /ˈsensə(r)/ *n* censor *m*. ● *vt* censurar. **~ship** *n* censura *f*. **~ure** /ˈsenʃə(r)/ *vt* censurar

census /ˈsensəs/ *n* censo *m*

cent /sent/ *n* centavo *m*

centenary /senˈtiːnərɪ/ *n* centenario *m*

centi|grade /ˈsentɪgreɪd/ *a* centígrado. **~litre** *n* centilitro *m*. **~metre** *n* centímetro *m*. **~pede** /-piːd/ *n* ciempiés *m*

central /ˈsentrəl/ *a* central; (of town) céntrico. **~ heating** *n* calefacción *f* central. **~ize** *vt* centralizar

centre /ˈsentə(r)/ *n* centro *m*. ● *vt* (*pt* **centred**) centrar. ● *vi* centrarse (**on** en)

century /ˈsentʃərɪ/ *n* siglo *m*

cereal /ˈsɪərɪəl/ *n* cereal *m*

ceremon|ial /serɪˈməʊnɪəl/ *a* & *n* ceremonial (*m*). **~y** /ˈserɪmənɪ/ *n* ceremonia *f*

certain /ˈsɜːtn/ *a* cierto. **for ~** seguro. **make ~ of** asegurarse de. **~ly** *adv* desde luego. **~ty** *n* certeza *f*

certificate /səˈtɪfɪkət/ *n* certificado *m*; (of birth, death etc) partida *f*

certify /ˈsɜːtɪfaɪ/ *vt* certificar

chafe /tʃeɪf/ *vt* rozar. ● *vi* rozarse

chaffinch /ˈtʃæfɪntʃ/ *n* pinzón *m*

chagrin /ˈʃægrɪn/ *n* disgusto *m*

chain /tʃeɪn/ *n* cadena *f*. ● *vt* encadenar. **~ reaction** *n* reacción *f* en cadena. **~-smoker** *n* fumador *m* que siempre tiene un cigarrillo encendido. **~ store** *n* tienda *f* de una cadena

chair /tʃeə(r)/ *n* silla *f*; (Univ) cátedra *f*. ● *vt* presidir. **~lift** *n* telesquí *m*, telesilla *m* (LAm). **~man** /-mən/ *n* presidente *m*

chalet /'ʃæleɪ/ *n* chalé *m*

chalk /tʃɔ:k/ *n* (Geol) creta *f*; (stick) tiza *f*, gis *m* (Mex)

challeng|e /'tʃælɪndʒ/ *n* desafío *m*; (fig) reto *m*. ● *vt* desafiar; (question) poner en duda. **~ing** *a* estimulante

chamber /'tʃeɪmbə(r)/ *n* (*old use*) cámara *f*. **~maid** *n* camarera *f*. **~pot** *n* orinal *m*

champagne /ʃæm'peɪn/ *n* champaña *m*, champán *m*

champion /'tʃæmpɪən/ *n* campeón *m*. ● *vt* defender. **~ship** *n* campeonato *m*

chance /tʃɑ:ns/ *n* casualidad *f*; (likelihood) posibilidad *f*; (opportunity) oportunidad *f*; (risk) riesgo *m*. **by ~** por casualidad. ● *a* fortuito

chancellor /'tʃɑ:nsələ(r)/ *n* canciller *m*; (Univ) rector *m*. **C~ of the Exchequer** Ministro *m* de Hacienda

chandelier /ʃændə'lɪə(r)/ *n* araña *f* (de luces)

chang|e /tʃeɪndʒ/ *vt* camb-iar; (substitute) reemplazar. **~ one's mind** cambiar de idea. ● *vi* cambiarse. ● *n* cambio *m*; (coins) cambio *m*, sencillo *m* (LAm), feria *f* (Mex); (money returned) cambio *m*, vuelta *f*, vuelto *m* (LAm). **~eable** *a* cambiable; <*weather*> variable. **~ing room** *n* (Sport) vestuario *m*, vestidor *m* (Mex); (in shop) probador *m*

channel /'tʃænl/ *n* canal *m*; (fig) medio *m*. ● *vt* (*pt* **channelled**) acanalar; (fig) encauzar. **the (English) C~** el Canal de la Mancha. **C~ Islands** *npl*. **the C~ Islands** las islas Anglonormandas. **C~ Tunnel** *n*. **the C~ Tunnel** el Eurotúnel

chant /tʃɑ:nt/ *n* canto *m*. ● *vt/i* cantar

chao|s /'keɪɒs/ *n* caos *m*. **~tic** /-'ɒtɪk/ *a* caótico

chap /tʃæp/ *n* 🄸 tipo *m*, tío *m* 🄸. ● *vt* (*pt* **chapped**) agrietar. ● *vi* agrietarse

chapel /'tʃæpl/ *n* capilla *f*

chaperon /'ʃæpərəʊn/ *n* acompañante *f*

chapter /'tʃæptə(r)/ *n* capítulo *m*

char /tʃɑ:(r)/ *vt* (*pt* **charred**) carbonizar

character /'kærəktə(r)/ *n* carácter *m*; (in book, play) personaje *m*. **in ~** característico. **~istic** /-'rɪstɪk/ *a* típico. ● *n* característica *f*. **~ize** *vt* caracterizar

charade /ʃə'rɑ:d/ *n* farsa *f*. **~s** *npl* (game) charada *f*

charcoal /'tʃɑ:kəʊl/ *n* carbón *m* vegetal; (for drawing) carboncillo *m*

charge /tʃɑ:dʒ/ *n* precio *m*; (Elec, Mil) carga *f*; (Jurid) acusación *f*; (task, custody) encargo *m*; (responsibility) responsabilidad *f*. **in ~ of** responsable de, encargado de. **the person in ~** la persona responsable. **take ~ of** encargarse de. ● *vt* pedir; (Elec, Mil) cargar; (Jurid) acusar. ● *vi* cargar; <*animal*> embestir (**at** contra)

charit|able /'tʃærɪtəbl/ *a* caritativo. **~y** /'tʃærɪtɪ/ *n* caridad *f*; (society) institución *f* benéfica

charm /tʃɑ:m/ *n* encanto *m*; (spell) hechizo *m*; (on bracelet) dije *m*, amuleto *m*. ● *vt* encantar. **~ing** *a* encantador

chart /tʃɑ:t/ *n* (Aviat, Naut) carta *f* de navegación; (table) tabla *f*

charter /'tʃɑ:tə(r)/ *n* carta *f*. ● *vt* alquilar <*bus, train*>; fletar <*plane, ship*>. **~ flight** *n* vuelo *m* chárter

chase /tʃeɪs/ *vt* perseguir. ● *vi* correr (after tras). ● *n* persecución *f*. □ **~ away**, **~ off** *vt* ahuyentar

chassis /ˈʃæsɪ/ *n* chasis *m*

chastise /tʃæsˈtaɪz/ *vt* castigar

chastity /ˈtʃæstətɪ/ *n* castidad *f*

chat /tʃæt/ *n* charla *f*, conversación *f* (LAm), plática *f* (Mex). ● *vi* (*pt* **chatted**) charlar, conversar (LAm), platicar (Mex)

chatter /ˈtʃætə(r)/ *n* charla *f*. ● *vi* charlar. **his teeth are ~ing** le castañetean los dientes. **~box** *n* parlanchín *m*

chauffeur /ˈʃəʊfə(r)/ *n* chófer *m*

chauvinis|m /ˈʃəʊvɪnɪzəm/ *n* patriotería *f*; (male) machismo *m*. **~t** *n* patriotero *m*; (male) machista *m*

cheap /tʃiːp/ *a* (**-er**, **-est**) barato; (poor quality) de baja calidad; <*rate*> económico. **~(ly)** *adv* barato, a bajo precio

cheat /ˈtʃiːt/ *vt* defraudar; (deceive) engañar. ● *vi* (at cards) hacer trampas. ● *n* trampa *f*; (person) tramposo *m*

check /tʃek/ *vt* comprobar; (examine) inspeccionar; (curb) frenar. ● *vi* comprobar. ● *n* comprobación *f*; (of tickets) control *m*; (curb) freno *m*; (Chess) jaque *m*; (pattern) cuadro *m*; (Amer, bill) cuenta *f*; (Amer, cheque) cheque *m*. □ **~ in** *vi* registrarse; (at airport) facturar el equipaje, chequear el equipaje (LAm), registrar el equipaje (Mex). □ **~ out** *vi* pagar la cuenta y marcharse. □ **~ up** *vi* confirmar. □ **~ up on** *vt* investigar. **~book** *n* (Amer) ⇒CHEQUEBOOK. **~ered** /ˈtʃekəd/ *a* (Amer) ⇒CHEQUERED

checkers /ˈtʃekəz/ *n* (Amer) damas *fpl*

check: ~mate *n* jaque *m* mate. ● *vt* dar mate a. **~out** *n* caja *f*. **~point** control *m*. **~up** *n* chequeo *m*, revisión

cheek /tʃiːk/ *n* mejilla *f*; (fig) descaro *m*. **~bone** *n* pómulo *m*. **~y** *a* descarado

cheep /tʃiːp/ *vi* piar

cheer /tʃɪə(r)/ *n* alegría *f*; (applause) viva *m*. **~s!** ¡salud!. ● *vt* alegrar; (applaud) aplaudir. ● *vi* alegrarse; (applaud) aplaudir. **~ up!** ¡anímate! **~ful** *a* alegre

cheerio /tʃɪərɪˈəʊ/ *int* 🅸 ¡adiós!, ¡hasta luego!

cheerless /ˈtʃɪəlɪs/ *a* triste

cheese /tʃiːz/ *n* queso *m*

cheetah /ˈtʃiːtə/ *n* guepardo *m*

chef /ʃef/ *n* jefe *m* de cocina

chemical /ˈkemɪkl/ *a* químico. ● *n* producto *m* químico

chemist /ˈkemɪst/ *n* farmacéutico *m*; (scientist) químico *m*. **~ry** *n* química *f*. **~'s (shop)** *n* farmacia *f*

cheque /tʃek/ *n* cheque *m*, talón *m*. **~book** *n* chequera *f*, talonario *m*

cherish /ˈtʃerɪʃ/ *vt* cuidar; (love) querer; abrigar <*hope*>

cherry /ˈtʃerɪ/ *n* cereza *f*. **~ tree** *n* cerezo *m*

chess /tʃes/ *n* ajedrez *m*. **~board** *n* tablero *m* de ajedrez

chest /tʃest/ *n* pecho *m*; (box) cofre *m*, cajón *m*

chestnut /ˈtʃesnʌt/ *n* castaña *f*. ● *a* castaño. **~ tree** *n* castaño *m*

chest of drawers *n* cómoda *f*

chew /tʃuː/ *vt* masticar. **~ing gum** *n* chicle *m*

chic /ʃiːk/ *a* elegante

chick /tʃɪk/ *n* polluelo *m*. **~en** /ˈtʃɪkɪn/ *n* pollo *m*. ● *a* 🅸 cobarde. □ **~en out** *vi* 🅸 acobardarse.

~enpox /'tʃɪkɪnpɒks/ *n* varicela *f*. **~pea** *n* garbanzo *m*

chicory /'tʃɪkərɪ/ *n* (in coffee) achicoria *f*; (in salad) escarola *f*

chief /tʃi:f/ *n* jefe *m*. ● *a* principal. **~ly** *adv* principalmente

chilblain /'tʃɪlbleɪn/ *n* sabañón *m*

child /tʃaɪld/ *n* (*pl* **children** /'tʃɪldrən/) niño *m*; (offspring) hijo *m*. **~birth** *n* parto *m*. **~hood** *n* niñez *f*. **~ish** *a* infantil. **~less** *a* sin hijos. **~like** *a* ingenuo, de niño

Chile /'tʃɪlɪ/ *n* Chile *m*. **~an** *a & n* chileno (*m*)

chill /tʃɪl/ *n* frío *m*; (illness) resfriado *m*. ● *a* frío. ● *vt* enfriar; refrigerar <*food*>

chilli /'tʃɪlɪ/ *n* (*pl* **-ies**) chile *m*

chilly /'tʃɪlɪ/ *a* frío

chime /tʃaɪm/ *n* carillón *m*. ● *vt* tocar <*bells*>; dar <*hours*>. ● *vi* repicar

chimney /'tʃɪmnɪ/ *n* (*pl* **-eys**) chimenea *f*. **~ sweep** *n* deshollinador *m*

chimpanzee /tʃɪmpæn'zi:/ *n* chimpancé *m*

chin /tʃɪn/ *n* barbilla *f*

china /'tʃaɪnə/ *n* porcelana *f*

Chin|a /'tʃaɪnə/ *n* China *f*. **~ese** /-'ni:z/ *a & n* chino (*m*)

chink /tʃɪŋk/ *n* (crack) grieta *f*; (sound) tintín *m*. ● *vi* tintinear

chip /tʃɪp/ *n* pedacito *m*; (splinter) astilla *f*; (Culin) patata *f* frita, papa *f* frita (LAm); (in gambling) ficha *f*; (Comp) chip *m*. **have a ~ on one's shoulder** guardar rencor. ● *vt* (*pt* **chipped**) desportillar. □ **~ in** *vi* 🅸 interrumpir; (with money) contribuir

chiropodist /kɪ'rɒpədɪst/ *n* callista *m & f*, pedicuro *m*

chirp /tʃɜ:p/ *n* pío *m*. ● *vi* piar. **~y** *a* alegre

chisel /'tʃɪzl/ *n* formón *m*. ● *vt* (*pt* **chiselled**) cincelar

chivalr|ous /'ʃɪvəlrəs/ *a* caballeroso. **~y** /-rɪ/ *n* caballerosidad *f*

chlorine /'klɔ:ri:n/ *n* cloro *m*

chock /tʃɒk/ *n* cuña *f*. **~-a-block** *a*, **~-full** *a* atestado

chocolate /'tʃɒklət/ *n* chocolate *m*; (individual sweet) bombón *m*, chocolate *m* (LAm)

choice /tʃɔɪs/ *n* elección *f*; (preference) preferencia *f*. ● *a* escogido

choir /'kwaɪə(r)/ *n* coro *m*

choke /tʃəʊk/ *vt* sofocar. ● *vi* sofocarse. ● *n* (Auto) choke *m*, estárter *m*, ahogador *m* (Mex)

cholera /'kɒlərə/ *n* cólera *m*

cholesterol /kə'lestərɒl/ *n* colesterol *m*

choose /tʃu:z/ *vt/i* (*pt* **chose**, *pp* **chosen**) elegir, escoger. **~y** *a* 🅸 exigente

chop /tʃɒp/ *vt* (*pt* **chopped**) cortar. ● *n* (Culin) chuleta *f*. □ **~ down** *vt* talar. □ **~ off** *vt* cortar. **~per** *n* hacha *f*; (butcher's) cuchilla *f*. **~py** *a* picado

chord /kɔ:d/ *n* (Mus) acorde *m*

chore /tʃɔ:(r)/ *n* tarea *f*, faena *f*. **household ~s** *npl* quehaceres *mpl* domésticos

chorus /'kɔ:rəs/ *n* coro *m*; (of song) estribillo *m*

chose /tʃəʊz/, **chosen** /'tʃəʊzn/ ⇒CHOOSE

Christ /kraɪst/ *n* Cristo *m*

christen /'krɪsn/ *vt* bautizar. **~ing** *n* bautizo *m*

Christian /'krɪstjən/ *a & n* cristiano (*m*). **~ity** /krɪstɪ'ænətɪ/ *n* cristianismo *m*. ~ **name** *n* nombre *m* de pila

Christmas /'krɪsməs/ *n* Navidad *f*. **Merry** ~! ¡Feliz Navidad!, ¡Felices Pascuas! **Father** ~ Papá *m* Noel. ● *a* de Navidad, navideño. ~ **card** *n* tarjeta *f* de Navidad *f*. ~ **day** *n* día *m* de Navidad. ~ **Eve** *n* Nochebuena *f*. ~ **tree** *n* árbol *m* de Navidad

chrom|e /krəʊm/ *n* cromo *m*. ~**ium** /'krəʊmɪəm/ *n* cromo *m*

chromosome /'krəʊməsəʊm/ *n* cromosoma *m*

chronic /'krɒnɪk/ *a* crónico; (Ⓘ, bad) terrible

chronicle /'krɒnɪkl/ *n* crónica *f*. ● *vt* historiar

chronological /krɒnə'lɒdʒɪkl/ *a* cronológico

chubby /'tʃʌbɪ/ *a* (**-ier**, **-iest**) regordete; <*person*> gordinflón Ⓘ

chuck /tʃʌk/ *vt* Ⓘ tirar. □ ~ **out** *vt* tirar

chuckle /'tʃʌkl/ *n* risa *f* ahogada. ● *vi* reírse entre dientes

chug /tʃʌg/ *vi* (*pt* **chugged**) (of motor) traquetear

chum /tʃʌm/ *n* amigo *m*, compinche *m*, cuate *m* (Mex)

chunk /tʃʌŋk/ *n* trozo *m* grueso. ~**y** *a* macizo

church /'tʃɜ:tʃ/ *n* iglesia *f*. ~**yard** *n* cementerio *m*

churn /'tʃɜ:n/ *n* (for milk) lechera *f*, cántara *f*; (for making butter) mantequera *f*. ● *vt* agitar. □ ~ **out** *vt* producir en profusión

chute /ʃu:t/ *n* tobogán *m*

cider /'saɪdə(r)/ *n* sidra *f*

cigar /sɪ'gɑ:(r)/ *n* puro *m*

cigarette /sɪgə'ret/ *n* cigarrillo *m*. ~ **end** *n* colilla *f*. ~ **holder** *n* boquilla *f*. ~ **lighter** *n* mechero *m*, encendedor *m*

cinecamera /'sɪnɪkæmərə/ *n* tomavistas *m*, filmadora *f* (LAm)

cinema /'sɪnəmə/ *n* cine *m*

cipher /'saɪfə(r)/ *n* (Math, fig) cero *m*; (code) clave *f*

circle /'sɜ:kl/ *n* círculo *m*; (in theatre) anfiteatro *m*. ● *vt* girar alrededor de. ● *vi* dar vueltas

circuit /'sɜ:kɪt/ *n* circuito *m*

circular /'sɜ:kjʊlə(r)/ *a* & *n* circular (*f*)

circulat|e /'sɜ:kjʊleɪt/ *vt* hacer circular. ● *vi* circular. ~**ion** /-'leɪʃn/ *n* circulación *f*; (number of copies) tirada *f*

circumcise /'sɜ:kəmsaɪz/ *vt* circuncidar

circumference /sə'kʌmfərəns/ *n* circunferencia *f*

circumstance /'sɜ:kəmstəns/ *n* circunstancia *f*. ~**s** (means) *npl* situación *f* económica

circus /'sɜ:kəs/ *n* circo *m*

cistern /'sɪstən/ *n* cisterna *f*

cite /saɪt/ *vt* citar

citizen /'sɪtɪzn/ *n* ciudadano *m*; (inhabitant) habitante *m* & *f*

citrus /'sɪtrəs/ *n*. ~ **fruits** cítricos *mpl*

city /'sɪtɪ/ *n* ciudad *f*; **the C**~ el centro *m* financiero de Londres

civic /'sɪvɪk/ *a* cívico

civil /'sɪvl/ *a* civil; (polite) cortés

civilian /sɪ'vɪlɪən/ *a* & *n* civil (*m* & *f*)

civiliz|ation /sɪvɪlaɪ'zeɪʃn/ *n* civilización *f*. ~**ed** /'sɪvəlaɪzd/ *a* civilizado.

civil: ~ **servant** *n* funcionario *m* (del Estado), burócrata *m* & *f* (Mex).

~ service *n* administración *f* pública. **~ war** *n* guerra *f* civil

clad /klæd/ ⇒CLOTHE

claim /kleɪm/ *vt* reclamar; (assert) pretender. ● *n* reclamación *f*; (right) derecho *m*; (Jurid) demanda *f*

clairvoyant /kleəˈvɔɪənt/ *n* clarividente *m* & *f*

clam /klæm/ *n* almeja *f*. ● *vi* (*pt* **clammed**). **~ up** [T] ponerse muy poco comunicativo

clamber /ˈklæmbə(r)/ *vi* trepar a gatas

clammy /ˈklæmɪ/ *a* (**-ier**, **-iest**) húmedo

clamour /ˈklæmə(r)/ *n* clamor *m*. ● *vi*. **~ for** pedir a gritos

clamp /klæmp/ *n* abrazadera *f*; (Auto) cepo *m*. ● *vt* sujetar con abrazadera; poner cepo a <*car*>. □ **~ down on** *vt* reprimir

clan /klæn/ *n* clan *m*

clang /klæŋ/ *n* sonido *m* metálico

clap /klæp/ *vt* (*pt* **clapped**) aplaudir; batir <*hands*>. ● *vi* aplaudir. ● *n* palmada *f*; (of thunder) trueno *m*

clarif|ication /klærɪfɪˈkeɪʃn/ *n* aclaración *f*. **~y** /ˈklærɪfaɪ/ *vt* aclarar. ● *vi* aclararse

clarinet /klærɪˈnet/ *n* clarinete *m*

clarity /ˈklærətɪ/ *n* claridad *f*

clash /klæʃ/ *n* choque *m*; (noise) estruendo *m*; (contrast) contraste *m*; (fig) conflicto *m*. ● *vt* golpear. ● *vi* encontrarse; <*colours*> desentonar

clasp /klɑːsp/ *n* cierre *m*. ● *vt* agarrar; apretar <*hand*>

class /klɑːs/ *n* clase *f*. **evening ~** *n* clase nocturna. ● *vt* clasificar

classic /ˈklæsɪk/ *a* & *n* clásico (*m*). **~al** *a* clásico. **~s** *npl* estudios *mpl* clásicos

classif|ication /klæsɪfɪˈkeɪʃn/ *n* clasificación *f*. **~y** /ˈklæsɪfaɪ/ *vt* clasificar

class: ~room *n* aula *f*, clase *f*. **~y** *a* [T] elegante

clatter /ˈklætə(r)/ *n* ruido *m*; (of train) traqueteo *m*. ● *vi* hacer ruido

clause /klɔːz/ *n* cláusula *f*; (Gram) oración *f*

claustrophobia /klɔːstrəˈfəʊbɪə/ *n* claustrofobia *f*

claw /klɔː/ *n* garra *f*; (of cat) uña *f*; (of crab) pinza *f*. ● *vt* arañar

clay /kleɪ/ *n* arcilla *f*

clean /kliːn/ *a* (**-er**, **-est**) limpio; <*stroke*> bien definido. ● *adv* completamente. ● *vt* limpiar. ● *vi* limpiar. □ **~ up** *vt* hacer la limpieza. **~er** *n* persona *f* quehace la limpieza. **~liness** /ˈklenlɪnɪs/ *n* limpieza *f*

cleans|e /klenz/ *vt* limpiar. **~er** *n* producto *m* de limpieza; (for skin) crema *f* de limpieza. **~ing cream** *n* crema *f* de limpieza

clear /klɪə(r)/ *a* (**-er**, **-est**) claro; (transparent) transparente; (without obstacles) libre; <*profit*> neto; <*sky*> despejado. **keep ~ of** evitar. ● *adv* claramente. ● *vt* despejar; liquidar <*goods*>; (Jurid) absolver; (jump over) saltar por encima de; quitar, levantar (LAm) <*table*>. □ **~ off** *vi* [x], **~ out** *vi* [T], (go away) largarse. □ **~ up** *vt* (tidy) ordenar; aclarar <*mystery*>. *vi* <*weather*> despejarse. **~ance** *n* (removal of obstructions) despeje *m*; (authorization) permiso *m*; (by security) acreditación *f*. **~ing** *n* claro *m*. **~ly** *adv* evidentemente. **~way** *n* carretera *f* en la que no se permite parar

cleavage /ˈkliːvɪdʒ/ *n* escote *m*

clef /klef/ *n* (Mus) clave *f*

clench /klentʃ/ *vt* apretar

clergy /ˈklɜːdʒɪ/ *n* clero *m*. **~man** /-mən/ *n* clérigo *m*

cleric /ˈklerɪk/ *n* clérigo *m*. **~al** *a* clerical; (of clerks) de oficina

clerk /klɑːk/ *n* empleado *m*; (Amer, salesclerk) dependiente *m*, vendedor *m*

clever /ˈklevə(r)/ *a* (**-er**, **-est**) inteligente; (skilful) hábil. **~ly** *adv* inteligentemente; (with skill) hábilmente. **~ness** *n* inteligencia *f*

cliché /ˈkliːʃeɪ/ *n* lugar *m* común *m*, cliché *m*

click /klɪk/ *n* golpecito *m*. ● *vi* chascar; 🅸 llevarse bien. ● *vt* chasquear

client /ˈklaɪənt/ *n* cliente *m*

cliff /klɪf/ *n* acantilado *m*

climat|e /ˈklaɪmət/ *n* clima *m*. **~ic** /-ˈmætɪk/ *a* climático

climax /ˈklaɪmæks/ *n* clímax *m*; (orgasm) orgasmo *m*

climb /klaɪm/ *vt* subir *<stairs>*; trepar *<tree>*; escalar *<mountain>*. ● *vi* subir. ● *n* subida *f*. □ **~ down** *vi* bajar; (fig) ceder. **~er** *n* (Sport) alpinista *m* & *f*, andinista *m* & *f* (LAm); (plant) trepadora *f*

clinch /klɪntʃ/ *vt* cerrar *<deal>*

cling /klɪŋ/ *vi* (*pt* **clung**) agarrarse; (stick) pegarse

clinic /ˈklɪnɪk/ *n* centro *m* médico; (private hospital) clínica *f*. **~al** *a* clínico

clink /klɪŋk/ *n* tintineo *m*. ● *vt* hacer tintinear. ● *vi* tintinear

clip /klɪp/ *n* *<fastener>* clip *m*; (for paper) sujetapapeles *m*; (for hair) horquilla *f*. ● *vt* (*pt* **clipped**) (cut) cortar; (join) sujetar. **~pers** /ˈklɪpəz/ *npl* (for hair) maquinilla *f* para cortar el pelo; (for nails) cortaúñas *m*. **~ping** *n* recorte *m*

cloak /kləʊk/ *n* capa *f*. **~room** *n* guardarropa *m*; (toilet) lavabo *m*, baño *m* (LAm)

clock /klɒk/ *n* reloj *m*. **~wise** *a/adv* en el sentido de las agujas del reloj. **~work** *n* mecanismo *m* de relojería. **like ~work** con precisión

clog /klɒg/ *n* zueco *m*. ● *vt* (*pt* **clogged**) atascar

cloister /ˈklɔɪstə(r)/ *n* claustro *m*

close[1] /kləʊs/ *a* (**-er**, **-est**) cercano; (together) apretado; *<friend>* íntimo; *<weather>* bochornoso; *<link etc>* estrecho; *<game, battle>* reñido. **have a ~ shave** (fig) escaparse de milagro. ● *adv* cerca. ● *n* recinto *m*

close[2] /kləʊz/ *vt* cerrar. ● *vi* cerrarse; (end) terminar. **~ down** *vt/i* cerrar. ● *n* fin *m*. **~d** *a* cerrado

closely /ˈkləʊslɪ/ *adv* estrechamente; (at a short distance) de cerca; (with attention) detenidamente; (precisely) rigurosamente

closet /ˈklɒzɪt/ *n* (Amer) armario *m*; (for clothes) armario *m*, closet *m* (LAm)

close-up /ˈkləʊsʌp/ *n* (Cinema etc) primer plano *m*

closure /ˈkləʊʒə(r)/ *n* cierre *m*

clot /klɒt/ *n* (Med) coágulo *m*; 🅸 tonto *m*. ● *vi* (*pt* **clotted**) cuajarse; *<blood>* coagularse

cloth /klɒθ/ *n* tela *f*; (duster) trapo *m*; (tablecloth) mantel *m*

cloth|e /kləʊð/ *vt* (*pt* **clothed** *or* **clad**) vestir. **~es** /kləʊðz/ *npl* ropa. **~espeg**, **~espin** (Amer) *n* pinza *f* (para tender la ropa). **~ing** *n* ropa *f*

cloud /klaʊd/ *n* nube *f*. ● **~ over** *vi* nublarse. **~y** *a* (**-ier**, **-iest**) nublado; *<liquid>* turbio

clout /klaʊt/ *n* bofetada *f.* ● *vt* abofetear

clove /kləʊv/ *n* clavo *m.* ~ **of garlic** *n* diente *m* de ajo

clover /ˈkləʊvə(r)/ *n* trébol *m*

clown /klaʊn/ *n* payaso *m.* ● *vi* hacer el payaso

club /klʌb/ *n* club *m*; (weapon) porra *f*; (golf club) palo *m* de golf; (at cards) trébol *m.* ● *vt* (*pt* **clubbed**) aporrear. □ ~ **together** *vi* contribuir con dinero (**to** para)

cluck /klʌk/ *vi* cloquear

clue /kluː/ *n* pista *f*; (in crosswords) indicación *f.* **not to have a** ~ no tener la menor idea

clump /klʌmp/ *n* grupo *m.* ● *vt* agrupar

clums|iness /ˈklʌmzɪnɪs/ *n* torpeza *f.* ~**y** /ˈklʌmzɪ/ *a* (**-ier**, **-iest**) torpe

clung /klʌŋ/ ⇒CLING

cluster /ˈklʌstə(r)/ *n* grupo *m.* ● *vi* agruparse

clutch /klʌtʃ/ *vt* agarrar. ● *n* (Auto) embrague *m*

clutter /ˈklʌtə(r)/ *n* desorden *m.* ● *vt.* ~ (**up**) abarrotar. ~**ed** /ˈklʌtəd/ *a* abarratado de cosas

coach /kəʊtʃ/ *n* autocar *m*, autobús *m*; (of train) vagón *m*; (horse-drawn) coche *m*; (Sport) entrenador *m.* ● *vt* (Sport) entrenar

coal /kəʊl/ *n* carbón *m*

coalition /kəʊəˈlɪʃn/ *n* coalición *f*

coarse /kɔːs/ *a* (**-er**, **-est**) grueso; <*material*> basto; (person, language) ordinario

coast /kəʊst/ *n* costa *f.* ● *vi* (with cycle) deslizarse sin pedalear; (with car) ir en punto muerto. ~**al** *a* costero. ~**guard** *n* guardacostas *m.* ~**line** *n* litoral *m*

coat /kəʊt/ *n* abrigo *m*; (jacket) chaqueta *f*; (of animal) pelo *m*; (of paint) mano *f.* ● *vt* cubrir, revestir. ~**hanger** *n* percha *f*, gancho *m* (LAm). ~**ing** *n* capa *f.* ~ **of arms** *n* escudo *m* de armas

coax /kəʊks/ *vt* engatusar

cobbler /ˈkɒblə(r)/ *n* zapatero *m* (remendón)

cobblestone /ˈkɒbəlstəʊn/ *n* adoquín *m*

cobweb /ˈkɒbweb/ *n* telaraña *f*

cocaine /kəˈkeɪn/ *n* cocaína *f*

cock /kɒk/ *n* (cockerel) gallo *m*; (male bird) macho *m.* ● *vt* amartillar <*gun*>; aguzar <*ears*>. ~**erel** /ˈkɒkərəl/ *n* gallo *m.* ~**-eyed** /-aɪd/ *a* [I] torcido

cockney /ˈkɒknɪ/ *a* & *n* (*pl* **-eys**) londinense (*m* & *f*) (del este de Londres)

cockpit /ˈkɒkpɪt/ *n* (in aircraft) cabina *f* del piloto

cockroach /ˈkɒkrəʊtʃ/ *n* cucaracha *f*

cocktail /ˈkɒkteɪl/ *n* cóctel *m*

cock-up /ˈkɒkʌp/ *n* [⊠] lío *m*

cocky /ˈkɒkɪ/ *a* (**-ier**, **-iest**) engreído

cocoa /ˈkəʊkəʊ/ *n* cacao *m*; (drink) chocolate *m*, cocoa *f* (LAm)

coconut /ˈkəʊkənʌt/ *n* coco *m*

cocoon /kəˈkuːn/ *n* capullo *m*

cod /kɒd/ *n invar* bacalao *m*

code /kəʊd/ *n* código *m*; (secret) clave *f*; **in** ~ en clave

coeducational /kəʊedʒʊˈkeɪʃənl/ *a* mixto

coerc|e /kəʊˈɜːs/ *vt* coaccionar. ~**ion** /-ʃn/ *n* coacción *f*

coffee /ˈkɒfɪ/ *n* café *m.* ~ **bean** *n* grano *m* de café. ~ **maker** *n* cafetera *f.* ~**pot** *n* cafetera *f*

coffin /ˈkɒfɪn/ *n* ataúd *m*, cajón *m* (LAm)

cog /kɒg/ *n* diente *m*; (fig) pieza *f*

coherent /kəʊˈhɪərənt/ *a* coherente

coil /kɔɪl/ *vt* enrollar. ● *n* rollo *m*; (one ring) vuelta *f*

coin /kɔɪn/ *n* moneda *f*. ● *vt* acuñar

coincide /kəʊɪnˈsaɪd/ *vi* coincidir. **~nce** /kəʊˈɪnsɪdəns/ *n* casualidad *f*. **~ntal** /kəʊɪnsɪˈdentl/ *a* casual

coke /kəʊk/ *n* (coal) coque *m*. **C~** (P) Coca-Cola *f* (P)

colander /ˈkʌləndə(r)/ *n* colador *m*

cold /kəʊld/ *a* (**-er**, **-est**) frío. **be ~** <*person*> tener frío. **it is ~** (weather) hace frío. ● *n* frío *m*; (Med) resfriado *m*. **have a ~** estar resfriado. **~-blooded** /-ˈblʌdɪd/ *a* <*animal*> de sangre fría; <*murder*> a sangre fría. **~-shoulder** /-ˈʃəʊldə(r)/ *vt* tratar con frialdad. **~ sore** *n* herpes *m* labial. **~ storage** *n* conservación *f* en frigorífico

coleslaw /ˈkəʊlslɔː/ *n* ensalada *f* de col

collaborat|e /kəˈlæbəreɪt/ *vi* colaborar. **~ion** /-ˈreɪʃn/ *n* colaboración *f*. **~or** *n* colaborador *m*

collaps|e /kəˈlæps/ *vi* derrumbarse; (Med) sufrir un colapso. ● *n* derrumbamiento *m*; (Med) colapso *m*. **~ible** /-əbl/ *a* plegable

collar /ˈkɒlə(r)/ *n* cuello *m*; (for animals) collar *m*. ● *vt* ⊞ hurtar. **~bone** *n* clavícula *f*

colleague /ˈkɒliːg/ *n* colega *m* & *f*

collect /kəˈlekt/ *vt* reunir; (hobby) coleccionar, juntar (LAm); (pick up) recoger; cobrar <*rent*>. ● *vi* <*people*> reunirse; <*things*> acumularse. **~ion** /-ʃn/ *n* colección *f*; (in church) colecta *f*; (of post) recogida *f*. **~or** *n* coleccionista *m* & *f*

college /ˈkɒlɪdʒ/ *n* colegio *m*; (of art, music etc) escuela *f*; (Amer) universidad *f*

colli|de /kəˈlaɪd/ *vi* chocar. **~sion** /-ˈlɪʒn/ *n* choque *m*

colloquial /kəˈləʊkwɪəl/ *a* coloquial

Colombia /kəˈlʌmbɪə/ *n* Colombia *f*. **~n** *a* & *n* colombiano (*m*)

colon /ˈkəʊlən/ *n* (Gram) dos puntos *mpl*; (Med) colon *m*

colonel /ˈkɜːnl/ *n* coronel *m*

colon|ial /kəˈləʊnɪəl/ *a* colonial. **~ize** /ˈkɒlənaɪz/ *vt* colonizar. **~y** /ˈkɒlənɪ/ *n* colonia *f*

colossal /kəˈlɒsl/ *a* colosal

colour /ˈkʌlə(r)/ *n* color *m*. **off ~** (fig) indispuesto. ● *a* de color(es), en color(es) ● *vt* colorear; (dye) teñir. **~-blind** *a* daltoniano. **~ed** /ˈkʌləd/ *a* de color. **~ful** *a* lleno de color; (fig) pintoresco. **~ing** *n* color; (food colouring) colorante *m*. **~less** *a* incoloro

column /ˈkɒləm/ *n* columna *f*. **~ist** *n* columnista *m* & *f*

coma /ˈkəʊmə/ *n* coma *m*

comb /kəʊm/ *n* peine *m*. ● *vt* (search) registrar. **~ one's hair** peinarse

combat /ˈkɒmbæt/ *n* combate *m*. ● *vt* (*pt* **combated**) combatir

combination /kɒmbɪˈneɪʃn/ *n* combinación *f*

combine /kəmˈbaɪn/ *vt* combinar. ● *vi* combinarse. ● /ˈkɒmbaɪn/ *n* asociación *f*. **~ harvester** *n* cosechadora *f*

combustion /kəm'bʌstʃən/ *n* combustión *f*

come /kʌm/ *vi* (*pt* **came**, *pp* **come**) venir; (occur) pasar. □ ~ **across** *vt* encontrarse con <*person*>; encontrar <*object*>. □ ~ **apart** *vi* deshacerse. □ ~ **away** *vi* (leave) salir; (become detached) salirse. □ ~ **back** *vi* volver. □ ~ **by** *vt* obtener. □ ~ **down** *vi* bajar. □ ~ **in** *vi* entrar; (arrive) llegar. □ ~ **into** *vt* entrar en; heredar <*money*>. □ ~ **off** *vi* desprenderse; (succeed) tener éxito. *vt*. ~ **off it!** 🅸 ¡no me vengas con eso! □ ~ **on** *vi* (start to work) encenderse. ~ **on, hurry up!** ¡vamos, date prisa! □ ~ **out** *vi* salir. □ ~ **round** *vi* (after fainting) volver en sí; (be converted) cambiar de idea; (visit) venir. □ ~ **to** *vt* llegar a <*decision etc*>. □ ~ **up** *vi* subir; (fig) surgir. □ ~ **up with** *vt* proponer <*idea*>. ~**back** *n* retorno *m*; (retort) réplica *f*

comedian /kə'mi:dɪən/ *n* cómico *m*

comedy /'kɒmədɪ/ *n* comedia *f*

comet /'kɒmɪt/ *n* cometa *m*

comfort /'kʌmfət/ *n* comodidad *f*; (consolation) consuelo *m*. ● *vt* consolar. ~**able** *a* cómodo. ~**er** *n* (for baby) chupete *m*, chupón *m* (LAm); (Amer, for bed) edredón *m*

comic /'kɒmɪk/ *a* cómico. ● *n* cómico *m*; (periodical) revista *f* de historietas, tebeo *m*. ~**al** *a* cómico. ~ **strip** *n* tira *f* cómica

coming /'kʌmɪŋ/ *n* llegada *f*. ~**s and goings** idas *fpl* y venidas. ● *a* próximo; <*week, month etc*> que viene

comma /'kɒmə/ *n* coma *f*

command /kə'mɑ:nd/ *n* orden *f*; (mastery) dominio *m*. ● *vt* ordenar; imponer <*respect*>

commandeer /kɒmən'dɪə(r)/ *vt* requisar

command: ~**er** *n* comandante *m*. ~**ing** *a* imponente. ~**ment** *n* mandamiento *m*

commando /kə'mɑ:ndəʊ/ *n* (*pl* **-os**) comando *m*

commemorat|e /kə'meməreɪt/ *vt* conmemorar. ~**ion** /-'reɪʃn/ *n* conmemoración *f*. ~**ive** /-ətɪv/ *a* conmemorativo

commence /kə'mens/ *vt* dar comienzo a. ● *vi* iniciarse

commend /kə'mend/ *vt* alabar. ~**able** *a* loable. ~**ation** /kɒmen'deɪʃn/ *n* elogio *m*

comment /'kɒment/ *n* observación *f*. ● *vi* hacer observaciones (**on** sobre)

commentary /'kɒməntrɪ/ *n* comentario *m*; (Radio, TV) reportaje *m*

commentat|e /'kɒmənteɪt/ *vi* narrar. ~**or** *n* (Radio, TV) locutor *m*

commerc|e /'kɒmɜ:s/ *n* comercio *m*. ~**ial** /kə'mɜ:ʃl/ *a* comercial. ● *n* anuncio *m*; aviso *m* (LAm). ~**ialize** *vt* comercializar

commiserat|e /kə'mɪzəreɪt/ *vi* compadecerse (**with** de). ~**ion** /-'reɪʃn/ *n* conmiseración *f*

commission /kə'mɪʃn/ *n* comisión *f*. **out of** ~ fuera de servicio. ● *vt* encargar; (Mil) nombrar oficial

commissionaire /kəmɪʃə'neə(r)/ *n* portero *m*

commit /kə'mɪt/ *vt* (*pt* **committed**) cometer; (entrust) confiar. ~ **o.s.** comprometerse. ~**ment** *n* compromiso *m*

committee /kə'mɪtɪ/ *n* comité *m*

commodity /kə'mɒdətɪ/ *n* producto *m*, artículo *m*

common /'kɒmən/ *a* (**-er**, **-est**) común; (usual) corriente; (vulgar) ordinario. ● *n*. in ~ en común. ~**er** *n* plebeyo *m*. ~ **law** *n* derecho *m* consuetudinario. ~**ly** *adv* comúnmente. **C~ Market** *n* Mercado *m* Común. ~**place** *a* banal. ● *n* banalidad *f*. ~ **room** *n* sala *f* común, salón *m* común. **C~s** *n*. the (House of) **C~s** la Cámara de los Comunes. ~ **sense** *n* sentido *m* común. **C~wealth** *n*. the **C~wealth** la Mancomunidad *f* Británica

commotion /kə'məʊʃn/ *n* confusión *f*

commune /'kɒmju:n/ *n* comuna *f*

communicat|e /kə'mju:nɪkeɪt/ *vt* comunicar. ● *vi* comunicarse. ~**ion** /-'keɪʃn/ *n* comunicación *f*. ~**ive** /-ətɪv/ *a* comunicativo

communion /kə'mju:nɪən/ *n* comunión *f*

communis|m /'kɒmjʊnɪsəm/ *n* comunismo *m*. ~**t** *n* comunista *m* & *f*

community /kə'mju:nətɪ/ *n* comunidad *f*. ~ **centre** *n* centro *m* social

commute /kə'mju:t/ *vi* viajar diariamente (entre el lugar de residencia y el trabajo). ● *vt* (Jurid) conmutar. ~**r** *n* viajero *m* diario

compact /kəm'pækt/ *a* compacto. ● /'kɒmpækt/ *n* (for powder) polvera *f*. ~ **disc**, ~ **disk** /'kɒmpækt/ *n* disco *m* compacto, compact-disc *m*. ~ **disc player** *n* (reproductor *m* de) compact-disc

companion /kəm'pænɪən/ *n* compañero *m*. ~**ship** *n* compañía *f*

company /'kʌmpənɪ/ *n* compañía *f*; (guests) visita *f*; (Com) sociedad *f*

compar|able /'kɒmpərəbl/ *a* comparable. ~**ative** /kəm'pærətɪv/ *a* comparativo; (fig) relativo. ● *n* (Gram) comparativo *m*. ~**e** /kəm'peə(r)/ *vt* comparar. ~**ison** /kəm'pærɪsn/ *n* comparación *f*

compartment /kəm'pɑ:tmənt/ *n* compartim(i)ento *m*

compass /'kʌmpəs/ *n* brújula *f*. ~**es** *npl* compás *m*

compassion /kəm'pæʃn/ *n* compasión *f*. ~**ate** /-ət/ *a* compasivo

compatible /kəm'pætəbl/ *a* compatible

compel /kəm'pel/ *vt* (*pt* **compelled**) obligar. ~**ling** *a* irresistible

compensat|e /'kɒmpənseɪt/ *vt* compensar; (for loss) indemnizar. ● *vi*. ~**e for sth** compensar algo. ~**ion** /-'seɪʃn/ *n* compensación *f*; (financial) indemnización *f*

compère /'kɒmpeə(r)/ *n* presentador *m*. ● *vt* presentar

compete /kəm'pi:t/ *vi* competir

competen|ce /'kɒmpətəns/ *n* competencia *f*. ~**t** *a* competente

competit|ion /kɒmpə'tɪʃn/ *n* (contest) concurso *m*; (Sport) competición *f*, competencia *f* (LAm); (Com) competencia *f*. ~**ive** /kəm'petətɪv/ *a* competidor; <*price*> competitivo. ~**or** /kəm'petɪtə(r)/ *n* competidor *m*; (in contest) concursante *m* & *f*

compile /kəm'paɪl/ *vt* compilar

complacen|cy /kəm'pleɪsənsɪ/ *n* autosuficiencia *f*. ~**t** *a* satisfecho de sí mismo

complain /kəm'pleɪn/ *vi*. ~ (about) quejarse (de). ● *vt*. ~ **that** quejarse de que. ~**t** *n* queja *f*; (Med) enfermedad *f*

complement /'kɒmplɪmənt/ *n* complemento *m.* ● *vt* complementar. **~ary** /-'mentrɪ/ *a* complementario

complet|e /kəm'pli:t/ *a* completo; (finished) acabado; (downright) total. ● *vt* acabar; llenar <*a form*>. **~ely** *adv* completamente. **~ion** /-ʃn/ *n* finalización *f*

complex /'kɒmpleks/ *a* complejo. ● *n* complejo *m*

complexion /kəm'plekʃn/ *n* tez *f*; (fig) aspecto *m*

complexity /kəm'pleksətɪ/ *n* complejidad *f*

complicat|e /'kɒmplɪkeɪt/ *vt* complicar. **~ed** *a* complicado. **~ion** /-'keɪʃn/ *n* complicación *f*

compliment /'kɒmplɪmənt/ *n* cumplido *m*; (amorous) piropo *m*. ● *vt* felicitar. **~ary** /-'mentrɪ/ *a* halagador; (given free) de regalo. **~s** *npl* saludos *mpl*

comply /kəm'plaɪ/ *vi*. **~ with** conformarse con

component /kəm'pəʊnənt/ *a* & *n* componente (*m*)

compos|e /kəm'pəʊz/ *vt* componer. **be ~ed of** estar compuesto de. **~er** *n* compositor *m*. **~ition** /kɒmpə'zɪʃn/ *n* composición *f*

compost /'kɒmpɒst/ *n* abono *m*

composure /kəm'pəʊʒə(r)/ *n* serenidad *f*

compound /'kɒmpaʊnd/ *n* compuesto *m*; (enclosure) recinto *m*. ● *a* compuesto; <*fracture*> complicado

comprehen|d /kɒmprɪ'hend/ *vt* comprender. **~sion** /kɒmprɪ'henʃn/ *n* comprensión *f*. **~sive** /kɒmprɪ'hensɪv/ *a* extenso; <*insurance*> contra todo riesgo. **~sive (school)** *n* instituto *m* de enseñanza secundaria

compress /'kɒmpres/ *n* (Med) compresa *f*. ● /kəm'pres/ *vt* comprimir. **~ion** /-'preʃn/ *n* compresión *f*

comprise /kəm'praɪz/ *vt* comprender

compromis|e /'kɒmprəmaɪz/ *n* acuerdo *m*, compromiso *m*, arreglo *m*. ● *vt* comprometer. ● *vi* llegar a un acuerdo. **~ing** *a* <*situation*> comprometido

compuls|ion /kəm'pʌlʃn/ *n* (force) coacción *f*; (obsession) compulsión *f*. **~ive** /kəm'pʌlsɪv/ *a* compulsivo. **~ory** /kəm'pʌlsərɪ/ *a* obligatorio

comput|er /kəm'pju:tə(r)/ *n* ordenador *m*, computadora *f* (LAm). **~erize** *vt* computarizar, computerizar. **~er studies** *n*, **~ing** *n* informática *f*, computación *f*

comrade /'kɒmreɪd/ *n* camarada *m & f*

con /kɒn/ *vt* (*pt* **conned**) 🅸 estafar. ● *n* (fraud) estafa *f*; (objection) ⇨PRO

concave /'kɒŋkeɪv/ *a* cóncavo

conceal /kən'si:l/ *vt* ocultar

concede /kən'si:d/ *vt* conceder

conceit /kən'si:t/ *n* vanidad *f*. **~ed** *a* engreído

conceiv|able /kən'si:vəbl/ *a* concebible. **~e** /kən'si:v/ *vt/i* concebir

concentrat|e /'kɒnsəntreɪt/ *vt* concentrar. ● *vi* concentrarse (on en). **~ion** /-'treɪʃn/ *n* concentración *f*

concept /'kɒnsept/ *n* concepto *m*

conception /kən'sepʃn/ *n* concepción *f*

concern /kən'sɜ:n/ *n* asunto *m*; (worry) preocupación *f*; (Com) empresa *f*. ● *vt* tener que ver con;

(deal with) tratar de. **as far as I'm ~ed** en cuanto a mí. **be ~ed about** preocuparse por. **~ing** *prep* acerca de

concert /'kɒnsət/ *n* concierto *m*. **~ed** /kən'sɜ:tɪd/ *a* concertado

concertina /kɒnsə'ti:nə/ *n* concertina *f*

concerto /kən'tʃɜ:təʊ/ *n* (*pl* **-os** *or* **-ti** /-tɪ/) concierto *m*

concession /kən'seʃn/ *n* concesión *f*

concise /kən'saɪs/ *a* conciso

conclu|de /kən'klu:d/ *vt/i* concluir. **~ding** *a* final. **~sion** /-ʃn/ *n* conclusión *f*.. **~sive** /-sɪv/ *a* decisivo. **~sively** *adv* concluyentemente

concoct /kən'kɒkt/ *vt* confeccionar; (fig) inventar. **~ion** /-ʃn/ *n* mezcla *f*; (drink) brebaje *m*

concrete /'kɒŋkri:t/ *n* hormigón *m*, concreto *m* (LAm). ● *a* concreto

concussion /kən'kʌʃn/ *n* conmoción *f* cerebral

condemn /kən'dem/ *vt* condenar. **~ation** /kɒndem'neɪʃn/ *n* condena *f*

condens|ation /kɒnden'seɪʃn/ *n* condensación *f*. **~e** /kən'dens/ *vt* condensar. ● *vi* condensarse

condescend /kɒndɪ'send/ *vi* dignarse (to a). **~ing** *a* superior

condition /kən'dɪʃn/ *n* condición *f*. **on ~ that** a condición de que. ● *vt* condicionar. **~al** *a* condicional. **~er** *n* (for hair) suavizante *m*, enjuague *m* (LAm)

condo /'kɒndəʊ/ *n* (*pl* **-os**) (Amer [!]) ⇒CONDOMINIUM

condolences /kən'dəʊlənsɪz/ *npl* pésame *m*

condom /'kɒndɒm/ *n* condón *m*

condominium /kɒndə'mɪnɪəm/ *n* (Amer) apartamento *m*, piso *m* (*en régimen de propiedad horizontal*)

condone /kən'dəʊn/ *vt* condonar

conduct /kən'dʌkt/ *vt* llevar a cabo <*business, experiment*>; conducir <*electricity*>; dirigir <*orchestra*>. ● /'kɒndʌkt/ *n* conducta *f*. **~or** /kən'dʌktə(r)/ *n* director *m*; (of bus) cobrador *m*. **~ress** /kən'dʌktrɪs/ *n* cobradora *f*

cone /kəʊn/ *n* cono *m*; (for ice cream) cucurucho *m*, barquillo *m* (Mex)

confectionery /kən'fekʃənrɪ/ *n* productos *mpl* de confitería

confederation /kənfedə'reɪʃn/ *n* confederación *f*

confess /kən'fes/ *vt* confesar. ● *vi* confesarse. **~ion** /-ʃn/ *n* confesión *f*

confetti /kən'fetɪ/ *n* confeti *m*

confide /kən'faɪd/ *vt/i* confiar

confiden|ce /'kɒnfɪdəns/ *n* confianza *f*; (self-confidence) confianza *f* en sí mismo; (secret) confidencia *f*. **~ce trick** *n* estafa *f*, timo *m*. **~t** /'kɒnfɪdənt/ *a* seguro de sí mismo. **be ~t of** confiar en

confidential /kɒnfɪ'denʃl/ *a* confidencial. **~ity** /-denʃɪ'ælətɪ/ *n* confidencialidad *f*

confine /kən'faɪn/ *vt* confinar; (limit) limitar. **~ment** *n* (imprisonment) prisión *f*

confirm /kən'fɜ:m/ *vt* confirmar. **~ation** /kɒnfə'meɪʃn/ *n* confirmación *f*. **~ed** *a* inveterado

confiscat|e /'kɒnfɪskeɪt/ *vt* confiscar. **~ion** /-'keɪʃn/ *n* confiscación *f*

conflict /'kɒnflɪkt/ *n* conflicto *m*. ● /kən'flɪkt/ *vi* chocar. **~ing** /kən'flɪktɪŋ/ *a* contradictorio

conform /kən'fɔ:m/ *vi* conformarse. **~ist** *n* conformista *m & f*

confound /kən'faʊnd/ *vt* confundir. **~ed** *a* [T] maldito

confront /kən'frʌnt/ *vt* hacer frente a; (face) enfrentarse con. **~ation** /kɒnfrʌn'teɪʃn/ *n* confrontación *f*

confus|e /kən'fju:z/ *vt* confundir. **~ed** *a* confundido. **get ~ed** confundirse. **~ing** *a* confuso. **~ion** /-ʒn/ *n* confusión *f*

congeal /kən'dʒi:l/ *vi* coagularse

congest|ed /kən'dʒestɪd/ *a* congestionado. **~ion** /-tʃən/ *n* congestión *f*

congratulat|e /kən'grætjʊleɪt/ *vt* felicitar. **~ions** /-'leɪʃnz/ *npl* enhorabuena *f*, felicitaciones *fpl* (LAm)

congregat|e /'kɒŋgrɪgeɪt/ *vi* congregarse. **~ion** /-'geɪʃn/ *n* asamblea *f*; (Relig) fieles *mpl*, feligreses *mpl*

congress /'kɒŋgres/ *n* congreso *m*. **C~** (Amer) el Congreso. **~man** /-mən/ *n* (Amer) miembro *m* del Congreso. **~woman** *n* (Amer) miembro *f* del Congreso.

conifer /'kɒnɪfə(r)/ *n* conífera *f*

conjugat|e /'kɒndʒʊgeɪt/ *vt* conjugar. **~ion** /-'geɪʃn/ *n* conjugación *f*

conjunction /kən'dʒʌŋkʃn/ *n* conjunción *f*

conjur|e /'kʌndʒə(r)/ *vi* hacer juegos de manos. ● *vt*. □ **~e up** *vt* evocar. **~er**, **~or** *n* prestidigitador *m*

conk /kɒŋk/ *vi*. **~ out** [T] fallar; <*person*> desmayarse

conker /'kɒŋkə(r)/ *n* [T] castaña *f* de Indias

conman /'kɒnmæn/ *n* (*pl* **-men**) [T] estafador *m*, timador *m*

connect /kə'nekt/ *vt* conectar; (associate) relacionar. ● *vi* (be fitted) estar conectado (**to** a). □ **~ with** *vt* <*train*> enlazar con. **~ed** *a* unido; (related) relacionado. **be ~ed with** tener que ver con, estar emparentado con. **~ion** /-ʃn/ *n* conexión *f*; (Rail) enlace *m*; (fig) relación *f*. **in ~ion with** a propósito de, con respecto a

connive /kə'naɪv/ *vi*. **~e at** ser cómplice en

connoisseur /kɒnə'sɜ:(r)/ *n* experto *m*

connotation /kɒnə'teɪʃn/ *n* connotación *f*

conquer /'kɒŋkə(r)/ *vt* conquistar; (fig) vencer. **~or** *n* conquistador *m*

conquest /'kɒŋkwest/ *n* conquista *f*

conscience /'kɒnʃəns/ *n* conciencia *f*

conscientious /kɒnʃɪ'enʃəs/ *a* concienzudo

conscious /'kɒnʃəs/ *a* consciente; (deliberate) intencional. **~ly** *adv* a sabiendas. **~ness** *n* consciencia *f*; (Med) conocimiento *m*

conscript /'kɒnskrɪpt/ *n* recluta *m & f*, conscripto *m* (LAm). ● /kən'skrɪpt/ *vt* reclutar. **~ion** /kən'skrɪpʃn/ *n* reclutamiento *m*, conscripción *f* (LAm)

consecrate /'kɒnsɪkreɪt/ *vt* consagrar

consecutive /kən'sekjʊtɪv/ *a* sucesivo

consensus /kən'sensəs/ *n* consenso *m*

consent /kən'sent/ *vi* consentir. ● *n* consentimiento *m*

consequen|ce /ˈkɒnsɪkwəns/ *n* consecuencia *f*. **~t** *a* consiguiente. **~tly** *adv* por consiguiente

conservation /kɒnsəˈveɪʃn/ *n* conservación *f*, preservación *f*. **~ist** *n* conservacionista *m & f*

conservative /kənˈsɜːvətɪv/ *a* conservador; (modest) prudente, moderado. **C~** *a & n* conservador (*m*)

conservatory /kənˈsɜːvətrɪ/ *n* invernadero *m*

conserve /kənˈsɜːv/ *vt* conservar

consider /kənˈsɪdə(r)/ *vt* considerar; (take into account) tomar en cuenta. **~able** *a* considerable. **~ably** *adv* considerablemente

considerat|e /kənˈsɪdərət/ *a* considerado. **~ion** /-ˈreɪʃn/ *n* consideración *f*. **take sth into ~ion** tomar algo en cuenta

considering /kənˈsɪdərɪŋ/ *prep* teniendo en cuenta. ● *conj*. **~** (that) teniendo en cuenta que

consign /kənˈsaɪn/ *vt* consignar; (send) enviar. **~ment** *n* envío *m*

consist /kənˈsɪst/ *vi*. **~ of** consistir en. **~ency** *n* consistencia *f*; (fig) coherencia *f*. **~ent** *a* coherente; (unchanging) constante. **~ent with** compatible con. **~ently** *adv* constantemente

consolation /kɒnsəˈleɪʃn/ *n* consuelo *m*

console /kənˈsəʊl/ *vt* consolar. ● /ˈkɒnsəʊl/ *n* consola *f*

consolidate /kənˈsɒlɪdeɪt/ *vt* consolidar

consonant /ˈkɒnsənənt/ *n* consonante *f*

conspicuous /kənˈspɪkjʊəs/ *a* (easily seen) visible; (showy) llamativo; (noteworthy) notable

conspir|acy /kənˈspɪrəsɪ/ *n* conspiración *f*. **~ator** /kənˈspɪrətə(r)/ *n* conspirador *m*. **~e** /kənˈspaɪə(r)/ *vi* conspirar

constable /ˈkʌnstəbl/ *n* agente *m & f* de policía

constant /ˈkɒnstənt/ *a* constante. **~ly** *adv* constantemente

constellation /kɒnstəˈleɪʃn/ *n* constelación *f*

consternation /kɒnstəˈneɪʃn/ *n* consternación *f*

constipat|ed /ˈkɒnstɪpeɪtɪd/ *a* estreñido. **~ion** /-ˈpeɪʃn/ *n* estreñimiento *m*

constituen|cy /kənˈstɪtjʊənsɪ/ *n* distrito *m* electoral. **~t** *n* (Pol) elector *m*. ● *a* constituyente, constitutivo

constitut|e /ˈkɒnstɪtjuːt/ *vt* constituir. **~ion** /-ˈtjuːʃn/ *n* constitución *f*. **~ional** /-ˈtjuːʃənl/ *a* constitucional. ● *n* paseo *m*

constrict /kənˈstrɪkt/ *vt* apretar. **~ion** /-ʃn/ *n* constricción *f*

construct /kənˈstrʌkt/ *vt* construir. **~ion** /-ʃn/ *n* construcción *f*. **~ive** *a* constructivo

consul /ˈkɒnsl/ *n* cónsul *m & f*. **~ate** /ˈkɒnsjʊlət/ *n* consulado *m*

consult /kənˈsʌlt/ *vt/i* consultar. **~ancy** *n* asesoría. **~ant** *n* asesor *m*; (Med) especialista *m & f*; (Tec) consejero *m* técnico. **~ation** /kɒnsəlˈteɪʃn/ *n* consulta *f*

consume /kənˈsjuːm/ *vt* consumir. **~r** *n* consumidor *m*. ● *a* de consumo

consummate /ˈkɒnsəmət/ *a* consumado. ● /ˈkɒnsəmeɪt/ *vt* consumar

consumption /kənˈsʌmpʃn/ *n* consumo *m*

contact /ˈkɒntækt/ *n* contacto *m*. ● *vt* ponerse en contacto con. **~ lens** *n* lentilla *f*, lente *f* de contacto (LAm)

contagious /kənˈteɪdʒəs/ *a* contagioso

contain /kənˈteɪn/ *vt* contener. **~ o.s.** contenerse. **~er** *n* recipiente *m*; (Com) contenedor *m*

contaminat|e /kənˈtæmɪneɪt/ *vt* contaminar. **~ion** /-ˈneɪʃn/ *n* contaminación *f*

contemplate /ˈkɒntəmpleɪt/ *vt* contemplar; (consider) considerar

contemporary /kənˈtempərərɪ/ *a* & *n* contemporáneo (*m*)

contempt /kənˈtempt/ *n* desprecio *m*. **~ible** *a* despreciable. **~uous** /-tjʊəs/ *a* desdeñoso

contend /kənˈtend/ *vt* competir. **~er** *n* aspirante *m* & *f* (for a)

content /kənˈtent/ *a* satisfecho. ● /ˈkɒntent/ *n* contenido *m*. ● /kənˈtent/ *vt* contentar. **~ed** /kənˈtentɪd/ *a* satisfecho. **~ment** /kənˈtentmənt/ *n* satisfacción *f*. **~s** /ˈkɒntents/ *n* contenido *m*; (of book) índice *m* de materias

contest /ˈkɒntest/ *n* (competition) concurso *m*; (Sport) competición *f*, competencia *f* (LAm). ● /kənˈtest/ *vt* disputar. **~ant** /kənˈtestənt/ *n* concursante *m* & *f*

context /ˈkɒntekst/ *n* contexto *m*

continent /ˈkɒntɪnənt/ *n* continente *m*. **the C~** Europa *f*. **~al** /-ˈnentl/ *a* continental. **~al quilt** *n* edredón *m*

contingen|cy /kənˈtɪndʒənsɪ/ *n* contingencia *f*. **~t** *a* & *n* contingente (*m*)

continu|al /kənˈtɪnjʊəl/ *a* continuo. **~ally** *adv* continuamente. **~ation** /-ˈeɪʃn/ *n* continuación *f*. **~e** /kənˈtɪnjuː/ *vt/i* continuar, seguir. **~ed** *a* continuo. **~ity** /kɒntɪˈnjuːətɪ/ *n* continuidad *f*. **~ous** /kənˈtɪnjʊəs/ *a* continuo. **~ously** *adv* continuamente

contort /kənˈtɔːt/ *vt* retorcer. **~ion** /-ʃn/ *n* contorsión *f*. **~ionist** /-ʃənɪst/ *n* contorsionista *m* & *f*

contour /ˈkɒntʊə(r)/ *n* contorno *m*

contraband /ˈkɒntrəbænd/ *n* contrabando *m*

contracepti|on /kɒntrəˈsepʃn/ *n* anticoncepción *f*. **~ve** /-tɪv/ *a* & *n* anticonceptivo (*m*)

contract /ˈkɒntrækt/ *n* contrato *m*. ● /kənˈtrækt/ *vt* contraer. ● *vi* contraerse. **~ion** /kənˈtrækʃn/ *n* contracción *f*. **~or** /kənˈtræktə(r)/ *n* contratista *m* & *f*

contradict /kɒntrəˈdɪkt/ *vt* contradecir. **~ion** /-ʃn/ *n* contradicción *f*. **~ory** *a* contradictorio

contraption /kənˈtræpʃn/ *n* **I** artilugio *m*

contrary /ˈkɒntrərɪ/ *a* contrario. **the ~** lo contrario. **on the ~** al contrario. ● *adv*. **~ to** contrariamente a. ● /kənˈtreərɪ/ *a* (obstinate) terco

contrast /ˈkɒntrɑːst/ *n* contraste *m*. ● /kənˈtrɑːst/ *vt/i* contrastar. **~ing** *a* contrastante

contravene /kɒntrəˈviːn/ *vt* contravenir

contribut|e /kənˈtrɪbjuːt/ *vt* contribuir con. ● *vi* contribuir. **~e to** escribir para <*newspaper*>. **~ion** /kɒntrɪˈbjuːʃn/ *n* contribución *f*. **~or** *n* contribuyente *m* & *f*; (to newspaper) colaborador *m*

contrite /ˈkɒntraɪt/ *a* arrepentido, pesaroso

contriv|e /kən'traɪv/ *vt* idear. **~e to** conseguir. **~ed** *a* artificioso

control /kən'trəʊl/ *vt* (*pt* **controlled**) controlar. ● *n* control *m*. **~ler** *n* director *m*. **~s** *npl* (Mec) mandos *mpl*

controvers|ial /kɒntrə'vɜ:ʃl/ controvertido. **~y** /'kɒntrəvɜ:sɪ/ *n* controversia *f*

conundrum /kə'nʌndrəm/ *n* adivinanza *f*

convalesce /kɒnvə'les/ *vi* convalecer. **~nce** *n* convalecencia *f*

convector /kən'vektə(r)/ *n* estufa *f* de convección

convene /kən'vi:n/ *vt* convocar. ● *vi* reunirse

convenien|ce /kən'vi:nɪəns/ *n* conveniencia *f*, comodidad *f*. **all modern ~ces** todas las comodidades. **at your ~ce** según le convenga. **~ces** *npl* servicios *mpl*, baños *mpl* (LAm). **~t** *a* conveniente; <*place*> bien situado; <*time*> oportuno. **be ~t** convenir. **~tly** *adv* convenientemente

convent /'kɒnvənt/ *n* convento *m*

convention /kən'venʃn/ *n* convención *f*. **~al** *a* convencional

converge /kən'vɜ:dʒ/ *vi* converger

conversation /kɒnvə'seɪʃn/ *n* conversación *f*. **~al** *a* familiar, coloquial.

converse /kən'vɜ:s/ *vi* conversar. ● /'kɒnvɜ:s/ *a* inverso. ● *n* lo contrario. **~ly** *adv* a la inversa

conver|sion /kən'vɜ:ʃn/ *n* conversión *f*. **~t** /kən'vɜ:t/ *vt* convertir. ● /'kɒnvɜ:t/ *n* converso *m*. **~tible** /kən'vɜ:tɪbl/ *a* convertible. ● *n* (Auto) descapotable *m*, convertible *m* (LAm)

convex /'kɒnveks/ *a* convexo

convey /kən'veɪ/ *vt* transportar <*goods, people*>; comunicar <*idea, feeling*>. **~or belt** *n* cinta *f* transportadora, banda *f* transportadora (LAm)

convict /kən'vɪkt/ *vt* condenar. ● /'kɒnvɪkt/ *n* presidiario *m*. **~ion** /kən'vɪkʃn/ *n* condena *f*; (belief) creencia *f*

convinc|e /kən'vɪns/ *vt* convencer. **~ing** *a* convincente

convoluted /'kɒnvəlu:tɪd/ *a* <*argument*> intrincado

convoy /'kɒnvɔɪ/ *n* convoy *m*

convuls|e /kən'vʌls/ *vt* convulsionar. **be ~ed with laughter** desternillarse de risa. **~ion** /-ʃn/ *n* convulsión *f*

coo /ku:/ *vi* arrullar

cook /kʊk/ *vt* hacer, preparar. ● *vi* cocinar; <*food*> hacerse. ● *n* cocinero *m*. □ **~ up** *vt* [I] inventar. **~book** *n* libro *m* de cocina. **~er** *n* cocina *f*, estufa *f* (Mex). **~ery** *n* cocina *f*

cookie /'kʊkɪ/ *n* (Amer) galleta *f*

cool /ku:l/ *a* (**-er**, **-est**) fresco; (calm) tranquilo; (unfriendly) frío. ● *n* fresco *m*; ☒ calma *f*. ● *vt* enfriar. ● *vi* enfriarse. □ **~ down** *vi* <*person*> calmarse. **~ly** *adv* tranquilamente

coop /ku:p/ *n* gallinero *m*. □ **~ up** *vt* encerrar

co-op /'kəʊɒp/ *n* cooperativa *f*

cooperat|e /kəʊ'ɒpəreɪt/ *vi* cooperar. **~ion** /-'reɪʃn/ *n* cooperación *f*. **~ive** /kəʊ'ɒpərətɪv/ *a* cooperativo. ● *n* cooperativa *f*

co-opt /kəʊ'ɒpt/ *vt* cooptar

co-ordinat|e /kəʊ'ɔ:dɪneɪt/ *vt* coordinar. ● /kəʊ'ɔ:dɪnət/ *n* (Math) coordenada *f*. **~es** *npl* prendas *fpl* para combinar. **~ion** /kəʊɔ:dɪˈneɪʃn/ *n* coordinación *f*

cop /kɒp/ *n* [I] poli *m & f* [I], tira *m & f* (Mex, [I])

cope /kəʊp/ *vi* arreglárselas. **~** with hacer frente a

copious /ˈkəʊpɪəs/ *a* abundante

copper /ˈkɒpə(r)/ *n* cobre *m*; (coin) perra *f*; [I] poli *m & f* [I], tira *m & f* (Mex, [I]). ● *a* de cobre

copy /ˈkɒpɪ/ *n* copia *f*; (of book, newspaper) ejemplar *m*. ● *vt* copiar. **~right** *n* derechos *mpl* de reproducción

coral /ˈkɒrəl/ *n* coral *m*

cord /kɔ:d/ *n* cuerda *f*; (fabric) pana *f*; (Amer, Elec) cordón *m*, cable *m*

cordial /ˈkɔ:dɪəl/ *a* cordial. ● *n* refresco *m* (concentrado)

cordon /ˈkɔ:dn/ *n* cordón *m*. □ **~ off** *vt* acordonar

core /kɔ:(r)/ *n* (of apple) corazón *m*; (of Earth) centro *m*; (of problem) meollo *m*

cork /kɔ:k/ *n* corcho *m*. **~screw** *n* sacacorchos *m*

corn /kɔ:n/ *n* (wheat) trigo *m*; (Amer) maíz *m*; (hard skin) callo *m*

corned beef /kɔ:nd ˈbi:f/ *n* carne *f* de vaca en lata

corner /ˈkɔ:nə(r)/ *n* ángulo *m*; (inside) rincón *m*; (outside) esquina *f*; (football) córner *m*. ● *vt* arrinconar; (Com) acaparar

cornet /ˈkɔ:nɪt/ *n* (Mus) corneta *f*; (for ice cream) cucurucho *m*, barquillo *m* (Mex)

corn: ~flakes *npl* copos *mpl* de maíz. **~flour** *n* maizena *f* (P)

Cornish /ˈkɔ:nɪʃ/ *a* de Cornualles

cornstarch /ˈkɔ:nstɑ:tʃ/ *n* (Amer) maizena *f* (P)

corny /ˈkɔ:nɪ/ *a* ([I], trite) gastado

coronation /kɒrəˈneɪʃn/ *n* coronación *f*

coroner /ˈkɒrənə(r)/ *n* juez *m* de primera instancia

corporal /ˈkɔ:pərəl/ *n* cabo *m*. ● *a* corporal

corporate /ˈkɔ:pərət/ *a* corporativo

corporation /kɔ:pəˈreɪʃn/ *n* corporación *f*; (Amer) sociedad *f* anónima

corps /kɔ:(r)/ *n* (*pl* **corps** /kɔ:z/) cuerpo *m*

corpse /kɔ:ps/ *n* cadáver *m*

corpulent /ˈkɔ:pjʊlənt/ *a* corpulento

corral /kəˈrɑ:l/ *n* (Amer) corral *m*

correct /kəˈrekt/ *a* correcto; <*time*> exacto. ● *vt* corregir. **~ion** /-ʃn/ *n* corrección *f*

correspond /kɒrɪˈspɒnd/ *vi* corresponder; (write) escribirse. **~ence** *n* correspondencia *f*. **~ent** *n* corresponsal *m & f*

corridor /ˈkɒrɪdɔ:(r)/ *n* pasillo *m*

corro|de /kəˈrəʊd/ *vt* corroer. ● *vi* corroerse. **~sion** /-ʒn/ *n* corrosión *f*. **~sive** /-sɪv/ *a* corrosivo

corrugated /ˈkɒrəgeɪtɪd/ *a* ondulado. **~ iron** *n* chapa *f* de zinc

corrupt /kəˈrʌpt/ *a* corrompido. ● *vt* corromper. **~ion** /-ʃn/ *n* corrupción *f*

corset /ˈkɔ:sɪt/ *n* corsé *m*

cosmetic /kɒzˈmetɪk/ *a & n* cosmético (*m*)

cosmic /ˈkɒzmɪk/ *a* cósmico

cosmopolitan /kɒzməˈpɒlɪtən/ *a & n* cosmopolita (*m & f*)

cosmos /ˈkɒzmɒs/ *n* cosmos *m*

cosset /ˈkɒsɪt/ *vt* (*pt* **cosseted**) mimar

cost /kɒst/ *vt* (*pt* **cost**) costar; (*pt* **costed**) calcular el coste de, calcular el costo de (LAm). ● *n* coste *m*, costo *m* (LAm). **at all ~s** cueste lo que cueste. **to one's ~** a sus expensas. **~s** *npl* (Jurid) costas *fpl*

Costa Rica /kɒstəˈri:kə/ *n* Costa *f* Rica. **~n** *a* & *n* costarricense (*m* & *f*), costarriqueño (*m* & *f*)

cost: ~-effective *a* rentable. **~ly** *a* (**-ier**, **-iest**) costoso

costume /ˈkɒstju:m/ *n* traje *m*; (for party, disguise) disfraz *m*

cosy /ˈkəʊzɪ/ *a* (**-ier**, **-iest**) acogedor. ● *n* cubreteras *m*

cot /kɒt/ *n* cuna *f*

cottage /ˈkɒtɪdʒ/ *n* casita *f*. **~ cheese** *n* requesón *m*. **~ pie** *n* pastel *m* de carne cubierta con puré

cotton /ˈkɒtn/ *n* algodón *m*; (thread) hilo *m*; (Amer) ⇒**~** WOOL. □ **~ on** *vi* 🅸 comprender. **~ bud** *n* bastoncillo *m*, cotonete *m* (Mex). **~ candy** *n* (Amer) algodón *m* de azúcar. **~ swab** *n* (Amer) ⇒**~** BUD. **~ wool** *n* algodón *m* hidrófilo

couch /kaʊtʃ/ *n* sofá *m*

cough /kɒf/ *vi* toser. ● *n* tos *f*. □ **~ up** *vt* 🅸 pagar. **~ mixture** *n* jarabe *m* para la tos

could /kʊd/ *pt of* CAN[1]

couldn't /ˈkʊdnt/ = **could not**

council /ˈkaʊnsl/ *n* consejo *m*; (of town) ayuntamiento *m*. **~ house** *n* vivienda *f* subvencionada. **~lor** *n* concejal *m*

counsel /ˈkaʊnsl/ *n* consejo *m*; (*pl invar*) (Jurid) abogado *m*. ● *vt* (*pt* **counselled**) aconsejar. **~ling** *n* terapia *f* de apoyo. **~lor** *n* consejero *m*

count /kaʊnt/ *n* recuento *m*; (nobleman) conde *m*. ● *vt/i* contar. □ **~ on** *vt* contar. **~down** *n* cuenta *f* atrás

counter /ˈkaʊntə(r)/ *n* (in shop) mostrador *m*; (in bank, post office) ventanilla *f*; (token) ficha *f*. ● *adv*. **~ to** en contra de. ● *a* opuesto. ● *vt* oponerse a; parar <*blow*>

counter... /ˈkaʊntə(r)/ *pref* contra.... **~act** /-ˈækt/ *vt* contrarrestar. **~-attack** *n* contraataque *m*. ● *vt/i* contraatacar. **~balance** *n* contrapeso *m*. ● *vt/i* contrapesar. **~clockwise** /-ˈklɒkwaɪz/ *a/adv* (Amer) en sentido contrario al de las agujas del reloj

counterfeit /ˈkaʊntəfɪt/ *a* falsificado. ● *n* falsificación *f*. ● *vt* falsificar

counterfoil /ˈkaʊntəfɔɪl/ *n* matriz *f*, talón *m* (LAm)

counter-productive /kaʊntəprəˈdʌktɪv/ *a* contraproducente

countess /ˈkaʊntɪs/ *n* condesa *f*

countless /ˈkaʊntlɪs/ *a* innumerable

country /ˈkʌntrɪ/ *n* (native land) país *m*; (countryside) campo *m*; (Mus) (música *f*) country *m*. **~-and-western** /-enˈwestən/ (música *f*) country *m*. **~man** /-mən/ *n* (of one's own country) compatriota *m*. **~side** *n* campo *m*; (landscape) paisaje *m*

county /ˈkaʊntɪ/ *n* condado *m*

coup /ku:/ *n* golpe *m*

couple /ˈkʌpl/ *n* (of things) par *m*; (of people) pareja *f*; (married) matrimonio *m*. **a ~ of** un par de

coupon /ˈku:pɒn/ *n* cupón *m*

courage /ˈkʌrɪdʒ/ *n* valor *m*. **~ous** /kəˈreɪdʒəs/ *a* valiente

courgette /kʊəˈʒet/ *n* calabacín *m*

courier /ˈkʊrɪə(r)/ *n* mensajero *m*; (for tourists) guía *m & f*

course /kɔːs/ *n* curso *m*; (behaviour) conducta *f*; (Aviat, Naut) rumbo *m*; (Culin) plato *m*; (for golf) campo *m*. **in due ∼** a su debido tiempo. **in the ∼ of** en el transcurso de, durante. **of ∼** claro, por supuesto. **of ∼ not** claro que no, por supuesto que no

court /kɔːt/ *n* corte *f*; (tennis) pista *f*; cancha *f* (LAm); (Jurid) tribunal *m*. ● *vt* cortejar; buscar <*danger*>

courteous /ˈkɜːtɪəs/ *a* cortés

courtesy /ˈkɜːtəsɪ/ *n* cortesía *f*

courtier /ˈkɔːtɪə(r)/ *n* (old use) cortesano *m*

court: ∼ martial *n* (*pl* **∼s martial**) consejo *m* de guerra. **∼-martial** *vt* (*pt* **∼-martialled**) juzgar en consejo de guerra. **∼ship** *n* cortejo *m*. **∼yard** *n* patio *m*

cousin /ˈkʌzn/ *n* primo *m*. **first ∼** primo carnal. **second ∼** primo segundo

cove /kəʊv/ *n* ensenada *f*, cala *f*

Coventry /ˈkɒvntrɪ/ *n*. **send s.o. to ∼** hacer el vacío a uno

cover /ˈkʌvə(r)/ *vt* cubrir. ● *n* cubierta *f*; (shelter) abrigo *m*; (lid) tapa *f*; (for furniture) funda *f*; (pretext) pretexto *m*; (of magazine) portada *f*. □ **∼ up** *vt* cubrir; (fig) ocultar. **∼ charge** *n* precio *m* del cubierto. **∼ing** *n* cubierta *f*. **∼ing letter** *n* carta *f* adjunta

covet /ˈkʌvɪt/ *vt* codiciar

cow /kaʊ/ *n* vaca *f*

coward /ˈkaʊəd/ *n* cobarde *m*. **∼ice** /ˈkaʊədɪs/ *n* cobardía *f*. **∼ly** *a* cobarde.

cowboy /ˈkaʊbɔɪ/ *n* vaquero *m*

cower /ˈkaʊə(r)/ *vi* encogerse, acobardarse

coxswain /ˈkɒksn/ *n* timonel *m*

coy /kɔɪ/ *a* (**-er**, **-est**) (shy) tímido; (evasive) evasivo

crab /kræb/ *n* cangrejo *m*, jaiba *f* (LAm)

crack /kræk/ *n* grieta *f*; (noise) crujido *m*; (of whip) chasquido *m*; (drug) crack *m*. ● *a* 🄸 de primera. ● *vt* agrietar; chasquear <*whip, fingers*>; cascar <*nut*>; gastar <*joke*>; resolver <*problem*>. ● *vi* agrietarse. **get ∼ing** 🄸 darse prisa. □ **∼ down on** *vt* 🄸 tomar medidas enérgicas contra

cracker /ˈkrækə(r)/ *n* (Culin) cracker *f*, galleta *f* (salada); (Christmas cracker) sorpresa *f* (*que estalla al abrirla*)

crackle /ˈkrækl/ *vi* crepitar. ● *n* crepitación *f*, crujido *m*

crackpot /ˈkrækpɒt/ *n* 🄸 chiflado *m*

cradle /ˈkreɪdl/ *n* cuna *f*. ● *vt* acunar

craft /krɑːft/ *n* destreza *f*; (technique) arte *f*; (cunning) astucia *f*. ● *n* *invar* (boat) barco *m*

craftsman /ˈkrɑːftsmən/ *n* (*pl* **-men**) artesano *m*. **∼ship** *n* artesanía *f*

crafty /ˈkrɑːftɪ/ *a* (**-ier**, **-iest**) astuto

cram /kræm/ *vt* (*pt* **crammed**) rellenar. **∼ with** llenar de. ● *vi* (for exams) memorizar, empollar, zambutir (Mex)

cramp /kræmp/ *n* calambre *m*

cramped /kræmpt/ *a* apretado

crane /kreɪn/ *n* grúa *f*. ● *vt* estirar <*neck*>

crank /kræŋk/ *n* manivela *f*; (person) excéntrico *m*. **∼y** *a* excéntrico

cranny /ˈkrænɪ/ *n* grieta *f*

crash /kræʃ/ *n* accidente *m*; (noise) estruendo *m*; (collision) choque *m*;

(Com) quiebra *f*. ● *vt* estrellar. ● *vi* quebrar con estrépito; (have accident) tener un accidente; <*car etc*> estrellarse, chocar; (fail) fracasar. ~ **course** *n* curso *m* intensivo. ~ **helmet** *n* casco *m* protector. ~**-land** *vi* hacer un aterrizaje forzoso

crass /kræs/ *a* craso, burdo

crate /kreɪt/ *n* cajón *m*. ● *vt* embalar

crater /'kreɪtə(r)/ *n* cráter *m*

crav|e /kreɪv/ *vt* ansiar. ~**ing** *n* ansia *f*

crawl /krɔ:l/ *vi* <*baby*> gatear; (move slowly) avanzar lentamente; (drag o.s.) arrastrarse. ~ **to** humillarse ante. ~ **with** hervir de. ● *n* (swimming) crol *m*. **at a** ~ a paso lento

crayon /'kreɪən/ *n* lápiz *m* de color; (made of wax) lápiz *m* de cera, crayola *f* (P), crayón *m* (Mex)

craz|e /kreɪz/ *n* manía *f*. ~**y** /'kreɪzɪ/ *a* (**-ier**, **-iest**) loco. **be** ~**y about** estar loco por

creak /kri:k/ *n* crujido *m*; (of hinge) chirrido *m*. ● *vi* crujir; <*hinge*> chirriar

cream /kri:m/ *n* crema *f*; (fresh) nata *f*, crema *f* (LAm). ● *a* (colour) color crema. ● *vt* (beat) batir. ~ **cheese** *n* queso *m* para untar, queso *m* crema (LAm). ~**y** *a* cremoso

crease /kri:s/ *n* raya *f*, pliegue *m* (Mex); (crumple) arruga *f*. ● *vt* plegar; (wrinkle) arrugar. ● *vi* arrugarse

creat|e /kri:'eɪt/ *vt* crear. ~**ion** /-ʃn/ *n* creación *f*. ~**ive** *a* creativo. ~**or** *n* creador *m*

creature /'kri:tʃə(r)/ *n* criatura *f*

crèche /kreʃ/ *n* guardería *f* (infantil)

credib|ility /kredə'bɪlətɪ/ *n* credibilidad *f*. ~**le** /'kredəbl/ *a* creíble

credit /'kredɪt/ *n* crédito *m*; (honour) mérito *m*. **take the** ~ **for** atribuirse el mérito de. ● *vt* (*pt* **credited**) acreditar; (believe) creer. ~ **s.o. with** atribuir a uno. ~ **card** *n* tarjeta *f* de crédito. ~**or** *n* acreedor *m*

creed /kri:d/ *n* credo *m*

creek /kri:k/ *n* ensenada *f*. **up the** ~ ☒ en apuros

creep /kri:p/ *vi* (*pt* **crept**) arrastrarse; (plant) trepar. ● *n* 🄸 adulador. ~**s** /kri:ps/ *npl*. **give s.o. the** ~**s** poner los pelos de punta a uno. ~**er** *n* enredadera *f*

cremat|e /krɪ'meɪt/ *vt* incinerar. ~**ion** /-ʃn/ *n* cremación *f*. ~**orium** /kremə'tɔ:rɪəm/ *n* (*pl* **-ia** /-ɪə/) crematorio *m*

crept /krept/ ⇒CREEP

crescendo /krɪ'ʃendəʊ/ *n* (*pl* **-os**) crescendo *m*

crescent /'kresnt/ *n* media luna *f*; (street) calle *f* en forma de media luna

crest /krest/ *n* cresta *f*; (on coat of arms) emblema *m*

crevice /'krevɪs/ *n* grieta *f*

crew /kru:/ *n* tripulación *f*; (gang) pandilla *f*. ~ **cut** *n* corte *m* al rape

crib /krɪb/ *n* (Amer) cuna *f*; (Relig) belén *m*. ● *vt/i* (*pt* **cribbed**) copiar

crick /krɪk/ *n* calambre *m*; (in neck) tortícolis *f*

cricket /'krɪkɪt/ *n* (Sport) críquet *m*; (insect) grillo *m*

crim|e /kraɪm/ *n* delito *m*; (murder) crimen *m*; (acts) delincuencia *f*. ~**inal** /'krɪmɪnl/ *a* & *n* criminal (*m* & *f*)

crimson /ˈkrɪmzn/ *a & n* carmesí (*m*)

cringe /krɪndʒ/ *vi* encogerse; (fig) humillarse

crinkle /ˈkrɪŋkl/ *vt* arrugar. ● *vi* arrugarse. ● *n* arruga *f*

cripple /ˈkrɪpl/ *n* lisiado *m*. ● *vt* lisiar; (fig) paralizar

crisis /ˈkraɪsɪs/ *n* (*pl* **crises** /-si:z/) crisis *f*

crisp /krɪsp/ *a* (**-er**, **-est**) (Culin) crujiente; <*air*> vigorizador. **~s** *npl* patatas *fpl* fritas, papas *fpl* fritas (LAm) (de bolsa)

crisscross /ˈkrɪskrɒs/ *a* entrecruzado. ● *vt* entrecruzar. ● *vi* entrecruzarse

criterion /kraɪˈtɪərɪən/ *n* (*pl* **-ia** /-ɪə/) criterio *m*

critic /ˈkrɪtɪk/ *n* crítico *m*. **~al** *a* crítico. **~ally** *adv* críticamente; (ill) gravemente

critici|sm /ˈkrɪtɪsɪzəm/ *n* crítica *f*. **~ze** /ˈkrɪtɪsaɪz/ *vt/i* criticar

croak /krəʊk/ *n* (of person) gruñido *m*; (of frog) canto *m*. ● *vi* gruñir; <*frog*> croar

Croat /ˈkrəʊæt/ *n* croata *m & f*. **~ia** /krəʊˈeɪʃə/ *n* Croacia *f*. **~ian** *a* croata

crochet /ˈkrəʊʃeɪ/ *n* crochet *m*, ganchillo *m*. ● *vt* tejer a crochet *or* a ganchillo

crockery /ˈkrɒkərɪ/ *n* loza *f*

crocodile /ˈkrɒkədaɪl/ *n* cocodrilo *m*. **~ tears** *npl* lágrimas *fpl* de cocodrilo

crocus /ˈkrəʊkəs/ *n* (*pl* **-es**) azafrán *m* de primavera

crook /krʊk/ *n* [I] sinvergüenza *m & f*. **~ed** /ˈkrʊkɪd/ *a* torcido, chueco (LAm); (winding) tortuoso; (dishonest) deshonesto

crop /krɒp/ *n* cosecha *f*; (haircut) corte *m* de pelo muy corto. ● *vt* (*pt* **cropped**) cortar. □ **~ up** *vi* surgir

croquet /ˈkrəʊkeɪ/ *n* croquet *m*

cross /krɒs/ *n* cruz *f*; (of animals) cruce *m*. ● *vt* cruzar; (oppose) contrariar. **~ s.o.'s mind** ocurrírsele a uno. ● *vi* cruzar. **~ o.s.** santiguarse. ● *a* enfadado, enojado (esp LAm). □ **~ out** *vt* tachar. **~bar** *n* travesaño *m*. **~-examine** /-ɪgˈzæmɪn/ *vt* interrogar. **~-eyed** *a* bizco. **~fire** *n* fuego *m* cruzado. **~ing** *n* (by boat) travesía *f*; (on road) cruce *m* peatonal. **~ly** *adv* con enfado, con enojo (esp LAm). **~-purposes** /-ˈpɜ:pəsɪz/ *npl*. **talk at ~-purposes** hablar sin entenderse. **~-reference** /-ˈrefrəns/ *n* remisión *f*. **~roads** *n invar* cruce *m*. **~-section** /-ˈsekʃn/ *n* sección *f* transversal; (fig) muestra *f* representativa. **~walk** *n* (Amer) paso de peatones. **~word** *n* **~word (puzzle)** crucigrama *m*

crotch /krɒtʃ/ *n* entrepiernas *fpl*

crouch /kraʊtʃ/ *vi* agacharse

crow /krəʊ/ *n* cuervo *m*. **as the ~ flies** en línea recta. ● *vi* cacarear. **~bar** *n* palanca *f*

crowd /kraʊd/ *n* muchedumbre *f*. ● *vt* amontonar; (fill) llenar. ● *vi* amontonarse; (gather) reunirse. **~ed** *a* atestado

crown /kraʊn/ *n* corona *f*; (of hill) cumbre *f*; (of head) coronilla *f*. ● *vt* coronar

crucial /ˈkru:ʃl/ *a* crucial

crucifix /ˈkru:sɪfɪks/ *n* crucifijo *m*. **~ion** /-ˈfɪkʃn/ *n* crucifixión *f*

crucify /ˈkru:sɪfaɪ/ *vt* crucificar

crude /kru:d/ *a* (**-er**, **-est**) (raw) crudo; (rough) tosco; (vulgar) ordinario

cruel /'krʊəl/ *a* (**crueller**, **cruellest**) cruel. **~ty** *n* crueldad *f*

cruet /'kru:ɪt/ *n* vinagrera *f*

cruise /kru:z/ *n* crucero *m*. ● *vi* hacer un crucero; (of car) circular lentamente. **~r** *n* crucero *m*

crumb /krʌm/ *n* miga *f*

crumble /'krʌmbl/ *vt* desmenuzar. ● *vi* desmenuzarse; (collapse) derrumbarse

crummy /'krʌmɪ/ *a* (**-ier**, **-iest**) ☒ miserable

crumpet /'krʌmpɪt/ *n* bollo *m* blando

crumple /'krʌmpl/ *vt* arrugar. ● *vi* arrugarse

crunch /krʌntʃ/ *vt* hacer crujir; (bite) masticar. **~y** *a* crujiente

crusade /kru:'seɪd/ *n* cruzada *f*. **~r** *n* cruzado *m*

crush /krʌʃ/ *vt* aplastar; arrugar <*clothes*>. ● *n* (crowd) aglomeración *f*. **have a ~ on** Ⓘ estar chiflado por

crust /krʌst/ *n* corteza *f*. **~y** *a* <*bread*> de corteza dura

crutch /krʌtʃ/ *n* muleta *f*; (Anat) entrepiernas *fpl*

crux /krʌks/ *n* (*pl* **cruxes**). **the ~ (of the matter)** el quid (de la cuestión)

cry /kraɪ/ *n* grito *m*. **be a far ~ from** (fig) distar mucho de. ● *vi* llorar; (call out) gritar. □ **~ off** *vi* echarse atrás, rajarse. **~baby** *n* llorón *m*

crypt /krɪpt/ *n* cripta *f*

cryptic /'krɪptɪk/ *a* enigmático

crystal /'krɪstl/ *n* cristal *m*. **~lize** *vi* cristalizarse

cub /kʌb/ *n* cachorro *m*. **C~ (Scout)** *n* lobato *m*

Cuba /'kju:bə/ *n* Cuba *f*. **~n** *a* & *n* cubano (*m*)

cubbyhole /'kʌbɪhəʊl/ *n* cuchitril *m*

cub|e /kju:b/ *n* cubo *m*. **~ic** *a* cúbico

cubicle /'kju:bɪkl/ *n* cubículo *m*; (changing room) probador *m*

cuckoo /'kʊku:/ *n* cuco *m*, cuclillo *m*

cucumber /'kju:kʌmbə(r)/ *n* pepino *m*

cuddl|e /'kʌdl/ *vt* abrazar. ● *vi* abrazarse. ● *n* abrazo *m*. **~y** *a* adorable

cue /kju:/ *n* (Mus) entrada *f*; (in theatre) pie *m*; (in snooker) taco *m*

cuff /kʌf/ *n* puño *m*; (Amer, of trousers) vuelta *f*, dobladillo *m*; (blow) bofetada *f*. **speak off the ~** hablar de improviso. ● *vt* abofetear. **~link** *n* gemelo *m*, mancuerna *f* (Mex)

cul-de-sac /'kʌldəsæk/ *n* callejón *m* sin salida

culinary /'kʌlɪnərɪ/ *a* culinario

cull /kʌl/ *vt* sacrificar en forma selectiva <*animals*>

culminat|e /'kʌlmɪneɪt/ *vi* culminar. **~ion** /-'neɪʃn/ *n* culminación *f*

culprit /'kʌlprɪt/ *n* culpable *m* & *f*

cult /kʌlt/ *n* culto *m*

cultivat|e /'kʌltɪveɪt/ *vt* cultivar. **~ion** /-'veɪʃn/ *n* cultivo *m*

cultur|al /'kʌltʃərəl/ *a* cultural. **~e** /'kʌltʃə(r)/ *n* cultura *f*; (Bot etc) cultivo *m*. **~ed** *a* cultivado; <*person*> culto

cumbersome /'kʌmbəsəm/ *a* incómodo; (heavy) pesado

cunning /'kʌnɪŋ/ *a* astuto. ● *n* astucia *f*

cup /kʌp/ *n* taza *f*; (trophy) copa *f*

cupboard /'kʌbəd/ *n* armario *m*

curator /kjʊə'reɪtə(r)/ *n* (of museum) conservador *m*

curb /kɜːb/ *n* freno *m*; (Amer) bordillo *m* (de la acera), borde *m* de la banqueta (Mex). ● *vt* refrenar

curdle /'kɜːdl/ *vt* cuajar. ● *vi* cuajarse; (go bad) cortarse

cure /kjʊə(r)/ *vt* curar. ● *n* cura *f*

curfew /'kɜːfjuː/ *n* toque *m* de queda

curio|sity /kjʊərɪ'ɒsətɪ/ *n* curiosidad *f*. **~us** /'kjʊərɪəs/ *a* curioso

curl /kɜːl/ *vt* rizar, enchinar (Mex). **~ o.s. up** acurrucarse. ● *vi* <*hair*> rizarse, enchinarse (Mex); <*paper*> ondularse. ● *n* rizo *m*, chino *m* (Mex). **~er** *n* rulo *m*, chino *m* (Mex). **~y** *a* (**-ier**, **-iest**) rizado, chino (Mex)

currant /'kʌrənt/ *n* pasa *f* de Corinto

currency /'kʌrənsɪ/ *n* moneda *f*

current /'kʌrənt/ *a* & *n* corriente (*f*); (existing) actual. **~ affairs** *npl* sucesos de actualidad. **~ly** *adv* actualmente

curriculum /kə'rɪkjʊləm/ *n* (*pl* **-la**) programa *m* de estudios. **~ vitae** *n* currículum *m* vitae

curry /'kʌrɪ/ *n* curry *m*. ● *vt* preparar al curry

curse /kɜːs/ *n* maldición *f*; (oath) palabrota *f*. ● *vt* maldecir. ● *vi* decir palabrotas

cursory /'kɜːsərɪ/ *a* superficial

curt /kɜːt/ *a* brusco

curtain /'kɜːtn/ *n* cortina *f*; (in theatre) telón *m*

curtsey, **curtsy** /'kɜːtsɪ/ *n* reverencia *f*. ● *vi* hacer una reverencia

curve /kɜːv/ *n* curva *f*. ● *vi* estar curvado; <*road*> torcerse

cushion /'kʊʃn/ *n* cojín *m*, almohadón *m*. ● *vt* amortiguar <*blow*>; (fig) proteger

cushy /'kʊʃɪ/ *a* (**-ier**, **-iest**) 🅸 fácil

custard /'kʌstəd/ *n* natillas *fpl*

custody /'kʌstədɪ/ *n* custodia *f*. **be in ~** (Jurid) estar detenido

custom /'kʌstəm/ *n* costumbre *f*; (Com) clientela *f*. **~ary** /-ərɪ/ *a* acostumbrado. **~er** *n* cliente *m*. **~s** *npl* aduana *f*. **~s officer** *n* aduanero *m*

cut /kʌt/ *vt/i* (*pt* **cut**, *pres p* **cutting**) cortar; reducir <*prices*>. ● *n* corte *m*; (reduction) reducción *f*. □ **~ across** *vt* cortar camino por. □ **~ back**, **~ down** *vt* reducir. □ **~ in** *vi* interrumpir. □ **~ off** *vt* cortar; (phone) desconectar; (fig) aislar. □ **~ out** *vt* recortar; (omit) suprimir. □ **~ through** *vt* cortar camino por. □ **~ up** *vt* cortar en pedazos

cute /kjuːt/ *a* (**-er**, **-est**) 🅸 mono, amoroso (LAm); (Amer, attractive) guapo, buen mozo (LAm)

cutlery /'kʌtlərɪ/ *n* cubiertos *mpl*

cutlet /'kʌtlɪt/ *n* chuleta *f*

cut: ~-price, (Amer) **~-rate** *a* a precio reducido. **~-throat** *a* despiadado. **~ting** *a* cortante; <*remark*> mordaz. ● *n* (from newspaper) recorte *m*; (of plant) esqueje *m*

CV *n* (= **curriculum vitae**) currículum *m* (vitae)

cycl|e /'saɪkl/ *n* ciclo *m*; (bicycle) bicicleta *f*. ● *vi* ir en bicicleta. **~ing** *n* ciclismo *m*. **~ist** *n* ciclista *m & f*

cylind|er /'sɪlɪndə(r)/ *n* cilindro *m*. **~er head** (Auto) *n* culata *f*. **~rical** /-'lɪndrɪkl/ *a* cilíndrico

cymbal /'sɪmbl/ *n* címbalo *m*

cynic /'sɪnɪk/ *n* cínico *m*. **~al** *a* cínico. **~ism** /-sɪzəm/ *n* cinismo *m*

Czech /tʃek/ *a & n* checo (*m*). **~oslovakia** /-əslə'vækɪə/ *n* (History) Checoslovaquia *f*. **~ Republic** *n*. **the ~ Republic** *n* la República Checa

Dd

dab /dæb/ *vt* (*pt* **dabbed**) tocar ligeramente. ● *n* toque *m* suave. **a ~ of** un poquito de

dad /dæd/ *n* [I] papá *m*. **~dy** *n* papi *m*. **~dy-long-legs** *n invar* (cranefly) típula *f*; (Amer, harvestman) segador *m*, falangio *m*

daffodil /'dæfədɪl/ *n* narciso *m*

daft /dɑ:ft/ *a* (**-er**, **-est**) [I] tonto

dagger /'dægə(r)/ *n* daga *f*, puñal *m*

daily /'deɪlɪ/ *a* diario. ● *adv* diariamente, cada día

dainty /'deɪntɪ/ *a* (**-ier**, **-iest**) delicado

dairy /'deərɪ/ *n* vaquería *f*; (shop) lechería *f*

daisy /'deɪzɪ/ *n* margarita *f*

dam /dæm/ *n* presa *f*, represa *f* (LAm)

damag|e /'dæmɪdʒ/ *n* daño *m*; **~s** (*npl*, Jurid) daños *mpl* y perjuicios *mpl*. ● *vt* (fig) dañar, estropear. **~ing** *a* perjudicial

dame /deɪm/ *n* (old use) dama *f*; (Amer, [x]) chica *f*

damn /dæm/ *vt* condenar; (curse) maldecir. ● *int* [I] ¡caray! [I]. ● *a* maldito. ● *n* **I don't give a ~** (no) me importa un comino

damp /dæmp/ *n* humedad *f*. ● *a* (**-er**, **-est**) húmedo. ● *vt* mojar. **~ness** *n* humedad *f*

danc|e /dɑ:ns/ *vt/i* bailar. ● *n* baile *m*. **~e hall** *n* salón *m* de baile. **~er** *n* bailador *m*; (professional) bailarín *m*. **~ing** *n* baile *m*

dandelion /'dændɪlaɪən/ *n* diente *m* de león

dandruff /'dændrʌf/ *n* caspa *f*

dandy /'dændɪ/ *n* petimetre *m*

Dane /deɪn/ *n* danés *m*

danger /'deɪndʒə(r)/ *n* peligro *m*; (risk) riesgo *m*. **~ous** *a* peligroso

dangle /'dæŋgl/ *vt* balancear. ● *vi* suspender, colgar

Danish /'deɪnɪʃ/ *a* danés. ● *m* (Lang) danés *m*

dar|e /deə(r)/ *vt* desafiar. ● *vi* atreverse a. **I ~ say** probablemente. ● *n* desafío *m*. **~edevil** *n* atrevido *m*. **~ing** *a* atrevido

dark /dɑ:k/ *a* (**-er**, **-est**) oscuro; *<skin, hair>* moreno. ● *n* oscuridad *f*; (nightfall) atardecer. **in the ~** a oscuras. **~en** *vt* oscurecer. ● *vi* oscurecerse. **~ness** *n* oscuridad *f*. **~room** *n* cámara *f* oscura

darling /'dɑ:lɪŋ/ *a* querido. ● *n* cariño *m*

darn /dɑ:n/ *vt* zurcir

dart /dɑ:t/ *n* dardo *m*. ● *vi* lanzarse; (run) precipitarse. **~board** *n* diana *f*. **~s** *npl* los dardos *mpl*

dash /dæʃ/ *vi* precipitarse. ● *vt* tirar; (break) romper; defraudar *<hopes>*. ● *n* (small amount) poquito *m*; (punctuation mark) guión *m*. □ **~ off** *vi* marcharse apresuradamente. **~ out** *vi* salir corriendo. **~board** *n* tablero *m* de mandos

data /'deɪtə/ *npl* datos *mpl*. **~base** *n* base *f* de datos. **~ processing** *n* proceso *m* de datos

date /deɪt/ *n* fecha *f*; (appointment) cita *f*; (fruit) dátil *m*. **to ~** hasta la fecha. ● *vt* fechar. ● *vi* datar; datar <*remains*>; (be old-fashioned) quedar anticuado. **~d** *a* pasado de moda

daub /dɔ:b/ *vt* embadurnar

daughter /ˈdɔ:tə(r)/ *n* hija *f*. **~-in-law** *n* nuera *f*

dawdle /ˈdɔ:dl/ *vi* andar despacio; (waste time) perder el tiempo

dawn /dɔ:n/ *n* amanecer *m*. ● *vi* amanecer; (fig) nacer. **it ~ed on me that** caí en la cuenta de que

day /deɪ/ *n* día *m*; (whole day) jornada *f*; (period) época *f*. **~break** *n* amanecer *m*. **~ care center** *n* (Amer) guardería *f* infantil. **~dream** *n* ensueño *m*. ● *vi* soñar despierto. **~light** *n* luz *f* del día. **~time** *n* día *m*

daze /deɪz/ *vt* aturdir. ● *n* aturdimiento *m*. **in a ~** aturdido. **~d** *a* aturdido

dazzle /ˈdæzl/ *vt* deslumbrar

dead /ded/ *a* muerto; (numb) dormido. ● *adv* justo; (Ⓘ, completely) completamente. **~ beat** rendido. **~ slow** muy lento. **stop ~** parar en seco. **~en** *vt* amortiguar <*sound, blow*>; calmar <*pain*>. **~ end** *n* callejón *m* sin salida. **~line** *n* fecha *f* tope, plazo *m* de entrega. **~lock** *n* punto *m* muerto. **~ly** *a* (**-ier, -iest**) mortal

deaf /def/ *a* (**-er, -est**) sordo. **~en** *vt* ensordecer. **~ness** *n* sordera *f*

deal /di:l/ *n* (agreement) acuerdo *m*; (treatment) trato *m*. **a good ~** bastante. **a great ~ (of)** muchísimo. ● *vt* (*pt* **dealt**) dar <*a blow, cards*>. ● *vi* (cards) dar, repartir. □ **~ in** *vt* comerciar en. □ **~ out** *vt* repartir, distribuir. □ **~ with** *vt* tratar con <*person*>; tratar de <*subject*>; ocuparse de <*problem*>. **~er** *n* comerciante *m*. **drug ~er** traficante *m & f* de drogas

dean /di:n/ *n* deán *m*; (Univ) decano *m*

dear /dɪə(r)/ *a* (**-er, -est**) querido; (expensive) caro. ● *n* querido *m*. ● *adv* caro. ● *int*. **oh ~!** ¡ay por Dios! **~ me!** ¡Dios mío! **~ly** *adv* (pay) caro; (very much) muchísimo

death /deθ/ *n* muerte *f*. **~ sentence** *n* pena *f* de muerte. **~ trap** *n* lugar *m* peligroso.

debat|able /dɪˈbeɪtəbl/ *a* discutible. **~e** /dɪˈbeɪt/ *n* debate *m*. ● *vt* debatir, discutir

debauchery /dɪˈbɔ:tʃərɪ/ *vt* libertinaje *m*

debit /ˈdebɪt/ *n* débito *m*. ● *vt* debitar, cargar. **~ card** *n* tarjeta *f* de cobro automático

debris /ˈdebri:/ *n* escombros *mpl*

debt /det/ *n* deuda *f*. **be in ~** tener deudas. **~or** *n* deudor *m*

decade /ˈdekeɪd/ *n* década *f*

decaden|ce /ˈdekədəns/ *n* decadencia *f*. **~t** *a* decadente

decay /dɪˈkeɪ/ *vi* descomponerse; <*tooth*> cariarse. ● *n* descomposición *f*; (of tooth) caries *f*

deceased /dɪˈsi:st/ *a* difunto

deceit /dɪˈsi:t/ *n* engaño *m*. **~ful** *a* falso. **~fully** *adv* falsamente

deceive /dɪˈsi:v/ *vt* engañar

December /dɪˈsembə(r)/ *n* diciembre *m*

decen|cy /ˈdi:sənsɪ/ *n* decencia *f*. **~t** *a* decente; (Ⓘ, good) bueno; (Ⓘ, kind) amable. **~tly** *adv* decentemente

decepti|on /dɪˈsepʃn/ *n* engaño *m*. **~ve** /-tɪv/ *a* engañoso

decibel /ˈdesɪbel/ *n* decibel(io) *m*

decide /dɪ'saɪd/ *vt/i* decidir. **~d** *a* resuelto; (unquestionable) indudable. **~dly** *adv* decididamente; (unquestionably) indudablemente

decimal /'desɪml/ *a & n* decimal (*m*). **~ point** *n* coma *f* (decimal), punto *m* decimal

decipher /dɪ'saɪfə(r)/ *vt* descifrar

decis|ion /dɪ'sɪʒn/ *n* decisión *f*. **~ive** /dɪ'saɪsɪv/ *a* decisivo; <*manner*> decidido

deck /dek/ *n* (Naut) cubierta *f*; (Amer, of cards) baraja *f*; (of bus) piso *m*. ● *vt* adornar. **~chair** *n* tumbona *f*, silla *f* de playa

declar|ation /deklə'reɪʃn/ *n* declaración *f*. **~e** /dɪ'kleə(r)/ *vt* declarar

decline /dɪ'klaɪn/ *vt* rehusar; (Gram) declinar. ● *vi* disminuir; (deteriorate) deteriorarse. ● *n* decadencia *f*; (decrease) disminución *f*

decode /di:'kəʊd/ *vt* descifrar

decompose /di:kəm'pəʊz/ *vi* descomponerse

décor /'deɪkɔ:(r)/ *n* decoración *f*

decorat|e /'dekəreɪt/ *vt* adornar, decorar (LAm); empapelar y pintar <*room*>. **~ion** /-'reɪʃn/ *n* (act) decoración *f*; (ornament) adorno *m*. **~ive** /-ətɪv/ *a* decorativo. **~or** *n* pintor *m* decorador

decoy /'di:kɔɪ/ *n* señuelo *m*. ● /dɪ'kɔɪ/ *vt* atraer con señuelo

decrease /dɪ'kri:s/ *vt/i* disminuir. ● /'di:kri:s/ *n* disminución *f*

decree /dɪ'kri:/ *n* decreto *m*. ● *vt* decretar

decrepit /dɪ'krepɪt/ *a* decrépito

dedicat|e /'dedɪkeɪt/ *vt* dedicar. **~ion** /-'keɪʃn/ *n* dedicación *f*

deduce /dɪ'dju:s/ *vt* deducir

deduct /dɪ'dʌkt/ *vt* deducir. **~ion** /-ʃn/ *n* deducción *f*

deed /di:d/ *n* hecho *m*; (Jurid) escritura *f*

deem /di:m/ *vt* juzgar, considerar

deep /di:p/ *a* (**-er**, **-est**) *adv* profundo. ● *adv* profundamente. **be ~ in thought** estar absorto en sus pensamientos. **~en** *vt* hacer más profundo. ● *vi* hacerse más profundo. **~freeze** *n* congelador *m*, freezer *m* (LAm). **~ly** *adv* profundamente

deer /dɪə(r)/ *n invar* ciervo *m*

deface /dɪ'feɪs/ *vt* desfigurar

default /dɪ'fɔ:lt/ *vi* faltar. ● *n*. **by ~** en rebeldía

defeat /dɪ'fi:t/ *vt* vencer; (frustrate) frustrar. ● *n* derrota *f*. **~ism** *n* derrotismo *m*. **~ist** *n* derrotista *a & (m & f)*

defect /'di:fekt/ *n* defecto *m*. ● /dɪ'fekt/ *vi* desertar. **~ to** pasar a. **~ion** /dɪ'fekʃn/ *n* (Pol) defección *f*. **~ive** /dɪ'fektɪv/ *a* defectuoso

defence /dɪ'fens/ *n* defensa *f*. **~less** *a* indefenso

defen|d /dɪ'fend/ *vt* defender. **~dant** *n* (Jurid) acusado *m*. **~sive** /-sɪv/ *a* defensivo. ● *n* defensiva *f*

defer /dɪ'fɜ:(r)/ *vt* (*pt* **deferred**) aplazar. **~ence** /'defərəns/ *n* deferencia *f*. **~ential** /defə'renʃl/ *a* deferente

defian|ce /dɪ'faɪəns/ *n* desafío *m*. **in ~ce of** a despecho de. **~t** *a* desafiante. **~tly** *adv* con actitud desafiante

deficien|cy /dɪ'fɪʃənsɪ/ *n* falta *f*. **~t** *a* deficiente. **be ~t in** carecer de

deficit /'defɪsɪt/ *n* déficit *m*

define /dɪ'faɪn/ *vt* definir

definite /'defɪnɪt/ *a* (final) definitivo; (certain) seguro; (clear) claro; (firm) firme. **~ly** *adv* seguramente; (definitively) definitivamente

definition /defɪ'nɪʃn/ *n* definición *f*

definitive /dɪ'fɪnətɪv/ *a* definitivo

deflate /dɪ'fleɪt/ *vt* desinflar. ● *vi* desinflarse

deflect /dɪ'flekt/ *vt* desviar

deform /dɪ'fɔ:m/ *vt* deformar. **~ed** *a* deforme. **~ity** *n* deformidad *f*

defrost /di:'frɒst/ *vt* descongelar. ● *vi* descongelarse

deft /deft/ *a* (**-er**, **-est**) hábil. **~ly** *adv* hábilmente *f*

defuse /di:'fju:z/ *vt* desactivar <*bomb*>; (fig) calmar

defy /dɪ'faɪ/ *vt* desafiar

degenerate /dɪ'dʒenəreɪt/ *vi* degenerar. ● /dɪ'dʒenərət/ *a & n* degenerado (*m*)

degrad|ation /degrə'deɪʃn/ *n* degradación *f*. **~e** /dɪ'greɪd/ *vt* degradar

degree /dɪ'gri:/ *n* grado *m*; (Univ) licenciatura *f*; (rank) rango *m*. **to a certain ~** hasta cierto punto

deign /deɪn/ *vi*. **~ to** dignarse

deity /'di:ɪtɪ/ *n* deidad *f*

deject|ed /dɪ'dʒektɪd/ *a* desanimado. **~ion** /-ʃn/ *n* abatimiento *m*

delay /dɪ'leɪ/ *vt* retrasar, demorar (LAm). ● *vi* tardar, demorar (LAm). ● *n* retraso *m*, demora *f* (LAm)

delegat|e /'delɪgeɪt/ *vt/i* delegar. ● /'delɪgət/ *n* delegado *m*. **~ion** /-'geɪʃn/ *n* delegación *f*

delet|e /dɪ'li:t/ *vt* tachar. **~ion** /-ʃn/ *n* supresión *f*

deliberat|e /dɪ'lɪbəreɪt/ *vt/i* deliberar. ● /dɪ'lɪbərət/ *a* intencionado; <*steps etc*> pausado. **~ely** *adv* a propósito. **~ion** /-'reɪʃn/ *n* deliberación *f*

delica|cy /'delɪkəsɪ/ *n* delicadeza *f*; (food) manjar *m*. **~te** /'delɪkət/ *a* delicado

delicatessen /delɪkə'tesn/ *n* charcutería *f*, salchichonería *f* (Mex)

delicious /dɪ'lɪʃəs/ *a* delicioso

delight /dɪ'laɪt/ *n* placer *m*. ● *vt* encantar. ● *vi* deleitarse. **~ed** *a* encantado. **~ful** *a* delicioso

deliri|ous /dɪ'lɪrɪəs/ *a* delirante. **~um** /-əm/ *n* delirio *m*

deliver /dɪ'lɪvə(r)/ *vt* entregar; (distribute) repartir; (aim) lanzar; (Med) **he ~ed the baby** la asistió en el parto. **~ance** *n* liberación *f*. **~y** *n* entrega *f*; (of post) reparto *m*; (Med) parto *m*

delta /'deltə/ *n* (Geog) delta *m*

delude /dɪ'lu:d/ *vt* engañar. **~ o.s.** engañarse

deluge /'delju:dʒ/ *n* diluvio *m*

delusion /dɪ'lu:ʒn/ *n* ilusión *f*

deluxe /dɪ'lʌks/ *a* de lujo

delve /delv/ *vi* hurgar. **~ into** (investigate) ahondar en

demand /dɪ'mɑ:nd/ *vt* exigir. ● *n* petición *f*, pedido *m* (LAm); (claim) exigencia *f*; (Com) demanda *f*. **in ~** muy popular, muy solicitado. **on ~** a solicitud. **~ing** *a* exigente. **~s** *npl* exigencias *fpl*

demented /dɪ'mentɪd/ *a* demente

demo /'deməʊ/ *n* (*pl* **-os**) 🅸 manifestación *f*

democra|cy /dɪ'mɒkrəsɪ/ *n* democracia *f*. **~t** /'deməkræt/ *n* demócrata *m & f*. **D~t** *a & n* (in US) demócrata (*m & f*). **~tic** /demə'krætɪk/ *a* democrático

demoli|sh /dɪ'mɒlɪʃ/ *vt* derribar. **~tion** /demə'lɪʃn/ *n* demolición *f*

demon /'di:mən/ *n* demonio *m*

demonstrat|e /'demənstreɪt/ *vt* demostrar. ● *vi* manifestarse, hacer una manifestación. **~ion** /-'streɪʃn/ *n* demostración *f*; (Pol) manifestación *f*. **~or** /'demənstreɪtə(r)/*n* (Pol) manifestante *m* & *f*; (marketing) demostrador *m*

demoralize /dɪ'mɒrəlaɪz/ *vt* desmoralizar

demote /dɪ'məʊt/ *vt* bajar de categoría

demure /dɪ'mjʊə(r)/ *a* recatado

den /den/ *n* (of animal) guarida *f*, madriguera *f*

denial /dɪ'naɪəl/ *n* denegación *f*; (statement) desmentimiento *m*

denim /'denɪm/ *n* tela *f* vaquera *or* de jeans, mezclilla (Mex) *f*. **~s** *npl* vaqueros *mpl*, jeans *mpl*, tejanos *mpl*, pantalones *mpl* de mezclilla (Mex)

Denmark /'denmɑ:k/ *n* Dinamarca *f*

denote /dɪ'nəʊt/ *vt* denotar

denounce /dɪ'naʊns/ *vt* denunciar

dens|e /dens/ *a* (**-er**, **-est**) espeso; <*person*> torpe. **~ely** *adv* densamente. **~ity** *n* densidad *f*

dent /dent/ *n* abolladura *f*. ● *vt* abollar

dental /'dentl/ *a* dental. **~ floss** /flɒs/ *n* hilo *m or* seda *f* dental. **~ surgeon** *n* dentista *m* & *f*

dentist /'dentɪst/ *n* dentista *m* & *f*. **~ry** *n* odontología *f*

dentures /'dentʃəz/ *npl* dentadura *f* postiza

deny /dɪ'naɪ/ *vt* negar; desmentir <*rumour*>; denegar <*request*>

deodorant /dɪ'əʊdərənt/ *a* & *n* desodorante (*m*)

depart /dɪ'pɑ:t/ *vi* partir, salir. **~ from** (deviate from) apartarse de

department /dɪ'pɑ:tment/ *n* departamento *m*; (Pol) ministerio *m*, secretaría *f* (Mex). **~ store** *n* grandes almacenes *mpl*, tienda *f* de departamentos (Mex)

departure /dɪ'pɑ:tʃə(r)/ *n* partida *f*; (of train etc) salida *f*

depend /dɪ'pend/ *vi* depender. **~ on** depender de. **~able** *a* digno de confianza. **~ant** /dɪ'pendənt/ *n* familiar *m* & *f* dependiente. **~ence** *n* dependencia *f*. **~ent** *a* dependiente. **be ~ent on** depender de

depict /dɪ'pɪkt/ *vt* representar; (in words) describir

deplete /dɪ'pli:t/ *vt* agotar

deplor|able /dɪ'plɔ:rəbl/ *a* deplorable. **~e** /dɪ'plɔ:(r)/ *vt* deplorar

deploy /dɪ'plɔɪ/ *vt* desplegar

deport /dɪ'pɔ:t/ *vt* deportar. **~ation** /-'teɪʃn/ *n* deportación *f*

depose /dɪ'pəʊz/ *vt* deponer

deposit /dɪ'pɒzɪt/ *vt* (*pt* **deposited**) depositar. ● *n* depósito *m*

depot /'depəʊ/ *n* depósito *m*; (Amer) estación *f* de autobuses

deprav|ed /dɪ'preɪvd/ *a* depravado. **~ity** /dɪ'prævətɪ/ *n* depravación *f*

depress /dɪ'pres/ *vt* deprimir; (press down) apretar. **~ed** *a* deprimido. **~ing** *a* deprimente. **~ion** /-ʃn/ *n* depresión *f*

depriv|ation /deprɪ'veɪʃn/ *n* privación *f*. **~e** /dɪ'praɪv/ *vt*. **~e of** privar de. **~d** *a* carenciado

depth /depθ/ *n* profundidad *f*. **be out of one's ~** perder pie; (fig) meterse en honduras. **in ~** a fondo

deput|ize /'depjʊtaɪz/ *vi.* **~ize for** sustituir a. **~y** /'depjʊtɪ/ *n* sustituto *m*. **~y chairman** *n* vicepresidente *m*

derail /dɪ'reɪl/ *vt* hacer descarrilar. **~ment** *n* descarrilamiento *m*

derelict /'derəlɪkt/ *a* abandonado y en ruinas

deri|de /dɪ'raɪd/ *vt* mofarse de. **~sion** /dɪ'rɪʒn/ *n* mofa *f*. **~sive** /dɪ'raɪsɪv/ *a* burlón. **~sory** /dɪ'raɪsərɪ/ *a* <*offer etc*> irrisorio

deriv|ation /derɪ'veɪʃn/ *n* derivación *f*. **~ative** /dɪ'rɪvətɪv/ *n* derivado *m*. **~e** /dɪ'raɪv/ *vt/i* derivar

derogatory /dɪ'rɒgətrɪ/ *a* despectivo

descen|d /dɪ'send/ *vt/i* descender, bajar. **~dant** *n* descendiente *m & f*. **~t** *n* descenso *m*, bajada *f*; (lineage) ascendencia *f*

descri|be /dɪs'kraɪb/ *vt* describir. **~ption** /-'krɪpʃn/ *n* descripción *f*. **~ptive** /-'krɪptɪv/ *a* descriptivo

desecrate /'desɪkreɪt/ *vt* profanar

desert[1] /dɪ'zɜ:t/ *vt* abandonar. ● *vi* (Mil) desertar. **~er** /dɪ'zɜ:tə(r)/ *n* desertor *m*

desert[2] /'dezət/ *a & n* desierto (*m*)

deserts /dɪ'zɜ:ts/ *npl* lo merecido. **get one's just ~** llevarse su merecido

deserv|e /dɪ'zɜ:v/ *vt* merecer. **~ing** *a* <*cause*> meritorio

design /dɪ'zaɪn/ *n* diseño *m*; (plan) plan *m*. **~s** (intentions) propósitos *mpl*. ● *vt* diseñar; (plan) planear

designate /'dezɪgneɪt/ *vt* designar

designer /dɪ'zaɪnə(r)/ *n* diseñador *m*; (fashion **~**) diseñador *m* de modas. ● *a* <*clothes*> de diseño exclusivo

desirable /dɪ'zaɪərəbl/ *a* deseable

desire /dɪ'zaɪə(r)/ *n* deseo *m*. ● *vt* desear

desk /desk/ *n* escritorio *m*; (at school) pupitre *m*; (in hotel) recepción *f*; (Com) caja *f*. **~top publishing** *n* autoedición *f*, edición *f* electrónica

desolat|e /'desələt/ *a* desolado; (uninhabited) deshabitado. **~ion** /-'leɪʃn/ *n* desolación *f*

despair /dɪ'speə(r)/ *n* desesperación *f*. **be in ~** estar desesperado. ● *vi*. **~ of** desesperarse de

despatch /dɪ'spætʃ/ *vt, n* ⇒DISPATCH

desperat|e /'despərət/ *a* desesperado. **~ely** *adv* desesperadamente. **~ion** /-'reɪʃn/ *n* desesperación *f*

despicable /dɪ'spɪkəbl/ *a* despreciable

despise /dɪ'spaɪz/ *vt* despreciar

despite /dɪ'spaɪt/ *prep* a pesar de

despondent /dɪ'spɒndənt/ *a* abatido

despot /'despɒt/ *n* déspota *m*

dessert /dɪ'zɜ:t/ *n* postre *m*. **~spoon** *n* cuchara *f* de postre

destination /destɪ'neɪʃn/ *n* destino *m*

destiny /'destɪnɪ/ *n* destino *m*

destitute /'destɪtju:t/ *a* indigente

destroy /dɪ'strɔɪ/ *vt* destruir. **~er** *n* destructor *m*

destructi|on /dɪ'strʌkʃn/ *n* destrucción *f*. **~ve** /-ɪv/ *a* destructivo

desultory /'desəltrɪ/ *a* desganado

detach /dɪ'tætʃ/ *vt* separar. **~able** *a* separable. **~ed** *a* (aloof) distante; (house) no adosado. **~ment** *n* desprendimiento *m*; (Mil) destacamento *m*; (aloofness) indiferencia *f*

detail /'di:teɪl/ *n* detalle *m*. **explain sth in ~** explicar algo detalladamente. ● *vt* detallar; (Mil) destacar. **~ed** *a* detallado

detain /dɪ'teɪn/ *vt* detener; (delay) retener. **~ee** /di:teɪ'ni:/ *n* detenido *m*

detect /dɪ'tekt/ *vt* percibir; (discover) descubrir. **~ive** *n* (private) detective *m*; (in police) agente *m* & *f*. **~or** *n* detector *m*

detention /dɪ'tenʃn/ *n* detención *f*

deter /dɪ'tɜ:(r)/ *vt* (*pt* **deterred**) disuadir; (prevent) impedir

detergent /dɪ'tɜ:dʒənt/ *a* & *n* detergente (*m*)

deteriorat|e /dɪ'tɪərɪəreɪt/ *vi* deteriorarse. **~ion** /-'reɪʃn/ *n* deterioro *m*

determin|ation /dɪtɜ:mɪ'neɪʃn/ *n* determinación *f*. **~e** /dɪ'tɜ:mɪn/ *vt* determinar; (decide) decidir. **~ed** *a* determinado; (resolute) decidido

deterrent /dɪ'terənt/ *n* fuerza *f* de disuasión

detest /dɪ'test/ *vt* aborrecer. **~able** *a* odioso

detonat|e /'detəneɪt/ *vt* hacer detonar. ● *vi* detonar. **~ion** /-'neɪʃn/ *n* detonación *f*. **~or** *n* detonador *m*

detour /'di:tʊə(r)/ *n* rodeo *m*; (Amer, of transport) desvío *m*, desviación *f*. ● *vt* (Amer) desviar

detract /dɪ'trækt/ *vi*. **~ from** disminuir

detriment /'detrɪmənt/ *n*. **to the ~ of** en perjuicio de. **~al** /-'mentl/ *a* perjudicial

devalue /di:'vælju:/ *vt* desvalorizar

devastat|e /'devəsteɪt/ *vt* devastar. **~ing** *a* devastador; (fig) arrollador. **~ion** /-'steɪʃn/ *n* devastación *f*

develop /dɪ'veləp/ *vt* desarrollar; contraer <*illness*>; urbanizar <*land*>. ● *vi* desarrollarse; (appear) surgir. **~ing** *a* <*country*> en vías de desarrollo. **~ment** *n* desarrollo *m*. (new) **~ment** novedad *f*

deviant /'di:vɪənt/ *a* desviado

deviat|e /'di:vɪeɪt/ *vi* desviarse. **~ion** /-'eɪʃn/ *n* desviación *f*

device /dɪ'vaɪs/ *n* dispositivo *m*; (scheme) estratagema *f*

devil /'devl/ *n* diablo *m*

devious /'di:vɪəs/ *a* taimado

devise /dɪ'vaɪz/ *vt* idear

devoid /dɪ'vɔɪd/ *a*. **be ~ of** carecer de

devolution /di:və'lu:ʃn/ *n* descentralización *f*; (of power) delegación *f*

devot|e /dɪ'vəʊt/ *vt* dedicar. **~ed** *a* <*couple*> unido; <*service*> leal. **~ee** /devə'ti:/ *n* partidario *m*. **~ion** /-ʃn/ *n* devoción *f*

devour /dɪ'vaʊə(r)/ *vt* devorar

devout /dɪ'vaʊt/ *a* devoto

dew /dju:/ *n* rocío *m*

dexterity /dek'sterətɪ/ *n* destreza *f*

diabet|es /daɪə'bi:ti:z/ *n* diabetes *f*. **~ic** /-'betɪk/ *a* & *n* diabético (*m*)

diabolical /daɪə'bɒlɪkl/ *a* diabólico

diagnos|e /'daɪəgnəʊz/ *vt* diagnosticar. **~is** /-'nəʊsɪs/ *n* (*pl* **-oses** /-si:z/) diagnóstico *m*

diagonal /daɪ'ægənl/ *a* & *n* diagonal (*f*)

diagram /'daɪəgræm/ *n* diagrama *m*

dial /'daɪəl/ *n* cuadrante *m*; (on clock, watch) esfera *f*; (on phone) disco *m*. ● *vt* (*pt* **dialled**) marcar, discar (LAm)

dialect /'daɪəlekt/ *n* dialecto *m*

dialling: ~ **code** *n* prefijo *m*, código *m* de la zona (LAm). ~ **tone** *n* tono *m* de marcar, tono *m* de discado (LAm)

dialogue /'daɪəlɒg/ *n* diálogo *m*

dial tone *n* (Amer) ⇨DIALLING TONE

diameter /daɪ'æmɪtə(r)/ *n* diámetro *m*

diamond /'daɪəmənd/ *n* diamante *m*; (shape) rombo *m*. ~**s** *npl* (Cards) diamantes *mpl*

diaper /'daɪəpə(r)/ *n* (Amer) pañal *m*

diaphragm /'daɪəfræm/ *n* diafragma *m*

diarrhoea /daɪə'rɪə/ *n* diarrea *f*

diary /'daɪərɪ/ *n* diario *m*; (book) agenda *f*

dice /daɪs/ *n invar* dado *m*. ● *vt* (Culin) cortar en cubitos

dictat|e /dɪk'teɪt/ *vt/i* dictar. ~**ion** /dɪk'teɪʃn/ *n* dictado *m*. ~**or** *n* dictador *m*. ~**orship** *n* dictadura *f*

dictionary /'dɪkʃənərɪ/ *n* diccionario *m*

did /dɪd/ ⇨DO

didn't /'dɪdnt/ = **did not**

die /daɪ/ *vi* (*pres p* **dying**) morir. **be dying to** morirse por. □ ~ **down** *vi* irse apagando. □ ~ **out** *vi* extinguirse

diesel /'di:zl/ *n* (fuel) gasóleo *m*. ~ **engine** *n* motor *m* diesel

diet /'daɪət/ *n* alimentación *f*; (restricted) régimen *m*. **be on a** ~ estar a régimen. ● *vi* estar a régimen

differ /'dɪfə(r)/ *vi* ser distinto; (disagree) no estar de acuerdo. ~**ence** /'dɪfrəns/ *n* diferencia *f*; (disagreement) desacuerdo *m*. ~**ent** /'dɪfrənt/ *a* distinto, diferente. ~**ently** *adv* de otra manera

difficult /'dɪfɪkəlt/ *a* difícil. ~**y** *n* dificultad *f*

diffus|e /dɪ'fju:s/ *a* difuso. ● /dɪ'fju:z/ *vt* difundir. ● *vi* difundirse. ~**ion** /-ʒn/ *n* difusión *f*

dig /dɪg/ *n* (poke) empujón *m*; (poke with elbow) codazo *m*; (remark) indirecta *f*. ~**s** *npl* 🅸 alojamiento *m* ● *vt* (*pt* **dug**, *pres p* **digging**) cavar; (thrust) empujar. ● *vi* cavar. □ ~ **out** *vt* extraer. □ ~ **up** *vt* desenterrar

digest /'daɪdʒest/ *n* resumen *m*. ● /daɪ'dʒest/ *vt* digerir. ~**ion** /-'dʒestʃn/ *n* digestión *f*. ~**ive** /-'dʒestɪv/ *a* digestivo

digger /'dɪgə(r)/ *n* (Mec) excavadora *f*

digit /'dɪdʒɪt/ *n* dígito *m*; (finger) dedo *m*. ~**al** /'dɪdʒɪtl/ *a* digital

dignified /'dɪgnɪfaɪd/ *a* solemne

dignitary /'dɪgnɪtərɪ/ *n* dignatario *m*

dignity /'dɪgnətɪ/ *n* dignidad *f*

digress /daɪ'gres/ *vi* divagar. ~ **from** apartarse de. ~**ion** /-ʃn/ *n* digresión *f*

dike /daɪk/ *n* dique *m*

dilapidated /dɪ'læpɪdeɪtɪd/ *a* ruinoso

dilate /daɪ'leɪt/ *vt* dilatar. ● *vi* dilatarse

dilemma /daɪ'lemə/ *n* dilema *m*

diligent /'dɪlɪdʒənt/ *a* diligente

dilute /daɪ'lju:t/ *vt* diluir

dim /dɪm/ *a* (**dimmer**, **dimmest**) <light> débil; <room> oscuro; (🅸, stupid) torpe. ● *vt* (*pt* **dimmed**) atenuar. ~ **one's headlights** (Amer) poner las (luces) cortas *or* de cruce, poner las (luces) bajas (LAm). ● *vi* <*light*> irse atenuando

dime /daɪm/ *n* (Amer) *moneda de diez centavos*

dimension /daɪ'menʃn/ *n* dimensión *f*

diminish /dɪ'mɪnɪʃ/ *vt/i* disminuir

dimple /'dɪmpl/ *n* hoyuelo *m*

din /dɪn/ *n* jaleo *m*

dine /daɪn/ *vi* cenar. **~r** *n* comensal *m* & *f*; (Amer, restaurant) cafetería *f*

dinghy /'dɪŋgɪ/ *n* bote *m*; (inflatable) bote *m* neumático

dingy /'dɪndʒɪ/ *a* (**-ier**, **-iest**) miserable, sucio

dining: /'daɪnɪŋ/**~ car** *n* coche *m* restaurante. **~ room** *n* comedor *m*

dinner /'dɪnə(r)/ *n* cena *f*, comida *f* (LAm). **have ~** cenar, comer (LAm). **~ party** *n* cena *f*, comida *f* (LAm)

dinosaur /'daɪnəsɔ:(r)/ *n* dinosaurio *m*

dint /dɪnt/ *n*. **by ~ of** a fuerza de

dip /dɪp/ *vt* (*pt* **dipped**) meter; (in liquid) mojar. **~ one's headlights** poner las (luces) cortas *or* de cruce, poner las (luces) bajas (LAm). ● *vi* bajar. ● *n* (slope) inclinación *f*; (in sea) baño *m*. □ **~ into** *vt* hojear <*book*>

diphthong /'dɪfθɒŋ/ *n* diptongo *m*

diploma /dɪ'pləʊmə/ *n* diploma *m*

diploma|cy /dɪ'pləʊməsɪ/ *n* diplomacia *f*. **~t** /'dɪpləmæt/ *n* diplomático *m*. **~tic** /-'mætɪk/ *a* diplomático

dipstick /'dɪpstɪk/ *n* (Auto) varilla *f* del nivel de aceite

dire /daɪə(r)/ *a* (**-er**, **-est**) terrible; <*need, poverty*> extremo

direct /dɪ'rekt/ *a* directo. ● *adv* directamente. ● *vt* dirigir; (show the way) indicar. **~ion** /-ʃn/ *n* dirección *f*. **~ions** *npl* instrucciones *fpl*. **~ly** *adv* directamente; (at once) en seguida. ● *conj* 🅸 en cuanto. **~or** *n* director *m*; (of company) directivo *m*

directory /dɪ'rektərɪ/ *n* guía *f*; (Comp) directorio *m*

dirt /dɜ:t/ *n* suciedad *f*. **~y** *a* (**-ier**, **-iest**) sucio. ● *vt* ensuciar

disab|ility /dɪsə'bɪlətɪ/ *n* invalidez *f*. **~le** /dɪs'eɪbl/ *vt* incapacitar. **~led** *a* minusválido

disadvantage /dɪsəd'vɑ:ntɪdʒ/ *n* desventaja *f*. **~d** *a* desfavorecido

disagree /dɪsə'gri:/ *vi* no estar de acuerdo (**with** con). **~ with** <*food, climate*> sentarle mal a. **~able** *a* desagradable. **~ment** *n* desacuerdo *m*; (quarrel) riña *f*

disappear /dɪsə'pɪə(r)/ *vi* desaparecer. **~ance** *n* desaparición *f*

disappoint /dɪsə'pɔɪnt/ *vt* decepcionar. **~ing** *a* decepcionante. **~ment** *n* decepción *f*

disapprov|al /dɪsə'pru:vl/ *n* desaprobación *f*. **~e** /dɪsə'pru:v/ *vi*. **~e of** desaprobar. **~ing** *a* de reproche

disarm /dɪs'ɑ:m/ *vt* desarmar. ● *vi* desarmarse. **~ament** *n* desarme *m*

disarray /dɪsə'reɪ/ *n* desorden *m*

disast|er /dɪ'zɑ:stə(r)/ *n* desastre *m*. **~rous** /-strəs/ *a* catastrófico

disband /dɪs'bænd/ *vt* disolver. ● *vi* disolverse

disbelief /dɪsbɪ'li:f/ *n* incredulidad *f*

disc /dɪsk/ *n* disco *m*

discard /dɪs'kɑ:d/ *vt* descartar; abandonar <*beliefs etc*>

discern /dɪ'sɜːn/ *vt* percibir. **~ing** *a* exigente; *<ear, eye>* educado

discharge /dɪs'tʃɑːdʒ/ *vt* descargar; cumplir *<duty>*; (Mil) licenciar. ● /'dɪstʃɑːdʒ/ *n* descarga *f*; (Med) secreción *f*; (Mil) licenciamiento *m*

disciple /dɪ'saɪpl/ *n* discípulo *m*

disciplin|ary /dɪsə'plɪnərɪ/ *a* disciplinario. **~e** /'dɪsɪplɪn/ *n* disciplina *f*. ● *vt* disciplinar; (punish) sancionar

disc jockey /'dɪskdʒɒkɪ/ *n* pinchadiscos *m & f*

disclaim /dɪs'kleɪm/ *vt* desconocer. **~er** *n* (Jurid) descargo *m* de responsabilidad

disclos|e /dɪs'kləʊz/ *vt* revelar. **~ure** /-ʒə(r)/ *n* revelación *f*

disco /'dɪskəʊ/ *n* (*pl* **-os**) 🅸 discoteca *f*

discolour /dɪs'kʌlə(r)/ *vt* decolorar. ● *vi* decolorarse

discomfort /dɪs'kʌmfət/ *n* malestar *m*; (lack of comfort) incomodidad *f*

disconcert /dɪskən'sɜːt/ *vt* desconcertar

disconnect /dɪskə'nekt/ *vt* separar; (Elec) desconectar

disconsolate /dɪs'kɒnsələt/ *a* desconsolado

discontent /dɪskən'tent/ *n* descontento *m*. **~ed** *a* descontento

discontinue /dɪskən'tɪnjuː/ *vt* interrumpir

discord /'dɪskɔːd/ *n* discordia *f*; (Mus) disonancia *f*. **~ant** /-'skɔːdənt/ *a* discorde; (Mus) disonante

discotheque /'dɪskətek/ *n* discoteca *f*

discount /'dɪskaʊnt/ *n* descuento *m*. ● /dɪs'kaʊnt/ *vt* hacer caso omiso de; (Com) descontar

discourag|e /dɪs'kʌrɪdʒ/ *vt* desanimar; (dissuade) disuadir. **~ing** *a* desalentador

discourteous /dɪs'kɜːtɪəs/ *a* descortés

discover /dɪs'kʌvə(r)/ *vt* descubrir. **~y** *n* descubrimiento *m*

discredit /dɪs'kredɪt/ *vt* (*pt* **discredited**) desacreditar. ● *n* descrédito *m*

discreet /dɪs'kriːt/ *a* discreto. **~ly** *adv* discretamente

discrepancy /dɪ'skrepənsɪ/ *n* discrepancia *f*

discretion /dɪ'skreʃn/ *n* discreción *f*

discriminat|e /dɪs'krɪmɪneɪt/ *vt* discriminar. **~e between** distinguir entre. **~ing** *a* perspicaz. **~ion** /-'neɪʃn/ *n* discernimiento *m*; (bias) discriminación *f*

discus /'dɪskəs/ *n* disco *m*

discuss /dɪ'skʌs/ *vt* discutir. **~ion** /-ʃn/ *n* discusión *f*

disdain /dɪs'deɪn/ *n* desdén *m*. **~ful** *a* desdeñoso

disease /dɪ'ziːz/ *n* enfermedad *f*

disembark /dɪsɪm'bɑːk/ *vi* desembarcar

disenchant|ed /dɪsɪn'tʃɑːntɪd/ *a* desilusionado. **~ment** *n* desencanto *m*

disentangle /dɪsɪn'tæŋgl/ *vt* desenredar

disfigure /dɪs'fɪgə(r)/ *vt* desfigurar

disgrace /dɪs'greɪs/ *n* vergüenza *f*. ● *vt* deshonrar. **~ful** *a* vergonzoso

disgruntled /dɪs'grʌntld/ *a* descontento

disguise /dɪs'gaɪz/ *vt* disfrazar. ● *n* disfraz *m*. **in ~** disfrazado

disgust /dɪs'gʌst/ *n* repugnancia *f*, asco *m*. ● *vt* dar asco a. **~ed** *a* indignado; (stronger) asqueado. **~ing** *a* repugnante, asqueroso

dish /dɪʃ/ *n* plato *m*. **wash** *or* **do the ~es** fregar los platos, lavar los trastes (Mex). □ **~ up** *vt/i* servir. **~cloth** *n* bayeta *f*

disheartening /dɪs'hɑ:tnɪŋ/ *a* desalentador

dishonest /dɪs'ɒnɪst/ *a* deshonesto. **~y** *n* falta *f* de honradez

dishonour /dɪs'ɒnə(r)/ *n* deshonra *f*

dish: ~ soap *n* (Amer) lavavajillas *m*. **~ towel** *n* paño *m* de cocina. **~washer** *n* lavaplatos *m*, lavavajillas *m*. **~washing liquid** *n* (Amer) ⇒**~** SOAP

disillusion /dɪsɪ'lu:ʒn/ *vt* desilusionar. **~ment** *n* desilusión *f*

disinfect /dɪsɪn'fekt/ *vt* desinfectar. **~ant** *n* desinfectante *m*

disintegrate /dɪs'ɪntɪgreɪt/ *vt* desintegrar. ● *vi* desintegrarse

disinterested /dɪs'ɪntrəstɪd/ *a* desinteresado

disjointed /dɪs'dʒɔɪntɪd/ *a* inconexo

disk /dɪsk/ *n* disco *m*. **~ drive** (Comp) unidad *f* de discos. **~ette** /dɪs'ket/ *n* disquete *m*

dislike /dɪs'laɪk/ *n* aversión *f*. ● *vt*. **I ~ dogs** no me gustan los perros

dislocate /'dɪsləkeɪt/ *vt* dislocar(se) *<limb>*

dislodge /dɪs'lɒdʒ/ *vt* sacar

disloyal /dɪs'lɔɪəl/ *a* desleal. **~ty** *n* deslealtad *f*

dismal /'dɪzməl/ *a* triste; (bad) fatal

dismantle /dɪs'mæntl/ *vt* desmontar

dismay /dɪs'meɪ/ *n* consternación *f*. ● *vt* consternar

dismiss /dɪs'mɪs/ *vt* despedir; (reject) rechazar. **~al** *n* despido *m*; (of idea) rechazo *m*

dismount /dɪs'maʊnt/ *vi* desmontar

disobe|dience /dɪsə'bi:dɪəns/ *n* desobediencia *f*. **~dient** *a* desobediente. **~y** /dɪsə'beɪ/ *vt/i* desobedecer

disorder /dɪs'ɔ:də(r)/ *n* desorden *m*; (ailment) afección *f*. **~ly** *a* desordenado

disorganized /dɪs'ɔ:gənaɪzd/ *a* desorganizado

disorientate /dɪs'ɔ:rɪənteɪt/ *vt* desorientar

disown /dɪs'əʊn/ *vt* repudiar

disparaging /dɪs'pærɪdʒɪŋ/ *a* despreciativo

dispatch /dɪs'pætʃ/ *vt* despachar. ● *n* despacho *m*. **~ rider** *n* mensajero *m*

dispel /dɪs'pel/ *vt* (*pt* **dispelled**) disipar

dispens|able /dɪs'pensəbl/ *a* prescindible. **~e** *vt* distribuir; (Med) preparar. □ **~ with** *vt* prescindir de

dispers|al /dɪ'spɜ:sl/ *n* dispersión *f*. **~e** /dɪ'spɜ:s/ *vt* dispersar. ● *vi* dispersarse

dispirited /dɪs'pɪrɪtɪd/ *a* desanimado

display /dɪs'pleɪ/ *vt* exponer *<goods>*; demostrar *<feelings>*. ● *n* exposición *f*; (of feelings) demostración *f*

displeas|e /dɪs'pli:z/ *vt* desagradar. **be ~ed with** estar disgustado con. ~**ure** /-'pleʒə(r)/ *n* desagrado *m*

dispos|able /dɪs'pəʊzəbl/ *a* desechable. ~**al** /dɪs'pəʊzl/ *n* (of waste) eliminación *f*. **at s.o.'s** ~**al** a la disposición de uno. ~**e of** /dɪs'pəʊz/ *vt* deshacerse de

disproportionate /dɪsprə'pɔ:ʃənət/ *a* desproporcionado

disprove /dɪs'pru:v/ *vt* desmentir <*claim*>; refutar <*theory*>

dispute /dɪs'pju:t/ *vt* discutir. ● *n* disputa *f*. **in** ~ disputado

disqualif|ication /dɪskwɒlɪfɪ'keɪʃn/ *n* descalificación *f*. ~**y** /dɪs'kwɒlɪfaɪ/ *vt* incapacitar; (Sport) descalificar

disregard /dɪsrɪ'gɑ:d/ *vt* no hacer caso de. ● *n* indiferencia *f* (**for** a)

disreputable /dɪs'repjʊtəbl/ *a* de mala fama

disrespect /dɪsrɪ'spekt/ *n* falta *f* de respeto

disrupt /dɪs'rʌpt/ *vt* interrumpir; trastornar <*plans*>. ~**ion** /-ʃn/ *n* trastorno *m*. ~**ive** *a* <*influence*> perjudicial, negativo

dissatis|faction /dɪsætɪs'fækʃn/ *n* descontento *m*. ~**fied** /dɪ'sætɪsfaɪd/ *a* descontento

dissect /dɪ'sekt/ *vt* disecar

dissent /dɪ'sent/ *vi* disentir. ● *n* disentimiento *m*

dissertation /dɪsə'teɪʃn/ *n* (Univ) tesis *f*

dissident /'dɪsɪdənt/ *a & n* disidente (*m & f*)

dissimilar /dɪ'sɪmɪlə(r)/ *a* distinto

dissolute /'dɪsəlu:t/ *a* disoluto

dissolve /dɪ'zɒlv/ *vt* disolver. ● *vi* disolverse

dissuade /dɪ'sweɪd/ *vt* disuadir

distan|ce /'dɪstəns/ *n* distancia *f*. **from a** ~**ce** desde lejos. **in the** ~**ce** a lo lejos. ~**t** *a* distante, lejano; (aloof) distante

distaste /dɪs'teɪst/ *n* desagrado *m*. ~**ful** *a* desagradable

distil /dɪs'tɪl/ *vt* (*pt* **distilled**) destilar. ~**lery** /dɪs'tɪlərɪ/ *n* destilería *f*

distinct /dɪs'tɪŋkt/ *a* distinto; (clear) claro; (marked) marcado. ~**ion** /-ʃn/ *n* distinción *f*; (in exam) sobresaliente *m*. ~**ive** *a* distintivo

distinguish /dɪs'tɪŋgwɪʃ/ *vt/i* distinguir. ~**ed** *a* distinguido

distort /dɪs'tɔ:t/ *vt* torcer. ~**ion** /-ʃn/ *n* deformación *f*

distract /dɪs'trækt/ *vt* distraer. ~**ed** *a* distraído. ~**ion** /-ʃn/ *n* distracción *f*; (confusion) aturdimiento *m*

distraught /dɪs'trɔ:t/ *a* consternado, angustiado

distress /dɪs'tres/ *n* angustia *f*. ● *vt* afligir. ~**ed** *a* afligido. ~**ing** *a* penoso

distribut|e /dɪ'strɪbju:t/ *vt* repartir, distribuir. ~**ion** /-'bju:ʃn/ *n* distribución *f*. ~**or** *n* distribuidor *m*; (Auto) distribuidor *m* (del encendido)

district /'dɪstrɪkt/ *n* zona *f*, región *f*; (of town) barrio *m*

distrust /dɪs'trʌst/ *n* desconfianza *f*. ● *vt* desconfiar de

disturb /dɪs'tɜ:b/ *vt* molestar; (perturb) inquietar; (move) desordenar; (interrupt) interrumpir. ~**ance** *n* disturbio *m*; (tumult) alboroto *m*. ~**ed** *a* trastornado. ~**ing** *a* inquietante

disused /dɪs'ju:zd/ *a* fuera de uso

ditch /dɪtʃ/ *n* zanja *f*; (for irrigation) acequia *f*. ● *vt* [I] abandonar

dither /ˈdɪðə(r)/ *vi* vacilar

ditto /ˈdɪtəʊ/ *adv* ídem

divan /dɪˈvæn/ *n* diván *m*

dive /daɪv/ *vi* tirarse (al agua), zambullirse; (rush) meterse (precipitadamente). ● *n* (into water) zambullida *f*; (Sport) salto *m* (de trampolín); (of plane) descenso *m* en picado, descenso *m* en picada (LAm); (🅘, place) antro *m*. **~r** *n* saltador *m*; (underwater) buzo *m*

diverge /daɪˈvɜːdʒ/ *vi* divergir. **~nt** *a* divergente

divers|e /daɪˈvɜːs/ *a* diverso. **~ify** *vt* diversificar. **~ity** *n* diversidad *f*

diver|sion /daɪˈvɜːʃn/ *n* desvío *m*; desviación *f*; (distraction) diversión *f*. **~t** /daɪˈvɜːt/ *vt* desviar; (entertain) divertir

divide /dɪˈvaɪd/ *vt* dividir. ● *vi* dividirse. **~d highway** *n* (Amer) autovía *f*, carretera *f* de doble pista

dividend /ˈdɪvɪdend/ *n* dividendo *m*

divine /dɪˈvaɪn/ *a* divino

diving /ˈdaɪvɪŋ/: **~ board** *n* trampolín *m*. **~ suit** *n* escafandra *f*

division /dɪˈvɪʒn/ *n* división *f*

divorce /dɪˈvɔːs/ *n* divorcio *m*. ● *vt* divorciarse de. **get ~d** divorciarse. ● *vi* divorciarse. **~e** /dɪvɔːˈsiː/ *n* divorciado *m*

divulge /daɪˈvʌldʒ/ *vt* divulgar

DIY *abbr* ⇒DO-IT-YOURSELF

dizz|iness /ˈdɪzɪnɪs/ *n* vértigo *m*. **~y** *a* (**-ier**, **-iest**) mareado. **be** *or* **feel ~y** marearse

DJ *abbr* ⇒DISC JOCKEY

do /duː/, *unstressed forms* /dʊ, də/

3rd pers sing present **does**; past **did**; past participle **done**

● *transitive verb*

····➤ hacer. **he does what he wants** hace lo que quiere. **to do one's homework** hacer los deberes. **to do the cooking** preparar la comida, cocinar. **well done!** ¡muy bien!

····➤ (clean) lavar <*dishes*>. limpiar <*windows*>

····➤ (as job) **what does he do?** ¿en qué trabaja?

····➤ (swindle) estafar. **I've been done!** ¡me han estafado!

····➤ (achieve) **she's done it!** ¡lo ha logrado!

● *intransitive verb*

····➤ hacer. **do as you're told!** ¡haz lo que se te dice!

····➤ (fare) **how are you doing?** (with a task) ¿qué tal te va? **how do you do?** (as greeting) mucho gusto, encantado

····➤ (perform) **she did well/badly** le fue bien/mal

····➤ (be suitable) **will this do?** ¿esto sirve?

····➤ (be enough) ser suficiente, bastar. **one box will do** con una caja basta, con una caja es suficiente

● *auxiliary verb*

····➤ (to form interrogative and negative) **do you speak Spanish?** ¿hablas español?. **I don't want to** no quiero. **don't shut the door** no cierres la puerta

····➤ (in tag questions) **you eat meat, don't you?** ¿comes carne, ¿verdad? *or* ¿no? **he lives in London, doesn't he?** vive en Londres, ¿no? *or* ¿verdad? *or* ¿no es cierto?

····➤ (in short answers) **do you like it? - yes, I do** ¿te gusta? - sí. **who wrote it? - I did** ¿quién lo escribió? - yo

····➤ (emphasizing) **do come in!** ¡pase Ud!. **you do exaggerate!** ¡cómo exageras!

□ **do away with** *vt* abolir. □ **do in** *vt* (☒, kill) eliminar. □ **do up** *vt* abrochar <*coat etc*>; arreglar <*house*>. □ **do with** *vt* (need) (with can, could) necesitar; (expressing connection) **it has nothing to do with that** no tiene nada que ver con eso. □ **do without** *vt* prescindir de

docile /'dəʊsaɪl/ *a* dócil

dock /dɒk/ *n* (Naut) dársena *f*; (wharf, quay) muelle *m*; (Jurid) banquillo *m* de los acusados. **~s** *npl* (port) puerto *m*. ● *vt* cortar <*tail*>; atracar <*ship*>. ● *vi* <*ship*> atracar. **~er** *n* estibador *m*. **~yard** *n* astillero *m*

doctor /'dɒktə(r)/ *n* médico *m*, doctor *m*

doctrine /'dɒktrɪn/ *n* doctrina *f*

document /'dɒkjʊmənt/ *n* documento *m*. **~ary** /-'mentrɪ/ *a* & *n* documental (*m*)

dodg|e /dɒdʒ/ *vt* esquivar. ● *vi* esquivarse. ● *n* treta *f*. **~ems** /'dɒdʒəmz/ *npl* autos *mpl* de choque. **~y** *a* (**-ier**, **-iest**) [I] (awkward) difícil

does /dʌz/ ⇒DO

doesn't /'dʌznt/ = **does not**

dog /dɒg/ *n* perro *m*. ● *vt* (*pt* **dogged**) perseguir

dogged /'dɒgɪd/ *a* obstinado

doghouse /'dɒghaʊs/ *n* (Amer) casa *f* del perro. **in the ~** [I] en desgracia

dogma /'dɒgmə/ *n* dogma *m*. **~tic** /-'mætɪk/ *a* dogmático

do|ings *npl* actividades *fpl*. **~-it-yourself** /du:ɪtjɔ:'self/ *n* bricolaje *m*

dole /dəʊl/ *n* [I] subsidio *m* de paro, subsidio *m* de desempleo. **on the ~** parado, desempleado. □ **~ out** *vt* distribuir

doleful /'dəʊlfl/ *a* triste

doll /dɒl/ *n* muñeca *f*

dollar /'dɒlə(r)/ *n* dólar *m*

dollop /'dɒləp/ *n* [I] porción *f*

dolphin /'dɒlfɪn/ *n* delfín *m*

domain /dəʊ'meɪn/ *n* dominio *m*; (fig) campo *m*

dome /dəʊm/ *n* cúpula *f*

domestic /də'mestɪk/ *a* doméstico; <*trade, flights, etc*> nacional. **~ated** /də'mestɪkeɪtɪd/ *a* <*animal*> domesticado. **~ science** *n* economía *f* doméstica

domin|ance /'dɒmɪnəns/ *n* dominio *m*. **~ant** *a* dominante. **~ate** /-eɪt/ *vt/i* dominar. **~ation** /-'neɪʃn/ *n* dominación *f*. **~eering** *a* dominante

Dominican Republic /də'mɪnɪkən/ *n* República *f* Dominicana

dominion /də'mɪnjən/ *n* dominio *m*

domino /'dɒmɪnəʊ/ *n* (*pl* **-oes**) ficha *f* de dominó. **~es** *npl* (game) dominó *m*

donat|e /dəʊ'neɪt/ *vt* donar. **~ion** /-ʃn/ *n* donativo *m*, donación *f*

done /dʌn/ ⇒DO

donkey /'dɒŋkɪ/ *n* burro *m*, asno *m*. **~'s years** [I] siglos *mpl*

donor /'dəʊnə(r)/ *n* donante *m* & *f*

don't /dəʊnt/ = **do not**

doodle /'du:dl/ *vi/t* garrapatear

doom /du:m/ *n* destino *m*; (death) muerte *f*. ● *vt*. **be ~ed to** ser condenado a

door /dɔ:(r)/ *n* puerta *f*. **~bell** *n* timbre *m*. **~ knob** *n* pomo *m* (de la puerta). **~mat** *n* felpudo *m*. **~step** *n* peldaño *m*. **~way** *n* entrada *f*

dope /dəʊp/ *n* 🅸 droga *f*; (🆇, idiot) imbécil *m*. ● *vt* 🅸 drogar

dormant /'dɔ:mənt/ *a* aletargado, <*volcano*> inactivo

dormice /'dɔ:maɪs/ ⇒DORMOUSE

dormitory /'dɔ:mɪtrɪ/ *n* dormitorio *m*

dormouse /'dɔ:maʊs/ *n* (*pl* **-mice**) lirón *m*

DOS /dɒs/ *abbr* (= **disc-operating system**) DOS *m*

dos|age /'dəʊsɪdʒ/ *n* dosis *f*. **~e** /dəʊs/ *n* dosis *f*

dot /dɒt/ *n* punto *m*. **on the ~** en punto

dote /dəʊt/ *vi*. **~ on** adorar

dotty /'dɒtɪ/ *a* (**-ier**, **-iest**) 🅸 chiflado

double /'dʌbl/ *a* doble. ● *adv* el doble. ● *n* doble *m*; (person) doble *m* & *f*. **at the ~** corriendo. ● *vt* doblar; redoblar <*efforts etc*>. ● *vi* doblarse. **~ bass** /beɪs/ *n* contrabajo *m*. **~ bed** *n* cama *f* de matrimonio, cama *f* de doa plazas (LAm). **~ chin** *n* papada *f*. **~-cross** /-'krɒs/ *vt* traicionar. **~-decker** /-'dekə(r)/ *n* autobús *m* de dos pisos. **~ Dutch** *n* 🅸 chino *m*. **~ glazing** /-gleɪzɪŋ/ *n* doble ventana *f*. **~s** *npl* (tennis) dobles *mpl*

doubly /'dʌblɪ/ *adv* doblemente

doubt /daʊt/ *n* duda *f*. ● *vt* dudar; (distrust) dudar de. **~ful** *a* dudoso. **~less** *adv* sin duda

dough /dəʊ/ *n* masa *f*; (🆇, money) pasta *f* 🅸, lana *f* (LAm 🅸). **~nut** *n* donut *m*, dona *f* (Mex)

dove /dʌv/ *n* paloma *f*

down /daʊn/ *adv* abajo. **~ with** abajo. **come ~** bajar. **go ~** bajar; <*sun*> ponerse. ● *prep* abajo. ● *a* 🅸 deprimido. ● *vt* derribar; (🅸, drink) beber. ● *n* (feathers) plumón *m*. **~ and out** *a* en la miseria. **~cast** *a* abatido. **~fall** *n* perdición *f*; (of king, dictator) caída *f*. **~-hearted** /-'hɑ:tɪd/ *a* abatido. **~hill** /-'hɪl/ *adv* cuesta abajo. **~load** /-'ləʊd/ *vt* (Comp) trasvasar. **~market** /-'mɑ:kɪt/ *a* <*newspaper*> popular; <*store*> barato. **~ payment** *n* depósito *m*. **~pour** *n* aguacero *m*. **~right** *a* completo. ● *adv* completamente. **~s** *npl* colinas *fpl*. **~stairs** /-'steəz/ *adv* abajo. ● /-steəz/ *a* de abajo. **~stream** *adv* río abajo. **~-to-earth** /-tʊ'ɜ:θ/ *a* práctico. **~town** /-'taʊn/ *n* centro *m* (*de la ciudad*). ● *adv*. **go ~town** ir al centro. **~ under** *adv* en las antípodas; (in Australia) en Australia. **~ward** /-wəd/ *a* & *adv*, **~wards** *adv* hacia abajo

dowry /'daʊərɪ/ *n* dote *f*

doze /dəʊz/ *vi* dormitar. □ **~ off** *vi* dormirse

dozen /'dʌzn/ *n* docena *f*. **a ~ eggs** una docena de huevos. **~s of** 🅸 miles de, muchos

Dr /'dɒktə(r)/ *abbr* (= **Doctor**) Dr **~. Broadley** (el) Doctor Broadley

drab /dræb/ *a* monótono

draft /drɑ:ft/ *n* borrador *m*; (Com) letra *f* de cambio; (Amer, Mil) reclutamiento *m*; (Amer, of air) corriente *f* de aire. ● *vt* redactar el borrador de; (Amer, conscript) reclutar

drag /dræg/ *vt* (*pt* **dragged**) arrastrar. ● *n* 🅸 lata *f*

dragon /'drægən/ *n* dragón *m*. **~fly** *n* libélula *f*

drain /dreɪn/ *vt* vaciar <*tank, glass*>; drenar <*land*>; (fig) agotar.

● *vi* escurrirse. ● *n* (pipe) sumidero *m*, resumidero *m* (LAm); (plughole) desagüe *m*. **~board** (Amer), **~ing board** *n* escurridero *m*

drama /ˈdrɑːmə/ *n* drama *m*; (art) arte *m* teatral. **~tic** /drəˈmætɪk/ *a* dramático. **~tist** /ˈdræmətɪst/ *n* dramaturgo *m*. **~tize** /ˈdræmətaɪz/ *vt* adaptar al teatro; (fig) dramatizar

drank /dræŋk/ ⇒DRINK

drape /dreɪp/ *vt* cubrir; (hang) colgar. **~s** *npl* (Amer) cortinas *fpl*

drastic /ˈdræstɪk/ *a* drástico

draught /drɑːft/ *n* corriente *f* de aire. **~ beer** *n* cerveza *f* de barril. **~s** *npl* (game) juego *m* de damas *fpl*. **~y** *a* lleno de corrientes de aire

draw /drɔː/ *vt* (*pt* **drew**, *pp* **drawn**) tirar; (attract) atraer; dibujar <*picture*>; trazar <*line*>. **~ the line** trazar el límite. ● *vi* (Art) dibujar; (Sport) empatar; **~ near** acercarse. ● *n* (Sport) empate *m*; (in lottery) sorteo *m*. □ **~ in** *vi* <*days*> acortarse. □ **~ out** *vt* sacar <*money*>. □ **~ up** *vi* pararse. *vt* redactar <*document*>; acercar <*chair*>. **~back** *n* desventaja *f*. **~bridge** *n* puente *m* levadizo

drawer /drɔː(r)/ *n* cajón *m*, gaveta *f* (Mex). **~s** *npl* calzones *mpl*

drawing /ˈdrɔːɪŋ/ *n* dibujo *m*. **~ pin** *n* tachuela *f*, chincheta *f*, chinche *f*. **~ room** *n* salón *m*

drawl /drɔːl/ *n* habla *f* lenta

drawn /drɔːn/ ⇒DRAW

dread /dred/ *n* terror *m*. ● *vt* temer. **~ful** *a* terrible. **~fully** *adv* terriblemente

dream /driːm/ *n* sueño *m*. ● *vt/i* (*pt* **dreamed** *or* **dreamt** /dremt/) soñar. □ **~ up** *vt* idear. *a* ideal. **~er** *n* soñador *m*

dreary /ˈdrɪərɪ/ *a* (**-ier**, **-iest**) triste; (boring) monótono

dredge /dredʒ/ *n* draga *f*. ● *vt* dragar. **~r** *n* draga *f*

dregs /dregz/ *npl* posos *mpl*, heces *fpl*; (fig) hez *f*

drench /drentʃ/ *vt* empapar

dress /dres/ *n* vestido *m*; (clothing) ropa *f*. ● *vt* vestir; (decorate) adornar; (Med) vendar. ● *vi* vestirse. □ **~ up** *vi* ponerse elegante. **~ up as** disfrazarse de. **~ circle** *n* primer palco *m*

dressing /ˈdresɪŋ/ *n* (sauce) aliño *m*; (bandage) vendaje *m*. **~-down** /-ˈdaʊn/ *n* rapapolvo *m*, reprensión *f*. **~ gown** *n* bata *f*. **~ room** *n* vestidor *m*; (in theatre) camarín *m*. **~ table** *n* tocador *m*

dress: ~maker *n* modista *m* & *f*. **~making** *n* costura *f*. **~ rehearsal** *n* ensayo *m* general

drew /druː/ ⇒DRAW

dribble /ˈdrɪbl/ *vi* <*baby*> babear; (in football) driblar, driblear

drie|d /draɪd/ *a* <*food*> seco; <*milk*> en polvo. **~r** /ˈdraɪə(r)/ *n* secador *m*

drift /drɪft/ *vi* ir a la deriva; <*snow*> amontonarse. ● *n* (movement) dirección *f*; (of snow) montón *m*

drill /drɪl/ *n* (tool) taladro *m*; (of dentist) torno *m*; (training) ejercicio *m*. ● *vt* taladrar, perforar; (train) entrenar. ● *vi* entrenarse

drink /drɪŋk/ *vt/i* (*pt* **drank**, *pp* **drunk**) beber, tomar (LAm). ● *n* bebida *f*. **~able** *a* bebible; <*water*> potable. **~er** *n* bebedor *m*. **~ing water** *n* agua *f* potable

drip /drɪp/ *vi* (*pt* **dripped**) gotear. ● *n* gota *f*; (Med) goteo *m* intraveno so; (⊠, person) soso *m*. **~-dry** /-'draɪ/ *a* de lava y pon. **~ping** *a*. **be ~ping wet** estar chorreando

drive /draɪv/ *vt* (*pt* **drove**, *pp* **driven**) conducir, manejar (LAm) *<car etc>*. **~ s.o. mad** volver loco a uno. **~ s.o. to do sth** llevar a uno a hacer algo. ● *vi* conducir, manejar (LAm). **~ at** querer decir. **~ in** (in car) entrar en coche. ● *n* paseo *m*; (road) calle *f*; (private road) camino *m* de entrada; (fig) empuje *m*. **~r** *n* conductor *m*, chofer *m* (LAm). **~r's license** *n* (Amer) ⇒DRIVING LICENCE

drivel /'drɪvl/ *n* tonterías *fpl*

driving /'draɪvɪŋ/ *n* conducción *f*. **~ licence** *n* permiso *m* de conducir, licencia *f* de conducción (LAm), licencia *f* (de manejar) (Mex). **~ test** *n* examen *m* de conducir, examen *m* de manejar (LAm)

drizzle /'drɪzl/ *n* llovizna *f*. ● *vi* lloviznar

drone /drəʊn/ *n* zumbido *m*. ● *vi* zumbar

drool /dru:l/ *vi* babear

droop /dru:p/ *vi* inclinarse; *<flowers>* marchitarse

drop /drɒp/ *n* gota *f*; (fall) caída *f*; (decrease) descenso *m*. ● *vt* (*pt* **dropped**) dejar caer; (lower) bajar. ● *vi* caer. □ **~ in on** *vt* pasar por casa de. □ **~ off** *vi* (sleep) dormirse. □ **~ out** *vi* retirarse; *<student>* abandonar los estudios. **~out** *n* marginado *m*

drought /draʊt/ *n* sequía *f*

drove /drəʊv/ ⇒DRIVE. ● *n* manada *f*

drown /draʊn/ *vt* ahogar. ● *vi* ahogarse

drowsy /'draʊzɪ/ *a* soñoliento

drudgery /'drʌdʒərɪ/ *n* trabajo *m* pesado

drug /drʌg/ *n* droga *f*; (Med) medicamento *m*. ● *vt* (*pt* **drugged**) drogar. **~ addict** *n* drogadicto *m*. **~gist** *n* (Amer) farmacéutico *m*. **~store** *n* (Amer) farmacia *f* (*que vende otros artículos también*)

drum /drʌm/ *n* tambor *m*; (for oil) bidón *m*. ● *vi* (*pt* **drummed**) tocar el tambor. ● *vt*. **~ sth into s.o.** hacerle aprender algo a uno a fuerza de repetírselo. **~mer** *n* tambor *m*; (in group) batería *f*. **~s** *npl* batería *f*. **~stick** *n* baqueta *f*; (Culin) muslo *m*

drunk /drʌŋk/ ⇒DRINK. ● *a* borracho. **get ~** emborracharse. ● *n* borracho *m*. **~ard** /-əd/ *n* borracho *m*. **~en** *a* borracho

dry /draɪ/ *a* (**drier**, **driest**) seco. ● *vt* secar. ● *vi* secarse. □ **~ up** *vi* *<stream>* secarse; *<funds>* agotarse. **~-clean** *vt* limpiar en seco. **~-cleaner's** tintorería *f*. **~er** *n* ⇒DRIER

dual /'dju:əl/ *a* doble. **~ carriageway** *n* autovía *f*, carretera *f* de doble pista

dub /dʌb/ *vt* (*pt* **dubbed**) doblar *<film>*

dubious /'dju:bɪəs/ *a* dudoso; *<person>* sospechoso

duchess /'dʌtʃɪs/ *n* duquesa *f*

duck /dʌk/ *n* pato *m*. ● *vt* sumergir; bajar *<head>*. ● *vi* agacharse. **~ling** /'dʌklɪŋ/ *n* patito *m*

duct /dʌkt/ *n* conducto *m*

dud /dʌd/ *a* inútil; *<cheque>* sin fondos

due /dju:/ *a* debido; (expected) esperado. **~ to** debido a. ● *adv*. **~ north** derecho hacia el norte. **~s** *npl* derechos *mpl*

duel /'dju:əl/ *n* duelo *m*

duet /dju:'et/ *n* dúo *m*

duffel, **duffle** /'dʌfl/: ~ **bag** *n* bolsa *f* de lona. ~ **coat** *n* trenca *f*

dug /dʌg/ ⇒DIG

duke /dju:k/ *n* duque *m*

dull /dʌl/ *a* (**-er**, **-est**) <*weather*> gris; <*colour*> apagado; <*person, play, etc*> pesado; <*sound*> sordo

dumb /dʌm/ *a* (**-er**, **-est**) mudo; 🅸 estúpido. ~**found** /dʌm'faʊnd/ *vt* pasmar

dummy /'dʌmɪ/ *n* muñeco *m*; (of tailor) maniquí *m*; (for baby) chupete *m*. ● *a* falso. ~ **run** prueba *f*

dump /dʌmp/ *vt* tirar, botar (LAm). ● *n* vertedero *m*; (Mil) depósito *m*; 🅸 lugar *m* desagradable. **be down in the ~s** estar deprimido

dumpling /'dʌmplɪŋ/ *n* bola *f* de masa hervida

Dumpster /'dʌmpstə(r)/ *n* (Amer, P) contenedor *m* (*para escombros*)

dumpy /'dʌmpɪ/ *a* (**-ier**, **-iest**) regordete

dunce /dʌns/ *n* burro *m*

dung /dʌŋ/ *n* (manure) estiércol *m*

dungarees /dʌŋgə'ri:z/ *npl* mono *m*, peto *m*

dungeon /'dʌndʒən/ *n* calabozo *m*

dunk /dʌŋk/ *vt* remojar

dupe /dju:p/ *vt* engañar. ● *n* inocentón *m*

duplicat|e /'dju:plɪkət/ *a & n* duplicado (*m*). ● /'dju:plɪkeɪt/ *vt* duplicar; (on machine) reproducir. ~**ing machine**, ~**or** *n* multicopista *f*

durable /'djʊərəbl/ *a* durable

duration /djʊ'reɪʃn/ *n* duración *f*

duress /djʊ'res/ *n*. **under** ~ bajo coacción

during /'djʊərɪŋ/ *prep* durante

dusk /dʌsk/ *n* anochecer *m*

dust /dʌst/ *n* polvo *m*. ● *vt* quitar el polvo a; (sprinkle) espolvorear (with con). ~**bin** *n* cubo *m* de la basura, bote *m* de la basura (Mex). ~ **cloth** (Amer), ~**er** *n* trapo *m*. ~**jacket** *n* sobrecubierta *f*. ~**man** /-mən/ *n* basurero *m*. ~**pan** *n* recogedor *m*. ~**y** *a* (**-ier**, **-iest**) polvoriento

Dutch /dʌtʃ/ *a* holandés. ● *n* (Lang) holandés *m*. **the** ~ (people) los holandeses. ~**man** /-mən/ *m* holandés *m*. ~**woman** *n* holandesa *f*

duty /'dju:tɪ/ *n* deber *m*; (tax) derechos *mpl* de aduana. **on** ~ de servicio. ~**-free** /-'fri:/ *a* libre de impuestos

duvet /'dju:veɪ/ *n* edredón *m*

dwarf /dwɔ:f/ *n* (*pl* **-s** *or* **dwarves**) enano *m*

dwell /dwel/ *vi* (*pt* **dwelt** *or* **dwelled**) morar.□ ~ **on** *vt* detenerse en. ~**ing** *n* morada *f*

dwindle /'dwɪndl/ *vi* disminuir

dye /daɪ/ *vt* (*pres p* **dyeing**) teñir. ● *n* tinte *m*

dying /'daɪɪŋ/ ⇒DIE

dynamic /daɪ'næmɪk/ *a* dinámico. ~**s** *npl* dinámica *f*

dynamite /'daɪnəmaɪt/ *n* dinamita *f*. ● *vt* dinamitar

dynamo /'daɪnəməʊ/ *n* (*pl* **-os**) dinamo *f*, dínamo *f*, dinamo *m* (LAm), dínamo *m* (LAm)

dynasty /'dɪnəstɪ/ *n* dinastía *f*

Ee

E *abbr* (= **East**) E

each /i:tʃ/ *a* cada. ● *pron* cada uno. **~ one** cada uno. **~ other** uno a otro, el uno al otro. **they love ~ other** se aman

eager /'i:gə(r)/ *a* impaciente; (enthusiastic) ávido. **~ness** *n* impaciencia *f*; (enthusiasm) entusiasmo *m*

eagle /'i:gl/ *n* águila *f*

ear /ɪə(r)/ *n* oído *m*; (outer) oreja *f*; (of corn) espiga *f*. **~ache** *n* dolor *m* de oído. **~drum** *n* tímpano *m*

earl /ɜ:l/ *n* conde *m*

early /'ɜ:lɪ/ *a* (**-ier**, **-iest**) temprano; (before expected time) prematuro. ● *adv* temprano; (ahead of time) con anticipación

earn /ɜ:n/ *vt* ganar; (deserve) merecer

earnest /'ɜ:nɪst/ *a* serio. **in ~** en serio

earnings /'ɜ:nɪŋz/ *npl* ingresos *mpl*; (Com) ganancias *fpl*

ear: ~phone *n* audífono *m*. **~ring** *n* pendiente *m*, arete *m* (LAm). **~shot** *n*. **within ~shot** al alcance del oído

earth /ɜ:θ/ *n* tierra *f*. **the E~** (planet) la Tierra. ● *vt* (Elec) conectar a tierra. **~quake** *n* terremoto *m*

earwig /'ɪəwɪg/ *n* tijereta *f*

ease /i:z/ *n* facilidad *f*; (comfort) tranquilidad *f*. **at ~** a gusto; (Mil) en posición de descanso. **ill at ~** molesto. **with ~** fácilmente. ● *vt* calmar; aliviar <*pain*>. ● *vi* calmarse; (lessen) disminuir

easel /'i:zl/ *n* caballete *m*

easily /'i:zɪlɪ/ *adv* fácilmente

east /i:st/ *n* este *m*. ● *a* este, oriental; <*wind*> del este. ● *adv* hacia el este.

Easter /'i:stə(r)/ *n* Semana *f* Santa; (Relig) Pascua *f* de Resurrección. **~ egg** *n* huevo *m* de Pascua

east: ~erly /-əli/ *a* <*wind*> del este. **~ern** /-ən/ *a* este, oriental. **~ward** /-wəd/, **~wards** *adv* hacia el este

easy /'i:zɪ/ *a* (**-ier**, **-iest**) fácil. ● *adv*. **go ~ on sth** Ⓘ no pasarse con algo. **take it ~** tomarse las cosas con calma. ● *int* ¡despacio! **~ chair** *n* sillón *m*. **~going** /-'gəʊɪŋ/ *a* acomodadizo

eat /i:t/ *vt/i* (*pt* **ate**, *pp* **eaten**) comer. □ **~ into** *vt* corroer. **~er** *n* comedor *m*

eaves /i:vz/ *npl* alero *m*. **~drop** *vi* (*pt* **-dropped**). **~drop (on)** escuchar a escondidas

ebb /eb/ *n* reflujo *m*. ● *vi* bajar; (fig) decaer

ebony /'ebənɪ/ *n* ébano *m*

EC /i:'si:/ *abbr* (= **European Community**) CE *f* (Comunidad *f* Europea)

eccentric /ɪk'sentrɪk/ *a* & *n* excéntrico (*m*). **~ity** /eksen'trɪsətɪ/ *n* excentricidad *f*

echo /'ekəʊ/ *n* (*pl* **-oes**) eco *m*. ● *vi* hacer eco

eclipse /ɪ'klɪps/ *n* eclipse *m*. ● *vt* eclipsar

ecolog|ical /i:kə'lɒdʒɪkl/ *a* ecológico. **~y** /ɪ'kɒlədʒɪ/ *n* ecología *f*

econom|ic /iːkəˈnɒmɪk/ *a* económico. **~ical** *a* económico. **~ics** *n* economía *f.* **~ist** /ɪˈkɒnəmɪst/ *n* economista *m & f.* **~ize** /ɪˈkɒnəmaɪz/ *vi* economizar. **~ize on sth** economizar algo. **~y** /ɪˈkɒnəmɪ/ *n* economía *f*

ecsta|sy /ˈekstəsɪ/ *n* éxtasis *f.* **~tic** /ɪkˈstætɪk/ *a* extático

Ecuador /ˈekwədɔː(r)/ *n* Ecuador *m.* **~ean** /ekwəˈdɔːrɪən/ *a & n* ecuatoriano (*m*)

edg|e /edʒ/ *n* borde *m*; (of knife) filo *m*; (of town) afueras *fpl*. **have the ~e on** 🅸 llevar la ventaja a. **on ~e** nervioso. ● *vt* ribetear; (move) mover poco a poco. ● *vi* avanzar cautelosamente. **~eways** *adv* de lado. **~y** *a* nervioso

edible /ˈedɪbl/ *a* comestible

edit /ˈedɪt/ *vt* dirigir <*newspaper*>; preparar una edición de <*text*>; editar <*film*>. **~ion** /ɪˈdɪʃn/ *n* edición *f.* **~or** *n* (of newspaper) director *m*; (of text) redactor *m.* **~orial** /edɪˈtɔːrɪəl/ *a* editorial. ● *n* artículo *m* de fondo

educat|e /ˈedʒʊkeɪt/ *vt* educar. **~ed** *a* culto. **~ion** /-ˈkeɪʃn/ *n* educación *f*; (knowledge, culture) cultura *f.* **~ional** /-ˈkeɪʃənl/ *a* instructivo

EEC /iːiːˈsiː/ *abbr* (= **European Economic Community**) CEE *f* (Comunidad *f* Económica Europea)

eel /iːl/ *n* anguila *f*

eerie /ˈɪərɪ/ *a* (**-ier**, **-iest**) misterioso

effect /ɪˈfekt/ *n* efecto *m.* **in ~** efectivamente. **take ~** entrar en vigor. **~ive** *a* eficaz; (striking) impresionante; (real) efectivo. **~ively** *adv* eficazmente. **~iveness** *n* eficacia *f*

effeminate /ɪˈfemɪnət/ *a* afeminado

efficien|cy /ɪˈfɪʃənsɪ/ *n* eficiencia *f*; (Mec) rendimiento *m.* **~t** *a* eficiente. **~tly** *adv* eficientemente

effort /ˈefət/ *n* esfuerzo *m.* **~less** *a* fácil

e.g. /iːˈdʒiː/ *abbr* (= **exempli gratia**) p.ej., por ejemplo

egg /eg/ *n* huevo *m.* □ **~ on** *vt* 🅸 incitar. **~cup** *n* huevera *f.* **~plant** *n* (Amer) berenjena *f.* **~shell** *n* cáscara *f* de huevo

ego /ˈiːgəʊ/ *n* (*pl* **-os**) yo *m.* **~ism** *n* egoísmo *m.* **~ist** *n* egoísta *m & f.* **~centric** /iːgəʊˈsentrɪk/ *a* egocéntrico. **~tism** *n* egotismo *m.* **~tist** *n* egotista *m & f*

eh /eɪ/ *int* 🅸 ¡eh!

eiderdown /ˈaɪdədaʊn/ *n* edredón *m*

eight /eɪt/ *a & n* ocho (*m*). **~een** /eɪˈtiːn/ *a & n* dieciocho (*m*). **~eenth** *a* decimoctavo. ● *n* dieciochavo *m.* **~h** /eɪtθ/ *a & n* octavo (*m*) **~ieth** /ˈeɪtɪəθ/ *a* octogésimo. ● *n* ochentavo *m.* **~y** /ˈeɪtɪ/ *a & n* ochenta (*m*)

either /ˈaɪðə(r)/ *a* cualquiera de los dos; (negative) ninguno de los dos; (each) cada. ● *pron* uno u otro; (with negative) ni uno ni otro. ● *adv* (negative) tampoco. ● *conj* o. **~ Tuesday or Wednesday** o el martes o el miércoles; (with negative) ni el martes ni el miércoles

eject /ɪˈdʒekt/ *vt* expulsar

eke /iːk/ *vt.* **~ out** hacer alcanzar <*resources*>. **~ out a living** ganarse la vida a duras penas

elaborate /ɪˈlæbərət/ *a* complicado. ● /ɪˈlæbəreɪt/ *vt* elaborar. ● /ɪˈlæbəreɪt/ *vi* explicarse

elapse /ɪˈlæps/ *vi* transcurrir

elastic /ɪ'læstɪk/ *a & n* elástico (*m*). **~ band** *n* goma *f* (elástica), liga *f* (Mex)

elat|ed /ɪ'leɪtɪd/ *a* regocijado. **~ion** /-ʃn/ *n* regocijo *m*

elbow /'elbəʊ/ *n* codo *m*. ● *vt* dar un codazo a

elder /'eldə(r)/ *a* mayor. ● *n* mayor *m & f*; (tree) saúco *m*. **~ly** /'eldəlɪ/ *a* mayor, anciano

eldest /'eldɪst/ *a & n* mayor (*m & f*)

elect /ɪ'lekt/ *vt* elegir. **~ to do** decidir hacer. ● *a* electo. **~ion** /-ʃn/ *n* elección *f*. **~or** *n* elector *m*. **~oral** *a* electoral. **~orate** /-ət/ *n* electorado *m*

electric /ɪ'lektrɪk/ *a* eléctrico. **~al** *a* eléctrico. **~ blanket** *n* manta *f* eléctrica. **~ian** /ɪlek'trɪʃn/ *n* electricista *m & f*. **~ity** /ɪlek'trɪsətɪ/ *n* electricidad *f*

electrify /ɪ'lektrɪfaɪ/ *vt* electrificar; (fig) electrizar

electrocute /ɪ'lektrəkju:t/ *vt* electrocutar

electrode /ɪ'lektrəʊd/ *n* electrodo *m*

electron /ɪ'lektrɒn/ *n* electrón *m*

electronic /ɪlek'trɒnɪk/ *a* electrónico. **~ mail** *n* correo *m* electrónico. **~s** *n* electrónica *f*

elegan|ce /'elɪgəns/ *n* elegancia *f*. **~t** *a* elegante. **~tly** *adv* elegantemente

element /'elɪmənt/ *n* elemento *m*. **~ary** /-'mentrɪ/ *a* elemental. **~ary school** *n* (Amer) escuela *f* primaria

elephant /'elɪfənt/ *n* elefante *m*

elevat|e /'elɪveɪt/ *vt* elevar. **~ion** /-'veɪʃn/ *n* elevación *f*. **~or** *n* (Amer) ascensor *m*

eleven /ɪ'levn/ *a & n* once (*m*). **~th** *a* undécimo. ● *n* onceavo *m*

elf /elf/ *n* (*pl* **elves**) duende *m*

eligible /'elɪdʒəbl/ *a* elegible. **be ~ for** tener derecho a

eliminat|e /ɪ'lɪmɪneɪt/ *vt* eliminar. **~ion** /-'neɪʃn/ *n* eliminación *f*

élite /eɪ'li:t/ *n* elite *f*, élite *f*

ellip|se /ɪ'lɪps/ *n* elipse *f*. **~tical** *a* elíptico

elm /elm/ *n* olmo *m*

elope /ɪ'ləʊp/ *vi* fugarse con el amante

eloquen|ce /'eləkwəns/ *n* elocuencia *f*. **~t** *a* elocuente

El Salvador /el'sælvədɔ:(r)/ *n* El Salvador

else /els/ *adv*. **somebody ~** otra persona. **everybody ~** todos los demás. **nobody ~** ningún otro, nadie más. **nothing ~** nada más. **or ~** o bien. **somewhere ~** en otra parte. **~where** *adv* en otra parte

elu|de /ɪ'lu:d/ *vt* eludir. **~sive** /-sɪv/ *a* esquivo

elves /elvz/ ⇒ELF

emaciated /ɪ'meɪʃɪeɪtɪd/ *a* consumido

email, e-mail /'i:meɪl/ *n* correo *m* electrónico, correo-e *m*. ● *vt* mandar por correo electrónico, emailear. **~ address** *n* casilla *f* electrónica, dirección *f* de correo electrónico

emancipat|e /ɪ'mænsɪpeɪt/ *vt* emancipar. **~ion** /-'peɪʃn/ *n* emancipación *f*

embankment /ɪm'bæŋkmənt/ *n* terraplén *m*; (of river) dique *m*

embargo /ɪm'bɑ:gəʊ/ *n* (*pl* **-oes**) embargo *m*

embark /ɪm'bɑ:k/ *vi* embarcarse. **~ on** (fig) emprender. **~ation** /embɑ:'keɪʃn/ *n* embarque *m*

embarrass /ɪm'bærəs/ *vt* avergonzar. **~ed** *a* avergonzado. **~ing** *a* embarazoso. **~ment** *n* vergüenza *f*

embassy /'embəsɪ/ *n* embajada *f*

embellish /ɪm'belɪʃ/ *vt* adornar. **~ment** *n* adorno *m*

embers /'embəz/ *npl* ascuas *fpl*

embezzle /ɪm'bezl/ *vt* desfalcar. **~ment** *n* desfalco *m*

emblem /'embləm/ *n* emblema *m*

embrace /ɪm'breɪs/ *vt* abrazar; (fig) abarcar. ● *vi* abrazarse. ● *n* abrazo *m*

embroider /ɪm'brɔɪdə(r)/ *vt* bordar. **~y** *n* bordado *m*

embroil /ɪm'brɔɪl/ *vt* enredar

embryo /'embrɪəʊ/ *n* (*pl* **-os**) embrión *m*. **~nic** /-'ɒnɪk/ *a* embrionario

emend /ɪ'mend/ *vt* enmendar

emerald /'emərəld/ *n* esmeralda *f*

emerge /ɪ'mɜ:dʒ/ *vi* salir. **~nce** /-əns/ *n* aparición *f*

emergency /ɪ'mɜ:dʒənsɪ/ *n* emergencia *f*; (Med) urgencia *f*. **in an ~** en caso de emergencia. **~ exit** *n* salida *f* de emergencia

emigra|nt /'emɪgrənt/ *n* emigrante *m & f*. **~te** /'emɪgreɪt/ *vi* emigrar. **~tion** /-'greɪʃn/ *n* emigración *f*

eminen|ce /'emɪnəns/ *n* eminencia *f*. **~t** *a* eminente. **~tly** *adv* eminentemente

emi|ssion /ɪ'mɪʃn/ *n* emisión *f*. **~t** *vt* (*pt* **emitted**) emitir

emoti|on /ɪ'məʊʃn/ *n* emoción *f*. **~onal** *a* emocional; <*person*> emotivo; (moving) conmovedor. **~ve** /ɪ'məʊtɪv/ *a* emotivo

empathy /'empəθɪ/ *n* empatía *f*

emperor /'empərə(r)/ *n* emperador *m*

empha|sis /'emfəsɪs/ *n* (*pl* **~ses** /-si:z/) énfasis *m*. **~size** /'emfəsaɪz/ *vt* enfatizar. **~tic** /ɪm'fætɪk/ *a* <*gesture*> enfático; <*assertion*> categórico

empire /'empaɪə(r)/ *n* imperio *m*

empirical /ɪm'pɪrɪkl/ *a* empírico

employ /ɪm'plɔɪ/ *vt* emplear. **~ee** /emplɔɪ'i:/ *n* empleado *m*. **~er** *n* patrón *m*. **~ment** *n* empleo *m*. **~ment agency** *n* agencia *f* de trabajo

empower /ɪm'paʊə(r)/ *vt* autorizar (**to do** a hacer)

empress /'emprɪs/ *n* emperatriz *f*

empty /'emptɪ/ *a* vacío; <*promise*> vano. **on an ~y stomach** con el estómago vacío. ● *n* [I] envase *m* (vacío). ● *vt* vaciar. ● *vi* vaciarse

emulate /'emjʊleɪt/ *vt* emular

emulsion /ɪ'mʌlʃn/ *n* emulsión *f*

enable /ɪ'neɪbl/ *vt*. **~ s.o. to do sth** permitir a uno hacer algo

enact /ɪ'nækt/ *vt* (Jurid) decretar; (in theatre) representar

enamel /ɪ'næml/ *n* esmalte *m*. ● *vt* (*pt* **enamelled**) esmaltar

enchant /ɪn'tʃɑ:nt/ *vt* encantar. **~ing** *a* encantador. **~ment** *n* encanto *m*

encircle /ɪn'sɜ:kl/ *vt* rodear

enclave /'enkleɪv/ *n* enclave *m*

enclos|e /ɪn'kləʊz/ *vt* cercar <*land*>; (Com) adjuntar. **~ed** *a* <*space*> cerrado; (Com) adjunto. **~ure** /ɪn'kləʊʒə(r)/ *n* cercamiento *m*

encode /ɪn'kəʊd/ *vt* codificar, cifrar

encore /'ɒŋkɔ:(r)/ *int* ¡otra! ● *n* bis *m*, repetición *f*

encounter /ɪn'kaʊntə(r)/ *vt* encontrar. ● *n* encuentro *m*

encourag|e /ɪn'kʌrɪdʒ/ *vt* animar; (stimulate) fomentar. **~ement** *n* ánimo *m*. **~ing** *a* alentador

encroach /ɪn'krəʊtʃ/ *vi*. **~ on** invadir <*land*>; quitar <*time*>

encyclopaedi|a /ɪnsaɪklə'pi:dɪə/ *n* enciclopedia *f*. **~c** *a* enciclopédico

end /end/ *n* fin *m*; (furthest point) extremo *m*. **in the ~** por fin. **make ~s meet** poder llegar a fin de mes. **put an ~ to** poner fin a. **no ~ of** muchísimos. **on ~** de pie; (consecutive) seguido. ● *vt/i* terminar, acabar

endanger /ɪn'deɪndʒə(r)/ *vt* poner en peligro. **~ed** *a* <*species*> en peligro

endearing /ɪn'dɪərɪŋ/ *a* simpático

endeavour /ɪn'devə(r)/ *n* esfuerzo *m*, intento *m*. ● *vi*. **~ to** esforzarse por

ending /'endɪŋ/ *n* fin *m*

endless /'endlɪs/ *a* interminable

endorse /ɪn'dɔ:s/ *vt* endosar; (fig) aprobar. **~ment** *n* endoso *m*; (fig) aprobación *f*; (Auto) nota *f* de inhabilitación

endur|ance /ɪn'djʊərəns/ *n* resistencia *f*. **~e** /ɪn'djʊə(r)/ *vt* aguantar. **~ing** *a* perdurable

enemy /'enəmɪ/ *n* & *a* enemigo (*m*)

energ|etic /enə'dʒetɪk/ *a* enérgico. **~y** /'enədʒɪ/ *n* energía *f*

enforce /ɪn'fɔ:s/ *vt* hacer cumplir <*law*>; hacer valer <*claim*>. **~d** *a* forzado

engag|e /ɪn'geɪdʒ/ *vt* emplear <*staff*>; captar <*attention*>; (Mec) hacer engranar. ● *vi* (Mec) engranar. **~e in** dedicarse a. **~ed** *a* prometido, comprometido (LAm); (busy) ocupado. **be ~ed** (of phone) estar comunicando, estar ocupado (LAm). **get ~ed** prometerse, comprometerse (LAm). **~ement** *n* compromiso *m*

engine /'endʒɪn/ *n* motor *m*; (of train) locomotora *f*. **~ driver** *n* maquinista *m*

engineer /endʒɪ'nɪə(r)/ *n* ingeniero *m*; (mechanic) mecánico *m*; (Amer, Rail) maquinista *m*. ● *vt* (contrive) fraguar. **~ing** *n* ingeniería *f*

England /'ɪŋglənd/ *n* Inglaterra *f*

English /'ɪŋglɪʃ/ *a* inglés. ● *n* (Lang) inglés *m*. ● *npl*. **the ~** los ingleses. **~man** /-mən/ *n* inglés *m*. **~woman** *n* inglesa *f*

engrav|e /ɪn'greɪv/ *vt* grabar. **~ing** *n* grabado *m*

engrossed /ɪn'grəʊst/ *a* absorto

engulf /ɪn'gʌlf/ *vt* envolver

enhance /ɪn'hɑ:ns/ *vt* realzar; aumentar <*value*>

enigma /ɪ'nɪgmə/ *n* enigma *m*. **~tic** /enɪg'mætɪk/ *a* enigmático

enjoy /ɪn'dʒɔɪ/ *vt*. **I ~ reading** me gusta la lectura. **~ o.s.** divertirse. **~able** *a* agradable. **~ment** *n* placer *m*

enlarge /ɪn'lɑ:dʒ/ *vt* agrandar; (Photo) ampliar. ● *vi* agrandarse. **~ upon** extenderse sobre. **~ment** *n* (Photo) ampliación *f*

enlighten /ɪn'laɪtn/ *vt* ilustrar. **~ment** *n*. **the E~ment** el siglo de la luces

enlist /ɪn'lɪst/ *vt* alistar; conseguir <*support*>. ● *vi* alistarse

enliven /ɪn'laɪvn/ *vt* animar

enorm|ity /ɪ'nɔ:mətɪ/ *n* enormidad *f*. **~ous** /ɪ'nɔ:məs/ *a* enorme. **~ously** *adv* enormemente

enough /ɪ'nʌf/ *a & adv* bastante. ● *n* bastante *m*, suficiente *m*. ● *int* ¡basta!

enquir|e /ɪn'kwaɪə(r)/ *vt/i* preguntar. **~e about** informarse de. **~y** *n* pregunta *f*; (investigation) investigación *f*

enrage /ɪn'reɪdʒ/ *vt* enfurecer

enrol /ɪn'rəʊl/ *vt* (*pt* **enrolled**) inscribir, matricular *<student>*. ● *vi* inscribirse, matricularse

ensue /ɪn'sju:/ *vi* seguir

ensure /ɪn'ʃʊə(r)/ *vt* asegurar

entail /ɪn'teɪl/ *vt* suponer; acarrear *<expense>*

entangle /ɪn'tæŋgl/ *vt* enredar. **~ment** *n* enredo *m*

enter /'entə(r)/ *vt* entrar en, entrar a (esp LAm); presentarse a *<competition>*; inscribirse en *<race>*; (write) escribir. ● *vi* entrar

enterpris|e /'entəpraɪz/ *n* empresa *f*; (fig) iniciativa *f*. **~ing** *a* emprendedor

entertain /entə'teɪn/ *vt* entretener; recibir *<guests>*; abrigar *<ideas, hopes>*; (consider) considerar. **~ing** *a* entretenido. **~ment** *n* entretenimiento *m*; (show) espectáculo *m*

enthral /ɪn'θrɔ:l/ *vt* (*pt* **enthralled**) cautivar

enthuse /ɪn'θju:z/ *vi*. **~ over** entusiasmarse por

enthusias|m /ɪn'θju:zɪæzəm/ *n* entusiasmo *m*. **~t** *n* entusiasta *m & f*. **~tic** /-'æstɪk/ *a* entusiasta. **~tically** *adv* con entusiasmo

entice /ɪn'taɪs/ *vt* atraer

entire /ɪn'taɪə(r)/ *a* entero. **~ly** *adv* completamente. **~ty** /ɪn'taɪərətɪ/ *n*. **in its ~ty** en su totalidad

entitle /ɪn'taɪtl/ *vt* titular; (give a right) dar derecho a. **be ~d to** tener derecho a. **~ment** *n* derecho *m*

entity /'entətɪ/ *n* entidad *f*

entrails /'entreɪlz/ *npl* entrañas *fpl*

entrance /'entrəns/ *n* entrada *f*. ● /ɪn'trɑ:ns/ *vt* encantar

entrant /'entrənt/ *n* participante *m & f*; (in exam) candidato *m*

entreat /ɪn'tri:t/ *vt* suplicar. **~y** *n* súplica *f*

entrenched /ɪn'trentʃt/ *a <position>* afianzado

entrust /ɪn'trʌst/ *vt* confiar

entry /'entrɪ/ *n* entrada *f*

entwine /ɪn'twaɪn/ *vt* entrelazar

enumerate /ɪ'nju:məreɪt/ *vt* enumerar

envelop /ɪn'veləp/ *vt* envolver

envelope /'envələʊp/ *n* sobre *m*

enviable /'envɪəbl/ *a* envidiable

envious /'envɪəs/ *a* envidioso

environment /ɪn'vaɪərənmənt/ *n* medio *m* ambiente. **~al** /-'mentl/ *a* ambiental

envisage /ɪn'vɪzɪdʒ/ *vt* prever; (imagine) imaginar

envision /ɪn'vɪʒn/ *vt* (Amer) prever

envoy /'envɔɪ/ *n* enviado *m*

envy /'envɪ/ *n* envidia *f*. ● *vt* envidiar

enzyme /'enzaɪm/ *n* enzima *f*

ephemeral /ɪ'femərəl/ *a* efímero

epic /'epɪk/ *n* épica *f*. ● *a* épico

epidemic /epɪ'demɪk/ *n* epidemia *f*. ● *a* epidémico

epilep|sy /'epɪlepsɪ/ *n* epilepsia *f*. **~tic** /-'leptɪk/ *a & n* epiléptico (*m*)

epilogue /'epɪlɒg/ *n* epílogo *m*

episode /'epɪsəʊd/ *n* episodio *m*

epitaph /'epɪtɑ:f/ *n* epitafio *m*

epitom|e /ɪ'pɪtəmɪ/ *n* personificación *f*, epítome *m*. **~ize** *vt* ser la personificación de

epoch /'i:pɒk/ *n* época *f*

equal /'i:kwəl/ *a & n* igual (*m & f*). **~ to** (a task) a la altura de. ● *vt* (*pt* **equalled**) ser igual a; (Math) ser. **~ity** /ɪ'kwɒlətɪ/ *n* igualdad *f*. **~ize** *vt* igualar. ● *vi* (Sport) emapatar. **~izer** *n* (Sport) gol *m* del empate. **~ly** *adv* igualmente; <*share*> por igual

equation /ɪ'kweɪʒn/ *n* ecuación *f*

equator /ɪ'kweɪtə(r)/ *n* ecuador *m*. **~ial** /ekwə'tɔ:rɪəl/ *a* ecuatorial

equilibrium /i:kwɪ'lɪbrɪəm/ *n* equilibrio *m*

equinox /'i:kwɪnɒks/ *n* equinoccio *m*

equip /ɪ'kwɪp/ *vt* (*pt* **equipped**) equipar. **~ sth with** proveer algo de. **~ment** *n* equipo *m*

equivalen|ce /ɪ'kwɪvələns/ *n* equivalencia *f*. **~t** *a & n* equivalente (*m*). **be ~t to** equivaler

equivocal /ɪ'kwɪvəkl/ *a* equívoco

era /'ɪərə/ *n* era *f*

eradicate /ɪ'rædɪkeɪt/ *vt* erradicar, extirpar

erase /ɪ'reɪz/ *vt* borrar. **~r** *n* goma *f* (de borrar)

erect /ɪ'rekt/ *a* erguido. ● *vt* levantar. **~ion** /-ʃn/ *n* construcción *f*; (Anat) erección *f*

ero|de /ɪ'rəʊd/ *vt* erosionar. **~sion** /-ʒn/ *n* erosión *f*

erotic /ɪ'rɒtɪk/ *a* erótico

err /ɜ:(r)/ *vi* errar; (sin) pecar

errand /'erənd/ *n* recado *m*, mandado *m* (LAm)

erratic /ɪ'rætɪk/ *a* desigual; <*person*> voluble

erroneous /ɪ'rəʊnɪəs/ *a* erróneo

error /'erə(r)/ *n* error *m*

erudit|e /'eru:daɪt/ *a* erudito. **~ion** /-'dɪʃn/ *n* erudición *f*

erupt /ɪ'rʌpt/ *vi* entrar en erupción; (fig) estallar. **~ion** /-ʃn/ *n* erupción *f*

escalat|e /'eskəleɪt/ *vt* intensificar. ● *vi* intensificarse. **~ion** /-'leɪʃn/ *n* intensificación *f*. **~or** *n* escalera *f* mecánica

escapade /eskə'peɪd/ *n* aventura *f*

escap|e /ɪ'skeɪp/ *vi* escaparse. ● *vt* evitar. ● *n* fuga *f*; (of gas, water) escape *m*. **have a narrow ~e** escapar por un pelo. **~ism** /-ɪzəm/ *n* escapismo *m*

escort /'eskɔ:t/ *n* acompañante *m*; (Mil) escolta *f*. ● /ɪ'skɔ:t/ *vt* acompañar; (Mil) escoltar

Eskimo /'eskɪməʊ/ *n* (*pl* **-os** *or invar*) esquimal *m & f*

especial /ɪ'speʃl/ *a* especial. **~ly** *adv* especialmente

espionage /'espɪənɑ:ʒ/ *n* espionaje *m*

Esq. /ɪ'skwaɪə(r)/ *abbr* (= **Esquire**) (in address) **E. Ashton, ~** Sr. Don E. Ashton

essay /'eseɪ/ *n* ensayo *m*; (at school) composición *f*

essence /'esns/ *n* esencia *f*. **in ~** esencialmente

essential /ɪ'senʃl/ *a* esencial. ● *n* elemento *m* esencial. **~ly** *adv* esencialmente

establish /ɪ'stæblɪʃ/ *vt* establecer. **~ment** *n* establecimiento *m*. **the E~ment** los que mandan, el sistema

estate /ɪ'steɪt/ *n* finca *f*; (housing estate) complejo *m* habitacional, urbanización *f*, fraccionamiento *m* (Mex); (possessions) bienes *mpl*.

~ **agent** *n* agente *m* inmobiliario. ~ **car** *n* ranchera *f*, (coche *m*) familiar *m*, camioneta *f* (LAm)

esteem /ɪ'sti:m/ *n* estimación *f*, estima *f*

estimat|e /'estɪmət/ *n* cálculo *m*; (Com) presupuesto *m*. ● /'estɪmeɪt/ *vt* calcular. ~**ion** /-'meɪʃn/ *n* estima *f*, estimación *f*; (opinion) opinión *f*

estranged /ɪs'treɪndʒd/ *a* alejado

estuary /'estʃʊərɪ/ *n* estuario *m*

etc /et'setrə/ *abbr* (= **et cetera**) etc., etcétera

etching /'etʃɪŋ/ *n* aguafuerte *m*

etern|al /ɪ'tɜ:nl/ *a* eterno. ~**ity** /-ətɪ/ *n* eternidad *f*

ether /'i:θə(r)/ *n* éter *m*

ethic /'eθɪk/ *n* ética *f*. ~**al** *a* ético. ~**s** *npl* ética *f*

ethnic /'eθnɪk/ *a* étnico

ethos /'i:θɒs/ *n* carácter *m* distintivo

etiquette /'etɪket/ *n* etiqueta *f*

etymology /etɪ'mɒlədʒɪ/ *n* etimología *f*

euphemism /'ju:fəmɪzəm/ *n* eufemismo *m*

euphoria /ju:'fɔ:rɪə/ *n* euforia *f*

Europe /'jʊərəp/ *n* Europa *f*. ~**an** /-'pɪən/ *a* & *n* europeo (*m*). ~**an Union** *n* Unión *f* Europea

euthanasia /ju:θə'neɪzɪə/ *n* eutanasia *f*

evacuat|e /ɪ'vækjʊeɪt/ *vt* evacuar; desocupar <*building*>. ~**ion** /-'eɪʃn/ *n* evacuación *f*

evade /ɪ'veɪd/ *vt* evadir

evaluate /ɪ'væljʊeɪt/ *vt* evaluar

evangelical /i:væn'dʒelɪkl/ *a* evangélico

evaporat|e /ɪ'væpəreɪt/ *vi* evaporarse. ~**ion** /-'reɪʃn/ *n* evaporación *f*

evasi|on /ɪ'veɪʒn/ *n* evasión *f*. ~**ve** /ɪ'veɪsɪv/ *a* evasivo

eve /i:v/ *n* víspera *f*

even /'i:vn/ *a* (flat, smooth) plano; <*colour*> uniforme; <*distribution*> equitativo; <*number*> par. **get** ~ **with** desquitarse con. ● *vt* nivelar. □ ~ **up** *vt* equilibrar. ● *adv* aun, hasta, incluso. ~ **if** aunque. ~ **so** aun así. **not** ~ ni siquiera

evening /'i:vnɪŋ/ *n* tarde *f*; (after dark) noche *f*. ~ **class** *n* clase *f* nocturna

event /ɪ'vent/ *n* acontecimiento *m*; (Sport) prueba *f*. **in the** ~ **of** en caso de. ~**ful** *a* lleno de acontecimientos

eventual /ɪ'ventʃʊəl/ *a* final, definitivo. ~**ity** /-'ælətɪ/ *n* eventualidad *f*. ~**ly** *adv* finalmente

ever /'evə(r)/ *adv* (negative) nunca, jamás; (at all times) siempre. **have you** ~ **been to Greece?** ¿has estado (alguna vez) en Grecia? ~ **after** desde entonces. ~ **since** desde entonces. ~ **so** 🅸 muy. **for** ~ para siempre. **hardly** ~ casi nunca. ~**green** *a* de hoja perenne. ● *n* árbol *m* de hoja perenne. ~**lasting** *a* eterno.

every /'evrɪ/ *a* cada, todo. ~ **child** todos los niños. ~ **one** cada uno. ~ **other day** un día sí y otro no. ~**body** *pron* todos, todo el mundo. ~**day** *a* de todos los días. ~**one** *pron* todos, todo el mundo. ~**thing** *pron* todo. ~**where** *adv* (be) en todas partes; (go) a todos lados

evict /ɪ'vɪkt/ *vt* desahuciar. ~**ion** /-ʃn/ *n* desahucio *m*

eviden|ce /'evɪdəns/ *n* evidencia *f*; (proof) pruebas *fpl*; (Jurid) testimonio *m*; **give ~ce** prestar declaración. **~ce of** señales de. **in ~ce** visible. **~t** *a* evidente. **~tly** *adv* evidentemente

evil /'i:vl/ *a* malvado. ● *n* mal *m*

evo|cative /ɪ'vɒkətɪv/ *a* evocador. **~ke** /ɪ'vəʊk/ *vt* evocar

evolution /i:və'lu:ʃn/ *n* evolución *f*

evolve /ɪ'vɒlv/ *vt* desarrollar. ● *vi* evolucionar

ewe /ju:/ *n* oveja *f*

exact /ɪg'zækt/ *a* exacto. ● *vt* exigir (from a). **~ing** *a* exigente. **~ly** *adv* exactamente

exaggerat|e /ɪg'zædʒəreɪt/ *vt* exagerar. **~ion** /-'reɪʃn/ *n* exageración *f*

exam /ɪg'zæm/ *n* examen *m*. **~ination** /ɪgzæmɪ'neɪʃn/ *n* examen *m*. **~ine** /ɪg'zæmɪn/ *vt* examinar; interrogar *<witness>*. **~iner** *n* examinador *m*

example /ɪg'zɑ:mpl/ *n* ejemplo *m*. **for ~** por ejemplo. **make an ~ of s.o.** darle un castigo ejemplar a uno

exasperat|e /ɪg'zæspəreɪt/ *vt* exasperar. **~ing** *a* exasperante. **~ion** /-'reɪʃn/ *n* exasperación *f*

excavat|e /'ekskəveɪt/ *vt* excavar. **~ion** /-'veɪʃn/ *n* excavación *f*

exceed /ɪk'si:d/ *vt* exceder. **~ingly** *adv* sumamente

excel /ɪk'sel/ *vi* (*pt* **excelled**) sobresalir. ● *vt*. **~ o.s.** lucirse. **~lence** /'eksələns/ *n* excelencia *f*. **~lent** *a* excelente

except /ɪk'sept/ *prep* menos, excepto. **~ for** si no fuera por. ● *vt* exceptuar. **~ing** *prep* con excepción de

exception /ɪk'sepʃən/ *n* excepción *f*. **take ~ to** ofenderse por. **~al** *a* excepcional. **~ally** *adv* excepcionalmente

excerpt /'eksɜ:pt/ *n* extracto *m*

excess /ɪk'ses/ *n* exceso *m*. ● /'ekses/ *a* excedente. **~ fare** suplemento *m*. **~ luggage** exceso *m* de equipaje. **~ive** *a* excesivo

exchange /ɪk'stʃeɪndʒ/ *vt* cambiar. ● *n* intercambio *m*; (of money) cambio *m*. **(telephone) ~** central *f* telefónica

excise /'eksaɪz/ *n* impuestos *mpl* interos. ● /ek'saɪz/ *vt* quitar

excit|able /ɪk'saɪtəbl/ *a* excitable. **~e** /ɪk'saɪt/ *vt* emocionar; (stimulate) excitar. **~ed** *a* entusiasmado. **get ~ed** entusiasmarse. **~ement** *n* emoción *f*; (enthusiasm) entusiasmo *m*. **~ing** *a* emocionante

excla|im /ɪk'skleɪm/ *vi/t* exclamar. **~mation** /eksklə'meɪʃn/ *n* exclamación *f*. **~mation mark** *n* signo *m* de admiración *f*

exclu|de /ɪk'sklu:d/ *vt* excluir. **~sion** /-ʒən/ *n* exclusión *f*. **~sive** /ɪk'sklu:sɪv/ *a* exclusivo; *<club>* selecto. **~sive of** excluyendo. **~sively** *adv* exclusivamente

excruciating /ɪk'skru:ʃɪeɪtɪŋ/ *a* atroz, insoportable

excursion /ɪk'skɜ:ʃn/ *n* excursión *f*

excus|able /ɪk'skju:zəbl/ *a* perdonable. **~e** /ɪk'skju:z/ *vt* perdonar. **~e from** dispensar de. **~e me!** ¡perdón! ● /ɪk'skju:s/ *n* excusa *f*

ex-directory /eksdɪ'rektərɪ/ *a* que no figura en la guía telefónica, privado (Mex)

execut|e /'eksɪkju:t/ *vt* ejecutar. **~ion** /eksɪ'kju:ʃn/ *n* ejecución *f.* **~ioner** *n* verdugo *m*

executive /ɪg'zekjʊtɪv/ *a & n* ejecutivo (*m*)

exempt /ɪg'zempt/ *a* exento (**from** de). ● *vt* dispensar. **~ion** /-ʃn/ *n* exención *f*

exercise /'eksəsaɪz/ *n* ejercicio *m.* ● *vt* ejercer. ● *vi* hacer ejercicio. **~ book** *n* cuaderno *m*

exert /ɪg'zɜ:t/ *vt* ejercer. **~ o.s.** hacer un gran esfuerzo. **~ion** /-ʃn/ *n* esfuerzo *m*

exhale /eks'heɪl/ *vt/i* exhalar

exhaust /ɪg'zɔ:st/ *vt* agotar. ● *n* (Auto) tubo *m* de escape. **~ed** *a* agotado. **~ion** /-stʃən/ *n* agotamiento *m.* **~ive** *a* exhaustivo

exhibit /ɪg'zɪbɪt/ *vt* exponer; (fig) mostrar. ● *n* objeto *m* expuesto; (Jurid) documento *m.* **~ion** /eksɪ'bɪʃn/ *n* exposición. **~ionist** *n* exhibicionista *m & f.* **~or** /ɪg'zɪbɪtə(r)/ *n* expositor *m*

exhilarat|ing /ɪg'zɪləreɪtɪŋ/ *a* excitante. **~ion** /-'reɪʃn/ *n* regocijo *m*

exhort /ɪg'zɔ:t/ *vt* exhortar

exile /'eksaɪl/ *n* exilio *m*; (person) exiliado *m.* ● *vt* desterrar

exist /ɪg'zɪst/ *vi* existir. **~ence** *n* existencia *f.* **in ~ence** existente

exit /'eksɪt/ *n* salida *f*

exorbitant /ɪg'zɔ:bɪtənt/ *a* exorbitante

exorcis|e /'eksɔ:saɪz/ *vt* exorcizar. **~m** /-sɪzəm/ *n* exorcismo *m.* **~t** *n* exorcista *m & f*

exotic /ɪg'zɒtɪk/ *a* exótico

expand /ɪk'spænd/ *vt* expandir; (develop) desarrollar. ● *vi* expandirse

expanse /ɪk'spæns/ *n* extensión *f*

expansion /ɪk'spænʃn/ *n* expansión *f*

expatriate /eks'pætrɪət/ *a & n* expatriado (*m*)

expect /ɪk'spekt/ *vt* esperar; (suppose) suponer; (demand) contar con. **I ~ so** supongo que sí. **~ancy** *n* esperanza *f.* **life ~ancy** esperanza *f* de vida. **~ant** *a* expectante. **~ant mother** *n* futura madre *f*

expectation /ekspek'teɪʃn/ *n* expectativa *f*

expedient /ɪk'spi:dɪənt/ *a* conveniente. ● *n* expediente *m*

expedition /ekspɪ'dɪʃn/ *n* expedición *f*

expel /ɪk'spel/ *vt* (*pt* **expelled**) expulsar

expend /ɪk'spend/ *vt* gastar. **~able** *a* prescindible. **~iture** /-ɪtʃə(r)/ *n* gastos *mpl*

expens|e /ɪk'spens/ *n* gasto *m.* **at s.o.'s ~e** a costa de uno. **~es** *npl* (Com) gastos *mpl.* **~ive** *a* caro

experience /ɪk'spɪərɪəns/ *n* experiencia. ● *vt* experimentar. **~d** *a* con experiencia; <*driver*> experimentado

experiment /ɪk'sperɪmənt/ *n* experimento *m.* ● *vi* experimentar. **~al** /-'mentl/ *a* experimental

expert /'ekspɜ:t/ *a & n* experto (*m*). **~ise** /ekspɜ:'ti:z/ *n* pericia *f.* **~ly** *adv* hábilmente

expir|e /ɪk'spaɪə(r)/ *vi* <*passport, ticket*> caducar; <*contract*> vencer. **~y** *n* vencimiento *m*, caducidad *f*

expla|in /ɪk'spleɪn/ *vt* explicar. **~nation** /eksplə'neɪʃn/ *n* explicación *f.* **~natory** /ɪks'plænətərɪ/ *a* explicativo

explicit /ɪk'splɪsɪt/ *a* explícito

explode /ɪk'spləʊd/ *vt* hacer explotar. ● *vi* estallar

exploit /'eksplɔɪt/ *n* hazaña *f*. ● /ɪk'splɔɪt/ *vt* explotar. **~ation** /eksplɔɪ'teɪʃn/ *n* explotación *f*

explor|ation /eksplə'reɪʃn/ *n* exploración *f*. **~atory** /ɪk'splɒrətrɪ/ *a* exploratorio. **~e** /ɪk'splɔ:(r)/ *vt* explorar. **~er** *n* explorador *m*

explosi|on /ɪk'spləʊʒn/ *n* explosión *f*. **~ve** /-sɪv/ *a* & *n* explosivo (*m*)

export /ɪk'spɔ:t/ *vt* exportar. ● /'ekspɔ:t/ *n* exportación *f*; (item) artículo *m* de exportación. **~er** /ɪks'pɔ:tə(r)/ exportador *m*

expos|e /ɪk'spəʊz/ *vt* exponer; (reveal) descubrir. **~ure** /-ʒə(r)/ *n* exposición *f*. **die of ~ure** morir de frío

express /ɪk'spres/ *vt* expresar. ● *a* expreso; <*letter*> urgente. ● *adv* (by express post) por correo urgente. ● *n* (train) rápido *m*, expreso *m*. **~ion** *n* expresión *f*. **~ive** *a* expresivo. **~ly** *adv* expresadamente. **~way** *n* (Amer) autopista *f*

expulsion /ɪk'spʌlʃn/ *n* expulsión *f*

exquisite /'ekskwɪzɪt/ *a* exquisito

exten|d /ɪk'stend/ *vt* extender; (prolong) prolongar; ampliar <*house*>. ● *vi* extenderse. **~sion** /-ʃn/ *n* extensión *f*; (of road, time) prolongación *f*; (building) anejo *m*. **~sive** /-sɪv/ *a* extenso. **~sively** *adv* extensamente. **~t** *n* extensión *f*; (fig) alcance. **to a certain ~t** hasta cierto punto

exterior /ɪk'stɪərɪə(r)/ *a* & *n* exterior (*m*)

exterminat|e /ɪk'stɜ:mɪneɪt/ *vt* exterminar. **~ion** /-'neɪʃn/ *n* exterminio *m*

external /ɪk'stɜ:nl/ *a* externo

extinct /ɪk'stɪŋkt/ *a* extinto. **~ion** /-ʃn/ *n* extinción *f*

extinguish /ɪk'stɪŋgwɪʃ/ *vt* extinguir. **~er** *n* extintor *m*, extinguidor *m* (LAm)

extol /ɪk'stəʊl/ *vt* (*pt* **extolled**) alabar

extort /ɪk'stɔ:t/ *vt* sacar por la fuerza. **~ion** /-ʃn/ *n* exacción *f*. **~ionate** /-ənət/ *a* exorbitante

extra /'ekstrə/ *a* de más. ● *adv* extraordinariamente. ● *n* suplemento *m*; (Cinema) extra *m* & *f*

extract /'ekstrækt/ *n* extracto *m*. ● /ɪk'strækt/ *vt* extraer. **~ion** /ɪk'strækʃn/ *n* extracción *f*

extradit|e /'ekstrədaɪt/ *vt* extraditar. **~ion** /-'dɪʃn/ *n* extradición *f*

~ordinary /ɪk'strɔ:dnrɪ/ *a* extraordinario. **~-sensory** /ekstrə'sensərɪ/ *a* extrasensorial

extravagan|ce /ɪk'strævəgəns/ *n* prodigalidad *f*; (of gestures, dress) extravagancia *f*. **~t** *a* pródigo; <*behaviour*> extravagante. **~za** *n* gran espectáculo *m*

extrem|e /ɪk'stri:m/ *a* & *n* extremo (*m*). **~ely** *adv* extremadamente. **~ist** *n* extremista *m* & *f*

extricate /'ekstrɪkeɪt/ *vt* desenredar, librar

extrovert /'ekstrəvɜ:t/ *n* extrovertido *m*

exuberan|ce /ɪg'zju:bərəns/ *n* exuberancia *f*. **~t** *a* exuberante

exude /ɪg'zju:d/ *vt* rezumar

exult /ɪg'zʌlt/ *vi* exultar. **~ation** /egzʌl'teɪʃn/ *n* exultación *f*

eye /aɪ/ *n* ojo *m*. **keep an ~ on** no perder de vista. **see ~ to ~ with**

s.o. estar de acuerdo con uno. ● *vt* (*pt* **eyed**, *pres p* **eyeing**) mirar. **~ball** *n* globo *m* ocular. **~brow** *n* ceja *f*. **~drops** *npl* colirio *m*. **~lash** *n* pestaña *f*. **~lid** *n* párpado *m*. **~-opener** *n* [I] revelación *f*. **~-shadow** *n* sombra *f* de ojos. **~sight** *n* vista *f*. **~sore** *n* (fig, [I]) monstruosidad *f*, adefesio *m*. **~witness** *n* testigo *m* ocular

Ff

fable /'feɪbl/ *n* fábula *f*

fabric /'fæbrɪk/ *n* tejido *m*, tela *f*

fabricate /'fæbrɪkeɪt/ *vt* inventar. **~ation** /-'keɪʃn/ *n* invención *f*

fabulous /'fæbjʊləs/ *a* fabuloso

facade /fə'sɑːd/ *n* fachada *f*

face /feɪs/ *n* cara *f*, rostro *m*; (of watch) esfera *f*, carátula *f* (Mex); (aspect) aspecto *m*. **~ down(wards)** boca abajo. **~ up(wards)** boca arriba. **in the ~ of** frente a. **lose ~** quedar mal. **pull ~s** hacer muecas. ● *vt* mirar hacia; <*house*> dar a; (confront) enfrentarse con. ● *vi* volverse. □ **~ up to** *vt* enfrentarse con. **~ flannel** *n* paño *m* (para lavarse la cara). **~less** *a* anónimo. **~ lift** *n* cirugía *f* estética en la cara

facetious /fə'siːʃəs/ *a* burlón

facial /'feɪʃl/ *a* facial

facile /'fæsaɪl/ *a* superficial, simplista

facilitate /fə'sɪlɪteɪt/ *vt* facilitar

facility /fə'sɪlɪtɪ/ *n* facilidad *f*

fact /fækt/ *n* hecho *m*. **as a matter of ~, in ~** en realidad, de hecho

faction /'fækʃn/ *n* facción *f*

factor /'fæktə(r)/ *n* factor *m*

factory /'fæktərɪ/ *n* fábrica *f*

factual /'fæktʃʊəl/ *a* basado en hechos, factual

faculty /'fækəltɪ/ *n* facultad *f*

fad /fæd/ *n* manía *f*, capricho *m*

fade /feɪd/ *vi* <*colour*> desteñirse; <*flowers*> marchitarse; <*light*> apagarse; <*memory, sound*> desvanecerse

fag /fæg/ *n* ([I], chore) faena *f*; ([X], cigarette) cigarillo *m*, pitillo *m*

Fahrenheit /'færənhaɪt/ *a* Fahrenheit

fail /feɪl/ *vi* fracasar; <*brakes*> fallar; (in an exam) suspender, ser reprobado (LAm). **he ~ed to arrive** no llegó. ● *vt* suspender, ser reprobado en (LAm) <*exam*>; suspender, reprobar (LAm) <*candidate*>. ● *n*. **without ~** sin falta. **~ing** *n* defecto *m*. ● *prep*. **~ing that, ...** si eso no resulta.... **~ure** /'feɪljə(r)/ *n* fracaso *m*

faint /feɪnt/ *a* (**-er**, **-est**) (weak) débil; (indistinct) indistinto. **feel ~** estar mareado. **the ~est idea** la más remota idea. ● *vi* desmayarse. ● *n* desmayo *m*. **~-hearted** /-'hɑːtɪd/ *a* pusilánime, cobarde. **~ly** *adv* (weakly) débilmente; (indistinctly) indistintamente; (slightly) ligeramente

fair /feə(r)/ *a* (**-er**, **-est**) (just) justo; <*weather*> bueno; <*amount*> razonable; <*hair*> rubio, güero (Mex [I]); <*skin*> blanco. ● *adv* limpio. ● *n* feria *f*. **~-haired** /-'heəd/ *a* rubio, güero (Mex [I]). **~ly** *adv* (justly) justamente; (rather) bastante. **~ness** *n* justicia *f*. **in all ~ness** sinceramente. **~ play** *n* juego *m* limpio

fairy /ˈfeərɪ/ *n* hada *f*. ~ **story**, ~ **tale** *n* cuento *m* de hadas

faith /feɪθ/ *n* (trust) confianza *f*; (Relig) fe *f*. ~**ful** *a* fiel. ~**fully** *adv* fielmente. **yours** ~**fully** (in letters) (le saluda) atentamente

fake /feɪk/ *n* falsificación *f*; (person) farsante *m*. ● *a* falso. ● *vt* falsificar

falcon /ˈfɔːlkən/ *n* halcón *m*

Falkland Islands /ˈfɔːlklənd/ *npl*. **the Falkland Islands, the Falklands** las (Islas) Malvinas

fall /fɔːl/ *vi* (*pt* **fell**, *pp* **fallen**) caer; (decrease) bajar. ● *n* caída *f*; (Amer, autumn) otoño *m*; (in price) bajada *f*. □ ~ **apart** *vi* deshacerse. □ ~ **back on** *vt* recurrir a. □ ~ **down** *vi* (fall) caerse. □ ~ **for** *vt* [T] enamorarse de *<person>*; dejarse engañar por *<trick>*. □ ~ **in** *vi* (Mil) formar filas. □ ~ **off** *vi* caerse; (diminish) disminuir. □ ~ **out** *vi* (quarrel) reñir (**with** con); (drop out) caerse; (Mil) romper filas. □ ~ **over** *vi* caerse. *vt* tropezar con. □ ~ **through** *vi* no salir adelante

fallacy /ˈfæləsɪ/ *n* falacia *f*

fallible /ˈfælɪbl/ *a* falible

fallout /ˈfɔːlaʊt/ *n* lluvia *f* radiactiva. ~ **shelter** *n* refugio *m* antinuclear

fallow /ˈfæləʊ/ *a* en barbecho

false /fɔːls/ *a* falso. ~ **alarm** *n* falsa alarma. ~**hood** *n* mentira *f*. ~**ly** *adv* falsamente. ~ **teeth** *npl* dentadura *f* postiza

falsify /ˈfɔːlsɪfaɪ/ *vt* falsificar

falter /ˈfɔːltə(r)/ *vi* vacilar

fame /feɪm/ *n* fama *f*. ~**d** *a* famoso

familiar /fəˈmɪlɪə(r)/ *a* familiar. **the name sounds** ~ el nombre me suena. **be** ~ **with** conocer. ~**ity** /-ˈærətɪ/ *n* familiaridad *f*. ~**ize** *vt* familiarizar

family /ˈfæməlɪ/ *n* familia *f*. ● *a* de (la) familia, familiar. ~ **tree** *n* árbol *m* genealógico

famine /ˈfæmɪn/ *n* hambre *f*, hambruna *f*

famished /ˈfæmɪʃt/ *a* hambriento

famous /ˈfeɪməs/ *a* famoso

fan /fæn/ *n* abanico *m*; (Mec) ventilador *m*; (enthusiast) aficionado *m*; (of group, actor) fan *m* & *f*; (of sport, team) hincha *m* & *f*. ● *vt* (*pt* **fanned**) abanicar; avivar *<interest>*. □ ~ **out** *vi* desparramarse en forma de abanico

fanatic /fəˈnætɪk/ *n* fanático *m*. ~**al** *a* fanático. ~**ism** /-sɪzəm/ *n* fanatismo *m*

fan belt *n* correa *f* de ventilador, banda *f* del ventilador (Mex)

fanciful /ˈfænsɪfl/ *a* (imaginative) imaginativo; (impractical) extravagante

fancy /ˈfænsɪ/ *n* imaginación *f*; (liking) gusto *m*. **take a** ~ **to** tomar cariño a *<person>*; aficionarse a *<thing>*. ● *a* de lujo. ● *vt* (imagine) imaginar; (believe) creer; ([T], want) apetecer a. ~ **dress** *n* disfraz *m*

fanfare /ˈfænfeə(r)/ *n* fanfarria *f*

fang /fæŋ/ *n* (of animal) colmillo *m*; (of snake) diente *m*

fantasize /ˈfæntəsaɪz/ *vi* fantasear

fantastic /fænˈtæstɪk/ *a* fantástico

fantasy /ˈfæntəsɪ/ *n* fantasía *f*

far /fɑː(r)/ *adv* lejos; (much) mucho. **as** ~ **as** hasta. **as** ~ **as I know** que yo sepa. **by** ~ con mucho. ● *a* (**further**, **furthest** *or* **farther**, **farthest**) lejano. ~ **away** lejano

farc|e /fɑːs/ *n* farsa *f*. ~**ical** *a* ridículo

fare /feə(r)/ *n* (on bus) precio *m* del billete, precio *m* del boleto (LAm); (on train, plane) precio *m* del billete, precio *m* del pasaje (LAm); (food) comida *f*

Far East /fɑ:r'i:st/ *n* Extremo *or* Lejano Oriente *m*

farewell /feə'wel/ *int & n* adiós (*m*)

far-fetched /fɑ:'fetʃt/ *a* improbable

farm /fɑ:m/ *n* granja *f*. ● *vt* cultivar. □ ~ **out** *vt* encargar (*a terceros*). ● *vi* ser agricultor. **~er** *n* agricultor *m*, granjero *m*. **~house** *n* granja *f*. **~ing** *n* agricultura *f*. **~yard** *n* corral *m*

far: **~-off** *a* lejano. **~-reaching** /fɑ:'ri:tʃɪŋ/ *a* trascendental. **~-sighted** /fɑ:'saɪtɪd/ *a* con visión del futuro; (Med, Amer) hipermétrope

farther, farthest /'fɑ:ðə(r), 'fɑ:ðəst/ ⇒FAR

fascinat|e /'fæsɪneɪt/ *vt* fascinar. **~ed** *a* fascinado. **~ing** *a* fascinante. **~ion** /-'neɪʃn/ *n* fascinación *f*

fascis|m /'fæʃɪzəm/ *n* fascismo *m*. **~t** *a & n* fascista (*m & f*)

fashion /'fæʃn/ *n* (manner) manera *f*; (vogue) moda *f*. **be in/out of ~** estar de moda/estar pasado de moda. **~able** *a* de moda

fast /fɑ:st/ *a* (**-er**, **-est**) rápido; <*clock*> adelantado; (secure) fijo; <*colours*> sólido. ● *adv* rápidamente; (securely) firmemente. **~ asleep** profundamente dormido. ● *vi* ayunar. ● *n* ayuno *m*

fasten /'fɑ:sn/ *vt* sujetar; cerrar <*case*>; abrochar <*belt etc*>. ● *vi* <*case*> cerrar; <*belt etc*> cerrarse. **~er**, **~ing** *n* (on box, window) cierre *m*; (on door) cerrojo *m*

fat /fæt/ *n* grasa *f*. ● *a* (**fatter**, **fattest**) gordo; <*meat*> que tiene mucha grasa; (thick) grueso. **get ~** engordar

fatal /'feɪtl/ *a* mortal; (fateful) fatídico. **~ity** /fə'tæləti/ muerto *m*. **~ly** *adv* mortalmente

fate /feɪt/ *n* destino *m*; (one's lot) suerte *f*. **~d** *a* predestinado. **~ful** *a* fatídico

father /'fɑ:ðə(r)/ *n* padre *m*. **~hood** *m* paternidad *f*. **~-in-law** *m* (*pl* **~s-in-law**) *m* suegro *m*. **~ly** *a* paternal

fathom /'fæðəm/ *n* braza *f*. ● *vt*. ~ (out) comprender

fatigue /fə'ti:g/ *n* fatiga *f*. ● *vt* fatigar

fat|ten *vt*. **~ten** (up) cebar <*animal*>. **~tening** *a* que engorda. **~ty** *a* graso, grasoso (LAm). ● *n* 🄸 gordinflón *m*

fatuous /'fætjʊəs/ *a* fatuo

faucet /'fɔ:sɪt/ *n* (Amer) grifo *m*, llave *f* (LAm)

fault /fɔ:lt/ *n* defecto *m*; (blame) culpa *f*; (tennis) falta *f*; (Geol) falla *f*. **at ~** culpable. ● *vt* encontrarle defectos a. **~less** *a* impecable. **~y** *a* defectuoso

favour /'feɪvə(r)/ *n* favor *m*. ● *vt* favorecer; (support) estar a favor de; (prefer) preferir. **~able** *a* favorable. **~ably** *adv* favorablemente. **~ite** *a & n* preferido (*m*). **~itism** *n* favoritismo *m*

fawn /fɔ:n/ *n* cervato *m*. ● *a* beige, beis. ● *vi*. ~ **on** adular

fax /fæks/ *n* fax *m*. ● *vt* faxear

fear /fɪə(r)/ *n* miedo *m*. ● *vt* temer. **~ful** *a* (frightening) espantoso; (frightened) temeroso. **~less** *a* intrépido. **~some** /-səm/ *a* espantoso

feasib|ility /fi:zə'bɪlətɪ/ *n* viabilidad *f*. **~le** /'fi:zəbl/ *a* factible; (likely) posible

feast /fi:st/ *n* (Relig) fiesta *f*; (meal) banquete *m*

feat /fi:t/ *n* hazaña *f*

feather /'feðə(r)/ *n* pluma *f*. **~weight** *n* peso *m* pluma

feature /'fi:tʃə(r)/ *n* (on face) rasgo *m*; (characteristic) característica *f*; (in newspaper) artículo *m*; **~ (film)** película *f* principal, largometraje *m*. ● *vt* presentar; (give prominence to) destacar

February /'februərɪ/ *n* febrero *m*

fed /fed/ ⇒FEED

feder|al /'fedərəl/ *a* federal. **~ation** /fedə'reɪʃn/ *n* federación *f*

fed up *a* [I] harto (**with** de)

fee /fi:/ *n* (professional) honorarios *mpl*; (enrolment) derechos *mpl*; (club) cuota *f*

feeble /'fi:bl/ *a* (**-er**, **-est**) débil

feed /fi:d/ *vt* (*pt* **fed**) dar de comer a; (supply) alimentar. ● *vi* comer. ● *n* (for animals) pienso *m*; (for babies) comida *f*. **~back** *n* reacción *f*

feel /fi:l/ *vt* (*pt* **felt**) sentir; (touch) tocar; (think) considerar. **do you ~ it's a good idea?** ¿te parece buena idea? **~ as if** tener la impresión de que. **~ hot/hungry** tener calor/hambre. **~ like** ([I], want) tener ganas de. ● *n* sensación *f*. **get the ~ of sth** acostumbrarse a algo. **~er** *n* (of insect) antena *f*. **~ing** *n* sentimiento *m*; (physical) sensación *f*

feet /fi:t/ ⇒FOOT

feign /feɪn/ *vt* fingir

feint /feɪnt/ *n* finta *f*

fell /fel/ ⇒FALL. ● *vt* derribar; talar <*tree*>

fellow /'feləʊ/ *n* [I] tipo *m*; (comrade) compañero *m*; (of society) socio *m*. **~ countryman** *n* compatriota *m*. **~ passenger/traveller** *n* compañero *m* de viaje

felony /'felənɪ/ *n* delito *m* grave

felt /felt/ *n* ⇒FEEL. ● *n* fieltro *m*

female /'fi:meɪl/ *a* hembra; <*voice, sex etc*> femenino. ● *n* mujer *f*; (animal) hembra *f*

femini|ne /'femənɪn/ *a* & *n* femenino (*m*). **~nity** /-'nɪnətɪ/ *n* feminidad *f*. **~st** *a* & *n* feminista *m* & *f*

fenc|e /fens/ *n* cerca *f*, cerco *m* (LAm). ● *vt*. **~e (in)** encerrar, cercar. ● *vi* (Sport) practicar la esgrima. **~er** *n* esgrimidor *m*. **~ing** *n* (Sport) esgrima *f*

fend /fend/ *vi*. **~ for o.s.** valerse por sí mismo. □ **~ off** *vt* defenderse de

fender /'fendə(r)/ *n* rejilla *f*; (Amer, Auto) guardabarros *m*, salpicadera *f* (Mex)

ferment /fə'ment/ *vt/i* fermentar. **~ation** /-'teɪʃn/ *n* fermentación *f*

fern /fɜ:n/ *n* helecho *m*

feroci|ous /fə'rəʊʃəs/ *a* feroz. **~ty** /fə'rɒsətɪ/ *n* ferocidad *f*

ferret /'ferɪt/ *n* hurón *m*. ● *vi* (*pt* **ferreted**) **~ about** husmear. ● *vt*. **~ out** descubrir

ferry /'ferɪ/ *n* ferry *m*. ● *vt* transportar

fertil|e /'fɜ:taɪl/ *a* fértil. **~ity** /-'tɪlətɪ/ *n* fertilidad *f*. **~ize** /'fɜ:təlaɪz/ *vt* fecundar, abonar <*soil*>. **~izer** *n* fertilizante *m*

ferv|ent /'fɜ:vənt/ *a* ferviente. **~our** /-və(r)/ *n* fervor *m*

fester /'festə(r)/ *vi* enconarse

festival /'festəvl/ *n* fiesta *f*; (of arts) festival *m*

festiv|e /'festɪv/ *a* festivo. **the ~e season** *n* las Navidades. **~ity** /fe'stɪvətɪ/ *n* festividad *f*

fetch /fetʃ/ *vt* (go for) ir a buscar; (bring) traer; (be sold for) venderse en. **~ing** *a* atractivo

fête /feɪt/ *n* fiesta *f*. ● *vt* festejar

fetish /'fetɪʃ/ *n* fetiche *m*

fetter /'fetə(r)/ *vt* encadenar

feud /fju:d/ *n* contienda *f*

feudal /'fju:dl/ *a* feudal. **~ism** *n* feudalismo m

fever /'fi:və(r)/ *n* fiebre *f*. **~ish** *a* febril

few /fju:/ *a* pocos. **a ~ houses** algunas casas. ● *n* pocos *mpl*. **a ~** unos (pocos). **a good ~, quite a ~** [I] muchos. **~er** *a* & *n* menos. **~est** *a* el menor número de

fiancé /fɪ'ɒnseɪ/ *n* novio *m*. **~e** /fɪ'ɒnseɪ/ *n* novia *f*

fiasco /fɪ'æskəʊ/ *n* (*pl* **-os**) fiasco *m*

fib /fɪb/ *n* [I] mentirilla *f*. ● *vi* [I] mentir, decir mentirillas

fibre /'faɪbə(r)/ *n* fibra *f*. **~glass** *n* fibra *f* de vidrio

fickle /'fɪkl/ *a* inconstante

ficti|on /'fɪkʃn/ *n* ficción *f*. (**works of**) **~on** novelas *fpl*. **~onal** *a* novelesco. **~tious** /fɪk'tɪʃəs/ *a* ficticio

fiddle /'fɪdl/ *n* [I] violín *m*; ([I], swindle) trampa *f*. ● *vt* [I] falsificar. **~ with** juguetear con

fidget /'fɪdʒɪt/ *vi* (*pt* **fidgeted**) moverse, ponerse nervioso. **~ with** juguetear con. ● *n* persona *f* inquieta. **~y** *a* inquieto

field /fi:ld/ *n* campo *m*. **~ day** *n*. **have a ~ day** hacer su agosto. **~ glasses** *npl* gemelos *mpl*. **F~ Marshal** *n* mariscal *m* de campo. **~ trip** *n* viaje *m* de estudio. **~work** *n* investigaciones *fpl* en el terreno

fiend /fi:nd/ *n* demonio *m*. **~ish** *a* diabólico

fierce /fɪəs/ *a* (**-er**, **-est**) feroz; *<attack>* violento. **~ly** *adv* *<growl>* con ferocidad; *<fight>* con fiereza

fiery /'faɪərɪ/ *a* (**-ier**, **-iest**) ardiente; *<temper>* exaltado

fifteen /fɪf'ti:n/ *a* & *n* quince (*m*). **~th** *a* decimoquinto. ● *n* quinceavo *m*

fifth /fɪfθ/ *a* & *n* quinto (*m*)

fift|ieth /'fɪftɪəθ/ *a* quincuagésimo. ● *n* cincuentavo *m*. **~y** *a* & *n* cincuenta (*m*). **~y-~y** *adv* mitad y mitad, a medias. ● *a*. **a ~y-~y chance** una posibilidad de cada dos

fig /fɪg/ *n* higo *m*

fight /faɪt/ *vi* (*pt* **fought**) luchar; (quarrel) disputar. ● *vt* luchar contra. ● *n* pelea *m*; (struggle) lucha *f*; (quarrel) disputa *f*; (Mil) combate *m*. □ **~ back** *vi* defenderse. □ **~ off** *vt* rechazar *<attack>*; luchar contra *<illness>*. **~er** *n* luchador *m*; (aircraft) avión *m* de caza. **~ing** *n* luchas *fpl*

figment /'fɪgmənt/ *n*. **~ of the imagination** producto *m* de la imaginación

figurative /'fɪgjʊrətɪv/ *a* figurado

figure /'fɪgə(r)/ *n* (number) cifra *f*; (person) figura *f*; (shape) forma *f*; (of woman) tipo *m*. ● *vt* imaginar; (Amer [I], reckon) calcular. ● *vi* figurar. **that ~s** [I] es lógico. □ **~ out** *vt* entender. **~head** *n* testaferro *m*, mascarón *m* de proa. **~ of speech** *n* figura *f* retórica

filch /fɪltʃ/ *vt* [I] hurtar

file /faɪl/ *n* (tool, for nails) lima *f*; (folder) carpeta *f*; (set of papers) expediente *m*; (Comp) archivo *m*; (row) fila *f*. **in single ~** en fila india. ● *vt* archivar <*papers*>; limar <*metal, nails*>. ● **~ in** *vi* entrar en fila. **~ past** *vt* desfilar ante

filing cabinet /ˈfaɪlɪŋ/ *n* archivador *m*

fill /fɪl/ *vt* llenar. ● *vi* llenarse. ● *n*. **eat one's ~** hartarse de comer. **have had one's ~ of** estar harto de □ **~ in** *vt* rellenar <*form, hole*>. □ **~ out** *vt* rellenar <*form*>. *vi* (get fatter) engordar. □ **~ up** *vt* llenar. *vi* llenarse

fillet /ˈfɪlɪt/ *n* filete *m*. ● *vt* (*pt* **filleted**) cortar en filetes <*meat*>; quitar la espina a <*fish*>

filling /ˈfɪlɪŋ/ *n* (in tooth) empaste *m*, tapadura *f* (Mex). **~ station** *n* gasolinera *f*

film /fɪlm/ *n* película *f*. ● *vt* filmar. **~ star** *n* estrella *f* de cine

filter /ˈfɪltə(r)/ *n* filtro *m*. ● *vt* filtrar. ● *vi* filtrarse. **~-tipped** *a* con filtro

filth /fɪlθ/ *n* mugre *f*. **~y** *a* mugriento

fin /fɪn/ *n* aleta *f*

final /ˈfaɪnl/ *a* último; (conclusive) decisivo. ● *n* (Sport) final *f*. **~s** *npl* (Schol) exámenes *mpl* de fin de curso

finale /fɪˈnɑːlɪ/ *n* final *m*

final|ist *n* finalista *m & f*. **~ize** *vt* ultimar. **~ly** *adv* (lastly) finalmente, por fin

financ|e /ˈfaɪnæns/ *n* finanzas *fpl*. ● *vt* financiar. **~ial** /faɪˈnænʃl/ *a* financiero; <*difficulties*> económico

find /faɪnd/ *vt* (*pt* **found**) encontrar. **~ out** *vt* descubrir. ● *vi* (learn) enterarse. **~ings** *npl* conclusiones *fpl*

fine /faɪn/ *a* (**-er**, **-est**) (delicate) fino; (excellent) excelente. ● *adv* muy bien. ● *n* multa *f*. ● *vt* multar. **~ arts** *npl* bellas artes *fpl*. **~ly** *adv* (cut) en trozos pequeños; <*adjust*> con precisión

finger /ˈfɪŋgə(r)/ *n* dedo *m*. ● *vt* tocar. **~nail** *n* uña *f*. **~print** *n* huella *f* digital. **~tip** *n* punta *f* del dedo

finish /ˈfɪnɪʃ/ *vt/i* terminar, acabar. **~ doing** terminar de hacer. ● *n* fin *m*; (of race) llegada *f*

finite /ˈfaɪnaɪt/ *a* finito

Fin|land /ˈfɪnlənd/ *n* Finlandia *f*. **~n** *n* finlandés *m*. **~nish** *a & n* finlandés (*m*)

fiord /fjɔːd/ *n* fiordo *m*

fir /fɜː(r)/ *n* abeto *m*

fire /faɪə(r)/ *n* fuego *m*; (conflagration) incendio *m*. ● *vt* disparar <*gun*>; (dismiss) despedir; avivar <*imagination*>. ● *vi* disparar. **~ alarm** *n* alarma *f* contra incendios. **~arm** *n* arma *f* de fuego. **~ brigade**, **~ department** (Amer) *n* cuerpo *m* de bomberos. **~ engine** *n* coche *m* de bomberos, carro *m* de bomberos (Mex). **~-escape** *n* escalera *f* de incendios. **~ extinguisher** *n* extintor *m*, extinguidor *m* (LAm). **~fighter** *n* bombero *m*. **~man** /-mən/ *n* bombero *m*. **~place** *n* chimenea *f*. **~side** *n* hogar *m*. **~ truck** *n* (Amer) ⇨**~** ENGINE. **~wood** *n* leña *f*. **~work** *n* fuego *m* artificial

firm /fɜːm/ *n* empresa *f*. ● *a* (**-er**, **-est**) firme. **~ly** *adv* firmemente

first /fɜːst/ *a* primero, (before masculine singular noun) primer. **at ~ hand** directamente. ● *n* primero *m*. ● *adv* primero; (first time) por primera vez. **~ of all** primero. **~ aid** *n* primeros auxilios *mpl*. ~ **aid kit** *n* botiquín *m*. ~ **class** /-'klɑːs/ *adv* *<travel>* en primera clase. ~**-class** *a* de primera clase. ~ **floor** *n* primer piso *m*; (Amer) planta *f* baja. **F~ Lady** *n* (Amer) Primera Dama *f*. ~**ly** *adv* en primer lugar. ~ **name** *n* nombre *m* de pila. ~**-rate** /-'reɪt/ *a* excelente

fish /fɪʃ/ *n* (*pl invar or* **-es**) pez *m*; (as food) pescado *m*. ● *vi* pescar. **go ~ing** ir de pesca. □ ~ **out** *vt* sacar. ~**erman** *n* pescador *m*. ~**ing** *n* pesca *f*. ~**ing pole** (Amer), ~**ing rod** *n* caña *f* de pesca. ~**monger** *n* pescadero *m*. ~ **shop** *n* pescadería *f*. ~**y** *a* *<smell>* a pescado; (🅸, questionable) sospechoso

fission /'fɪʃn/ *n* fisión *f*

fist /fɪst/ *n* puño *m*

fit /fɪt/ *a* (**fitter**, **fittest**) (healthy) en forma; (good enough) adecuado; (able) capaz. ● *n* (attack) ataque; (of clothes) corte *m*. ● *vt* (*pt* **fitted**) (adapt) adaptar; (be the right size for) quedarle bien a; (install) colocar. ● *vi* encajar; (in certain space) caber; *<clothes>* quedarle bien a uno. □ ~ **in** *vi* caber. ~**ful** *a* irregular. ~**ness** *n* salud *f*; (Sport) (buena) forma *f* física. ~**ting** *a* apropiado. ● *n* (of clothes) prueba *f*. ~**ting room** *n* probador *m*

five /faɪv/ *a & n* cinco (*m*)

fix /fɪks/ *vt* fijar; (mend, deal with) arreglar. ● *n*. **in a ~** en un aprieto. ~**ed** *a* fijo. ~**ture** /'fɪkstʃə(r)/ *n* (Sport) partido *m*

fizz /fɪz/ *vi* burbujear. ● *n* efervescencia *f*. ~**le** /fɪzl/ *vi*. ~**le out** fracasar. ~**y** *a* efervescente; *<water>* con gas

fjord /fjɔːd/ *n* fiordo *m*

flabbergasted /'flæbəgɑːstɪd/ *a* estupefacto

flabby /'flæbɪ/ *a* flojo

flag /flæg/ *n* bandera *f*. ● *vi* (*pt* **flagged**) (weaken) flaquear; *<conversation>* languidecer

flagon /'flægən/ *n* botella *f* grande, jarro *m*

flagpole /'flægpəʊl/ *n* asta *f* de bandera

flagrant /'fleɪgrənt/ *a* flagrante

flair /fleə(r)/ *n* don *m* (**for** de)

flak|e /fleɪk/ *n* copo *m*; (of paint, metal) escama *f*. ● *vi* desconcharse. ~**y** *a* escamoso

flamboyant /flæm'bɔɪənt/ *a* *<clothes>* vistoso; *<manner>* extravagante

flame /fleɪm/ *n* llama *f*. **go up in ~s** incendiarse

flamingo /flə'mɪŋgəʊ/ *n* (*pl* **-o(e)s**) flamenco *m*

flammable /'flæməbl/ *a* inflamable

flan /flæn/ *n* tartaleta *f*

flank /flæŋk/ *n* (of animal) ijada *f*; (of person) costado *m*; (Mil, Sport) flanco *m*

flannel /'flænl/ *n* franela *f*; (for face) paño *m* (para lavarse la cara).

flap /flæp/ *vi* (*pt* **flapped**) ondear; *<wings>* aletear. ● *vt* batir *<wings>*; agitar *<arms>*. ● *n* (cover) tapa *f*; (of pocket) cartera *f*; (of table) ala *f*. **get into a ~** 🅸 ponerse nervioso

flare /fleə(r)/ ● *n* llamarada *f*; (Mil) bengala *f*; (in skirt) vuelo *m*. □ ~ **up** *vi* llamear; *<fighting>* estallar; *<person>* encolerizarse

flash /flæʃ/ ● *vi* destellar. ● *vt* (aim torch) dirigir; (flaunt) hacer ostentación de. ~ **past** pasar como un rayo. ● *n* destello *m*; (Photo) flash *m*. ~**back** *n* escena *f* retrospectiva.

~**light** *n* (Amer, torch) linterna *f*. ~**y** *a* ostentoso

flask /flɑ:sk/ *n* frasco *m*; (vacuum flask) termo *m*

flat /flæt/ *a* (**flatter, flattest**) plano; <*tyre*> desinflado; <*refusal*> categórico; <*fare, rate*> fijo; (Mus) bemol. ● *adv* (Mus) demasiado bajo. ~ **out** (at top speed) a toda velocidad. ● *n* (rooms) apartamento *m*, piso *m*; (Auto, esp Amer) [I] pinchazo *m*; (Mus) bemol *m*. ~**ly** *adv* categóricamente. ~**ten** *vt* allanar, aplanar

flatter /flætə(r)/ *vt* adular. ~**ing** *a* <*person*> lisonjero; <*clothes*> favorecedor. ~**y** *n* adulación *f*

flaunt /flɔ:nt/ *vt* hacer ostentación de

flavour /'fleɪvə(r)/ *n* sabor *m*. ● *vt* sazonar. ~**ing** *n* condimento *m*

flaw /flɔ:/ *n* defecto *m*. ~**less** *a* perfecto

flea /fli:/ *n* pulga *f*

fleck /flek/ *n* mancha *f*, pinta *f*

fled /fled/ ⇒FLEE

flee /fli:/ *vi* (*pt* **fled**) huir. ● *vt* huir de

fleece /fli:s/ *n* vellón *m*. ● *vt* [I] desplumar

fleet /fli:t/ *n* flota *f*; (of cars) parque *m* móvil

fleeting /'fli:tɪŋ/ *a* fugaz

Flemish /'flemɪʃ/ *a* & *n* flamenco (*m*)

flesh /fleʃ/ *n* carne *f*. **in the** ~ en persona

flew /flu:/ ⇒FLY

flex /fleks/ *vt* doblar; flexionar <*muscle*>. ● *n* (Elec) cable *m*

flexib|ility /fleksə'bɪlətɪ/ *n* flexibilidad *f*. ~**le** /'fleksəbl/ *a* flexible

flexitime /'fleksɪtaɪm/, (Amer) **flextime** /'flekstaɪm/ *n* horario *m* flexible

flick /flɪk/ *n* golpecito *m*. ● *vt* dar un golpecito a. □ ~ **through** *vt* hojear

flicker /'flɪkə(r)/ *vi* parpadear. ● *n* parpadeo *m*; (of hope) resquicio *m*

flies /flaɪz/ *npl* ([I], on trousers) bragueta *f*

flight /flaɪt/ *n* vuelo *m*; (fleeing) huida *f*, fuga *f*. ~ **of stairs** tramo *m* de escalera *f*. **take (to)** ~ darse a la fuga. ~ **attendant** *n* (male) sobrecargo *m*, aeromozo *m* (LAm); (female) azafata *f*, aeromoza *f* (LAm). ~**-deck** *n* cubierta *f* de vuelo

flimsy /'flɪmzɪ/ *a* (**-ier, -iest**) flojo, débil, poco sólido

flinch /flɪntʃ/ *vi* retroceder (**from** ante)

fling /flɪŋ/ *vt* (*pt* **flung**) arrojar. ● *n* (love affair) aventura *f*; (wild time) juerga *f*

flint /flɪnt/ *n* pedernal *m*; (for lighter) piedra *f*

flip /flɪp/ *vt* (*pt* **flipped**) dar un golpecito a. ● *n* golpecito *m*. □ ~ **through** *vt* hojear.

flippant /'flɪpənt/ *a* poco serio

flipper /'flɪpə(r)/ *n* aleta *f*

flirt /flɜ:t/ *vi* coquetear. ● *n* (woman) coqueta *f*; (man) coqueto *m*

flit /flɪt/ *vi* (*pt* **flitted**) revolotear

float /fləʊt/ *vi* flotar. ● *vt* hacer flotar; introducir en Bolsa <*company*>. ● *n* flotador *m*; (cash) caja *f* chica

flock /flɒk/ *n* (of birds) bandada *f*; (of sheep) rebaño *m*. ● *vi* congregarse

flog /flɒg/ *vt* (*pt* **flogged**) (beat) azotar; ([I], sell) vender

flood /flʌd/ *n* inundación *f*; (fig) avalancha *f*. ● *vt* inundar. ● *vi*

<building etc> inundarse; *<river>* desbordar. **~light** *n* foco *m*. ● *vt* (*pt* **~lit**) iluminar (con focos)

floor /flɔː(r)/ *n* suelo *m*; (storey) piso *m*; (for dancing) pista *f*. ● *vt* derribar; (baffle) confundir

flop /flɒp/ *vi* (*pt* **flopped**) dejarse caer pesadamente; (I, fail) fracasar. ● *n* I fracaso *m*. **~py** *a* flojo. ● *n* ⇒~PY DISK. **~py disk** *n* disquete *m*, floppy (disk) *m*

floral /ˈflɔːrəl/ *a* floral

florid /ˈflɒrɪd/ *a* florido

florist /ˈflɒrɪst/ *n* florista *m* & *f*

flounder /ˈflaʊndə(r)/ *vi* (in water) luchar para mantenerse a flote; *<speaker>* quedar sin saber qué decir

flour /flaʊə(r)/ *n* harina *f*

flourish /ˈflʌrɪʃ/ *vi* florecer; *<business>* prosperar. ● *vt* blandir. ● *n* ademán *m* elegante; (in handwriting) rasgo *m*. **~ing** *a* próspero

flout /flaʊt/ *vt* burlarse de

flow /fləʊ/ *vi* fluir; *<blood>* correr; (hang loosely) caer. ● *n* flujo *m*; (stream) corriente *f*; (of traffic, information) circulación *f*. **~ chart** *n* organigrama *m*

flower /ˈflaʊə(r)/ *n* flor *f*. ● *vi* florecer, florear (Mex). **~ bed** *n* macizo *m* de flores. **~y** *a* florido

flown /fləʊn/ ⇒FLY

flu /fluː/ *n* gripe *f*

fluctuat|e /ˈflʌktjʊeɪt/ *vi* fluctuar. **~ion** /-ˈeɪʃn/ *n* fluctuación *f*

flue /fluː/ *n* tiro *m*

fluen|cy /ˈfluːənsɪ/ *n* fluidez *f*. **~t** *a* *<style>* fluido; *<speaker>* elocuente. **be ~t in a language** hablar un idioma con fluidez. **~tly** *adv* con fluidez

fluff /flʌf/ *n* pelusa *f*. **~y** *a* (**-ier**, **-iest**) velloso

fluid /ˈfluːɪd/ *a* & *n* fluido (*m*)

flung /flʌŋ/ ⇒FLING

fluorescent /flʊəˈresnt/ *a* fluorescente

flush /flʌʃ/ *vi* ruborizarse. ● *vt*. **~ the toilet** tirar de la cadena, jalarle a la cadena (LAm). ● *n* (blush) rubor *m*

fluster /ˈflʌstə(r)/ *vt* poner nervioso

flute /fluːt/ *n* flauta *f*

flutter /ˈflʌtə(r)/ *vi* ondear; *<bird>* revolotear. ● *n* (of wings) revoloteo *m*; (fig) agitación *f*

flux /flʌks/ *n* flujo *m*. **be in a state of ~** estar siempre cambiando

fly /flaɪ/ *vi* (*pt* **flew**, *pp* **flown**) volar; *<passenger>* ir en avión; *<flag>* flotar; (rush) correr. ● *vt* pilotar, pilotear (LAm) *<aircraft>*; transportar en avión *<passengers, goods>*; izar *<flag>*. ● *n* mosca *f*; (of trousers) ⇒FLIES. **~ing** *a* volante. **~ing visit** visita *f* relámpago. ● *n* (activity) aviación *f*. **~leaf** *n* guarda *f*. **~over** *n* paso *m* elevado

foal /fəʊl/ *n* potro *m*

foam /fəʊm/ *n* espuma *f*. ● *vi* espumar. **~ rubber** *n* goma *f* espuma, hule *m* espuma (Mex)

fob /fɒb/ *vt* (*pt* **fobbed**). **~ sth off onto s.o.** (palm off) encajarle algo a uno

focal /ˈfəʊkl/ *a* focal

focus /ˈfəʊkəs/ *n* (*pl* **-cuses** *or* **-ci** /-saɪ/) foco *m*; (fig) centro *m*. **in ~** enfocado. **out of ~** desenfocado. ● *vt* (*pt* **focused**) enfocar (fig) concentrar. ● *vi* enfocar; (fig) concentrarse (**on** en)

fodder /ˈfɒdə(r)/ *n* forraje *m*

foe /fəʊ/ *n* enemigo *m*

foetus /ˈfiːtəs/ *n* (*pl* **-tuses**) feto *m*

fog /fɒg/ *n* niebla *f*

fog|gy *a* (**-ier**, **-iest**) nebuloso. **it is ~gy** hay niebla. **~horn** *n* sirena *f* de niebla

foible /ˈfɔɪbl/ *n* punto *m* débil

foil /fɔɪl/ *vt* (thwart) frustrar. ● *n* papel *m* de plata

foist /fɔɪst/ *vt* encajar (**on** a)

fold /fəʊld/ *vt* doblar; cruzar <*arms*>. ● *vi* doblarse; (fail) fracasar. ● *n* pliegue *m*. (for sheep) redil *m*. **~er** *n* carpeta *f*. **~ing** *a* plegable

foliage /ˈfəʊlɪɪdʒ/ *n* follaje *m*

folk /fəʊk/ *n* gente *f*. ● *a* popular. **~lore** /-lɔ:(r)/ *n* folklore *m*. **~ music** *n* música *f* folklórica; (modern) música *f* folk. **~s** *npl* (one's relatives) familia *f*

follow /ˈfɒləʊ/ *vt/i* seguir. □ **~ up** *vt* seguir. **~er** *n* seguidor *m*. **~ing** *n* partidarios *mpl*. ● *a* siguiente. ● *prep* después de

folly /ˈfɒlɪ/ *n* locura *f*

fond /fɒnd/ *a* (**-er**, **-est**) (loving) cariñoso; <*hope*> vivo. **be ~ of s.o.** tener(le) cariño a uno. **be ~ of sth** ser aficionado a algo

fondle /ˈfɒndl/ *vt* acariciar

fondness /ˈfɒndnɪs/ *n* cariño *m*; (for things) afición *f*

font /fɒnt/ *n* pila *f* bautismal

food /fu:d/ *n* comida *f*. **~ processor** *n* robot *m* de cocina

fool /fu:l/ *n* idiota *m* & *f* ● *vt* engañar. □ **~ about** *vi* hacer payasadas. **~hardy** *a* temerario. **~ish** *a* tonto. **~ishly** *adv* tontamente. **~ishness** *n* tontería *f*. **~proof** *a* infalible

foot /fʊt/ *n* (*pl* **feet**) pie *m*; (measure) pie *m* (= 30,48cm); (of animal, furniture) pata *f*. **get under s.o.'s feet** estorbar a uno. **on ~** a pie. **on/to one's feet** de pie. **put one's ~ in it** meter la pata. ● *vt* pagar <*bill*>. **~age** /-ɪdʒ/ *n* (of film) secuencia *f*. **~ball** *n* (ball) balón *m*; (game) fútbol *m*, futbol *m* (Mex); (American **~ball**) fútbol *m* americano, futbol *m* americano (Mex). **~baller** *n* futbolista *m* & *f*. **~bridge** *n* puente *m* para peatones. **~hills** *npl* estribaciones *fpl*. **~hold** *n* punto *m* de apoyo. **~ing** *n* pie *m*. **on an equal ~ing** en igualdad de condiciones. **~lights** *npl* candilejas *fpl*. **~man** /-mən/ *n* lacayo *m*. **~note** *n* nota *f* (al pie de la página). **~path** *n* (in country) senda *f*; (in town) acera *f*, banqueta *f* (Mex). **~print** *n* huella *f*. **~step** *n* paso *m*. **~wear** *n* calzado *m*

---

for /fɔ:(r)/, *unstressed form* /fə(r)/

● *preposition*

····➤ (intended for) para. **it's ~ my mother** es para mi madre. **she works ~ a multinational** trabaja para una multinacional

····➤ (on behalf of) por. **I did it ~ you** lo hice por ti

⇨ See entries **para** and **por** for further information

····➤ (expressing purpose) para. **I use it ~ washing the car** lo uso para limpiar el coche. **what ~?** ¿para qué?. **to go out ~ a meal** salir a comer fuera

····➤ (in favour of) a favor de. **are you ~ or against the idea?** estás a favor o en contra de la idea?

····➤ (indicating cost, in exchage for) por. **I bought it ~ 30 pounds** lo compré por 30 libras. **she left him ~ another man** lo dejó por otro. **thanks ~ everything** gracias por todo. **what's the Spanish ~**

'toad'? ¿cómo se dice 'toad' en español?

····➤ (expressing duration) **he read ~ two hours** leyó durante dos horas. **how long are you going ~?** ¿por cuánto tiempo vas? **I've been waiting ~ three hours** hace tres horas que estoy esperando, llevo tres horas esperando

····➤ (in the direction of) para. **the train ~ Santiago** el tren para Santiago

● *conjunction*

····➤ (because) porque, pues (literary usage). **she left at once, ~ it was getting late** se fue en seguida, porque *or* pues se hacía tarde

forage /ˈfɒrɪdʒ/ *vi* forrajear. ● *n* forraje *m*

forbade /fəˈbæd/ ⇒FORBID

forbearance /fɔːˈbeərəns/ *n* paciencia *f*

forbid /fəˈbɪd/ *vt* (*pt* **forbade**, *pp* **forbidden**) prohibir (**s.o. to do** a uno hacer). **~ s.o. sth** prohibir algo a uno. **~ding** *a* imponente

force /fɔːs/ *n* fuerza *f*. **by ~** a la fuerza. **come into ~** entrar en vigor. **the ~s** las fuerzas *fpl* armadas. ● *vt* forzar; (compel) obligar (**s.o. to do sth** a uno a hacer algo). **~ on** imponer a. **~ open** forzar. **~d** *a* forzado. **~-feed** *vt* alimentar a la fuerza. **~ful** *a* enérgico

forceps /ˈfɔːseps/ *n* fórceps *m*

forcibl|e /ˈfɔːsəbl/ *a* a la fuerza. **~y** *adv* a la fuerza

ford /fɔːd/ *n* vado *m* ● *vt* vadear

fore /fɔː(r)/ *a* anterior. ● *n*. **come to the ~** hacerse evidente

forearm /ˈfɔːrɑːm/ *n* antebrazo *m*

foreboding /fɔːˈbəʊdɪŋ/ *n* presentimiento *m*

forecast /ˈfɔːkɑːst/ *vt* (*pt* **forecast**) pronosticar <*weather*>; prever <*result*>. ● *n* pronóstico *m*. **weather ~** pronóstico *m* del tiempo

forecourt /ˈfɔːkɔːt/ *n* patio *m* delantero

forefinger /ˈfɔːfɪŋgə(r)/ *n* (dedo *m*) índice *m*

forefront /ˈfɔːfrʌnt/ *n* vanguardia *f*. **in the ~** a la vanguardia

forego /fɔːˈgəʊ/ *vt* (*pt* **forewent**, *pp* **foregone**) ⇒FORGO

foregone /ˈfɔːgɒn/ *a*. **~ conclusion** resultado *m* previsto

foreground /ˈfɔːgraʊnd/ *n*. **in the ~** en primer plano

forehead /ˈfɒrɪd/ *n* frente *f*

foreign /ˈfɒrən/ *a* extranjero; <*trade*> exterior; <*travel*> al extranjero, en el extranjero. **~er** *n* extranjero *m*

foreman /ˈfɔːmən/ (*pl* **-men** /-mən/) *n* capataz *m*

foremost /ˈfɔːməʊst/ *a* primero. ● *adv*. **first and ~** ante todo

forerunner /ˈfɔːrʌnə(r)/ *n* precursor *m*

foresee /fɔːˈsiː/ *vt* (*pt* **-saw**, *pp* **-seen**) prever. **~able** *a* previsible

foresight /ˈfɔːsaɪt/ *n* previsión *f*

forest /ˈfɒrɪst/ *n* bosque *m*

forestall /fɔːˈstɔːl/ *vt* (prevent) prevenir; (preempt) anticiparse a

forestry /ˈfɒrɪstrɪ/ *n* silvicultura *f*

foretaste /ˈfɔːteɪst/ *n* anticipo *m*

foretell /fɔːˈtel/ *vt* (*pt* **foretold**) predecir

forever /fəˈrevə(r)/ *adv* para siempre; (always) siempre

forewarn /fɔːˈwɔːn/ *vt* advertir

forewent /fɔːˈwent/ ⇒FOREGO

foreword /'fɔ:wɜ:d/ *n* prefacio *m*

forfeit /'fɔ:fɪt/ *n* (penalty) pena *f*; (in game) prenda *f*. ● *vt* perder; perder el derecho a <*property*>

forgave /fə'geɪv/ ⇒FORGIVE

forge /fɔ:dʒ/ *n* fragua *f*. ● *vt* fraguar; (copy) falsificar. □ ~ **ahead** *vi* adelantarse rápidamente. ~**r** *n* falsificador *m*. ~**ry** *n* falsificación *f*

forget /fə'get/ *vt* (*pt* **forgot**, *pp* **forgotten**) olvidar, olvidarse de. ● *vi* olvidarse (**about** de). **I forgot** se me olvidó. ~**ful** *a* olvidadizo

forgive /fə'gɪv/ *vt* (*pt* **forgave**, *pp* **forgiven**) perdonar. ~ **s.o. for sth** perdonar algo a uno. ~**ness** *n* perdón *m*

forgo /fɔ:'gəʊ/ *vt* (*pt* **forwent**, *pp* **forgone**) renunciar a

fork /fɔ:k/ *n* tenedor *m*; (for digging) horca *f*; (in road) bifurcación *f*. ● *vi* <*road*> bifurcarse. □ ~ **out** *vt* Ⓘ desembolsar, aflojar Ⓘ. ~**lift truck** *n* carretilla *f* elevadora

forlorn /fə'lɔ:n/ *a* <*hope, attempt*> desesperado; <*smile*> triste

form /fɔ:m/ *n* forma *f*; (document) formulario *m*; (Schol) clase *f*. ● *vt* formar. ● *vi* formarse

formal /'fɔ:ml/ *a* formal; <*person*> formalista; <*dress*> de etiqueta. ~**ity** /-'mælətɪ/ *n* formalidad *f*. ~**ly** *adv* oficialmente

format /'fɔ:mæt/ *n* formato *m*. ● *vt* (*pt* **formatted**) (Comp) formatear

formation /fɔ:'meɪʃn/ *n* formación *f*

former /'fɔ:mə(r)/ *a* anterior; (first of two) primero. ● *n*. **the** ~ el primero *m*, la primera *f*, los primeros *mpl*, las primeras *fpl*. ~**ly** *adv* antes

formidable /'fɔ:mɪdəbl/ *a* formidable

formula /'fɔ:mjʊlə/ *n* (*pl* **-ae** /-i:/ or **-as**) fórmula *f*. ~**te** /-leɪt/ *vt* formular

forsake /fə'seɪk/ *vt* (*pt* **forsook**, *pp* **forsaken**) abandonar

fort /fɔ:t/ *n* fuerte *m*

forth /fɔ:θ/ *adv*. **and so** ~ y así sucesivamente. ~**coming** /-'kʌmɪŋ/ *a* próximo, venidero; (sociable) comunicativo. ~**right** *a* directo. ~**with** /-'wɪθ/ *adv* inmediatamente

fortieth /'fɔ:tɪɪθ/ *a* cuadragésimo. ● *n* cuadragésima parte *f*

fortnight /'fɔ:tnaɪt/ *n* quince días *mpl*, quincena *f*. ~**ly** *a* bimensual. ● *adv* cada quince días

fortress /'fɔ:trɪs/ *n* fortaleza *f*

fortunate /'fɔ:tʃənət/ *a* afortunado. **be** ~ tener suerte. ~**ly** *adv* afortunadamente

fortune /'fɔ:tʃu:n/ *n* fortuna *f*. ~**-teller** *n* adivino *m*

forty /'fɔ:tɪ/ *a* & *n* cuarenta (*m*). ~ **winks** un sueñecito

forum /'fɔ:rəm/ *n* foro *m*

forward /'fɔ:wəd/ *a* <*movement*> hacia adelante; (advanced) precoz; (pert) impertinente. ● *n* (Sport) delantero *m*. ● *adv* adelante. **go** ~ avanzar. ● *vt* hacer seguir <*letter*>; enviar <*goods*>. ~**s** *adv* adelante

forwent /fɔ:'went/ ⇒FORGO

fossil /'fɒsl/ *a* & *n* fósil (*m*)

foster /'fɒstə(r)/ *vt* (promote) fomentar; criar <*child*>. ~ **child** *n* hijo *m* adoptivo

fought /fɔ:t/ ⇒FIGHT

foul /faʊl/ *a* (**-er**, **-est**) <*smell*> nauseabundo; <*weather*> pésimo; <*person*> asqueroso; (dirty) sucio; <*language*> obsceno. ● *n* (Sport) falta *f*. ● *vt* contaminar; (entangle) enredar. ~ **play** *n* (Sport) jugada *f* sucia; (crime) delito *m*

found /faʊnd/ ⇒FIND. ● *vt* fundar.

foundation /faʊn'deɪʃn/ *n* fundación *f*; (basis) fundamento. (cosmetic) base *f* (de maquillaje). ~**s** *npl* (Archit) cimientos *mpl*

founder /'faʊndə(r)/ *n* fundador *m*. ● *vi* <*ship*> hundirse

fountain /'faʊntɪn/ *n* fuente *f*. ~ **pen** *n* pluma *f* (estilográfica) *f*, estilográfica *f*

four /fɔ:(r)/ *a* & *n* cuatro (*m*). ~**fold** *a* cuádruple. ● *adv* cuatro veces. ~**some** /-səm/ *n* grupo *m* de cuatro personas ~**teen** /'fɔ:ti:n/ *a* & *n* catorce (*m*). ~**teenth** *a* & *n* decimocuarto (*m*). ~**th** /fɔ:θ/ *a* & *n* cuarto (*m*). ~**-wheel drive** *n* tracción *f* integral

fowl /faʊl/ *n* ave *f*

fox /fɒks/ *n* zorro *m*, zorra *f*. ● *vt* 🅸 confundir

foyer /'fɔɪeɪ/ *n* (of theatre) foyer *m*; (of hotel) vestíbulo *m*

fraction /'frækʃn/ *n* fracción *f*

fracture /'fræktʃə(r)/ *n* fractura *f*. ● *vt* fracturar. ● *vi* fracturarse

fragile /'frædʒaɪl/ *a* frágil

fragment /'frægmənt/ *n* fragmento *m*. ~**ary** /-ərɪ/ *a* fragmentario

fragran|ce /'freɪgrəns/ *n* fragancia *f*. ~**t** *a* fragante

frail /freɪl/ *a* (**-er**, **-est**) frágil

frame /freɪm/ *n* (of picture, door, window) marco *m*; (of spectacles) montura *f*; (fig, structure) estructura *f*. ● *vt* enmarcar <*picture*>; formular <*plan, question*>; 🅸, (incriminate unjustly) incriminar falsamente. ~**work** *n* estructura *f*; (context) marco *m*

France /frɑ:ns/ *n* Francia *f*

frank /fræŋk/ *a* franco. ● *vt* franquear. ~**ly** *adv* francamente

frantic /'fræntɪk/ *a* frenético. ~ with loco de

fratern|al /frə'tɜ:nl/ *a* fraternal. ~**ity** /frə'tɜ:nɪtɪ/ *n* fraternidad *f*; (club) asociación *f*. ~**ize** /'frætənaɪz/ *vi* fraternizar

fraud /frɔ:d/ *n* fraude *m*; (person) impostor *m*. ~**ulent** /-jʊlənt/*a* fraudulento

fraught /frɔ:t/ *a* (tense) tenso. ~ with cargado de

fray /freɪ/ *n* riña *f*

freak /fri:k/ *n* fenómeno *m*; (monster) monstruo *m*. ● *a* anormal. ~**ish** *a* anormal

freckle /'frekl/ *n* peca *f*. ~**d** *a* pecoso

free /fri:/ *a* (**freer** /'fri:ə(r)/, **freest** /'fri:ɪst/) libre; (gratis) gratuito. ~ **of charge** gratis. ● *vt* (*pt* **freed**) (set at liberty) poner en libertad; (relieve from) liberar (**from/of** de); (untangle) desenredar. ~**dom** *n* libertad *f*. ~**hold** *n* propiedad *f* absoluta. ~ **kick** *n* tiro *m* libre. ~**lance** *a* & *adv* por cuenta propia. ~**ly** *adv* libremente. ~**mason** *n* masón *m*. ~**-range** *a* <*eggs*> de granja. ~ **speech** *n* libertad *f* de expresión. ~**style** *n* estilo *m* libre. ~**way** *n* (Amer) autopista *f*

freez|e /'fri:z/ *vt* (*pt* **froze**, *pp* **frozen**) helar; congelar <*food, wages*>. ● *vi* helarse; (become motionless) quedarse inmóvil. ● *n* (on wages, prices) congelación *f*. ~**er** *n* congelador *m*. ~**ing** *a* glacial. ● *n*. ~**ing** (**point**) punto *m* de congelación *f*. **below** ~**ing** bajo cero

freight /freɪt/ *n* (goods) mercancías *fpl*. **~er** *n* buque *m* de carga

French /frentʃ/ *a* francés. ● *n* (Lang) francés *m*. ● *npl*. **the ~** (people) los franceses. **~ fries** *npl* patatas *fpl* fritas, papas *fpl* fritas (LAm). **~man** /-mən/ *n* francés *m*. **~ window** *n* puerta *f* ventana. **~woman** *f* francesa *f*

frenz|ied /ˈfrenzɪd/ *a* frenético. **~y** *n* frenesí *m*

frequency /ˈfriːkwənsɪ/ *n* frecuencia *f*

frequent /frɪˈkwent/ *vt* frecuentar. ● /ˈfriːkwənt/ *a* frecuente. **~ly** *adv* frecuentemente

fresh /freʃ/ *a* (**-er**, **-est**) fresco; (different, additional) nuevo; <*water*> dulce. **~en** *vi* refrescar. □ **~en up** *vi* <*person*> refrescarse. **~er** *n* Ⓘ ⇒~MAN. **~ly** *adv* recientemente. **~man** *n* /-mən/ estudiante *m* de primer año. **~ness** *n* frescura *f*

fret /fret/ *vi* (*pt* **fretted**) preocuparse. **~ful** *a* (discontented) quejoso; (irritable) irritable

friction /ˈfrɪkʃn/ *n* fricción *f*

Friday /ˈfraɪdeɪ/ *n* viernes *m*

fridge /frɪdʒ/ *n* Ⓘ frigorífico *m*, nevera *f*, refrigerador *m* (LAm)

fried /fraɪd/ ⇒FRY. ● *a* frito

friend /frend/ *n* amigo *m*. **~liness** *n* simpatía *f*. **~ly** *a* (**-ier**, **-iest**) simpático. **~ship** *n* amistad *f*

fries /fraɪz/ *npl* ⇒FRENCH FRIES

frieze /friːz/ *n* friso *m*

frigate /ˈfrɪgət/ *n* fragata *f*

fright /fraɪt/ *n* miedo *m*; (shock) susto *m*. **~en** *vt* asustar. □ **~ off** *vt* ahuyentar. **~ened** *a* asustado. **be ~ened** tener miedo (**of** de.) **~ful** *a* espantoso, horrible. **~fully** *adv* terriblemente

frigid /ˈfrɪdʒɪd/ *a* frígido

frill /frɪl/ *n* volante *m*, olán *m* (Mex). **~s** *npl* (fig) adornos *mpl*. **with no ~s** sencillo

fringe /frɪndʒ/ *n* (sewing) fleco *m*; (ornamental border) franja *f*; (of hair) flequillo *m*, cerquillo *m* (LAm), fleco *m* (Mex); (of area) periferia *f*; (of society) margen *m*

fritter /ˈfrɪtə(r)/ *vt*. □ **~ away** *vt* desperdiciar <*time*>; malgastar <*money*>

frivol|ity /frɪˈvɒlətɪ/ *n* frivolidad *f*. **~ous** /ˈfrɪvələs/ *a* frívolo

fro /frəʊ/ ⇒TO AND FRO

frock /frɒk/ *n* vestido *m*

frog /frɒg/ *n* rana *f*. **have a ~ in one's throat** tener carraspera. **~man** /-mən/ *n* hombre *m* rana. **~spawn** *n* huevos *mpl* de rana

frolic /ˈfrɒlɪk/ *vi* (*pt* **frolicked**) retozar

from /frɒm/, *unstressed* /frəm/ *prep* de; (indicating starting point) desde; (habit, conviction) por; **~ then on** a partir de ahí

front /frʌnt/ *n* parte *f* delantera; (of building) fachada *f*; (of clothes) delantera *f*; (Mil, Pol) frente *f*; (of book) principio *m*; (fig, appearance) apariencia *f*; (seafront) paseo *m* marítimo, malecón *m* (LAm). **in ~ of** delante de. ● *a* delantero; (first) primero. **~al** *a* frontal; <*attack*> de frente. **~ door** *n* puerta *f* principal

frontier /ˈfrʌntɪə(r)/ *n* frontera *f*

front page *n* (of newspaper) primera plana *f*

frost /frɒst/ *n* (freezing) helada *f*; (frozen dew) escarcha *f*. **~bite** *n* congelación *f*. **~bitten** *a* congelado. **~ed** *a* <*glass*> esmerilado.

~ing *n* (Amer) glaseado *m*. **~y** *a* <*weather*> helado; <*night*> de helada; (fig) glacial

froth /frɒθ/ *n* espuma *f*. ● *vi* espumar. **~y** *a* espumoso

frown /fraʊn/ *vi* fruncir el entrecejo ● *n* ceño *m*. □ **~ on** *vt* desaprobar.

froze /frəʊz/ ⇒FREEZE. **~n** /'frəʊzn/ ⇒FREEZE. ● *a* congelado; <*region*> helado

frugal /'fru:gl/ *a* frugal

fruit /fru:t/ *n* (Bot, on tree, fig) fruto *m*; (as food) fruta *f*. **~ful** /'fru:tfl/ *a* fértil; (fig) fructífero. **~ion** /fru:'ɪʃn/ *n*. **come to ~ion** realizarse. **~less** *a* infructuoso. **~ salad** *n* macedonia *f* de frutas. **~y** *a* que sabe a fruta

frustrat|e /frʌ'streɪt/ *vt* frustrar. **~ion** /-ʃn/ *n* frustración *f*. **~ed** *a* frustrado. **~ing** *a* frustrante

fry /fraɪ/ *vt* (*pt* **fried**) freír. ● *vi* freírse. **~ing pan** *n* sárten *f*, sartén *m* (LAm)

fudge /fʌdʒ/ *n* dulce *m* de azúcar

fuel /'fju:əl/ *n* combustible *m*

fugitive /'fju:dʒɪtɪv/ *a* & *n* fugitivo (*m*)

fulfil /fʊl'fɪl/ *vt* (*pt* **fulfilled**) cumplir (con) <*promise, obligation*>; satisfacer <*condition*>; hacer realidad <*ambition*>. **~ment** *n* (of promise, obligation) cumplimiento *m*; (of conditions) satisfacción *f*; (of hopes, plans) realización *f*

full /fʊl/ *a* (**-er**, **-est**) lleno; <*bus, hotel*> completo; <*account*> detallado. **at ~ speed** a máxima velocidad. **be ~ (up)** (with food) no poder más. ● *n*. **in ~** sin quitar nada. **to the ~** completamente. **write in ~** escribir con todas las letras. **~back** *n* (Sport) defensa *m* & *f*. **~-blown** /fʊl'bləʊn/ *a* verdadero. **~-fledged** /-'fledʒd/ *a* (Amer) ⇒FULLY-FLEDGED. **~ moon** *n* luna *f* llena. **~-scale** /-'skeɪl/ *a* <*drawing*> de tamaño natural; (fig) amplio. **~ stop** *n* punto *m*. **~-time** *a* <*employment*> de jornada completa. ● /-'taɪm/ *adv* a tiempo completo. **~y** *adv* completamente. **~-fledged** /-'fledʒd/ *a* <*chick*> capaz de volar; <*lawyer, nurse*> hecho y derecho

fulsome /'fʊlsəm/ *a* excesivo

fumble /'fʌmbl/ *vi* buscar (a tientas)

fume /fju:m/ *vi* despedir gases; (fig, be furious) estar furioso. **~s** *npl* gases *mpl*

fumigate /'fju:mɪgeɪt/ *vt* fumigar

fun /fʌn/ *n* (amusement) diversión *f*; (merriment) alegría *f*. **for ~** en broma. **have ~** divertirse. **make ~ of** burlarse de

function /'fʌŋkʃn/ *n* (purpose, duty) función *f*; (reception) recepción *f*. ● *vi* funcionar. **~al** *a* funcional

fund /fʌnd/ *n* fondo *m*. ● *vt* financiar

fundamental /fʌndə'mentl/ *a* fundamental. **~ist** *a* & *n* fundamentalista (*m* & *f*)

funeral /'fju:nərəl/ *n* entierro *m*, funerales *mpl*. **~ director** *n* director *m* de pompas fúnebres

funfair /'fʌnfeə(r)/ *n* feria *f*; (permanent) parque *m* de atracciones, parque *m* de diversiones (LAm)

fungus /'fʌŋgəs/ *n* (*pl* **-gi** /-gaɪ/) hongo *m*

funnel /'fʌnl/ *n* (for pouring) embudo *m*; (of ship) chimenea *f*

funn|ily /'fʌnɪlɪ/ *adv* (oddly) curiosamente. **~y** *a* (**-ier**, **-iest**) divertido, gracioso; (odd) curioso, raro

fur /fɜ:(r)/ *n* pelo *m*; (pelt) piel *f*

furious /ˈfjʊərɪəs/ *a* furioso. **~ly** *adv* furiosamente

furlough /ˈfɜ:ləʊ/ *n* (Amer) permiso *m*. **on ~** de permiso

furnace /ˈfɜ:nɪs/ *n* horno *m*

furnish /ˈfɜ:nɪʃ/ *vt* amueblar, amoblar (LAm); (supply) proveer. **~ings** *npl* muebles *mpl*, mobiliario *m*

furniture /ˈfɜ:nɪtʃə(r)/ *n* muebles *mpl*, mobiliario *m*. **a piece of ~** un mueble

furrow /ˈfʌrəʊ/ *n* surco *m*

furry /ˈfɜ:rɪ/ *a* peludo

furthe|r /ˈfɜ:ðə(r)/ *a* más lejano; (additional) nuevo. ● *adv* más lejos; (more) además. ● *vt* fomentar. **~rmore** *adv* además. **~st** *a* más lejano. ● *adv* más lejos

furtive /ˈfɜ:tɪv/ *a* furtivo

fury /ˈfjʊərɪ/ *n* furia *f*

fuse /fju:z/ *vt* (melt) fundir; (fig, unite) fusionar. **~ the lights** fundir los plomos. ● *vi* fundirse; (fig) fusionarse. ● *n* fusible *m*, plomo *m*; (of bomb) mecha *f*. **~box** *n* caja *f* de fusibles

fuselage /ˈfju:zəlɑ:ʒ/ *n* fuselaje *m*

fusion /ˈfju:ʒn/ *n* fusión *f*

fuss /fʌs/ *n* (commotion) jaleo *m*. **kick up a ~** armar un lío, armar una bronca. **make a ~ of** tratar con mucha atención. ● *vi* preocuparse. **~y** *a* (**-ier**, **-iest**) (finicky) remilgado; (demanding) exigente

futil|e /ˈfju:taɪl/ *a* inútil, vano. **~ity** /fju:ˈtɪlətɪ/ *n* inutilidad *f*

futur|e /ˈfju:tʃə(r)/ *a* futuro. ● *n* futuro *m*. **in ~e** de ahora en adelante. **~istic** /fju:tʃəˈrɪstɪk/ *a* futurista

fuzz /fʌz/ *n* pelusa *f*. **~y** *a* <*hair*> crespo; <*photograph*> borroso

Gg

gab /gæb/ *n*. **have the gift of the ~** tener un pico de oro

gabardine /gæbəˈdi:n/ *n* gabardina *f*

gabble /ˈgæbl/ *vi* hablar atropelladamente

gable /ˈgeɪbl/ *n* aguilón *m*

gad /gæd/ *vi* (*pt* **gadded**). **~ about** callejear

gadget /ˈgædʒɪt/ *n* chisme *m*

Gaelic /ˈgeɪlɪk/ *a* & *n* gaélico (*m*)

gaffe /gæf/ *n* plancha *f*, metedura *f* de pata, metida *f* de pata (LAm)

gag /gæg/ *n* mordaza *f*; (joke) chiste *m*. ● *vt* (*pt* **gagged**) amordazar. ● *vi* hacer arcadas

gaiety /ˈgeɪətɪ/ *n* alegría *f*

gaily /ˈgeɪlɪ/ *adv* alegremente

gain /geɪn/ *vt* ganar; (acquire) adquirir; (obtain) conseguir. ● *vi* <*clock*> adelantar. ● *n* ganancia *f*; (increase) aumento *m*

gait /geɪt/ *n* modo *m* de andar

gala /ˈgɑ:lə/ *n* fiesta *f*. **~ performance** (función *f* de) gala *f*

galaxy /ˈgæləksɪ/ *n* galaxia *f*

gale /geɪl/ *n* vendaval *m*

gall /gɔ:l/ *n* bilis *f*; (fig) hiel *f*; (impudence) descaro *m*

gallant /ˈgælənt/ *a* (brave) valiente; (chivalrous) galante. **~ry** *n* valor *m*

gall bladder /ˈgɔ:lblædə(r)/ *n* vesícula *f* biliar

gallery /ˈgælərɪ/ *n* galería *f*

galley /ˈgælɪ/ *n* (ship) galera *f*; (ship's kitchen) cocina *f*. ~ (**proof**) *n* galerada *f*

gallivant /ˈgælɪvænt/ *vi* 🅃 callejear

gallon /ˈgælən/ *n* galón *m* (imperial = 4,546l; Amer = 3,785l)

gallop /ˈgæləp/ *n* galope *m*. ● *vi* (*pt* **galloped**) galopar

gallows /ˈgæləʊz/ *n* horca *f*

galore /gəˈlɔː(r)/ *a* en abundancia

galvanize /ˈgælvənaɪz/ *vt* galvanizar

gambl|e /ˈgæmbl/ *vi* jugar. ~**e on** contar con. ● *vt* jugarse. ● *n* (venture) empresa *f* arriesgada; (bet) apuesta *f*; (risk) riesgo *m*. ~**er** *n* jugador *m*. ~**ing** *n* juego *m*

game /geɪm/ *n* juego *m*; (match) partido *m*; (animals, birds) caza *f*. ● *a* valiente. ~ **for** listo para. ~**keeper** *n* guardabosque *m*. ~**s** *n* (in school) deportes *mpl*

gammon /ˈgæmən/ *n* jamón *m* fresco

gamut /ˈgæmət/ *n* gama *f*

gander /ˈgændə(r)/ *n* ganso *m*

gang /gæŋ/ *n* pandilla *f*; (of workmen) equipo *m*. □ ~ **up** *vi* unirse (on contra)

gangling /ˈgæŋglɪŋ/ *a* larguirucho

gangrene /ˈgæŋgriːn/ *n* gangrena *f*

gangster /ˈgæŋstə(r)/ *n* bandido *m*, gángster *m* & *f*

gangway /ˈgæŋweɪ/ *n* pasillo *m*; (of ship) pasarela *f*

gaol /dʒeɪl/ *n* cárcel *f*. ~**er** *n* carcelero *m*

gap /gæp/ *n* espacio *m*; (in fence, hedge) hueco *m*; (in time) intervalo *m*; (in knowledge) laguna *f*; (difference) diferencia *f*

gap|e /ˈgeɪp/ *vi* quedarse boquiabierto; (be wide open) estar muy abierto. ~**ing** *a* abierto; (person) boquiabierto

garage /ˈgærɑːʒ/ *n* garaje *m*, garage *m* (LAm), cochera *f* (Mex); (petrol station) gasolinera *f*; (for repairs, sales) taller *m*, garage *m* (LAm)

garbage /ˈgɑːbɪdʒ/ *n* basura *f*. ~ **can** *n* (Amer) cubo *m* de la basura, bote *m* de la basura (Mex). ~ **collector**, ~ **man** *n* (Amer) basurero *m*

garble /ˈgɑːbl/ *vt* tergiversar, embrollar

garden /ˈgɑːdn/ *n* (of flowers) jardín *m*; (of vegetables/fruit) huerto *m*. ● *vi* trabajar en el jardín. ~**er** /ˈgɑːdnə(r)/ *n* jardinero *m*. ~**ing** *n* jardinería *f*; (vegetable growing) horticultura *f*

gargle /ˈgɑːgl/ *vi* hacer gárgaras

gargoyle /ˈgɑːgɔɪl/ *n* gárgola *f*

garish /ˈgeərɪʃ/ *a* chillón

garland /ˈgɑːlənd/ *n* guirnalda *f*

garlic /ˈgɑːlɪk/ *n* ajo *m*

garment /ˈgɑːmənt/ *n* prenda *f* (de vestir)

garnish /ˈgɑːnɪʃ/ *vt* adornar, decorar. ● *n* adorno *m*

garret /ˈgærət/ *n* buhardilla *f*

garrison /ˈgærɪsn/ *n* guarnición *f*

garrulous /ˈgærələs/ *a* hablador

garter /ˈgɑːtə(r)/ *n* liga *f*

gas /gæs/ *n* (*pl* **gases**) gas *m*; (anaesthetic) anestésico *m*; (Amer, petrol) gasolina *f*. ● *vt* (*pt* **gassed**) asfixiar con gas

gash /gæʃ/ *n* tajo *m*. ● *vt* hacer un tajo de

gasket /ˈgæskɪt/ *n* junta *f*

gas: ~ **mask** *n* careta *f* antigás. ~ **meter** *n* contador *m* de gas

gasoline /ˈgæsəliːn/ *n* (Amer) gasolina *f*

gasp /gɑːsp/ *vi* jadear; (with surprise) dar un grito ahogado. ● *n* exclamación *f*, grito *m*

gas: ~ ring *n* hornillo *m* de gas. **~ station** *n* (Amer) gasolinera *f*

gastric /ˈgæstrɪk/ *a* gástrico

gate /geɪt/ *n* puerta *f*; (of metal) verja *f*; (barrier) barrera *f*

gate: ~crash *vt* colarse en. **~crasher** *n* intruso *m* (*que ha entrado sin ser invitado*). **~way** *n* puerta *f*

gather /ˈgæðə(r)/ *vt* reunir <*people, things*>; (accumulate) acumular; (pick up) recoger; recoger <*flowers*>; (fig, infer) deducir; (sewing) fruncir. **~ speed** acelerar. ● *vi* <*people*> reunirse; <*things*> acumularse. **~ing** *n* reunión *f*

gaudy /ˈgɔːdɪ/ *a* (**-ier**, **-iest**) chillón

gauge /geɪdʒ/ *n* (measurement) medida *f*; (Rail) entrevía *f*; (instrument) indicador *m*. ● *vt* medir; (fig) estimar

gaunt /gɔːnt/ *a* descarnado; (from illness) demacrado

gauntlet /ˈgɔːntlɪt/ *n*. **run the ~ of** aguantar el acoso de

gauze /gɔːz/ *n* gasa *f*

gave /geɪv/ ⇨GIVE

gawky /ˈgɔːkɪ/ *a* (**-ier**, **-iest**) torpe

gawp /gɔːp/ *vi*. **~ at** mirar como un tonto

gay /geɪ/ *a* (**-er**, **-est**) ([I], homosexual) homosexual, gay [I]; (dated, joyful) alegre

gaze /geɪz/ *vi*. **~** (**at**) mirar (fijamente). ● *n* mirada *f* (fija)

gazelle /gəˈzel/ *n* (*pl invar or* **-s**) gacela *f*

GB *abbr* ⇨GREAT BRITAIN

gear /gɪə(r)/ *n* equipo *m*; (Tec) engranaje *m*; (Auto) marcha *f*, cambio *m*. **in ~** engranado. **out of ~** desengranado. **change ~, shift ~** (Amer) cambiar de marcha. ● *vt* adaptar. **~box** *n* (Auto) caja *f* de cambios

geese /giːs/ ⇨GOOSE

gel /dʒel/ *n* gel *m*

gelatine /ˈdʒelətiːn/ *n* gelatina *f*

gelignite /ˈdʒelɪgnaɪt/ *n* gelignita *f*

gem /dʒem/ *n* piedra *f* preciosa

Gemini /ˈdʒemɪnaɪ/ *n* Géminis *mpl*

gender /ˈdʒendə(r)/ *n* género *m*

gene /dʒiːn/ *n* gen *m*, gene *m*

genealogy /dʒiːnɪˈælədʒɪ/ *n* genealogía *f*

general /ˈdʒenərəl/ *a* general. ● *n* general *m*. **in ~** en general. **~ election** *n* elecciones *fpl* generales. **~ization** /-ˈzeɪʃn/ *n* generalización *f*. **~ize** *vt/i* generalizar. **~ knowledge** *n* cultura *f* general. **~ly** *adv* generalmente. **~ practitioner** *n* médico *m* de cabecera

generat|e /ˈdʒenəreɪt/ *vt* generar. **~ion** /-ˈreɪʃn/ *n* generación *f*. **~ion gap** *n* brecha *f* generacional. **~or** *n* generador *m*

genero|sity /dʒenəˈrɒsətɪ/ *n* generosidad *f*. **~us** /ˈdʒenərəs/ *a* generoso; (plentiful) abundante

genetic /dʒɪˈnetɪk/ *a* genético. **~s** *n* genética *f*

Geneva /dʒɪˈniːvə/ *n* Ginebra *f*

genial /ˈdʒiːnɪəl/ *a* simpático, afable

genital /ˈdʒenɪtl/ *a* genital. **~s** *npl* genitales *mpl*

genitive /ˈdʒenɪtɪv/ *a* & *n* genitivo (*m*)

genius /ˈdʒi:nɪəs/ *n* (*pl* **-uses**) genio *m*

genocide /ˈdʒenəsaɪd/ *n* genocidio *m*

genre /ʒɑ:ŋr/ *n* género *m*

gent /dʒent/ *n* 🄸 señor *m*. **~s** *n* aseo *m* de caballeros

genteel /dʒenˈti:l/ *a* distinguido

gentl|e /ˈdʒentl/ *a* (**-er**, **-est**) <*person*> dulce; <*murmur, breeze*> suave; <*hint*> discreto. **~eman** *n* señor *m*; (well-bred) caballero *m*. **~eness** *n* amabilidad *f*. **~y** *adv* amablemente

genuine /ˈdʒenjʊɪn/ *a* verdadero; <*person*> sincero

geograph|er /dʒɪˈɒgrəfə(r)/ *n* geógrafo *m*. **~ical** /dʒɪəˈgræfɪkl/ *a* geográfico. **~y** /dʒɪˈɒgrəfɪ/ *n* geografía *f*

geolog|ical /dʒɪəˈlɒdʒɪkl/ *a* geológico. **~ist** /dʒɪˈɒlədʒɪst/ *n* geólogo *m*. **~y** /dʒɪˈɒlədʒɪ/ *n* geología *f*

geometr|ic(al) /dʒɪəˈmetrɪk(l)/ *a* geométrico. **~y** /dʒɪˈɒmətrɪ/ *n* geometría *f*

geranium /dʒəˈreɪnɪəm/ *n* geranio *m*

geriatric /dʒerɪˈætrɪk/ *a* <*patient*> anciano; <*ward*> de geriatría. **~s** *n* geriatría *f*

germ /dʒɜ:m/ *n* microbio *m*, germen *m*

German /ˈdʒɜ:mən/ *a* & *n* alemán (*m*). **~ic** /dʒɜ:ˈmænɪk/ *a* germánico. **~ measles** *n* rubéola *f*. **~y** *n* Alemania *f*

germinate /ˈdʒɜ:mɪneɪt/ *vi* germinar

gesticulate /dʒeˈstɪkjʊleɪt/ *vi* hacer ademanes, gesticular

gesture /ˈdʒestʃə(r)/ *n* gesto *m*, ademán *m*; (fig) gesto *m*. ● *vi* hacer gestos

get /get/

past **got**; past participle **got**, **gotten** (Amer); present participle **getting**

● *transitive verb*

····➤ (obtain) conseguir, obtener. **did you get the job?** ¿conseguiste el trabajo?

····➤ (buy) comprar. **I got it in the sales** lo compré en las rebajas

····➤ (achieve, win) sacar. **she got very good marks** sacó muy buenas notas

····➤ (receive) recibir. **I got a letter from Alex** recibí una carta de Alex

····➤ (fetch) ir a buscar. **~ your coat** vete a buscar tu abrigo

····➤ (experience) llevarse. **I got a terrible shock** me llevé un shock espantoso

····➤ (🄸, understand) entender. **I don't ~ what you mean** no entiendo lo que quieres decir

····➤ (ask or persuade) **to ~ s.o. to do sth** hacer que uno haga algo

Note that *hacer que* is followed by the subjunctive form of the verb

····➤ (cause to be done or happen) **I must ~ this watch fixed** tengo quellevar a arreglar este reloj. **they got the roof mended** hicieron arreglar el techo

● *intransitive verb*

····➤ (arrive, reach) llegar. **I got there late** llegué tarde. **how do you ~ to Paddington?** ¿cómo se llega a Paddington?

····➤ (become) **to ~ tired** cansarse. **she got very angry** se puso furio sa. **it's ~ting late** se está haciendo tarde

⇨ For translations of expressions such as **get better, get old** see entries **better, old** etc. See also **got**

····➤ **to get to do sth** (manage to) llegar a. **did you ~ to see him?** ¿llegaste a verlo?

□ **get along** *vi* (manage) arreglárselas; (progress) hacer progresos. □ **get along with** *vt* llevarse bien con. □ **get at** *vt* (reach) llegar a; (imply) querer decir. □ **get away** *vi* salir; (escape) escaparse. □ **get back** *vi* volver. *vt* (recover) recobrar. □ **get by** *vi* (manage) arreglárselas; (pass) pasar. □ **get down** *vi* bajar. *vt* (make depressed) deprimir. □ **get in** *vi* entrar. □ **get into** *vt* entrar en; subir a <*car*> □ **get off** *vt* bajar(se) de <*train etc*>. *vi* (from train etc) bajarse; (Jurid) salir absuelto. □ **get on** *vi* (progress) hacer progresos; (succeed) tener éxito. *vt* subirse a <*train etc*>. □ **get on with** *vt* (be on good terms with) llevarse bien con; (continue) seguir con. □ **get out** *vi* salir. *vt* (take out) sacar. □ **get out of** *vt* (fig) librarse de. □ **get over** *vt* reponerse de <*illness*>. □ **get round** *vt* soslayar <*difficulty etc*>; engatusar <*person*>. □ **get through** *vi* pasar; (on phone) comunicarse (to con). □ **get together** *vi* (meet up) reunirse. *vt* (assemble) reunir. □ **get up** *vi* levantarse; (climb) subir

geyser /ˈgiːzə(r)/ *n* géiser *m*

ghastly /ˈgɑːstlɪ/ *a* (**-ier, -iest**) horrible

gherkin /ˈgɜːkɪn/ *n* pepinillo *m*

ghetto /ˈgetəʊ/ *n* (*pl* **-os**) gueto *m*

ghost /gəʊst/ *n* fantasma *m*. **~ly** *a* espectral

giant /ˈdʒaɪənt/ *n* gigante *m*. ● *a* gigantesco

gibberish /ˈdʒɪbərɪʃ/ *n* jerigonza *f*

gibe /dʒaɪb/ *n* pulla *f*

giblets /ˈdʒɪblɪts/ *npl* menudillos *mpl*

gidd|iness /ˈgɪdɪnɪs/ *n* vértigo *m*. **~y** *a* (**-ier, -iest**) mareado. **be/feel ~y** estar/sentirse mareado

gift /gɪft/ *n* regalo *m*; (ability) don *m*. **~ed** *a* dotado de talento. **~-wrap** *vt* envolver para regalo

gigantic /dʒaɪˈgæntɪk/ *a* gigantesco

giggle /ˈgɪgl/ *vi* reírse tontamente. ● *n* risita *f*

gild /gɪld/ *vt* dorar

gills /gɪlz/ *npl* agallas *fpl*

gilt /gɪlt/ *n* dorado *m*. ● *a* dorado

gimmick /ˈgɪmɪk/ *n* truco *m*

gin /dʒɪn/ *n* ginebra *f*

ginger /ˈdʒɪndʒə(r)/ *n* jengibre *m*. ● *a* rojizo. **he has ~ hair** es pelirrojo. **~bread** *n* pan *m* de jengibre

gipsy /ˈdʒɪpsɪ/ *n* gitano *m*

giraffe /dʒɪˈrɑːf/ *n* jirafa *f*

girder /ˈgɜːdə(r)/ *n* viga *f*

girdle /ˈgɜːdl/ *n* (belt) cinturón *m*; (corset) corsé *m*

girl /gɜːl/ *n* chica *f*, muchacha *f*; (child) niña *f*. **~friend** *n* amiga *f*; (of boy) novia *f*. **~ish** *a* de niña; <*boy*> afeminado. **~ scout** *n* (Amer) exploradora *f*, guía *f*

giro /ˈdʒaɪrəʊ/ *n* (*pl* **-os**) giro *m* (bancario)

girth /gɜːθ/ *n* circunferencia *f*

gist /dʒɪst/ *n* lo esencial

give /gɪv/ *vt* (*pt* **gave**, *pp* **given**) dar; (deliver) entregar; regalar <*present*>; prestar <*aid, attention*>. ~ **o.s. to** darse a. ● *vi* dar; (yield) ceder; (stretch) dar de sí. ● *n* elasticidad *f*. □ ~ **away** *vt* regalar; revelar <*secret*>. □ ~ **back** *vt* devolver. □ ~ **in** *vi* ceder. □ ~ **off** *vt* emitir. □ ~ **out** *vt* distribuir. (become used up) agotarse. □ ~ **up** *vt* renunciar a; (yield) ceder. ~ **up doing sth** dejar de hacer algo. ~ **o.s. up** entregarse (**to** a). *vi* rendirse. **~n** /ˈgɪvn/ ⇒GIVE. ● *a* dado. **~n name** *n* nombre *m* de pila

glacier /ˈglæsɪə(r)/ *n* glaciar *m*

glad /glæd/ *a* contento. **be** ~ alegrarse (**about** de). **~den** *vt* alegrar

gladly /ˈglædlɪ/ *adv* alegremente; (willingly) con mucho gusto

glamo|rous /ˈglæmərəs/ *a* glamoroso. **~ur** /ˈglæmə(r)/ *n* glamour *m*

glance /glɑːns/ *n* ojeada *f*. ● *vi*. ~ **at** dar un vistazo a

gland /glænd/ *n* glándula *f*

glar|e /gleə(r)/ *vi* <*light*> deslumbrar; (stare angrily) mirar airadamente. ● *n* resplandor *m*; (stare) mirada *f* airada. **~ing** *a* deslumbrante; (obvious) manifiesto

glass /glɑːs/ *n* (material) cristal *m*, vidrio *m*; (without stem or for wine) vaso *m*; (with stem) copa *f*; (for beer) caña *f*; (mirror) espejo *m*. **~es** *npl* (spectacles) gafas *fpl*, lentes *fpl* (LAm), anteojos *mpl* (LAm). **~y** *a* vítreo

glaze /gleɪz/ *vt* poner cristal(es) *or* vidrio(s) a <*windows, doors*>; vidriar <*pottery*>. ● *vi*. ~ (**over**) <*eyes*> vidriarse. ● *n* barniz *m*; (for pottery) esmalte *m*

gleam /gliːm/ *n* destello *m*. ● *vi* destellar

glean /gliːn/ *vt* espigar; recoger <*information*>

glee /gliː/ *n* regocijo *m*

glib /glɪb/ *a* de mucha labia; <*reply*> fácil

glid|e /glaɪd/ *vi* deslizarse; (plane) planear. **~er** *n* planeador *m*. **~ing** *n* planeo *m*

glimmer /ˈglɪmə(r)/ *n* destello *m*. ● *vi* destellar

glimpse /glɪmps/ *n*. **catch a** ~ **of** vislumbrar, ver brevemente. ● *vt* vislumbrar

glint /glɪnt/ *n* destello *m*. ● *vi* destellar

glisten /ˈglɪsn/ *vi* brillar

glitter /ˈglɪtə(r)/ *vi* brillar. ● *n* brillo *m*

gloat /gləʊt/ *vi*. ~ **on/over** regodearse sobre

glob|al /ˈgləʊbl/ *a* (worldwide) mundial; (all-embracing) global. **~al warming** *n* calentamiento *m* global. **~e** /gləʊb/ *n* globo *m*

gloom /gluːm/ *n* oscuridad *f*; (sadness, fig) tristeza *f*. **~y** *a* (**-ier**, **-iest**) triste; (pessimistic) pesimista

glor|ify /ˈglɔːrɪfaɪ/ *vt* glorificar. **~ious** /ˈglɔːrɪəs/ *a* espléndido; <*deed, hero etc*> glorioso. **~y** /ˈglɔːrɪ/ *n* gloria *f*

gloss /glɒs/ *n* lustre *m*. ~ (paint) (pintura *f* al *or* de) esmalte *m*. □ ~ **over** *vt* (make light of) minimizar; (cover up) encubrir

glossary /ˈglɒsərɪ/ *n* glosario *m*

glossy /ˈglɒsɪ/ *a* brillante

glove /glʌv/ *n* guante *m*. ~ **compartment** *n* (Auto) guantera *f*, gaveta *f*

glow /gləʊ/ *vi* brillar. ● *n* brillo *m*. **~ing** /ˈgləʊɪŋ/ *a* incandescente; <*account*> entusiasta; <*complexion*> rojo

glucose /ˈgluːkəʊs/ *n* glucosa *f*

glue /gluː/ *n* cola *f*, goma *f* de pegar. ● *vt* (*pres p* **gluing**) pegar

glum /glʌm/ *a* (**glummer**, **glummest**) triste

glutton /ˈglʌtn/ *n* glotón *m*

gnarled /nɑːld/ *a* nudoso

gnash /næʃ/ *vt*. ~ **one's teeth** rechinar los dientes

gnat /næt/ *n* jején *m*, mosquito *m*

gnaw /nɔː/ *vt* roer. ● *vi*. ~ **at** roer

gnome /nəʊm/ *n* gnomo *m*

---

go /gəʊ/

3rd pers sing present **goes**; past **went**; past participle **gone**

● *intransitive verb*

⟶ ir. **I'm going to France** voy a Francia. **to go shopping** ir de compras. **to go swimming** ir a nadar

⟶ (leave) irse. **we're going on Friday** nos vamos el viernes

⟶ (work, function) *<engine, clock>* funcionar

⟶ (become) **to go deaf** quedarse sordo. **to go mad** volverse loco. **his face went red** se puso colorado

⟶ (stop) *<headache, pain>* irse (+ *me/te/le*). **the pain's gone** se me ha ido el dolor

⟶ (turn out, progress) ir. **everything's going very well** todo va muy bien. **how did the exam go?** ¿qué tal te fue en el examen?

⟶ (match, suit) combinar. **the jacket and the trousers go well together** la chaqueta y los pantalones combinan bien.

⟶ (cease to function) *<bulb, fuse>* fundirse. **the brakes have gone** los frenos no funcionan

● *auxiliary verb*

to be going to + *infinitive* ir a + *infinitivo*. **it's going to rain** va a llover. **she's going to win!** ¡va a ganar!

● *noun* (*pl* **goes**)

⟶ (turn) turno *m*. **you have three goes** tienes tres turnos. **it's your go** te toca a ti

⟶ (attempt) **to have a go at doing sth** intentar hacer algo. **have another go** inténtalo de nuevo

⟶ (energy, drive) empuje *m*. **she has a lot of go** tiene mucho empuje

⟶ (in phrases) **I've been on the go all day** no he parado en todo el día. **to make a go of sth** sacar algo adelante

□ **go across** *vt/vi* cruzar. □ **go after** *vt* perseguir. □ **go away** *vi* irse. □ **go back** *vi* volver. □ **go back on** *vt* faltar a *<promise etc>*. □ **go by** *vi* pasar. □ **go down** *vi* bajar; *<sun>* ponerse. □ **go for** *vt* (I, attack) atacar. □ **go in** *vi* entrar. □ **go in for** *vt* presentarse para *<exam>*; participar en *<competition>*. □ **go off** *vi* (leave) irse; (go bad) pasarse; (explode) estallar; *<lights>* apagarse. □ **go on** *vi* seguir; (happen) pasar; (be switched on) encenderse, prenderse (LAm). □ **go out** *vi* salir; *<fire, light>* apagarse. □ **go over** *vt* (check) revisar; (revise) repasar. □ **go through** *vt* pasar por; (search) registrar; (check) examinar. □ **go up** *vi/vt* subir. □ **go without** *vt* pasar sin

---

goad /gəʊd/ *vt* aguijonear

go-ahead /'gəʊəhed/ *n* luz *f* verde. ● *a* dinámico

goal /gəʊl/ *n* (Sport) gol *m*; (objective) meta *f*. **~ie** /'gəʊlɪ/ *n* 🅸, **~keeper** *n* portero *m*, arquero *m* (LAm). **~post** *n* poste *m* de la portería, poste *m* del arco (LAm)

goat /gəʊt/ *n* cabra *f*

gobble /'gɒbl/ *vt* engullir

goblin /'gɒblɪn/ *n* duende *m*

god /gɒd/ *n* dios *m*. **G~** *n* Dios *m*. **~child** *n* ahijado *m*. **~-daughter** *n* ahijada *f*. **~dess** /'gɒdes/ *n* diosa *f*. **~father** *n* padrino *m*. **~forsaken** *a* olvidado de Dios. **~mother** *n* madrina *f*. **~send** *n* beneficio *m* inesperado. **~son** *n* ahijado *m*

going /'gəʊɪŋ/ *n* camino *m*; (racing) (estado *m* del) terreno *m*. **it is slow/hard ~** es lento/difícil. ● *a* <*price*> actual; <*concern*> en funcionamiento

gold /gəʊld/ *n* oro *m*. ● *a* de oro. **~en** *a* de oro; (in colour) dorado; <*opportunity*> único. **~en wedding** *n* bodas *fpl* de oro. **~fish** *n* *invar* pez *m* de colores. **~mine** *n* mina *f* de oro; (fig) fuente *f* de gran riqueza. **~-plated** /-'pleɪtɪd/ *a* chapado en oro. **~smith** *n* orfebre *m*

golf /gɒlf/ *n* golf *m*. **~ ball** *n* pelota *f* de golf. **~ club** *n* palo *m* de golf; (place) club *m* de golf. **~course** *n* campo *m* de golf. **~er** *n* jugador *m* de golf

gondola /'gɒndələ/ *n* góndola *f*

gone /gɒn/ ⇒GO. ● *a* pasado. **~ six o'clock** después de las seis

gong /gɒŋ/ *n* gong(o) *m*

good /gʊd/ *a* (**better**, **best**) bueno, (*before masculine singular noun*) buen. **~ afternoon** buenas tardes. **~ evening** (before dark) buenas tardes; (after dark) buenas noches. **~ morning** buenos días. **~ night** buenas noches. **as ~ as** (almost) casi. **feel ~** sentirse bien. **have a ~ time** divertirse. ● *n* bien *m*. **for ~** para siempre. **it is no ~ shouting** es inútil gritar *etc*. **~bye** /-'baɪ/ *int* ¡adiós! ● *n* adiós *m*. **say ~bye to** despedirse de. **~-for-nothing** /-fənʌθɪŋ/ *a* & *n* inútil (*m*). **G~ Friday** *n* Viernes *m* Santo. **~-looking** /-'lʊkɪŋ/ *a* guapo, buen mozo *m* (LAm), buena moza *f* (LAm). **~ness** *n* bondad *f*. **~ness!**, **~ness gracious!**, **~ness me!**, **my ~ness!** ¡Dios mío! **~s** *npl* mercancías *fpl*. **~will** /-'wɪl/ *n* buena voluntad *f*. **~y** *n* (Culin, 🅸) golosina *f*; (in film) bueno *m*

gooey /'gu:ɪ/ *a* (**gooier**, **gooiest**) 🅸 pegajoso; (fig) sentimental

goofy /'gu:fɪ/ *a* (Amer) necio

goose /gu:s/ *n* (*pl* **geese**) oca *f*, ganso *m*. **~berry** /'gʊzbərɪ/ *n* uva *f* espina, grosella *f* espinosa. **~-flesh** *n*, **~-pimples** *npl* carne *f* de gallina

gore /gɔ:(r)/ *n* sangre *f*. ● *vt* cornear

gorge /gɔ:dʒ/ *n* (Geog) garganta *f*. ● *vt*. **~ o.s.** hartarse (**on** de)

gorgeous /'gɔ:dʒəs/ *a* precioso; (splendid) magnífico

gorilla /gə'rɪlə/ *n* gorila *m*

gorse /gɔ:s/ *n* aulaga *f*

gory /'gɔ:rɪ/ *a* (**-ier**, **-iest**) 🅸 sangriento

gosh /gɒʃ/ *int* ¡caramba!

go-slow /gəʊ'sləʊ/ *n* huelga *f* de celo, huelga *f* pasiva

gospel /'gɒspl/ *n* evangelio *m*

gossip /'gɒsɪp/ *n* (chatter) chismorreo *m*; (person) chismoso *m*. ● *vi* (*pt* **gossiped**) (chatter) chismorrear; (repeat scandal) conta chismes

got /gɒt/ ⇒GET. **have ~** tener. **I've ~ to do it** tengo quehacerlo.

gotten /'gɒtn/ ⇒GET

gouge /gaʊdʒ/ *vt* abrir <*hole*>. □ **~ out** *vt* sacar

gourmet /'gʊəmeɪ/ *n* gastrónomo *m*

govern /'gʌvən/ *vt/i* gobernar. **~ess** *n* institutriz *f*. **~ment** *n* gobierno *m*. **~or** *n* gobernador *m*

gown /gaʊn/ *n* vestido *m*; (of judge, teacher) toga *f*

GP *abbr* ⇒GENERAL PRACTITIONER

grab /græb/ *vt* (*pt* **grabbed**) agarrar

grace /greɪs/ *n* gracia *f*. **~ful** *a* elegante

gracious /'greɪʃəs/ *a* (kind) amable; (elegant) elegante

grade /greɪd/ *n* clase *f*, categoría *f*; (of goods) clase *f*, calidad *f*; (on scale) grado *m*; (school mark) nota *f*; (Amer, class) curso *m*, año *m*

gradient /'greɪdɪənt/ *n* pendiente *f*, gradiente *f* (LAm)

gradual /'grædʒʊəl/ *a* gradual. **~ly** *adv* gradualmente, poco a poco

graduat|e /'grædjʊət/ *n* (Univ) licenciado. ● /'grædjʊeɪt/ *vi* licenciarse. **~ion** /-'eɪʃn/ *n* graduación *f*

graffiti /grə'fi:tɪ/ *npl* graffiti *mpl*, pintadas *fpl*

graft /grɑ:ft/ *n* (Med, Bot) injerto *m*; (Amer 🅸, bribery) chanchullos *mpl*. ● *vt* injertar

grain /greɪn/ *n* grano *m*

gram /græm/ *n* gramo *m*

gramma|r /'græmə(r)/ *n* gramática *f*. **~tical** /grə'mætɪkl/ *a* gramatical

gramme /græm/ *n* gramo *m*

grand /grænd/ *a* (**-er**, **-est**) magnífico; (🅸, excellent) estupendo. **~child** *n* nieto *m*. **~daughter** *n* nieta *f*. **~eur** /'grændʒə(r)/ *n* grandiosidad *f*. **~father** *n* abuelo *m*. **~father clock** *n* reloj *m* de caja. **~iose** /'grændɪəʊs/ *a* grandioso. **~mother** *n* abuela *f*. **~parents** *npl* abuelos *mpl*. **~ piano** *n* piano *m* de cola. **~son** *n* nieto *m*. **~stand** /'grænstænd/ *n* tribuna *f*

granite /'grænɪt/ *n* granito *m*

granny /'grænɪ/ *n* 🅸 abuela *f*

grant /grɑ:nt/ *vt* conceder; (give) donar; (admit) admitir (**that** que). **take for ~ed** dar por sentado. ● *n* concesión *f*; (Univ) beca *f*

granule /'grænu:l/ *n* gránulo *m*

grape /greɪp/ *n* uva *f*. **~fruit** *n invar* pomelo *m*, toronja *f* (LAm)

graph /grɑ:f/ *n* gráfica *f*

graphic /'græfɪk/ *a* gráfico. **~s** *npl* diseño *m* gráfico; (Comp) gráficos *mpl*

grapple /'græpl/ *vi*. **~ with** forcejear con; (mentally) lidiar con

grasp /grɑ:sp/ *vt* agarrar. ● *n* (hold) agarro *m*; (fig) comprensión *f*. **~ing** *a* avaro

grass /grɑ:s/ *n* hierba *f*. **~hopper** *n* saltamontes *m*. **~ roots** *npl* base *f* popular. ● *a* de las bases. **~y** *a* cubierto de hierba

grate /greɪt/ *n* rejilla *f*; (fireplace) chimenea *f*. ● *vt* rallar. ● *vi* rechinar; (be irritating) ser crispante

grateful /'greɪtfl/ *a* agradecido. **~ly** *adv* con gratitud

grater /'greɪtə(r)/ *n* rallador *m*

gratif|ied /'grætɪfaɪd/ *a* contento. **~y** /'grætɪfaɪ/ *vt* satisfacer; (please) agradar a. **~ying** *a* agradable

grating /'greɪtɪŋ/ *n* reja *f*

gratitude /'grætɪtju:d/ *n* gratitud *f*

gratuitous /grə'tju:ɪtəs/ *a* gratuito

gratuity /grə'tju:ətɪ/ *n* (tip) propina *f*

grave /greɪv/ *n* sepultura *f*. ● *a* (**-er**, **-est**) (serious) grave

gravel /'grævl/ *n* grava *f*

gravely /'greɪvlɪ/ *adv* (seriously) seriamente; (solemnly) con gravedad

grave: ~stone *n* lápida *f*. **~yard** *n* cementerio *m*

gravitate /'grævɪteɪt/ *vi* gravitar

gravity /'grævətɪ/ *n* gravedad *f*

gravy /'greɪvɪ/ *n* salsa *f*

gray /greɪ/ *a* & *n* (Amer) ⇒GREY

graze /greɪz/ *vi* (eat) pacer. ● *vt* (touch) rozar; (scrape) raspar. ● *n* rasguño *m*

greas|e /gri:s/ *n* grasa *f*. ● *vt* engrasar. **~eproof paper** *n* papel *m* encerado *or* de cera. **~y** *a* <*hands*> grasiento; <*food*> graso; <*hair, skin*> graso, grasoso (LAm)

great /greɪt/ *a* (**-er**, **-est**) grande, (*before singular noun*) gran; (🅸, very good) estupendo. **G~ Britain** *n* Gran Bretaña *f*. **~-grandfather** /-'grænfɑ:ðə(r)/ *n* bisabuelo *m*. **~-grandmother** /-'grænmʌðə(r)/ *n* bisabuela *f*. **~ly** *adv* (very) muy; (much) mucho

Greece /gri:s/ *n* Grecia *f*

greed /gri:d/ *n* avaricia *f*; (for food) glotonería *f*. **~y** *a* avaro; (for food) glotón

Greek /gri:k/ *a* & *n* griego (*m*)

green /gri:n/ *a* (**-er**, **-est**) verde. ● *n* verde *m*; (grass) césped *m*. **~ belt** *n* zona *f* verde. **~ card** *n* (Amer) permiso *m* de residencia y trabajo. **~ery** *n* verdor *m*. **~gage** /-geɪdʒ/ *n* claudia *f*. **~grocer** *n* verdulero *m*. **~house** *n* invernadero *m*. **the ~house effect** el efecto invernadero. **~ light** *n* luz *f* verde. **~s** *npl* verduras *fpl*

greet /gri:t/ *vt* saludar; (receive) recibir. **~ing** *n* saludo *m*

gregarious /grɪ'geərɪəs/ *a* gregario; <*person*> sociable

grenade /grɪ'neɪd/ *n* granada *f*

grew /gru:/ ⇒GROW

grey /greɪ/ *a* (**-er**, **-est**) gris. **have ~ hair** ser canoso. ● *n* gris *m*. **~hound** *n* galgo *m*

grid /grɪd/ *n* reja *f*; (Elec, network) red *f*; (on map) cuadriculado *m*

grief /gri:f/ *n* dolor *m*. **come to ~** <*person*> acabar mal; (fail) fracasar

grievance /'gri:vns/ *n* queja *f* formal

grieve /gri:v/ *vt* apenar. ● *vi* afligirse. **~ for** llorar

grievous /'gri:vəs/ *a* doloroso; (serious) grave. **~ bodily harm** (Jurid) lesiones *fpl* (corporales) graves

grill /grɪl/ *n* parrilla *f*. ● *vt* asar a la parrilla; (🅸, interrogate) interrogar

grille /grɪl/ *n* rejilla *f*

grim /grɪm/ *a* (**grimmer**, **grimmest**) severo

grimace /'grɪməs/ *n* mueca *f*. ● *vi* hacer muecas

grim|e /graɪm/ *n* mugre *f*. **~y** *a* mugriento

grin /grɪn/ *vt* (*pt* **grinned**) sonreír. ● *n* sonrisa *f* (abierta)

grind /graɪnd/ *vt* (*pt* **ground**) moler <*coffee, corn etc*>; (pulverize) pulverizar; (sharpen) afilar; (Amer) picar, moler <*meat*>

grip /grɪp/ *vt* (*pt* **gripped**) agarrar; (interest) captar. ● *n* (hold) agarro *m*; (strength of hand) apretón *m*; (hairgrip) horquilla *f*, pasador *m*

(Mex). **come to ~s with** entender *<subject>*

grisly /'grɪzlɪ/ *a* (**-ier**, **-iest**) horrible

gristle /'grɪsl/ *n* cartílago *m*

grit /grɪt/ *n* arenilla *f*; (fig) agallas *fpl*. ● *vt* (*pt* **gritted**) echar arena en *<road>*. **~ one's teeth** (fig) acorazarse

groan /grəʊn/ *vi* gemir. ● *n* gemido *m*

grocer /'grəʊsə(r)/ *n* tendero *m*, abarrotero *m* (Mex). **~ies** *npl* comestibles *mpl*. **~y** *n* tienda *f* de comestibles, tienda *f* de abarrotes (Mex)

groggy /'grɒgɪ/ *a* (weak) débil; (unsteady) inseguro; (ill) malucho

groin /grɔɪn/ *n* ingle *f*

groom /gru:m/ *n* mozo *m* de caballos; (bridegroom) novio *m*. ● *vt* almohazar *<horses>*; (fig) preparar

groove /gru:v/ *n* ranura *f*; (in record) surco *m*

grope /grəʊp/ *vi* (find one's way) moverse a tientas. **~ for** buscar a tientas

gross /grəʊs/ *a* (**-er**, **-est**) (coarse) grosero; (Com) bruto; (fat) grueso; (flagrant) flagrante. ● *n invar* gruesa *f*. **~ly** *adv* (very) enormemente

grotesque /grəʊ'tesk/ *a* grotesco

ground /graʊnd/ ⇒GRIND. ● *n* suelo *m*; (area) terreno *m*; (reason) razón *f*; (Amer, Elec) toma *f* de tierra. ● *vt* fundar *<theory>*; retirar del servicio *<aircraft>*. **~s** *npl* jardines *mpl*; (sediment) poso *m*. **~ beef** *n* (Amer) carne *f* picada, carne *f* molida. **~ cloth** *n* (Amer) ⇒~SHEET. **~ floor** *n* planta *f* baja. **~ing** *n* base *f*, conocimientos *mpl* (in de). **~less** *a* infundado. **~sheet** *n* suelo *m* impermeable (de una tienda de campaña). **~work** *n* trabajo *m* preparatorio

group /gru:p/ *n* grupo *m*. ● *vt* agrupar. ● *vi* agruparse

grouse /graʊs/ *n invar* (bird) urogallo *m*. ● *vi* 🅸 rezongar

grovel /'grɒvl/ *vi* (*pt* **grovelled**) postrarse; (fig) arrastrarse

grow /grəʊ/ *vi* (*pt* **grew**, *pp* **grown**) crecer; (become) volverse, ponerse. ● *vt* cultivar. **~ a beard** dejarse (crecer) la barba. □ **~ up** *vi* hacerse mayor. **~ing** *a* *<quantity>* cada vez mayor; *<influence>* creciente

growl /graʊl/ *vi* gruñir. ● *n* gruñido *m*

grown /grəʊn/ ⇒GROW. ● *a* adulto. **~-up** *a* & *n* adulto (*m*)

growth /grəʊθ/ *n* crecimiento *m*; (increase) aumento *m*; (development) desarrollo *m*; (Med) bulto *m*, tumor *m*

grub /grʌb/ *n* (larva) larva *f*; (🅸, food) comida *f*

grubby /'grʌbɪ/ *a* (**-ier**, **-iest**) mugriento

grudg|e /grʌdʒ/ *vt* ⇒BEGRUDGE. ● *n* rencilla *f*. **bear/have a ~e against s.o.** guardarle rencor a uno. **~ingly** *adv* de mala gana

gruelling /'gru:əlɪŋ/ *a* agotador

gruesome /'gru:səm/ *a* horrible

gruff /grʌf/ *a* (**-er**, **-est**) *<manners>* brusco; *<voice>* ronco

grumble /'grʌmbl/ *vi* rezongar

grumpy /'grʌmpɪ/ *a* (**-ier**, **-iest**) malhumorado

grunt /grʌnt/ *vi* gruñir. ● *n* gruñido *m*

guarant|ee /gærən'ti:/ *n* garantía *f*. ● *vt* garantizar. **~or** *n* garante *m* & *f*

guard /gɑːd/ *vt* proteger; (watch) vigilar. ● *n* (vigilance, Mil group) guardia *f*; (person) guardia *m*; (on train) jefe *m* de tren. □ ~ **against** *vt* evitar; protegerse contra <*risk*>. **~ed** *a* cauteloso. **~ian** /-ɪən/ *n* guardián *m*; (of orphan) tutor *m*

Guatemala /gwɑːtəˈmɑːlə/ *n* Guatemala *f*. **~n** *a* & *n* guatemalteco (*m*)

guer(r)illa /gəˈrɪlə/ *n* guerrillero *m*. ~ **warfare** *n* guerrilla *f*

guess /ges/ *vt* adivinar; (Amer, suppose) suponer. ● *n* conjetura *f*. **~work** *n* conjeturas *fpl*

guest /gest/ *n* invitado *m*; (in hotel) huésped *m*. ~ **house** *n* casa *f* de huéspedes

guffaw /gʌˈfɔː/ *n* carcajada *f*. ● *vi* reírse a carcajadas

guidance /ˈgaɪdəns/ *n* (advice) consejos *mpl*; (information) información *f*

guide /gaɪd/ *n* (person) guía *m* & *f*; (book) guía *f*. **Girl G~** exploradora *f*, guía *f*. ● *vt* guiar. **~book** *n* guía *f*. ~ **dog** *n* perro *m* guía, perro *m* lazarillo. **~d missile** *n* proyectil *m* teledirigido. **~lines** *npl* pauta *f*

guild /gɪld/ *n* gremio *m*

guile /gaɪl/ *n* astucia *f*

guillotine /ˈgɪlətiːn/ *n* guillotina *f*

guilt /gɪlt/ *n* culpa *f*; (Jurid) culpabilidad *f*. **~y** *a* culpable

guinea pig /ˈgɪnɪ/ *n* (also fig) cobaya *f*

guitar /gɪˈtɑː(r)/ *n* guitarra *f*. **~ist** *n* guitarrista *m* & *f*

gulf /gʌlf/ *n* (part of sea) golfo *m*; (gap) abismo *m*

gull /gʌl/ *n* gaviota *f*

gullet /ˈgʌlɪt/ *n* garganta *f*, gaznate *m* 🅘

gullible /ˈgʌləbl/ *a* crédulo

gully /ˈgʌlɪ/ *n* (ravine) barranco *m*

gulp /gʌlp/ *vt*. □ ~ (**down**) tragarse de prisa. ● *vi* tragar saliva. ● *n* trago *m*

gum /gʌm/ *n* (Anat) encía *f*; (glue) goma *f* de pegar; (for chewing) chicle *m*. ● *vt* (*pt* **gummed**) engomar

gun /gʌn/ *n* (pistol) pistola *f*; (rifle) fusil *m*, escopeta *f*; (artillery piece) cañón *m*. ● *vt* (*pt* **gunned**). □ ~ **down** *vt* abatir a tiros. **~fire** *n* tiros *mpl*

gun: **~man** /-mən/ *n* pistolero *m*, gatillero *m* (Mex). **~powder** *n* pólvora *f*. **~shot** *n* disparo *m*

gurgle /ˈgɜːgl/ *vi* <*liquid*> gorgotear; <*baby*> gorjear

gush /gʌʃ/ *vi*. ~ (**out**) salir a borbotones. ● *n* (of liquid) chorro *m*; (fig) torrente *m*

gusset /ˈgʌsɪt/ *n* entretela *f*

gust /gʌst/ *n* ráfaga *f*

gusto /ˈgʌstəʊ/ *n* entusiasmo *m*

gusty /ˈgʌstɪ/ *a* borrascoso

gut /gʌt/ *n* intestino *m*. ● *vt* (*pt* **gutted**) destripar; <*fire*> destruir. **~s** *npl* tripas *fpl*; (🅘, courage) agallas *fpl*

gutter /ˈgʌtə(r)/ *n* (on roof) canalón *m*, canaleta *f*; (in street) cuneta *f*; (fig, 🅧) arroyo *m*

guttural /ˈgʌtərəl/ *a* gutural

guy /gaɪ/ *n* (🅘, man) tipo *m* 🅘, tío *m* 🅘

guzzle /ˈgʌzl/ *vt* (drink) chupar 🅘; (eat) tragarse

gym /dʒɪm/ *n* 🅘 (gymnasium) gimnasio *m*; (gymnastics) gimnasia *f*

gymnasium /dʒɪmˈneɪzɪəm/ *n* gimnasio *m*

gymnast /ˈdʒɪmnæst/ *n* gimnasta *m* & *f*. **~ics** /dʒɪmˈnæstɪks/ *npl* gimnasia *f*

gymslip /'dʒɪmslɪp/ *n* túnica *f* (de gimnasia)

gynaecolog|ist /gaɪnɪ'kɒlədʒɪst/ *n* ginecólogo *m*. **~y** *n* ginecología *f*

gypsy /'dʒɪpsɪ/ *n* gitano *m*

gyrate /dʒaɪə'reɪt/ *vi* girar

Hh

haberdashery /'hæbədæʃərɪ/ *n* mercería *f*; (Amer, clothes) ropa *f* y accesorios *mpl* para caballeros

habit /'hæbɪt/ *n* costumbre *f*; (Relig, costume) hábito *m*. **be in the ~ of** (+ *gerund*) tener la costumbre de (+ *infinitivo*), soler (+ *infinitivo*). **get into the ~ of** (+ *gerund*) acostumbrarse a (+ *infinitivo*)

habitable /'hæbɪtəbl/ *a* habitable

habitat /'hæbɪtæt/ *n* hábitat *m*

habitation /hæbɪ'teɪʃn/ *n* habitación *f*

habitual /hə'bɪtjʊəl/ *a* habitual; <*liar*> inveterado. **~ly** *adv* de costumbre

hack /hæk/ *n* (old horse) jamelgo *m*; (writer) escritorzuelo *m*. ● *vt* cortar. **~er** *n* (Comp) pirata *m* informático

hackneyed /'hæknɪd/ *a* manido

had /hæd/ ⇒HAVE

haddock /'hædək/ *n invar* eglefino *m*

haemorrhage /'hemərɪdʒ/ *n* hemorragia *f*

haemorrhoids /'hemərɔɪdz/ *npl* hemorroides *fpl*

hag /hæg/ *n* bruja *f*

haggard /'hægəd/ *a* demacrado

hail /heɪl/ *n* granizo *m*. ● *vi* granizar. ● *vt* (greet) saludar; llamar <*taxi*>. □ **~ from** *vt* venir de. **~stone** *n* grano *m* de granizo

hair /heə(r)/ *n* pelo *m*. **~band** *n* cinta *f*, banda *f* (Mex). **~brush** *n* cepillo *m* (para el pelo). **~cut** *n* corte *m* de pelo. **have a ~cut** cortarse el pelo. **~do** *n* 🅸 peinado *m*. **~dresser** *n* peluquero *m*. **~dresser's (shop)** *n* peluquería *f*. **~-dryer** *n* secador *m*, secadora *f* (Mex). **~grip** *n* horquilla *f*, pasador *m* (Mex). **~pin** *n* horquilla *f*. **~pin bend** *n* curva *f* cerrada. **~-raising** *a* espeluznante. **~spray** *n* laca *f*, fijador *m* (para el pelo). **~style** *n* peinado *m*. **~y** *a* (**-ier**, **-iest**) peludo

half /hɑːf/ *n* (*pl* **halves**) mitad *f*. ● *a* medio. **~ a dozen** media docena *f*. **~ an hour** media hora *f*. ● *adv* medio, a medias. **~-hearted** /-'hɑːtɪd/ *a* poco entusiasta. **~-mast** /-'mɑːst/ *n*. **at ~-mast** a media asta. **~ term** *n* vacaciones *fpl* de medio trimestre. **~-time** *n* (Sport) descanso *m*, medio tiempo *m* (LAm). **~way** *a* medio. ● *adv* a medio camino

hall /hɔːl/ *n* (entrance) vestíbulo *m*; (for public events) sala *f*, salón *m*. **~ of residence** residencia *f* universitaria, colegio *m* mayor. **~mark** /-mɑːk/ *n* (on gold, silver) contraste *m*; (fig) sello *m* (distintivo)

hallo /hə'ləʊ/ *int* ⇒HELLO

Hallowe'en /'hæləʊ'iːn/ *n* víspera *f* de Todos los Santos

hallucination /həluːsɪ'neɪʃn/ *n* alucinación *f*

halo /'heɪləʊ/ *n* (*pl* **-oes**) aureola *f*

halt /hɔːlt/ *n*. **come to a ~** pararse. ● *vt* parar. ● *vi* pararse

halve /hɑːv/ *vt* reducir a la mitad; (divide into halves) partir por la mitad

halves /hɑːvz/ ⇒HALF

ham /hæm/ *n* jamón *m*

hamburger /ˈhæmbɜːgə(r)/ *n* hamburguesa *f*

hammer /ˈhæmə(r)/ *n* martillo *m*. ● *vt* martill(e)ar

hammock /ˈhæmək/ *n* hamaca *f*

hamper /ˈhæmpə(r)/ *n* cesta *f*. ● *vt* estorbar

hamster /ˈhæmstə(r)/ *n* hámster *m*

hand /ˈhænd/ *n* mano *f*; (of clock, watch) manecilla *f*; (worker) obrero *m*. **by ~** a mano. **lend a ~** echar una mano. **on ~** a mano. **on the one ~... on the other d** por un lado... por otro. **out of ~** fuera de control. **to ~** a mano. ● *vt* pasar. □ **~ down** *vt* pasar. □ **~ in** *vt* entregar. □ **~ over** *vt* entregar. □ **~ out** *vt* distribuir. **~bag** *n* bolso *m*, cartera *f* (LAm), bolsa *f* (Mex). **~brake** *n* (in car) freno *m* de mano. **~cuffs** *npl* esposas *fpl*. **~ful** *n* puñado *m*; (Ⓘ, person) persona *f* difícil

handicap /ˈhændɪkæp/ *n* desventaja *f*; (Sport) hándicap *m*. **~ped** *a* minusválido

handicraft /ˈhændɪkrɑːft/ *n* artesanía *f*

handkerchief /ˈhæŋkətʃɪf/ *n* (*pl* **-fs** *or* **-chieves** /-ˈtʃiːvz/) pañuelo *m*

handle /ˈhændl/ *n* (of door) picaporte *m*; (of drawer) tirador *m*; (of implement) mango *m*; (of cup, bag, jug) asa *f*. ● *vt* manejar; (touch) tocar. **~bars** *npl* manillar *m*, manubrio *m* (LAm).

hand: ~out *n* folleto *m*; (of money, food) dádiva *f*. **~shake** *n* apretón *m* de manos

handsome /ˈhænsəm/ *a* (good-looking) guapo, buen mozo, buena moza (LAm); (generous) generoso

handwriting /ˈhændraɪtɪŋ/ *n* letra *f*

handy /ˈhændɪ/ *a* (**-ier**, **-iest**) (useful) práctico; <*person*> diestro; (near) a mano. **come in ~** venir muy bien. **~man** *n* hombre *m* habilidoso

hang /hæŋ/ *vt* (*pt* **hung**) colgar; (*pt* **hanged**) (capital punishment) ahorcar. ● *vi* colgar; <*clothing*> caer. ● *n*. **get the ~ of sth** coger el truco de algo. □ **~ about, ~ around** *vi* holgazanear. □ **~ on** *vi* (wait) esperar. □ **~ out** *vt* tender <*washing*>. □ **~ up** *vi* (also telephone) colgar

hangar /ˈhæŋə(r)/ *n* hangar *m*

hang: ~er *n* (for clothes) percha *f*. **~-glider** *n* alta *f* delta, deslizador *m* (Mex). **~over** (after drinking) resaca *f*. **~-up** *n* Ⓘ complejo *m*

hankie, hanky /ˈhæŋkɪ/ *n* Ⓘ pañuelo *m*

haphazard /hæpˈhæzəd/ *a* fortuito. **~ly** *adv* al azar

happen /ˈhæpən/ *vi* pasar, suceder, ocurrir. **if he ~s to come** si acaso viene. **~ing** *n* acontecimiento *m*

happ|ily /ˈhæpɪlɪ/ *adv* alegremente; (fortunately) afortunadamente. **~iness** *n* felicidad *f*. **~y** *a* (**-ier**, **-iest**) feliz; (satisfied) contento

harass /ˈhærəs/ *vt* acosar. **~ment** *n* acoso *m*

harbour /ˈhɑːbə(r)/ *n* puerto *m*

hard /hɑːd/ *a* (**-er**, **-est**) duro; (difficult) difícil. ● *adv* <*work*> mucho; (pull) con fuerza. **~ done by** tratado injustamente. **~-boiled egg** /-'bɔɪld/ *n* huevo *m* duro. **~ disk** *n* disco *m* duro. **~en** *vt* endurecer. ● *vi* endurecerse. **~-headed** /-'hedɪd/ *a* realista

hardly /'hɑːdlɪ/ *adv* apenas. **~ ever** casi nunca

hard: ~ness *n* dureza *f*. **~ship** *n* apuro *m*. **~ shoulder** *n* arcén *m*, acotamiento *m* (Mex). **~ware** *n* /-weə(r)/ ferretería *f*; (Comp) hardware *m*. **~ware store** *n* (Amer) ferretería *f*. **~-working** /-'wɜːkɪŋ/ *a* trabajador

hardy /'hɑːdɪ/ *a* (**-ier**, **-iest**) fuerte; (Bot) resistente

hare /heə(r)/ *n* liebre *f*

hark /hɑːk/ *vi* escuchar. □ **~ back to** *vt* volver a

harm /hɑːm/ *n* daño *m*. **there is no ~ in asking** con preguntar no se pierde nada. ● *vt* hacer daño a <*person*>; dañar <*thing*>; perjudicar <*interests*>. **~ful** *a* perjudicial. **~less** *a* inofensivo

harmonica /hɑː'mɒnɪkə/ *n* armónica *f*

harmon|ious /hɑː'məʊnɪəs/ *a* armonioso. **~y** /'hɑːmənɪ/ *n* armonía *f*

harness /'hɑːnɪs/ *n* arnés *m*. ● *vt* poner el arnés a <*horse*>; (fig) aprovechar

harp /hɑːp/ *n* arpa *f*. ● *vi*. **~ on** (about) machacar (con)

harpoon /hɑː'puːn/ *n* arpón *m*

harpsichord /'hɑːpsɪkɔːd/ *n* clavicémbalo *m*, clave *m*

harrowing / 'hærəʊɪŋ/ *a* desgarrador

harsh /hɑːʃ/ *a* (**-er**, **-est**) duro, severo; <*light*> fuerte; <*climate*> riguroso. **~ly** *adv* severamente. **~ness** *n* severidad *f*

harvest /'hɑːvɪst/ *n* cosecha *f*. ● *vt* cosechar

has /hæz/ ⇒HAVE

hassle /'hæsl/ *n* [I] lío *m* [I], rollo *m* [I]. ● *vt* (harass) fastidiar

hast|e /heɪst/ *n* prisa *f*, apuro *m* (LAm). **make ~e** darse prisa. **~ily** /'heɪstɪlɪ/ *adv* de prisa. **~y** /'heɪstɪ/ *a* (**-ier**, **-iest**) rápido; (rash) precipitado

hat /hæt/ *n* sombrero *m*

hatch /hætʃ/ *n* (for food) ventanilla *f*; (Naut) escotilla *f*. ● *vt* empollar <*eggs*>; tramar <*plot*>. ● *vi* salir del cascarón. **~back** *n* coche *m* con tres/cinco puertas; (door) puerta *f* trasera

hatchet /'hætʃɪt/ *n* hacha *f*

hat|e /heɪt/ *n* odio *m*. ● *vt* odiar. **~eful** *a* odioso. **~red** /'heɪtrɪd/ *n* odio *m*

haughty /'hɔːtɪ/ *a* (**-ier**, **-iest**) altivo

haul /hɔːl/ *vt* arrastrar; transportar <*goods*>. ● *n* (catch) redada *f*; (stolen goods) botín *m*; (journey) recorrido *m*. **~age** /-ɪdʒ/ *n* transporte *m*. **~er** (Amer), **~ier** *n* transportista *m & f*

haunt /hɔːnt/ *vt* frecuentar; <*ghost*> rondar. ● *n* sitio *m* preferido. **~ed** *a* <*house*> embrujado; <*look*> angustiado

have /hæv/, *unstressed forms*: /həv, əv/

3rd pers sing present **has**; past **had**

● *transitive verb*

····➤ tener. **I ~ three sisters** tengo tres hermanas. **do you ~ a credit card?** ¿tiene una tarjeta de crédito?

····➤ (in requests) **can I ~ a kilo of apples, please?** ¿me da un kilo de manzanas, por favor?

····➤ (eat) comer. **I had a pizza** comí una pizza

····➤ (drink) tomar. **come and ~ a drink** ven a tomar una copa

····➤ (smoke) fumar *<cigarette>*

····➤ (hold, organize) hacer *<party, meeting>*

····➤ (get, receive) **I had a letter from Tony yesterday** recibí una carta de Tony ayer. **we've had no news of her** no hemos tenido noticias suyas

····➤ (illness) tener *<flu, headache>*. **to ~ a cold** estar resfriado, tener catarro

····➤ **to have sth done: we had it painted** lo hicimos pintar. **I had my hair cut** me corté el pelo

····➤ **to have it in for s.o.** tenerle manía a uno

● *auxiliary verb*

····➤ haber. **I've seen her already** ya la he visto, ya la vi (LAm)

····➤ **to have just done sth** acabar de hacer algo. **I've just seen her** acabo de verla

····➤ **to have to do sth** tener quehacer algo. **I ~ to** *or* **I've got to go to the bank** tengo que ir al banco

····➤ (in tag questions) **you've met her, ~n't you?** ya la conoces, ¿no? *or* ¿verdad? *or* ¿no es cierto?

····➤ (in short answers) **you've forgotten something - have I?** has olvidado algo - ¿sí?

haven /ˈheɪvn/ *n* puerto *m*; (refuge) refugio *m*

haversack /ˈhævəsæk/ *n* mochila *f*

havoc /ˈhævək/ *n* estragos *mpl*

hawk /hɔːk/ *n* halcón *m*

hawthorn /ˈhɔːθɔːn/ *n* espino *m*

hay /heɪ/ *n* heno *m*. **~ fever** *n* fiebre *f* del heno. **~stack** *n* almiar *m*. **~wire** *a*. **go ~wire** (plans) desorganizarse; *<machine>* estropearse

hazard /ˈhæzəd/ *n* riesgo *m*. **~ous** *a* arriesgado

haze /heɪz/ *n* neblina *f*

hazel /ˈheɪzl/ *n* avellano *m*. **~nut** *n* avellana *f*

hazy /ˈheɪzɪ/ *a* (**-ier**, **-iest**) nebuloso

he /hiː/ *pron* él

head /hed/ *n* cabeza *f*; (of family, government) jefe *m*; (of organization) director *m*; (of beer) espuma *f*. **~s or tails** cara o cruz. ● *a* principal. ● *vt* encabezar, cabecear *<ball>*. □ **~ for** *vt* dirigirse a. **~ache** *n* dolor *m* de cabeza. **~er** *n* (football) cabezazo *m*. **~first** /-ˈfɜːst/ *adv* de cabeza. **~ing** *n* título *m*, encabezamiento *m*. **~lamp** *n* faro *m*, foco *m* (LAm). **~land** /-lənd/ *n* promontorio *m*. **~line** *n* titular *m*. **the news ~lines** el resumen informativo. **~long** *adv* de cabeza; (precipitately) precipitadamente. **~master** *n* director *m*. **~mistress** *n* directora *f*. **~-on** /-ˈɒn/ *a & adv* de frente. **~phones** *npl* auriculares *mpl*, cascos *mpl*. **~quarters** /-ˈkwɔːtəz/ *n* (of business) oficina *f* central; (Mil) cuartel *m* general. **~strong** *a* testarudo. **~teacher** /-ˈtiːtʃə(r)/ *n* director *m*. **~y** *a* (**-ier**, **-iest**) *<scent>* embriagador

heal /hiːl/ *vt* curar. ● *vi* cicatrizarse

health /helθ/ *n* salud *f*. **~y** *a* sano

heap /hiːp/ *n* montón *m*. ● *vt* amontonar.

hear /hɪə(r)/ *vt/i* (*pt* **heard** /hɜːd/) oír. **~, ~!** ¡bravo! **~ about** oír hablar de. **~ from** recibir noticias de. **~ing** *n* oído *m*; (Jurid) vista *f*. **~ing-aid** *n* audífono *m*. **~say** *n* rumores *mpl*

hearse /hɜːs/ *n* coche *m* fúnebre

heart /hɑːt/ *n* corazón *m*. **at ~** en el fondo. **by ~** de memoria. **lose ~** descorazonarse. **~ache** *n* congoja *f*. **~ attack** *n* ataque *m* al corazón, infarto *m*. **~break** *n* congoja *f*. **~breaking** *a* desgarrador. **~burn** *n* ardor *m* de estómago. **~felt** *a* sincero

hearth /hɑːθ/ *n* hogar *m*

heart: ~ily *adv* de buena gana. **~less** *a* cruel. **~y** *a* (welcome) caluroso; <*meal*> abundante

heat /hiːt/ *n* calor *m*; (contest) (prueba *f*) eliminatoria *f*. ● *vt* calentar. ● *vi* calentarse. **~ed** *a* (fig) acalorado. **~er** *n* calentador *m*

heath /hiːθ/ *n* brezal *m*, monte *m*

heathen /ˈhiːðn/ *n & a* pagano (*m*)

heather /ˈheðə(r)/ *n* brezo *m*

heat: ~ing *n* calefacción *f*. **~stroke** *n* insolación *f*. **~wave** *n* ola *f* de calor

heave /hiːv/ *vt* (lift) levantar; exhalar <*sigh*>; (!, throw) tirar. ● *vi* (pull) tirar, jalar (LAm); (!, retch) dar arcadas

heaven /ˈhevn/ *n* cielo *m*. **~ly** *a* celestial; (astronomy) celeste; (!, excellent) divino

heav|ily /ˈhevɪlɪ/ *adv* pesadamente; (smoke, drink) mucho. **~y** *a* (**-ier**, **-iest**) pesado; <*rain*> fuerte; <*traffic*> denso. **~yweight** *n* peso *m* pesado

heckle /ˈhekl/ *vt* interrumpir

hectic /ˈhektɪk/ *a* febril

he'd /hiːd/ = **he had, he would**

hedge /hedʒ/ *n* seto *m* (vivo). ● *vi* escaparse por la tangente. **~hog** *n* erizo *m*

heed /hiːd/ *vt* hacer caso de. ● *n*. **take ~** tener cuidado

heel /hiːl/ *n* talón *m*; (of shoe) tacón *m*

hefty /ˈheftɪ/ *a* (**-ier**, **-iest**) (sturdy) fuerte; (heavy) pesado

heifer /ˈhefə(r)/ *n* novilla *f*

height /haɪt/ *n* altura *f*; (of person) estatura *f*; (of fame, glory) cumbre *f*. **~en** *vt* elevar; (fig) aumentar

heir /eə(r)/ *n* heredero *m*. **~ess** *n* heredera *f*. **~loom** *n* reliquia *f* heredada

held /held/ ⇒HOLD

helicopter /ˈhelɪkɒptə(r)/ *n* helicóptero *m*

hell /hel/ *n* infierno *m*

he'll /hiːl/ = **he will**

hello /həˈləʊ/ *int* ¡hola!; (Telephone, caller) ¡oiga!, ¡bueno! (Mex); (Telephone, person answering) ¡diga!, ¡bueno! (Mex). **say ~ to** saludar

helm /helm/ *n* (Naut) timón *m*

helmet /ˈhelmɪt/ *n* casco *m*

help /help/ *vt/i* ayudar. **he cannot ~ laughing** no puede menos de reír. **~ o.s. to** servirse. **it cannot be ~ed** no hay más remedio. ● *n* ayuda *f*. ● *int* ¡socorro! **~er** *n* ayudante *m*. **~ful** *a* útil; <*person*> amable. **~ing** *n* porción *f*. **~less** *a* (unable to manage) incapaz; (defenceless) indefenso

hem /hem/ *n* dobladillo *m*

hemisphere /ˈhemɪsfɪə(r)/ *n* hemisferio *m*

hen /hen/ *n* (chicken) gallina *f*; (female bird) hembra *f*

hence /hens/ *adv* de aquí. **~forth** *adv* de ahora en adelante

henpecked /ˈhenpekt/ *a* dominado por su mujer

her /hɜ:(r)/ *pron* (direct object) la; (indirect object) le; (*after prep*) ella. **I know ~** la conozco. ● *a* su, sus *pl*

herb /hɜ:b/ *n* hierba *f*. **~al** *a* de hierbas

herd /hɜ:d/ *n* (of cattle, pigs) manada *f*; (of goats) rebaño *m*. ● *vt* arrear. **~ together** reunir

here /hɪə(r)/ *adv* aquí, acá (esp LAm). **~!** (take this) ¡tenga! **~abouts** /-əˈbaʊts/ *adv* por aquí. **~after** /-ˈɑ:ftə(r)/ *adv* en el futuro. **~by** /-ˈbaɪ/ *adv* por este medio

heredit|ary /hɪˈredɪtərɪ/ *a* hereditario

here|sy /ˈherəsɪ/ *n* herejía *f*. **~tic** *n* hereje *m & f*

herewith /hɪəˈwɪð/ *adv* adjunto

heritage /ˈherɪtɪdʒ/ *n* herencia *f*; (fig) patrimonio *m*

hermetically /hɜ:ˈmetɪklɪ/ *adv*. **~ sealed** herméticamente cerrado

hermit /ˈhɜ:mɪt/ *n* ermitaño *m*, eremita *m*

hernia /ˈhɜ:nɪə/ *n* hernia *f*

hero /ˈhɪərəʊ/ *n* (*pl* **-oes**) héroe *m*. **~ic** /hɪˈrəʊɪk/ *a* heroico

heroin /ˈherəʊɪn/ *n* heroína *f*

hero: ~ine /ˈherəʊɪn/ *n* heroína *f*. **~ism** /ˈherəʊɪzm/ *n* heroismo *m*

heron /ˈherən/ *n* garza *f* (real)

herring /ˈherɪŋ/ *n* arenque *m*

hers /hɜ:z/ *poss pron* (el) suyo *m*, (la) suya *f*, (los) suyos *mpl*, (las) suyas *fpl*

herself /hɜ:ˈself/ *pron* ella misma; (*reflexive*) se; (*after prep*) sí misma

he's /hi:z/ = **he is, he has**

hesit|ant /ˈhezɪtənt/ *a* vacilante. **~ate** /-teɪt/ *vi* vacilar. **~ation** /-ˈteɪʃn/ *n* vacilación *f*

heterosexual /hetərəʊˈseksjʊəl/ *a & n* heterosexual (*m & f*)

het up /hetˈʌp/ *a* 🅸 nervioso

hew /hju:/ *vt* (*pp* **hewed** *or* **hewn**) cortar; (cut into shape) tallar

hexagon /ˈheksəgən/ *n* hexágono *m*. **~al** /-ˈægənl/ *a* hexagonal

hey /heɪ/ *int* ¡eh!; (expressing dismay, protest) ¡oye!

heyday /ˈheɪdeɪ/ *n* apogeo *m*

hi /haɪ/ *int* 🅸 ¡hola!

hibernat|e /ˈhaɪbəneɪt/ *vi* hibernar. **~ion** /-ˈneɪʃn/ *n* hibernación *f*

hiccough, hiccup /ˈhɪkʌp/ *n* hipo *m*. **have (the) ~s** tener hipo. ● *vi* hipar

hide /haɪd/ *vt* (*pt* **hid**, *pp* **hidden**) esconder. ● *vi* esconderse. ● *n* piel *f*; (tanned) cuero *m*. **~-and-seek** /ˈhaɪdnsi:k/ *n*. **play ~-and-seek** jugar al escondite, jugar a las escondidas (LAm)

hideous /ˈhɪdɪəs/ *a* (dreadful) horrible; (ugly) feo

hideout /ˈhaɪdaʊt/ *n* escondrijo *m*

hiding /ˈhaɪdɪŋ/ *n* (🅸, thrashing) paliza *f*. **go into ~** esconderse. **~ place** *n* escondite *m*, escondrijo *m*

hierarchy /ˈhaɪərɑ:kɪ/ *n* jerarquía *f*

hieroglyphics /haɪərəˈglɪfɪks/ *n* jeroglíficos *mpl*

hi-fi /ˈhaɪfaɪ/ *a* de alta fidelidad. ● *n* equipo *m* de alta fidelidad, hi-fi *m*

high /haɪ/ *a* (**-er, -est**) alto; <*ideals*> elevado; <*wind*> fuerte;

(⊞, drugged) drogado, colocado ⊞; <voice> agudo; <meat> pasado. ● *n* alto nivel *m*. **a** (**new**) **~** un récord. ● *adv* alto. **~er education** *n* enseñanza *f* superior. **~-handed** /-'hændɪd/ *a* prepotente. **~ heels** *npl* zapatos *mpl* de tacón alto. **~lands** /-ləndz/ *npl* tierras *fpl* altas. **~-level** *a* de alto nivel. **~light** *n* punto *m* culminante. ● *vt* destacar; (Art) realzar. **~ly** *adv* muy; <paid> muy bien. **~ly strung** *a* nervioso. **H~ness** *n* (title) alteza *f*. **~-rise** *a* <building> alto. **~ school** *n* (Amer) instituto *m*, colegio *m* secundario. **~ street** *n* calle *f* principal. **~-strung** *a* (Amer) nervioso. **~way** *n* carretera *f*

hijack /'haɪdʒæk/ *vt* secuestrar. ● *n* secuestro *m*. **~er** *n* secuestrador

hike /haɪk/ *n* caminata *f*. ● *vi* ir de caminata. **~r** *n* excursionista *m & f*

hilarious /hɪ'leərɪəs/ *a* muy divertido

hill /hɪl/ *n* colina *f*; (slope) cuesta *f*. **~side** *n* ladera *f*. **~y** *a* accidentado

hilt /hɪlt/ *n* (of sword) puño *m*. **to the ~** (fig) totalmente

him /hɪm/ *pron* (*direct object*) lo, le (only Spain); (*indirect object*) le; (*after prep*) él. **I know ~** lo/le conozco. **~self** *pron* él mismo; (*reflexive*) se; (*after prep*) sí mismo

hind|er /'hɪndə(r)/ *vt* estorbar. **~rance** /'hɪndrəns/ *n* obstáculo *m*

hindsight /'haɪnsaɪt/ *n*. **with ~** retrospectivamente

Hindu /'hɪndu:/ *n & a* hindú (*m & f*). **~ism** *n* hinduismo *m*

hinge /hɪndʒ/ *n* bisagra *f*

hint /hɪnt/ *n* indirecta *f*; (advice) consejo *m*. ● *vi* soltar una indirecta. **~ at** dar a entender

hip /hɪp/ *n* cadera *f*

hippie /'hɪpɪ/ *n* hippy *m & f*

hippopotamus /hɪpə'pɒtəməs/ *n* (*pl* **-muses** *or* **-mi** /-maɪ/) hipopótamo *m*

hire /haɪə(r)/ *vt* alquilar <thing>; contratar <person>. ● *n* alquiler *m*. **car ~** alquiler *m* de coches. **~ purchase** *n* compra *f* a plazos

his /hɪz/ *a* su, sus *pl*. ● *poss pron* (el) suyo *m*, (la) suya *f*, (los) suyos *mpl*, (las) suyas *fpl*

Hispan|ic /hɪ'spænɪk/ *a* hispánico. ● *n* (Amer) hispano *m*. **~ist** /'hɪspənɪst/ *n* hispanista *m & f*

hiss /hɪs/ *n* silbido. ● *vt/i* silbar

histor|ian /hɪ'stɔ:rɪən/ *n* historiador *m*. **~ic(al)** /hɪ'stɒrɪkl/ *a* histórico. **~y** /'hɪstərɪ/ *n* historia *f*.

hit /hɪt/ *vt* (*pt* **hit**, *pres p* **hitting**) golpear <object>; pegarle a <person>; (collide with) chocar con; (affect) afectar. **~ it off with** hacer buenas migas con. □ **~ on** *vt* dar con. ● *n* (blow) golpe *m*; (success) éxito *m*

hitch /hɪtʃ/ *vt* (fasten) enganchar. ● *n* (snag) problema *m*. **~ a lift**, **~ a ride** (Amer) ⇒~HIKE. **~hike** *vi* hacer autostop, hacer dedo, ir de aventón (Mex). **~hiker** *n* autoestopista *m & f*

hither /'hɪðə(r)/ *adv* aquí, acá. **~ and thither** acá y allá. **~to** *adv* hasta ahora

hit-or-miss /hɪtɔ:'mɪs/ *a* <approach> poco científico

hive /haɪv/ *n* colmena *f*

hoard /hɔ:d/ *vt* acumular. ● *n* provisión *f*; (of money) tesoro *m*

hoarding /ˈhɔːdɪŋ/ *n* valla *f* publicitaria

hoarse /hɔːs/ *a* (**-er**, **-est**) ronco. **~ly** *adv* con voz ronca

hoax /həʊks/ *n* engaño *m*. ● *vt* engañar

hob /hɒb/ *n* (of cooker) hornillos *mpl*, hornillas *fpl* (LAm)

hobble /ˈhɒbl/ *vi* cojear, renguear (LAm)

hobby /ˈhɒbɪ/ *n* pasatiempo *m*. **~horse** *n* (toy) caballito *m* (de niño); (fixation) caballo *m* de batalla

hockey /ˈhɒkɪ/ *n* hockey *m*; (Amer) hockey *m* sobre hielo

hoe /həʊ/ *n* azada *f*. ● *vt* (*pres p* **hoeing**) azadonar

hog /hɒg/ *n* (Amer) cerdo *m*. ● *vt* (*pt* **hogged**) 🄸 acaparar

hoist /hɔɪst/ *vt* levantar; izar <*flag*>. ● *n* montacargas *m*

hold /həʊld/ *vt* (*pt* **held**) tener; (grasp) coger (esp Spain), agarrar; (contain) contener; mantener <*interest*>; (believe) creer. ● *vi* mantenerse. ● *n* (influence) influencia *f*; (Naut, Aviat) bodega *f*. **get ~ of** agarrar; (fig, acquire) adquirir. □ **~ back** *vt* (contain) contener. □ **~ on** *vi* (stand firm) resistir; (wait) esperar. □ **~ on to** *vt* (keep) guardar; (cling to) agarrarse a. □ **~ out** *vt* (offer) ofrecer. *vi* (resist) resistir. □ **~ up** *vt* (raise) levantar; (support) sostener; (delay) retrasar; (rob) atracar. **~all** *n* bolsa *f* (de viaje). **~er** *n* tenedor *m*; (of post) titular *m*; (wallet) funda *f*. **~up** atraco *m*

hole /həʊl/ *n* agujero *m*; (in ground) hoyo *m*; (in road) bache *m*. ● *vt* agujerear

holiday /ˈhɒlɪdeɪ/ *n* vacaciones *fpl*; (public) fiesta *f*. **go on ~** ir de vacaciones. **~maker** *n* veraneante *m & f*

holiness /ˈhəʊlɪnɪs/ *n* santidad *f*

Holland /ˈhɒlənd/ *n* Holanda *f*

hollow /ˈhɒləʊ/ *a & n* hueco (*m*)

holly /ˈhɒlɪ/ *n* acebo *m*

holocaust /ˈhɒləkɔːst/ *n* holocausto *m*

holster /ˈhəʊlstə(r)/ *n* pistolera *f*

holy /ˈhəʊlɪ/ *a* (**-ier**, **-iest**) santo, sagrado. **H~ Ghost** *n*, **H~ Spirit** *n* Espíritu *m* Santo. **~ water** *n* agua *f* bendita

homage /ˈhɒmɪdʒ/ *n* homenaje *m*. **pay ~ to** rendir homenaje a

home /həʊm/ *n* casa *f*; (for old people) residencia *f* de ancianos; (native land) patria *f*. ● *a* <*cooking*> casero; (address) particular; <*background*> familiar; (Pol) interior; <*match*> de casa. ● *adv*. (at) **~** en casa. **~land** *n* patria *f*. **~less** *a* sin hogar. **~ly** *a* (**-ier**, **-iest**) casero; (Amer, ugly) feo. **~-made** *a* hecho en casa. **~ page** *n* (Comp) página *f* frontal. **~sick** *a*. **be ~sick** echar de menos a su familia/su país, extrañar a su familia/su país (LAm). **~ town** *n* ciudad *f* natal. **~work** *n* deberes *mpl*

homicide /ˈhɒmɪsaɪd/ *n* homicidio *m*

homoeopathic /həʊmɪəʊˈpæθɪk/ *a* homeopático

homogeneous /hɒməʊˈdʒiːnɪəs/ *a* homogéneo

homosexual /həʊməʊˈseksjʊəl/ *a & n* homosexual (*m*)

honest /ˈɒnɪst/ *a* honrado; (frank) sincero. **~ly** *adv* honradamente. **~y** *n* honradez *f*

honey /ˈhʌnɪ/ *n* miel *f*. **~comb** *n* panal *m*. **~moon** *n* luna *f* de miel. **~suckle** *n* madreselva *f*

honorary /ˈɒnərərɪ/ *a* honorario

honour /ˈɒnə(r)/ *n* honor *m*. ● *vt* honrar; cumplir (con) <*promise*>. **~able** *a* honorable

hood /hʊd/ *n* capucha *f*; (car roof) capota *f*; (Amer, car bonnet) capó *m*, capote *m* (Mex)

hoodwink /ˈhʊdwɪŋk/ *vt* engañar

hoof /hu:f/ *n* (*pl* **hoofs** *or* **hooves**) (of horse) casco *m*, pezuña *f* (Mex); (of cow) pezuña *f*

hook /hʊk/ *n* gancho *m*; (on garment) corchete *m*; (for fishing) anzuelo *m*. **let s.o. off the ~** dejar salir a uno del atolladero. **off the ~** <*telephone*> descolgado. ● *vt*. **~ed on** 🅸 adicto a. □ **~ up** *vt* enganchar. **~ed** *a* <*tool*> en forma de gancho; <*nose*> aguileño

hookey /ˈhʊkɪ/ *n*. **play ~** (Amer 🅸) faltar a clase, hacer novillos

hooligan /ˈhu:lɪgən/ *n* vándalo *m*, gamberro *m*

hoop /hu:p/ *n* aro *m*

hooray /hʊˈreɪ/ *int & n* ¡viva! (*m*)

hoot /hu:t/ *n* (of horn) bocinazo *m*; (of owl) ululato *m*. ● *vi* tocar la bocina; <*owl*> ulular

Hoover /ˈhu:və(r)/ *n* (P) aspiradora *f*. ● *vt* pasar la aspiradora por, aspirar (LAm)

hooves /hu:vz/ ⇒HOOF

hop /hɒp/ *vi* (*pt* **hopped**) saltar a la pata coja; <*frog, rabbit*> brincar, saltar; <*bird*> dar saltitos. ● *n* salto *m*; (flight) etapa *f*. **~(s)** (Bot) lúpulo *m*

hope /həʊp/ *n* esperanza *f*. ● *vt/i* esperar. **~ for** esperar. **~ful** *a* (optimistic) esperanzado; (promising) esperanzador. **~fully** *adv* con optimismo; (it is hoped) se espera. **~less** *a* desesperado

horde /hɔ:d/ *n* horda *f*

horizon /həˈraɪzn/ *n* horizonte *m*

horizontal /hɒrɪˈzɒntl/ *a* horizontal. **~ly** *adv* horizontalmente

hormone /ˈhɔ:məʊn/ *n* hormona *f*

horn /hɔ:n/ *n* cuerno *m*, asta *f*, cacho *m* (LAm); (of car) bocina *f*; (Mus) trompa *f*. **~ed** *a* con cuernos

hornet /ˈhɔ:nɪt/ *n* avispón *m*

horoscope /ˈhɒrəskəʊp/ *n* horóscopo *m*

horrible /ˈhɒrəbl/ *a* horrible

horrid /ˈhɒrɪd/ *a* horrible

horrific /həˈrɪfɪk/ *a* horroroso

horrify /ˈhɒrɪfaɪ/ *vt* horrorizar

horror /ˈhɒrə(r)/ *n* horror *m*

hors-d'oeuvre /ɔ:ˈdɜ:vr/ *n* (*pl* **-s** /-ˈdɜ:vr/) entremés *m*, botana *f* (Mex)

horse /hɔ:s/ *n* caballo *m*. **~back** *n*. **on ~back** a caballo. **~power** *n* (unit) caballo *m* (de fuerza). **~racing** *n* carreras *fpl* de caballos. **~shoe** *n* herradura *f*

horticultur|al /hɔ:tɪˈkʌltʃərəl/ *a* hortícola. **~e** /ˈhɔ:tɪkʌltʃə(r)/ *n* horticultura *f*

hose /həʊz/ *n* manguera *f*, manga *f*. ● *vt*. **~ down** lavar (con manguera). **~pipe** *n* manga *f*

hosiery /ˈhəʊzɪərɪ/ *n* calcetería *f*

hospice /ˈhɒspɪs/ *n* residencia *f* para enfermos desahuciados

hospitable /hɒˈspɪtəbl/ *a* hospitalario

hospital /ˈhɒspɪtl/ *n* hospital *m*

hospitality /hɒspɪˈtælətɪ/ *n* hospitalidad *f*

host /həʊst/ *n* (master of house) anfitrión *m*; (Radio, TV) presentador *m*; (multitude) gran cantidad *f*; (Relig) hostia *f*

hostage /ˈhɒstɪdʒ/ *n* rehén *m*

hostel /'hɒstl/ *n* (for students) residencia *f*; (for homeless people) hogar *m*

hostess /'həʊstɪs/ *n* anfitriona *f*

hostil|e /'hɒstaɪl/ *a* hostil. **~ity** /-'tɪlətɪ/ *n* hostilidad *f*

hot /hɒt/ *a* (**hotter**, **hottest**) caliente; <*weather, day*> caluroso; <*climate*> cálido; (Culin) picante; <*news*> de última hora. **be/feel ~** tener calor. **get ~** calentarse. **it is ~** hace calor. **~bed** *n* (fig) semillero *m*

hotchpotch /'hɒtʃpɒtʃ/ *n* mezcolanza *f*

hot dog *n* perrito *m* caliente

hotel /həʊ'tel/ *n* hotel *m*. **~ier** /-ɪeɪ/*n* hotelero *m*

hot: ~house *n* invernadero *m*. **~plate** *n* placa *f*, hornilla *f* (LAm). **~-water bottle** /-'wɔ:tə(r)/ *n* bolsa *f* de agua caliente

hound /haʊnd/ *n* perro *m* de caza. ● *vt* perseguir

hour /aʊə(r)/ *n* hora *f*. **~ly** *a* <*rate*> por hora. ● *adv* (every hour) cada hora; (by the hour) por hora

house /haʊs/ *n* (*pl* **-s** /'haʊzɪz/) casa *f*; (Pol) cámara *f*. ● /haʊz/ *vt* alojar; (keep) guardar. **~hold** *n* casa *f*. **~holder** *n* dueño *m* de una casa. **~keeper** *n* ama *f* de llaves. **~maid** *n* criada *f*, mucama *f* (LAm). **~-proud** *a* meticuloso. **~warming** (party) *n fiesta de inauguración de una casa*. **~wife** *n* ama *f* de casa. **~work** *n* tareas *fpl* domésticas

housing /'haʊzɪŋ/ *n* alojamiento *m*. **~ development** (Amer), **~ estate** *n* complejo *m* habitacional, urbanización *f*

hovel /'hɒvl/ *n* casucha *f*

hover /'hɒvə(r)/ *vi* <*bird, threat etc*> cernerse; (loiter) rondar. **~craft** *n* (*pl invar or* **-crafts**) aerodeslizador *m*

how /haʊ/ *adv* cómo. **~ about a walk?** ¿qué te parece si damos un paseo? **~ are you?** ¿cómo está Vd? **~ do you do?** (in introduction) mucho gusto. **~ long?** (in time) ¿cuánto tiempo? **~ long is the room?** ¿cuánto mide de largo el cuarto? **~ often?** ¿cuántas veces?

however /haʊ'evə(r)/ *adv* (nevertheless) no obstante, sin embargo; (with verb) de cualquier manera que (+ *subjunctive*); (with adjective or adverb) por... que (+ *subjunctive*). **~ much it rains** por mucho que llueva

howl /haʊl/ *n* aullido. ● *vi* aullar

hp *abbr* ⇒HORSEPOWER

HP *abbr* ⇒HIRE PURCHASE

hub /hʌb/ *n* (of wheel) cubo *m*; (fig) centro *m*

hubcap /'hʌbkæp/ *n* tapacubos *m*

huddle /'hʌdl/ *vi* apiñarse

hue /hju:/ *n* (colour) color *m*

huff /hʌf/ *n*. **be in a ~** estar enfurruñado

hug /hʌg/ *vt* (*pt* **hugged**) abrazar. ● *n* abrazo *m*

huge /hju:dʒ/ *a* enorme. **~ly** *adv* enormemente

hulk /hʌlk/ *n* (of ship) barco *m* viejo

hull /hʌl/ *n* (of ship) casco *m*

hullo /hə'ləʊ/ *int* ⇒HELLO

hum /hʌm/ *vt/i* (*pt* **hummed**) <*person*> canturrear; <*insect, engine*> zumbar. ● *n* zumbido *m*

human /'hju:mən/ *a* & *n* humano (*m*). **~ being** *n* ser *m* humano. **~e** /hju:'meɪn/ *a* humano. **~itarian** /hju:mænɪ'teərɪən/ *a* humanitario. **~ity** /hju:'mænətɪ/ *n* humanidad *f*

humbl|e /ˈhʌmbl/ *a* (**-er**, **-est**) humilde. ● *vt* humillar. **~y** *adv* humildemente

humdrum /ˈhʌmdrʌm/ *a* monótono

humid /ˈhju:mɪd/ *a* húmedo. **~ity** /hju:ˈmɪdətɪ/ *n* humedad *f*

humiliat|e /hju:ˈmɪlɪeɪt/ *vt* humillar. **~ion** /-ˈeɪʃn/ *n* humillación *f*

humility /hju:ˈmɪlətɪ/ *n* humildad *f*

humo|rist /ˈhju:mərɪst/ *n* humorista *m & f*. **~rous** /-rəs/ *a* humorístico. **~rously** *adv* con gracia. **~ur** /ˈhju:mə(r)/ *n* humor *m*. **sense of ~ur** sentido *m* del humor

hump /hʌmp/ *n* (of person, camel) joroba *f*; (in ground) montículo *m*. ● *vt* encorvar. **~** (**about**) (🄸, carry) cargar

hunch /hʌntʃ/ *vt* encorvar. ● *n* presentimiento *m*; (lump) joroba *f*. **~back** *n* jorobado *m*

hundred /ˈhʌndrəd/ *a* ciento, (before noun) cien. **one ~ and ninety-eight** ciento noventa y ocho. **two ~** doscientos. **three ~ pages** trescientas páginas. **four ~** cuatrocientos. **five ~** quinientos. ● *n* ciento *m*. **~s of** centenares de. **~th** *a & n* centésimo (*m*). **~weight** *n* 50,8kg; (Amer) 45,36kg

hung /hʌŋ/ ⇒HANG

Hungar|ian /hʌŋˈgeərɪən/ *a & n* húngaro (*m*). **~y** /ˈhʌŋgərɪ/ *n* Hungría *f*

hung|er /ˈhʌŋgə(r)/ *n* hambre *f*. ● *vi*. **~er for** tener hambre de. **~rily** /ˈhʌŋgrəlɪ/ *adv* ávidamente. **~ry** *a* (**-ier**, **-iest**) hambriento. **be ~ry** tener hambre

hunk /hʌŋk/ *n* (buen) pedazo *m*

hunt /hʌnt/ *vt* cazar. ● *vi* cazar. **~ for** buscar. ● *n* caza *f*. **~er** *n* cazador *m*. **~ing** *n* caza *f*. **go ~ing** ir de caza

hurl /hɜ:l/ *vt* lanzar

hurrah /hʊˈrɑ:/, **hurray** /hʊˈreɪ/ *int & n* ¡viva! (*m*)

hurricane /ˈhʌrɪkən/ *n* huracán *m*

hurr|ied /ˈhʌrɪd/ *a* apresurado. **~iedly** *adv* apresuradamente. **~y** *vi* darse prisa, apurarse (LAm). ● *vt* meter prisa a, apurar (LAm). ● *n* prisa *f*. **be in a ~y** tener prisa, estar apurado (LAm)

hurt /hɜ:t/ *vt* (*pt* **hurt**) hacer daño a, lastimar (LAm). **~ s.o.'s feelings** ofender a uno. ● *vi* doler. **my head ~s** me duele la cabeza. **~ful** *a* hiriente

hurtle /ˈhɜ:tl/ *vt* ir volando. ● *vi*. **~ along** mover rápidamente

husband /ˈhʌzbənd/ *n* marido *m*, esposo *m*

hush /hʌʃ/ *vt* acallar. ● *n* silencio *m*. □ **~ up** *vt* acallar <*affair*>. **~-hush** *a* 🄸 super secreto

husk /hʌsk/ *n* cáscara *f*

husky /ˈhʌskɪ/ *a* (**-ier**, **-iest**) (hoarse) ronco

hustle /ˈhʌsl/ *vt* (jostle) empujar. ● *vi* (hurry) darse prisa, apurarse (LAm). ● *n* empuje *m*

hut /hʌt/ *n* cabaña *f*

hutch /hʌtʃ/ *n* conejera *f*

hybrid /ˈhaɪbrɪd/ *a & n* híbrido (*m*)

hydrangea /haɪˈdreɪndʒə/ *n* hortensia *f*

hydrant /ˈhaɪdrənt/ *n*. (**fire**) **~** *n* boca *f* de riego, boca *f* de incendios (LAm)

hydraulic /haɪˈdrɔ:lɪk/ *a* hidráulico

hydroelectric /haɪdrəʊɪˈlektrɪk/ *a* hidroeléctrico

hydrofoil /ˈhaɪdrəfɔɪl/ *n* hidrodeslizador *m*

hydrogen /ˈhaɪdrədʒən/ *n* hidrógeno *m*

hyena /haɪˈiːnə/ *n* hiena *f*

hygien|e /ˈhaɪdʒiːn/ *n* higiene *f*. **~ic** /haɪˈdʒiːnɪk/ *a* higiénico

hymn /hɪm/ *n* himno *m*

hyper... /ˈhaɪpə(r)/ *pref* hiper...

hyphen /ˈhaɪfn/ *n* guión *m*. **~ate** /-eɪt/ *vt* escribir con guión

hypno|sis /hɪpˈnəʊsɪs/ *n* hipnosis *f*. **~tic** /-ˈnɒtɪk/ *a* hipnótico. **~tism** /ˈhɪpnətɪzəm/ *n* hipnotismo *m*. **~tist** /ˈhɪpnətɪst/ *n* hipnotista *m & f*. **~tize** /ˈhɪpnətaɪz/ *vt* hipnotizar

hypochondriac /haɪpəˈkɒndrɪæk/ *n* hipocondríaco *m*

hypocri|sy /hɪˈpɒkrəsɪ/ *n* hipocresía *f*. **~te** /ˈhɪpəkrɪt/ *n* hipócrita *m & f*. **~tical** /hɪpəˈkrɪtɪkl/ *a* hipócrita

hypodermic /haɪpəˈdɜːmɪk/ *a* hipodérmico. ● *n* hipodérmica *f*

hypothe|sis /haɪˈpɒθəsɪs/ *n* (*pl* **-theses** /-siːz/) hipótesis *f*. **~tical** /-əˈθetɪkl/ *a* hipotético

hysteri|a /hɪˈstɪərɪə/ *n* histerismo *m*. **~cal** /-ˈterɪkl/ *a* histérico. **~cs** /hɪˈsterɪks/ *npl* histerismo *m*. **have ~cs** ponerse histérico; (laugh) morir de risa

Ii

I /aɪ/ *pron* yo

ice /aɪs/ *n* hielo *m*. ● *vt* helar; glasear <*cake*>. ● *vi*. **~ (up)** helarse, congelarse. **~berg** /-bɜːg/ *n* iceberg *m*. **~ box** *n* (compartment) congelador; (Amer ⓘ, refrigerator) frigorífico *m*, refrigerador *m* (LAm). **~cream** *n* helado *m*. **~ cube** *n* cubito *m* de hielo

Iceland /ˈaɪslənd/ *n* Islandia *f*

ice: ~ lolly polo *m*, paleta *f* helada (LAm). **~ rink** *n* pista *f* de hielo. **~ skating** *n* patinaje *m* sobre hielo

icicle /ˈaɪsɪkl/ *n* carámbano *m*

icing /ˈaɪsɪŋ/ *n* glaseado *m*

icon /ˈaɪkɒn/ *n* icono *m*

icy /ˈaɪsɪ/ *a* (**-ier**, **-iest**) helado; (fig) glacial

I'd /aɪd/ = **I had, I would**

idea /aɪˈdɪə/ *n* idea *f*

ideal /aɪˈdɪəl/ *a & n* ideal (*m*). **~ism** *n* idealismo *m*. **~ist** *n* idealista *m & f*. **~istic** /-ˈlɪstɪk/ *a* idealista. **~ize** *vt* idealizar. **~ly** *adv* idealmente

identical /aɪˈdentɪkl/ *a* idéntico. **~ twins** *npl* gemelos *mpl* idénticos, gemelos *mpl* (LAm)

identif|ication /aɪdentɪfɪˈkeɪʃn/ *n* identificación *f*. **~y** /aɪˈdentɪfaɪ/ *vt* identificar. ● *vi*. **~y with** identificarse con

identity /aɪˈdentɪtɪ/ *n* identidad *f*. **~ card** *n* carné *m* de identidad

ideolog|ical /aɪdɪəˈlɒdʒɪkl/ *a* ideológico. **~y** /aɪdɪˈɒlədʒɪ/ *n* ideología *f*

idiocy /ˈɪdɪəsɪ/ *n* idiotez *f*

idiom /ˈɪdɪəm/ *n* locución *f*. **~atic** /-ˈmætɪk/ *a* idiomático

idiot /ˈɪdɪət/ *n* idiota *m & f*. **~ic** /-ˈɒtɪk/ *a* idiota

idle /ˈaɪdl/ *a* (**-er**, **-est**) ocioso; (lazy) holgazán; (out of work) desocupado; <*machine*> parado. ● *vi* <*engine*> andar al ralentí. **~ness** *n* ociosidad *f*; (laziness) holgazanería *f*

idol /ˈaɪdl/ *n* ídolo *m*. **~ize** *vt* idolatrar

idyllic /ɪˈdɪlɪk/ *a* idílico

i.e. *abbr* (= **id est**) es decir

if /ɪf/ *conj* si

igloo /ˈɪglu:/ *n* iglú *m*

ignit|e /ɪgˈnaɪt/ *vt* encender. ● *vi* encenderse. **~ion** /-ˈnɪʃn/ *n* ignición *f*; (Auto) encendido *m*. **~ion key** *n* llave *f* de contacto

ignoramus /ɪgnəˈreɪməs/ *n* (*pl* **-muses**) ignorante

ignoran|ce /ˈɪgnərəns/ *n* ignorancia *f*. **~t** *a* ignorante

ignore /ɪgˈnɔ:(r)/ *vt* no hacer caso de; hacer caso omiso de <*warning*>

ill /ɪl/ *a* enfermo. ● *adv* mal. ● *n* mal *m*

I'll /aɪl/ = **I will**

ill: ~-advised /-ədˈvaɪzd/ *a* imprudente. **~ at ease** /-ətˈi:z/ *a* incómodo. **~-bred** /-ˈbred/ *a* mal educado

illegal /ɪˈli:gl/ *a* ilegal

illegible /ɪˈledʒəbl/ *a* ilegible

illegitima|cy /ɪlɪˈdʒɪtɪməsɪ/ *n* ilegitimidad *f*. **~te** /-ət/ *a* ilegítimo

illitera|cy /ɪˈlɪtərəsɪ/ *n* analfabetismo *m*. **~te** /-ət/ *a* analfabeto

illness /ˈɪlnɪs/ *n* enfermedad *f*

illogical /ɪˈlɒdʒɪkl/ *a* ilógico

illuminat|e /ɪˈlu:mɪneɪt/ *vt* iluminar. **~ion** /-ˈneɪʃn/ *n* iluminación *f*

illus|ion /ɪˈlu:ʒn/ *n* ilusión *f*. **~sory** /-serɪ/ *a* ilusorio

illustrat|e /ˈɪləstreɪt/ *vt* ilustrar. **~ion** /-ˈstreɪʃn/ *n* ilustración *f*; (example) ejemplo *m*

illustrious /ɪˈlʌstrɪəs/ *a* ilustre

ill will /ɪlˈwɪl/ *n* mala voluntad *f*

I'm /aɪm/ = **I am**

image /ˈɪmɪdʒ/ *n* imagen *f*. **~ry** *n* imágenes *fpl*

imagin|able /ɪˈmædʒɪnəbl/ *a* imaginable. **~ary** *a* imaginario. **~ation** /-ˈneɪʃn/ *n* imaginación *f*. **~ative** *a* imaginativo. **~e** /ɪˈmædʒɪn/ *vt* imaginar(se)

imbalance /ɪmˈbæləns/ *n* desequilibrio *m*

imbecile /ˈɪmbəsi:l/ *n* imbécil *m & f*

imitat|e /ˈɪmɪteɪt/ *vt* imitar. **~ion** /-ˈteɪʃn/ *n* imitación *f*. ● *a* de imitación. **~or** *n* imitador *m*

immaculate /ɪˈmækjʊlət/ *a* inmaculado

immatur|e /ɪməˈtjʊə(r)/ *a* inmaduro. **~ity** *n* inmadurez *f*

immediate /ɪˈmi:dɪət/ *a* inmediato. **~ly** *adv* inmediatamente. ● *conj* en cuanto (+ *subjunctive*)

immens|e /ɪˈmens/ *a* inmenso. **~ely** *adv* inmensamente; (🅸, very much) muchísimo

immers|e /ɪˈmɜ:s/ *vt* sumergir. **~ion** /-ʃn/ *n* inmersión *f*. **~ion heater** *n* calentador *m* de inmersión

immigra|nt /ˈɪmɪgrənt/ *a & n* inmigrante (*m & f*). **~tion** /-ˈgreɪʃn/ *n* inmigración *f*

imminent /ˈɪmɪnənt/ *a* inminente

immobil|e /ɪ'məʊbaɪl/ *a* inmóvil. **~ize** /-bɪlaɪz/ *vt* inmovilizar

immoderate /ɪ'mɒdərət/ *a* inmoderado

immodest /ɪ'mɒdɪst/ *a* inmodesto

immoral /ɪ'mɒrəl/ *a* inmoral. **~ity** /ɪmə'rælətɪ/ *n* inmoralidad *f*

immortal /ɪ'mɔ:tl/ *a* inmortal. **~ity** /-'tælətɪ/ *n* inmortalidad *f*. **~ize** *vt* inmortalizar

immun|e /ɪ'mju:n/ *a* inmune (**to** a). **~ity** *n* inmunidad *f*. **~ization** /ɪmjʊnaɪ'zeɪʃn/ *n* inmunización *f*. **~ize** /'ɪmjʊnaɪz/ *vt* inmunizar

imp /ɪmp/ *n* diablillo *m*

impact /'ɪmpækt/ *n* impacto *m*

impair /ɪm'peə(r)/ *vt* perjudicar

impale /ɪm'peɪl/ *vt* atravesar (**on** con)

impart /ɪm'pɑ:t/ *vt* comunicar <*news*>; impartir <*knowledge*>

impartial /ɪm'pɑ:ʃl/ *a* imparcial. **~ity** /-ɪ'ælətɪ/ *n* imparcialidad *f*

impassable /ɪm'pɑ:səbl/ *a* <*barrier etc*> infranqueable; <*road*> intransitable

impassive /ɪm'pæsɪv/ *a* impasible

impatien|ce /ɪm'peɪʃəns/ *n* impaciencia *f*. **~t** *a* impaciente. **get ~t** impacientarse. **~tly** *adv* con impaciencia

impeccable /ɪm'pekəbl/ *a* impecable

impede /ɪm'pi:d/ *vt* estorbar

impediment /ɪm'pedɪmənt/ *n* obstáculo *m*. (**speech**) **~** defecto *m* del habla

impending /ɪm'pendɪŋ/ *a* inminente

impenetrable /ɪm'penɪtrəbl/ *a* impenetrable

imperative /ɪm'perətɪv/ *a* imprescindible. ● *n* (Gram) imperativo *m*

imperceptible /ɪmpə'septəbl/ *a* imperceptible

imperfect /ɪm'pɜ:fɪkt/ *a* imperfecto. **~ion** /ɪmpə'fekʃn/ *n* imperfección *f*

imperial /ɪm'pɪərɪəl/ *a* imperial. **~ism** *n* imperialismo *m*

impersonal /ɪm'pɜ:sənl/ *a* impersonal

impersonat|e /ɪm'pɜ:səneɪt/ *vt* hacerse pasar por; (mimic) imitar. **~ion** /-'neɪʃn/ *n* imitación *f*. **~or** *n* imitador *m*

impertinen|ce /ɪm'pɜ:tɪnəns/ *n* impertinencia *f*. **~t** *a* impertinente

impervious /ɪm'pɜ:vɪəs/ *a*. **~ to** impermeable a

impetuous /ɪm'petjʊəs/ *a* impetuoso

impetus /'ɪmpɪtəs/ *n* ímpetu *m*

implacable /ɪm'plækəbl/ *a* implacable

implant /ɪm'plɑ:nt/ *vt* implantar

implement /'ɪmplɪmənt/ *n* instrumento *m*, implemento *m* (LAm). ● /'ɪmplɪment/ *vt* implementar

implicat|e /'ɪmplɪkeɪt/ *vt* implicar. **~ion** /-'keɪʃn/ *n* implicación *f*

implicit /ɪm'plɪsɪt/ *a* (implied) implícito; (unquestioning) absoluto

implore /ɪm'plɔ:(r)/ *vt* implorar

imply /ɪm'plaɪ/ *vt* (involve) implicar; (insinuate) dar a entender, insinuar

impolite /ɪmpə'laɪt/ *a* mal educado

import /ɪm'pɔ:t/ *vt* importar. ● /'ɪmpɔ:t/ *n* importación *f*, (item) artículo *m* de importación; (meaning) significación *f*

importan|ce /ɪm'pɔ:təns/ *n* importancia *f*. **~t** *a* importante

importer /ɪm'pɔ:tə(r)/ *n* importador *m*

impos|e /ɪm'pəʊz/ *vt* imponer. ● *vi*. **~e on** abusar de la amabilidad de. **~ing** *a* imponente. **~ition** /ɪmpə'zɪʃn/ *n* imposición *f*; (fig) abuso *m*

impossib|ility /ɪmpɒsə'bɪlətɪ/ *n* imposibilidad *f*. **~le** /ɪm'pɒsəbl/ *a* imposible

impostor /ɪm'pɒstə(r)/ *n* impostor *m*

impoten|ce /'ɪmpətəns/ *n* impotencia *f*. **~t** *a* impotente

impound /ɪm'paʊnd/ *vt* confiscar

impoverished /ɪm'pɒvərɪʃt/ *a* empobrecido

impractical /ɪm'præktɪkl/ *a* poco práctico

impregnable /im'pregnəbl/ *a* inexpugnable

impregnate /'ɪmpregneɪt/ *vt* impregnar (**with** con, de)

impress /ɪm'pres/ *vt* impresionar; (make good impression) causar una buena impresión a. ● *vi* impresionar

impression /ɪm'preʃn/ *n* impresión *f*. **~able** *a* impresionable. **~ism** *n* impresionismo *m*

impressive /ɪm'presɪv/ *a* impresionante

imprint /'ɪmprɪnt/ *n* impresión *f*. ● /ɪm'prɪnt/ *vt* imprimir

imprison /ɪm'prɪzn/ *vt* encarcelar. **~ment** *n* encarcelamiento *m*

improbab|ility /ɪmprɒbə'bɪlətɪ/ *n* improbabilidad *f*. **~le** /ɪm'prɒbəbl/ *a* improbable

impromptu /ɪm'prɒmptju:/ *a* improvisado. ● *adv* de improviso

improper /ɪm'prɒpə(r)/ *a* impropio; (incorrect) incorrecto

improve /ɪm'pru:v/ *vt* mejorar. ● *vi* mejorar. **~ment** *n* mejora *f*

improvis|ation /ɪmprəvaɪ'zeɪʃn/ *n* improvisación *f*. **~e** /'ɪmprəvaɪz/ *vt/i* improvisar

impuden|ce /'ɪmpjʊdəns/ *n* insolencia *f*. **~t** *a* insolente

impuls|e /'ɪmpʌls/ *n* impulso *m*. **on ~e** sin reflexionar. **~ive** *a* irreflexivo

impur|e /ɪm'pjʊə(r)/ *a* impuro. **~ity** *n* impureza *f*

in /ɪn/ *prep* en; (within) dentro de. **~ a firm manner** de una manera terminante. **~ an hour('s time)** dentro de una hora. **~ doing** al hacer. **~ so far as** en la medida en que. **~ the evening** por la tarde. **~ the rain** bajo la lluvia. **~ the sun** al sol. **one ~ ten** uno de cada diez. **the best ~ the world** el mejor del mundo. ● *adv* (inside) dentro; (at home) en casa. **come ~** entrar. ● *n*. **the ~s and outs of** los detalles de

inability /ɪnə'bɪlətɪ/ *n* incapacidad *f*

inaccessible /ɪnæk'sesəbl/ *a* inaccesible

inaccura|cy /ɪn'ækjʊrəsɪ/ *n* inexactitud *f*. **~te** /-ət/ *a* inexacto

inactiv|e /ɪn'æktɪv/ *a* inactivo. **~ity** /-'tɪvətɪ/ *n* inactividad *f*

inadequa|cy /ɪn'ædɪkwəsɪ/ *a* insuficiencia *f*. **~te** /-ət/ *a* insuficiente

inadvertently /ɪnəd'vɜ:təntlɪ/ *adv* sin querer

inadvisable /ɪnəd'vaɪzəbl/ *a* desaconsejable

inane /ɪ'neɪn/ *a* estúpido

inanimate /ɪn'ænɪmət/ *a* inanimado

inappropriate /ɪnə'prəʊprɪət/ *a* inoportuno

inarticulate /ɪnɑ:'tɪkjʊlət/ *a* incapaz de expresarse claramente

inattentive /ɪnə'tentɪv/ *a* desatento

inaudible /ɪn'ɔ:dəbl/ *a* inaudible

inaugurate /ɪ'nɔ:gjʊreɪt/ *vt* inaugurar

inborn /'ɪnbɔ:n/ *a* innato

inbred /ɪn'bred/ *a* (inborn) innato; *<social group>* endogámico

Inc /ɪŋk/ *abbr* (Amer) (= **Incorporated**) S.A., Sociedad Anónima

incalculable /ɪn'kælkjʊləbl/ *a* incalculable

incapable /ɪn'keɪpəbl/ *a* incapaz

incapacit|ate /ɪnkə'pæsɪteɪt/ *vt* incapacitar. **~y** *n* incapacidad *f*

incarcerate /ɪn'kɑ:səreɪt/ *vt* encarcelar

incarnat|e /ɪn'kɑ:nət/ *a* encarnado. **~ion** /-'neɪʃn/ *n* encarnación *f*

incendiary /ɪn'sendɪərɪ/ *a* incendiario. **~ bomb** bomba *f* incendiaria

incense /'ɪnsens/ *n* incienso *m*. ● /ɪn'sens/ *vt* enfurecer

incentive /ɪn'sentɪv/ *n* incentivo *m*

incessant /ɪn'sesnt/ *a* incesante. **~ly** *adv* sin cesar

incest /'ɪnsest/ *n* incesto *m*. **~uous** /ɪn'sestjʊəs/ *a* incestuoso

inch /ɪntʃ/ *n* pulgada *f*; (= 2,54cm). ● *vi*. **~ forward** avanzar lentamente

incidence /'ɪnsɪdəns/ *n* frecuencia *f*

incident /'ɪnsɪdənt/ *n* incidente *m*

incidental /ɪnsɪ'dentl/ *a* *<effect>* secundario; (minor) incidental. **~ly** *adv* a propósito

incinerat|e /ɪn'sɪnəreɪt/ *vt* incinerar. **~or** *n* incinerador *m*

incision /ɪn'sɪʒn/ *n* incisión *f*

incite /ɪn'saɪt/ *vt* incitar. **~ment** *n* incitación *f*

inclination /ɪnklɪ'neɪʃn/ *n* inclinación *f*. **have no ~ to** no tener deseos de

incline /ɪn'klaɪn/ *vt* inclinar. **be ~d to** tener tendencia a. ● *vi* inclinarse. ● /'ɪnklaɪn/ *n* pendiente *f*

inclu|de /ɪn'klu:d/ *vt* incluir. **~ding** *prep* incluso. **~sion** /-ʒn/ *n* inclusión *f*. **~sive** /-sɪv/ *a* inclusivo

incognito /ɪnkɒg'ni:təʊ/ *adv* de incógnito

incoherent /ɪnkəʊ'hɪərənt/ *a* incoherente

incom|e /'ɪnkʌm/ *n* ingresos *mpl*. **~e tax** *n* impuesto *m* sobre la renta. **~ing** *a* *<tide>* ascendente

incomparable /ɪn'kɒmpərəbl/ *a* incomparable

incompatible /ɪnkəm'pætəbl/ *a* incompatible

incompeten|ce /ɪn'kɒmpɪtəns/ *n* incompetencia *f*. **~t** *a* incompetente

incomplete /ɪnkəm'pli:t/ *a* incompleto

incomprehensible /ɪnkɒmprɪ'hensəbl/ *a* incomprensible

inconceivable /ɪnkən'si:vəbl/ *a* inconcebible

inconclusive /ɪnkən'klu:sɪv/ *a* no concluyente

incongruous /ɪn'kɒŋgrʊəs/ *a* incongruente

inconsiderate /ɪnkən'sɪdərət/ *a* desconsiderado

inconsisten|cy /ɪnkən'sɪstənsɪ/ *n* inconsecuencia *f*. **~t** *a* inconsecuente. **be ~t with** no concordar con

inconspicuous /ɪnkən'spɪkjʊəs/ *a* que no llama la atención. **~ly** *adv* sin llamar la atención

incontinent /ɪn'kɒntɪnənt/ *a* incontinente

inconvenien|ce /ɪnkən'vi:nɪəns/ *a* inconveniencia *f*; (drawback) inconveniente *m*. **~t** *a* inconveniente

incorporate /ɪn'kɔ:pəreɪt/ *vt* incorporar; (include) incluir; (Com) constituir (en sociedad)

incorrect /ɪnkə'rekt/ *a* incorrecto

increas|e /'ɪnkri:s/ *n* aumento *m* (in de). ● /ɪn'kri:s/ *vt/i* aumentar. **~ing** /ɪn'kri:sɪŋ/ *a* creciente. **~ingly** *adv* cada vez más

incredible /ɪn'kredəbl/ *a* increíble

incredulous /ɪn'kredjʊləs/ *a* incrédulo

incriminat|e /ɪn'krɪmɪneɪt/ *vt* incriminar. **~ing** *a* comprometedor

incubat|e /'ɪŋkjʊbeɪt/ *vt* incubar. **~ion** /-'beɪʃn/ *n* incubación *f*. **~or** *n* incubadora *f*

incur /ɪn'kɜ:(r)/ *vt* (*pt* **incurred**) incurrir en; contraer *<debts>*

incurable /ɪn'kjʊərəbl/ *a* *<disease>* incurable; *<romantic>* empedernido

indebted /ɪn'detɪd/ *a*. **be ~ to s.o.** estar en deuda con uno

indecen|cy /ɪn'di:snsɪ/ *n* indecencia *f*. **~t** *a* indecente

indecisi|on /ɪndɪ'sɪʒn/ *n* indecisión *f*. **~ve** /-'saɪsɪv/ *a* indeciso

indeed /ɪn'di:d/ *adv* en efecto; (really?) ¿de veras?

indefinable /ɪndɪ'faɪnəbl/ *a* indefinible

indefinite /ɪn'defɪnət/ *a* indefinido. **~ly** *adv* indefinidamente

indelible /ɪn'delɪbl/ *a* indeleble

indemni|fy /ɪn'demnɪfaɪ/ *vt* (insure) asegurar; (compensate) indemnizar. **~ty** /-ətɪ/ *n* (insurance) indemnidad *f*; (payment) indemnización *f*

indent /ɪn'dent/ *vt* sangrar *<text>*. **~ation** /-'teɪʃn/ *n* mella *f*

independen|ce /ɪndɪ'pendəns/ *n* independencia *f*. **~t** *a* independiente. **~tly** *adv* independientemente

in-depth /ɪn'depθ/ *a* a fondo

indescribable /ɪndɪ'skraɪbəbl/ *a* indescriptible

indestructible /ɪndɪ'strʌktəbl/ *a* indestructible

indeterminate /ɪndɪ'tɜ:mɪnət/ *a* indeterminado

index /'ɪndeks/ *n* (*pl* **indexes**) (in book) índice *m*; (*pl* **indexes** *or* **indices**) (Com, Math) índice *m*. ● *vt* poner índice a; (enter in index) poner en un índice. **~ finger** *n* (dedo *m*) índice *m*. **~-linked** /-'lɪŋkt/ *a* indexado

India /'ɪndɪə/ *n* la India. **~n** *a* & *n* indio (*m*)

indicat|e /'ɪndɪkeɪt/ *vt* indicar. **~ion** /-'keɪʃn/ *n* indicación *f*. **~ive** /ɪn'dɪkətɪv/ *a* & *n* indicativo (*m*). **~or** /'ɪndɪkeɪtə(r)/ *n* indicador *m*; (Auto) intermitente *m*

indices /'ɪndɪsi:z/ ⇒INDEX

indict /ɪn'daɪt/ *vt* acusar. **~ment** *n* acusación *f*

indifferen|ce /ɪn'dɪfrəns/ *n* indiferencia *f*. **~t** *a* indiferente; (not good) mediocre

indigesti|ble /ɪndɪ'dʒestəbl/ *a* indigesto. **~on** /-tʃən/ *n* indigestión *f*

indigna|nt /ɪn'dɪgnənt/ *a* indignado. **~tion** /-'neɪʃn/ *n* indignación *f*

indirect /ɪndɪ'rekt/ *a* indirecto. **~ly** *adv* indirectamente

indiscre|et /ɪndɪ'skri:t/ *a* indiscreto. **~tion** /-'kreʃn/ *n* indiscreción *f*

indiscriminate /ɪndɪ'skrɪmɪnət/ *a* indistinto. **~ly** *adv* indistintamente

indispensable /ɪndɪ'spensəbl/ *a* indispensable, imprescindible

indisposed /ɪndɪ'spəʊzd/ *a* indispuesto

indisputable /ɪndɪ'spju:təbl/ *a* indiscutible

indistinguishable /ɪndɪ'stɪŋgwɪʃəbl/ *a* indistinguible (**from** de)

individual /ɪndɪ'vɪdjʊəl/ *a* individual. ● *n* individuo *m*. **~ly** *adv* individualmente

indoctrinat|e /ɪn'dɒktrɪneɪt/ *vt* adoctrinar. **~ion** /-'neɪʃn/ *n* adoctrinamiento *m*

indolen|ce /'ɪndələns/ *n* indolencia *f*. **~t** *a* indolente

indomitable /ɪn'dɒmɪtəbl/ *a* indómito

indoor /'ɪndɔ:(r)/ *a* interior; <*clothes etc*> de casa; (covered) cubierto. **~s** *adv* dentro, adentro (LAm)

induc|e /ɪn'dju:s/ *vt* inducir. **~ement** *n* incentivo *m*

indulge /ɪn'dʌldʒ/ *vt* satisfacer <*desires*>; complacer <*person*>. ● *vi*. **~ in** permitirse. **~nce** /-əns/ *n* (of desires) satisfacción *f*; (extravagance) lujo *m*. **~nt** *a* indulgente

industrial /ɪn'dʌstrɪəl/ *a* industrial; <*unrest*> laboral. **~ist** *n* industrial *m & f*. **~ized** *a* industrializado

industrious /ɪn'dʌstrɪəs/ *a* trabajador

industry /'ɪndəstrɪ/ *n* industria *f*; (zeal) aplicación *f*

inebriated /ɪ'ni:brɪeɪtɪd/ *a* beodo, ebrio

inedible /ɪn'edɪbl/ *a* incomible

ineffective /ɪnɪ'fektɪv/ *a* ineficaz; <*person*> incompetente

ineffectual /ɪnɪ'fektjʊəl/ *a* ineficaz

inefficien|cy /ɪnɪ'fɪʃnsɪ/ *n* ineficacia *f*; (of person) incompetencia *f*. **~t** *a* ineficaz; <*person*> incompetente

ineligible /ɪn'elɪdʒəbl/ *a* inelegible. **be ~ for** no tener derecho a

inept /ɪ'nept/ *a* inepto

inequality /ɪnɪ'kwɒlətɪ/ *n* desigualdad *f*

inert /ɪ'nɜ:t/ *a* inerte. **~ia** /ɪ'nɜ:ʃə/ *n* inercia *f*

inescapable /ɪnɪ'skeɪpəbl/ *a* ineludible

inevitabl|e /ɪn'evɪtəbl/ *a* inevitable. ● *n*. **the ~e** lo inevitable. **~y** *adv* inevitablemente

inexact /ɪnɪg'zækt/ *a* inexacto

inexcusable /ɪnɪk'skju:səbl/ *a* imperdonable

inexpensive /ɪnɪk'spensɪv/ *a* económico, barato

inexperience /ɪnɪk'spɪərɪəns/ *n* falta *f* de experiencia. **~d** *a* inexperto

inexplicable /ɪnɪk'splɪkəbl/ *a* inexplicable

infallib|ility /ɪnfælə'bɪlətɪ/ *n* infalibilidad *f*. **~le** /ɪn'fæləbl/ *a* infalible

infam|ous /'ɪnfəməs/ *a* infame. **~y** *n* infamia *f*

infan|cy /'ɪnfənsɪ/ *n* infancia *f*. **~t** *n* niño *m*. **~tile** /'ɪnfəntaɪl/ *a* infantil

infantry /'ɪnfəntrɪ/ *n* infantería *f*

infatuat|ed /ɪn'fætjʊeɪtɪd/ *a*. **be ~ed with** estar encaprichado con. **~ion** /-'eɪʃn/ *n* encaprichamiento *m*

infect /ɪn'fekt/ *vt* infectar; (fig) contagiar. **~ s.o. with sth** contagiarle algo a uno. **~ion** /-ʃn/ *n* infección *f*. **~ious** /-ʃəs/ *a* contagioso

infer /ɪn'fɜ:(r)/ *vt* (*pt* **inferred**) deducir

inferior /ɪn'fɪərɪə(r)/ *a* & *n* inferior (*m* & *f*). **~ity** /-'ɒrətɪ/ *n* inferioridad *f*

inferno /ɪn'fɜ:nəʊ/ *n* (*pl* **-os**) infierno *m*

infertil|e /ɪn'fɜ:taɪl/ *a* estéril. **~ity** /-'tɪlətɪ/ *n* esterilidad *f*

infest /ɪn'fest/ *vt* infestar

infidelity /ɪnfɪ'delətɪ/ *n* infidelidad *f*

infiltrat|e /'ɪnfɪltreɪt/ *vt* infiltrarse en. ● *vi* infiltrarse. **~or** *n* infiltrado *m*

infinite /'ɪnfɪnət/ *a* infinito. **~ly** *adv* infinitamente

infinitesimal /ɪnfɪnɪ'tesɪml/ *a* infinitesimal

infinitive /ɪn'fɪnətɪv/ *n* infinitivo *m*

infinity /ɪn'fɪnətɪ/ *n* (infinite distance) infinito *m*; (infinite quantity) infinidad *f*

infirm /ɪn'fɜ:m/ *a* enfermizo. **~ity** *n* enfermedad *f*

inflam|e /ɪn'fleɪm/ *vt* inflamar. **~mable** /ɪn'flæməbl/ *a* inflamable. **~mation** /-ə'meɪʃn/ *n* inflamación *f*

inflat|e /ɪn'fleɪt/ *vt* inflar. **~ion** /-ʃn/ *n* inflación *f*. **~ionary** *a* inflacionario

inflection /ɪn'flekʃn/ *n* inflexión *f*

inflexible /ɪn'fleksəbl/ *a* inflexible

inflict /ɪn'flɪkt/ *vt* infligir (**on** a)

influen|ce /'ɪnflʊəns/ *n* influencia *f*. **under the ~ce** (Ⓣ, drunk) borracho. ● *vt* influir (en). **~tial** /-'enʃl/ *a* influyente

influenza /ɪnflʊ'enzə/ *n* gripe *f*

influx /'ɪnflʌks/ *n* afluencia *f*

inform /ɪn'fɔ:m/ *vt* informar. **keep ~ed** tener al corriente. ● *vi*. **~ on s.o.** delatar a uno

informal /ɪn'fɔ:ml/ *a* informal; <*language*> familiar. **~ity** /-'mælətɪ/ *n* falta *f* de ceremonia. **~ly** *adv* (casually) de manera informal; (unofficially) informalmente

inform|ation /ɪnfə'meɪʃn/ *n* información *f*. **~ation technology** *n* informática *f*. **~ative** *a* /ɪn'fɔ:mətɪv/ informativo. **~er** /ɪb'fɔ:mə(r)/ *n* informante *m*

infrared /ɪnfrə'red/ *a* infrarrojo

infrequent /ɪn'fri:kwənt/ *a* poco frecuente. **~ly** *adv* raramente

infringe /ɪn'frɪndʒ/ *vt* infringir. **~ on** violar. **~ment** *n* violación *f*

infuriat|e /ɪn'fjʊərɪeɪt/ *vt* enfurecer. **~ing** *a* exasperante

ingen|ious /ɪn'dʒi:niəs/ *a* ingenioso. **~uity** /ɪndʒɪ'nju:ətɪ/ *n* ingeniosidad *f*

ingot /'ɪŋgət/ *n* lingote *m*

ingrained /ɪn'greɪnd/ *a* (belief) arraigado

ingratiate /ɪn'greɪʃɪeɪt/ *vt*. **~ o.s. with** congraciarse con

ingratitude /ɪnˈgrætɪtjuːd/ *n* ingratitud *f*

ingredient /ɪnˈgriːdɪənt/ *n* ingrediente *m*

ingrowing /ˈɪngrəʊɪŋ/, **ingrown** /ˈɪngrəʊn/ *a*. ~ **nail** *n* uñero *m*, uña *f* encarnada

inhabit /ɪnˈhæbɪt/ *vt* habitar. **~able** *a* habitable. **~ant** *n* habitante *m*

inhale /ɪnˈheɪl/ *vt* aspirar. ● *vi* (when smoking) aspirar el humo. **~r** *n* inhalador *m*

inherent /ɪnˈhɪərənt/ *a* inherente. **~ly** *adv* intrínsecamente

inherit /ɪnˈherɪt/ *vt* heredar. **~ance** /-əns/ *n* herencia *f*

inhibit /ɪnˈhɪbɪt/ *vt* inhibir. **~ed** *a* inhibido. **~ion** /-ˈbɪʃn/ *n* inhibición *f*

inhospitable /ɪnhəˈspɪtəbl/ *a* <*place*> inhóspito; <*person*> inhospitalario

inhuman /ɪnˈhjuːmən/ *a* inhumano. **~e** /ɪnhjuːˈmeɪn/ *a* inhumano. **~ity** /ɪnhjuːˈmænətɪ/ *n* inhumanidad *f*

initial /ɪˈnɪʃl/ *n* inicial *f*. ● *vt* (*pt* **initialled**) firmar con iniciales. ● *a* inicial. **~ly** *adv* al principio

initiat|e /ɪˈnɪʃɪeɪt/ *vt* iniciar; promover <*scheme etc*>. **~ion** /-ˈeɪʃn/ *n* iniciación *f*

initiative /ɪˈnɪʃətɪv/ *n* iniciativa *f*. **on one's own ~** por iniciativa propia. **take the ~** tomar la iniciativa

inject /ɪnˈdʒekt/ *vt* inyectar. **~ion** /-ʃn/ *n* inyección *f*

injur|e /ˈɪndʒə(r)/ *vt* herir. **~y** *n* herida *f*

injustice /ɪnˈdʒʌstɪs/ *n* injusticia *f*

ink /ɪŋk/ *n* tinta *f*

ink: ~well *n* tintero *m*. **~y** *a* manchado de tinta

inland /ˈɪnlənd/ *a* interior. ● /ɪnˈlænd/ *adv* tierra adentro. **I~ Revenue** /ˈɪnlənd/ *n* Hacienda *f*

in-laws /ˈɪnlɔːz/ *npl* parientes *mpl* políticos

inlay /ɪnˈleɪ/ *vt* (*pt* **inlaid**) taracear, incrustar. ● /ˈɪnleɪ/ *n* taracea *f*, incrustación *f*

inlet /ˈɪnlet/ *n* (in coastline) ensenada *f*; (of river, sea) brazo *m*

inmate /ˈɪnmeɪt/ *n* (of asylum) interno *m*; (of prison) preso *m*

inn /ɪn/ *n* posada *f*

innate /ɪˈneɪt/ *a* innato

inner /ˈɪnə(r)/ *a* interior; (fig) íntimo. **~most** *a* más íntimo. **~ tube** *n* cámara *f*

innocen|ce /ˈɪnəsns/ *n* inocencia *f*. **~t** *a* & *n* inocente (*m* & *f*)

innocuous /ɪˈnɒkjʊəs/ *a* inocuo

innovat|e /ˈɪnəveɪt/ *vi* innovar. **~ion** /-ˈveɪʃn/ *n* innovación *f*. **~ive** /ˈɪnəvətɪv/ *a* innovador. **~or** *n* innovador *m*

innuendo /ɪnjuːˈendəʊ/ *n* (*pl* **-oes**) insinuación *f*

innumerable /ɪˈnjuːmərəbl/ *a* innumerable

inoculat|e /ɪˈnɒkjʊleɪt/ *vt* inocular. **~ion** /-ˈleɪʃn/ *n* inoculación *f*

inoffensive /ɪnəˈfensɪv/ *a* inofensivo

inopportune /ɪnˈɒpətjuːn/ *a* inoportuno

input /ˈɪnpʊt/ *n* aportación *f*, aporte *m* (LAm); (Comp) entrada *f*. ● *vt* (*pt* **input**, *pres p* **inputting**) entrar <*data*>

inquest /ˈɪnkwest/ *n* investigación *f* judicial

inquir|e /ɪnˈkwaɪə(r)/ *vt/i* preguntar. **~e about** informarse de. **~y** *n* pregunta *f*; (investigation) investigación *f*

inquisition /ɪnkwɪˈzɪʃn/ *n* inquisición *f*

inquisitive /ɪnˈkwɪzətɪv/ *a* inquisitivo

insan|e /ɪnˈseɪn/ *a* loco. **~ity** /ɪnˈsænətɪ/ *n* locura *f*

insatiable /ɪnˈseɪʃəbl/ *a* insaciable

inscri|be /ɪnˈskraɪb/ *vt* inscribir *<letters>*; grabar *<design>*. **~ption** /-ɪpʃn/ *n* inscripción *f*

inscrutable /ɪnˈskru:təbl/ *a* inescrutable

insect /ˈɪnsekt/ *n* insecto *m*. **~icide** /ɪnˈsektɪsaɪd/ *n* insecticida *f*

insecur|e /ɪnsɪˈkjʊə(r)/ *a* inseguro. **~ity** *n* inseguridad *f*

insensitive /ɪnˈsensətɪv/ *a* insensible

inseparable /ɪnˈsepərəbl/ *a* inseparable

insert /ˈɪnsɜ:t/ *n* materia *f* insertada. ● /ɪnˈsɜ:t/ *vt* insertar. **~ion** /ɪnˈsɜ:ʃn/ *n* inserción *f*

inside /ɪnˈsaɪd/ *n* interior *m*. **~ out** al revés; (thoroughly) a fondo. ● *a* interior. ● *adv* dentro, adentro (LAm). ● *prep* dentro de. **~s** *npl* tripas *fpl*

insight /ˈɪnsaɪt/ *n* perspicacia *f*. **gain an ~ into** llegar a comprender bien

insignificant /ɪnsɪgˈnɪfɪkənt/ *a* insignificante

insincer|e /ɪnsɪnˈsɪə(r)/ *a* poco sincero. **~ity** /-ˈserətɪ/ *n* falta *f* de sinceridad

insinuat|e /ɪnˈsɪnjʊeɪt/ *vt* insinuar. **~ion** /-ˈeɪʃn/ *n* insinuación *f*

insipid /ɪnˈsɪpɪd/ *a* insípido

insist /ɪnˈsɪst/ *vt* insistir (**that** en que). ● *vi* insistir. **~ on** insistir en. **~ence** /-əns/ *n* insistencia *f*. **~ent** *a* insistente. **~ently** *adv* con insistencia

insolen|ce /ˈɪnsələns/ *n* insolencia *f*. **~t** *a* insolente

insoluble /ɪnˈsɒljʊbl/ *a* insoluble

insolvent /ɪnˈsɒlvənt/ *a* insolvente

insomnia /ɪnˈsɒmnɪə/ *n* insomnio *m*. **~c** /-ɪæk/ *n* insomne *m & f*

inspect /ɪnˈspekt/ *vt* (officially) inspeccionar; (look at closely) revisar, examinar . **~ion** /-ʃn/ *n* inspección *f*. **~or** *n* inspector *m*; (on train, bus) revisor *m*, inspector *m* (LAm)

inspir|ation /ɪnspəˈreɪʃn/ *n* inspiración *f*. **~e** /ɪnˈspaɪə(r)/ *vt* inspirar. **~ing** *a* inspirador

instability /ɪnstəˈbɪlətɪ/ *n* inestabilidad *f*

install /ɪnˈstɔ:l/ *vt* instalar. **~ation** /-əˈleɪʃn/ *n* instalación *f*

instalment /ɪnˈstɔ:lmənt/ *n* (payment) plazo *m*; (of publication) entrega *f*; (of radio, TV serial) episodio *m*

instance /ˈɪnstəns/ *n* ejemplo *m*; (case) caso *m*. **for ~** por ejemplo. **in the first ~** en primer lugar

instant /ˈɪnstənt/ *a* instantáneo. ● *n* instante *m*. **~aneous** /ɪnstənˈteɪmɪəs/ *a* instantáneo

instead /ɪnˈsted/ *adv* en cambio. **~ of** en vez de, en lugar de

instigat|e /ˈɪnstɪgeɪt/ *vt* instigar. **~ion** /-ˈgeɪʃn/ *n* instigación *f*

instinct /ˈɪnstɪŋkt/ *n* instinto *m*. **~ive** *a* instintivo

institut|e /ˈɪnstɪtju:t/ *n* instituto *m*. ● *vt* instituir; iniciar *<enquiry*

etc>. **~ion** /-'tjuːʃn/ *n* institución *f*. **~ional** *a* institucional

instruct /ɪn'strʌkt/ *vt* instruir; (order) mandar. **~ s.o. in sth** enseñar algo a uno. **~ion** /-ʃn/ *n* instrucción *f*. **~ions** *npl* (for use) modo *m* de empleo. **~ive** *a* instructivo. **~or** *n* instructor *m*

instrument /'ɪnstrəmənt/ *n* instrumento *m*. **~al** /ɪnstrə'mentl/ *a* instrumental. **be ~al in** jugar un papel decisivo en

insubordinat|e /ɪnsə'bɔːdɪnət/ *a* insubordinado. **~ion** /-'neɪʃn/ *n* insubordinación *f*

insufferable /ɪn'sʌfərəbl/ *a* <*person*> insufrible; <*heat*> insoportable

insufficient /ɪnsə'fɪʃnt/ *a* insuficiente

insular /'ɪnsjʊlə(r)/ *a* insular; (narrow-minded) estrecho de miras

insulat|e /'ɪnsjʊleɪt/ *vt* aislar. **~ion** /-'leɪʃn/ *n* aislamiento *m*

insulin /'ɪnsjʊlɪn/ *n* insulina *f*

insult /ɪn'sʌlt/ *vt* insultar. ● /'ɪnsʌlt/ *n* insulto *m*. **~ing** /ɪn'sʌltɪŋ/ *a* insultante

insur|ance /ɪn'ʃʊərəns/ *n* seguro *m*. **~e** /ɪn'ʃʊə(r)/ *vt* (Com) asegurar; (Amer) ⇒ENSURE

insurmountable /ɪnsə'maʊntəbl/ *a* insuperable

intact /ɪn'tækt/ *a* intacto

integral /'ɪntɪgrəl/ *a* integral

integrat|e /'ɪntɪgreɪt/ *vt* integrar. ● *vi* integrarse. **~ion** /-'greɪʃn/ *n* integración *f*

integrity /ɪn'tegrətɪ/ *n* integridad *f*

intellect /'ɪntəlekt/ *n* intelecto *m*. **~ual** /ɪntə'lektʃʊəl/ *a & n* intelectual (*m*)

intelligen|ce /ɪn'telɪdʒəns/ *n* inteligencia *f*. **~t** *a* inteligente. **~tly** *adv* inteligentemente

intelligible /ɪn'telɪdʒəbl/ *a* inteligible

intend /ɪn'tend/ *vt*. **~ to do** pensar hacer

intens|e /ɪn'tens/ *a* intenso; <*person*> apasionado. **~ely** *adv* intensamente; (very) sumamente. **~ify** /-ɪfaɪ/ *vt* intensificar. ● *vi* intensificarse. **~ity** /-ɪtɪ/ *n* intensidad *f*

intensive /ɪn'tensɪv/ *a* intensivo. **~ care** *n* cuidados *mpl* intensivos

intent /ɪn'tent/ *n* propósito *m*. ● *a* atento. **~ on** absorto en. **~ on doing** resuelto a hacer

intention /ɪn'tenʃn/ *n* intención *f*. **~al** *a* intencional

intently /ɪn'tentlɪ/ *adv* atentamente

interact /ɪntər'ækt/ *vi* relacionarse. **~ion** /-ʃn/ *n* interacción *f*

intercept /ɪntə'sept/ *vt* interceptar. **~ion** /-ʃn/ *n* interceptación *f*

interchange /ɪntə'tʃeɪndʒ/ *vt* intercambiar. ● /'ɪntətʃeɪndʒ/ *n* intercambio *m*; (road junction) cruce *m*. **~able** /-'tʃeɪndʒəbl/ *a* intercambiable

intercity /ɪntə'sɪtɪ/ *a* rápido interurbano *m*

intercourse /'ɪntəkɔːs/ *n* trato *m*; (sexual) acto *m* sexual

interest /'ɪntrest/ *n* interés *m*. ● *vt* interesar. **~ed** *a* interesado. **be ~ed in** interesarse por. **~ing** *a* interesante

interfere /ɪntə'fɪə(r)/ *vi* entrometerse. **~ in** entrometerse en. **~ with** afectar (a); interferir <*radio*>. **~nce** /-rəns/ *n* intromisión *f*; (Radio) interferencia *f*

interior /ɪn'tɪərɪə(r)/ *a & n* interior (*m*)

interjection /ɪntə'dʒekʃn/ *n* interjección *f*

interlude /'ɪntəlu:d/ *n* intervalo *m*; (theatre, music) interludio *m*

intermediary /ɪntə'mi:dɪərɪ/ *a & n* intermediario (*m*)

interminable /ɪn'tɜ:mɪnəbl/ *a* interminable

intermittent /ɪntə'mɪtnt/ *a* intermitente. **~ly** *adv* con discontinuidad

intern /ɪn'tɜ:n/ *vt* internar. ● /'ɪntɜ:n/ *n* (Amer, doctor) interno *m*

internal /ɪn'tɜ:nl/ *a* interno. **~ly** *adv* internamente. **I~ Revenue Service** *n* (Amer) Hacienda *f*

international /ɪntə'næʃənl/ *a* internacional

Internet /'ɪntənet/ *n*. **the ~** el Internet

interpret /ɪn'tɜ:prɪt/ *vt/i* interpretar. **~ation** /-'teɪʃn/ *n* interpretación *f*. **~er** *n* intérprete *m & f*

interrogat|e /ɪn'terəgeɪt/ *vt* interrogar. **~ion** /-'geɪʃn/ *n* interrogatorio *m*. **~ive** /-'rɒgətɪv/ *a* interrogativo

interrupt /ɪntə'rʌpt/ *vt/i* interrumpir. **~ion** /-ʃn/ *n* interrupción *f*

intersect /ɪntə'sekt/ *vt* cruzar. ● *vi* <*roads*> cruzarse; (geometry) intersecarse. **~ion** /-ʃn/ *n* (roads) cruce *m*; (geometry) intersección *f*

intersperse /ɪntə'spɜ:s/ *vt* intercalar

interstate (highway) /'ɪntəsteɪt/ *n* (Amer) carretera *f* interestatal

intertwine /ɪntə'twaɪn/ *vt* entrelazar. ● *vi* entrelazarse

interval /'ɪntəvl/ *n* intervalo *m*; (theatre) descanso *m*. **at ~s** a intervalos

interven|e /ɪntə'vi:n/ *vi* intervenir. **~tion** /-'venʃn/ *n* intervención *f*

interview /'ɪntəvju:/ *n* entrevista *f*. ● *vt* entrevistar. **~ee** /-'i:/ *n* entrevistado *m*. **~er** *n* entrevistador *m*

intestine /ɪn'testɪn/ *n* intestino *m*

intimacy /'ɪntɪməsɪ/ *n* intimidad *f*

intimate /'ɪntɪmət/ *a* íntimo. ● /'ɪntɪmeɪt/ *vt* (state) anunciar; (imply) dar a entender. **~ly** /'ɪntɪmətlɪ/ *adv* íntimamente

intimidat|e /ɪn'tɪmɪdeɪt/ *vt* intimidar. **~ion** /-'deɪʃn/ *n* intimidación *f*

into /'ɪntu:/, *before consonant* /'ɪntə/ *prep* en; <*translate*> a

intolerable /ɪn'tɒlərəbl/ *a* intolerable

intoleran|ce /ɪn'tɒlərəns/ *n* intolerancia *f*. **~t** *a* intolerante

intoxicat|e /ɪn'tɒksɪkeɪt/ *vt* embriagar; (Med) intoxicar. **~ed** *a* ebrio. **~ing** *a* <*substance*> estupefaciente. **~ion** /-'keɪʃn/ *n* embriaguez *f*; (Med) intoxicación *f*

intransitive /ɪn'trænsɪtɪv/ *a* intransitivo

intravenous /ɪntrə'vi:nəs/ *a* intravenoso

intrepid /ɪn'trepɪd/ *a* intrépido

intrica|cy /'ɪntrɪkəsɪ/ *n* complejidad *f*. **~te** /-ət/ *a* complejo

intrigu|e /ɪn'tri:g/ *vt/i* intrigar. ● /'ɪntri:g/ *n* intriga *f*. **~ing** /ɪn'tri:gɪŋ/ *a* intrigante

intrinsic /ɪn'trɪnsɪk/ *a* intrínseco. **~ally** *adv* intrínsecamente

introduc|e /ɪntrə'dju:s/ *vt* introducir; presentar <*person*>. **~tion**

/ɪntrə'dʌkʃn/ *n* introducción *f*; (to person) presentación *f*. **~tory** /ɪntrə'dʌktərɪ/ *a* preliminar; <*course*> de introducción

introvert /'ɪntrəvɜ:t/ *n* introvertido *m*

intru|de /ɪn'tru:d/ *vi* entrometerse; (disturb) importunar. **~der** *n* intruso *m*. **~sion** /-ʒn/ *n* intrusión *f*. **~sive** /-sɪv/ *a* impertinente

intuiti|on /ɪntju:'ɪʃn/ *n* intuición *f*. **~ve** /ɪn'tju:ɪtɪv/ *a* intuitivo

inundat|e /'ɪnʌndeɪt/ *vt* inundar. **~ion** /-'deɪʃn/ *n* inundación *f*

invade /ɪn'veɪd/ *vt* invadir. **~r** *n* invasor *m*

invalid /'ɪnvəlɪd/ *n* inválido *m*. ● /ɪn'vælɪd/ *a* inválido. **~ate** /ɪn'vælɪdeɪt/ *vt* invalidar

invaluable /ɪn'væljʊəbl/ *a* inestimable, invalorable (LAm)

invariabl|e /ɪn'veərɪəbl/ *a* invariable. **~y** *adv* invariablemente

invasion /ɪn'veɪʒn/ *n* invasión *f*

invent /ɪn'vent/ *vt* inventar. **~ion** /-'venʃn/ *n* invención *f*. **~ive** *a* inventivo. **~or** *n* inventor *m*

inventory /'ɪnvəntrɪ/ *n* inventario *m*

invertebrate /ɪn'vɜ:tɪbrət/ *n* invertebrado *m*

inverted commas /ɪnvɜ:tɪd 'kɒməz/ *npl* comillas *fpl*

invest /ɪn'vest/ *vt* invertir. ● *vi*. **~ in** hacer una inversión *f*

investigat|e /ɪn'vestɪgeɪt/ *vt* investigar. **~ion** /-'geɪʃn/ *n* investigación *f*. **under ~ion** sometido a examen. **~or** *n* investigador *m*

inveterate /ɪn'vetərət/ *a* inveterado

invidious /ɪn'vɪdɪəs/ *a* (hateful) odioso; (unfair) injusto

invigorating /ɪn'vɪgəreɪtɪŋ/ *a* vigorizante; (stimulating) estimulante

invincible /ɪn'vɪnsɪbl/ *a* invencible

invisible /ɪn'vɪzəbl/ *a* invisible

invit|ation /ɪnvɪ'teɪʃn/ *n* invitación *f*. **~e** /ɪn'vaɪt/ *vt* invitar; (ask for) pedir. ● /'ɪnvaɪt/ *n* Ⓘ invitación *f*. **~ing** /ɪn'vaɪtɪŋ/ *a* atrayente

invoice /'ɪnvɔɪs/ *n* factura *f*. ● *vt*. **~ s.o.** (**for sth**) pasarle a uno factura (por algo)

involuntary /ɪn'vɒləntərɪ/ *a* involuntario

involve /ɪn'vɒlv/ *vt* (entail) suponer; (implicate) implicar. **~d in** envuelto en. **~d** *a* (complex) complicado. **~ment** *n* participación *f*; (relationship) enredo *m*

inward /'ɪnwəd/ *a* interior. ● *adv* hacia adentro. **~s** *adv* hacia dentro

iodine /'aɪədi:n/ *n* yodo *m*

ion /'aɪən/ *n* ion *m*

iota /aɪ'əʊtə/ *n* (amount) pizca *f*

IOU /aɪəʊ'ju:/ *abbr* (= **I owe you**) pagaré *m*

IQ *abbr* (= **intelligence quotient**) CI *m*, cociente *m* intelectual

Iran /ɪ'rɑ:n/ *n* Irán *m*. **~ian** /ɪ'reɪnɪən/ *a* & *n* iraní (*m*)

Iraq /ɪ'rɑ:k/ *n* Irak *m*. **~i** *a* & *n* iraquí (*m*)

irate /aɪ'reɪt/ *a* colérico

Ireland /'aɪələnd/ *n* Irlanda *f*

iris /'aɪərɪs/ *n* (Anat) iris *m*; (Bot) lirio *m*

Irish /'aɪərɪʃ/ *a* irlandés. ● *n* (Lang) irlandés *m*. *npl*. **the ~** (people) los irlandeses. **~man** /-mən/ *n* irlandés *m*. **~woman** *n* irlandesa *f*

iron /'aɪən/ *n* hierro *m*; (appliance) plancha *f*. ● *a* de hierro. ● *vt* planchar. □ **~ out** *vt* allanar

ironic /aɪ'rɒnɪk/ *a* irónico. **~ally** *adv* irónicamente

ironing board /'aɪənɪŋ/ *n* tabla *f* de planchar, burro *m* de planchar (Mex)

iron: ~monger /-mʌŋgə(r)/ *n* ferretero *m*. **~monger's** *n* ferretería *f*

irony /'aɪərənɪ/ *n* ironía *f*

irrational /ɪ'ræʃənl/ *a* irracional

irrefutable /ɪrɪ'fju:təbl/ *a* irrefutable

irregular /ɪ'regjʊlə(r)/ *a* irregular. **~ity** /-'lærətɪ/ *n* irregularidad *f*

irrelevan|ce /ɪ'reləvəns/ *n* irrelevancia *f*. **~t** *a* irrelevante

irreparable /ɪ'repərəbl/ *a* irreparable

irreplaceable /ɪrɪ'pleɪsəbl/ *a* irreemplazable

irresistible /ɪrɪ'zɪstəbl/ *a* irresistible

irrespective /ɪrɪ'spektɪv/ *a*. **~ of** sin tomar en cuenta

irresponsible /ɪrɪ'spɒnsəbl/ *a* irresponsable

irretrievable /ɪrɪ'tri:vəbl/ *a* irrecuperable

irreverent /ɪ'revərənt/ *a* irreverente

irrevocable /ɪ'revəkəbl/ *a* irrevocable

irrigat|e /'ɪrɪgeɪt/ *vt* regar, irrigar. **~ion** /-'geɪʃn/ *n* riego *m*, irrigación *f*

irritable /'ɪrɪtəbl/ *a* irritable

irritat|e /'ɪrɪteɪt/ *vt* irritar. **~ed** *a* <*expression*> de impaciencia; <*skin*> irritado. **be ~ed with** estar irritado con. **~ing** *a* irritante. **~ion** /-'teɪʃn/ *n* irritación *f*

IRS *abbr* (Amer) ⇒INTERNAL REVENUE SERVICE

is /ɪz/ ⇒BE

Islam /'ɪzlɑ:m/ *n* el Islam. **~ic** /ɪz'læmɪk/ *a* islámico

island /'aɪlənd/ *n* isla *f*. **~er** *n* isleño *m*

isolat|e /'aɪsəleɪt/ *vt* aislar. **~ion** /-'leɪʃn/ *n* aislamiento *m*

Israel /'ɪzreɪl/ *n* Israel *m*. **~i** /ɪz'reɪlɪ/ *a* & *n* israelí (*m*)

issue /'ɪʃu:/ *n* tema *m*, asunto *m*; (of magazine etc) número *m*; (of stamps, bank notes) emisión *f*; (of documents) expedición *f*. **take ~ with** discrepar de. ● *vt* hacer público <*statement*>; expedir <*documents*>; emitir <*stamps etc*>; prestar <*library book*>

it /ɪt/

● *pronoun*

····➤ (as subject) *generally not translated.* **it's huge** es enorme. **where is it?** ¿dónde está? **it's all lies** son todas mentiras

····➤ (as direct object) lo (*m*), la (*f*). **he read it to me** me lo/la leyó. **give it to me** dámelo/dámela

····➤ (as indirect object) le. **I gave it another coat of paint** le di otra mano de pintura

····➤ (after a preposition) *generally not translated.* **there's nothing behind it** no hay nada detrás

! Note, however, that in some cases *él* or *ella* must be used e.g. **he picked**

up the spoon and hit me with it agarró la cuchara y me golpeó con ella

····➤ (at door) **who is it?** ¿quién es?. **it's me** soy yo; (on telephone) **who is it, please?** ¿quién habla, por favor?; (before passing on to sb else) ¿de parte de quién, por favor? **it's Carol** soy Carol (Spain), habla Carol

····➤ (in impersonal constructions) **it is well known that ...** bien se sabe que ... **it's five o'clock** son las cinco. **so it seems** así parece

····➤ **that's it** (that's right) eso es; (that's enough, that's finished) ya está

Italian /ɪ'tæljən/ *a & n* italiano (*m*)

italics /ɪ'tælɪks/ *npl* (letra *f*) cursiva *f*

Italy /'ɪtəlɪ/ *n* Italia *f*

itch /ɪtʃ/ *n* picazón *f*. ● *vi* picar. **I'm ~ing to** estoy que me muero por. **my arm ~es** me pica el brazo. **~y** *a* que pica. **I've got an ~y nose** me pica la nariz

it'd /ɪtəd/ = **it had, it would**

item /'aɪtəm/ *n* artículo *m*; (on agenda) punto *m*. **news ~** *n* noticia *f*. **~ize** *vt* detallar

itinerary /aɪ'tɪnərərɪ/ *n* itinerario *m*

it'll /'ɪtl/ = **it will**

its /ɪts/ *a* su, sus (*pl*). ● *pron* (el) suyo *m*, (la) suya *f*, (los) suyos *mpl*, (las) suyas *fpl*

it's /ɪts/ = **it is, it has**

itself /ɪt'self/ *pron* él mismo, ella misma, ello mismo; (*reflexive*) se; (*after prep*) sí mismo, sí misma

I've /aɪv/ = **I have**

ivory /'aɪvərɪ/ *n* marfil *m*. **~ tower** *n* torre *f* de marfil

ivy /'aɪvɪ/ *n* hiedra *f*

Jj

jab /dʒæb/ *vt* (*pt* **jabbed**) pinchar; (thrust) hurgonear. ● *n* pinchazo *m*

jack /dʒæk/ *n* (Mec) gato *m*; (socket) enchufe *m* hembra; (Cards) sota *f*. □ **~ up** *vt* alzar con gato

jackal /'dʒækl/ *n* chacal *m*

jackdaw /'dʒækdɔ:/ *n* grajilla *f*

jacket /'dʒækɪt/ *n* chaqueta *f*; (casual) americana *f*, saco *m* (LAm); (Amer, of book) sobrecubierta *f*; (of record) funda *f*, carátula *f*

jack: ~ knife *vi* <*lorry*> plegarse. **~pot** *n* premio *m* gordo. **hit the ~pot** sacar el premio gordo

jade /dʒeɪd/ *n* (stone) jade *m*

jagged /'dʒægɪd/ *a* <*edge, cut*> irregular; <*rock*> recortado

jaguar /'dʒægjʊə(r)/ *n* jaguar *m*

jail /dʒeɪl/ *n* cárcel *m*, prisión *f*. ● *vt* encarcelar. **~er** *n* carcelero *m*. **~house** *n* (Amer) cárcel *f*

jam /dʒæm/ *vt* (*pt* **jammed**) interferir con <*radio*>; atestar <*road*>. **~ sth into sth** meter algo a la fuerza en algo. ● *vi* <*brakes*> bloquearse; <*machine*> trancarse. ● *n* mermelada *f*; (🅘, situation) apuro *m*

jangle /'dʒæŋgl/ *n* sonido *m* metálico (y áspero). ● *vi* hacer ruido (metálico)

janitor /'dʒænɪtə(r)/ *n* portero *m*

January /'dʒænjʊərɪ/ *n* enero *m*

Japan /dʒə'pæn/ *n* (el) Japón *m*. **~ese** /dʒæpə'ni:z/ *a & n invar* japonés (*m*)

jar /dʒɑ:(r)/ *n* tarro *m*, bote *m*. ● *vi* (*pt* **jarred**) <*clash*> desentonar. ● *vt* sacudir

jargon /'dʒɑ:gən/ *n* jerga *f*

jaundice /'dʒɔ:ndɪs/ *n* ictericia *f*

jaunt /dʒɔ:nt/ *n* excursión *f*

jaunty /'dʒɔ:ntɪ/ *a* (**-ier**, **-iest**) garboso

jaw /dʒɔ:/ *n* mandíbula *f*. **~s** *npl* fauces *fpl*. **~bone** *n* mandíbula *f*, maxilar *m*; (of animal) quijada *f*

jay /dʒeɪ/ *n* arrendajo *m*. **~walk** *vi* cruzar la calle descuidadamente. **~walker** *n* peatón *m* imprudente

jazz /dʒæz/ *n* jazz *m*. □ **~ up** *vt* animar. **~y** *a* chillón

jealous /dʒeləs/ *a* celoso; (envious) envidioso. **~y** *n* celos *mpl*

jeans /dʒi:nz/ *npl* vaqueros *mpl*, jeans *mpl*, tejanos *mpl*, pantalones *mpl* de mezclilla (Mex)

Jeep (*P*), **jeep** /dʒi:p/ *n* Jeep *m* (*P*)

jeer /dʒɪə(r)/ *vi*. **~ at** mofarse de; (boo) abuchear. ● *n* burla *f*; (boo) abucheo *m*

Jell-O /'dʒeləʊ/ *n* (*P*) (Amer) gelatina *f* (*con sabor a frutas*)

jelly /dʒelɪ/ *n* (clear jam) jalea *f*; (pudding) ⇒JELL-O; (substance) gelatina *f*. **~fish** *n* (*pl invar or* **-es**) medusa *f*

jeopardize /'dʒepədaɪz/ *vt* arriesgar

jerk /dʒɜ:k/ *n* sacudida *f*; (⊠, fool) idiota *m* & *f*. ● *vt* sacudir

jersey /'dʒɜ:zɪ/ *n* (*pl* **-eys**) jersey *m*, suéter *m*, pulóver *m*

jest /dʒest/ *n* broma *f*. ● *vi* bromear

Jesus /'dʒi:zəs/ *n* Jesús *m*

jet /dʒet/ *n* (stream) chorro *m*; (plane) avión *m* (*con motor a reacción*); (mineral) azabache *m*. **~-black** /-'blæk/ *a* azabache negro *a invar*. **~ lag** *n* jet lag *m*, desfase *f* horario. **have ~ lag** estar desfasado. **~-propelled** /-prə'peld/ *a* (de propulsión) a reacción

jettison /'dʒetɪsn/ *vt* echar al mar; (fig, discard) deshacerse de

jetty /'dʒetɪ/ *n* muelle *m*

Jew /dʒu:/ *n* judío *m*

jewel /'dʒu:əl/ *n* joya *f*. **~ler** *n* joyero *m*. **~lery** *n* joyas *fpl*

Jewish /'dʒu:ɪʃ/ *a* judío

jiffy /'dʒɪfɪ/ *n* momentito *m*. **do sth in a ~** hacer algo en un santiamén

jig /dʒɪg/ *n* (dance) giga *f*

jigsaw /'dʒɪgsɔ:/ *n*. **~** (**puzzle**) rompecabezas *m*

jilt /dʒɪlt/ *vt* dejar plantado

jingle /'dʒɪŋgl/ *vt* hacer sonar. ● *vi* tintinear. ● *n* tintineo *m*; (advert) jingle *m* (publicitario)

job /dʒɒb/ *n* empleo *m*, trabajo *m*; (piece of work) trabajo *m*. **it is a good ~ that** menos mal que. **~less** *a* desempleado

jockey /'dʒɒkɪ/ *n* jockey *m*

jocular /'dʒɒkjʊlə(r)/ *a* jocoso

jog /dʒɒg/ *vt* (*pt* **jogged**) empujar; refrescar <*memory*>. ● *vi* hacer footing, hacer jogging. **~er** *n* persona *f* quehace footing. **~ging** *n* footing *m*, jogging *m*. **go ~ging** salir a hacer footing *or* jogging

join /dʒɔɪn/ *vt* (link) unir; hacerse socio de <*club*>; hacerse miembro de <*political group*>; alistarse en <*army*>; reunirse con <*another person*>. ● *n* juntura. ● *vi*. **~ together** <*parts*> unirse; <*roads etc*> empalmar; <*rivers*> confluir. □ **~ in** *vi* participar (en). □ **~ up** *vi* (Mil) alistarse. **~er** *n* carpintero *m*

joint /dʒɔɪnt/ *a* conjunto. ● *n* (join) unión *f*, junta *f*; (Anat) articulación *f.* (Culin) trozo *m* de carne (para asar). **out of ~** descoyuntado. **~ account** *n* cuenta *f* conjunta. **~ly** *adv* conjuntamente. **~ owner** *n* copropietario *m.*

joist /dʒɔɪst/ *n* viga *f*

jok|e /dʒəʊk/ *n* (story) chiste *m*; (practical joke) broma *f.* ● *vi* bromear. **~er** *n* bromista *m* & *f*; (Cards) comodín *m.* **~y** *a* jocoso

jolly /'dʒɒlɪ/ *a* (**-ier**, **-iest**) alegre. ● *adv* 🅘 muy

jolt /dʒɒlt/ *vt* sacudir. ● *vi* <*vehicle*> dar una sacudida. ● *n* sacudida *f*

jostle /'dʒɒsl/ *vt* empujar. ● *vi* empujarse

jot /dʒɒt/ *n* pizca *f.* ● *vt* (*pt* **jotted**). □ **~ down** *vt* apuntar (rápidamente). **~ter** *n* bloc *m*

journal /'dʒɜ:nl/ *n* (diary) diario *m*; (newspaper) periódico *m*; (magazine) revista *f.* **~ism** *n* periodismo *m.* **~ist** *n* periodista *m* & *f*

journey /'dʒɜ:nɪ/ *n* viaje *m.* **go on a ~** hacer un viaje. ● *vi* viajar

jovial /'dʒəʊvɪəl/ *a* jovial

joy /dʒɔɪ/ *n* alegría *f.* **~ful** *a* feliz. **~ous** *a* feliz. **~rider** *n* joven *m* que roba un coche para dar una vuelta. **~stick** *n* (Aviat) palanca *f* de mando; (Comp) mando *m*, joystick *m*

jubila|nt /'dʒu:bɪlənt/ *a* jubiloso. **~tion** /-'leɪʃn/ *n* júbilo *m*

jubilee /'dʒu:bɪli:/ *n* aniversario *m* especial

Judaism /'dʒu:deɪɪzəm/ *n* judaísmo *m*

judge /dʒʌdʒ/ *n* juez *m.* ● *vt* juzgar. **~ment** *n* juicio *m*

judicia|l /dʒu:'dɪʃl/ *a* judicial. **~ry** /-ərɪ/ *n* judicatura *f*

judo /'dʒu:dəʊ/ *n* judo *m*

jug /dʒʌg/ *n* jarra *f*

juggernaut /'dʒʌgənɔ:t/ *n* camión *m* grande

juggle /'dʒʌgl/ *vi* hacer malabarismos. ● *vt* hacer malabarismos con. **~r** *n* malabarista *m* & *f*

juic|e /dʒu:s/ *n* jugo *m*, zumo *m.* **~y** *a* jugoso, zumoso; <*story etc*> 🅘 picante

jukebox /'dʒu:kbɒks/ *n* máquina *f* de discos, rocola *f* (LAm)

July /dʒu:'laɪ/ *n* julio *m*

jumble /'dʒʌmbl/ *vt.* **~** (up) mezclar. ● *n* (muddle) revoltijo *m.* **~ sale** *n* venta *f* de objetos usados *m*

jumbo /'dʒʌmbəʊ/ *a* gigante. **~ jet** *n* jumbo *m*

jump /dʒʌmp/ *vt* saltar. **~ rope** (Amer) saltar a la comba, saltar a la cuerda. **~ the gun** obrar prematuramente. **~ the queue** colarse. ● *vi* saltar; (start) sobresaltarse; <*prices*> alzarse. **~ at an opportunity** apresurarse a aprovechar una oportunidad. ● *n* salto *m*; (start) susto *m*; (increase) aumento *m.* **~er** *n* jersey *m*, suéter *m*, pulóver *m*; (Amer, dress) pichi *m*, jumper *m* & *f* (LAm). **~er cables** (Amer), **~ leads** *npl* cables *mpl* de arranque. **~ rope** (Amer) comba *f*, cuerda *f*, reata *f* (Mex). **~suit** *n* mono *m.* **~y** *a* nervioso

junction /'dʒʌŋkʃn/ *n* (of roads, rails) cruce *m*; (Elec) empalme *m*

June /dʒu:n/ *n* junio *m*

jungle /'dʒʌŋgl/ *n* selva *f*, jungla *f*

junior /'dʒu:nɪə(r)/ *a* (in age) más joven (**to** que); (in rank) subalterno. ● *n* menor *m*

junk /dʒʌŋk/ *n* trastos *mpl* viejos; (worthless stuff) basura *f.* ● *vt* 🅘 tirar. **~ food** *n* comida *f* basura, alimento *m* chatarra (Mex). **~ie**

/'dʒʌŋkɪ/ *n* Ⓘ drogadicto *m*, yonqui *m & f* Ⓘ. **~ mail** *n* propaganda *f* que se recibe por correo. **~ shop** *n* tienda *f* de trastos viejos

junta /'dʒʌntə/ *n* junta *f* militar

Jupiter /'dʒu:pɪtə(r)/ *n* Júpiter *m*

jurisdiction /dʒʊərɪs'dɪkʃn/ *n* jurisdicción *f*

jur|or /'dʒʊərə(r)/ *n* (miembro *m* de un) jurado *m*. **~y** *n* jurado *m*

just /dʒʌst/ *a* (fair) justo. ● *adv* exactamente, justo; (barely) justo; (only) sólo, solamente. **~ as tall** tan alto (**as** como). **~ listen!** ¡escucha! **he has ~ arrived** acaba de llegar, recién llegó (LAm)

justice /'dʒʌstɪs/ *n* justicia *f*. **J~ of the Peace** juez *m* de paz

justif|iable /dʒʌstɪ'faɪəbl/ *a* justificable. **~iably** *adv* con razón. **~ication** /dʒʌstɪfɪ'keɪʃn/ *n* justificación *f*. **~y** /'dʒʌstɪfaɪ/ *vt* justificar

jut /dʒʌt/ *vi* (*pt* **jutted**). **~ (out)** sobresalir

juvenile /'dʒu:vənaɪl/ *a* juvenil; (childish) infantil. ● *n* (Jurid) menor *m & f*

Kk

kaleidoscope /kə'laɪdəskəʊp/ *n* caleidoscopio *m*

kangaroo /kæŋgə'ru:/ *n* canguro *m*

karate /kə'rɑ:tɪ/ *n* kárate *m*, karate *m* (LAm)

keel /ki:l/ *n* (of ship) quilla *f*. □ **~ over** *vi* volcar(se)

keen /ki:n/ *a* (**-er**, **-est**) *<interest, feeling>* vivo; *<wind, mind, analysis>* penetrante; *<eyesight>* agudo; (eager) entusiasta. **I'm ~ on golf** me encanta el golf. **he's ~ on Shostakovich** le gusta Shostakovich. **~ly** *adv* vivamente; (enthusiastically) con entusiasmo. **~ness** *n* intensidad *f*; (enthusiasm) entusiasmo *m*.

keep /ki:p/ *vt* (*pt* **kept**) guardar; cumplir *<promise>*; tener *<shop, animals>*; mantener *<family>*; observar *<rule>*; (celebrate) celebrar; (delay) detener; (prevent) impedir. ● *vi* *<food>* conservarse; (remain) quedarse; (continue) seguir. **~ doing** seguir haciendo. ● *n* subsistencia *f*; (of castle) torreón *m*. **for ~s** Ⓘ para siempre. □ **~ back** *vt* retener. ● *vi* no acercarse. □ **~ in** *vt* no dejar salir. □ **~ off** *vt* mantenerse alejado de *<land>*. **'d off the grass'** 'prohibido pisar el césped'. □ **~ on** *vi* seguir. **~ on doing sth** seguir haciendo. □ **~ out** *vt* no dejar entrar. □ **~ up** *vt* mantener. □ **~ up with** *vt* estar al día en

kennel /'kenl/ *n* casa *f* del perro; (Amer, for boarding) residencia *f* canina. **~s** *n invar* residencia *f* canina

kept /kept/ ⇒KEEP

kerb /kɜ:b/ *n* bordillo *m* (de la acera), borde *m* de la banqueta (Mex)

kerosene /'kerəsi:n/ *n* queroseno *m*

ketchup /'ketʃʌp/ *n* salsa *f* de tomate

kettle /'ketl/ *n* pava *f*, tetera *f* (para calentar agua)

key /ki:/ *n* llave *f*; (of computer, piano) tecla *f*; (Mus) tono *m*. **be off ~** no estar en el tono. ● *a* clave. □ **~ in** *vt* teclear. **~board** *n* teclado *m*.

~hole *n* ojo *m* de la cerradura. **~ring** *n* llavero *m*

khaki /ˈkɑːkɪ/ *a* caqui

kick /kɪk/ *vt* dar una patada a <*person*>; patear <*ball*>. ● *vi* dar patadas; <*horse*> cocear. ● *n* patada *f*; (of horse) coz *f*; (I, thrill) placer *m*. □ **~ out** *vt* I echar. □ **~ up** *vt* armar <*fuss etc*>. **~off** *n* (Sport) saque *m* inicial. **~ start** *vt* arrancar (*con el pedal de arranque*) <*engine*>

kid /kɪd/ *n* (young goat) cabrito *m*; (I, child) niño *m*, chaval *m*, escuincle *m* (Mex). ● *vt* (*pt* **kidded**) tomar el pelo a. ● *vi* bromear

kidnap /ˈkɪdnæp/ *vt* (*pt* **kidnapped**) secuestrar. **~per** *n* secuestrador *m*. **~ping** *n* secuestro *m*

kidney /ˈkɪdnɪ/ *n* riñón *m*

kill /kɪl/ *vt* matar; (fig) acabar con. ● *n* matanza *f*. □ **~ off** *vt* matar. **~er** *n* asesino *m*. **~ing** *n* matanza *f*; (murder) asesinato *m*. **make a ~ing** (fig) hacer un gran negocio

kiln /kɪln/ *n* horno *m*

kilo /ˈkiːləʊ/ *n* (*pl* **-os**) kilo *m*. **~gram(me)** /ˈkɪləgræm/ *n* kilogramo *m*. **~metre** /ˈkɪləmiːtə(r)/, /kɪˈlɒmɪtə(r)/ *n* kilómetro *m*. **~watt** /ˈkɪləwɒt/ *n* kilovatio *m*

kilt /kɪlt/ *n* falda *f* escocesa

kin /kɪn/ *n* familiares *mpl*

kind /kaɪnd/ *n* tipo *m*, clase *f*. **~ of** (I, somewhat) un poco. **in ~** en especie. **be two of a ~** ser tal para cual. ● *a* amable

kindergarten /ˈkɪndəgɑːtn/ *n* jardín *m* de infancia

kind-hearted /kaɪndˈhɑːtɪd/ *a* bondadoso

kindle /ˈkɪndl/ *vt* encender

kind|ly *a* (**-ier**, **-iest**) bondadoso. ● *adv* amablemente; (please) haga el favor de. **~ness** *n* bondad *f*; (act) favor *m*

king /kɪŋ/ *n* rey *m*. **~dom** *n* reino *m*. **~fisher** *n* martín *m* pescador. **~-size(d)** *a* extragrande

kink /kɪŋk/ *n* (in rope) vuelta *f*, curva *f*; (in hair) onda *f*. **~y** *a* I pervertido

kiosk /ˈkiːɒsk/ *n* quiosco *m*

kipper /ˈkɪpə(r)/ *n* arenque *m* ahumado

kiss /kɪs/ *n* beso *m*. ● *vt* besar. ● *vi* besarse

kit /kɪt/ *n* avíos *mpl*. **tool ~** caja *f* de herramientas. □ **~ out** *vt* (*pt* **kitted**) equipar

kitchen /ˈkɪtʃɪn/ *n* cocina *f*

kite /kaɪt/ *n* cometa *f*, papalote *m* (Mex)

kitten /ˈkɪtn/ *n* gatito *m*

knack /næk/ *n* truco *m*

knapsack /ˈnæpsæk/ *n* mochila *f*

knead /niːd/ *vt* amasar

knee /niː/ *n* rodilla *f*. **~cap** *n* rótula *f*

kneel /niːl/ *vi* (*pt* **kneeled** *or* **knelt**). **~ (down)** arrodillarse; (be on one's knees) estar arrodillado

knelt /nelt/ ⇨KNEEL

knew /njuː/ ⇨KNOW

knickers /ˈnɪkəz/ *npl* bragas *fpl*, calzones *mpl* (LAm), pantaletas *fpl* (Mex)

knife /naɪf/ *n* (*pl* **knives**) cuchillo *m*. ● *vt* acuchillar

knight /naɪt/ *n* caballero *m*; (Chess) caballo *m*. ● *vt* conceder el título de Sir a. **~hood** *n* título *m* de Sir

knit /nɪt/ *vt* (*pt* **knitted** *or* **knit**) hacer, tejer (LAm). ● *vi* tejer, hacer punto. **~ one's brow** fruncir el ce ño. **~ting** *n* tejido *m*, punto *m*. **~ting needle** *n* aguja *f* de hacer punto, aguja *f* de tejer

knives /naɪvz/ ⇒KNIFE

knob /nɒb/ *n* botón *m*; (of door, drawer etc) tirador *m*. **~bly** *a* nudoso

knock /nɒk/ *vt* golpear; (criticize) criticar. ● *vi* golpear; (at door) llamar, golpear (LAm). ● *n* golpe *m*. □ **~ about** *vt* maltratar. □ **~ down** *vt* derribar; atropellar <*person*>. □ **~ off** *vt* hacer caer. *vi* (🄸, finish work) terminar, salir del trabajo. □ **~ out** *vt* (by blow) dejar sin sentido; (eliminate) eliminar. □ **~ over** *vt* tirar; atropellar <*person*>. **~er** *n* aldaba *f*. **~-kneed** /-'ni:d/ *a* patizambo. **~out** *n* (Boxing) nocaut *m*

knot /nɒt/ *n* nudo *m*. ● *vt* (*pt* **knotted**) anudar

know /nəʊ/ *vt* (*pt* **knew**) saber; (be acquainted with) conocer. **let s.o. ~ sth** decirle algo a uno; (warn) avisarle algo a uno. ● *vi* saber. **~ how to do sth** saber hacer algo. **~ about** entender de <*cars etc*>. **~ of** saber de. ● *n*. **be in the ~** estar enterado. **~-all** *n n* sabelotodo *m* & *f*. **~-how** *n* know-how *m*, conocimientos *mpl* y experiencia. **~ingly** *adv* a sabiendas. **~-it-all** *n* (Amer) ⇒~-ALL

knowledge /'nɒlɪdʒ/ *n* saber *m*; (awareness) conocimiento *m*; (learning) conocimientos *mpl*. **~able** *a* informado

known /nəʊn/ ⇒KNOW. ● *a* conocido

knuckle /'nʌkl/ *n* nudillo *m*. □ **~ under** *vi* someterse

Korea /kə'rɪə/ *n* Corea *f*. **~n** *a* & *n* coreano (*m*)

kudos /'kju:dɒs/ *n* prestigio *m*

Ll

lab /læb/ *n* 🄸 laboratorio *m*

label /'leɪbl/ *n* etiqueta *f*. ● *vt* (*pt* **labelled**) poner etiqueta a; (fig, describe as) tachar de

laboratory /lə'bɒrətərɪ/ *n* laboratorio *m*

laborious /lə'bɔ:rɪəs/ *a* penoso

labour /'leɪbə(r)/ *n* trabajo *m*; (workers) mano *f* de obra; (Med) parto *m*. **in ~** de parto. ● *vi* trabajar. ● *vt* insistir en. **L~** *n* el partido *m* laborista. ● *a* laborista. **~er** *n* peón *m*

lace /leɪs/ *n* encaje *m*; (of shoe) cordón *m*, agujeta *f* (Mex). ● *vt* (fasten) atar

lacerate /'læsəreɪt/ *vt* lacerar

lack /læk/ *n* falta *f*. **for ~ of** por falta de. ● *vt* faltarle a uno. **he ~s confidence** le falta confianza en sí mismo. **~ing** *a*. **be ~ing** faltar. **be ~ing in** no tener

lad /læd/ *n* muchacho *m*

ladder /'lædə(r)/ *n* escalera *f* (de mano); (in stocking) carrera *f*. ● *vt* hacerse una carrera en. ● *vi* hacérsele una carrera a

laden /'leɪdn/ *a* cargado (**with** de)

ladle /'leɪdl/ *n* cucharón *m*

lady /'leɪdɪ/ *n* señora *f*. **young ~** señorita *f*. **~bird** *n*, **~bug** *n* (Amer) mariquita *f*, catarina *f* (Mex). **~-in-waiting** *n* dama *f* de honor. **~like** *a* fino

lag /læg/ *vi* (*pt* **lagged**). **~ (behind)** retrasarse. ● *vt* revestir <*pipes*>. ● *n* (interval) intervalo *m*

lager /'lɑ:gə(r)/ *n* cerveza *f* (rubia)

lagging /'lægɪŋ/ *n* revestimiento *m*

lagoon /lə'gu:n/ *n* laguna *f*

laid /leɪd/ ⇒LAY

lain /leɪn/ ⇒LIE[1]

lair /leə(r)/ *n* guarida *f*

lake /leɪk/ *n* lago *m*

lamb /læm/ *n* cordero *m*

lame /leɪm/ *a* (**-er**, **-est**) cojo, rengo (LAm); <*excuse*> pobre, malo

lament /lə'ment/ *n* lamento *m*. ● *vt* lamentar. **~able** /'læmən təbl/ *a* lamentable

lamp /læmp/ *n* lámpara *f*

lamp: ~post *n* farol *m*. **~shade** *n* pantalla *f*

lance /lɑ:ns/ *n* lanza *f*

land /lænd/ *n* tierra *f*; (country) país *m*; (plot) terreno *m*. ● *vt* desembarcar; (obtain) conseguir; dar <*blow*>. ● *vi* (from ship) desembarcar; <*aircraft*> aterrizar. □ **~ up** *vi* ir a parar. **~ing** *n* desembarque *m*; (Aviat) aterrizaje *m*; (top of stairs) descanso *m*. **~lady** *n* casera *f*; (of inn) dueña *f*. **~lord** *n* casero *m*, dueño *m*; (of inn) dueño *m*. **~mark** *n* punto *m* destacado. **~scape** /-skeɪp/ *n* paisaje *m*. **~slide** *n* desprendimiento *m* de tierras; (Pol) victoria *f* arrolladora

lane /leɪn/ *n* (path, road) camino *m*, sendero *m*; (strip of road) carril *m*

language /'læŋgwɪdʒ/ *n* idioma *m*; (speech, style) lenguaje *m*

lank /læŋk/ *a* <*hair*> lacio. **~y** *a* (**-ier**, **-iest**) larguirucho

lantern /'læntən/ *n* linterna *f*

lap /læp/ *n* (of body) rodillas *fpl*; (Sport) vuelta *f*. ● *vi* (*pt* **lapped**) <*waves*> chapotear. □ **~up** beber a lengüetazos; (fig) aceptar con entusiasmo

lapel /lə'pel/ *n* solapa *f*

lapse /læps/ *vi* (decline) degradarse; (expire) caducar; <*time*> transcurrir. **~ into silence** callarse. ● *n* error *m*; (of time) intervalo *m*

laptop /'læptɒp/ *n*. **~** (**computer**) laptop *m*, laptop *f* (LAm)

lard /lɑ:d/ *n* manteca *f* de cerdo

larder /'lɑ:də(r)/ *n* despensa *f*

large /lɑ:dʒ/ *a* (**-er**, **-est**) grande, (before singular noun) gran. ● *n*. **at ~** en libertad. **~ly** *adv* en gran parte

lark /lɑ:k/ *n* (bird) alondra *f*; (joke) broma *f*; (bit of fun) travesura *f*. □ **~ about** *vt* hacer el tonto Ⓘ

larva /'lɑ:və/ *n* (*pl* **-vae** /-vi:/) larva *f*

laser /'leɪzə(r)/ *n* láser *m*. **~ beam** *n* rayo *m* láser. **~ printer** *n* impresora *f* láser

lash /læʃ/ *vt* azotar. □ **~ out** *vi* atacar. **~ out against** *vt* atacar. ● *n* latigazo *m*; (eyelash) pestaña *f*; (whip) látigo *m*

lashings /'læʃɪŋz/ *npl*. **~ of** (⊠, cream etc) montones de

lass /læs/ *n* muchacha *f*

lasso /læ'su:/ *n* (*pl* **-os**) lazo *m*

last /lɑ:st/ *a* último; <*week etc*> pasado. **~ Monday** el lunes pasado. **~ night** anoche. ● *adv* por último; (most recently) la última vez. **he came ~** llegó el último. ● *n* último *m*; (remainder) lo que queda. **~ but one** penúltimo. **at** (**long**) **~** por fin. ● *vi/t* durar. □ **~ out** *vi* sobrevivir. **~ing** *a* duradero. **~ly** *adv* por último

latch /lætʃ/ *n* pestillo *m*

late /leɪt/ *a* (**-er**, **-est**) (not on time) tarde; (recent) reciente; (former) antiguo, ex. **be ~** llegar tarde. **in ~ July** a fines de julio. **the ~ Dr Phillips** el difunto Dr. Phillips. ● *adv* tarde. **~ly** *adv* últimamente

latent /ˈleɪtnt/ *a* latente

later /ˈleɪtə(r)/ *adv* más tarde

lateral /ˈlætərəl/ *a* lateral

latest /ˈleɪtɪst/ *a* último. ● *n*. **at the ~** a más tardar

lathe /leɪð/ *n* torno *m*

lather /ˈlɑːðə(r)/ *n* espuma *f*

Latin /ˈlætɪn/ *n* (Lang) latín *m*. ● *a* latino. **~ America** *n* América *f* Latina, Latinoamérica *f*. **~ American** *a & n* latinoamericano *f*

latitude /ˈlætɪtjuːd/ *n* latitud *m*

latter /ˈlætə(r)/ *a* último; (of two) segundo. ● *n*. **the ~** éste *m*, ésta *f*, éstos *mpl*, éstas *fpl*

laugh /lɑːf/ *vi* reír(se). **~ at** reírse de. ● *n* risa *f*. **~able** *a* ridículo. **~ing stock** *n* hazmerreír *m*. **~ter** *n* risas *fpl*

launch /lɔːntʃ/ *vt* lanzar; botar <*new vessel*>. ● *n* lanzamiento *m*; (of new vessel) botadura; (boat) lancha *f* (a motor). **~ing pad**, **~ pad** *n* plataforma *f* de lanzamiento

laund|er /ˈlɔːndə(r)/ *vt* lavar (y planchar). **~erette** /-et/, **L~romat** /ˈlɔːndrəmæt/ (Amer) (*P*) *n* lavandería *f* automática. **~ry** *n* (place) lavandería *f*; (dirty clothes) ropa *f* sucia; (clean clothes) ropa *f* limpia

lava /ˈlɑːvə/ *n* lava *f*

lavatory /ˈlævətərɪ/ *n* (cuarto *m* de) baño *m*. **public ~** servicios *mpl*, baños *mpl* (LAm)

lavish /ˈlævɪʃ/ *a* <*lifestyle*> de derroche; (meal) espléndido; (production) fastuoso. ● *vt* prodigar (**on** a)

law /lɔː/ *n* ley *f*; (profession, subject of study) derecho *m*. **~ and order** *n* orden *m* público. **~ court** *n* tribunal *m*

lawn /lɔːn/ *n* césped *m*, pasto *m* (LAm). **~mower** *n* cortacésped *f*, cortadora *f* de pasto (LAm)

lawsuit /ˈlɔːsuːt/ *n* juicio *m*

lawyer /ˈlɔjə(r)/ *n* abogado *m*

lax /læks/ *a* descuidado; <*morals etc*> laxo

laxative /ˈlæksətɪv/ *n* laxante *m*

lay /leɪ/ ⇒LIE. ● *vt* (*pt* **laid**) poner <*also table, eggs*>; tender <*trap*>; formar <*plan*>. **~ hands on** echar mano a. **~ hold of** agarrar. ● *a* (non-clerical) laico; <*opinion etc*> profano. □ **~ down** *vt* dejar a un lado; imponer <*condition*>. □ **~ into** *vt* ▣ dar una paliza a. □ **~ off** *vt* despedir <*worker*>. *vi* ▣ terminar. □ **~ on** *vt* (provide) proveer. □ **~ out** *vt* (design) disponer; (display) exponer; gastar <*money*>. **~about** *n* holgazán. **~-by** *n* área *f* de reposo

layer /ˈleɪə(r)/ *n* capa *f*

layette /leɪˈet/ *n* canastilla *f*

layman /ˈleɪmən/ *n* (*pl* **-men**) lego *m*

layout /ˈleɪaʊt/ *n* disposición *f*

laz|e /leɪz/ *vi* holgazanear; (relax) descansar. **~iness** *n* pereza *f*. **~y** *a* perezoso. **~ybones** *n* holgazán *m*

lead[1] /liːd/ *vt* (*pt* **led**) conducir; dirigir <*team*>; llevar <*life*>; encabezar <*parade, attack*>. **I was led to believe that ...** me dieron a entender que .... ● *vi* (go first) ir delante; (in race) aventajar. ● *n* mando *m*; (clue) pista *f*; (leash) correa *f*; (wire) cable *m*. **be in the ~** llevar la delantera

lead[2] /led/ *n* plomo *m*; (of pencil) mina *f*. **~ed** *a* <*fuel*> con plomo

lead /liːd/: **~er** *n* jefe *m*; (Pol) líder *m* & *f*; (of gang) cabecilla *m*. **~ership** *n* dirección *f*. **~ing** *a* principal; (in front) delantero

leaf /liːf/ *n* (*pl* **leaves**) hoja *f*. □ **~ through** *vi* hojear **~let** /ˈliːflɪt/ *n* folleto *m*. **~y** *a* frondoso

league /liːg/ *n* liga *f*. **be in ~ with** estar aliado con

leak /liːk/ *n* (hole) agujero *m*; (of gas, liquid) escape *m*; (of information) filtración *f*; (in roof) gotera *f*; (in boat) vía *f* de agua. ● *vi* gotear; <*liquid*> salirse; <*boat*> hacer agua. ● *vt* perder; filtrar <*information*>. **~y** *a* <*receptacle*> agujereado; <*roof*> que tiene goteras

lean /liːn/ (*pt* **leaned** *or* **leant** /lent/) *vt* apoyar. ● *vi* inclinarse. □ **~ against** *vt* apoyarse en. □ **~ on** *vt* apoyarse en. □ **~ out** *vt* asomarse (**of** a). □ **~ over** *vi* inclinarse ● *a* (**-er**, **-est**) <*person*> delgado; <*animal*> flaco; <*meat*> magro. **~ing** *a* inclinado. **~-to** *n* colgadizo *m*

leap /liːp/ *vi* (*pt* **leaped** *or* **leapt** /lept/) saltar. ● *n* salto *m*. **~frog** *n*. **play ~frog** saltar al potro, jugar a la pídola, brincar al burro (Mex). ● *vi* (*pt* **-frogged**) saltar. **~ year** *n* año *m* bisiesto

learn /lɜːn/ *vt/i* (*pt* **learned** *or* **learnt**) aprender (**to do** a hacer). **~ed** /-ɪd/ *a* culto. **~er** *n* principiante *m* & *f*; (apprentice) aprendiz *m*. **~ing** *n* saber *m*

lease /liːs/ *n* arriendo *m*. ● *vt* arrendar

leash /liːʃ/ *n* correa *f*

least /liːst/ *a* (smallest amount of) mínimo; (slightest) menor; (smallest) más pequeño. ● *n*. **the ~** lo menos. **at ~** por lo menos. **not in the ~** en absoluto. ● *adv* menos

leather /ˈleðə(r)/ *n* piel *f*, cuero *m*

leave /liːv/ *vt* (*pt* **left**) dejar; (depart from) salir de. **~ alone** dejar de tocar <*thing*>; dejar en paz <*person*>. ● *vi* marcharse; <*train*> salir. ● *n* permiso *m*. □ **~ behind** *vt* dejar. □ **~ out** *vt* omitir. □ **~ over** *vt*. **be left over** quedar. **on ~** (Mil) de permiso

leaves /liːvz/ ⇒LEAF

lecture /ˈlektʃə(r)/ *n* conferencia *f*; (Univ) clase *f*; (rebuke) sermón *m*. ● *vi* dar clase. ● *vt* (scold) sermonear. **~r** *n* conferenciante *m* & *f*, conferencista *m* & *f* (LAm); (Univ) profesor *m* universitario

led /led/ ⇒LEAD[1]

ledge /ledʒ/ *n* cornisa *f*; (of window) alféizar *m*

leek /liːk/ *n* puerro *m*

leer /ˈlɪə(r)/ *vi*. **~ at** mirar impúdicamente. ● *n* mirada impúdica *f*

left /left/ ⇒LEAVE. *a* izquierdo. ● *adv* a la izquierda. ● *n* izquierda *f*. **~-handed** /-ˈhændɪd/ *a* zurdo. **~ luggage** *n* consigna *f*. **~overs** *npl* restos *mpl*. **~-wing** /-ˈwɪŋ/ *a* izquierdista

leg /leg/ *n* pierna *f*; (of animal, furniture) pata *f*; (of pork) pernil *m*; (of lamb) pierna *f*; (of journey) etapa *f*. **on its last ~s** en las últimas. **pull s.o.'s ~** [T] tomarle el pelo a uno

legacy /ˈlegəsɪ/ *n* herencia *f*

legal /ˈliːgl/ *a* (permitted by law) lícito; (recognized by law) legítimo; <*system etc*> jurídico. **~ity** /liːˈgælətɪ/ *n* legalidad *f*. **~ize** *vt* legalizar. **~ly** *adv* legalmente

legend /ˈledʒənd/ *n* leyenda *f*. **~ary** *a* legendario

legible /ˈledʒəbl/ *a* legible

legislat|e /ˈledʒɪsleɪt/ *vi* legislar. **~ion** /-ˈleɪʃn/ *n* legislación *f*

legitimate /lɪ'dʒɪtɪmət/ *a* legítimo

leisure /'leʒə(r)/ *n* ocio *m*. **at your ~** cuando le venga bien. **~ly** *a* lento, pausado

lemon /'lemən/ *n* limón *m*. **~ade** /-'neɪd/ *n* (fizzy) gaseosa *f* (de limón); (still) limonada *f*

lend /lend/ *vt* (*pt* **lent**) prestar. **~ing** *n* préstamo *m*

length /leŋθ/ *n* largo *m*; (of time) duración *f*; (of cloth) largo *m*. **at ~** (at last) por fin. **at (great) ~** detalladamente. **~en** /'leŋθən/ *vt* alargar. ● *vi* alargarse. **~ways** *adv* a lo largo. **~y** *a* largo

lenient /'li:nɪənt/ *a* indulgente

lens /lens/ *n* lente *f*; (of camera) objetivo *m*. **(contact) ~es** *npl* lentillas *fpl*, lentes *mpl* de contacto (LAm)

lent /lent/ ⇒LEND

Lent /lent/ *n* cuaresma *f*

Leo /'li:əʊ/ *n* Leo *m*

leopard /'lepəd/ *n* leopardo *m*

leotard /'li:ətɑ:d/ *n* malla *f*

lesbian /'lezbɪən/ *n* lesbiana *f*. ● *a* lesbiano

less /les/ *a & n & adv & prep* menos. **~ than** menos que; (with numbers) menos de. **~ and ~** cada vez menos. **none the ~** sin embargo. **~en** *vt/i* disminuir

lesson /'lesn/ *n* clase *f*

lest /lest/ *conj* no sea que (+ *subjunctive*)

let /let/ *vt* (*pt* **let**, *pres p* **letting**) dejar; (lease) alquilar. **~ me do it** déjame hacerlo. ● *v aux*. **~'s go!** ¡vamos!, ¡vámonos! **~'s see** (vamos) a ver. **~'s talk/drink** hablemos/bebamos. □ **~ down** *vt* bajar; (deflate) desinflar; (fig) defraudar. □ **~ go** *vt* soltar. □ **~ in** *vt* dejar entrar. □ **~ off** *vt* disparar <*gun*>; (cause to explode) hacer explotar; hacer estallar <*firework*>; (excuse) perdonar. □ **~ out** *vt* dejar salir. □ **~ through** *vt* dejar pasar. □ **~ up** *vi* disminuir. **~down** *n* desilusión *f*

lethal /'li:θl/ *a* <*dose, wound*> mortal; <*weapon*> mortífero

letharg|ic /lɪ'θɑ:dʒɪk/ *a* letárgico. **~y** /'leθədʒɪ/ *n* letargo *m*

letter /'letə(r)/ *n* (of alphabet) letra *f*; (written message) carta *f*. **~ bomb** *n* carta *f* bomba. **~box** *n* buzón *m*. **~ing** *n* letras *fpl*

lettuce /'letɪs/ *n* lechuga *f*

let-up /'letʌp/ *n* interrupción *f*

leukaemia /lu:'ki:mɪə/ *n* leucemia *f*

level /'levl/ *a* (flat, even) plano, parejo (LAm); <*spoonful*> raso. **~ with** (at same height) al nivel de. ● *n* nivel *m*. ● *vt* (*pt* **levelled**) nivelar; (aim) apuntar. **~ crossing** *n* paso *m* a nivel, crucero *m* (Mex)

lever /'li:və(r)/ *n* palanca *f*. ● *vt* apalancar. **~ open** abrir haciendo palanca. **~age** /-ɪdʒ/ *n* apalancamiento *m*

levy /'levɪ/ *vt* imponer <*tax*>. ● *n* impuesto *m*

lewd /lu:d/ *a* (**-er**, **-est**) lascivo

liab|ility /laɪə'bɪlətɪ/ *n* responsabilidad *f*; (🅸, disadvantage) lastre *m*. **~ilities** *npl* (debts) deudas *fpl*. **~le** /'laɪəbl/ *a*. **be ~le to do** tener tendencia a hacer. **~le for** responsable de. **~le to** susceptible de; expuesto a <*fine*>

liais|e /lɪ'eɪz/ *vi* actuar de enlace (with con). **~on** /-ɒn/ *n* enlace *m*

liar /'laɪə(r)/ *n* mentiroso *m*

libel /'laɪbl/ *n* difamación *f*. ● *vt* (*pt* **libelled**) difamar (por escrito)

liberal /'lɪbərəl/ *a* liberal; (generous) generoso. **L~** (Pol) del Partido Liberal. ● *n* liberal *m & f*. **~ly** *adv* liberalmente; (generously) generosamente

liberat|e /'lɪbəreɪt/ *vt* liberar. **~ion** /-'reɪʃn/ *n* liberación *f*

liberty /'lɪbətɪ/ *n* libertad *f*. **take liberties** tomarse libertades. **take the ~ of** tomarse la libertad de

Libra /'li:brə/ *n* Libra *f*

librar|ian /laɪ'breərɪən/ *n* bibliotecario *m*. **~y** /'laɪbrərɪ/ *n* biblioteca *f*

lice /laɪs/ ⇒LOUSE

licence /'laɪsns/ *n* licencia *f*, permiso *m*

license /'laɪsns/ *vt* autorizar. ● *n* (Amer) ⇒LICENCE. **~ number** *n* (Amer) (número *m* de) matrícula *f*. **~ plate** *n* (Amer) matrícula *f*, placa *f* (LAm)

lick /lɪk/ *vt* lamer; (⊠, defeat) dar una paliza a. ● *n* lametón *m*

licorice /'lɪkərɪs/ *n* (Amer) regaliz *m*

lid /lɪd/ *n* tapa *f*; (eyelid) párpado *m*

lie[1] /laɪ/ *vi* (*pt* **lay**, *pp* **lain**, *pres p* **lying**) echarse, tenderse; (be in lying position) estar tendido; (be) estar, encontrarse. **~ low** quedarse escondido. □ **~ down** *vi* echarse, tenderse

lie[2] /laɪ/ *n* mentira *f*. ● *vi* (*pt* **lied**, *pres p* **lying**) mentir

lie-in /laɪ'ɪn/ *n*. **have a ~** quedarse en la cama

lieutenant /lef'tenənt/ *n* (Mil) teniente *m*

life /laɪf/ *n* (*pl* **lives**) vida *f*. **~ belt** *n* salvavidas *m*. **~boat** *n* lancha *f* de salvamento; (on ship) bote *m* salvavidas. **~buoy** *n* boya *f* salvavidas. **~guard** *n* salvavidas *m & f*. **~ jacket** *n* chaleco *m* salvavidas. **~less** *a* sin vida. **~like** *a* verosímil. **~line** *n* cuerda *f* de salvamento; (fig) tabla *f* de salvación. **~long** *a* de toda la vida. **~ preserver** *n* (Amer, buoy) ⇒~BUOY; (jacket) ⇒~ JACKET. **~ ring** *n* (Amer) ⇒~ BELT. **~saver** *n* (person) salvavidas *m & f*; (fig) salvación *f*. **~-size(d)** *a* (de) tamaño natural. **~time** *n* vida *f*. **~ vest** *n* (Amer) ⇒~ JACKET

lift /lɪft/ *vt* levantar. ● *vi* <*fog*> disiparse. ● *n* ascensor *m*. **give a ~ to s.o.** llevar a uno en su coche, dar aventón a uno (Mex). □ **~ up** *vt* levantar. **~-off** *n* despegue *m*

light /laɪt/ *n* luz *f*; (lamp) lámpara *f*, luz *f*; (flame) fuego *m*. **come to ~** salir a la luz. **have you got a ~?** ¿tienes fuego? **the ~s** *npl* (traffic signals) el semáforo; (on vehicle) las luces. ● *a* (**-er**, **-est**) (in colour) claro; (not heavy) ligero. ● *vt* (*pt* **lit** *or* **lighted**) encender, prender (LAm); (illuminate) iluminar. ● *vi* encenderse, prenderse (LAm). **~ up** *vt* iluminar. ● *vi* iluminarse. **~ bulb** *n* bombilla *f*, foco *m* (Mex). **~en** *vt* (make less heavy) aligerar, alivianar (LAm); (give light to) iluminar; (make brighter) aclarar. **~er** *n* (for cigarettes) mechero *m*, encendedor *m*. **~-hearted** /-'hɑ:tɪd/ *a* alegre. **~house** *n* faro *m*. **~ly** *adv* ligeramente

lightning /'laɪtnɪŋ/ *n*. **flash of ~** relámpago *m*. ● *a* relámpago

lightweight *a* ligero, liviano (LAm)

like /laɪk/ *a* parecido. ● *prep* como. ● *conj* 🅸 como. ● *vt*. **I ~ chocolate** me gusta el chocolate. **they ~ swimming** (a ellos) les gusta nadar. **would you ~ a coffee?** ¿quieres un café? **~able** *a* simpático.

like|lihood /'laɪklɪhʊd/ *n* probabilidad *f*. **~ly** *a* (**-ier**, **-iest**) probable. **he is ~ly to come** es probable que venga. ● *adv* probablemente. **not ~ly!** ¡ni hablar! **~n** *vt* comparar (**to** con, a). **~ness** *n* parecido *m*. **be a good ~ness** parecerse mucho. **~wise** *adv* (also) también; (the same way) lo mismo

liking /'laɪkɪŋ/ *n* (for thing) afición *f*; (for person) simpatía *f*

lilac /'laɪlək/ *a* lila. ● *n* lila *f*; (color) lila *m*

lily /'lɪlɪ/ *n* lirio *m*; (white) azucena *f*

limb /lɪm/ *n* miembro *m*. **out on a ~** aislado

lime /laɪm/ *n* (white substance) cal *f*; (fruit) lima *f*. **~light** *n*. **be in the ~light** ser el centro de atención

limerick /'lɪmərɪk/ *n* quintilla *f* humorística

limit /'lɪmɪt/ *n* límite *m*. ● *vt* limitar. **~ation** /-'teɪʃn/ *n* limitación *f*. **~ed** *a* limitado. **~ed company** *n* sociedad *f* anónima

limousine /'lɪməziːn/ *n* limusina *f*

limp /lɪmp/ *vi* cojear, renguear (LAm). ● *n* cojera *f*, renguera *f* (LAm). **have a ~** cojear. ● *a* (**-er**, **-est**) flojo

linden /'lɪndn/ *n* (Amer) tilo *m*

line /laɪn/ *n* línea *f*; (track) vía *f*; (wrinkle) arruga *f*; (row) fila *f*; (of poem) verso *m*; (rope) cuerda *f*; (of goods) surtido *m*; (Amer, queue) cola *f*. **stand in ~** (Amer) hacer cola. **get in ~** (Amer) ponerse en la cola. **cut in ~** (Amer) colarse. **in ~ with** de acuerdo con. ● *vt* forrar <*skirt, box*>; bordear <*streets etc*>. □ **~ up** *vi* alinearse; (in queue) hacer cola. *vt* (form into line) poner en fila; (align) alinear. **~d** /laɪnd/ *a* <*paper*> con renglones; (with fabric) forrado

linen /'lɪnɪn/ *n* (sheets etc) ropa *f* blanca; (material) lino *m*

liner /'laɪnə(r)/ *n* (ship) transatlántico *m*

linger /'lɪŋgə(r)/ *vi* tardar en marcharse. **~** (**on**) <*smells etc*> persistir. □ **~ over** *vt* dilatarse en

lingerie /'lænʒərɪ/ *n* lencería *f*

linguist /'lɪŋgwɪst/ *n* políglota *m* & *f*; lingüista *m* & *f*. **~ic** /lɪŋ'gwɪstɪk/ *a* lingüístico. **~ics** *n* lingüística *f*

lining /'laɪnɪŋ/ *n* forro *m*

link /lɪŋk/ *n* (of chain) eslabón *m*; (connection) conexión *f*; (bond) vínculo *m*; (transport, telecommunications) conexión *f*, enlace *m*. ● *vt* conectar; relacionar <*facts, events*>. □ **~ up** *vt/i* conectar

lino /'laɪnəʊ/ *n* (*pl* **os**) linóleo *m*

lint /lɪnt/ *n* (Med) hilas *fpl*

lion /'laɪən/ *n* león *m*. **~ess** /-nɪs/ *n* leona *f*

lip /lɪp/ *n* labio *m*; (edge) borde *m*. **~read** *vi* leer los labios. **~salve** *n* crema *f* para los labios. **~ service** *n*. **pay ~ service to** aprobar de boquilla, aprobar de los dientes para afuera (Mex). **~stick** *n* lápiz *m* de labios

liqueur /lɪ'kjʊə(r)/ *n* licor *m*

liquid /'lɪkwɪd/ *a* & *n* líquido (*m*)

liquidate /'lɪkwɪdeɪt/ *vt* liquidar

liquidize /'lɪkwɪdaɪz/ *vt* licuar. **~r** *n* licuadora *f*

liquor /'lɪkə(r)/ *n* bebidas *fpl* alcohólicas

liquorice /'lɪkərɪs/ *n* regaliz *m*

liquor store *n* (Amer) tienda *f* de bebidas alcohólicas

lisp /lɪsp/ *n* ceceo *m*. **speak with a ~** cecear. ● *vi* cecear

list /lɪst/ *n* lista *f*. ● *vt* hacer una lista de; (enter in a list) inscribir. ● *vi* (ship) escorar

listen /ˈlɪsn/ *vi* escuchar. **~ in (to)** escuchar. **~ to** escuchar. **~er** *n* oyente *m & f*

listless /ˈlɪstlɪs/ *a* apático

lit /lɪt/ ⇒LIGHT

literacy /ˈlɪtərəsɪ/ *n* alfabetismo *m*

literal /ˈlɪtərəl/ *a* literal. **~ly** *adv* literalmente

literary /ˈlɪtərərɪ/ *a* literario

literate /ˈlɪtərət/ *a* alfabetizado

literature /ˈlɪtərətʃə(r)/ *n* literatura *f*; (fig) folletos *mpl*

lithe /laɪð/ *a* ágil

litre /ˈli:tə(r)/ *n* litro *m*

litter /ˈlɪtə(r)/ *n* basura *f*; (of animals) camada *f*. ● *vt* ensuciar; (scatter) esparcir. **~ed with** lleno de. **~ bin** *n* papelera *f*. **~bug**, **~ lout** *n* persona *f* que tira basura en lugares públicos

little /ˈlɪtl/ *a* pequeño; (not much) poco. **a ~ water** un poco de agua. ● *pron* poco, poca. **a ~** un poco. ● *adv* poco. **~ by ~** poco a poco. **~ finger** *n* (dedo *m*) meñique *m*

live /lɪv/ *vt/i* vivir. □ **~ down** *vt* lograr borrar. □ **~ off** *vt* vivir a costa de <*family, friends*>; (feed on) alimentarse de. □ **~ on** *vt* (feed o.s. on) vivir de. *vi* <*memory*> seguir presente; <*tradition*> seguir existiendo. □ **~ up** *vt*. **~ it up** [I] darse la gran vida. □ **~ up to** *vt* vivir de acuerdo con; cumplir <*promise*>. ● /laɪv/ *a* vivo; <*wire*> con corriente; <*broadcast*> en directo

livelihood /ˈlaɪvlɪhʊd/ *n* sustento *m*

lively /ˈlaɪvlɪ/ *a* (**-ier**, **-iest**) vivo

liven up /ˈlaɪvn/ *vt* animar. ● *vi* animar(se)

liver /ˈlɪvə(r)/ *n* hígado *m*

lives /laɪvz/ ⇒LIFE

livestock /ˈlaɪvstɒk/ *n* animales *mpl* (de cría); (cattle) ganado *m*

livid /ˈlɪvɪd/ *a* lívido; ([I], angry) furioso

living /ˈlɪvɪŋ/ *a* vivo. ● *n* vida *f*. **make a ~** ganarse la vida. **~ room** *n* salón *m*, sala *f* (de estar), living *m* (LAm)

lizard /ˈlɪzəd/ *n* lagartija *f*; (big) lagarto *m*

load /ləʊd/ *n* (also Elec) carga *f*; (quantity) cantidad *f*; (weight, strain) peso *m*. **~s of** [I] montones de. ● *vt* cargar. **~ed** *a* cargado

loaf /ləʊf/ *n* (*pl* **loaves**) pan *m*; (stick of bread) barra *f* de pan. ● *vi*. **~ (about)** holgazanear

loan /ləʊn/ *n* préstamo *m*. **on ~** prestado. ● *vt* prestar

loath|e /ləʊð/ *vt* odiar. **~ing** *n* odio *m* (**of** a). **~esome** /-səm/ *a* repugnante

lobby /ˈlɒbɪ/ *n* vestíbulo *m*; (Pol) grupo *m* de presión. ● *vt* ejercer presión sobre. ● *vi*. **~ for sth** ejercer presión para obtener algo

lobe /ləʊb/ *n* lóbulo *m*

lobster /ˈlɒbstə(r)/ *n* langosta *f*, bogavante m

local /ˈləʊkl/ *a* local. **~ (phone) call** llamada *f* urbana. ● *n* ([I], pub) bar *m*. **the ~s** los vecinos *mpl*

local: ~ government *n* administración *f* municipal. **~ity** /-ˈkælətɪ/ *n* localidad *f*. **~ly** *adv* <*live, work*> en la zona

locat|e /ləʊˈkeɪt/ *vt* (situate) situar, ubicar (LAm); (find) localizar, ubicar (LAm). **~ion** /-ʃn/ *n* situación *f*, ubicación *f* (LAm). **on ~ion** fuera del estudio. **to film on ~ion in Andalusia** rodar en Andalucía

lock /lɒk/ *n* (of door etc) cerradura *f*; (on canal) esclusa *f*; (of hair) mechón *m*. ● *vt* cerrar con llave. ● *vi* cerrarse con llave. □ **~ in** *vt* encerrar. □ **~ out** *vt* cerrar la puerta a. □ **~ up** *vt* encerrar <*person*>; cerrar con llave <*building*>

locker /ˈlɒkə(r)/ *n* armario *m*, locker *m* (LAm). **~ room** *n* (Amer) vestuario *m*, vestidor *m* (Mex)

locket /ˈlɒkɪt/ *n* medallón *m*

lock: ~out /ˈlɒkaʊt/ *n* cierre *m* patronal, paro *m* patronal (LAm). **~smith** *n* cerrajero *m*

locomotive /ləʊkəˈməʊtɪv/ *n* locomotora *f*

lodg|e /lɒdʒ/ *n* (of porter) portería *f*. ● *vt* alojar; presentar <*complaint*>. **~er** *n* huésped *m*. **~ings** *n* alojamiento *m*; (room) habitación *f* alquilada

loft /lɒft/ *n* desván *m*, altillo *m* (LAm)

lofty /ˈlɒftɪ/ *a* (**-ier, -iest**) elevado; (haughty) altanero

log /lɒg/ *n* (of wood) tronco *m*; (as fuel) leño *m*; (record) diario *m*. **sleep like a ~** dormir como un tronco. ● *vt* (*pt* **logged**) registrar. □ **~ in, ~ on** *vi* (Comp) entrar (al sistema). □ **~ off, ~ out** *vi* (Comp) salir (del sistema)

logarithm /ˈlɒgərɪðəm/ *n* logaritmo *m*

loggerheads /ˈlɒgəhedz/ *npl*. **be at ~ with** estar a matar con

logic /ˈlɒdʒɪk/ *a* lógica *f*. **~al** *a* lógico. **~ally** *adv* lógicamente

logistics /ləˈdʒɪstɪks/ *n* logística *f*. ● *npl* (practicalities) problemas *mpl* logísticos

logo /ˈləʊgəʊ/ *n* (*pl* **-os**) logo *m*

loin /lɔɪn/ *n* (Culin) lomo *m*. **~s** *npl* entrañas *fpl*

loiter /ˈlɔɪtə(r)/ *vi* perder el tiempo

loll /lɒl/ *vi* repantigarse

loll|ipop /ˈlɒlɪpɒp/ *n* pirulí *m*. **~y** *n* polo *m*, paleta *f* (helada) (LAm)

London /ˈlʌndən/ *n* Londres *m*. ● *a* londinense. **~er** *n* londinense *m & f*

lone /ləʊn/ *a* solitario. **~ly** *a* (**-ier, -iest**) solitario. **feel ~ly** sentirse muy solo. **~r** *n* solitario *m*. **~some** /-səm/ *a* solitario

long /lɒŋ/ *a* (**-er, -est**) largo. **a ~ time** mucho tiempo. **how ~ is it?** ¿cuánto tiene de largo? ● *adv* largo/mucho tiempo. **as ~ as** (while) mientras; (provided that) con tal que (+ *subjunctive*). **before ~** dentro de poco. **so ~!** ¡hasta luego! **so ~ as** (provided that) con tal que (+ *subjunctive*). □ **~ for** *vi* anhelar. **~ to do** estar deseando hacer. **~-distance** /-ˈdɪstəns/ *a* de larga distancia. **~-distance phone call** llamada *f* de larga distancia, conferencia *f*. **~er** *adv*. **no ~er** ya no

long: ~-haul /-ˈhɔːl/ *a* de larga distancia. **~ing** *n* anhelo *m*, ansia *f*

longitude /ˈlɒŋgɪtjuːd/ *n* longitud *f*

long: ~ jump *n* salto *m* de longitud. **~-playing record** *n* elepé *m*. **~-range** *a* de largo alcance. **~-sighted** /-ˈsaɪtɪd/ *a* hipermétrope. **~-term** *a* a largo plazo. **~-winded** /-ˈwɪndɪd/ *a* prolijo

loo /luː/ *n* 🅸 váter *m*, baño *m* (LAm)

look /lʊk/ *vt* mirar; representar <*age*>. ● *vi* mirar; (seem) parecer; (search) buscar. ● *n* mirada *f*; (appearance) aspecto *m*. **good ~s** belleza *f*. □ **~ after** *vt* cuidar <*person*>;

(be responsible for) encargarse de. □~ **at** *vt* mirar; (consider) considerar. □~ **down on** *vt* despreciar. □~ **for** *vt* buscar. □~ **forward to** *vt* esperar con ansia. □~ **into** *vt* investigar. □~ **like** *vt* parecerse a. □~ **on** *vi* mirar. □~ **out** *vi* tener cuidado. □~ **out for** *vt* buscar; (watch) tener cuidado con. □~ **round** *vi* volver la cabeza. □~ **through** *vt* hojear. □~ **up** *vt* buscar <*word*>; (visit) ir a ver. □~ **up to** *vt* admirar. **~-alike** *n* 🅘 doble *m & f*. **~out** *n* (Mil, person) vigía *m*. **be on the ~out for** andar a la caza de. **~s** *npl* belleza *f*

loom /lu:m/ *n* telar *m*. ● *vi* aparecerse

looney, **loony** /ˈlu:nɪ/ *a & n* 🅧 chiflado (*m*) 🅘, loco (*m*)

loop /lu:p/ *n* (shape) curva *f* ; (in string) lazada *f*. ● *vt* hacer una lazada con. **~hole** *n* (in rule) escapatoria *f*

loose /lu:s/ *a* (**-er**, **-est**) suelto; <*garment, thread, hair*> flojo; (inexact) vago; (not packed) suelto. **be at a ~ end** no tener nada quehacer. **~ly** *adv* sueltamente; (roughly) aproximadamente. **~n** *vt* aflojar

loot /lu:t/ *n* botín *m*. ● *vt/i* saquear. **~er** *n* saqueador *m*

lop /lɒp/ *vt* (*pt* **lopped**). **~ off** cortar

lop-sided /-ˈsaɪdɪd/ *a* ladeado

lord /lɔ:d/ *n* señor *m*; (British title) lord *m*. (**good**) **L~!** ¡Dios mío! **the L~** el Señor. **the** (**House of**) **L~s** la Cámara de los Lores

lorry /ˈlɒrɪ/ *n* camión *m*. **~ driver** *n* camionero *m*

lose /lu:z/ *vt/i* (*pt* **lost**) perder. **~r** *n* perdedor *m*

loss /lɒs/ *n* pérdida *f*. **be at a ~** estar perplejo. **be at a ~ for words** no encontrar palabras

lost /lɒst/ ⇒LOSE. ● *a* perdido. **get ~** perderse. **~ property** *n*, **~ and found** (Amer) oficina *f* de objetos perdidos

lot /lɒt/ *n* (fate) suerte *f*; (at auction) lote *m*; (land) solar *m*. **a ~** (**of**) muchos. **quite a ~ of** 🅘 bastante. **~s** (**of**) 🅘 muchos. **they ate the ~** se lo comieron todo

lotion /ˈləʊʃn/ *n* loción *f*

lottery /ˈlɒtərɪ/ *n* lotería *f*

loud /laʊd/ *a* (**-er**, **-est**) fuerte; (noisy) ruidoso; (gaudy) chillón. **out ~** en voz alta. **~hailer** /-ˈheɪlə(r)/ *n* megáfono *m*. **~ly** *adv* <*speak*> en voz alta; <*shout*> fuerte; <*complain*> a voz en grito. **~speaker** /-ˈspi:kə(r)/ *n* altavoz *m*, altoparlante *m* (LAm)

lounge /laʊndʒ/ *vi* repantigarse. ● *n* salón *m*, sala *f* (de estar), living *m* (LAm)

lous|e /laʊs/ *n* (*pl* **lice**) piojo *m*. **~y** /ˈlaʊzɪ/ *a* (**-ier**, **-iest**) (🅧, bad) malísimo

lout /laʊt/ *n* patán *m*

lov|able /ˈlʌvəbl/ *a* adorable. **~e** /lʌv/ *n* amor *m*; (tennis) cero *m*. **be in ~e** (**with**) estar enamorado (de). **fall in ~e** (**with**) enamorarse (de). ● *vt* querer, amar <*person*>. **I ~e milk** me encanta la leche. **~e affair** *n* aventura *f*, amorío *m*

lovely /ˈlʌvlɪ/ *a* (**-ier**, **-iest**) <*appearance*> precioso, lindo (LAm); <*person*> encantador, amoroso (LAm)

lover /ˈlʌvə(r)/ *n* amante *m & f*

loving /ˈlʌvɪŋ/ *a* cariñoso

low /ləʊ/ *a & adv* (**-er**, **-est**) bajo. ● *vi* <*cattle*> mugir. **~er** *vt* bajar.

~er o.s. envilecerse. **~-level** *a* a bajo nivel. **~ly** *a* (**-ier**, **-iest**) humilde

loyal /'lɔɪəl/ *a* leal, fiel. **~ty** *n* lealtad *f*

lozenge /'lɒzɪŋdʒ/ *n* (shape) rombo *m*; (tablet) pastilla *f*

LP *abbr* (= **long-playing record**) elepé *m*

Ltd /'lɪmɪtɪd/ *abbr* (= **Limited**) S.A., Sociedad Anónima

lubricate /'lu:brɪkeɪt/ *vt* lubricar

lucid /'lu:sɪd/ *a* lúcido

luck /lʌk/ *n* suerte *f*. **good ~!** ¡(buena) suerte! **~ily** *adv* por suerte. **~y** *a* (**-ier**, **-iest**) <*person*> con suerte. **be ~y** tener suerte. **~y number** número *m* de la suerte

lucrative /'lu:krətɪv/ *a* lucrativo

ludicrous /'lu:dɪkrəs/ *a* ridículo

lug /lʌg/ *vt* (*pt* **lugged**) [I] arrastrar

luggage /'lʌgɪdʒ/ *n* equipaje *m*. **~ rack** *n* rejilla *f*

lukewarm /'lu:kwɔ:m/ *a* tibio; (fig) poco entusiasta

lull /lʌl/ *vt* (soothe, send to sleep) adormecer; (calm) calmar. ● *n* periodo *m* de calma

lullaby /'lʌləbaɪ/ *n* canción *f* de cuna

lumber /'lʌmbə(r)/ *n* trastos *mpl* viejos; (wood) maderos *mpl*. ● *vt*. **~ s.o. with sth** [I] endilgar algo a uno. **~jack** *n* leñador *m*

luminous /'lu:mɪnəs/ *a* luminoso

lump /'lʌmp/ *n* (swelling) bulto *m*; (as result of knock) chichón *m*; (in liquid) grumo *m*; (of sugar) terrón *m*. ● *vt*. **~ together** agrupar. **~ it** [I] aguantarse. **~ sum** *n* suma *f* global. **~y** *a* <*sauce*> grumoso; <*mattress, cushions*> lleno de protuberancias

lunacy /'lu:nəsɪ/ *n* locura *f*

lunar /'lu:nə(r)/ *a* lunar

lunatic /'lu:nətɪk/ *n* loco *m*

lunch /lʌntʃ/ *n* comida *f*, almuerzo *m*. **have ~** comer, almorzar

luncheon /'lʌntʃən/ *n* comida *f*, almuerzo *m*. **~ voucher** *n* vale *m* de comida

lung /lʌŋ/ *n* pulmón *m*

lunge /lʌndʒ/ *n* arremetida *f*. ● *vi*. **~ at** arremeter contra

lurch /lɜ:tʃ/ *vi* tambalearse. ● *n*. **leave in the ~** dejar plantado

lure /ljʊə(r)/ *vt* atraer

lurid /'ljʊərɪd/ *a* <*colour*> chillón; (shocking) morboso

lurk /lɜ:k/ *vi* merodear; (in ambush) estar al acecho

luscious /'lʌʃəs/ *a* delicioso

lush /lʌʃ/ *a* exuberante

lust /lʌst/ *n* lujuria *f*; (craving) deseo *m*. ● *vi*. **~ after** codiciar

lute /lu:t/ *n* laúd *m*

Luxembourg, **Luxemburg** /'lʌksəmbɜ:g/ *n* Luxemburgo *m*

luxuriant /lʌg'zjʊərɪənt/ *a* exuberante

luxur|ious /lʌg'zjʊərɪəs/ *a* lujoso. **~y** /'lʌkʃərɪ/ *n* lujo *m*. ● *a* de lujo

lying /'laɪɪŋ/ ⇒LIE[1], LIE[2]. ● *n* mentiras *fpl*. ● *a* mentiroso

lynch /lɪntʃ/ *vt* linchar

lyric /'lɪrɪk/ *a* lírico. **~al** *a* lírico. **~s** *npl* letra *f*

Mm

MA /em'eɪ/ *abbr* ⇒MASTER

mac /mæk/ *n* [I] impermeable *m*

macabre /mə'kɑ:brə/ *a* macabro

macaroni /mækə'rəʊnɪ/ *n* macarrones *mpl*

mace /meɪs/ *n* (staff) maza *f*; (spice) macis *f*. **M~** (*P*) (Amer) gas *m* para defensa personal

machine /mə'ʃi:n/ *n* máquina *f*. **~ gun** *n* ametralladora *f*. **~ry** *n* maquinaria *f*; (working parts, fig) mecanismo *m*

mackintosh /'mækɪntɒʃ/ *n* impermeable *m*

macro /'mækrəʊ/ *n* (*pl* **-os**) (Comp) macro *m*

macrobiotic /mækrəʊbaɪ'ɒtɪk/ *a* macrobiótico

mad /mæd/ *a* (**madder**, **maddest**) loco; ([I], angry) furioso. **be ~ about** estar loco por

madam /'mædəm/ *n* señora *f*

mad: ~cap *a* atolondrado. **~den** *vt* (make mad) enloquecer; (make angry) enfurecer

made /meɪd/ ⇒MAKE. **~-to-measure** hecho a (la) medida

mad: ~house *n* manicomio *m*. **~ly** *adv* (interested, in love etc) locamente; (frantically) como un loco. **~man** /-mən/ *n* loco *m*. **~ness** *n* locura *f*

Madonna /mə'dɒnə/ *n*. **the ~** (Relig) la Virgen

maestro /'maɪstrəʊ/ *n* (*pl* **maestri** /-stri:/ *or* **-os**) maestro *m*

Mafia /'mæfɪə/ *n* mafia *f*

magazine /mægə'zi:n/ *n* revista *f*; (of gun) recámara *f*

magenta /mə'dʒentə/ *a* magenta, morado

maggot /'mægət/ *n* gusano *m*

magic /'mædʒɪk/ *n* magia *f*. ● *a* mágico. **~al** *a* mágico. **~ian** /mə'dʒɪʃn/ *n* mago *m*

magistrate /'mædʒɪstreɪt/ *n* juez *m* que conoce de faltas y asuntos civiles de menor importancia

magnet /'mægnɪt/ *n* imán *m*. **~ic** /-'netɪk/ *a* magnético; (fig) lleno de magnetismo. **~ism** *n* magnetismo *m*. **~ize** *vt* imantar, magnetizar

magnif|ication /mægnɪfɪ'keɪʃn/ *n* aumento *m*. **~y** /'mægnɪfaɪ/ *vt* aumentar. **~ying glass** *n* lupa *f*

magnificen|ce /mæg'nɪfɪsns/ *a* magnificencia *f*. **~t** *a* magnífico

magnitude /'mægnɪtju:d/ *n* magnitud *f*

magpie /'mægpaɪ/ *n* urraca *f*

mahogany /mə'hɒgənɪ/ *n* caoba *f*

maid /meɪd/ *n* (servant) criada *f*, sirvienta *f*; (girl, old use) doncella *f*. **old ~** solterona *f*

maiden /'meɪdn/ *n* doncella *f*. ● *a* <*voyage*> inaugural. **~ name** *n* apellido *m* de soltera

mail /meɪl/ *n* correo *m*; (armour) (cota *f* de) malla *f*. ● *a* correo. ● *vt* echar al correo <*letter*>; (send) enviar por correo. **~box** *n* (Amer) buzón m. **~ing list** *n* lista *f* de direcciones. **~man** /-mən/ *n* (Amer) cartero *m*. **~ order** *n* venta *f* por correo

maim /meɪm/ *vt* mutilar

main /meɪn/ *n*. (water/gas) **~** cañería *f* principal. **in the ~** en su mayor parte. **the ~s** *npl* (Elec) la red *f* de suministro. ● *a* principal. **~ course** *n* plato *m* principal, plato *m* fuerte. **~ frame** *n* (Comp) unidad *f* central. **~land** *n*. **the ~land** la masa territorial de un país excluyendo sus islas. ● *a*. **~land China** (la) China continental. **~ly** *adv* principalmente. **~ road** *n* carretera *f* principal. **~stream** *a* <*culture*> establecido. **~ street** *n* calle *f* principal

maint|ain /meɪn'teɪn/ *vt* mantener. **~enance** /'meɪntənəns/ *n* mantenimiento *m*

maisonette /meɪzə'net/ *n* (small house) casita *f*; (part of house) dúplex *m*

maize /meɪz/ *n* maíz *m*

majestic /mə'dʒestɪk/ *a* majestuoso

majesty /'mædʒəstɪ/ *n* majestad *f*

major /'meɪdʒə(r)/ *a* (important) muy importante; (Mus) mayor. **a ~ road** una calle prioritaria. ● *n* comandante *m & f*, mayor *m & f* (LAm). ● *vi*. **~ in** (Amer, Univ) especializarse en

Majorca /mə'jɔːkə/ *n* Mallorca *f*

majority /mə'dʒɒrətɪ/ *n* mayoría *f*. ● *a* mayoritario

make /meɪk/ *vt* (*pt* **made**) hacer; (manufacture) fabricar; ganar <*money*>; tomar <*decision*>; llegar a <*destination*>. **~ s.o. do sth** obligar a uno a hacer algo. **be made of** estar hecho de. **I ~ it two o'clock** yo tengo las dos. **~ believe** fingir. **~ do** (manage) arreglarse. **~ do with** (content o.s.) contentarse con. **~ it** llegar; (succeed) tener éxito. ● *n* marca *f*. **~ for** *vt* dirigirse a. □ **~ good** *vt* compensar; (repair) reparar. □ **~ off** *vi* escaparse (**with** con). □ **~ out** *vt* distinguir; (understand) entender; (write out) hacer; (assert) dar a entender. *vi* (cope) arreglárselas. □ **~ up** *vt* (constitute) formar; (prepare) preparar; inventar <*story*>; **~ it up** (become reconciled) hacer las paces. **~ up** (**one's face**) maquillarse. □ **~ up for** *vt* compensar. **~-believe** *a* fingido, simulado. *n* ficción *f*. **~over** *n* (Amer) maquillaje *m*. **~r** *n* fabricante *m & f*. **~shift** *a* (temporary) provisional, provisorio (LAm); (improvised) improvisado. **~up** *n* maquillaje *m*. **put on ~up** maquillarse.

making /'meɪkɪŋ/ *n*. **he has the ~s of** tiene madera de. **in the ~** en vías de formación

maladjusted /mælə'dʒʌstɪd/ *a* inadaptado

malaria /mə'leərɪə/ *n* malaria *f*, paludismo *m*

Malaysia /mə'leɪzɪə/ *n* Malasia *f*. **~n** *a & n* malaisio (*m*)

male /meɪl/ *a* macho; <*voice, attitude*> masculino. ● *n* macho *m*; (man) varón *m*

malevolent /mə'levələnt/ *a* malévolo

malfunction /mæl'fʌŋkʃn/ *vi* fallar, funcionar mal

malic|e /'mælɪs/ *n* mala intención *f*, maldad *f*. **bear s.o. ~e** guardar rencor a uno. **~ious** /mə'lɪʃəs/ *a* malintencionado. **~iously** *adv* con malevolencia

malignant /mə'lɪgnənt/ *a* maligno

mallet /'mælɪt/ *n* mazo *m*

malnutrition /mælnju:'trɪʃn/ *n* desnutrición *f*

malpractice /mæl'præktɪs/ *n* mala práctica *f* (en el ejercicio de una profesión)

malt /mɔ:lt/ *n* malta *f*

Malt|a /'mɔ:ltə/ *n* Malta *f*. **~ese** /-'ti:z/ *a & n* maltés (*m*)

mammal /'mæml/ *n* mamífero *m*

mammoth /'mæməθ/ *n* mamut *m*. ● *a* gigantesco

man /mæn/ *n* (*pl* **men** /men/) hombre *m*; (Chess) pieza *f*. **~ in the street** hombre *m* de la calle. ● *vt* (*pt* **manned**) encargarse de <*switchboard*>; tripular <*ship*>; servir <*guns*>

manacles /'mænəklz/ *n* (for wrists) esposas *fpl*; (for legs) grillos *mpl*

manag|e /'mænɪdʒ/ *vt* dirigir; administrar <*land, finances*>; (handle) manejar. ● *vi* (Com) dirigir; (cope) arreglárselas. **~e to do** lograr hacer. **~eable** *a* <*task*> posible de alcanzar; <*size*> razonable. **~ement** *n* dirección *f*. **~er** *n* director *m*; (of shop) encargado *m*; (of soccer team) entrenador *m*, director *m* técnico (LAm). **~eress** /-'res/ *n* encargada *f*. **~erial** /-'dʒɪərɪəl/ *a* directivo, gerencial (LAm). **~ing director** *n* director *m* ejecutivo

mandate /'mændeɪt/ *n* mandato *m*

mandatory /'mændətərɪ/ *a* obligatorio

mane /meɪn/ *n* (of horse) crin(es) *f(pl)*; (of lion) melena *f*

mangle /'mæŋgl/ *n* rodillo *m* (escurridor). ● *vt* destrozar

man: ~handle *vt* mover a pulso; (treat roughly) maltratar. **~hole** *n* registro *m*. **~hood** *n* madurez *f*; (quality) virilidad *f*. **~-hour** *n* hora *f* hombre. **~-hunt** *n* persecución *f*

mania /'meɪnɪə/ *n* manía *f*. **~c** /-ɪæk/ *n* maníaco *m*

manicure /'mænɪkjʊə(r)/ *n* manicura *f*, manicure *f* (LAm)

manifest /'mænɪfest/ *a* manifiesto. ● *vt* manifestar. **~ation** /-'steɪʃn/ *n* manifestación *f*

manifesto /mænɪ'festəʊ/ *n* (*pl* **-os**) manifiesto *m*

manipulat|e /mə'nɪpjʊleɪt/ *vt* manipular. **~ion** /-'leɪʃn/ *n* manipulación *f*. **~ive** /-lətɪv/ *a* manipulador

man: ~kind *n* humanidad *f*. **~ly** *a* viril. **~-made** *a* artificial

manner /'mænə(r)/ *n* manera *f*; (demeanour) actitud *f*; (kind) clase *f*. **~ed** *a* amanerado. **~s** *npl* modales *mpl*, educación *f*. **bad ~s** mala educación

manoeuvre /mə'nu:və(r)/ *n* maniobra *f*. ● *vt/i* maniobrar

manor /'mænə(r)/ *n*. **~ house** casa *f* solariega

manpower *n* mano *f* de obra

mansion /'mænʃn/ *n* mansión *f*

man: ~-size(d) *a* grande. **~slaughter** *n* homicidio *m* sin premeditación

mantelpiece /'mæntlpi:s/ *n* repisa *f* de la chimenea

manual /'mænjʊəl/ *a* manual. ● *n* (handbook) manual *m*

manufacture /mænjʊ'fæktʃə(r)/ *vt* fabricar. ● *n* fabricación *f*. **~r** *n* fabricante *m & f*

manure /mə'njʊə(r)/ *n* estiércol *m*

manuscript /'mænjʊskrɪpt/ *n* manuscrito *m*

many /'menɪ/ *a & pron* muchos, muchas. **~ people** mucha gente. **a great/good ~** muchísimos. **how ~?** ¿cuántos? **so ~** tantos. **too ~** demasiados

map /mæp/ *n* mapa *m*; (of streets etc) plano *m*

mar /mɑ:(r)/ *vt* (*pt* **marred**) estropear

marathon /ˈmærəθən/ *n* maratón *m & f*

marble /ˈmɑːbl/ *n* mármol *m*; (for game) canica *f*

march /mɑːtʃ/ *vi* (Mil) marchar. **~ off** *vi* irse. ● *n* marcha *f*

March /mɑːtʃ/ *n* marzo *m*

march-past /ˈmɑːtʃpɑːst/ *n* desfile *m*

mare /meə(r)/ *n* yegua *f*

margarine /mɑːdʒəˈriːn/ *n* margarina *f*

margin /ˈmɑːdʒɪn/ *n* margen *f*. **~al** *a* marginal

marijuana /mærɪˈhwɑːnə/ *n* marihuana *f*

marina /məˈriːnə/ *n* puerto *m* deportivo

marine /məˈriːn/ *a* marino. ● *n* (sailor) infante *m* de marina

marionette /mærɪəˈnet/ *n* marioneta *f*

marital status /mærɪtl ˈsteɪtəs/ *n* estado *m* civil

mark /mɑːk/ *n* marca *f*; (stain) mancha *f*; (Schol) nota *f*; (target) blanco *m*. ● *vt* (indicate) señalar, marcar; (stain) manchar; corregir <*exam*>. **~ time** marcar el paso. □ **~ out** *vt* (select) señalar; (distinguish) distinguir. **~ed** *a* marcado. **~edly** /-kɪdlɪ/ *adv* marcadamente. **~er** *n* marcador *m*. **~er (pen)** *n* rotulador *m*, marcador *m* (LAm)

market /ˈmɑːkɪt/ *n* mercado *m*. **on the ~** en venta. ● *vt* comercializar. **~ garden** *n* huerta *f*. **~ing** *n* marketing *m*

marking /ˈmɑːkɪŋ/ *n* marcas *fpl*; (on animal, plant) mancha *f*

marksman /ˈmɑːksmən/ *n* (*pl* **-men**) tirador *m*. **~ship** *n* puntería *f*

marmalade /ˈmɑːməleɪd/ *n* mermelada *f* (de cítricos)

maroon /məˈruːn/ *a & n* granate (*m*). ● *vt* abandonar (en una isla desierta)

marquee /mɑːˈkiː/ *n* toldo *m*, entoldado *m*; (Amer, awning) marquesina *f*

marriage /ˈmærɪdʒ/ *n* matrimonio *m*; (ceremony) casamiento *m*

married /ˈmærɪd/ *a* casado; <*life*> conyugal

marrow /ˈmærəʊ/ *n* (of bone) tuétano *m*; (vegetable) calabaza *f* verde alargada. **~ squash** *n* (Amer) calabaza *f* verde alargada

marry /ˈmærɪ/ *vt* casarse con; (give or unite in marriage) casar. ● *vi* casarse. **get married** casarse (**to** con)

Mars /mɑːz/ *n* Marte *m*

marsh /mɑːʃ/ *n* pantano *m*

marshal /ˈmɑːʃl/ *n* (Mil) mariscal *m*; (Amer, police chief) jefe *m* de policía. ● *vt* (*pt* **marshalled**) reunir; poner en orden <*thoughts*>

marsh: ~ mallow /-ˈmæləʊ/ *n* malvavisco *m*, bombón *m* (LAm). **~y** *a* pantanoso

martial /ˈmɑːʃl/ *a* marcial. **~ arts** *npl* artes *fpl* marciales. **~ law** *n* ley *f* marcial

martyr /ˈmɑːtə(r)/ *n* mártir *m & f*

marvel /ˈmɑːvl/ *n* maravilla *f*. ● *vi* (*pt* **marvelled**) maravillarse (**at** de). **~lous** *a* maravilloso

Marxis|m /ˈmɑːksɪzəm/ *n* marxismo *m*. **~t** *a & n* marxista (*m & f*)

marzipan /ˈmɑːzɪpæn/ *n* mazapán *m*

mascara /mæˈskɑːrə/ *n* rímel *m* (*P*)

mascot /ˈmæskɒt/ *n* mascota *f*

masculin|e /ˈmæskjʊlm/ *a* & *n* masculino (*m*). **~ity** /-ˈlmətɪ/ *n* masculinidad *f*

mash /mæʃ/ *n* (Br ⊞, potatoes) puré *m* de patatas, puré *m* de papas (LAm). ● *vt* hacer puré de, moler (Mex). **~ed potatoes** *npl* puré *m* de patatas, puré *m* de papas (LAm)

mask /mɑːsk/ *n* máscara *f*; (Sport) careta *f*. ● *vt* ocultar

masochis|m /ˈmæsəkɪzəm/ *n* masoquismo *m*. **~t** *n* masoquista *m* & *f*. **~tic** /-ˈkɪstɪk/ *a* masoquista

mason /ˈmeɪsn/ *n* (stone **~**) mampostero *m*. **M~** (freemason) masón *m*. **~ry** /ˈmeɪsnrɪ/ *n* albañilería *f*

masquerade /mɑːskəˈreɪd/ *n* mascarada *f*. ● *vi*. **~ as** hacerse pasar por

mass /mæs/ *n* masa *f*; (Relig) misa *f*; (large quantity) montón *m*. **the ~es** las masas. ● *vi* concentrarse

massacre /ˈmæsəkə(r)/ *n* masacre *f*, matanza *f*. ● *vt* masacrar

mass|age /ˈmæsɑːʒ/ *n* masaje *m*. ● *vt* masajear. **~eur** /mæˈsɜː(r)/ *n* masajista *m*. **~euse** /mæˈsɜːz/ *n* masajista *f*

massive /ˈmæsɪv/ *a* masivo; (heavy) macizo; (huge) enorme

mass: ~ media *n* medios *mpl* de comunicación. **~-produce** /-prəˈdjuːs/ *vt* fabricar en serie

mast /mɑːst/ *n* mástil *m*; (for radio, TV) antena *f* repetidora

master /ˈmɑːstə(r)/ *n* amo *m*; (expert) maestro *m*; (in secondary school) profesor *m*; (of ship) capitán *m*; (master copy) original *m*. **~'s degree** master *m*, maestría *f*. **M~ of Arts** (**MA**) poseedor *m* de una maestría en folosofía y letras. **M~ of Science** (**MSc**) poseedor *m* de una maestría en ciencias. ● *vt* llegar a dominar. **~ key** *n* llave *f* maestra. **~mind** *n* cerebro *m*. ● *vt* dirigir. **~piece** *n* obra *f* maestra. **~stroke** *n* golpe *m* de maestro. **~y** *n* dominio *m*; (skill) maestría *f*

masturbat|e /ˈmæstəbeɪt/ *vi* masturbarse. **~ion** /-ˈbeɪʃn/ *n* masturbación *f*

mat /mæt/ *n* estera *f*; (at door) felpudo *m*. ● *a* (Amer) ⇨MATT

match /mætʃ/ *n* (Sport) partido *m*; (for fire) cerilla *f*, fósforo *m* (LAm), cerillo *m* (Mex); (equal) igual *m*. ● *vt* emparejar; (equal) igualar; <*clothes, colours*> hacer juego con. ● *vi* hacer juego. **~box** *n* caja *f* de cerillas, caja *f* de fósforos (LAm), caja *f* de cerillos (Mex). **~ing** *a* quehace juego. **~stick** *n* cerilla *f*, fósforo *m* (LAm), cerillo *m* (Mex)

mate /meɪt/ *n* (of person) pareja *f*; (of animals, male) macho *m*; (of animals, female) hembra *f*; (assistant) ayudante *m*; (⊞, friend) amigo *m*, cuate *m* (Mex); (Chess) (jaque *m*) mate *m*. ● *vi* aparearse

material /məˈtɪərɪəl/ *n* material *m*; (cloth) tela *f*. ● *a* material. **~istic** /-ˈlɪstɪk/ *a* materialista. **~ize** *vi* materializarse. **~s** *npl* materiales *mpl*

matern|al /məˈtɜːnl/ *a* maternal. **~ity** /-ətɪ/ *n* maternidad *f*. ● *a* <*ward*> de obstetricia; <*clothes*> premamá, de embarazada

math /mæθ/ *n* (Amer) ⇨MATHS

mathematic|ian /mæθəməˈtɪʃn/ *n* matemático *m*. **~al** /-ˈmætɪkl/ *a* matemático. **~s** /-ˈmætɪks/ *n* matemática(s) *f(pl)*

maths /mæθs/ *n* matemática(s) *f(pl)*

matinée, matinee /ˈmætɪneɪ/ *n* (Theatre) función *f* de tarde; (Cinema) primera sesión *f* (de la tarde)

matrices /'meɪtrɪsi:z/ ⇒MATRIX

matriculat|e /mə'trɪkjʊleɪt/ *vi* matricularse. **~ion** /-'leɪʃn/ *n* matrícula *f*

matrimon|ial /mætrɪ'məʊnɪəl/ *a* matrimonial. **~y** /'mætrɪmənɪ/ *n* matrimonio *m*

matrix /'meɪtrɪks/ *n* (*pl* **matrices**) matriz *f*

matron /'meɪtrən/ *n* (married, elderly) matrona *f*; (in school) ama *f* de llaves; (former use, in hospital) enfermera *f* jefe

matt, **matte** (Amer) /mæt/ *a* mate

matted /'mætɪd/ *a* enmarañado y apelmazado

matter /'mætə(r)/ *n* (substance) materia *f*; (affair) asunto *m*; (pus) pus *m*. **as a ~ of fact** en realidad. **no ~** no importa. **what is the ~?** ¿qué pasa? **to make ~s worse** para colmo (de males). ● *vi* importar. **it doesn't ~** no importa. **~-of-fact** /-əv'fækt/ *a* <*person*> práctico

mattress /'mætrɪs/ *n* colchón *m*

matur|e /mə'tjʊə(r)/ *a* maduro. ● *vi* madurar. **~ity** *n* madurez *f*

maudlin /'mɔ:dlɪn/ *a* llorón

maul /mɔ:l/ *vt* atacar (y herir)

mauve /məʊv/ *a* & *n* malva (*m*)

maverick /'mævərɪk/ *n* inconformista *m* & *f*

maxim /'mæksɪm/ *n* máxima *f*

maxim|ize /'mæksɪmaɪz/ *vt* maximizar. **~um** /-əm/ *a* & *n* máximo (*m*)

---

may /meɪ/, past **might**

● *auxiliary verb*

····➤ (expressing possibility) **he ~ come** puede que venga, es posible que venga. **it ~ be true** puede ser verdad. **she ~ not have seen him** es posible que *or* puede que no lo haya visto

····➤ (asking for or giving permission) **~ I smoke?** ¿puedo fumar?, ¿se puede fumar? **~ I have your name and address, please?** ¿quiere darme su nombre y dirección, por favor?

····➤ (expressing a wish) **~ he be happy** que sea feliz

····➤ (conceding) **he ~ not have much experience, but he's very hard-working** no tendrá mucha experiencia, pero es muy trabajador. **that's as ~ be** puede ser

····➤ **I ~ as well stay** más vale quedarme

May /meɪ/ *n* mayo *m*

maybe /'meɪbɪ/ *adv* quizá(s), tal vez, a lo mejor

May Day *n* el primero de mayo

mayhem /'meɪhem/ *n* caos *m*

mayonnaise /meɪə'neɪz/ *n* mayonesa *f*, mahonesa *f*

mayor /meə(r)/ *n* alcalde *m*, alcaldesa *f*. **~ess** /-ɪs/ *n* alcaldesa *f*

maze /meɪz/ *n* laberinto *m*

me /mi:/ *pron* me; (*after prep*) mí. **he knows ~** me conoce. **it's ~** soy yo

meadow /'medəʊ/ *n* prado *m*, pradera *f*

meagre /'mi:gə(r)/ *a* escaso

meal /mi:l/ *n* comida *f*. **~time** *n* hora *f* de comer

mean /mi:n/ *vt* (*pt* **meant**) (intend) tener la intención de, querer; (signify) querer decir, significar. **~ to do** tener la intención de hacer. **~ well** tener buenas intenciones. **be meant for** estar destinado a. ● *a*

(**-er**, **-est**) (miserly) tacaño; (unkind) malo; (Math) medio. ● *n* media *f*; (average) promedio *m*

meander /mɪ'ændə(r)/ *vi* <*river*> serpentear

meaning /'mi:nɪŋ/ *n* sentido *m*. **~ful** *a* significativo. **~less** *a* sin sentido

meanness /'mi:nnɪs/ *n* (miserliness) tacañería *f*, (unkindness) maldad *f*

means /mi:nz/ *n* medio *m*. **by ~ of** por medio de, mediante. **by all ~** por supuesto. **by no ~** de ninguna manera. ● *npl* (wealth) medios *mpl*, recursos *mpl*. **~ test** *n* investigación *f* de ingresos

meant /ment/ ⇒MEAN

meantime /'mi:ntaɪm/ *adv* mientras tanto, entretanto. ● *n*. **in the ~** mientras tanto, entretanto

meanwhile /'mi:nwaɪl/ *adv* mientras tanto, entretanto

measl|es /'mi:zlz/ *n* sarampión *m*. **~y** /'mi:zlɪ/ *a* Ⓘ miserable

measure /'meʒə(r)/ *n* medida *f*; (ruler) regla *f*. ● *vt/i* medir. □ **~ up to** *vt* estar a la altura de. **~ment** *n* medida *f*

meat /mi:t/ *n* carne *f*. **~ball** *n* albóndiga *f*. **~y** *a* <*taste, smell*> a carne; <*soup, stew*> con mucha carne

mechan|ic /mɪ'kænɪk/ *n* mecánico *m*. **~ical** *a* mecánico. **~ics** *n* mecánica *f*. **~ism** /'mekənɪzəm/ *n* mecanismo *m*. **~ize** /'mekənaɪz/ *vt* mecanizar

medal /'medl/ *n* medalla *f*. **~list** /'medəlɪst/ *n* medallista *m* & *f*. **be a gold ~list** ganar una medalla de oro

meddle /'medl/ *vi* meterse, entrometerse (**in** en). **~ with** (tinker) toquetear

media /'mi:dɪə/ ⇒MEDIUM. ● *npl*. **the ~** los medios de comunicación

mediat|e /'mi:dɪeɪt/ *vi* mediar. **~ion** /-'eɪʃn/ *n* mediación *f*. **~or** *n* mediador *m*

medical /'medɪkl/ *a* médico; <*student*> de medicina. ● *n* revisión *m* médica

medicat|ed /'medɪkeɪtɪd/ *a* medicinal. **~ion** /-'keɪʃn/ *n* medicación *f*

medicin|al /mɪ'dɪsɪnl/ *a* medicinal. **~e** /'medsɪn/ *n* medicina *f*

medieval /medɪ'i:vl/ *a* medieval

mediocre /mi:dɪ'əʊkə(r)/ *a* mediocre

meditat|e /'medɪteɪt/ *vi* meditar. **~ion** /-'teɪʃn/ *n* meditación *f*

Mediterranean /medɪtə'reɪnɪən/ *a* mediterráneo. ● *n*. **the ~** el Mediterráneo

medium /'mi:dɪəm/ *n* (*pl* **media**) medio *m*. **happy ~** término *m* medio. ● *a* mediano. **~-size(d)** /-saɪz(d)/ *a* de tamaño mediano

medley /'medlɪ/ *n* (Mus) popurrí *m*; (mixture) mezcla *f*

meek /mi:k/ *a* (**-er**, **-est**) dócil

meet /mi:t/ *vt* (*pt* **met**) encontrar; (bump into s.o.) encontrarse con; (fetch) ir a buscar; (get to know, be introduced to) conocer. ● *vi* encontrarse; (get to know) conocerse; (have meeting) reunirse. **~ up** *vi* encontrarse (**with** con). □ **~ with** *vt* ser recibido con; (Amer, meet) encontrarse con. **~ing** *n* reunión *f*; (accidental between two people) encuentro *m*

megabyte /'megəbaɪt/ *n* (Comp) megabyte *m*, megaocteto *m*

megaphone /'megəfəʊn/ *n* megáfono *m*

melanchol|ic /melən'kɒlɪk/ *a* melancólico. **~y** /'melənkɒlɪ/ *n* melancolía *f*. ● *a* melancólico

mellow /'meləʊ/ *a* (**-er**, **-est**) <*fruit*> maduro; <*sound*> dulce; <*colour*> tenue; <*person*> apacible

melodrama /'melədrɑ:mə/ *n* melodrama *m*. **~tic** /melədrə'mætɪk/ *a* melodramático

melody /'melədɪ/ *n* melodía *f*

melon /'melən/ *n* melón *m*

melt /melt/ *vt* (make liquid) derretir; fundir <*metals*>. ● *vi* (become liquid) derretirse; <*metals*> fundirse. □ **~ down** *vt* fundir

member /'membə(r)/ *n* miembro *m* & *f*; (of club) socio *m*. **~ of staff** empleado *m*. **M~ of Congress** *n* (Amer) miembro *m* & *f* del Congreso. **M~ of Parliament** *n* diputado *m*. **~ship** *n* calidad *f* de socio; (members) socios *mpl*, membresía *f* (LAm)

membrane /'membreɪn/ *n* membrana *f*

memento /mɪ'mentəʊ/ *n* (*pl* **-os** *or* **-oes**) recuerdo *m*

memo /'meməʊ/ *n* (*pl* **-os**) memorándum *m*, memo *m*

memoir /'memwɑ:(r)/ *n* memoria *f*

memorable /'memərəbl/ *a* memorable

memorandum /memə'rændəm/ *n* (*pl* **-ums** *or* **-da** /-də/) memorándum *m*

memorial /mɪ'mɔ:rɪəl/ *n* monumento *m*. ● *a* conmemorativo

memor|ize /'meməraɪz/ *vt* aprender de memoria. **~y** /'memərɪ/ *n* (faculty) memoria *f*; (thing remembered) recuerdo *m*. **from ~y** de memoria. **in ~y of** a la memoria de

men /men/ ⇒MAN

menac|e /'menəs/ *n* amenaza *f*; ([I], nuisance) peligro *m* público. ● *vt* amenazar. **~ing** *a* amenazador

mend /mend/ *vt* reparar; arreglar <*garment*>. **~ one's ways** enmendarse. ● *n* remiendo *m*. **be on the ~** ir mejorando

menfolk /'menfəʊk/ *n* hombres *mpl*

menial /'mi:nɪəl/ *a* servil

meningitis /menɪn'dʒaɪtɪs/ *n* meningitis *f*

menopause /'menəpɔ:z/ *n* menopausia *f*

menstruat|e /'menstrʊeɪt/ *vi* menstruar. **~ion** /-'eɪʃn/ *n* menstruación *f*

mental /'mentl/ *a* mental; <*hospital*> psiquiátrico. **~ity** /-'tælətɪ/ *n* mentalidad *f*. **~ly** *adv* mentalmente. **be ~ly ill** ser un enfermo mental

mention /'menʃn/ *vt* mencionar. **don't ~ it!** ¡no hay de qué! ● *n* mención *f*

mentor /'mentɔ:(r)/ *n* mentor *m*

menu /'menju:/ *n* menú *m*

meow /mɪ'aʊ/ *n* & *vi* ⇒MEW

mercenary /'mɜ:sɪnərɪ/ *a* & *n* mercenario (*m*)

merchandise /'mɜ:tʃəndaɪz/ *n* mercancías *fpl*, mercadería *f* (LAm)

merchant /'mɜ:tʃənt/ *n* comerciante *m*. ● *a* <*ship, navy*> mercante. **~ bank** *n* banco *m* mercantil

merci|ful /'mɜ:sɪfl/ *a* misericordioso. **~less** *a* despiadado

mercury /'mɜ:kjʊrɪ/ *n* mercurio *m*. **M~y** (planet) Mercurio *m*

mercy /'mɜːsɪ/ *n* compasión *f*. **at the ~ of** a merced de

mere /mɪə(r)/ *a* simple. **~ly** *adv* simplemente

merge /mɜːdʒ/ *vt* unir; fusionar <*companies*>. ● *vi* unirse; <*companies*> fusionarse. **~r** *n* fusión *f*

meridian /mə'rɪdɪən/ *n* meridiano *m*

meringue /mə'ræŋ/ *n* merengue *m*

merit /'merɪt/ *n* mérito *m*. ● *vt* (*pt* **merited**) merecer

mermaid /'mɜːmeɪd/ *n* sirena *f*

merr|ily /'merəlɪ/ *adv* alegremente. **~iment** /'merɪmənt/ *n* alegría *f*. **~y** /'merɪ/ *a* (**-ier**, **-iest**) alegre. **make ~** divertirse. **~y-go-round** *n* tiovivo *m*, carrusel *m* (LAm). **~y-making** *n* jolgorio *m*

mesh /meʃ/ *n* malla *f*

mesmerize /'mezməraɪz/ *vt* hipnotizar; (fascinate) cautivar

mess /mes/ *n* desorden *m*; (dirt) suciedad *f*; (Mil) rancho *m*. **make a ~ of** estropear. □ **~ up** *vt* desordenar; (dirty) ensuciar; estropear <*plans*>. □ **~ about** *vi* tontear. □ **~ with** *vt* (tinker with) manosear

mess|age /'mesɪdʒ/ *n* mensaje *m*; (when phoning) recado *m*. **~enger** /'mesɪndʒə(r)/ *n* mensajero *m*

Messiah /mɪ'saɪə/ *n* Mesías *m*

Messrs /'mesəz/ *npl*. **~ Smith** los señores Smith, los Sres. Smith

messy /'mesɪ/ *a* (**-ier**, **-iest**) en desorden; (dirty) sucio

met /met/ ⇒MEET

metabolism /mɪ'tæbəlɪzəm/ *n* metabolismo *m*

metal /'metl/ *n* metal. ● *a* de metal. **~lic** /mə'tælɪk/ *a* metálico

metaphor /'metəfə(r)/ *n* metáfora *f*. **~ical** /-'fɒrɪkl/ *a* metafórico

mete /miːt/ *vt*. **~ out** repartir; dar <*punishment*>

meteor /'miːtɪə(r)/ *n* meteoro *m*. **~ic** /-'ɒrɪk/ *a* meteórico. **~ite** /'miːtɪəraɪt/ *n* meteorito *m*

meteorolog|ical /miːtɪərə'lɒdʒɪkl/ *a* meteorológico. **~ist** /-'rɒlədʒɪst/ *n* meteorólogo *m*. **~y** /-'rɒlədʒɪ/ *n* meteorología *f*

meter /'miːtə(r)/ *n* contador *m*, medidor *m* (LAm); (Amer) ⇒METRE

method /'meθəd/ *n* método *m*. **~ical** /mɪ'θɒdɪkl/ *a* metódico. **M~ist** /'meθədɪst/ *a* & *n* metodista (*m* & *f*)

methylated /'meθɪleɪtɪd/ *a*. **~ spirit(s)** *n* alcohol *m* desnaturalizado

meticulous /mɪ'tɪkjʊləs/ *a* meticuloso

metre /'miːtə(r)/ *n* metro *m*

metric /'metrɪk/ *a* métrico

metropoli|s /mɪ'trɒpəlɪs/ *n* metrópoli(s) *f*. **~tan** /metrə'pɒlɪtən/ *a* metropolitano

mettle /'metl/ *n*. **be on one's ~** (fig) estar dispuesto a dar lo mejor de sí

mew /mjuː/ *n* maullido *m*. ● *vi* maullar

Mexic|an /'meksɪkən/ *a* & *n* mejicano (*m*), mexicano (*m*). **~o** /-kəʊ/ *n* Méjico *m*, México *m*

miaow /miː'aʊ/ *n* & *vi* ⇒MEW

mice /maɪs/ ⇒MOUSE

mickey /'mɪkɪ/ *n*. **take the ~ out of** 🄸 tomar el pelo a

micro... /'maɪkrəʊ/ *pref* micro...

microbe /'maɪkrəʊb/ *n* microbio *m*

micro: ~chip *n* pastilla *f*. **~film** *n* microfilme *m*. **~phone** *n* micrófono *m*. **~processor** /-'prəʊsesə(r)/ *n* microprocesador *m*. **~scope** *n* microscopio *m*.

~scopic /-'skɒpɪk/ *a* microscópico. **~wave** *n* microonda *f*. **~wave oven** *n* horno *m* de microondas

mid- /mɪd/ *pref.* **in ~ air** en pleno aire. **in ~ March** a mediados de marzo

midday /mɪd'deɪ/ *n* mediodía *m*

middl|e /'mɪdl/ *a* de en medio. ● *n* medio *m*. **in the ~e of** en medio de. **~e-aged** /-'eɪdʒd/ *a* de mediana edad. **M~e Ages** *npl* Edad *f* Media. **~e class** *n* clase *f* media. **~e-class** *a* de la clase media. **M~e East** *n* Oriente *m* Medio. **~eman** *n* intermediario *m*. **~e name** *n* segundo nombre *m*. **~ing** *a* regular

midge /mɪdʒ/ *n* mosquito *m*

midget /'mɪdʒɪt/ *n* enano *m*. ● *a* minúsculo

Midlands /'mɪdləndz/ *npl* región *f* central de Inglaterra

midnight /'mɪdnaɪt/ *n* medianoche *f*

midriff /'mɪdrɪf/ *n* diafragma *m*

midst /mɪdst/ *n*. **in our ~** entre nosotros. **in the ~ of** en medio de

midsummer /mɪd'sʌmə(r)/ *n* pleno verano *m*; (solstice) solsticio *m* de verano

midway /mɪd'weɪ/ *adv* a mitad de camino

Midwest /'mɪd'west/ región *f* central de los EE.UU.

midwife /'mɪdwaɪf/ *n* comadrona *f*, partera *f*

midwinter /mɪd'wɪntə(r)/ *n* pleno invierno *m*

might /maɪt/ ⇒MAY. ● *n* (strength) fuerza *f*; (power) poder *m*. **~y** *a* (strong) fuerte; (powerful) poderoso. ● *adv* [I] muy

migraine /'mi:greɪn/ *n* jaqueca *f*

migra|nt /'maɪgrənt/ *a* migratorio. ● *n* (person) emigrante *m & f*. **~te** /maɪ'greɪt/ *vi* emigrar. **~tion** /-'greɪʃn/ *n* migración *f*

mild /maɪld/ *a* (**-er**, **-est**) *<person>* afable; *<climate>* templado; (slight) ligero; *<taste, manner>* suave

mildew /'mɪldju:/ *n* moho *m*; (on plants) mildeu *m*, mildiu *m*

mildly /'maɪldlɪ/ *adv* (gently) suavemente; (slightly) ligeramente

mile /maɪl/ *n* milla *f*. **~s better** [I] mucho mejor. **~s too big** [I] demasiado grande. **~age** /-ɪdʒ/ *n* (loosely) kilometraje *m*. **~ometer** /maɪ'lɒmɪtə(r)/ *n* (loosely) cuentakilómetros *m*. **~stone** *n* mojón *m*; (event, stage, fig) hito *m*

militant /'mɪlɪtənt/ *a & n* militante (*m & f*)

military /'mɪlɪtərɪ/ *a* militar

militia /mɪ'lɪʃə/ *n* milicia *f*

milk /mɪlk/ *n* leche *f*. ● *a <product>* lácteo; *<chocolate>* con leche. ● *vt* ordeñar *<cow>*. **~man** /-mən/ *n* lechero *m*. **~ shake** *n* batido *m*, (leche *f*) malteada *f* (LAm), licuado *m* con leche (LAm). **~y** *a* lechoso. **M~y Way** *n* Vía *f* Láctea

mill /mɪl/ *n* molino *m*; (for coffee, pepper) molinillo *m*; (factory) fábrica *f* de tejidos de algodón. ● *vt* moler. □ **~ about, mill around** *vi* dar vueltas

millennium /mɪ'lenɪəm/ *n* (*pl* **-ia** /-ɪə/ *or* **-iums**) milenio *m*

miller /'mɪlə(r)/ *n* molinero *m*

milli... /'mɪlɪ/ *pref* mili... **~gram(me)** *n* miligramo *m*. **~metre** *n* milímetro *m*

milliner /'mɪlɪnə(r)/ *n* sombrerero *m*

million /ˈmɪlɪən/ *n* millón *m*. **a ~ pounds** un millón de libras. **~aire** /-ˈeə(r)/ *n* millonario *m*

millstone /ˈmɪlstəʊn/ *n* muela *f* (de molino); (fig, burden) carga *f*

mime /maɪm/ *n* mímica *f*. ● *vt* imitar, hacer la mímica de. ● *vi* hacer la mímica

mimic /ˈmɪmɪk/ *vt* (*pt* **mimicked**) imitar. ● *n* imitador *m*. **~ry** *n* imitación *f*

mince /mɪns/ *vt* picar, moler (LAm) <*meat*>. **not to ~ matters/words** no andar(se) con rodeos. ● *n* carne *f* picada, carne *f* molida (LAm). **~ pie** *n* pastelito *m* de Navidad (*pastelito relleno de picadillo de frutos secos*). **~r** *n* máquina *f* de picar carne, máquina *f* de moler carne (LAm)

mind /maɪnd/ *n* mente *f*; (sanity) juicio *m*. **to my ~** a mi parecer. **be on one's mind** preocuparle a uno. **make up one's ~** decidirse. ● *vt* (look after) cuidar (de); atender <*shop*>. d **the steps!** ¡cuidado con las escaleras! **never ~ him** no le hagas caso. **I don't ~ the noise** no me molesta el ruido. **would you ~ closing the door?** ¿le importaría cerrar la puerta? ● *vi*. **never ~** no importa, no te preocupes. **I don't ~** (don't object) me da igual. **do you ~ if I smoke?** ¿le importa si fumo? **~ful** *a* atento (**of** a). **~less** *a* <*activity*> mecánico; <*violence*> ciego

mine[1] /maɪn/ *poss pron* (*sing*) mío, mía; (*pl*) míos, mías. **it is ~** es mío. **~ are blue** los míos/las mías son azules. **a friend of ~** un amigo mío/ una amiga mía

mine[2] /maɪn/ *n* mina *f*; (Mil) mina *f*. ● *vt* extraer. **~field** *n* campo *m* de minas. **~r** *n* minero *m*

mineral /ˈmɪnərəl/ *a* & *n* mineral (*m*). **~ water** *n* agua *f* mineral

mingle /ˈmɪŋgl/ *vi* mezclarse

mini... /ˈmɪnɪ/ *pref* mini...

miniature /ˈmɪnɪtʃə(r)/ *n* miniatura *f*. ● *a* en miniatura

mini: ~bus *n* microbús *m*. **~cab** *n* taxi *m* (*que se pide por teléfono*)

minim|al /ˈmɪnɪml/ *a* mínimo. **~ize** *vt* reducir al mínimo. **~um** /-məm/ *a* & *n* (*pl* **-ima** /-mə/) mínimo (*m*)

mining /ˈmaɪnɪŋ/ *n* minería *f*. ● *a* minero

miniskirt /ˈmɪnɪskɜːt/ *n* minifalda *f*

minist|er /ˈmɪnɪstə(r)/ *n* ministro *m*, secretario *m* (Mex); (Relig) pastor *m*. **~erial** /-ˈstɪərɪəl/ *a* ministerial. **~ry** *n* ministerio *m*, secretaría *f* (Mex)

mink /mɪŋk/ *n* visón *m*

minor /ˈmaɪnə(r)/ *a* (also Mus) menor; <*injury*> leve; <*change*> pequeño; <*operation*> de poca importancia. ● *n* menor *m* & *f* de edad. **~ity** /maɪˈnɒrətɪ/ *n* minoría *f*. ● *a* minoritario

minstrel /ˈmɪnstrəl/ *n* juglar *m*

mint /mɪnt/ *n* (plant) menta *f*; (sweet) pastilla *f* de menta; (Finance) casa *f* de la moneda. **in ~ condition** como nuevo. ● *vt* acuñar

minus /ˈmaɪnəs/ *prep* menos; (🅘, without) sin. ● *n* (sign) menos *m*. **five ~ three is two** cinco menos tres es igual a dos. **~ sign** *n* (signo *m* de) menos *m*

minute[1] /ˈmɪnɪt/ *n* minuto *m*. **the ~s** *npl* (of meeting) el acta *f*

minute[2] /maɪˈnjuːt/ *a* diminuto; (detailed) minucioso

mirac|le /'mɪrəkl/ *n* milagro *m*. **~ulous** /mɪ'rækjʊləs/ *a* milagroso

mirage /'mɪrɑ:ʒ/ *n* espejismo *m*

mirror /'mɪrə(r)/ *n* espejo *m*; (driving **~**) (espejo *m*) retrovisor *m*. ● *vt* reflejar

mirth /mɜ:θ/ *n* regocijo *m*; (laughter) risas *fpl*

misapprehension /mɪsæprɪ'henʃn/ *n* malentendido *m*

misbehav|e /mɪsbɪ'heɪv/ *vi* portarse mal. **~iour** *n* mala conducta

miscalculat|e /mɪs'kælkjʊleɪt/ *vt/i* calcular mal. **~ion** /-'leɪʃn/ *n* error *m* de cálculo

miscarr|iage /'mɪskærɪdʒ/ *n* aborto *m* espontáneo. **~iage of justice** *n* injusticia *f*. **~y** *vi* abortar

miscellaneous /mɪsə'leɪnɪəs/ *a* heterogéneo

mischie|f /'mɪstʃɪf/ *n* (foolish conduct) travesura *f*; (harm) daño *m*. **get into ~f** hacer travesuras. **make ~f** causar daños. **~vous** /'mɪstʃɪvəs/ *a* travieso; <*grin*> pícaro

misconception /mɪskən'sepʃn/ *n* equivocación *f*

misconduct /mɪs'kɒndʌkt/ *n* mala conducta *f*

misdeed /mɪs'di:d/ *n* fechoría *f*

misdemeanour /mɪsdɪ'mi:nə(r)/ *n* delito *m* menor, falta *f*

miser /'maɪzə(r)/ *n* avaro *m*

miserable /'mɪzərəbl/ *a* (sad) triste; (in low spirits) abatido; (wretched, poor) mísero; <*weather*> pésimo

miserly /'maɪzəlɪ/ *a* avariento

misery /'mɪzərɪ/ *n* (unhappiness) tristeza *f*; (pain) sufrimiento *m*

misfire /mɪs'faɪə(r)/ *vi* fallar

misfit /'mɪsfɪt/ *n* inadaptado *m*

misfortune /mɪs'fɔ:tʃu:n/ *n* desgracia *f*

misgiving /mɪs'gɪvɪŋ/ *n* recelo *m*

misguided /mɪs'gaɪdɪd/ *a* equivocado

mishap /'mɪshæp/ *n* percance *m*

misinform /mɪsɪn'fɔ:m/ *vt* informar mal

misinterpret /mɪsɪn'tɜ:prɪt/ *vt* interpretar mal

misjudge /mɪs'dʒʌdʒ/ *vt* juzgar mal; (miscalculate) calcular mal

mislay /mɪs'leɪ/ *vt* (*pt* **mislaid**) extraviar, perder

mislead /mɪs'li:d/ *vt* (*pt* **misled** /mɪs'led/) engañar. **~ing** *a* engañoso

mismanage /mɪs'mænɪdʒ/ *vt* administrar mal. **~ment** *n* mala administración *f*

misplace /mɪs'pleɪs/ *vt* (lose) extraviar, perder

misprint /'mɪsprɪnt/ *n* errata *f*

miss /mɪs/ *vt* (fail to hit) no dar en; (regret absence of) echar de menos, extrañar (LAm); perder <*train, party*>; perder <*chance*>. **~ the point** no comprender. ● *vi* errar el tiro, fallar; <*bullet*> no dar en el blanco. ● *n* fallo *m*, falla *f* (LAm); (title) señorita *f*. □ **~ out** *vt* saltarse <*line*>. **~out on sth** perderse algo

misshapen /mɪs'ʃeɪpən/ *a* deforme

missile /'mɪsaɪl/ *n* (Mil) misil *m*

missing /'mɪsɪŋ/ *a* (lost) perdido. **be ~** faltar. **go ~** desaparecer. **~ person** desaparecido *m*

mission /'mɪʃn/ *n* misión *f*. **~ary** /'mɪʃənərɪ/ *n* misionero *m*

mist /mɪst/ *n* neblina *f*; (at sea) bruma *f*. □ **~ up** *vi* empañarse

mistake /mɪ'steɪk/ *n* error *m*. **make a ~** cometer un error. **by ~** por error. ● *vt* (*pt* **mistook**, *pp* **mistaken**) confundir. **~ for** confundir con. **~n** /-ən/ *a* equivocado. **be ~n** equivocarse

mistletoe /'mɪsltəʊ/ *n* muérdago *m*

mistreat /mɪs'triːt/ *vt* maltratar

mistress /'mɪstrɪs/ *n* (of house) señora *f*; (lover) amante *f*

mistrust /mɪs'trʌst/ *vt* desconfiar de. ● *n* desconfianza *f*. **~ful** *a* desconfiado

misty /'mɪstɪ/ *a* (**-ier**, **-iest**) neblinoso; <*day*> de neblina. **it's ~** hay neblina

misunderstand /mɪsʌndə'stænd/ *vt* (*pt* **-stood**) entender mal. **~ing** *n* malentendido *m*

misuse /mɪs'juːz/ *vt* emplear mal; malversar <*funds*>. ● /mɪs'juːs/ *n* mal uso *m*; (unfair use) abuso *m*; (of funds) malversación *f*

mite /maɪt/ *n* (insect) ácaro *m*

mitten /'mɪtn/ *n* mitón *m*

mix /mɪks/ *vt* mezclar. ● *vi* mezclarse; (go together) combinar. **~ with** tratarse con <*people*>. ● *n* mezcla *f*. □ **~ up** *vt* mezclar; (confuse) confundir. **~ed** *a* <*school etc*> mixto; (assorted) mezclado. **be ~ed up** estar confuso. **~er** *n* (Culin) batidora *f*; (TV, machine) mezcladora *f*. **~ture** /'mɪkstʃə(r)/ *n* mezcla *f*. **~-up** *n* lío *m*

moan /məʊn/ *n* gemido *m*. ● *vi* gemir; (complain) quejarse (**about** de)

moat /məʊt/ *n* foso *m*

mob /mɒb/ *n* turba *f*. ● *vt* (*pt* **mobbed**) acosar

mobil|e /'məʊbaɪl/ *a* móvil. **~e home** *n* caravana *f* fija, trailer *m* (LAm). **~e (phone)** *n* (teléfono *m*) móvil *m*, (teléfono *m*) celular *m* (LAm). ● *n* móvil *m*. **~ize** /'məʊbɪlaɪz/ *vt* movilizar. ● *vi* movilizarse

mock /mɒk/ *vt* burlarse de. ● *a* <*anger*> fingido; <*exam*> de práctica. **~ery** /'mɒkərɪ/ *n* burla *f*. **make a ~ery of sth** ridiculizar algo

model /'mɒdl/ *n* (example) modelo *m*; (mock-up) maqueta *f*; (person) modelo *m*. ● *a* (exemplary) modelo; <*car etc*> en miniatura. ● *vt* (*pt* **modelled**) modelar. **~ o.s. on s.o.** tomar a uno como modelo

modem /'məʊdem/ *n* (Comp) módem *m*

moderat|e /'mɒdərət/ *a* & *n* moderado (*m*). ● /'mɒdəreɪt/ *vt* moderar. **~ely** /'mɒdərətlɪ/ *adv* (fairly) medianamente. **~ion** /-'reɪʃn/ *n* moderación *f*. **in ~ion** con moderación

modern /'mɒdn/ *a* moderno. **~ize** *vt* modernizar

modest /'mɒdɪst/ *a* modesto. **~y** *n* modestia *f*

modif|ication /mɒdɪfɪ'keɪʃn/ *n* modificación *f*. **~y** /-faɪ/ *vt* modificar

module /'mɒdjuːl/ *n* módulo *m*

moist /mɔɪst/ *a* (**-er**, **-est**) húmedo. **~en** /'mɔɪsn/ *vt* humedecer

moistur|e /'mɔɪstʃə(r)/ *n* humedad *f*. **~ize** *vt* hidratar. **~izer**, **~izing cream** *n* crema *f* hidratante

mole /məʊl/ *n* (animal) topo *m*; (on skin) lunar *m*

molecule /'mɒlɪkjuːl/ *n* molécula *f*

molest /mə'lest/ *vt* abusar (sexualmente) de

mollify /'mɒlɪfaɪ/ *vt* aplacar

mollusc /'mɒləsk/ *n* molusco *m*

mollycoddle /ˈmɒlɪkɒdl/ *vt* mimar

molten /ˈməʊltən/ *a* fundido; <*lava*> líquido

mom /mɒm/ *n* (Amer, [I]) mamá *f* [I]

moment /ˈməʊmənt/ *n* momento *m*. **at the ~** en este momento. **for the ~** de momento. **~ary** /ˈməʊməntərɪ/ *a* momentáneo

momentous /məˈmentəs/ *a* trascendental

momentum /məˈmentəm/ *n* momento *m*; (speed) velocidad *f*

mommy /ˈmɒmɪ/ *n* (Amer, [I]) mamá *m* [I]

monarch /ˈmɒnək/ *n* monarca *m*. **~y** *n* monarquía *f*

monastery /ˈmɒnəstərɪ/ *n* monasterio *m*

Monday /ˈmʌndeɪ/ *n* lunes *m*

money /ˈmʌnɪ/ *n* dinero *m*, plata *f* (LAm). **~box** *n* hucha *f*, alcancía *f* (LAm). **~ order** *n* giro *m* postal

mongrel /ˈmʌŋgrəl/ *n* perro *m* mestizo, chucho *m* [I]

monitor /ˈmɒnɪtə(r)/ *n* (Tec) monitor *m*. ● *vt* observar <*elections*>; seguir <*progress*>; (electronically) monitorizar; escuchar <*broadcast*>

monk /mʌŋk/ *n* monje *m*

monkey /ˈmʌŋkɪ/ *n* mono *m*. **~-nut** *n* cacahuete *m*, cacahuate *m* (Mex), maní *m* (LAm). **~wrench** *n* llave *f* inglesa

mono /ˈmɒnəʊ/ *n* monofonía *f*

monologue /ˈmɒnəlɒg/ *n* monólogo *m*

monopol|ize /məˈnɒpəlaɪz/ *vt* monopolizar; acaparar <*conversation*>. **~y** *n* monopolio *m*

monoton|e /ˈmɒnətəʊn/ *n* tono *m* monocorde. **~ous** /məˈnɒtənəs/ *a* monótono. **~y** *n* monotonía *f*

monsoon /mɒnˈsuːn/ *n* monzón *m*

monst|er /ˈmɒnstə(r)/ *n* monstruo *m*. **~rous** /-strəs/ *a* monstruoso

month /mʌnθ/ *n* mes *m*. **£200 a ~** 200 libras mensuales *or* al mes. **~ly** *a* mensual. **~ly payment** mensualidad *f*, cuota *f* mensual (LAm). ● *adv* mensualmente

monument /ˈmɒnjʊmənt/ *n* monumento *m*. **~al** /-ˈmentl/ *a* monumental

moo /muː/ *n* mugido *m*. ● *vi* mugir

mood /muːd/ *n* humor *m*. **be in a good/bad ~** estar de buen/mal humor. **~y** *a* (**-ier**, **-iest**) temperamental; (bad-tempered) malhumorado

moon /muːn/ *n* luna *f*. **~light** *n* luz *f* de la luna. **~lighting** *n* pluriempleo *m*. **~lit** *a* iluminado por la luna; <*night*> de luna

moor /mʊə(r)/ *n* páramo *m*; (of heather) brezal *m*. ● *vt* amarrar. **~ing** *n* (place) amarradero *m*. **~ings** *npl* (ropes) amarras *fpl*

moose /muːs/ *n invar* alce *m* americano

mop /mɒp/ *n* fregona *f*, trapeador *m* (LAm). **~ of hair** pelambrera *f*. ● *vt* (*pt* **mopped**). **~ (up)** limpiar

mope /məʊp/ *vi* estar abatido

moped /ˈməʊped/ *n* ciclomotor *m*

moral /ˈmɒrəl/ *a* moral. ● *n* (of tale) moraleja *f*

morale /məˈrɑːl/ *n* moral *f*

moral|ity /məˈrælətɪ/ *n* moralidad *f*. **~ly** *adv* moralmente. **~s** *npl* moralidad *f*

morbid /ˈmɔːbɪd/ *a* morboso

more /mɔː(r)/ *a* más. **two ~ bottles** dos botellas más ● *pron* más. **you ate ~ than me** comiste más que yo. **some ~** más. **~ than six** más de seis. **the ~ he has, the ~ he wants** cuánto más tiene, más quiere. ● *adv* más. **~ and ~** cada vez más. **~ or less** más o menos. **once ~** una vez más. **she doesn't live here any ~** ya no vive aquí. **~over** /mɔːˈrəʊvə(r)/ *adv* además

morgue /mɔːg/ *n* depósito *m* de cadáveres, morgue *f* (LAm)

morning /ˈmɔːnɪŋ/ *n* mañana *f*; (early hours) madrugada *f*. **at 11 o'clock in the ~** a las once de la mañana. **in the ~** por la mañana, en la mañana (LAm). **tomorrow/ yesterday ~** mañana/ayer por la mañana *or* (LAm) en la mañana. (**good**) **~!** ¡buenos días!

Morocc|an /məˈrɒkən/ *a & n* marroquí (*m & f*). **~o** /-kəʊ/ *n* Marruecos *m*

moron /ˈmɔːrɒn/ *n* imbécil *m & f*

morose /məˈrəʊs/ *a* taciturno

Morse /mɔːs/ *n* Morse *m*. **in ~** (**code**) *n* en (código) morse

morsel /ˈmɔːsl/ *n* bocado *m*

mortal /ˈmɔːtl/ *a & n* mortal (*m*). **~ity** /-ˈtælətɪ/ *n* mortalidad *f*

mortar /ˈmɔːtə(r)/ *n* (all senses) mortero *m*

mortgage /ˈmɔːgɪdʒ/ *n* hipoteca *f*. ● *vt* hipotecar

mortify /ˈmɔːtɪfaɪ/ *vt* darle mucha vergüenza a

mortuary /ˈmɔːtjʊərɪ/ *n* depósito *m* de cadáveres, morgue *f* (LAm)

mosaic /məʊˈzeɪk/ *n* mosaico *m*

mosque /mɒsk/ *n* mezquita *f*

mosquito /mɒsˈkiːtəʊ/ *n* (*pl* **-oes**) mosquito *m*, zancudo *m* (LAm)

moss /mɒs/ *n* musgo *m*

most /məʊst/ *a* la mayoría de, la mayor parte de. **~ days** casi todos los días. ● *pron* la mayoría, la mayor parte. **at ~** como máximo. **make the ~ of** aprovechar al máximo. ● *adv* más; (very) muy; (Amer, almost) casi. **~ly** *adv* principalmente

MOT *n*. **~** (**test**) ITV *f*, inspección *f* técnica de vehículos

motel /məʊˈtel/ *n* motel *m*

moth /mɒθ/ *n* mariposa *f* de la luz, palomilla *f*; (in clothes) polilla *f*

mother /ˈmʌðə(r)/ *n* madre *f*. ● *vt* mimar. **~-in-law** *n* (*pl* **~s-in-law**) suegra *f*. **~land** *n* patria *f*. **~ly** *a* maternal. **~-of-pearl** *n* nácar *m*, madreperla *f*. **M~'s Day** *n* el día *m* de la Madre. **~-to-be** *n* futura madre *f*. **~ tongue** *n* lengua *f* materna

motif /məʊˈtiːf/ *n* motivo *m*

motion /ˈməʊʃn/ *n* movimiento *m*; (proposal) moción *f*. **put** *or* **set in ~** poner algo en marcha. ● *vt/i*. **~** (**to**) **s.o. to** hacerle señas a uno para que. **~less** *a* inmóvil

motiv|ate /ˈməʊtɪveɪt/ *vt* motivar. **~ation** /-ˈveɪʃn/ *n* motivación *f*. **~e** /ˈməʊtɪv/ *n* motivo *m*

motley /ˈmɒtlɪ/ *a* variopinto

motor /ˈməʊtə(r)/ *n* motor *m*. ● *a* motor; (fem) motora, motriz. **~ bike** *n* ⊡ motocicleta *f*, moto *f* ⊡. **~ boat** *n* lancha *f* a motor. **~ car** *n* automóvil *m*. **~ cycle** *n* motocicleta *f*. **~cyclist** *n* motociclista *m & f*. **~ing** *n* automovilismo *m*. **~ist** *n* automovilista *m & f*. **~way** *n* autopista *f*

motto /ˈmɒtəʊ/ *n* (*pl* **-oes**) lema *m*

mould /məʊld/ *n* molde *m*; (fungus) moho *m*. ● *vt* moldear; formar <*character*>. **~ing** *n* (on wall etc) moldura *f* **~y** *a* mohoso

moult /məʊlt/ *vi* mudar de pelo/ piel/plumas

mound /maʊnd/ *n* montículo *m*; (pile, fig) montón *m*

mount /maʊnt/ *vt* montar *<horse>*; engarzar *<gem>*; preparar *<attack>*. ● *vi* subir, crecer. ● *n.* montura *f*; (mountain) monte *m*. □ ~ **up** *vi* irse acumulando

mountain /ˈmaʊntɪn/ *n* montaña *f*. ~**eer** /maʊntɪˈnɪə(r)/ *n* alpinista *m & f*. ~**eering** *n* alpinismo *m*. ~**ous** *a* montañoso

mourn /mɔːn/ *vt* llorar. ● *vi* lamentarse. ~ **for s.o.** llorar a uno. ~**er** *n* doliente *m & f*. ~**ful** *a* triste. ~**ing** *n* duelo *m*, luto *m*. **be in** ~**ing** estar de duelo

mouse /maʊs/ *n* (*pl* **mice**) ratón *m*. ~**trap** *n* ratonera *f*

mousse /muːs/ *n* (Culin) mousse *f* or *m*; (for hair) mousse *f*

moustache /məˈstɑːʃ/ *n* bigote *m*

mouth /maʊθ/ *n* boca *f*; (of cave) entrada *f*; (of river) desembocadura *f*. ~**ful** *n* bocado *m*. ~**-organ** *n* armónica *f*. ~**wash** *n* enjuague *m* bucal

move /muːv/ *vt* mover; (relocate) trasladar; (with emotion) conmover; (propose) proponer. ~ **the television** cambiar de lugar la televisión. ~ **house** mudarse de casa. ● *vi* moverse; (be in motion) estar en movimiento; (take action) tomar medidas. ● *n* movimiento *m*; (in game) jugada *f*; (player's turn) turno *m*; (removal) mudanza *f*. □ ~ **away** *vi* alejarse. □ ~ **in** *vi* instalarse. ~ **in with s.o.** irse a vivir con uno. □ ~ **over** *vi* correrse. ~**ment** *n* movimiento *m*

movie /ˈmuːvɪ/ *n* (Amer) película *f*. **the** ~**s** *npl* el cine. ~ **camera** *n* (Amer) tomavistas *m*, filmadora *f* (LAm)

moving /ˈmuːvɪŋ/ *a* en movimiento; (touching) conmovedor

mow /məʊ/ *vt* (*pt* **mowed** or **mown** /məʊn/) cortar *<lawn>*; segar *<hay>*. □ ~ **down** *vt* acribillar. ~**er** *n* (for lawn) cortacésped *m*

MP *abbr* ⇒MEMBER OF PARLIAMENT

Mr /ˈmɪstə(r)/ *abbr* (*pl* **Messrs**) (= **Mister**) Sr. ~ **Coldbeck** Sr. Coldbeck

Mrs /ˈmɪsɪz/ *abbr* (*pl* **Mrs**) (= **Missis**) Sra. ~ **Andrews** Sra. Andrews

Ms /mɪz/ *abbr* (*title of married or unmarried woman*)

MSc *abbr* ⇒MASTER

much /mʌtʃ/ *a & pron* mucho, mucha. ● *adv* mucho; (before pp) muy. ~ **as** por mucho que. ~ **the same** más o menos lo mismo. **how** ~? ¿cuánto?. **so** ~ tanto. **too** ~ demasiado

muck /mʌk/ *n* estiércol *m*; ([I], dirt) mugre *f*. □ ~ **about** *vi* [I] tontear

mud /mʌd/ *n* barro *m*, lodo *m*

muddle /ˈmʌdl/ *vt* embrollar. ● *n* desorden *m*; (mix-up) lío *m*. □ ~ **through** *vi* salir del paso

muddy *a* lodoso; *<hands etc>* cubierto de lodo. ~**guard** *n* guardabarros *m*, salpicadera *f* (Mex)

muffle /ˈmʌfl/ *vt* amortiguar *<sound>*. ~**r** *n* (scarf) bufanda *f*; (Amer, Auto) silenciador *m*

mug /mʌg/ *n* taza *f* (*alta y sin platillo*), tarro *m* (Mex); (for beer) jarra *f*; ([I], face) cara *f*, jeta *f* [x]; ([I], fool) idiota *m & f*. ● *vt* (*pt* **mugged**) asaltar. ~**ger** *n* asaltante *m & f*. ~**ging** *n* asalto *m*

muggy /ˈmʌgɪ/ *a* bochornoso

mule /mjuːl/ *n* mula *f*

mull /mʌl/ (Amer), ~ **over** *vt* reflexionar sobre

multi|coloured /mʌltɪˈkʌləd/ *a* multicolor. ~**national** /-ˈnæʃənl/ *a & n* multinacional (*f*)

multipl|e /ˈmʌltɪpl/ *a* múltiple. ● *n* múltiplo *m*. **~ication** /mʌltɪplɪˈkeɪʃn/ *n* multiplicación *f*. **~y** /ˈmʌltɪplaɪ/ *vt* multiplicar. ● *vi* (Math) multiplicar; (increase) multiplicarse

multitude /ˈmʌltɪtjuːd/ *n*. **a ~ of problems** múltiples problemas

mum /mʌm/ *n* Ⓘ mamá *f* Ⓘ

mumble /ˈmʌmbl/ *vt* mascullar. ● *vi* hablar entre dientes

mummy /ˈmʌmɪ/ *n* (Ⓘ, mother) mamá *f* Ⓘ; (archaeology) momia *f*

mumps /mʌmps/ *n* paperas *fpl*

munch /mʌntʃ/ *vt/i* mascar

mundane /mʌnˈdeɪn/ *a* mundano

municipal /mjuːˈnɪsɪpl/ *a* municipal

mural /ˈmjʊərəl/ *a & n* mural (*f*)

murder /ˈmɜːdə(r)/ *n* asesinato *m*. ● *vt* asesinar. **~er** *n* asesino *m*

murky /ˈmɜːkɪ/ *a* (**-ier**, **-iest**) turbio

murmur /ˈmɜːmə(r)/ *n* murmullo *m*. ● *vt/i* murmurar

musc|le /ˈmʌsl/ *n* músculo *m*. **~ular** /ˈmʌskjʊlə(r)/ *a* muscular; *<arm, body>* musculoso

muse /mjuːz/ *vi* meditar (on sobre)

museum /mjuːˈzɪəm/ *n* museo *m*

mush /mʌʃ/ *n* papilla *f*

mushroom /ˈmʌʃrʊm/ *n* champiñón *m*; (Bot) seta *f*. ● *vi* aparecer como hongos

mushy /ˈmʌʃɪ/ *a* blando

music /ˈmjuːzɪk/ *n* música *f*. **~al** *a* musical. **be ~** tener sentido musical. ● *n* musical *m*. **~ian** /mjuːˈzɪʃn/ *n* músico *m*

Muslim /ˈmʊzlɪm/ *a & n* musulmán (*m*)

mussel /ˈmʌsl/ *n* mejillón *m*

must /mʌst/ *v aux* deber, tener que; (expressing supposition) deber (de). **he ~ be old** debe (de) ser viejo. **I ~ have done it** debo (de) haberlo hecho. ● *n*. **be a ~** ser imprescindible

mustache /ˈmʌstæʃ/ *n* (Amer) bigote *m*

mustard /ˈmʌstəd/ *n* mostaza *f*

muster /ˈmʌstə(r)/ *vt* reunir

musty /ˈmʌstɪ/ *a* (**-ier**, **-iest**) que huele a humedad

mutation /mjuːˈteɪʃn/ *n* mutación *f*

mute /mjuːt/ *a* mudo

mutilate /ˈmjuːtɪleɪt/ *vt* mutilar

mutiny /ˈmjuːtɪnɪ/ *n* motín *m*. ● *vi* amotinarse

mutter /ˈmʌtə(r)/ *vt/i* murmurar

mutton /ˈmʌtn/ *n* carne *f* de ovino

mutual /ˈmjuːtʃʊəl/ *a* mutuo; (Ⓘ, common) común

muzzle /ˈmʌzl/ *n* (snout) hocico *m*; (device) bozal *m*

my /maɪ/ *a* (*sing*) mi; (*pl*) mis

myself /maɪˈself/ *pron* (*reflexive*) me; (used for emphasis) yo mismo *m*, yo misma *f*. **I cut ~** me corté. **I made it ~** lo hice yo mismo/misma. **I was by ~** estaba solo/sola

myster|ious /mɪˈstɪərɪəs/ *a* misterioso. **~y** /ˈmɪstərɪ/ *n* misterio *m*

mystical /ˈmɪstɪkl/ *a* místico

mystify /ˈmɪstɪfaɪ/ *vt* dejar perplejo

mystique /mɪˈstiːk/ *n* mística *f*

myth /mɪθ/ *n* mito *m*. **~ical** *a* mítico. **~ology** /mɪˈθɒlədʒɪ/ *n* mitología *f*

Nn

N *abbr* (= **north**) N

nab /næb/ *vt* (*pt* **nabbed**) (⊠, arrest) pescar; (snatch) agarrar

nag /næg/ *vt* (*pt* **nagged**) fastidiar; (scold) estarle encima a. ● *vi* criticar

nail /neɪl/ *n* clavo *m*; (of finger, toe) uña *f*. ~ **polish** esmalte *m* para las uñas. ● *vt*. ~ (**down**) clavar

naive /naɪ'i:v/ *a* ingenuo

naked /'neɪkɪd/ *a* desnudo. **to the ~ eye** a simple vista

name /neɪm/ *n* nombre *m*; (of book, film) título *m*; (fig) fama *f*. **my ~ is Chris** me llamo Chris. **good ~** buena reputación. ● *vt* ponerle nombre a; (appoint) nombrar. **a man ~d Jones** un hombre llamado Jones. **she was ~d after** *or* (Amer) **for her grandmother** le pusieron el nombre de su abuela. **~less** *a* anónimo. **~ly** *adv* a saber. **~sake** *n* (person) tocayo *m*

nanny /'nænɪ/ *n* niñera *f*

nap /næp/ *n* (sleep) sueñecito *m*; (after lunch) siesta *f*. **have a ~** echarse un sueño

napkin /'næpkɪn/ *n* servilleta *f*

nappy /'næpɪ/ *n* pañal *m*

narcotic /nɑ:'kɒtɪk/ *a* & *n* narcótico (*m*)

narrat|e /nə'reɪt/ *vt* narrar. **~ive** /'nærətɪv/ *n* narración *f*. **~or** /nə'reɪtə(r)/ *n* narrador *m*

narrow /'nærəʊ/ *a* (**-er**, **-est**) estrecho, angosto (LAm). **have a ~ escape** salvarse de milagro. ● *vt* estrechar; (limit) limitar. ● *vi* estrecharse. **~ly** *adv* (just) por poco. **~-minded** /-'maɪndɪd/ *a* de miras estrechas

nasal /'neɪzl/ *a* nasal; <*voice*> gangoso

nasty /'nɑ:stɪ/ *a* (**-ier**, **-iest**) desagradable; (spiteful) malo (**to** con); <*taste, smell*> asqueroso; <*cut*> feo

nation /'neɪʃn/ *n* nación *f*

national /'næʃənl/ *a* nacional. ● *n* ciudadano *m*. ~ **anthem** *n* himno *m* nacional. **~ism** *n* nacionalismo *m*. **~ity** /næʃə'nælətɪ/ *n* nacionalidad *f*. **~ize** *vt* nacionalizar. **~ly** *adv* a escala nacional

nationwide /'neɪʃnwaɪd/ *a* & *adv* a escala nacional

native /'neɪtɪv/ *n* natural *m* & *f*. **be a ~ of** ser natural de. ● *a* nativo; <*country, town*> natal; <*language*> materno; <*plant, animal*> autóctono. **N~ American** indio *m* americano

nativity /nə'tɪvətɪ/ *n*. **the N~** la Natividad *f*

NATO /'neɪtəʊ/ *abbr* (= **North Atlantic Treaty Organization**) OTAN *f*

natter /'nætə(r)/ 🄸 *vi* charlar. ● *n* charla *f*

natural /'nætʃərəl/ *a* natural. ~ **history** *n* historia *f* natural. **~ist** *n* naturalista *m* & *f*. **~ized** *a* <*citizen*> naturalizado. **~ly** *adv* (of course) naturalmente; (by nature) por naturaleza

nature /'neɪtʃə(r)/ *n* naturaleza *f*; (of person) carácter *m*; (of things) naturaleza *f*

naught /nɔ:t/ *n* cero *m*

naughty /'nɔ:tɪ/ *a* (**-ier**, **-iest**) malo, travieso

nause|a /'nɔ:zɪə/ *n* náuseas *fpl.* **~ous** /-ɪəs/ *a* nauseabundo

nautical /'nɔ:tɪkl/ *a* náutico. **~ mile** *n* milla *f* marina

naval /'neɪvl/ *a* naval; *<officer>* de marina

nave /neɪv/ *n* nave *f*

navel /'neɪvl/ *n* ombligo *m*

naviga|ble /'nævɪgəbl/ *a* navegable. **~te** /'nævɪgeɪt/ *vt* navegar por *<sea etc>*; gobernar *<ship>*. ● *vi* navegar. **~tion** /-'geɪʃn/ *n* navegación *f.* **~tor** *n* oficial *m* & *f* de derrota

navy /'neɪvɪ/ *n* marina *f* de guerra. **~ (blue)** *a* & *n* azul (*m*) marino

NE *abbr* (= **north-east**) NE

near /'nɪə(r)/ *adv* cerca. **draw ~** acercarse. ● *prep.* **~ (to)** cerca de. **go ~ (to) sth** acercarse a algo. ● *a* cercano. ● *vt* acercarse a. **~by** *a* cercano. **~ly** *adv* casi. **he ~ly died** por poco se muere, casi se muere. **not ~ly** ni con mucho. **~sighted** /-'saɪtɪd/ *a* miope, corto de vista

neat /ni:t/ *a* (**-er**, **-est**) *<person>* pulcro; *<room etc>* bien arreglado; (ingenious) hábil; *<whisky, gin>* solo; (Amer [I], great) fantástico [I]. **~ly** *adv* pulcramente; *<organized>* cuidadosamente

necessar|ily /nesə'serɪlɪ/ *adv* necesariamente. **~y** /'nesəserɪ/ *a* necesario

necessit|ate /nə'sesɪteɪt/ *vt* exigir. **~y** /nɪ'sesətɪ/ *n* necesidad *f.* **the bare ~ies** lo indispensable

neck /nek/ *n* (of person, bottle, dress) cuello *m*; (of animal) pescuezo *m.* **~ and ~** a la par, parejos (LAm). **~lace** /'nekləs/ *n* collar *m.* **~line** *n* escote *m*

nectar /'nektə(r)/ *n* néctar *m*

nectarine /'nektərɪn/ *n* nectarina *f*

née /neɪ/ *a* de soltera

need /ni:d/ *n* necesidad *f* (**for** de). ● *vt* necesitar; (demand) exigir. **you ~ not speak** no tienes que hablar

needle /'ni:dl/ *n* aguja *f.* ● *vt* ([I], annoy) pinchar

negotianeedless /'ni:dlɪs/ *a* innecesario

needlework /'ni:dlwɜ:k/ *n* labores *fpl* de aguja; (embroidery) bordado *m*

needy /'ni:dɪ/ *a* (**-ier**, **-iest**) necesitado

negative /'negətɪv/ *a* negativo. ● *n* (of photograph) negativo *m*; (no) negativa *f*

neglect /nɪ'glekt/ *vt* descuidar *<house>*; desatender *<children>*; no cumplir con *<duty>*. ● *n* negligencia *f.* (**state of**) **~** abandono *m.* **~ful** *a* negligente

neglig|ence /'neglɪdʒəns/ *n* negligencia *f*, descuido *m.* **~ent** *a* negligente. **~ible** /'neglɪdʒəbl/ *a* insignificante

negotia|ble /nɪ'gəʊʃəbl/ *a* negociable. **~te** /nɪ'gəʊʃɪeɪt/ *vt/i* negociar. **~tion** /-'eɪʃn/ *n* negociación *f.* **~tor** *n* negociador *m*

neigh /neɪ/ *vi* relinchar

neighbour /'neɪbə(r)/ *n* vecino *m.* **~hood** *n* vecindad *f*, barrio *m.* **in the ~hood of** alrededor de. **~ing** *a* vecino

neither /'naɪðə(r)/ *a.* **~ book** ninguno de los libros. ● *pron* ninguno, -na. ● *conj.* **neither...nor** ni...ni. **~ do I** yo tampoco

neon /'ni:ɒn/ *n* neón *m.* ● *a* *<lamp etc>* de neón

nephew /'nevju:/ *n* sobrino *m*

Neptune /'neptju:n/ *n* Neptuno *m*

nerv|e /nɜ:v/ *n* nervio *m*; (courage) valor *m*; (calm) sangre *f* fría; (▣, impudence) descaro *m*. **~es** *npl* (before exams etc) nervios *mpl*. **get on s.o.'s ~es** ponerle los nervios de punta a uno. **~e-racking** *a* exasperante. **~ous** /'nɜ:vəs/ *a* nervioso. **be/feel ~ous** estar nervioso. **~ousness** *n* nerviosismo *m*. **~y** /'nɜ:vɪ/ *a* nervioso; (Amer ▣) descarado

nest /nest/ *n* nido *m*. ● *vi* anidar

nestle /'nesl/ *vi* acurrucarse

net /net/ *n* red *f*. **the N~** (Comp) la Red. ● *vt* (*pt* **netted**) pescar (con red) <*fish*>. ● *a* neto. **~ball** *n* baloncesto *m*

Netherlands /'neðələndz/ *npl*. **the ~** los Países Bajos

netting /'netɪŋ/ *n* redes *fpl*. **wire ~** tela *f* metálica

nettle /'netl/ *n* ortiga *f*

network /'netwɜ:k/ *n* red *f*; (TV) cadena *f*

neuro|sis /njʊə'rəʊsɪs/ *n* (*pl* **-oses** /-si:z/) neurosis *f*. **~tic** /-'rɒtɪk/ *a* & *n* neurótico (*m*)

neuter /'nju:tə(r)/ *a* & *n* neutro (*m*). ● *vt* castrar <*animals*>

neutral /'nju:trəl/ *a* neutral; <*colour*> neutro; (Elec) neutro. **~ (gear)** (Auto) punto *m* muerto. **~ize** *vt* neutralizar

neutron /'nju:trɒn/ *n* neutrón *m*

never /nevə(r)/ *adv* nunca; (more emphatic) jamás; (▣, not) no. **~ again** nunca más. **he ~ smiles** no sonríe nunca, nunca sonríe. **I ~ saw him** ▣ no lo vi. **~-ending** *a* interminable. **~theless** /-ðə'les/ *adv* sin embargo, no obstante

new /nju:/ *a* (**-er**, **-est**) nuevo. **~born** *a* recién nacido. **~comer** *n* recién llegado *m*. **~fangled** /-'fæŋgld/ *a* (pej) moderno. **~ly** *adv* recién. **~ly-weds** *npl* recién casados *mpl*

news /nju:z/ *n*. **a piece of ~** una noticia. **good/bad ~** buenas/malas noticias. **the ~** (TV, Radio) las noticias. **~agent** *n* vendedor *m* de periódicos. **~caster** *n* locutor *m*. **~dealer** *n* (Amer) ⇒~AGENT. **~flash** *n* información *f* de última hora. **~letter** *n* boletín *m*, informativo *m*. **~paper** *n* periódico *m*, diario *m*. **~reader** *n* locutor *m*

newt /nju:t/ *n* tritón *m*

New Year /nju:'jɪə(r)/ *n* Año *m* Nuevo. **~'s Day** *n* día *m* de Año Nuevo. **~'s Eve** *n* noche *f* vieja, noche *f* de fin de Año

New Zealand /njʊ:'zi:lənd/ *n* Nueva Zeland(i)a *f*

next /nekst/ *a* próximo; <*week, month etc*> que viene, próximo; (adjoining) vecino; (following) siguiente. ● *adv* luego, después. **~ to** al lado de. **when you see me ~** la próxima vez que me veas. **~ to nothing** casi nada. **~ door** al lado (**to** de). **~-door** *a* de al lado. **~ of kin** *n* familiar(es) *m(pl)* más cercano(s)

nib /nɪb/ *n* plumilla *f*

nibble /'nɪbl/ *vt/i* mordisquear. ● *n* mordisco *m*

Nicaragua /nɪkə'rægjʊə/ *n* Nicaragua *f*. **~n** *a* & *n* nicaragüense (*m* & *f*)

nice /naɪs/ *a* (**-er**, **-est**) agradable; (likeable) simpático; (kind) amable; <*weather, food*> bueno. **we had a ~ time** lo pasamos bien. **~ly** *adv* (kindly) amablemente; (politely) con buenos modales

niche /nɪtʃ, ni:ʃ/ *n* nicho *m*

nick /nɪk/ *n* corte *m* pequeño. **in the ~ of time** justo a tiempo. ● *vt* (⊠ steal) afanar ⊠

nickel /ˈnɪkl/ *n* (metal) níquel *m*; (Amer) moneda *f* de cinco centavos

nickname /ˈnɪkneɪm/ *n* apodo *m*. ● *vt* apodar

nicotine /ˈnɪkətiːn/ *n* nicotina *f*

niece /niːs/ *n* sobrina *f*

niggling /ˈnɪglɪŋ/ *a* <doubt> constante

night /naɪt/ *n* noche *f*; (evening) tarde *f*. **at ~** por la noche, de noche. **good ~** ¡buenas noches! ● *a* nocturno, de noche. **~cap** *n* (drink) bebida *f* (tomada antes de acostarse). **~club** *n* club *m* nocturno. **~dress** *n* camisón *m*. **~fall** *n* anochecer *m*. **~gown**, **~ie** /ˈnaɪtɪ/ ⓘ *n* camisón *m*. **~life** *n* vida *f* nocturna. **~ly** *a* de todas las noches. **~mare** *n* pesadilla *f*. **~ school** *n* escuela *f* nocturna. **~-time** *n* noche *f*. **~watchman** *n* sereno *m*

nil /nɪl/ *n* nada *f*; (Sport) cero *m*

nimble /ˈnɪmbl/ *a* (**-er**, **-est**) ágil

nine /naɪn/ *a* & *n* nueve (*m*). **~teen** /naɪnˈtiːn/ *a* & *n* diecinueve (*m*). **~teenth** *a* decimonoveno. ● *n* diecinueveavo *m*. **~tieth** /ˈnaɪntɪəθ/ *a* nonagésimo. ● *n* noventavo *m*. **~ty** *a* & *n* noventa (*m*)

ninth /ˈnaɪnθ/ *a* & *n* noveno (*m*)

nip /nɪp/ *vt* (*pt* **nipped**) (pinch) pellizcar; (bite) mordisquear. ● *vi* (ⓘ, rush) correr

nipple /ˈnɪpl/ *n* (of woman) pezón *m*; (of man) tetilla *f*; (of baby's bottle) tetina *f*, chupón *m* (Mex)

nippy /ˈnɪpɪ/ *a* (**-ier**, **-iest**) (ⓘ, chilly) fresquito

nitrogen /ˈnaɪtrədʒən/ *n* nitrógeno *m*

no /nəʊ/ *a* ninguno, (before masculine singular noun) ningún. **I have ~ money** no tengo dinero. **there's ~ food left** no queda nada de comida. **it has ~ windows** no tiene ventanas. **I'm ~ expert** no soy ningún experto. **~ smoking** prohibido fumar. **~ way!** ⓘ ¡ni hablar! ● *adv* & *int* no. ● *n* (*pl* **noes**) no *m*

noble /ˈnəʊbl/ *a* (**-er**, **-est**) noble. **~man** /-mən/ *n* noble *m*

nobody /ˈnəʊbədɪ/ *pron* nadie. **there's ~ there** no hay nadie

nocturnal /nɒkˈtɜːnl/ *a* nocturno

nod /nɒd/ *vt* (*pt* **nodded**). **~ one's head** asentir con la cabeza. ● *vi* (in agreement) asentir con la cabeza; (in greeting) saludar con la cabeza. □ **~ off** *vi* dormirse

nois|e /nɔɪz/ *n* ruido *m*. **~ily** *adv* ruidosamente. **~y** *a* (**-ier**, **-iest**) ruidoso. **it's too ~y here** hay demasiado ruido aquí

nomad /ˈnəʊmæd/ *n* nómada *m* & *f*. **~ic** /-ˈmædɪk/ *a* nómada

no man's land *n* tierra *f* de nadie

nominat|e /ˈnɒmɪneɪt/ *vt* (put forward) proponer; postular (LAm); (appoint) nombrar. **~ion** /-ˈneɪʃn/ *n* nombramiento *m*; (Amer, Pol) proclamación *f*

non-... /nɒn/ *pref* no ...

nonchalant /ˈnɒnʃələnt/ *a* despreocupado

non-committal /nɒnkəˈmɪtl/ *a* evasivo

nondescript /ˈnɒndɪskrɪpt/ *a* anodino

none /nʌn/ *pron* ninguno, ninguna. **there were ~ left** no quedaba ninguno/ninguna. **~ of us** ninguno de nosotros. ● *adv* no, de ninguna manera. **he is ~ the happier** no está más contento

nonentity /nɒ'nentətɪ/ *n* persona *f* insignificante

non-existent /nɒnɪg'zɪstənt/ *a* inexistente

nonplussed /nɒn'plʌst/ *a* perplejo

nonsens|e /'nɒnsns/ *n* tonterías *fpl*, disparates *mpl*. **~ical** /-'sensɪkl/ *a* disparatado

non-smoker /nɒn'sməʊkə(r)/ *n* no fumador *m*. **I'm a ~** no fumo

non-stop /nɒn'stɒp/ *a* <*train*> directo; <*flight*> sin escalas. ● *adv* sin parar; (by train) directamente; (by air) sin escalas

noodles /'nu:dlz/ *npl* fideos *mpl*

nook /nʊk/ *n* rincón *m*

noon /nu:n/ *n* mediodía *m*

no-one /'nəʊwʌn/ *pron* nadie

noose /nu:s/ *n* soga *f*

nor /nɔ:(r)/ *conj* ni, tampoco. **neither blue ~ red** ni azul ni rojo. **he doesn't play the piano, ~ do I** no sabe tocar el piano, ni yo tampoco

norm /nɔ:m/ *n* norma *f*

normal /'nɔ:ml/ *a* normal. **~cy** *n* (Amer) normalidad *f*. **~ity** /-'mælətɪ/ *n* normalidad *f*. **~ly** *adv* normalmente

north /nɔ:θ/ *n* norte *m*. ● *a* norte. ● *adv* hacia el norte. **N~ America** *n* América *f* del Norte, Norteamérica *f*. **N~ American** *a* & *n* norteamericano (*m*). **~east** *n* nor(d)este *m*. ● *a* nor(d)este. ● *adv* <*go*> hacia el nor(d)este. **it's ~east of Leeds** está al nor(d)este de Leeds. **~erly** /'nɔ:ðəlɪ/ *a* <*wind*> del norte. **~ern** /'nɔ:ðən/ *a* del norte. **~erner** *n* norteño *m*. **N~ern Ireland** *n* Irlanda *f* del Norte. **N~ Sea** *n* mar *m* del Norte. **~ward** /'nɔ:θwəd/, **~wards** *adv* hacia el norte. **~west** *n* noroeste *m*. ● *a* noroeste. ● *adv* hacia el noroeste

Norw|ay /'nɔ:weɪ/ *n* Noruega *f*. **~egian** /-'wi:dʒən/ *a* & *n* noruego (*m*)

nose /nəʊz/ *n* nariz *f*. **~bleed** *n* hemorragia *f* nasal. **~dive** *vi* descender en picado, descender en picada (LAm)

nostalgi|a /nɒ'stældʒə/ *n* nostalgia *f*. **~c** *a* nostálgico

nostril /'nɒstrɪl/ *n* ventana *f* de la nariz *f*

nosy /'nəʊzɪ/ *a* (**-ier**, **-iest**) [!] entrometido, metiche (LAm)

not /nɒt/

Cuando **not** va precedido del verbo auxiliar **do** or **have** o de un verbo modal como **should** etc se suele emplear la forma contraída **don't, haven't, shouldn't** etc

● *adverb*

····➤ no. **I don't know** no sé. **~ yet** todavía no. **~ me** yo no

····➤ (replacing a clause) **I suppose ~** supongo que no. **of course ~** por supuesto que no. **are you going to help me or ~?** ¿me vas a ayudar o no?

····➤ (emphatic) ni. **~ a penny more!** ¡ni un penique más!

····➤ (in phrases) **certainly ~** de ninguna manera . **~ you again!** ¡tú otra vez!

notabl|e /'nəʊtəbl/ *a* notable; <*author*> distinguido. **~y** /'nəʊtəblɪ/ *adv* notablemente; (in particular) particularmente

notch /nɒtʃ/ *n* muesca *f*. □ **~ up** *vt* apuntarse

note /nəʊt/ *n* (incl Mus) nota *f*; (banknote) billete *m*. **take ~s** tomar apuntes. ● *vt* (notice) observar; (record) anotar. □ **~ down** *vt* apuntar. **~book** *n* cuaderno *m*. **~d** *a* célebre. **~paper** *n* papel *m* de carta(s)

nothing /ˈnʌθɪŋ/ *pron* nada. **he eats ~** no come nada. **for ~** (free) gratis; (in vain) en vano. **~ else** nada más. **~ much happened** no pasó gran cosa. **he does ~ but complain** no hace más que quejarse

notice /ˈnəʊtɪs/ *n* (sign) letrero *m*; (item of information) anuncio *m*; (notification) aviso *m*; (of termination of employment) preaviso *m*; **~ (of dismissal)** despido *m*. **take ~ of** hacer caso a <*person*>. ● *vt* notar. ● *vi* darse cuenta. **~able** *a* perceptible. **~ably** *adv* perceptiblemente. **~board** *n* tablón *m* de anuncios, tablero *m* de anuncios (LAm)

notif|ication /nəʊtɪfɪˈkeɪʃn/ *n* notificación *f*. **~y** /ˈnəʊtɪfaɪ/ *vt* informar; (in writing) notificar. **~y s.o. of sth** comunicarle algo a uno

notion /ˈnəʊʃn/ *n* (concept) concepto *m*; (idea) idea *f*

notorious /nəʊˈtɔːrɪəs/ *a* notorio

notwithstanding /nɒtwɪθˈstændɪŋ/ *prep* a pesar de. ● *adv* no obstante

nougat /ˈnuːgɑː/ *n* turrón *m*

nought /nɔːt/ *n* cero *m*

noun /naʊn/ *n* sustantivo *m*, nombre *m*

nourish /ˈnʌrɪʃ/ *vt* alimentar. **~ment** *n* alimento *m*

novel /ˈnɒvl/ *n* novela *f*. ● *a* original, novedoso. **~ist** *n* novelista *m* & *f*. **~ty** *n* novedad *f*

November /nəʊˈvembə(r)/ *n* noviembre *m*

novice /ˈnɒvɪs/ *n* principiante *m* & *f*

now /naʊ/ *adv* ahora. **~ and again, ~ and then** de vez en cuando. **right ~** ahora mismo. **from ~ on** a partir de ahora. ● *conj*. **~ (that)** ahora que. **~adays** /ˈnaʊədeɪz/ *adv* hoy (en) día

nowhere /ˈnəʊweə(r)/ *adv* por ninguna parte, por ningún lado; (after motion towards) a ninguna parte, a ningún lado

nozzle /ˈnɒzl/ *n* (on hose) boca *f*; (on fire extinguisher) boquilla *f*

nuance /ˈnjʊɑːns/ *n* matiz *m*

nuclear /ˈnjuːklɪə(r)/ *a* nuclear

nucleus /ˈnjuːklɪəs/ *n* (*pl* **-lei** /-lɪaɪ/) núcleo *m*

nude /njuːd/ *a* & *n* desnudo (*m*). **in the ~** desnudo

nudge /nʌdʒ/ *vt* codear (ligeramente). ● *n* golpe *m* (suave) con el codo

nudi|st /ˈnjuːdɪst/ *n* nudista *m* & *f*. **~ty** /ˈnjuːdətɪ/ *n* desnudez *f*

nuisance /ˈnjuːsns/ *n* (thing, event) molestia *f*, fastidio *m*; (person) pesado *m*

null /nʌl/ *a* nulo

numb /nʌm/ *a* entumecido. **go ~** entumecerse ● *vt* entumecer

number /ˈnʌmbə(r)/ *n* número *m*; (telephone number) número *m* de teléfono. **a ~ of people** varias personas. ● *vt* numerar; (count, include) contar. **~plate** *n* matrícula *f*, placa *f* (LAm)

numer|al /ˈnjuːmərəl/ *n* número *m*. **~ical** /njuːˈmerɪkl/ *a* numérico. **~ous** /ˈnjuːmərəs/ *a* numeroso

nun /nʌn/ *n* monja *f*

nurse /nɜ:s/ *n* enfermero *m*, enfermera *f*; (nanny) niñera *f*. ● *vt* cuidar; abrigar *<hope etc>*

nursery /'nɜ:sərɪ/ *n* (for plants) vivero *m*; (day ~) guardería *f*. ~ **rhyme** *n* canción *f* infantil. ~ **school** *n* jardín *m* de infancia, jardín *m* infantil (LAm)

nursing home /'nɜ:sɪŋ/ *n* (for older people) residencia *f* de ancianos (*con mayor nivel de asistencia médica*)

nut /nʌt/ *n* fruto *m* seco (nuez, almendra, avellana etc); (Tec) tuerca *f*. ~**case** *n* [I] chiflado *m*. ~**crackers** *npl* cascanueces *m*. ~**meg** /-meg/ *n* nuez *f* moscada

nutri|ent /'nju:trɪənt/ *n* nutriente *m*. ~**tion** /nju:'trɪʃn/ *n* nutrición *f*. ~**tious** /nju:'trɪʃəs/ *a* nutritivo

nuts /nʌts/ *a* ([I], crazy) chiflado

nutshell /'nʌtʃel/ *n* cáscara *f* de nuez. **in a** ~ en pocas palabras

NW *abbr* (= **north-west**) NO

nylon /'naɪlɒn/ *n* nylon *m*

Oo

oaf /əʊf/ *n* zoquete *m*

oak /əʊk/ *n* roble *m*

OAP /əʊer'pi:/ *abbr* (= **old-age pensioner**) *n* pensionista *m & f*, pensionado *m*

oar /ɔ:(r)/ *n* remo *m*

oasis /əʊ'eɪsɪs/ *n* (*pl* **oases** /-si:z/) oasis *m*

oath /əʊθ/ *n* juramento *m*

oat|meal /'əʊtmi:l/ *n* harina *f* de avena; (Amer, flakes) avena *f* (en copos). ~**s** /əʊts/ *npl* avena *f*

obedien|ce /əʊ'bi:dɪəns/ *n* obediencia *f*. ~**t** *a* obediente. ~**tly** *adv* obedientemente

obes|e /əʊ'bi:s/ *a* obeso. ~**ity** *n* obesidad *f*

obey /əʊ'beɪ/ *vt/i* obedecer

obituary /ə'bɪtʃʊərɪ/ *n* nota *f* necrológica, obituario *m*

object /'ɒbdʒɪkt/ *n* objeto *m*; (aim) objetivo *m*. ● /əb'dʒekt/ *vi* oponerse (**to** a). ~**ion** /əb'dʒekʃn/ *n* objeción *f*. ~**ionable** *a* censurable; (unpleasant) desagradable. ~**ive** /əb'dʒektɪv/ *a & n* objetivo (*m*)

oblig|ation /ɒblɪ'geɪʃn/ *n* obligación *f*. **be under an** ~**ation to** estar obligado a. ~**atory** /ə'blɪgətrɪ/ *a* obligatorio. ~**e** /ə'blaɪdʒ/ *vt* obligar. **I'd be much** ~**ed if you could help me** le quedaría muy agradecido si pudiera ayudarme. ● *vi* hacer un favor. ~**ing** *a* atento

oblique /ə'bli:k/ *a* oblicuo

obliterate /ə'blɪtəreɪt/ *vt* arrasar; (erase) borrar

oblivio|n /ə'blɪvɪən/ *n* olvido *m*. ~**us** /-vɪəs/ *a* (unaware) inconsciente (**to, of** de)

oblong /'ɒblɒŋ/ *a* oblongo. ● *n* rectángulo *m*

obnoxious /əb'nɒkʃəs/ *a* odioso

oboe /'əʊbəʊ/ *n* oboe *m*

obscen|e /əb'si:n/ *a* obsceno. ~**ity** /əb'senətɪ/ *n* obscenidad *f*

obscur|e /əb'skjʊə(r)/ *a* oscuro. ● *vt* ocultar; impedir ver claramente *<issue>*. ~**ity** *n* oscuridad *f*

obsequious /əb'siːkwɪəs/ *a* servil

observ|ant /əb'zɜːvənt/ *a* observador. **~ation** /ɒbzə'veɪʃn/ *n* observación *f*. **~atory** /əb'zɜːvətrɪ/ *n* observatorio *m*. **~e** /əb'zɜːv/ *vt* observar. **~er** *n* observador *m*

obsess /əb'ses/ *vt* obsesionar. **~ed** /əb'sest/ *a* obsesionado. **~ion** /-ʃn/ *n* obsesión *f*. **~ive** *a* obsesivo

obsolete /'ɒbsəliːt/ *a* obsoleto

obstacle /'ɒbstəkl/ *n* obstáculo *m*

obstina|cy /'ɒbstɪnəsɪ/ *n* obstinación *f*. **~te** /-ət/ *a* obstinado. **~tely** *adv* obstinadamente

obstruct /əb'strʌkt/ *vt* obstruir; bloquear *<traffic>*. **~ion** /-ʃn/ *n* obstrucción *f*

obtain /əb'teɪn/ *vt* conseguir, obtener. **~able** *a* asequible

obtrusive /əb'truːsɪv/ *a* *<presence>* demasiado prominente; *<noise>* molesto

obtuse /əb'tjuːs/ *a* obtuso

obvious /'ɒbvɪəs/ *a* obvio. **~ly** *adv* obviamente

occasion /ə'keɪʒn/ *n* ocasión *f*. **~al** *a* esporádico. **~ally** *adv* de vez en cuando

occult /ɒ'kʌlt/ *a* oculto

occup|ant /'ɒkjʊpənt/ *n* ocupante *m* & *f*. **~ation** /ɒkjʊ'peɪʃn/ *n* ocupación *f*. **~ier** /'ɒkjʊpaɪə(r)/ *n* ocupante *m* & *f*. **~y** /'ɒkjʊpaɪ/ *vt* ocupar. **keep o.s. ~ied** entretenerse

occur /ə'kɜː(r)/ *vi* (*pt* **occurred**) tener lugar, ocurrir; *<change>* producirse; (exist) encontrarse. **it ~red to me that** se me ocurrió que. **~rence** /ə'kʌrəns/ *n* (incidence) incidencia *f*. **it is a rare ~rence** no es algo frecuente

ocean /'əʊʃn/ *n* océano *m*

o'clock /ə'klɒk/ *adv*. **it is 7 ~** son las siete. **it's one ~** es la una

octagon /'ɒktəgən/ *n* octágono *m*

octave /'ɒktɪv/ *n* octava *f*

October /ɒk'təʊbə(r)/ *n* octubre *m*

octopus /'ɒktəpəs/ *n* (*pl* **-puses**) pulpo *m*

odd /ɒd/ *a* (**-er**, **-est**) extraño, raro; *<number>* impar; (one of pair) desparejado. **smoke the ~ cigarette** fumarse algún que otro cigarrillo. **fifty-~** unos cincuenta, cincuenta y pico. **the ~ one out** la excepción. **~ity** *n* (thing) rareza *f*; (person) bicho *m* raro. **~ly** *adv* de una manera extraña. **~ly enough** por extraño que parezca. **~ment** *n* retazo *m*. **~s** *npl* probabilidades *fpl*; (in betting) apuesta *f*. **be at ~s** estar en desacuerdo. **~s and ends** *mpl* [I] cosas *fpl* sueltas

odious /'əʊdɪəs/ *a* odioso

odometer /ɒ'dɒmətə(r)/ *n* (Amer) cuentakilómetros *m*

odour /'əʊdə(r)/ *n* olor *m*

---

of /ɒv/, *unstressed form* /əv/

● *preposition*

····▸ de. **a pound of cheese** una libra de queso. **it's made of wood** es de madera. **a girl of ten** una niña de diez años

····▸ (in dates) de. **the fifth of November** el cinco de noviembre

····▸ (Amer, when telling the time) **it's ten (minutes) of five** son las cinco menos diez, son diez para las cinco (LAm)

! of is not translated in cases such as the following: **a colleague of mine** *un colega mío;* **there were six of us** *éramos seis;* **that's very kind of you** *es Ud muy amable*

off /ɒf/ *prep* (from) de. **he picked it up ~ the floor** lo recogió del suelo; (distant from) **just ~ the coast of Texas** a poca distancia de la costa de Tejas. **2 ft ~ the ground** a dos pies del suelo; (absent from) **I've been ~ work for a week** hace una semana que no voy a trabajar. ● *adv* (removed) **the lid was ~** la tapa no estaba puesta; (distant) **some way ~** a cierta distancia; (leaving) **I'm ~** me voy; (switched off) *<light, TV>* apagado; *<water>* cortado; (cancelled) *<match>* cancelado; (not on duty) *<day>* libre. ● *adj.* **be ~** *<meat>* estar malo, estar pasado; *<milk>* estar cortado. **~-beat** *a* poco convencional. **~ chance** *n.* **on the ~ chance** por si acaso

offen|ce /ə'fens/ *n* (breach of law) infracción *f*; (criminal **~ce**) delito *m*; (cause of outrage) atentado *m*; (Amer, attack) ataque *m*. **take ~ce** ofenderse. **~d** *vt* ofender. **~der** *n* delincuente *m & f*. **~sive** /-sɪv/ *a* ofensivo; (disgusting) desagradable

offer /'ɒfə(r)/ *vt* ofrecer. **~ to do sth** ofrecerse a hacer algo. ● *n* oferta *f*. **on ~** de oferta

offhand /ɒf'hænd/ *a* (brusque) brusco. **say sth in an ~ way** decir algo a la ligera. ● *adv* de improviso

office /'ɒfɪs/ *n* oficina *f*; (post) cargo *m*. **doctor's ~** (Amer) consultorio *m*, consulta *m*. **~ block** *n* edificio *m* de oficinas **~r** *n* oficial *m & f*; (police **~r**) policía *m & f*; (as form of address) agente

offici|al /ə'fɪʃl/ *a* oficial. ● *n* funcionario *m* del Estado; (of party, union) dirigente *m & f*. **~ally** *adv* oficialmente. **~ous** /ə'fɪʃəs/ *a* oficioso

offing /'ɒfɪŋ/ *n.* **in the ~** en perspectiva

off: ~-licence *n* tienda *f* de vinos y licores. **~-putting** *a* (disconcerting) desconcertante; (disagreeable) desagradable. **~set** *vt* (*pt* **-set**, *pres p* **-setting**) compensar. **~side** /ɒf'saɪd/ *a* (Sport) fuera de juego. **~spring** *n invar* prole *f*. **~-stage** /-'steɪdʒ/ *adv* fuera del escenario. **~-white** *a* color hueso

often /'ɒfn/ *adv* a menudo, con frecuencia. **how ~?** ¿con qué frecuencia? **more ~** con más frecuencia

ogle /'əʊgl/ *vt* comerse con los ojos

ogre /'əʊgə(r)/ *n* ogro *m*

oh /əʊ/ *int* ¡ah!; (expressing dismay) ¡ay!

oil /ɔɪl/ *n* aceite *m*; (petroleum) petróleo *m*. ● *vt* lubricar. **~field** *n* yacimiento *m* petrolífero. **~ painting** *n* pintura *f* al óleo; (picture) óleo *m*. **~ rig** *n* plataforma *f* petrolífera. **~y** *a* *<substance>* oleaginoso; *<food>* aceitoso

ointment /'ɔɪntmənt/ *n* ungüento *m*

OK /əʊ'keɪ/ *int* ¡vale!, ¡de acuerdo!, ¡bueno! (LAm). ● *a* **~, thanks** bien, gracias. **the job's ~** el trabajo no está mal

old /əʊld/ *a* (**-er**, **-est**) viejo; (not modern) antiguo; (former) antiguo; **an ~ friend** un viejo amigo. **how ~ is she?** ¿cuántos años tiene? **she is ten years ~** tiene diez años. **his ~er sister** su hermana mayor.

~**age** *n* vejez *f*. ~**-fashioned** /-'fæʃənd/ *a* anticuado

olive /'ɒlɪv/ *n* aceituna *f*.

Olympic /ə'lɪmpɪk/ *a* olímpico. **the ~s** *npl*, **the ~ Games** *npl* los Juegos Olímpicos

omelette /'ɒmlɪt/ *n* tortilla *f* francesa, omelette *m* (LAm)

omen /'əʊmen/ *n* agüero *m*

omi|ssion /ə'mɪʃn/ *n* omisión *f*. ~**t** /əʊ'mɪt/ *vt* (*pt* **omitted**) omitir

on /ɒn/ *prep* en, sobre; (about) sobre. ~ **foot** a pie. ~ **Monday** el lunes. ~ **seeing** al ver. **I heard it ~ the radio** lo oí por la radio. ● *adv* (light etc) encendido, prendido (LAm); (machine) en marcha; (tap) abierto. ~ **and** ~ sin cesar. **and so** ~ y así sucesivamente. **have a hat** ~ llevar (puesto) un sombrero. **further** ~ un poco más allá. **what's ~ at the Odeon?** ¿qué dan en el Odeon? **go** ~ continuar. **later** ~ más tarde

once /wʌns/ *adv* una vez; (formerly) antes. **at** ~ inmediatamente. ~ **upon a time there was...** érase una vez.... ~ **and for all** de una vez por todas. ● *conj* una vez que

one /wʌn/ *a* uno, (before masculine singular noun) un. **the ~ person I trusted** la única persona en la que confiaba. ● *n* uno *m*. ~ **by** ~ uno a uno.. ● *pron* uno (*m*), una (*f*). **the blue** ~ el/la azul. **this** ~ éste/ésta. ~ **another** el uno al otro.

onerous /'ɒnərəs/ *a* <*task*> pesado

one: ~self /-'self/ *pron* (reflexive) se; (*after prep*) sí (mismo); (emphatic use) uno mismo, una misma. **by ~self** solo. ~**-way** *a* <*street*> de sentido único; <*ticket*> de ida, sencillo

onion /'ʌnɪən/ *n* cebolla *f*

onlooker /'ɒnlʊkə(r)/ *n* espectador *m*

only /'əʊnlɪ/ *a* único. **she's an ~ child** es hija única. ● *adv* sólo, solamente. ~ **just** (barely) apenas. **I've ~ just arrived** acabo de llegar. ● *conj* pero, sólo que

onset /'ɒnset/ *n* comienzo *m*; (of disease) aparición *f*

onslaught /'ɒnslɔ:t/ *n* ataque *m*

onus /'əʊnəs/ *n* responsabilidad *f*

onward(s) /'ɒnwəd(z)/ *a & adv* hacia adelante

ooze /u:z/ *vt/i* rezumar

opaque /əʊ'peɪk/ *a* opaco

open /'əʊpən/ *a* abierto; <*question*> discutible. ● *n*. **in the** ~ al aire libre. ● *vt/i* abrir. ~**ing** *n* abertura *f*; (beginning) principio *m*. ~**ly** *adv* abiertamente. ~**-minded** /-'maɪndɪd/ *a* de actitud abierta

opera /'ɒprə/ *n* ópera *f*

operate /'ɒpəreɪt/ *vt* manejar, operar (Mex) <*machine*>. ● *vi* funcionar; <*company*> operar. ~ **(on)** (Med) operar (a)

operatic /ɒpə'rætɪk/ *a* operístico

operation /ɒpə'reɪʃn/ *n* operación *f*; (Mec) funcionamiento *m*; (using of machine) manejo *m*. **he had an** ~ lo operaron. **in** ~ en vigor. ~**al** *a* operacional

operative /'ɒpərətɪv/ *a*. **be** ~ estar en vigor

operator *n* operador *m*

opinion /ə'pɪnɪən/ *n* opinión *f*. **in my** ~ en mi opinión, a mi parecer

opponent /ə'pəʊnənt/ *n* adversario *m*; (in sport) contrincante *m & f*

opportun|e /'ɒpətju:n/ *a* oportuno. ~**ist** /ɒpə'tju:nɪst/ *n* oportunista *m & f*. ~**ity** /ɒpə'tju:nətɪ/ *n* oportunidad *f*

oppos|e /ə'pəʊz/ *vt* oponerse a. **be ~ed to** oponerse a, estar en contra de. ~**ing** *a* opuesto. ~**ite** /'ɒpəzɪt/

a (contrary) opuesto; (facing) de enfrente. ● *n*. **the ~ite** lo contrario. **quite the ~ite** al contrario. ● *adv* enfrente. ● *prep* enfrente de. **~ite number** *n* homólogo *m*. **~ition** /ɒpəˈzɪʃn/ *n* oposición *f*; (resistence) resistencia *f*

oppress /əˈpres/ *vt* oprimir. **~ion** /-ʃn/ *n* opresión *f*. **~ive** *a* (cruel) opresivo; <*heat*> sofocante

opt /ɒpt/ *vi*. **~ to** optar por. □ **~ out** *vi* decidir no tomar parte

optic|al /ˈɒptɪkl/ *a* óptico. **~ian** /ɒpˈtɪʃn/ *n* óptico *m*

optimis|m /ˈɒptɪmɪzəm/ *n* optimismo *m*. **~t** *n* optimista *m* & *f*. **~tic** /-ˈmɪstɪk/ *a* optimista

option /ˈɒpʃn/ *n* opción *f*. **~al** *a* facultativo

or /ɔ:(r)/ *conj* o; (before **o-** and **ho-**) u; (*after negative*) ni. **~ else** si no, o bien

oral /ˈɔ:rəl/ *a* oral. ● *n* ◻ examen *m* oral

orange /ˈɒrɪndʒ/ *n* naranja *f*; (colour) naranja *m*. ● *a* naranja. **~ade** /-ˈeɪd/ *n* naranjada *f*

orbit /ˈɔ:bɪt/ *n* órbita *f*. ● *vt* orbitar

orchard /ˈɔ:tʃəd/ *n* huerto *m*

orchestra /ˈɔ:kɪstrə/ *n* orquesta *f*; (Amer, in theatre) platea *f*. **~l** /-ˈkestrəl/ *a* orquestal. **~te** /-eɪt/ *vt* orquestar

orchid /ˈɔ:kɪd/ *n* orquídea *f*

ordain /ɔ:ˈdeɪn/ *vt* (Relig) ordenar; (decree) decretar

ordeal /ɔ:ˈdi:l/ *n* dura prueba *f*

order /ˈɔ:də(r)/ *n* orden *m*; (Com) pedido *m*; (command) orden *f*. **in ~ that** para que. **in ~ to** para. ● *vt* (command) ordenar, mandar; (Com) pedir; (in restaurant) pedir, ordenar (LAm); encargar <*book*>; llamar, ordenar (LAm) <*taxi*>. **~ly** *a* ordenado. ● *n* camillero *m*

ordinary /ˈɔ:dɪnrɪ/ *a* corriente; (average) medio; (mediocre) ordinario

ore /ɔ:(r)/ *n* mena *f*

organ /ˈɔ:gən/ *n* órgano *m*

organ|ic /ɔ:ˈgænɪk/ *a* orgánico. **~ism** /ˈɔ:gənɪzəm/ *n* organismo *m*. **~ist** /ˈɔ:gənɪst/ *n* organista *m* & *f*. **~ization** /ɔ:gənaɪˈzeɪʃn/ *n* organización *f*. **~ize** /ˈɔ:gənaɪz/ *vt* organizar. **~izer** *n* organizador *m*

orgasm /ˈɔ:gæzəm/ *n* orgasmo *m*

orgy /ˈɔ:dʒɪ/ *n* orgía *f*

Orient /ˈɔ:rɪənt/ *n* Oriente *m*. **~al** /-ˈentl/ *a* oriental

orientat|e /ˈɔ:rɪənteɪt/ *vt* orientar. **~ion** /-ˈteɪʃn/ *n* orientación *f*

origin /ˈɒrɪdʒɪn/ *n* origen *m*. **~al** /əˈrɪdʒənl/ *a* original. **~ally** *adv* originariamente. **~ate** /əˈrɪdʒɪneɪt/ *vi*. **~ate from** provenir de

ornament /ˈɔ:nəmənt/ *n* adorno *m*. **~al** /-ˈmentl/ *a* de adorno

ornate /ɔ:ˈneɪt/ *a* ornamentado; <*style*> recargado

ornithology /ɔ:nɪˈθɒlədʒɪ/ *n* ornitología *f*

orphan /ˈɔ:fn/ *n* huérfano *m*. ● *vt*. **be ~ed** quedar huérfano. **~age** /-ɪdʒ/ *n* orfanato *m*

orthodox /ˈɔ:θədɒks/ *a* ortodoxo

oscillate /ˈɒsɪleɪt/ *vi* oscilar

ostentatious /ɒstenˈteɪʃəs/ *a* ostentoso

osteopath /ˈɒstɪəpæθ/ *n* osteópata *m* & *f*

ostracize /ˈɒstrəsaɪz/ *vt* hacerle vacío a

ostrich /ˈɒstrɪtʃ/ *n* avestruz *m*

other /ˈʌðə(r)/ *a & pron* otro. **~ than** aparte de. **the ~ one** el otro. **~wise** *adv* de lo contrario, si no

otter /ˈɒtə(r)/ *n* nutria *f*

ouch /aʊtʃ/ *int* ¡ay!

ought /ɔːt/ *v aux*. **I ~ to see it** debería verlo. **he ~ to have done it** debería haberlo hecho

ounce /aʊns/ *n* onza *f* (= 28.35 gr.)

our /ˈaʊə(r)/ *a* (*sing*) nuestro, nuestra, (*pl*) nuestros, nuestras. **~s** /ˈaʊəz/ *poss pron* (*sing*) nuestro, nuestra; (*pl*) nuestros, nuestras. **~s is red** el nuestro es rojo. **a friend of ~s** un amigo nuestro. **~selves** /-ˈselvz/ *pron* (reflexive) nos; (used for emphasis and after prepositions) nosotros mismos, nosotras mismas. **we behaved ~selves** nos portamos bien. **we did it ~selves** lo hicimos nosotros mismos/nosotras mismas

oust /aʊst/ *vt* desbancar; derrocar <*government*>

out /aʊt/ *adv* (outside) fuera, afuera (LAm). (not lighted, not on) apagado; (in blossom) en flor; (in error) equivocado. **he's ~** (not at home) no está; **be ~ to** estar resuelto a. **~ of** *prep* (from inside) de; (outside) fuera, afuera (LAm). **five ~ of six** cinco de cada seis. **made ~ of** hecho de. **we're ~ of bread** nos hemos quedado sin pan. **~break** *n* (of war) estallido *m*; (of disease) brote *m*. **~burst** *n* arrebato *m*. **~cast** *n* paria *m & f*. **~come** *n* resultado *m*. **~cry** *n* protesta *f*. **~dated** /-ˈdeɪtɪd/ *a* anticuado. **~do** /-ˈduː/ *vt* (*pt* **-did**, *pp* **-done**) superar. **~door** *a* <*clothes*> de calle; <*pool*> descubierto. **~doors** /-ˈdɔːz/ *adv* al aire libre

outer /ˈaʊtə(r)/ *a* exterior

out: ~fit *n* equipo *m*; (clothes) conjunto *m*. **~going** *a* <*minister etc*> saliente; (sociable) abierto. **~goings** *npl* gastos *mpl*. **~grow** /-ˈgrəʊ/ *vt* (*pt* **-grew**, *pp* **-grown**) crecer más que <*person*>. **he's ~grown his new shoes** le han quedado pequeños los zapatos nuevos. **~ing** *n* excursión *f*

outlandish /aʊtˈlændɪʃ/ *a* extravagante

out: ~law *n* forajido *m*. ● *vt* proscribir. **~lay** *n* gastos *mpl*. **~let** *n* salida *f*; (Com) punto *m* de venta; (Amer, Elec) toma *f* de corriente. **~line** *n* contorno *m*; (summary) resumen *m*; (plan of project) esquema *m*. ● *vt* trazar; (summarize) esbozar. **~live** /-ˈlɪv/ *vt* sobrevivir a. **~look** *n* perspectivas *fpl*; (attitude) punto *m* de vista. **~lying** *a* alejado. **~number** /-ˈnʌmbə(r)/ *vt* superar en número. **~-of-date** *a* <*ideas*> desfasado; <*clothes*> pasado de moda. **~patient** *n* paciente *m* externo. **~post** *n* avanzada *f*. **~put** *n* producción *f*; (of machine, worker) rendimiento *m*. **~right** *adv* completamente; (frankly) abiertamente; <*kill*> en el acto. ● *a* completo; <*refusal*> rotundo. **~set** *n* principio *m*. **~side** *a & n* exterior (*m*). **at the ~side** como máximo. ● /-ˈsaɪd/ *adv* fuera, afuera (LAm). ● *prep* fuera de. **~size** *a* de talla gigante. **~skirts** *npl* afueras *fpl*. **~spoken** /-ˈspəʊkn/ *a* directo, franco. **~standing** /-ˈstændɪŋ/ *a* excepcional; <*debt*> pendiente. **~stretched** /aʊt ˈstretʃt/ *a* extendido. **~strip** /-ˈstrɪp/ *vt* (*pt* **-stripped**) (run faster than) tomarle la delantera a; (exceed)sobrepasar. **~ward** /-wəd/ *a* <*appearance*> exterior; <*sign*> externo; <*journey*> de ida.

~wardly *adv* por fuera, exteriormente. **~(s)** *adv* hacia afuera. **~weigh** /-'weɪ/ *vt* ser mayor que. **~wit** /-'wɪt/ *vt* (*pt* **-witted**) burlar

oval /'əʊvl/ *a* ovalado, oval. ● *n* óvalo *m*

ovary /'əʊvərɪ/ *n* ovario *m*

ovation /əʊ'veɪʃn/ *n* ovación *f*

oven /'ʌvn/ *n* horno *m*

over /'əʊvə(r)/ *prep* por encima de; (across) al otro lado de; (during) durante; (more than) más de. **~ and above** por encima de. ● *adv* por encima; (ended) terminado; (more) más; (in excess) de sobra. **~ again** otra vez. **~ and ~** una y otra vez. **~ here** por aquí. **~ there** por allí. **all ~** (finished) acabado; (everywhere) por todas partes

over... /'əʊvə(r)/ *pref* excesivamente, demasiado

over: ~all /-'ɔ:l/ *a* global; <*length, cost*> total. ● *adv* en conjunto. ● /'əʊvərɔ:l/ *n*, **~alls** *npl* mono *m*, overol *m* (LAm); (Amer, dungarees) peto *m*, overol *m*. **~awe** /-'ɔ:/ *vt* intimidar. **~balance** /-'bæləns/ *vi* perder el equilibrio. **~bearing** /-'beərɪŋ/ *a* dominante. **~board** *adv* <*throw*> por la borda. **~cast** /-'kɑ:st/ *a* <*day*> nublado; <*sky*> cubierto. **~charge** /-'tʃɑ:dʒ/ *vt* cobrarle de más. **~coat** *n* abrigo *m*. **~come** /-'kʌm/ *vt* (*pt* **-came**, *pp* **-come**) superar, vencer. **~crowded** /-'kraʊdɪd/ *a* abarrotado (de gente). **~do** /-'du:/ *vt* (*pt* **-did**, *pp* **-done**) exagerar; (Culin) recocer. **~dose** *n* sobredosis *f*. **~draft** *n* descubierto *m*. **~draw** /-'drɔ:/ *vt* (*pt* **-drew**, *pp* **-drawn**) girar en descubierto. **be ~drawn** tener un descubierto. **~due** /-'dju:/ *a*. **the book is a month ~due** el plazo de devolución del libro venció hace un mes. **~estimate** /-'estɪmeɪt/ *vt* sobreestimar. **~flow** /-'fləʊ/ *vi* desbordarse. ● *n* /-fləʊ/ (excess) exceso *m*; (outlet) rebosadero *m*. **~grown** /-'grəʊn/ *a* demasiado grande; <*garden*> lleno de maleza. **~haul** /-'hɔ:l/ *vt* revisar. ● /-hɔ:l/ *n* revisión *f*. **~head** /-'hed/ *adv* por encima. ● /-hed/ *a* de arriba. **~heads** /-hedz/ *npl*, **~head** *n* (Amer) gastos *mpl* indirectos. **~hear** /-'hɪə(r)/ *vt* (*pt* **-heard**) oír por casualidad. **~joyed** /-'dʒɔɪd/ *a* encantado. **~land** *a*/*adv* por tierra. **~lap** /-'læp/ *vi* (*pt* **-lapped**) traslaparse. **~leaf** /-'li:f/ *adv* al dorso. **~load** /-'ləʊd/ *vt* sobrecargar. **~look** /-'lʊk/ *vt* <*room*> dar a; (not notice) pasar por alto; (disregard) disculpar. **~night** /-'naɪt/ *adv* durante la noche. **stay ~night** quedarse a pasar la noche. ● *a* <*journey*> de noche; <*stay*> de una noche. **~pass** *n* paso *m* elevado, paso *m* a desnivel (Mex). **~pay** /-'peɪ/ *vt* (*pt* **-paid**) pagar demasiado. **~power** /-'paʊə(r)/ *vt* dominar <*opponent*>; <*emotion*> abrumar. **~powering** /-'paʊərɪŋ/ *a* <*smell*> muy fuerte; <*desire*> irresistible. **~priced** /-'praɪst/ *a* demasiado caro. **~rated** /-'reɪtɪd/ *a* sobrevalorado. **~react** /-rɪ'ækt/ *vi* reaccionar en forma exagerada. **~ride** /-'raɪd/ *vt* (*pt* **-rode**, *pp* **-ridden**) invalidar. **~riding** /-'raɪdɪŋ/ *a* dominante. **~rule** /-'ru:l/ *vt* anular; rechazar <*objection*>. **~run** /-'rʌn/ *vt* (*pt* **-ran**, *pp* **-run**, *pres p* **-running**) invadir; exceder <*limit*>. **~seas** /-'si:z/ *a* <*trade*> exterior; <*investments*> en el exterior; <*visitor*> extranjero. ● *adv* al extranjero. **~see** /-'si:/ *vt* (*pt* **-saw**, *pp* **-seen**) supervisar.

~seer /-sɪə(r)/ *n* capataz *m & f*, supervisor *m*. **~shadow** /-ˈʃædəʊ/ *vt* eclipsar. **~shoot** /-ˈʃuːt/ *vt* (*pt* **-shot**) excederse. **~sight** *n* descuido *m*. **~sleep** /-ˈsliːp/ *vi* (*pt* **-slept**) quedarse dormido. **~step** /-ˈstep/ *vt* (*pt* **-stepped**) sobrepasar. **~step the mark** pasarse de la raya

overt /ˈəʊvɜːt/ *a* manifiesto

over: ~take /-ˈteɪk/ *vt/i* (*pt* **-took**, *pp* **-taken**) sobrepasar; (Auto) adelantar, rebasar (Mex). **~throw** /-ˈθrəʊ/ *vt* (*pt* **-threw**, *pp* **-thrown**) derrocar. **~time** *n* horas *fpl* extra

overture /ˈəʊvətjʊə(r)/ *n* obertura *f*

over: ~turn /-ˈtɜːn/ *vt* darle la vuelta a. ● *vi* volcar. **~weight** /-ˈweɪt/ *a* demasiado gordo. **be ~weight** pesar demasiado. **~whelm** /-ˈwelm/ *vt* aplastar; (with emotion) abrumar. **~whelming** *a* aplastante; (fig) abrumador. **~work** /-ˈwɜːk/ *vt* hacer trabajar demasiado. ● *vi* trabajar demasiado. ● *n* agotamiento *m*

ow|e /əʊ/ *vt* deber. **~ing to** debido a

owl /aʊl/ *n* búho *m*

own /əʊn/ *a* propio. **my ~ house** mi propia casa. ● *pron*. **it's my ~** es mío (propio)/mía (propia). **on one's ~** solo. **get one's ~ back** Ⓘ desquitarse. ● *vt* tener. □ **~ up** *vi*. Ⓘ confesarse culpable. **~er** *n* propietario *m*, dueño *m*. **~ership** *n* propiedad *f*

oxygen /ˈɒksɪdʒən/ *n* oxígeno *m*

oyster /ˈɔɪstə(r)/ *n* ostra *f*

Pp

p *abbr* (= **pence, penny**) penique(s) *m(pl)*

p. (*pl* **pp.**) (= **page**) pág., p.

pace /peɪs/ *n* paso *m*. **keep ~ with s.o.** seguirle el ritmo a uno. ● *vi*. **~ up and down** andar de un lado para otro. **~maker** *n* (runner) liebre *f*; (Med) marcapasos *m*

Pacific /pəˈsɪfɪk/ *n*. **the ~ (Ocean)** el (Océano) Pacífico *m*

pacif|ist /ˈpæsɪfɪst/ *n* pacifista *m & f*. **~y** /ˈpæsɪfaɪ/ *vt* apaciguar

pack /pæk/ *n* fardo *m*; (of cigarettes) paquete *m*, cajetilla *f*; (of cards) baraja *f*; (of hounds) jauría *f*; (of wolves) manada *f*. **a ~ of lies** una sarta de mentiras. ● *vt* empaquetar; hacer *<suitcase>*; (press down) apisonar. ● *vi* hacer la maleta, empacar (LAm). **~age** /-ɪdʒ/ *n* paquete *m*. **~age holiday** *n* vacaciones *fpl* organizadas. **~ed** /pækt/ *a* lleno (de gente). **~et** /ˈpækɪt/ *n* paquete *m*

pact /pækt/ *n* pacto *m*, acuerdo *m*

pad /pæd/ *n* (for writing) bloc *m*. **shoulder ~s** hombreras *fpl*. ● *vt* (*pt* **padded**) rellenar

paddle /ˈpædl/ *n* pala *f*. ● *vi* mojarse los pies; (in canoe) remar (*con pala*)

paddock /ˈpædək/ *n* prado *m*

padlock /ˈpædlɒk/ *n* candado *m*. ● *vt* cerrar con candado

paed|iatrician /piːdɪəˈtrɪʃn/ *n* pediatra *m & f*. **~ophile** /ˈpiːdəfaɪl/ *n* pedófilo *m*

pagan /ˈpeɪgən/ *a & n* pagano (*m*)

page /peɪdʒ/ *n* página *f*; (attendant) paje *m*; (in hotel) botones *m*. ● *vt* llamar por megafonía/por buscapersonas

paid /peɪd/ ⇒PAY. ● *a*. **put ~ to** 🅸 acabar con

pail /peɪl/ *n* balde *m*, cubo *m*

pain /peɪn/ *n* dolor *m*. **I have a ~ in my back** me duele la espalda. *m*. **be in ~** tener dolores. **be a ~ in the neck** 🅸 ser un pesado; (thing) ser una lata. ● *vt* doler. **~ful** *a* doloroso. **it's very ~ful** duele mucho. **~-killer** *n* analgésico *m*. **~less** *a* indoloro. **~staking** /ˈpeɪnzteɪkɪŋ/ *a* concienzudo

paint /peɪnt/ *n* pintura *f*. ● *vt/i* pintar. **~er** *n* pintor *m*. **~ing** *n* (medium) pintura *f*; (picture) cuadro *m*

pair /peə(r)/ *n* par *m*; (of people) pareja *f*. **a ~ of trousers** unos pantalones. □ **~off, ~ up** *vi* formar parejas

pajamas /pəˈdʒɑːməz/ *npl* (Amer) pijama *m*

Pakistan /pɑːkɪˈstɑːn/ *n* Pakistán *m*. **~i** *a & n* paquistaní (*m & f*)

pal /pæl/ *n* 🅸 amigo *m*

palace /ˈpælɪs/ *n* palacio *m*

palat|able /ˈpælətəbl/ *a* agradable. **~e** /ˈpælət/ *n* paladar *m*

pale /peɪl/ *a* (**-er**, **-est**) pálido. **go ~, turn ~** palidecer. **~ness** *n* palidez *f*

Palestin|e /ˈpælɪstaɪn/ *n* Palestina *f*. **~ian** /-ˈstɪnɪən/ *a & n* palestino (*m*)

palette /ˈpælɪt/ *n* paleta *f*

palm /pɑːm/ *n* palma *f*. □ **~ off** *vt* encajar (**on** a). **P~ Sunday** *n* Domingo *m* de Ramos

palpable /ˈpælpəbl/ *a* palpable

palpitat|e /ˈpælpɪteɪt/ *vi* palpitar. **~ion** /-ˈteɪʃn/ *n* palpitación *f*

pamper /ˈpæmpə(r)/ *vt* mimar

pamphlet /ˈpæmflɪt/ *n* folleto *m*

pan /pæn/ *n* cacerola *f*; (for frying) sartén *f*

panacea /pænəˈsɪə/ *n* panacea *f*

Panama /ˈpænəmɑː/ *n* Panamá *m*. **~nian** /-ˈmeɪnɪən/ *a & n* panameño (*m*)

pancake /ˈpænkeɪk/ *n* crep(e) *m*, panqueque *m* (LAm)

panda /ˈpændə/ *n* panda *m*

pandemonium /pændɪˈməʊnɪəm/ *n* pandemonio *m*

pander /ˈpændə(r)/ *vi*. **~ to s.o.** consentirle los caprichos a uno

pane /peɪn/ *n* vidrio *m*, cristal *m*

panel /ˈpænl/ *n* panel *m*; (group of people) jurado *m*. **~ling** *n* paneles *mpl*

pang /pæŋ/ *n* punzada *f*

panic /ˈpænɪk/ *n* pánico *m*. ● *vi* (*pt* **panicked**) dejarse llevar por el pánico. **~-stricken** *a* aterrorizado

panoram|a /pænəˈrɑːmə/ *n* panorama *m*. **~ic** /-ˈræmɪk/ *a* panorámico

pansy /ˈpænzɪ/ *n* (Bot) pensamiento *m*

pant /pænt/ *vi* jadear

panther /ˈpænθə(r)/ *n* pantera *f*

panties /ˈpæntɪz/ *npl* bragas *fpl*, calzones *mpl* (LAm), pantaletas *fpl* (Mex)

pantihose /ˈpæntɪhəʊz/ *npl* ⇒PANTYHOSE

pantomime /ˈpæntəmaɪm/ *n* pantomima *f*

pantry /ˈpæntrɪ/ *n* despensa *f*

pants /pænts/ *npl* (man's) calzoncillos *mpl*; (woman's) bragas *fpl*, calzones *mpl* (LAm), pantaletas *fpl* (Mex); (Amer, trousers) pantalones *mpl*

pantyhose /'pæntɪhəʊz/ *npl* (Amer) panty *m*, medias *fpl*, pantimedias *fpl* (Mex)

paper /'peɪpə(r)/ *n* papel *m*; (newspaper) diario *m*, periódico *m*; (exam) examen *m*; (document) documento *m*. ● *vt* empapelar, tapizar (Mex). **~back** *n* libro *m* en rústica. **~ clip** *n* sujetapapeles *m*, clip *m*. **~weight** *n* pisapapeles *m*. **~work** *n* papeleo *m*, trabajo *m* administrativo

parable /'pærəbl/ *n* parábola *f*

parachut|e /'pærəʃu:t/ *n* paracaídas *m*. ● *vi* saltar en paracaídas. **~ist** *n* paracaidista *m & f*

parade /pə'reɪd/ *n* desfile *m*; (Mil) formación *f*. ● *vi* desfilar. ● *vt* hacer alarde de

paradise /'pærədaɪs/ *n* paraíso *m*

paraffin /'pærəfɪn/ *n* queroseno *m*

paragraph /'pærəgrɑ:f/ *n* párrafo *m*

Paraguay /'pærəgwaɪ/ *n* Paraguay *m*. **~an** *a & n* paraguayo (*m*)

parallel /'pærəlel/ *a* paralelo. ● *n* paralelo *m*; (line) paralela *f*

paraly|se /'pærəlaɪz/ *vt* paralizar. **~sis** /pə'ræləsɪs/ *n* (*pl* **-ses** /-si:z/) parálisis *f*

paranoia /pærə'nɔɪə/ *n* paranoia *f*

parapet /'pærəpɪt/ *n* parapeto *m*

paraphernalia /pærəfə'neɪlɪə/ *n* trastos *mpl*

parasite /'pærəsaɪt/ *n* parásito *m*

paratrooper /'pærətru:pə(r)/ *n* paracaidista *m* (*del ejército*)

parcel /'pɑ:sl/ *n* paquete *m*

parch /pɑ:tʃ/ *vt* resecar. **be ~ed** 🄸 estar muerto de sed

parchment /'pɑ:tʃmənt/ *n* pergamino *m*

pardon /'pɑ:dn/ *n* perdón *m*; (Jurid) indulto *m*. **I beg your ~** perdón. (**I beg your**) **~?** ¿cómo?, ¿mande? (Mex). ● *vt* perdonar; (Jurid) indultar. **~ me?** (Amer) ¿cómo?

parent /'peərənt/ *n* (father) padre *m*; (mother) madre *f*. **my ~s** mis padres. **~al** /pə'rentl/ *a* de los padres

parenthesis /pə'renθəsɪs/ *n* (*pl* **-theses** /-si:z/) paréntesis *m*

parenthood /'peərənthʊd/ *n* el ser padre/madre

Paris /'pærɪs/ *n* París *m*

parish /'pærɪʃ/ *n* parroquia *f*; (municipal) distrito *m*. **~ioner** /pə'rɪʃənə(r)/ *n* feligrés *m*

park /pɑ:k/ *n* parque *m*. ● *vt/i* aparcar, estacionar (LAm)

parking /'pɑ:kɪŋ/: **~ lot** *n* (Amer) aparcamiento *m*, estacionamiento *m* (LAm). **~ meter** *n* parquímetro *m*

parkway /'pɑ:kweɪ/ *n* (Amer) carretera *f* ajardinada

parliament /'pɑ:ləmənt/ *n* parlamento *m*. **~ary** /-'mentrɪ/ *a* parlamentario

parlour /'pɑ:lə(r)/ *n* salón *m*

parochial /pə'rəʊkɪəl/ *a* (fig) provinciano

parody /'pærədɪ/ *n* parodia *f*. ● *vt* parodiar

parole /pə'rəʊl/ *n* libertad *f* condicional

parrot /'pærət/ *n* loro *m*, papagayo *m*

parsley /'pɑ:slɪ/ *n* perejil *m*

parsnip /'pɑ:snɪp/ *n* pastinaca *f*

part /pɑ:t/ *n* parte *f*; (of machine) pieza *f*; (of serial) episodio *m*; (in play) papel *m*; (Amer, in hair) raya *f*. **take ~ in** tomar parte en, participar en. **for the most ~** en su mayor parte. ● *adv* en parte. ● *vt* separar. ● *vi* separarse. □ **~ with** *vt* desprenderse de

partial /'pɑ:ʃl/ *a* parcial. **be ~ to** tener debilidad por. **~ly** *adv* parcialmente

participa|nt /pɑ:'tɪsɪpənt/ *n* participante *m & f*. **~te** /-peɪt/ *vi* participar. **~tion** /-'peɪʃn/ *n* participación *f*

particle /'pɑ:tɪkl/ *n* partícula *f*

particular /pə'tɪkjʊlə(r)/ *a* particular; (precise) meticuloso; (fastidious) quisquilloso. **in ~** en particular. ● *n* detalle *m*. **~ly** *adv* particularmente; (specifically) específicamente

parting /'pɑ:tɪŋ/ *n* despedida *f*; (in hair) raya *f*. ● *a* de despedida

partition /pɑ:'tɪʃn/ *n* partición *f*; (wall) tabique *m*. ● *vt* dividir

partly /'pɑ:tlɪ/ *adv* en parte

partner /'pɑ:tnə(r)/ *n* socio *m*; (Sport) pareja *f*. **~ship** *n* asociación *f*; (Com) sociedad *f*

partridge /'pɑ:trɪdʒ/ *n* perdiz *f*

part-time /pɑ:t'taɪm/ *a & adv* a tiempo parcial, de medio tiempo (LAm)

party /'pɑ:tɪ/ *n* reunión *f*, fiesta *f*; (group) grupo *m*; (Pol) partido *m*; (Jurid) parte *f*

pass /pɑ:s/ *vt* (hand, convey) pasar; (go past) pasar por delante de; (overtake) adelantar, rebasar (Mex); (approve) aprobar <*exam, bill, law*>; pronunciar <*judgement*>. ● *vi* pasar; <*pain*> pasarse; (Sport) pasar la pelota. □ **~ away** *vi* fallecer. □ **~ down** *vt* transmitir. □ **~ out** *vi* desmayarse. □ **~ round** *vt* distribuir. □ **~ up** *vt* ⓘ dejar pasar. ● *n* (permit) pase *m*; (ticket) abono *m*; (in mountains) puerto *m*, desfiladero *m*; (Sport) pase *m*; (in exam) aprobado *m*. **make a ~ at** ⓘ intentar besar. **~able** *a* pasable; <*road*> transitable

passage /'pæsɪdʒ/ *n* (voyage) travesía *f*; (corridor) pasillo *m*; (alleyway) pasaje *m*; (in book) pasaje *m*

passenger /'pæsɪndʒə(r)/ *n* pasajero *m*

passer-by /pɑ:sə'baɪ/ *n* (*pl* **passers-by**) transeúnte *m & f*

passion /'pæʃn/ *n* pasión *f*. **~ate** /-ət/ *a* apasionado. **~ately** *adv* apasionadamente

passive /'pæsɪv/ *a* pasivo

Passover /'pɑ:səʊvə(r)/ *n* Pascua *f* de los hebreos

pass: ~port *n* pasaporte *m*. **~word** *n* contraseña *f*

past /pɑ:st/ *a* anterior; <*life*> pasado; <*week, year*> último. **in times ~** en tiempos pasados. ● *n* pasado *m*. **in the ~** (formerly) antes, antiguamente. ● *prep* por delante de; (beyond) más allá de. **it's twenty ~ four** son las cuatro y veinte. ● *adv*. **drive ~** pasar en coche. **go ~** pasar

paste /peɪst/ *n* pasta *f*; (glue) engrudo *m*; (wallpaper ~) pegamento *m*; (jewellery) estrás *m*

pastel /'pæstl/ *a & n* pastel (*m*)

pasteurize /'pɑ:stʃəraɪz/ *vt* pasteurizar

pastime /'pɑ:staɪm/ *n* pasatiempo *m*

pastry /'peɪstrɪ/ *n* masa *f*; (cake) pastelito *m*

pasture /'pɑ:stʃə(r)/ *n* pasto(s) *m*(*pl*)

pasty /'pæstɪ/ *n* empanadilla *f*, empanada *f* (LAm)

pat /pæt/ *vt* (*pt* **patted**) darle palmaditas. ● *n* palmadita *f*; (of butter) porción *f*

patch /pætʃ/ *n* (on clothes) remiendo *m*, parche *m*; (over eye) parche *m*. **a bad ~** una mala racha. ● *vt* remendar. □ **~ up** *vt* hacerle un arreglo a

patent /'peɪtnt/ *a* patente. ● *n* patente *f*. ● *vt* patentar. **~ leather** *n* charol *m*. **~ly** *adv*. **it's ~ly obvious that...** está clarísimo que...

patern|al /pə'tɜːnl/ *a* paterno. **~ity** /-ətɪ/ *n* paternidad *f*

path /pɑːθ/ *n* (*pl* **-s** /pɑːðz/) sendero *m*; (Sport) pista *f*; (of rocket) trayectoria *f*; (fig) camino *m*

pathetic /pə'θetɪk/ *a* (pitiful) patético; <*excuse*> pobre. **don't be so ~** no seas tan pusilánime

patien|ce /'peɪʃns/ *n* paciencia *f*. **~t** *a* & *n* paciente (*m* & *f*). **be ~t with s.o.** tener paciencia con uno. **~tly** *adv* pacientemente

patio /'pætɪəʊ/ *n* (*pl* **-os**) patio *m*

patriot /'pætrɪət/ *n* patriota *m* & *f*. **~ic** /-'ɒtɪk/ *a* patriótico. **~ism** *n* patriotismo *m*

patrol /pə'trəʊl/ *n* patrulla *f*. ● *vt/i* patrullar

patron /'peɪtrən/ *n* (of the arts) mecenas *m* & *f*; (of charity) patrocinador *m*; (customer) cliente *m* & *f*. **~age** /'pætrənɪdʒ/ *n* (sponsorship) patrocinio *m*; (of the arts) mecenazgo *m*. **~ize** /'pætrənaɪz/ *vt* ser cliente de; (fig) tratar con condescendencia. **~izing** *a* condescendiente

pattern /'pætn/ *n* diseño *m*; (sample) muestra *f*; (in dressmaking) patrón *m*

paunch /pɔːntʃ/ *n* panza *f*

pause /pɔːz/ *n* pausa *f*. ● *vi* hacer una pausa

pave /peɪv/ *vt* pavimentar; (with flagstones) enlosar. **~ment** *n* pavimento *m*; (at side of road) acera *f*, banqueta *f* (Mex)

paving stone /'peɪvɪŋstəʊn/ *n* losa *f*

paw /pɔː/ *n* pata *f*

pawn /pɔːn/ *n* (Chess) peón *m*; (fig) títere *m*. ● *vt* empeñar. **~broker** *n* prestamista *m* & *f*

pay /peɪ/ *vt* (*pt* **paid**) pagar; prestar <*attention*>; hacer <*compliment, visit*>. **~ cash** pagar al contado. ● *vi* pagar; (be profitable) rendir. ● *n* paga *f*. **in the ~ of** al servicio de. □ **~ back** *vt* devolver; pagar <*loan*>. □ **~ in** *vt* ingresar, depositar (LAm). □ **~ off** *vt* cancelar, saldar <*debt*>. *vi* valer la pena. □ **~ up** *vi* pagar. **~able** *a* pagadero. **~ment** *n* pago *m*. **~roll** *n* nómina *f*

pea /piː/ *n* guisante *m*, arveja *f* (LAm), chícharo *m* (Mex)

peace /piːs/ *n* paz *f*. **~ of mind** tranquilidad *f*. **~ful** *a* tranquilo. **~maker** *n* conciliador *m*

peach /piːtʃ/ *n* melocotón *m*, durazno *m* (LAm)

peacock /'piːkɒk/ *n* pavo *m* real

peak /piːk/ *n* cumbre *f*; (of career) apogeo *m*; (maximum) máximo *m*. **~ hours** *npl* horas *fpl* de mayor demanda (*o consumo etc*)

peal /piːl/ *n* repique *m*. **~s of laughter** risotadas *fpl*

peanut /'piːnʌt/ *n* cacahuete *m*, maní *m* (LAm), cacahuate *m* (Mex)

pear /peə(r)/ *n* pera *f*. **~ (tree)** peral *m*

pearl /pɜːl/ *n* perla *f*

peasant /ˈpeznt/ *n* campesino *m*
peat /piːt/ *n* turba *f*
pebble /ˈpebl/ *n* guijarro *m*
peck /pek/ *vt* picotear. ● *n* picotazo *m*; (kiss) besito *m*
peculiar /prˈkjuːlɪə(r)/ *a* raro; (special) especial. **~ity** /-ˈærətɪ/ *n* rareza *f*; (feature) particularidad *f*
pedal /ˈpedl/ *n* pedal *m*. ● *vi* pedalear
pedantic /prˈdæntɪk/ *a* pedante
peddle /ˈpedl/ *vt* vender por las calles
pedestal /ˈpedɪstl/ *n* pedestal *m*
pedestrian /prˈdestrɪən/ *n* peatón *m*. **~ crossing** paso *m* de peatones. ● *a* pedestre; (dull) prosaico
pedigree /ˈpedɪgriː/ linaje *m*; (of animal) pedigrí *m*. ● *a* <*animal*> de raza
peek /piːk/ *vi* mirar a hurtadillas
peel /piːl/ *n* piel *f*, cáscara *f*. ● *vt* pelar <*fruit, vegetables*>. ● *vi* pelarse
peep /piːp/ *vi*. **~ at** echarle un vistazo a. ● *n* (look) vistazo *m*; (bird sound) pío *m*
peer /pɪə(r)/ *vi* mirar. **~ at** escudriñar. ● *n* (equal) par *m* & *f*; (contemporary) coetáneo *m*; (lord) par *m*. **~age** /-ɪdʒ/ *n* nobleza *f*
peg /peg/ *n* (in ground) estaca *f*; (on violin) clavija *f*; (for washing) pinza *f*; (hook) gancho *m*; (for tent) estaquilla *f*. **off the ~** de confección. ● *vt* (*pt* **pegged**) sujetar (*con estacas, etc*); fijar <*precios*>
pejorative /prˈdʒɒrətɪv/ *a* peyorativo, despectivo
pelican /ˈpelɪkən/ *n* pelícano *m*
pellet /ˈpelɪt/ *n* bolita *f*; (for gun) perdigón *m*
pelt /pelt/ *n* pellejo *m*. ● *vt*. **~ s.o. with sth** lanzarle algo a uno. ● *vi*. **~ with rain, ~ down** llover a cántaros
pelvis /ˈpelvɪs/ *n* pelvis *f*
pen /pen/ (for writing) pluma *f*; (ball-point) bolígrafo *m*; (sheep **~**) redil *m*; (cattle **~**) corral *m*
penal /ˈpiːnl/ *a* penal. **~ize** *vt* sancionar. **~ty** /ˈpenltɪ/ *n* pena *f*; (fine) multa *f*; (in soccer) penalty *m*; (in US football) castigo *m*. **~ty kick** *n* (in soccer) penalty *m*
penance /ˈpenəns/ *n* penitencia *f*
pence /pens/ ⇒PENNY
pencil /ˈpensl/ *n* lápiz *m*. ● *vt* (*pt* **pencilled**) escribir con lápiz. **~-sharpener** *n* sacapuntas *m*
pendulum /ˈpendjʊləm/ *n* péndulo *m*
penetrat|e /ˈpenɪtreɪt/ *vt/i* penetrar. **~ing** *a* penetrante. **~ion** /-ˈtreɪʃn/ *n* penetración *f*
penguin /ˈpeŋgwɪn/ *n* pingüino *m*
penicillin /penɪˈsɪlɪn/ *n* penicilina *f*
peninsula /pəˈnɪnsjʊlə/ *n* península *f*
penis /ˈpiːnɪs/ *n* pene *m*
pen: ~knife /ˈpennaɪf/ *n* (*pl* **penknives**) navaja *f*. **~-name** *n* seudónimo *m*
penn|iless /ˈpenɪlɪs/ *a* sin un céntimo. **~y** /ˈpenɪ/ *n* (*pl* **pennies** *or* **pence**) penique *m*
pension /ˈpenʃn/ *n* pensión *f*; (for retirement) pensión *f* de jubilación. **~er** *n* jubilado *m*
pensive /ˈpensɪv/ *a* pensativo
Pentecost /ˈpentɪkɒst/ *n* Pentecostés *m*
penthouse /ˈpenthaʊs/ *n* penthouse *m*

pent-up /pent'ʌp/ *a* reprimido; (confined) encerrado

penultimate /pen'ʌltɪmət/ *a* penúltimo

people /'pi:pl/ *npl* gente *f*; (citizens) pueblo *m*. ~ **say (that)** se dice que, dicen que. **English** ~ los ingleses. **young** ~ los jóvenes. **the** ~ (nation) el pueblo. ● *vt* poblar

pepper /'pepə(r)/ *n* pimienta *f*; (vegetable) pimiento *m*. ● *vt* (intersperse) salpicar (**with** de). ~**box** *n* (Amer) pimentero *m*. ~**corn** *n* grano *m* de pimienta. ~**mint** *n* menta *f*; (sweet) caramelo *m* de menta. ~**pot** *n* pimentero *m*

per /pɜ:(r)/ *prep* por. ~ **annum** al año. ~ **cent** ⇒PERCENT. ~ **head** por cabeza, por persona. **ten miles** ~ **hour** diez millas por hora

perceive /pə'si:v/ *vt* percibir; (notice) darse cuenta de

percent, **per cent** /pə'sent/ *n* (*no pl*) porcentaje *m*. ● *adv* por ciento. ~**age** /-ɪdʒ/ *n* porcentaje *m*

percepti|ble /pə'septəbl/ *a* perceptible. ~**on** /-ʃn/ *n* percepción *f*. ~**ve** /-tɪv/ *a* perspicaz

perch /pɜ:tʃ/ *n* (of bird) percha *f*; (fish) perca *f*. ● *vi* <*bird*> posarse. ~ **on** <*person*> sentarse en el borde de

percolat|e /'pɜ:kəleɪt/ *vi* filtrarse. ~**or** *n* cafetera *f* eléctrica

percussion /pə'kʌʃn/ *n* percusión *f*

perfect /'pɜ:fɪkt/ *a* perfecto; <*place, day*> ideal. ● /pə'fekt/ *vt* perfeccionar. ~**ion** /pə'fekʃn/ *n* perfección *f*. **to** ~**ion** a la perfección. ~**ly** /'pɜ:fɪktlɪ/ *adv* perfectamente

perform /pə'fɔ:m/ *vt* desempeñar <*function, role*>; ejecutar <*task*>; realizar <*experiment*>; representar <*play*>; (Mus) interpretar. ~ **an operation** (Med) operar. ● *vi* <*actor*> actuar; <*musician*> tocar; (produce results) <*vehicle*> responder; <*company*> rendir. ~**ance** /-əns/ *n* ejecución *f*; (of play) representación *f*; (of actor, musician) interpretación *f*; (of team) actuación *f*; (of car) rendimiento *m*. ~**er** *n* (actor) actor *m*; (entertainer) artista *m & f*

perfume /'pɜ:fju:m/ *n* perfume *m*

perhaps /pə'hæps/ *adv* quizá(s), tal vez, a lo mejor

peril /'perəl/ *n* peligro *m*. ~**ous** *a* arriesgado, peligroso

perimeter /pə'rɪmɪtə(r)/ *n* perímetro *m*

period /'pɪərɪəd/ *n* período *m*; (in history) época *f*; (lesson) clase *f*; (Amer, Gram) punto *m*; (menstruation) período *m*, regla *f*. ● *a* de (la) época. ~**ic** /-'ɒdɪk/ *a* periódico. ~**ical** /pɪərɪ'ɒdɪkl/ *n* revista *f*. ~**ically** *adv* periódico

peripher|al /pə'rɪfərəl/ *a* secundario; (Comp) periférico. ~**y** /pə'rɪfərɪ/ *n* periferia *f*

perish /'perɪʃ/ *vi* perecer; (rot) deteriorarse. ~**able** *a* perecedero. ~**ing** *a* 🅸 glacial

perjur|e /'pɜ:dʒə(r)/ *vr*. ~**e o.s.** perjurarse. ~**y** *n* perjurio *m*

perk /pɜ:k/ *n* gaje *m*. □ ~ **up** *vt* reanimar. *vi* reanimarse

perm /pɜ:m/ *n* permanente *f*. ● *vt*. **have one's hair** ~**ed** hacerse la permanente

permanen|ce /'pɜ:mənəns/ *n* permanencia *f*. ~**t** *a* permanente. ~**tly** *adv* permanentemente

permissible /pə'mɪsəbl/ *a* permisible

permission /pə'mɪʃn/ *n* permiso *m*

permit /pə'mɪt/ *vt* (*pt* **permitted**) permitir. ● /'pɜ:mɪt/ *n* permiso *m*

peroxide /pə'rɒksaɪd/ *n* peróxido *m*

perpendicular /pɜ:pən'dɪkjʊlə(r)/ *a & n* perpendicular (*f*)

perpetrat|e /'pɜ:pɪtreɪt/ *vt* cometer. **~or** *n* autor *m*

perpetua|l /pə'petʃʊəl/ *a* perpetuo. **~te** /pə'petʃʊeɪt/ *vt* perpetuar

perplex /pə'pleks/ *vt* dejar perplejo. **~ed** *a* perplejo

persecut|e /'pɜ:sɪkju:t/ *vt* perseguir. **~ion** /-'kju:ʃn/ *n* persecución *f*

persever|ance /pɜ:sɪ'vɪərəns/ *n* perseverancia *f*. **~e** /pɜ:sɪ'vɪə(r)/ *vi* perseverar, persistir

Persian /'pɜ:ʃn/ *a* persa. **the ~ Gulf** *n* el golfo Pérsico

persist /pə'sɪst/ *vi* persistir. **~ence** /-əns/ *n* persistencia *f*. **~ent** *a* persistente; (continual) continuo

person /'pɜ:sn/ *n* persona *f*. **in ~** en persona. **~al** *a* personal; <*call*> particular; <*property*> privado. **~al assistant** *n* secretario *m* personal. **~ality** /-'nælətɪ/ *n* personalidad *f*. **~ally** *adv* personalmente. **~nel** /pɜ:sə'nel/ *n* personal *m*. **P~** (department) sección *f* de personal

perspective /pə'spektɪv/ *n* perspectiva *f*

perspir|ation /pɜ:spə'reɪʃn/ *n* transpiración *f*. **~e** /pəs'paɪə(r)/ *vi* transpirar

persua|de /pə'sweɪd/ *vt* convencer, persuadir. **~e s.o. to do sth** convencer a uno para quehaga algo. **~sion** *n* /-ʃn/ persuasión *f*. **~sive** /-sɪv/ *a* persuasivo

pertinent /'pɜ:tɪnənt/ *a* pertinente. **~ly** *adv* pertinentemente

perturb /pə'tɜ:b/ *vt* perturbar

Peru /pə'ru:/ *n* el Perú *m*

peruse /pə'ru:z/ *vt* leer cuidadosamente

Peruvian /pə'ru:vɪan/ *a & n* peruano (*m*)

perver|se /pə'vɜ:s/ *a* retorcido; (stubborn) obstinado. **~sion** *n* perversión *f*. **~t** /pə'vɜ:t/ *vt* pervertir. ● /'pɜ:vɜ:t/ *n* pervertido *m*

pessimis|m /'pesɪmɪzəm/ *n* pesimismo *m*. **~t** *n* pesimista *m & f*. **~tic** /-'mɪstɪk/ *a* pesimista

pest /pest/ *n* plaga *f*; (Ⓘ, person, thing) peste *f*

pester /'pestə(r)/ *vt* importunar

pesticide /'pestɪsaɪd/ *n* pesticida *f*

pet /pet/ *n* animal *m* doméstico; (favourite) favorito *m*. ● *a* preferido. **my ~ hate** lo que más odio. ● *vt* (*pt* **petted**) acariciar

petal /'petl/ *n* pétalo *m*

petition /pɪ'tɪʃn/ *n* petición *f*

pet name *n* apodo *m*

petrified /'petrɪfaɪd/ *a* (terrified) muerto de miedo; (Geol) petrificado

petrol /'petrəl/ *n* gasolina *f*. **~eum** /pɪ'trəʊlɪəm/ *n* petróleo *m*. **~ pump** *n* surtidor *m*. **~ station** *n* gasolinera *f*. **~ tank** *n* depósito *m* de gasolina

petticoat /'petɪkəʊt/ *n* enagua *f*; (slip) combinación *f*

petty /'petɪ/ *a* (**-ier, -iest**) insignificante; (mean) mezquino. **~y cash** *n* dinero *m* para gastos menores

petulant /'petjʊlənt/ *a* irritable

pew /pjuː/ *n* banco *m* (de iglesia)

phantom /'fæntəm/ *n* fantasma *m*

pharma|ceutical /fɑːmə'sjuːtɪkl/ *a* farmacéutico. **~cist** /'fɑːməsɪst/ *n* farmacéutico *m*. **~cy** /'fɑːməsɪ/ *n* farmacia *f*

phase /feɪz/ *n* etapa *f*. ◻ **~ out** *vt* retirar progresivamente

PhD *abbr* (= **Doctor of Philosophy**) *n* doctorado *m*; (person) Dr., Dra.

pheasant /'feznt/ *n* faisán *m*

phenomen|al /fɪ'nɒmɪnl/ *a* fenomenal. **~on** /-ɪnən/ *n* (*pl* **-ena** /-inə/) fenómeno *m*

philistine /'fɪlɪstaɪn/ *a* & *n* filisteo (*m*)

philosoph|er /fɪ'lɒsəfə(r)/ *n* filósofo *m*. **~ical** /-ə'sɒfɪkl/ *a* filosófico. **~y** /fɪ'lɒsəfɪ/ *n* filosofía *f*

phlegm /flem/ *n* flema *f*. **~atic** /fleg'mætɪk/ *a* flemático

phobia /'fəʊbɪə/ *n* fobia *f*

phone /fəʊn/ *n* [I] teléfono *m*. ● *vt/i* llamar (por teléfono). **~ back** (call again) volver a llamar; (return call) llamar (más tarde). **~ book** *n* guía *f* telefónica, directorio *m* (LAm). **~ booth**, **~ box** *n* cabina *f* telefónica. **~ call** *n* llamada *f* (telefónica). **~ card** *n* tarjeta *f* telefónica. **~ number** *n* número *m* de teléfono

phonetic /fə'netɪk/ *a* fonético. **~s** *n* fonética *f*

phoney /'fəʊnɪ/ *a* (**-ier**, **-iest**) [I] falso

phosph|ate /'fɒsfeɪt/ *n* fosfato *m*. **~orus** /'fɒsfərəs/ *n* fósforo *m*

photo /'fəʊtəʊ/ *n* (*pl* **-os**) [I] foto *f*. **take a ~** sacar una foto. **~copier** /-kɒpɪə(r)/ *n* fotocopiadora *f*. **~copy** *n* fotocopia *f*. ● *vt* fotocopiar. **~genic** /-'dʒenɪk/ *a* fotogénico. **~graph** /-grɑːf/ *n* fotografía *f*. ● *vt* fotografiar, sacarle una fotografía a. **~grapher** /fə'tɒgrəfə(r)/ *n* fotógrafo *m*. **~graphic** /-'græfɪk/ *a* fotográfico. **~graphy** /fə'tɒgrəfɪ/ *n* fotografía *f*

phrase /freɪz/ *n* frase *f*. ● *vt* expresar. **~ book** *n* manual *m* de conversación

physi|cal /'fɪzɪkl/ *a* físico. **~cian** /fɪ'zɪʃn/ *n* médico *m*. **~cist** /'fɪzɪsɪst/ *n* físico *m*. **~cs** /'fɪzɪks/ *n* física *f*. **~ology** /fɪzɪ'ɒlədʒɪ/ *n* fisiología *f*. **~otherapist** /fɪzɪəʊ'θerəpɪst/ *n* fisioterapeuta *m* & *f*. **~otherapy** /fɪzɪəʊ'θerəpɪ/ *n* fisioterapia *f*. **~que** /fɪ'ziːk/ *n* físico *m*

pian|ist /'pɪənɪst/ *n* pianista *m* & *f*. **~o** /pɪ'ænəʊ/ *n* (*pl* **-os**) piano *m*

pick /pɪk/ (*tool*) pico *m*. ● *vt* escoger; cortar <*flowers*>; recoger <*fruit, cotton*>; abrir con una ganzúa <*lock*>. **~ a quarrel** buscar camorra. **~ holes in** criticar. ◻ **~ on** *vt* meterse con. ◻ **~ out** *vt* escoger; (identify) reconocer. ◻ **~ up** *vt* recoger; (lift) levantar; (learn) aprender; adquirir <*habit, etc*>; contagiarse de <*illness*>. ● *vi* mejorar; <*sales*> subir. **~axe** *n* pico *m*

picket /'pɪkɪt/ *n* (group) piquete *m*. **~ line** *n* piquete *m*. ● *vt* formar un piquete frente a

pickle /'pɪkl/ *n* (in vinegar) encurtido *m*; (Amer, gherkin) pepinillo *m*; (relish) salsa *f* (a base de encurtidos). ● *vt* encurtir

pick: ~pocket *n* carterista *m* & *f*. **~-up** *n* (truck) camioneta *f*

picnic /'pɪknɪk/ *n* picnic *m*

picture /'pɪktʃə(r)/ *n* (painting) cuadro *m*; (photo) foto *f*; (drawing) dibujo *m*; (illustration) ilustración *f*; (film) película *f*; (fig) descripción *f*. ● *vt* imaginarse. **~sque** /-'resk/ *a* pintoresco

pie /paɪ/ *n* empanada *f*; (sweet) pastel *m*, tarta *f*

piece /pi:s/ *n* pedazo *m*, trozo *m*; (part of machine) pieza *f*; (coin) moneda *f*; (in chess) figura *f*. **a ~ of advice** un consejo. **a ~ of furniture** un mueble. **a ~ of news** una noticia. **take to ~s** desmontar. □**~ together** *vt* juntar. **~meal** *a* gradual; (unsystematic) poco sistemático. ● *adv* poco a poco

pier /pɪə(r)/ *n* muelle *m*; (with amusements) *paseo con atracciones sobre un muelle*

pierc|e /pɪəs/ *vt* perforar. **~ing** *a* penetrante

piety /'paɪətɪ/ *n* piedad *f*

pig /pɪg/ *n* cerdo *m*, chancho *m* (LAm)

pigeon /'pɪdʒɪn/ *n* paloma *f*; (Culin) pichón *m*. **~-hole** *n* casillero *m*; (fig) casilla *f*

piggy /'pɪgɪ/ *n* cerdito *m*. **~back** *n*. **give s.o. a ~back** llevar a uno a cuestas. **~ bank** *n* hucha *f*

pig-headed /-'hedɪd/ *a* terco

pigment /'pɪgmənt/ *n* pigmento *m*

pig|sty /'pɪgstaɪ/ *n* pocilga *f*. **~tail** *n* (plait) trenza *f*; (bunch) coleta *f*

pike /paɪk/ *n invar* (fish) lucio *m*

pilchard /'pɪltʃəd/ *n* sardina *f*

pile /paɪl/ *n* (heap) montón *m*; (of fabric) pelo *m*. ● *vt* amontonar. **~ it on** exagerar. ● *vi* amontonarse. □**~ up** *vt* amontonar. ● *vi* amontonarse. **~s** /paɪlz/ *npl* (Med) almorranas *fpl*. **~-up** *n* choque *m* múltiple

pilgrim /'pɪlgrɪm/ *n* peregrino. **~age** /-ɪdʒ/ *n* peregrinación *f*

pill /pɪl/ *n* pastilla *f*

pillar /'pɪlə(r)/ *n* columna *f*. **~ box** *n* buzón *m*

pillow /'pɪləʊ/ *n* almohada *f*. **~case** *n* funda *f* de almohada

pilot /'paɪlət/ *n* piloto *m*. ● *vt* pilotar. **~ light** *n* fuego *m* piloto

pimple /'pɪmpl/ *n* grano *m*, espinilla *f* (LAm)

pin /pɪn/ *n* alfiler *m*; (Mec) perno *m*. **~s and needles** hormigueo *m*. ● *vt* (*pt* **pinned**) prender con alfileres; (fix) sujetar

PIN /pɪn/ *n* (= **personal identification number**) PIN *m*

pinafore /'pɪnəfɔ:(r)/ *n* delantal *m*. **~ dress** *n* pichi *m*, jumper *m* & *f* (LAm)

pincers /'pɪnsəz/ *npl* tenazas *fpl*

pinch /pɪntʃ/ *vt* pellizcar; ([I], steal) hurtar. ● *vi* <*shoe*> apretar. ● *n* pellizco *m*; (small amount) pizca *f*. **at a ~** si fuera necesario

pine /paɪn/ *n* pino *m*. ● *vi*. **~ for sth** suspirar por algo. □**~ away** *vi* languidecer de añoranza. **~apple** /'paɪnæpl/ *n* piña *f*

ping-pong /'pɪŋpɒŋ/ *n* ping-pong *m*

pink /pɪŋk/ *a* & *n* rosa (*m*), rosado (*m*)

pinnacle /'pɪnəkl/ *n* pináculo *m*

pin: ~point *vt* determinar con precisión *f*. **~stripe** *n* raya *f* fina

pint /paɪnt/ *n* pinta *f* (= 0.57 litros)

pioneer /paɪə'nɪə(r)/ *n* pionero *m*

pious /'paɪəs/ *a* piadoso

pip /pɪp/ *n* (seed) pepita *f*; (time signal) señal *f*

pipe /paɪp/ *n* tubo *m*; (Mus) caramillo *m*; (for smoking) pipa *f*. ● *vt* llevar por tuberías. **~-dream** *n* ilusión *f*. **~line** *n* conducto *m*; (for oil) oleoducto *m*. **in the ~line** en preparación *f*

piping /ˈpaɪpɪŋ/ *n* tubería *f*. ● *adv*. **~ hot** muy caliente, hirviendo

pira|cy /ˈpaɪərəsɪ/ *n* piratería *f*. **~te** /ˈpaɪərət/ *n* pirata *m*

Pisces /ˈpaɪsi:z/ *n* Piscis *m*

piss /pɪs/ *vi* ☒ mear. □ **~ off** *vi* ☒. **~ off!** ¡vete a la mierda! **~ed** /pɪst/ *a* (☒, drunk) como una cuba; (Amer, fed up) cabreado

pistol /ˈpɪstl/ *n* pistola *f*

piston /ˈpɪstən/ *n* pistón *m*

pit /pɪt/ *n* hoyo *m*; (mine) mina *f*; (Amer, in fruit) hueso *m*

pitch /pɪtʃ/ *n* (substance) brea *f*; (degree) grado *m*; (Mus) tono *m*; (Sport) campo *m*. ● *vt* (throw) lanzar; armar <*tent*>. ● *vi* <*ship*> cabecear. **~-black** /-ˈblæk/ *a* oscuro como boca de lobo. **~er** *n* jarra *f*

pitfall /ˈpɪtfɔ:l/ *n* trampa *f*

pith /pɪθ/ *n* (of orange, lemon) médula *f*; (fig) meollo *m*

pitiful /ˈpɪtɪfl/ *a* lastimoso

pittance /ˈpɪtns/ *n* miseria *f*

pity /ˈpɪtɪ/ *n* lástima *f*, pena *f*; (compassion) piedad *f*. **it's a ~ you can't come** es una lástima que no puedas venir. ● *vt* tenerle lástima a

pivot /ˈpɪvət/ *n* pivote *m*. ● *vi* pivotar; (fig) depender (**on** de)

placard /ˈplækɑ:d/ *n* pancarta *f*; (sign) letrero *m*

placate /pləˈkeɪt/ *vt* apaciguar

place /pleɪs/ *n* lugar *m*; (seat) asiento *m*; (in firm, team) puesto *m*; ([T], house) casa *f*. **feel out of ~** sentirse fuera de lugar. **take ~** tener lugar. ● *vt* poner, colocar; (identify) identificar. **be ~d** (in race) colocarse. **~ mat** *n* mantel *m* individual

placid /ˈplæsɪd/ *a* plácido

plague /pleɪg/ *n* peste *f*; (fig) plaga *f*. ● *vt* atormentar

plaice /pleɪs/ *n invar* platija *f*

plain /pleɪn/ *a* (**-er, -est**) (clear) claro; (simple) sencillo; (candid) franco; (ugly) feo. **in ~ clothes** de civil. ● *adv* totalmente. ● *n* llanura *f*. **~ly** *adv* claramente; (frankly) francamente; (simply) con sencillez

plait /plæt/ *vt* trenzar. ● *n* trenza *f*

plan /plæn/ *n* plan *m*; (map) plano *m*; (of book, essay) esquema *f*. ● *vt* (*pt* **planned**) planear; planificar <*strategies*>. **I'm ~ning to go to Greece** pienso ir a Grecia

plane /pleɪn/ *n* (tree) plátano *m*; (level) nivel *m*; (Aviat) avión *m*; (tool) cepillo *m*. ● *vt* cepillar

planet /ˈplænɪt/ *n* planeta *m*. **~ary** *a* planetario

plank /plæŋk/ *n* tabla *f*

planning /ˈplænɪŋ/ *n* planificación *f*. **family ~** planificación familiar. **town ~** urbanismo *m*

plant /plɑ:nt/ *n* planta *f*; (Mec) maquinaria *f*; (factory) fábrica *f*. ● *vt* plantar; (*place in position*) colocar. **~ation** /plænˈteɪʃn/ *n* plantación *f*

plaque /plæk/ *n* placa *f*

plasma /ˈplæzmə/ *n* plasma *m*

plaster /ˈplɑ:stə(r)/ *n* yeso *m*; (on walls) revoque *m*; (sticking plaster) tirita *f* (P), curita *f* (P) (LAm); (for setting bones) yeso *m*, escayola *f*. ● *vt* revocar; rellenar con yeso <*cracks*>

plastic /ˈplæstɪk/ *a & n* plástico (*m*)

Plasticine /ˈplæstɪsi:n/ *n* (P) plastilina *f* (P)

plastic surgery /plæstɪk ˈsɜ:dʒərɪ/ *n* cirugía *f* estética

plate /pleɪt/ *n* plato *m*; (of metal) chapa *f*; (silverware) vajilla *f* de plata; (in book) lámina *f*. ● *vt* recubrir (with de)

platform /ˈplætfɔːm/ *n* plataforma *f*; (Rail) andén *m*

platinum /ˈplætɪnəm/ *n* platino *m*

platitude /ˈplætɪtjuːd/ *n* lugar *m* común

platonic /pləˈtɒnɪk/ *a* platónico

plausible /ˈplɔːzəbl/ *a* verosímil; <*person*> convincente

play /pleɪ/ *vt* jugar a <*game, cards*>; jugar a, jugar (LAm) <*football, chess*>; tocar <*instrument*>; (act role) representar el papel de. ● *vi* jugar. ● *n* juego *m*; (drama) obra *f* de teatro. □ ~ **down** *vt* minimizar. □ ~ **up** *vi* [I] <*child*> dar guerra; <*car, TV*> no funcionar bien. ~**er** *n* jugador *m*; (Mus) músico *m*. ~**ful** *a* juguetón. ~**ground** *n* parque *m* de juegos infantiles; (in school) patio *m* de recreo. ~**group** *n* jardín *m* de la infancia. ~**ing card** *n* naipe *m*. ~**ing field** *n* campo *m* de deportes. ~**pen** *n* corralito *m*. ~**wright** /-raɪt/ *n* dramaturgo *m*

plc *abbr* (= **public limited company**) S.A.

plea /pliː/ *n* súplica *f*; (excuse) excusa *f*; (Jurid) defensa *f*

plead /pliːd/ *vt* (Jurid) alegar; (as excuse) pretextar. ● *vi* suplicar. ~ **with** suplicarle a. ~ **guilty** declararse culpable

pleasant /ˈpleznt/ *a* agradable

pleas|e /pliːz/ *int* por favor. ● *vt* complacer; (satisfy) contentar. ● *vi* agradar; (wish) querer. ~**ed** *a* (satisfied) satisfecho; (happy) contento. ~**ed with** satisfecho de. ~**ing** *a* agradable; (news) grato. ~**ure** /ˈpleʒə(r)/ *n* placer *m*

pleat /pliːt/ *n* pliegue *m*

pledge /pledʒ/ *n* cantidad *f* prometida

plent|iful /ˈplentɪfl/ *a* abundante. ~**y** /ˈplentɪ/ *n* abundancia *f*. ● *pron*. ~**y of** muchos, -chas; (of sth uncountable) mucho, -cha

pliable /ˈplaɪəbl/ *a* flexible

pliers /ˈplaɪəz/ *npl* alicates *mpl*

plight /plaɪt/ *n* situación *f* difícil

plimsolls /ˈplɪmsəlz/ *npl* zapatillas *fpl* de lona

plod /plɒd/ *vi* (*pt* **plodded**) caminar con paso pesado

plot /plɒt/ *n* complot *m*; (of novel etc) argumento *m*; (piece of land) parcela *f*. ● *vt* (*pt* **plotted**) tramar; (mark out) trazar. ● *vi* conspirar

plough /plaʊ/ *n* arado *m*. ● *vt/i* arar. □ ~ **into** *vt* estrellarse contra. □ ~ **through** *vt* avanzar laboriosamente por

ploy /plɔɪ/ *n* treta *f*

pluck /plʌk/ *vt* arrancar; depilarse <*eyebrows*>; desplumar <*bird*>. ~ **up courage to** armarse de valor para. ● *n* valor *m*. ~**y** *a* (**-ier, -iest**) valiente

plug /plʌg/ *n* (in bath) tapón *m*; (Elec) enchufe *m*; (spark ~) bujía *f*. ● *vt* (*pt* **plugged**) tapar; ([I], advertise) hacerle propaganda a. □ ~ **in** *vt* (Elec) enchufar. ~**hole** *n* desagüe *m*

plum /plʌm/ *n* ciruela *f*

plumage /ˈpluːmɪdʒ/ *n* plumaje *m*

plumb|er /ˈplʌmə(r)/ *n* fontanero *m*, plomero *m* (LAm). ~**ing** *n* instalación *f* sanitaria, instalación *f* de cañerías

plume /pluːm/ *n* pluma *f*

plump /plʌmp/ *a* (**-er, -est**) rechoncho

plunge /plʌndʒ/ *vt* hundir *<knife>*; (in water) sumergir; (into state, condition) sumir. ● *vi* zambullirse; (fall) caer. ● *n* zambullida *f*

plural /'plʊərəl/ *n* plural *m*. ● *a* en plural

plus /plʌs/ *prep* más. ● *a* positivo. ● *n* signo *m* de más; (fig) ventaja *f*

plush /plʌʃ/ *a* lujoso

Pluto /'plu:təʊ/ *n* Plutón *m*

plutonium /plu:'təʊnɪəm/ *n* plutonio *m*

ply /plaɪ/ *vt* manejar *<tool>*; ejercer *<trade>*. **~ s.o. with drink** dar continuamente de beber a uno. **~wood** *n* contrachapado *m*

p.m. *abbr* (= **post meridiem**) de la tarde

pneumatic drill /nju:'mætɪk/ *a* martillo *m* neumático

pneumonia /nju:'məʊnjə/ *n* pulmonía *f*

poach /pəʊtʃ/ *vt* escalfar *<egg>*; cocer *<fish etc>*; (steal) cazar furtivamente. **~er** *n* cazador *m* furtivo

PO box /pi:'əʊ/ *n* Apdo. postal

pocket /'pɒkɪt/ *n* bolsillo *m*; (of air, resistance) bolsa *f*. ● *vt* poner en el bolsillo. **~book** *n* (notebook) libro *m* de bolsillo; (Amer, wallet) cartera *f*; (Amer, handbag) bolso *m*, cartera *f* (LAm), bolsa *f* (Mex). **~ money** *n* dinero *m* de bolsillo, mesada *f* (LAm)

pod /pɒd/ *n* vaina *f*

poem /'pəʊɪm/ *n* poema *f*

poet /'pəʊɪt/ *n* poeta *m*. **~ic** /-'etɪk/ *a* poético. **~ry** /'pəʊɪtrɪ/ *n* poesía *f*

poignant /'pɔɪnjənt/ *a* conmovedor

point /pɔɪnt/ *n* (dot, on scale) punto *m*; (sharp end) punta *f*; (in time) momento *m*; (statement) observación; (on agenda, in discussion) punto *m*; (Elec) toma *f* de corriente. **to the ~** pertinente. **up to a ~** hasta cierto punto. **be on the ~ of** estar a punto de. **get to the ~** ir al grano. **there's no ~ (in) arguing** no sirve de nada discutir. ● *vt* (aim) apuntar; (show) indicar. ● *vi* señalar. **~ at/to sth** señalar algo. □ **~ out** *vt* señalar. **~-blank** *a & adv* a quemarropa. **~ed** *a* (chin, nose) puntiagudo; (fig) mordaz. **~less** *a* inútil

poise /pɔɪz/ *n* porte *m*; (composure) desenvoltura *f*

poison /'pɔɪzn/ *n* veneno *m*. ● *vt* envenenar. **~ous** *a* venenoso; *<chemical etc>* tóxico

poke /pəʊk/ *vt* empujar; atizar *<fire>*. ● *vi* hurgar; (pry) meterse. ● *n* golpe *m*. □ **~ about** *vi* fisgonear. **~r** /'pəʊkə(r)/ *n* atizador *m*; (Cards) póquer *m*

poky /'pəʊkɪ/ *a* (**-ier**, **-iest**) diminuto

Poland /'pəʊlənd/ *n* Polonia *f*

polar /'pəʊlə(r)/ *a* polar. **~ bear** *n* oso *m* blanco

pole /pəʊl/ *n* palo *m*; (fixed) poste *m*; (for flag) mástil *m*; (Geog) polo *m*

police /pə'li:s/ *n* policía *f*. **~man** /-mən/ *n* policía *m*, agente *m*. **~ station** *n* comisaría *f*. **~woman** *n* policía *f*, agente *f*

policy /'pɒlɪsɪ/ *n* política *f*; (insurance) póliza *f* (de seguros)

polish /'pɒlɪʃ/ *n* (for shoes) betún *m*; (furniture ~) cera *f* para muebles; (floor ~) abrillantador *m* de suelos; (shine) brillo *m*; (fig) finura *f*. ● *vt* darle brillo a; limpiar *<shoes>*; (refine) pulir. □ **~ off** *vt* despachar. **~ed** *a* pulido

Polish /'pəʊlɪʃ/ *a & n* polaco (*m*)

polite /pə'laɪt/ *a* cortés. **~ly** *adv* cortésmente. **~ness** *n* cortesía *f*

politic|al /pə'lɪtɪkl/ *a* político. **~ian** /pɒlɪ'tɪʃn/ *n* político *m*. **~s** /'pɒlətɪks/ *n* política *f*

poll /pəʊl/ *n* elección *f*; (survey) encuesta *f*. ● *vt* obtener *<votes>*

pollen /'pɒlən/ *n* polen *m*

polling booth *n* cabina *f* de votar

pollut|e /pə'lu:t/ *vt* contaminar. **~ion** /-ʃn/ *n* contaminación *f*

polo /'pəʊləʊ/ *n* polo *m*. **~ neck** *n* cuello *m* vuelto

poly|styrene /pɒlɪ'staɪri:n/ *n* poliestireno *m*. **~thene** /'pɒlɪθi:n/ *n* plástico, polietileno *m*

pomp /pɒmp/ *n* pompa *f*. **~ous** *a* pomposo

pond /pɒnd/ *n* (natural) laguna *f*; (artificial) estanque *m*

ponder /'pɒndə(r)/ *vt* considerar. **~ous** *a* pesado

pony /'pəʊnɪ/ *n* poni *m*. **~-tail** *n* cola *f* de caballo

poodle /'pu:dl/ *n* caniche *m*

pool /pu:l/ *n* charca *f*; (artificial) estanque *m*; (puddle) charco *m*. (common fund) fondos *mpl* comunes; (snooker) billar *m* americano. (**swimming**) **~** *n* piscina *f*, alberca *f* (Mex). **~s** *npl* quinielas *fpl*. ● *vt* aunar

poor /pʊə(r)/ *a* (**-er**, **-est**) pobre; *<quality, diet>* malo. **be in ~ health** estar mal de salud. **~ly** *a* Ⅱ malito. ● *adv* mal

pop /pɒp/ *n* (Mus) música *f* pop; (Amer Ⅱ, father) papá *m*. ● *vt* (*pt* **popped**) hacer reventar; (put) poner. □ **~ in** *vi* (visit) pasar por. □ **~ out** *vi* saltar; *<person>* salir un rato. □ **~ up** *vi* surgir, aparecer

popcorn /'pɒpkɔ:n/ *n* palomitas *fpl*

pope /pəʊp/ *n* papa *m*

poplar /'pɒplə(r)/ *n* álamo *m* (blanco)

poppy /'pɒpɪ/ *n* amapola *f*

popular /'pɒpjʊlə(r)/ *a* popular. **~ity** /-'lærətɪ/ *n* popularidad *f*. **~ize** *vt* popularizar

populat|e /'pɒpjʊleɪt/ *vt* poblar. **~ion** /-'leɪʃn/ *n* población *f*

porcelain /'pɔ:səlɪn/ *n* porcelana *f*

porch /pɔ:tʃ/ *n* porche *m*

porcupine /'pɔ:kjʊpaɪn/ *n* puerco *m* espín

pore /pɔ:(r)/ *n* poro *m*

pork /pɔ:k/ *n* carne *f* de cerdo *m*, carne *f* de puerco *m* (Mex)

porn /pɔ:n/ *n* Ⅱ pornografía *f*. **~ographic** /-ə'græfɪk/ *a* pornográfico. **~ography** /pɔ:'nɒgrəfɪ/ *n* pornografía *f*

porpoise /'pɔ:pəs/ *n* marsopa *f*

porridge /'pɒrɪdʒ/ *n* avena *f* (*cocida*)

port /pɔ:t/ *n* puerto *m*; (Naut) babor *m*; (Comp) puerto *m*; (Culin) oporto *m*

portable /'pɔ:təbl/ *a* portátil

porter /'pɔ:tə(r)/ *n* (for luggage) maletero *m*; (concierge) portero *m*

porthole /'pɔ:thəʊl/ *n* portilla *f*

portion /'pɔ:ʃn/ *n* porción *f*; (part) parte *f*

portrait /'pɔ:trɪt/ *n* retrato *m*

portray /pɔ:'treɪ/ *vt* representar. **~al** *n* representación *f*

Portug|al /'pɔ:tjʊgl/ *n* Portugal *m*. **~uese** /-'gi:z/ *a* & *n* portugués (*m*)

pose /pəʊz/ *n* pose *f*, postura *f*. ● *vt* representar *<threat>*; plantear *<problem, question>*. ● *vi* posar. **~ as** hacerse pasar por

posh /pɒʃ/ *a* Ⅱ elegante

position /pə'zɪʃn/ *n* posición *f*; (job) puesto *m*; (situation) situación *f*. ● *vt* colocar

positive /'pɒzətɪv/ *a* positivo; (real) auténtico; (certain) seguro. ● *n* (Photo) positiva *f*. **~ly** *adv* positivamente

possess /pə'zes/ *vt* poseer. **~ion** /-ʃn/ *n* posesión *f*; (Jurid) bien *m*. **~ive** *a* posesivo

possib|ility /pɒsə'bɪlətɪ/ *n* posibilidad *f*. **~le** /'pɒsəbl/ *a* posible. **~ly** *adv* posiblemente

post /pəʊst/ *n* (pole) poste *m*; (job) puesto *m*; (mail) correo *m*. ● *vt* echar al correo <*letter*>; (send) enviar por correo. **keep s.o. ~ed** mantener a uno al corriente

post... /pəʊst/ *pref* post, pos

post: ~age /-ɪdʒ/ *n* franqueo *m*. **~al** *a* postal. **~al order** *n* giro *m* postal. **~ box** *n* buzón *m*. **~card** *n* (tarjeta *f*) postal *f*. **~code** *n* código *m* postal

poster /'pəʊstə(r)/ *n* cartel *m*, póster *m*

posterity /pɒs'terətɪ/ *n* posteridad *f*

posthumous /'pɒstjʊməs/ *a* póstumo

post: ~man /-mən/ *n* cartero *m*. **~mark** *n* matasellos *m*

post mortem /pəʊst'mɔːtəm/ *n* autopsia *f*

post office *n* oficina *f* de correos, correos *mpl*, correo *m* (LAm)

postpone /pəʊst'pəʊn/ *vt* aplazar, posponer. **~ment** *n* aplazamiento *m*

postscript /'pəʊstskrɪpt/ *n* posdata *f*

posture /'pɒstʃə(r)/ *n* postura *f*

posy /'pəʊzɪ/ *n* ramillete *m*

pot /pɒt/ *n* (for cooking) olla *f*; (for jam, honey) tarro *m*; (for flowers) tiesto *m*; (in pottery) vasija *f*. **~s and pans** cacharros *mpl*

potato /pə'teɪtəʊ/ *n* (*pl* **-oes**) patata *f*, papa *f* (LAm)

potent /'pəʊtnt/ *a* potente; <*drink*> fuerte

potential /pəʊ'tenʃl/ *a* & *n* potencial (*m*). **~ly** *adv* potencialmente

pot: ~hole *n* cueva *f* subterránea; (in road) bache *m*. **~holing** *n* espeleología *f*

potion /'pəʊʃn/ *n* poción *f*

pot-shot *n* tiro *m* al azar

potter /'pɒtə(r)/ *n* alfarero *m*. ● *vi* hacer pequeños trabajos agradables. **~y** *n* (pots) cerámica *f*; (workshop, craft) alfarería *f*

potty /'pɒtɪ/ *a* (**-ier**, **-iest**) ◻ chiflado. ● *n* orinal *m*

pouch /paʊtʃ/ *n* bolsa *f* pequeña; (for correspondence) valija *f*

poultry /'pəʊltrɪ/ *n* aves *fpl* de corral

pounce /paʊns/ *vi* saltar. **~ on** abalanzarse sobre

pound /paʊnd/ *n* (weight) libra *f* (= 454g); (money) libra *f* (esterlina); (for cars) depósito *m*. ● *vt* (crush) machacar. ● *vi* aporrear; <*heart*> palpitar; <*sound*> retumbar

pour /pɔː(r)/ *vt* verter; echar <*salt*>. **~ (out)** servir <*drink*>. ● *vi* <*blood*> manar; <*water*> salir; (rain) llover a cántaros. □ **~ out** *vi* <*people*> salir en tropel. **~ing** *a*. **~ing rain** lluvia *f* torrencial

pout /paʊt/ *vi* hacer pucheros

poverty /'pɒvətɪ/ *n* pobreza *f*

powder /'paʊdə(r)/ *n* polvo *m*; (cosmetic) polvos *mpl*. ● *vt* empolvar. **~ one's face** ponerse polvos en la cara. **~y** *a* como polvo

power /'paʊə(r)/ *n* poder *m*; (energy) energía *f*; (electricity) electricidad *f*; (nation) potencia *f*. ● *vt*. **~ed by** impulsado por **~ cut** *n* apagón *m*. **~ed** *a* con motor. **~ful** *a* poderoso. **~less** *a* impotente. **~ plant**, **~-station** *n* central *f* eléctrica

PR = **public relations**

practicable /'præktɪkəbl/ *a* practicable

practical /'præktɪkl/ *a* práctico. **~ joke** *n* broma *f*. **~ly** *adv* prácticamente

practi|ce /'præktɪs/ *n* práctica *f*; (custom) costumbre *f*; (exercise) ejercicio *m*; (Sport) entrenamiento *m*; (clients) clientela *f*. **he's out of ~ce** le falta práctica. **in ~ce** (in fact) en la práctica. **~se** /'præktɪs/ *vt* practicar; ensayar <*act*>; ejercer <*profession*>. ● *vi* practicar; <*professional*> ejercer. **~tioner** /-'tɪʃənə(r)/ *n* médico *m*

prairie /'preərɪ/ *n* pradera *f*

praise /preɪz/ *vt* (Relig) alabar; (compliment) elogiar. ● *n* (credit) elogios *mpl*. **~worthy** *a* loable

pram /præm/ *n* cochecito *m*

prank /præŋk/ *n* travesura *f*

prawn /prɔ:n/ *n* gamba *f*, camarón *m* (LAm)

pray /preɪ/ *vi* rezar (**for** por). **~er** /preə(r)/ *n* oración *f*

pre.. /pri:/ *pref* pre...

preach /pri:tʃ/ *vt/i* predicar. **~er** *n* predicador *m*; (Amer, minister) pastor *m*

pre-arrange /pri:ə'reɪndʒ/ *vt* concertar de antemano

precarious /prɪ'keərɪəs/ *a* precario. **~ly** *adv* precariamente

precaution /prɪ'kɔ:ʃn/ *n* precaución *f*

precede /prɪ'si:d/ *vt* preceder. **~nce** /'presədəns/ *n* precedencia *f*. **~nt** /'presədənt/ *n* precedente *m*

preceding /prɪ'si:dɪŋ/ *a* anterior

precept /'pri:sept/ *n* precepto *m*

precinct /'pri:sɪŋkt/ *n* recinto *m*; (Amer, police district) distrito *m* policial; (Amer, voting district) circunscripción *f*. **pedestrian ~** zona *f* peatonal. **~s** (of city) límites *mpl*

precious /'preʃəs/ *a* precioso. ● *adv* Ⓘ muy

precipice /'presɪpɪs/ *n* precipicio *m*

precipitate /prɪ'sɪpɪteɪt/ *vt* precipitar. ● /prɪ'sɪpɪtət/ *n* precipitado *m*. ● /prɪ'sɪpɪtət/ *a* precipitado

precis|e /prɪ'saɪs/ *a* (accurate) exacto; (specific) preciso; (meticulous) minucioso. **~ely** *adv* con precisión. **~!** ¡exacto! **~ion** /-'sɪʒn/ *n* precisión *f*

preclude /prɪ'klu:d/ *vt* excluir

precocious /prɪ'kəʊʃəs/ *a* precoz. **~ly** *adv* precozmente

preconce|ived /pri:kən'si:vd/ *a* preconcebido. **~ption** /-'sepʃn/ *n* preconcepción *f*

precursor /pri:'kɜ:sə(r)/ *n* precursor *m*

predator /'predətə(r)/ *n* depredador *m*. **~y** *a* predador

predecessor /'pri:dɪsesə(r)/ *n* predecesor *m*, antecesor *m*

predicament /prɪ'dɪkəmənt/ *n* aprieto *m*

predict /prɪ'dɪkt/ *vt* predecir. **~ion** /-ʃn/ *n* predicción *f*

preen /pri:n/ *vt* arreglar. **~ o.s.** atildarse

prefab /'pri:fæb/ *n* Ⓘ casa *f* prefabricada. **~ricated** /-'fæbrɪkeɪtɪd/ *a* prefabricado

preface /ˈprefəs/ *n* prefacio *m*; (to event) prólogo *m*

prefect /ˈpri:fekt/ *n* (Schol) monitor *m*; (official) prefecto *m*

prefer /prɪˈfɜ:(r)/ *vt* (*pt* **preferred**) preferir. ~ **sth to sth** preferir algo a algo. ~**able** /ˈprefrəbl/ *a* preferible. ~**ence** /ˈprefrəns/ *n* preferencia *f*. ~**ential** /-əˈrenʃl/ *a* preferente

pregnan|cy /ˈpregnənsɪ/ *n* embarazo *m*. ~**t** *a* embarazada

prehistoric /pri:hɪˈstɒrɪk/ *a* prehistórico

prejudge /pri:ˈdʒʌdʒ/ *vt* prejuzgar

prejudice /ˈpredʒʊdɪs/ *n* prejuicio *m*. ● *vt* predisponer; (harm) perjudicar. ~**d** *a* lleno de prejuicios

preliminary /prɪˈlɪmɪnərɪ/ *a* preliminar

prelude /ˈprelju:d/ *n* preludio *m*

premature /ˈpremətjʊə(r)/ *a* prematuro

premeditated /pri:ˈmedɪteɪtɪd/ *a* premeditado

premier /ˈpremɪə(r)/ *n* (Pol) primer ministro *m*

première /ˈpremɪeə(r)/ *n* estreno *m*

premise /ˈpremɪs/ *n* premisa *f*. ~**s** /ˈpremɪsɪz/ *npl* local *m*. **on the** ~**s** en el local

premium /ˈpri:mɪəm/ *n* (insurance ~) prima *f* de seguro. **be at a** ~ escasear

premonition /pri:məˈnɪʃn/ *n* premonición *f*, presentimiento *m*

preoccup|ation /pri:ɒkjʊˈpeɪʃn/ *n* (obsession) obsesión *f*; (concern) preocupación *f*. ~**ied** /-ˈɒkjʊpaɪd/ *a* absorto; (worried) preocupado

preparat|ion /prepəˈreɪʃn/ *n* preparación *f*. ~**ions** *npl* preparativos *mpl*. ~**ory** /prɪˈpærətrɪ/ *a* preparatorio

prepare /prɪˈpeə(r)/ *vt* preparar. ● *vi* prepararse. ● *a* preparado (willing). **be** ~**d to** estar dispuesto a

preposition /prepəˈzɪʃn/ *n* preposición *f*

preposterous /prɪˈpɒstərəs/ *a* absurdo

prerequisite /pri:ˈrekwɪzɪt/ *n* requisito *m* esencial

prerogative /prɪˈrɒgətɪv/ *n* prerrogativa *f*

Presbyterian /prezbɪˈtɪərɪən/ *a* & *n* presbiteriano (*m*)

prescri|be /prɪˈskraɪb/ *vt* prescribir; (Med) recetar. ~**ption** /-ˈɪpʃn/ *n* (Med) receta *f*

presence /ˈprezns/ *n* presencia *f*. ~ **of mind** presencia *f* de ánimo

present /ˈpreznt/ *n* (gift) regalo *m*; (current time) presente *m*. **at** ~ actualmente. **for the** ~ por ahora. ● *a* presente. ● /prɪˈzent/ *vt* presentar; (give) obsequiar. ~ **s.o. with** obsequiar a uno con. ~**able** /prɪˈzentəbl/ *a* presentable. ~**ation** /preznˈteɪʃn/ *n* presentación *f*; (ceremony) ceremonia *f* de entrega. ~**er** /prɪˈzentə(r)/ *n* presentador *m*. ~**ly** /ˈprezntlɪ/ *adv* dentro de poco

preserv|ation /prezəˈveɪʃn/ *n* conservación *f*. ~**ative** /prɪˈzɜ:vətɪv/ *n* conservante *m*. ~**e** /prɪˈzɜ:v/ *vt* conservar; (maintain) mantener; (Culin) hacer conserva de. ● *n* coto *m*; (jam) confitura *f*. **wildlife** ~**e** (Amer) reserva *f* de animales

preside /prɪˈzaɪd/ *vi* presidir. ~ **over** presidir

presiden|cy /'prezɪdənsɪ/ *n* presidencia *f*. **~t** *n* presidente *m*. **~tial** /-'denʃl/ *a* presidencial

press /pres/ *vt* apretar; prensar <*grapes*>; (put pressure on) presionar; (iron) planchar. **be ~ed for time** andar escaso de tiempo. ● *vi* apretar; <*time*> apremiar; (fig) urgir. ● *n* (Mec, newspapers) prensa *f*; (printing) imprenta *f*. □ **~ on** *vi* seguir adelante (**with** con). **~ conference** *n* rueda *f* de prensa. **~ cutting** *n* recorte *m* de periódico. **~ing** *a* urgente. **~-up** *n* flexión *f*, fondo *m*

pressur|e /'preʃə(r)/ *n* presión *f*. ● *vt* presionar. **~e-cooker** *n* olla *f* a presión. **~ize** *vt* presionar

prestig|e /pre'sti:ʒ/ *n* prestigio *m*. **~ious** /-'stɪdʒəs/ *a* prestigioso

presum|ably /prɪ'zju:məblɪ/ *adv*. **~...** supongo que..., me imagino que... **~e** /prɪ'zju:m/ *vt* suponer. **~ptuous** /prɪ'zʌmptʃʊəs/ *a* impertinente

presuppose /pri:sə'pəʊz/ *vt* presuponer

preten|ce /prɪ'tens/ *n* fingimiento *m*; (claim) pretensión *f*; (pretext) pretexto *m*. **~d** /-'tend/ *vt/i* fingir. **~sion** /-'tenʃən/ *n* pretensión *f*. **~tious** /-'tenʃəs/ *a* pretencioso

pretext /'pri:tekst/ *n* pretexto *m*

pretty /'prɪtɪ/ *a* (**-ier**, **-iest**) *adv* bonito, lindo (esp LAm)

prevail /prɪ'veɪl/ *vi* predominar; (win) prevalecer. □ **~ on** *vt* persuadir

prevalen|ce /'prevələns/ *n* (occurrence) preponderancia *f*; (predominance) predominio *m*. **~t** *a* extendido

prevent /prɪ'vent/ *vt* (hinder) impedir; (forestall) prevenir, evitar. **~ion** /-ʃn/ *n* prevención *f*. **~ive** *a* preventivo

preview /'pri:vju:/ *n* preestreno *m*; (trailer) avance *m*

previous /'pri:vɪəs/ *a* anterior. **~ to** antes de. **~ly** *adv* antes

prey /preɪ/ *n* presa *f*. **bird of ~** ave *f* de rapiña

price /praɪs/ *n* precio *m*. ● *vt* fijar el precio de. **~less** *a* inestimable; ([I], amusing) muy divertido. **~y** *a* [I] carito

prick /prɪk/ *vt/i* pinchar. ● *n* pinchazo *m*

prickl|e /'prɪkl/ *n* (Bot) espina *f*; (of animal) púa *f*; (sensation) picor *m*. **~y** *a* espinoso; <*animal*> con púas; (touchy) quisquilloso

pride /praɪd/ *n* orgullo *m*. ● *vr*. **~ o.s. on** enorgullecerse de

priest /pri:st/ *n* sacerdote *m*. **~hood** *n* sacerdocio *m*

prim /prɪm/ *a* (**primmer**, **primmest**) mojigato; (affected) remilgado

primar|ily /'praɪmərɪlɪ/ *adv* en primer lugar. **~y** /'praɪmərɪ/ *a* (principal) primordial; (first, basic) primario. **~ school** *n* escuela *f* primaria

prime /praɪm/ *vt* cebar <*gun*>; (prepare) preparar; aprestar <*surface*>. ● *a* principal; (first rate) excelente. **~ minister** *n* primer ministro *m*. ● *n*. **be in one's ~** estar en la flor de la vida. **~r** *n* (paint) imprimación *f*

primeval /praɪ'mi:vl/ *a* primigenio

primitive /'prɪmɪtɪv/ *a* primitivo

primrose /'prɪmrəʊz/ *n* primavera *f*

prince /prɪns/ *n* príncipe *m*. **~ss** /prɪn'ses/ *n* princesa *f*

principal /ˈprɪnsəpl/ *a* principal. ● *n* (of school) director *m*; (of university) rector *m*. **~ly** /ˈprɪnsɪpəlɪ/ *adv* principalmente

principle /ˈprɪnsəpl/ *n* principio *m*. **in ~** en principio. **on ~** por principio

print /prɪnt/ *vt* imprimir; (write in capitals) escribir con letras de molde. **~ed matter** impresos *mpl*. ● *n* (characters) letra *f*; (picture) grabado *m*; (Photo) copia *f*; (fabric) estampado *m*. **in ~** (published) publicado; (available) a la venta. **out of ~** agotado. **~er** /ˈprɪntə(r)/ *n* impresor *m*; (machine) impresora *f*. **~ing** *n* impresión *f*; (trade) imprenta *f*. **~out** *n* listado *m*

prior /ˈpraɪə(r)/ *n* prior *m*. ● *a* previo. **~ to** antes de. **~ity** /praɪˈɒrətɪ/ *n* prioridad *f*. **~y** *n* priorato *m*

prise /praɪz/ *vt*. **~ open** abrir haciendo palanca

prison /ˈprɪzn/ *n* cárcel *m*. **~er** *n* prisionero *m*; (in prison) preso *m*; (under arrest) detenido *m*. **~ officer** *n* funcionario *m* de prisiones

priva|cy /ˈprɪvəsɪ/ *n* privacidad *f*. **~te** /ˈpraɪvɪt/ *a* privado; (confidential) personal; <*lessons, house*> particular. **in ~te** en privado; (secretly) en secreto. ● *n* soldado *m* raso. **~te detective** *n* detective *m* & *f* privado. **~tely** *adv* en privado. **~tion** /praɪˈveɪʃn/ *n* privación *f*

privilege /ˈprɪvəlɪdʒ/ *n* privilegio *m*. **~d** *a* privilegiado. **be ~d to** tener el privilegio de

prize /praɪz/ *n* premio *m*. ● *a* <*idiot etc*> de remate. ● *vt* estimar

pro /prəʊ/ *n*. **~s and cons** los pros *m* y los contras

probab|ility /prɒbəˈbɪlətɪ/ *n* probabilidad *f*. **~le** /ˈprɒbəbl/ *a* probable. **~ly** *adv* probablemente

probation /prəˈbeɪʃn/ *n* período *m* de prueba; (Jurid) libertad *f* condicional

probe /prəʊb/ *n* sonda *f*; (fig) investigación *f*. ● *vt* sondar. ● *vi*. **~ into** investigar

problem /ˈprɒbləm/ *n* problema *m*. ● *a* difícil. **~atic** /-ˈmætɪk/ *a* problemático

procedure /prəˈsiːdʒə(r)/ *n* procedimiento *m*

proceed /prəˈsiːd/ *vi* proceder; (move forward) avanzar. **~ings** *npl* (report) actas *fpl*; (Jurid) proceso *m*. **~s** /ˈprəʊsiːdz/ *npl*. **the ~s** lo recaudado

process /ˈprəʊses/ *n* proceso *m*. **in the ~ of** en vías de. ● *vt* tratar; revelar <*photo*>; tramitar <*order*>. **~ion** /prəˈseʃn/ *n* desfile *m*; (Relig) procesión *f*

procla|im /prəˈkleɪm/ *vt* proclamar. **~mation** /prɒkləˈmeɪʃn/ *n* proclamación *f*

procure /prəˈkjʊə(r)/ *vt* obtener

prod /prɒd/ *vt* (*pt* **prodded**) (with sth sharp) pinchar; (with elbow) darle un codazo a. ● *n* (with sth sharp) pinchazo *m*; (with elbow) codazo *m*

produc|e /prəˈdjuːs/ *vt* producir; surtir <*effect*>; sacar <*gun*>; producir <*film*>; poner en escena <*play*>. ● /ˈprɒdjuːs/ *n* productos *mpl*. **~er** /prəˈdjuːsə(r)/ *n* (TV, Cinema) productor *m*; (in theatre) director *m*; (manufacturer) fabricante *m* & *f*. **~t** /ˈprɒdʌkt/ *n* producto *m*. **~tion** /prəˈdʌkʃn/ *n* (manufacture) fabricación *f*; (output) producción *f*; (of play) producción *f*. **~tive** /prəˈdʌktɪv/ *a* productivo. **~tivity** /prɒdʌkˈtɪvətɪ/ *n* productividad *f*

profess /prə'fes/ *vt* profesar; (pretend) pretender. **~ion** /-'feʃn/ *n* profesión *f*. **~ional** *a & n* profesional (*m & f*). **~or** /-'fesə(r)/ *n* catedrático *m*; (Amer) profesor *m*

proficien|cy /prə'fɪʃənsɪ/ *n* competencia *f*. **~t** *a* competente

profile /'prəʊfaɪl/ *n* perfil *m*

profit /'prɒfɪt/ *n* (Com) ganancia *f*; (fig) provecho *m*. ● *vi*. **~ from** sacar provecho de. **~able** *a* provechoso

profound /prə'faʊnd/ *a* profundo. **~ly** *adv* profundamente

profus|e /prə'fju:s/ *a* profuso. **~ely** *adv* profusamente

prognosis /prɒg'nəʊsɪs/ *n* (*pl* **-oses**) pronóstico *m*

program /'prəʊgræm/ *n* (Comp) programa *m*; (Amer, course) curso *m*. **~me** /'prəʊgræm/ *n* programa *m*. ● *vt* (*pt* **-med**) programar. **~mer** *n* programador *m*

progress /'prəʊgres/ *n* progreso *m*; (development) desarrollo *m*. **make ~** hacer progresos. **in ~** en curso. ● /prə'gres/ *vi* hacer progresos; (develop) desarrollarse. **~ion** /prə'greʃn/ *n* progresión *f*; (advance) evolución *f*. **~ive** /prə'gresɪv/ *a* progresivo; (reforming) progresista. **~ively** *adv* progresivamente

prohibit /prə'hɪbɪt/ *vt* prohibir; (prevent) impedir. **~ive** *a* prohibitivo

project /prə'dʒekt/ *vt* proyectar. ● *vi* (stick out) sobresalir. ● /'prɒdʒekt/ *n* proyecto *m*; (Schol) trabajo *m*; (Amer, housing **~**) complejo *m* de viviendas subvencionadas. **~or** /prə'dʒektə(r)/ *n* proyector *m*

prolific /prə'lɪfɪk/ *a* prolífico

prologue /'prəʊlɒg/ *n* prólogo *m*

prolong /prə'lɒŋ/ *vt* prolongar

prom /prɒm/ *n* (Amer) baile *m* del colegio. **~enade** /prɒmə'nɑ:d/ *n* paseo *m* marítimo. ● *vi* pasearse.

prominen|ce /'prɒmɪnəns/ *n* prominencia *f*; (fig) importancia *f*. **~t** *a* prominente; (important) importante; (conspicuous) destacado

promiscu|ity /prɒmɪ'skju:ətɪ/ *n* promiscuidad *f*. **~ous** /prə'mɪskjʊəs/ *a* promiscuo

promis|e /'prɒmɪs/ *n* promesa *f*. ● *vt/i* prometer. **~ing** *a* prometedor; <*future*> halagüeño

promot|e /prə'məʊt/ *vt* promover; promocionar <*product*>; (in rank) ascender. **~ion** /-'məʊʃn/ *n* promoción *f*; (in rank) ascenso *m*

prompt /prɒmpt/ *a* rápido; (punctual) puntual. ● *adv* en punto. ● *n* (Comp) presto *m*. ● *vt* incitar; apuntar <*actor*>. **~ly** *adv* puntualmente

prone /prəʊn/ *a* (tendido) boca abajo. **be ~ to** ser propenso a

pronoun /'prəʊnaʊn/ *n* pronombre *m*

pronounc|e /prə'naʊns/ *vt* pronunciar; (declare) declarar. **~ement** *n* declaración *f*. **~ed** *a* pronunciado; (noticeable) marcado

pronunciation /prənʌnsɪ'eɪʃn/ *n* pronunciación *f*

proof /pru:f/ *n* prueba *f*, pruebas *fpl*; (of alcohol) graduación *f* normal. ● *a*. **~ against** a prueba de. **~-reading** *n* corrección *f* de pruebas

propaganda /prɒpə'gændə/ *n* propaganda *f*

propagate /'prɒpəgeɪt/ *vt* propagar. ● *vi* propagarse

propel /prə'pel/ *vt* (*pt* **propelled**) propulsar. **~ler** *n* hélice *f*

proper /'prɒpə(r)/ *a* correcto; (suitable) apropiado; (Gram) propio; (🅸, real) verdadero. **~ly** *adv* correctamente; <*eat, work*> bien

property /'prɒpətɪ/ *n* propiedad *f*; (things owned) bienes *mpl*. ● *a* inmobiliario

prophe|cy /'prɒfəsɪ/ *n* profecía *f*. **~sy** /'prɒfɪsaɪ/ *vt/i* profetizar. **~t** /'prɒfɪt/ *n* profeta *m*. **~tic** /prə'fetɪk/ *a* profético

proportion /prə'pɔ:ʃn/ *n* proporción *f*. **~al** *a*, **~ate** /-ət/ *a* proporcional

propos|al /prə'pəʊzl/ *n* propuesta *f*; (of marriage) proposición *f* matrimonial. **~e** /prə'pəʊz/ *vt* proponer. ● *vi*. **~e to s.o.** hacerle una oferta de matrimonio a una. **~ition** /prɒpə'zɪʃn/ *n* propuesta *f*; (offer) oferta *f*

proprietor /prə'praɪətə(r)/ *n* propietario *m*

pro rata /'prəʊ'rɑ:tə/ *adv* a prorrata

prose /prəʊz/ *n* prosa *f*

prosecut|e /'prɒsɪkju:t/ *vt* procesar (**for** por); (carry on) proseguir. **~ion** /-'kju:ʃn/ *n* proceso *m*. **the ~** (side) la acusación. **~or** *n* fiscal *m* & *f*; (in private prosecutions) abogado *m* de la acusación

prospect /'prɒspekt/ *n* (possibility) posibilidad *f* (**of** de); (situation envisaged) perspectiva *f*. **~s** (chances) perspectivas *fpl*. **~ive** /prə'spektɪv/ *a* posible; (future) futuro. **~or** /prə'spektə(r)/ *n* prospector *m*. **~us** /prə'spektəs/ *n* folleto *m* informativo

prosper /'prɒspə(r)/ *vi* prosperar. **~ity** /-'sperətɪ/ *n* prosperidad *f*. **~ous** *a* próspero

prostitut|e /'prɒstɪtju:t/ *n* prostituta *f*. **~ion** /-'tju:ʃn/ *n* prostitución *f*

prostrate /'prɒstreɪt/ *a* postrado

protagonist /prə'tægənɪst/ *n* protagonista *m* & *f*

protect /prə'tekt/ *vt* proteger. **~ion** /-ʃn/ *n* protección *f*. **~ive** *a* protector. **~or** *n* protector *m*

protein /'prəʊti:n/ *n* proteína *f*

protest /'prəʊtest/ *n* protesta *f*. **in ~ (against)** en señal de protesta (contra). **under ~** bajo protesta. ● /prə'test/ *vt/i* protestar

Protestant /'prɒtɪstənt/ *a* & *n* protestante (*m* & *f*)

protester /prə'testə(r)/ *n* manifestante *m* & *f*

protocol /'prəʊtəkɒl/ *n* protocolo *m*

protrud|e /prə'tru:d/ *vi* sobresalir. **~ing** *a* <*chin*> prominente. **~ing eyes** ojos saltones

proud /praʊd/ *a* orgulloso. **~ly** *adv* con orgullo; (arrogantly) orgullosamente

prove /pru:v/ *vt* probar; demostrar <*loyalty*>. ● *vi* resultar. **~n** *a* probado

proverb /'prɒvɜ:b/ *n* refrán *m*, proverbio *m*

provide /prə'vaɪd/ *vt* proporcionar; dar <*accommodation*>. **~ s.o. with sth** proveer a uno de algo. ● *vi*. **~ for** (allow for) prever; mantener <*person*>. **~d** *conj*. **~d (that)** con tal de que, siempre que

providen|ce /'prɒvɪdəns/ *n* providencia *f*. **~tial** /-'denʃl/ *a* providencial

providing /prə'vaɪdɪŋ/ *conj*. **~ that** con tal de que, siempre que

provinc|e /'prɒvɪns/ *n* provincia *f*; (fig) competencia *f*. **~ial** /prə'vɪnʃl/ *a* provincial

provision /prə'vɪʒn/ *n* provisión *f*; (supply) suministro *m*; (stipulation) disposición *f*. **~s** *npl* provisiones *fpl*, víveres *mpl*. **~al** *a* provisional

provo|cation /prɒvə'keɪʃn/ *n* provocación *f*. **~cative** /-'vɒkətɪv/ *a* provocador. **~ke** /prə'vəʊk/ *vt* provocar

prow /praʊ/ *n* proa *f*

prowess /'praʊɪs/ *n* destreza *f*; (valour) valor *m*

prowl /praʊl/ *vi* merodear. **~er** *n* merodeador *m*

proximity /prɒk'sɪmətɪ/ *n* proximidad *f*

prude /pru:d/ *n* mojigato *m*

pruden|ce /'pru:dəns/ *n* prudencia *f*. **~t** *a* prudente. **~tly** *adv* prudentemente

prudish /'pru:dɪʃ/ *a* mojigato

prune /pru:n/ *n* ciruela *f* pasa. ● *vt* podar

pry /praɪ/ *vi* curiosear. **~ into sth** entrometerse en algo. *vt* (Amer) ⇨PRISE

PS *n* (postscript) P.D.

psalm /sɑ:m/ *n* salmo *m*

psychiatr|ic /saɪkɪ'ætrɪk/ *a* psiquiátrico. **~ist** /saɪ'kaɪətrɪst/ *n* psiquiatra *m* & *f*. **~y** /saɪ'kaɪətrɪ/ *n* psiquiatría *f*

psychic /'saɪkɪk/ *a* para(p)sicológico

psycho|analysis /saɪkəʊə'næləsɪs/ *n* (p)sicoanálisis *m*. **~logical** /saɪkə'lɒdʒɪkl/ *a* (p)sicológico. **~logist** /saɪ'kɒlədʒɪst/ *n* (p)sicólogo *m*. **~logy** /saɪ'kɒlədʒɪ/ *n* (p)sicología *f*. **~therapy** /-'θerəpɪ/ *n* (p)sicoterapia *f*

pub /pʌb/ *n* bar *m*

puberty /'pju:bətɪ/ *n* pubertad *f*

pubic /'pju:bɪk/ *a* pubiano, púbico

public /'pʌblɪk/ *a* público. **~an** *n* tabernero *m*. **~ation** /-'keɪʃn/ *n* publicación *f*. **~ holiday** *n* día *m* festivo, día *m* feriado (LAm). **~ house** *n* bar *m*. **~ity** /pʌb'lɪsətɪ/ *n* publicidad *f*. **~ize** /'pʌblɪsaɪz/ *vt* hacer público. **~ly** *adv* públicamente. **~ school** *n* colegio *m* privado; (Amer) instituto *m*, escuela *f* pública

publish /'pʌblɪʃ/ *vt* publicar. **~er** *n* editor *m*. **~ing** *n* publicación *f*. **~ing house** editorial *f*

pudding /'pʊdɪŋ/ *n* postre *m*; (steamed) budín *m*

puddle /'pʌdl/ *n* charco *m*

Puerto Ric|an /pwɜ:təʊ'ri:kən/ *a* & *n* portorriqueño (*m*), puertorriqueño (*m*). **~o** /-əʊ/ *n* Puerto Rico *m*

puff /pʌf/ *n* (of wind) ráfaga *f*; (of smoke) nube *f*; (action) soplo *m*; (on cigarette) chupada *f*, calada *f*. ● *vt/i* soplar. **~ at** dar chupadas a <*pipe*>. **~ out** (swell up) inflar, hinchar. **~ed** *a* (out of breath) sin aliento. **~ paste** (Amer), **~ pastry** *n* hojaldre *m*. **~y** *a* hinchado

pull /pʊl/ *vt* tirar de, jalar (LAm); desgarrarse <*muscle*>. **~ a face** hacer una mueca. **~ a fast one** hacer una mala jugada. ● *vi* tirar, jalar (LAm). **~ at** tirar de, jalar (LAm). ● *n* tirón *m*, jalón *m* (LAm); (pulling force) fuerza *f*; (influence) influencia *f*. □ **~ away** *vi* (Auto) alejarse. □ **~ back** *vi* retirarse. □ **~ down** *vt* echar abajo <*building*>; (lower) bajar. □ **~ in** *vi* (Auto) parar. □ **~ off** *vt* (remove) quitar; (achieve) conseguir. □ **~ out** *vt* sacar; retirar <*team*>. *vi* (Auto) salirse. □ **~ through** *vi* recobrar la salud. □ **~ up** *vi* (Auto) parar. *vt* (uproot) arrancar; (reprimand) regañar

pullover /'pʊləʊvə(r)/ *n* suéter *m*, pulóver *m*, jersey *m*

pulp /pʌlp/ *n* pulpa *f*; (for paper) pasta *f*

pulpit /'pʊlpɪt/ *n* púlpito *m*

pulse /pʌls/ *n* (Med) pulso *m*; (Culin) legumbre *f*

pummel /'pʌml/ *vt* (*pt* **pummelled**) aporrear

pump /pʌmp/ *n* bomba *f*; (for petrol) surtidor *m*. ● *vt* sacar con una bomba. □ ~ **up** *vt* inflar

pumpkin /'pʌmpkɪn/ *n* calabaza *f*

pun /pʌn/ *n* juego *m* de palabras

punch /pʌntʃ/ *vt* darle un puñetazo a; (perforate) perforar; hacer <*hole*>. ● *n* puñetazo *m*; (vigour) fuerza *f*; (device) perforadora *f*; (drink) ponche *m*. ~ **in** *vi* (Amer) fichar (al entrar al trabajo). ~ **out** *vi* (Amer) fichar (al salir del trabajo)

punctual /'pʌŋktʃʊəl/ *a* puntual. **~ity** /-'ælətɪ/ *n* puntualidad *f*. **~ly** *adv* puntualmente

punctuat|e /'pʌŋkʃʊeɪt/ *vt* puntuar. **~ion** /-'eɪʃn/ *n* puntuación *f*

puncture /'pʌŋktʃə(r)/ *n* (in tyre) pinchazo *m*. **have a ~** pinchar. ● *vt* pinchar. ● *vi* pincharse

punish /'pʌnɪʃ/ *vt* castigar. **~ment** *n* castigo *m*

punk /pʌŋk/ *n* punk *m & f*, punki *m & f*; (Music) punk *m*; (Amer, hoodlum) vándalo *m*

punt /pʌnt/ *n* (boat) batea *f*. **~er** *n* apostante *m & f*

puny /'pju:nɪ/ *a* (**-ier**, **-iest**) enclenque

pup /pʌp/ *n* cachorro *m*

pupil /'pju:pl/ *n* alumno *m*; (of eye) pupila *f*

puppet /'pʌpɪt/ *n* marioneta *f*, títere *m*; (glove ~) títere *m*

puppy /'pʌpɪ/ *n* cachorro *m*

purchase /'pɜ:tʃəs/ *vt* adquirir. ● *n* adquisición *f*. **~r** *n* comprador *m*

pur|e /'pjʊə(r)/ *a* (**-er**, **-est**) puro. **~ity** *n* pureza *f*

purgatory /'pɜ:gətrɪ/ *n* purgatorio *m*

purge /pɜ:dʒ/ *vt* purgar. ● *n* purga *f*

purif|ication /pjʊərɪfɪ'keɪʃn/ *n* purificación *f*. **~y** /'pjʊərɪfaɪ/ *vt* purificar

purist /'pjʊərɪst/ *n* purista *m & f*

puritan /'pjʊərɪtən/ *n* puritano *m*. **~ical** /-'tænɪkl/ *a* puritano

purple /'pɜ:pl/ *a* morado. ● *n* morado *m*, púrpura *f*

purport /pə'pɔ:t/ *vt*. ~ **to be** pretender ser

purpose /'pɜ:pəs/ *n* propósito *m*; (determination) resolución *f*. **on ~** a propósito. **serve a ~** servir de algo. **~ful** *a* (resolute) resuelto. **~ly** *adv* a propósito

purr /pɜ:(r)/ *vi* ronronear

purse /pɜ:s/ *n* monedero *m*; (Amer) bolso *m*, cartera *f* (LAm), bolsa *f* (Mex)

pursu|e /pə'sju:/ *vt* perseguir, continuar con <*course of action*>. **~it** /pə'sju:t/ *n* persecución *f*; (pastime) actividad *f*

pus /pʌs/ *n* pus *m*

push /pʊʃ/ *vt* empujar; apretar (button). ● *vi* empujar. ● *n* empujón *m*; (effort) esfuerzo *m*. □ ~ **back** *vt* hacer retroceder. □ ~ **off** *vi* ☒ largarse. **~chair** *n* sillita *f* de paseo, carreola *f* (Mex). **~y** *a* (pej) ambicioso

pussy /pʊsɪ/ (*pl* **-sies**), **pussycat** /'pʊsɪkæt/ *n* ☐ minino *m*

put /pʊt/ *vt* (*pt* **put**, *pres p* **putting**) poner; (with care, precision) colocar; (inside sth) meter; (express) decir. □ **~ across** *vt* comunicar. □ **~ away** *vt* guardar. □ **~ back** *vt* volver a poner; retrasar <*clock*>. □ **~ by** *vt* guardar; ahorrar <*money*>. □ **~ down** *vt* (on a surface) dejar; colgar <*phone*>; (suppress) sofocar; (write) apuntar; (kill) sacrificar. □ **~ forward** *vt* presentar <*plan*>; proponer <*candidate*>; adelantar <*clocks*>; adelantar <*meeting*>. □ **~ in** *vt* (instal) poner; presentar <*claim*>. □ **~ in for** *vt* solicitar. □ **~ off** *vt* aplazar, posponer; (disconcert) desconcertar. □ **~ on** *vt* (wear) ponerse; poner <*CD, music*>; encender <*light*>. □ **~ out** *vt* (extinguish) apagar; (inconvenience) incomodar; extender <*hand*>; (disconcert) desconcertar. □ **~ through** *vt* (phone) poner, pasar (**to** con). □ **~ up** *vt* levantar; aumentar <*rent*>; subir <*price*>; poner <*sign*>; alojar <*guest*>. □ **~ up with** *vt* aguantar, soportar

putrid /'pju:trɪd/ *a* putrefacto

putt /pʌt/ *n* (golf) golpe *m* suave

puzzl|e /'pʌzl/ *n* misterio *m*; (game) rompecabezas *m*. ● *vt* dejar perplejo. **~ed** *a* <*expression*> de desconcierto. **I'm ~ed about it** me tiene perplejo. **~ing** *a* incomprensible; (odd) curioso

pygmy /'pɪgmɪ/ *n* pigmeo *m*

pyjamas /pə'dʒɑ:məz/ *npl* pijama *m*, piyama *m or f* (LAm)

pylon /'paɪlɒn/ *n* pilón *m*

pyramid /'pɪrəmɪd/ *n* pirámide *f*

python /'paɪθn/ *n* pitón *m*

Qq

quack /kwæk/ *n* (of duck) graznido *m*; (person) charlatán *m*. **~ doctor** *n* curandero *m*

quadrangle /'kwɒdræŋgl/ *n* cuadrilátero *m*

quadruped /'kwɒdrʊped/ *n* cuadrúpedo *m*

quadruple /'kwɒdrʊpl/ *a* & *n* cuádruplo (*m*). ● *vt* cuadruplicar

quagmire /'kwægmaɪə(r)/ *n* lodazal *m*

quaint /kweɪnt/ *a* (**-er**, **-est**) pintoresco; (odd) curioso

quake /kweɪk/ *vi* temblar. ● *n* [I] terremoto *m*

qualif|ication /kwɒlɪfɪ'keɪʃn/ *n* título *m*; (requirement) requisito *m*; (ability) capacidad *f*; (Sport) clasificación *f*; (fig) reserva *f*. **~ied** /'kwɒlɪfaɪd/ *a* cualificado; (with degree, diploma) titulado; (competent) capacitado. **~y** /'kwɒlɪfaɪ/ *vt* calificar; (limit) limitar. ● *vi* titularse; (Sport) clasificarse. **~y for sth** (be entitled to) tener derecho a algo

qualit|ative /'kwɒlɪtətɪv/ *a* cualitativo. **~y** /'kwɒlɪtɪ/ *n* calidad *f*; (attribute) cualidad *f*

qualm /kwɑ:m/ *n* reparo *m*

quandary /'kwɒndrɪ/ *n* dilema *m*

quanti|fy /'kwɒntɪfaɪ/ *vt* cuantificar. **~ty** /-tɪ/ *n* cantidad *f*

quarantine /'kwɒrənti:n/ *n* cuarentena *f*. ● *vt* poner en cuarentena

quarrel /ˈkwɒrəl/ *n* pelea *f.* ● *vi* (*pt* **quarrelled**) pelearse, discutir. **~some** /-səm/ *a* pendenciero

quarry /ˈkwɒrɪ/ *n* (excavation) cantera *f*; (prey) presa *f*

quart /kwɔ:t/ *n* cuarto *m* de galón

quarter /ˈkwɔ:tə(r)/ *n* cuarto *m*; (of year) trimestre *m*; (district) barrio *m*. **a ~ of an hour** un cuarto de hora. ● *vt* dividir en cuartos; (Mil) acuartelar. **~-final** *n* cuarto *m* de final. **~ly** *a* trimestral. ● *adv* trimestralmente

quartz /kwɔ:ts/ *n* cuarzo *m*

quay /ki:/ *n* muelle *m*

queasy /ˈkwi:zɪ/ *a* mareado

queen /kwi:n/ *n* reina *f*. **~ mother** *n* reina *f* madre

queer /kwɪə(r)/ *a* (**-er**, **-est**) extraño

quench /kwentʃ/ *vt* quitar <*thirst*>; sofocar <*desire*>

query /ˈkwɪərɪ/ *n* pregunta *f*. ● *vt* preguntar; (doubt) poner en duda

quest /kwest/ *n* busca *f*

question /ˈkwestʃən/ *n* pregunta *f*; (for discussion) cuestión *f*. **in ~** en cuestión. **out of the ~** imposible. **without ~** sin duda. ● *vt* hacer preguntas a; <*police etc*> interrogar; (doubt) poner en duda. **~able** *a* discutible. **~ mark** *n* signo *m* de interrogación. **~naire** /-ˈneə(r)/ *n* cuestionario *m*

queue /kju:/ *n* cola *f*. ● *vi* (*pres p* **queuing**) hacer cola

quibble /ˈkwɪbl/ *vi* discutir; (split hairs) sutilizar

quick /kwɪk/ *a* (**-er**, **-est**) rápido. **be ~!** ¡date prisa! ● *adv* rápido. **~en** *vt* acelerar. ● *vi* acelerarse. **~ly** *adv* rápido. **~sand** *n* arena *f* movediza. **~-tempered** /-ˈtempəd/ *a* irascible

quid /kwɪd/ *n invar* 🅘 libra *f* (esterlina)

quiet /ˈkwaɪət/ *a* (**-er**, **-est**) tranquilo; (silent) callado; (discreet) discreto. ● *n* tranquilidad *f*. ● *vt/i* (Amer) ⇒QUIETEN. **~en** *vt* calmar. ● *n* calmarse. **~ly** *adv* tranquilamente; (silently) silenciosamente; (discreetly) discretamente. **~ness** *n* tranquilidad *f*

quilt /kwɪlt/ *n* edredón *m*. **~ed** *a* acolchado

quintet /kwɪnˈtet/ *n* quinteto *m*

quirk /kwɜ:k/ *n* peculiaridad *f*

quit /kwɪt/ *vt* (*pt* **quitted**) dejar. **~ doing** (Amer, cease) dejar de hacer. ● *vi* (give in) abandonar; (stop) parar; (resign) dimitir

quite /kwaɪt/ *adv* bastante; (completely) totalmente; (really) verdaderamente. **~ (so!)** ¡claro! **~ a few** bastante

quits /kwɪts/ *a*. **be ~** estar en paz. **call it ~** darlo por terminado

quiver /ˈkwɪvə(r)/ *vi* temblar

quiz /kwɪz/ *n* (*pl* **quizzes**) serie *f* de preguntas; (game) concurso *m*. ● *vt* (*pt* **quizzed**) interrogar. **~zical** *a* burlón

quota /ˈkwəʊtə/ *n* cuota *f*

quot|ation /kwəʊˈteɪʃn/ *n* cita *f*; (price) presupuesto *m*. **~ation marks** *npl* comillas *fpl*. **~e** /kwəʊt/ *vt* citar; (Com) cotizar. ● *n* 🅘 cita *f*; (price) presupuesto *m*. **in ~es** *npl* entre comillas.

Rr

rabbi /'ræbaɪ/ *n* rabino *m*

rabbit /'ræbɪt/ *n* conejo *m*

rabi|d /'ræbɪd/ *a* feroz; *<dog>* rabioso. **~es** /'reɪbi:z/ *n* rabia *f*

race /reɪs/ *n* (in sport) carrera *f*; (ethnic group) raza *f*. ● *vt* hacer correr *<horse>*. ● *vi* (run) correr, ir corriendo; (rush) ir de prisa. **~course** *n* hipódromo *m*. **~horse** *n* caballo *m* de carreras. **~ relations** *npl* relaciones *fpl* raciales. **~track** *n* hipódromo *m*

racial /'reɪʃl/ *a* racial

racing /'reɪsɪŋ/ *n* carreras *fpl*. **~ car** *n* coche *m* de carreras

racis|m /'reɪsɪzəm/ *n* racismo *m*. **~t** *a & n* racista (*m & f*)

rack[1] /ræk/ *n* (shelf) estante *m*; (for luggage) rejilla *f*; (for plates) escurreplatos *m*. ● *vt*. **~ one's brains** devanarse los sesos

rack[2] /ræk/ *n*. **go to ~ and ruin** quedarse en la ruina

racket /'rækɪt/ *n* (for sports) raqueta; (din) alboroto *m*; (swindle) estafa *f*. **~eer** /-ə'tɪə(r)/ *n* estafador *m*

racy /'reɪsɪ/ *a* (**-ier**, **-iest**) vivo

radar /'reɪdɑ:(r)/ *n* radar *m*

radian|ce /'reɪdɪəns/ *n* resplandor *m*. **~t** *a* radiante

radiat|e /'reɪdɪeɪt/ *vt* irradiar. ● *vi* divergir. **~ion** /-'eɪʃn/ *n* radiación *f*. **~or** *n* radiador *m*

radical /'rædɪkl/ *a & n* radical (*m*)

radio /'reɪdɪəʊ/ *n* (*pl* **-os**) radio *f or m*. ● *vt* transmitir por radio. **~active** /reɪdɪəʊ'æktɪv/ *a* radiactivo. **~activity** /-'tɪvətɪ/ *n* radiactividad *f*

radish /'rædɪʃ/ *n* rábano *m*

radius /'reɪdɪəs/ *n* (*pl* **-dii** /-dɪaɪ/) radio *m*

raffle /'ræfl/ *n* rifa *f*

raft /rɑ:ft/ *n* balsa *f*

rafter /'rɑ:ftə(r)/ *n* cabrio *m*

rag /ræg/ *n* andrajo *m*; (for wiping) trapo *m*. **in ~s** *<person>* andrajoso

rage /reɪdʒ/ *n* rabia *f*; (fashion) moda *f*. ● *vi* estar furioso; *<storm>* bramar

ragged /'rægɪd/ *a* *<person>* andrajoso; *<clothes>* hecho jirones

raid /reɪd/ *n* (Mil) incursión *f*; (by police, etc) redada *f*; (by thieves) asalto *m*. ● *vt* (Mil) atacar; *<police>* hacer una redada en; *<thieves>* asaltar. **~er** *n* invasor *m*; (thief) ladrón *m*

rail /reɪl/ *n* barandilla *f*; (for train) riel *m*; (rod) barra *f*. **by ~** por ferrocarril. **~ing** *n* barandilla *f*; (fence) verja *f*. **~road** *n* (Amer), **~way** *n* ferrocarril *m*. **~way station** *n* estación *f* de ferrocarril

rain /reɪn/ *n* lluvia *f*. ● *vi* llover. **~bow** /-bəʊ/ *n* arco *m* iris. **~coat** *n* impermeable *m*. **~fall** *n* precipitación *f*. **~y** *a* (**-ier**, **-iest**) lluvioso

raise /reɪz/ *vt* levantar; (breed) criar; obtener *<money etc>*; formular *<question>*; plantear *<problem>*; subir *<price>*. ● *n* (Amer) aumento *m*

raisin /'reɪzn/ *n* (uva *f*) pasa *f*

rake /reɪk/ *n* rastrillo *m*. ● *vt* rastrillar; (search) buscar en. □ **~ up** *vt* remover

rally /'rælɪ/ *vt* reunir; (revive) reanimar. ● *n* reunión *f*; (Auto) rally *m*

ram /ræm/ *n* carnero *m*. ● *vt* (*pt* **rammed**) (thrust) meter por la fuerza; (crash into) chocar con

RAM /ræm/ *n* (Comp) RAM *f*

rambl|e /'ræmbl/ *n* excursión *f* a pie. ● *vi* ir de paseo; (in speech) divagar. □ **~e on** *vi* divagar. **~er** *n* excursionista *m* & *f*. **~ing** *a* <*speech*> divagador

ramp /ræmp/ *n* rampa *f*

rampage /ræm'peɪdʒ/ *vi* alborotarse. ● /'ræmpeɪdʒ/ *n*. **go on the ~** alborotarse

ramshackle /'ræmʃækl/ *a* desvencijado

ran /ræn/ ⇒RUN

ranch /rɑːntʃ/ *n* hacienda *f*

random /'rændəm/ *a* hecho al azar; (chance) fortuito. ● *n*. **at ~** al azar

rang /ræŋ/ ⇒RING[2]

range /reɪndʒ/ *n* alcance *m*; (distance) distancia *f*; (series) serie *f*; (of mountains) cordillera *f*; (extent) extensión *f*; (Com) surtido *m*; (stove) cocina *f* económica. ● *vi* extenderse; (vary) variar. **~r** *n* guardabosque *m*

rank /ræŋk/ *n* posición *f*, categoría *f*; (row) fila *f*; (for taxis) parada *f*. **the ~ and file** la masa *f*. **~s** *npl* soldados *mpl* rasos. ● *a* (**-er**, **-est**) (smell) fétido; (fig) completo. ● *vt* clasificar. ● *vi* clasificarse

ransack /'rænsæk/ *vt* registrar; (pillage) saquear

ransom /'rænsəm/ *n* rescate *m*. **hold s.o. to ~** exigir rescate por uno. ● *vt* rescatar; (redeem) redimir

rant /rænt/ *vi* despotricar

rap /ræp/ *n* golpe *m* seco. ● *vt/i* (*pt* **rapped**) golpear

rape /reɪp/ *vt* violar. ● *n* violación *f*

rapid /'ræpɪd/ *a* rápido. **~s** *npl* rápidos *mpl*

rapist /'reɪpɪst/ *n* violador *m*

raptur|e /'ræptʃə(r)/ *n* éxtasis *m*. **~ous** /-rəs/ *a* extático

rare /reə(r)/ *a* (**-er**, **-est**) raro; (Culin) poco hecho. **~fied** /'reərɪfaɪd/ *a* enrarecido. **~ly** *adv* raramente

raring /'reərɪŋ/ *a* 🄸. **~ to** impaciente por

rarity /'reərətɪ/ *n* rareza *f*

rascal /'rɑːskl/ *n* granuja *m* & *f*

rash /ræʃ/ *a* (**-er**, **-est**) precipitado, imprudente. ● *n* erupción *f*

rasher /'ræʃə(r)/ *n* loncha *f*

rashly /'ræʃlɪ/ *adv* precipitadamente, imprudentemente

rasp /rɑːsp/ *n* (file) escofina *f*

raspberry /'rɑːzbrɪ/ *n* frambuesa *f*

rat /ræt/ *n* rata *f*

rate /reɪt/ *n* (ratio) proporción *f*; (speed) velocidad *f*; (price) precio *m*; (of interest) tipo *m*. **at any ~** de todas formas. **at this ~** así. **~s** *npl* (taxes) impuestos *mpl* municipales. ● *vt* valorar; (consider) considerar; (Amer, deserve) merecer. ● *vi* ser considerado

rather /'rɑːðə(r)/ *adv* mejor dicho; (fairly) bastante; (a little) un poco. ● *int* claro. **I would ~ not** prefiero no

rating /'reɪtɪŋ/ *n* clasificación *f*; (sailor) marinero *m*; (number, TV) índice *m*

ratio /'reɪʃɪəʊ/ *n* (*pl* **-os**) proporción *f*

ration /'ræʃn/ *n* ración *f*. **~s** *npl* (provisions) víveres *mpl*. ● *vt* racionar

rational /'ræʃənəl/ *a* racional. **~ize** *vt* racionalizar

rattle /'rætl/ *vi* traquetear. ● *vt* (shake) agitar; Ⓘ desconcertar. ● *n* traqueteo *m*; (toy) sonajero *m*. □ **~ off** *vt* (fig) decir de corrida

raucous /'rɔ:kəs/ *a* estridente

ravage /'rævɪdʒ/ *vt* estragar

rave /reɪv/ *vi* delirar; (in anger) despotricar. **~ about sth** poner a algo por las nubes

raven /'reɪvn/ *n* cuervo *m*

ravenous /'rævənəs/ *a* voraz; <*person*> hambriento. **be ~** morirse de hambre

ravine /rə'vi:n/ *n* barranco *m*

raving /'reɪvɪŋ/ *a*. **~ mad** loco de atar

ravishing /'rævɪʃɪŋ/ *a* (enchanting) encantador

raw /rɔ:/ *a* (**-er**, **-est**) crudo; <*sugar*> sin refinar; (inexperienced) inexperto. **~ deal** *n* tratamiento *m* injusto, injusticia *f*. **~ materials** *npl* materias *fpl* primas

ray /reɪ/ *n* rayo *m*

raze /reɪz/ *vt* arrasar

razor /'reɪzə(r)/ *n* navaja *f* de afeitar; (electric) maquinilla *f* de afeitar

Rd /rəʊd/ *abbr* (= **Road**) C/, Calle *f*

re /ri:/ *prep* con referencia a. ● *pref* re.

reach /ri:tʃ/ *vt* alcanzar; (extend) extender; (arrive at) llegar a; (achieve) lograr; (hand over) pasar, dar. ● *vi* extenderse. ● *n* alcance *m*. **within ~ of** al alcance de; (close to) a corta distancia de. □ **~ out** *vi* alargar la mano

react /rɪ'ækt/ *vi* reaccionar. **~ion** /rɪ'ækʃn/ *n* reacción *f*. **~ionary** *a* & *n* reaccionario (*m*). **~or** /rɪ'æk tə(r)/ *n* reactor *m*

read /ri:d/ *vt* (*pt* **read** /red/) leer; (study) estudiar; (interpret) interpretar. ● *vi* leer; <*instrument*> indicar. □ **~ out** *vt* leer en voz alta. **~able** *a* (clear) legible. **~er** *n* lector *m*

readily /'redɪlɪ/ *adv* (willingly) de buena gana; (easily) fácilmente

reading /'ri:dɪŋ/ *n* lectura *f*

readjust /ri:ə'dʒʌst/ *vt* reajustar. ● *vi* readaptarse (**to** a)

ready /'redɪ/ *a* (**-ier**, **-iest**) listo, preparado. **get ~** prepararse. **~-made** *a* confeccionado

real /rɪəl/ *a* verdadero. ● *adv* (Amer Ⓘ) verdaderamente. **~ estate** *n* bienes *mpl* raíces, propiedad *f* inmobiliaria. **~ estate agent** ⇒REALTOR. **~ism** *n* realismo *m*. **~ist** *n* realista *m* & *f*. **~istic** /-'lɪstɪk/ *a* realista. **~ity** /rɪ'ælətɪ/ *n* realidad *f*. **~ization** /rɪəlaɪ'zeɪʃn/ *n* comprensión *f*. **~ize** /'rɪəlaɪz/ *vt* darse cuenta de; (fulfil, Com) realizar. **~ly** /'rɪəlɪ/ *adv* verdaderamente

realm /relm/ *n* reino *m*

realtor /'ri:əltə(r)/ *n* (Amer) agente *m* inmobiliario

reap /ri:p/ *vt* segar; (fig) cosechar

reappear /ri:ə'pɪə(r)/ *vi* reaparecer

rear /rɪə(r)/ *n* parte *f* de atrás. ● *a* posterior, trasero. ● *vt* (bring up, breed) criar. ● *vi* **~ (up)** <*horse*> encabritarse

rearguard /'rɪəgɑ:d/ *n* retaguardia *f*

rearrange /ri:ə'reɪndʒ/ *vt* arreglar de otra manera

reason /'ri:zn/ *n* razón *f*, motivo *m*. **within ~** dentro de lo razonable. ● *vi* razonar. **~able** *a* razonable. **~ing** *n* razonamiento *m*

reassur|ance /ri:ə'ʃʊərəns/ *n* promesa *f* tranquilizadora; (guarantee) garantía *f*. **~e** /ri:ə'ʃʊə(r)/ *vt* tranquilizar

rebate /'ri:beɪt/ *n* (discount) rebaja *f*

rebel /'rebl/ *n* rebelde *m* & *f*. ● /rɪ'bel/ *vi* (*pt* **rebelled**) rebelarse. **~lion** /rɪ'belɪən/ *n* rebelión *f*. **~lious** *a* rebelde

rebound /rɪ'baʊnd/ *vi* rebotar; (fig) recaer. ● /'ri:baʊnd/ *n* rebote *m*

rebuff /rɪ'bʌf/ *vt* rechazar. ● *n* desaire *m*

rebuild /ri:'bɪld/ *vt* (*pt* **rebuilt**) reconstruir

rebuke /rɪ'bju:k/ *vt* reprender. ● *n* reprimenda *f*

recall /rɪ'kɔ:l/ *vt* (call s.o. back) llamar; (remember) recordar. ● *n* /'ri:kɔ:l/ (of goods, ambassador) retirada *f*; (memory) memoria *f*

recap /'ri:kæp/ *vt/i* (*pt* **recapped**) ⓘ resumir

recapitulate /ri:kə'pɪtʃʊleɪt/ *vt/i* resumir

recapture /ri:'kæptʃə(r)/ *vt* recobrar; (recall) hacer revivir

recede /rɪ'si:d/ *vi* retroceder

receipt /rɪ'si:t/ *n* recibo *m*. **~s** *npl* (Com) ingresos *mpl*

receive /rɪ'si:v/ *vt* recibir. **~r** *n* (of stolen goods) perista *m* & *f*; (part of phone) auricular *m*

recent /'ri:snt/ *a* reciente. **~ly** *adv* recientemente

recept|ion /rɪ'sepʃn/ *n* recepción *f*; (welcome) acogida *f*. **~ionist** *n* recepcionista *m* & *f*. **~ive** /-tɪv/ *a* receptivo

recess /rɪ'ses/ *n* hueco *m*; (holiday) vacaciones *fpl*. **~ion** /rɪ'seʃn/ *n* recesión *f*

recharge /ri:'tʃɑ:dʒ/ *vt* cargar de nuevo, recargar

recipe /'resəpɪ/ *n* receta *f*. **~ book** *n* libro *m* de cocina

recipient /rɪ'sɪpɪənt/ *n* recipiente *m* & *f*; (of letter) destinatario *m*

recit|al /rɪ'saɪtl/ *n* (Mus) recital *m*. **~e** /rɪ'saɪt/ *vt* recitar; (list) enumerar

reckless /'reklɪs/ *a* imprudente. **~ly** *adv* imprudentemente

reckon /'rekən/ *vt/i* calcular; (consider) considerar; (think) pensar. □ **~ on** *vt* (rely) contar con

reclaim /rɪ'kleɪm/ *vt* reclamar; recuperar <*land*>

reclin|e /rɪ'klaɪn/ *vi* recostarse. **~ing** *a* acostado; <*seat*> reclinable

recluse /rɪ'klu:s/ *n* ermitaño *m*

recogni|tion /rekəg'nɪʃn/ *n* reconocimiento *m*. **beyond ~tion** irreconocible. **~ze** /'rekəgnaɪz/ *vt* reconocer

recoil /rɪ'kɔɪl/ *vi* retroceder. ● /'ri:kɔɪl/ *n* (of gun) culatazo *m*

recollect /rekə'lekt/ *vt* recordar. **~ion** /-ʃn/ *n* recuerdo *m*

recommend /rekə'mend/ *vt* recomendar. **~ation** /-'deɪʃn/ *n* recomendación *f*

reconcil|e /'rekənsaɪl/ *vt* reconciliar <*people*>; conciliar <*facts*>. **~e o.s.** resignarse (**to** a). **~iation** /-sɪlɪ'eɪʃn/ *n* reconciliación *f*

reconnaissance /rɪ'kɒnɪsns/ *n* reconocimiento *m*

reconnoitre /rekə'nɔɪtə(r)/ *vt* (*pres p* **-tring**) (Mil) reconocer

re: ~consider /ri:kən'sɪdə(r)/ *vt* volver a considerar. **~construct** /ri:kən'strʌkt/ *vt* reconstruir

record /rɪ'kɔ:d/ *vt* (in register) registrar; (in diary) apuntar; (Mus) grabar. ● /'rekɔ:d/ *n* (document) do cumento *m*; (of events) registro *m*; (Mus) disco *m*; (Sport) récord *m*. **off the ~** en confianza. **~er** /rɪ'kɔ:də(r)/ *n* registrador *m*; (Mus) flauta *f* dulce. **~ing** /rɪ'kɔ:dɪŋ/ *n* grabación *f*. **~-player** /'rekɔ:d-/ *n* tocadiscos *m* invar

recount /rɪ'kaʊnt/ *vt* contar, relatar

re-count /'ri:kaʊnt/ *vt* volver a contar; recontar <*votes*>. ● /'ri:kaʊnt/ *n* (Pol) recuento *m*

recover /rɪ'kʌvə(r)/ *vt* recuperar. ● *vi* reponerse. **~y** *n* recuperación *f*

recreation /rekrɪ'eɪʃn/ *n* recreo *m*. **~al** *a* de recreo

recruit /rɪ'kru:t/ *n* recluta *m*. ● *vt* reclutar; contratar <*staff*>. **~ment** *n* reclutamiento *m*

rectang|le /'rektæŋgl/ *n* rectángulo *m*. **~ular** /-'tæŋgjʊlə(r)/ *a* rectangular

rectify /'rektɪfaɪ/ *vt* rectificar

rector /'rektə(r)/ *n* párroco *m*; (of college) rector *m*. **~y** *n* rectoría *f*

recuperat|e /rɪ'ku:pəreɪt/ *vt* recuperar. ● *vi* reponerse. **~ion** /-'reɪʃn/ *n* recuperación *f*

recur /rɪ'kɜ:(r)/ *vi* (*pt* **recurred**) repetirse. **~rence** /rɪ'kʌrns/ *n* repetición *f*. **~rent** /rɪ'kʌrənt/ *a* repetido

recycle /ri:'saɪkl/ *vt* reciclar

red /red/ *a* (**redder**, **reddest**) rojo. ● *n* rojo. **be in the ~** estar en números rojos. **~den** *vi* enrojecerse. **~dish** *a* rojizo

redecorate /ri:'dekəreɪt/ *vt* pintar de nuevo

rede|em /rɪ'di:m/ *vt* redimir. **~mption** /-'dempʃn/ *n* redención *f*

red: ~-handed /-'hændɪd/ *a*. **catch s.o. ~handed** agarrar a uno con las manos en la masa. **~ herring** *n* (fig) pista *f* falsa. **~-hot** *a* al rojo vivo; **~ light** *n* luz *f* roja

redo /ri:'du:/ *vt* (*pt* **redid**, *pp* **redone**) rehacer

redouble /rɪ'dʌbl/ *vt* redoblar

red tape /red'teɪp/ *n* (fig) papeleo *m*

reduc|e /rɪ'dju:s/ *vt* reducir; aliviar <*pain*>. ● *vi* (Amer, slim) adelgazar. **~tion** /rɪ'dʌkʃn/ *n* reducción *f*

redundan|cy /rɪ'dʌndənsɪ/ *n* superfluidad *f*; (unemployment) despido *m*. **~t** superfluo. **she was made ~t** la despidieron por reducción de plantilla

reed /ri:d/ *n* caña *f*; (Mus) lengüeta *f*

reef /ri:f/ *n* arrecife *m*

reek /ri:k/ *n* mal olor *m*. ● *vi*. **~** (of) apestar (a)

reel /ri:l/ *n* carrete *m*. ● *vi* dar vueltas; (stagger) tambalearse. □ **~ off** *vt* (fig) enumerar

refectory /rɪ'fektərɪ/ *n* refectorio *m*

refer /rɪ'fɜ:(r)/ *vt* (*pt* **referred**) remitir. ● *vi* referirse. **~ to** referirse a; (consult) consultar. **~ee** /refə'ri:/ *n* árbitro *m*; (for job) referencia *f*. ● *vi* (*pt* **refereed**) arbitrar. **~ence** /'refrəns/ *n* referencia *f*. **~ence book** *n* libro *m* de consulta. **in ~ence to, with ~ence to** con referencia a; (Com) respecto a. **~endum** /refə'rendəm/ *n* (*pl* **-ums** *or* **-da**) referéndum *m*

refill /ri:'fɪl/ *vt* volver a llenar. ● /'ri:fɪl/ *n* recambio *m*

refine /rɪ'faɪn/ *vt* refinar. **~d** *a* refinado. **~ry** /-ərɪ/ *n* refinería *f*

reflect /rɪ'flekt/ *vt* reflejar. ● *vi* reflejarse; (think) reflexionar. □ ~ badly upon perjudicar. **~ion** /-ʃn/ *n* reflexión *f*; (image) reflejo *m*. **~or** *n* reflector *m*

reflex /'ri:fleks/ *a* & *n* reflejo (*m*). **~ive** /rɪ'fleksɪv/ *a* (Gram) reflexivo

reform /rɪ'fɔ:m/ *vt* reformar. ● *vi* reformarse. ● *n* reforma *f*

refrain /rɪ'freɪn/ *n* estribillo *m*. ● *vi* abstenerse (**from** de)

refresh /rɪ'freʃ/ *vt* refrescar. **~ing** *a* refrescante. **~ments** *npl* (food and drink) refrigerio *m*

refrigerat|e /rɪ'frɪdʒəreɪt/ *vt* refrigerar. **~or** *n* frigorífico *m*, refrigerador *m* (LAm)

refuel /ri:'fju:əl/ *vt/i* (*pt* **refuelled**) repostar

refuge /'refju:dʒ/ *n* refugio *m*. **take ~** refugiarse. **~e** /refjʊ'dʒi:/ *n* refugiado *m*

refund /rɪ'fʌnd/ *vt* reembolsar. ● /'ri:fʌnd/ *n* reembolso *m*

refusal /rɪ'fju:zl/ *n* negativa *f*

refuse /rɪ'fju:z/ *vt* rehusar. ● *vi* negarse. ● /'refju:s/ *n* residuos *mpl*

refute /rɪ'fju:t/ *vt* refutar

regain /rɪ'geɪn/ *vt* recobrar

regal /'ri:gl/ *a* real

regard /rɪ'gɑ:d/ *vt* considerar; (look at) contemplar. **as ~s** en lo que se refiere a. ● *n* (consideration) consideración *f*; (esteem) estima *f*. **~s** *npl* saludos *mpl*. **kind ~s** recuerdos. **~ing** *prep* en lo que se refiere a. **~less** *adv* a pesar de todo. **~less of** sin tener en cuenta

regatta /rɪ'gætə/ *n* regata *f*

regime /reɪ'ʒi:m/ *n* régimen *m*

regiment /'redʒɪmənt/ *n* regimiento *m*. **~al** /-'mentl/ *a* del regimiento

region /'ri:dʒən/ *n* región *f*. **in the ~ of** alrededor de. **~al** *a* regional

register /'redʒɪstə(r)/ *n* registro *m*. ● *vt* registrar; matricular <*vehicle*>; declarar <*birth*>; certificar <*letter*>; facturar <*luggage*>. ● *vi* (enrol) inscribirse; (fig) producir impresión

registrar /redʒɪ'strɑ:(r)/ *n* secretario *m* del registro civil; (Univ) secretario *m* general

registration /redʒɪ'streɪʃn/ *n* registración *f*; (in register) inscripción *f*. **~ number** *n* (Auto) (número de) matrícula *f*

registry /'redʒɪstrɪ/ *n*. **~ office** *n* registro *m* civil

regret /rɪ'gret/ *n* pesar *m*; (remorse) arrepentimiento *m*. ● *vt* (*pt* **regretted**) lamentar. **I ~ that** siento (que). **~table** *a* lamentable

regula|r /'regjʊlə(r)/ *a* regular; (usual) habitual. ● *n* Ⓘ cliente *m* habitual. **~rity** /-'lærətɪ/ *n* regularidad *f*. **~rly** *adv* con regularidad. **~te** /'regjʊleɪt/ *vt* regular. **~tion** /-'leɪʃn/ *n* regulación *f*; (rule) regla *f*

rehears|al /rɪ'hɜ:sl/ *n* ensayo *m*. **~e** /rɪ'hɜ:s/ *vt* ensayar

reign /reɪn/ *n* reinado *m*. ● *vi* reinar

reindeer /'reɪndɪə(r)/ *n invar* reno *m*

reinforce /ri:ɪn'fɔ:s/ *vt* reforzar. **~ment** *n* refuerzo *m*

reins /reɪnz/ *npl* riendas *fpl*

reiterate /ri:'ɪtəreɪt/ *vt* reiterar

reject /rɪ'dʒekt/ *vt* rechazar. ● /'ri:dʒekt/ *n* producto *m* defectuoso. **~ion** /rɪ'dʒekʃn/ *n* rechazo *m*; (after job application) respuesta *f* negativa

rejoice /rɪ'dʒɔɪs/ *vi* regocijarse

rejoin /rɪ'dʒɔɪn/ *vt* reunirse con

rejuvenate /rɪ'dʒu:vəneɪt/ *vt* rejuvenecer

relapse /rɪ'læps/ *n* recaída *f*. ● *vi* recaer; (into crime) reincidir

relat|e /rɪ'leɪt/ *vt* contar; (connect) relacionar. ● *vi* relacionarse (to con). **~ed** *a* emparentado; *<ideas etc>* relacionado. **~ion** /rɪ'leɪʃn/ *n* relación *f*; (person) pariente *m & f*. **~ionship** *n* relación *f*; (blood tie) parentesco *m*; (affair) relaciones *fpl*. **~ive** /'relətɪv/ *n* pariente *m & f*. ● *a* relativo. **~ively** *adv* relativamente

relax /rɪ'læks/ *vt* relajar. ● *vi* relajarse. **~ation** /-'seɪʃn/ *n* relajación *f*; (rest) descanso *m*; (recreation) recreo *m*. **~ing** *a* relajante

relay /'ri:leɪ/ *n* relevo *m*. **~** (race) *n* carrera *f* de relevos. ● /rɪ'leɪ/ *vt* transmitir

release /rɪ'li:s/ *vt* soltar; poner en libertad *<prisoner>*; estrenar *<film>*; (Mec) soltar; publicar *<news>*. ● *n* liberación *f*; (of film) estreno *m*; (record) disco *m* nuevo

relent /rɪ'lent/ *vi* ceder. **~less** *a* implacable; (continuous) incesante

relevan|ce /'reləvəns/ *n* pertinencia *f*. **~t** *a* pertinente

relia|bility /rɪlaɪə'bɪlətɪ/ *n* fiabilidad *f*. **~ble** /rɪ'laɪəbl/ *a <person>* de confianza; *<car>* fiable. **~nce** /rɪ'laɪəns/ *n* dependencia *f*; (trust) confianza *f*. **~nt** /rɪ'laɪənt/ *a* confiado

relic /'relɪk/ *n* reliquia *f*

relie|f /rɪ'li:f/ *n* alivio *m*; (assistance) socorro *m*. **be on ~f** (Amer) recibir prestaciones de la seguridad social. **~ve** /rɪ'li:v/ *vt* aliviar; (take over from) relevar. **~ved** *a* aliviado. **feel ~ved** sentir un gran alivio

religio|n /rɪ'lɪdʒən/ *n* religión *f*. **~us** /rɪ'lɪdʒəs/ *a* religioso

relinquish /rɪ'lɪŋkwɪʃ/ *vt* abandonar, renunciar

relish /'relɪʃ/ *n* gusto *m*; (Culin) salsa *f*. ● *vt* saborear

reluctan|ce /rɪ'lʌktəns/ *n* desgana *f*. **~t** *a* mal dispuesto. **be ~t to** no tener ganas de. **~tly** *adv* de mala gana

rely /rɪ'laɪ/ *vi*. **~ on** contar con; (trust) fiarse de; (depend) depender

remain /rɪ'meɪn/ *vi* (be left) quedar; (stay) quedarse; (continue to be) seguir. **~der** *n* resto *m*. **~s** *npl* restos *mpl*; (left-overs) sobras *fpl*

remand /rɪ'mɑ:nd/ *vt*. **~ in custody** mantener bajo custodia. ● *n*. **on ~** en prisión preventiva

remark /rɪ'mɑ:k/ *n* observación *f*. ● *vt* observar. **~able** *a* notable

remarry /ri:'mærɪ/ *vi* volver a casarse

remedy /'remədɪ/ *n* remedio *m*. ● *vt* remediar

remember /rɪ'membə(r)/ *vt* acordarse de, recordar. ● *vi* acordarse

remind /rɪ'maɪnd/ *vt* recordar. **~er** *n* recordatorio *m*

reminisce /remɪ'nɪs/ *vi* rememorar los viejos tiempos. **~nces** /-ənsɪz/ *npl* recuerdos *mpl*. **~nt** /-'nɪsnt/ *a*. **be ~nt of** recordar

remnant /'remnənt/ *n* resto *m*; (of cloth) retazo *m*; (trace) vestigio *m*

remorse /rɪ'mɔ:s/ *n* remordimiento *m*. **~ful** *a* arrepentido. **~less** *a* implacable

remote /rɪ'məʊt/ *a* remoto. **~ control** *n* mando *m* a distancia. **~ly** *adv* remotamente

remov|able /rɪ'mu:vəbl/ *a* (detachable) de quita y pon; *<handle>* desmontable. **~al** *n* eliminación *f*; (from house) mudanza *f*. **~e**

/rɪ'mu:v/ *vt* quitar; (dismiss) destituir; (get rid of) eliminar

render /'rendə(r)/ *vt* rendir <*homage*>; prestar <*help etc*>. ~ **sth useless** hacer que algo resulte inútil

rendezvous /'rɒndɪvu:/ *n* (*pl* **-vous** /-vu:z/) cita *f*

renegade /'renɪgeɪd/ *n* renegado

renew /rɪ'nju:/ *vt* renovar; (resume) reanudar. **~al** *n* renovación *f*

renounce /rɪ'naʊns/ *vt* renunciar a

renovat|e /'renəveɪt/ *vt* renovar. **~ion** /-'veɪʃn/ *n* renovación *f*

renown /rɪ'naʊn/ *n* renombre *m*. **~ed** *a* de renombre

rent /rent/ *n* alquiler *m*. ● *vt* alquilar. **~al** *n* alquiler *m*. **car ~** (Amer) alquiler *m* de coche

renunciation /rɪnʌnsɪ'eɪʃn/ *n* renuncia *f*

reopen /ri:'əʊpən/ *vt* volver a abrir. ● *vi* reabrirse

reorganize /ri:'ɔ:gənaɪz/ *vt* reorganizar

rep /rep/ *n* (Com) representante *m* & *f*

repair /rɪ'peə(r)/ *vt* arreglar, reparar; arreglar <*clothes, shoes*>. ● *n* reparación *f*; (patch) remiendo *m*. **in good ~** en buen estado. **it's beyond ~** ya no tiene arreglo

repatriate /ri:'pætrɪeɪt/ *vt* repatriar

repay /ri:'peɪ/ *vt* (*pt* **repaid**) reembolsar; pagar <*debt*>; corresponder a <*kindness*>. **~ment** *n* pago *m*

repeal /rɪ'pi:l/ *vt* revocar. ● *n* revocación *f*

repeat /rɪ'pi:t/ *vt* repetir. ● *vi* repetir(se). ● *n* repetición *f*. **~edly** *adv* repetidas veces

repel /rɪ'pel/ *vt* (*pt* **repelled**) repeler. **~lent** *a* repelente

repent /rɪ'pent/ *vi* arrepentirse. **~ant** *a* arrepentido

repercussion /ri:pə'kʌʃn/ *n* repercusión *f*

repertoire /'repətwɑ:(r)/ *n* repertorio *m*

repetit|ion /repɪ'tɪʃn/ *n* repetición *f*. **~ious** /-'tɪʃəs/ *a*, **~ive** /rɪ'petətɪv/ *a* repetitivo

replace /rɪ'pleɪs/ *vt* reponer; cambiar <*battery*>; (take the place of) sustituir. **~ment** *n* sustitución *f*; (person) sustituto *m*

replay /'ri:pleɪ/ *n* (Sport) repetición *f* del partido; (recording) repetición *f* inmediata

replenish /rɪ'plenɪʃ/ *vt* reponer

replica /'replɪkə/ *n* réplica *f*

reply /rɪ'plaɪ/ *vt/i* responder, contestar. ~ **to sth** responder a algo, contestar algo. ● *n* respuesta *f*

report /rɪ'pɔ:t/ *vt* <*reporter*> informar sobre; informar de <*accident*>; (denounce) denunciar. ● *vi* informar; (present o.s.) presentarse. ● *n* informe *m*; (Schol) boletín *m* de notas; (rumour) rumor *m*; (in newspaper) reportaje *m*. ~ **card** (Amer) *n* boletín *m* de calificaciones. **~edly** *adv* según se dice. **~er** *n* periodista *m* & *f*, reportero *m*

reprehensible /reprɪ'hensəbl/ *a* reprensible

represent /reprɪ'zent/ *vt* representar. **~ation** /-'teɪʃn/ *n* representación *f*. **~ative** *a* representativo. ● *n* representante *m* & *f*; (Amer, in government) diputado *m*

repress /rɪ'pres/ *vt* reprimir. **~ion** /-ʃn/ *n* represión *f*. **~ive** *a* represivo

reprieve /rɪ'pri:v/ *n* indulto *m*; (fig) respiro *m*. ● *vt* indultar

reprimand /'reprɪmɑ:nd/ *vt* reprender. ● *n* reprensión *f*

reprisal /rɪ'praɪzl/ *n* represalia *f*

reproach /rɪ'prəʊtʃ/ *vt* reprochar. ● *n* reproche *m*. **~ful** *a* de reproche

reproduc|e /ri:prə'dju:s/ *vt* reproducir. ● *vi* reproducirse. **~tion** /-'dʌkʃn/ *n* reproducción *f*. **~tive** /-'dʌktɪv/ *a* reproductor

reprove /rɪ'pru:v/ *vt* reprender

reptile /'reptaɪl/ *n* reptil *m*

republic /rɪ'pʌblɪk/ *n* república *f*. **~an** *a* & *n* republicano (*m*). **R~** *a* & *n* (in US) republicano (*m*)

repugnan|ce /rɪ'pʌgnəns/ *n* repugnancia *f*. **~t** *a* repugnante

repuls|e /rɪ'pʌls/ *vt* rechazar, repulsar. **~ion** /-ʃn/ *n* repulsión *f*. **~ive** *a* repulsivo

reput|able /'repjʊtəbl/ *a* acreditado, reputado. **~ation** /repjʊ'teɪʃn/ *n* reputación *f*

request /rɪ'kwest/ *n* petición *f*. ● *vt* pedir

require /rɪ'kwaɪə(r)/ *vt* requerir; (need) necesitar; (demand) exigir. **~d** *a* necesario. **~ment** *n* requisito *m*

rescue /'reskju:/ *vt* rescatar, salvar. ● *n* rescate *m*. **~r** *n* salvador *m*

research /rɪ'sɜ:tʃ/ *n* investigación *f*. ● *vt* investigar. **~er** *n* investigador *m*

resembl|ance /rɪ'zembləns/ *n* parecido *m*. **~e** /rɪ'zembl/ *vt* parecerse a

resent /rɪ'zent/ *vt* guardarle rencor a <*person*>. **she ~ed his success** le molestaba que él tuviera éxito. **~ful** *a* resentido. **~ment** *n* resentimiento *m*

reserv|ation /rezə'veɪʃn/ *n* reserva *f*; (booking) reserva *f*. **~e** /rɪ'zɜ:v/ *vt* reservar. ● *n* reserva *f*; (in sports) suplente *m* & *f*. **~ed** *a* reservado. **~oir** /'rezəvwɑ:(r)/ *n* embalse *m*

reshuffle /ri:'ʃʌfl/ *n* (Pol) reorganización *f*

residen|ce /'rezɪdəns/ *n* residencia *f*. **~t** *a* & *n* residente (*m* & *f*). **~tial** /rezɪ'denʃl/ *a* residencial

residue /'rezɪdju:/ *n* residuo *m*

resign /rɪ'zaɪn/ *vt/i* dimitir. **~ o.s. to** resignarse a. **~ation** /rezɪg'neɪʃn/ *n* resignación *f*; (from job) dimisión *f*. **~ed** *a* resignado

resilien|ce /rɪ'zɪlɪəns/ *n* elasticidad *f*; (of person) resistencia *f*. **~t** *a* elástico; <*person*> resistente

resin /'rezɪn/ *n* resina *f*

resist /rɪ'zɪst/ *vt* resistir. ● *vi* resistirse. **~ance** *n* resistencia *f*. **~ant** *a* resistente

resolut|e /'rezəlu:t/ *a* resuelto. **~ion** /-'lu:ʃn/ *n* resolución *f*

resolve /rɪ'zɒlv/ *vt* resolver. **~ to do** resolver a hacer. ● *n* resolución *f*

resort /rɪ'zɔ:t/ *n* recurso *m*; (place) lugar *m* turístico. **in the last ~** como último recurso. □ **~ to** *vt* recurrir a.

resource /rɪ'sɔ:s/ *n* recurso *m*. **~ful** *a* ingenioso

respect /rɪ'spekt/ *n* (esteem) respeto *m*; (aspect) respecto *m*. **with ~ to** con respecto a. ● *vt* respetar. **~able** *a* respetable. **~ful** *a* respetuoso. **~ive** *a* respectivo. **~ively** *adv* respectivamente

respiration /respə'reɪʃn/ *n* respiración *f*

respite /ˈrespaɪt/ *n* respiro *m*

respon|d /rɪˈspɒnd/ *vi* responder. **~se** /rɪˈspɒns/ *n* respuesta *f*; (reaction) reacción *f*

responsib|ility /rɪspɒnsəˈbɪlətɪ/ *n* responsabilidad *f*. **~le** /rɪˈspɒnsəbl/ *a* responsable; <*job*> de responsabilidad. **~ly** *adv* con formalidad

responsive /rɪˈspɒnsɪv/ *a* que reacciona bien. **~ to** sensible a

rest /rest/ *vt* descansar; (lean) apoyar. ● *vi* descansar; (lean) apoyarse. ● *n* descanso *m*; (Mus) pausa *f*; (remainder) resto *m*, lo demás; (people) los demás, los otros *mpl*. **to have a ~** tomarse un descanso. □ **~ up** *vi* (Amer) descansar

restaurant /ˈrestərɒnt/ *n* restaurante *m*

rest: ~ful *a* sosegado. **~ive** *a* impaciente. **~less** *a* inquieto

restor|ation /restəˈreɪʃn/ *n* restablecimiento *m*; (of building, monarch) restauración *f*. **~e** /rɪˈstɔː(r)/ *vt* restablecer; restaurar <*building*>; devolver <*confidence, health*>

restrain /rɪˈstreɪn/ *vt* contener. **~ o.s.** contenerse. **~ed** *a* (moderate) moderado; (in control of self) comedido. **~t** *n* restricción *f*; (moderation) compostura *f*

restrict /rɪˈstrɪkt/ *vt* restringir. **~ion** /-ʃn/ *n* restricción *f*. **~ive** *a* restrictivo

rest room *n* (Amer) baño *m*, servicio *m*

result /rɪˈzʌlt/ *n* resultado *m*. **as a ~ of** como consecuencia de. ● *vi*. **~ from** resultar de. **~ in** dar como resultado

resume /rɪˈzjuːm/ *vt* reanudar. ● *vi* reanudarse

résumé /ˈrezjʊmeɪ/ *n* resumen *m*; (Amer, CV) currículum *m*, historial *m* personal

resurrect /rezəˈrekt/ *vt* resucitar. **~ion** /-ʃn/ *n* resurrección *f*

resuscitat|e /rɪˈsʌsɪteɪt/ *vt* resucitar. **~ion** /-ˈteɪʃn/ *n* resucitación *f*

retail /ˈriːteɪl/ *n* venta *f* al por menor. ● *a & adv* al por menor. ● *vt* vender al por menor. ● *vi* venderse al por menor. **~er** *n* minorista *m & f*

retain /rɪˈteɪn/ *vt* retener; conservar <*heat*>

retaliat|e /rɪˈtælɪeɪt/ *vi* desquitarse; (Mil) tomar represalias. **~ion** /-ˈeɪʃn/ *n* represalias *fpl*

retarded /rɪˈtɑːdɪd/ *a* retrasado

rethink /riːˈθɪŋk/ *vt* (*pt* **rethought**) reconsiderar

reticen|ce /ˈretɪsns/ *n* reticencia *f*. **~t** *a* reticente

retina /ˈretɪnə/ *n* retina *f*

retinue /ˈretɪnjuː/ *n* séquito *m*

retir|e /rɪˈtaɪə(r)/ *vi* (from work) jubilarse; (withdraw) retirarse; (go to bed) acostarse. **~ed** *a* jubilado. **~ement** *n* jubilación *f*. **~ing** *a* retraído

retort /rɪˈtɔːt/ *vt/i* replicar. ● *n* réplica *f*

retrace /riːˈtreɪs/ *vt*. **~ one's steps** volver sobre sus pasos

retract /rɪˈtrækt/ *vt* retirar <*statement*>. ● *vi* retractarse

retrain /riːˈtreɪn/ *vi* hacer un curso de reciclaje

retreat /rɪˈtriːt/ *vi* retirarse. ● *n* retirada *f*; (place) refugio *m*

retrial /riːˈtraɪəl/ *n* nuevo juicio *m*

retriev|al /rɪˈtriːvl/ *n* recuperación *f*. **~e** /rɪˈtriːv/ *vt* recuperar. **~er** *n* (dog) perro *m* cobrador

retro|grade /'retrəgreɪd/ *a* retrógrado. **~spect** /-spekt/ *n.* **in ~** en retrospectiva. **~spective** /-'spektɪv/ *a* retrospectivo

return /rɪ'tɜ:n/ *vi* volver, regresar; *<symptom>* reaparecer. ● *vt* devolver; corresponder a *<affection>*. ● *n* regreso *m*, vuelta *f*; (Com) rendimiento *m*; (to owner) devolución *f*. **in ~ for** a cambio de. **many happy ~s!** ¡feliz cumpleaños! **~ ticket** *n* billete *m or* (LAm) boleto *m* de ida y vuelta, boleto *m* redondo (Mex). **~s** *npl* (Com) ingresos *mpl*

reun|ion /ri:'ju:nɪən/ *n* reunión *f*. **~ite** /ri:ju:'naɪt/ *vt* reunir

rev /rev/ *n* (Auto, [I]) revolución *f*. ● *vt/i*. **~ (up)** (*pt* **revved**) (Auto, [I]) acelerar(se)

reveal /rɪ'vi:l/ *vt* revelar. **~ing** *a* revelador

revel /'revl/ *vi* (*pt* **revelled**) tener un jolgorio. **~ in** deleitarse en. **~ry** *n* jolgorio *m*

revelation /revə'leɪʃn/ *n* revelación *f*

revenge /rɪ'vendʒ/ *n* venganza *f*. **take ~** vengarse. ● *vt* vengar

revenue /'revənju:/ *n* ingresos *mpl*

revere /rɪ'vɪə(r)/ *vt* venerar. **~nce** /'revərəns/ *n* reverencia *f*.

Reverend /'revərənd/ *a* reverendo

reverent /'revərənt/ *a* reverente

reverie /'revərɪ/ *n* ensueño *m*

revers|al /rɪ'vɜ:sl/ *n* inversión *f*. **~e** /rɪ'vɜ:s/ *a* inverso. ● *n* contrario *m*; (back) revés *m*; (Auto) marcha *f* atrás. ● *vt* invertir; anular *<decision>*; (Auto) dar marcha atrás a. ● *vi* (Auto) dar marcha atrás

revert /rɪ'vɜ:t/ *vi.* **~ to** volver a; (Jurid) revertir a

review /rɪ'vju:/ *n* revisión *f*; (Mil) revista *f*; (of book, play, etc) crítica *f*. ● *vt* examinar *<situation>*; reseñar *<book, play, etc>*; (Amer, for exam) repasar

revis|e /rɪ'vaɪz/ *vt* revisar; (Schol) repasar. **~ion** /rɪ'vɪʒn/ *n* revisión *f*; (Schol) repaso *m*

revive /rɪ'vaɪv/ *vt* resucitar *<person>*

revolt /rɪ'vəʊlt/ *vi* sublevarse. ● *n* revuelta *f*. **~ing** *a* asqueroso

revolution /revə'lu:ʃn/ *n* revolución *f*. **~ary** *a & n* revolucionario (*m*). **~ize** *vt* revolucionar

revolv|e /rɪ'vɒlv/ *vi* girar. **~r** *n* revólver *m*. **~ing** /rɪ'vɒlvɪŋ/ *a* giratorio

revue /rɪ'vju:/ *n* revista *f*

revulsion /rɪ'vʌlʃn/ *n* asco *m*

reward /rɪ'wɔ:d/ *n* recompensa *f*. ● *vt* recompensar. **~ing** *a* gratificante

rewrite /ri:'raɪt/ *vt* (*pt* **rewrote**, *pp* **rewritten**) volver a escribir *or* redactar; (copy out) escribir otra vez

rhetoric /'retərɪk/ *n* retórica *f*. **~al** /rɪ'tɒrɪkl/ *a* retórico

rheumatism /'ru:mətɪzəm/ *n* reumatismo *m*

rhinoceros /raɪ'nɒsərəs/ *n* (*pl* **-oses** *or invar*) rinoceronte *m*

rhubarb /'ru:bɑ:b/ *n* ruibarbo *m*

rhyme /raɪm/ *n* rima *f*; (poem) poesía *f*. ● *vt/i* rimar

rhythm /'rɪðəm/ *n* ritmo *m*. **~ic(al)** /'rɪðmɪk(l)/ *a* rítmico

rib /rɪb/ *n* costilla *f*

ribbon /'rɪbən/ *n* cinta *f*

rice /raɪs/ *n* arroz *m*. **~ pudding** *n* arroz con leche

rich /rɪtʃ/ *a* (**-er**, **-est**) rico. ● *n* ricos *mpl*. **~es** *npl* riquezas *fpl*

ricochet /ˈrɪkəʃeɪ/ *vi* rebotar

rid /rɪd/ *vt* (*pt* **rid**, *pres p* **ridding**) librar (**of** de). **get ~ of** deshacerse de. **~dance** /ˈrɪdns/ *n*. **good ~dance!** ¡adiós y buen viaje!

ridden /ˈrɪdn/ ⇒RIDE

riddle /ˈrɪdl/ *n* acertijo *m*. ● *vt* acribillar. **be ~d with** estar lleno de

ride /raɪd/ *vi* (*pt* **rode**, *pp* **ridden**) (on horseback) montar a caballo; (go) ir (en bicicleta, a caballo etc). ● *vt* montar a <*horse*>; ir en <*bicycle*>; (Amer) ir en <*bus, tren*>; recorrer <*distance*>. ● *n* (on horse) cabalgata *f*; (in car) paseo *m* en coche. **take s.o. for a ~** ⊞ engañarle a uno. **~r** *n* (on horse) jinete *m*; (cyclist) ciclista *m & f*

ridge /rɪdʒ/ *n* (of hills) cadena *f*; (hilltop) cresta *f*

ridicul|e /ˈrɪdɪkjuːl/ *n* burlas *fpl*. ● *vt* ridiculizar. **~ous** /rɪˈdɪkjʊləs/ *a* ridículo

rife /raɪf/ *a* difundido

rifle /ˈraɪfl/ *n* fusil *m*

rift /rɪft/ *n* grieta *f*; (fig) ruptura *f*

rig /rɪg/ *vt* (*pt* **rigged**) (pej) amañar. ● *n* (at sea) plataforma *f* de perforación. □ **~ up** *vt* improvisar

right /raɪt/ *a* <*answer*> correcto; (morally) bueno; (not left) derecho; (suitable) adecuado. **be ~** <*person*> tener razón; <*clock*> estar bien. **it is ~** (just, moral) es justo. **put ~** rectificar. **the ~ person for the job** la persona indicada para el puesto. ● *n* (entitlement) derecho *m*; (not left) derecha *f*; (not evil) bien *m*. **~ of way** (Auto) prioridad *f*. **be in the ~** tener razón. **on the ~** a la derecha. ● *vt* enderezar; (fig) reparar. ● *adv* a la derecha; (directly) derecho; (completely) completamente. **~ away** *adv* inmediatamente. **~ angle** *n* ángulo *m* recto. **~eous** /ˈraɪtʃəs/ *a* recto; <*cause*> justo. **~ful** /ˈraɪtfl/ *a* legítimo. **~-handed** /-ˈhændɪd/ *a* diestro. **~-hand man** *n* brazo *m* derecho. **~ly** *adv* justamente. **~ wing** *a* (Pol) derechista

rigid /ˈrɪdʒɪd/ *a* rígido

rig|orous /ˈrɪgərəs/ *a* riguroso. **~our** /ˈrɪgə(r)/ *n* rigor *m*

rim /rɪm/ *n* borde *m*; (of wheel) llanta *f*; (of glasses) montura *f*

rind /raɪnd/ *n* corteza *f*; (of fruit) cáscara *f*

ring[1] /rɪŋ/ *n* (circle) círculo *m*; (circle of metal etc) aro *m*; (on finger) anillo *m*; (on finger with stone) sortija *f*; (Boxing) cuadrilátero *m*; (bullring) ruedo *m*; (for circus) pista *f*; ● *vt* cercar

ring[2] /rɪŋ/ *n* (of bell) toque *m*; (tinkle) tintineo *m*; (telephone call) llamada *f*. ● *vt* (*pt* **rang**, *pp* **rung**) hacer sonar; (telephone) llamar por teléfono. **~ the bell** tocar el timbre. ● *vi* sonar. **~ back** *vt/i* volver a llamar. □ **~ up** *vt* llamar por teléfono

ring: ~leader /ˈrɪŋliːdə(r)/ *n* cabecilla *m & f*. **~ road** *n* carretera *f* de circunvalación

rink /rɪŋk/ *n* pista *f*

rinse /rɪns/ *vt* enjuagar. ● *n* aclarado *m*; (of dishes) enjuague *m*; (for hair) tintura *f* (no permanente)

riot /ˈraɪət/ *n* disturbio *m*; (of colours) profusión *f*. **run ~** desenfrenarse. ● *vi* causar disturbios

rip /rɪp/ *vt* (*pt* **ripped**) rasgar. ● *vi* rasgarse. ● *n* rasgón *m*. □ **~ off** *vt* (pull off) arrancar; (⊠, cheat) robar

ripe /raɪp/ *a* (**-er**, **-est**) maduro. **~n** /ˈraɪpn/ *vt/i* madurar

rip-off /ˈrɪpɒf/ *n* ⊠ timo *m*

ripple /ˈrɪpl/ *n* (on water) onda *f*

ris|e /raɪz/ *vi* (*pt* **rose**, *pp* **risen**) subir; <*sun*> salir; <*river*> crecer; <*prices*> subir; <*land*> elevarse; (get up) levantarse. ● *n* subida *f*; (land) altura *f*; (increase) aumento *m*; (to power) ascenso *m*. **give ~e to** ocasionar. **~er** *n*. **early ~er** *n* madrugador *m*. **~ing** *n*. ● *a* <*sun*> naciente; <*number*> creciente; <*prices*> en alza

risk /rɪsk/ *n* riesgo *m*. ● *vt* arriesgar. **~y** *a* (**-ier**, **-iest**) arriesgado

rite /raɪt/ *n* rito *m*

ritual /'rɪtʃʊəl/ *a & n* ritual (*m*)

rival /'raɪvl/ *a & n* rival (*m*). **~ry** *n* rivalidad *f*

river /'rɪvə(r)/ *n* río *m*

rivet /'rɪvɪt/ *n* remache *m*. **~ing** *a* fascinante

road /rəʊd/ *n* (in town) calle *f*; (between towns) carretera *f*; (route, way) camino *m*. **~ map** *n* mapa *m* de carreteras. **~side** *n* borde *m* de la carretera. **~works** *npl* obras *fpl*. **~worthy** *a* <*vehicle*> apto para circular

roam /rəʊm/ *vi* vagar

roar /rɔː(r)/ *n* rugido *m*; (laughter) carcajada *f*. ● *vt/i* rugir. **~ past** <*vehicles*> pasar con estruendo. **~ with laughter** reírse a carcajadas. **~ing** *a* <*trade etc*> activo

roast /rəʊst/ *vt* asar; tostar <*coffee*>. ● *a & n* asado (*m*). **~ beef** *n* rosbif *m*

rob /rɒb/ *vt* (*pt* **robbed**) atracar, asaltar <*bank*>; robarle a <*person*>. **~ of** (deprive of) privar de. **~ber** *n* ladrón *m*; (of bank) atracador *m*. **~bery** *n* robo *m*; (of bank) atraco *m*

robe /rəʊb/ *n* bata *f*; (Univ etc) toga *f*

robin /'rɒbɪn/ *n* petirrojo *m*

robot /'rəʊbɒt/ *n* robot *m*, autómata *m*

robust /rəʊ'bʌst/ *a* robusto

rock /rɒk/ *n* roca *f*; (crag, cliff) peñasco *m*. ● *vt* mecer; (shake) sacudir. ● *vi* mecerse; (shake) sacudirse. ● *n* (Mus) música *f* rock. **~-bottom** /-'bɒtəm/ *a* Ⓘ bajísimo

rocket /'rɒkɪt/ *n* cohete *m*

rock: ~ing-chair *n* mecedora *f*. **~y** *a* (**-ier**, **-iest**) rocoso; (fig, shaky) bamboleante

rod /rɒd/ *n* vara *f*; (for fishing) caña *f*; (metal) barra *f*

rode /rəʊd/ ⇒RIDE

rodent /'rəʊdnt/ *n* roedor *m*

rogue /rəʊg/ *n* pícaro *m*

role /rəʊl/ *n* papel *m*

roll /rəʊl/ *vt* hacer rodar; (roll up) enrollar; allanar <*lawn*>; aplanar <*pastry*>. ● *vi* rodar; <*ship*> balancearse; (on floor) revolcarse. **be ~ing in money** Ⓘ nadar en dinero ● *n* rollo *m*; (of ship) balanceo *m*; (of drum) redoble *m*; (of thunder) retumbo *m*; (bread) panecillo *m*, bolillo *m* (Mex). □ **~ over** *vi* (turn over) dar una vuelta. □ **~ up** *vt* enrollar; arremangar <*sleeve*>. *vi* Ⓘ llegar. **~-call** *n* lista *f*

roller /'rəʊlə(r)/ *n* rodillo *m*; (wheel) rueda *f*; (for hair) rulo *m*. **~-coaster** *n* montaña *f* rusa. **~-skate** *n* patín *m* de ruedas. **~-skating** patinaje *m (sobre ruedas)*

rolling /'rəʊlɪŋ/ *a* ondulado. **~-pin** *n* rodillo *m*

ROM /rɒm/ *n* (= **read-only memory**) ROM *f*

Roman /'rəʊmən/ *a & n* romano (*m*). **~ Catholic** *a & n* católico (*m*) (romano)

romance /rəʊ'mæns/ *n* novela *f* romántica; (love) amor *m*; (affair) aventura *f*

Romania /ru:'meɪnɪə/ *n* Rumania *f*, Rumanía *f*. **~n** *a* & *n* rumano (*m*)

romantic /rəʊ'mæntɪk/ *a* romántico

Rome /'rəʊm/ *n* Roma *f*

romp /rɒmp/ *vi* retozar

roof /ru:f/ *n* techo *m*, tejado *m*; (of mouth) paladar *m*. ● *vt* techar. **~ rack** *n* baca *f*. **~top** *n* tejado *m*

rook /rʊk/ *n* grajo *m*; (*in chess*) torre *f*

room /ru:m/ *n* cuarto *m*, habitación *f*; (bedroom) dormitorio *m*; (space) espacio *m*; (large hall) sala *f*. **~y** *a* espacioso

roost /ru:st/ *vi* posarse. **~er** *n* gallo *m*

root /ru:t/ *n* raíz *f*. **take ~** echar raíces; <*idea*> arraigarse. ● *vi* echar raíces. **~ about** *vi* hurgar. □ **~ for** *vt* [I] alentar. □ **~ out** *vt* extirpar

rope /rəʊp/ *n* cuerda *f*. **know the ~s** estar al corriente. ● *vt* atar; (Amer, lasso) enlazar. □ **~ in** *vt* agarrar

rose[1] /rəʊz/ *n* rosa *f*; (nozzle) roseta *f*

rose[2] /rəʊz/ ⇒RISE

rosé /'rəʊzeɪ/ *n* (vino *m*) rosado *m*

rot /rɒt/ *vt* (*pt* **rotted**) pudrir. ● *vi* pudrirse. ● *n* putrefacción *f*

rota /'rəʊtə/ *n* lista *f* (de turnos)

rotary /'rəʊtərɪ/ *a* rotatorio

rotat|e /rəʊ'teɪt/ *vt* girar; (change round) alternar. ● *vi* girar; (change round) alternarse. **~ion** /-ʃn/ *n* rotación *f*

rote /rəʊt/ *n*. **by ~** de memoria

rotten /'rɒtn/ *a* podrido; [I] pésimo [I]; <*weather*> horrible

rough /rʌf/ *a* (**-er**, **-est**) áspero; <*person*> tosco; (bad) malo; <*ground*> accidentado; (violent) brutal; (approximate) aproximado; <*diamond*> bruto. ● *adv* duro. **~ copy**, **~ draft** borrador *m*. ● *vt*. **~ it** vivir sin comodidades. **~age** /'rʌfɪdʒ/ *n* fibra *f*. **~-and-ready** *a* improvisado. **~ly** *adv* bruscamente; (more or less) aproximadamente

roulette /ru:'let/ *n* ruleta *f*

round /raʊnd/ *a* (**-er**, **-est**) redondo. ● *n* círculo *m*; (of visits, drinks) ronda *f*; (of competition) vuelta *f*; (Boxing) asalto *m*. ● *prep* alrededor de. ● *adv* alrededor. **~ about** (approximately) aproximadamente. **come ~ to**, **go ~ to** (a friend etc) pasar por casa de. ● *vt* doblar <*corner*>. □ **~ off** *vt* terminar; redondear <*number*>. □ **~ up** *vt* rodear <*cattle*>; hacer una redada de <*suspects*>. **~about** *n* tiovivo *m*, carrusel *m* (LAm); (for traffic) glorieta *f*, rotonda *f*. ● *a* indirecto. **~ trip** *n* viaje *m* de ida y vuelta. **~-up** *n* resumen *m*; (of suspects) redada *f*

rous|e /raʊz/ *vt* despertar. **~ing** *a* enardecedor

route /ru:t/ *n* ruta *f*; (Naut, Aviat) rumbo *m*; (of bus) línea *f*

routine /ru:'ti:n/ *n* rutina *f*. ● *a* rutinario

row[1] /rəʊ/ *n* fila *f*. ● *vi* remar

row[2] /raʊ/ *n* ([I], noise) bulla *f* [I]; (quarrel) pelea *f*. ● *vi* [I] pelearse

rowboat /'rəʊbəʊt/ (Amer) *n* bote *m* de remos

rowdy /'raʊdɪ/ *a* (**-ier**, **-iest**) *n* escandaloso, alborotador

rowing /'rəʊɪŋ/ *n* remo *m*. **~ boat** *n* bote *m* de remos

royal /ˈrɔɪəl/ *a* real. **~ist** *a & n* monárquico (*m*). **~ly** *adv* magníficamente. **~ty** *n* realeza *f*

rub /rʌb/ *vt* (*pt* **rubbed**) frotar. □ **~ out** *vt* borrar

rubber /ˈrʌbə(r)/ *n* goma *f*, caucho *m*, hule *m* (Mex); (eraser) goma *f* (de borrar). **~ band** *n* goma *f* (elástica). **~-stamp** *vt* (fig) autorizar. **~y** *a* parecido al caucho

rubbish /ˈrʌbɪʃ/ *n* basura *f*; (junk) trastos *mpl*; (fig) tonterías *fpl*. **~ bin** *n* cubo *m* de la basura, bote *m* de la basura (Mex). **~y** *a* sin valor

rubble /ˈrʌbl/ *n* escombros *mpl*

ruby /ˈruːbɪ/ *n* rubí *m*

rucksack /ˈrʌksæk/ *n* mochila *f*

rudder /ˈrʌdə(r)/ *n* timón *m*

rude /ruːd/ *a* (**-er**, **-est**) grosero, mal educado; (improper) indecente; (brusque) brusco. **~ly** *adv* groseramente. **~ness** *n* mala educación *f*

rudimentary /ruːdɪˈmentrɪ/ *a* rudimentario

ruffian /ˈrʌfɪən/ *n* rufián *m*

ruffle /ˈrʌfl/ *vt* despeinar <*hair*>; arrugar <*clothes*>

rug /rʌg/ *n* alfombra *f*, tapete *m* (Mex); (blanket) manta *f* de viaje

rugged /ˈrʌgɪd/ *a* <*coast*> escarpado; <*landscape*> escabroso

ruin /ˈruːɪn/ *n* ruina *f*. ● *vt* arruinar; (spoil) estropear

rul|e /ruːl/ *n* regla *f*; (Pol) dominio *m*. **as a ~** por regla general. ● *vt* gobernar; (master) dominar; (Jurid) dictaminar. **~e out** *vt* descartar. **~ed paper** *n* papel *m* rayado. **~er** *n* (sovereign) soberano *m*; (leader) gobernante *m & f*; (measure) regla *f*. **~ing** *a* <*class*> dirigente. ● *n* decisión *f*

rum /rʌm/ *n* ron *m*

rumble /ˈrʌmbl/ *vi* retumbar; <*stomach*> hacer ruidos

rummage /ˈrʌmɪdʒ/ *vi* hurgar

rumour /ˈruːmə(r)/ *n* rumor *m*. ● *vt*. **it is ~ed that** se rumorea que

rump steak /rʌmpsteɪk/ *n* filete *m* de cadera

run /rʌn/ *vi* (*pt* **ran**, *pp* **run**, *pres p* **running**) correr; <*water*> correr; (function) funcionar; (melt) derretirse; <*makeup*> correrse; <*colour*> desteñir; <*bus etc*> circular; (in election) presentarse. ● *vt* correr <*race*>; dirigir <*business*>; correr <*risk*>; (move, pass) pasar; tender <*wire*>; preparar <*bath*>. **~ a temperature** tener fiebre. ● *n* corrida *f*, carrera *f*; (outing) paseo *m* (en coche); (ski) pista *f*. **in the long ~** a la larga. **be on the ~** estar prófugo. □ **~ away** *vi* huir, escaparse. □ **~ down** *vi* bajar corriendo; <*battery*> descargarse. *vt* (Auto) atropellar; (belittle) denigrar. □ **~ in** *vi* entrar corriendo. □ **~ into** *vt* toparse con <*friend*>; (hit) chocar con. □ **~ off** *vt* sacar <*copies*>. □ **~ out** *vi* salir corriendo; <*liquid*> salirse; (fig) agotarse. □ **~ out of** *vt* quedarse sin. □ **~ over** *vt* (Auto) atropellar. □ **~ through** *vt* (review) ensayar; (rehearse) repasar. □ **~ up** *vt* ir acumulando <*bill*>. *vi* subir corriendo. **~away** *n* fugitivo *m*. **~ down** *a* <*person*> agotado

rung[1] /rʌŋ/ *n* (of ladder) peldaño *m*

rung[2] /rʌŋ/ ⇒RING[2]

run: ~ner /ˈrʌnə(r)/ *n* corredor *m*; (on sledge) patín *m*. **~ner bean** *n* judía *f* escarlata. **~ner-up** *n*. **be ~er up** quedar en segundo lugar. **~ning** *n*. **be in the ~ning** tener posibilidades de ganar. ● *a* <*water*>

corriente; <*commentary*> en directo. **four times ~ning** cuatro veces seguidas. **~ny** /ˈrʌnɪ/ *a* líquido; <*nose*> que moquea. **~way** *n* pista *f* de aterrizaje

rupture /ˈrʌptʃə(r)/ *n* ruptura *f*. ● *vt* romper

rural /ˈrʊərəl/ *a* rural

ruse /ru:z/ *n* ardid *m*

rush /rʌʃ/ *n* (haste) prisa *f*; (crush) bullicio *m*; (plant) junco *m*. ● *vi* precipitarse. ● *vt* apresurar; (Mil) asaltar. **~-hour** *n* hora *f* punta, hora *f* pico (LAm)

Russia /ˈrʌʃə/ *n* Rusia *f*. **~n** *a* & *n* ruso (*m*)

rust /rʌst/ *n* orín *m*. ● *vt* oxidar. ● *vi* oxidarse

rustle /ˈrʌsl/ *vt* hacer susurrar; (Amer) robar. ● *vi* susurrar □ **~ up** *vt* [I] preparar.

rust: ~proof *a* inoxidable. **~y** (**-ier, -iest**) oxidado

rut /rʌt/ *n* surco *m*. **be in a ~** estar anquilosado

ruthless /ˈru:θlɪs/ *a* despiadado

rye /raɪ/ *n* centeno *m*

Ss

S *abbr* (= **south**) S

sabot|age /ˈsæbətɑ:ʒ/ *n* sabotaje *m*. ● *vt* sabotear. **~eur** /-ˈtɜ:(r)/ *n* saboteador *m*

saccharin /ˈsækərɪn/ *n* sacarina *f*

sachet /ˈsæʃeɪ/ *n* bolsita *f*

sack /sæk/ *n* saco *m*. **get the ~** [I] ser despedido. ● *vt* [I] despedir.

sacrament /ˈsækrəmənt/ *n* sacramento *m*

sacred /ˈseɪkrɪd/ *a* sagrado

sacrifice /ˈsækrɪfaɪs/ *n* sacrificio *m*. ● *vt* sacrificar

sacrileg|e /ˈsækrɪlɪdʒ/ *n* sacrilegio *m*. **~ious** /-ˈlɪdʒəs/ *a* sacrílego

sad /sæd/ *a* (**sadder**, **saddest**) triste. **~den** *vt* entristecer

saddle /ˈsædl/ *n* silla *f* de montar. ● *vt* ensillar <*horse*>. **~ s.o. with sth** (fig) endilgarle algo a uno

sadist /ˈseɪdɪst/ *n* sádico *m*. **~tic** /səˈdɪstɪk/ *a* sádico

sadly /ˈsædlɪ/ *adv* tristemente; (fig) desgraciadamente. **~ness** *n* tristeza *f*

safe /seɪf/ *a* (**-er**, **-est**) seguro; (out of danger) salvo; (cautious) prudente. **~ and sound** sano y salvo. ● *n* caja *f* fuerte. **~ deposit** *n* caja *f* de seguridad. **~guard** *n* salvaguardia *f*. ● *vt* salvaguardar. **~ly** *adv* sin peligro; (in safe place) en lugar seguro. **~ty** *n* seguridad *f*. **~ty belt** *n* cinturón *m* de seguridad. **~ty pin** *n* imperdible *m*

sag /sæg/ *vi* (*pt* **sagged**) <*ceiling*> combarse; <*bed*> hundirse

saga /ˈsɑ:gə/ *n* saga *f*

Sagittarius /sædʒɪˈteərɪəs/ *n* Sagitario *m*

said /sed/ ⇒SAY

sail /seɪl/ *n* vela *f*; (trip) paseo *m* (en barco). **set ~** zarpar. ● *vi* navegar; (leave) partir; (Sport) practicar la vela; (fig) deslizarse. **go ~ing** salir a navegar. *vt* gobernar <*boat*>. **~boat** *n* (Amer) barco *m* de vela. **~ing** *n* (Sport) vela *f*. **~ing boat** *n*, **~ing ship** *n* barco *m* de vela. **~or** *n* marinero *m*

saint /seɪnt/, *before name* /sənt/ *n* santo *m*. **~ly** *a* santo

sake /seɪk/ *n*. **for the ~ of** por. **for God's ~** por el amor de Dios

salad /'sæləd/ *n* ensalada *f*. **~ bowl** *n* ensaladera *f*. **~ dressing** *n* aliño *m*

salary /'sælərɪ/ *n* sueldo *m*

sale /seɪl/ *n* venta *f*; (at reduced prices) liquidación *f*. **for ~** (sign) se vende. **be for ~** estar a la venta. **be on ~** (Amer, reduced) estar en liquidación. **~able** *a* vendible. (for sale) estar a la venta. **~s clerk** *n* (Amer) dependiente *m*, dependienta *f*. **~sman** /-mən/ *n* vendedor *m*; (in shop) dependiente *m*. **~swoman** *n* vendedora *f*; (in shop) dependienta *f*

saliva /sə'laɪvə/ *n* saliva *f*

salmon /'sæmən/ *n invar* salmón *m*

saloon /sə'lu:n/ *n* (on ship) salón *m*; (Amer, bar) bar *m*; (Auto) turismo *m*

salt /sɔ:lt/ *n* sal *f*. ● *vt* salar. **~ cellar** *n* salero *m*. **~y** *a* salado

salute /sə'lu:t/ *n* saludo *m*. ● *vt* saludar. ● *vi* hacer un saludo

Salvadorean, Salvadorian /sælvə'dɔ:rɪən/ *a* & *n* salvadoreño (*m*)

salvage /'sælvɪdʒ/ *vt* salvar

salvation /sæl'veɪʃn/ *n* salvación *f*

same /seɪm/ *a* igual (**as** que); (*before noun*) mismo (**as** que). **at the ~ time** al mismo tiempo. ● *pron*. **the ~** lo mismo. **all the ~** de todas formas. ● *adv*. **the ~** igual

sample /'sɑ:mpl/ *n* muestra *f*. ● *vt* degustar <*food*>

sanct|ify /'sæŋktɪfaɪ/ *vt* santificar. **~ion** /'sæŋkʃn/ *n* sanción *f*. ● *vt* sancionar. **~uary** /'sæŋktʃʊərɪ/ *n* (Relig) santuario *m*; (for wildlife) reserva *f*; (refuge) asilo *m*

sand /sænd/ *n* arena *f*. ● *vt* pulir <*floor*>. □ **~ down** *vt* lijar <*wood*>

sandal /'sændl/ *n* sandalia *f*

sand: ~castle *n* castillo *m* de arena. **~paper** *n* papel *m* de lija. ● *vt* lijar. **~storm** *n* tormenta *f* de arena

sandwich /'sænwɪdʒ/ *n* bocadillo *m*, sandwich *m*. ● *vt*. **be ~ed between** <*person*> estar apretujado entre

sandy /'sændɪ/ *a* arenoso

sane /seɪn/ *a* (**-er**, **-est**) <*person*> cuerdo; (sensible) sensato

sang /sæŋ/ ⇒SING

sanitary /'sænɪtrɪ/ *a* higiénico; <*system etc*> sanitario. **~ towel**, **~ napkin** *n* (Amer) compresa *f* (higiénica)

sanitation /sænɪ'teɪʃn/ *n* higiene *f*; (drainage) sistema *m* sanitario

sanity /'sænɪtɪ/ *n* cordura *f*; (good sense) sensatez *f*

sank /sæŋk/ ⇒SINK

Santa (Claus) /'sæntə(klɔ:z)/ *n* Papá *m* Noel

sap /sæp/ *n* (in plants) savia *f*. ● *vt* (*pt* **sapped**) minar

sapling /'sæplɪŋ/ *n* árbol *m* joven

sapphire /'sæfaɪə(r)/ *n* zafiro *m*

sarcas|m /'sɑ:kæzəm/ *n* sarcasmo *m*. **~tic** /-'kæstɪk/ *a* sarcástico

sardine /sɑ:'di:n/ *n* sardina *f*

sash /sæʃ/ *n* (over shoulder) banda *f*; (round waist) fajín *m*.

sat /sæt/ ⇒SIT

satchel /'sætʃl/ *n* cartera *f*

satellite /'sætəlaɪt/ *n* & *a* satélite (*m*). **~ TV** *n* televisión *f* por satélite

satin /'sætɪn/ *n* raso *m*. ● *a* de raso

satir|e /'sætaɪə(r)/ *n* sátira *f*. **~ical** /sə'tɪrɪkl/ *a* satírico. **~ize** /'sætəraɪz/ *vt* satirizar

satis|faction /sætɪs'fækʃn/ *n* satisfacción *f*. **~factorily** /-'fæktərɪlɪ/ *adv* satisfactoriamente. **~factory** /-'fæktərɪ/ *a* satisfactorio. **~fy** /'sætɪsfaɪ/ *vt* satisfacer; (convince) convencer. **~fying** *a* satisfactorio

saturat|e /'sætʃəreɪt/ *vt* saturar. **~ed** *a* saturado; (drenched) empapado

Saturday /'sætədeɪ/ *n* sábado *m*

Saturn /'sætən/ *n* Saturno *m*

sauce /sɔ:s/ *n* salsa *f*; (cheek) descaro *m*. **~pan** /'sɔ:spən/ *n* cazo *m*, cacerola *f*. **~r** /'sɔ:sə(r)/ *n* platillo *m*

saucy /'sɔ:sɪ/ *a* (**-ier**, **-iest**) descarado

Saudi /'saʊdɪ/ *a* & *n* saudita (*m* & *f*). **~ Arabia** /-ə'reɪbɪə/ *n* Arabia *f* Saudí

sauna /'sɔ:nə/ *n* sauna *f*

saunter /'sɔ:ntə(r)/ *vi* pasearse

sausage /'sɒsɪdʒ/ *n* salchicha *f*

savage /'sævɪdʒ/ *a* salvaje; (fierce) feroz. ● *n* salvaje *m* & *f*. ● *vt* atacar. **~ry** *n* ferocidad *f*

sav|e /seɪv/ *vt* (rescue) salvar; ahorrar <*money, time*>; (prevent) evitar; (Comp) guardar. ● *n* (football) parada *f*. ● *prep* salvo, excepto. □ **~e up** *vi/t* ahorrar. **~er** *n* ahorrador *m*. **~ing** *n* ahorro *m*. **~ings** *npl* ahorros *mpl*

saviour /'seɪvɪə(r)/ *n* salvador *m*

savour /'seɪvə(r)/ *vt* saborear. **~y** *a* (appetizing) sabroso; (not sweet) no dulce

saw[1] /sɔ:/ ⇒SEE[1]

saw[2] /sɔ:/ *n* sierra *f*. ● *vt* (*pt* **sawed**, *pp* **sawn**) serrar. **~dust** *n* serrín *m*. **~n** /sɔ:n/ ⇒SAW[2]

saxophone /'sæksəfəʊn/ *n* saxofón *m*, saxófono *m*

say /seɪ/ *vt/i* (*pt* **said** /sed/) decir; rezar <*prayer*>. ● *n*. **have a ~** expresar una opinión; (in decision) tener voz en capítulo. **have no ~** no tener ni voz ni voto. **~ing** *n* refrán *m*

scab /skæb/ *n* costra *f*; (Ⓘ, blackleg) esquirol *m*

scaffolding /'skæfəldɪŋ/ *n* andamios *mpl*

scald /skɔ:ld/ *vt* escaldar

scale /skeɪl/ *n* (also Mus) escala *f*; (of fish) escama *f*. ● *vt* (climb) escalar. **~ down** *vt* reducir (a escala) <*drawing*>; recortar <*operation*>. **~s** *npl* (for weighing) balanza *f*, peso *m*

scallion /'skæljən/ *n* (Amer) cebolleta *f*

scalp /skælp/ *vt* quitar el cuero cabelludo a

scamper /'skæmpə(r)/ *vi*. **~ away** irse correteando

scan /skæn/ *vt* (*pt* **scanned**) escudriñar; (quickly) echar un vista zo a; <*radar*> explorar

scandal /'skændl/ *n* escándalo *m* (gossip) chismorreo *m*. **~ize** *vt* escandalizar. **~ous** *a* escandaloso

Scandinavia /skændɪ'neɪvɪə/ *n* Escandinavia *f*. **~n** *a* & *n* escandinavo (*m*)

scant /skænt/ *a* escaso. **~y** *a* (**-ier**, **-iest**) escaso

scapegoat /'skeɪpgəʊt/ *n* cabeza *f* de turco

scar /skɑ:(r)/ *n* cicatriz *f*

scarc|e /skeəs/ *a* (**-er**, **-est**) escaso. **be ~e** escasear. **make o.s. ~** Ⓘ mantenerse lejos. **~ely** *adv* apenas. **~ity** *n* escasez *f*

scare /'skeə(r)/ *vt* asustar. **be ~** tener miedo. **be ~d of sth** tener miedo a algo. ● *n* susto *m*. **~crow** *n* espantapájaros *m*

scarf /skɑ:f/ *n* (*pl* **scarves**) bufanda *f*; (over head) pañuelo *m*

scarlet /ˈskɑ:lət/ *a* escarlata *f*. **~ fever** *n* escarlatina *f*

scarves /skɑ:vz/ ⇒SCARF

scary /ˈskeərɪ/ *a* (**-ier**, **-iest**) que da miedo

scathing /ˈskeɪðɪŋ/ *a* mordaz

scatter /ˈskætə(r)/ *vt* (throw) esparcir; (disperse) dispersar. ● *vi* dispersarse. **~ed** /ˈskætəd/ *a* disperso; (occasional) esporádico

scavenge /ˈskævɪndʒ/ *vi* escarbar (en la basura)

scenario /sɪˈnɑ:rɪəʊ/ *n* (*pl* **-os**) perspectiva *f*; (of film) guión *m*

scen|e /si:n/ *n* escena *f*; (sight) vista *f*; (fuss) lío *m*. **behind the ~es** entre bastidores. **~ery** /ˈsi:nərɪ/ *n* paisaje *m*; (in theatre) decorado *m*. **~ic** /ˈsi:nɪk/ *a* pintoresco

scent /sent/ *n* olor *m*; (perfume) perfume *m*; (trail) pista *f*. ● *vt* intuir; (make fragrant) perfumar

sceptic /ˈskeptɪk/ *n* escéptico *m*. **~al** *a* escéptico. **~ism** /-sɪzəm/ *n* escepticismo *m*

sceptre /ˈseptə(r)/ *n* cetro *m*

schedule /ˈʃedju:l, ˈskedju:l/ *n* programa *f*; (timetable) horario *m*. **behind ~** atrasado. **it's on ~** va de acuerdo a lo previsto. ● *vt* proyectar. **~d flight** *n* vuelo *m* regular

scheme /ski:m/ *n* proyecto *m*; (plot) intriga *f*. ● *vi* (pej) intrigar

schizophrenic /skɪtsəˈfrenɪk/ *a* & *n* esquizofrénico (*m*)

scholar /ˈskɒlə(r)/ *n* erudito *m*. **~ly** *a* erudito. **~ship** *n* erudición *f*; (grant) beca *f*

school /sku:l/ *n* escuela *f*; (Univ) facultad *f*. ● *a* <*age, holidays, year*> escolar. ● *vt* instruir; (train) capacitar. **~boy** *n* colegial *m*. **~girl** *n* colegiala *f*. **~ing** *n* instrucción *f*. **~master** *n* (primary) maestro *m*; (secondary) profesor *m*. **~mistress** *n* (primary) maestra *f*; (secondary) profesora *f*. **~teacher** *n* (primary) maestro *m*; (secondary) profesor *m*

scien|ce /ˈsaɪəns/ *n* ciencia *f*. **study ~ce** estudiar ciencias. **~ce fiction** *n* ciencia *f* ficción. **~tific** /-ˈtɪfɪk/ *a* científico. **~tist** /ˈsaɪəntɪst/ *n* científico *m*

scissors /ˈsɪsəz/ *npl* tijeras *fpl*

scoff /skɒf/ *vt* 🅸 zamparse. ● *vi*. **~ at** mofarse de

scold /skəʊld/ *vt* regañar

scoop /sku:p/ *n* pala *f*; (news) primicia *f*. □ **~ out** *vt* sacar; excavar <*hole*>

scooter /ˈsku:tə(r)/ *n* escúter *m*; (for child) patinete *m*

scope /skəʊp/ *n* alcance *m*; (opportunity) oportunidad *f*

scorch /skɔ:tʃ/ *vt* chamuscar. **~ing** *a* 🅸 de mucho calor

score /skɔ:(r)/ *n* tanteo *m*; (Mus) partitura *f*; (twenty) veintena *f*. **on that ~** en cuanto a eso. **know the ~** 🅸 saber cómo son las cosas. ● *vt* marcar <*goal*>; anotarse <*points*>; (cut, mark) rayar; conseguir <*success*>. ● *vi* marcar

scorn /skɔ:n/ *n* desdén *m*. ● *vt* desdeñar. **~ful** *a* desdeñoso

Scorpio /ˈskɔ:pɪəʊ/ *n* Escorpio *m*, Escorpión *m*

scorpion /ˈskɔ:pɪən/ *n* escorpión *m*

Scot /skɒt/ *n* escocés *m*. **~ch** /skɒtʃ/ *n* whisky *m*, güisqui *m*

scotch /skɒtʃ/ *vt* frustrar; acallar *<rumours>*

Scotch tape *n* (Amer) celo *m*, cinta *f* Scotch

Scot: ~land /'skɒtlənd/ *n* Escocia *f*. **~s** *a* escocés. **~tish** *a* escocés

scoundrel /'skaʊndrəl/ *n* canalla *f*

scour /'skaʊə(r)/ *vt* fregar; (search) registrar. **~er** *n* estropajo *m*

scourge /skɜ:dʒ/ *n* azote *m*

scout /skaʊt/ *n* explorador *m*. **Boy S~** explorador *m*

scowl /skaʊl/ *n* ceño *m* fruncido. ● *vi* fruncir el ceño

scram /skræm/ *vi* [I] largarse

scramble /'skræmbl/ *vi* (clamber) gatear. ● *n* (difficult climb) subida *f* difícil; (struggle) rebatiña *f*. **~d egg** *n* huevos *mpl* revueltos

scrap /skræp/ *n* pedacito *m*; ([I], fight) pelea *f*. ● *vt* (*pt* **scrapped**) desechar. **~book** *n* álbum *m* de recortes. **~s** *npl* sobras *fpl*

scrape /skreɪp/ *n* (fig) apuro *m*. ● *vt* raspar; (graze) rasparse; (rub) rascar. □ **~ through** *vi/t* aprobar por los pelos *<exam>*. □ **~ together** *vt* reunir. **~r** *n* rasqueta *f*

scrap: ~heap *n* montón *m* de deshechos. **~ yard** *n* chatarrería *f*

scratch /skrætʃ/ *vt* rayar *<furniture, record>*; (with nail etc) arañar; rascarse *<itch>*. ● *vi* arañar. ● *n* rayón *m*; (from nail etc) arañazo *m*. **start from ~** empezar desde cero. **be up to ~** dar la talla

scrawl /skrɔ:l/ *n* garabato *m*. ● *vt/i* garabatear

scream /skri:m/ *vt/i* gritar. ● *n* grito *m*

screech /skri:tʃ/ *vi* chillar; *<brakes etc>* chirriar. ● *n* chillido *m*; (of brakes etc) chirrido *m*

screen /skri:n/ *n* pantalla *f*; (folding) biombo *m*. ● *vt* (hide) ocultar; (protect) proteger; proyectar *<film>*

screw /skru:/ *n* tornillo *m*. ● *vt* atornillar. □ **~ up** *vt* atornillar; entornar *<eyes>*; torcer *<face>*; ([✱], ruin) fastidiar. **~driver** *n* destornillador *m*

scribble /'skrɪbl/ *vt/i* garrabatear. ● *n* garrabato *m*

script /skrɪpt/ *n* escritura *f*; (of film etc) guión *m*

scroll /skrəʊl/ *n* rollo *m* (de pergamino)

scrounge /skraʊndʒ/ *vt/i* gorronear. **~r** *n* gorrón *m*

scrub /skrʌb/ *n* (land) maleza *f*. ● *vt/i* (*pt* **scrubbed**) fregar

scruff /skrʌf/ *n*. **by the ~ of the neck** por el pescuezo. **~y** *a* (**-ier, -iest**) desaliñado

scrup|le /'skru:pl/ *n* escrúpulo *m*. **~ulous** /-jʊləs/ *a* escrupuloso

scrutin|ize /'skru:tɪnaɪz/ *vt* escudriñar; inspeccionar *<document>*. **~y** /'skru:tɪnɪ/ *n* examen *m* minucioso

scuffle /'skʌfl/ *n* refriega *f*

sculpt /skʌlpt/ *vt/i* esculpir. **~or** *n* escultor *m*. **~ure** /-tʃə(r)/ *n* escultura *f*. ● *vt/i* esculpir

scum /skʌm/ *n* espuma *f*; (people, pej) escoria *f*

scupper /'skʌpə(r)/ *vt* echar por tierra *<plans>*

scurry /'skʌrɪ/ *vi* corretear

scuttle /'skʌtl/ *n* cubo *m* del carbón. ● *vt* barrenar *<ship>*. ● *vi*. **~ away** escabullirse rápidamente

scythe /saɪð/ *n* guadaña *f*

SE *abbr* (= **south-east**) SE

sea /si:/ *n* mar *m*. **at ~** en el mar; (fig) confuso. **by ~** por mar. **~food** *n* mariscos *mpl*. **~ front** *n* paseo *m* marítimo, malecón *m* (LAm). **~gull** *n* gaviota *f*. **~horse** *n* caballito *m* de mar

seal /si:l/ *n* sello *m*; (animal) foca *f*. ● *vt* sellar. □ **~ off** *vt* acordonar <*area*>

sea level *n* nivel *m* del mar

sea lion *n* león *m* marino

seam /si:m/ *n* costura *f*; (of coal) veta *f*

seaman /'si:mən/ *n* (*pl* **-men**) marinero *m*

seamy /'si:mɪ/ *a* sórdido

seance /'seɪɑ:ns/ *n* sesión *f* de espiritismo

search /sɜ:tʃ/ *vt* registrar; buscar en <*records*>. ● *vi* buscar. ● *n* (for sth) búsqueda *f*; (of sth) registro *m*; (Comp) búsqueda *f*. **in ~ of** en busca de. □ **~ for** *vt* buscar. **~ing** *a* penetrante. **~light** *n* reflector *m*. **~ party** *n* partida *f* de rescate

sea: ~shore *n* orilla *f* del mar. **~sick** *a* mareado. **be ~sick** marearse. **~side** *n* playa *f*

season /'si:zn/ *n* estación *f*; (period) temporada *f*. **high/low ~** temporada *f* alta/baja. ● *vt* (Culin) sazonar. **~al** *a* estacional; <*demand*> de estación. **~ed** *a* (fig) avezado. **~ing** *n* condimento *m*. **~ ticket** *n* abono *m* (de temporada)

seat /si:t/ *n* asiento *m*; (place) lugar *m*; (in cinema, theatre) localidad *f*; (of trousers) fondillos *mpl*. **take a ~** sentarse. ● *vt* sentar; (have seats for) <*auditorium*> tener capacidad para; <*bus*> tener asientos para. **~belt** *n* cinturón *m* de seguridad

sea: ~-urchin *n* erizo *m* de mar. **~weed** *n* alga *f* marina. **~worthy** *a* en condiciones de navegar

seclu|ded /sɪ'klu:dɪd/ *a* aislado. **~sion** /-ʒn/ *n* aislamiento *m*

second /'sekənd/ *a* & *n* segundo (*m*). **on ~ thoughts** pensándolo bien. ● *adv* (in race etc) en segundo lugar. ● *vt* secundar. **~s** *npl* (goods) artículos *mpl* de segunda calidad; (Ⓘ, more food) **have ~s** repetir. ● /sɪ'kɒnd/ *vt* (transfer) trasladar temporalmente. **~ary** /'sekəndrɪ/ *a* secundario. **~ary school** *n* instituto *m* (de enseñanza secundaria)

second: ~-class *a* de segunda (clase). **~-hand** *a* de segunda mano. **~ly** *adv* en segundo lugar. **~-rate** *a* mediocre

secre|cy /'si:krəsɪ/ *n* secreto *m*. **~t** *a* & *n* secreto (*m*). **in ~t** en secreto

secretar|ial /sekrə'teərɪəl/ *a* de secretario; <*course*> de secretariado. **~y** /'sekrətrɪ/ *n* secretario *m*. **S~y of State** (in UK) ministro *m*: (in US) secretario *m* de Estado

secretive /'si:krɪtɪv/ *a* reservado

sect /sekt/ *n* secta *f*. **~arian** /-'teərɪən/ *a* sectario

section /'sekʃn/ *n* sección *f*; (part) parte *f*

sector /'sektə(r)/ *n* sector *m*

secular /'sekjʊlə(r)/ *a* secular

secur|e /sɪ'kjʊə(r)/ *a* seguro; <*shelf*> firme. ● *vt* asegurar; (obtain) obtener. **~ely** *adv* seguramente. **~ity** *n* seguridad *f*; (for loan) garantía *f*

sedat|e /sɪ'deɪt/ *a* reposado. ● *vt* sedar. **~ion** /sɪ'deɪʃn/ *n* sedación *f*. **~ive** /'sedətɪv/ *a* & *n* sedante (*m*)

sediment /'sedɪmənt/ *n* sedimento *m*

seduc|e /sɪ'dju:s/ *vt* seducir. **~er** *n* seductor *m*. **~tion** /sɪ'dʌkʃn/ *n* seducción *f*. **~tive** /sɪ'dʌktɪv/ *a* seductor

see /si:/ ● *vt* (*pt* **saw**, *pp* **seen**) ver; (understand) comprender; (escort) acompañar. **~ing that** visto que. **~ you later!** ¡hasta luego! ● *vi* ver. □ **~ off** *vt* (say goodbye to) despedirse de. □ **~ through** *vt* llevar a cabo; calar <*person*>. □ **~ to** *vt* ocuparse de

seed /si:d/ *n* semilla *f*; (fig) germen *m*; (Amer, pip) pepita *f*. **go to ~** granar; (fig) echarse a perder. **~ling** *n* planta *f* de semillero. **~y** *a* (**-ier**, **-iest**) sórdido

seek /si:k/ *vt* (*pt* **sought**) buscar; pedir <*approval*>. □ **~ out** *vt* buscar

seem /si:m/ *vi* parecer

seen /si:n/ ⇒SEE

seep /si:p/ *vi* filtrarse

see-saw /ˈsi:sɔ:/ *n* balancín *m*

seethe /si:ð/ *vi* (fig) estar furioso. **I was seething with anger** me hervía la sangre

see-through /ˈsi:θru:/ *a* transparente

segment /ˈsegmənt/ *n* segmento *m*; (of orange) gajo *m*

segregat|e /ˈsegrɪgeɪt/ *vt* segregar. **~ion** /-ˈgeɪʃn/ *n* segregación *f*

seiz|e /si:z/ *vt* agarrar; (Jurid) incautar. **~e on** *vt* aprovechar <*chance*>. □ **~e up** *vi* (Tec) agarrotarse. **~ure** /ˈsi:ʒə(r)/ *n* incautación *f*; (Med) ataque *m*

seldom /ˈseldəm/ *adv* rara vez

select /sɪˈlekt/ *vt* escoger; (Sport) seleccionar. ● *a* selecto; (exclusive) exclusivo. **~ion** /-ʃn/ *n* selección *f*. **~ive** *a* selectivo

self /self/ *n* (*pl* **selves**). **he's his old ~ again** vuelve a ser el de antes. **~-addressed** *a* con el nombre y la dirección del remitente. **~-catering** *a* con facilidades para cocinar. **~-centred** *a* egocéntrico. **~-confidence** *n* confianza *f* en sí mismo. **~-confident** *a* seguro de sí mismo. **~-conscious** *a* cohibido. **~-contained** *a* independiente. **~-control** *n* dominio *m* de sí mismo. **~-defence** *n* defensa *f* propia. **~-employed** *a* que trabaja por cuenta propia. **~-evident** *a* evidente. **~-important** *a* presumido. **~-indulgent** *a* inmoderado. **~-interest** *n* interés *m* (personal). **~ish** *a* egoísta. **~ishness** *n* egoísmo *m*. **~-pity** *n* autocompasión. **~-portrait** *n* autorretrato *m*. **~-respect** *n* amor *m* propio. **~-righteous** *a* santurrón. **~-sacrifice** *n* abnegación *f*. **~-satisfied** *a* satisfecho de sí mismo. **~-serve** (Amer), **~-service** *a* & *n* autoservicio (*m*). **~-sufficient** *a* independiente

sell /sel/ *vt* (*pt* **sold**) vender. ● *vi* venderse. □ **~ off** *vt* liquidar. **~ out** *vi*. **we've sold out of gloves** los guantes están agotados. **~-by date** *n* fecha *f* límite de venta. **~er** *n* vendedor *m*

Sellotape /ˈseləteɪp/ *n* (P) celo *m*, cinta *f* Scotch

sell-out /ˈselaʊt/ *n* (performance) éxito *m* de taquilla; (Ⓘ, betrayal) capitulación *f*

semblance /ˈsembləns/ *n* apariencia *f*

semester /sɪˈmestə(r)/ *n* (Amer) semestre *m*

semi... /ˈsemɪ/ *pref* semi...

semi|breve /-bri:v/ *n* redonda *f* **~circle** *n* semicírculo *m* **~colon** /-ˈkəʊlən/ *n* punto *m* y coma. **~-detached** /-dɪˈtætʃt/ *a* <*house*> adosado. **~final** /-ˈfaɪnl/ *n* semifinal *f*

seminar /'semɪnɑ:(r)/ *n* seminario *m*

senat|e /'senɪt/ *n* senado *m*. **the S~e** (Amer) el Senado. **~or** /-ətə(r)/ *n* senador *m*

send /send/ *vt/i* (*pt* **sent**) mandar, enviar. □ **~ away** *vt* despedir. □ **~ away for** *vt* pedir (por correo). □ **~ for** *vt* enviar a buscar. □ **~ off for** *vt* pedir (por correo). □ **~ up** *vt* [I] parodiar. **~er** *n* remitente *m*. **~-off** *n* despedida *f*

senile /'si:naɪl/ *a* senil

senior /'si:nɪə(r)/ *a* mayor; (in rank) superior; <*partner etc*> principal. ● *n* mayor *m & f*. **~ citizen** *n* jubilado *m*. **~ high school** *n* (Amer) colegio *m* secundario. **~ity** /-'ɒrətɪ/ *n* antigüedad *f*

sensation /sen'seɪʃn/ *n* sensación *f*. **~al** *a* sensacional

sens|e /sens/ *n* sentido *m*; (common sense) juicio *m*; (feeling) sensación *f*. **make ~e** *vt* tener sentido. **make ~e of sth** entender algo. **~eless** *a* sin sentido. **~ible** /'sensəbl/ *a* sensato; <*clothing*> práctico. **~itive** /'sensɪtɪv/ *a* sensible; (touchy) susceptible. **~itivity** /-'tɪvətɪ/ *n* sensibilidad *f*. **~ual** /'senʃʊəl/ *a* sensual. **~uous** /'sensʊəs/ *a* sensual

sent /sent/ ⇒SEND

sentence /'sentəns/ *n* frase *f*; (judgment) sentencia *f*; (punishment) condena *f*. ● *vt*. **~ to** condenar a

sentiment /'sentɪmənt/ *n* sentimiento *m*; (opinion) opinión *f*. **~al** /-'mentl/ *a* sentimental. **~ality** /-'tælətɪ/ *n* sentimentalismo *m*

sentry /'sentrɪ/ *n* centinela *f*

separa|ble /'sepərəbl/ *a* separable. **~te** /'sepərət/ *a* separado; (independent) independiente. ● *vt* /'sepəreɪt/ separar. ● *vi* separarse. **~tely** /'sepərətlɪ/ *adv* por separado. **~tion** /-'reɪʃn/ *n* separación *f*. **~tist** /'sepərətɪst/ *n* separatista *m & f*

September /sep'tembə(r)/ *n* se(p)tiembre *m*

septic /'septɪk/ *a* séptico

sequel /'si:kwəl/ *n* continuación *f*; (later events) secuela *f*

sequence /'si:kwəns/ *n* sucesión *f*; (of film) secuencia *f*

Serb /sɜ:b/ *a & n* ⇒SERBIAN. **~ia** /'sɜ:bɪə/ *n* Serbia *f* **~ian** *a & n* serbio (*m*)

serenade /serə'neɪd/ *n* serenata *f*. ● *vt* dar serenata a

serene /sɪ'ri:n/ *a* sereno

sergeant /'sɑ:dʒənt/ *n* sargento *m*

serial /'sɪərɪəl/ *n* serie *f*. **~ize** *vt* serializar

series /'sɪəri:z/ *n* serie *f*

serious /'sɪərɪəs/ *a* serio. **~ly** *adv* seriamente; (ill) gravemente. **take ~ly** tomar en serio

sermon /'sɜ:mən/ *n* sermón *m*

serum /'sɪərəm/ *n* (*pl* **-a**) suero *m*

servant /'sɜ:vənt/ *n* criado *m*

serve /sɜ:v/ *vt* servir; servir a <*country*>; cumplir <*sentence*>. **~ as** servir de. **it ~s you right** ¡bien te lo mereces! ● *vi* servir; (in tennis) sacar. ● *n* (in tennis) saque *m*. **~r** *n* (Comp) servidor *m*

service /'sɜ:vɪs/ *n* servicio *m*; (of car etc) revisión *f*. ● *vt* revisar <*car etc*>. **~ charge** *n* (in restaurant) servicio *m*. **~s** *npl* (Mil) fuerzas *fpl* armadas. **~ station** *n* estación *f* de servicio

serviette /sɜ:vɪ'et/ *n* servilleta *f*

servile /'sɜ:vaɪl/ *a* servil

session /'seʃn/ *n* sesión *f*

set /set/ *vt* (*pt* **set**, *pres p* **setting**) poner; poner en hora <*clock etc*>; fijar <*limit etc*>; (typeset) componer. **~ fire to** prender fuego a. **~ free** *vt* poner en libertad. ● *vi* <*sun*> ponerse; <*jelly*> cuajarse. ● *n* serie *f*; (of cutlery etc) juego *m*; (tennis) set *m*; (TV, Radio) aparato *m*; (in theatre) decorado *m*; (of people) círculo *m*. ● *a*. fijo. **be ~ on** estar resuelto a. □ **~ back** *vt* (delay) retardar; ([I], cost) costar. □ **~ off** *vi* salir. *vt* hacer sonar <*alarm*>; hacer explotar <*bomb*>. □ **~ out** *vt* exponer <*argument*>. *vi* (leave) salir. □ **~ up** *vt* establecer. **~back** *n* revés *m*

settee /se'ti:/ *n* sofá *m*

setting /'setɪŋ/ *n* (of dial, switch) posición *f*

settle /'setl/ *vt* (arrange) acordar; arreglar <*matter*>; resolver <*dispute*>; pagar <*bill*>; saldar <*debt*>. ● *vi* (live) establecerse. □ **~ down** *vi* calmarse; (become more responsible) sentar (la) cabeza. □ **~ for** *vt* aceptar. □ **~ up** *vi* arreglar cuentas. **~ment** *n* establecimiento *m*; (agreement) acuerdo *m*; (of debt) liquidación *f*; (colony) colonia *f*. **~r** *n* colono *m*

set: ~-to *n* pelea *f*. **~-up** *n* [I] sistema *m*; (con) tinglado *m*

seven /'sevn/ *a* & *n* siete (*m*). **~teen** /sevn'ti:n/ *a* & *n* diecisiete (*m*). **~teenth** *a* decimoséptimo. ● *n* diecisietavo *m*. **~th** *a* & *n* séptimo (*m*). **~tieth** /'sevəntɪɪθ/ *a* septuagésimo. ● *n* setentavo *m*. **~ty** /'sevntɪ/ *a* & *n* setenta (*m*)

sever /'sevə(r)/ *vt* cortar; (fig) romper

several /'sevrəl/ *a* & *pron* varios

sever|e /sɪ'vɪə(r)/ *a* (**-er**, **-est**) severo; (serious) grave; <*weather*> riguroso. **~ely** *adv* severamente. **~ity** /sɪ'verətɪ/ *n* severidad *f*; (seriousness) gravedad *f*

sew /səʊ/ *vt/i* (*pt* **sewed**, *pp* **sewn**, *or* **sewed**) coser. □ **~ up** *vt* coser

sew|age /'su:ɪdʒ/ *n* aguas *fpl* residuales. **~er** /'su:ə(r)/ *n* cloaca *f*

sewing /'səʊɪŋ/ *n* costura *f*. **~-machine** *n* máquina *f* de coser

sewn /səʊn/ ⇨SEW

sex /seks/ *n* sexo *m*. **have ~** tener relaciones sexuales. ● *a* sexual. **~ist** *a* & *n* sexista (*m* & *f*). **~ual** /'sekʃʊəl/ *a* sexual. **~ual intercourse** *n* relaciones *fpl* sexuales. **~uality** /-'ælətɪ/ *n* sexualidad *f*. **~y** *a* (**-ier**, **-iest**) excitante, sexy, provocativo

shabby /'ʃæbɪ/ *a* (**-ier**, **-iest**) <*clothes*> gastado; <*person*> pobremente vestido

shack /ʃæk/ *n* choza *f*

shade /ʃeɪd/ *n* sombra *f*; (of colour) tono *m*; (for lamp) pantalla *f*; (nuance) matiz *m*; (Amer, over window) persiana *f*

shadow /'ʃædəʊ/ *n* sombra *f*. ● *vt* (follow) seguir de cerca a. **~y** *a* (fig) vago

shady /'ʃeɪdɪ/ *a* (**-ier**, **-iest**) sombreado; (fig) turbio; <*character*> sospechoso

shaft /ʃɑ:ft/ *n* (of arrow) astil *m*; (Mec) eje *m*; (of light) rayo *m*; (of lift, mine) pozo *m*

shaggy /'ʃægɪ/ *a* (**-ier**, **-iest**) peludo

shake /ʃeɪk/ *vt* (*pt* **shook**, *pp* **shaken**) sacudir; agitar <*bottle*>; (shock) desconcertar. **~ hands with** estrechar la mano a. **~ one's head** negar con la cabeza; (Amer, meaning yes) asentir con la cabeza. ● *vi* temblar. □ ~ **off** *vi* deshacerse de. ● *n* sacudida *f*

shaky /'ʃeɪkɪ/ *a* (**-ier**, **-iest**) tembloroso; <*table etc*> inestable

shall /ʃæl/ *v aux*. **we ~ see** veremos. **~ we go to the cinema?** ¿vamos al cine?

shallow /'ʃæləʊ/ *a* (**-er**, **-est**) poco profundo; (fig) superficial

sham /ʃæm/ *n* farsa *f*. ● *a* fingido

shambles /'ʃæmblz/ *npl* (Ⓘ, mess) caos *m*

shame /ʃeɪm/ *n* (feeling) vergüenza *f*. **what a ~!** ¡qué lástima! ● *vt* avergonzar. **~ful** *a* vergonzoso. **~less** *a* desvergonzado

shampoo /ʃæm'pu:/ *n* champú *m*. ● *vt* lavar

shan't /ʃɑ:nt/ = **shall not**

shape /ʃeɪp/ *n* forma *f*. ● *vt* formar; determinar <*future*>. ● *vi* tomar forma. **~less** *a* informe

share /ʃeə(r)/ *n* porción *f*; (Com) acción *f*. ● *vt* compartir; (divide) dividir. ● *vi* compartir. **~ in sth** participar en algo. □ **~ out** *vt* repartir. **~holder** *n* accionista *m & f*. **~-out** *n* reparto *m*

shark /ʃɑ:k/ *n* tiburón *m*

sharp /ʃɑ:p/ *a* (**-er**, **-est**) <*knife etc*> afilado; <*pin etc*> puntiagudo; <*pain, sound*> agudo; <*taste*> ácido; <*bend*> cerrado; <*contrast*> marcado; (clever) listo; (Mus) sostenido. ● *adv* en punto. **at seven o'clock ~** a las siete en punto. ● *n* (Mus) sostenido *m*. **~en** *vt* afilar; sacar punta a <*pencil*>. **~ener** *n* (Mec) afilador *m*; (for pencils) sacapuntas *m*. **~ly** *adv* bruscamente

shatter /'ʃætə(r)/ *vt* hacer añicos. **he was ~ed by the news** la noticia lo dejó destrozado. ● *vi* hacerse añicos. **~ed** /'ʃætəd/*a* (exhausted) agotado

shav|e /ʃeɪv/ *vt* afeitar, rasurar (Mex). ● *vi* afeitarse, rasurarse (Mex). ● *n* afeitada *f*, rasurada *f* (Mex). **have a ~e** afeitarse. **~er** *n* maquinilla *f* (de afeitar). **~ing brush** *n* brocha *f* de afeitar. **~ing cream** *n* crema *f* de afeitar

shawl /ʃɔ:l/ *n* chal *m*

she /ʃi:/ *pron* ella

sheaf /ʃi:f/ *n* (*pl* **sheaves** /ʃi:vz/) gavilla *f*

shear /ʃɪə(r)/ *vt* (*pp* **shorn** *or* **sheared**) esquilar. **~s** /ʃɪəz/ *npl* tijeras *fpl* grandes

shed /ʃed/ *n* cobertizo *m*. ● *vt* (*pt* **shed**, *pres p* **shedding**) perder; derramar <*tears*>; despojarse de <*clothes*>. **~ light on** arrojar luz sobre

she'd /ʃi:(ə)d/ = **she had**, **she would**

sheep /ʃi:p/ *n invar* oveja *f*. **~dog** *n* perro *m* pastor. **~ish** *a* avergonzado

sheer /ʃɪə(r)/ *a* (as intensifier) puro; (steep) perpendicular

sheet /ʃi:t/ *n* sábana *f*; (of paper) hoja *f*; (of glass) lámina *f*; (of ice) capa *f*

shelf /ʃelf/ *n* (*pl* **shelves**) estante *m*. **a set of shelves** unos estantes

shell /ʃel/ *n* concha *f*; (of egg) cáscara *f*; (of crab, snail, tortoise) caparazón *m or f*; (explosive) proyectil *m*, obús *m*. ● *vt* pelar <*peas etc*>; (Mil) bombardear

she'll /'ʃi:(ə)l/ = SHE HAD, SHE WOULD

shellfish /'ʃelfɪʃ/ *n invar* marisco *m*; (collectively) mariscos *mpl*

shelter /'ʃeltə(r)/ *n* refugio *m*. **take ~** refugiarse. ● *vt* darle cobijo a <*fugitive*>; (protect from weather) resguardar. ● *vi* refugiarse. **~ed** /ˈʃeltəd/ *a* <*spot*> abrigado; <*life*> protegido

shelv|e /ʃelv/ *vt* (fig) dar carpetazo a. **~ing** *n* estantería *f*

shepherd /ˈʃepəd/ *n* pastor *m*. **~ess** /-ˈdes/ *n* pastora *f*

sherbet /ˈʃɜ:bət/ *n* (Amer, water ice) sorbete *m*

sheriff /ˈʃerɪf/ *n* (in US) sheriff *m*

sherry /ˈʃerɪ/ *n* (vino *m* de) jerez *m*

she's /ʃi:z/ = **she is**, **she has**

shield /ʃi:ld/ *n* escudo *m*. ● *vt* proteger

shift /ʃɪft/ *vt* cambiar; correr <*furniture etc*>. ● *vi* <*wind*> cambiar; <*attention, opinion*> pasar a; (Amer, change gear) cambiar de velocidad. ● *n* cambio *m*; (work) turno *m*; (workers) tanda *f*. **~y** *a* (**-ier**, **-iest**) furtivo

shilling /ˈʃɪlɪŋ/ *n* chelín *m*

shimmer /ˈʃɪmə(r)/ *vi* rielar, relucir

shin /ʃɪn/ *n* espinilla *f*

shine /ʃaɪn/ *vi* (*pt* **shone**) brillar. ● *vt* sacar brillo a. **~ a light on sth** alumbrar algo con una luz. ● *n* brillo *m*

shingle /ˈʃɪŋgl/ *n* (pebbles) guijarros *mpl*

shin|ing /ˈʃaɪnɪŋ/ *a* brillante. **~y** /ˈʃaɪnɪ/ *a* (**-ier**, **-iest**) brillante

ship /ʃɪp/ *n* barco *m*, buque *m*. ● *vt* (*pt* **shipped**) transportar; (send) enviar; (load) embarcar. **~building** *n* construcción *f* naval. **~ment** *n* envío *m*. **~ping** *n* transporte *m*; (ships) barcos *mpl*. **~shape** *a* limpio y ordenado. **~wreck** *n* naufragio *m*. **~wrecked** *a* naufragado. **be ~wrecked** naufragar. **~yard** *n* astillero *m*

shirk /ʃɜ:k/ *vt* esquivar

shirt /ʃɜ:t/ *n* camisa *f*. **in ~-sleeves** en mangas de camisa

shit /ʃɪt/ *n* & *int* (vulg) mierda (*f*). ● *vi* (vulg) (*pt* **shat**, *pres p* **shitting**) cagar

shiver /ˈʃɪvə(r)/ *vi* temblar. ● *n* escalofrío *m*

shoal /ʃəʊl/ *n* banco *m*

shock /ʃɒk/ *n* (of impact) choque *m*; (of earthquake) sacudida *f*; (surprise) shock *m*; (scare) susto *m*; (Elec) descarga *f*; (Med) shock *m*. **get a ~** llevarse un shock. ● *vt* escandalizar; (apall) horrorizar. **~ing** *a* escandaloso; 🅸 espantoso

shod /ʃɒd/ ⇒SHOE

shoddy /ˈʃɒdɪ/ *a* (**-ier**, **-iest**) mal hecho, de pacotilla

shoe /ʃu:/ *n* zapato *m*; (of horse) herradura *f*. ● *vt* (*pt* **shod**, *pres p* **shoeing**) herrar <*horse*>. **~horn** *n* calzador *m*. **~lace** *n* cordón *m* (de zapato). **~ polish** *n* betún *m*

shone /ʃɒn/ ⇒SHINE

shoo /ʃu:/ *vt* ahuyentar

shook /ʃʊk/ ⇒SHAKE

shoot /ʃu:t/ *vt* (*pt* **shot**) disparar; rodar <*film*>. ● *vi* (hunt) cazar. ● *n* (Bot) retoño *m*. □ **~ down** *vt* derribar. □ **~ out** *vi* (rush) salir disparado. □ **~ up** *vi* <*prices*> dispararse; (grow) crecer mucho

shop /ʃɒp/ *n* tienda *f*. **go to the ~** ir de compras. **talk ~** hablar de trabajo. ● *vi* (*pt* **shopping**) hacer compras. **go ~ping** ir de compras. □ **~ around** *vi* buscar el mejor precio. **~ assistant** *n* dependiente *m*, dependienta *f*, empleado *m*, empleada *f* (LAm). **~keeper** *n* comerciante *m*, tendero *m*. **~lifter** *n* ladrón *m* (*que roba en las tiendas*). **~lifting** *n* hurto *m* (*en las tiendas*)

das). **~per** *n* comprador *m*. **~ping** *n* (purchases) compras *fpl*. **do the ~ping** hacer la compra, hacer el mandado (Mex). **~ping bag** *n* bolsa *f* de la compra. **~ping cart** *n* (Amer) carrito *m* (de la compra). **~ping centre**, **~ping mall** (Amer) *n* centro *m* comercial. **~ping trolley** *n* carrito *m* de la compra. **~ steward** *n* enlace *m* sindical. **~ window** *n* escaparate *m*, vidriera *f* (LAm), aparador *m* (Mex)

shore /ʃɔ:(r)/ *n* orilla *f*

shorn /ʃɔ:n/ ⇒SHEAR

short /ʃɔ:t/ *a* (**-er**, **-est**) corto; (not lasting) breve; <*person*> bajo; (curt) brusco. **a ~ time ago** hace poco. **be ~ of time/money** andar corto de tiempo/dinero. **Mick is ~ for Michael** Mick es el diminutivo de Michael. ● *adv* <*stop*> en seco. **we never went ~ of food** nunca nos faltó comida. ● *n*. **in ~** en resumen. **~age** /-ɪdʒ/ *n* escasez *f*, falta *f*. **~bread** *n* galleta *f* (*de mantequilla*). **~ circuit** *n* cortocircuito *m*. **~coming** *n* defecto *m*. **~ cut** *n* atajo *m*. **~en** *vt* acortar. **~hand** *n* taquigrafía *f*. **~ly** *adv* (soon) dentro de poco. **~ly before midnight** poco antes de la medianoche. **~s** *npl* pantalones *m* cortos, shorts *mpl*; (Amer, underwear) calzoncillos *mpl*. **~-sighted** /-'saɪtɪd/ *a* miope

shot /ʃɒt/ ⇒SHOOT. ● *n* (from gun) disparo *m*; tiro *m*; (in soccer) tiro *m*, disparo *m*; (in other sports) tiro *m*; (Photo) foto *f*. **be a good/poor ~** ser un buen/mal tirador. **be off like a ~** salir disparado. **~gun** *n* escopeta *f*

should /ʃʊd, ʃəd/ *v aux*. **I ~ go** debería ir. **you ~n't have said that** no deberías haber dicho eso. **I ~ like to see her** me gustaría verla. **if he ~ come** si viniese

shoulder /'ʃəʊldə(r)/ *n* hombro *m*. ● *vt* cargar con <*responsibility*>; ponerse al hombro <*burden*>. **~ blade** *n* omóplato *m*

shout /ʃaʊt/ *n* grito *m*. ● *vt/i* gritar. **~ at s.o.** gritarle a uno

shove /ʃʌv/ *n* empujón *m*. ● *vt* empujar; ([I], put) poner. ● *vi* empujar. □ **~ off** *vi* [I] largarse

shovel /'ʃʌvl/ *n* pala *f*. ● *vt* (*pt* **shovelled**) palear <*coal*>; espalar <*snow*>

show /ʃəʊ/ *vt* (*pt* **showed**, *pp* **shown**) mostrar; (put on display) exponer; poner <*film*>. **I'll ~ you to your room** lo acompaño a su cuarto. ● *vi* (be visible) verse. ● *n* muestra *f*; (exhibition) exposición *f*; (in theatre) espectáculo *m*; (on TV, radio) programa *m*; (ostentation) pompa *f*. **be on ~** estar expuesto. □ **~ off** *vt* (pej) lucir, presumir de. *vi* presumir, lucirse. □ **~ up** *vi* (be visible) notarse; (arrive) aparecer. *vt* (reveal) poner de manifiesto; (embarrass) hacer quedar mal. **~case** *n* vitrina *f*. **~down** *n* confrontación *f*

shower /'ʃaʊə(r)/ *n* (of rain) chaparrón *m*; (for washing) ducha *f*. **have a ~, take a ~** ducharse. ● *vi* ducharse

showjumping *n* concursos *mpl* hípicos.

shown /ʃəʊn/ ⇒SHOW

show: **~-off** *n* fanfarrón *m*. **~room** *n* sala *f* de exposición *f*. **~y** *a* (**-ier**, **-iest**) llamativo; (attractive) ostentoso

shrank /ʃræŋk/ ⇒SHRINK

shred /ʃred/ *n* pedazo *m*; (fig) pizca *f*. ● *vt* (*pt* **shredded**) hacer tiras; destruir, triturar <*documents*>.

~der *n* (for paper) trituradora *f*; (for vegetables) cortadora *f*

shrewd /ʃru:d/ *a* (**-er**, **-est**) astuto

shriek /ʃri:k/ *n* chillido *m*; (of pain) alarido *m*. ● *vt/i* chillar

shrift /ʃrɪft/ *n*. **give s.o. short ~** despachar a uno con brusquedad. **give sth short ~** desestimar algo de plano

shrill /ʃrɪl/ *a* agudo

shrimp /ʃrɪmp/ *n* gamba *f*, camarón *m* (LAm); (Amer, large) langostino *m*

shrine /ʃraɪn/ *n* (place) santuario *m*; (tomb) sepulcro *m*

shrink /ʃrɪŋk/ *vt* (*pt* **shrank**, *pp* **shrunk**) encoger. ● *vi* encogerse; <*amount*> reducirse; retroceder (recoil)

shrivel /ˈʃrɪvl/ *vi* (*pt* **shrivelled**). **~** (**up**) <*plant*> marchitarse; <*fruit*> resecarse y arrugarse

shroud /ʃraʊd/ *n* mortaja *f*; (fig) velo *m*. ● *vt* envolver

Shrove /ʃrəʊv/ *n*. **~ Tuesday** *n* martes *m* de carnaval

shrub /ʃrʌb/ *n* arbusto *m*

shrug /ʃrʌg/ *vt* (*pt* **shrugged**) encogerse de hombros

shrunk /ʃrʌŋk/ ⇒SHRINK. **~en** *a* encogido

shudder /ˈʃʌdə(r)/ *vi* estremecerse. ● *n* estremecimiento *m*

shuffle /ˈʃʌfl/ *vi* andar arrastrando los pies. ● *vt* barajar <*cards*>. **~ one's feet** arrastrar los pies

shun /ʃʌn/ *vt* (*pt* **shunned**) evitar

shunt /ʃʌnt/ *vt* cambiar de vía

shush /ʃʊʃ/ *int* ¡chitón!

shut /ʃʌt/ *vt* (*pt* **shut**, *pres p* **shutting**) cerrar. ● *vi* cerrarse. ● *a*. **be ~** estar cerrado. □ **~ down** *vt/i* cerrar. □ **~ up** *vt* cerrar; [I] hacer callar. *vi* callarse. **~ter** *n* contraventana *f*; (Photo) obturador *m*

shuttle /ˈʃʌtl/ *n* lanzadera *f*; (Aviat) puente *m* aéreo; (space **~**) transbordador *m* espacial. ● *vi*. **~** (back and forth) ir y venir. **~cock** *n* volante *m*. **~ service** *n* servicio *m* de enlace

shy /ʃaɪ/ *a* (**-er**, **-est**) tímido. ● *vi* (*pt* **shied**) asustarse. **~ness** *n* timidez *f*

sick /sɪk/ *a* enfermo; <*humour*> negro; ([I], fed up) harto. **be ~** estar enfermo; (vomit) vomitar. **be ~ of** (fig) estar harto de. **feel ~** sentir náuseas. **get ~** (Amer) caer enfermo, enfermarse (LAm). **~ leave** *n* permiso *m* por enfermedad, baja *f* por enfermedad. **~ly** /ˈsɪklɪ/ *a* (**-lier**, **-liest**) enfermizo; <*taste, smell etc*> nauseabundo. **~ness** /ˈsɪknɪs/ *n* enfermedad *f*

side /saɪd/ *n* lado *m*; (of hill) ladera *f*; (of person) costado *m*; (team) equipo *m*; (fig) parte *f*. **~ by ~** uno al lado del otro. **take ~s** tomar partido. ● *a* lateral. □ **~ with** *vt* ponerse de parte de. **~board** *n* aparador *m*. **~ dish** *n* acompañamiento *m*. **~-effect** *n* efecto *m* secundario; (fig) consecuencia *f* indirecta. **~line** *n* actividad *f* suplementaria. **~ road** *n* calle *f* secundaria. **~-step** *vt* eludir. **~-track** *vt* desviar del tema. **~walk** *n* (Amer) acera *f*, vereda *f* (LAm), banqueta *f* (Mex). **~ways** *a & adv* de lado

siding /ˈsaɪdɪŋ/ *n* apartadero *m*

sidle /ˈsaɪdl/ *vi*. **~ up to s.o.** acercarse furtivamente a uno

siege /si:dʒ/ *n* sitio *m*

sieve /sɪv/ *n* tamiz *m*. ● *vt* tamizar, cernir

sift /sɪft/ *vt* tamizar, cernir. ● *vi*. ~ **through sth** pasar algo por el tamiz

sigh /saɪ/ *n* suspiro. ● *vi* suspirar

sight /saɪt/ *n* vista *f*; (spectacle) espectáculo *m*; (on gun) mira *f*. **at first** ~ a primera vista. **catch** ~ **of** ver; (in distance) avistar. **lose** ~ **of** perder de vista. **see the** ~**s** visitar los lugares de interés. **within** ~ **of** (near) cerca de. ● *vt* ver; divisar <*land*>. ~**-seeing** *n*. **go** ~ ir a visitar los lugares de interés. ~**seer** /-siːə(r)/ *n* turista *m & f*

sign /saɪn/ *n* (indication) señal *f*, indicio *m*; (gesture) señal *f*, seña *f*; (notice) letrero *m*; (Astr) signo *m*. ● *vt* firmar. □ ~ **on** *vi* (for unemployment benefit) anotarse para recibir el seguro de desempleo

signal /'sɪgnəl/ *n* señal *f*. ● *vt* (*pt* **signalled**) señalar. ● *vi*. ~ (**to s.o.**) hacer señas (a uno); (Auto) poner el intermitente, señalizar

signature /'sɪgnətʃə(r)/ *n* firma *f*. ~ **tune** *n* sintonía *f*

significan|ce /sɪg'nɪfɪkəns/ *n* importancia *f*. ~**t** *a* (important) importante; <*fact, remark*> significativo

signify /'sɪgnɪfaɪ/ *vt* significar

signpost /'saɪnpəʊst/ *n* señal *f*, poste *m* indicador

silen|ce /'saɪləns/ *n* silencio *m*. ● *vt* hacer callar. ~**cer** *n* (on gun and on car) silenciador *m*. ~**t** *a* silencioso; <*film*> mudo. **remain** ~**t** quedarse callado. ~**tly** *adv* silenciosamente

silhouette /sɪluː'et/ *n* silueta *f*. ● *vt*. **be** ~**d** perfilarse (**against** contra)

silicon /'sɪlɪkən/ *n* silicio *m*. ~ **chip** *n* pastilla *f* de silicio

silk /sɪlk/ *n* seda *f*. ~**y** *a* (of silk) de seda; (like silk) sedoso

silly /'sɪlɪ/ *a* (**-ier**, **-iest**) tonto

silt /sɪlt/ *n* cieno *m*

silver /'sɪlvə(r)/ *n* plata *f*. ● *a* de plata. ~**-plated** *a* bañado en plata, plateado. ~**ware** /-weə(r)/ *n* platería *f*

simil|ar /'sɪmɪlə(r)/ *a* parecido, similar. ~**arity** /-'lærətɪ/ *n* parecido *m*. ~**arly** *adv* de igual manera. ~**e** /'sɪmɪlɪ/ *n* símil *m*

simmer /'sɪmə(r)/ *vt/i* hervir a fuego lento. □ ~ **down** *vi* calmarse

simpl|e /'sɪmpl/ *a* (**-er**, **-est**) sencillo, simple; <*person*> (humble) simple; (backward) simple. ~**e-minded** /-'maɪndɪd/ *a* ingenuo. ~**icity** /-'plɪsətɪ/ *n* simplicidad *f*, sencillez *f*. ~**ify** /'sɪmplɪfaɪ/ *vt* simplificar. ~**y** *adv* sencillamente, simplemente; (absolutely) realmente

simulate /'sɪmjʊleɪt/ *vt* simular

simultaneous /sɪml'teɪnɪəs/ *a* simultáneo. ~**ly** *adv* simultáneamente

sin /sɪn/ *n* pecado *m*. ● *vi* (*pt* **sinned**) pecar

since /sɪns/

● *preposition*

····➤ desde. **he's been living here** ~ **1991** vive aquí desde 1991. ~ **Christmas** desde Navidad. ~ **then** desde entonces. **I haven't been feeling well** ~ **Sunday** desde el domingo que no me siento bien. **how long is it** ~ **your interview?** ¿cuánto (tiempo) hace de la entrevista?

● *adverb*

····➤ desde entonces. **I haven't spoken to her ~** no he hablado con ella desde entonces

● *conjunction*

····➤ desde que. **I haven't seen her ~ she left** no la he visto desde que se fue. **~ coming to Manchester** desde que vine (*or* vino *etc*) a Manchester. **it's ten years ~ he died** hace diez años que se murió

····➤ (because) como, ya que. **~ it was quite late, I decided to stay** como *or* ya que era bastante tarde, decidí quedarme

sincer|e /sɪn'sɪə(r)/ *a* sincero. **~ely** *adv* sinceramente. **yours ~ely, ~ely (yours)** (in letters) (saluda) a usted atentamente. **~ity** /-'serətɪ/ *n* sinceridad *f*

sinful /'sɪnfl/ *a* <*person*> pecador; <*act*> pecaminoso

sing /sɪŋ/ *vt/i* (*pt* **sang**, *pp* **sung**) cantar

singe /sɪndʒ/ *vt* (*pres p* **singeing**) chamuscar

singer /'sɪŋə(r)/ *n* cantante *m & f*

single /'sɪŋgl/ *a* solo; (not double) sencillo; (unmarried) soltero; <*bed, room*> individual, de una plaza (LAm); <*ticket*> de ida, sencillo. **not a ~ house** ni una sola casa. **every ~ day** todos los días sin excepción. ● *n* (ticket) billete *m* sencillo, boleto *m* de ida (LAm). □ **~ out** *vt* escoger; (distinguish) distinguir. **~-handed** /-'hændɪd/ *a & adv* sin ayuda. **~s** *npl* (Sport) individuales *mpl*

singular /'sɪŋgjʊlə(r)/ *n* singular *f*. ● *a* singular; (unusual) raro; <*noun*> en singular

sinister /'sɪnɪstə(r)/ *a* siniestro

sink /sɪŋk/ *vt* (*pt* **sank**, *pp* **sunk**) hundir. ● *vi* hundirse. ● *n* fregadero *m* (Amer, in bathroom) lavabo *m*, lavamanos *m*. □ **~ in** *vi* penetrar

sinner /'sɪnə(r)/ *n* pecador *m*

sip /sɪp/ *n* sorbo *m*. ● *vt* (*pt* **sipped**) sorber

siphon /'saɪfən/ *n* sifón *m*. **~ (out)** sacar con sifón. □ **~ off** *vt* desviar <*money*>.

sir /sɜ:(r)/ *n* señor *m*. **S~** *n* (title) sir *m*. **Dear S~,** (in letters) De mi mayor consideración:

siren /'saɪərən/ *n* sirena *f*

sister /'sɪstə(r)/ *n* hermana *f*; (nurse) enfermera *f* jefe. **~-in-law** *n* (*pl* **~s-in-law**) cuñada *f*

sit /sɪt/ *vi* (*pt* **sat**, *pres p* **sitting**) sentarse; <*committee etc*> reunirse en sesión. **be ~ting** estar sentado. ● *vt* sentar; hacer <*exam*>. □ **~ back** *vi* (fig) relajarse. □ **~ down** *vi* sentarse. **be ~ting down** estar sentado. □ **~ up** *vi* (from lying) incorporarse; (straighten back) ponerse derecho. **~-in** *n* (strike) encierro *m*, ocupación *f*

site /saɪt/ *n* emplazamiento *m* (piece of land) terreno *m*; (archaeological) yacimiento *m*. **building ~** *n* solar *m*. ● *vt* situar

sit: ~ting *n* sesión *f*; (in restaurant) turno *m*. **~ting room** *n* sala *f* de estar, living *m*

situat|e /'sɪtjʊeɪt/ *vt* situar. **~ion** /-'eɪʃn/ *n* situación *f*

six /sɪks/ *a & n* seis (*m*). **~teen** /sɪk'sti:n/ *a & n* dieciséis (*m*). **~teenth** *a* decimosexto. ● *n* dieciseisavo *m*. **~th** *a & n* sexto (*m*). **~tieth** /'sɪkstɪɪθ/ *a* sexagésimo. ● *n* sesentavo *m*. **~ty** /'sɪkstɪ/ *a & n* sesenta (*m*)

size /saɪz/ *n* tamaño *m*; (of clothes) talla *f*; (of shoes) número *m*; (of problem, operation) magnitud *f*. **what ~ do you take?** (clothes) ¿qué talla tiene (shoes) ¿qué número calza?. □~ **up** *vt* [I] evaluar <*problem*>; calar <*person*>

sizzle /ˈsɪzl/ *vi* crepitar

skat|e /skeɪt/ *n* patín *m*. ● *vi* patinar. **~eboard** *n* monopatín *m*, patineta *f* (Mex). **~er** *n* patinador *m*. **~ing** *n* patinaje *m*. **~ing-rink** *n* pista *f* de patinaje

skeleton /ˈskelɪtn/ *n* esqueleto *m*. **~ key** *n* llave *f* maestra

sketch /sketʃ/ *n* (drawing) dibujo *m*; (rougher) esbozo *m*; (TV, Theatre) sketch *m*. ● *vt* esbozar. ● *vi* dibujar. **~y** *a* (**-ier**, **-iest**) incompleto

ski /skiː/ *n* (*pl* **skis**) esquí *m*. ● *vi* (*pt* **skied**, *pres p* **skiing**) esquiar. **go ~ing** ir a esquiar

skid /skɪd/ *vi* (*pt* **skidded**) patinar. ● *n* patinazo *m*

ski: ~er *n* esquiador *m*. **~ing** *n* esquí *m*

skilful /ˈskɪlfl/ *a* diestro

ski-lift /ˈskiːlɪft/ *n* telesquí *m*

skill /skɪl/ *n* habilidad *f*; (technical) destreza *f*. **~ed** *a* hábil; <*worker*> cualificado

skim /skɪm/ *vt* (*pt* **skimmed**) espumar <*soup*>; desnatar, descremar <*milk*>; (glide over) pasar casi rozando. **~ milk** (Amer), **~med milk** *n* leche *f* desnatada, leche *f* descremada. **~ through** *vt* leer por encima

skimp /skɪmp/ *vi*. **~ on sth** escatimar algo. **~y** *a* (**-ier**, **-iest**) escaso; <*skirt, dress*> brevísimo

skin /skɪn/ *n* piel *f*. ● *vt* (*pt* **skinned**) despellejar. **~-deep** *a* superficial. **~-diving** *n* submarinismo *m*. **~ny** *a* (**-ier**, **-iest**) flaco

skip /skɪp/ *vi* (*pt* **skipped**) *vi* saltar; (with rope) saltar a la comba, saltar a la cuerda. ● *vt* saltarse <*chapter*>; faltar a <*class*>. ● *n* brinco *m*; (container) contenedor *m* (*para escombros*). **~per** *n* capitán *m*. **~ping-rope**, **~rope** (Amer) *n* comba *f*, cuerda *f* de saltar, reata *f* (Mex)

skirmish /ˈskɜːmɪʃ/ *n* escaramuza *f*

skirt /skɜːt/ *n* falda *f*. ● *vt* bordear; (go round) ladear. **~ing-board** *n* rodapié *m*, zócalo *m*

skittle /ˈskɪtl/ *n* bolo *m*

skive off /skaɪv/ (*vi* [I], disappear) escurrir el bulto; (stay away from work) no ir a trabajar

skulk /skʌlk/ *vi* (hide) esconderse. **~ around** *vi* merodear

skull /skʌl/ *n* cráneo *m*; (remains) calavera *f*

sky /skaɪ/ *n* cielo *m*. **~lark** *n* alondra *f*. **~light** *n* tragaluz *m*. **~scraper** *n* rascacielos *m*

slab /slæb/ *n* (of concrete) bloque *m*; (of stone) losa *f*

slack /slæk/ *a* (**-er**, **-est**) flojo; <*person*> poco aplicado; <*period*> de poca actividad. ● *vi* flojear. **~en** *vt* aflojar. ● *vi* <*person*> descansar. □ **~en off** *vt/i* aflojar

slain /sleɪn/ ⇒SLAY

slake /sleɪk/ *vt* apagar

slam /slæm/ *vt* (*pt* **slammed**). **~ the door** dar un portazo. **~ the door shut** cerrar de un portazo. **~ on the brakes** pegar un frenazo; (⊠, criticize) atacar violentamente. ● *vi* cerrarse de un portazo

slander /ˈslɑːndə(r)/ *n* calumnia *f*. ● *vt* difamar

slang /slæŋ/ *n* argot *m*

slant /slɑ:nt/ *vt* inclinar. ● *n* inclinación *f*

slap /slæp/ *vt* (*pt* **slapped**) (on face) pegarle una bofetada a; (put) tirar. ~ **s.o. on the back** darle una palmada a uno en la espalda ● *n* bofetada *f*; (on back) palmada *f*. ● *adv* de lleno. **~dash** *a* descuidado; <*work*> chapucero

slash /slæʃ/ *vt* acuchillar; (fig) rebajar drásticamente. ● *n* cuchillada *f*

slat /slæt/ *n* tablilla *f*

slate /sleɪt/ *n* pizarra *f*. ● *vt* [I] poner por los suelos

slaughter /ˈslɔ:tə(r)/ *vt* matar salvajemente; matar <*animal*>. ● *n* carnicería *f*; (of animals) matanza *f*

slave /sleɪv/ *n* esclavo *m*. ● *vi* ~ (**away**) trabajar como un negro. **~-driver** *n* [I] negrero *m*. **~ry** /-ərɪ/ *n* esclavitud *f*

slay /sleɪ/ *vt* (*pt* **slew**, *pp* **slain**) dar muerte a

sleazy /ˈsli:zɪ/ *a* (**-ier**, **-iest**) [I] sórdido

sled /sled/ (Amer), **sledge** /sledʒ/ *n* trineo *m*

sledge-hammer *n* mazo *m*, almádena *f*

sleek /sli:k/ *a* (**-er**, **-est**) liso, brillante

sleep /sli:p/ *n* sueño *m*. **go to** ~ dormirse. ● *vi* (*pt* **slept**) dormir. ● *vt* poder alojar. **~er** *n* (on track) traviesa *f*, durmiente *m*. **be a light/heavy ~er** tener el sueño ligero/pesado. **~ing bag** *n* saco *m* de dormir. **~ing pill** *n* somnífero *m*. **~less** *a*. **have a ~less night** pasar la noche en blanco. **~walk** *vi* caminar dormido. **~y** *a* (**-ier**, **-iest**) soñoliento. **be/feel ~y** tener sueño

sleet /sli:t/ *n* aguanieve *f*

sleeve /sli:v/ *n* manga *f*; (for record) funda *f*, carátula *f*. **up one's ~** en reserva. **~less** *a* sin mangas

sleigh /sleɪ/ *n* trineo *m*

slender /ˈslendə(r)/ *a* delgado; (fig) escaso

slept /slept/ ⇒SLEEP

slew /slu:/ ⇒SLAY

slice /slaɪs/ *n* (of ham) lonja *f*; (of bread) rebanada *f*; (of meat) tajada *f*; (of cheese) trozo *m*; (of sth round) rodaja *f*. ● *vt* cortar (en rebanadas, tajadas etc)

slick /slɪk/ *a* <*performance*> muy pulido. ● *n*. (**oil**) ~ marea *f* negra

slid|e /slaɪd/ *vt* (*pt* **slid**) deslizar. ● *vi* (intentionally) deslizarse; (unintentionally) resbalarse. ● *n* resbalón *m*; (in playground) tobogán *m*, resbaladilla *f* (Mex); (for hair) pasador *m*, broche *m* (Mex); (Photo) diapositiva *f*. **~ing scale** *n* escala *f* móvil

slight /slaɪt/ *a* (**-er**, **-est**) ligero; (slender) delgado. ● *vt* desairar. ● *n* desaire *m*. **~est** *a* mínimo. **not in the ~est** en absoluto. **~ly** *adv* un poco, ligeramente

slim /slɪm/ *a* (**slimmer**, **slimmest**) delgado. ● *vi* (*pt* **slimmed**) (become slimmer) adelgazar; (diet) hacer régimen

slim|e /slaɪm/ *n* limo *m*; (of snail, slug) baba *f*. **~y** *a* viscoso; (fig) excesivamente obsequioso

sling /slɪŋ/ *n* (Med) cabestrillo *m*. ● *vt* (*pt* **slung**) lanzar

slip /slɪp/ *vt* (*pt* **slipped**) deslizar. ~ **s.o.'s mind** olvidársele a uno. ● *vi* resbalarse. **it ~ped out of my hands** se me resbaló de las manos. **he ~ped out the back door** se deslizó por la puerta trasera ● *n* resbalón *m*; (mistake) error *m*; (pet coat) combinación *f*; (paper) trozo *m*. **give s.o. the ~** lograr zafarse de uno. **~ of the tongue** *n* lapsus *m* linguae. □ **~ away** *vi* escabullirse. □ **~ up** *vi* [I] equivocarse

slipper /ˈslɪpə(r)/ *n* zapatilla *f*

slippery /ˈslɪpərɪ/ *a* resbaladizo

slip: ~ road *n* rampa *f* de acceso. **~shod** /ˈslɪpʃɒd/ *a* descuidado. **~-up** *n* [I] error *m*

slit /slɪt/ *n* raja *f*; (cut) corte *m*. ● *vt* (*pt* **slit**, *pres p* **slitting**) rajar; (cut) cortar

slither /ˈslɪðə(r)/ *vi* deslizarse

slobber /ˈslɒbə(r)/ *vi* babear

slog /slɒg/ *vt* (*pt* **slogged**) golpear. ● *vi* caminar trabajosamente. ● *n* golpetazo *m*; (hard work) trabajo *m* penoso. □ **~ away** *vi* sudar tinta [I]

slogan /ˈsləʊgən/ *n* eslogan *m*

slop /slɒp/ *vt* (*pt* **slopped**) derramar. ● *vi* derramarse

slop|e /sləʊp/ *vi* inclinarse. ● *vt* inclinar. ● *n* declive *m*, pendiente *f*. **~ing** *a* inclinado

sloppy /ˈslɒpɪ/ *a* (**-ier**, **-iest**) *<work>* descuidado; *<person>* desaliñado

slosh /slɒʃ/ *vi* [I] chapotear

slot /slɒt/ *n* ranura *f*. ● *vt* (*pt* **slotted**) encajar

slot-machine *n* distribuidor *m* automático; (for gambling) máquina *f* tragamonedas

slouch /slaʊtʃ/ *vi* andar cargado de espaldas; (in chair) repanchigarse

Slovak /ˈsləʊvæk/ *a* & *n* eslovaco (*m*). **~ia** *n* Eslovaquia *f*

slovenly /ˈslʌvnlɪ/ *a* *<work>* descuidado; *<person>* desaliñado

slow /sləʊ/ *a* (**-er**, **-est**) lento. **be ~** *<clock>* estar atrasado. **in ~ motion** a cámara lenta. ● *adv* despacio. ● *vt* retardar. ● *vi* ir más despacio. □ **~ down**, **~ up** *vt* retardar. *vi* ir más despacio. **~ly** *adv* despacio, lentamente

sludge /slʌdʒ/ *n* fango *m*

slug /slʌg/ *n* babosa *f*. **~gish** *a* lento

slum /slʌm/ *n* barrio *m* bajo

slumber /ˈslʌmbə(r)/ *vi* dormir

slump /slʌmp/ *n* baja *f* repentina; (in business) depresión *f*. ● *vi* bajar repentinamente; (collapse) desplomarse

slung /slʌŋ/ ⇨SLING

slur /slɜː(r)/ *vt* (*pt* **slurred**). **~ one's words** arrastrar las palabras. ● *n*. **a racist ~** un comentario racista

slush /slʌʃ/ *n* nieve *f* medio derretida

sly /slaɪ/ *a* (**slyer**, **slyest**) (crafty) astuto. ● *n*. **on the ~** a hurtadillas. **~ly** *adv* astutamente

smack /smæk/ *n* manotazo *m*. ● *adv* [I] **~ in the middle** justo en el medio. **he went ~ into a tree** se dio contra un árbol. ● *vt* pegarle a (*con la mano*)

small /smɔːl/ *a* (**-er**, **-est**) pequeño, chico (LAm). ● *n*. **the ~ of the back** la región lumbar. **~ ads** *npl* anuncios *mpl* (clasificados), avisos *mpl* (clasificados) (LAm). **~ change** *n* suelto *m*. **~pox** /-pɒks/ *n* viruela *f*. **~ talk** *n* charla *f* sobre temas triviales

smart /smɑːt/ *a* (**-er**, **-est**) elegante; (clever) listo; (brisk) rápido. ● *vi* escocer. □ **~en up** *vt* arreglar. *vi* *<person>* mejorar su aspecto, arreglarse. **~ly** *adv* elegantemente; (quickly) rápidamente

smash /smæʃ/ *vt* romper; (into little pieces) hacer pedazos; batir *<record>*. ● *vi* romperse; (collide) chocar (**into** con). ● *n* (noise) estrépito *m*; (collision) choque *m*; (in sport) smash *m*. □ ~ **up** *vt* destrozar. ~**ing** *a* [T] estupendo

smattering /ˈsmætərɪŋ/ *n* nociones *fpl*

smear /smɪə(r)/ *vt* untar (**with** de); (stain) manchar (**with** de); (fig) difamar. ● *n* mancha *f*

smell /smel/ *n* olor *m*; (sense) olfato *m*. ● *vt* (*pt* **smelt**) oler; *<animal>* olfatear. ● *vi* oler. ~ **of sth** oler a algo. ~**y** *a* maloliente. **be** ~**y** oler mal

smelt /smelt/ ⇒SMELL. ● *vt* fundir

smile /smaɪl/ *n* sonrisa *f*. ● *vi* sonreír. ~ **at s.o.** sonreírle a uno

smirk /smɜːk/ *n* sonrisita *f* (*de suficiencia etc*)

smith /smɪθ/ *n* herrero *m*

smithereens /smɪðəˈriːnz/ *npl*. **smash sth to** ~ hacer algo añicos

smock /smɒk/ *n* blusa *f*, bata *f*

smog /smɒg/ *n* smog *m*

smok|e /sməʊk/ *n* humo *m*. ● *vt* fumar *<tobacco>*; ahumar *<food>*. ● *vi* fumar. ~**eless** *a* que arde sin humo. ~**er** *n* fumador *m*. ~**y** *a* *<room>* lleno de humo

smooth /smuːð/ *a* (**-er**, **-est**) *<texture/stone>* liso; *<skin>* suave; *<movement>* suave; *<sea>* tranquilo. ● *vt* alisar. □ ~ **out** *vt* allanar *<problems>*. ~**ly** *adv* suavemente; (without problems) sin problemas

smother /ˈsmʌðə(r)/ *vt* asfixiar *<person>*. ~ **s.o. with kisses** cubrir a uno de besos

smoulder /ˈsməʊldə(r)/ *vi* arder sin llama

smudge /smʌdʒ/ *n* borrón *m*. ● *vi* tiznarse

smug /smʌg/ *a* (**smugger**, **smuggest**) pagado de sí mismo; *<expression>* de suficiencia

smuggl|e /ˈsmʌgl/ *vt* pasar de contrabando. ~**er** *n* contrabandista *m & f*. ~**ing** *n* contrabando *m*

snack /snæk/ *n* tentempié *m*. ~ **bar** *n* cafetería *f*

snag /snæg/ *n* problema *m*

snail /sneɪl/ *n* caracol *m*. **at a** ~**'s pace** a paso de tortuga

snake /sneɪk/ *n* culebra *f*, serpiente *f*

snap /snæp/ *vt* (*pt* **snapped**) (break) romper. ~ **one's fingers** chasquear los dedos. ● *vi* romperse; *<dog>* intentar morder; (say) contestar bruscamente. ~ **at** *<dog>* intentar morder; (say) contestar bruscamente. ● *n* chasquido *m*; (Photo) foto *f*. ● *a* instantáneo. □ ~ **up** *vt* no dejar escapar *<offer>*. ~**py** *a* (**-ier**, **-iest**) [T] rápido. **make it** ~**py!** ¡date prisa! ~**shot** *n* foto *f*

snare /sneə(r)/ *n* trampa *f*

snarl /snɑːl/ *vi* gruñir

snatch /snætʃ/ *vt*. ~ **sth from s.o** arrebatarle algo a uno; (steal) robar. ● *n* (short part) fragmento *m*

sneak /sniːk/ *n* soplón *m*. ● *v* (*past & pp* **sneaked** *or* [T] **snuck**) ~ **in** entrar a hurtadillas. ~ **of** escabullirse. ~**ers** /ˈsniːkəz/ *np* zapatillas *fpl* de deporte. ~**y** artero

sneer /snɪə(r)/ *n* expresión desdeñosa. ● *vi* hacer una mueca de desprecio. ~ **at** hablar con desprecio a

sneeze /sni:z/ *n* estornudo *m*. ● *vi* estornudar

snide /snaɪd/ *a* insidioso

sniff /snɪf/ *vt* oler. ● *vi* sorberse la nariz

snigger /ˈsnɪgə(r)/ *n* risilla *f*. ● *vi* reírse (*por lo bajo*)

snip /snɪp/ *vt* (*pt* **snipped**) dar un tijeretazo a. ● *n* tijeretazo *m*

sniper /ˈsnaɪpə(r)/ *n* francotirador *m*

snippet /ˈsnɪpɪt/ *n* (of conversation) trozo *m*. **~s of information** datos *mpl* aislados

snivel /ˈsnɪvl/ *vi* (*pt* **snivelled**) lloriquear

snob /snɒb/ *n* esnob *m & f*. **~bery** *n* esnobismo *m*. **~bish** *a* esnob

snooker /ˈsnu:kə(r)/ *n* snooker *m*

snoop /snu:p/ *vi* 🄸 husmear

snooze /snu:z/ *n* sueñecito *m*. ● *vi* dormitar

snore /snɔ:(r)/ *n* ronquido *m*. ● *vi* roncar

snorkel /ˈsnɔ:kl/ *n* esnórkel *m*

snort /snɔ:t/ *n* bufido *m*. ● *vi* bufar

snout /snaʊt/ *n* hocico *m*

snow /snəʊ/ *n* nieve *f*. ● *vi* nevar. **be ~ed in** estar aislado por la nieve. **be ~ed under with work** estar agobiado de trabajo. **~ball** *n* bola *f* de nieve. **~drift** *n* nieve *f* amontonada. **~fall** *n* nevada *f*. **~flake** *n* copo *m* de nieve. **~man** *n* muñeco *m* de nieve. **~plough** *n* quitanieves *m*. **~storm** *n* tormenta *f* de nieve. **~y** *a* <*day, weather*> nevoso; <*landscape*> nevado

snub /snʌb/ *vt* (*pt* **snubbed**) desairar. ● *n* desaire *m*. **~-nosed** *a* chato

snuck /snʌk/ ⇨SNEAK

snuff out /snʌf/ *vt* apagar <*candle*>

snug /snʌg/ *a* (**snugger**, **snuggest**) cómodo; (tight) ajustado

snuggle (up) /ˈsnʌgl/ *vi* acurrucarse

so /səʊ/ *adv* (before a or adv) tan; (thus) así. ● *conj* (therefore) así que. **~ am I** yo también. **~ as to** para. **~ far** *adv* (time) hasta ahora. **~ far as I know** que yo sepa. **~ long!** ¡hasta luego! **and ~ on, and ~ forth** etcétera (etcétera). **I think ~** creo que sí. **or ~** más o menos **~ that** *conj* para que.

soak /səʊk/ *vt* remojar. ● *vi* remojarse. □ **~ in** *vi* penetrar. □ **~ up** *vt* absorber. **~ing** *a* empapado.

so-and-so /ˈsəʊənsəʊ/ *n* fulano *m*

soap /səʊp/ *n* jabón *m*. ● *vt* enjabonar. **~ opera** *n* telenovela *f*, culebrón *m*. **~ powder** *n* jabón *m* en polvo. **~y** *a* jabonoso

soar /sɔ:(r)/ *vi* <*bird/plane*> planear; (rise) elevarse; <*price*> dispararse. **~ing** *a* <*inflation*> galopante

sob /sɒb/ *n* sollozo *m*. ● *vi* (*pt* **sobbed**) sollozar

sober /ˈsəʊbə(r)/ *a* (not drunk) sobrio

so-called /ˈsəʊkɔ:ld/ *a* llamado; (pej) supuesto

soccer /ˈsɒkə(r)/ *n* fútbol *m*, futbol *m* (Mex)

sociable /ˈsəʊʃəbl/ *a* sociable

social /ˈsəʊʃl/ *a* social; (sociable) sociable. **~ism** *n* socialismo *m*. **~ist** *a & n* socialista (*m & f*). **~ize** *vt* socializar. **~ security** *n* seguridad *f* social. **~ worker** *n* asistente *m* social

society /səˈsaɪətɪ/ *n* sociedad *f*

sociolog|ical /səʊsɪə'lɒdʒɪkl/ *a* sociológico. **~ist** /-'ɒlədʒɪst/ *n* sociólogo *m*. **~y** /-'ɒlədʒɪ/ *n* sociología *f*

sock /sɒk/ *n* calcetín *m*

socket /'sɒkɪt/ *n* (of joint) hueco *m*; (of eye) cuenca *f*; (wall plug) enchufe *m*; (for bulb) portalámparas *m*

soda /'səʊdə/ *n* soda *f*. **~-water** *n* soda *f*

sodium /'səʊdɪəm/ *n* sodio *m*

sofa /'səʊfə/ *n* sofá *m*

soft /sɒft/ *a* (**-er**, **-est**) blando; <*light, colour*> suave; (gentle) dulce, tierno; (not strict) blando. **~ drink** *n* refresco *m*. **~en** /'sɒfn/ *vt* ablandar; suavizar <*skin*>. ● *vi* ablandarse. **~ly** *adv* dulcemente; <*speak*> bajito. **~ware** /-weə(r)/ *n* software *m*

soggy /'sɒgɪ/ *a* (**-ier**, **-iest**) empapado

soil /sɔɪl/ *n* tierra *f*; (Amer, dirt) suciedad *f*. ● *vt* ensuciar

solar /'səʊlə(r)/ *a* solar

sold /səʊld/ ⇒SELL

solder /'sɒldə(r)/ *vt* soldar

soldier /'səʊldʒə(r)/ *n* soldado *m*. □ **~ on** *vi* Ⓘ seguir al pie del cañon

sole /səʊl/ *n* (of foot) planta *f*; (of shoe) suela *f*. ● *a* único, solo. **~ly** *adv* únicamente

solemn /'sɒləm/ *a* solemne

solicitor /sə'lɪsɪtə(r)/ *n* abogado *m*; (notary) notario *m*

solid /'sɒlɪd/ *a* sólido; <*gold etc*> macizo; (unanimous) unánime; <*meal*> sustancioso. ● *n* sólido *m*. **~s** *npl* alimentos *mpl* sólidos. **~arity** /sɒlɪ'dærətɪ/ *n* solidaridad *f*. **~ify** /sə'lɪdɪfaɪ/ *vi* solidificarse

solitary /'sɒlɪtrɪ/ *a* solitario

solitude /'sɒlɪtju:d/ *n* soledad *f*

solo /'səʊləʊ/ *n* (*pl* **-os**) (Mus) solo *m*. **~ist** *n* solista *m & f*

solstice /'sɒlstɪs/ *n* solsticio *m*

solu|ble /'sɒljʊbl/ *a* soluble. **~tion** /sə'lu:ʃn/ *n* solución *f*

solve /sɒlv/ *vt* solucionar <*problem*>; resolver <*mystery*>. **~nt** /-vənt/ *a & n* solvente (*m*)

sombre /'sɒmbə(r)/ *a* sombrío

---

some /sʌm/, *unstressed form* /səm/

● *adjective*

····➤ (unspecified number) unos, unas. **he ate ~ olives** comió unas aceitunas

····➤ (unspecified amount) *not translated*. **I have to buy ~ bread** tengo que comprar pan. **would you like ~ coffee?** ¿quieres café?

····➤ (certain, not all) algunos, -nas. **I like ~ modern writers** algunos escritores modernos me gustan

····➤ (a little) algo de. **I eat ~ meat, but not much** como algo de carne, pero no mucho

····➤ (considerable amount of) **we've known each other for ~ time** ya hace tiempo que nos conocemos

····➤ (expressing admiration) **that's ~ car you've got!** ¡vaya coche que tienes!

● *pronoun*

····➤ (a number of things or people) algunos, -nas, unos, unas. **~ are mine and ~ aren't** algunos *or* unos son míos y otros no. **aren't there any apples? we bought ~ yesterday** ¿no hay manzanas? compramos algunas ayer

····➤ (part of an amount) **he wants ~** quiere un poco. **~ of what he said** parte *or* algo de lo que dijo

....➤ (certain people) algunos, -nas. **~ say that...** algunos dicen que...

● *adverb*

....➤ (approximately) unos, unas, alrededor de. **there were ~ fifty people there** había unas cincuenta personas, había alrededor de cincuenta personas

some: ~body /-bədɪ/ *pron* alguien. **~how** *adv* de algún modo. **~how or other** de una manera u otra. **~one** *pron* alguien

somersault /ˈsʌməsɔ:lt/ *n* salto *m* mortal. ● *vi* dar un salto mortal

some: ~thing *pron* algo *m*. **~thing like** (approximately) alrededor de. **~time** *a* ex. ● *adv* algún día. **~time next week** un día de la semana que viene. **~times** *adv* a veces. **~where** *adv* en alguna parte, en algún lado

son /sʌn/ *n* hijo *m*

sonata /səˈnɑ:tə/ *n* sonata *f*

song /sɒŋ/ *n* canción *f*

sonic /ˈsɒnɪk/ *a* sónico

son-in-law /ˈsʌnɪnlɔ:/ *n* (*pl* **sons-in-law**) yerno *m*

sonnet /ˈsɒnɪt/ *n* soneto *m*

son of a bitch *n* (*pl* **sons of bitches**) (esp Amer ☒) hijo *m* de puta

soon /su:n/ *adv* (**-er**, **-est**) pronto; (in a short time) dentro de poco. **~ after** poco después. **~er or later** tarde o temprano. **as ~ as** en cuanto; **as ~ as possible** lo antes posible. **the ~er the better** cuanto antes mejor

soot /sʊt/ *n* hollín *m*

sooth|e /su:ð/ *vt* calmar; aliviar <*pain*>. **~ing** *a* <*medicine*> calmante; <*words*> tranquilizador

sooty /ˈsʊtɪ/ *a* cubierto de hollín

sophisticated /səˈfɪstɪkeɪtɪd/ *a* sofisticado; (complex) complejo

sophomore /ˈsɒfəmɔ:(r)/ *n* (Amer) estudiante *m & f* de segundo curso (*en la universidad*)

sopping /ˈsɒpɪŋ/ *a*. **~** (wet) empapado

soppy /ˈsɒpɪ/ *a* (**-ier**, **-iest**) 🅸 sentimental

soprano /səˈprɑ:nəʊ/ *n* (*pl* **-os**) soprano *f*

sordid /ˈsɔ:dɪd/ *a* sórdido

sore /ˈsɔ:(r)/ *a* (**-er**, **-est**) dolorido; (Amer 🅸, angry) **be ~ at s.o.** estar picado con uno. **~ throat** *n* dolor *m* de garganta. **I've got a ~ throat** me duele la garganta. ● *n* llaga *f*.

sorrow /ˈsɒrəʊ/ *n* pena *f*, pesar *m*

sorry /ˈsɒrɪ/ *a* (**-ier**, **-ier**) arrepentido; (wretched) lamentable. **I'm ~** lo siento. **be ~ for s.o.** (pity) compadecer a uno. **I'm ~ you can't come** siento que no puedas venir. **say ~** pedir perdón. **~!** (apologizing) ¡lo siento!, ¡perdón!. **~?** (asking s.o. to repeat) ¿cómo?

sort /sɔ:t/ *n* tipo *m*, clase *f*; (🅸, person) tipo *m*. **a ~ of** una especie de. ● *vt* clasificar. ▫ **~ out** *vt* (organize) ordenar; organizar <*finances*>; (separate out) separar; solucionar <*problem*>

so-so /ˈsəʊsəʊ/ *a* regular

soufflé /ˈsu:fleɪ/ *n* suflé *m*

sought /sɔ:t/ ⇒SEEK

soul /səʊl/ *n* alma *f*

sound /saʊnd/ *n* sonido *m*; (noise) ruido *m*. ● *vt* tocar. ● *vi* sonar; (seem) parecer (**as if** que). **it ~s interesting** suena interesante.. ● *a* (**-er**, **-est**) sano; <*argument*> lógico; (secure) seguro. ● *adv*. **~ asleep** profundamente dormido. **~ barrier** *n* barrera *f* del sonido. **~ly**

adv sólidamente; (asleep) profundamente. **~proof** *a* insonorizado. **~track** *n* banda *f* sonora

soup /su:p/ *n* sopa *f*

sour /'saʊə(r)/ *a* (**-er**, **-est**) agrio; <*milk*> cortado

source /sɔ:s/ *n* fuente *f*

south /saʊθ/ *n* sur *m*. ● *a* sur *a invar*; <*wind*> del sur. ● *adv* <*go*> hacia el sur. **it's ~ of** está al sur de. **S~ Africa** *n* Sudáfrica *f*. **S~ America** *n* América *f* (del Sur), Sudamérica *f*. **S~ American** *a* & *n* sudamericano (*m*). **~-east** *n* sudeste *m*, sureste *m*. **~erly** /'sʌðəlɪ/ <*wind*> del sur. **~ern** /'sʌðən/ *a* del sur, meridional. **~erner** *n* sureño *m*. **~ward** /-wəd/, **~wards** *adv* hacia el sur. **~-west** *n* sudoeste *m*, suroeste *m*

souvenir /su:və'nɪə(r)/ *n* recuerdo *m*

sovereign /'sɒvrɪn/ *n* & *a* soberano (*m*)

Soviet /'səʊvɪət/ *a* (History) soviético. **the ~ Union** *n* la Unión *f* Soviética

sow[1] /səʊ/ *vt* (*pt* **sowed**, *pp* **sowed** *or* **sown** /səʊn/) sembrar

sow[2] /saʊ/ *n* cerda *f*

soy (esp Amer), **soya** /'sɔɪə/ *n*. **~ bean** *n* soja *f*

spa /spɑ:/ *n* balneario *m*

space /speɪs/ *n* espacio *m*; (room) espacio *m*, lugar *m*. ● *a* <*research etc*> espacial. ● *vt* espaciar. □ **~ out** *vt* espaciar. **~craft**, **~ship** *n* nave *f* espacial

spacious /'speɪʃəs/ *a* espacioso

spade /speɪd/ *n* pala *f*. **~s** *npl* (Cards) picas *fpl*

spaghetti /spə'getɪ/ *n* espaguetis *mpl*

Spain /speɪn/ *n* España *f*

span /spæn/ *n* (of arch) luz *f*; (of time) espacio *m*; (of wings) envergadura *f*. ● *vt* (*pt* **spanned**) extenderse sobre. ● *a* ⇒SPICK

Spaniard /'spænjəd/ *n* español *m*

spaniel /'spænjəl/ *n* spaniel *m*

Spanish /'spænɪʃ/ *a* español; (Lang) castellano, español. ● *n* (Lang) castellano *m*, español *m*. *npl*. **the ~** (people) los españoles

spank /spæŋk/ *vt* pegarle a (*en las nalgas*)

spanner /'spænə(r)/ *n* llave *f*

spare /speə(r)/ *vt*. **if you can ~ the time** si tienes tiempo. **can you ~ me a pound?** ¿tienes una libra que me des? **~ no effort** no escatimar esfuerzos. **have money to ~** tener dinero de sobra. ● *a* (not in use) de más; (replacement) de repuesto; (free) libre. **~ (part)** *n* repuesto *m*. **~ room** *n* cuarto *m* de huéspedes. **~ time** *n* tiempo *m* libre. **~ tyre** *n* neumático *m* de repuesto

sparingly /'speərɪŋlɪ/ *adv* <*use*> con moderación

spark /spɑ:k/ *n* chispa *f*. ● *vt* provocar <*criticism*>; suscitar <*interest*>. **~ing plug** *n* (Auto) bujía *f*

sparkl|e /'spɑ:kl/ *vi* centellear. ● *n* destello *m*. **~ing** *a* centelleante; <*wine*> espumoso

spark plug *n* (Auto) bujía *f*

sparrow /'spærəʊ/ *n* gorrión *m*

sparse /spɑ:s/ *a* escaso. **~ly** *adv* escasamente

spasm /'spæzəm/ *n* espasmo *m*; (of cough) acceso *m*. **~odic** /-'mɒdɪk/ *a* espasmódico; (Med) irregular

spat /spæt/ ⇒SPIT

spate /speɪt/ *n* racha *f*

spatial /'speɪʃl/ *a* espacial

spatter /'spætə(r)/ *vt* salpicar (with de)

spawn /spɔ:n/ *n* huevas *fpl.* ● *vt* generar. ● *vi* desovar

speak /spi:k/ *vt/i* (*pt* **spoke**, *pp* **spoken**) hablar. ~ **for s.o.** hablar en nombre de uno. □ ~ **up** *vi* hablar más fuerte. ~**er** *n* (in public) orador *m*; (loudspeaker) altavoz *m*; (of language) hablante *m & f*

spear /spɪə(r)/ *n* lanza *f.* ~**head** *vt* (lead) encabezar

special /'speʃl/ *a* especial. ~**ist** /'speʃəlɪst/ *n* especialista *m & f.* ~**ity** /-ɪ'ælətɪ/ *n* especialidad *f.* ~**ization** /-əlar'zeɪʃn/ *n* especialización *f.* ~**ize** /-əlaɪz/ *vi* especializarse. ~**ized** *a* especializado. ~**ly** *adv* especialmente. ~**ty** *n* (Amer) especialidad *f*

species /'spi:ʃi:z/ *n* especie *f*

specif|ic /spə'sɪfɪk/ *a* específico. ~**ically** *adv* específicamente; <*state*> explícitamente. ~**ication** /-ɪ'keɪʃn/ *n* especificación *f.* ~**y** /'spesɪfaɪ/ *vt* especificar

specimen /'spesɪmɪn/ *n* muestra *f*

speck /spek/ *n* (of dust) mota *f*; (in distance) punto *m*

specs /speks/ *npl* 🅸 ⇒SPECTACLES

spectac|le /'spektəkl/ *n* espectáculo *m.* ~**les** *npl* gafas *fpl*, lentes *fpl* (LAm), anteojos *mpl* (LAm). ~**ular** /-'tækjʊlə(r)/ *a* espectacular

spectator /spek'teɪtə(r)/ *n* espectador *m*

spectr|e /'spektə(r)/ *n* espectro *m.* ~**um** /'spektrəm/ *n* (*pl* **-tra** /-trə/) espectro *m*; (of views) gama *f*

speculat|e /'spekjʊleɪt/ *vi* especular. ~**ion** /-'leɪʃn/ *n* especulación *f.* ~**or** *n* especulador *m*

sped /sped/ ⇒SPEED

speech /spi:tʃ/ *n* (faculty) habla *f*; (address) discurso *m.* ~**less** *a* mudo

speed /spi:d/ *n* velocidad *f*; (rapidity) rapidez *f.* ● *vi* (*pt* **speeded**) (drive too fast) ir a exceso de velocidad. □ ~ **off,** ~ **away** (*pt* **sped**) *vi* alejarse a toda velocidad. □ ~ **by** (*pt* **sped**) *vi* <*time*> pasar volando. □ ~ **up** (*pt* **speeded**) *vt* acelerar. *vi* acelerarse. ~**boat** *n* lancha *f* motora. ~ **limit** *n* velocidad *f* máxima. ~**ometer** /spi:'dɒmɪtə(r)/ *n* velocímetro *m.* ~**way** *n* (Amer) autopista *f.* ~**y** *a* (**-ier**, **-iest**) rápido

spell /spel/ *n* (magic) hechizo *m*; (of weather, activity) período *m.* **go through a bad** ~ pasar por una mala racha. ● *vt/i* (*pt* **spelled** *or* **spelt**) escribir. □ ~ **out** *vt* deletrear; (fig) explicar. ~**ing** *n* ortografía *f*

spellbound /'spelbaʊnd/ *a* embelesado

spelt /spelt/ ⇒SPELL

spend /spend/ *vt* (*pt* **spent** /spent/) gastar <*money*>; pasar <*time*>; dedicar <*care*>. ● *vi* gastar dinero

sperm /spɜ:m/ *n* (*pl* **sperms** *or* **sperm**) esperma *f*; (individual) espermatozoide *m*

spew /spju:/ *vt/i* vomitar

spher|e /sfɪə(r)/ *n* esfera *f.* ~**ical** /'sferɪkl/ *a* esférico

spice /spaɪs/ *n* especia *f*

spick /spɪk/ *a.* ~ **and span** limpio y ordenado

spicy /'spaɪsɪ/ *a* picante

spider /'spaɪdə(r)/ *n* araña *f*

spik|e /spaɪk/ *n* (of metal etc) punta *f.* ~**y** *a* puntiagudo

spill /spɪl/ *vt* (*pt* **spilled** *or* **spilt**) derramar. ● *vi* derramarse. ~ **over** *vi* <*container*> desbordarse; <*liquid*> rebosar

spin /spɪn/ *vt* (*pt* **spun**, *pres p* **spinning**) hacer girar; hilar <*wool*>; centrifugar <*washing*>. ● *vi* girar. ● *n*. **give sth a** ~ hacer girar algo. **go for a** ~ (Auto) ir a dar un paseo en coche

spinach /'spɪnɪdʒ/ *n* espinacas *fpl*

spindly /'spɪndlɪ/ *a* larguirucho

spin-drier /spɪn'draɪə(r)/ *n* centrifugadora *f* (*de ropa*)

spine /spaɪn/ *n* columna *f* vertebral; (of book) lomo *m*; (on animal) púa *f*. ~**less** *a* (fig) sin carácter

spinning wheel /'spɪnɪŋ/ *n* rueca *f*

spin-off /'spɪnɒf/ *n* resultado *m* indirecto; (by-product) producto *m* derivado

spinster /'spɪnstə(r)/ *n* soltera *f*

spiral /'spaɪərəl/ *a* espiral; <*shape*> de espiral. ● *n* espiral *f*. ● *vi* (*pt* **spiralled**) <*unemployment*> escalar; <*prices*> dispararse. ~ **staircase** *n* escalera *f* de caracol

spire /'spaɪə(r)/ *n* aguja *f*

spirit /'spɪrɪt/ *n* espíritu *m*. **be in good** ~**s** estar animado. **in low** ~**s** abatido. ~**ed** *a* animado, fogoso. ~**s** *npl* (drinks) bebidas *fpl* alcohólicas (*de alta graduación*). ~**ual** /'spɪrɪtjʊəl/ *a* espiritual

spit /spɪt/ *vt* (*pt* **spat** *or* (Amer) **spit**, *pres p* **spitting**) escupir. ● *vi* escupir. **it's** ~**ting** caen algunas gotas. ● *n* saliva *f*; (for roasting) asador *m*

spite /spaɪt/ *n* rencor *m*. **in** ~ **of** a pesar de. ● *vt* fastidiar. ~**ful** *a* rencoroso

spittle /'spɪtl/ *n* baba *f*

splash /splæʃ/ *vt* salpicar. ● *v* <*person*> chapotear. ● *n* salpicadu ra *f*. **a** ~ **of paint** un poco de pintu ra. □ ~ **about** *vi* chapotear. □ ~ **down** *vi* <*spacecraft*> amerizar □ ~ **out** *vi* gastarse un dineral (o en)

splend|id /'splendɪd/ *a* espléndi do. ~**our** /-ə(r)/ *n* esplendor *m*

splint /splɪnt/ *n* tablilla *f*

splinter /'splɪntə(r)/ *n* astilla *f* ● *vi* astillarse

split /splɪt/ *vt* (*pt* **split**, *pres p* **splitting**) partir; fisionar <*atom*> reventar <*trousers*>; (divide) di vidir. ● *vi* partirse; (divide) di vidirse. **a** ~**ting headache** un dolo de cabeza espantoso. ● *n* (in gar ment) descosido *m*; (in wood, glass) ra jadura *f*. □ ~ **up** *vi* separarse. ~ **second** *n* fracción *f* de segundo

splutter /'splʌtə(r)/ *vi* chisporro tear; <*person*> farfullar

spoil /spɔɪl/ *vt* (*pt* **spoilt** o **spoiled**) estropear, echar a perder; (indulge) consentir, mal criar. ~**s** *npl* botín *m*. ~**-sport** *n* aguafiestas *m & f*

spoke[1] /spəʊk/ ⇒SPEAK

spoke[2] /spəʊk/ *n* (of wheel) rayo *m*

spoken /spəʊkən/ ⇒SPEAK

spokesman /'spəʊksmən/ *n* (*p* **-men**) portavoz *m*

sponge /spʌndʒ/ *n* esponja *f*. ● *v* limpiar con una esponja. ~ **off**, ~ **on** *vt* vivir a costillas de. ~ **cake** *n* bizcocho *m*

sponsor /'spɒnsə(r)/ *n* patrocina dor *m*; (of the arts) mecenas *m & f* (surety) garante *m*. ● *vt* patrocinar ~**ship** *n* patrocinio *m*; (of the arts mecenazgo *m*

spontaneous /spɒn'teɪmɪəs/ *a* espontáneo. **~ously** *adv* espontáneamente

spoof /spu:f/ *n* [I] parodia *f*

spooky /'spu:kɪ/ *a* (**-ier**, **-iest**) [I] espeluznante

spool /spu:l/ *n* carrete *m*

spoon /spu:n/ *n* cuchara *f*. **~ful** *n* cucharada *f*

sporadic /spə'rædɪk/ *a* esporádico

sport /spɔ:t/ *n* deporte *m*. **~s car** *n* coche *m* deportivo. **~s centre** *n* centro *m* deportivo. **~sman** /-mən/ *n*, (*pl* **-men**), **~swoman** *n* deportista *m & f*

spot /spɒt/ *n* mancha *f*; (pimple) grano *m*; (place) lugar *m*; (in pattern) lunar *m*. **be in a ~** [I] estar en apuros. **on the ~** allí mismo; <*decide*> en ese mismo momento. ● *vt* (*pt* **spotted**) manchar; ([I], notice) ver, divisar; descubrir <*mistake*>. **~ check** *n* control *m* hecho al azar. **~less** *a* <*clothes*> impecable; <*house*> limpísimo. **~light** *n* reflector *m*; (in theatre) foco *m*. **~ted** *a* moteado; <*material*> de lunares. **~ty** *a* (**-ier, -iest**) <*skin*> lleno de granos; <*youth*> con la cara llena de granos

spouse /spaʊz/ *n* cónyuge *m & f*

spout /spaʊt/ *n* pico *m*; (jet) chorro *m*

sprain /spreɪn/ *vt* hacerse un esguince en. ● *n* esguince *m*

sprang /spræŋ/ ⇒SPRING

spray /spreɪ/ *n* (of flowers) ramillete *m*; (from sea) espuma *f*; (liquid in spray form) espray *m*; (device) rociador *m*. ● *vt* rociar

spread /spred/ *vt* (*pt* **spread**) (stretch, extend) extender; desplegar <*wings*>; difundir <*idea, news*>. **~ butter on a piece of toast** untar una tostada con mantequilla. ● *vi* extenderse; <*disease*> propagarse; <*idea, news*> difundirse. ● *n* (of ideas) difusión *f*; (of disease, fire) propagación *f*; ([I], feast) festín *m*. □ **~ out** *vi* (move apart) desplegarse

spree /spri:/ *n*. **go on a shopping ~** ir de expedición a las tiendas

sprightly /'spraɪtlɪ/ *a* (**-ier**, **-iest**) vivo

spring /sprɪŋ/ *n* (season) primavera *f*; (device) resorte *m*; (in mattress) muelle *m*, resorte *m* (LAm); (elasticity) elasticidad *f*; (water) manantial *m*. ● *a* primaveral. ● *vi* (*pt* **sprang**, *pp* **sprung**) saltar; (issue) brotar. **~ from sth** <*problem*> provenir de algo. □ **~ up** *vi* surgir. **~board** *n* trampolín *m*. **~-clean** /-'kli:n/ *vi* hacer una limpieza general. **~ onion** *n* cebolleta *f*. **~time** *n* primavera *f*. **~y** *a* (**-ier**, **-iest**) <*mattress, grass*> mullido

sprinkle /'sprɪŋkl/ *vt* salpicar; (with liquid) rociar. ● *n* salpicadura *f*; (of liquid) rociada *f*. **~r** *n* regadera *f*

sprint /sprɪnt/ *n* carrera *f* corta. ● *vi* (Sport) esprintar; (run fast) correr. **~er** *n* corredor *m*

sprout /spraʊt/ *vi* brotar. ● *n* brote *m*. (**Brussels**) **~s** *npl* coles *fpl* de Bruselas

sprung /sprʌŋ/ ⇒SPRING

spud /spʌd/ *n* [I] patata *f*, papa *f* (LAm)

spun /spʌn/ ⇒SPIN

spur /spɜ:(r)/ *n* espuela *f*; (stimulus) acicate *m*. **on the ~ of the moment** sin pensarlo. ● *vt* (*pt* **spurred**). **~** (**on**) espolear; (fig) estimular

spurn /spɜ:n/ *vt* desdeñar; (reject) rechazar

spurt /spɜ:t/ *vi* <*liquid*> salir a chorros. ● *n* chorro *m*; (of activity) racha *f*

spy /spaɪ/ *n* espía *m* & *f*. ● *vt* descubrir, ver. ● *vi* espiar. **~ on s.o.** espiar a uno

squabble /'skwɒbl/ *vi* reñir

squad /skwɒd/ *n* (Mil) pelotón *m*; (of police) brigada *f*; (Sport) equipo *m*. **~ car** *m* coche *m* patrulla. **~ron** /'skwɒdrən/ *n* (Mil, Aviat) escuadrón *m*; (Naut) escuadra *f*

squalid /'skwɒlɪd/ *a* miserable

squall /skwɔ:l/ *n* turbión *m*

squalor /'skwɒlə(r)/ *n* miseria *f*

squander /'skwɒndə(r)/ *vt* derrochar; desaprovechar <*opportunity*>

square /skweə(r)/ *n* cuadrado *m*; (in town) plaza *f*. ● *a* cuadrado; <*meal*> decente; (□, old-fashioned) chapado a la antigua. ● *vt* (settle) arreglar; (Math) elevar al cuadrado. ● *vi* (agree) cuadrar. □ **~ up**. *vi* arreglar cuentas (**with** con). **~ly** *adv* directamente

squash /skwɒʃ/ *vt* aplastar; (suppress) acallar. ● *n*. **it was a terrible ~** íbamos (*or* iban) terriblemente apretujados; (drink) **orange ~** naranjada *f*; (Sport) squash *m*; (vegetable) calabaza *f*. **~y** *a* blando

squat /skwɒt/ *vi* (*pt* **squatted**) ponerse en cuclillas; (occupy illegally) ocupar sin autorización. ● *a* rechoncho y bajo. **~ter** *n* ocupante *m* & *f* ilegal, okupa *m* & *f*

squawk /skwɔ:k/ *n* graznido *m*. ● *vi* graznar

squeak /skwi:k/ *n* chillido *m*; (of door) chirrido *m*. ● *vi* chillar; <*door*> chirriar; <*shoes*> crujir. **~y** *a* chirriante

squeal /skwi:l/ *n* chillido *m* ● *vi* chillar

squeamish /'skwi:mɪʃ/ *a* impresionable, delicado

squeeze /skwi:z/ *vt* apretar; exprimir <*lemon etc*>. ● *vi*. **~ in** meterse. ● *n* estrujón *m*; (of hand) apretón *m*

squid /skwɪd/ *n* calamar *m*

squiggle /'skwɪgl/ *n* garabato *m*

squint /skwɪnt/ *vi* bizquear; (trying to see) entrecerrar los ojos. ● *n* estrabismo *m*

squirm /skwɜ:m/ *vi* retorcerse

squirrel /'skwɪrəl/ *n* ardilla *f*

squirt /skwɜ:t/ *vt* <*liquid*> echar un chorro de. ● *vi* salir a chorros. ● *n* chorrito *m*

St /sənt/ *abbr* (= **saint**) /sənt/ S, San(to); (= **street**) C/, Calle *f*

stab /stæb/ *vt* (*pt* **stabbed**) apuñalar. ● *n* puñalada *f*; (pain) punzada *f*. **have a ~ at sth** intentar algo

stabili|ty /stə'bɪlətɪ/ *n* estabilidad *f*. **~ze** /'steɪbɪlaɪz/ *vt/i* estabilizar

stable /'steɪbl/ *a* (**-er**, **-est**) estable. ● *n* caballeriza *f*, cuadra *f*

stack /stæk/ *n* montón *m*. ● *vt*. **~ (up)** amontonar

stadium /'steɪdɪəm/ *n* (*pl* **-diums** *or* **-dia** /-dɪə/) estadio *m*

staff /stɑ:f/ *n* (stick) palo *m*; (employees) personal *m*. **teaching ~** personal *m* docente. **a member of ~** un empleado

stag /stæg/ *n* ciervo *m*. **~-night**, **~-party** *n* (before wedding) fiesta *f* de despedida de soltero; (men-only party) fiesta *f* para hombres

stage /steɪdʒ/ *n* (in theatre) escenario *f*; (platform) plataforma *f*; (phase) etapa *f*. **the ~** (profession, medium) el teatro. ● *vt* poner en escena

<*play*>; (arrange) organizar; (pej) orquestar. **~coach** *n* diligencia *f*

stagger /'stægə(r)/ *vi* tambalearse. ● *vt* dejar estupefacto; escalonar <*holidays etc*>. **~ing** *a* asombroso

stagna|nt /'stægnənt/ *a* estancado. **~te** /stæg'neɪt/ *vi* estancarse

staid /steɪd/ *a* serio, formal

stain /steɪn/ *vt* manchar; (colour) teñir. ● *n* mancha *f*; (dye) tintura *f*. **~ed glass window** *n* vidriera *f* de colores. **~less steel** *n* acero *m* inoxidable. **~ remover** *n* quitamanchas *m*

stair /steə(r)/ *n* escalón *m*. **~s** *npl* escalera *f*. **~case**, **~way** *n* escalera *f*

stake /steɪk/ *n* estaca *f*; (wager) apuesta *f*; (Com) intereses *mpl*. **be at ~** estar en juego. ● *vt* estacar; jugarse <*reputation*>. **~ a claim** reclamar

stala|ctite /'stæləktaɪt/ *n* estalactita *f*. **~gmite** /'stæləgmaɪt/ *n* estalagmita *f*

stale /steɪl/ *a* (**-er**, **-est**) no fresco; <*bread*> duro; <*smell*> viciado. **~mate** *n* (Chess) ahogado *m*; (deadlock) punto *m* muerto

stalk /stɔ:k/ *n* tallo *m*. ● *vt* acechar. ● *vi* irse indignado

stall /stɔ:l/ *n* (in stable) compartimiento *m*; (in market) puesto *m*. **~s** *npl* (in theatre) platea *f*, patio *m* de butacas. ● *vt* parar <*engine*>. ● *vi* <*engine*> pararse; (fig) andar con rodeos

stallion /'stæljən/ *n* semental *m*

stalwart /'stɔ:lwət/ *a* <*supporter*> leal, incondicional

stamina /'stæmɪnə/ *n* resistencia *f*

stammer /'stæmə(r)/ *vi* tartamudear. ● *n* tartamudeo *m*

stamp /stæmp/ *vt* (with feet) patear; (press) estampar; (with rubber stamp) sellar; (fig) señalar. ● *vi* dar patadas en el suelo. ● *n* sello *m*, estampilla *f* (LAm), timbre *m* (Mex); (on passport) sello *m*; (with foot) patada *f*; (mark) marca *f*, señal *f*. □ **~ out** *vt* (fig) erradicar. **~ed addressed envelope** *n* sobre *m* franqueado con su dirección

stampede /stæm'pi:d/ *n* estampida *f*. ● *vi* salir en estampida

stance /stɑ:ns/ *n* postura *f*

stand /stænd/ *vi* (*pt* **stood**) estar de pie, estar parado (LAm); (rise) ponerse de pie, pararse; (be) encontrarse; (Pol) presentarse como candidato (**for** en). **the offer ~s** la oferta sigue en pie. **~ to reason** ser lógico. ● *vt* (endure) soportar; (place) colocar. **~ a chance** tener una posibilidad. ● *n* posición *f*, postura *f*; (for lamp etc) pie *m*, sostén *m*; (at market) puesto *m*; (booth) quiosco *m*; (Sport) tribuna *f*. **make a ~ against sth** oponer resistencia a algo. □ **~ back** *vi* apartarse. □ **~ by** *vi* estar preparado. *vt* (support) apoyar. □ **~ down** *vi* retirarse. □ **~ for** *vt* significar. □ **~ in for** *vt* suplir a. □ **~ out** *vi* destacarse. □ **~ up** *vi* ponerse de pie, pararse (LAm). □ **~ up for** *vt* defender. **~ up for oneself** defenderse. □ **~ up to** *vt* resistir a

standard /'stændəd/ *n* norma *f*; (level) nivel *m*; (flag) estandarte *m*. ● *a* estándar *a invar*, normal. **~ize** *vt* estandarizar. **~ lamp** *n* lámpara *f* de pie. **~s** *npl* principios *mpl*

stand: ~-by *n* (at airport) stand-by *m*. **be on ~-by** <*police*> estar en estado de alerta. **~-in** *n* suplente *m*

& f. **~ing** *a* de pie, parado (LAm); (permanent) permanente *f.* ● *n* posición *f*; (prestige) prestigio *m.* **~off** *n* (Amer, draw) empate *m*; (deadlock) callejón *m* sin salida. **~point** *n* punto *m* de vista. **~still** *n.* **be at a ~still** estar paralizado. **come to a ~still** *<vehicle>* parar; *<city>* quedar paralizado

stank /stæŋk/ ⇒STINK

staple /'steɪpl/ *a* principal. ● *n* grapa *f.* ● *vt* sujetar con una grapa. **~r** *n* grapadora *f*

star /stɑ:(r)/ *n* (incl Cinema, Theatre) estrella *f*; (asterisk) asterisco *m.* ● *vi* (*pt* **starred**). **~ in a film** protagonizar una película. **~board** *n* estribor *m.*

starch /stɑ:tʃ/ *n* almidón *m*; (in food) fécula *f.* ● *vt* almidonar. **~y** *a* *<food>* a base de féculas

stardom /'stɑ:dəm/ *n* estrellato *m*

stare /steə(r)/ *n* mirada *f* fija. ● *vi.* **~ (at)** mirar fijamente

starfish /'stɑ:fɪʃ/ *n* estrella *f* de mar

stark /stɑ:k/ *a* (**-er**, **-est**) escueto. ● *adv* completamente

starling /'stɑ:lɪŋ/ *n* estornino *m*

starry /'stɑ:rɪ/ *a* estrellado

start /stɑ:t/ *vt* empezar, comenzar; encender *<engine>*; arrancar *<car>*; (cause) provocar; abrir *<business>*. ● *vi* empezar; *<car etc>* arrancar; (jump) dar un respingo. **to ~ with** (as linker) para empezar. **~ off by doing sth** empezar por hacer algo. ● *n* principio *m*; (Sport) ventaja *f*; (jump) susto *m.* **make an early ~** (on journey) salir temprano. **~er** *n* (Auto) motor *m* de arranque; (Culin) primer plato *m.* **~ing-point** *n* punto *m* de partida

startle /'stɑ:tl/ *vt* asustar

starv|ation /stɑ:'veɪʃn/ *n* hambre *f*, inanición *f.* **~e** /stɑ:v/ *vt* hacer morir de hambre. ● *vi* morirse de hambre. **I'm ~ing** me muero de hambre

state /steɪt/ *n* estado *m.* **be in a ~** estar agitado. **the S~** los Estados *mpl* Unidos. ● *vt* declarar; expresar *<views>*; (fix) fijar. ● *a* del Estado; (Schol) público; (with ceremony) de gala. **~ly** *a* (**-ier**, **-iest**) majestuoso. **~ly home** *n* casa *f* solariega. **~ment** *n* declaración *f*; (account) informe *m.* **~sman** /-mən/ *n* estadista *m*

static /'stætɪk/ *a* estacionario. ● *n* (interference) estática *f*

station /'steɪʃn/ *n* estación *f*; (on radio) emisora *f*; (TV) canal *m.* ● *vt* colocar; (Mil) estacionar. **~ary** *a* estacionario. **~er's (shop)** *n* papelería *f.* **~ery** *n* artículos *mpl* de papelería. **~ wagon** *n* (Amer) ranchera *f*, (coche *m*) familiar *m*, camioneta *f* (LAm)

statistic /stə'tɪstɪk/ *n* estadística *f.* **~al** *a* estadístico. **~s** *n* (science) estadística *f*

statue /'stætʃu:/ *n* estatua *f*

stature /'stætʃə(r)/ *n* talla *f*, estatura *f*

status /'steɪtəs/ *n* posición *f* social; (prestige) categoría *f*; (Jurid) estado *m*

statut|e /'stætʃu:t/ *n* estatuto *m.* **~ory** /-ʊtrɪ/ *a* estatutario

staunch /stɔ:nʃ/ *a* (**-er**, **-est**) leal

stave /'steɪv/ *n* (Mus) pentagrama *m.* □ **~ off** *vt* evitar

stay /steɪ/ *n* (of time) estancia *f*, estadía *f* (LAm); (Jurid) suspensión *f.* ● *vi* quedarse; (reside) alojarse. **I'm ~ing in a hotel** estoy en un hotel. □ **~ in** *vi* quedarse en casa. □ **~ up** *vi* quedarse levantado

stead /sted/ *n*. **in s.o.'s ~** en lugar de uno. **stand s.o. in good ~** resultarle muy útil a uno. **~ily** *adv* firmemente; (regularly) regularmente. **~y** *a* (**-ier**, **-iest**) firme; (regular) regular; <*flow*> continuo; <*worker*> serio

steak /steɪk/ *n*. **a ~** un filete. **some ~** carne para guisar

steal /sti:l/ *vt* (*pt* **stole**, *pp* **stolen**) robar. **~ in** *vi* entrar a hurtadillas

stealth /stelθ/ *n*. **by ~** sigilosamente. **~y** *a* sigiloso

steam /sti:m/ *n* vapor *m*. **let off ~** (fig) desahogarse. ● *vt* (cook) cocer al vapor. ● *vi* echar vapor. □ **~ up** *vi* empañarse. **~ engine** *n* máquina *f* de vapor. **~er** *n* (ship) barco *m* de vapor. **~roller** *n* apisonadora *f*. **~y** *a* lleno de vapor

steel /sti:l/ *n* acero *m*. ● *vt*. **~ o.s.** armarse de valor. **~ industry** *n* industria *f* siderúrgica

steep /sti:p/ ● *a* (**-er**, **-est**) empinado; <*increase*> considerable; <*price*> [I] excesivo

steeple /'sti:pl/ *n* aguja *f*, campanario *m*

steeply /'sti:plɪ/ *adv* abruptamente; <*increase*> considerablemente

steer /stɪə(r)/ *vt* dirigir; gobernar <*ship*>. ● *vi* (in ship) estar al timón. **~ clear of** evitar. **~ing** *n* (Auto) dirección *f*. **~ing wheel** *n* volante *m*

stem /stem/ *n* (of plant) tallo *m*; (of glass) pie *m*; (of word) raíz *f*. ● *vt* (*pt* **stemmed**) contener <*bleeding*>. ● *vi*. **~ from** provenir de

stench /stentʃ/ *n* hedor *m*

stencil /'stensl/ *n* plantilla *f*

stenographer /ste'nɒgrəfə(r)/ *n* estenógrafo *m*

step /step/ *vi* (*pt* **stepped**). **~ in sth** pisar algo. □ **~ aside** *vi* hacerse a un lado. □ **~ down** *vi* retirarse. □ **~ in** *vi* (fig) intervenir. □ **~ up** *vt* intensificar; redoblar <*security*>. ● *n* paso *m*; (stair) escalón *m*; (fig) medida *f*. **take ~s** tomar medidas. **be in ~** llevar el paso. **be out of ~** no llevar el paso. **~brother** *n* hermanastro *m*. **~daughter** *n* hijastra *f*. **~father** *n* padrastro *m*. **~ladder** *n* escalera *f* de tijera. **~mother** *n* madrastra *f*. **~ping-stone** *n* peldaño *m*. **~sister** *n* hermanastra *f*. **~son** *n* hijastro *m*

stereo /'sterɪəʊ/ *n* (*pl* **-os** estéreo *m*. ● *a* estéreo *a invar*. **~type** *n* estereotipo *m*

steril|e /'steraɪl/ *a* estéril. **~ize** /'sterɪlaɪz/ *vt* esterilizar

sterling /'stɜ:lɪŋ/ *n* libras *fpl* esterlinas. ● *a* <*pound*> esterlina

stern /stɜ:n/ *n* (of boat) popa *f*. ● *a* (**-er**, **-est**) severo

stethoscope /'steθəskəʊp/ *n* estetoscopio *m*

stew /stju:/ *vt/i* guisar. ● *n* estofado *m*, guiso *m*

steward /'stjʊu:əd/ *n* administrador *m*; (on ship) camarero *m*; (air steward) sobrecargo *m*, aeromozo *m* (LAm). **~ess** /-'des/ *n* camarera *f*; (on aircraft) auxiliar *f* de vuelo, azafata *f*

stick /stɪk/ *n* palo *m*; (for walking) bastón *m*; (of celery etc) tallo *m*. ● *vt* (*pt* **stuck**) (glue) pegar; ([I], put) poner; (thrust) clavar; ([I], endure) soportar. ● *vi* pegarse; (jam) atascarse. □ **~ out** *vi* sobresalir. □ **~ to** *vt* ceñirse a. □ **~ up for** *vt* [I] defender. **~er** *n* pegatina *f*.

~ing plaster *n* esparadrapo *m*; (individual) tirita *f*, curita *f* (LAm). **~ler** /'stɪklə(r)/ *n*. **be a ~ler for** insistir en. **~y** /'stɪkɪ/ *a* (**-ier**, **-iest**) *<surface>* pegajoso; *<label>* engomado

stiff /stɪf/ *a* (**-er**, **-est**) rígido; *<joint, fabric>* tieso; *<muscle>* entumecido; (difficult) difícil; *<manner>* estirado; *<drink>* fuerte. **have a ~ neck** tener tortícolis. **~en** *vi* (become rigid) agarrotarse; (become firm) endurecerse. **~ly** *adv* rígidamente.

stifl|e /'staɪfl/ *vt* sofocar. **~ing** *a* sofocante

stiletto (heel) /stɪ'letəʊ/ *n* (*pl* **-os**) tacón *m* de aguja

still /stɪl/ *a* inmóvil; (peaceful) tranquilo; *<drink>* sin gas. **sit ~, stand ~** quedarse tranquilo. ● *adv* todavía, aún; (nevertheless) sin embargo. **~born** *a* nacido muerto. **~ life** *n* (*pl* **-s**) bodegón *m*. **~ness** *n* tranquilidad *f*

stilted /'stɪltɪd/ *a* rebuscado; *<conversation>* forzado

stilts /stɪlts/ *npl* zancos *mpl*

stimul|ant /'stɪmjʊlənt/ *n* estimulante *m*. **~ate** /-leɪt/ *vt* estimular. **~ation** /-'leɪʃn/ *n* estímulo *m*. **~us** /-əs/ *n* (*pl* **-li** /-laɪ/) estímulo *m*

sting /stɪŋ/ *n* picadura *f*; (organ) aguijón *m*. ● *vt/i* (*pt* **stung**) picar

stingy /'stɪndʒɪ/ *a* (**-ier**, **-iest**) tacaño

stink /stɪŋk/ *n* hedor *m*. ● *vi* (*pt* **stank** *or* **stunk**, *pp* **stunk**) apestar, oler mal

stipulat|e /'stɪpjʊleɪt/ *vt/i* estipular. **~ion** /-'leɪʃn/ *n* estipulación *f*

stir /stɜː(r)/ *vt* (*pt* **stirred**) remover, revolver; (move) agitar; estimular *<imagination>*. ● *vi* moverse. **~ up trouble** armar lío 🅸. ● *n* revuelo *m*, conmoción *f*

stirrup /'stɪrəp/ *n* estribo *m*

stitch /stɪtʃ/ *n* (in sewing) puntada *f*; (in knitting) punto *m*; (pain) dolor *m* costado. **be in ~es** 🅸 desternillarse de risa. ● *vt* coser

stock /stɒk/ *n* (Com, supplies) existencias *fpl*; (Com, variety) surtido *m*; (livestock) ganado *m*; (Culin) caldo *m*. **~s and shares, ~s and bonds** (Amer) acciones *fpl*. **out of ~** agotado. **take ~ of sth** (fig) hacer un balance de algo. ● *a* estándar *a invar*; (fig) trillado. ● *vt* surtir, abastecer (**with** de). ◻ **~ up** *vi* abastecerse (**with** de). **~broker** /-brəʊkə(r)/ *n* corredor *m* de bolsa. **S~ Exchange** *n* bolsa *f*. **~ing** *n* media *f*. **~pile** *n* reservas *fpl*. ● *vt* almacenar. **~-still** *a* inmóvil. **~-taking** *n* (Com) inventario *m*. **~y** *a* (**-ier**, **-iest**) bajo y fornido

stodgy /'stɒdʒɪ/ (**-dgier**, **-dgiest**) *a* pesado

stoke /stəʊk/ *vt* echarle carbón (*or* leña) a

stole /stəʊl/ ⇒STEAL

stolen /'stəʊlən/ ⇒STEAL

stomach /'stʌmək/ *n* estómago *m*. ● *vt* soportar. **~-ache** *n* dolor *m* de estómago

ston|e /stəʊn/ *n* piedra *f*; (in fruit) hueso *m*; (weight, *pl* **stone**) *unidad de peso equivalente a 14 libras o 6,35 kg*. ● *a* de piedra. ● *vt* apedrear. **~e-deaf** *a* sordo como una tapia. **~y** *a* *<silence>* sepulcral

stood /stʊd/ ⇒STAND

stool /stuːl/ *n* taburete *m*

stoop /stu:p/ *vi* agacharse; (fig) rebajarse. ● *n*. **have a ~** ser cargado de espaldas

stop /stɒp/ *vt* (*pt* **stopped**) (halt, switch off) parar; (cease) terminar; (prevent) impedir; (interrupt) interrumpir. **~ doing sth** dejar de hacer algo. **~ it!** ¡basta ya! ● *vi* <*bus*> parar, detenerse; <*clock*> pararse. **it's ~ped raining** ha dejado de llover. ● *n* (bus etc) parada *f*; (break on journey) parada *f*. **put a ~ to sth** poner fin a algo. **come to a ~** detenerse. **~gap** *n* remedio *m* provisional. **~over** *n* escala *f*. **~page** /ˈstɒpɪdʒ/ *n* suspensión *f*, paradero *m* (LAm); (of work) huelga *f*, paro *m* (LAm); (interruption) interrupción *f*. **~per** *n* tapón *m*. **~watch** *n* cronómetro *m*

storage /ˈstɔ:rɪdʒ/ *n* almacenamiento *m*

store /stɔ:(r)/ *n* provisión *f*; (depot) almacén *m*; (Amer, shop) tienda *f*; (fig) reserva *f*. **in ~** en reserva. ● *vt* (for future) poner en reserva; (in warehouse) almacenar. □ **~ up** *vt* (fig) ir acumulando. **~keeper** *n* (Amer) tendero *m*, comerciante *m & f*. **~room** *n* almacén *m*; (for food) despensa *f*

storey /ˈstɔ:rɪ/ *n* (*pl* **-eys**) piso *m*, planta *f*

stork /stɔ:k/ *n* cigüeña *f*

storm /stɔ:m/ *n* tempestad *f*. ● *vi* rabiar. ● *vt* (Mil) asaltar. **~y** *a* tormentoso; <*sea, relationship*> tempestuoso

story /ˈstɔ:rɪ/ *n* historia *f*; (in newspaper) artículo *m*; (rumour) rumor *m*; (Ⓘ, lie) mentira *f*, cuento *m*. **~-teller** *n* cuentista *m & f*

stout /staʊt/ *a* (**-er**, **-est**) robusto, corpulento. ● *n* cerveza *f* negra

stove /stəʊv/ *n* estufa *f*

stow /stəʊ/ *vt* guardar; (hide) esconder. □ **~ away** *vi* viajar de polizón. **~away** *n* polizón *m & f*

straggl|e /ˈstrægl/ *vi* rezagarse. **~y** *a* desordenado

straight /streɪt/ *a* (**-er**, **-est**) recto; (tidy) en orden; (frank) franco; <*hair*> lacio; (Ⓘ, conventional) convencional. **be ~** estar derecho. ● *adv* <*sit up*> derecho; (direct) directamente; (without delay) inmediatamente. **~ away** en seguida, inmediatamente. **~ on** todo recto. **~ out** sin rodeos. ● *n* recta *f*. **~en** *vt* enderezar. □ **~en up** *vt* ordenar. **~forward** /-ˈfɔ:wəd/ *a* franco; (easy) sencillo

strain /streɪn/ *n* (tension) tensión *f*; (injury) torcedura *f*. ● *vt* forzar <*voice, eyesight*>; someter a demasiada tensión <*relations*>; (sieve) colar. **~ one's back** hacerse daño en la espalda. **~ a muscle** hacerse un esguince. **~ed** *a* forzado; <*relations*> tirante. **~er** *n* colador *m*. **~s** *npl* (Mus) acordes *mpl*

strait /streɪt/ *n* estrecho *m*. **be in dire ~s** estar en grandes apuros. **~jacket** *n* camisa *f* de fuerza

strand /strænd/ *n* (thread) hebra *f*. **a ~ of hair** un pelo. ● *vt*. **be ~ed** <*ship*> quedar encallado. **I was left ~ed** me abandonaron a mi suerte

strange /streɪndʒ/ *a* (**-er**, **-est**) raro, extraño; (not known) desconocido. **~ly** *adv* de una manera rara. **~ly enough** aunque parezca mentira. **~r** *n* desconocido *m*; (from another place) forastero *m*

strangle /ˈstræŋgl/ *vt* estrangular

strap /stræp/ *n* correa *f*; (of garment) tirante *m*. ● *vt* (*pt* **strapped**) atar con una correa

strat|egic /strə'tiːdʒɪk/ *a* estratégico. **~egy** /'strætədʒɪ/ *n* estrategia *f*

straw /strɔː/ *n* paja *f*; (drinking ~) pajita *f*, paja *f*, popote *m* (Mex). **the last ~** el colmo. **~berry** /-bərɪ/ *n* fresa *f*; (large) fresón *m*

stray /streɪ/ *vi* (wander away) apartarse; (get lost) extraviarse; (deviate) desviarse (**from** de). ● *a* <*animal*> (without owner) callejero; (lost) perdido. ● *n* (without owner) perro *m*/gato *m* callejero; (lost) perro *m*/gato *m* perdido

streak /striːk/ *n* lista *f*, raya *f*; (in hair) reflejo *m*; (in personality) veta *f*

stream /striːm/ *n* arroyo *m*; (current) corriente *f*. **a ~ of abuse** una sarta de insultos. ● *vi* correr. □ **~ out** *vi* <*people*> salir en tropel. **~er** *n* (paper) serpentina *f*; (banner) banderín *m*. **~line** *vt* dar líneaaerodinámica a; (simplify) racionalizar. **~lined** *a* aerodinámico

street /striːt/ *n* calle *f*. **~car** *n* (Amer) tranvía *m*. **~ lamp** *n* farol *m*. **~ map**, **~ plan** *n* plano *m*

strength /streŋθ/ *n* fuerza *f*; (of wall etc) solidez *f*. **~en** *vt* reforzar <*wall*>; fortalecer <*muscle*>

strenuous /'strenjʊəs/ *a* enérgico; (arduous) arduo; (tiring) fatigoso

stress /stres/ *n* énfasis *f*; (Gram) acento *m*; (Mec, Med, tension) tensión *f*. ● *vt* insistir en

stretch /stretʃ/ *vt* estirar; (extend) extender; forzar <*truth*>; estirar <*resources*>. ● *vi* estirarse; (when sleepy) desperezarse; (extend) extenderse; (be elastic) estirarse. ● *n* (period) período *m*; (of road) tramo *m*. **at a ~** sin parar. □ **~ out** *vi* <*person*> tenderse. **~er** *n* camilla *f*

strict /strɪkt/ *a* (**-er**, **-est**) estricto; <*secrecy*> absoluto. **~ly** *adv* con severidad; <*rigorously*> terminantemente. **~ly speaking** en rigor

stridden /strɪdn/ ⇒STRIDE

stride /straɪd/ *vi* (*pt* **strode**, *pp* **stridden**) andar a zancadas. ● *n* zancada *f*. **take sth in one's ~** tomarse algo con calma. **~nt** /'straɪdnt/ *a* estridente

strife /straɪf/ *n* conflicto *m*

strike /straɪk/ *vt* (*pt* **struck**) golpear; encender <*match*>; encontrar <*gold, oil*>; <*clock*> dar. **it ~s me as odd** me parece raro. ● *vi* golpear; (go on strike) declararse en huelga; (be on strike) estar en huelga; (attack) atacar; <*clock*> dar la hora. ● *n* (of workers) huelga *f*, paro *m*; (attack) ataque *m*. **come out on ~** ir a la huelga. □ **~ off**, **~ out** *vt* tachar. **~ up a friendship** trabar amistad. **~r** *n* huelguista *m* & *f*; (Sport) artillero *m*

striking /'straɪkɪŋ/ *a* <*resemblance*> sorprendente; <*colour*> llamativo

string /strɪŋ/ *n* cordel *m*, mecate *m* (Mex); (Mus) cuerda *f*; (of lies, pearls) sarta *f*; (of people) sucesión *f*. □ **~ along** *vt* Ⓘ engañar

stringent /'strɪndʒənt/ *a* riguroso

strip /strɪp/ *vt* (*pt* **stripped**) desnudar <*person*>; deshacer <*bed*>. ● *vi* desnudarse. ● *n* tira *f*; (of land) franja *f*. **~ cartoon** *n* historieta *f*

stripe /straɪp/ *n* raya *f*. **~d** *a* a rayas, rayado

strip lighting *n* luz *f* fluorescente

strive /straɪv/ *vi* (*pt* **strove**, *pp* **striven**). **~ to** esforzarse por

strode /strəʊd/ ⇒STRIDE

stroke /strəʊk/ *n* golpe *m*; (in swimming) brazada *f*; (Med) ataque *m* de apoplejía; (of pen etc) trazo *m*; (of clock) campanada *f*; (caress) caricia *f*. **a ~ of luck** un golpe de suerte. ● *vt* acariciar

stroll /strəʊl/ *vi* pasearse. ● *n* paseo *m*. **~er** *n* (Amer) sillita *f* de paseo, cochecito *m*

strong /strɒŋ/ *a* (**-er**, **-est**) fuerte. **~hold** *n* fortaleza *f*; (fig) baluarte *m*. **~ly** *adv* (greatly) fuertemente; <*protest*> enérgicamente; (deeply) profundamente. **~room** *n* cámara *f* acorazada

strove /strəʊv/ ⇒STRIVE

struck /strʌk/ ⇒STRIKE

structur|al /'strʌktʃərəl/ *a* estructural. **~e** /'strʌktʃə(r)/ *n* estructura *f*

struggle /'strʌgl/ *vi* luchar; (thrash around) forcejear. ● *n* lucha *f*

strum /strʌm/ *vt* (*pt* **strummed**) rasguear

strung /strʌŋ/ ⇒STRING

strut /strʌt/ *n* (in building) puntal *m*. ● *vi* (*pt* **strutted**) pavonearse

stub /stʌb/ *n* (of pencil, candle) cabo *m*; (counterfoil) talón *m*; (of cigarette) colilla. □ **~ out** (*pt* **stubbed**) *vt* apagar

stubble /'stʌbl/ *n* rastrojo *m*; (beard) barba *f* de varios días

stubborn /'stʌbən/ *a* terco

stuck /stʌk/ ⇒STICK. ● *a*. **the drawer is ~** el cajón se ha atascado. **the door is ~** la puerta se ha atrancado. **~-up** *a* [I] estirado

stud /stʌd/ *n* tachuela *f*; (for collar) gemelo *m*.

student /'stju:dənt/ *n* estudiante *m & f*; (at school) alumno *m*. **~ driver** *n* (Amer) *persona que está aprendiendo a conducir*

studio /'stju:dɪəʊ/ *n* (*pl* **-os**) estudio *m*. **~ apartment**, **~ flat** *n* estudio *m*

studious /'stju:dɪəs/ *a* estudioso

study /'stʌdɪ/ *n* estudio *m*. ● *vt/i* estudiar

stuff /stʌf/ *n* [I] cosas *fpl*. **what's this ~ called?** ¿cómo se llama esta cosa? ● *vt* rellenar; disecar <*animal*>; (cram) atiborrar; (put) meter de prisa. **~ o.s.** [I] darse un atracón. **~ing** *n* relleno *m*. **~y** *a* (**-ier**, **-iest**) mal ventilado; (old-fashioned) acartonado. **it's ~y in here** está muy cargado el ambiente

stumbl|e /'stʌmbl/ *vi* tropezar. **~e across**, **~e on** *vt* dar con. **~ing-block** *n* tropiezo *m*, impedimento *m*

stump /stʌmp/ *n* (of limb) muñón *m*; (of tree) tocón *m*

stun /stʌn/ *vt* (*pt* **stunned**) (daze) aturdir; (bewilder) dejar atónito. **~ning** *a* sensacional

stung /stʌŋ/ ⇒STING

stunk /stʌŋk/ ⇒STINK

stunt /stʌnt/ *n* [I] ardid *m* publicitario. ● *vt* detener, atrofiar. **~ed** *a* (growth) atrofiado; (body) raquítico. **~man** *n* especialista *m*. **~woman** *n* especialista *f*

stupendous /stju:'pendəs/ *a* estupendo

stupid /'stju:pɪd/ *a* (foolish) tonto; (unintelligent) estúpido. **~ity** /-'pɪdətɪ/ *n* estupidez *f*. **~ly** *adv* estúpidamente

stupor /'stju:pə(r)/ *n* estupor *m*

sturdy /'stɜ:dɪ/ *a* (**-ier**, **-iest**) robusto

stutter /'stʌtə(r)/ *vi* tartamudear. ● *n* tartamudeo *m*

sty /staɪ/ *n* (*pl* **sties**) pocilga *f*; (Med) orzuelo *m*

styl|e /staɪl/ *n* estilo *m*; (fashion) moda *f*; (design, type) diseño *m*. **in ~** a lo grande. ● *vt* diseñar. **~ish** *a* elegante. **~ist** *n* estilista *m & f*. **hair ~ist** estilista *m & f*

stylus /'staɪləs/ *n* (*pl* **-uses**) aguja *f* (*de tocadiscos*)

suave /swɑːv/ *a* elegante y desenvuelto

subconscious /sʌb'kɒnʃəs/ *a & n* subconsciente (*m*)

subdivide /sʌbdɪ'vaɪd/ *vt* subdividir

subdued /səb'djuːd/ *a* apagado

subject /'sʌbdʒɪkt/ *a* sometido. **~ to** sujeto a. ● *n* (theme) tema *m*; (Schol) asignatura *f*, materia *f* (LAm); (Gram) sujeto *m*; (Pol) súbdito *m*. ● /səb'dʒekt/ *vt* someter. **~ive** /səb'dʒektɪv/ *a* subjetivo

subjunctive /səb'dʒʌŋktɪv/ *a & n* subjuntivo (*m*)

sublime /sə'blaɪm/ *a* sublime

submarine /sʌbmə'riːn/ *n* submarino *m*

submerge /səb'mɜːdʒ/ *vt* sumergir. ● *vi* sumergirse

submi|ssion /səb'mɪʃn/ *n* sumisión *f*. **~t** /səb'mɪt/ *vt* (*pt* **submitted**) (subject) someter; presentar <*application*>. ● *vi* rendirse

subordinate /sə'bɔːdɪnət/ *a & n* subordinado (*m*). ● /sə'bɔːdɪneɪt/ *vt* subordinar

subscri|be /səb'skraɪb/ *vi* suscribir. **~be to** suscribirse a <*magazine*>. **~ber** *n* suscriptor *m*. **~ption** /-rɪpʃn/ *n* (to magazine) suscripción *f*

subsequent /'sʌbsɪkwənt/ *a* posterior, subsiguiente. **~ly** *adv* posteriormente

subside /səb'saɪd/ *vi* <*land*> hundirse; <*flood*> bajar; <*storm, wind*> amainar. **~nce** /'sʌbsɪdəns/ *n* hundimiento *m*

subsidiary /səb'sɪdɪərɪ/ *a* secundario; <*subject*> complementario. ● *n* (Com) filial

subsid|ize /'sʌbsɪdaɪz/ *vt* subvencionar, subsidiar (LAm). **~y** /'sʌbsədɪ/ *n* subvención *f*, subsidio *m*

substance /'sʌbstəns/ *n* sustancia *f*

substandard /sʌb'stændəd/ *a* de calidad inferior

substantial /səb'stænʃl/ *a* (sturdy) sólido; <*meal*> sustancioso; (considerable) considerable

substitut|e /'sʌbstɪtjuːt/ *n* (person) substituto *m*; (thing) sucedáneo *m*. ● *vt/i* sustituir. **~ion** /-'tjuːʃn/ *n* sustitución *f*

subterranean /sʌbtə'reɪnjən/ *a* subterráneo

subtitle /'sʌbtaɪtl/ *n* subtítulo *m*

subtle /'sʌtl/ *a* (**-er**, **-est**) sutil; (tactful) discreto. **~ty** *n* sutileza *f*

subtract /səb'trækt/ *vt* restar. **~ion** /-ʃn/ *n* resta *f*

suburb /'sʌbɜːb/ *n* barrio *m* residencial de las afueras, colonia *f*. **the ~s** las afueras *fpl*. **~an** /sə'bɜːbən/ *a* suburbano. **~ia** /sə'bɜːbɪə/ *n zonas residenciales de las afueras de una ciudad*

subversive /səb'vɜːsɪv/ *a* subversivo

subway /'sʌbweɪ/ *n* paso *m* subterráneo; (Amer) metro *m*

succeed /sək'siːd/ *vi* <*plan*> dar resultado; <*person*> tener éxito. **~ in doing** lograr hacer. ● *vt* suceder

success /sək'ses/ *n* éxito *m*. **~ful** *a* <*person*> de éxito, exitoso (LAm). **the ~ful applicant** el candidato que obtenga el puesto. **~fully** *a* satisfactoriamente. **~ion** /-ʃn/ *n* sucesión *f*. **for 3 years in ~ion** du rante tres años consecutivos. **in rapid ~ion** uno tras otro. **~ive** *a* sucesivo. **~or** *n* sucesor *m*

succulent /'sʌkjʊlənt/ *a* suculento

succumb /sə'kʌm/ *vi* sucumbir

such /sʌtʃ/ *a* tal (+ *noun*), tan (+ *adj*). **~ a big house** una casa tan grande. ● *pron* tal. **~ and ~** tal o cual. **~ as** como. **~ as it is** tal como es

suck /sʌk/ *vt* chupar <*sweet, thumb*>; sorber <*liquid*>. □ **~ up** *vt* <*vacuum cleaner*> aspirar; <*pump*> succionar. □ **~ up to** *vt* [I] dar coba a. **~er** *n* (plant) chupón *m*; ([I], person) imbécil *m*

suckle /sʌkl/ *vt* amamantar

suction /'sʌkʃn/ *n* succión *f*

sudden /'sʌdn/ *a* repentino. **all of a ~** de repente. **~ly** *adv* de repente

suds /sʌds/ *npl* espuma *f* de jabón

sue /su:/ *vt* (*pres p* **suing**) demandar (**for** por)

suede /sweɪd/ *n* ante *m*

suet /'su:ɪt/ *n* sebo *m*

suffer /'sʌfə(r)/ *vt* sufrir; (tolerate) aguantar. ● *vi* sufrir; (be affected) resentirse

suffic|e /sə'faɪs/ *vi* bastar. **~ient** /sə'fɪʃnt/ *a* suficiente, bastante. **~iently** *adv* (lo) suficientemente

suffix /'sʌfɪks/ *n* (*pl* **-ixes**) sufijo *m*

suffocat|e /'sʌfəkeɪt/ *vt* asfixiar. ● *vi* asfixiarse. **~ion** /-'keɪʃn/ *n* asfixia *f*

sugar /'ʃʊgə(r)/ *n* azúcar *m* & *f*. **~ bowl** *n* azucarero *m*. **~y** *a* azucarado.

suggest /sə'dʒest/ *vt* sugerir. **~ion** /-tʃən/ *n* sugerencia *f*

suicid|al /su:ɪ'saɪdl/ *a* suicida. **~e** /'su:ɪsaɪd/ *n* suicidio *m*. **commit ~e** suicidarse

suit /su:t/ *n* traje *m*; (woman's) traje *m* de chaqueta; (Cards) palo *m*; (Jurid) pleito *m*. ● *vt* venirle bien a, convenirle a; <*clothes*> quedarle bien a; (adapt) adaptar. **be ~ed to** <*thing*> ser apropiado para. **I'm not ~ed to this kind of work** no sirvo para este tipo de trabajo. **~able** *a* apropiado, adecuado. **~ably** *adv* <*dressed*> apropiadamente; <*qualified*> adecuadamente. **~case** *n* maleta *f*, valija *f* (LAm)

suite /swi:t/ *n* (of furniture) juego *m*; (of rooms) suite *f*

sulk /sʌlk/ *vi* enfurruñarse

sullen /'sʌlən/ *a* hosco

sulphur /'sʌlfə(r)/ *n* azufre *m*. **~ic acid** /sʌl'fjʊərɪk/ *n* ácido *m* sulfúrico

sultan /'sʌltən/ *n* sultán *m*

sultana /sʌl'tɑ:nə/ *n* pasa *f* de Esmirna

sultry /'sʌltrɪ/ *a* (**-ier**, **-iest**) <*weather*> bochornoso; (fig) sensual

sum /sʌm/ *n* (of money) suma *f*, cantidad *f*; (Math) suma *f*. ● □ **~ up** (*pt* **summed**) *vt* resumir. ● *vi* recapitular

summar|ily /'sʌmərɪlɪ/ *adv* sumariamente. **~ize** *vt* resumir. **~y** *n* resumen *m*

summer /'sʌmə(r)/ *n* verano *m*. **~ camp** *n* (in US) colonia *f* de vacaciones. **~time** *n* verano *m*. **~y** *a* veraniego

summit /'sʌmɪt/ *n* (of mountain) cumbre *f*. **~ conference** *n* conferencia *f* cumbre

summon /'sʌmən/ *vt* llamar; convocar <*meeting, s.o. to meeting*>;

(Jurid) citar. □ ~ **up** *vt* armarse de. ~**s** *n* (Jurid) citación *f.* ● *vt* citar

sumptuous /'sʌmptjʊəs/ *a* suntuoso

sun /sʌn/ *n* sol *m.* ~**bathe** *vi* tomar el sol, asolearse (LAm). ~**beam** *n* rayo *m* de sol. ~**burn** *n* quemadura *f* de sol. ~**burnt** *a* quemado por el sol

Sunday /'sʌndeɪ/ *n* domingo *m*

sunflower /'sʌnflaʊə(r)/ *n* girasol *m*

sung /sʌŋ/ ⇒SING

sunglasses /'sʌnglɑ:sɪz/ *npl* gafas *fpl* de sol, lentes *mpl* de sol (LAm)

sunk /sʌŋk/ ⇒SINK. ~**en** /'sʌŋkən/ ● *a* hundido

sun: ~**light** *n* luz *f* del sol. ~**ny** *a* (**-ier**, **-iest**) <*day*> de sol; (place) soleado. **it is** ~**ny** hace sol. ~**rise** *n* salida *f* del sol. **at** ~**rise** al amanecer. ~**roof** *n* techo *m* corredizo. ~**set** *n* puesta *f* del sol. ~**shine** *n* sol *m.* ~**stroke** *n* insolación *f.* ~**tan** *n* bronceado *m.* **get a** ~**tan** broncearse. ~**tan lotion** *n* bronceador *m*

super /'su:pə(r)/ *a* [I] genial, super *a invar*

superb /su:'pɜ:b/ *a* espléndido

supercilious /su:pə'sɪlɪəs/ *a* desdeñoso

superficial /su:pə'fɪʃl/ *a* superficial

superfluous /su:'pɜ:flʊəs/ *a* superfluo

superhighway /'su:pəhaɪweɪ/ *n* (Amer, Auto) autopista *f*; (Comp) **information** ~ autopista *f* de la comunicación

superhuman /su:pə'hju:mən/ *a* sobrehumano

superintendent /su:pərɪn'tendənt/ *n* director *m*; (Amer, of building) portero *m*; (of police) comisario *m*; (in US) superintendente *m & f*

superior /su:'pɪərɪə(r)/ *a & n* superior (*m*). ~**ity** /-'ɒrətɪ/ *n* superioridad *f*

superlative /su:'pɜ:lətɪv/ *a* inigualable. ● *n* superlativo *m*

supermarket /'su:pəmɑ:kɪt/ *n* supermercado *m*

supernatural /su:pə'nætʃrəl/ *a* sobrenatural

superpower /'su:pəpaʊə(r)/ *n* superpotencia *f*

supersede /su:pə'si:d/ *vt* reemplazar, sustituir

supersonic /su:pə'sɒnɪk/ *a* supersónico

superstitio|n /su:pə'stɪʃn/ *n* superstición *f.* ~**us** *a* /-əs/ supersticioso

supervis|e /'su:pəvaɪz/ *vt* supervisar. ~**ion** /-'vɪʒn/ *n* supervisión *f.* ~**or** *n* supervisor *m*

supper /'sʌpə(r)/ *n* cena *f* (ligera), comida *f* (ligera) (LAm)

supple /sʌpl/ *a* flexible

supplement /'sʌplɪmənt/ *n* suplemento *m*; (to diet, income) complemento *m.* ● *vt* complementar <*diet, income*>. ~**ary** /-'mentərɪ/ *a* suplementario

suppl|ier /sə'plaɪə(r)/ *n* (Com) proveedor *m.* ~**y** /sə'plaɪ/ *vt* suministrar; proporcionar <*information*>. ~**y s.o. with sth** <*equipment*> proveer a uno de algo; (in business) abastecer a uno de algo. ● *n* suministro *m.* ~**y and demand** oferta *f* y demanda. ~**ies** *npl* provisiones *mpl*, víveres *mpl*; (Mil) pertrechos *mpl.* **office ~ies** artículos *mpl* de oficina

support /sə'pɔ:t/ *vt* (hold up) sostener; (back) apoyar; mantener *<family>*. ● *n* apoyo *m*; (Tec) soporte *m*. **~er** *n* partidario *m*; (Sport) hincha *m & f*

suppos|e /sə'pəʊz/ *vt* suponer, imaginarse; (think) creer. **I'm ~ed to start work at nine** se supone que tengo que empezar a trabajar a las nueve. **~edly** *adv* supuestamente. **~ition** /sʌpə'zɪʃn/ *n* suposición *f*

suppress /sə'pres/ *vt* reprimir *<feelings>*; sofocar *<rebellion>*. **~ion** /-ʃn/*n* represión *f*

suprem|acy /su:'preməsɪ/ *n* supremacía *f*. **~e** /su:'pri:m/ *a* supremo

sure /ʃʊə(r)/ *a* (**-er**, **-est**) seguro. **make ~ that** asegurarse de que. ● *adv* ¡claro! **~ly** *adv* (undoubtedly) seguramente; (gladly) desde luego. **~ly you don't believe that!** ¡no te creerás eso! **~ty** /-ətɪ/ *n* garantía *f*

surf /sɜ:f/ *n* oleaje *m*; (foam) espuma *f*. ● *vi* hacer surf. ● *vt* (Comp) surfear, navegar

surface /'sɜ:fɪs/ *n* superficie *f*. ● *a* superficial. ● *vt* recubrir (**with** de). ● *vi* salir a la superficie; *<problems>* aflorar

surfboard /'sɜ:fbɔ:d/ *n* tabla *f* de surf

surfeit /'sɜ:fɪt/ *n* exceso *m*

surf: ~er *n* surfista *m & f* **~ing** *n* surf *m*

surge /sɜ:dʒ/ *vi* *<crowd>* moverse en tropel; *<sea>* hincharse. ● *n* oleada *f*; (in demand, sales) aumento *m*

surg|eon /'sɜ:dʒən/ *n* cirujano *m*. **~ery** *n* cirugía *f*; (consulting room) consultorio *m*; (consulting hours) consulta *f*. **~ical** *a* quirúrgico

surly /'sɜ:lɪ/ *a* (**-ier**, **-iest**) hosco

surmise /sə'maɪz/ *vt* conjeturar

surmount /sə'maʊnt/ *vt* superar

surname /'sɜ:neɪm/ *n* apellido *m*

surpass /sə'pɑ:s/ *vt* superar

surplus /'sɜ:pləs/ *a & n* excedente (*m*)

surpris|e /sə'praɪz/ *n* sorpresa *f*. ● *vt* sorprender. **~ed** *a* sorprendido. **~ing** *a* sorprendente. **~ingly** *adv* sorprendentemente

surrender /sə'rendə(r)/ *vt* entregar. ● *vi* rendirse. ● *n* rendición *f*

surreptitious /sʌrəp'tɪʃəs/ *a* furtivo

surround /sə'raʊnd/ *vt* rodear; (Mil) rodear, cercar. **~ing** *a* circundante. **~ings** *npl* alrededores *mpl*; (environment) ambiente *m*

surveillance /sɜ:'veɪləns/ *n* vigilancia *f*

survey /'sɜ:veɪ/ *n* inspección *f*; (report) informe *m*; (general view) vista *f* general. ● /sə'veɪ/ *vt* inspeccionar; (measure) medir; (look at) contemplar. **~or** *n* topógrafo *m*, agrimensor *m*; (of building) perito *m*

surviv|al /sə'vaɪvl/ *n* supervivencia *f*. **~e** /sə'vaɪv/ *vt/i* sobrevivir. **~or** *n* superviviente *m & f*

susceptible /sə'septəbl/ *a*. **~ to** propenso a

suspect /sə'spekt/ *vt* sospechar; sospechar de *<person>*. ● /'sʌspekt/ *a & n* sospechoso (*m*)

suspen|d /sə'spend/ *vt* suspender. **~ders** *npl* (Amer, braces) tirantes *mpl*. **~se** /-s/ *n* (in film etc) suspense *m*, suspenso *m* (LAm). **keep s.o. in ~se** mantener a uno sobre ascuas. **~sion** /-ʃn/ *n* suspensión *f*. **~sion bridge** *n* puente *m* colgante

suspici|on /sə'spɪʃn/ *n* (belief) sospecha *f*; (mistrust) desconfianza *f*. **~ous** /-ʃəs/ *a* desconfiado; (causing suspicion) sospechoso

sustain /sə'steɪn/ *vt* sostener; mantener *<conversation, interest>*; (suffer) sufrir

SW *abbr* (= **south-west**) SO

swab /swɒb/ *n* (specimen) muestra *f*, frotis *m*

swagger /'swægə(r)/ *vi* pavonearse

swallow /'swɒləʊ/ *vt/i* tragar. ● *n* trago *m*; (bird) golondrina *f*

swam /swæm/ ⇒SWIM

swamp /swɒmp/ *n* pantano *m*, ciénaga *f*. ● *vt* inundar. **~y** *a* pantanoso

swan /swɒn/ *n* cisne *m*

swap /swɒp/ *vt/i* (*pt* **swapped**) intercambiar. **~ sth for sth** cambiar algo por algo. ● *n* cambio *m*

swarm /swɔːm/ *n* enjambre *m*. ● *vi* *<bees>* enjambrar; (fig) hormiguear

swarthy /'swɔːðɪ/ *a* (**-ier**, **-iest**) moreno

swat /swɒt/ *vt* (*pt* **swatted**) matar (*con matamoscas etc*)

sway /sweɪ/ *vi* balancearse; (gently) mecerse. ● *vt* (influence) influir en

swear /sweə(r)/ *vt/i* (*pt* **swore**, *pp* **sworn**) jurar. **~word** *n* palabrota *f*

sweat /swet/ *n* sudor *m*, transpiración *f*. ● *vi* sudar

sweat|er /'swetə(r)/ *n* jersey *m*, suéter *m*. **~shirt** *n* sudadera *f*. **~suit** *n* (Amer) chándal *m*, equipo *m* de deportes

swede /swiːd/ *n* nabo *m* sueco

Swede /swiːd/ *n* sueco *m*. **~n** /'swiːdn/ *n* Suecia *f*. **~ish** *a* sueco. ● *n* (Lang) sueco *m*. ● *npl*. **the ~** (people) los suecos

sweep /swiːp/ *vt* (*pt* **swept**) barrer; deshollinar *<chimney>*. ● *vi* barrer. ● *n* barrido *m*. **~ away** *vt* (carry away) arrastrar; (abolish) erradicar. **~er** *n* barrendero *m*. **~ing** *a* *<gesture>* amplio; *<changes>* radical; *<statement>* demasiado general

sweet /swiːt/ *a* (**-er**, **-est**) dulce; (fragrant) fragante; (pleasant) agradable; (kind, gentle) dulce; (cute) rico. **have a ~ tooth** ser dulcero. ● *n* caramelo *m*, dulce *m* (Mex); (dish) postre *m*. **~en** *vt* endulzar. **~heart** *n* enamorado *m*; (as form of address) amor *m*. **~ly** *adv* dulcemente. **~ potato** *n* boniato *m*, batata *f*

swell /swel/ *vt* (*pt* **swelled**, *pp* **swollen** *or* **swelled**) hinchar; (increase) aumentar. ● *vi* hincharse; (increase) aumentar. ● *a* (Amer [I]) fenomenal. ● *n* (of sea) oleaje *m*. **~ing** *n* hinchazón *m*

sweltering /'sweltərɪŋ/ *adj* sofocante

swept /swept/ ⇒SWEEP

swerve /swɜːv/ *vi* virar bruscamente

swift /swɪft/ *a* (**-er**, **-est**) veloz, rápido; *<reply>* rápido. ● *n* (bird) vencejo *m*. **~ly** *adv* rápidamente

swig /swɪg/ *vt* (*pt* **swigged**) [I] beber a grandes tragos. ● *n* [I] trago *m*

swim /swɪm/ *vi* (*pt* **swam**, *pp* **swum**) nadar. ● *n* baño *m*. **~mer** *n* nadador *m*. **~ming** *n* natación *f*. **~ming bath(s)** *n(pl)* piscina *f* cubierta, alberca *f* techada (Mex). **~ming pool** *n* piscina *f*, alberca *f* (Mex). **~ming trunks** *npl* bañador *m*, traje *m* de baño **~suit** *n* traje *m* de baño, bañador *m*

swindle /'swɪndl/ *vt* estafar. ● *n* estafa *f*. **~r** *n* estafador *m*

swine /swaɪn/ *npl* cerdos *mpl*. ● *n* (*pl* **swine**) (🅸, person) canalla *m* & *f*

swing /swɪŋ/ *vt* (*pt* **swung**) balancear; (object on rope) hacer oscilar. ● *vi* (dangle) balancearse; (swing on a swing) columpiarse; <*pendulum*> oscilar. **~ open/shut** abrirse/cerrarse. ● *n* oscilación *f*, vaivén *m*; (seat) columpio *m*; (in opinion) cambio *m*. **in full ~** en plena actividad

swipe /swaɪp/ *vt* darle un golpe a; (🅴, snatch) birlar. ● *n* golpe *m*

Swiss /swɪs/ *a* suizo (*m*). ● *npl*. **the ~** los suizos

switch /swɪtʃ/ *n* (Elec) interruptor *m*; (exchange) intercambio *m*; (Amer, Rail) agujas *fpl*. ● *vt* cambiar; (deviate) desviar. □ **~ off** *vt* (Elec) apagar <*light, TV, heating*>; desconectar <*electricity*>. □ **~ on** *vt* encender, prender (LAm); arrancar <*engine*>. **~board** *n* centralita *f*

Switzerland /'swɪtsələnd/ *n* Suiza *f*

swivel /'swɪvl/ *vi* (*pt* **swivelled**) girar. ● *vt* hacer girar

swollen /'swəʊlən/ ⇒SWELL. ● *a* hinchado

swoop /swu:p/ *vi* <*bird*> abatirse; <*police*> llevar a cabo una redada. ● *n* (of bird) descenso *m* en picado *or* (LAm) en picada; (by police) redada *f*

sword /sɔ:d/ *n* espada *f*

swore /swɔ:(r)/ ⇒SWEAR

sworn /swɔ:n/ ⇒SWEAR. ● *a* <*enemy*> declarado; <*statement*> jurado

swot /swɒt/ *vt/i* (*pt* **swotted**) (Schol, 🅸) empollar, estudiar como loco. ● *n* (Schol, 🅸) empollón *m*, matado *m* (Mex)

swum /swʌm/ ⇒SWIM

swung /swʌŋ/ ⇒SWING

syllable /'sɪləbl/ *n* sílaba *f*

syllabus /'sɪləbəs/ *n* (*pl* **-buses**) plan *m* de estudios; (of a particular subject) programa *m*

symbol /'sɪmbl/ *n* símbolo *m*. **~ic**(al) /-'bɒlɪk(l)/ *a* simbólico. **~ism** *n* simbolismo *m*. **~ize** *vt* simbolizar

symmetr|ical /sɪ'metrɪkl/ *a* simétrico. **~y** /'sɪmətrɪ/ *n* simetría *f*

sympath|etic /sɪmpə'θetɪk/ *a* comprensivo; (showing pity) compasivo. **~ize** /'sɪmpəθaɪz/ *vi* comprender; (commiserate) **~ize with s.o.** compadecer a uno. **~y** /'sɪmpəθɪ/ *n* comprensión *f*; (pity) compasión *f*; (condolences) pésame *m*

symphony /'sɪmfənɪ/ *n* sinfonía *f*

symptom /'sɪmptəm/ *n* síntoma *m*. **~atic** /-'mætɪk/ *a* sintomático

synagogue /'sɪnəgɒg/ *n* sinagoga *f*

synchronize /'sɪŋkrənaɪz/ *vt* sincronizar

syndicate /'sɪndɪkət/ *n* agrupación *f*; (Amer, TV) agencia *f* de distribución periodística

synonym /'sɪnənɪm/ *n* sinónimo *m*. **~ous** /-'nɒnɪməs/ *a* sinónimo

syntax /'sɪntæks/ *n* sintaxis *f*

synthesi|s /'sɪnθəsɪs/ *n* (*pl* **-theses** /-si:z/) síntesis *f*. **~ze** /-aɪz/ *vt* sintetizar

synthetic /sɪn'θetɪk/ *a* sintético

syringe /'sɪrɪndʒ/ *n* jeringa *f*, jeringuilla *f*

syrup /'sɪrəp/ *n* (sugar solution) almíbar *m*; (with other ingredients) jarabe *m*; (medicine) jarabe *m*

system /'sɪstəm/ *n* sistema *m*, método *m*; (Tec, Mec, Comp) sistema *m*. **the digestive ~** el aparato digestivo. **~atic** /-ə'mætɪk/ *a* sistemático. **~atically** /-ə'mætɪklɪ/ *adv* sistemáticamente. **~s analyst** *n* analista *m & f* de sistemas

Tt

tab /tæb/ *n* (flap) lengüeta *f*; (label) etiqueta *f*

table /'teɪbl/ *n* mesa *f*; (list) tabla *f*. **~cloth** *n* mantel *m*. **~ mat** *n* salvamanteles *m*. **~spoon** *n* cuchara *f* grande; (measure) cucharada *f* (grande)

tablet /'tæblɪt/ *n* pastilla *f*; (pill) comprimido *m*

table tennis *n* tenis *m* de mesa, ping-pong *m*

tabloid /'tæblɔɪd/ *n* tabloide *m*

taboo /tə'bu:/ *a & n* tabú (*m*)

tacit /'tæsɪt/ *a* tácito

taciturn /'tæsɪtɜ:n/ *a* taciturno

tack /tæk/ *n* tachuela *f*; (stitch) hilván *m*. ● *vt* clavar con tachuelas; (sew) hilvanar. ● *vi* (Naut) virar □ **~ on** *vt* añadir.

tackle /'tækl/ *n* (equipment) equipo *m*; (soccer) entrada *f* fuerte; (US football, Rugby) placaje *m*. **fishing ~** aparejo *m* de pesca. ● *vt* abordar <*problem*>; (in soccer) entrarle a; (in US football, Rugby) placar

tacky /'tækɪ/ *a* pegajoso

tact /tækt/ *n* tacto *m*. **~ful** *a* diplomático

tactic|al /'tæktɪkl/ *a* táctico. **~s** *npl* táctica *f*

tactless /'tæktləs/ *a* indiscreto

tadpole /'tædpəʊl/ *n* renacuajo *m*

tag /tæg/ *n* (label) etiqueta *f*. □ **~ along** (*pt* **tagged**) *vt* Ⅰ seguir

tail /teɪl/ *n* (of horse, fish, bird) cola *f*; (of dog, pig) rabo *m*. **~s** *npl* (tailcoat) frac *m*; (of coin) cruz *f*. ● *vt* seguir. □ **~ off** *vi* disminuir.

tailor /'teɪlə(r)/ *n* sastre *m*. **~ed** /'teɪləd/ *a* entallado. **~-made** *n* hecho a (la) medida

taint /teɪnt/ *vt* contaminar

take /teɪk/ *vt* (*pt* **took**, *pp* **taken**) tomar, coger (esp Spain), agarrar (esp LAm); (capture) capturar; (endure) aguantar; (require) requerir; llevar <*time*>; tomar <*bath*>; tomar <*medicine*>; (carry) llevar; aceptar <*cheque*>. **I ~ a size 10** uso la talla 14. ● *n* (Cinema) toma *f*. □ **~ after** *vt* parecerse a. □ **~ away** *vt* llevarse; (confiscate) quitar. □ **~ back** *vt* retirar <*statement etc*>. □ **~ in** *vt* achicar <*garment*>; (understand) asimilar; (deceive) engañar. □ **~ off** *vt* (remove) quitar, sacar; quitarse <*shoes, jacket*>; (mimic) imitar. *vi* (Aviat) despegar. □ **~ on** *vt* contratar <*employee*>. □ **~ out** *vt* sacar. □ **~ over** *vt* tomar posesión de; hacerse cargo de <*job*>. *vi* (assume control) asumir el poder. □ **~ up** *vt* empezar a hacer <*hobby*>; aceptar <*challenge*>; subir <*hem*>; llevar <*time*>; ocupar <*space*>. **~-off** *n* despegue *m*. **~-over** *n* (Com) absorción *f*

takings /'teɪkɪŋz/ *npl* recaudación *f*; (at box office) taquilla *f*

talcum powder /'tælkəm/ *n* polvos *mpl* de talco, talco *m* (LAm)

tale /teɪl/ *n* cuento *m*

talent /'tælənt/ *n* talento *m*. **~ed** *a* talentoso

talk /tɔ:k/ *vt/i* hablar. **~ to s.o.** hablar con uno. **~ about** hablar de. ● *n* conversación *f*; (lecture) charla *f*. □ **~ over** *vt* discutir. **~ative** /-ətɪv/ *a* hablador

tall /tɔ:l/ *a* (**-er**, **-est**) alto. **~ story** *n* [I] cuento *m* chino

tally /'tælɪ/ *vi* coincidir (**with** con)

talon /'tælən/ *n* garra *f*

tambourine /tæmbə'ri:n/ *n* pandereta *f*

tame /teɪm/ *a* (**-er**, **-est**) <*animal*> (by nature) manso; (tamed) domado. ● *vt* domar <*wild animal*>

tamper /'tæmpə(r)/ *vi*. **~ with** tocar; (alter) alterar, falsificar

tampon /'tæmpɒn/ *n* tampón *m*

tan /tæn/ *vi* (*pt* **tanned**) broncearse. ● *n* bronceado *m*. **get a ~** broncearse. ● *a* habano

tang /tæŋ/ *n* sabor *m* fuerte

tangent /'tændʒənt/ *n* tangente *f*

tangerine /tændʒə'ri:n/ *n* mandarina *f*

tangible /'tændʒəbl/ *a* tangible

tangle /'tæŋgl/ *vt* enredar. **get ~d** (**up**) enredarse. ● *n* enredo *m*, maraña *f*

tango /'tæŋgəʊ/ *n* (*pl* **-os**) tango *m*

tank /tæŋk/ *n* depósito *m*; (Auto) tanque *m*; (Mil) tanque *m*

tanker /'tæŋkə(r)/ *n* (ship) buque *m* cisterna; (truck) camión *m* cisterna

tantrum /'tæntrəm/ *n* berrinche *m*, rabieta *f*

tap /tæp/ *n* grifo *m*, llave *f* (LAm); (knock) golpecito *m*. ● *vt* (*pt* **tapped**) (knock) dar un golpecito en; interceptar <*phone*>. ● *vi* dar golpecitos (**on** en). **~ dancing** *n* claqué *m*

tape /teɪp/ *n* cinta *f*; (Med) esparadrapo *m*. ● *vt* (record) grabar. **~-measure** *n* cinta *f* métrica

taper /'teɪpə(r)/ *vt* afilar. ● *vi* afilarse. □ **~ off** *vi* disminuir

tape recorder *n* magnetofón *m*, magnetófono *m*

tapestry /'tæpɪstrɪ/ *n* tapiz *m*

tar /tɑ:(r)/ *n* alquitrán *m*. ● *vt* (*pt* **tarred**) alquitranar

target /'tɑ:gɪt/ *n* blanco *m*; (fig) objetivo *m*

tarmac /'tɑ:mæk/ *n* pista *f*. **T~** *n* (Amer, P) asfalto *m*

tarnish /'tɑ:nɪʃ/ *vt* deslustrar; empañar <*reputation*>

tart /tɑ:t/ *n* pastel *m*; (individual) pastelillo *m*; ([x], woman) prostituta *f*, fulana *f* [I]. ● *vt*. **~ o.s. up** [I] engalanarse. ● *a* (**-er**, **-est**) ácido

tartan /'tɑ:tn/ *n* tartán *m*, tela *f* escocesa

task /tɑ:sk/ *n* tarea *f*. **take to ~** reprender

tassel /'tæsl/ *n* borla *f*

tast|e /teɪst/ *n* sabor *m*, gusto *m*; (liking) gusto *m*. ● *vt* probar. ● *vi*. **~e of** saber a. **~eful** *a* de buen gusto. **~eless** *a* soso; (fig) de mal gusto. **~y** *a* (**-ier**, **-iest**) sabroso

tat /tæt/ ⇒TIT FOR TAT

tatter|ed /'tætəd/ *a* hecho jirones. **~s** /'tætəz/ *npl* andrajos *mpl*

tattoo /tæ'tu:/ *n* (on body) tatuaje *m*. ● *vt* tatuar

tatty /'tætɪ/ *a* (**-ier**, **-iest**) gastado, estropeado

taught /tɔ:t/ ⇒TEACH

taunt /tɔ:nt/ *vt* provocar mediante burlas. ● *n* pulla *f*

Taurus /'tɔ:rəs/ *n* Tauro *m*

taut /tɔ:t/ *a* tenso

tavern /'tævən/ *n* taberna *f*

tax /tæks/ *n* impuesto *m*. ● *vt* imponer contribuciones a <*person*>; gravar <*thing*>; (strain) poner a prueba. **~able** *a* imponible. **~ation** /-'seɪʃn/ *n* impuestos *mpl*; (system) sistema *m* tributario. **~ collector** *n* recaudador *m* de impuestos. **~-free** *a* libre de impuestos

taxi /'tæksɪ/ *n* (*pl* **-is**) taxi *m*. ● *vi* (*pt* **taxied**, *pres p* **taxiing**) <*aircraft*> rodar por la pista

taxpayer /'tækspeɪə(r)/ *n* contribuyente *m & f*

tea /ti:/ *n* té *m*; (afternoon tea) merienda *f*, té *m*. **~ bag** *n* bolsita *f* de té

teach /ti:tʃ/ *vt* (*pt* **taught**) dar clases de, enseñar <*subject*>; dar clase a <*person*>. **~ school** (Amer) dar clase(s) en un colegio. ● *vi* dar clase(s). **~er** *n* profesor *m*; (primary) maestro *m*. **~ing** *n* enseñanza *f*. ● *a* docente

tea: ~cup *n* taza *f* de té. **~ leaf** *n* hoja *f* de té

team /ti:m/ *n* equipo *m*. □ **~ up** *vi* asociarse (with con). **~ work** *n* trabajo *m* de equipo

teapot /'ti:pɒt/ *n* tetera *f*

tear[1] /teə(r)/ *vt* (*pt* **tore**, *pp* **torn**) romper, rasgar. ● *vi* romperse, rasgarse. ● *n* rotura *f*; (rip) desgarrón *m*. □ **~ along** *vi* ir a toda velocidad. □ **~ apart** *vt* desgarrar. □ **~ off**, **~ out** *vt* arrancar. □ **~ up** *vt* romper

tear[2] /tɪə(r)/ *n* lágrima *f*. **be in ~s** estar llorando. **~ful** *a* lloroso <*farewell*> triste. **~ gas** *n* gas *m* lacrimógeno

tease /ti:z/ *vt* tomarle el pelo a

tea: ~ set *n* juego *m* de té. **~spoon** *n* cucharita *f*, cucharilla *f*; (amount) cucharadita *f*

teat /ti:t/ *n* (of animal) tetilla *f*; (for bottle) tetina *f*

tea towel /'ti:taʊəl/ *n* paño *m* de cocina

techni|cal /'teknɪkl/ *a* técnico. **~cality** *n* /-'kæləti/ *n* detalle *m* técnico. **~cally** *adv* técnicamente. **~cian** /tek'nɪʃn/ *n* técnico *m*.

technique /tek'ni:k/ *n* técnica *f*

technolog|ical /teknə'lɒdʒɪkl/ *a* tecnológico. **~y** /tek'nɒlədʒɪ/ *n* tecnología *f*

teddy bear /'tedɪ/ *n* osito *m* de peluche

tedi|ous /'ti:dɪəs/ *a* tedioso. **~um** /'ti:dɪəm/ *n* tedio *m*

teem /ti:m/ *vi* abundar (with en), estar repleto (with de)

teen|age /'ti:neɪdʒ/ *a* adolescente; (for teenagers) para jóvenes. **~ager** *n* adolescente *m & f*. **~s** /ti:nz/ *npl* adolescencia *f*

teeny /'ti:nɪ/ *a* (**-ier**, **-iest**) 🄸 chiquito

teeter /'ti:tə(r)/ *vi* balancearse

teeth /ti:θ/ ⇒TOOTH. **~e** /ti:ð/ *vi*. **he's ~ing** le están saliendo los dientes. **~ing troubles** *npl* (fig) problemas *mpl* iniciales

tele|communications /telɪkəmju:nɪ'keɪʃnz/ *npl* telecomunicaciones *fpl*. **~gram** /'telɪgræm/ *n* telegrama *m*. **~pathic** /telɪ'pæθɪk/ *a* telepático. **~pathy** /tə'lepəθɪ/ *n* telepatía *f*

telephon|e /'telɪfəʊn/ *n* teléfono *m*. ● *vt* llamar por teléfono.

~e booth, **~e box** *n* cabina *f* telefónica. **~e call** *n* llamada *f* telefónica. **~e directory** *n* guía *f* telefónica. **~e exchange** *n* central *f* telefónica. **~ist** /tɪ'lefənɪst/ *n* telefonista *m & f*

tele|sales /'telɪseɪlz/ *npl* televentas *fpl*. **~scope** *n* telescopio *m*. **~scopic** /-'skɒpɪk/ *a* telescópico. **~text** *n* teletex(to) *m*

televis|e /'telɪvaɪz/ *vt* televisar. **~ion** /'telɪvɪʒn/ *n* (medium) televisión *f*. **~ion (set)** *n* televisor *m*

telex /'teleks/ *n* télex *m*

tell /tel/ *vt* (*pt* **told**) decir; contar <*story, joke*>; (distinguish) distinguir. **~ the difference** notar la diferencia. **~ the time** decir la hora. ● *vi* (produce an effect) tener efecto; (know) saber. □ **~ off** *vt* regañar. **~ing** *a* revelador. **~-tale** *n* soplón *m*. ● *a* revelador

telly /'telɪ/ *n* [I] tele *f*

temp /temp/ *n* empleado *m* eventual *or* temporal

temper /'tempə(r)/ *n* (mood) humor *m*; (disposition) carácter *m*; (fit of anger) cólera *f*. **be in a ~** estar furioso. **lose one's ~** perder los estribos. **~ament** /'temprəmənt/ *n* temperamento *m*. **~amental** /-'mentl/ *a* temperamental. **~ate** /'tempərət/ *a* templado. **~ature** /'temprɪtʃə(r)/ *n* temperatura *f*. **have a ~ature** tener fiebre

tempestuous /tem'pestjʊəs/ *a* tempestuoso

temple /'templ/ *n* templo *m*; (Anat) sien *f*

tempo /'tempəʊ/ *n* (*pl* **-os** *or* **tempi**) ritmo *m*

temporar|ily /'tempərərəlɪ/ *adv* temporalmente, temporariamente (LAm). **~y** /'tempərərɪ/ *a* temporal, provisional; <*job*> eventual, temporal

tempt /tempt/ *vt* tentar. **~ation** /-'teɪʃn/ *n* tentación *f*. **~ing** *a* tentador

ten /ten/ *a & n* diez (*m*)

tenaci|ous /tɪ'neɪʃəs/ *a* tenaz. **~ty** /tɪ'næsətɪ/ *n* tenacidad *f*

tenan|cy /'tenənsɪ/ *n* inquilinato *m*. **~t** *n* inquilino *m*, arrendatorio *m*

tend /tend/ *vi*. **~ to** tender a. ● *vt* cuidar (de). **~ency** /'tendənsɪ/ *n* tendencia *f*

tender /'tendə(r)/ *a* tierno; (painful) sensible. ● *n* (Com) oferta *f*. **legal ~** *n* moneda *f* de curso legal. ● *vt* ofrecer, presentar. **~ly** *adv* tiernamente

tendon /'tendən/ *n* tendón *m*

tennis /'tenɪs/ *n* tenis *m*

tenor /'tenə(r)/ *n* tenor *m*

tens|e /tens/ *a* (**-er**, **-est**) (taut) tenso, tirante; <*person*> tenso. ● *n* (Gram) tiempo *m*. **~ion** /'tenʃn/ *n* tensión *f*; (between two parties) conflicto *m*

tent /tent/ *n* tienda *f* (de campaña), carpa *f* (LAm)

tentacle /'tentəkl/ *n* tentáculo *m*

tentative /'tentətɪv/ *a* <*plan*> provisional; <*offer*> tentativo; <*person*> indeciso

tenterhooks /'tentəhʊks/ *npl*. **be on ~** estar en ascuas

tenth /tenθ/ *a & n* décimo (*m*)

tenuous /'tenjʊəs/ *a* <*claim*> poco fundado; <*link*> indirecto

tenure /'tenjʊə(r)/ *n* tenencia *f*; (period of office) ejercicio *m*

tepid /'tepɪd/ *a* tibio

term /tɜːm/ *n* (of time) período *m*; (Schol) trimestre *m*; (word etc) término *m*. **~s** *npl* condiciones *fpl*; (Com) precio *m*. **on good/bad ~s** en buenas/malas relaciones. ● *vt* calificar de

termin|al /ˈtɜːmɪnl/ *a* terminal. ● (transport) terminal *f*; (Comp, Elec) terminal *m*. **~ate** /-eɪt/ *vt* poner fin a; poner término a <*contract*>; (Amer, fire) despedir. ● *vi* terminarse. **~ology** /-ˈnɒlədʒɪ/ *n* terminología *f*

terrace /ˈterəs/ *n* terraza *f*; (houses) hilera *f* de casas

terrain /təˈreɪn/ *n* terreno *m*

terrestrial /tɪˈrestrɪəl/ *a* terrestre

terribl|e /ˈterəbl/ *a* espantoso. **~y** *adv* terriblemente

terrif|ic /təˈrɪfɪk/ *a* (🅸, excellent) estupendo; (🅸, huge) enorme. **~ied** /ˈterɪfaɪd/ *a* aterrorizado. **~y** /ˈterɪfaɪ/ *vt* aterrorizar. **~ying** *a* aterrador

territor|ial /terɪˈtɔːrɪəl/ *a* territorial. **~y** /ˈterɪtrɪ/ *n* territorio *m*

terror /ˈterə(r)/ *n* terror *m*. **~ism** *n* terrorismo *m*. **~ist** *n* terrorista *m & f*. **~ize** *vt* aterrorizar

terse /tɜːs/ *a* seco, lacónico

test /test/ *n* (of machine, drug) prueba *f*; (exam) prueba *f*, test *m*; (of blood) análisis *m*; (for eyes, hearing) examen *m*. ● *vt* probar, poner a prueba <*product*>; hacerle una prueba a <*student*>; evaluar <*knowledge*>; examinar <*sight*>

testament /ˈtestəmənt/ *n* (will) testamento *m*. **Old/New T~** Antiguo/Nuevo Testamento

testicle /ˈtestɪkl/ *n* testículo *m*

testify /ˈtestɪfaɪ/ *vt* atestiguar. ● *vi* declarar

testimon|ial /testɪˈməʊnɪəl/ *n* recomendación *f*. **~y** /ˈtestɪmənɪ/ *n* testimonio *m*

test: ~ match *n* partido *m* internacional. **~ tube** *n* tubo *m* de ensayo, probeta *f*

tether /ˈteðə(r)/ *vt* atar. ● *n*. **be at the end of one's ~** no poder más

text /tekst/ *n* texto *m*. **~book** *n* libro *m* de texto

textile /ˈtekstaɪl/ *a & n* textil (*m*)

texture /ˈtekstʃə(r)/ *n* textura *f*

Thames /temz/ *n* Támesis *m*

than /ðæn, ðən/ *conj* que; (with quantity) de

thank /θæŋk/ *vt* darle las gracias a, agradecer. **~ you** gracias. **~ful** *a* agradecido. **~fully** *adv* (happily) gracias a Dios. **~less** *a* ingrato. **~s** *npl* agradecimiento *m*. **~s!** 🅸 ¡gracias!. **~s to** gracias a

Thanksgiving (Day) /θæŋksˈgɪvɪŋ/ *n* (in US) el día de Acción de Gracias

that /ðæt, ðət/ *a* (*pl* **those**) ese, aquel, esa, aquella. ● *pron* (*pl* **those**) ése, aquél, ésa, aquélla. **~ is** es decir. **~'s not true** eso no es cierto. **~'s why** por eso. **is ~ you?** ¿eres tú? **like ~** así. ● *adv* tan. ● *rel pron* que; (with prep) el que, la que, el cual, la cual. ● *conj* que

thatched /θætʃt/ *a* <*roof*> de paja; <*cottage*> con techo de paja

thaw /θɔː/ *vt* descongelar. ● *vi* descongelarse; <*snow*> derretirse. ● *n* deshielo *m*

the *before vowel* /ðɪ/, *before consonant* /ðə/, *stressed form* /ðiː/

● *definite article*

····➤el (*m*), la (*f*), los (*mpl*), las (*fpl*). ~ **building** el edificio. ~ **windows** las ventanas

> **!** Feminine singular nouns beginning with a stressed or accented *a* or *ha* take the article *el* instead of *la*, e.g. ~ **soul** *el alma;* ~ **axe** *el hacha.* ~ **eagle** *el águila*
>
> Note that when *el* follows the prepositions *de* and *a*, it combines to form *del* and *al*, e.g. **of** ~ **group** *del grupo.* **I went to** ~ **bank** *fui al banco*

····➤(before an ordinal number in names, titles) *not translated.* **Henry** ~ **Eighth** Enrique Octavo. **Elizabeth** ~ **Second** Isabel Segunda

····➤(in abstractions) lo. ~ **impossible** lo imposible

theatr|e /'θɪətə(r)/ *n* teatro *m;* (Amer, movie theatre) cine *m.* **~ical** /-'ætrɪkl/ *a* teatral

theft /θeft/ *n* hurto *m*

their /ðeə(r)/ *a* su, sus *pl.* **~s** /ðeəz/ *poss pron* (el) suyo *m*, (la) suya *f*, (los) suyos *mpl*, (las) suyas *fpl*

them /ðem, ðəm/ *pron* (accusative) los *m*, las *f;* (dative) les; (*after prep*) ellos *m*, ellas *f*

theme /θi:m/ *n* tema *m.* ~ **park** *n* parque *m* temático. ~ **song** *n* motivo *m* principal

themselves /ðəm'selvz/ *pron* ellos mismos *m*, ellas mismas *f;* (*reflexive*) se; (*after prep*) sí mismos *m*, sí mismas *f*

then /ðen/ *adv* entonces; (next) luego, después. **by** ~ para entonces. **now and** ~ de vez en cuando. **since** ~ desde entonces. ● *a* entonces

theology /θɪ'ɒlədʒɪ/ *n* teología *f*

theor|etical /θɪə'retɪkl/ *a* teórico. **~y** /'θɪərɪ/ *n* teoría *f*

therap|eutic /θerə'pju:tɪk/ *a* terapéutico. **~ist** /'θerəpɪst/ *n* terapeuta *m & f.* **~y** /θerəpɪ/ *n* terapia *f*

there /ðeə(r)/ *adv* ahí; (further away) allí, ahí; (less precise, further) allá. ~ **is,** ~ **are** hay. ~ **it is** ahí está. **down** ~ ahí abajo. **up** ~ ahí arriba. ● *int.* **~! that's the last box** ¡listo! ésa es la última caja. **~, ~, don't cry!** vamos, no llores. **~abouts** *adv* por ahí. **~fore** /-fɔ:(r)/ *adv* por lo tanto.

thermometer /θə'mɒmɪtə(r)/ *n* termómetro *m*

Thermos /'θɜ:məs/ *n* (P) termo *m*

thermostat /'θɜ:məstæt/ *n* termostato *m*

thesaurus /θɪ'sɔ:rəs/ *n* (*pl* **-ri** /-raɪ/) diccionario *m* de sinónimos

these /ði:z/ *a* estos, estas. ● *pron* éstos, éstas

thesis /'θi:sɪs/ *n* (*pl* **theses** /-si:z/) tesis *f*

they /ðeɪ/ *pron* ellos *m*, ellas *f.* ~ **say that** dicen *or* se dice que

they'd /ðeɪ(ə)d/ = **they had, they would**

they'll /ðeɪl/ = **they will**

they're /ðeɪə(r)/ = **they are**

they've /ðeɪv/ = **they have**

thick /θɪk/ *a* (**-er, -est**) *<layer, sweater>* grueso, gordo; *<sauce>* espeso; *<fog, smoke>* espeso, denso; *<fur>* tupido; (**Ⓘ**, stupid) burro. ● *adv* espesamente, densamente. ● *n.* **in the** ~ **of** en medio de. **~en** *vt* espesar. ● *vi* espesarse. **~et** /-ɪt/ *n* matorral *m.* **~ness** *n* (of fabric) grosor *m*; (of paper, wood, wall) espesor *m*

thief /θi:f/ *n* (*pl* **thieves** /θi:vz/) ladrón *m*

thigh /θaɪ/ *n* muslo *m*

thimble /ˈθɪmbl/ *n* dedal *m*

thin /θɪn/ *a* (**thinner**, **thinnest**) *<person>* delgado, flaco; *<layer, slice>* fino; *<hair>* ralo

thing /θɪŋ/ *n* cosa *f*. **it's a good ~ (that)**... menos mal que.... **just the ~** exactamente lo que se necesita. **poor ~!** ¡pobrecito!

think /θɪŋk/ *vt* (*pt* **thought**) pensar, creer. ● *vi* pensar (**about** en); (carefully) reflexionar; (imagine) imaginarse. **I ~ so** creo que sí. **~ of s.o.** pensar en uno. **I hadn't thought of that** eso no se me ha ocurrido. **~ over** *vt* pensar bien. **~ up** *vt* idear, inventar. **~er** *n* pensador *m*. **~-tank** *n* gabinete *m* estratégico

third /θɜ:d/ *a* tercero, (before masculine singular noun) tercer. ● *n* tercio *m*, tercera parte *f*. **~ (gear)** *n* (Auto) tercera *f*. **~-rate** *a* muy inferior. **T~ World** *n* Tercer Mundo *m*

thirst /θɜ:st/ *n* sed *f*. **~y** *a* sediento. **be ~y** tener sed

thirt|een /θɜ:ˈti:n/ *a* & *n* trece (*m*). **~teenth** *a* decimotercero. ● *n* treceavo *m* **~ieth** /ˈθɜ:tɪəθ/ *a* trigésimo. ● *n* treintavo *m*. **~y** /ˈθɜ:tɪ/ *a* & *n* treinta (*m*)

this /ðɪs/ *a* (*pl* **these**) este, esta. **~ one** éste, ésta. ● *pron* (*pl* **these**) éste, ésta, esto. **like ~** así

thistle /ˈθɪsl/ *n* cardo *m*

thong /θɒŋ/ *n* correa *f*; (Amer, sandal) chancla *f*

thorn /θɔ:n/ *n* espina *f*. **~y** *a* espinoso

thorough /ˈθʌrə/ *a* *<investigation>* riguroso; *<cleaning etc>* a fondo; *<person>* concienzudo. **~bred** /-bred/ *a* de pura sangre. **~fare** *n* vía *f* pública; (street) calle *f*. **no ~fare** prohibido el paso. **~ly** *adv* *<clean>* a fondo; *<examine>* minuciosamente; (completely) perfectamente

those /ðəʊz/ *a* esos, esas, aquellos, aquellas. ● *pron* ésos, ésas, aquéllos, aquéllas

though /ðəʊ/ *conj* aunque. ● *adv* sin embargo. **as ~** como si

thought /θɔ:t/ ⇒THINK. ● *n* pensamiento *m*; (idea) idea *f*. **~ful** *a* pensativo; (considerate) atento. **~fully** *adv* pensativamente; (considerately) atentamente. **~less** *a* desconsiderado

thousand /ˈθaʊznd/ *a* & *n* mil (*m*). **~th** *a* & *n* milésimo (*m*)

thrash /θræʃ/ *vt* azotar; (defeat) derrotar

thread /θred/ *n* hilo *m*; (of screw) rosca *f*. ● *vt* enhebrar *<needle>*; ensartar *<beads>*. **~bare** *a* gastado, raído

threat /θret/ *n* amenaza *f*. **~en** *vt/i* amenazar. **~ening** *a* amenazador

three /θri:/ *a* & *n* tres (*m*). **~fold** *a* triple. ● *adv* tres veces

threshold /ˈθreʃhəʊld/ *n* umbral *m*

threw /θru:/ ⇒THROW

thrift /θrɪft/ *n* economía *f*, ahorro *m*. **~y** *a* frugal

thrill /θrɪl/ *n* emoción *f*. ● *vt* emocionar. **~ed** *a* contentísimo (**with** con). **~er** *n* (book) libro *m* de suspense *or* (LAm) suspenso; (film) película *f* de suspense *or* (LAm) suspenso. **~ing** *a* emocionante

thriv|e /θraɪv/ *vi* prosperar. **~ing** *a* próspero

throat /θrəʊt/ *n* garganta *f*

throb /θrɒb/ *vi* (*pt* **throbbed**) palpitar; (with pain) dar punzadas; *<engine>* vibrar. **~bing** *a* *<pain>* punzante

throes /θrəʊz/ *npl*. **be in one's death ~** estar agonizando

throne /θrəʊn/ *n* trono *m*

throng /θrɒŋ/ *n* multitud *f*

throttle /ˈθrɒtl/ *n* (Auto) acelerador *m* (*que se acciona con la mano*). ● *vt* estrangular

through /θru:/ *prep* por, a través de; (during) durante; (by means of) a través de; (Amer, until and including) **Monday ~ Friday** de lunes a viernes. ● *adv* de parte a parte, de un lado a otro; (entirely) completamente; (to the end) hasta el final. **be ~** (finished) haber terminado. ● *a* *<train etc>* directo. **no ~ road** calle sin salida. **~out** /-ˈaʊt/ *prep* por todo; (time) durante todo. **~out his career** a lo largo de su carrera

throve /θrəʊv/ ⇒THRIVE

throw /θrəʊ/ *vt* (*pt* **threw**, *pp* **thrown**) tirar, aventar (Mex); lanzar *<grenade, javelin>*; (disconcert) desconcertar; 🅸 hacer, dar *<party>*. ● *n* (of ball) tiro *m*; (of dice) tirada *f*. □ **~ away** *vt* tirar. □ **~ up** *vi* (vomit) vomitar.

thrush /θrʌʃ/ *n* tordo *m*

thrust /θrʌst/ *vt* (*pt* **thrust**) empujar; (push in) clavar. ● *n* empujón *m*; (of sword) estocada *f*

thud /θʌd/ *n* ruido *m* sordo

thug /θʌg/ *n* matón *m*

thumb /θʌm/ *n* pulgar *m*. ● *vt*. **~ a lift** ir a dedo. **~tack** *n* (Amer) chincheta *f*, tachuela *f*, chinche *f* (Mex)

thump /θʌmp/ *vt* golpear. ● *vi* *<heart>* latir fuertemente. ● *n* golpazo *m*

thunder /ˈθʌndə(r)/ *n* truenos *mpl*, (of traffic) estruendo *m*. ● *vi* tronar. **~bolt** *n* rayo *m*. **~storm** *n* tormenta *f* eléctrica. **~y** *a* con truenos

Thursday /ˈθɜ:zdeɪ/ *n* jueves *m*

thus /ðʌs/ *adv* así

thwart /θwɔ:t/ *vt* frustrar

tic /tɪk/ *n* tic *m*

tick /tɪk/ *n* (sound) tic *m*; (insect) garrapata *f*, (mark) marca *f*, visto *m*, palomita *f* (Mex); (🅸, instant) momentito *m*. ● *vi* hacer tictac. ● *vt*. **~ (off)** marcar

ticket /ˈtɪkɪt/ *n* (for bus, train) billete *m*, boleto *m* (LAm); (for plane) pasaje *m*, billete *m*; (for theatre, museum) entrada *f*; (for baggage, coat) ticket *m*; (fine) multa *f*. **~ collector** *n* revisor *m*. **~ office** *n* (transport) mostrador *m* de venta de billetes *or* (LAm) boletos; (in theatre) taquilla *f*, boletería *f* (LAm)

tickl|e /ˈtɪkl/ *vt* hacerle cosquillas a. ● *n* cosquilleo *m*. **~ish** /ˈtɪklɪʃ/ *a*. **be ~ish** tener cosquillas

tidal wave /ˈtaɪdl/ *n* maremoto *m*

tide /taɪd/ *n* marea *f*. **high/low ~** marea alta/baja. □ **~ over** *vt* ayudar a salir de un apuro

tid|ily /ˈtaɪdɪlɪ/ *adv* ordenadamente. **~iness** *n* orden *m*. **~y** *a* (**-ier**, **-iest**) ordenado. ● *vt/i* **~y (up)** ordenar, arreglar

tie /taɪ/ *vt* (*pres p* **tying**) atar, amarrar (LAm); hacer *<knot>*. ● *vi* (Sport) empatar. ● *n* (constraint) atadura *f*; (bond) lazo *m*; (necktie) corbata *f*; (Sport) empate *m*. **~ in with** *vt* concordar con. □ **~ up** *vt* atar. **be ~d up** (busy) estar ocupado

tier /tɪə(r)/ *n* hilera *f* superpuesta; (in stadium etc) grada *f*; (of cake) piso *m*

tiger /ˈtaɪgə(r)/ *n* tigre *m*

tight /taɪt/ *a* (**-er**, **-est**) <*clothes*> ajustado, ceñido; (taut) tieso; <*control*> estricto; <*knot, nut*> apretado; ([I], drunk) borracho. **~en** *vt* apretar. □ **~en up** *vt* hacer más estricto. **~-fisted** /-ˈfɪstɪd/ *a* tacaño. **~ly** *adv* bien, fuerte; <*fastened*> fuertemente. **~rope** *n* cuerda *f* floja. **~s** *npl* (for ballet etc) leotardo(s) *m(pl)*; (pantyhose) medias *fpl*

tile /taɪl/ *n* (decorative) azulejo *m*; (on roof) teja *f*; (on floor) baldosa *f*. ● *vt* azulejar; tejar <*roof*>; embaldosar <*floor*>

till /tɪl/ *prep* hasta. ● *conj* hasta que. ● *n* caja *f*. ● *vt* cultivar

tilt /tɪlt/ *vt* inclinar. ● *vi* inclinarse. ● *n* inclinación *f*

timber /ˈtɪmbə(r)/ *n* madera *f* (*para construcción*)

time /taɪm/ *n* tiempo *m*; (moment) momento *m*; (occasion) ocasión *f*; (by clock) hora *f*; (epoch) época *f*; (rhythm) compás *m*. **at ~s** a veces. **for the ~ being** por el momento. **from ~ to ~** de vez en cuando. **have a good ~** divertirse, pasarlo bien. **in a year's ~** dentro de un año. **in no ~** en un abrir y cerrar de ojos. **in ~** a tiempo; (eventually) con el tiempo. **arrive on ~** llegar a tiempo. **it's ~ we left** es hora de irnos. ● *vt* tomar el tiempo a <*runner*>; cronometrar <*race*>. **~ bomb** *n* bomba *f* de tiempo. **~ly** *a* oportuno. **~r** *n* cronómetro *m*; (Culin) avisador *m*; (with sand) reloj *m* de arena; (Elec) interruptor *m* de reloj. **~s** /ˈtaɪmz/ *prep*. **2 ~s 4 is 8** 2 (multiplicado) por 4 son 8. **~table** *n* horario *m*

timid /ˈtɪmɪd/ *a* tímido; (fearful) miedoso

tin /tɪn/ *n* estaño *m*; (container) lata *f*. **~ foil** *n* papel *m* de estaño

tinge /tɪndʒ/ *vt*. **be ~d with sth** estar matizado de algo. ● *n* matiz *m*

tingle /ˈtɪŋgl/ *vi* sentir un hormigueo

tinker /ˈtɪŋkə(r)/ *vi*. **~ with** juguetear con

tinkle /ˈtɪŋkl/ *vi* tintinear

tinned /tɪnd/ *a* en lata, enlatado

tin opener *n* abrelatas *m*

tint /tɪnt/ *n* matiz *m*

tiny /ˈtaɪnɪ/ *a* (**-ier**, **-iest**) minúsculo, diminuto

tip /tɪp/ *n* punta *f*. ● *vt* (*pt* **tipped**) (tilt) inclinar; (overturn) volcar; (pour) verter; (give gratuity to) darle (una) propina a. □ **~ off** *vt* avisar. □ **~ out** *vt* verter. □ **~ over** *vi* caerse. *n* propina *f*; (advice) consejo *m* (práctico); (for rubbish) vertedero *m*. **~ped** *a* <*cigarette*> con filtro

tipsy /ˈtɪpsɪ/ *a* achispado

tiptoe /ˈtɪptəʊ/ *n*. **on ~** de puntillas

tiptop /ˈtɪptɒp/ *a* [I] de primera. **in ~ condition** en excelente estado

tire /ˈtaɪə(r)/ *n* (Amer) ⇒TYRE. ● *vt* cansar. ● *vi* cansarse. **~d** /ˈtaɪəd/ *a* cansado. **get ~d** cansarse. **~d of** harto de. **~d out** agotado. **~less** *a* incansable; <*efforts*> inagotable. **~some** /-səm/ *a* <*person*> pesado; <*task*> tedioso

tiring /ˈtaɪərɪŋ/ *a* cansado, cansador (LAm)

tissue /ˈtɪʃuː/ *n* (Anat, Bot) tejido *m*; (paper handkerchief) pañuelo *m* de papel. **~ paper** *n* papel *m* de seda

tit /tɪt/ *n* (bird) paro *m*; ([x], breast) teta *f*

titbit /ˈtɪtbɪt/ *n* exquisitez *f*

tit for tat *n*: **it was ~** fue ojo por ojo, diente por diente

title /ˈtaɪtl/ *n* título *m*

to /tu:, tə/ *prep* a; (towards) hacia; (in order to) para; (as far as) hasta; (of) de. **give it ~ me** dámelo. **what did you say ~ him?** ¿qué le dijiste?; **I don't want ~** no quiero. **it's twenty ~ seven** (by clock) son las siete menos veinte, son veinte para las siete (LAm). ● *adv*. **pull ~** cerrar. **~ and fro** *adv* de un lado a otro

toad /təʊd/ *n* sapo *m*. **~stool** *n* hongo *m* (*no comestible*)

toast /təʊst/ *n* pan *m* tostado, tostadas *fpl*; (drink) brindis *m*. **a piece of ~** una tostada, un pan tostado (Mex). **drink a ~ to** brindar por. ● *vt* (Culin) tostar; (drink to) brindar por. **~er** *n* tostadora *f* (eléctrica), tostador *m*

tobacco /təˈbækəʊ/ *n* tabaco *m*. **~nist** /-ənɪst/ *n* estanquero *m*

toboggan /təˈbɒgən/ *n* tobogán *m*

today /təˈdeɪ/ *n & adv* hoy (*m*)

toddler /ˈtɒdlə(r)/ *n* niño *m* pequeño (*entre un año y dos años y medio de edad*)

toe /təʊ/ *n* dedo *m* (del pie); (of shoe) punta *f*. **big ~** dedo *m* gordo (del pie). **on one's ~s** (fig) alerta. ● *vt*. **~ the line** acatar la disciplina

toffee /ˈtɒfɪ/ *n* toffee *m* (*golosina hecha con azúcar y mantequilla*)

together /təˈgeðə(r)/ *adv* juntos; (at same time) a la vez. **~ with** junto con

toil /tɔɪl/ *vi* afanarse. ● *n* trabajo *m* duro

toilet /ˈtɔɪlɪt/ *n* servicio *m*, baño *m* (LAm). **~ paper** *n* papel *m* higiénico. **~ries** /ˈtɔɪlɪtrɪz/ *npl* artículos *mpl* de tocador. **~ roll** *n* rollo *m* de papel higiénico

token /ˈtəʊkən/ *n* muestra *f*; (voucher) vale *m*; (coin) ficha *f*. ● *a* simbólico

told /təʊld/ ⇒TELL

tolera|ble /ˈtɒlərəbl/ *a* tolerable; (not bad) pasable. **~nce** /ˈtɒlərəns/ *n* tolerancia *f*. **~nt** *a* tolerante. **~te** /-reɪt/ *vt* tolerar. **~tion** /-ˈreɪʃən/ *n* tolerancia *f*

toll /təʊl/ *n* (on road) peaje *m*, cuota *f* (Mex). **death ~** número *m* de muertos. **~ call** *n* (Amer) llamada *f* interurbana, conferencia *f*. ● *vi* doblar, tocar a muerto

tomato /təˈmɑːtəʊ/ *n* (*pl* **-oes**) tomate *m*, jitomate *m* (Mex)

tomb /tu:m/ *n* tumba *f*, sepulcro *m*. **~stone** *n* lápida *f*

tomorrow /təˈmɒrəʊ/ *n & adv* mañana (*f*). **see you ~!** ¡hasta mañana!

ton /tʌn/ *n* tonelada *f* (= 1,016kg). **~s of** Ⓘ montones de. **metric ~** tonelada *f* (métrica) (= 1,000kg)

tone /təʊn/ *n* tono *m*. □ **~ down** *vt* atenuar; moderar <*language*>. **~-deaf** *a* que no tiene oído (musical)

tongs /tɒŋz/ *npl* tenacillas *fpl*

tongue /tʌŋ/ *n* lengua *f*. **say sth ~ in cheek** decir algo medio burlándose. **~-tied** *a* cohibido. **~-twister** *n* trabalenguas *m*

tonic /ˈtɒnɪk/ *a* tónico. ● *n* (Med, fig) tónico *m*. **~ (water)** *n* tónica *f*

tonight /təˈnaɪt/ *adv & n* esta noche (*f*); (evening) esta tarde (*f*)

tonne /tʌn/ *n* tonelada *f* (métrica)

tonsil /ˈtɒnsl/ *n* amígdala *f*. **~litis** /-ˈlaɪtɪs/ *n* amigdalitis *f*

too /tu:/ *adv* (excessively) demasiado; (also) también. **I'm not ~ sure**

no estoy muy seguro. ~ **many** demasiados. ~ **much** demasiado

took /tʊk/ ⇒TAKE

tool /tu:l/ *n* herramienta *f*

tooth /tu:θ/ *n* (*pl* **teeth**) diente *m*; (molar) muela *f*. **~ache** *n* dolor *m* de muelas. **~brush** *n* cepillo *m* de dientes. **~paste** *n* pasta *f* dentífrica, pasta *f* de dientes. **~pick** *n* palillo *m* (de dientes)

top /tɒp/ *n* parte *f* superior, parte *f* de arriba; (of mountain) cima *f*; (of tree) copa *f*; (of page) parte *f* superior; (lid, of bottle) tapa *f*; (of pen) capuchón *m*; (spinning ~) trompo *m*, peonza *f*. **be ~ of the class** ser el primero de la clase. **from ~ to bottom** de arriba abajo. **on ~ of** encima de; (besides) además de. ● *a* más alto; <*shelf*> superior; <*speed*> máximo; (in rank) superior; (leading) más destacado. ● *vt* (*pt* **topped**) cubrir; (exceed) exceder. □ **~ up** *vt* llenar. **~ floor** *n* último piso *m*. **~ hat** *n* chistera *f*. **~-heavy** /-ˈhevɪ/ *a* inestable (*por ser más pesado en su parte superior*)

topic /ˈtɒpɪk/ *n* tema *m*. **~al** *a* de actualidad

topless /tɒples/ *a* topless

topple /ˈtɒpl/ *vi* (Pol) derribar; (overturn) volcar. ● *vi* caerse

top secret /tɒpˈsi:krɪt/ *a* secreto, reservado

torch /tɔ:tʃ/ *n* linterna *f*; (flaming) antorcha *f*

tore /tɔ:(r)/ ⇒TEAR[1]

torment /ˈtɔ:ment/ *n* tormento *m*. ● /tɔ:ˈment/ *vt* atormentar

torn /tɔ:n/ ⇒TEAR[1]

tornado /tɔ:ˈneɪdəʊ/ *n* (*pl* **-oes**) tornado *m*

torpedo /tɔ:ˈpi:dəʊ/ *n* (*pl* **-oes**) torpedo *m*. ● *vt* torpedear

torrent /ˈtɒrənt/ *n* torrente *m*. **~ial** /təˈrenʃl/ *a* torrencial

torrid /ˈtɒrɪd/ *a* tórrido; <*affair*> apasionado

tortoise /ˈtɔ:təs/ *n* tortuga *f*. **~shell** *n* carey *m*

tortuous /ˈtɔ:tjʊəs/ *a* tortuoso

torture /ˈtɔ:tʃə(r)/ *n* tortura *f*. ● *vt* torturar

Tory /ˈtɔ:rɪ/ *a* & *n* tory *m* & *f*

toss /tɒs/ *vt* tirar, lanzar <*ball*>; (shake) sacudir. ● *vi*. **~ and turn** (in bed) dar vueltas

tot /tɒt/ *n* pequeño *m*; (Ⓘ, of liquor) trago *m*. ● *vt* (*pt* **totted**). **~ up** Ⓘ sumar

total /ˈtəʊtl/ *a* & *n* total (*m*). ● *vi* (*pt* **totalled**) ascender a un total de; (add up) totalizar. **~itarian** /təʊtælɪˈteərɪən/ *a* totalitario. **~ly** *adv* totalmente

totter /ˈtɒtə(r)/ *vi* tambalearse

touch /tʌtʃ/ *vt* tocar; (move) conmover; (concern) afectar. ● *vi* tocar; <*wires*> tocarse. ● *n* toque *m*; (sense) tacto *m*; (contact) contacto *m*. **be/get/stay in ~ with** estar/ponerse/mantenerse en contacto con. □ **~ down** *vi* <*aircraft*> aterrizar. □ **~ up** *vt* retocar. **~ing** *a* enternecedor. **~y** *a* quisquilloso

tough /tʌf/ *a* (**-er**, **-est**) duro; (strong) fuerte, resistente; (difficult) difícil; (severe) severo. **~en**. **~ (up)** *vt* endurecer; hacer más fuerte <*person*>

tour /tʊə(r)/ *n* viaje *m*; (visit) visita *f*; (excursion) excursión *f*; (by team etc) gira *f*. **be on ~** estar de gira. ● *vt* recorrer; (visit) visitar. **~ guide** *n* guía de turismo

touris|m /ˈtʊərɪzəm/ *n* turismo *m*. **~t** /ˈtʊərɪst/ *n* turista *m* & *f*. ● *a* turístico. **~t office** *n* oficina *f* de turismo

tournament /'tɔ:nəmənt/ *n* torneo *m*

tousle /'taʊzl/ *vt* despeinar

tout /taʊt/ *vi*. ~ (**for**) solicitar

tow /təʊ/ *vt* remolcar. ● *n* remolque *m*

toward(s) /tə'wɔ:d(z)/ *prep* hacia. **his attitude ~ her** su actitud para con ella

towel /'taʊəl/ *n* toalla *f*

tower /'taʊə(r)/ *n* torre *f*. ● *vi*. ~ **above** <*building*> descollar sobre; <*person*> destacar sobre. **~ block** *n* edificio *m or* bloque *m* de apartamentos. **~ing** *a* altísimo; <*rage*> violento

town /taʊn/ *n* ciudad *f*; (smaller) pueblo *m*. **go to ~** 🅸 no escatimar dinero. **~ hall** *n* ayuntamiento *m*

toxic /'tɒksɪk/ *a* tóxico

toy /tɔɪ/ *n* juguete *m*. □ **~ with** *vt* juguetear con <*object*>; darle vueltas a <*idea*>. **~shop** *n* juguetería *f*

trac|e /treɪs/ *n* señal *f*, rastro *m*. ● *vt* trazar; (draw) dibujar; (with tracing paper) calcar; (track down) localizar. **~ing paper** *n* papel *m* de calcar

track /træk/ *n* pista *f*, huellas *fpl*; (path) sendero *m*; (Sport) pista *f*. **the ~(s)** la vía férrea; (Rail) vía *f*. **keep ~ of** seguirle la pista a <*person*>. ● *vt* seguirle la pista a. □ **~ down** *vt* localizar. **~ suit** *n* equipo *m* (de deportes), chándal *m*

tract /trækt/ *n* (land) extensión *f*; (pamphlet) tratado *m* breve

traction /'trækʃn/ *n* tracción *f*

tractor /'træktə(r)/ *n* tractor *m*

trade /treɪd/ *n* comercio *m*; (occupation) oficio *m*; (exchange) cambio *m*; (industry) industria *f*. ● *vt*. **~ sth for sth** cambiar algo por algo. ● *vi* comerciar. □ **~ in** *vt* (give in part-exchange) entregar como parte del pago. **~ mark** *n* marca *f* (de fábrica). **~r** *n* comerciante *m & f*. **~ union** *n* sindicato *m*

tradition /trə'dɪʃn/ *n* tradición *f*. **~al** *a* tradicional

traffic /'træfɪk/ *n* tráfico *m*. ● *vi* (*pt* **trafficked**) comerciar (**in** en). **~ circle** *n* (Amer) glorieta *f*, rotonda *f*. **~ island** *n* isla *f* peatonal. **~ jam** *n* embotellamiento *m*, atasco *m*. **~ lights** *npl* semáforo *m*. **~ warden** *n* guardia *m*, controlador *m* de tráfico

trag|edy /'trædʒɪdɪ/ *n* tragedia *f*. **~ic** /'trædʒɪk/ *a* trágico

trail /treɪl/ *vi* arrastrarse; (lag) rezagarse. ● *vt* (track) seguir la pista de. ● *n* (left by animal, person) huellas *fpl*; (path) sendero *m*. **be on the ~ of s.o./sth** seguir la pista de uno/algo **~er** *n* remolque *m*; (Amer, caravan) caravana *f*, rulot *m*; (film) avance *m*

train /treɪn/ *n* (Rail) tren *m*; (of events) serie *f*; (of dress) cola *f*. ● *vt* capacitar <*employee*>; adiestrar <*soldier*>; (Sport) entrenar; educar <*voice*>; guiar <*plant*>; amaestrar <*animal*>. ● *vi* estudiar; (Sport) entrenarse. **~ed** *a* (skilled) cualificado, calificado; <*doctor*> diplomado. **~ee** /treɪ'ni:/ *n* aprendiz *m*; (Amer, Mil) recluta *m & f*. **~er** *n* (Sport) entrenador *m*; (of animals) amaestrador *m*. **~ers** *mpl* zapatillas *fpl* de deporte. **~ing** *n* capacitación *f*; (Sport) entrenamiento *m*

trait /treɪ(t)/ *n* rasgo *m*

traitor /'treɪtə(r)/ *n* traidor *m*

tram /træm/ *n* tranvía *m*

tramp /træmp/ *vi*. ~ (**along**) caminar pesadamente. ● *n* vagabundo *m*

trample /'træmpl/ *vt* pisotear. ● *vi.* ~ on pisotear

trampoline /'træmpəli:n/ *n* trampolín *m*

trance /trɑ:ns/ *n* trance *m*

tranquil /'træŋkwɪl/ *a* tranquilo. **~lity** /-'kwɪlətɪ/ *n* tranquilidad *f*; (of person) serenidad *f*. **~lize** /'træŋkwɪlaɪz/ *vt* sedar, dar un sedante a. **~lizer** *n* sedante *m*, tranquilizante *m*

transaction /træn'zækʃən/ *n* transacción *f*, operación *f*

transatlantic /trænzət'læntɪk/ *a* transatlántico

transcend /træn'send/ *vt* (go beyond) exceder

transcript /'trænskrɪpt/ *n* transcripción *f*

transfer /træns'fɜ:(r)/ *vt* (*pt* **transferred**) trasladar; traspasar <*player*>; transferir <*funds, property*>; pasar <*call*>. ● *vi* trasladarse. ● /'trænsfɜ:(r)/ *n* traslado *m*; (of player) traspaso *m*; (of funds, property) transferencia *f*; (paper) calcomanía *f*

transform /træns'fɔ:m/ *vt* transformar. **~ation** /-ə'meɪʃn/ *n* transformación *f*. **~er** *n* transformador *m*

transfusion /træns'fju:ʒn/ *n* transfusión *f*

transient /'trænzɪənt/ *a* pasajero

transistor /træn'zɪstə(r)/ *n* transistor *m*

transit /'trænsɪt/ *n* tránsito *m*. **~ion** /træn'zɪʒn/ *n* transición *f*. **~ive** /'trænsɪtɪv/ *a* transitivo

translat|e /trænz'leɪt/ *vt* traducir. **~ion** /-ʃn/ *n* traducción *f*. **~or** *n* traductor *m*

transmission /træns'mɪʃn/ *n* transmisión *f*

transmit /trænz'mɪt/ *vt* (*pt* **transmitted**) transmitir. **~ter** *n* transmisor *m*

transparen|cy /træns'pærənsɪ/ *n* transparencia *f*; (Photo) diapositiva *f*. **~t** *a* transparente

transplant /træns'plɑ:nt/ *vt* trasplantar. ● /'trænsplɑ:nt/ *n* trasplante *m*

transport /træn'spɔ:t/ *vt* transportar. ● /'trænspɔ:t/ *n* transporte *m*. **~ation** /-'teɪʃn/ *n* transporte *m*

trap /træp/ *n* trampa *f*. ● *vt* (*pt* **trapped**) atrapar; (jam) atascar; (cut off) bloquear. **~door** *n* trampilla *f*

trapeze /trə'pi:z/ *n* trapecio *m*

trash /træʃ/ *n* basura *f*; (Amer, worthless people) escoria *f*. **~ can** *n* (Amer) cubo *m* de la basura, bote *m* de la basura (Mex). **~y** *a* <*souvenir*> de porquería; <*magazine*> malo

travel /'trævl/ *vi* (*pt* **travelled**) viajar; <*vehicle*> desplazarse. ● *vt* recorrer. ● *n* viajes *mpl*. **~ agency** *n* agencia *f* de viajes. **~ler** *n* viajero *m*. **~ler's cheque** *n* cheque *m* de viaje *or* viajero. **~ling expenses** *npl* gastos *mpl* de viaje

trawler /'trɔ:lə(r)/ *n* barca *f* pesquera

tray /treɪ/ *n* bandeja *f*

treacher|ous *a* traidor; (deceptive) engañoso. **~y** *n* traición *f*

treacle /'tri:kl/ *n* melaza *f*

tread /tred/ *vi* (*pt* **trod**, *pp* **trodden**) pisar. **~ on sth** pisar algo. **~ carefully** andarse con cuidado. ● *n* (step) paso *m*; (of tyre) banda *f* de rodamiento

treason /'tri:zn/ *n* traición *f*

treasur|e /'treʒə(r)/ *n* tesoro *m*. **~ed** /'treʒəd/ *a* <*possession*> preciado. **~er** /'treʒərə(r)/ *n* tesorero *m*. **~y** *n* erario *m*, tesoro *m*. **the T~y** el fisco, la hacienda pública. **Department of the T~y** (in US) Departamento *m* del Tesoro

treat /tri:t/ *vt* tratar; (Med) tratar. **~ s.o.** (to meal etc) invitar a uno. ● *n* placer *m*; (present) regalo *m*

treatise /'tri:tɪz/ *n* tratado *m*

treatment /'tri:tmənt/ *n* tratamiento *m*

treaty /'tri:tɪ/ *n* tratado *m*

treble /'trebl/ *a* triple; <*clef*> de sol; <*voice*> de tiple. ● *vt* triplicar. ● *vi* triplicarse. ● *n* tiple *m* & *f*

tree /tri:/ *n* árbol *m*

trek /trek/ *n* caminata *f*. ● *vi* (*pt* **trekked**) caminar

trellis /'trelɪs/ *n* enrejado *m*

tremble /'trembl/ *vi* temblar

tremendous /trɪ'mendəs/ *a* formidable; (Ⓘ, huge) tremendo. **~ly** *adv* tremendamente

tremor /'tremə(r)/ *n* temblor *m*

trench /trentʃ/ *n* zanja *f*; (Mil) trinchera *f*

trend /trend/ *n* tendencia *f*; (fashion) moda *f*. **~y** *a* (**-ier**, **-iest**) Ⓘ moderno

trepidation /trepɪ'deɪʃn/ *n* inquietud *f*

trespass /'trespəs/ *vi*. **~ on** entrar sin autorización (*en propiedad ajena*). **~er** *n* intruso *m*

trial /'traɪəl/ *n* prueba *f*; (Jurid) proceso *m*, juicio *m*; (ordeal) prueba *f* dura. **by ~ and error** por ensayo y error. **be on ~** estar a prueba; (Jurid) estar siendo procesado

triang|le /'traɪæŋgl/ *n* triángulo *m*. **~ular** /-'æŋgjʊlə(r)/ *a* triangular

trib|al /'traɪbl/ *a* tribal. **~e** /traɪb/ *n* tribu *f*

tribulation /trɪbjʊ'leɪʃn/ *n* tribulación *f*

tribunal /traɪ'bju:nl/ *n* tribunal *m*

tributary /'trɪbjʊtrɪ/ *n* (Geog) afluente *m*

tribute /'trɪbju:t/ *n* tributo *m*; (acknowledgement) homenaje *m*. **pay ~ to** rendir homenaje a

trick /trɪk/ *n* trampa *f*, ardid *m*; (joke) broma *f*; (feat) truco *m*; (in card games) baza *f*. **play a ~ on** gastar una broma a. ● *vt* engañar. **~ery** *n* engaño *m*

trickle /'trɪkl/ *vi* gotear. **~ in** (fig) entrar poco a poco

trickster /'trɪkstə(r)/ *n* estafador *m*

tricky /'trɪkɪ/ *a* delicado, difícil

tricycle /'traɪsɪkl/ *n* triciclo *m*

tried /traɪd/ ⇒TRY

trifl|e /'traɪfl/ *n* nimiedad *f*; (Culin) *postre de bizcocho, jerez, frutas y nata*. ● *vi*. □ **~e with** *vt* jugar con. **~ing** *a* insignificante

trigger /'trɪgə(r)/ *n* (of gun) gatillo *m*. ● *vt*. **~** (off) desencadenar

trim /trɪm/ *a* (**trimmer**, **trimmest**) (slim) esbelto; (neat) elegante. ● *vt* (*pt* **trimmed**) (cut) recortar; (adorn) adornar. ● *n* (cut) recorte *m*. **in ~** en buen estado. **~mings** *npl* recortes *mpl*

trinity /'trɪnɪtɪ/ *n*. **the (Holy) T~** la (Santísima) Trinidad

trinket /'trɪŋkɪt/ *n* chuchería *f*

trio /'tri:əʊ/ *n* (*pl* **-os**) trío *m*

trip /trɪp/ (*pt* **tripped**) *vt* **~** (up) hacerle una zancadilla a, hacer tropezar ● *vi* tropezar. ● *n* (journey) viaje *m*; (outing) excursión *f*; (stumble) traspié *m*

tripe /traɪp/ *n* callos *mpl*, mondongo *m* (LAm), pancita *f* (Mex); (🅃, nonsense) paparruchas *fpl*

triple /ˈtrɪpl/ *a* triple. ● *vt* triplicar. ● *vi* triplicarse. **~t** /ˈtrɪplɪt/ *n* trillizo *m*

triplicate /ˈtrɪplɪkət/ *a* triplicado. **in ~** por triplicado

tripod /ˈtraɪpɒd/ *n* trípode *m*

trite /traɪt/ *a* trillado

triumph /ˈtraɪʌmf/ *n* triunfo *m*. ● *vi* triunfar (**over** sobre). **~al** /-ˈʌmfl/ *a* triunfal. **~ant** /-ˈʌmfnt/ *a* <*troops*> triunfador; <*moment*> triunfal; <*smile*> de triunfo

trivial /ˈtrɪvɪəl/ *a* insignificante; <*concerns*> trivial. **~ity** /-ˈælətɪ/ *n* trivialidad *f*

trod, trodden /trɒd, trɒdn/ ⇨TREAD

trolley /ˈtrɒlɪ/ *n* (*pl* **-eys**) carretón *m*; (in supermarket, airport) carrito *m*; (for food, drink) carrito *m*, mesa *f* rodante. **~ car** *n* (Amer) tranvía *f*

trombone /trɒmˈbəʊn/ *n* trombón *m*

troop /tru:p/ *n* compañía *f*; (of cavalry) escuadrón *m*. ● *vi*. **~ in** entrar en tropel. **~ out** salir en tropel. **~er** *n* soldado *m* de caballería; (Amer, state police officer) agente *m* & *f*. **~s** *npl* (Mil) tropas *fpl*

trophy /ˈtrəʊfɪ/ *n* trofeo *m*

tropic /ˈtrɒpɪk/ *n* trópico *m*. **~al** *a* tropical. **~s** *npl* trópicos *mpl*

trot /trɒt/ *n* trote *m*. ● *vi* (*pt* **trotted**) trotar

trouble /ˈtrʌbl/ *n* problemas *mpl*; (awkward situation) apuro *m*; (inconvenience) molestia *f*. **be in ~** estar en apuros. **get into ~** meterse en problemas. **look for ~** buscar camorra. **take the ~ to do sth** molestarse en hacer algo. ● *vt* (bother) molestar; (worry) preocupar. **~-maker** *n* alborotador *m*. **~some** /-səm/ *a* problemático. **~ spot** *n* punto *m* conflictivo

trough /trɒf/ *n* (for drinking) abrevadero *m*; (for feeding) comedero *m*

troupe /tru:p/ *n* compañía *f* teatral

trousers /ˈtraʊzəz/ *npl* pantalón *m*, pantalones *mpl*

trout /traʊt/ *n* (*pl* **trout**) trucha *f*

trowel /ˈtraʊəl/ *n* (garden) desplantador *m*; (for mortar) paleta *f*

truant /ˈtru:ənt/ *n*. **play ~** hacer novillos

truce /tru:s/ *n* tregua *f*

truck /trʌk/ *n* camión *m*; (Rail) vagón *m*, furgón *m*; (Amer, vegetables, fruit) productos *mpl* de la huerta. **~ driver**, **~er** (Amer) *n* camionero *m*. **~ing** *n* transporte *m* por carretera

trudge /trʌdʒ/ *vi* andar penosamente

true /tru:/ *a* (**-er, -est**) verdadero; <*story, account*> verídico; <*friend*> auténtico, de verdad. **~ to sth/s.o.** fiel a algo/uno. **be ~** ser cierto. **come ~** hacerse realidad

truffle /ˈtrʌfl/ *n* trufa *f*; (chocolate) trufa *f* de chocolate

truly /ˈtru:lɪ/ *adv* verdaderamente; (sincerely) sinceramente. **yours ~** (in letters) cordiales saludos

trump /trʌmp/ *n* (Cards) triunfo *m*; (fig) baza *f*

trumpet /ˈtrʌmpɪt/ *n* trompeta *f*. **~er** *n* trompetista *m* & *f*, trompeta *m* & *f*

truncheon /ˈtrʌntʃən/ *n* porra *f*

trunk /trʌŋk/ *n* (of tree) tronco *m*; (box) baúl *m*; (of elephant) trompa *f*; (Amer, Auto) maletero *m*, cajuela *f*

(Mex). **~s** *npl* bañador *m*, traje *m* de baño

truss /trʌs/. **truss** (**up**) *vt* atar

trust /trʌst/ *n* confianza *f*; (money, property) fondo *m* de inversiones; (institution) fundación *f*. **on ~** a ojos cerrados; (Com) al fiado. ● *vi*. **~ in s.o./sth** confiar en uno/algo. ● *vt* confiar en; (in negative sentences) fiarse; (hope) esperar. **~ed** *a* leal. **~ee** /trʌ'sti:/ *n* fideicomisario *m*. **~ful** *a* confiado. **~ing** *a* confiado. **~worthy**, **~y** *a* digno de confianza

truth /tru:θ/ *n* (*pl* **-s** /tru:ðz/) verdad *f*; (of account, story) veracidad *f*. **~ful** *a* veraz.

try /traɪ/ *vt* (*pt* **tried**) intentar; probar <*food, product*>; (be a strain on) poner a prueba; (Jurid) procesar. **~ to do sth** tratar de hacer algo, intentar hacer algo. **~ not to forget** procura no olvidarte. ● *n* tentativa *f*, prueba *f*; (Rugby) ensayo *m*. □ **~ on** *vt* probarse <*garment*>. □ **~ out** *vt* probar. **~ing** *a* duro; (annoying) molesto

tsar /zɑ:(r)/ *n* zar *m*

T-shirt /'ti:ʃɜ:t/ *n* camiseta *f*

tub /tʌb/ *n* cuba *f*; (for washing clothes) tina *f*; (bathtub) bañera *f*; (for ice cream) envase *m*, tarrina *f*

tuba /'tju:bə/ *n* tuba *f*

tubby /'tʌbɪ/ *a* (**-ier**, **-iest**) rechoncho

tube /tju:b/ *n* tubo *m*; (Ⓘ, Rail) metro *m*; (Amer Ⓘ, television) tele *f*. **inner ~** *n* cámara *f* de aire

tuberculosis /tju:bɜ:kjʊ'ləʊsɪs/ *n* tuberculosis *f*

tub|ing /'tju:bɪŋ/ *n* tubería *f*. **~ular** /-jʊlə(r)/ *a* tubular

tuck /tʌk/ *n* (fold) jareta *f*. ● *vt* plegar; (put) meter. □ **~ in(to)** *vi* (Ⓘ, eat) ponerse a comer. □ **~ up** *vt* arropar <*child*>

Tuesday /'tju:zdeɪ/ *n* martes *m*

tuft /tʌft/ *n* (of hair) mechón *m*; (of feathers) penacho *m*; (of grass) mata *f*

tug /tʌg/ *vt* (*pt* **tugged**) tirar de. ● *vi*. **~ at sth** tirar de algo. ● *n* tirón *m*; (Naut) remolcador *m*. **~-of-war** *n juego de tira y afloja*

tuition /tju:'ɪʃn/ *n* clases *fpl*

tulip /'tju:lɪp/ *n* tulipán *m*

tumble /'tʌmbl/ *vi* caerse. ● *n* caída *f*. **~down** *a* en ruinas. **~-drier** *n* secadora *f*. **~r** *n* (glass) vaso *m* (*de lados rectos*)

tummy /'tʌmɪ/ *n* Ⓘ barriga *f*

tumour /'tju:mə(r)/ *n* tumor *m*

tumult /'tju:mʌlt/ *n* tumulto *m*. **~uous** /-'mʌltjʊəs/ *a* <*applause*> apoteósico

tuna /'tju:nə/ *n* (*pl* **tuna**) atún *m*

tune /tju:n/ *n* melodía *f*; (piece) tonada *f*. **be in ~** estar afinado. **be out of ~** estar desafinado. ● *vt* afinar, sintonizar <*radio, TV*>; (Mec) poner a punto. ● *vi*. **~ in** (**to**) sintonizar (con). □ **~ up** *vt/i* afinar. **~ful** *a* melodioso. **~r** *n* afinador *m*; (Radio) sintonizador *m*

tunic /'tju:nɪk/ *n* túnica *f*

tunnel /'tʌnl/ *n* túnel *m*. ● *vi* (*pt* **tunnelled**) abrir un túnel

turban /'tɜ:bən/ *n* turbante *m*

turbine /'tɜ:baɪn/ *n* turbina *f*

turbo /'tɜ:bəʊ/ *n* (*pl* **-os**) turbo(compresor) *m*

turbulen|ce /'tɜ:bjʊləns/ *n* turbulencia *f*. **~t** *a* turbulento

turf /tɜ:f/ *n* (*pl* **turfs** *or* **turves**) césped *m*; (segment of grass) tepe *m*. □ **~ out** *vt* Ⓘ echar

turgid /'tɜ:dʒɪd/ *a* <*language*> ampuloso

turkey /'tɜːkɪ/ *n* (*pl* **-eys**) pavo *m*

Turk|ey /'tɜːkɪ/ *f* Turquía *f.* **~ish** *a & n* turco (*m*)

turmoil /'tɜːmɔɪl/ *n* confusión *f*

turn /tɜːn/ *vt* hacer girar; volver *<head, page>*; doblar *<corner>*; (change) cambiar; (deflect) desviar. **~ sth into sth** convertir *or* transformar algo en algo. ● *vi* *<handle>* girar, dar vueltas; *<person>* volverse, darse la vuelta. **~ right** girar *or* doblar *or* torcer a la derecha. **~ red** ponerse rojo. **~ into sth** convertirse en algo. ● *n* vuelta *f*; (in road) curva *f*; (change) giro *m*; (sequence) turno *m*; (🅸, of illness) ataque *m*. **good ~** favor *m*. **in ~** a su vez. □ **~ down** *vt* (fold) doblar; (reduce) bajar; (reject) rechazar. □ **~ off** *vt* cerrar *<tap>*; apagar *<light, TV, etc>*. *vi* (from road) doblar. □ **~ on** *vt* abrir *<tap>*; encender, prender (LAm) *<light etc>*. □ **~ out** *vt* apagar *<light etc>*. *vi* (result) resultar. □ **~ round** *vi* darse la vuelta. □ **~ up** *vi* aparecer. *vt* (find) encontrar; levantar *<collar>*; subir *<hem>*; acortar *<trousers>*; poner más fuerte *<gas>*. **~ed-up** *a* *<nose>* respingón. **~ing** *n* (in town) bocacalle *f*. **we've missed the ~ing** nos hemos pasado la calle (*or* carretera). **~ing-point** *n* momento *m* decisivo.

turnip /'tɜːnɪp/ *n* nabo *m*

turn: ~over *n* (Com) facturación *f*; (of staff) movimiento *m*. **~pike** *n* (Amer) autopista *f* de peaje. **~stile** *n* torniquete *m*. **~table** *n* platina *f*. **~-up** *n* (of trousers) vuelta *f*, valenciana *f* (Mex)

turquoise /'tɜːkwɔɪz/ *a & n* turquesa (*f*)

turret /'tʌrɪt/ *n* torrecilla *f*

turtle /'tɜːtl/ *n* tortuga *f* de mar (Amer, tortoise) tortuga *f*

turves /tɜːvz/ ⇒TURF

tusk /tʌsk/ *n* colmillo *m*

tussle /'tʌsl/ *n* lucha *f*

tutor /'tjuːtə(r)/ *n* profesor *m* particular

tuxedo /tʌk'siːdəʊ/ *n* (*pl* **-os**) (Amer) esmoquin *m*, smoking *m*

TV /tiː'viː/ *n* televisión *f*, tele *f* 🅸

twang /twæŋ/ *n* tañido *m*; (in voice) gangueo *m*

tweet /twiːt/ *n* piada *f*. ● *vi* piar

tweezers /'twiːzəz/ *npl* pinzas *fpl*

twel|fth /twelfθ/ *a* duodécimo. ● *n* doceavo *m*. **~ve** /twelv/ *a & n* doce (*m*)

twent|ieth /'twentɪəθ/ *a* vigésimo. ● *n* veinteavo *m*. **~y** /'twentɪ/ *a & n* veinte (*m*)

twice /twaɪs/ *adv* dos veces. **~ as many people** el doble de gente

twiddle /'twɪdl/ *vt* (hacer) girar

twig /twɪg/ *n* ramita *f*. ● *vi* (*p* **twigged**) 🅸 caer, darse cuenta

twilight /'twaɪlaɪt/ *n* crepúsculo *m*

twin /twɪn/ *a & n* gemelo (*m*), mellizo (*m*) (LAm)

twine /twaɪn/ *n* cordel *m*, bramante *m*

twinge /twɪndʒ/ *n* punzada *f*; (of remorse) punzada *f*

twinkle /'twɪŋkl/ *vi* centellear ● *n* centelleo *m*; (in eye) brillo *m*

twirl /twɜːl/ *vt* (hacer) girar. ● *vi* girar. ● *n* vuelta *f*

twist /twɪst/ *vt* retorcer; (roll) enrollar; girar *<knob>*; tergiversar *<words>*; (distort) retorcer. **~ one's ankle** torcerse el tobillo. ● *vi* *<rope, wire>* enrollarse; *<road, river>*

serpentear. ● *n* torsión *f*; (curve) vuelta *f*

twit /twɪt/ *n* [T] imbécil *m*

twitch /twɪtʃ/ *vi* moverse. ● *n* tic *m*

twitter /ˈtwɪtə(r)/ *vi* gorjear

two /tuː/ *a* & *n* dos (*m*). **~-bit** *a* (Amer) de tres al cuarto. **~-faced** *a* falso, insincero. **~fold** *a* doble. ● *adv* dos veces. **~pence** /ˈtʌpəns/ *n* dos peniques *mpl*. **~-piece** (**suit**) *n* traje *m* de dos piezas. **~-way** *a* <*traffic*> de doble sentido

tycoon /taɪˈkuːn/ *n* magnate *m*

tying /ˈtaɪɪŋ/ ⇒TIE

type /taɪp/ *n* tipo *m*. ● *vt/i* escribir a máquina. **~-cast** *a* <*actor*> encasillado. **~script** *n* texto *m* mecanografiado, manuscrito *m* (*de una obra, novela etc*). **~writer** *n* máquina *f* de escribir. **~written** *a* escrito a máquina, mecanografiado

typhoon /taɪˈfuːn/ *n* tifón *m*

typical /ˈtɪpɪkl/ *a* típico. **~ly** *adv* típicamente

typify /ˈtɪpɪfaɪ/ *vt* tipificar

typi|ng /ˈtaɪpɪŋ/ *n* mecanografía *f*. **~st** *n* mecanógrafo *m*

tyran|nical /tɪˈrænɪkl/ *a* tiránico. **~ny** /ˈtɪrənɪ/ *n* tiranía *f*. **~t** /ˈtaɪərənt/ *n* tirano *m*

tyre /ˈtaɪə(r)/ *n* neumático *m*, llanta *f* (LAm)

Uu

udder /ˈʌdə(r)/ *n* ubre *f*

UFO /ˈjuːfəʊ/ *abbr* (= **unidentified flying object**) OVNI *m* (*objeto volante no identificado*)

ugly /ˈʌglɪ/ *a* (**-ier**, **-iest**) feo

UK /juːˈkeɪ/ *abbr* (= **United Kingdom**) Reino *m* Unido

Ukraine /juːˈkreɪn/ *n* Ucrania *f*

ulcer /ˈʌlsə(r)/ *n* úlcera *f*; (external) llaga *f*

ultimate /ˈʌltɪmət/ *a* (eventual) final; (utmost) máximo. **~ly** *adv* en última instancia; (in the long run) a la larga

ultimatum /ʌltɪˈmeɪtəm/ *n* (*pl* **-ums**) ultimátum *m*

ultra... /ˈʌltrə/ *pref* ultra... **~violet** /-ˈvaɪələt/ *a* ultravioleta

umbilical cord /ʌmˈbɪlɪkl/ *n* cordón *m* umbilical

umbrella /ʌmˈbrelə/ *n* paraguas *m*

umpire /ˈʌmpaɪə(r)/ *n* árbitro *m*. ● *vt* arbitrar

umpteen /ˈʌmptiːn/ *a* [T] tropecientos [T]. **~th** *a* [T] enésimo

un... /ʌn/ *pref* in..., des..., no, poco, sin

UN /juːˈen/ *abbr* (= **United Nations**) ONU *f* (*Organización de las Naciones Unidas*)

unable /ʌnˈeɪbl/ *a*. **be ~ to** no poder; (be incapable of) ser incapaz de

unacceptable /ʌnək'septəbl/ *a* <*behaviour*> inaceptable; <*terms*> inadmisible

unaccompanied /ʌnə'kʌmpənɪd/ *a* <*luggage*> no acompañado; <*person, instrument*> solo; <*singing*> sin acompañamiento

unaccustomed /ʌnə'kʌstəmd/ *a* desacostumbrado. **be ~ to** *a* no estar acostumbrado a

unaffected /ʌnə'fektɪd/ *a* natural

unaided /ʌn'eɪdɪd/ *a* sin ayuda

unanimous /ju:'nænɪməs/ *a* unánime. **~ly** *adv* unánimemente; <*elect*> por unanimidad

unarmed /ʌn'ɑ:md/ *a* desarmado

unattended /ʌnə'tendɪd/ *a* sin vigilar

unattractive /ʌnə'træktɪv/ *a* poco atractivo

unavoidabl|e /ʌnə'vɔɪdəbl/ *a* inevitable. **~y** *adv*. **I was ~y delayed** no pude evitar llegar tarde

unaware /ʌnə'weə(r)/ *a*. **be ~ of** ignorar, no ser consciente de. **~s** /-eəz/ *adv* desprevenido

unbearabl|e /ʌn'beərəbl/ *a* insoportable, inaguantable. **~y** *adv* inaguantablemente

unbeat|able /ʌn'bi:təbl/ *a* <*quality*> insuperable; <*team*> invencible. **~en** *a* no vencido; <*record*> insuperado

unbelievabl|e /ʌnbɪ'li:vəbl/ *a* increíble. **~y** *adv* increíblemente

unbiased /ʌn'baɪəst/ *a* imparcial

unblock /ʌn'blɒk/ *vt* desatascar

unbolt /ʌn'bəʊlt/ *vt* descorrer el pestillo de

unborn /ʌn'bɔ:n/ *a* que todavía no ha nacido

unbreakable /ʌn'breɪkəbl/ *a* irrompible

unbroken /ʌn'brəʊkən/ *a* (intact) intacto; (continuous) ininterrumpido

unbutton /ʌn'bʌtn/ *vt* desabotonar, desabrochar

uncalled-for /ʌn'kɔ:ldfɔ:(r)/ *a* fuera de lugar

uncanny /ʌn'kænɪ/ *a* (**-ier, -iest**) raro, extraño

uncertain /ʌn'sɜ:tn/ *a* incierto; (hesitant) vacilante. **be ~ of/about sth** no estar seguro de algo. **~ty** *n* incertidumbre *f*

uncharitable /ʌn'tʃærɪtəbl/ *a* severo

uncivilized /ʌn'sɪvɪlaɪzd/ *a* incivilizado

uncle /'ʌŋkl/ *n* tío *m*

unclean /ʌn'kli:n/ *a* impuro

unclear /ʌn'klɪə(r)/ *a* poco claro

uncomfortable /ʌn'kʌmfətəbl/ *a* incómodo

uncommon /ʌn'kɒmən/ *a* poco común

uncompromising /ʌn'kɒmprəmaɪzɪŋ/ *a* intransigente

unconcerned /ʌnkən'sɜ:nd/ *a* indiferente

unconditional /ʌnkən'dɪʃənl/ *a* incondicional

unconnected /ʌnkə'nektɪd/ *a* (unrelated) sin conexión. **the events are ~** estos acontecimientos no guardan ninguna relación (entre sí)

unconscious /ʌn'kɒnʃəs/ *a* (Med) inconsciente. **~ly** *adv* inconscientemente

unconventional /ʌnkən'venʃənl/ *a* poco convencional

uncork /ʌn'kɔ:k/ *vt* descorchar

uncouth /ʌn'ku:θ/ *a* zafio

uncover /ʌn'kʌvə(r)/ *vt* destapar; revelar <*plot, scandal*>

undaunted /ʌn'dɔ:ntɪd/ *a* impertérrito

undecided /ʌndɪ'saɪdɪd/ *a* indeciso

undeniabl|e /ʌndɪ'naɪəbl/ *a* innegable. **~y** *adv* sin lugar a dudas

under /'ʌndə(r)/ *prep* debajo de; (less than) menos de; <*heading*> bajo; (according to) según; (expressing movement) por debajo de. ● *adv* debajo, abajo

under... *pref* sub...

under: ~carriage *n* (Aviat) tren *m* de aterrizaje. **~charge** *vt* /-'tʃɑ:dʒ/ cobrarle de menos a. **~clothes** *npl* ropa *f* interior. **~coat**, **~coating** (Amer) *n* (paint) pintura *f* base; (first coat) primera mano *f* de pintura. **~cover** *a* /-'kʌvə(r)/ secreto. **~current** *n* corriente *f* submarina. **~dog** *n*. **the ~dog** el que tiene menos posibilidades. **the ~dogs** *npl* los de abajo. **~done** *a* /-'dʌn/ <*meat*> poco hecho. **~estimate** /-'estɪmeɪt/ *vt* (underrate) subestimar. **~fed** /-'fed/ *a* subalimentado. **~foot** /-'fʊt/ *adv* debajo de los pies. **~go** *vt* (*pt* **-went**, *pp* **-gone**) sufrir. **~graduate** /-'grædjʊət/ *n* estudiante *m* & *f* universitario (no licenciado). **~ground** /-'graʊnd/ *adv* bajo tierra; (in secret) clandestinamente. ● /-graʊnd/ *a* subterráneo; (secret) clandestino. ● *n* metro *m*. **~growth** *n* maleza *f*. **~hand** /-'hænd/ *a* (secret) clandestino; (deceptive) fraudulento. **~lie** /-'laɪ/ *vt* (*pt* **-lay**, *pp* **-lain**, *pres p* **-lying**) subyacer a. **~line** /-'laɪn/ *vt* subrayar. **~lying** /-'laɪɪŋ/ *a* subyacente. **~mine** /-'maɪn/ *vt* socavar. **~neath** /-'ni:θ/ *prep* debajo de, abajo de (LAm). ● *adv* por debajo. **~paid** /-'peɪd/ *a* mal pagado. **~pants** *npl* calzoncillos *mpl*. **~pass** *n* paso *m* subterráneo; (for traffic) paso *m* inferior. **~privileged** /-'prɪvəlɪdʒd/ *a* desfavorecido. **~rate** /-'reɪt/ *vt* subestimar. **~rated** /-'reɪtɪd/ *a* no debidamente apreciado. **~shirt** *n* (Amer) camiseta *f* (interior).

understand /ʌndə'stænd/ *vt* (*pt* **-stood**) entender; (empathize with) comprender, entender. ● *vi* entender, comprender. **~able** *a* comprensible. **~ing** *a* comprensivo. ● *n* (grasp) entendimiento *m*; (sympathy) comprensión *f*; (agreement) acuerdo *m*

under: ~statement *n* subestimación *f*. **~take** /-'teɪk/ (*pt* **-took**, *pp* **-taken**) emprender <*task*>; asumir <*responsibility*>. **~take to do sth** comprometerse a hacer algo. **~taker** *n* director *m* de pompas fúnebres. **~taking** /-'teɪkɪŋ/ *n* empresa *f*; (promise) promesa *f*. **~tone** *n*. **in an ~tone** en voz baja. **~value** /-'vælju:/ *vt* subvalorar. **~water** /-'wɔ:tə(r)/ *a* submarino. ● *adv* debajo del agua. **~wear** *n* ropa *f* interior. **~weight** /-'weɪt/ *a* de peso más bajo que el normal. **~went** /-'went/ ⇒UNDERGO. **~world** *n* (criminals) hampa *f*. **~write** /-'raɪt/ *vt* (*pt* **-wrote**, *pp* **-written**) (Com) asegurar; (guarantee financially) financiar

undeserved /ʌndɪ'zɜ:vd/ *a* inmerecido

undesirable /ʌndɪ'zaɪərəbl/ *a* indeseable

undignified /ʌn'dɪgnɪfaɪd/ *a* indecoroso

undisputed /ʌndɪs'pju:tɪd/ *a* *<champion>* indiscutido; *<facts>* innegable

undo /ʌn'du:/ *vt* (*pt* **-did**, *pp* **-done**) desabrochar *<button, jacket>*; abrir *<zip>*; desatar *<knot, laces>*

undoubted /ʌn'daʊtɪd/ *a* indudable. **~ly** *adv* indudablemente, sin duda

undress /ʌn'dres/ *vt* desvestir, desnudar. ● *vi* desvestirse, desnudarse

undue /ʌn'dju:/ *a* excesivo

undulate /'ʌndjʊleɪt/ *vi* ondular

unduly /ʌn'dju:lɪ/ *adv* excesivamente

unearth /ʌn'ɜ:θ/ *vt* desenterrar; descubrir *<document>*

unearthly /ʌn'ɜ:θlɪ/ *a* sobrenatural. **at an ~ hour** a estas horas intempestivas

uneasy /ʌn'i:zɪ/ *a* incómodo

uneconomic /ʌni:kə'nɒmɪk/ *a* poco económico

uneducated /ʌn'edjʊkeɪtɪd/ *a* sin educación

unemploy|ed /ʌnɪm'plɔɪd/ *a* desempleado, parado. **~ment** *n* desempleo *m*, paro *m*

unending /ʌn'endɪŋ/ *a* interminable, sin fin

unequal /ʌn'i:kwəl/ *a* desigual

unequivocal /ʌnɪ'kwɪvəkl/ *a* inequívoco

unethical /ʌn'eθɪkl/ *a* poco ético, inmoral

uneven /ʌn'i:vn/ *a* desigual

unexpected /ʌnɪk'spektɪd/ *a* inesperado; *<result>* imprevisto. **~ly** *adv* *<arrive>* de improviso; *<happen>* de forma imprevista

unfair /ʌn'feə(r)/ *a* injusto; improcedente *<dismissal>*. **~ly** *adv* injustamente

unfaithful /ʌn'feɪθfl/ *a* infiel

unfamiliar /ʌnfə'mɪlɪə(r)/ *a* desconocido. **be ~ with** desconocer

unfasten /ʌn'fɑ:sn/ *vt* desabrochar *<clothes>*; (untie) desatar

unfavourable /ʌn'feɪvərəbl/ *a* desfavorable

unfeeling /ʌn'fi:lɪŋ/ *a* insensible

unfit /ʌn'fɪt/ *a*. **I'm ~** no estoy en forma. **~ for human consumption** no apto para el consumo

unfold /ʌn'fəʊld/ *vt* desdoblar; desplegar *<wings>*; (fig) revelar. ● *vi* *<leaf>* abrirse; *<events>* desarrollarse

unforeseen /ʌnfɔ:'si:n/ *a* imprevisto

unforgettable /ʌnfə'getəbl/ *a* inolvidable

unforgivable /ʌnfə'gɪvəbl/ *a* imperdonable

unfortunate /ʌn'fɔ:tʃənət/ *a* desafortunado; (regrettable) lamentable. **~ly** *adv* desafortunadamente; (stronger) por desgracia, desgraciadamente

unfounded /ʌn'faʊndɪd/ *a* infundado

unfriendly /ʌn'frendlɪ/ *a* poco amistoso; (stronger) antipático

unfurl /ʌn'fɜ:l/ *vt* desplegar

ungainly /ʌn'geɪnlɪ/ *a* desgarbado

ungrateful /ʌn'greɪtfl/ *a* desagradecido, ingrato

unhapp|iness /ʌn'hæpɪnes/ *n* infelicidad *f*, tristeza *f*. **~y** *a* (**-ier**, **-iest**) infeliz, triste; (unsuitable) inoportuno. **be ~y about sth** no estar contento con algo

unharmed /ʌn'hɑ:md/ *a* *<person>* ileso

unhealthy /ʌn'helθɪ/ *a* (**-ier**, **-iest**) *<person>* de mala salud; *<complexion>* enfermizo; *<conditions>* poco saludable

unhurt /ʌn'hɜːt/ *a* ileso

unification /juːnɪfɪ'keɪʃn/ *n* unificación *f*

uniform /'juːnɪfɔːm/ *a & n* uniforme (*m*). **~ity** /-'fɔːmətɪ/ *n* uniformidad *f*

unify /'juːnɪfaɪ/ *vt* unir

unilateral /juːnɪ'lætərəl/ *a* unilateral

unimaginable /ʌnɪ'mædʒɪnəbl/ *a* inimaginable

unimaginative /ʌnɪ'mædʒɪnətɪv/ *a* *<person>* poco imaginativo

unimportant /ʌnɪm'pɔːtnt/ *a* sin importancia

uninhabited /ʌnɪn'hæbɪtɪd/ *a* deshabitado; *<island>* despoblado

unintelligible /ʌnɪn'telɪdʒəbl/ *a* ininteligible

unintentional /ʌnɪn'tenʃənl/ *a* involuntario

union /'juːnjən/ *n* unión *f*; (trade union) sindicato *m*; (student ~) asociación *f* de estudiantes. **U~ Jack** *n* bandera *f* del Reino Unido

unique /juː'niːk/ *a* único

unison /'juːnɪsn/ *n*. **in ~** al unísono

unit /'juːnɪt/ *n* unidad *f*; (of furniture etc) módulo *m*; (in course) módulo *m*

unite /juː'naɪt/ *vt* unir. ● *vi* unirse. **U~d Kingdom** *n* Reino *m* Unido. **U~d Nations** *n* Organización *f* de las Naciones Unidas (ONU). **U~d States (of America)** *n* Estados *mpl* Unidos (de América)

unity /'juːnɪtɪ/ *n* unidad *f*

univers|al /juːnɪ'vɜːsl/ *a* universal. **~e** /'juːnɪvɜːs/ *n* universo *m*

university /juːnɪ'vɜːsətɪ/ *n* universidad *f*. ● *a* universitario

unjust /ʌn'dʒʌst/ *a* injusto. **~ified** /-ɪfaɪd/ *a* injustificado

unkind /ʌn'kaɪnd/ *a* poco amable; (cruel) cruel; *<remark>* hiriente

unknown /ʌn'nəʊn/ *a* desconocido

unlawful /ʌn'lɔːfl/ *a* ilegal

unleaded /ʌn'ledɪd/ *a* *<fuel>* sin plomo

unleash /ʌn'liːʃ/ *vt* soltar

unless /ʌn'les, ən'les/ *conj* a menos que, a no ser que

unlike /ʌn'laɪk/ *prep* diferente de. (in contrast to) a diferencia de. **~ly** *a* improbable

unlimited /ʌn'lɪmɪtɪd/ *a* ilimitado

unlisted /ʌn'lɪstɪd/ *a* (Amer) que no figura en la guía telefónica, privado (Mex)

unload /ʌn'ləʊd/ *vt* descargar

unlock /ʌn'lɒk/ *vt* abrir (con llave)

unluck|ily /ʌn'lʌkɪlɪ/ *adv* desgraciadamente. **~y** *a* (**-ier**, **-iest**) *<person>* sin suerte, desafortunado. **be ~y** tener mala suerte; (bring bad luck) traer mala suerte

unmarried /ʌn'mærɪd/ *a* soltero

unmask /ʌn'mɑːsk/ *vt* desenmascarar

unmentionable /ʌn'menʃənəbl/ *a* inmencionable

unmistakable /ʌnmɪ'steɪkəbl/ *a* inconfundible

unnatural /ʌn'nætʃərəl/ *a* poco natural; (not normal) anormal

unnecessar|ily /ʌn'nesəsərɪlɪ/ *adv* innecesariamente. **~y** *a* innecesario

unnerve /ʌn'nɜːv/ *vt* desconcertar

unnoticed /ʌn'nəʊtɪst/ *a* inadvertido

unobtainable /ʌnəb'teɪnəbl/ *a* imposible de conseguir

unobtrusive /ʌnəb'tru:sɪv/ *a* discreto

unofficial /ʌnə'fɪʃl/ *a* no oficial. **~ly** *adv* extraoficialmente

unpack /ʌn'pæk/ *vt* sacar las cosas de <*bags*>; deshacer, desempacar (LAm) <*suitcase*>. ● *vi* deshacer las maletas

unpaid /ʌn'peɪd/ *a* <*work*> no retribuido, no remunerado; <*leave*> sin sueldo

unperturbed /ʌnpə'tɜ:bd/ *a* impasible. **he carried on ~** siguió sin inmutarse

unpleasant /ʌn'pleznt/ *a* desagradable

unplug /ʌn'plʌg/ *vt* desenchufar

unpopular /ʌn'pɒpjʊlə(r)/ *a* impopular

unprecedented /ʌn'presɪdentɪd/ *a* sin precedentes

unpredictable /ʌnprɪ'dɪktəbl/ *a* imprevisible

unprepared /ʌnprɪ'peəd/ *a* no preparado; (unready) desprevenido

unprofessional /ʌnprə'feʃənəl/ *a* poco profesional

unprofitable /ʌn'prɒfɪtəbl/ *a* no rentable

unprotected /ʌnprə'tektɪd/ *a* sin protección; <*sex*> sin el uso de preservativos

unqualified /ʌn'kwɒlɪfaɪd/ *a* sin título; (fig) absoluto

unquestion|able /ʌn'kwestʃənəbl/ *a* incuestionable, innegable. **~ing** *a* <*obedience*> ciego; <*loyalty*> incondicional

unravel /ʌn'rævl/ *vt* (*pt* **unravelled**) desenredar; desentrañar <*mystery*>

unreal /ʌn'rɪəl/ *a* irreal. **~istic** /-'lɪstɪk/ *a* poco realista

unreasonable /ʌn'ri:zənəbl/ *a* irrazonable

unrecognizable /ʌnrekəg'naɪzəbl/ *a* irreconocible

unrelated /ʌnrɪ'leɪtɪd/ *a* <*facts*> no relacionados (entre sí); <*people*> no emparentado

unreliable /ʌnrɪ'laɪəbl/ *a* <*person*> informal; <*machine*> poco fiable; <*information*> poco fidedigno

unrepentant /ʌnrɪ'pentənt/ *a* impenitente

unrest /ʌn'rest/ *n* (discontent) descontento *m*; (disturbances) disturbios *mpl*

unrivalled /ʌn'raɪvld/ *a* incomparable

unroll /ʌn'rəʊl/ *vt* desenrollar. ● *vi* desenrollarse

unruffled /ʌn'rʌfld/ <*person*> sereno

unruly /ʌn'ru:lɪ/ *a* <*class*> indisciplinado; <*child*> revoltoso

unsafe /ʌn'seɪf/ *a* inseguro

unsatisfactory /ʌnsætɪs'fæktərɪ/ *a* insatisfactorio

unsavoury /ʌn'seɪvərɪ/ *a* desagradable

unscathed /ʌn'skeɪðd/ *a* ileso

unscheduled /ʌn'ʃedju:ld/ *a* no programado, no previsto

unscrew /ʌn'skru:/ *vt* destornillar; desenroscar <*lid*>

unscrupulous /ʌn'skru:pjʊləs/ *a* inescrupuloso

unseemly /ʌn'si:mlɪ/ *a* indecoroso

unseen /ʌn'si:n/ *a* *<danger>* oculto; (unnoticed) sin ser visto

unselfish /ʌn'selfɪʃ/ *a* *<act>* desinteresado; *<person>* nada egoísta

unsettle /ʌn'setl/ *vt* desestabilizar *<situation>*; alterar *<plans>*. **~d** *a* agitado; *<weather>* inestable; (undecided) pendiente (de resolución)

unshakeable /ʌn'ʃeɪkəbl/ *a* inquebrantable

unshaven /ʌn'ʃeɪvn/ *a* sin afeitar, sin rasurar (Mex)

unsightly /ʌn'saɪtlɪ/ *a* feo

unskilled /ʌn'skɪld/ *a* *<work>* no especializado; *<worker>* no cualificado, no calificado

unsociable /ʌn'səʊʃəbl/ *a* insociable

unsolved /ʌn'sɒlvd/ *a* no resuelto; *<murder>* sin esclarecerse

unsophisticated /ʌnsə'fɪstɪkeɪtɪd/ *a* sencillo

unsound /ʌn'saʊnd/ *a* poco sólido

unspecified /ʌn'spesɪfaɪd/ *a* no especificado

unstable /ʌn'steɪbl/ *a* inestable

unsteady /ʌn'stedɪ/ *a* inestable, poco firme

unstuck /ʌn'stʌk/ *a* despegado. **come ~** despegarse; (fail) fracasar

unsuccessful /ʌnsək'sesfʊl/ *a* *<attempt>* infructuoso. **be ~** no tener éxito, fracasar

unsuitable /ʌn'su:təbl/ *a* *<clothing>* poco apropiado, poco adecuado; *<time>* inconveniente. **she is ~ for the job** no es la persona indicada para el trabajo

unsure /ʌn'ʃʊə(r)/ *a* inseguro

unthinkable /ʌn'θɪŋkəbl/ *a* inconcebible

untid|iness /ʌn'taɪdɪnəs/ *n* desorden *m*. **~y** *a* (**-ier**, **-iest**) desordenado; *<appearance, writing>* descuidado

untie /ʌn'taɪ/ *vt* desatar, desamarrar (LAm)

until /ən'tɪl, ʌn'tɪl/ *prep* hasta. ● *conj* hasta que

untold /ʌn'təʊld/ *a* incalculable

untouched /ʌn'tʌtʃt/ *a* intacto

untried /ʌn'traɪd/ *a* no probado

untrue /ʌn'tru:/ *a* falso

unused /ʌn'ju:zd/ *a* nuevo. ● /ʌn'ju:st/ *a*. **~ to** no acostumbrado a

unusual /ʌn'ju:ʒʊəl/ *a* poco común, poco corriente. **it's ~ to see so many people** es raro ver a tanta gente. **~ly** *adv* excepcionalmente, inusitadamente

unveil /ʌn'veɪl/ *vt* descubrir

unwanted /ʌn'wɒntɪd/ *a* superfluo; *<child>* no deseado

unwelcome /ʌn'welkəm/ *a* *<news>* poco grato; *<guest>* inoportuno

unwell /ʌn'wel/ *a* indispuesto

unwieldy /ʌn'wi:ldɪ/ *a* pesado y difícil de manejar

unwilling /ʌn'wɪlɪŋ/ *a* mal dispuesto. **be ~** no querer

unwind /ʌn'waɪnd/ *vt* (*pt* **unwound**) desenrollar. ● *vi* (◻, relax) relajarse

unwise /ʌn'waɪz/ *a* poco sensato

unworthy /ʌn'wɜ:ðɪ/ *a* indigno

unwrap /ʌn'ræp/ *vt* (*pt* **unwrapped**) desenvolver

unwritten /ʌn'rɪtn/ *a* no escrito; *<agreement>* verbal

up /ʌp/ *adv* arriba; (upwards) hacia arriba; (higher) más arriba. **~ here** aquí arriba. **~ there** allí arriba. **~**

to hasta. **he's not ~ yet** todavía no se ha levantado. **be ~ against** enfrentarse con. **come ~** subir. **go ~** subir. **he's not ~ to the job** no tiene las condiciones necesarias para el trabajo. **it's ~ to you** depende de ti. **what's ~?** ¿qué pasa? ● *prep*. **go ~ the stairs** subir la escalera. **it's just ~ the road** está un poco más allá. ● *vt* (*pt* **upped**) aumentar. ● *n*. **~s and downs** *npl* altibajos *mpl*; (of life) vicisitudes *fpl*. **~bringing** /'ʌpbrɪŋɪŋ/ *n* educación *f*. **~date** /ʌp'deɪt/ *vt* poner al día. **~grade** /ʌp'greɪd/ *vt* elevar de categoría <*person*>; mejorar <*equipment*>. **~heaval** /ʌp'hi:vl/ *n* trastorno *m*. **~hill** /ʌp'hɪl/ *adv* cuesta arriba. **~hold** /ʌp'həʊld/ *vt* (*pt* **upheld**) mantener <*principle*>; confirmar <*decision*>. **~holster** /ʌp'həʊlstə(r)/ *vt* tapizar. **~holstery** *n* tapicería *f*. **~keep** *n* mantenimiento *m*. **~-market** /ʌp'mɑ:kɪt/ *a* de categoría

upon /ə'pɒn/ *prep* sobre. **once ~ a time** érase una vez

upper /'ʌpə(r)/ *a* superior. **~ class** *n* clase *f* alta

up: ~right *a* vertical; <*citizen*> recto. **place sth ~right** poner algo de pie. **~rising** /'ʌpraɪzɪŋ/ *n* levantamiento *m*. **~roar** *n* tumulto *m*

upset /ʌp'set/ *vt* (*pt* **upset**, *pres p* **upsetting**) (hurt) disgustar; (offend) ofender; (distress) alterar; desbaratar <*plans*>. ● *a* (hurt) disgustado; (distressed) alterado; (offended) ofendido; (disappointed) desilusionado. ● /'ʌpset/ *n* trastorno *m*. **have a stomach ~** estar mal del estómago

up: ~shot *n* resultado *m*. **~side down** /ʌpsaɪd'daʊn/ *adv* al revés (*con la parte de arriba abajo*); (in disorder) patas arriba. **turn sth ~side down** poner algo boca abajo. **~stairs** /ʌp'steəz/ *adv* arriba. **go ~stairs** subir. ● /'ʌpsteəz/ *a* de arriba. **~start** *n* advenedizo *m*. **~state** *adv* (Amer). **I live ~state** vivo en el norte del estado. **~stream** /ʌp'stri:m/ *adv* río arriba. **~take** *n*. **be quick on the ~take** agarrar las cosas al vuelo. **~-to-date** /ʌptə'deɪt/ *a* al día; <*news*> de última hora. **~turn** *n* repunte *m*, mejora *f*. **~ward** /'ʌpwəd/ *a* <*movement*> ascendente; <*direction*> hacia arriba. ● *adv* hacia arriba. **~wards** *adv* hacia arriba

uranium /jʊ'reɪnɪəm/ *n* uranio *m*

Uranus /'jʊərənəs/, /jʊə'reɪnəs/ *n* Urano *m*

urban /'ɜ:bən/ *a* urbano

urchin /'ɜ:tʃɪn/ *n* pilluelo *m*

urge /ɜ:dʒ/ *vt* instar. **~ s.o. to do sth** instar a uno a quehaga algo ● *n* impulso *m*; (wish, whim) ganas *fpl*. □ **~ on** *vt* animar

urgen|cy /'ɜ:dʒənsɪ/ *n* urgencia *f*. **~t** *a* urgente. **~tly** *adv* urgentemente, con urgencia

urin|ate /'jʊərɪneɪt/ *vi* orinar. **~e** /'jʊərɪn/ *n* orina *f*

Uruguay /jʊərəgwaɪ/ *n* Uruguay *m*. **~an** *a* & *n* uruguayo (*m*)

us /ʌs, əs/ *pron* nos; (*after prep*) nosotros *m*, nosotras *f*

US(A) /ju:es'eɪ/ *abbr* (= **United States (of America)**) EE.UU (*only written*), Estados *mpl* Unidos

usage /'ju:zɪdʒ/ *n* uso *m*

use /ju:z/ *vt* usar; utilizar <*service, facilities*>; consumir <*fuel*> ● /ju:s/ *n* uso *m*, empleo *m*. **be of ~** servir. **it is no ~** es inútil. □ **~ up**

vt agotar, consumir. **~d** /ju:zd/ *a* usado. ● /ju:st/ *v mod* **~ to. he ~d to say** decía, solía decir. **there ~d to be** (antes) había. ● *a* /ju:st/. **be ~d to** estar acostumbrado a. **~ful** /ˈju:sfl/ *a* útil. **~fully** *adv* útilmente. **~less** *a* inútil; *<person>* incompetente. **~r** /-zə(r)/ *n* usuario *m*. **drug ~** *n* consumidor *m* de drogas

usher /ˈʌʃə(r)/ *n* (in theatre etc) acomodador *m*. □ **~ in** *vt* hacer pasar; marcar el comienzo de *<new era>*. **~ette** /-ˈret/ *n* acomodadora *f*

USSR *abbr* (History) (= **Union of Soviet Socialist Republics**) URSS

usual /ˈju:ʒʊəl/ *a* usual; (habitual) acostumbrado, habitual; *<place, route>* de siempre. **as ~** como de costumbre, como siempre. **~ly** *adv* normalmente. **he ~ly wakes up early** suele despertarse temprano

utensil /ju:ˈtensl/ *n* utensilio *m*

utilize /ˈju:tɪlaɪz/ *vt* utilizar

utmost /ˈʌtməʊst/ *a* sumo. ● *n*. **do one's ~** hacer todo lo posible (to para)

utter /ˈʌtə(r)/ *a* completo. ● *vt* pronunciar *<word>*; dar *<cry>*. **~ly** *adv* totalmente

U-turn /ˈju:tɜ:n/ *n* cambio *m* de sentido

Vv

vacan|cy /ˈveɪkənsɪ/ *n* (job) vacante *f*; (room) habitación *f* libre. **~t** *a* *<building>* desocupado; *<seat>* libre; *<post>* vacante; *<look>* ausente

vacate /vəˈkeɪt/ *vt* dejar

vacation /vəˈkeɪʃn/ *n* (Amer) vacaciones *fpl*. **go on ~** ir de vacaciones. **~er** *n* (Amer) veraneante *m & f*

vaccin|ate /ˈvæksɪmeɪt/ *vt* vacunar. **~ation** /-ˈneɪʃn/ *n* vacunación *f*. **~e** /ˈvæksi:n/ *n* vacuna *f*

vacuum /ˈvækjʊəm/ *n* vacío *m*. **~ cleaner** *n* aspiradora *f*

vagina /vəˈdʒaɪnə/ *n* vagina *f*

vague /veɪg/ *a* (**-er**, **-est**) vago; *<outline>* borroso; *<person, expression>* despistado. **~ly** *adv* vagamente

vain /veɪn/ *a* (**-er**, **-est**) vanidoso; (useless) vano. **in ~** en vano

Valentine's Day /ˈvæləntaɪnz/ *n* el día de San Valentín

valiant /ˈvælɪənt/ *a* valeroso

valid /ˈvælɪd/ *a* válido. **~ate** /-eɪt/ *vt* dar validez a; validar *<contract>*. **~ity** /-ˈɪdətɪ/ *n* validez *f*

valley /ˈvælɪ/ *n* (*pl* **-eys**) valle *m*

valour /ˈvælə(r)/ *n* valor *m*

valu|able /ˈvæljʊəbl/ *a* valioso. **~ables** *npl* objetos *mpl* de valor. **~ation** /-ˈeɪʃn/ *n* valoración *f*. **~e** /ˈvælju:/ *n* valor *m*. ● *vt* valorar; tasar, valorar, avaluar (LAm) *<property>*. **~e added tax** *n* impuesto *m* sobre el valor añadido

valve /vælv/ *n* válvula *f*

vampire /'væmpaɪə(r)/ *n* vampiro *m*

van /væn/ *n* furgoneta *f*, camioneta *f*; (Rail) furgón *m*

vandal /'vændl/ *n* vándalo *m*. **~ism** *n* vandalismo *m*. **~ize** *vt* destruir

vanilla /və'nɪlə/ *n* vainilla *f*

vanish /'vænɪʃ/ *vi* desaparecer

vanity /'vænɪtɪ/ *n* vanidad *f*. **~ case** *n* neceser *m*

vapour /'veɪpə(r)/ *n* vapor *m*

varia|ble /'veərɪəbl/ *a* variable. **~nce** /-əns/ *n*. **at ~ce** en desacuerdo. **~nt** *n* variante *f*. **~tion** /-'eɪʃn/ *n* variación *f*

vari|ed /'veərɪd/ *a* variado. **~ety** /və'raɪətɪ/ *n* variedad *f*. **~ety show** *n* espectáculo *m* de variedades. **~ous** /'veərɪəs/ *a* (several) varios; (different) diversos

varnish /'vɑ:nɪʃ/ *n* barniz *m*; (for nails) esmalte *m*. ● *vt* barnizar; pintar <*nails*>

vary /'veərɪ/ *vt/i* variar

vase /vɑ:z/, (Amer) /veɪs/ *n* (for flowers) florero *m*; (ornamental) jarrón *m*

vast /vɑ:st/ *a* vasto, extenso; <*size*> inmenso. **~ly** *adv* infinitamente

vat /væt/ *n* cuba *f*

VAT /vi:er'ti:/ *abbr* (= **value added tax**) IVA *m*

vault /vɔ:lt/ *n* (roof) bóveda *f*; (in bank) cámara *f* acorazada; (tomb) cripta *f*. ● *vt/i* saltar

VCR *n* = **videocassette recorder**

VDU *n* = **visual display unit**

veal /vi:l/ *n* ternera *f*

veer /vɪə(r)/ *vi* dar un viraje, virar

vegeta|ble /'vedʒɪtəbl/ *a* vegetal. ● *n* verdura *f*. **~rian** /vedʒɪ'teərɪən/ *a* & *n* vegetariano (*m*). **~tion** /vedʒɪ'teɪʃn/ *n* vegetación *f*

vehement /'vi:əmənt/ *a* vehemente. **~tly** *adv* con vehemencia

vehicle /'vi:ɪkl/ *n* vehículo *m*

veil /veɪl/ *n* velo *m*

vein /veɪn/ *n* vena *f*; (in marble) veta *f*

velocity /vɪ'lɒsɪtɪ/ *n* velocidad *f*

velvet /'velvɪt/ *n* terciopelo *m*

vendetta /ven'detə/ *n* vendetta *f*

vend|ing machine /'vendɪŋ/ distribuidor *m* automático. **~or** /'vendə(r)/ *n* vendedor *m*

veneer /və'nɪə(r)/ *n* chapa *f*, enchapado *m*; (fig) barniz *m*, apariencia *f*

venerate /'venəreɪt/ *vt* venerar

venereal /və'nɪərɪəl/ *a* venéreo

Venetian blind /və'ni:ʃn/ *n* persiana *f* veneciana

Venezuela /venə'zweɪlə/ *n* Venezuela *f*. **~n** *a* & *n* venezolano (*m*)

vengeance /'vendʒəns/ venganza *f*. **with a ~** (fig) con ganas

venom /'venəm/ *n* veneno *m*. **~ous** *a* venenoso

vent /vent/ *n* (conducto *m* de) ventilación; (air ~) respiradero *m*. give ~ to dar rienda suelta a. ● descargar

ventilat|e /'ventɪleɪt/ *vt* ventilar. **~ion** /-'leɪʃn/ *n* ventilación *f*

ventriloquist /ven'trɪləkwɪst/ ventrílocuo *m*

venture /'ventʃə(r)/ *n* empresa *f*. ● *vt* aventurar. ● *vi* atreverse

venue /'venju:/ *n* (for concert) lugar *m* de actuación

Venus /'vi:nəs/ *n* Venus *m*

veranda /və'rændə/ *n* galería *f*

verb /vɜ:b/ *n* verbo *m*. **~al** *a* verbal.

verdict /ˈvɜ:dɪkt/ *n* veredicto *m*; (opinion) opinión *f*

verge /vɜ:dʒ/ *n* borde *m*. □ **~ on** *vt* rayar en

verify /ˈverɪfaɪ/ *vt* (confirm) confirmar; (check) verificar

vermin /ˈvɜ:mɪn/ *n* alimañas *fpl*

versatil|e /ˈvɜ:sətaɪl/ *a* versátil. **~ity** /-ˈtɪlətɪ/ *n* versatilidad *f*

verse /vɜ:s/ *n* estrofa *f*; (poetry) poesías *fpl*. **~d** /vɜ:st/ *a*. **be well-~ed in** ser muy versado en. **~ion** /ˈvɜ:ʃn/ *n* versión *f*

versus /ˈvɜ:səs/ *prep* contra

vertebra /ˈvɜ:tɪbrə/ *n* (*pl* **-brae** /-bri:/) vértebra *f*. **~te** /-brət/ *n* vertebrado *m*

vertical /ˈvɜ:tɪkl/ *a* & *n* vertical (*f*). **~ly** *adv* verticalmente

vertigo /ˈvɜ:tɪgəʊ/ *n* vértigo *m*

verve /vɜ:v/ *n* brío *m*

very /ˈverɪ/ *adv* muy. **~ much** muchísimo. **~ well** muy bien. **the ~ first** el primero de todos. ● *a* mismo. **the ~ thing** exactamente lo quehace falta

vessel /ˈvesl/ *n* (receptacle) recipiente *m*; (ship) navío *m*, nave *f*

vest /vest/ *n* camiseta *f*; (Amer) chaleco *m*.

vestige /ˈvestɪdʒ/ *n* vestigio *m*

vet /vet/ *n* veterinario *m*; (Amer 🄸, veteran) veterano *m*. ● *vt* (*pt* **vetted**) someter a investigación <*applicant*>

veteran /ˈvetərən/ *n* veterano *m*

veterinary /ˈvetərɪnərɪ/ *a* veterinario. **~ surgeon** *n* veterinario *m*

veto /ˈvi:təʊ/ *n* (*pl* **-oes**) veto *m*. ● *vt* vetar

vex /veks/ *vt* fastidiar

via /ˈvaɪə/ *prep* por, por vía de

viable /ˈvaɪəbl/ *a* viable

viaduct /ˈvaɪədʌkt/ *n* viaducto *m*

vibrat|e /vaɪˈbreɪt/ *vt/i* vibrar. **~ion** /-ʃn/ *n* vibración *f*

vicar /ˈvɪkə(r)/ *n* párroco *m*. **~age** /-rɪdʒ/ *n* casa *f* del párroco

vice /vaɪs/ *n* vicio *m*; (Tec) torno *m* de banco

vice versa /vaɪsɪˈvɜ:sə/ *adv* viceversa

vicinity /vɪˈsɪnɪtɪ/ *n* vecindad *f*. **in the ~ of** cerca de

vicious /ˈvɪʃəs/ *a* <*attack*> feroz; <*dog*> fiero; <*rumour*> malicioso. **~ circle** *n* círculo *m* vicioso

victim /ˈvɪktɪm/ *n* víctima *f*. **~ize** *vt* victimizar

victor /ˈvɪktə(r)/ *n* vencedor *m*

Victorian /vɪkˈtɔ:rɪən/ *a* victoriano

victor|ious /vɪkˈtɔ:rɪəs/ *a* <*army*> victorioso; <*team*> vencedor. **~y** /ˈvɪktərɪ/ *n* victoria *f*

video /ˈvɪdɪəʊ/*n* (*pl* **-os**) vídeo *m*, video *m* (LAm). **~ camera** *n* videocámara *f*. **~(cassette) recorder** *n* magnetoscopio *m*. **~tape** *n* videocassette *f*

vie /vaɪ/ *vi* (*pres p* **vying**) rivalizar

Vietnam /vjetˈnæm/ *n* Vietnam *m*. **~ese** *a* & *n* vietnamita (*m* & *f*)

view /vju:/ *n* vista *f*; (mental survey) visión *f* de conjunto; (opinion) opinión *f*. **in my ~** a mi juicio. **in ~ of** en vista de. **on ~** expuesto. ● *vt* ver <*scene, property*>; (consider) considerar. **~er** *n* (TV) televidente *m* & *f*. **~finder** *n* visor *m*. **~point** *n* punto *m* de vista

vigilance *n* vigilancia *f*. **~ant** *a* vigilante

vigo|rous /'vɪgərəs/ *a* enérgico; <*growth*> vigoroso. **~ur** /'vɪgə(r)/ *n* vigor *m*

vile /vaɪl/ *a* (base) vil; <*food*> asqueroso; <*weather, temper*> horrible

village /'vɪlɪdʒ/ *n* pueblo *m*; (small) aldea *f*. **~r** *n* vecino *m* del pueblo; (of small village) aldeano *m*

villain /'vɪlən/ *n* maleante *m & f*; (in story etc) villano *m*

vindicate /'vɪndɪkeɪt/ *vt* justificar

vindictive /vɪn'dɪktɪv/ *a* vengativo

vine /vaɪn/ *n* (on ground) vid *f*; (climbing) parra *f*

vinegar /'vɪnɪgə(r)/ *n* vinagre *m*

vineyard /'vɪnjəd/ *n* viña *f*

vintage /'vɪntɪdʒ/ *n* (year) cosecha *f*. ● *a* <*wine*> añejo; <*car*> de época

vinyl /'vaɪnɪl/ *n* vinilo *m*

viola /vɪ'əʊlə/ *n* viola *f*

violat|e /'vaɪəleɪt/ *vt* violar. **~ion** /-'leɪʃn/ *n* violación *f*

violen|ce /'vaɪələns/ *n* violencia *f*. **~t** *a* violento. **~tly** *adv* violentamente

violet /'vaɪələt/ *a & n* violeta (*f*); (colour) violeta (*m*)

violin /'vaɪəlɪn/ *n* violín *m*. **~ist** *n* violinista *m & f*

VIP /vi:aɪ'pi:/ *abbr* (= **very important person**) VIP *m*

viper /'vaɪpə(r)/ *n* víbora *f*

virgin /'vɜ:dʒɪn/ *a & n* virgen (*f*)

Virgo /'vɜ:gəʊ/ *n* Virgo *f*

virile /'vɪraɪl/ *a* viril

virtual /'vɜ:tʃʊəl/ *a*. **traffic is at a ~ standstill** el tráfico está prácticamente paralizado. **~ reality** *n* realidad *f* virtual. **~ly** *adv* prácticamente

virtue /'vɜ:tʃu:/ *n* virtud *f*. **by ~ of** en virtud de

virtuous /'vɜ:tʃʊəs/ *a* virtuoso

virulent /'vɪrʊlənt/ *a* virulento

virus /'vaɪərəs/ *n* (*pl* **-uses**) virus *m*

visa /'vi:zə/ *n* visado *m*, visa *f* (LAm)

vise /vaɪs/ *n* (Amer) torno *m* de banco

visib|ility /vɪzɪ'bɪlətɪ/ *n* visibilidad *f*. **~le** /'vɪzɪbl/ *a* visible; <*sign, improvement*> evidente

vision /'vɪʒn/ *n* visión *f*; (sight) vista *f*

visit /'vɪzɪt/ *vt* visitar; hacer una visita a <*person*>. ● *vi* hacer visitas. **~ with s.o.** (Amer) ir a ver a uno. ● *n* visita *f*. **pay s.o. a ~** hacerle una visita a uno. **~or** *n* visitante *m & f*; (guest) visita *f*

visor /'vaɪzə(r)/ *n* visera *f*

visual /'vɪʒjʊəl/ *a* visual. **~ize** *v* imaginar(se); (foresee) prever

vital /'vaɪtl/ *a* (essential) esencial; <*factor*> de vital importancia; <*organ*> vital. **~ity** /vaɪ'tælətɪ/ *n* vitalidad *f*

vitamin /'vɪtəmɪn/ *n* vitamina *f*.

vivacious /vɪ'veɪʃəs/ *a* vivaz

vivid /'vɪvɪd/ *a* vivo. **~ly** *adv* intensamente; (describe) gráficamente

vivisection /vɪvɪ'sekʃn/ *n* vivisección *f*

vocabulary /və'kæbjʊlərɪ/ *n* vocabulario *m*

vocal /'vəʊkl/ *a* vocal. **~ist** cantante *m & f*

vocation /vəʊ'keɪʃn/ *n* vocación *f*. **~al** *a* profesional

vociferous /və'sɪfərəs/ *a* vociferador

vogue /vəʊg/ *n* moda *f*, boga *f*

voice /vɔɪs/ *n* voz *f*. ● *vt* expresar

void /vɔɪd/ *a* (not valid) nulo. ● *n* vacío *m*

volatile /'vɒlətaɪl/ *a* volátil; <*person*> imprevisible

volcan|ic /vɒl'kænɪk/ *a* volcánico. **~o** /vɒl'keɪnəʊ/ *n* (*pl* **-oes**) volcán *m*

volley /'vɒlɪ/ *n* (*pl* **-eys**) (of gunfire) descarga *f* cerrada; (sport) volea *f*. **~ball** *n* vóleibol *m*

volt /vəʊlt/ *n* voltio *m*. **~age** /-ɪdʒ/ *n* voltaje *m*

volume /'vɒljuːm/ *n* volumen *m*; (book) tomo *m*

voluntar|ily /'vɒləntərəlɪ/ *adv* voluntariamente. **~y** *a* voluntario; <*organization*> de beneficencia

volunteer /vɒlən'tɪə(r)/ *n* voluntario *m*. ● *vt* ofrecer. ● *vi*. **~** (to) ofrecerse (a)

vomit /'vɒmɪt/ *vt/i* vomitar. ● *n* vómito *m*

voracious /və'reɪʃəs/ *a* voraz

vot|e /vəʊt/ *n* voto *m*; (right) derecho *m* al voto; (act) votación *f*. ● *vi* votar. **~er** *n* votante *m & f*. **~ing** *n* votación *f*

vouch /vaʊtʃ/ *vi*. **~ for s.o.** responder por uno. **~er** /-ə(r)/ *n* vale *m*

vow /vaʊ/ *n* voto *m*. ● *vi* jurar

vowel /'vaʊəl/ *n* vocal *f*

voyage /'vɔɪɪdʒ/ *n* viaje *m*; (by sea) travesía *f*

vulgar /'vʌlgə(r)/ *a* (coarse) grosero, vulgar; (tasteless) de mal gusto. **~ity** /-'gærətɪ/ *n* vulgaridad *f*

vulnerable /'vʌlnərəbl/ *a* vulnerable

vulture /'vʌltʃə(r)/ *n* buitre *m*

vying /'vaɪɪŋ/ ⇒VIE

Ww

W *abbr* (= **West**) O

wad /wɒd/ *n* (of notes) fajo *m*; (tied together) lío *m*; (papers) montón *m*

waddle /'wɒdl/ *vi* contonearse

wade /weɪd/ *vi* caminar (*por el agua etc*)

wafer /'weɪfə(r)/ *n* galleta *f* de barquillo

waffle /'wɒfl/ *n* [I] palabrería *f*. ● *vi* [I] divagar; (in essay, exam) meter paja [I]. ● *n* (Culin) gofre *m*, wafle *m* (LAm)

waft /wɒft/ *vi* flotar

wag /wæg/ *vt* (*pt* **wagged**) menear. ● *vi* menearse

wage /weɪdʒ/ *n* sueldo *m*. **~s** *npl* salario *m*, sueldo *m*. **~r** *n* apuesta *f*

waggle /'wægl/ *vt* menear. ● *vi* menearse

wagon /'wægən/ *n* carro *m*; (Rail) vagón *m*; (Amer, delivery truck) furgoneta *f* de reparto

wail /weɪl/ *vi* llorar

waist /weɪst/ *n* cintura *f*. **~coat** *n* chaleco *m*. **~line** *n* cintura *f*

wait /weɪt/ *vi* esperar; (at table) servir. **~ for** esperar. **~ on s.o.** atender a uno. ● *vt* (await) esperar <*chance, turn*>. **~ table** (Amer) servir a la mesa. **I can't ~ to see him** me muero de ganas de verlo. ● *n* espera *f*. **lie in ~** acechar

waiter /'weɪtə(r)/ *n* camarero *m*, mesero *m* (LAm)

wait: ~ing-list *n* lista *f* de espera. **~ing-room** *n* sala *f* de espera

waitress /'weɪtrɪs/ *n* camarera *f*, mesera *f* (LAm)

waive /weɪv/ *vt* renunciar a

wake /weɪk/ *vt* (*pt* **woke**, *pp* **woken**) despertar. ● *vi* despertarse. ● *n* (Naut) estela *f*. **in the ~ of** como resultado de. □ **~ up** *vt* despertar. *vi* despertarse

Wales /weɪlz/ *n* (el país de) Gales

walk /wɔ:k/ *vi* andar, caminar; (not ride) ir a pie; (stroll) pasear. ● *vt* andar por <*streets*>; llevar de paseo <*dog*>. ● *n* paseo *m*; (long) caminata *f*; (gait) manera *f* de andar. □ **~ out** *vi* salir; <*workers*> declararse en huelga. □ **~ out on** *vt* abandonar. **~er** *n* excursionista *m & f*

walkie-talkie /wɔ:kɪ'tɔ:kɪ/ *n* walkie-talkie *m*

walk: ~ing-stick *n* bastón *m*. **W~man** /-mən/ *n* Walkman *m* (*P*). **~-out** *n retirada en señal de protesta*; (strike) abandono *m* del trabajo

wall /wɔ:l/ *n* (interior) pared *f*; (exterior) muro *m*

wallet /'wɒlɪt/ *n* cartera *f*, billetera *f*

wallop /'wɒləp/ *vt* (*pt* **walloped**) ◻ darle un golpazo a.

wallow /'wɒləʊ/ *vi* revolcarse

wallpaper /'wɔ:lpeɪpə(r)/ *n* papel *m* pintado

walnut /'wɔ:lnʌt/ *n* nuez *f*; (tree) nogal *m*

walrus /'wɔ:lrəs/ *n* morsa *f*

waltz /wɔ:ls/ *n* vals *m*. ● *vi* valsar

wand /wɒnd/ *n* varita *f* (mágica)

wander /'wɒndə(r)/ *vi* vagar; (stroll) pasear; (digress) divagar. ● *n* vuelta *f*, paseo *m*. **~er** *n* trotamundos *m*

wane /weɪn/ *vi* <*moon*> menguar; <*interest*> decaer. ● *n*. **be on the ~** <*popularity*> estar decayendo

wangle /wæŋgl/ *vt* ◻ agenciarse

want /wɒnt/ *vt* querer; (need) necesitar. ● *vi*. **~ for** carecer de. ● *n* necesidad *f*; (lack) falta *f*. **~ed** *a* <*criminal*> buscado

war /wɔ:(r)/ *n* guerra *f*. **at ~** en guerra

warble /'wɔ:bl/ *vi* trinar, gorjear

ward /wɔ:d/ *n* (in hospital) sala *f*; (child) pupilo *m*. □ **~ off** *vt* conjurar <*danger*>; rechazar <*attack*>

warden /'wɔ:dn/ *n* guarda *m*

warder /'wɔ:də(r)/ *n* celador *m* (*de una cárcel*)

wardrobe /'wɔ:drəʊb/ *n* armario *m*; (clothes) guardarropa *f*, vestuario *m*

warehouse /'weəhaʊs/ *n* depósito *m*, almacén *m*

wares /weəz/ *npl* mercancía(s) *f(pl)*

war: ~fare *n* guerra *f*. **~head** *n* cabeza *f*, ojiva *f*

warm /wɔ:m/ *a* (**-er**, **-est**) <*water, day*> tibio, templado; <*room*> caliente; <*climate, wind*> cálido; <*clothes*> de abrigo; <*welcome*> caluroso. **be ~** <*person*> tener calor. **it's ~ today** hoy hace calor. ● *vt*. **~ (up)** calentar <*room*>; recalentar <*food*>; (fig) animar. ● *vi*. **~ (up)** calentarse; (fig) animarse. **~-blooded** /-'blʌdɪd/ *a* de sangre caliente. **~ly** *adv* (heartily) calurosamente. **~th** *n* calor *m*; (of colour, atmosphere) calidez *f*

warn /wɔ:n/ *vt* advertir. **~ing** *n* advertencia *f*; (notice) aviso *m*

warp /wɔ:p/ *vt* alabear. **~ed** /'wɔ:pt/ *a* <*wood*> alabeado; <*mind*> retorcido

warrant /'wɒrənt/ *n* orden *f* judicial; (search ~) orden *f* de registro; (for arrest) orden *f* de arresto. ● *vt* justificar. **~y** *n* garantía *f*

warrior /'wɒrɪə(r)/ *n* guerrero *m*

warship /'wɔ:ʃɪp/ *n* buque *m* de guerra

wart /wɔ:t/ *n* verruga *f*

wartime /'wɔ:taɪm/ *n* tiempo *m* de guerra

wary /'weərɪ/ *a* (**-ier**, **-iest**) cauteloso. **be ~ of** recelar de

was /wəz, wɒz/ ⇒BE

wash /wɒʃ/ *vt* lavar; fregar, lavar (LAm) <*floor*>. **~ one's face** lavarse la cara. ● *vi* lavarse. ● *n* (in washing machine) lavado *m*. **have a ~** lavarse. **I gave the car a ~** lavé el coche. □ **~ out** *vt* (clean) lavar; (rinse) enjuagar. □ **~ up** *vi* fregar los platos, lavar los trastes (Mex); (Amer, wash face and hands) lavarse. **~able** *a* lavable. **~basin**, **~bowl** (Amer) *n* lavabo *m*. **~er** *n* arandela *f*. **~ing** *n* lavado *m*; (dirty clothes) ropa *f* para lavar; (wet clothes) ropa *f* lavada. **do the ~ing** lavar la ropa, hacer la colada. **~ing-machine** *n* máquina *f* de lavar, lavadora *f*. **~ing-powder** *n* jabón *m* en polvo. **~ing-up** *n*. **do the ~ing-up** lavar los platos, fregar (los platos). **~ing-up liquid** *n* lavavajillas *m*. **~out** *n* 🅸 desastre *m*. **~room** *n* (Amer) baños *mpl*, servicios *mpl*

wasp /wɒsp/ *n* avispa *f*

waste /weɪst/ ● *a* <*matter*> de desecho; <*land*> (barren) yermo; (uncultivated) baldío. ● *n* (of materials) desperdicio *m*; (of time) pérdida *f*; (refuse) residuos *mpl*. ● *vt* despilfarrar <*electricity, money*>; desperdiciar <*talent, effort*>; perder <*time*>. ● *vi*. **~-disposal unit** *n* trituradora *f* de desperdicios. **~ful** *a* poco económico; <*person*> despilfarrador. **~-paper basket** *n* papelera *f*

watch /wɒtʃ/ *vt* mirar; observar <*person, expression*>; ver <*TV*>; (keep an eye on) vigilar; (take heed) tener cuidado con. ● *vi* mirar. ● *n* (observation) vigilancia *f*; (period of duty) guardia *f*; (timepiece) reloj *m*. **~ out** *vi* (be careful) tener cuidado; (look carefully) estarse atento. **~dog** *n* perro *m* guardián. **~man** /-mən/ *n* (*pl* **-men**) vigilante *m*.

water /'wɔ:tə(r)/ *n* agua *f*. ● *vt* regar <*plants etc*>. ● *vi* <*eyes*> llorar. **make s.o.'s mouth ~** hacérsele la boca agua, hacérsele agua la boca (LAm). **~ down** *vt* diluir; aguar <*wine*>. **~-colour** *n* acuarela *f*. **~cress** *n* berro *m*. **~fall** *n* cascada *f*; (large) catarata *f*. **~ing-can** *n* regadera *f*. **~ lily** *n* nenúfar *m*. **~logged** /-lɒgd/ *a* anegado; <*shoes*> empapado. **~proof** *a* impermeable; <*watch*> sumergible. **~-skiing** *n* esquí *m* acuático. **~tight** *a* hermético; <*boat*> estanco; <*argument*> irrebatible. **~way** *n* canal *m* navegable. **~y** *a* acuoso; <*eyes*> lloroso

watt /wɒt/ *n* vatio *m*

wave /weɪv/ *n* onda *f*; (of hand) señal *f*; (fig) oleada *f*. ● *vt* agitar; (curl) ondular <*hair*>. ● *vi* (signal) hacer señales con la mano; ondear <*flag*>. **~band** *n* banda *f* de frecuencia. **~length** *n* longitud *f* de onda

waver /'weɪvə(r)/ *vi* (be indecisive) vacilar; (falter) flaquear

wavy /'weɪvɪ/ *a* (**-ier**, **-iest**) ondulado

wax /wæks/ *n* cera *f.* ● *vi* <*moon*> crecer. **~work** *n* figura *f* de cera. **~works** *npl* museo *m* de cera

way /weɪ/ *n* (route) camino *m*; (manner) manera *f*, forma *f*, modo *m*; (direction) dirección *f*; (habit) costumbre *f*. **it's a long ~ from here** queda muy lejos de aquí. **be in the ~** estorbar. **by the ~** a propósito. **either ~** de cualquier manera. **give ~** (collapse) ceder, romperse; (Auto) ceder el paso. **in a ~** en cierta manera. **in some ~s** en ciertos modos. **make ~** dejar paso a. **no ~!** ¡ni hablar! **on my ~ to** de camino a. **out of the ~** remoto; (extraordinary) fuera de lo común. **that ~** por allí. **this ~** por aquí. **~ in** *n* entrada *f*. **~lay** /weɪ'leɪ/ *vt* (*pt* **-laid**) abordar. **~ out** *n* salida *f*. **~-out** *a* ultramoderno, original. **~s** *npl* costumbres *fpl*

we /wi:/ *pron* nosotros *m*, nosotras *f*

weak /wi:k/ *a* (**-er**, **-est**) débil; <*structure*> poco sólido; <*performance, student*> flojo; <*coffee*> poco cargado; <*solution*> diluido; <*beer*> suave; (pej) aguado. **~en** *vt* debilitar. ● *vi* <*resolve*> flaquear. **~ling** *n* alfeñique *m*. **~ness** *n* debilidad *f*

wealth /welθ/ *n* riqueza *f*. **~y** *a* (**-ier**, **-iest**) rico

weapon /'wepən/ *n* arma *f*

wear /weə(r)/ *vt* (*pt* **wore**, *pp* **worn**) llevar; vestirse de <*black, red, etc*>; (usually) usar. **I've got nothing to ~** no tengo nada que ponerme. ● *vi* (through use) gastarse; (last) durar. ● *n* uso *m*; (damage) desgaste *m*; **~ and tear** desgaste *m* natural. □ **~ out** *vt* gastar; (tire) agotar. *vi* gastarse

weary /'wɪərɪ/ *a* (**-ier**, **-iest**) cansado. ● *vt* cansar. ● *v*[...] cansarse. **~ of** cansarse de

weather /'weðə(r)/ *n* tiempo *m*. **what's the ~ like?** ¿qué tiempo hace?. **the ~ was bad** hizo mal tiempo. **be under the ~** [I] no andar muy bien [I]. ● *vt* (survive) sobrellevar. **~-beaten** *a* curtido. **~ forecast** *n* pronóstico *m* del tiempo. **~-vane** *n* veleta *f*

weave /wi:v/ *vt* (*pt* **wove**, *p*[*p*] **woven**) tejer; entreteje[r] <*threads*>. **~ one's way** abrirse pa[so]. ● *vi* <*person*> zigzaguea[r]; <*road*> serpentear. **~r** *n* tejedor *m*

web /web/ *n* (of spider) telaraña *f*; ([...]) intrigue) red *f*. **~ site** *n* (Comp) siti[o] web *m*

wed /wed/ *vt* (*pt* **wedded**) ca[...]sarse con. ● *vi* casarse.

we'd /wi:d/, /wɪəd/ = **we had**, **we would**

wedding /'wedɪŋ/ *n* boda *f*, casamiento *m*. **~-cake** *n* pastel *m* d[e] boda. **~-ring** *n* anillo *m* de boda

wedge /wedʒ/ *n* cuña *f*

Wednesday /'wenzdeɪ/ *n* miércoles *m*

wee /wi:/ *a* [I] pequeñito. ● *n*. **hav[e] a ~** [I] hacer pis [I]

weed /wi:d/ *n* mala hierba *f*. ● [...] desherbar. □ **~ out** *vt* elimina[r]. **~killer** *n* herbicida *m*. **~y** *a* <*person*> enclenque; (Amer, lanky) largu[i]rucho [I]

week /wi:k/ *n* semana *f*. **~day** día *m* de semana. **~end** *n* fin *m* d[e] semana. **~ly** *a* semanal. ● *n* semanario *m*. ● *adv* semanalment[e]

weep /wi:p/ *vi* (*pt* **wept**) llorar

weigh /weɪ/ *vt/i* pesar. **~ anch[or]** levar anclas. □ **~ down** *vt* (fi[...]

oprimir. □~ **up** *vt* pesar; (fig) considerar

weight /weɪt/ *n* peso *m*; (sport) pesa *f*. **put on** ~ engordar. **lose** ~ adelgazar. **~-lifting** *n* halterofilia *f*, levantamiento *m* de pesos

weir /wɪə(r)/ *n* presa *f*

weird /wɪəd/ *a* (**-er**, **-est**) raro, extraño; (unearthly) misterioso

welcom|e /'welkəm/ *a* bienvenido. **you're ~e!** (after thank you) ¡de nada! ● *n* bienvenida *f*; (reception) acogida *f*. ● *vt* dar la bienvenida a; (appreciate) alegrarse de. **~ing** *a* acogedor

weld /weld/ *vt* soldar. ● *n* soldadura *f*. **~er** *n* soldador *m*

welfare /'welfeə(r)/ *n* bienestar *m*; (aid) asistencia *f* social. **W~ State** *n* estado *m* benefactor

well /wel/ *adv* (**better**, **best**) bien. **~ done!** ¡muy bien!, ¡bravo! **as ~** también. **as ~ as** además de. **we may as ~ go tomorrow** más vale que vayamos mañana. **do ~** (succeed) tener éxito. **very ~** muy bien. ● *a* bien. **I'm very ~** estoy muy bien. ● *int* (introducing, continuing sentence) bueno; (surprise) ¡vaya!; (indignation, resignation) bueno. **~ I never!** ¡no me digas! ● *n* pozo *m*

we'll /wi:l/, /wɪəl/ = WE WILL

well: ~-behaved /-bɪ'heɪvd/ *a* que se porta bien, bueno. **~-educated** /-'edjʊkeɪtɪd/ *a* culto.

wellington (boot) /'welɪŋtən/ *n* bota *f* de goma *or* de agua; (Amer, short boot) botín *m*

well: ~-known /-'nəʊn/ *a* conocido. **~ off** *a* adinerado. **~-stocked** /-'stɒkt/ *a* bien provisto. **~-to-do** /-tə'du:/ *a* adinerado

Welsh /welʃ/ *a* & *n* galés (*m*). **the ~** *n* los galeses

went /went/ ⇒GO

wept /wept/ ⇒WEEP

were /wɜ:(r), wə(r)/ ⇒BE

we're /wɪə(r)/ = **we are**

west /west/ *n* oeste *m*. **the W~** el Occidente *m*. ● *a* oeste; <*wind*> del oeste. ● *adv* <*go*> hacia el oeste, al oeste. **it's ~ of York** está al oeste de York. **~erly** /-əlɪ/ *a* <*wind*> del oeste. **~ern** /-ən/ *a* occidental. ● *n* (film) película *f* del Oeste. **~erner** *n* occidental *m* & *f*. **W~ Indian** *a* & *n* antillano (*m*). **W~ Indies** *npl* Antillas *fpl*. **~ward(s)** /-wəd(z)/ *adv* hacia el oeste

wet /wet/ *a* (**wetter**, **wettest**) mojado; (rainy) lluvioso; ([I], person) soso. **'~ paint'** 'pintura fresca'. **get ~** mojarse. **he got his feet ~** se mojó los pies. ● *vt* (*pt* **wetted**) mojar; (dampen) humedecer. **~ o.s.** orinarse. **~ blanket** *n* aguafiestas *m* & *f*. **~ suit** *n* traje *m* de neopreno

we've /wi:v/ = WE HAVE

whack /wæk/ *vt* [I] golpear. ● *n* [I] golpe *m*.

whale /weɪl/ *n* ballena *f*. **we had a ~ of a time** [I] lo pasamos bomba [I]

wham /wæm/ *int* ¡zas!

wharf /wɔ:f/ *n* (*pl* **wharves** *or* **wharfs**) muelle *m*

what /wɒt/

● *adjective*

····➤ (in questions) qué. **~ perfume are you wearing?** ¿qué perfume llevas?. **~ colour are the walls?** ¿de qué color son las paredes?

····➤ (in exclamations) qué. **~ a beautiful house!** ¡qué casa más linda!. **~ a lot of people!** ¡cuánta gente!

····➤ (in indirect speech) qué. **I'll ask him ~ bus to take** le preguntaré qué autobús hay que tomar. **do you know ~ time it leaves?** ¿sabes a qué hora sale?

● *pronoun*

····➤ (in questions) qué. **~ is it?** ¿qué es? **~ for?** ¿para qué?. **~'s the problem?** ¿cuál es el problema? **~'s he like?** ¿cómo es? **what?** (say that again) ¿cómo?, ¿qué?

····➤ (in indirect questions) qué. **I didn't know ~ to do** no sabía qué hacer

····➤ (relative) lo que. **I did ~ I could** hice lo que pude. **~ I need is a new car** lo que necesito es un coche nuevo

····➤ (in phrases) **~ about me?** ¿y yo qué? **~ if she doesn't come?** ¿y si no viene?

whatever /wɒt'evə(r)/ *a* cualquiera. ● *pron* (todo) lo que, cualquier cosa que

whatsoever /wɒtsəʊ'evə(r)/ *a & pron* = **whatever**

wheat /wi:t/ *n* trigo *m*

wheel /wi:l/ *n* rueda *f*. **at the ~** al volante. ● *vt* empujar <*bicycle etc*>; llevar (*en silla de ruedas etc*) <*person*>. **~barrow** *n* carretilla *f*. **~chair** *n* silla *f* de ruedas

wheeze /wi:z/ *vi* respirar con dificultad

when /wen/ *adv* cuándo. ● *conj* cuando. **~ever** /-'evə(r)/ *adv* (every time that) cada vez que, siempre que; (at whatever time) **we'll go ~ever you're ready** saldremos cuando estés listo

where /weə(r)/ *adv & conj* donde; (interrogative) dónde. **~ are you going?** ¿adónde vas? **~ are you from?** ¿de dónde eres?. **~abouts** /-əbaʊts/ *adv* en qué parte. ● *n* paradero *m*. **~as** /-'æz/ *conj* por cuanto; (in contrast) mientras (que). **~ver** /weər'evə(r)/ *adv* (in questions) dónde; (no matter where) en cualquier parte. ● *conj* donde (+ *subjunctive*), dondequiera (+ *subjunctive*)

whet /wet/ *vt* (*pt* **whetted**) abrir <*appetite*>

whether /'weðə(r)/ *conj* si. **I don't know ~ she will like it** no sé si le gustará. **~ you like it or not** te guste o no te guste

which /wɪtʃ/ *a* (in questions) (*sing*) qué, cuál; (*pl*) qué, cuáles. **~ one** cuál. **~ one of you** cuál de ustedes. ● *pron* (in questions) (*sing*) cuál; (*pl*) cuáles; (relative) que; (object) el cual, la cual, lo cual, los cuales, las cuales. **~ever** /-'evə(r)/ *a* cualquier. ● *pron* cualquiera que, el que, la que; (in questions) cuál; (*pl*) cuáles

while /waɪl/ *n* rato *m*. **a ~ ago** hace un rato. ● *conj* mientras; (although) aunque. □ **~ away** *vt* pasar <*time*>

whilst /waɪlst/ *conj* ⇒WHILE

whim /wɪm/ *n* capricho *m*

whimper /'wɪmpə(r)/ *vi* gimotear. ● *n* quejido *m*

whine /waɪn/ *vi* <*person*> gemir; <*child*> lloriquear; <*dog*> aullar

whip /wɪp/ *n* látigo *m*; (for punishment) azote *m*. ● *vt* (*pt* **whipped** /wɪpt/) fustigar, pegarle a (*con la fusta*) <*horse*>; azotar <*person*>; (Culin) batir

whirl /wɜ:l/ *vi* girar rápidamente. **~pool** *n* remolino *m*. **~wind** torbellino *m*

whirr /wɜ:(r)/ *n* zumbido *m*. ● *vi* zumbar

whisk /wɪsk/ *vt* (Culin) batir. ● *n* (Culin) batidor *m*. ~ **away** llevarse

vhisker /ˈwɪskə(r)/ *n* pelo *m*. ~**s** *npl* (of cat etc) bigotes *mpl*

vhisky /ˈwɪskɪ/ *n* whisky *m*, güisqui *m*

vhisper /ˈwɪspə(r)/ *vt* susurrar. ● *vi* cuchichear. ● *n* susurro *m*

vhistle /ˈwɪsl/ *n* silbido *m*; (loud) chiflado *m*; (instrument) silbato *m*, pito *m*. ● *vi* silbar; (loudly) chiflar

vhite /waɪt/ *a* (**-er**, **-est**) blanco. **go** ~ ponerse pálido. ● *n* blanco; (of egg) clara *f*. ~ **coffee** *n* café *m* con leche. ~**-collar worker** *n* empleado *m* de oficina. ~ **elephant** *n* objeto *m* inútil y costoso. ~**-hot** *a* <*metal*> al rojo blanco. ~ **lie** *n* mentirijilla *f*. ~**n** *vt/i* blanquear. ~**wash** *n* cal *f*; (cover-up) tapadera *f* [I]. ● *vt* blanquear, encalar

/hitsun /ˈwɪtsn/ *n* Pentecostés *m*

hiz /wɪz/ *vi* (*pt* **whizzed**). ~ **by**, ~ **past** pasar zumbando. ~**-kid** *n* [I] lince *m* [I]

ho /huː/ *pron* (in questions) quién; *pl*) quiénes; (as relative) que; **the girl** ~ **lives there** la chica que vive allí. **those** ~ **can't come tomorrow** os que no puedan venir mañana. ~**ever** /huːˈevə(r)/ *pron* quienquiera que; (interrogative) quién

hole /həʊl/ *a*. **the** ~ **country** todo l país. **there's a** ~ **bottle left** queda na botella entera. ● *n* todo *m*, onjunto *m*; (total) total *m*. **on the** ~ n general. ~**-hearted** /-ˈhɑːtɪd/ *a* <*support*> incondicional; <*approval*> sin reservar. ~**meal** *a* integral. ~**sale** *n* venta *f* al por mayor. ● *a* & *adv* al por mayor. ~**some** /-səm/ *a* sano

holly /ˈhəʊlɪ/ *adv* completamente

whom /huːm/ *pron* que, a quien; (in questions) a quién

whooping cough /ˈhuːpɪŋ/ *n* tos *f* convulsa

whore /hɔː(r)/ *n* puta *f*

whose /huːz/ *pron* de quién; (*pl*) de quiénes. ● *a* (in questions) de quién; (*pl*) de quiénes; (relative) cuyo; (*pl*) cuyos

why /waɪ/ *adv* por qué. ~ **not?** ¿por qué no? **that's** ~ **I couldn't go** por eso no pude ir. ● *int* ¡vaya!

wick /wɪk/ *n* mecha *f*

wicked /ˈwɪkɪd/ *a* malo; (mischievous) travieso; ([I], very bad) malísimo

wicker /ˈwɪkə(r)/ *n* mimbre *m* & *f*. ● *a* de mimbre. ~**work** *n* artículos *mpl* de mimbre

wicket /ˈwɪkɪt/ *n* (cricket) rastrillo *m*

wide /waɪd/ *a* (**-er**, **-est**) ancho; <*range, experience*> amplio; (off target) desviado. **it's four metres** ~ tiene cuatro metros de ancho. ● *adv*. **open** ~! abra bien la boca. ~ **awake** *a* completamente despierto; (fig) despabilado. **I left the door** ~ **open** dejé la puerta abierta de par en par. ~**ly** *adv* extensamente; (believed) generalmente; (different) muy. ~**n** *vt* ensanchar. ● *vi* ensancharse. ~**spread** *a* extendido; (fig) difundido

widow /ˈwɪdəʊ/ *n* viuda *f*. ~**er** *n* viudo *m*.

width /wɪdθ/ *n* anchura *f*. **in** ~ de ancho

wield /wiːld/ *vt* manejar; ejercer <*power*>

wife /waɪf/ *n* (*pl* **wives**) mujer *f*, esposa *f*

wig /wɪg/ *n* peluca *f*

wiggle /ˈwɪgl/ *vt* menear. ● *vi* menearse

wild /waɪld/ *a* (**-er, -est**) *<animal>* salvaje; *<flower>* silvestre; *<country>* agreste; (enraged) furioso; *<idea>* extravagante; (with joy) loco. **a ~ guess** una conjetura hecha totalmente al azar. **I'm not ~ about the idea** la idea me enloquece. ● *adv* en estado salvaje. **run ~** *<children>* criarse como salvajes. **~s** *npl* regiones *fpl* salvajes. **~erness** /ˈwɪldənɪs/ *n* páramo *m*. **~fire** *n*. **spread like ~fire** correr como un reguero de pólvora. **~-goose chase** *n* empresa *f* inútil. **~life** *n* fauna *f*. **~ly** *adv* violentamente; (fig) locamente

will /wɪl/

● *auxiliary verb*

past **would**; contracted forms **I'll, you'll, etc = I will, you will, etc.; won't = will not**

····▸ (talking about the future)

! The Spanish future tense is not always the first option for translating the English future tense. The present tense of *ir + a + verb* is commonly used instead, particularly in Latin American countries. **he'll be here on Tuesday** *estará el martes, va a estar el martes;* **she won't agree** *no va a aceptar, no aceptará*

····▸ (in invitations and requests) **~ you have some wine?** ¿quieres (un poco de) vino? **you'll stay for dinner, won't you?** te quedas a cenar, ¿no?

····▸ (in tag questions) **you ~ be bac soon, won't you?** vas a volve pronto, ¿no?

····▸ (in short answers) **will it be read by Monday? - yes, it ~** ¿estar listo para el lunes? - sí

● *noun*

····▸ (mental power) voluntad *f*

····▸ (document) testamento *m*

willing /ˈwɪlɪŋ/ *a* complaciente. ~ **to** dispuesto a. **~ly** *adv* de buen gana

willow /ˈwɪləʊ/ *n* sauce *m*

will-power /ˈwɪlpaʊə(r)/ *n* fuerz *f* de voluntad

wilt /wɪlt/ *vi* marchitarse

win /wɪn/ *vt* (*pt* **won**, *pres p* **wir ning**) ganar; (achieve, obtain) cons guir. ● *vi* ganar. ● *n* victoria *f*. □ **over** *vt* ganarse a

wince /wɪns/ *vi* hacer una mue de dolor

winch /wɪntʃ/ *n* cabrestante *r* ● *vt* levantar con un cabrestant

wind[1] /wɪnd/ *n* viento *m*; (in sto ach) gases *mpl*. **~ instrume** instrumento *m* de viento. ● *vt* d jar sin aliento; *<blow>* cortarle respiración a

wind[2] /waɪnd/ *vt* (*pt* **wound**) (wr around) enrollar; dar cuerda *<clock etc>*. ● *vi* *<road etc>* serpe tear. □ **~ up** *vt* dar cuerda *<watch, clock>*; (fig) termina concluir

wind /wɪnd/ **: ~-cheater** *n* zadora *f*. **~fall** *n* (fig) suerte inesperada

winding /ˈwaɪndɪŋ/ *a* tortuoso

windmill /ˈwɪndmɪl/ *n* molino (de viento)

vindow /ˈwɪndəʊ/ *n* ventana *f*; (in shop) escaparate *m*, vitrina *f* (LAm), vidriera *f* (LAm), aparador *m* (Mex); (of vehicle, booking-office) ventanilla *f*; (Comp) ventana *f*, window *m*. **~ box** *n* jardinera *f*. **~-shop** *vi* mirar los escaparates. **~sill** *n* alféizar *m* *or* repisa *f* de la ventana

'ind /wɪnd/**: ~pipe** *n* tráquea *f*. **~screen** *n*, **~shield** *n* (Amer) parabrisas *m*. **~screen wiper** *n* limpiaparabrisas *m*. **~-swept** *a* azotado por el viento. **~y** *a* (**-ier**, **-iest**) <*day*> ventoso, de viento. **it's ~y** hace viento

'ine /waɪn/ *n* vino *m*. **~-cellar** *n* bodega *f*. **~glass** *n* copa *f* de vino. **~-growing** *n* vinicultura *f*. ● *a* vinícola. **~ list** *n* lista *f* de vinos. **~-tasting** *n* cata *f* de vinos

'ing /wɪŋ/ *n* ala *f*; (Auto) aleta *f*. **under one's ~** bajo la protección de uno. **~er** *n* (Sport) ala *m* & *f*. **~s** *npl* (in theatre) bastidores *mpl*

'ink /wɪŋk/ *vi* guiñar el ojo; <*light etc*> centellear. ● *n* guiño *m*. **not to sleep a ~** no pegar ojo

'in: ~ner *n* ganador *m*. **~ning-post** *n* poste *m* de llegada. **~nings** *npl* ganancias *fpl*

'int|er /ˈwɪntə(r)/ *n* invierno *m*. ● *vi* invernar. **~ry** *a* invernal

'ipe /waɪp/ *vt* limpiar, pasarle un trapo a; (dry) secar. **~ one's nose** limpiarse la nariz. ● *n*. **give sth a ~** limpiar algo, pasarle un trapo a algo. □ **~ out** *vt* (cancel) cancelar; (destroy) destruir; (obliterate) borrar. □ **~ up** *vt* limpiar

'ir|e /ˈwaɪə(r)/ *n* alambre *m*; (Elec) cable *m*. **~ing** *n* instalación *f* eléctrica

'isdom /ˈwɪzdəm/ *n* sabiduría *f*. **~ tooth** *n* muela *f* del juicio

wise /waɪz/ *a* (**-er**, **-est**) sabio; (sensible) prudente; <*decision, choice*> acertado. **~ly** *adv* sabiamente; (sensibly) prudentemente

wish /wɪʃ/ *n* deseo *m*; (greeting) saludo *m*. **make a ~** pedir un deseo. **best ~es, John** (in letters) saludos de John, un abrazo de John. ● *vt* desear. **~ s.o. well** desear buena suerte a uno. **I ~ I were rich** ¡ojalá fuera rico! **he ~ed he hadn't told her** lamentó habérselo dicho. **~ful thinking** *n* ilusiones *fpl*

wistful /ˈwɪstfl/ *a* melancólico

wit /wɪt/ *n* gracia *f*; (intelligence) ingenio *m*. **be at one's ~s' end** no saber más qué hacer

witch /wɪtʃ/ *n* bruja *f*. **~craft** *n* brujería *f*.

with /wɪð/ *prep* con; (cause, having) de. **come ~ me** ven conmigo. **take it ~ you** llévalo contigo; (formal) llévelo consigo. **the man ~ the beard** el hombre de la barba. **trembling ~ fear** temblando de miedo

withdraw /wɪðˈdrɔː/ *vt* (*pt* **withdrew**, *pp* **withdrawn**) retirar. ● *vi* apartarse. **~al** *n* retirada *f*. **~n** *a* <*person*> retraído

wither /ˈwɪðə(r)/ *vi* marchitarse

withhold /wɪðˈhəʊld/ *vt* (*pt* **withheld**) retener; (conceal) ocultar (from a)

within /wɪðˈɪn/ *prep* dentro de. ● *adv* dentro. **~ sight** a la vista

without /wɪðˈaʊt/ *prep* sin. **~ paying** sin pagar

withstand /wɪðˈstænd/ *vt* (*pt* **-stood**) resistir

witness /ˈwɪtnɪs/ *n* testigo *m*; (proof) testimonio *m*. ● *vt* presenciar; atestiguar <*signature*>. **~-box** *n* tribuna *f* de los testigos

witt|icism /ˈwɪtɪsɪzəm/ *n* ocurrencia *f*. **~y** /ˈwɪtɪ/ *a* (**-ier**, **-iest**) gracioso

wives /waɪvz/ ⇒WIFE

wizard /ˈwɪzəd/ *n* hechicero *m*

wizened /ˈwɪznd/ *a* arrugado

wobbl|e /ˈwɒbl/ *vi* <*chair*> tambalearse; <*bicycle*> bambolearse; <*voice, jelly, hand*> temblar. **~y** *a* <*chair etc*> cojo

woe /wəʊ/ *n* aflicción *f*

woke /wəʊk/, **woken** /ˈwəʊkən/ ⇒WAKE

wolf /wʊlf/ *n* (*pl* **wolves** /wʊlvz/) lobo *m*

woman /ˈwʊmən/ *n* (*pl* **women**) mujer *f*

womb /wu:m/ *n* matriz *f*

women /ˈwɪmɪn/ *npl* ⇒WOMAN

won /wʌn/ ⇒WIN

wonder /ˈwʌndə(r)/ *n* maravilla *f*; (bewilderment) asombro *m*. **no ~** no es de extrañarse (**that** que). ● *vt* (ask oneself) preguntarse. **I ~ whose book this is** me pregunto de quién será este libro; (in polite requests) **I ~ if you could help me?** ¿me podría ayudar? **~ful** *a* maravilloso. **~fully** *adv* maravillosamente

won't /wəʊnt/ = **will not**

wood /wʊd/ *n* madera *f*; (for burning) leña *f*; (area) bosque *m*. **~ed** *a* poblado de árboles, boscoso. **~en** *a* de madera. **~land** *n* bosque *m*. **~wind** /-wɪnd/ *n* instrumentos *mpl* de viento de madera. **~work** *n* carpintería *f*; (in room etc) maderaje *m*. **~worm** *n* carcoma *f*. **~y** *a* leñoso

wool /wʊl/ *n* lana *f*. **pull the ~ over s.o.'s eyes** engañar a uno. **~len** *a* de lana. **~ly** *a* (**-ier**, **-iest**) de lana; (unclear) vago. ● *n* jersey *m*

word /wɜ:d/ *n* palabra *f*; (news) ticia *f*. **by ~ of mouth** de palabr **didn't say a ~** yo no dije nada other **~s** es decir. ● *vt* expres **~ing** *n* redacción *f*; (of questi formulación *f*. **~ processor** procesador *m* de textos. **~y** *a* p lijo

wore /wɔ:(r)/ ⇒WEAR

work /wɜ:k/ *n* trabajo *m*; (arts) ol *f*. **be out of ~** estar sin traba estar desocupado. ● *vt* hacer bajar; manejar <*machine*>. ● trabajar; <*machine*> funcion <*student*> estudiar; <*drug etc*> s tir efecto. □ **~ off** *vt* desahog □ **~ out** *vt* resolver <*problen* (calculate) calcular; (understa entender. *vi* (succeed) salir b (Sport) entrenarse. □ **~ up** *vt*. **~ed up** exaltarse. **~able** *a* <*p ect, solution*> factible. **~er** *n* bajador *m*; (manual) obrero *m*; office, bank) empleado *m*. **~ing** <*day*> laborable; <*clothes etc*> trabajo. **in ~ing order** en estado funcionamiento. **~ing class** clase *f* obrera. **~ing-class** *a* d clase obrera. **~man** /-mən/ *n* **-men**) obrero *m*. **~manship** destreza *f*. **~s** *npl* (building) fábr *f*; (Mec) mecanismo *m*. **~shop** *n* ller *m*

world /wɜ:ld/ *n* mundo *m*. **ou this ~** maravilloso. ● *a* mund **W~ Cup** *n*. **the W~ Cup** la C del Mundo. **~ly** *a* munda **~wide** *a* universal. **W~ W Web** *n* World Wide Web *m*

worm /wɜ:m/ *n* gusano *m*, lom *f*

worn /wɔ:n/ ⇒WEAR. ● *a* gast **~-out** *a* gastado; <*person*> re do

vorr|ied /ˈwʌrɪd/ *a* preocupado. **~y** /ˈwʌrɪ/ *vt* preocupar; (annoy) molestar. ● *vi* preocuparse. ● *n* preocupación *f*. **~ying** *a* inquietante

vorse /wɜːs/ *a* peor. **get ~** empeorar. ● *adv* peor; (more) más. **~n** *vt/i* empeorar

vorship /ˈwɜːʃɪp/ *n* culto *m*; (title) Su Señoría. ● *vt* (*pt* **worshipped**) adorar

vorst /wɜːst/ *a* peor. **he's the ~ in the class** es el peor de la clase. ● *adv* peor. ● *n*. **the ~** lo peor

vorth /wɜːθ/ *n* valor *m*. ● *a*. **be ~** valer. **it's ~ trying** vale la pena probarlo. **it was ~ my while** (me) valió la pena. **~less** *a* sin valor. **~while** /-ˈwaɪl/ *a* que vale la pena. **~y** /ˈwɜːðɪ/ *a* meritorio; (respectable) respetable; (laudable) loable

'ould /wʊd/ *v aux*. (in conditional sentences) **~ you go?** ¿irías tú? **he ~ come if he could** vendría si pudiera; (in reported speech) **I thought you'd forget** pensé que te olvidarías; (in requests, invitations) **~ you come here, please?** ¿quieres venir aquí? **~ you switch the television off?** ¿podrías apagar la televisión?; be prepared to) **he ~n't listen to me** o me quería escuchar

ound[1] /wuːnd/ *n* herida *f*. ● *vt* erir

ound[2] /waʊnd/ ⇒WIND[2]

ove, woven /wəʊv, ˈwəʊvn/ ⇒WEAVE

ow /waʊ/ *int* ¡ah!

'angle /ˈræŋgl/ *vi* reñir. ● *n* riña *f*

ap /ræp/ *vt* (*pt* **wrapped**) envolver. ● *n* bata *f*; (shawl) chal *m*. **per** *n*, **~ping** *n* envoltura *f*

ath /rɒθ/ *n* ira *f*

wreak /riːk/ *vt* sembrar. **~ havoc** causar estragos

wreath /riːθ/ *n* (*pl* **-ths** /-ðz/) corona *f*

wreck /rek/ *n* (ship) restos *mpl* de un naufragio; (vehicle) restos *mpl* de un avión siniestrado. **be a nervous ~** tener los nervios destrozados. ● *vt* provocar el naufragio de <*ship*>; destrozar <*car*>; (Amer, demolish) demoler; (fig) destrozar. **~age** /-ɪdʒ/ *n* restos *mpl*; (of building) ruinas *fpl*

wrench /rentʃ/ *vt* arrancar; (sprain) desgarrarse; dislocarse <*joint*>. ● *n* tirón *m*; (emotional) dolor *m* (*causado por una separación*); (tool) llave *f* inglesa

wrestl|e /ˈresl/ *vi* luchar. **~er** *n* luchador *m*. **~ing** *n* lucha *f*

wretch /retʃ/ *n* (despicable person) desgraciado *m*; (unfortunate person) desdichado *m & f*. **~ed** /-ɪd/ *a* desdichado; <*weather*> horrible

wriggle /ˈrɪgl/ *vi* retorcerse. **~ out of** escaparse de

wring /rɪŋ/ *vt* (*pt* **wrung**) retorcer <*neck*>. **~ out of** (obtain from) arrancar. □ **~ out** *vt* retorcer

wrinkl|e /ˈrɪŋkl/ *n* arruga *f*. ● *vt* arrugar. ● *vi* arrugarse. **~y** *a* arrugado

wrist /rɪst/ *n* muñeca *f*. **~watch** *n* reloj *m* de pulsera

writ /rɪt/ *n* orden *m* judicial

write /raɪt/ *vt/i* (*pt* **wrote**, *pp* **written**, *pres p* **writing**) escribir. □ **~ down** *vt* anotar. □ **~ off** *vt* cancelar <*debt*>. **~-off** *n*. **the car was a ~-off** el coche fue declarado un siniestro total. **~r** *n* escritor *m*

writhe /raɪð/ *vi* retorcerse

writing /ˈraɪtɪŋ/ *n* (script) escritura *f*; (handwriting) letra *f*. **in ~** por escrito. **~s** *npl* obra *f*, escritos *mpl*. **~ desk** *n* escritorio *m*. **~ pad** *n* bloc *m*. **~ paper** *n* papel *m* de escribir

written /ˈrɪtn/ ⇒WRITE

wrong /rɒŋ/ *a* equivocado, incorrecto; (not just) injusto; (mistaken) equivocado. **be ~** no tener razón; (be mistaken) equivocarse. **what's ~?** ¿qué pasa? **it's ~ to steal** robar está mal. **what's ~ with that?** ¿qué hay de malo en eso?. ● *adv* mal. **go ~** equivocarse; <*plan*> salir mal. ● *n* injusticia *f*; (evil) mal *m*. **in the ~** equivocado. ● *vt* ser injusto con. **~ful** *a* injusto. **~ly** *adv* mal; (unfairly) injustamente

wrote /rəʊt/ ⇒WRITE

wrought iron /rɔːt/ *n* hierro *m* forjado

wrung /rʌŋ/ ⇒WRING

wry /raɪ/ *a* (**wryer**, **wryest**) irónico. **make a ~ face** torcer el gesto

Xx

xerox /ˈzɪərɒks/ *vt* fotocopiar, xerografiar

Xmas /ˈkrɪsməs/ *n abbr* (**Christmas**) Navidad *f*

X-ray /ˈeksreɪ/ *n* (ray) rayo *m* X; (photograph) radiografía *f*. **~s** *npl* rayos *mpl*. ● *vt* hacer una radiografía de

xylophone /ˈzaɪləfəʊn/ *n* xilofón *m*, xilófono *m*

Yy

yacht /jɒt/ *n* yate *m*. **~ing** *n* na vegación *f* a vela

yank /jæŋk/ *vt* [I] tirar de (*violentamente*)

Yankee /ˈjæŋkɪ/ *n* [I] yanqui *m* &

yap /jæp/ *vi* (*pt* **yapped**) <*dog* ladrar (*con ladridos agudos*)

yard /jɑːd/ *n* patio *m*; (Amer, garden jardín *m*; (measurement) yarda *f* 0.9144 metre)

yarn /jɑːn/ *n* hilo *m*; ([I], tale) cuent *m*

yawn /jɔːn/ *vi* bostezar. ● *n* bost zo *m*

year /jɪə(r)/ *n* año *m*. **be three ~ old** tener tres años. **~ly** *a* anua ● *adv* cada año

yearn /ˈjɜːn/ *vi*. **~ to do sth** anh lar hacer algo. **~ for sth** añor algo. **~ing** *n* anhelo *m*, ansia *f*

yeast /jiːst/ *n* levadura *f*

yell /jel/ *vi* gritar. ● *n* grito *m*

yellow /ˈjeləʊ/ *a* & *n* amarillo (

yelp /jelp/ *n* gañido *m*. ● *vi* gañ

yes /jes/ *int* & *n* sí (*m*)

yesterday /ˈjestədeɪ/ *adv* & ayer (*m*). **the day before ~** an ayer *m*. **~ morning** ayer por la m ñana, ayer en la mañana (LAm)

yet /jet/ *adv* todavía, aún; (alrea ya. **as ~** hasta ahora; (as a linker) s embargo. ● *conj* pero

Yiddish /ˈjɪdɪʃ/ *n* yidish *m*

yield /jiːld/ *vt* (surrender) ceder; p ducir <*crop/mineral*>; dar < *sults*>. ● *vi* ceder. **'yield'** (Amer, tra sign) ceda el paso. ● *n* rendimiento *m*

yoga /'jəʊgə/ *n* yoga *m*

yoghurt /'jɒgət/ *n* yogur *m*

yoke /jəʊk/ *n* (fig also) yugo *m*

yokel /'jəʊkl/ *n* palurdo *m*

yolk /jəʊk/ *n* yema *f* (de huevo)

you /ju:/

● *pronoun*

····➤ (as the subject) (familiar form) (*sing*) tú, vos (River Plate and parts of Central America); (*pl*) vosotros, -tras (Spain), ustedes (LAm); (formal) (*sing*) usted; (*pl*) ustedes

! In Spanish the subject pronoun is usually only used to give emphasis or mark contrast.

····➤ (as the direct object) (familiar form) (*sing*) te; (*pl*) os (Spain), los, las (LAm); (formal) (*sing*) lo *or* (Spain) le, la; (*pl*) los *or* (Spain) les, las. **I love ~** te quiero

····➤ (as the indirect object) (familiar form) (*sing*) te; (*pl*) os (Spain), les (LAm); (formal) (*sing*) le; (*pl*) les. **I sent ~ the book yesterday** te mandé el libro ayer

! The pronoun *se* replaces the indirect object pronoun *le* or *les* when the latter is used with the direct object pronoun (*lo*, *la* etc), e.g. **I gave it to ~** *se lo di*

····➤ (when used after a preposition) (familiar form) (*sing*) ti, vos (River Plate and parts of Central America); (*pl*) vosotros, -tras (Spain), ustedes (LAm); (formal) (*sing*) usted; (*pl*) ustedes

····➤ (generalizing) uno, tú (esp Spain). **~ feel very proud** uno se siente muy orgulloso, te sientes muy orgulloso (esp Spain). **~ have to be patient** hay que tener paciencia

you'd /ju:d/, /jʊəd/ = **you had, you would**

you'll /ju:l/, /jʊəl/ = **you will**

young /jʌŋ/ *a* (**-er, -est**) joven. **my ~er sister** mi hermana menor. **he's a year ~er than me** tiene un año menos que yo. **~ lady** *n* señorita *f*. **~ man** *n* joven *m*. **~ster** /-stə(r)/ *n* joven *m*

your /jɔ:(r)/ *a* (belonging to one person) (*sing, familiar*) tu; (*pl, familiar*) tus; (*sing, formal*) su; (*pl, formal*) sus; (belonging to more than one person) (*sing, familiar*) vuestro, -tra, su (LAm); (*pl, familiar*) vuestros, -tras, sus (LAm); (*sing, formal*) su; (*pl, formal*) sus

you're /jʊə(r)/, /jɔ:(r)/ = **you are**

yours /jɔ:z/ *poss pron* (belonging to one person) (*sing, familiar*) tuyo, -ya; (*pl, familiar*) tuyos, -yas; (*sing, formal*) suyo, -ya; (*pl, formal*) suyos, -yas. (belonging to more than one person) (*sing, familiar*) vuestro, -tra; (*pl, familiar*) vuestros, -tras, suyos, -yas (LAm); (*sing, formal*) suyo, -ya; (*pl, formal*) suyos, -yas. **an aunt of ~** una tía tuya; **~ is here** el tuyo está aquí

yoursel|f /jɔ:'self/ *pron* (*reflexive*). (emphatic use) Ⓘ tú mismo, tú misma; (formal) usted mismo, usted misma. **describe ~f** descríbete; (Ud form) descríbase. **stop thinking about ~f** deja de pensar en ti mismo; (formal) deje de pensar en sí mismo; **by ~f** solo, sola. **~ves** /jɔ:'selvz/ *pron* vosotros mismos, vosotras mismas (familiar), ustedes mismos, ustedes mismas (LAm familiar), ustedes mismos, ustedes mismas (formal); (*reflexive*). **behave ~ves** ¡portaos bien (familiar), ¡pórtense bien! (formal, LAm familiar). **by ~ves** so·los, solas

youth /ju:θ/ *n* (*pl* **youths** /ju:ðz/) (early life) juventud *f*; (boy) joven *m*; (young people) juventud *f*. **~ful** *a* joven, juvenil. **~ hostel** *n* albergue *m* juvenil

you've /ju:v/ = **you have**

Yugoslav /ˈju:gəslɑ:v/ *a* & *n* yugoslavo (*m*). **~ia** /-ˈslɑ:vɪə/ *n* Yugoslavia *f*

Zz

zeal /zi:l/ *n* fervor *m*, celo *m*

zeal|ot /ˈzelət/ *n* fanático *m*. **~ous** /-əs/ *a* ferviente; (worker) que pone gran celo en su trabajo

zebra /ˈzebrə/ *n* cebra *f*. **~ crossing** *n* paso *m* de cebra

zenith /ˈzenɪθ/ *n* cenit *m*

zero /ˈzɪərəʊ/ *n* (*pl* **-os**) cero *m*

zest /zest/ *n* entusiasmo *m*; (peel) cáscara *f*

zigzag /ˈzɪgzæg/ *n* zigzag *m*. ● *vi* (*pt* **zigzagged**) zigzaguear

zilch /zɪltʃ/ *n* ☒ nada de nada

zinc /zɪŋk/ *n* cinc *m*

zip /zɪp/ *n* cremallera *f*, cierre *m* (LAm), zíper *m* (Mex). ● *vt*. **~ (up)** cerrar (la cremallera). **~ code** *n* (Amer) código *m* postal. **~ fastener** *n* cremallera *f*. **~per** *n/vt* ⇒zip

zodiac /ˈzəʊdɪæk/ *n* zodíaco *m*, zodiaco *m*

zombie /ˈzɒmbɪ/ *n* zombi *m* & *f*

zone /zəʊn/ *n* zona *f*. **time ~** *n* huso *m* horario

zoo /zu:/ *n* zoo *m*, zoológico *m*. **~logical** /zu:əˈlɒdʒɪkl/ *a* zoológico. **~logist** /zu:ˈɒlədʒɪst/ *n* zoólogo *m*. **~logy** /zu:ˈɒlədʒɪ/ *n* zoología *f*

zoom /zu:m/. □ **~ in** *vi* (Photo) hacer un zoom in (**on** sobre). □ **~ past** *vi/t* pasar zumbando. **~ lens** *n* teleobjetivo *m*, zoom *m*

zucchini /zʊˈki:nɪ/ *n* (*invar* o **~s**) (Amer) calabacín *m*

Numbers		Números
zero	0	cero
one (first)	1	uno (primero)
two (second)	2	dos (segundo)
three (third)	3	tres (tercero)
four (fourth)	4	cuatro (cuarto)
five (fifth)	5	cinco (quinto)
six (sixth)	6	seis (sexto)
seven (seventh)	7	siete (séptimo)
eight (eighth)	8	ocho (octavo)
nine (ninth)	9	nueve (noveno)
ten (tenth)	10	diez (décimo)
eleven (eleventh)	11	once (undécimo)
twelve (twelfth)	12	doce (duodécimo)
thirteen (thirteenth)	13	trece (decimotercero)
fourteen (fourteenth)	14	catorce (decimocuarto)
fifteen (fifteenth)	15	quince (decimoquinto)
sixteen (sixteenth)	16	dieciséis (decimosexto)
seventeen (seventeenth)	17	diecisiete (decimoséptimo)
eighteen (eighteenth)	18	dieciocho (decimoctavo)
nineteen (nineteenth)	19	diecinueve (decimonoveno)
twenty (twentieth)	20	veinte (vigésimo)
twenty-one (twenty-first)	21	veintiuno (vigésimo primero)
twenty-two (twenty-second)	22	veintidós (vigésimo segundo)
twenty-three (twenty-third)	23	veintitrés (vigésimo tercero)
twenty-four (twenty-fourth)	24	veinticuatro (vigésimo cuarto)
twenty-five (twenty-fifth)	25	veinticinco (vigésimo quinto)
twenty-six (twenty-sixth)	26	veintiséis (vigésimo sexto)
thirty (thirtieth)	30	treinta (trigésimo)
thirty-one (thirty-first)	31	treinta y uno (trigésimo primero)

forty (fortieth)	40	cuarenta (cuadragésimo)
fifty (fiftieth)	50	cincuenta (quincuagésimo)
sixty (sixtieth)	60	sesenta (sexagésimo)
seventy (seventieth)	70	setenta (septuagésimo)
eighty (eightieth)	80	ochenta (octogésimo)
ninety (ninetieth)	90	noventa (nonagésimo)
a/one hundred (hundredth)	100	cien (centésimo)
a/one hundred and one (hundred and first)	101	ciento uno (centésimo primero)
two hundred (two hundredth)	200	doscientos (ducentésimo)
three hundred (three hundredth)	300	trescientos (tricentésimo)
four hundred (four hundredth)	400	cuatrocientos (cuadringentésimo)
five hundred (five hundredth)	500	quinientos (quingentésimo)
six hundred (six hundredth)	600	seiscientos (sexcentésimo)
seven hundred (seven hundredth)	700	setecientos (septingentésimo)
eight hundred (eight hundredth)	800	ochocientos (octingentésimo)
nine hundred (nine hundredth)	900	novecientos (noningentésimo)
a/one thousand (thousandth)	1000	mil (milésimo)
two thousand (two thousandth)	2000	dos mil (dos milésimo)
a/one million (millionth)	1,000,000	un millón (millonésimo)

ꞏpanish Verbs

ꞏegular verbs:
ꞏ -ar (*e.g.* **comprar**)
ꞏresent; compr|o, **~as, ~a,**
ꞏamos, ~áis, ~an
ꞏuture: comprar|é, **~ás,**
ꞏá, ~emos, ~éis, ~án
ꞏnperfect: compr|aba,
ꞏabas, ~aba, ~ábamos,
ꞏabais, ~aban
ꞏreterite: compr|é, **~aste,**
ꞏó, ~amos, ~asteis,
ꞏaron
ꞏresent subjunctive:
ꞏmpr|e, **~es, ~e, ~emos,**
ꞏéis, ~en
ꞏnperfect subjunctive:
ꞏmpr|ara, **~aras ~ara,**
ꞏáramos, ~arais, ~aran
ꞏmpr|ase, **~ases, ~ase,**
ꞏásemos, ~aseis, ~asen
ꞏnditional: comprar|ía,
ꞏías, ~ía, ~íamos, ~íais,
ꞏían
ꞏesent participle:
ꞏmprando
ꞏast participle: comprado
ꞏnperative: compra,
ꞏmprad
ꞏ -er (*e.g.* **beber**)
ꞏesent: beb|o, **~es, ~e,**
ꞏemos, ~éis, ~en
ꞏuture: beber|é, **~ás, ~á,**
ꞏemos, ~éis, ~án
ꞏperfect: beb|ía, **~ías,**
ꞏa, ~íamos, ~íais, ~ían
Preterite: beb|í, **~iste, ~ió,**
~imos, ~isteis, ~ieron
Present subjunctive: beb|a,
~as, ~a, ~amos, ~áis,
~an
Imperfect subjunctive:
beb|iera, **~ieras, ~iera,**
~iéramos, ~ierais, ~ieran
beb|iese, **~ieses, ~iese,**
~iésemos, ~ieseis,
~iesen
Conditional: beber|ía, **~ías,**
~ía, ~íamos, ~íais, ~ían
Present participle:
bebiendo
Past participle: bebido
Imperative: bebe, bebed
in **-ir** (*e.g.* **vivir**)
Present: viv|o, **~es, ~e,**
~imos, ~ís, ~en
Future: vivir|é, **~ás, ~á,**
~emos, ~éis, ~án
Imperfect: viv|ía, **~ías,**
~ía, ~íamos, ~íais, ~ían
Preterite: viv|í, **~iste, ~ió,**
~imos, ~isteis, ~ieron
Present subjunctive: viv|a,
~as, ~a, ~amos, ~áis,
~an
Imperfect subjunctive:
viv|iera, **~ieras, ~iera,**
~iéramos, ~ierais, ~ieran
viv|iese, **~ieses, ~iese,**
~iésemos, ~ieseis,
~iesen

Conditional: vivir|ía, **~ías, ~ía, ~íamos, ~íais, ~ían**
Present participle: viviendo
Past participle: vivido
Imperative: vive, vivid

Irregular verbs:
[1] **cerrar**
Present: cierro, cierras, cierra, cerramos, cerráis, cierran
Present subjunctive: cierre, cierres, cierre, cerremos, cerréis, cierren
Imperative: cierra, cerrad

[2] **contar**, **mover**
Present: cuento, cuentas, cuenta, contamos, contáis, cuentan
muevo, mueves, mueve, movemos, movéis, mueven
Present subjunctive: cuente, cuentes, cuente, contemos, contéis, cuenten
mueva, muevas, mueva, movamos, mováis, muevan
Imperative: cuenta, contad
mueve, moved

[3] **jugar**
Present: juego, juegas, juega, jugamos, jugáis, juegan
Preterite: jugué, jugaste, jugó, jugamos, jugasteis, jugaron
Present subjunctive: juegue, juegues, juegue, juguemos, juguéis, jueguen

[4] **sentir**
Present: siento, sientes, siente, sentimos, sentís, sienten
Preterite: sentí, sentiste, sintió, sentimos, sentisteis, sintieron
Present subjunctive: sienta, sientas, sienta, sintamos, sintáis, sientan
Imperfect subjunctive: sint|iera, **~ieras, ~iera, ~iéramos, ~ierais, ~ieran**
sint|iese, **~ieses, ~iese, ~iésemos, ~ieseis, ~iesen**
Present participle: sintiendo
Imperative: siente, sentid

[5] **pedir**
Present: pido, pides, pide, pedimos, pedís, piden
Preterite: pedí, pediste, pidió, pedimos, pedisteis, pidieron
Present subjunctive: pid|a, **~as, ~a, ~amos, ~áis, ~an**
Imperfect subjunctive: pid|iera, **~ieras, ~iera,**

~iéramos, ~ierais, ~ieran
pid|iese, **~ieses, ~iese, ~iésemos, ~ieseis, ~iesen**
resent participle: pidiendo
nperative: pide, pedid

] **dormir**
resent: duermo, duermes, duerme, dormimos, dormís, duermen
reterite: dormí, dormiste, durmió, dormimos, dormisteis, durmieron
resent subjunctive: duerma, duermas, duerma, durmamos, durmáis, duerman
nperfect subjunctive: durm|iera, **~ieras, ~iera, ~iéramos, ~ierais, ~ieran**
durm|iese, **~ieses, ~iese, ~iésemos, ~ieseis, ~iesen**
resent participle: durmiendo
nperative: duerme, dormid

] **dedicar**
reterite: dediqué, dedicaste, dedicó, dedicamos, dedicasteis, dedicaron
resent subjunctive: dediqu|e, **~es, ~e, ~emos, ~éis, ~en**

[8] **delinquir**
Present: delinco, delinques, delinque, delinquimos, delinquís, delinquen
Present subjunctive: delinc|a, **~as, ~a, ~amos, ~áis, ~an**

[9] **vencer**, **esparcir**
Present: venzo, vences, vence, vencemos, vencéis, vencen
esparzo, esparces, esparce, esparcimos, esparcís, esparcen
Present subjunctive: venz|a, **~as, ~a, ~amos, ~áis, ~an**
esparz|a, **~as, ~a, ~amos, ~áis, ~an**

[10] **rechazar**
Preterite: rechacé, rechazaste, rechazó, rechazamos, rechazasteis, rechazaron
Present subjunctive: rechac|e, **~es, ~e, ~emos, ~éis, ~en**

[11] **conocer**, **lucir**
Present: conozco, conoces, conoce, conocemos, conocéis, conocen
luzco, luces, luce, lucimos, lucís, lucen
Present subjunctive: conozc|a, **~as, ~a,**

~amos, ~áis, ~an
luzc|a, **~as, ~a, ~amos, ~áis, ~an**

[12] **pagar**
Preterite: pagué, pagaste, pagó, pagamos, pagasteis, pagaron
Present subjunctive: pagu|e, **~es, ~e, ~emos, ~éis, ~en**

[13] **distinguir**
Present: distingo, distingues, distingue, distinguimos, distinguís, distinguen
Present subjunctive: disting|a, **~as, ~a, ~amos, ~áis, ~an**

[14] **acoger, afligir**
Present: acojo, acoges, acoge, acogemos, acogéis, acogen
aflijo, afliges, aflige, afligimos, afligís, afligen
Present subjunctive: acoj|a, **~as, ~a, ~amos, ~áis, ~an**
aflij|a, **~as, ~a, ~amos, ~áis, ~an**

[15] **averiguar**
Preterite: averigüé, averiguaste, averiguó, averiguamos, averiguasteis, averiguaron
Present subjunctive: averigü|e, **~es, ~e, ~emos, ~éis, ~en**

[16] **agorar**
Present: agüero, agüeras, agüera, agoramos, agorá agüeran
Present subjunctive: agüere, agüeres, agüere, agoremos, agoréis, agüeren
Imperative: agüera, agora

[17] **huir**
Present: huyo, huyes, huy huimos, huís, huyen
Preterite: huí, huiste, huy huimos, huisteis, huyero
Present subjunctive: huy|a **~as, ~a, ~amos, ~áis, ~an**
Imperfect subjunctive: huy|era, **~eras, ~era, ~éramos, ~erais, ~era**
huy|ese, **~eses, ~ese, ~ésemos, ~eseis, ~esen**
Present participle: huyen
Imperative: huye, huid

[18] **creer**
Preterite: creí, creíste, creyó, creímos, creísteis, creyeron
Imperfect subjunctive: crey|era, **~eras, ~era, ~éramos, ~erais, ~era**

crey|ese, **~eses, ~ese, ~ésemos, ~eseis, ~esen**
Present participle: creyendo
Past participle: creído

[19] **argüir**
Present: arguyo, arguyes, arguye, argüimos, argüís, arguyen
Preterite: argüí, argüiste, arguyó, argüimos, argüisteis, arguyeron
Present subjunctive: arguy|a, **~as, ~a, ~amos, ~áis, ~an**
Imperfect subjunctive: arguy|era, **~eras, ~era, ~éramos, ~erais, ~eran** arguy|ese, **~eses, ~ese, ~ésemos, ~eseis, ~esen**
Present participle: arguyendo
Imperative: arguye, argüid

[20] **vaciar**
Present: vacío, vacías, vacía, vaciamos, vaciáis, vacían
Present subjunctive: vacíe, vacíes, vacíe, vaciemos, vaciéis, vacíen
Imperative: vacía, vaciad

[21] **acentuar**
Present: acentúo, acentúas, acentúa, acentuamos, acentuáis, acentúan
Present subjunctive: acentúe, acentúes, acentúe, acentuemos, acentuéis, acentúen
Imperative: acentúa, acentuad

[22] **atañer**, **engullir**
Preterite: atañ|i, **~iste, ~ó, ~imos, ~isteis, ~eron** engull|í **~iste, ~ó, ~imos, ~isteis, ~eron**
Imperfect subjunctive: atañera, **~eras, ~era, ~éramos, ~erais, ~eran** atañese, **~eses, ~ese, ~ésemos, ~eseis, ~esen** engull|era, **~eras, ~era, ~éramos, ~erais, ~eran** engull|ese, **~eses, ~ese, ~ésemos, ~eseis, ~esen**
Present participle: atañendo engullendo

[23] **aislar**, **aullar**
Present: aíslo, aíslas, aísla, aislamos, aisláis, aíslan aúllo, aúllas, aúlla, aullamos aulláis, aúllan
Present subjunctive: aísle, aísles, aísle, aislemos, aisléis, aíslen

aúlle, aúlles, aúlle,
aullemos, aulléis, aúllen
Imperative: aísla, aislad
aúlla, aullad

[24] **abolir**
Present: abolimos, abolís
Present subjunctive: not used
Imperative: abolid

[25] **andar**
Preterite: anduv|e, **~iste, ~o, ~imos, ~isteis, ~ieron**
Imperfect subjunctive:
anduv|iera, **~ieras, ~iera, ~iéramos, ~ierais, ~ieran**
anduv|iese, **~ieses, ~iese, ~iésemos, ~ieseis, ~iesen**

[26] **dar**
Present: doy, das, da, damos, dais, dan
Preterite: di, diste, dio, dimos, disteis, dieron
Present subjunctive: dé, des, dé, demos, deis, den
Imperfect subjunctive:
diera, dieras, diera, diéramos, dierais, dieran
diese, dieses, diese, diésemos, dieseis, diesen

[27] **estar**
Present: estoy, estás, está, estamos, estáis, están
Preterite: estuv|e, **~iste, ~o, ~imos, ~isteis, ~ieron**
Present subjunctive: esté, estés, esté, estemos, estéis, estén
Imperfect subjunctive:
estuv|iera, **~ieras, ~iera, ~iéramos, ~ierais, ~ieran**
estuv|iese, **~ieses, ~iese, ~iésemos, ~ieseis, ~iesen**
Imperative: está, estad

[28] **caber**
Present: quepo, cabes, cabe, cabemos, cabéis, caben
Future: cabr|é, **~ás, ~á, ~emos, ~éis, ~án**
Preterite: cup|e, **~iste, ~o, ~imos, ~isteis, ~ieron**
Present subjunctive:
quep|a, **~as, ~a, ~amos, ~áis, ~an**
Imperfect subjunctive:
cup|iera, **~ieras, ~iera, ~iéramos, ~ierais, ~ieran**
cup|iese, **~ieses, ~iese, ~iésemos, ~ieseis, ~iesen**
Conditional: cabr|ía, **~ías, ~ía, ~íamos, ~íais, ~ían**

[29] **caer**
Present: caigo, caes, cae, caemos, caéis, caen
Preterite: caí, caiste, cayó, caímos, caísteis, cayeron
Present subjunctive: caig|a, **~as, ~a, ~amos, ~áis, ~an**
Imperfect subjunctive: cay|era, **~eras, ~era, ~éramos, ~erais, ~eran** cay|ese, **~eses, ~ese, ~ésemos, ~eseis, ~esen**
Present participle: cayendo
Past participle: caído

[30] **haber**
Present: he, has, ha, hemos, habéis, han
Future: habr|é **~ás, ~á, ~emos, ~éis, ~án**
Preterite: hub|e, **~iste, ~o, ~imos, ~isteis, ~ieron**
Present subjunctive: hay|a, **~as, ~a, ~amos, ~áis, ~an**
Imperfect subjunctive: hub|iera, **~ieras, ~iera, ~iéramos, ~ierais, ~ieran** hub|iese, **~ieses, ~iese, ~iésemos, ~ieseis, ~iesen**
Conditional: habr|ía, **~ías, ~ía, ~íamos, ~íais, ~ían**
Imperative: he, habed

[31] **hacer**
Present: hago, haces, hace, hacemos, hacéis, hacen
Future: har|é, **~ás, ~á, ~emos, ~éis, ~án**
Preterite: hice, hiciste, hizo, hicimos, hicisteis, hicieron
Present subjunctive: hag|a, **~as, ~a, ~amos, ~áis, ~an**
Imperfect subjunctive: hic|iera, **~ieras, ~iera, ~iéramos, ~ierais, ~ieran** hic|iese, **~ieses, ~iese, ~iésemos, ~ieseis, ~iesen**
Conditional: har|ía, **~ías, ~ía, ~íamos, ~íais, ~ían**
Past participle: hecho
Imperative: haz, haced

[32] **placer**
Present subjunctive: plazca
Imperfect subjunctive: placiera, placiese

[33] **poder**
Present: puedo, puedes, puede, podemos, podéis, pueden
Future: podr|é, **~ás, ~á, ~emos, ~éis, ~án**

Preterite: pud|e, **~iste, ~o, ~imos, ~isteis, ~ieron**
Present subjunctive: pueda, puedas, pueda, podamos, podáis, puedan
Imperfect subjunctive: pud|iera, **~ieras, ~iera, ~iéramos, ~ierais, ~ieran** pud|iese, **~ieses, ~iese, ~iésemos, ~ieseis, ~iesen**
Conditional: podr|ía, **~ías, ~ía, ~íamos, ~íais, ~ían**
Past participle: pudiendo

[34] **poner**
Present: pongo, pones, pone, ponemos, ponéis, ponen
Future: pondr|é, **~ás, ~á, ~emos, ~éis, ~án**
Preterite: pus|e, **~iste, ~o, ~imos, ~isteis, ~ieron**
Present subjunctive: pong|a, **~as, ~a, ~amos, ~áis, ~an**
Imperfect subjunctive: pus|iera, **~ieras, ~iera, ~iéramos, ~ierais, ~ieran** pus|iese, **~ieses, ~iese, ~iésemos, ~ieseis, ~iesen**
Conditional: pondr|ía, **~ías, ~ía, ~íamos, ~íais, ~ían**
Past participle: puesto
Imperative: pon, poned

[35] **querer**
Present: quiero, quieres, quiere, queremos, queréis, quieren
Future: querr|é, **~ás, ~á, ~emos, ~éis, ~án**
Preterite: quis|e, **~iste, ~o, ~imos, ~isteis, ~ieron**
Present subjunctive: quiera, quieras, quiera, queramos, queráis, quieran
Imperfect subjunctive: quis|iera, **~ieras, ~iera, ~iéramos, ~ierais, ~ieran** quis|iese, **~ieses, ~iese, ~iésemos, ~ieseis, ~iesen**
Conditional: querr|ía, **~ías, ~ía, ~íamos, ~íais, ~ían**
Imperative: quiere, quered

[36] **raer**
Present: raigo/rayo, raes, rae, raemos, raéis, raen
Preterite: raí, raíste, rayó, raímos, raísteis, rayeron

Present subjunctive: raig|a, **~as, ~a, ~amos, ~áis, ~an** ray|a, **~as, ~a, ~amos, ~áis, ~an**
Imperfect subjunctive: ray|era, **~eras, ~era, ~éramos, ~erais, ~eran** ray|ese, **~eses, ~ese, ~ésemos, ~eseis, ~esen**
Present participle: rayendo
Past participle: raído

[37] **roer**
Present: roo, roes, roe, roemos, roéis, roen
Preterite: roí, roíste, royó, roímos, roísteis, royeron
Present subjunctive: ro|a, **~as, ~a, ~amos, ~áis, ~an**
Imperfect subjunctive: roy|era, **~eras, ~era, ~éramos, ~erais, ~eran** roy|ese, **~eses, ~ese, ~ésemos, ~eseis, ~esen**
Present participle: royendo
Past participle: roído

[38] **saber**
Present: sé, sabes, sabe, sabemos, sabéis, saben
Future: sabr|é, **~ás, ~á, ~emos, ~éis, ~án**
Preterite: sup|e, **~iste, ~o, ~imos, ~isteis, ~ieron**
Present subjunctive: sep|a, **~as, ~a, ~amos, ~áis, ~an**
Imperfect subjunctive: sup|iera, **~ieras, ~iera, ~iéramos, ~ierais, ~ieran** sup|iese, **~ieses, ~iese, ~iésemos, ~ieseis, ~iesen**
Conditional: sabr|ía, **~ías, ~ía, ~íamos, ~íais, ~ían**

[39] **ser**
Present: soy, eres, es, somos, sois, son
Imperfect: era, eras, era, éramos, erais, eran
Preterite: fui, fuiste, fue, fuimos, fuisteis, fueron
Present subjunctive: se|a, **~as, ~a, ~amos, ~áis, ~an**
Imperfect subjunctive: fu|era, **~eras, ~era, ~éramos, ~erais, ~eran** fu|ese, **~eses, ~ese, ~ésemos, ~eseis, ~esen**
Imperative: sé, sed

[40] **tener**
Present: tengo, tienes, tiene, tenemos, tenéis, tienen
Future: tendr|é, **~ás, ~á, ~emos, ~éis, ~án**
Preterite: tuv|e, **~iste, ~o, ~imos, ~isteis, ~ieron**
Present subjunctive: teng|a, **~as, ~a, ~amos, ~áis, ~an**
Imperfect subjunctive: tuv|iera, **~ieras, ~iera, ~iéramos, ~ierais, ~ieran** tuv|iese, **~ieses, ~iese, ~iésemos, ~ieseis, ~iesen**
Conditional: tendr|ía, **~ías, ~ía, ~íamos, ~íais, ~ían**
Imperative: ten, tened

[41] **traer**
Present: traigo, traes, trae, traemos, traéis, traen
Preterite: traj|e, **~iste, ~o, ~imos, ~isteis, ~eron**
Present subjunctive: traig|a, **~as, ~a, ~amos, ~áis, ~an**
Imperfect subjunctive: traj|era, **~eras, ~era, ~éramos, ~erais, ~eran** traj|ese, **~eses, ~ese, ~ésemos, ~eseis, ~esen**
Present participle: trayendo
Past participle: traído

[42] **valer**
Present: valgo, vales, vale, valemos, valéis, valen
Future: vald|ré, **~ás, ~á, ~emos, ~éis, ~án**
Present subjunctive: valg|a, **~as, ~a, ~amos ~áis, ~an**
Conditional: vald|ría, **~ías, ~ía, ~íamos, ~íais, ~ían**
Imperative: vale, valed

[43] **ver**
Present: veo, ves, ve, vemos, veis, ven
Imperfect: ve|ía, **~ías, ~ía, ~íamos, ~íais, ~ían**
Preterite: vi, viste, vio, vimos, visteis, vieron
Present subjunctive: ve|a, **~as, ~a, ~amos, ~áis, ~an**
Past participle: visto

[44] **yacer**
Present: yazco, yaces, yace, yacemos, yacéis, yacen
Present subjunctive: yazc|a, **~as, ~a,**

~amos, ~áis, ~an
mperative: yace, yaced

[45] **asir**
Present: asgo, ases, ase, asimos, asís, asen
Present subjunctive: asg|a, **~as, ~a, ~amos, ~áis, ~an**

[46] **decir**
Present: digo, dices, dice, decimos, decís, dicen
Future: dir|é, **~ás, ~á, ~emos, ~éis, ~án**
Preterite: dij|e, **~iste, ~o, ~imos, ~isteis, ~eron**
Present subjunctive: dig|a, **~as, ~a, ~amos, ~áis, ~an**
Imperfect subjunctive: dij|era, **~eras, ~era, ~éramos, ~erais, ~eran**
dij|ese, **~eses, ~ese, ~ésemos, ~eseis, ~esen**
Conditional: dir|ía, **~ías, ~ía, ~íamos, ~íais, ~ían**
Present participle: dicho
Imperative: di, decid

[47] **reducir**
Present: reduzco, reduces, reduce, reducimos, reducís, reducen
Preterite: reduj|e, **~iste, ~o, ~imos, ~isteis, ~eron**
Present subjunctive: reduzc|a, **~as, ~a, ~amos, ~áis, ~an**
Imperfect subjunctive: reduj|era, **~eras, ~era, ~éramos, ~erais, ~eran**
reduj|ese, **~eses, ~ese, ~ésemos, ~eseis, ~esen**

[48] **erguir**
Present: yergo, yergues, yergue, erguimos, erguís, yerguen
Preterite: erguí, erguiste, irguió, erguimos, erguisteis, irguieron
Present subjunctive: yerg|a, **~as, ~a, ~amos, ~áis, ~an**
Imperfect subjunctive: irgu|iera, **~ieras, ~iera, ~iéramos, ~ierais, ~ieran**
irgu|iese, **~ieses, ~iese, ~iésemos, ~ieseis, ~iesen**
Present participle: irguiendo
Imperative: yergue, erguid

[49] **ir**
Present: voy, vas, va, vamos, vais, van

Imperfect: iba, ibas, iba, íbamos, ibais, iban
Preterite: fui, fuiste, fue, fuimos, fuisteis, fueron
Present subjunctive: vay|a, **~as, ~a, ~amos, ~áis, ~an**
Imperfect subjunctive: fu|era, **~eras, ~era, ~éramos, ~erais, ~eran**
fu|ese, **~eses, ~ese, ~ésemos, ~eseis, ~esen**
Present participle: yendo
Imperative: ve, id

[50] **oír**
Present: oigo, oyes, oye, oímos, oís, oyen
Preterite: oí, oíste, oyó, oímos, oísteis, oyeron
Present subjunctive: oig|a, **~as, ~a, ~amos, ~áis, ~an**
Imperfect subjunctive: oy|era, **~eras, ~era, ~éramos, ~erais, ~eran**
oy|ese, **~eses, ~ese, ~ésemos, ~eseis, ~esen**
Present participle: oyendo
Past participle: oído
Imperative: oye, oíd

[51] **reír**
Present: río, ríes, ríe, reímos, reís, ríen
Preterite: reí, reíste, rió, reímos, reísteis, rieron
Present subjunctive: ría, rías, ría, riamos, riáis, rían
Present participle: riendo
Past participle: reído
Imperative: ríe, reíd

[52] **salir**
Present: salgo, sales, sale, salimos, salís, salen
Future: saldr|é, **~ás, ~á, ~emos, ~éis, ~án**
Present subjunctive: salg|a, **~as, ~a, ~amos, ~áis, ~an**
Conditional: saldr|ía, **~ías, ~ía, ~íamos, ~íais, ~ían**
Imperative: sal, salid

[53] **venir**
Present: vengo, vienes, viene, venimos, venís, vienen
Future: vendr|é, **~ás, ~á, ~emos, ~éis, ~án**
Preterite: vin|e, **~iste, ~o, ~imos, ~isteis, ~ieron**
Present subjunctive: veng|a, **~as, ~a, ~amos, ~áis, ~an**

Imperfect subjunctive: vin|iera, **~ieras, ~iera, ~iéramos, ~ierais, ~ieran** vin|iese, **~ieses, ~iese, ~iésemos, ~ieseis, ~iesen**

Conditional: vendr|ía, **~ías, ~ía, ~íamos, ~íais, ~ían**
Present participle: viniendo
Imperative: ven, venid

Verbos Irregulares Ingleses

Infinitivo	*Pretérito*	*Participio pasado*
arise	arose	arisen
awake	awoke	awoken
be	was	been
bear	bore	borne
beat	beat	beaten
become	became	become
befall	befell	befallen
beget	begot	begotten
begin	began	begun
behold	beheld	beheld
bend	bent	bent
beset	beset	beset
bet	bet, betted	bet, betted
bid	bade, bid	bidden, bid
bind	bound	bound
bite	bit	bitten
bleed	bled	bled
blow	blew	blown
break	broke	broken
breed	bred	bred
bring	brought	brought
broadcast	broadcast(ed)	broadcast
build	built	built
burn	burnt, burned	burnt, burned
burst	burst	burst
buy	bought	bought
cast	cast	cast
catch	caught	caught
choose	chose	chosen
cleave	clove, cleft, cleaved	cloven, cleft, cleaved
cling	clung	clung
clothe	clothed, clad	clothed, clad
come	came	come

Infinitivo	*Pretérito*	*Participio pasado*
cost	cost	cost
creep	crept	crept
crow	crowed, crew	crowed
cut	cut	cut
leal	dealt	dealt
lig	dug	dug
lo	did	done
lraw	drew	drawn
lream	dreamt, dreamed	dreamt, dreamed
lrink	drank	drunk
lrive	drove	driven
well	dwelt	dwelt
at	ate	eaten
ll	fell	fallen
eed	fed	fed
eel	felt	felt
ght	fought	fought
nd	found	found
ee	fled	fled
ling	flung	flung
ly	flew	flown
orbear	forbore	forborne
orbid	forbad(e)	forbidden
orecast	forecast(ed)	forecast(ed)
oresee	foresaw	foreseen
oretell	foretold	foretold
orget	forgot	forgotten
orgive	forgave	forgiven
orsake	forsook	forsaken
reeze	froze	frozen
ainsay	gainsaid	gainsaid
et	got	got, gotten
ive	gave	given
o	went	gone
rind	ground	ground

Infinitivo	*Pretérito*	*Participio pasado*
grow	grew	grown
hang	hung, hanged	hung, hanged
have	had	had
hear	heard	heard
hew	hewed	hewn, hewed
hide	hid	hidden
hit	hit	hit
hold	held	held
hurt	hurt	hurt
inlay	inlaid	inlaid
keep	kept	kept
kneel	knelt	knelt
knit	knitted, knit	knitted, knit
know	knew	known
lay	laid	laid
lead	led	led
lean	leaned, leant	leaned, leant
leap	leaped, leapt	leaped, leapt
learn	learned, learnt	learned, learnt
leave	left	left
lend	lent	lent
let	let	let
lie	lay	lain
light	lit, lighted	lit, lighted
lose	lost	lost
make	made	made
mean	meant	meant
meet	met	met
mislay	mislaid	mislaid
mislead	misled	misled
misspell	misspelt	misspelt
mistake	mistook	mistaken
misunderstand	misunderstood	misunderstood
mow	mowed	mown
outbid	outbid	outbid

Infinitivo	*Pretérito*	*Participio pasado*
outdo	outdid	outdone
outgrow	outgrew	outgrown
overcome	overcame	overcome
overdo	overdid	overdone
overhang	overhung	overhung
overhear	overheard	overheard
override	overrode	overridden
overrun	overran	overrun
oversee	oversaw	overseen
overshoot	overshot	overshot
oversleep	overslept	overslept
overtake	overtook	overtaken
overthrow	overthrew	overthrown
partake	partook	partaken
pay	paid	paid
prove	proved	proved, proven
put	put	put
quit	quitted, quit	quitted, quit
read /ri:d/	read /red/	read /red/
rebuild	rebuilt	rebuilt
redo	redid	redone
rend	rent	rent
repay	repaid	repaid
rewrite	rewrote	rewritten
rid	rid	rid
ride	rode	ridden
ring	rang	rung
rise	rose	risen
run	ran	run
saw	sawed	sawn, sawed
say	said	said
see	saw	seen
seek	sought	sought
sell	sold	sold
send	sent	sent

Infinitivo	*Pretérito*	*Participio pasado*
set	set	set
sew	sewed	sewn, sewed
shake	shook	shaken
shear	sheared	shorn, sheared
shed	shed	shed
shine	shone	shone
shoe	shod	shod
shoot	shot	shot
show	showed	shown, showed
shrink	shrank	shrunk
shut	shut	shut
sing	sang	sung
sink	sank	sunk
sit	sat	sat
slay	slew	slain
sleep	slept	slept
slide	slid	slid
sling	slung	slung
slit	slit	slit
smell	smelt, smelled	smelt, smelled
smite	smote	smitten
sow	sowed	sown, sowed
speak	spoke	spoken
speed	speeded, sped	speeded, sped
spell	spelt, spelled	spelt, spelled
spend	spent	spent
spill	spilled, spilt	spilled, spilt
spin	spun	spun
spit	spat	spat
split	split	split
spoil	spoilt, spoiled	spoilt, spoiled
spread	spread	spread
spring	sprang	sprung
stand	stood	stood
steal	stole	stolen

Infinitivo	*Pretérito*	*Participio pasado*
stick	stuck	stuck
sting	stung	stung
stink	stank, stunk	stunk
strew	strewed	strewn, strewed
stride	strode	stridden
strike	struck	struck
string	strung	strung
strive	strove	striven
swear	swore	sworn
sweep	swept	swept
swell	swelled	swollen, swelled
swim	swam	swum
swing	swung	swung
take	took	taken
teach	taught	taught
tear	tore	torn
tell	told	told
think	thought	thought
thrive	thrived, throve	thrived, thriven
throw	threw	thrown
thrust	thrust	thrust
tread	trod	trodden, trod
unbend	unbent	unbent
undergo	underwent	undergone
understand	understood	understood
undertake	undertook	undertaken
undo	undid	undone
upset	upset	upset
wake	woke, waked	woken, waked
waylay	waylaid	waylaid
wear	wore	worn
weave	wove	woven
weep	wept	wept
win	won	won
wind	wound	wound

Infinitivo	*Pretérito*	*Participio pasado*
withdraw	withdrew	withdrawn
withhold	withheld	withheld
withstand	withstood	withstood
wring	wrung	wrung
write	wrote	written